Mind & Brain
The Science of Psychology

University of California, Santa Barbara

10th Edition

Alan J. Fridlund | James W. Kalat

Australia • Brazil • Japan • Korea • Mexico • Singapore • Spain • United Kingdom • United States

Mind & Brain : The Science of Psychology
University of California, Santa Barbara
10th Edition

INTRODUCTION TO PSYCHOLOGY, TENTH EDITION
Kalat

© 2014, 2011 Cengage Learning. All rights reserved.

BIOLOGICAL PSYCHOLOGY, ELEVENTH EDITION
Kalat

© 2013, 2009 Cengage Learning. All rights reserved.

MEANING AND THE TEMPORAL LOBES: IS GOD IN THE AMYGDALA?
Fridund

© 2007, 2009 by Alan J. Fridlund. All rights reserved.

WHATEVER HAPPENED TO "LITTLE ALBERT"?
Fridlund

© 2010 by Alan J. Fridlund. All rights reserved.

Senior Project Development Manager:
 Linda deStefano

Market Development Manager:
 Heather Kramer

Senior Production/Manufacturing Manager:
 Donna M. Brown

Production Editorial Manager:
 Kim Fry

Sr. Rights Acquisition Account Manager:
 Todd Osborne

For product information and technology assistance, contact us at
Cengage Learning Customer & Sales Support, 1-800-354-9706

For permission to use material from this text or product,
submit all requests online at **cengage.com/permissions**
Further permissions questions can be emailed to
permissionrequest@cengage.com

This book contains select works from existing Cengage Learning resources and was produced by Cengage Learning Custom Solutions for collegiate use. As such, those adopting and/or contributing to this work are responsible for editorial content accuracy, continuity and completeness.

Compilation © 2013 Cengage Learning

ISBN-13: 978-1-285-56312-1

ISBN-10: 1-285-56312-3

Cengage Learning
5191 Natorp Boulevard
Mason, Ohio 45040
USA
Cengage Learning is a leading provider of customized learning solutions with office locations around the globe, including Singapore, the United Kingdom, Australia, Mexico, Brazil, and Japan. Locate your local office at:
international.cengage.com/region.

Cengage Learning products are represented in Canada by Nelson Education, Ltd.
For your lifelong learning solutions, visit **www.cengage.com/custom.**
Visit our corporate website at **www.cengage.com.**

Printed in the United States of America

Custom Table of Contents

brief contents

contents

3 Biological Psychology 57

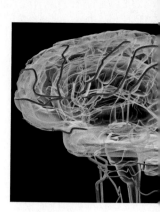

4 Sensation and Perception 101

5 Development 145

6 Learning 185

7 Memory 219

8 Cognition and Language 255

9 Intelligence 293

10 Consciousness 319

11 Motivated Behaviors 349

12 Emotions, Stress, and Health 383

13 Social Psychology 419

14 Personality 459

15 Abnormal Psychology: Disorders and Treatment 493

Some years ago, I was on a plane that had to turn around shortly after takeoff because one of its two engines had failed. When we were told to get into crash position, the first thing I thought was, "I don't want to die yet! I was looking forward to writing the next edition of my textbook!" True story.

I remember taking my first course in psychology as a freshman at Duke University in 1965. Frequently, I would describe the fascinating facts I had just learned to my roommate, friends, relatives, or anyone else who would listen. I haven't changed much since then. When I read about new research or think of a new example to illustrate some point, I want to tell my wife, children, colleagues, and students. Psychology is fun. I enjoy reading about it, writing about it, and teaching about it. Recently I retired from teaching after 35 years at North Carolina State University, but I still volunteer to "pinch hit" when any of my colleagues are ill or out of town. I wake up in the morning and think, "Wow! I get to teach about optical illusions today," or "Great! Today's topic is emotions!" Do professors in other fields enjoy teaching so much? Does someone in the French department wake up thinking how delightful it will be to teach about adverbs today? I doubt it.

Ideally, a course or textbook in psychology should accomplish two goals. The first is to instill a love of learning so that our graduates will continue to update their education. Even if students permanently remembered everything they learned—and of course they won't—their understanding would gradually go out of date unless they continue to learn about new developments. I hope that some of our students occasionally read *Scientific American Mind* or similar publications. The second goal is to teach students the skills of evaluating evidence and questioning assertions, so that when they do read about some new research, they will ask the right questions before drawing a conclusion. That skill can carry over to fields other than psychology.

Throughout this text, I have tried to model the habit of critical thinking or evaluating the evidence, particularly in the **What's the Evidence?** features that describe research studies in some detail. I have pointed out the limitations of the evidence and the possibilities for alternative interpretations. The goal is to help students ask their own questions, distinguish between good and weak evidence, and ultimately, appreciate the excitement of psychological inquiry.

Approaches, Features, and Student Aids

Many years ago, I read an educational psychology textbook that said children with learning disabilities and attention problems learn best from specific, concrete examples. I remember thinking, "Wait a minute. I do, too! Don't we *all* learn best from specific, concrete examples?" For this reason, science classes use laboratories to let students see for themselves. Few introductory psychology classes offer laboratories, but we can nevertheless encourage students to try procedures that require little or no equipment. At various points, the text describes simple **Try It Yourself** exercises, such as negative afterimages, binocular rivalry, encoding specificity, and the Stroop effect. Additional activities are available as **Online Try It Yourself** activities on Psychology CourseMate. Students who try these activities will understand and remember the concepts far better than if they merely read about them. A few of the online activities enable students to collect and report their own data.

Cognitive psychology researchers find that we learn more if we alternate between reading and testing than if we spend the same amount of time reading. The **Concept Checks** pose questions that attentive readers should be able to answer. Students who answer correctly can feel encouraged. Those who miss a question should use the feedback to reread the relevant passages.

Education was long a traditional field in which the procedures hardly changed since the invention of chalk. Today, however, educators use the power of new technologies, and this text offers several important technological enhancements. As noted above, Psychology CourseMate includes the Online Try It Yourself exercises as well as an integrated eBook, flash cards, quizzes, an online glossary, and videos. Each chapter of this text is divided into two to five modules, each with its own summary. Modules provide flexibility for the instructor who wishes to take sections in a different order—for example, operant conditioning before classical conditioning—or who wishes to omit a section. Modular format also breaks up the reading assignments so that a student reads one or two modules for each class. Key terms are listed at the end of each module and are also available as flash cards on Psychology

CourseMate. At the end of the text, a combined Subject Index and Glossary defines key terms and provides page references.

What's New in the Tenth Edition

Whenever I begin a new edition, my editor solicits both general and specific recommendations from many professors who teach the course. Frequently, text reviewers comment that the text is a bit too long for a one-semester course and their general recommendation is to streamline it. But then under specific recommendations, the same reviewers list important topics to be added. As the author, I find additional topics I want to add myself. The tendency, therefore, is for the text to grow longer and longer with each revision. This time, I made a deliberate effort to shorten the text, but without deleting any important content. In many cases I found it possible to rephrase a sentence in fewer words. I deleted some tangential material, illustrated certain concepts with two or three examples instead of three or four, and so forth. The most noticeable change is at the end, where this text has one chapter on psychopathology and treatment instead of two. I reorganized and condensed the material on those topics, but all of the key content remains.

This edition has more than 450 new references, most of them from 2009 or later. Several topics have been moved from one chapter to another, such as genetics and evolution from the developmental chapter to the biological chapter. Several new topics have been added, including blindsight, epigenetics, near and far transfer, probabilistic learning, and job burnout. Many of the figures are new or revised. Here are a few of my favorite new studies:

- "Hurt feelings" are surprisingly similar to physical pain. Hurt feelings activate some of the same brain areas as physical pain, and it is possible to relieve hurt feelings by taking acetaminophen (Tylenol)! (chapter 4)
- At least in Western cultures, women apologize more than men. However, men also report fewer times when they think they should have apologized, and fewer times when they think someone else should have apologized to them. (chapter 5)
- When a car driver hears a passenger talking on a cell phone, the driver hears half the conversation (a "halfalogue"), which is more distracting than hearing a full conversation. (chapter 8)
- Several studies show that people eat more when offered larger portions. They like a wine better if they are told it is from California than if they are told it is from North Dakota. (chapter 11)

- Researchers have successfully used measurements of penis erection to gauge men's sexual interest in heterosexual, homosexual, or pedophilic activities. They assumed that they could also use measurements of vaginal secretions to gauge women's sexual interests. New research shows that this method led to misleading conclusions, as women increase vaginal secretions in response to any depiction of sex, even if highly aversive—perhaps as a defense against damage, in the case of unwanted sex. (chapter 11)
- A woman with damage to her amygdala shows no fear of snakes, spiders, scary movies, or "monsters" who pop out in dark halls of a "haunted house." Also, she stands closer than normal to other people, and shows no discomfort if someone approaches virtually nose to nose. (chapter 12)

Teaching and Learning Supplements

You're familiar with those television advertisements that offer something, usually for $19.95, and then say, "But wait, there's more!" Same here. In addition to the text, the publisher offers many supplements:

Test Bank, revised by the author himself, includes many new or reworded items, with an emphasis on being short, clear, and important. That bank is also available in ExamView® electronic format. Many of the items have already been tested with classes at North Carolina State University. In those cases, the Test Bank indicates the percentage correct and point biserial. The Test Bank also includes a special file of items that cut across chapters, intended for a comprehensive final exam.

Instructor's Resource Manual is both thorough and creative. It includes suggestions for class demonstrations and lecture material.

PowerLecture with ExamView is designed to facilitate an instructor's assembly of PowerPoint® or similar demonstrations and contains lecture slides, figures, and tables from the text; the Instructor's Resource Manual; and the Test Bank. With PowerLecture, all of your media resources are in one place, including an image library with graphics from the book itself, video clips, and more. ExamView includes all of the test items from the printed Test Bank in electronic format and enables you to create customized tests in print or online.

Cengage Learning's Psychology CourseMate brings course concepts to life with interactive learning, study, and exam preparation tools that support the printed textbook. CourseMate includes an integrated eBook, glossaries, flash cards, quizzes, videos, Try It Yourself activities, and more—as well as EngagementTracker, a first-of-its-kind tool that monitors student engagement in the course. The accompanying instructor website, available through login .cengage.com, offers access to password-protected resources such as an electronic version of the instructor's manual, test bank files, and PowerPoint slides. CourseMate can be bundled with the student text. Contact your Cengage sales representative for information on getting access to CourseMate.

WebTutor™ helps you jump-start your course with customizable, rich, text-specific content within your Course Management System. Whether you want to Web-enable your class or put an entire course online, WebTutor delivers. WebTutor offers a wide array of resources, including access to the eBook, glossaries, flash cards, quizzes, videos, Try It Yourself activities, and more.

Acknowledgments

To begin the job of writing a textbook, a potential author needs self-confidence bordering on arrogance and, to complete it, the humility to accept criticism of favorite ideas and carefully written prose. A great many people provided helpful suggestions that made this a far better text than it would have been without them.

My acquisitions editor, Timothy Matray, has been very helpful and supportive throughout the preparation of this edition. I have been delighted to work with Arwen Petty, my developmental editor, who provided helpful, intelligent advice on everything from the big picture to the details. I thank them for their tireless help.

Nicole Richards and Casey Lozier supervised the supplements, a task that grows bigger with each edition. I greatly appreciate the detailed work of the copy editor at Graphic World Inc. Nicole Richards also secured numerous quality peer reviews and managed the test-item file. Cheryll Linthicum and Christy Frame did a marvelous job of supervising the production, a complicated task with a book such as this. Jennifer Wahi, the art director, and Jeanne Calabrese, who designed the cover and interior, had the patience and artistic judgment to counterbalance their very nonartistic author. Elisabeth Rhoden planned and executed the marketing strategies. Greg Piferi, the photo researcher, found wonderful photographs and managed the permissions requests. Pablo D'Stair researched and managed the text permissions requests. To each of these, my thanks and congratulations.

My wife, Jo Ellen Kalat, not only provided support and encouragement but also listened to my attempts to explain concepts and offered many helpful suggestions and questions. I thank my department head, Douglas Gillan, and my North Carolina State colleagues—especially David Martin—for their helpful suggestions.

Many reviewers provided helpful and insightful comments. I thank the following people: Rebecca Brand, Villanova University; Thomas Brothen, University of Minnesota; Carolyn Cohen, Northern Essex Community College; Alex Czopp, Western Washington University; Karen Douglas, San Antonio College–Alamo Colleges; Terry Trepper, Purdue University Calumet.

Each edition builds on contributions from reviewers of previous editions. I would also like to thank the following reviewers who contributed their insight to previous editions: Jennifer Ackil, Gustavus Adolphus College; Jeffrey Adams, Trent University; Judi Addelston, Valencia Community College; Mark Affeltranger, University of Pittsburgh; Catherine Anderson, Amherst College; Susan Anderson, University of South Alabama; Bob Arkin, Ohio State University; Melanie M. Arpaio, Sussex County Community College; Susan Baillet, University of Portland; Cynthia Bane, Denison University; Joe Bean, Shorter College; Mark Bodamer, John Carroll University; Richard W. Bowen, Loyola University Chicago; Michael Brislawn, Bellevue Community College; Delbert Brodie, St. Thomas University; John Broida, University of Southern Maine; Gordon Brow, Pasadena City College; Gregory Bushman, Beloit College; James Calhoun, University of Georgia; Bernardo Carducci, Indiana University Southeast; Thomas Carskadon, Mississippi State University; Mar Casteel, Pennsylvania State University, York Campus; Liz Coccia, Austin Community College; Karen Couture, Keene State College; Deana Davalos, Colorado State University; Patricia Deldin, Harvard University; Katherine Demitrakis, Albuquerque Technical Vocational Institute; Janet Dizinno, St. Mary University; Alicia M. Doerflinger, Marietta College; Kimberly Duff, Cerritos College; Darlene Earley-Hereford, Southern Union State Community College; David J. Echevarria, University of Southern Mississippi; Vanessa Edkins, University of Kansas; Susan Field, Georgian Court College; Deborah Frisch, University of Oregon; Gabriel Frommer, Indiana University; Rick Fry, Youngstown State University; Robe Gehring, University of Southern Indiana; Judy Gentry, Columbus State Community College; Anna L. Ghee, Xavier University; Bill P. Godsil, Santa Monica College; Kerri Goodwin, Loyola College in Maryland; Joel Grace, Mansfield University; Troianne Grayson, Florida Community College at Jacksonville; Joe Grisham, Indiana River

Community College; Julie A. Gurner, Quinnipiac University; Community College of Philadelphia; Alexandria E. Guzmán, University of New Haven; Richard Hanson, Fresno City College; Richard Harris, Kansas State University; Wendy Hart-Stravers, Arizona State University; W. Bruce Haslam, Weber State University; Christopher Hayashi, Southwestern College; Bert Hayslip, University of North Texas; Manda Helzer, Southern Oregon University; W. Elaine Hogan, University of North Carolina Wilmington; Debra Hollister, Valencia Community College; Susan Horton, Mesa Community College; Charles Huffman, James Madison University; Linda Jackson, Michigan State University; Alisha Janowsky, University of Central Florida; Robert Jensen, California State University, Sacramento; Andrew Johnson, Park University; James Johnson, Illinois State University; Craig Jones, Arkansas State University; Lisa Jordan, University of Maryland; Dale Jorgenson, California State University, Long Beach; Jon Kahane, Springfield College; Peter Kaplan, University of Colorado, Denver; Arthur Kemp, Central Missouri State University; Mark J. Kirschner, Quinnipiac University; Kristina T. Klassen, North Idaho College; Martha Kuehn, Central Lakes College; Cindy J. Lahar, University of Calgary; Chris Layne, University of Toledo; Cynthia Ann Lease, Virginia Polytechnic Institute and State University; Chantal Levesque, University of Rochester; John Lindsay, Georgia College and State University; Mary Livingston, Louisiana Technical University; Linda Lockwood, Metropolitan State College of Denver; Sanford Lopater, Christopher Newport University; Mark Ludorf, Stephen F. Austin State University; Jonathan Lytle, Temple University; Pamelyn M. MacDonald, Washburn University; Steve Madigan, University of Southern California; Don Marzoff, Louisiana State University; Christopher Mayhorn, North Carolina State University; Michael McCall, Ithaca College; David G. McDonald, University of Missouri; Tracy A. McDonough, College of Mount St. Joseph; J. Mark McKellop, Juniata College; Mary Meiners, San Diego Miramar College; Dianne Mello-Goldner, Pine Manor College; Nancy J. Melucci, Long Beach City College; Michelle Merwin, University of Tennessee at Martin; Rowland Miller, Sam Houston State University; Gloria Mitchell, De Anza College; Paul Moore, Quinnipiac University; Anne Moyer, Stony Brook University; Jeffrey Nagelbush, Ferris State University; Bethany Neal-Beliveau, Indiana University-Purdue University at Indianapolis; Todd Nelson, California State University, Stanislaus; Jan Ochman, Inver Hills Community College; Wendy Palmquist, Plymouth State College; Elizabeth Parks, Kennesaw State University; Gerald Peterson, Saginaw Valley State University; Brady Phelps, South Dakota State University; Shane Pitts, Birmingham Southern College; William Price, North Country Community College; Thomas Reig, Winona State University; David Reitman, Louisiana State University; Bridget Rivera, Loyola College in Maryland; Robert A. Rosellini, University at Albany; Jeffrey Rudski, Muhlenberg College; Linda Ruehlman, Arizona State University; Richard Russell, Santa Monica College; Mark Samuels, New Mexico Institute of Mining and Technology; Kim Sawrey, University of North Carolina at Wilmington; Troy Schiedenhelm, Rowan-Cabarrus Community College; Michele N. Shiota, University of California, Berkeley; Eileen Smith, Fairleigh Dickinson University; Noam Shpancer, Purdue University; James Spencer, West Virginia State College; Jim Stringham, University of Georgia; Robert Stawski, Syracuse University; Whitney Sweeney, Beloit College; Alan Swinkels, St. Edward's University; Natasha Tokowicz, University of Pittsburgh; Patricia Toney, Sandhills Community College; Warren W. Tryon, Fordham University; Katherine Urquhart, Lake Sumter Community College; Stavros Valenti, Hofstra University; Suzanne Valentine-French, College of Lake County; Douglas Wallen, Mankato State University; Michael Walraven, Jackson Community College; Donald Walter, University of Wisconsin–Parkside; Jeffrey Weatherly, University of North Dakota; Ellen Weissblum, State University of New York Albany; Fred Whitford, Montana State University; Don Wilson, Lane Community College; David Woehr, Texas A&M University; Jay Wright, Washington State University; John W. Wright, Washington State University.

James W. Kalat

Welcome to introductory psychology! I hope you will enjoy reading this text as much as I enjoyed writing it. I have tried to make this book interesting and as easy to study as possible.

Features of This Text

Modular Format

Each chapter is divided into two or more modules so that you can study a limited section at a time. Each chapter begins with a table of contents to orient you to the topics considered. At the end of each module is a list of key terms and a summary of important points, each with page references. At the end of a chapter, you will find suggestions for further reading, suggested Internet sites, and other suggestions.

Key Terms

When an important term first appears in the text, it is highlighted in **boldface** and defined in *italics*. All the boldface terms are listed alphabetically at the end of each module. They appear again with definitions in the combined Subject Index and Glossary at the end of the book. You might want to find the Subject Index and Glossary right now and familiarize yourself with it. You can also consult or download a list of key terms with their definitions from Psychology CourseMate.

I sometimes meet students who think they have mastered the course because they have memorized the definitions. You do need to understand the defined words, but don't memorize the definitions word for word. It would be better to try to use each word in a sentence or think of examples of each term. Better yet, when appropriate, think of evidence for or against the concept that the term represents.

Questions to Check Your Understanding

People remember material better if they alternate between reading and testing than if they spend the whole time reading. (We'll consider that point again in the chapter on memory.) At various points in this text are Concept Checks, questions that ask you to use or apply the information you just read. Try to answer each of them before reading the answer. If your answer is correct, you can feel encouraged. If it is incorrect, you should reread the section.

Try It Yourself Activities

The text includes many items marked Try It Yourself. Most of these can be done quickly with little or no equipment. Online Try It Yourself activities are also available at Psychology CourseMate. These are like the Try It Yourself activities in the text, except that they include sounds and motion. The description of a psychological principle will be easier to understand and remember after you have experienced it yourself.

What's the Evidence? Sections

Every chapter except the first includes a section titled What's the Evidence? These sections highlight research studies in more detail, specifying the hypothesis (idea being tested), research methods, results, and interpretation. In some cases, the discussion also mentions the limitations of the study. These sections provide examples of how to evaluate evidence.

CourseMate

The Psychology CourseMate can be accessed through http://www.cengagebrain.com. CourseMate includes an integrated eBook, glossaries, flash cards, quizzes, videos, Try It Yourself activities, and more. All of these opportunities are highly recommended.

Indexes and Reference List

A section at the back of the book lists the references cited in the text in case you want to check something for more details. The combined Subject Index and Glossary defines key terms and indicates where in the book to find more information. The name index provides the same information for all names mentioned in the text.

Answers to Some Frequently Asked Questions

Do you have any useful suggestions for improving study habits? Whenever students ask me why they did badly on the last test, I ask, "When did you read the assignment?" Many answer that they read it the night before the test. If you want to learn the subject matter well, read the assigned material before the lecture, review it again after the lecture, and quickly go over it again a few days later. Then reread the textbook assignments and your lecture notes before a test. Memory researchers have established that you will understand and remember something better by studying it several times spread out over days than by studying the same amount of time all at once. Also, of course, the more total time you spend studying, the better.

When you study, don't just read the text but stop and think about it. The more actively you use the material, the better you will remember it. One way to improve your studying is to read by the SPAR method: **S**urvey, **P**rocess meaningfully, **A**sk questions, **R**eview.

Survey: Know what to expect so that you can focus on the main points. When you start a chapter, first look over the outline to get a preview of the contents. When you start a new module, turn to the end and read the summary.

Process meaningfully: Read the chapter carefully, stopping to think from time to time. Tell your roommate something you learned. Think about how you might apply a concept to a real-life situation. Pause when you come to the Concept Checks and try to answer them. Do the Try It Yourself exercises. Try to monitor how well you understand the text and adjust your reading accordingly. Good readers read quickly through easy, familiar content but slowly through difficult material.

Ask questions: When you finish the chapter, try to anticipate what questions your instructor would ask on a test. What questions would you ask, if you were the professor? Write out the questions, think about them, and hold them for later.

Review: Pause for at least an hour, preferably a day. Now return to your questions and try to answer them. Check your answers against the text. Reinforcing your memory a day or two after you first read the chapter will help you retain the material longer and deepen your understanding. If you study the same material several times at lengthy intervals, you increase your chance of remembering it long after the course is over.

What do those parentheses mean, as in "(Williams & Bargh, 2008)"? Am I supposed to remember the names and dates? Psychologists generally cite references in the text in parentheses rather than in footnotes. "(Williams & Bargh, 2008)" refers to an article written by Williams and Bargh, published in 2008. All the references cited in the text are listed in alphabetical order (by the author's last name) in the References section at the back of the book.

You will also notice a few citations that include two dates separated by a slash, such as "(Wundt, 1862/1961)." This means that Wundt's document was originally published in 1862 and was republished in 1961.

No, you should not memorize the parenthetical source citations. They are provided so an interested reader can look up the source of a statement and check for further information. The names that *are* worth remembering, such as B. F. Skinner, Jean Piaget, and Sigmund Freud, are emphasized in the discussion itself.

Can you help me read and understand graphs?
You will encounter four kinds of graphs in this text: pie graphs, bar graphs, line graphs, and scatter plots. Let's look at each kind.

A pie graph shows the components of a whole. Figure 1 shows the proportion of psychologists who work in various settings. It shows that many are self-employed, almost as many work in colleges and other educational institutions, and a slightly smaller number work in hospitals and other health-care institutions.

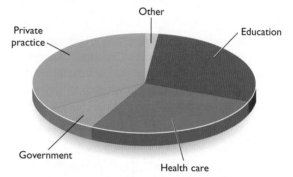

Figure 1

Bar graphs show measurements for two or more groups. Figure 2 shows how much unpleasantness three groups of women reported while they were waiting for a painful shock. The unpleasantness was least if a woman could hold her husband's hand while waiting, intermediate if she held a stranger's hand, and most if she was by herself.

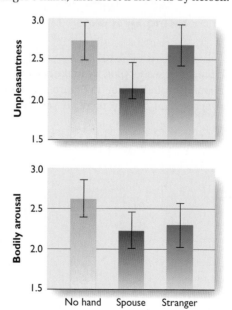

Figure 2

Line graphs show how one variable relates to another variable. Figure 3 shows measurements of conscientiousness in people from age 10 to 80. The upward slope of the line indicates that older people tend to be more conscientious than younger people, on average.

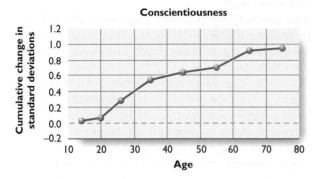

Conscientiousness

Figure 3

Scatter plots are similar to line graphs, with this difference: A line graph shows averages, whereas a scatter plot shows individual data points. By looking at a scatter plot, we can see how much variation occurs among individuals.

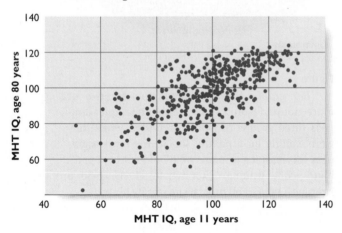

Figure 4

To prepare a scatter plot, we make two observations about each individual. In Figure 4, each person is represented by one point. If you take that point and scan down to the *x*-axis, you find that person's score on an IQ test at age 11. If you then scan across to the *y*-axis, you find that person's score on a similar test at age 80. You can see about how consistent most people's scores are over a lifetime.

We may have to take multiple-choice tests on this material. How can I do better on those tests?

1. Read each choice carefully. Do not choose the first answer that looks correct; first make sure that the other answers are wrong. If two answers fit with what you know, decide which of the two is better.

2. If you don't know the correct answer, make an educated guess. Eliminate answers that are clearly wrong. An answer that includes absolute words such as always or never is probably wrong. Also eliminate any answer that includes unfamiliar terms. If you have never heard of something, it is probably not the right answer. Remember, every test question is about something presented either in lecture or in the text.

3. After you finish, don't be afraid to go back and reconsider your answers. Students have been telling each other for decades that "you should stick with your first answer," but research says that most people who change their answers improve their scores. When you examine a question a second time, you sometimes discover that you misunderstood it the first time.

Last Words Before We Start . . .

Most of all, I hope you enjoy the text. I have tried to include the liveliest examples I can find. The goal is not just to teach you some facts but also to teach you a love of learning so that you will continue to read more and educate yourself about psychology long after your course is over.

James W. Kalat

1

tockphoto/kryczka

What Is Psychology?

If you are like most students, you start off assuming that nearly everything you read in your textbooks and everything your professors tell you must be true. What if it isn't? Suppose impostors have replaced your college's faculty. They pretend to know what they are talking about and they all vouch for one another's competence, but in fact, they are all unqualified. They managed to find textbooks that support their prejudices, but those textbooks are full of false information, too. If so, how would you know?

While we are entertaining such skeptical thoughts, why limit ourselves to colleges? When you read books and magazines or listen to political commentators, how do you know who has the right answers?

No one has the right answers all of the time. Professors, textbook authors, advice columnists, politicians, and others have strong reasons for some beliefs and weak reasons for others. Sometimes even the best and

Even when the people we trust seem very confident of their opinions, we should examine their evidence or reasoning.

most conscientious individuals discover to their embarrassment that a confident opinion was wrong. I don't mean to imply that you should disregard everything you read or hear. But you should expect people to tell you the reasons for their conclusions so that you can distinguish between an idea that is nearly certain and one that is little more than a guess.

You have just encountered the theme of this book: Evaluate the evidence. You will hear all sorts of claims concerning psychology, as well as medicine, politics, and other fields. Some are valid, others are wrong, many are valid under certain conditions, and some are too vague to be either right or wrong. When you finish this book, you will be in a better position to examine evidence and decide which claims to take seriously.

Psychologists' Goals

- What is psychology?
- What philosophical questions motivate psychologists?
- What do various kinds of psychologists do?
- Should you consider majoring in psychology?

Your history text probably doesn't spend much time discussing what the term *history* means, and I doubt that a course on English literature spends the first day defining literature. Psychology is different because so many people have misconceptions about this field. I remember a student who asked when we would get to the kind of psychology he could "use on" people. Another young man bluntly asked me (in my office, not publicly) whether I could teach him tricks to seduce his girlfriend. I told him that (a) psychologists don't try to trick people into doing something against their better judgment, (b) if I did know tricks like that, ethically I couldn't tell him about them, and (c) if I knew powerful tricks to control behavior *and* I had no ethics, I would probably use those powers for my own profit instead of teaching introduction to psychology!

The term *psychology* derives from the Greek roots *psyche*, meaning "soul" or "mind," and *logos*, meaning "word." Psychology is literally the study of the mind or soul, and people defined it that way until the early 1900s. Around 1920, psychologists became disenchanted with the idea of studying the mind. First, research deals with what we observe, and mind is unobservable. Second, talking about "the mind" implies it is a thing or object. Mental activity is a process. It is not like the river but like the flow of the river; not like the automobile but like the movement of the automobile. Beginning in the early 1900s, psychologists defined their field as the study of behavior.

Certainly the study of behavior is important, but is behavior all that we care about? When you look at this optical illusion and say that the horizontal part of the top line looks longer than that of the bottom line (although really they are the same length), we wonder why the line *looks* longer, not just why you *said* it looks longer. So as a compromise, let's define psychology as *the systematic study of behavior and experience*. The word *experience* lets us discuss your perceptions without implying that a mind exists independently of your body.

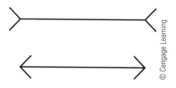

When most people think of psychologists, they think of clinical psychologists—those who try to help worried, depressed, or otherwise troubled people. Clinical psychology is only one part of psychology. Psychology also includes research on sensation and perception, learning and memory, hunger and thirst, sleep, attention, child development, and more. Perhaps you expect that a course in psychology will teach you to "analyze" people and decipher hidden aspects of their personality. It will not. You will learn to understand many aspects of behavior, but you will gain no dazzling powers. Ideally, you will become more skeptical of those who claim to analyze people's personality from small samples of their behavior.

General Points About Psychology

Let's start with three of the most general statements about psychology. Each of these will arise repeatedly throughout this text.

It Depends

Hardly anything is true about the psychology of all people all the time. Almost every aspect of behavior depends on age, for example. Infants differ from children, who differ from young adults, who differ from older adults. Behavior also varies with people's genetics, health, past experiences, and whether they are currently awake or asleep. In some ways, behavior differs between males and females or from one culture to another. Some aspects depend on the time of day, the temperature of the room, or how recently someone ate. How a person answers a question depends on the exact wording of the question, the wording of the previous question, and who is asking the questions.

If psychology regards "it depends" as a general truth, you may infer that psychology really doesn't know anything. On the contrary, "it depends" is a serious point. The key is to know *what* it depends on. The further you pursue your studies of psychology, the more you will become attuned to the wealth of subtle influences that most people overlook. For example, suppose you are about to take a test. At the top of the test, the instructor has put the instructions in bright red letters to make sure students read them. What will be the result? One result is that the students' test scores will be lower than usual! Ever since you started school, your teachers have been marking your errors with red ink. Just seeing red ink at the top of a test reminds you of times when you did badly, and that bit of discouragement may interfere with your performance. Even a small red letter or number at the top of a test slightly impairs students' performance, on average (Elliot, Maier, Moller, Friedman, & Meinhardt, 2007).

For another example of "it depends," imagine yourself in this study: A psychologist meets you on the bottom floor of a building, thanks you for agree-

If you're holding a hot cup, you tend to rate other people's personality as warm. Your ratings go the opposite way if you're holding a cold cup. We often overlook factors such as these that subtly influence our thinking and behavior.

ing to participate in her research study, and escorts you to the elevator to go to the top floor, where she has her lab. As you ride up the elevator, she asks you to hold her cup of coffee while she asks you a couple of questions about yourself and fills in the answers on her clipboard. When you reach the laboratory, your task is to read a brief description of a person and then rate that person's personality along several dimensions, such as intelligence, sense of humor, imagination, and warmth. Here, the key factor was the temperature of the coffee cup you held briefly while riding up the elevator. If it was a hot cup of coffee, you are more likely to rate this person as "warm." If it was a cold cup, you are more likely to rate the person as "cold" (Williams & Bargh, 2008). Naturally, you are unaware that holding the cup influenced you at all. Much of psychology attempts to identify the subtle, easily ignored factors that influence your actions.

Accurate Measurement Is Key

Nobel Prize–winning biologist Sidney Brenner was quoted as saying, "Progress in science depends on new techniques, new discoveries, and new ideas, probably in that order" (McElheny, 2004, p. 71). In any field, from astronomy to zoology, new discoveries and ideas depend on good measurements. Psychologists' understanding has advanced fastest on topics such as sensory processes, learning, and memory, which researchers can measure fairly easily and accurately. For example, research on the best ways to study requires good measures of how much people remember, and psychologists have developed many ways of taking those measurements.

Research progress has been slower in areas where we struggle to find clear definitions and accurate measurements. What is emotion? What is personality? Could you measure love? Psychologists have some interesting and important things to say about these topics, but the research progress is limited by the difficulty of measurement.

Confidence in the Conclusions Depends on the Strength of the Research

Is it all right for young children to spend hours a day watching television? How much is too much? Is it sometimes all right to spank a child? What should be the limits, if any, on teenagers playing violent video games? To what extent do the behavioral differences between men and women reflect biological influences? You probably have opinions on these questions, even if you don't know of any scientific evidence to support your opinions. Similarly, many psychologists have strong opinions on these and other issues. They might be able to cite some research support, but frankly, many of them hold more confident opinions than the data support. It is important to distinguish between opinions based on conclusive evidence and those based on less. When this text describes research studies in some detail, the reason is to give you an idea of how strong the research evidence is (or isn't) behind some conclusion.

Major Philosophical Issues in Psychology

Psychology began in the late 1800s as an attempt to apply scientific methods to the questions of philosophy of mind. Three of the most profound philosophical questions related to psychology are free will versus determinism, the mind–brain problem, and the nature–nurture issue.

Free Will Versus Determinism

The scientific approach to anything, including psychology, assumes that we live in a universe of cause and effect. If things "just happen" for no reason at all, then we have no hope of discovering scientific principles. That is, scientists assume determinism, *the idea that every event has a cause, or determinant, that one could observe or measure.* This view is an assumption, not an established fact, but the success of scientific research attests to its value.

Does it apply to human behavior? We are, after all, part of the physical world. According to the determinist assumption, everything we do has causes. This view seems to conflict with the impression all of us have that "*I* make the decisions about my actions. Sometimes, when I am deciding what to eat for lunch or which sweater to buy, I am in doubt right up to the last second. The decision could have gone either way." *The belief that behavior is caused by a person's independent decisions* is known as free will. This impression, right or wrong, is a strong one (Nichols, 2011). Do you think your behavior is predictable? How about other people's behavior? Questionnaires show that most people think their own behavior is less predictable than other people's. That is, you think you have free will, but other people, not so much (Pronin & Kugler, 2010).

Some psychologists maintain that free will is an illusion (Wegner, 2002): What you call a conscious intention is more a prediction than a cause of your

Behavior is guided by external forces, such as waves, and by forces within the individual. According to the determinist view, even those internal forces follow physical laws.

behavior. When you have the experience of deciding to move a finger, the behavior is already starting to happen. We shall explore the evidence for this idea later, in the module on consciousness.

Other psychologists and philosophers reply that you do make decisions, in the sense that something within you initiates the action (Baumeister, 2008). When a ball bounces down a hill, its motion depends on the shape of the hill. When you run down a hill, you could change direction if you saw a car coming toward you, or a snake lying in your path. The ball could not.

Nevertheless, the "you" that makes your decisions is itself a product of your heredity and the events of your life. (You did not create yourself.) In a sense, yes, you have a will, an ability to make choices. But your will is the product of your heredity and experiences. It did not emerge from nothing.

The test of determinism is ultimately empirical: If everything you do has a cause, your behavior should be predictable. Behavior is clearly predictable in some cases, such as reflexes. However, ordinarily psychologists' predictions are more like predicting the weather. The predictions are nearly accurate most of the time, but they can't be accurate in every detail, simply because so many small influences are operating.

Researchers admit one point: Although determinism makes sense theoretically and leads to good research, it doesn't work well as a philosophy of life. One study provides a good illustration of this point: Psychologists asked people to read one of two passages. Some read an argument for determinism, and others read a paper on an irrelevant topic. The study subjects were then put in a situation in which it would be easy to "cheat" to gain a personal advantage. A higher percentage of those who had read the determinism essay cheated (Vohs & Schooler, 2008). Apparently, they felt less sense of personal responsibility.

The Mind–Brain Problem

Given that we live in a universe of matter and energy, what, if anything, is the mind? And why does consciousness exist? The *philosophical question of how experience relates to the brain* is the mind–brain problem (or mind–body problem). One view, called dualism, holds that *the mind is separate from the brain but somehow controls the brain and therefore*

Why do different children develop different interests? They had different hereditary tendencies, but they also had different experiences. Separating the roles of nature and nurture is difficult.

Figure 1.1 These PET scans show the brain activity of normal people during different activities. Red indicates the highest activity, followed by yellow, green, and blue. Arrows indicate the most active areas.

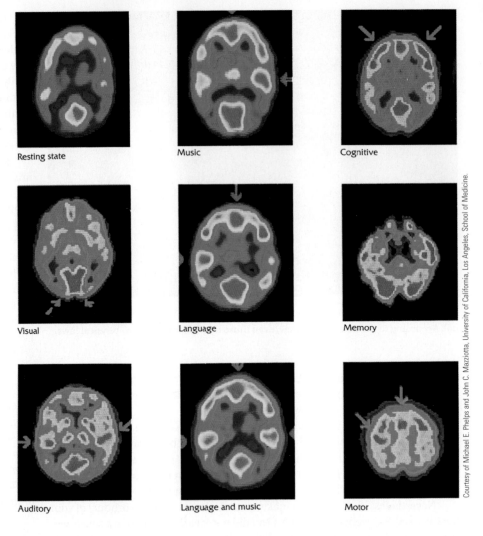

Resting state

Music

Cognitive

Visual

Language

Memory

Auditory

Language and music

Motor

Courtesy of Michael E. Phelps and John C. Mazziotta, University of California, Los Angeles, School of Medicine.

the rest of the body. However, dualism contradicts the law of conservation of matter and energy, one of the cornerstones of physics. According to that principle, the only way to influence any matter or energy, including the matter and energy that compose your body, is to act on it with other matter or energy. If the mind isn't composed of matter or energy, it can't *do* anything. For that reason, nearly all brain researchers and philosophers favor monism, *the view that conscious experience is inseparable from the physical brain.* That is, mental activity *is* brain activity. So far as we can tell, consciousness can't exist without brain activity, and it is presumably also true that certain kinds of brain activity can't exist without consciousness. The mind–brain problem inspires much research, some of which we shall consider in chapter 3 on the brain and chapter 10 on consciousness.

The photos in Figure 1.1 show brain activity while a person was engaged in nine tasks, as measured by a technique called positron-emission tomography (PET). Red indicates the highest degree of brain activity, followed by yellow, green, and blue.

As you can see, the various tasks increased activity in different brain areas, although all areas showed some activity at all times (Phelps & Mazziotta, 1985). You might ask: Did the brain activity cause the thoughts, or did the thoughts cause the brain activity? Most brain researchers reply, "Neither," because brain activity and mental activity are the same thing.

Even if we accept this position, we are still far from understanding the mind–brain relationship. What type of brain activity is associated with consciousness? Why does conscious experience exist at all? Could a brain get along without conscious experience? In the search for answers to these questions, research studies are not about to put philosophers out of business, but results do constrain the philosophical answers that we can seriously consider.

The Nature–Nurture Issue

Why do most little boys spend more time than little girls with toy guns and trucks and less time with dolls? Is it because of biological differences or because parents rear their sons and daughters differently?

Alcohol abuse is common in some cultures and rare in others. Are these differences entirely a matter of social custom, or do genes influence alcohol use also?

Certain psychological disorders are more common in large cities than in small towns and in the countryside. Does life in crowded cities cause psychological disorders? Or do people develop such disorders because of a genetic predisposition and then move to big cities in search of jobs, housing, and welfare services?

Each of these questions relates to the nature–nurture issue (or heredity-environment issue): *How do differences in behavior relate to differences in heredity and environment?* The nature–nurture issue shows up in various ways throughout psychology, and it seldom has a simple answer. Sometimes the answer is a complex version of "it depends": Hereditary differences might make a big difference for people in one environment and less difference in another.

concept check

1. In what way does all scientific research presuppose determinism?
2. What is one major objection to dualism?

Answers

2. Dualism conflicts with the principle of the conservation of matter and energy. A nonmaterial mind could not influence anything in the universe.

1. We could not discover scientific laws and principles if we did not live in a universe of cause and effect.

What Psychologists Do

We have considered some major philosophical issues related to psychology in general. However, most psychologists deal with smaller, more manageable questions. They work in many occupational settings, as shown in Figure 1.2. The most common settings are colleges and universities, private practice, hospitals and mental health clinics, and government agencies.

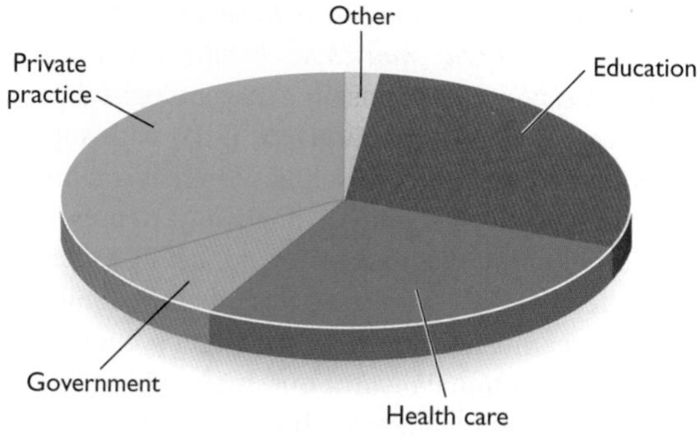

Service Providers to Individuals

It is important to distinguish among several types of mental health professionals. Some of the main kinds of service providers for people with psychological troubles are clinical psychologists, psychiatrists, social workers, and counseling psychologists.

Clinical Psychology

Clinical psychologists *have an advanced degree in psychology (master's degree, PhD, or PsyD), with a specialty in understanding and helping people with psychological problems.* Those problems range from depression, anxiety, and substance abuse to marriage conflicts, difficulties making decisions, or even the feeling that "I should be getting more out of life." Clinical psychologists try, in one way or another, to understand why a person is having problems and then help that person overcome the difficulties. Some clinical psychologists are college professors and researchers, but most are full-time practitioners.

Psychiatry

Psychiatry is a *branch of medicine that deals with emotional disturbances.* To become a psychiatrist, someone first earns an MD degree and then takes an additional 4 years of residency training in psychiatry. Because psychiatrists are medical doctors, they can prescribe drugs, such as tranquilizers and antidepressants, whereas most psychologists cannot. In the United States, a few states now permit psychologists with a couple years of additional training to prescribe drugs (Fox et al., 2009). More psychiatrists than clinical psychologists work in mental hospitals, and psychiatrists more often treat clients with severe disorders.

Figure 1.2 Psychologists work in a variety of settings. (Based on data from U.S. Department of Labor, 2008.)

Does psychiatrists' ability to prescribe drugs give them an advantage over psychologists in places where psychologists cannot prescribe them? Not always. Drugs can be useful, but relying entirely on them can be a mistake. Whereas a typical visit to a clinical psychologist includes an extensive discussion of the client's troubles, many visits to a psychiatrist focus mainly on checking the effectiveness of a drug and evaluating its side effects. A survey found that over the years, fewer and fewer psychiatrists have been providing talk therapy (Mojtabai & Olfson, 2008).

Other Mental Health Professionals

Several other kinds of professionals also provide help and counsel. Psychoanalysts are *therapy providers who rely heavily on the theories and methods pioneered by the early twentieth-century Viennese physician Sigmund Freud and later modified by others.* Freud and his followers attempted to infer the hidden, unconscious, symbolic meaning behind people's words and actions, and psychoanalysts today continue that effort.

There is some question about who may rightly call themselves psychoanalysts. Some people apply the term to anyone who attempts to uncover unconscious thoughts and feelings. Others apply the term only to graduates of a 6- to 8-year program at an institute of psychoanalysis. These institutes admit only people who are already either psychiatrists or clinical psychologists. (Do you see why you will never meet a *young* psychoanalyst?)

A clinical social worker *is similar to a clinical psychologist but with different training.* In most cases, a clinical social worker has a master's degree in social work with a specialization in psychological problems. Many health maintenance organizations (HMOs) steer most of their clients with psychological problems toward clinical social workers instead of psychologists or psychiatrists because the social workers, with less formal education, charge less per hour. Some psychiatric nurses (nurses with additional training in psychiatry) provide similar services.

Counseling psychologists *help people with educational, vocational, marriage, health-related, and other decisions.* A counseling psychologist has a doctorate degree (PhD, PsyD, or EdD) with supervised experience in counseling. Whereas a clinical psychologist deals mainly with anxiety, depression, and other emotional distress, a counseling psychologist deals mostly with life decisions and family or career readjustments. Counseling psychologists work in educational institutions, mental health centers, rehabilitation agencies, businesses, and private practice.

You may also have heard of forensic psychologists, *who provide advice and consultation to police, lawyers, and courts.* Forensic psychologists are clinical or counseling psychologists with additional training in legal issues. They advise on such decisions as whether a defendant is mentally competent to stand trial or whether someone eligible for parole is dangerous (Otto & Heilbrun, 2002). Several popular films and television series have depicted forensic psychologists helping police investigators develop a psychological profile of a serial killer. That may sound like an exciting, glamorous profession, but few psychologists engage in such activities (and the accuracy of their profiles is uncertain, as discussed in chapter 14). Most criminal profilers today have training and experience in law enforcement, not psychology.

Table 1.1 compares various types of mental health professionals.

Table 1.1 Mental Health Professionals

Type of Therapist	Education
Clinical psychologist	PhD with clinical emphasis or PsyD plus internship. Ordinarily, 5+ years after undergraduate degree.
Psychiatrist	MD plus psychiatric residency. Total of 8 years after undergraduate degree.
Psychoanalyst	Psychiatry or clinical psychology plus 6–8 years in a psychoanalytic institute. Many others who rely on Freudian methods also call themselves psychoanalysts.
Psychiatric nurse	From 2-year (AA) degree to master's degree plus supervised experience.
Clinical social worker	Master's degree plus 2 years of supervised experience. Total of at least 4 years after undergraduate degree.
Counseling psychologist	PhD, PsyD, or EdD plus supervised experience in counseling.
Forensic psychologist	Doctorate, ordinarily in clinical psychology or counseling psychology, plus additional training in legal issues.

© Cengage Learning

concept check

3. Can psychoanalysts prescribe drugs?

Answer

3. Psychoanalysts have a degree in either psychiatry or clinical psychology. Those trained in psychiatry can prescribe drugs because psychiatrists are medical doctors. However, in most states, psychoanalysts trained in clinical psychology cannot prescribe drugs.

Service Providers to Organizations

Psychologists also work in business, industry, and school systems, doing work you might not recognize as psychology. The job prospects in these fields have been good, and you might find these fields interesting.

Industrial/Organizational Psychology

The psychological study of people at work is known as industrial/organizational (I/O) psychology. This field deals with such issues as hiring the right person for a job, training people for jobs, developing work teams, determining salaries and bonuses, providing feedback to workers about their performance, planning an organizational structure, and organizing the workplace so that workers will be productive and satisfied. I/O psychologists attend to both the individual worker and the organization, including the impact of economic conditions and government regulations. We consider work motivation in chapter 11.

Here's an example of a concern for industrial/organizational psychologists (Campion & Thayer, 1989): A company that manufactures electronic equipment needed to publish reference and repair manuals for its products. The engineers who designed the devices did not want to spend their time writing the manuals, so the company hired a technical writer to prepare the manuals. After a year, she received an unsatisfactory performance rating because the manuals she wrote contained too many technical errors. She countered that, when she asked engineers in the company to explain technical details to her, they were always too busy. She found her job complicated and frustrating. Her office was badly lit, noisy, and overheated, and her chair was uncomfortable. Whenever she mentioned these problems, she was told that she "complained too much."

In a situation such as this, an industrial/organizational psychologist helps the company evaluate its options. One solution would be to fire her and hire an expert on electrical engineering who is also an outstanding writer who tolerates a badly lit, noisy, overheated, uncomfortable office. However, if the company cannot find or afford such a person, then it needs to improve the working conditions and provide the current employee with more training and help.

Human Factors Specialists

Learning to operate our increasingly complex machinery is one of the struggles of modern life. Sometimes, the consequences are serious. Imagine an airplane pilot who raises the wing flaps instead of lowering the landing gear, or a worker in a nuclear power plant who overlooks a warning signal. A type of psychologist known as a **human factors specialist** (or **ergonomist**) *tries to facilitate the operation of machinery so that ordinary people can use it efficiently and safely.* Human factors specialists first worked in military settings, where complex technologies sometimes require soldiers to spot nearly invisible targets, understand speech through deafening noise, track objects in three dimensions, and make life-or-death decisions in a split second. The military turned to psychologists to redesign the tasks to fit the skills that their personnel could master.

Human factors specialists soon applied their expertise to the design of everyday devices, such as cameras, computers, microwave ovens, and cell phones. The field combines features of psychology, engineering, and computer science. It is a growing field with many jobs available.

School Psychology

Many if not most children have school problems at one time or another. Some children have trouble sitting still or paying attention. Others get into trouble for misbehavior. Some have problems with reading or other academic skills. Others master their schoolwork quickly and become bored. They too need special attention.

School psychologists are *specialists in the psychological condition of students,* usually in kindergarten through the 12th grade. School psychologists identify children's educational needs, devise a plan to meet those needs, and then either implement the plan themselves or advise teachers how to implement it.

School psychology can be taught in a psychology department, an education department, or a department of educational psychology. In some countries, it is possible to practice school psychology with only a bachelor's degree. In the United States, the minimum education requirement for a school psychologist is

Human factors specialists help redesign machines to make them easier and safer to use. This field uses principles of both engineering and psychology.

usually a master's degree, but a doctorate may become necessary in the future. Most school psychologists work for a school system, but some work for mental health clinics, guidance centers, and other institutions.

Psychologists in Teaching and Research

Many psychologists, especially those who are not clinical psychologists, teach and conduct research in colleges and universities. To some extent, different kinds of psychologists study different topics. For example, developmental psychologists observe children, and biological psychologists examine the effects of brain damage. However, different kinds of psychologists also sometimes study the same questions, approaching them in different ways. To illustrate, let's consider one example: how we select what to eat. Different kinds of psychologists offer different explanations.

Developmental Psychology

Developmental psychologists *study how behavior changes with age,* "from womb to tomb." For example, they might examine language development from age 2 to 4 or memory from age 60 to 80, both describing the changes and trying to explain them.

With regard to food selection, some taste preferences are present from birth. Newborns prefer sweet tastes and avoid bitter and sour substances. However, they appear indifferent to salty tastes, as if they could not yet taste salts (Beauchamp, Cowart, Mennella, & Marsh, 1994). Toddlers will try to eat almost anything they can fit into their mouths, unless it tastes sour or bitter. For that reason, parents need to keep dangerous substances like furniture polish out of toddlers' reach. Older children become increasingly selective about the foods they accept, but up to age 7 or 8, usually the only reason children give for refusing something is that they think it would taste bad (Rozin, Fallon, & Augustoni-Ziskind, 1986). As they grow older, they cite more complex reasons for rejecting foods, such as health concerns.

Learning and Motivation

The research field of **learning and motivation** studies *how behavior depends on the outcomes of past behaviors and current motivations.* How often we engage in any particular behavior depends on the results of that behavior in the past.

We learn our food choices largely by learning what *not* to eat. For example, if you eat something and then feel sick, you form an aversion to the taste of that food, especially if it was unfamiliar. It doesn't matter whether you consciously think the food

Infants and young children will try to eat almost anything that tastes okay. As they grow older, they begin to avoid foods for reasons other than taste.

If you ate corn dogs and cotton candy and then got sick on a wild ride, something in your brain would blame the food, regardless of what you think consciously. This kind of learning helps us avoid harmful substances.

made you ill. If you eat something at an amusement park and then go on a wild ride and get sick, you may dislike that food, even though you know the ride was at fault. Chapter 6 discusses this point in more detail.

Cognitive Psychology

Cognition refers to *thought and knowledge*. A cognitive psychologist *studies those processes*. (The root *cogn-* also shows up in the word *recognize*, which literally means "to know again.") Typically, cognitive psychologists focus on how people make decisions, solve problems, and convert their thoughts into language. These psychologists study both the best (expert decision making) and the worst (why people make costly errors) of human cognition.

Most cognitive psychologists don't study anything related to food selection, but cognitions about food do enter into our food decisions. For example, people often refuse an edible food just because of the very idea of it (Rozin & Fallon, 1987; Rozin, Millman, & Nemeroff, 1986). Most people in the United States refuse to eat meat from dogs, cats, or horses. Vegetarians reject all meat, not because they think it would taste bad, but because they dislike the idea of eating animal parts. The longer people have been vegetarians, the more firmly they tend to regard meat eating as wrong (Rozin, Markwith, & Stoess, 1997).

How would you like to try the tasty morsels in Figure 1.3? Most people in North America are repulsed by the idea of eating insects or reptiles, even if they are germ-free (Rozin & Fallon, 1987). Would you be willing to drink a glass of apple juice after you watched someone dip a cockroach into it? What if the cockroach was carefully sterilized? Some people not only refuse to drink that cockroach-violated glass of apple juice but also say they have lost their taste for apple juice in general (Rozin et al., 1986).

Biological Psychology

A biopsychologist (or behavioral neuroscientist) *explains behavior in terms of biological factors, such as activities of the nervous system, the effects of drugs and hormones, genetics, and evolutionary pressures*. How would a biological psychologist approach the question of how people (or animals) select foods?

A small part of the difference among people in their taste preferences relates to the fact that some people have up to three times as many taste buds as others do, mostly for genetic reasons. The genes vary within each population, but the relative frequencies of strong tasters and weak tasters are fairly similar for Asia, Europe, and Africa (Wooding et al., 2004). People with the most taste buds usually have the least tolerance for strong tastes, including black coffee, black breads, hot peppers, grapefruit, radishes, and Brussels sprouts (Bartoshuk, Duffy, Lucchina, Prutkin, & Fast, 1998; Drewnowski, Henderson, Shore, & Barratt-Fornell, 1998). Most of them also dislike foods that are too sweet (Yeomans, Tepper, Rietzschel, & Prescott, 2007).

Hormones also affect taste preferences. Many years ago, there was a case in which a child showed a strong craving for salt. As an infant, he licked the salt off crackers and bacon without eating the food itself. He put a thick layer of salt on everything he ate. Sometimes he swallowed salt directly from the shaker. When deprived of salt, he stopped eating and began to waste away. At the age of 3½, he was taken to the hospital and fed the usual hospital fare. He soon died of salt deficiency (Wilkins & Richter, 1940).

The reason was that he had defective adrenal glands, which secrete the hormones that enable the body to retain salt (Verrey & Beron, 1996). He craved salt because he had to consume it fast enough to replace what he lost in his urine. (Too much salt is bad for your health, but too little salt is also dangerous.) Later research confirmed that salt-deficient animals immediately show an in-

Figure 1.3 Different cultures have different food taboos. Here is an assortment of insect and reptile dishes—maybe not your idea of tasty treats, but delicacies elsewhere in the world.

Cassava, a root vegetable native to South America, is now a staple food in much of Africa as well. It grows in climates not suitable for most other crops. However, people must pound and wash it for days to remove the cyanide.

creased preference for salty tastes (Rozin & Kalat, 1971). Becoming salt deficient causes salty foods to taste especially good (Jacobs, Mark, & Scott, 1988). People often report salt cravings after losing salt by bleeding or sweating, and many women crave salt during menstruation or pregnancy.

Evolutionary Psychology

An evolutionary psychologist *tries to explain behavior in terms of the evolutionary history of the species, including why evolution might have favored a tendency to act in particular ways.* For example, *why* do people and other animals crave sweets and avoid bitter tastes? Here, the answer is easy: Most sweets are nutritious and almost all bitter substances are poisonous (T. R. Scott & Verhagen, 2000). Ancient animals that ate fruits and other sweets survived to become our ancestors.

However, although some evolutionary explanations of behavior are persuasive, others are debatable (de Waal, 2002). Yes, the brain is the product of evolution, just as any other organ is, but the question is whether evolution has micromanaged our behavior. For example, men are more likely than women are to seek multiple sexual partners. Does that tendency reflect an evolutionary predisposition, as some evolutionary psychologists argue, or is it a custom that people learn? The research challenge is to separate the evolutionary influences on our behavior from what we have learned during a lifetime. Chapter 3 discusses this issue in more detail.

Social Psychology and Cross-Cultural Psychology

Social psychologists *study how an individual influences other people and how the group influences an individual.* For example, people usually eat together, and on the average we eat about twice as much when we are in a large group than we do when eating alone (de Castro, 2000). If you invite guests to your house, you offer them something to eat or drink as a way to strengthen a social relationship. Cross-cultural psychology *compares the behavior of people from different cultures.* Interests of cross-cultural psychologists overlap those of social psychologists, except that cross-cultural psychologists compare one culture to another. Comparing people from different cultures is central to determining what is truly characteristic of humans and what varies depending on our background.

Cuisine is one of the most stable and defining features of any culture. In one study, researchers interviewed Japanese high school and college students who had spent a year in another country as part of an exchange program. The students' satisfaction with their year abroad had little relationship to the educational system, religion, family life, recreation, or dating customs of the host country. The main determinant of their satisfaction was the food: Students who could sometimes eat Japanese food had a good time. Those who could not became homesick (Furukawa, 1997).

The similarity between the words *culture* and *agriculture* is no coincidence, as cultivating crops was a major step toward civilization. We learn from our culture what to eat and how to prepare it (Rozin, 1996). Consider, for example, cassava, a root vegetable that is poisonous unless someone washes and pounds it for 3 days. Can you imagine discovering that fact? Someone had to say, "So far, everyone who ate this plant died, but I bet that if I wash and pound it for 3 days, then it will be okay." That was a difficult and amazing discovery, but once someone discovered it, culture passed it on to later generations and eventually other countries and continents.

Table 1.2 summarizes some of the major fields of psychology, including several that have not been discussed.

concept check

4. a. Of the kinds of psychological research just described—developmental psychology, learning and motivation, cognitive psychology, biological psychology, evolu-

Table 1.2 Some Major Specializations in Psychology

Specialization	General Interest	Example of Interest or Research Topic
Biopsychologist	Relationship between brain and behavior	What body signals indicate hunger and satiety?
Clinical psychologist	Emotional difficulties	How can people be helped to overcome severe anxiety?
Cognitive psychologist	Memory, thinking	Do people have several kinds of memory?
Community psychologist	Organizations and social structures	Would improved job opportunities decrease psychological distress?
Counseling psychologist	Helping people make important decisions	Should this person consider changing careers?
Developmental psychologist	Changes in behavior over age	At what age can a child first distinguish between appearance and reality?
Educational psychologist	Improvement of learning in school	What is the best way to test a student's knowledge?
Environmental psychologist	How factors such as noise, heat, and crowding affect behavior	What building design can maximize the productivity of the people who use it?
Evolutionary psychologist	Evolutionary history of behavior	How did people evolve their facial expressions of emotion?
Human factors specialist	Communication between person and machine	How can an airplane cockpit be redesigned to increase safety?
Industrial/organizational psychologist	People at work	Should jobs be made simple and foolproof or interesting and challenging?
Learning and motivation specialist	Learning in humans and other species	What are the effects of reinforcement and punishment?
Personality psychologist	Personality differences	Why are certain people shy and others gregarious?
Psychometrician	Measuring intelligence, personality, interests	How fair are current IQ tests? Can we devise better tests?
School psychologist	Problems that affect schoolchildren	How should the school handle a child who regularly disrupts the classroom?
Social psychologist	Group behavior, social influences	What methods of persuasion are most effective for changing attitudes?

© Cengage Learning

tionary psychology, social psychology, and cross-cultural psychology—which field concentrates most on children?

b. Which two are most concerned with how people behave in groups?

c. Which concentrates most on thought and knowledge?

d. Which is most interested in the effects of brain damage?

e. Which is most concerned with studying the effect of a reward on future behavior?

5. Why do many menstruating women crave potato chips?

Answers

4. **a.** Developmental psychology. **b.** Social psychology and cross-cultural psychology. **c.** Cognitive psychology. **d.** Biological psychology. **e.** Learning and motivation.

5. By losing blood, they also lose salt, and a deficiency of salt triggers a craving for salty tastes.

Should You Major in Psychology?

Can you get a job if you major in psychology? Psychology is one of the most popular majors in the United States, Canada, and Europe. So if psychology majors cannot get jobs a huge number of people are going to be in trouble!

The bad news is that few jobs specifically advertise for college graduates with a bachelor's degree in psychology. According to one survey, only 20 to 25% of psychology majors took a job closely related to psychology, such as personnel work or social services (Borden & Rajecki, 2000). The good news is that an enormous variety of jobs are available for graduates with a bachelor's degree, not specifying any major. If you earn a degree in psychology, you will compete with everyone else for jobs in government, business, and industry. Even if you get a job that seems remote from psychology, your psychology courses will have taught you much about how to evaluate evidence, organize and write papers, handle statistics, listen carefully to what people say, and respect cultural differences.

Many students major in psychology and then apply to medical school, dental school, law school, divinity school, or other professional schools. Find out what coursework is expected for the professional program of your choice and then compare the coursework required for a psychology major. You will probably find that the psychology major is compatible with your professional preparation.

Suppose you want a career as a psychologist. The educational requirements vary among countries, but in the United States and Canada, nearly all jobs in psychology require education beyond the bachelor's degree. People with a master's degree can get jobs in mental health or educational counseling, but in most states, they must work under the supervision of someone with a doctorate. People with a PhD (doctor of philosophy) in clinical psychology or a PsyD (doctor of psychology) degree can provide mental health services. The main difference between the PhD and PsyD degrees is that the PhD includes an extensive research project, leading to a dissertation, whereas the PsyD degree does not. PsyD programs vary strikingly, including some that are academically strong and others with low standards (Norcross, Kohout, & Wicherski, 2005). A college teaching or research position almost always requires a PhD. An increasing percentage of doctorate-level psychologists now work in business, industry, and the military doing research related to practical problems.

For more information about majoring in psychology, prospects for graduate school, and a great variety of jobs for psychology graduates, visit the website of the American Psychological Association (www.apa.org/students).

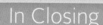

module 1.1

In Closing

Types of Psychologists

An experimental psychology researcher, a clinical psychologist, a human factors specialist, and an industrial/organizational psychologist are all psychologists, even though their daily activities have little in common. What unites psychologists is a dedication to progress through research.

This discussion of the various psychological approaches has been simplified in several ways. In particular, biological psychology, cognitive psychology, social psychology, and the other fields overlap significantly. Nearly all psychologists combine insights and information gained from several approaches. Many like to hyphenate their self-description to emphasize the overlap. For example, "I'm a social-developmental-cognitive neuroscientist."

As we proceed through this book, we shall consider one type of behavior at a time and, generally, one approach at a time. That is simply a necessity; we cannot talk intelligently about many topics at once. But bear in mind that all these processes do ultimately fit together. What you do at any given moment depends on a great many influences.

Summary

The page number after an item indicates where the topic is first discussed.

- *What is psychology?* Psychology is the systematic study of behavior and experience. Psychologists deal with both theoretical and practical questions. (page 3)
- *Three general themes.* Almost any behavior depends on many influences, and few statements apply to everyone all the time. Research progress depends on good measurement. Some conclusions in psychology are based on stronger evidence than others. (page 3)
- *Determinism–free will.* Determinism is the view that everything, including human behavior, has a physical cause. This view is difficult to reconcile with the feeling that humans have free will—that we deliberately, consciously decide what to do. (page 4)
- *Mind–brain.* The mind–brain problem is the question of how conscious experience relates to the activity of the brain. (page 5)
- *Nature–nurture.* Behavior depends on both nature (heredity) and nurture (environment). The relative contributions of nature and nurture vary from one behavior to another. (page 6)

- *Psychology and psychiatry.* Clinical psychologists have a PhD, PsyD, or master's degree. Psychiatrists are medical doctors. Both clinical psychologists and psychiatrists treat people with emotional problems, but psychiatrists can prescribe drugs and other medical treatments, whereas in most states, psychologists cannot. Counseling psychologists help people deal with difficult decisions, and less often deal with serious disorders. (page 7)
- *Service providers to organizations.* Nonclinical fields of application include industrial/ organizational psychology, human factors, and school psychology. (page 8)
- *Research fields in psychology.* Psychology as an academic field has many subfields, including biological psychology, learning and motivation, cognitive psychology, developmental psychology, and social psychology. (page 9)
- *Job prospects.* People with a bachelor's degree in psychology enter a wide variety of careers or continue their education in professional schools. Those with an advanced degree in psychology have additional possibilities depending on their area of specialization. (page 13)

Key Terms

You can check the page listed for a complete description of a term. You can also refer to the glossary/index at the end of the text for a definition of a given term, or you can download a list of all the terms and their definitions for any chapter at this website: http://psychology.wadsworth.com/kalat_intro10e.

biopsychologist (or behavioral neuroscientist) (page 10)
clinical psychologist (page 7)
clinical social worker (page 7)
cognition (page 10)
cognitive psychologist (page 10)
counseling psychologist (page 8)
cross-cultural psychology (page 11)
determinism (page 4)
developmental psychologist (page 9)
dualism (page 5)
evolutionary psychologist (page 11)
forensic psychologist (page 8)
free will (page 4)

human factors specialist (or ergonomist) (page 9)
industrial/organizational (I/O) psychology (page 8)
learning and motivation (page 9)
mind–brain problem (page 5)
monism (page 6)
nature–nurture issue (page 7)
psychiatry (page 7)
psychoanalyst (page 7)
psychology (page 3)
school psychologist (page 9)
social psychologist (page 11)

Psychology Then and Now

- How did psychology get started?
- What were the interests of early psychologists?
- How has psychology changed over the years?

Imagine yourself as a young scholar in 1880. Enthusiastic about the new scientific approach in psychology, you decide to become a psychologist. Like other early psychologists, you have a background in either biology or philosophy. You are determined to apply the scientific methods of biology to the problems of philosophy.

So far, so good. But what questions will you address? A good research question is interesting and answerable. (If it can't be both, it should at least be one or the other!) In 1880 how would you choose a research topic? You cannot get research ideas from a psychological journal because the first issue won't be published until next year. (Incidentally, it will be in German.) You cannot follow in the tradition of previous researchers because there haven't *been* any previous researchers. You are on your own.

In the next several pages, we shall explore some of the changes in what psychologists considered good research topics, including projects that dominated psychology for a while and then faded. We shall discuss additional historical developments in later chapters. Figure 1.4 outlines some major historical events inside and outside psychology. For additional information about the history of psychology, visit either of these websites: www.cwu.edu/~warren/today .html or www.uakron.edu/ahap.

The Early Era

The sciences of astronomy, physics, chemistry, and biology developed gradually over centuries. At first, all practitioners were amateurs. They worked in medicine, law, or other professions and did a little research in their spare time. Long before any people called themselves scientists, and long before universities began to include these fields as worthy areas of study, the amateur investigators had accumulated a great deal of knowledge.

In contrast to these "older" sciences, psychology began as a deliberate attempt to start a new science. In the late 1800s, several scholars noted the progress occurring in biology and other fields, and contrasted it to their perception that our understanding of mental processes had not advanced much since the time of Aristotle and other ancient thinkers. They proposed to attack the age-old questions of mind by using the methods of science. Whether a science of mind was even possible, many doubted. But the only way to find out was to try.

Wilhelm Wundt and the First Psychological Laboratory

In 1879, medical doctor and sensory researcher Wilhelm Wundt (pronounced voont) set up in Leipzig, Germany, the first laboratory intended exclusively for psychological research. Wundt's interests were wide-ranging (Zehr, 2000), but one of his goals was to find the elements of experience, comparable to those of chemistry. Psychology's elements were, he maintained, sensations and feelings (Wundt,

1896/1902).[1] At a given moment, you might experience the taste of a fine meal, the sound of good music, and a certain degree of pleasure. These elements would merge into a compound experience. Furthermore, Wundt maintained, your experience is partly under your voluntary control; you can shift your attention from one element to another and get a different experience. To test his idea about the components of experience, Wundt presented various kinds of lights, textures, and sounds and asked subjects to report the intensity and quality of their sensations. That is, he asked them to introspect—*to look within themselves.* He recorded the changes in people's reports as he changed the stimuli.

Wundt demonstrated the possibility of meaningful psychological research. For example, in one of his earliest studies, he set up a pendulum that struck metal balls and made a sound at two points on its swing. People would watch the pendulum and indicate where it appeared to be when they heard the sound. On average, people reported the pendulum to be about ⅛ of a second in front of or behind the ball when they heard the strike (Wundt, 1862/1961). Apparently, the time we think we see or hear something is not the same as when the event occurs. Wundt's interpretation was that a person needs about ⅛ of a second to shift attention from one stimulus to another.

Wundt and his students were prolific investigators, and the brief treatment here cannot do him justice. He wrote more than 50,000 pages about his research, but his main impact came from setting the precedent of collecting scientific data to answer psychological questions.

Edward Titchener and Structuralism

At first, most of the world's psychologists received their education from Wundt himself. One of his students, Edward Titchener, came to the United States

[1] A reference citation containing a slash between the years, such as this one, refers to a book originally published in the first year (1896) and reprinted in the second year (1902). All references are listed at the end of the book.

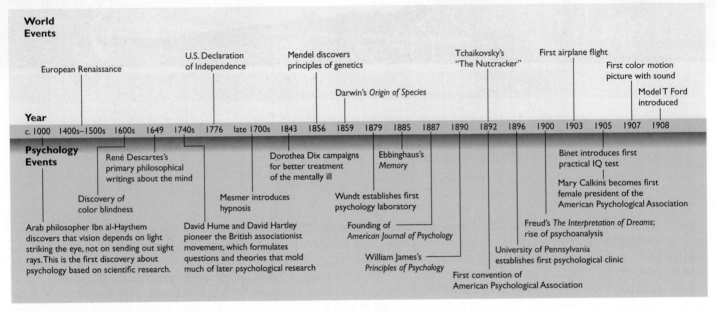

European Renaissance

U.S. Declaration of Independence

Mendel discovers principles of genetics

Tchaikovsky's "The Nutcracker"

First airplane flight

First color motion picture with sound

Darwin's *Origin of Species*

Model T Ford introduced

Year

c. 1000 1400s–1500s 1600s 1649 1740s 1776 late 1700s 1843 1856 1859 1879 1885 1887 1890 1892 1896 1900 1903 1905 1907 1908

Psychology Events

René Descartes's primary philosophical writings about the mind

Dorothea Dix campaigns for better treatment of the mentally ill

Ebbinghaus's *Memory*

Binet introduces first practical IQ test

Discovery of color blindness

Mesmer introduces hypnosis

Wundt establishes first psychology laboratory

Mary Calkins becomes first female president of the American Psychological Association

Arab philosopher Ibn al-Haythem discovers that vision depends on light striking the eye, not on sending out sight rays. This is the first discovery about psychology based on scientific research.

David Hume and David Hartley pioneer the British associationist movement, which formulates questions and theories that mold much of later psychological research

Founding of *American Journal of Psychology*

Freud's *The Interpretation of Dreams*; rise of psychoanalysis

William James's *Principles of Psychology*

University of Pennsylvania establishes first psychological clinic

First convention of American Psychological Association

Figure 1.4 Dates of some important events in psychology and elsewhere. (Based partly on Dewsbury, 2000a.)

in 1892 as a psychology professor at Cornell University. Like Wundt, Titchener believed that the main question of psychology was the nature of mental experiences.

Titchener (1910) typically presented a stimulus and asked his subject to analyze it into its separate features—for example, to look at a lemon and describe its yellowness, brightness, shape, and other characteristics. He called his approach structuralism, *an attempt to describe the structures that compose the mind*, particularly sensations, feelings, and images. For example, imagine you are the psychologist: I look at a lemon and try to describe my experience of its brightness to you separately from my experience of its yellowness.

You see the problem. How do you know whether my reports are accurate? After Titchener died in 1927, psychologists virtually abandoned both his questions and his methods. Why? Remember that a good scientific question is both interesting and an-

swerable. Regardless of whether Titchener's questions about the elements of the mind were interesting, they seemed unanswerable.

William James and Functionalism

In the same era as Wundt and Titchener, Harvard University's William James articulated some of the major issues of psychology and earned recognition as the founder of American psychology. James's book *The Principles of Psychology* (1890) defined many of the questions that still dominate psychology today.

James had little patience with searching for the elements of the mind. He focused on what the mind *does* rather than what it *is*. That is, instead of seeking the elements of consciousness, he preferred *to learn how people produce useful behaviors*. For this reason, we call his approach functionalism. He suggested the following examples of good psychological questions (James, 1890):

- How can people strengthen good habits?
- Can someone attend to more than one item at a time?
- How do people recognize that they have seen something before?
- How does an intention lead to action?

James proposed possible answers but did little research of his own. His main contribution was to inspire later researchers to address the questions that he posed.

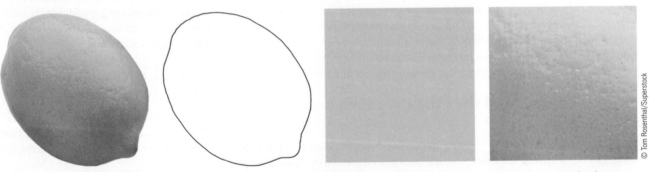

© Tom Rosenthal/Superstock

Edward Titchener asked subjects to describe their sensations. For example, they might describe their sensation of shape, their sensation of color, and their sensation of texture while looking at a lemon.

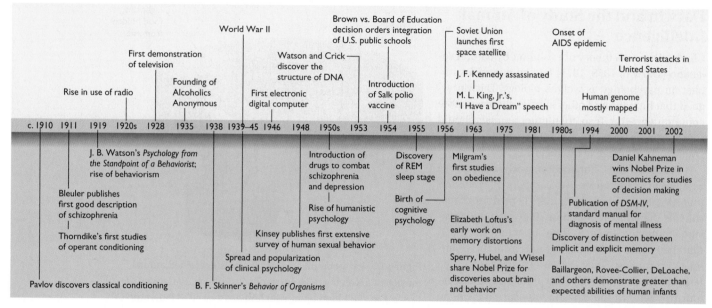

| c. 1910 | 1911 | 1919 | 1920s | 1928 | 1935 | 1938 | 1939–45 | 1946 | 1948 | 1950s | 1953 | 1954 | 1955 | 1956 | 1963 | 1975 | 1981 | 1980s | 1994 | 2000 | 2001 | 2002 |

Above the timeline:

Rise in use of radio

First demonstration of television

Founding of Alcoholics Anonymous

World War II

First electronic digital computer

Watson and Crick discover the structure of DNA

Brown vs. Board of Education decision orders integration of U.S. public schools

Introduction of Salk polio vaccine

Soviet Union launches first space satellite

J. F. Kennedy assassinated

M. L. King, Jr.'s, "I Have a Dream" speech

Onset of AIDS epidemic

Human genome mostly mapped

Terrorist attacks in United States

Below the timeline:

Bleuler publishes first good description of schizophrenia

J. B. Watson's *Psychology from the Standpoint of a Behaviorist*; rise of behaviorism

Thorndike's first studies of operant conditioning

Pavlov discovers classical conditioning

B. F. Skinner's *Behavior of Organisms*

Spread and popularization of clinical psychology

Kinsey publishes first extensive survey of human sexual behavior

Introduction of drugs to combat schizophrenia and depression

Rise of humanistic psychology

Discovery of REM sleep stage

Birth of cognitive psychology

Milgram's first studies on obedience

Elizabeth Loftus's early work on memory distortions

Sperry, Hubel, and Wiesel share Nobel Prize for discoveries about brain and behavior

Publication of *DSM-IV*, standard manual for diagnosis of mental illness

Discovery of distinction between implicit and explicit memory

Baillargeon, Rovee-Collier, DeLoache, and others demonstrate greater than expected abilities of human infants

Daniel Kahneman wins Nobel Prize in Economics for studies of decision making

Studying Sensation

In the late 1800s and early 1900s, psychologists paid little attention to abnormal behavior, leaving it to psychiatrists. They devoted much of their research to the study of vision and other sensations. Why? One reason was that they wanted to understand mental experience, and experience consists of sensations. Another reason was that it is best to start with relatively easy, answerable questions. It was certainly easier to study sensation than, say, personality.

Early psychologists discovered major differences between physical stimuli and psychological perceptions. For example, a light that is twice as intense as another one does not look twice as bright. Figure 1.5 shows the relationship between the intensity of light and its perceived brightness. *The mathematical description of the relationship between the physical stimulus and its perceived properties* is called the psychophysical function because it relates psychology to physics. Such research demonstrated the feasibility of scientific research on psychological questions.

concept check

6. What topic was the main focus of research for the earliest psychologists and why?
7. What was the difference between structuralists and functionalists?

Answers

6. Early psychological research focused mainly on sensation because sensation is central to experience and because the early researchers believed that sensation questions were answerable.

7. Structuralists wanted to understand the components of the mind. They based their research mainly on introspection. Functionalists wanted to explore what the mind could *do*, and they focused mainly on behavior.

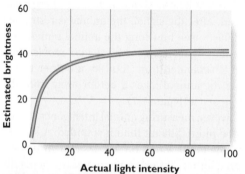

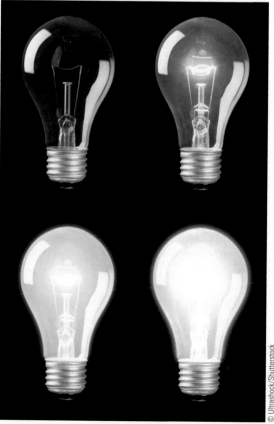

Figure 1.5 This graph relates the perceived intensity of light to its physical intensity. When a light becomes twice as intense physically, it does not seem twice as bright. (Adapted from Stevens, 1961.)

© Ultrashock/Shutterstock

Darwin and the Study of Animal Intelligence

Charles Darwin's theory of evolution by natural selection (Darwin, 1859, 1871) had an enormous impact on psychology as well as biology. Darwin argued that humans and other species share a remote common ancestor. If so, then other animals should share some features in common with humans, including some degree of intelligence.

Based on this implication, early comparative psychologists, *specialists who compare different animal species*, did something that seemed more reasonable then than it does now: They set out to measure animal intelligence. They apparently imagined that they could rank-order animals from the smartest to the dullest. They set various species to such tasks as the delayed-response problem and the detour problem. In the *delayed-response problem*, an animal sees or hears a signal indicating where it can find food. After the signal, the animal is restrained for a delay to see how long the animal remembers the signal (Figure 1.6). In the *detour problem*, an animal is separated from food by a barrier to see whether the animal takes a detour away from the food to reach it (Figure 1.7).

However, measuring animal intelligence turned out to be more difficult than it sounded. A species that seemed dull-witted on one task might be brilliant on another. For example, zebras are generally slow to learn to approach one pattern instead of another for food unless the patterns happen to be narrow stripes versus wide stripes, in which case they excel (Giebel, 1958; Figure 1.8). Rats don't learn to find food hidden under the object that looks different from the others, but they easily learn to choose the object that *smells* different from the others (Langworthy & Jennings, 1972).

Eventually, psychologists decided that the relative intelligence of nonhuman animals was a pointless question. Different species excel in different ways, and it doesn't make sense to rank-order them.

Psychologists today continue to study animal learning, but the emphasis has changed. The questions are now, "What can we learn from animal studies about the mechanisms of intelligent behavior?" and "How did each species evolve its behavioral tendencies?"

Measuring Human Intelligence

While some psychologists studied animal intelligence, others examined human intelligence. Francis Galton, a cousin of Charles Darwin, was among the first to try to measure intelligence and to ask whether intellectual variations were based on heredity. Galton was fascinated with measurement (Hergenhahn, 1992). For example, he invented the

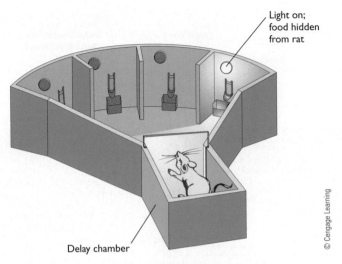

Figure 1.6 Early comparative psychologists assessed animal intelligence with the delayed-response problem. Variations on this task are still used today with humans as well as laboratory animals.

Figure 1.7 In the detour problem, an animal must go away from the food to move toward it.

weather map, measured degrees of boredom during lectures, suggested the use of fingerprints to identify individuals, and—in the name of science—attempted to measure the beauty of women in different countries.

In an effort to determine the role of heredity in human achievement, Galton (1869/1978) examined whether the sons of famous and accomplished men tended to become eminent themselves. (Women in nineteenth-century England had little opportunity for fame.) Galton found that the sons of judges, writers, politicians, and other noted men had a high probability of similar accomplishment themselves. He attributed this edge to heredity. (Do you think he had adequate evidence for his conclusion? If the sons of famous men become famous themselves, is heredity the only explanation?)

Galton tried to measure intelligence using simple sensory and motor tasks, but his measurements were unsatisfactory. In 1905 a French researcher named Alfred Binet devised the first useful intelligence test, which we shall discuss further in chapter 9. At this point, just note that the idea of testing intelligence became popular in the United States and other Western countries. Psycholo-

Figure 1.8 Zebras learn rapidly when they have to compare stripe patterns (Giebel, 1958).

gists, inspired by the popularity of intelligence tests, later developed tests of personality, interests, and other psychological characteristics. Scientists attempting to measure human intelligence face some of the same problems as those trying to measure animal intelligence: People have many intelligent abilities, and it is possible to be more adept at one than another. Much research goes into trying to make intelligence tests fair and accurate.

The Rise of Behaviorism

Today it seems reasonable to define psychology as "the systematic study of behavior and experience." For a substantial period of psychology's history, most experimental psychologists would have objected to the words "and experience." Some psychologists still object today, though less strenuously. During the mid-1900s, most researchers described psychology as the study of behavior, period. They had little to say about minds, experiences, or anything of the sort. (According to one quip, psychologists had "lost their minds.")

What was the objection to studying experience? Recall the failure of Titchener's effort to analyze experience into its components. Most psychologists concluded that questions about mind were unanswerable. Instead, they focused on observable behaviors. How do changes in the environment alter behavior? What is learning and how does it occur?

John B. Watson

Many regard John B. Watson as the founder of behaviorism, *a field of psychology that concentrates on observable, measurable behaviors and not on mental*

processes. Watson was not the first behaviorist, but he systematized the approach and popularized it (Watson, 1919, 1925). Here are two quotes from Watson:

> Psychology as the behaviorist views it is a purely objective experimental branch of natural science. Its theoretical goal is the prediction and control of behavior. (1913, p. 158)
>
> The goal of psychological study is the ascertaining of such data and laws that, given the stimulus, psychology can predict what the response will be; or, on the other hand, given the response, it can specify the nature of the effective stimulus. (1919, p. 10)

Studies of Learning

Inspired by Watson, many researchers set out to study animal behavior, especially animal learning. One advantage of studying nonhuman animals is that the researcher can control the animals' diet, waking/sleeping schedule, and so forth far more completely than with humans. The other supposed advantage was that nonhuman learning might be simpler to understand. Many psychologists optimistically expected to discover simple, basic laws of behavior. Just as physicists could study gravity by dropping any object in any location, many psychologists in the mid-1900s thought they could learn all about behavior by studying rats in mazes. One highly influential psychologist, Clark Hull, wrote, "One of the most persistently baffling problems which confronts modern psychologists is the finding of an adequate explanation of the phenomena of maze learning" (1932, p. 25). Another wrote, "I believe that everything important in psychology (except perhaps . . . such matters as involve society and words) can be investigated in essence through the continued experimental and theoretical analysis of

Early behaviorists studied rats in mazes. As they discovered that this behavior was more complicated than they supposed, behaviorists turned their interest to other topics.

© WILL & DENI MCINTYRE/Gettyimages

the determiners of rat behavior at a choice-point in a maze" (Tolman, 1938, p. 34).

As research progressed, psychologists found that the behavior of a rat in a maze was more complicated than they had expected. Just as psychologists of the 1920s abandoned the structuralist approach to the mind, later psychologists abandoned the hope that studying rats in mazes would quickly uncover universal principles of behavior. Psychologists continue to study animal learning, but the goals and methods have changed.

The behaviorist approach is still alive and well today, as we shall see in chapter 6, but it no longer dominates experimental psychology as it once did. The rise of computer science showed that it was possible to talk about memory, knowledge, and information processing in machines, and if machines can have such processes, presumably humans can, too. Psychologists demonstrated the possibilities of meaningful research on topics that behaviorists had avoided.

From Freud to Modern Clinical Psychology

In the early 1900s, clinical psychology was a small field devoted largely to visual, auditory, movement, and memory disorders (Routh, 2000). The treatment of psychological disorders (or mental illness) remained the province of psychiatry. The Austrian psychiatrist Sigmund Freud revolutionized and popularized psychotherapy with his methods of

Courtesy Wellesley College Archives © Notman

Figure 1.9 Mary Calkins, one of the first prominent women in U.S. psychology.

analyzing patients' dreams and memories. He tried to trace current behavior to early childhood experiences, including children's sexual fantasies. We shall examine Freud's theories in chapter 14. Freud was a persuasive speaker and writer, and his influence was enormous. By the mid-1900s, most psychiatrists in the United States and Europe were following his methods.

During World War II, many soldiers wanted help in dealing with the traumas caused by their war experiences. Because psychiatrists could not keep up with the need, psychologists began providing therapy, and clinical psychology as we now know it began to develop. Researchers began to evaluate treatments, and new treatment methods emerged, as we shall see in chapter 15.

Recent Trends

Psychology ranges from the study of simple sensory processes to interventions intended to change communities. Basic research *seeks theoretical knowledge for its own sake,* such as understanding the processes of learning and memory. Applied research *deals with practical problems,* such as how to help children with learning disabilities. The two kinds of research are mutually supportive. Understanding the basic processes helps applied researchers develop effective interventions. Those working toward practical solutions sometimes discover principles that are theoretically important.

Recall that some of the earliest psychological researchers wanted to study the conscious mind but became discouraged with Titchener's introspective methods. Since the 1960s, cognitive psychology (the study of thought and knowledge) has gradually gained in prominence. Although cognitive psychologists sometimes ask people to describe their thoughts, more often they measure the accuracy and speed of responses under various circumstances to draw inferences about the underlying processes.

Another rapidly growing field is neuroscience. New techniques of brain scanning now enable researchers to examine brain activity without opening the skull. Today, neuroscience influences nearly every aspect of psychology, and psychologists in almost any field of specialization need to be aware of the field's developments and their theoretical implications (Norcross et al., 2005).

Evolutionary psychology is another new emphasis. Animals that behaved in certain ways survived, reproduced, and became our ancestors. Those whose behaviors did not lead to reproductive success failed to pass on their genes. In some cases, we can cautiously infer the selective pressures that led to our current behaviors.

For many decades, researchers interested in personality concentrated mostly on what can go wrong, such as fear, anger, and sadness. The relatively new field of positive psychology *studies the predispositions and experiences that make people happy, productive, and successful.* We turn to this topic in chapter 12.

New fields of application have also arisen. Health psychologists *study how people's health is influenced by their behaviors,* such as smoking, drinking, sexual activities, exercise, diet, and reactions to stress. They also try to help people change their behaviors to promote better health. Sports psychologists *apply psychological principles to help athletes set goals, train, and concentrate their efforts.*

Psychologists today have also broadened their scope to include more of human diversity. In its early days, around 1900, psychology was more open to women than most other academic disciplines were, but even so, the opportunities for women were limited (Milar, 2000). Mary Calkins (Figure 1.9), an early memory researcher, was regarded as Harvard's best psychology graduate student, but she was denied a PhD because of Harvard's tradition of granting degrees only to men (Scarborough & Furomoto, 1987). She did, however, serve as president of the American Psychological Association, as did Margaret Washburn, another important woman in the early days of psychology.

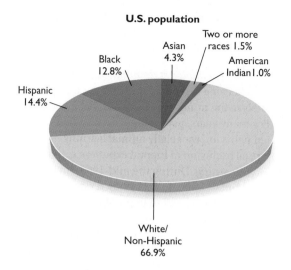

U.S. population

Black 12.8%

Hispanic 14.4%

Asian 4.3%

Two or more races 1.5%

American Indian 1.0%

White/ Non-Hispanic 66.9%

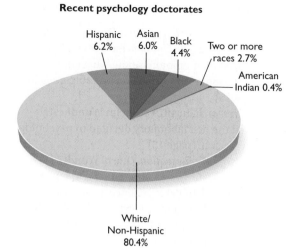

Recent psychology doctorates

Hispanic 6.2%

Asian 6.0%

Black 4.4%

Two or more races 2.7%

American Indian 0.4%

White/ Non-Hispanic 80.4%

Figure 1.10 Ethnic groups as a percentage of the U.S. population and as a percentage of people receiving doctorate degrees in psychology during 2005. (Source: Center for Psychology Workforce Analysis and Research, 2007.)

As of 2005, women were receiving more than 70% of new PhDs in psychology (Cynkar, 2007). Women heavily dominate some fields, such as developmental psychology, and hold many leadership roles in psychological organizations. Minority students receive bachelor's and master's degrees in psychology almost in proportion to their numbers in the total population. However, the number of African American and Hispanic students receiving PhD degrees in this discipline lags behind the population norms, as shown in Figure 1.10 (Center for Psychology Workforce Analysis and Research, 2007).

What will psychology be like in the future? A few likely trends are foreseeable. Because advances in medicine have enabled people to live longer, the psychology of aging is increasingly important. Because of depletion of natural resources and climate change, people will need to change their way of life in many ways that we cannot fully anticipate. Persuading people to change their behavior is a task for both politicians and psychologists.

module 1.2

In Closing

Psychology Through the Years

Throughout the early years of psychology, many psychologists devoted enormous efforts to projects that produced disappointing results, such as Titchener's search for the elements of the mind. Not all the efforts of early psychologists were fruitless, and in later chapters, you will encounter many classic studies that have withstood the test of time. Still, if some past psychologists spent their time on projects we now consider misguided, can we be sure that many of today's psychologists aren't on the wrong track?

We can't, of course. Of all the theories and research projects that we now respect most dearly, some will stand the test of time and others will not. That is not a reason for despair. Much like a rat in a maze, researchers make progress by trial and error. They advance in a certain direction, and sometimes it leads to progress, and sometimes it leads to a dead end. But even exploring a dead end and eliminating it is progress of a sort. Even when research doesn't lead to clear answers, at least it leads to better questions.

Summary

- *Choice of research questions.* During the history of psychology, researchers have several times changed their opinions about what constitutes an interesting, important, answerable question. (page 15)

- *First research.* In 1879 Wilhelm Wundt established the first laboratory devoted to psychological research. (page 15)

- *Limits of self-observation.* One of Wundt's students, Edward Titchener, attempted to analyze the elements of mental experience, relying on people's own observations. Other psychologists became discouraged with this approach. (page 15)

- *The founding of American psychology.* William James, the founder of American psychology, focused attention on how the mind guides useful behavior rather than on the contents of the mind. By doing so, he paved the way for the rise of behaviorism. (page 16)

- *Early sensory research.* In the late 1800s and early 1900s, many researchers concentrated on studies of the senses, partly because sensation is central to mental experience. (page 17)

- *Darwin's influence.* Charles Darwin's theory of evolution by natural selection influenced psychology in many ways. It prompted some prominent early psychologists to compare the intelligence of different species. That question turned out to be more complicated than expected. (page 18)

- *Intelligence testing.* The measurement of human intelligence was one concern of early psychologists that has persisted through the years. (page 18)

- *The era of behaviorist dominance.* As psychologists became discouraged with their attempts to analyze the mind, they turned to behaviorism. For many years, psychological researchers studied behavior, especially animal learning, to the virtual exclusion of mental experience. (page 19)

- *Maze learning.* During the mid-1900s, many experimental psychologists studied rats in mazes. As this approach failed to produce general laws of learning and behavior, researchers became discouraged with it and largely abandoned it. (page 19)

- *Freud.* Sigmund Freud's theories heavily influenced the early development of psychotherapy, although other methods are more widespread today. (page 20)

- *Clinical psychology.* At one time, psychiatrists provided nearly all the care for people with psychological disorders. After World War II, clinical psychologists began to assume much of this role. (page 20)

- *Psychological research today.* Today, psychologists study a wide variety of topics. Cognitive psychology has replaced behaviorist approaches to learning as the dominant field of experimental psychology. Neuroscience now influences researchers in almost all fields. Other new approaches are also becoming widespread. (page 20)

Key Terms

You can check the page listed for a complete description of a term. You can also refer to the glossary/index at the end of the text for a definition of a given term, or you can download a list of all the terms and their definitions for any chapter on your Psychology CourseMate at CengageBrain.com.

applied research (page 20)
basic research (page 20)
behaviorism (page 19)
comparative psychologist (page 18)
functionalism (page 16)
health psychologist (page 20)

introspection (page 15)
positive psychology (page 20)
psychophysical function (page 17)
sports psychologist (page 20)
structuralism (page 16)

exploration and study

Access an interactive eBook and chapter-specific learning tools, including
- **flashcards**
- **quizzes**
- **videos**

and more, in your Psychology CourseMate. Go to **CengageBrain.com**.

If your professor has assigned Aplia:
1. Sign in to your account.
2. Complete the corresponding exercises as required by your professor.
3. When finished, click "Grade It Now" to see which areas you have mastered, which areas need more work, and detailed explanations of every answer.

Isabella Bluesky/Photo Researchers

Scientific Methods in Psychology

© Panoramic Images / Getty Images

Years ago, I was watching a Discovery Channel nature documentary about elephants. After the narrator discussed the enormous amount of food elephants eat, he started on their digestive system. He commented that the average elephant passes enough gas in a day to propel a car for 20 miles (32 km). I thought, "Wow, isn't that amazing!" and I told a couple of other people about it.

Later I started to think, "Wait a minute. *How did someone measure that?* Did someone attach a balloon to an elephant's rear end and collect gas for 24 hours? And then put the gas into a car to see how far the car would go? Was it a full-sized car or an economy car? City traffic or highway? How do they know they measured a typical elephant? Did they determine the mean for a broad sample of elephants?" As I thought about it, my doubts grew.

"Oh, well," you might say. "Who cares?" You're right; how far you could propel a car on elephant gas doesn't matter. However, my point is not to ridicule the makers of this documentary but to ridicule *me*. Remember, I said I told two people about this claim before I started to doubt it. For decades, I have been teaching students to question assertions and evaluate the evidence, and here I was, uncritically accepting a silly statement and telling other people, who, for all I know, may have gone on to tell other people. The point is that all of us yield to the temptation to accept unsupported claims, and we all need to discipline ourselves to question the evidence, especially evidence supposedly backing the interesting or exciting claims that we would like to believe. This chapter concerns evaluating evidence in psychology.

module 2.1

Evaluating Evidence and Thinking Critically

- How do scientists evaluate theories?
- Why are most scientists so skeptical of theories and claims that contradict our current understanding?

What constitutes an explanation? Consider the following quote ("The Medals and the Damage Done," 2004, p. 604):

> In 2002, [Michael] Brennan was a British national rowing champion . . . As the UK Olympic trials loomed, Brennan was feeling confident. But . . . for much of the past 12 months, Brennan's performance has been eroded by constant colds, aching joints and fatigue . . . When the trials rolled round this April, Brennan . . . finished at the bottom of the heap. "I couldn't believe it," he says. To an experienced sports doctor, the explanation is obvious: Brennan has "unexplained underperformance syndrome" (UPS).

What do you think? Is "unexplained underperformance syndrome" an *explanation*?

Consider other examples: Birds fly south for the winter "because they have an instinct." Certain people get into fights "because they are aggressive." Certain students have trouble paying attention "because they have attention deficit disorder." Are these statements explanations? Or are they no better than unexplained underperformance syndrome?

A good explanation goes beyond giving something a name, and finding good explanations requires good research. Psychological researchers use scientific methods, but they face problems that chemists and physicists do not. One problem is sampling. A psychologist who studies a group of people has to worry about whether those people might be unusual in some way. A chemist studying, say, a methane molecule doesn't have that worry. If you see one methane molecule, you've seen them all. Another issue is ethics. Chemists can do whatever they want to a jar of chemicals, as long as they don't blow up the lab. Psychologists dealing with people have stringent limits. Still another problem is that people who know they are in a research study sometimes behave differently just because they know someone is watching them. Chemists don't have that worry about a jar of chemicals. In this chapter, we explore some general principles of science, and also some of the special ways that psychologists adapt those principles.

Gathering Evidence

The word *science* derives from a Latin word meaning "knowledge." Science is a search for knowledge based on carefully observed, replicable data. Let's first consider data collection, and then examine that word *replicable*.

Research starts with careful observation. For example, Robert Provine (2000) studied laughter by visiting shopping malls and recording who laughed and when. The sciences of astronomy and anatomy are based almost entirely on observation and description.

When we want to go beyond observations to find explanations, researchers form and test a hypothesis, which is *a clear predictive statement*. A test of a hypothesis goes through the series of steps described in the following four sec-

tions (and illustrated in Figure 2.1). Articles in most scientific publications follow this sequence, too. In each of the remaining chapters of this book, you will find at least one example of a psychological study described in a section entitled "What's the Evidence?" Each of those will go through the sequence from hypothesis to interpretation.

Hypothesis

A hypothesis can be based on observations, such as noticing that some children who watch much televised violence are themselves aggressive. You might then form a hypothesis that watching violence leads to violence. A hypothesis can also be based on a more general statement, such as "children tend to imitate the behavior they see," including televised violence.

A good hypothesis leads to predictions. For example, "if we let children watch violent television, they will behave more aggressively," or "if we decrease the amount of violence on television, the crime rate will decrease."

Method

Any hypothesis could be tested in many ways. One way to test the effects of televised violence would be to examine whether children who watch more violent programs are more violent themselves. However, that study could not tell us about cause and effect: Watching violence may lead to violence, but people who are already violent probably like to watch violence. A better method is to take a set of children, such as those attending a summer camp, randomly assign them to two groups and let one group watch violent programs while the other group watches nonviolent programs, and see whether the two groups differ in their violent behaviors (Parke, Berkowitz, Leyens, West, & Sebastian, 1977). The limitation is that researchers control what people watch for only a few days.

Because any method has strengths and weaknesses, researchers vary their methods. If studies using different methods all point to the same conclusion, we increase our confidence in that conclusion.

Results

Fundamental to any research is measuring the outcome. A phenomenon such as "violent behavior" is tricky to measure. (Do threats count? Does verbal

Figure 2.1 An experiment tests the predictions that follow from a hypothesis. Results either support the hypothesis or indicate a need to revise or abandon it.

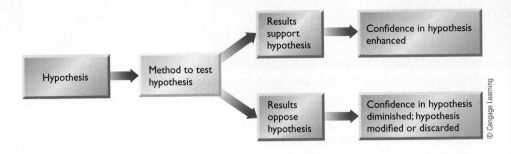

abuse? When does a push or shove cross the line between playfulness and violence?) It is important for an investigator to set clear rules about measurements. After making the measurements, the investigator determines whether the results are impressive enough to call for an explanation or whether the apparent trends might have been due to chance.

Interpretation

Researchers' final task is to consider what the results mean. If the results contradict the hypothesis, researchers should abandon or modify the original hypothesis. If the results match the prediction, investigators gain confidence in the hypothesis, but they also should consider other hypotheses that fit the results.

Replicability

Most scientific researchers are scrupulously honest in reporting their results. Distortions of data are rare and scandalous. A major reason for honesty is that other researchers can check their results. Anyone who reports a scientific study must include the methods in enough detail for other people to repeat the procedure and, we hope, get approximately the same results.

Replicable results are *those that anyone can obtain, at least approximately, by following the same procedures.* Consider an example of a nonreplicable result. In the 1960s and early 1970s, several researchers reported that they trained rats to do something, chopped up the rats' brains, extracted certain chemicals, and injected those chemicals into untrained animals. The recipients then apparently remembered what the first group of rats had learned to do. From what we know of brain functioning, theoretically this procedure shouldn't work, but if it did, imagine the possibilities. Some people proposed, semiseriously, that someday you could get an injection of European history or introduction to calculus instead of going to class. Alas, the results were not replicable. When other researchers repeated the procedures, most of them found no consistent effect (L. T. Smith, 1975).

So, what conclusion should we draw? Until or unless someone finds conditions under which the

phenomenon is replicable (consistently repeatable), we do not take it seriously. This rule may seem harsh, but it is our best defense against error. If a result is not replicable, we don't necessarily assume the original study was incompetent or fraudulent. Sometimes random data accidentally yield an apparently meaningful pattern, and the investigator innocently believes he or she has discovered something interesting. That sort of event happens somewhat frequently, and it would be helpful if researchers more frequently attempted to replicate others' published results (Lehrer, 2010; Simmons, Nelson, & Simonsohn, 2011).

Often, however, an effect is small but real. For example, one method of teaching might work better than another, but only slightly, so researchers do not replicate the advantage in every study. When looking at small trends in the data, researchers use a meta-analysis, *which combines the results of many studies and analyzes them as though they were all one huge study.* A meta-analysis also determines which variations in procedure increase or decrease the effects.

Evaluating Scientific Theories

If replicable data support a hypothesis, eventually researchers propose a theory. A scientific theory is more than a guess. It is *an explanation or model that fits many observations and makes accurate predictions.* A good theory starts with as few assumptions as possible and leads to many correct predictions. In that way, it reduces the amount of information we must remember. The periodic table in chemistry is an excellent example: From the information about the elements, we can predict the properties of an enormous number of compounds.

One important reason for scientific progress is that scientists generally agree on how to evaluate theories. Whereas most people can hardly imagine evidence that would change their religious or political views, scientists can generally imagine evidence that would abandon their favorite theories in favor of other ones. (Oh, not always, of course. Some people are stubborn.)

Burden of Proof

The philosopher Karl Popper emphasized scientists' willingness to disconfirm their theories by saying that the purpose of research is to find which theories are *incorrect.* That is, the point of research is to *falsify* the incorrect theories, and a good theory is one that withstands all attempts to falsify it. It wins by a process of elimination.

A well-formed theory is falsifiable—that is, *stated in such clear, precise terms that we can see what evidence would count against it*—if, of course, such evidence existed. For example, the theory of gravity makes precise predictions about falling objects. Because people have tested these predictions many times, and none of the observations have disconfirmed the predictions, we have high confidence in the theory.

This point is worth restating because "falsifiable" sounds like a bad thing. Falsifiable does not mean we actually have evidence against a theory. (If we did, it would be falsi*fied.*) Falsifiable means we can *imagine* something that would count as evidence against the theory. A theory that makes only vague predictions is not falsifiable. For example, Sigmund Freud claimed that all dreams are motivated by wish fulfillment, although a "censor" in the head disguises the wish. If you have a happy dream, it appears to be a wish fulfillment. If you have an unhappy dream, then evidently a censor in your brain disguised the wish. As Domhoff (2003) noted, Freud stated his theory in such a way that any observation counted for it or at least not against it (Figure 2.2).

However, when Popper wrote that research is *always* an attempt to falsify a theory, he went too far. "All objects fall" (the law of gravity) is falsifiable. "Some objects fall" is not falsifiable, although it is certainly true—a pitifully weak statement, but nevertheless true. If "some objects fall" *were* false, you could not *demonstrate* it to be false!

Instead of insisting that all research is an effort to falsify a theory, another approach is to discuss burden of proof, *the obligation to present evidence to support one's claim.* In a criminal trial, the burden of proof is on the prosecution. If the prosecution does not make a convincing case, the defendant goes free. The reason is that the prosecution should be able to find convincing evidence if someone is guilty, but many innocent defendants could not possibly demonstrate their innocence.

Similarly in science, the burden of proof is on anyone who makes a claim that should be demonstrable if it is true. For the claim "some objects fall," the burden of proof is on anyone who supports the claim. (It's easy to fulfill that burden of proof, of course.) For the claim "every object falls," we can't expect anyone to demonstrate it to be true for every object, and so the burden of proof is on anyone who doubts the claim. (We will continue to believe the statement unless someone shows an exception.) For a claim such as "UFOs from outer space have visited Earth" or "some people have psychic powers to perceive things without any sensory information," the burden of proof is on anyone who supports these statements. (If they are true, someone should be able to show clear evidence.)

Figure 2.2 According to Freud, every dream is based on wish fulfillment. If a dream seems unhappy, it is because a censor in your head disguised the wish. Can you imagine any observation that would contradict this theory?

Parsimony

What do we do if several theories fit the known facts? For example, suppose you notice that a picture on your wall is hanging on an angle. You consider three possible explanations:

- A mild earth tremor shook the picture.
- One of your friends bumped it without telling you.
- A ghost moved it.

All three explanations fit the observation, but we don't consider them on an equal basis. *When given a choice among explanations that seem to fit the facts, we prefer the one whose assumptions are fewer, simpler, or more consistent with other well-established theories.* This is known as the principle of parsimony (literally "stinginess") or *Occam's razor* (after the philosopher William of Occam). The principle of parsimony is a conservative idea: We stick with ideas that work and try as hard as we can to avoid new assumptions (e.g., ghosts).

Parsimony and Degrees of Open-Mindedness

The principle of parsimony tells us to adhere to what we already believe, to resist radically new hypotheses. You might protest: "Shouldn't we remain open-minded to new possibilities?" Yes, if open-mindedness means a willingness to consider proper evidence, but not if it means the assumption that "anything has as much chance of being true as anything else." The stronger the reasons behind our current opinion, the more evidence we should need before replacing it.

For example, many people have attempted to build a "perpetual motion machine," one that generates more energy than it uses. (Figure 2.3 shows one example.) The U.S. Patent Office is officially closed-minded on this issue, refus-

ing even to consider patent applications for such machines. Physicists are convinced, both for logical reasons and because of consistent observations, that any work wastes energy, and that keeping a machine going always requires energy. If someone shows you what appears to be a perpetual motion machine, look for a hidden battery or other power source. If you don't find one, you probably overlooked it. A claim as extraordinary as a perpetual motion machine requires extraordinary evidence.

Let's consider a couple of examples from psychology in which people have claimed very surprising results. Although it is fair to examine the evidence, it is also important to maintain a skeptical attitude and look as closely as possible for a simple, parsimonious explanation.

Applying Parsimony: Clever Hans, the Amazing Horse

Early in the twentieth century, Mr. von Osten, a German mathematics teacher, set out to demonstrate the intellectual ability of his horse, Hans. He first showed Hans an object, said "one," and lifted Hans's foot. He raised Hans's foot twice for two objects and so on. With practice, Hans learned to look at objects and tap the correct number of times. Soon it was no longer necessary for Hans to see the objects. He could just hear a number and tap the appropriate number.

Mr. von Osten moved on to addition, subtraction, multiplication, division, simple algebra, and far more. Hans caught on quickly, responding with 90 to 95% accuracy. Hans and von Osten began giving public demonstrations. Many people were ready to believe that Hans had great intellectual powers. But Oskar Pfungst (1911) observed that Hans could answer a question correctly only if he saw the questioner and the questioner knew the answer. Apparently, the questioner (who was not always von Osten) was giving away the answer.

Eventually, Pfungst observed that anyone who asked Hans a question would lean forward to watch Hans's foot. Hans had learned to start tapping whenever he saw that signal. After Hans reached the correct number of taps, the questioner would slightly change facial expression, anticipating that this might be the last tap. Hans simply continued tapping until he saw that cue.

Note that Pfungst did not demonstrate that Hans *didn't* understand mathematics. Pfungst merely demonstrated that he could explain Hans's behavior in the parsimonious terms of responses to facial expressions, and therefore, no one needed to assume anything more complex.

Applying Parsimony: Extrasensory Perception

The possibility of extrasensory perception (ESP) has long been controversial in psychology. Supporters of extrasensory perception claim that *at least some people, some of the time, acquire information without receiving energy through any sense organ.* Supporters claim that people with ESP can identify someone else's thoughts (telepathy) even from a great distance and despite barriers that would block any known form of energy. Supporters also claim that certain people can perceive objects that are hidden from sight (clairvoyance), predict the future (precognition), and influence such physical events as a roll of dice by mental concentration (psychokinesis).

Acceptance of any of these claims would require us not only to overhaul major concepts in psychology but also to discard the most fundamental tenets of physics. What evidence is there for ESP?

Anecdotes

Anecdotes are people's reports of isolated events, such as a dream or hunch that comes true. Such experiences often seem impressive, but they are not scientific evidence. Sooner or later, occasional bizarre coincidences are almost sure to occur, and people tend to remember them. At one point a com-

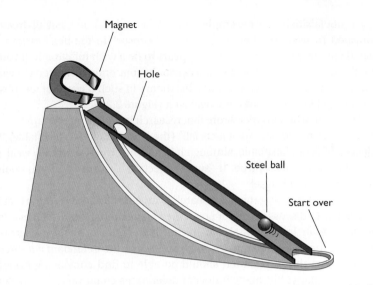

Figure 2.3 A proposed perpetual motion machine: The magnet pulls the metal ball up the inclined plane. When the ball reaches the top, it falls through the hole and returns to its starting point, from which the magnet will again pull the ball up. Can you see why this device is sure to fail? (See answer A on page 33.)

pany in North Carolina had two employees named Suresh C. Srivastava. What are the odds against that? Well, this is the wrong question. The odds against that particular coincidence may be high, but the chance of *some* strange coincidence occurring is highly likely, given a long enough wait.

Furthermore, we tend to remember, talk about, and sometimes exaggerate the hunches and dreams that *do* come true and forget the ones that don't. We could evaluate anecdotal evidence only if people recorded their hunches and dreams *before* the predicted events and then determined how many unlikely predictions actually came to pass.

You may have heard of the "prophet Nostradamus," a sixteenth-century French writer who allegedly predicted many events of later centuries. Figure 2.4 presents four samples of his writings. All of his "predictions" are at this level of vagueness. After something happens, people imaginatively reinterpret his writings to fit the event. (If we don't know what a prediction means until *after* it occurs, is it really a prediction?)

Clever Hans and his owner, Mr. von Osten, demonstrated that the horse could answer complex mathematical questions with great accuracy. The question was, "How?" (After Pfungst, 1911, in Fernald, 1984.)

1. The great man will be struck down in the day by a thunderbolt. An evil deed, foretold by the bearer of a petition. According to the prediction another falls at night time. Conflict at Reims, London, and pestilence in Tuscany.

2. When the fish that travels over both land and sea is cast up on to the shore by a great wave, its shape foreign, smooth, and frightful. From the sea the enemies soon reach the walls.

3. The bird of prey flying to the left, before battle is joined with the French, he makes preparations. Some will regard him as good, others bad or uncertain. The weaker party will regard him as a good omen.

4. Shortly afterwards, not a very long interval, a great tumult will be raised by land and sea. The naval battles will be greater than ever. Fires, creatures which will make more tumult.

Figure 2.4 According to the followers of Nostradamus, each of these statements is a specific prophecy of a twentieth-century event (Cheetham, 1973). What do you think the prophecies mean? Compare your answers to answer B on page 33.

concept check

1. How could someone scientifically evaluate the accuracy of Nostradamus's predictions?

Answer

1. To evaluate Nostradamus's predictions, we would need to ask someone to tell us precisely what his predictions mean before the events they supposedly predict. Then we would ask someone else to estimate the likelihood of those events. Eventually, we would compare the accuracy of the predictions to the advance estimates of their probability.

Professional Psychics

Various stage performers claim to read other people's minds and perform other amazing feats. The Amazing Kreskin prefers to talk of his "extremely sensitive" rather than "extrasensory" perception (Kreskin, 1991). Still, part of his success as a performer comes from allowing people to believe he has uncanny mental powers.

After carefully observing Kreskin and others, David Marks and Richard Kammann (1980) concluded that they used the same kinds of deception commonly employed in magic acts. For example, Kreskin sometimes begins his act by asking the audience to read his mind. Let's try this trick right now, using Kreskin's instructions: Try to read my mind. I am thinking of a number between 1 and 50. Both digits are odd numbers, but they are not the same. For example, it could be 15 but it could not be 11. Have you chosen a number? Please do.

All right, my number was 37. Did you think of 37? If not, how about 35? You see, I started to think 35 and then changed my mind, so you might have got 35.

If you successfully "read my mind," are you impressed? Don't be. At first, it seemed that you had many numbers to choose from (1 to 50), but by the end of the instructions, you had only a few. The first digit had to be 1 or 3, and the second had to be 1, 3, 5, 7, or 9. You eliminated 11 and 33 because both digits are the same, and you probably eliminated 15, the example. That leaves only seven possibilities. Most people stay far away from the example and avoid the highest and lowest possible choices. That leaves 37 as the most likely choice and 35 as the second most likely.

After a variety of other tricks (Marks & Kammann, 1980), Kreskin goes backstage while the mayor or some other dignitary hides Kreskin's paycheck in the

Magician Lance Burton can make people and animals seem to suddenly appear, disappear, float in the air, or do other things that we know are impossible. Even if we don't know how he accomplishes these feats, we take it for granted that they are based on methods of misleading the audience.

audience. Kreskin comes back, walks around, and eventually shouts, "The check is here!" If he guesses wrong, he does not get paid. (He hardly ever misses.)

How does he do it? It is a Clever Hans trick. Kreskin studies people's faces. Most people get more excited as he gets close to the check and more disappointed if he moves away.

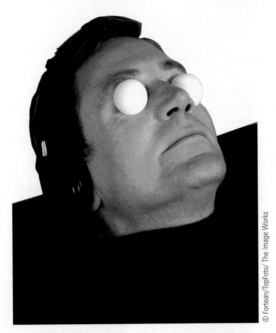

© Fortean/TopFoto/ The Image Works

Figure 2.5 In the *ganzfeld* procedure, a "receiver," who is deprived of most normal sensory information, tries to describe the photo or film that a "sender" is examining.

Of course, someone always objects, "Well, maybe you've explained what some professional psychics do. But there's this other guy you haven't investigated yet. Maybe he really does possess psychic powers." Well, maybe, but it is simpler (more parsimonious) to assume that other performers are also using illusion and deception.

Experiments

Because anecdotes and stage performances occur under uncontrolled conditions, they are nearly worthless as scientific evidence. Laboratory experiments provide the only evidence about ESP worth serious consideration.

Over the years, researchers have tried many procedures, including guessing the order of a deck of cards, guessing numbers generated by a random-number generator, and describing a remote setting currently viewed by someone else. In each case, initial studies generated excitement that subsided after other researchers failed to replicate the findings. For example, in the *ganzfeld* procedure (from German words meaning "entire field"), a "sender" views a photo or film, selected at random from four possibilities, and a "receiver" in another room is asked to describe the sender's thoughts and images. Typically, the receiver wears half Ping-Pong balls over the eyes and listens to static noise through earphones to minimize normal stimuli that might over-

power the presumably weak extrasensory stimuli (Figure 2.5). Later, a judge examines a transcript of what the receiver said and compares it to the four photos or films, determining which one it matches most closely. On average, it should match the target about one in four times. If a receiver "hits" more often than one in four, we can calculate the probability of accidentally doing that well. One review reported that 6 of the 10 laboratories using this method found positive results (Bem & Honorton, 1994). However, 14 later studies from 7 laboratories failed to find evidence that differed from chance (Milton & Wiseman, 1999).

In 2011, a prestigious journal published a series of studies claiming to show that people can foresee the future (Bem, 2011). In one study, college students clicked on the left or right side of the screen to predict which side would show a picture. After the guess, the computer randomly chose one side or the other. If it matched the student's guess, it displayed an erotic photograph of a couple engaged in a sex act. The experimenter reported that students' guesses matched the computer's choice 53% of the time, suggesting an ability to predict the future. In another of the studies, students read a list of words, tried to recall them, and then studied half of the list again. The claim was that the students remembered more of the words that they studied again afterwards. That is, you could improve your score on a test by studying the material after the test was over! (If you believe this can work, you are welcome to try it.)

Before you revise your study habits, however, you should know that other psychologists have noted many problems and oddities in both the research procedures and the statistical analysis of results (Alcock, 2011; Rouder & Morey, 2011). Also, laboratories at three universities repeated the procedures exactly and failed to replicate the results (Ritchie, Wiseman, & French, 2012). Given the long history of promising results that other researchers could not replicate, most psychologists remain skeptical of these and similar claims.

The lack of replicability is one major reason to be skeptical of ESP, but another reason is parsimony. If someone claims that a horse does mathematics or a person foresees random events, we should search thoroughly for a simple explanation.

Would you like to test your own ability to find a parsimonious explanation for apparent mind-reading? Go to your Psychology CourseMate at CengageBrain .com. Navigate to the Online Try It Yourself section, and click Psychic Phenomenon.

In Closing

Scientific Thinking in Psychology

What have we learned about science in general? Science does not deal with proof or certainty. All scientific conclusions are tentative and are subject to revision. Nevertheless, this tentativeness does not imply a willingness to abandon well-established theories without excellent reasons.

Scientists always prefer the most parsimonious theory. Before they accept any claim that requires a major new assumption, they insist that it be supported by replicable experiments that rule out simpler explanations and by a new theory that is superior to the theory it replaces.

Summary

- *Steps in a scientific study.* A scientific study goes through the following sequence of steps: hypothesis, method, results, and interpretation. Because almost any study is subject to more than one possible interpretation, we base our conclusions on a pattern of results from many studies. (page 27)
- *Replicability.* The results of a given study are taken seriously only if other investigators following the same method obtain similar results. (page 28)
- *Burden of proof.* In any dispute, the side that should be capable of presenting clear evidence has the obligation to do so. (page 28)

- *Parsimony.* All else being equal, scientists prefer the theory that relies on simpler assumptions, or assumptions consistent with other theories that are already accepted. (page 29)
- *Skepticism about extrasensory perception.* Psychologists carefully scrutinize claims of extrasensory perception because the evidence reported so far has been unreplicable and because the scientific approach includes a search for parsimonious explanations. (page 30)

Key Terms

burden of proof (page 29)
extrasensory perception (ESP) (page 30)
falsifiable (page 28)
hypothesis (page 27)

meta-analysis (page 28)
parsimony (page 29)
replicable result (page 28)
theory (page 28)

Answers to Other Questions in the Module

A. Any magnet strong enough to pull the metal ball up the inclined plane would not release the ball when it reached the hole at the top. It would pull the ball across the hole. (page 30)

B. The prophecies of Nostradamus (see page 31), as interpreted by Cheetham (1973), refer to the following: (1) the assassinations of John F. Kennedy and Robert F. Kennedy, (2) Polaris ballistic missiles shot from submarines, (3) Hitler's invasion of France, and (4) World War II.

Conducting Psychological Research

A radio talk show featured two psychologists as guests. The first argued that day care was bad for children because she had seen in her clinical practice many sadly disturbed adults who had been left in day care as children. The second psychologist, researcher Sandra Scarr (1997), pointed out that the clinician had no way of knowing about the well-adjusted adults who had also been left in day care as children. Scarr described eight well-designed research studies, examining thousands of people in four countries, which found no evidence of harmful consequences from day care.

Which type of evidence strikes you as stronger, the anecdotes or the eight research studies? To Scarr's dismay, the people who called in to the program seemed to find both kinds of evidence about equally convincing.

Psychology, like any other field, makes progress only when its practitioners distinguish between strong evidence and weak evidence. In this module, we consider some of the special problems researchers encounter when they investigate psychological phenomena.

General Principles of Psychological Research

The primary goal of this module is not to prepare you to conduct psychological research but to help you be an intelligent interpreter of research. When you hear about some new study, you should be able to ask pertinent questions to decide how good the evidence is and what conclusion (if any) the evidence justifies.

Operational Definitions

Suppose a physicist asks you to measure the effect of temperature on the length of an iron bar. You ask, "What do we *really mean* by temperature? And what do we *really mean* by length?" The physicist replies, "Don't worry about it. Here is a thermometer and a ruler. Go measure them."

Psychologists need to use the same strategy. If we want to measure the effect of temperature on, say, anger, we could debate what anger really is, or we could choose a way to measure it. We might ask people to tell us how angry they are, or we might count frowns per minute or swear words per minute, or we might find some other way to measure anger. In doing so, we are using an operational definition, *a definition that specifies the operations (or procedures) used to produce or measure something, ordinarily a way to give it a numerical value.* An operational definition is not like a dictionary definition. You might object that "frowns per minute" is not what anger really *is.* Of course not, but the reading on a thermometer is also not what temperature really is. An operational definition just says how to measure something. It lets us get on with research.

Suppose we want to investigate friendliness. We would need an operational definition of friendliness—that is, a way to measure it. We might define it as the number of people someone smiles at during an hour or the number of people someone lists as close friends. We might operationally define *love* as "how many hours you spend with someone who asks you to stay nearby."

concept check

2. Which of the following is an operational definition of intelligence?
   a. the ability to comprehend relationships
   b. a score on an IQ test
   c. the ability to survive in the real world
   d. the product of the cerebral cortex of the brain
3. What would you propose as an operational definition of *sense of humor*?

Answers

3. We might define *sense of humor* as the number of times someone laughs during a movie or the number of times someone says something that makes other people laugh. Other definitions are possible if they include a method of measurement.

2. A score on an IQ test (b) is an operational definition of intelligence. (Whether it is the *best* operational definition is a different question.) None of the other answer choices tells how to measure or produce intelligence.

Population Samples

In a chemistry lab, if you find the properties of some compound, your results apply to that same compound anywhere. Psychology is different. When psychologists study a group of people, they need to worry about whether those people might be unusual in some way.

For some purposes, the worry is small. For example, the eyes, ears, and other sense organs operate similarly in all people, with obvious exceptions of those with visual or hearing impairments. Indeed, for many purposes, researchers use laboratory animals. We refer to *a group chosen because of its ease of study* as a convenience sample. Unfortunately, many researchers overuse research on college students in the United States or similar countries, a convenience sample that is satisfactory for some purposes and not others.

Often it is important to get a better sample of the population, and if comparing two populations, such as the students in two states, researchers need similar samples of those populations. Consider this example: Every fall, the newspapers report the average SAT scores for different American states, and certain states do consistently better than others. However, in some states, most high school students take the SAT. In states where most colleges require the ACT instead, students take the SAT only if they plan to apply to out-of-state schools (often the most prestigious ones). The results are meaningless if we compare most students in one state to a select group from another.

A big improvement over a convenience sample is a representative sample, *one that resembles the population* in its percentage of males and females, Blacks and Whites, young and old, city dwellers and farmers, or whatever other characteristics are likely to affect the results. To get a representative sample of the people in a region, an investigator determines what percentage of the residents belong to each category and then selects people to match those percentages. Of course, a sample that is representative in some ways might not be representative in others.

Better yet is a random sample, *one in which every individual in the population has an equal chance of being selected.* To produce a random sample of Toronto residents, an investigator might start with a map of Toronto and select a certain number of city blocks at random, randomly select one house from each of those blocks, and then randomly choose one person from each of those households. *Random* here has a special meaning. If you simply say, "Okay, I'll pick this block, this block, and this block," the results are not random. You need to make sure that every block, or every person, has an equal chance of being chosen. A random sample has this advantage: The larger a random sample, the smaller the probability that its results differ substantially from the whole population. However, although a random sample is theoretically the best, it is difficult to achieve.

If we want results that apply to all of humanity, research becomes more difficult, because the population of one country may differ from other countries. Most people in the United States have been described as Western, Educated, Industrial, Rich (compared to most of the rest of the world), and Democratic—abbreviated WEIRD (Henrich, Heine,

College students are often used as convenience samples.

& Norenzayan, 2010). You might find the abbreviation insulting, but the point is that we need to take cultural differences seriously.

We know to expect cultural differences in matters of diet and leisure activities (Kobayashi, 2011), religion, politics, and sexual behavior. Differences also emerge where we might not expect them. Just to take one example: If you were asked to arrange a series of pictures in order from the first event to the most recent to tell a logical story, you would probably arrange the pictures from left to right, or possibly from top to bottom. Australian aborigines arrange the pictures from east to west, regardless of which direction the people themselves are facing (Boroditsky & Gaby, 2010). Doing so, of course, requires them to know exactly which direction is east. For them, the arrow of time goes east to west, just as Americans think of it as going from left to right.

A researcher who wants to talk about humans throughout the world, and not just one culture, needs a cross-cultural sample, *groups of people from at least two cultures.* Cross-cultural sampling is difficult because of the expense, language barriers, and reluctance of people in some cultures to participate in what they consider strange tasks. Table 2.1 reviews the major types of samples.

A psychological researcher tests generalizations about human behavior by comparing people from different cultures.

Table 2.1 Types of Samples

Sample	Individuals Included	Advantages and Disadvantages
Convenience sample	Anyone who is available	Easiest to get, but results may not generalize to the whole population
Representative sample	Same percentage of male/female, White/Black, etc., as the whole population	Results probably similar to whole population, although sample may be representative in some ways but not others
Random sample	Everyone in population has same chance of being chosen	Difficult to get this kind of sample, but it is the best suited for generalizing to the whole population
Cross-cultural sample	People from different cultures	Difficulties include language barriers, cooperation problems, etc., but essential for studying many issues

© Cengage Learning

concept check

4. Suppose you stand on a street and you interview every tenth person who walks by. What kind of sample is this—convenience, representative, or random?

Answer

4. This is a convenience sample. You made no effort to get a sample that matches the total population in age or anything else, so it is not a representative sample. Everyone in the population did not have an equal chance of participating, because not all kinds of people are equally likely to be walking down that street at that time of day.

Observational Research Designs

Operational definitions and sampling are important issues for many kinds of research. Psychologists use various methods of investigation, each with its advantages and disadvantages. Most research starts with description: What happens and under what circumstances? Let's first examine several kinds of observational studies. Later we consider experiments, which are designed to illuminate cause-and-effect relationships.

Naturalistic Observations

A naturalistic observation is *a careful examination of what happens under more or less natural conditions.* For example, biologist Jane Goodall (1971) spent years observing chimpanzees in the wild, recording their food habits, their social interactions, their gestures, and their whole way of life (Figure 2.6).

Figure 2.6 In a naturalistic study, observers record the behavior in a natural setting. Here noted biologist Jane Goodall records her observations on chimpanzees. By patiently staying with the chimps, Goodall gradually won their trust and learned to recognize individual animals.

Similarly, psychologists sometimes try to observe human behavior "as an outsider." A psychologist might observe how often strangers smile at each other when they pass on a street. How much does this behavior differ between small towns and crowded cities? Who smiles more, women or men? Young people or old people?

Case Histories

Some fascinating conditions are rare. For example, some people are almost completely insensitive to pain. People with Capgras syndrome believe that some of their relatives have been replaced with impostors, who look, sound, and act like the real people. People with Cotard's syndrome insist that they are dead or do not exist. A psychologist who encounters someone with a rare condition may report a case history, *a thorough description of a person, including abilities and disabilities, medical condition, life history, unusual experiences, and whatever else seems relevant.* A case history is a kind of naturalistic observation, but we distinguish it because it focuses on a single individual.

A case history can be valuable, but it runs the risk of being just an anecdote. Unless other observers examine this person or someone similar, we are at the mercy of the original investigator, who may have overlooked important points, exaggerated, or misunderstood. A good case history guides further research, but we should interpret a single report cautiously.

Surveys

A survey is *a study of the prevalence of certain beliefs, attitudes, or behaviors based on people's responses to questions.* No matter what your occupation, at some time you will probably conduct a survey of your employees, your customers, your neighbors, or fellow members of an organization. You will also frequently read and hear about survey results. You should understand how survey results can be misleading.

Sampling

Getting a random or representative sample is important in any research, but especially with surveys. In 1936 the *Literary Digest* mailed 10 million postcards, asking people their choice for president of the United States. Of the 2 million responses, 57% preferred the Republican candidate, Alfred Landon.

Later that year, the Democratic candidate, Franklin Roosevelt, defeated Landon by a wide margin. Why was the survey so far off the mark? The problem was that the *Literary Digest* had selected names from the telephone book and automobile registration lists. In 1936, near the end of the Great Depression, few poor people (who were mostly Democrats) owned telephones or cars.

The Seriousness of Those Being Interviewed

When taking a survey, how carefully do you consider your answers? In one survey, only 45% of the respondents said they believed in the existence of intelligent life on other planets. However, a few questions later on the survey, 82% said they believed the U.S. government was "hiding evidence of intelligent life in space" (Emery, 1997). Did 37% of the people *really* think that the U.S. government is hiding evidence of something that doesn't exist? Or did they answer impulsively without much thought?

try it ▶ yourself

Here's another example: Which of the following programs would you most like to see on television reruns? Rate your choices from highest (1) to lowest (10). (Please fill in your answers, either in the text or on a separate sheet of paper, before continuing to the next paragraph.)

___ South Park	___ Xena, Warrior Princess
___ Lost	___ The X-Files
___ Cheers	___ Teletubbies
___ Seinfeld	___ Space Doctor
___ I Love Lucy	___ Homicide

When I conducted this survey with my own students at North Carolina State University, nearly all did exactly what I asked—they gave every program a rating, including *Space Doctor*, a program that never existed. Most rated it toward the bottom, but more than 10% rated it in the top five, and a few ranked it as their top choice. (This survey was inspired by an old *Candid Camera* episode in which interviewers asked people their opinions of the nonexistent program *Space Doctor* and received many confident replies.)

Some odd survey results merely reflect the fact that people did not take the questions seriously or did not understand the questions.

Students who rated *Space Doctor* did nothing wrong, of course. I asked them to rank programs, and they did. The fault lies with anyone who interprets such survey results as if they represented informed opinions.

The Wording of the Questions

try it ▶ yourself

Let's start with a little demonstration. Please answer these two questions:

1. I oppose raising taxes. (Circle one.)
   1   2   3   4   5   6   7
   Strongly agree   Strongly disagree
2. I make it a practice to never lie. (Circle one.)
   1   2   3   4   5   6   7
   Strongly agree   Strongly disagree

Now cover up those answers and reply to these similar questions:

3. I would be willing to pay a few extra dollars in taxes to provide high-quality education to all children. (Circle one.)
   1   2   3   4   5   6   7
   Strongly agree   Strongly disagree
4. Like all human beings, I occasionally tell a white lie. (Circle one.)
   1   2   3   4   5   6   7
   Strongly agree   Strongly disagree

Most students at one college indicated agreement to all four items (Madson, 2005). Note that item 1 contradicts 3, and 2 contradicts 4. You can't be opposed to raising taxes and in favor of raising taxes. You can't be honest all the time and occasionally lie. However, the wording of a question changes its connotation. Question 3 talks about raising taxes "a few extra dollars" for a worthy cause. That differs from raising taxes by an unknown amount for unknown reasons. Similarly, depending on what you mean by a "white lie," you might tell one occasionally while still insisting that you "make it a practice

to never lie"—at least not much. The point is that someone can bias your answers one way or the other by rewording a question.

Here is another example. Imagine yourself as the judge in a divorce case, where you have to decide whether to give parent A or parent B primary custody of their child. Never mind which parent is the father and which is the mother. Parent A is more or less "okay." Parent B has some major positives and major negatives. B has a better house, a higher income, and a closer relationship with the child. However, B also has to do much work-related travel and has some minor health problems. To which parent would you award custody? Most people reply B. However, if asked to which parent would you *deny* custody, again most people reply B. The term "award" gets people to focus on the positives, and the word "deny" gets them to emphasize the negatives, resulting in a different outcome (Shafir, 1983).

In short, the next time you hear the results of some survey, ask how the question was worded and what choices were offered. Even a slightly different wording could yield a different percentage.

Surveyor Biases

Sometimes, an organization words the questions of a survey to encourage the answers they hope to receive. According to a 1993 survey, 92% of high school boys and 98% of high school girls said they were victims of sexual harassment (Shogren, 1993). Shocking, isn't it? However, perhaps the designers of the survey *wanted* to show that sexual harassment is rampant. The survey defined sexual harassment by a long list of acts ranging from major offenses (e.g., having someone rip your clothes off in public) to minor annoyances. For example, if you didn't like the sexual graffiti on the restroom wall, you could consider yourself sexually harassed. If you tried to make yourself look sexually attractive (as most teenagers do, right?) and then attracted a suggestive look

Stem cells are the basic cells from which all of a person's tissues and organs develop. Congress is considering whether to provide federal funding for experiments using stem cells from human embryos. The live embryos would be destroyed in their first week of development to obtain these cells. Do you support or oppose using your federal tax dollars for such experiments?

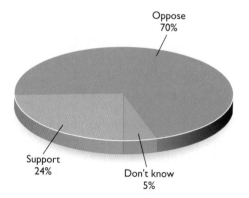

Sometimes fertility clinics produce extra fertilized eggs, also known as embryos, that are not implanted in a woman's womb. These extra embryos either are discarded, or couples can donate them for use in medical research called stem cell research. Some people support stem cell research, saying it's an important way to find treatments for many diseases. Other people oppose stem cell research, saying it's wrong to use any human embryos for research purposes. What about you—do you support or oppose stem cell research?

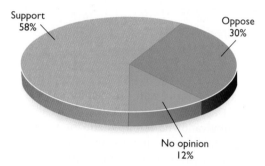

Figure 2.7 The question on the left, written by opponents of stem cell research, led most people to express opposition. The question on the right, worded differently, led most people to express support. (From ICR/National Conference of Catholic Bishops, 2001 and ABC News/Bellnet, June 2001, © 2004 by Public Agenda Foundation. Reprinted by permission.)

from someone you *didn't* want to attract, that stare would count as sexual harassment. (I worry about those who said they *weren't* sexually harassed! They liked *all* the graffiti on the restroom walls? No one *ever* looked at them in a sexual way?) Sexual harassment is, of course, a serious problem, but a survey that combines major and minor offenses is likely to mislead.

Figure 2.7 shows the results for two surveys conducted on similar populations at about the same time. The issue is whether stem cells derived from aborted fetuses can be used in medical research. The question on the left was written by an organization opposed to abortion and stem cell research. The question on the right was worded by an organization that is either neutral or favorable to stem cell research (Public Agenda, 2001). As you can see, the wording of the question influenced the answers.

Correlational Studies

Another type of research is a correlational study. A correlation is *a measure of the relationship between two variables.* (A variable is anything measurable that differs among individuals, such as age, years of education, or reading speed.) A correlational study is a procedure in which investigators measure the relation between two variables without controlling either variable. For example, one might measure the correlation between people's height and weight, or the correlation between scores on personality tests and how many friends someone has.

The Correlation Coefficient

Some pairs of variables are strongly related and others, weakly. To measure the strength of a correlation, researchers use a correlation coefficient, *a mathematical estimate of the relationship between two variables.* A correlation coefficient of zero indicates no consistent relationship. A coefficient of +1 or –1 indicates a perfect relationship—that is, if you know the value of one variable, you can predict the other with perfect accuracy. (In psychology you probably will never see a perfect +1 or –1 correlation coefficient.) A positive coefficient, such as +1, means that as one variable increases, the other increases also. A negative coefficient, such as –1, means that as one variable increases, the other decreases. A negative correlation is just as useful as a positive correlation. For example, the more often people practice golf, the lower their golf scores, so golf practice is negatively correlated with scores. In nations where people eat more seafood,

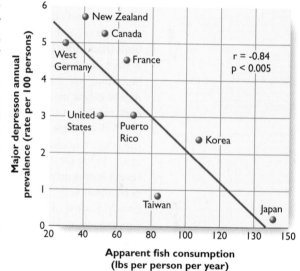

Figure 2.8 Each dot represents one country. The value along the *x*-axis indicates the amount of seafood that an average person eats in a year. The value along the *y*-axis indicates the probability of developing major depression. As seafood consumption increases, the probability of depression decreases. (© Cengage Learning)

depression is less common, so seafood consumption is negatively correlated with depression, as shown in Figure 2.8 (Gómez-Pinilla, 2008).

A 0 correlation indicates that as one variable goes up, the other does not consistently go up or down. A correlation near 0 can mean that two variables really are unrelated or that one or both variables were poorly measured. (If something is inaccurately measured, we can hardly expect it to predict anything else.) For example, if you ask students how eager they are to do well in school, their answers

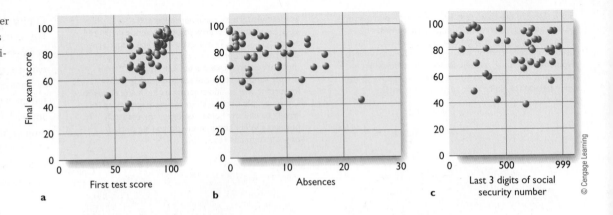

Figure 2.9 In these scatter plots, each dot represents measurements of two variables for one person.
(a) Scores on first test and scores on final exam (correlation = +.72).
(b) Times absent and scores on final exam (correlation = −.44).
(c) Last three digits of social security number and scores on final exam (correlation = −.08).

correlate almost zero with academic success (Dompnier, Darnon, & Butera, 2009). Does that mean that motivation is unimportant for school success? Hardly. It means that many students say they are highly motivated because they think they are supposed to say so. If a measurement is poor—in this case, answers to certain questions—the measurement won't correlate highly with anything else.

Figure 2.9 shows scatter plots for three correlations (real data). In a scatter plot, *each dot represents a given individual, with one measurement for that individual on the x-axis (horizontal) and another measurement on the y-axis (vertical).* In Figure 2.9, each dot represents one student in an introductory psychology class. The value for that student along the *y*-axis represents percentage correct on the final exam. In the first graph, values along the *x*-axis represent scores on the first test in the course. Here the correlation is +.72, indicating a fairly strong relationship. Most of the students who did well on the first test also did well on the final, and most who did poorly on the first test also did poorly on the final. In the second graph, the *x*-axis represents times absent out of 38 class meetings. Here you see a correlation of −.44, indicating that those with more absences generally had lower exam scores. The third graph shows how the final exam scores related to the last three digits of each student's social security number. As you would expect, the correlation is close to 0. If we examined the data for a larger population of students, the correlation would no doubt come closer and closer to 0.

concept check

5. Identify each of these as a positive, zero, or negative correlation:
   a. The more crowded a neighborhood, the lower the income.
   b. People with high IQ scores are neither more nor less likely than other people to have high telephone numbers.
   c. People who awaken frequently during the night are more likely than other people to feel depressed.
6. Which indicates a stronger relationship between two variables, a +.50 correlation or a −.75 correlation?
7. The correlation between students' grades and their scores on a self-esteem questionnaire is very low, not much above 0. Why might that be?

Answers

5. **a.** Negative correlation between crowdedness and income. **b.** Zero correlation between telephone numbers and IQ scores. **c.** Positive correlation between awakenings and depression.
6. The −.75 correlation indicates a stronger relationship—that is, a greater accuracy of predicting one variable based on measurements of the other. A negative correlation is just as useful as a positive one.
7. One possibility is that grades are unrelated to self-esteem. Another possibility is that we used an inaccurate measurement of either self-esteem or grades or both. If anything is measured poorly, it cannot correlate strongly with anything else.

Illusory Correlations

Sometimes with unsystematic observations, we think we see a correlation that doesn't really exist. For example, many people believe that consuming sugar makes children hyperactive. However, extensive research found little effect of sugar on activity levels, and some studies found that sugar *calms* behavior (Milich, Wolraich, & Lindgren, 1986; Wolraich et al., 1994). Why, then, do many people believe that sugar makes children hyperactive? Researchers watched two sets of mothers with their 5- to 7-year-old sons after telling one group that they had given the sons sugar and the other that they had given the sons a placebo, *a pill with no known pharmacological effects*. In fact, they had given both a placebo. The mothers who *thought* their sons had been given sugar rated their sons hyperactive during the observation period, whereas the other mothers did not (Hoover & Milich, 1994). That is, they saw what they expected to see.

When people expect to see a connection between two events (e.g., sugar and activity levels), they remember the cases that support the connection and disregard the exceptions, thus perceiving an illusory correlation, *an apparent relationship based on casual observations of unrelated or weakly related events.* Many stereotypes about groups of people are illusory correlations.

As another example, consider the widely held belief that a full moon affects human behavior. For hundreds of years, many people have believed that crime and various kinds of mental disturbance are more common under a full moon than at other times. In fact, the term *lunacy* (from the Latin word *luna*, meaning "moon") originally meant mental illness caused by the full moon. Some police officers claim that they receive more calls on nights with a full moon, and some hospital workers say they have more emergency cases on such nights. However, careful reviews of the data have found no relationship between the moon's phases and either crime or mental illness (Raison, Klein, & Steckler, 1999; Rotton & Kelly, 1985). Why, then, does the belief persist? People remember events that fit the belief and disregard those that do not.

Correlation ≠ Causation

"Correlation does not mean causation." That is a statement you will hear again and again in psychology and other fields. A correlation indicates how strongly two variables are related to each other. It does not tell us *why* they are related. If two variables—let's call them A and B—are positively correlated, it could be that A causes B, B causes A, or some third variable, C, causes both of them.

For example, how much sunscreen people use is positively correlated with their chance of getting skin cancer. Does that mean that sunscreen causes cancer? Hardly. It's more likely that people who are worried about skin cancer, because they spend much time in the sun, are the ones who use more sunscreen.

There is also a positive correlation between how often parents spank their children and how often the children misbehave. Does this correlation indicate that spankings lead to misbehavior? Or does misbehavior lead to spankings? Yet another possibility is that the parents had genes for "hostile" behavior that led them to spank, and the children inherited those genes, which led to misbehaviors. Because all these explanations are possible, we can't draw a conclusion about causation.

"Then what good is a correlation?" you might ask. First, correlations help us make predictions. Second, correlational studies pave the way for later experimentation that might lead to a conclusion. For example, we might persuade half the parents to stop spanking, and see whether their children's behavior improves.

Here are more examples of why we cannot draw conclusions regarding cause and effect from correlational data (see also Figure 2.10):

- *Political conservativeness correlates with happiness.* That is, political conservatives tend to be happier than liberals (Napier & Jost, 2008). Does being conservative make you happier? Or does being happy make you more conservative? Maybe it's neither. Maybe financially secure people are more likely than poor people to be political conservatives, and more likely to be happy. Without other kinds of research, we can't draw a conclusion.
- *According to one study, people who sleep about 7 hours a night are less likely to die within the next few years than those who sleep either more or less* (Kripke, Garfinkel, Wingard, Klauber, & Marler, 2002). Should we conclude (as some people did) that sleeping too much impairs your health? Here is

People's expectations and faulty memories produce illusory correlations, such as that between the full moon and abnormal behavior.

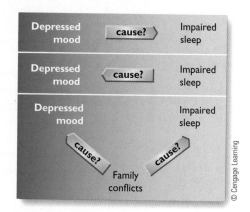

Figure 2.10 A strong correlation between depression and impaired sleep does not tell us whether depression interferes with sleep, poor sleep leads to depression, or whether another problem leads to both depression and sleep problems.

an alternative: People who already have life-threatening illnesses tend to sleep more than healthy people. So perhaps illness causes extra sleep rather than extra sleep causing illness. Or perhaps advancing age increases the probability of both illness and extra sleep. (The study included people ranging from young adulthood through age 101!)

Now, let me tell you a dirty little secret: In rare circumstances, correlational results *do* imply cause and effect. It is a "dirty little secret" because professors want students to avoid cause-and-effect conclusions from correlations, and mentioning the exceptions is risky. Still, consider the fact that people are generally in a better mood when the weather improves (Keller et al., 2005). A likely explanation is that the weather changes your mood. What other possibility is there? Your mood changes the weather? Hardly. Might something else control both the weather and your mood? If so, what? In the absence of any other hypothesis, we conclude that the weather changes your mood. Also consider that how often a U.S. congressional representative votes a pro-feminist position (as defined by the National Organization for Women) correlates with how many daughters the representative has (Washington, 2006). It is implausible that someone's voting record would influence the sex of his or her children. It is highly likely that having daughters could influence political views. Again, the results suggest cause and effect. Nevertheless, the point remains: We should almost always be skeptical of causal conclusions that anyone draws from a correlational study.

concept check

8. Suppose we find a +.8 correlation between students' reported interest in psychology and their grades on a psychology test. What conclusion can we draw?

9. On average, the more medicines people take, the more likely they are to die young. Propose alternative explanations for this correlation.

10. On average, drug addicts who regularly attend counseling sessions are more likely to stay drug-free than those who drop out. Propose alternative explanations for this correlation.

Answers

8. We can conclude only that if we know either someone's interest level or test score, we can predict the other with reasonably high accuracy. We *cannot* conclude that an interest in psychology will help someone learn the material or that doing well on psychology tests increases someone's interest in the material. Either conclusion might be true, of course, but neither conclusion follows from these results. A correlational study cannot demonstrate a cause-and-effect relationship.

9. Perhaps people get sick from complications caused by taking too many pills. Or maybe the people who take many medicines are those who already had serious illnesses.

10. Perhaps the counseling sessions are helpful to people who want to quit drugs. Or perhaps the people with the most serious addictions are the ones who quit.

Experiments

To determine causation, an investigator uses an ex-periment, *a study in which the investigator manipulates at least one variable while measuring at least one other variable.* The independent variable is *the item that an experimenter changes or controls*—for example, the type of training that people receive or the wording of the instructions before they start some task. The dependent variable is *the item that an experimenter measures to determine the outcome*—for example, how many questions people answer correctly or how rapidly they respond to signals. If the procedure causes different groups to behave differently, you can think of the independent variable as the cause and the dependent variable as the effect.

An experimental group *receives the treatment that an experiment is designed to test.* For example, the experimental group might receive some special experience that we think will influence later behavior. The control group is *a set of individuals treated in the same way as the experimental group except for the procedure that the experiment is designed to test.* If the people in the experimental group received a special experience, those in the control group do something else during the same time. If those in the experimental group receive a medication, those in the control group receive a placebo. Table 2.2 contrasts experiments with observational studies.

A key procedure for any experiment is random assignment of participants to groups: *The experimenter uses a chance procedure, such as drawing names out of a hat, to make sure that every participant has the same probability as any other participant of being assigned to a given group.* Why is this so important? Consider a couple of examples.

Women at menopause have decreased release of estrogens and related hormones. For years physicians recommended hormone replacement therapy, and the women receiving such therapy tended to be healthier than other women their age. However, women who follow their physicians' advice tend to be more health-conscious in other ways, such as diet and exercise, so they could be healthy for reasons other than the hormones. In an experiment, more than 160,000 women agreed to receive either the hormones or a placebo. The result: Women taking the hormones had decreased risk of hip fractures and colon cancer, but increased risk of

Table 2.2 Comparison of Five Methods of Research

Observational Studies

Case Study	Detailed description of single individual; suitable for studying rare conditions.
Naturalistic Observation	Description of behavior under natural conditions.
Survey	Study of attitudes, beliefs, or behaviors based on answers to questions.
Correlation	Description of the relationship between two variables that the investigator measures but does not control; determines whether two variables are closely related but does not address questions of cause and effect.

Experiment

	Determination of the effect of a variable controlled by the investigator on some other variable that is measured; the only method that can inform us about cause and effect.

© Cengage Learning

heart disease, stroke, and breast cancer (Writing Group, 2002). Overall, the harms were at least as great as the benefits.

Another example: Several studies have found that moderate alcohol drinkers (about one glass of beer or wine per day) tend in the long run to be healthier than heavy drinkers or non-drinkers. It's clear that heavy drinking would be bad, but if you are a non-drinker, should you take up beer or wine? We can't be sure. First, this is a small effect. In one study, non-drinkers constituted 22% of the healthier old people, compared to 25% of the less healthy old people (Sun et al., 2011). Second, non-drinkers could differ from moderate drinkers in other ways. Maybe healthy people are more likely to drink than are people who are prone to illness. Maybe people who belong to religions that forbid alcohol have health risks for other reasons. And we could imagine other possibilities. We can't be sure, unless someone does a study with random assignment to drinking and not drinking. (That would be a hard study to do.)

concept check

11. An instructor wants to find out whether the frequency of testing in an introductory psychology class influences students' final exam performance. The instructor gives weekly tests in one class, just three tests in a second class, and only a single midterm exam in the third class. All three classes take the same final exam, and the instructor then compares their performances. Identify the independent variable and the dependent variable in this example experiment.

Answer

11. The independent variable is the frequency of tests during the semester. The dependent variable is the students' performance on the final exam.

Reducing the Influence of Expectations

Experiments can go wrong in many ways, if we're not careful. Let's consider several possible problems and how researchers overcome them.

Experimenter Bias and Blind Studies

Experimenter bias is *the tendency of an experimenter (unintentionally, as a rule) to misperceive the results.* Imagine that you, as a psychological investigator, are testing the hypothesis that left-handed children are more creative than right-handed children. (I don't know why you would be testing this silly hypothesis, but suppose you are.) If the results support your hypothesis, you expect to be on your way to fame and success as a psychology researcher. Now you see a left-handed child do something, and you are trying to decide whether it counts as "creative." You want to be fair. You don't want your hypothesis to influence what you count as creative. Just try to ignore your hypothesis.

To minimize the influence of expectations, it is best to use a **blind observer**—*an observer who records data without knowing the researcher's predictions.* For example, you might ask someone to record creative acts by a group of children without knowing that you are interested in handedness. Observers who do not know the hypothesis record their observations fairly.

Ideally, the experimenter conceals the procedure from the participants also. Suppose experimenters give children a pill that is supposed to increase their creativity. If the children know the prediction, their expectations may influence their behavior.

In a **single-blind study**, *either the observer or the participants are unaware of which participants received which treatment* (Table 2.3). In a **double-blind study**, *both the observer and the participants are unaware of which participants received which treatment*. Of course, the experimenter who organized the study would need to keep records of which participants received which procedure. (If *everyone* loses track of the procedure, it is known jokingly as "triple blind.")

Demand Characteristics

Here is a problem that faces psychological researchers but not chemists: People in a psychological experiment know they are in an experiment. (Ethically, the researcher is required to tell them and to obtain their consent.) If you know you are in a study, and that someone is watching you, might that not influence your behavior? Furthermore, suppose you know (or guess) what the experimenter hopes to see. Might that expectation alter your behavior?

Table 2.3 Single-Blind and Double-Blind Studies

Who is aware of which participants are in which group?			
	Experimenter Who Organized the Study	Observer	Participants
Single-blind	aware	unaware	aware
Single-blind	aware	aware	unaware
Double-blind	aware	unaware	unaware

© Cengage Learning

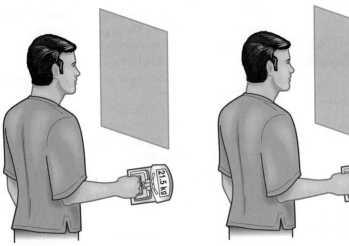

Told that pink increases strength   Told that pink decreases strength

© Cengage Learning

Figure 2.11 Men who expected to feel stronger while looking at pink were in fact stronger than those who expected to feel weaker while looking at pink.

Here is an example: Experimenters told one group of men that there was reason to believe that seeing the color pink decreases one's strength. They told another group that seeing the color pink increases one's strength. Then they tested the men's grip strength while looking at a pink panel. Those who expected pink to increase their strength showed a 10% stronger grip (Smith, Bell, & Fusco, 1986; Figure 2.11).

Even when researchers don't tell people what they expect, people's guesses influence their behavior. Martin Orne (1969) defined demand characteristics as *cues that tell participants what is expected of them and what the experimenter hopes to find.* To minimize demand characteristics, experimenters often try to conceal the purpose of the experiment. A double-blind study also serves the purpose: If two groups share the same expectations but behave differently because of a treatment, then the differences are not due to their expectations.

Problems With a Before-and-After Study

Imagine a chemist adding one clear liquid to another. Suddenly the first mixture turns green and explodes. We would conclude cause and effect, as we have no reason to expect that the first liquid was about to turn green and explode on its own. Now imagine some procedures in psychology: Researchers give children language training and find that their language skills improve over the next few months. They provide therapy for depressed patients and find that many of them become gradually less depressed. They provide special training for violent teenagers, and find that many of them become less violent. In any of these cases, can we conclude cause and effect? No, because it is possible, even likely, that many of these people would have improved over time without treatment.

Instead of a before-and-after study, a better design is to compare two groups: An investigator provides the treatment for one group (the *experimental group*) and not the other (the *control group*), with participants randomly assigned to the two groups. The difference, if any, that emerges between the groups is an indication of the treatment's effect. Even then, we should beware of generalizing the results too far. Maybe the procedure works only in one culture or under special circumstances. Psychologists have learned to be cautious about the results of any single study.

What's the Evidence?

Inheritance of Acquired Characteristics? Problems in a Before-and-After Study

Let's examine a specific study that illustrates the limitations of a before-and-after study. It pertains to evolution, but the point here is not so much evolution itself as some pitfalls of research.

Charles Darwin's theory of evolution by natural selection makes a simple point: If individuals with one kind of genes reproduce more than those with other genes, then the first set of genes will become more common from one generation to the next. Eventually, the whole population will resemble those who were most successful at reproducing. Prior to Darwin, Jean-Baptiste Lamarck had offered a different theory, evolution by inheritance of acquired characteristics. According to that theory, if you exercise your muscles, your children will be born with larger muscles. If you fail to use your little toe, your children will be born with a smaller little toe than you had. The evidence never supported that theory, and by the early 1900s nearly all biologists abandoned it in favor of Darwin's theory. However, a few holdouts continued defending Lamarckian evolution.

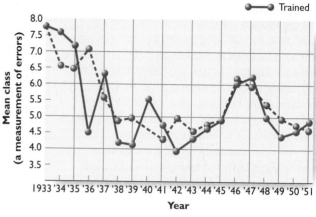

Figure 2.12 Rats in the experimental group and the control group improved at equal rates from one generation to the next. (From Agar, W. E., Drummond, F. H., Tiegs, O. W., & Gunson, M. M., "Fourth (final) report on a test of McDougall's Lamarckian experiment on the training of rats," *Journal of Experimental Biology, 31,* 307–321. Copyright © 1954 The Company of Biologists Ltd. Reprinted by permission.)

First Study (McDougall, 1938)

Hypothesis If rats learn to swim through a maze, their offspring will learn the maze more quickly.

Method Rats had to learn to swim a particular route to get out of a tank of water. The experimenter trained them until each rat was consistently swimming quickly the correct route. Then he let them breed. He did not select the best learners for breeding, but simply chose rats at random. When rats of the next generation were old enough, he trained them and let them reproduce. This procedure continued for one generation after another.

Results The average performance of the rats improved from one generation to the next for the first few generations. That is, the second generation learned faster than the first, the third faster than the second, and so on for a few generations. Later, the results fluctuated.

Interpretation These results are consistent with the hypothesis, but we should consider other hypotheses, too. If these results really indicate inheritance of acquired characteristics, we would have to imagine that the experience of learning the maze somehow directed the genes to mutate in the right way to help the next generation learn the same maze. It is difficult to imagine how this could happen.

When results conflict so strongly with what we think we know, scientists ask these questions: Are the results replicable? Is there a more parsimonious explanation? And is there any flaw in the design of the study?

Do you, in fact, see anything wrong with the procedure? At the time of this study, hardly anyone saw what was wrong. However, one group of researchers noticed that this is a before-and-after study with no control group. What would happen, they wondered, if they repeated the study using a control group that was not trained in the maze? Would their offspring improve as much as the offspring of the trained rats?

Second Study (Agar, Drummond, Tiegs, & Gunson, 1954)

Hypothesis If it is possible to replicate McDougall's results, the improvement will also occur in a control group that receives no training in the maze.

Method Rats in the trained group were treated the same as those in McDougall's study: Rats learned the maze and then mated. Rats of the next generation also learned the maze and then mated and so forth.

In the control group, the rats used for training were not used for breeding. Young, healthy rats typically have a litter of about 12 babies. In each generation, a few rats were trained in the maze but not used for breeding. Other rats from the same litter were not trained and were permitted to breed. In each generation, the researchers obtained a measure of maze learning, but because only untrained rats mated, all the rats in the control group were descended from untrained rats. Any improvement over generations could not be due to the training. The experiment continued for 18 years, with a few generations of rats per year. (Rats reach sexual maturity at about age 60 days.)

Results Figure 2.12 shows the results. For the first few years, on average, both the trained group and the control group improved from one generation to the next. In later years, the results fluctuated. The two groups performed similarly throughout the study.

Interpretation To most people's surprise, McDougall's results were replicable. However, because the trained group did not differ from the control group, training had nothing to do with the improvement over generations. That is, the results showed no evidence for inheritance of acquired characteristics.

How, then, can we explain the improvement over generations? One possibility is that rats of the first generation were stressed. They had just been shipped in by train, in crowded boxes, from rat-breeding facilities to McDougall's laboratory. (Yes, there are companies that specialize in breeding and selling rats.) The second generation grew up in the laboratory, but they were the offspring of highly stressed parents. Conceivably, those effects could persist for several generations.

Another possibility is that the experimenters gradually got better at taking care of rats and running the experiment. We might be seeing a change in the experimenters, not a change in the rats.

A third possibility is that because the experimenters always mated brother with sister, later generations may have become less vigorous. Ordinarily, we expect inbreeding to be a disadvantage, but perhaps less vigorous rats swam more slowly and therefore had more time to consider which direction to turn in the maze. This idea sounds a little far-fetched but not impossible.

We don't know which explanation is correct. The question isn't important enough for anyone to do the additional research necessary to find out. The main conclusion is that we can account for the results without assuming inheritance of acquired characteristics.

This episode illustrates several points about research: (a) If the results seem unlikely, look for a more parsimonious explanation. (b) Beware of before-and-after studies. Without a control group, we don't know what the results mean. (c) If behavior changes from one generation to the next, the explanation doesn't have to be genetic. It might reflect a change in the environment. (For example, your environment differs from the one in which your grandparents grew up.)

Ethical Considerations in Research

In any experiment, psychologists manipulate a variable to determine how it affects behavior. Perhaps you object to the idea of someone trying to alter your behavior. If so, consider that every time you talk to people, you are trying to alter their behavior at least slightly. Most experiments in psychology are no more manipulative than a conversation. Still, some experiments do raise difficult issues, and researchers are bound by both law and conscience to treat their participants ethically.

Ethical Concerns With Humans

Consider the question of televised violence. If psychologists believed that watching violent programs might really transform viewers into murderers, it would be unethical to conduct experiments to find out for sure. It is also unethical to perform procedures likely to cause significant pain, embarrassment, or any other harm.

Before conducting any study on people, researchers ask them to give their informed consent, *a statement that they have been told what to expect and that they agree to continue.* When researchers ask for volunteers, they describe what will happen. Most procedures are innocuous, such as tests of perception, memory, or attention. Occasionally, however, the procedure includes something that people might not wish to do, such as examining disgusting photographs, drinking concentrated sugar water, or receiving electrical shocks. Participants are told they have the right to quit if they find the procedure too disagreeable.

Special problems arise in research with children, people who are mentally retarded, or others who might not understand the instructions well enough to provide informed consent (Bonnie, 1997). Individuals with severe depression pose a special problem (Elliott, 1997) because some seem to have lost interest in protecting their own welfare. In such cases, researchers either consult the person's guardian or nearest relative or simply decide not to proceed.

Research at a college must first be approved by an Institutional Review Board (IRB). An IRB judges whether the proposed studies include procedures for informed consent and whether they safeguard each participant's confidentiality. An IRB also tries to prevent risky procedures. It probably would reject a proposal to offer cocaine, even if people were eager to give their informed consent. A committee would also ban procedures that they consider seriously embarrassing or degrading. Many "reality television" shows would be banned if they needed approval from an IRB (Spellman, 2005).

The committee also evaluates procedures in which investigators want to deceive participants temporarily. Suppose a researcher wants to test whether it is harder to persuade people who know someone is trying to persuade them. The researcher wants to use one group that is informed of the upcoming persuasion and one that is not. The researcher cannot fully inform all participants without losing the whole point of the study. The institutional committee would have to decide whether this temporary deception is acceptable.

The American Psychological Association (APA) published a book discussing the proper ethical treatment of volunteers in experiments (Sales & Folkman, 2000). The APA censures or expels any member who violates these principles.

Ethical Concerns With Nonhumans

Some psychological research deals with nonhuman animals, especially research on basic processes such as sensation, hunger, and learning (Figure 2.13). Researchers use nonhumans if they want to control aspects of life that people will not let them control (e.g., who mates with whom), if they want to study behavior continuously over months or years (longer than people are willing to participate), or if the research poses health risks. Animal research has long been essential for preliminary testing of most new drugs, surgical procedures, and methods of relieving pain. People with untreatable illnesses argue that they have the right to hope for cures that might result from animal research (Feeney, 1987). Much of our knowledge in psychology, biology, and medicine made use of animal studies at some point.

Nevertheless, some people oppose much or all of animal research. Animals, after all, cannot give informed consent. Some animal rights supporters insist that animals should have the same rights as humans, that keeping ani-

Figure 2.13 One example of animal research: A mirror mounted on a young owl's head enables investigators to track the owl's head movements and thereby discover how the owl localizes sounds with one ear plugged. The findings may help researchers understand how people with visual loss use their hearing to compensate.

example, animal rights advocates point to studies that exposed monkeys or puppies to painful procedures that seem difficult to justify. Researchers point to protesters who have vandalized laboratories, planted bombs, banged on a researcher's children's windows at night, and inserted a garden hose through a window to flood a house (G. Miller, 2007a). Some protesters have stated that they oppose using any drug, even a medication for AIDS, if its discovery came from research with animals. Unfortunately, when both sides concentrate on criticizing their most extreme opponents, they make points of agreement harder to find.

One careful study by a relatively unbiased outsider concluded that the truth is messy: Some research is painful to the animals *and* nevertheless valuable for scientific and medical progress (Blum, 1994). We must, most people conclude, seek a compromise.

Professional organizations such as the Neuroscience Society and the American Psychological Association publish guidelines for the proper use of animals in research. Colleges and other research institutions maintain laboratory animal care committees to ensure that laboratory animals are treated humanely, that their pain and discomfort are kept to a minimum, and that experimenters consider alternatives before imposing potentially painful procedures.

How can we determine in advance whether the value of the expected experimental results (which is hard to predict) will outweigh the pain the animals will endure (which is hard to measure)? As is common with ethical decisions, reasonable arguments can be raised on both sides of the question, and no compromise is fully satisfactory.

mals (even pets) in cages is slavery, and that killing any animal is murder. Others oppose some kinds of research but are willing to compromise about others.

Psychologists vary in their attitudes. Most support some kinds of animal research but draw a line somewhere separating acceptable from unacceptable research (Plous, 1996). Naturally, different psychologists draw that line at different places.

In this debate, as in so many other political controversies, one common tactic is for each side to criticize the most extreme actions of its opponents. For

module 2.2

In Closing

Psychological Research

Most scientists avoid the word *prove*, because it sounds too final. Psychologists certainly do. (The joke is that psychology courses don't have true–false tests, just maybe–perhaps tests.) The most complex and most interesting aspects of human behavior are products of genetics, a lifetime of experiences, and countless current influences. Given the practical and ethical limitations, it might seem that psychological researchers would become discouraged. However, because of these difficulties, researchers have been highly inventive in designing complex methods. A single study rarely answers a question decisively, but many studies converge to increase our total understanding.

Summary

- *Operational definitions.* For many purposes, psychologists use operational definitions, which state how to measure a phenomenon or how to produce it. (page 34)
- *Sampling.* Because psychologists hope to draw conclusions that apply to a large population, they try to select a sample that resembles the total population—either a representative sample or a random sample. To apply the results to people worldwide, they need a cross-cultural sample. (page 34)
- *Naturalistic observations.* Naturalistic observations provide descriptions of humans or other species under natural conditions. (page 36)
- *Case histories.* A case history is a detailed research study of a single individual, generally someone with unusual characteristics. (page 37)
- *Surveys.* A survey is a report of people's answers on a questionnaire. It is easy to conduct a survey and, unfortunately, easy to get misleading results. (page 37)
- *Correlations.* A correlational study examines the relationship between variables that are outside the investigator's control. The strength of this relationship is measured by a correlation coefficient that ranges from 0 (no relationship) to plus or minus 1 (a perfect relationship). (page 39)
- *Illusory correlations.* Beware of illusory correlations—relationships that people think they observe between variables after casual observation. (page 40)
- *Inferring causation.* A correlational study cannot uncover cause-and-effect relationships, but an experiment can. (page 41)
- *Experiments.* In an experiment, the investigator manipulates an independent variable to determine its effect on the dependent variable. A before-and-after study often leads to results that are hard to interpret. It is better to compare the results for different groups. (page 42)
- *Random assignment.* An experimenter randomly assigns individuals to the experimental and control groups. All participants should have an equal probability of being chosen for the experimental group. (page 42)
- *Overcoming experimenter bias.* An experimenter's expectations influence the interpretations of behavior and the recording of data. To ensure objectivity, investigators use blind observers who do not know what results are expected. In a double-blind study, neither the observer nor the participants know the researcher's predictions. (page 43)
- *Demand characteristics.* Researchers try to minimize the effects of demand characteristics, which are cues that tell participants what the experimenter expects them to do. (page 43)
- *Ethics of experimentation.* Research on human participants should not proceed until the participants have given their informed consent. Psychologists try to minimize risk to their participants, but they sometimes face difficult ethical decisions. (page 46)

Key Terms

blind observer (page 43)

case history (page 37)

control group (page 42)

convenience sample (page 35)

correlation (page 39)

correlation coefficient (page 39)

cross-cultural sample (page 35)

demand characteristics (page 44)

dependent variable (page 42)

double-blind study (page 43)

experiment (page 42)

experimental group (page 42)

experimenter bias (page 43)

illusory correlation (page 41)

independent variable (page 42)

informed consent (page 46)

naturalistic observation (page 36)

operational definition (page 34)

placebo (page 41)

random assignment (page 42)

random sample (page 35)

representative sample (page 35)

scatter plot (page 40)

single-blind study (page 43)

survey (page 37)

module 2.3

Measuring and Analyzing Results

- How can researchers state the "average" results of a study?
- How can researchers describe the variations among individuals?
- How can researchers determine whether the results represent something more than chance fluctuations?

Some years ago, a television program reported that 28 young people known to have played the game Dungeons and Dragons had committed suicide. Alarming, right?

Not necessarily. At that time, at least 3 million young people played the game regularly. The reported suicide rate among D&D players—28 per 3 million—was considerably *less* than the suicide rate among teenagers in general.

So do these results mean that playing D&D *prevents* suicide? Hardly. The 28 reported cases are probably an incomplete count. Besides, no matter what the correlation between playing D&D and committing suicide, it could not tell us about cause and effect. Maybe the kinds of young people who play D&D are simply different from those who do not.

Then what conclusion should we draw? *None.* When the data are incomplete or the method is flawed, no conclusion follows. (Even when the data are acceptable, people sometimes present them in a confusing or misleading manner, as shown in Figure 2.14.) In this module, we consider proper ways to analyze and interpret results.

Descriptive Statistics

To explain the meaning of a study, an investigator must summarize the results. If a researcher observes 100 people, we want to know the general trends or averages, not the details of each individual. An investigator provides descriptive sta-

tistics, which are *mathematical summaries of results.* The correlation coefficient, discussed earlier in this chapter, is an example of a descriptive statistic.

Measures of the Central Score

We care about the central score—that is, the middle or average score. Three ways of representing the central score are the mean, median, and mode. The mean is *the sum of all the scores divided by the total number of scores.* When people say "average," they generally refer to the mean. For example, the mean of 2, 10, and 3 is 5 (15 ÷ 3). The mean is especially useful if the scores approximate the normal distribution (or normal curve), *a symmetrical frequency of scores clustered around the mean.* For example, if we measure how long it takes various students to complete some task, their times usually follow a pattern close to the normal distribution.

The mean can be misleading, however. For example, *every* student in my class this semester has a greater than average number of arms and legs! It's true. Think about it. What is the average (mean) number of arms or legs for a human being? It is not 2, but 1.99 . . . because a few people have had an arm or leg amputated. So if the "average" refers to the mean, it is possible for almost everyone to be above or below average. Here is another example: A survey asked people how many sex partners they hoped to have, ideally, over the next 30 years. The mean for women was 2.8 and the mean for men was 64.3 (L. C.

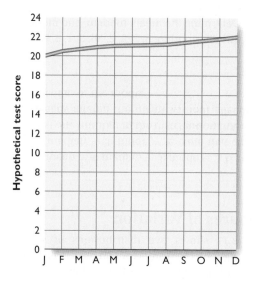

a

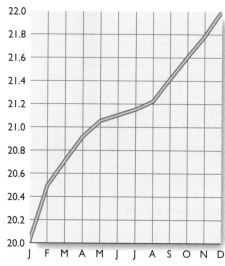

b

Figure 2.14 Statistics can be misleading: Both graphs present the same data, an increase from 20 to 22 over 1 year's time. But graph (**b**) makes that increase look dramatic by ranging from 20 to 22 (rather than from 0 to 22). (After Huff, 1954.)

Miller & Fishkin, 1997). But those means are extremely misleading. Almost two thirds of women and about half of men replied "1." They wanted a loving relationship with one partner. Most of the others said they hoped for a few partners during their lifetime, but a small number of men said they hoped for hundreds, thousands, or tens of thousands.

When the population distribution is far from symmetrical, we can better represent the typical scores by the median instead of the mean. To determine the median, *we arrange the scores in order from the highest to the lowest. The middle score is the median.* For example, for the set of scores 2, 10, and 3, the median is 3. For the set of scores 1, 1, 1, and 3.5 x 10^5, the median is 1. In short, extreme scores greatly affect the mean but not the median.

The third way to represent the central score is the mode, *the score that occurs most frequently.* For example, in the distribution of scores 2, 2, 3, 4, and 10, the mode is 2. The mode is seldom useful except under special circumstances. Suppose we asked college students how much they study and gathered the results shown in Figure 2.15. Half of the students at this college study a great deal, and half study very little. The mean for this distribution is 4.28 hours per day, a misleading number because all the students study either much more or much less than that. The median is no better as a representation of these results: Because we have an even number of students, there is no middle score. We could take a figure midway between the two scores nearest the middle, but in this case those scores are 2 and 7, so we would compute a median of 4.5, again misleading. A distribution like this is called a *bimodal distribution* (one with two common scores); the researcher might describe the two modes and not even mention the mean or the median.

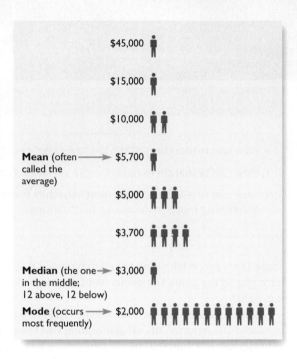

Figure 2.16 The monthly salaries of the 25 employees of company X, showing the mean, median, and mode. (After Huff, 1954.)

To summarize: The mean is what most people intend when they say "average." It is the sum of the scores divided by the number of scores. The median is the middle score after the scores are ranked from highest to lowest. The mode is the most common score (Figure 2.16).

concept check

13. **a.** For the following distribution of scores, determine the mean, the median, and the mode: 5, 2, 2, 2, 8, 3, 1, 6, 7.
    b. Determine the mean, median, and mode for this distribution: 5, 2, 2, 2, 35, 3, 1, 6, 7.

Answer

13. **a.** mean = 4; median = 3; mode = 2. **b.** mean = 7; median = 3; mode = 2. Note that changing just one number in the distribution from 8 to 35 greatly altered the mean without affecting the median or the mode.

Measures of Variation

Figure 2.17 shows two distributions of scores, which might be the results for two tests in an introductory psychology class. Both tests have the same mean, 70, but different distributions. If you had a

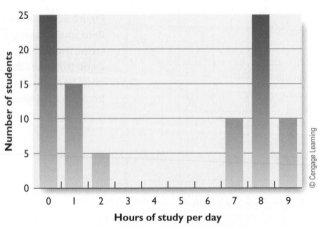

Figure 2.15 Results of an imaginary survey of study habits at one college. In this case, both the mean and the median are misleading. This distribution has two modes, which are 0 and 8.

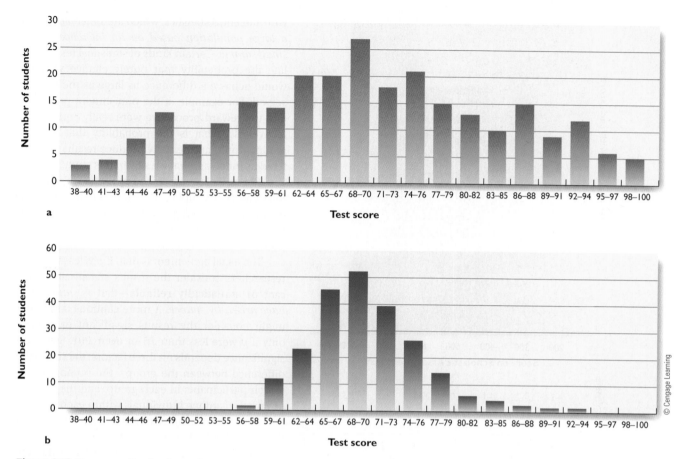

Figure 2.17 These two distributions of test scores have the same mean but different variances and different standard deviations.

score of 80, you would beat only 75% of the other students on the first test, but with the same score, you would beat 95% of the other students on the second test.

To describe the difference between the two graphs in Figure 2.17, we need a measurement of the variation (or spread) around the mean. The simplest such measurement is the range of a distribution, *a statement of the highest and lowest scores.* The range in Figure 2.17a is 38 to 100, and in Figure 2.17b, it is 56 to 94.

The range is a simple but not very useful calculation because it reflects only the extremes. The more useful measure is the standard deviation (SD), *a measurement of the amount of variation among scores in a normal distribution.* In the appendix to this chapter, you will find a formula for calculating the standard deviation. For present purposes, you can simply remember that when the scores are closely clustered near the mean, the standard deviation is small. When the scores are more widely scattered, the standard deviation is large. So, Figure 2.17a has a larger standard deviation, and Figure 2.17b has a smaller one.

As Figure 2.18 shows, the SAT was designed to produce a mean of 500 and a standard deviation of 100. Of all people taking the test, 68% score within 1 standard deviation above or below the mean (400–600), and 95% score within 2 standard deviations (300–700). Only 2.5% score above 700. Another 2.5% score below 300.

Standard deviations enable us to compare scores on different tests. For example, if you scored 1 standard deviation above the mean on the SAT, you tested about as well, relatively speaking, as someone who scored 1 standard deviation above the mean on a different test, such as the American College Test.

concept check

14. Suppose that you score 80 on your first psychology test. The mean for the class is 70, and the standard deviation is 5. On the second test, you receive a score of 90. This time the mean for the class is also 70, but the standard deviation is 20. Compared to the other students in your class, did your performance improve, deteriorate, or stay the same?

Answer

14. Even though your score rose from 80 on the first test to 90 on the second, your performance actually deteriorated in comparison to other students' scores. A score of 80 on the first test was 2 standard deviations above the mean, better than 98% of all other students. A 90 on the second test was only 1 standard deviation above the mean, a score that beats only 84% of the other students.

© Cengage Learning

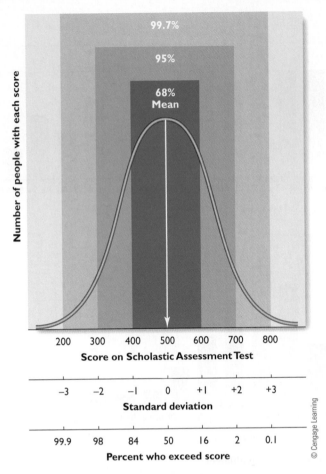

Figure 2.18 In a normal distribution of scores, the amount of variation from the mean can be measured in standard deviations. In this example, scores between 400 and 600 are said to be within 1 standard deviation from the mean; scores between 300 and 700 are within 2 standard deviations from the mean.

Evaluating Results: Inferential Statistics

Suppose researchers randomly assign people to two groups to help them quit smoking cigarettes. One group receives punishments for smoking, and the other group gets rewards for not smoking. Before treatment, both groups average about 10 cigarettes per day. At the end of 6 weeks of therapy, those in the punishment group average 7.5 cigarettes per day, whereas those in the reward group average 6.5 cigarettes per day. How seriously should we take this difference?

To answer this question, we obviously need to know more than just the numbers 7.5 and 6.5. How many smokers were in the study? (Just a few? Hundreds? Thousands?) Also, how much variation occurred within each group? Are most people's behaviors close to the group means, or did a few extreme scores distort the averages? We evaluate the results

with inferential statistics, which are *statements about a large population based on an inference from a small sample.* Certain kinds of statistical tests calculate the probability that purely chance variation would achieve a difference as large as the one observed. For example, if the punishment procedure and the reward procedure were really equal in effectiveness, what is the probability that the two groups would accidentally produce results that differed as much as what we saw in this study?

The result is summarized by a *p* (as in *probability*) value. For example, p < .05 indicates that *the probability that randomly generated results would resemble the observed results is less than 5%.* The smaller the *p* value, the more impressive the results.

The usual agreement is that, if *p* is less than .05, researchers consider the results statistically significant or **statistically reliable**—that is, *unlikely to have arisen by chance.* A more cautious researcher might consider the results significant or reliable only if *p* were less than .01 or even .001. Statistical significance depends on three factors: the size of the difference between the groups, the number of research participants in each group, and the amount of variation among individuals within each group.

If the results are not statistically significant, what then? We should draw no conclusion. We should *not* conclude that the hypothesis was wrong or that the procedure had no effect. Sometimes, a hypothesis is correct but difficult to demonstrate, and sometimes, a procedure appears to be ineffective just because our measurements are inaccurate. Of course, the more often researchers have failed to find a significant effect, the more skeptical we should become.

For a variety of reasons, many scientists recommend that instead of (or in addition to) stating the *p* value, researchers should show the means and 95% confidence intervals for each group, as shown in Figure 2.19 (Cumming, 2008). The 95% confidence interval is *the range within which the true population mean lies, with 95% certainty.*

"Wait a minute," you protest. "We already know the means: 7.5 and 6.5. Aren't *those* the 'true' population means?" No, those are the means for particular samples of the population. Someone who studies another group of smokers may not get the same results. What we care about is the mean for all smokers. It is impractical to measure that mean, but if we know the sample mean, the size of the sample, and the standard deviation, we can estimate how close the sample mean is to the population mean. Figure 2.19 presents two possibilities.

In Figure 2.19a, the 95% confidence intervals are small. In other words, the standard deviations were small, the samples were large, and the sample means are almost certainly close to the true population means. In Figure 2.19b, the confidence intervals are larger, so the sample means are just rough approximations of the true population means. Presenting data with confidence intervals enables readers to see how large and impressive the difference is between two groups (Hunter, 1997; Loftus, 1996).

concept check

15. Should we be more impressed with results when the 95% confidence intervals are large or small? Should we be more impressed if the *p* value is large or small?

Answer

15. In both cases, smaller. A small 95% confidence interval indicates high confidence in the results. A small *p* value indicates a low probability of getting such a large difference merely by chance.

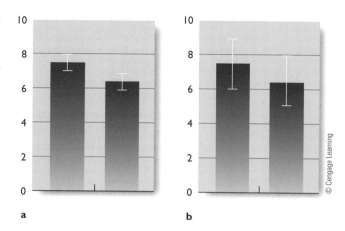

Figure 2.19 The vertical lines indicate 95% confidence intervals. The pair of graphs in part **a** indicate that the true mean has a 95% chance of falling within a very narrow range. The graphs in part **b** indicate a wider range.

module 2.3

In Closing

Statistics and Conclusions

Sometimes, psychological researchers get such consistent effects that they need no statistics: If you turn out the lights in a sealed room, people will no longer be able to see. If you add sugar to your iced tea, it tastes sweet. Statistical tests are critical for evaluating smaller effects: Does a change in wording alter people's responses to a survey? Does using an electronic study guide improve students' test scores? Does family therapy provide better results than individual therapy to treat drug abuse? Most psycho-

logical researchers deal with small effects and need a solid understanding of statistics.

Examining the statistics is only the first step toward drawing a conclusion. To say that an experiment has statistically significant or reliable results means only that we would be unlikely to get such results merely by chance. At that point, psychologists use their knowledge to seek the most likely interpretation of the results.

Summary

- *Mean, median, and mode.* One way of presenting the central score of a distribution is via the mean, determined by adding all the scores and dividing by the number of individuals. Another way is the median, which is the middle score after all the scores have been arranged from highest to lowest. The mode is the score that occurs most frequently. (page 49)

- *Standard deviation (SD).* To indicate whether most scores are clustered close to the mean or whether they are spread out, psychologists report the range of scores called the standard deviation. If we know that a given score is a certain number of standard deviations above or below the mean, then we can determine what percentage of other scores it exceeds. (page 51)

- *Inferential statistics.* Inferential statistics are attempts to deduce the properties of a large population based on the results from a small sample of that population. (page 52)
- *Probability of chance results.* The most common use of inferential statistics is to calculate the probability that a given research result could have arisen by chance. That probability is low if the difference between the two groups is large, if the variability within each group is small, and if the number of individuals in each group is large. (page 52)
- *Statistical significance.* When psychologists say $p < .05$, they mean that the probability that accidental fluctuations could produce the kind of results they obtained is less than 5%. They generally set a standard of 5% or less. If the results meet that standard, they are then said to be statistically significant or reliable. (page 52)

Key Terms

95% confidence interval (page 52)

descriptive statistics (page 49)

inferential statistics (page 52)

mean (page 49)

median (page 50)

mode (page 50)

normal distribution (or normal curve) (page 49)

$p < .05$ (page 52)

range (page 51)

standard deviation (SD) (page 51)

statistically significant (or statistically reliable) results (page 52)

exploration and study

Access an interactive eBook and chapter-specific learning tools, including
- **flashcards**
- **quizzes**
- **videos**

and more, in your Psychology CourseMate. Go to **CengageBrain.com.**

If your professor has assigned Aplia:
1. Sign in to your account.
2. Complete the corresponding exercises as required by your professor.
3. When finished, click "Grade It Now" to see which areas you have mastered, which areas need more work, and detailed explanations of every answer.

appendix 2

Statistical Calculations

This appendix shows you how to calculate a few of the statistics mentioned in chapter 2. It is intended primarily to satisfy your curiosity. Ask your instructor whether you should use this appendix for any other purpose.

Standard Deviation

To determine the standard deviation (SD):

1. Determine the mean of the scores.
2. Subtract the mean from each of the individual scores.
3. Square each of those results, add the squares together, and divide by the total number of scores.

The result is called the *variance*. The standard deviation is the square root of the variance. Here is an example:

Individual scores	Each score minus the mean	Difference squared
12.5	−2.5	6.25
17.0	+2.0	4.00
11.0	−4.0	16.00
14.5	−0.5	0.25
16.0	+1.0	1.00
16.5	+1.5	2.25
17.5	+2.5	6.25
105		36.00

The mean is 15.0 (the sum of the first column, divided by 7). The variance is 5.143 (the sum of the third column, divided by 7). The standard deviation is 2.268 (the square root of 5.143).

Correlation Coefficients

To determine the correlation coefficient, we designate one of the variables x and the other one y. We obtain pairs of measures, x_i and y_i. Then we use the following formula:

$$r = \frac{[(\sum x_i y_i)] - n \cdot \bar{x} \cdot \bar{y}}{n \cdot sx \cdot sy}$$

In this formula, $(\sum x_i y_i)$ is the sum of the products of x and y. For each pair of observations (x, y), we multiply x times y and then add together all the products. The term $n \cdot \bar{x} \cdot \bar{y}$ means n (the number of pairs) times the mean of x times the mean of y. The denominator, $n \cdot sx \cdot sy$, means n times the standard deviation of x times the standard deviation of y.

Web/Technology Resources

Introductory Statistics: Concepts, Models, and Applications

Access an interactive eBook and chapter-specific learning tools, including
- **flashcards**
- **quizzes**
- **videos**
  and more, in your Psychology CourseMate. Go to **CengageBrain.com.**

You can read an entire statistics textbook by David W. Stockburger, Southwest Missouri State University, on your Psychology CourseMate at CengageBrain.com. Navigate to Chapter 2.

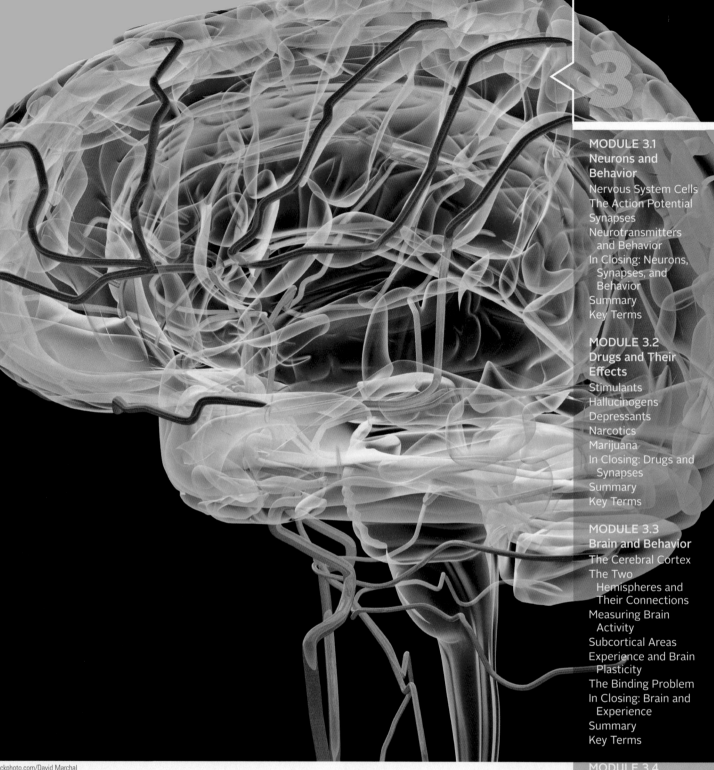

Biological Psychology

A human brain weighs only 1.2 to 1.4 kg (2.5 to 3 lb), and a bee's brain weighs only a milligram. A dollar bill weighs about a gram, so if you imagine a bill chopped into a thousand pieces, one of those pieces weighs about as much as a bee's brain. With that tiny brain, a bee locates food, evades predators, finds its way back to the hive, and then does a dance that directs other bees to the food. It also takes care of the queen bee and protects the hive against intruders.

Everything you perceive or do is a product of your brain activity. How does the brain do all that? We would like to know for both practical and theoretical reasons. Some of the practical issues relate to abnormal behavior. Are psychological disorders biological in origin? Can we treat them effectively with drugs or other biological interventions? Can we prevent deterioration in old age? Theoretical issues relate to what makes us tick. How does brain activity relate to consciousness? Do people differ in personality because of differences in their brains? The fascination of such questions impels researchers to tireless efforts.

© Townsend Dickinson/The Image Works

A bee has amazingly complex behavior, but we have no way to get inside the bee's experience to know what (if anything) it feels like to be a bee.

Neurons and Behavior

- To what extent can we explain our experiences and behavior in terms of the actions of individual cells in the nervous system?

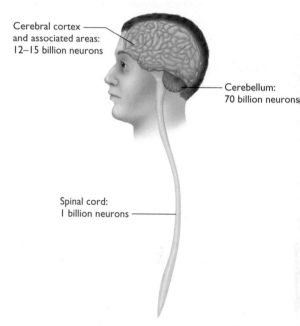

Cerebral cortex and associated areas: 12–15 billion neurons

Cerebellum: 70 billion neurons

Spinal cord: 1 billion neurons

Figure 3.1 Estimated distribution of the neurons in the adult human central nervous system. An exact count is not feasible, and the number varies from one person to another. (Based on data of R. W. Williams & Herrup, 1988.)

How do you differ from a machine? We usually think of a machine as something made of metal, but really a machine is anything that converts one type of energy into another, such as converting gasoline into the operation of a car. In that sense, you don't differ from a machine at all, because you are a machine. Your body converts the energy in your food into all the actions of your body. Your brain is part of that machine, and one way to understand your thoughts and actions is to analyze how your brain works. Researchers examine the functions of different parts of the brain, just as someone might study a car by examining what each of the car's parts does.

We start with the individual cells that compose the nervous system. Studying a single cell in your body doesn't take us far toward understanding your behavior, any more than studying a single silicon chip explains a computer. Still, it's a place to start, and it does shed light on a few matters of psychological interest.

Nervous System Cells

You experience your "self" as a single entity that senses, thinks, and remembers. However, your brain consists of an enormous number of separate cells called neurons (NOO-rons). Figure 3.1 shows estimates of the numbers of neurons in various parts of the human nervous system (R. W. Williams & Herrup, 1988). The nervous system also contains other kinds of cells called glia (GLEE-uh) *that support the neurons in many ways such as by insulating them, synchronizing activity among neighboring neurons, and removing waste products.* The glia are smaller but more numerous than neurons.

Neurons are similar to other body cells in most ways. The most distinctive feature of neurons is their shape, which varies depending on whether they receive information from a few sources or many and whether they send impulses over a short or a long distance (Figure 3.2). A neuron consists of three parts: a cell body, dendrites, and an axon (Figure 3.3). The cell body *contains the nucleus of the cell.* The dendrites (from a Greek word meaning "tree") are *widely branching structures that receive input from other neurons.* The axon is a *single, long, thin, straight fiber with branches near its tip.* Some vertebrate axons are covered with myelin, *an insulating sheath that speeds up the transmission of impulses along an axon.* As a rule, an axon transmits information to other cells, and the dendrites or cell body receives that information. The information can be either excitatory or inhibitory. That is, it can increase or decrease the probability that the next cell will send a message of its own. Inhibitory messages are essential for many purposes. For example, during a period of painful stimulation, your brain has mechanisms to inhibit further sensation of pain. If you step on a tack and reflexively raise your foot, inhibitory synapses prevent you from trying to raise your other foot at the same time.

concept check

1. Which part of a neuron receives input from other neurons? Which part sends messages to other cells?

Answer

1. Dendrites receive input from other neurons. Axons send messages.

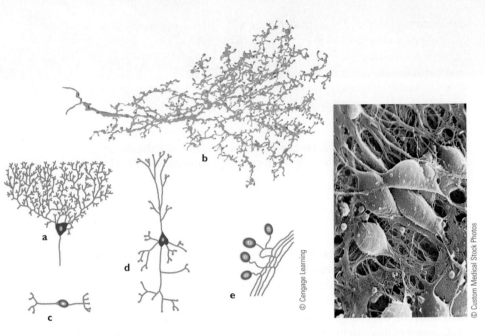

Figure 3.2 Neurons vary enormously in shape. The neurons in (**a**) and (**b**) receive input from many sources, the neuron in (**c**) from only a few sources, and the neuron in (**d**) from an intermediate number of sources. The sensory neurons (**e**) carry messages from sensory receptors to the brain or spinal cord. Inset: Electron micrograph showing cell bodies in brown and axons and dendrites in green. The color was added artificially; electron micrographs are made with electron beams, not light, and therefore they show no color.

The Action Potential

The function of an axon is to convey information over long distances, such as from the skin to the spinal cord. Electrical conduction would convey information almost instantaneously, but your body is a relatively poor conductor of electricity. If axons conducted electrically, impulses would get weaker and weaker as they traveled. Short people would feel a pinch on their toes more intensely than tall people would—if either felt their toes at all.

Instead, axons convey information by a process called an action potential, *an excitation that travels along an axon at a constant strength, no matter how far it travels.* An action potential is a yes–no or on–off message, like flicking a light switch (without a dimmer). This principle is known as the *all-or-none law.*

The advantage of an action potential over simple electrical conduction is that action potentials reach your brain at full strength. The disadvantage is that action potentials take time. Your knowledge of what is happening to your toes is at least a 20th of a second out of date. Pain and itch sensations are even slower. A 20th of a second will seldom inconvenience you, but that delay is theoretically interesting. When researchers first demonstrated that your touch perceptions are delayed while the message travels to the brain, they showed that percep-

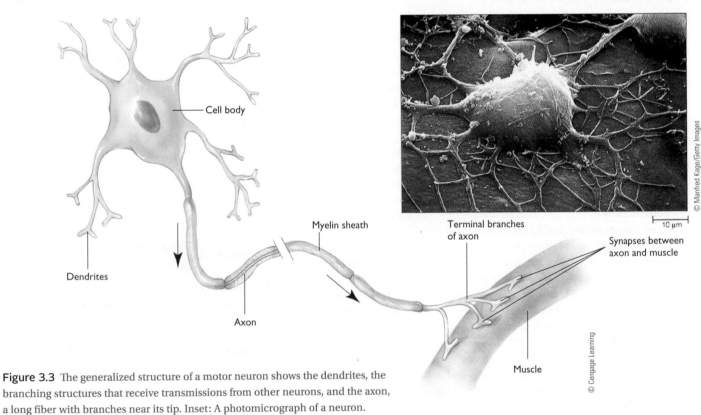

Figure 3.3 The generalized structure of a motor neuron shows the dendrites, the branching structures that receive transmissions from other neurons, and the axon, a long fiber with branches near its tip. Inset: A photomicrograph of a neuron.

tions occur in your head, not in your fingers. When you touch something, it *seems* that the sensation is in your finger, but no, it is in your head. Other evidence for this conclusion is that direct stimulation of certain brain areas produces touch sensation, even if a finger was amputated, and touching the finger produces no sensation if the relevant brain area is damaged.

Here is a quick description of how the action potential works:

1. When the axon is not stimulated, its membrane has a resting potential, *an electrical polarization across the membrane (or covering) of an axon.* Typically, the inside has a charge of about –70 millivolts relative to the outside. It gets this value from the negatively charged proteins inside the axon. In addition, a mechanism called the sodium-potassium pump pushes sodium ions out of the axon while pulling potassium ions in. Consequently, sodium ions are more concentrated outside the axon and potassium ions are more concentrated inside.

2. An action potential starts in either of two ways: First, many axons produce spontaneous activity. Second, input from other neurons can excite a neuron's membrane. In either case, if the excitation reaches the *threshold* of the axon (typically about −55 millivolts), it briefly opens some *gates* in the axon through which sodium and potassium ions can flow. Sodium ions, which are highly concentrated outside the membrane, rush into the cell, attracted by the negative charge inside. The influx of positively charged sodium ions is the action potential. As the positive charge enters the axon at one point, it stimulates the next point along the axon, which then starts opening sodium channels and repeating the process, as shown in Figure 3.4.

3. After the sodium gates have been open for a few milliseconds, they snap shut, but the potassium gates remain open a little longer. Because the sodium ions have brought positive charges into the cell, the inside of the cell no longer attracts potassium ions, and because they are more concentrated inside the cell than outside, they tend to flow out of the cell, carrying positive charges with them. Their exit drives the inside of the axon back to its resting potential (Figure 3.5b).

4. Eventually, the sodium-potassium pump removes the extra sodium ions and recaptures the escaped potassium ions.

These are the highlights: Sodium enters the cell (excitation). Then potassium leaves (return to the resting potential).

Conduction along an axon is analogous to a fire burning along a string: The fire at each point ignites

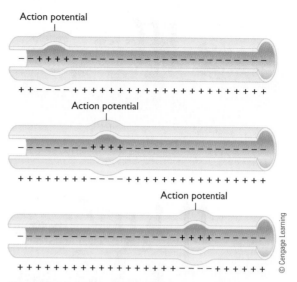

Figure 3.4 Ion movements conduct an action potential along an axon. At each point along the membrane, sodium ions enter the axon. As each point along the membrane returns to its original state, the action potential flows to the next point.

the next point, which in turn ignites the next point. In an axon, after sodium ions enter the membrane, some of them diffuse to the neighboring portion of the axon, exciting it enough to open its own sodium gates. The action potential spreads to this next area and so on down the axon, as shown in Figure 3.5. In this manner, the action potential remains equally strong all the way to the end of the axon.

How does this information relate to psychology? First, it explains why sensations from your fingers and toes do not fade away by the time they reach your brain. Second, an understanding of action potentials is one step toward understanding the communication between neurons. Third, anesthetic drugs (e.g., Novocain) operate by clogging sodium gates and therefore silencing neurons. When your dentist drills a tooth, the receptors in your tooth send out the message "Pain! Pain! Pain!" But that message does not reach your brain because the sodium gates are blocked.

concept check

2. If a mouse and a giraffe both get pinched on the toes at the same time, which will respond faster? Why?

3. Fill in these blanks: When the axon membrane is at rest, the inside has a _____ charge relative to the outside. When the membrane reaches its threshold, ____ ions enter from outside to inside, bringing with them a _____ charge. That flow of ions constitutes the ____ _____ of the axon.

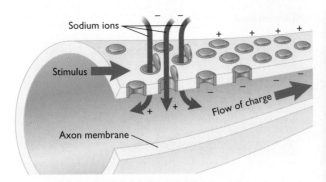

Sodium ions

Stimulus

Axon membrane

Flow of charge

a

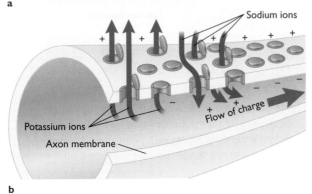

Sodium ions

Potassium ions

Axon membrane

Flow of charge

b

Figure 3.5 **(a)** During an action potential, sodium gates open, and sodium ions enter the axon, bearing a positive charge. **(b)** After an action potential occurs, the sodium gates close at that point and open at the next point along the axon. As the sodium gates close, potassium gates open, and potassium ions flow out of the axon. (Modified from Starr & Taggart, 1992.)

Answers

3. negative/sodium/positive/action potential.

2. The mouse will react faster because the action potentials have a shorter distance to travel in the mouse's nervous system than in the giraffe's.

Synapses

How do so many separate neurons combine forces to produce your stream of experiences? The answer is communication. Communication between one neuron and the next is not like transmission along an axon. At a synapse (SIN-aps), *the specialized junction between one neuron and another* (Figure 3.6), *a neuron releases a chemical that either excites or inhibits the next neuron.* That is, the chemical makes the next neuron either more or less likely to produce its own action potential.

A typical axon has several branches, each ending with a little bulge called a *presynaptic ending*, or terminal bouton, as shown in Figure 3.7. (*Bouton* is French for "button.") When an action potential reaches the terminal bouton, it releases a neu-

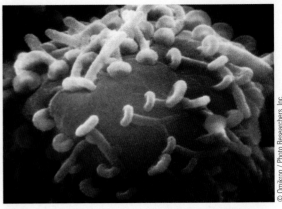

Figure 3.6 This synapse is magnified thousands of times in an electron micrograph. The tips of axons swell to form terminal boutons.

rotransmitter, *a chemical that activates receptors on other neurons* (Figure 3.7). Various brain areas use dozens of chemicals as neurotransmitters, but a given neuron releases only one or a few of them. The neurotransmitter molecules diffuse across a narrow gap to receptors on the postsynaptic neuron, *the neuron on the receiving end of the synapse.* A neurotransmitter fits into its receptor as a key fits into a lock, and it either excites or inhibits the postsynaptic neuron. The messages in a computer are simply on/off (represented as 1 or 0), and scientists used to assume that synaptic messages were like that, too. We now know that synaptic messages are highly variable. Depending on the transmitter and its receptor, the effect might have a sudden onset and last only a millisecond, or it might develop more gradually and last for seconds. *Peptide* transmitters diffuse to a wider brain area and produce effects that last many minutes. A quick, sudden message is important for vision and hearing. Slower, longer-lasting messages are more appropriate for taste and smell. Very slow, minutes-long messages are useful for hunger, thirst, and sex drive. Figure 3.8 summarizes synaptic transmission.

The inhibitory synapses are important. Inhibition is like stepping on the brakes. For example, when a pinch on your foot stimulates a reflex that contracts one set of muscles, inhibitory synapses in your spinal cord block activity in the muscles that would move your leg in the opposite direction.

After a neurotransmitter excites or inhibits a receptor, it separates from the receptor, ending the message. From that point on, the fate of the receptor molecule varies. It could return to re-excite the postsynaptic receptor, it could diffuse away from the synapse, or it could be reabsorbed by the axon that released it (through a process called *reuptake*). Most antidepressant drugs act by blocking reuptake, thus prolonging a transmitter's effects.

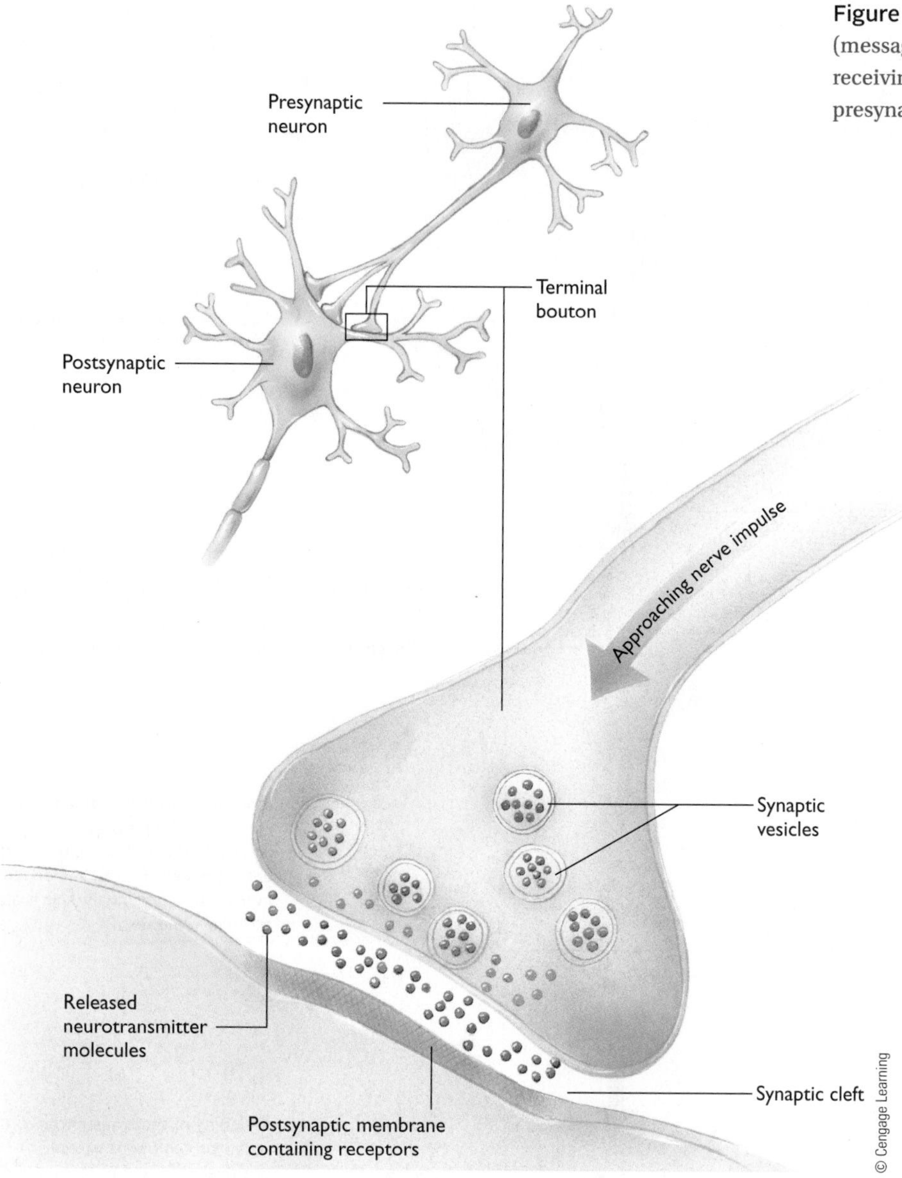

Figure 3.7 A synapse is a junction of a presynaptic (message-sending) cell and a postsynaptic (message-receiving) cell. The terminal bouton at the tip of the presynaptic axon contains the neurotransmitter.

Presynaptic neuron

Terminal bouton

Postsynaptic neuron

Approaching nerve impulse

Synaptic vesicles

Released neurotransmitter molecules

Synaptic cleft

Postsynaptic membrane containing receptors

© Cengage Learning

concept check

4. What is the difference between the presynaptic neuron and the postsynaptic neuron?
5. GABA is a neurotransmitter that inhibits postsynaptic neurons. If a drug prevents GABA from attaching to its receptors, what will happen to the postsynaptic neuron?

Answers

4. The presynaptic neuron releases a neurotransmitter that travels to the postsynaptic neuron, where it activates an excitatory or inhibitory receptor.

5. If a drug prevents GABA from attaching to its receptors, the postsynaptic neuron will receive less inhibition. It will therefore produce more action potentials than usual.

critical check

What's the Evidence?

Neurons Communicate Chemically
You have just learned that neurons communicate by releasing chemicals at synapses. What evidence led to this important conclusion?

Today, neuroscientists have a wealth of evidence that neurons release chemicals at synapses.

Figure 3.8 The complex process of neural communication takes only 1–2 milliseconds.

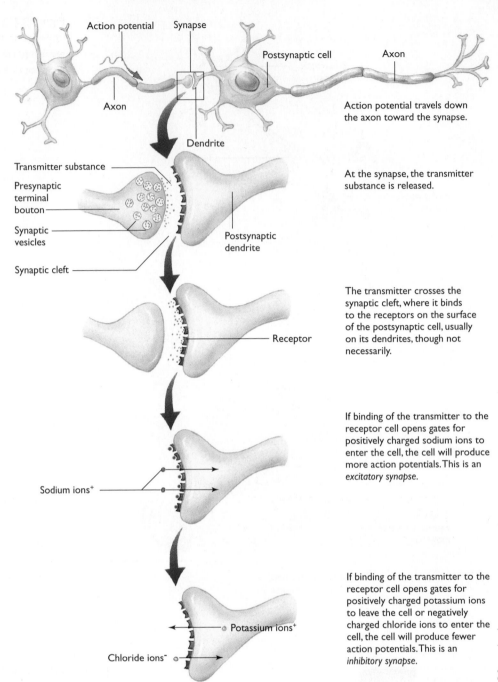

Action potential   Synapse

Postsynaptic cell   Axon

Axon

Action potential travels down the axon toward the synapse.

Dendrite

Transmitter substance
Presynaptic terminal bouton
Synaptic vesicles
Synaptic cleft

Postsynaptic dendrite

At the synapse, the transmitter substance is released.

Receptor

The transmitter crosses the synaptic cleft, where it binds to the receptors on the surface of the postsynaptic cell, usually on its dendrites, though not necessarily.

Sodium ions⁺

If binding of the transmitter to the receptor cell opens gates for positively charged sodium ions to enter the cell, the cell will produce more action potentials. This is an *excitatory synapse.*

Potassium ions⁺

Chloride ions⁻

If binding of the transmitter to the receptor cell opens gates for positively charged potassium ions to leave the cell or negatively charged chloride ions to enter the cell, the cell will produce fewer action potentials. This is an *inhibitory synapse.*

© Cengage Learning

They radioactively trace where chemicals go and what happens when they get there. They inject purified chemicals and use extremely fine electrodes to measure the responses of neurons. In 1920 Otto Loewi conducted a clever experiment with simple tools to demonstrate that neurons communicate with chemicals, as he later described in his autobiography (Loewi, 1960).

Hypothesis If a neuron releases chemicals, an investigator should be able to collect some of those chemicals, transfer them to another animal, and thereby get the second animal to do what the first animal had been doing. Loewi could not collect chemicals within the brain, so he worked with axons to the heart muscles. (A neuron stimulates a muscle at a junction that is like the synapse between two neurons.)

Method Loewi electrically stimulated certain axons that slowed a frog's heart. As he continued the stimulation, he collected fluid around that heart and transferred it to the heart of a second frog.

Results When Loewi transferred the fluid from the first frog's heart, the second frog's heart rate also slowed (Figure 3.9).

Interpretation Evidently, the stimulated axons had released a chemical that slows heart rate. At least in this case, neurons send messages by releasing chemicals.

Loewi won a Nobel Prize in physiology for this and related research. Even outstanding experiments have limitations, however. Loewi's results did not indicate whether axons release chemicals at all synapses, most, or only a few.

Table 3.1 Some of the Most Important Neurotransmitters

Neurotransmitter	Functions	Comment
Glutamate	The brain's main excitatory transmitter, present at most synapses. Essential for almost all brain activities, including learning.	Strokes kill neurons mostly by overstimulation, due to excess release of glutamate.
GABA (gamma-amino-butyric acid)	The brain's main inhibitory transmitter.	Antianxiety drugs and antiepileptic drugs increase activity at GABA synapses.
Acetylcholine	Increases brain arousal.	Acetylcholine is also released by motor neurons to stimulate skeletal muscles.
Dopamine	One path is important for movement (damaged in Parkinson's disease). Another path is important for memory and cognition.	Most antipsychotic drugs decrease activity at dopamine synapses. L-dopa, used for Parkinson's disease, increases availability of dopamine.
Serotonin	Modifies many types of motivated and emotional behavior.	Most antidepressant drugs prolong activity at serotonin synapses.
Norepinephrine	Enhances storage of memory of emotional or otherwise meaningful events.	All or nearly all axons releasing norepinephrine originate from one small brain area, called the locus coeruleus.
Histamine	Increases arousal and alertness.	Antihistamines (for allergies) block histamine and therefore lead to drowsiness.
Endorphins	Decrease pain and increase pleasure.	Morphine and heroin stimulate the same receptors as endorphins.
Nitric oxide	Dilates blood vessels in the most active brain areas.	The only known transmitter that is a gas.
Anandamide, 2AG, and others	Sent by the postsynaptic neuron back to the presynaptic neuron to decrease further release of transmitters.	THC, the active chemical in marijuana, stimulates these same presynaptic receptors.

© Cengage Learning

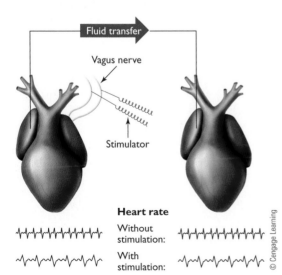

Figure 3.9 Otto Loewi stimulated axons known to decrease a frog's heart rate. He collected fluid from around the heart and transferred it to another frog's heart. When the second frog's heart slowed its beat, Loewi concluded that the axons in the first heart released a chemical that slows heart rate.

Answering that question required technologies not available until several decades later. The answer is that the great majority of synapses use chemicals, although a few communicate electrically.

Neurotransmitters and Behavior

The brain has dozens of neurotransmitters, each of which activates many kinds of receptors. Table 3.1 lists some of the most abundant transmitters. For example, serotonin activates at least 15 kinds, probably more (Roth, Lopez, & Kroeze, 2000). Each receptor type controls somewhat different aspects of behavior. For example, because serotonin type 3 receptors are responsible for nausea, researchers have developed drugs to block nausea (Perez, 1995). However, with a few exceptions, most complex behaviors rely on several transmitters and several types of receptors.

Still, a disorder that increases or decreases a particular transmitter or receptor alters behavior in predictable ways. One example is Parkinson's disease, *a condition that affects about 1% of people over the age of 50. The main symptoms are difficulty in initiating voluntary movement, slow movement, tremors, rigidity, and depressed mood.* All of these symptoms can be traced to a gradual decay of a pathway of axons that release *the neurotransmitter* dopamine (DOPE-uh-meen). Unlike so many medications discovered by accident, the treatment for Parkinson's disease emerged from knowledge of the underlying mechanism of the disease. Researchers knew they needed to increase dopamine levels in the brain. Dopamine pills or injections would not work because dopamine (like many other chemicals) is unable to cross from the blood into the brain.

However, a drug called L-dopa does cross into the brain. Neurons absorb L-dopa, convert it to dopamine, and thereby increase their supply of dopamine. As we shall see in chapter 15, drugs that alleviate depression and schizophrenia also act on dopamine and serotonin synapses.

concept check

6. Some people with schizophrenia take haloperidol, a drug that blocks dopamine synapses. How would haloperidol affect someone with Parkinson's disease?

Answer

6. Haloperidol would increase the severity of Parkinson's disease. In fact, large doses of haloperidol induce symptoms of Parkinson's disease in anyone.

module 3.1 >

In Closing

Neurons, Synapses, and Behavior

Even what seems a simple behavior, such as saying a few words, corresponds to a complicated sequence of well-timed movements. Those complex behaviors emerge from synapses, which in their basic outline are simple processes: A cell releases a chemical, which excites or inhibits a second cell for various periods of time. Then the chemical washes away or reenters the first cell to be used again.

Complex behavior is possible because of the connections among huge numbers of neurons. No one neuron or synapse does much by itself. Your experience results from dozens of types of neurotransmitters, billions of neurons, and trillions of synapses, each contributing in a small way.

Summary

- *Neuron structure.* A neuron, or nerve cell, consists of a cell body, dendrites, and an axon. The axon conveys information to other neurons. (page 59)
- *The action potential.* Information is conveyed along an axon by an action potential, which is regenerated without loss of strength at each point along the axon. (page 60)
- *Mechanism of the action potential.* An action potential depends on the entry of sodium into the axon. Anything that blocks this flow blocks the action potential. (page 61)
- *How neurons communicate.* A neuron communicates with another neuron by releasing a chemical called a neurotransmitter at a specialized junction called a synapse. A neurotransmitter can either excite or inhibit the next neuron. (page 62)
- *Neurotransmitters and behavioral disorders.* An excess or deficit of a particular neurotransmitter can lead to abnormal behavior, such as that exhibited by people with Parkinson's disease. (page 65)

Key Terms

action potential (page 60)

axon (page 59)

cell body (page 59)

dendrite (page 59)

dopamine (page 66)

glia (page 59)

myelin (page 59)

neuron (page 59)

neurotransmitter (page 62)

Parkinson's disease (page 66)

postsynaptic neuron (page 62)

resting potential (page 61)

synapse (page 62)

terminal bouton (page 62)

module 3.2

Drugs and Their Effects

- How do drugs affect synapses?
- How do they affect behavior?

If you were to change a few of a computer's connections at random, you could produce an "altered state," which would almost certainly not be an improvement. Giving drugs to a human brain is a little like changing the connections of a computer, and almost any drug at least temporarily impairs brain functioning in some way. By examining the effects of drugs on the brain, we gain greater insight into the brain's normal processes and functions. In chapter 15, we shall consider drug abuse and addiction, including alcoholism. Here the emphasis is on how drugs operate.

Psychoactive drugs *alter experience by altering activity at synapses*. Some attach to receptors and activate them. Some attach imperfectly, like an almost-fitting key that gets stuck in a lock. Drugs increase or decrease the release of transmitters or decrease reuptake (the return of released transmitters to the neuron that released them). A drug that increases activity at a synapse is called an *agonist*, based on the Greek word for a contestant or fighter. A drug that decreases activity at a synapse is an *antagonist*, from the Greek word for an enemy.

Stimulants

Stimulants are *drugs that increase energy, alertness, and activity*. Amphetamine, methamphetamine, and cocaine block the protein that the presynaptic neuron uses to reabsorb dopamine or serotonin after releasing them (Beuming et al., 2008). As a result, stimulant drugs prolong the effects of those transmitters at their receptors. Dopamine synapses are critical for almost anything that strongly motivates people, ranging from sex and food to gambling and video games (Koepp et al., 1998; Maldonado et al., 1997). By increasing the activity at dopamine synapses, stimulant drugs hijack the brain's motivational system.

Cocaine has long been available in the powdery form of cocaine hydrochloride, which can be sniffed. Before 1985, the only way to get a more intense effect from cocaine hydrochloride was to transform it into *freebase cocaine*—cocaine with the hydrochloride re-

Ritalin, a drug given to calm hyperactive children, has the same synaptic effects as cocaine. The difference is quantitative. A Ritalin pill slowly and slightly increases dopamine activity in the brain, whereas cocaine produces a sudden rush of effects.

moved. Freebase cocaine enters the brain rapidly, and fast entry intensifies the experience. *Crack cocaine*, which first became available in 1985, is cocaine that has already been converted into freebase rocks, ready to be smoked (Brower & Anglin, 1987; Kozel & Adams, 1986). It is called "crack" because it makes popping noises when smoked. Crack produces a rush of potent effects within a few seconds.

The behavioral effects of stimulant drugs depend on the dose. Low levels enhance attention. In fact, amphetamine is often prescribed for attention deficit disorder, under the trade name Adderall. At higher doses, amphetamine and cocaine lead to confusion, impaired attention, and impulsiveness (Simon, Mendez, & Setlow, 2007; Stalnaker et al., 2007). Physical effects include higher heart rate, blood pressure, and body temperature, and a risk of convulsions, lung damage, and heart attack.

As amphetamine or cocaine enters the brain, it increases arousal and produces mostly pleasant effects. However, because these drugs are inhibiting the reuptake of dopamine and other transmitters, the transmitters wash away from synapses faster than the presynaptic neurons can replace them. Over the next few hours, the presynaptic neurons' supply of transmitters dwindles and the user begins to experience mild lethargy and depression that last until the neurons rebuild their supply.

Methylphenidate (Ritalin), a drug often prescribed for attention deficit disorder, works the same way as cocaine, at the same synapses (Volkow et al., 1997, 1998). The difference is that methylphenidate, taken as pills, reaches the brain gradually over an hour or more and declines slowly over hours. Therefore, it does not produce the sudden "rush" that makes crack cocaine so addictive.

If people take methylphenidate for attention deficit disorder, do they become more likely to abuse drugs later? Many of those people do abuse alcohol and a variety of other drugs, but we can't necessarily attribute that abuse to

© Mart of Images / Alamy

methylphenidate. Those people might have been disposed to try drugs anyway. To answer the question clearly, someone would have to do random assignment of people to receive methylphenidate or not. Such a study has not been done, and would be difficult. Studies using less satisfactory methods have yielded inconclusive results. Some suggest that taking methylphenidate increases the probability of later drug abuse, and some suggest it decreases the probability (Golden, 2009). Taking methylphenidate probably has no big effect on later drug use, one way or the other.

Tobacco delivers nicotine, which increases wakefulness and arousal by stimulating synapses responsive to the neurotransmitter *acetylcholine*. Although nicotine is classed as a stimulant, most smokers say it relaxes them. The research suggests an explanation for this paradox. Although smoking increases tension levels, abstaining from cigarettes increases tension even more. Smoking another cigarette relieves the withdrawal symptoms and restores the usual mood (Parrott, 1999). One reason why it is difficult to quit smoking is that nicotine alters certain cells so that they become more responsive to nicotine and less responsive to other kinds of pleasant events (Changeux, 2010). As this happens, it becomes more and more difficult to give up smoking.

concept check

7. The drug AMPT (alpha-methyl-para-tyrosine) prevents the body from making dopamine. How would a large dose of AMPT affect someone's later responsiveness to cocaine, amphetamine, or methylphenidate?

8. Some people with attention deficit disorder report that they experience benefits for the first few hours after taking methylphenidate pills but begin to deteriorate in the late afternoon and evening. Why?

Answers

7. Someone who took AMPT would become less responsive than usual to amphetamine, cocaine, or methylphenidate. These drugs prolong the effects of dopamine, but if the neurons cannot make dopamine, they cannot release it. Remember what happens after taking cocaine: Neurons release dopamine and other transmitters faster than they resynthesize them. Because cocaine blocks reuptake, the supply of transmitters dwindles, and the result is lethargy and mild depression. The same process occurs with methylphenidate but more slowly and to a smaller degree.

Hallucinogens

Drugs that induce sensory distortions are called hallucinogens (Jacobs, 1987). Many of these drugs are derived from mushrooms or plants, and others are manufactured. Hallucinogenic drugs such as LSD (lysergic acid diethylamide) distort sensations and sometimes produce a dreamlike state or an intense mystical experience. Peyote, a hallucinogen derived from a cactus plant, has a long history of use in Native American religious ceremonies (Figure 3.10).

LSD attaches mainly to one kind of serotonin receptor (Jacobs, 1987). It stimulates those receptors at irregular times and prevents neurotransmitters from stimulating them at the normal times. We have an interesting gap in our knowledge at this point: We know *where* LSD exerts its effects, but we do not understand *how* altering those receptors leads to the experiences that LSD users report.

The drug MDMA (methylenedioxymethamphetamine), popularly known as "ecstasy," produces stimulant effects similar to amphetamine at low doses and hallucinogenic effects similar to LSD at higher doses. Many young adults use MDMA at parties to increase their energy. However, as the drug wears off, people feel depressed and lethargic. Re-

Figure 3.10 Tablas, or yarn paintings, created by members of the Huichol tribe (Mexico) evoke the beautiful lights, vivid colors, and "peculiar creatures" experienced after the people eat the hallucinogenic peyote cactus in ritualized ceremonies.

peated users show increased anxiety and depression and impairments of attention, memory, and sleep, which persist a year or more after they quit using the drug (Montoya, Sorrentino, Lukas, & Price, 2002; Reneman et al., 2001). MDMA also increases body temperature, sometimes to dangerous levels. Several studies have reported persisting depression, anxiety, and memory loss in heavy users of MDMA, although it is not certain how much of the damage comes from MDMA and how much from other drugs these people may have taken (Capela et al., 2009; Hanson & Luciana, 2010).

Depressants

Depressants are *drugs that decrease arousal*, such as alcohol and *anxiolytics* (anxiety-reducing drugs). People have been using alcohol since prehistoric times. When archeologists unearthed a Neolithic village in Iran's Zagros Mountains, they found a jar that had been constructed about 5500–5400 B.C., one of the oldest human-made crafts ever found (Figure 3.11). Inside the jar, especially at the bottom, the archeologists found a yellowish residue. They were curious to know what the jar had held, so they sent the residue for chemical analysis. The unambiguous answer came back: It was wine. The jar had been a wine vessel (McGovern, Glusker, Exner, & Voigt, 1996).

Alcohol is a *class of molecules that includes methanol, ethanol, propyl alcohol (rubbing alcohol), and others. Ethanol is the type that people drink.* At moderate doses, alcohol relaxes people by facilitating activity at inhibitory synapses. In greater amounts, it increases risk-taking behaviors, including aggression, by suppressing the fears and inhibitions that ordinarily limit such behaviors. In still greater amounts, as in binge drinking, alcohol suppresses breathing and heart rate to a dangerous degree. Excessive use damages the liver and other organs, aggravates medical conditions, and impairs memory and motor control. A woman who drinks alcohol during pregnancy risks damage to her baby's brain, health, and appearance.

In small amounts, alcohol relaxes people. In large amounts, it impairs judgment, suppresses breathing, and damages the liver and other organs.

Anxiolytic drugs or **tranquilizers** *help people relax.* The most common examples are *benzodiazepines*, including diazepam (Valium) and alprazolam (Xanax). Benzodiazepines calm people by facilitating transmission at inhibitory synapses. Taking these drugs at the same time as alcohol can produce dangerous suppression of breathing and heart rate.

One benzodiazepine drug, flunitrazepam (Rohypnol), has attracted attention as a "date rape drug." It dissolves quickly in water and has no color, odor, or taste to warn the person who is consuming it. As with other anxiolytics, it induces drowsiness, clumsiness, and memory impairment (Anglin, Spears, & Hutson, 1997; Woods & Winger, 1997). Someone under the influence of the drug does not have the strength to fight off an attacker and may not remember the event clearly. A hospital that suspects someone has been given this drug can detect its presence with a urine test. Another date rape drug, GHB (gamma hydroxybutyrate), has become widespread because it can be made easily (though impurely) with household ingredients. Like flunitrazepam, it relaxes the body and impairs muscle coordination. Large doses induce vomiting, tremors, coma, and death.

Figure 3.11 This wine jar, dated about 5500–5400 B.C., is one of the oldest human crafts ever found.

9. Which kind of synapses do alcohol and anxiolytic drugs (tranquilizers) facilitate?

Answer

9. They facilitate transmission at inhibitory synapses.

Narcotics

Narcotics are *drugs that produce drowsiness, insensitivity to pain, and decreased responsiveness.* Opiates are *either natural drugs derived from the opium poppy, or synthetic drugs with a chemical structure resembling natural opiates.* Opiates make people feel happy, warm, and content, with little anxiety or pain. Morphine (named after Morpheus, the Greek god of dreams) has important medical use as a painkiller. Undesirable consequences include nausea and withdrawal from the world. After the drug leaves the brain, elation gives way to anxiety, pain, and exaggerated responsiveness to sounds and other stimuli. These withdrawal symptoms become especially strong after habitual use.

Opiate drugs such as morphine, heroin, methadone, and codeine bind to specific receptors in the brain (Pert & Snyder, 1973). The discovery of neurotransmitter receptors demonstrated that opiates block pain in the brain, not in the skin. Neuroscientists then found that the brain produces several chemicals, called endorphins, that *bind to the opiate receptors* (Hughes et al., 1975). Endorphins inhibit chronic pain. The brain also releases endorphins during pleasant experiences, such as the "runner's high" or the chill you feel down your back when you hear especially thrilling music (A. Goldstein, 1980).

Although opiates have a strong potential to become addictive, people who take morphine for pain control under medical care almost never develop an addiction. Addiction depends not only on the drug itself, but also on the person, the setting, and the reasons for taking the drug.

Marijuana

Marijuana (*cannabis*) is difficult to classify. It is certainly not a stimulant. It has a calming effect but not like that of alcohol or tranquilizers. It softens pain but not as powerfully as opiates. It produces an illusion that time is passing more slowly than usual, but marijuana's effects do not include the more extreme sensory distortions that LSD causes.

Many studies report memory problems in marijuana users. One of the stronger studies found that a few months after people quit using marijuana, their memory improved (Pope, Gruber, Hudson, Huestis, & Yurgelun-Todd, 2001). This result strongly suggests that poor memory was a result of marijuana use, not a lifelong characteristic of those who chose to use marijuana.

Marijuana has several potential medical uses. It reduces nausea, suppresses tremors, reduces pressure in the eyes, and decreases cell loss in the brain after a stroke (Glass, 2001; Panikashvili et al., 2001). However, animal research shows that marijuana is most effective in protecting the brain from stroke damage if it is administered as quickly as possible after the stroke, or better yet *before* the stroke (Schomacher, Müller, Sommer, Schwab, & Schäbitz, 2008). (It's a little

impractical to recommend that everyone at risk for stroke should remain more or less permanently stoned.)

Because of legal restrictions, research on these medical uses has been limited. On the negative side, marijuana increases the risk of Parkinson's disease (Glass, 2001), and long-term use probably increases the risk of lung cancer, as tobacco cigarettes do.

You may have heard that marijuana is dangerous as a "gateway drug." That is, many heroin and cocaine users had used marijuana first. True, but they also tried cigarettes and alcohol first, as well as other risky experiences. It is unclear that the use of marijuana encourages the use of other drugs.

The active ingredient in marijuana is THC, or tetrahydrocannabinol. THC attaches to receptors that are abundant throughout the brain (Herkenham, Lynn, deCosta, & Richfield, 1991). The brain produces large amounts of its own chemicals, anandamide and 2-AG, that attach to those receptors (Devane et al., 1992; Stella, Schweitzer, & Piomelli, 1997). These receptors are abundant in brain areas that control memory and movement, but they are nearly absent from the medulla, which controls heart rate and breathing (Herkenham et al., 1990). In contrast, the medulla has many opiate receptors.

Unlike most other neurotransmitter receptors, those for anandamide and 2-AG (and therefore marijuana) are located on the *pre*synaptic neuron. When the presynaptic neuron releases a transmitter, such as glutamate or GABA, the postsynaptic (receiving) cell releases anandamide or 2-AG, which returns to the presynaptic cell to inhibit further re-

After California legalized marijuana for medical uses, many clubs and stores opened for the sale and distribution of the drug.

© Ted Soqui/CORBIS

lease (Kreitzer & Regehr, 2001; Oliet, Baimoukhametova, Piet, & Bains, 2007; R. I. Wilson & Nicoll, 2002). In effect it says, "I received your signal. You can slow down on sending any more of it." Marijuana, by resembling these natural reverse transmitters, has the same effect, except that it slows the signal even before it has been sent. It is as if the presynaptic cell "thinks" it has sent a signal when in fact it has not.

Marijuana has many behavioral effects, which researchers are beginning to explain. It decreases nausea by blocking the type of serotonin receptor responsible for nausea (Fan, 1995). It increases activity in brain areas responsible for feeding and appetite (DiMarzo et al., 2001). How it produces the illusion that time is passing slowly is hard to explain, but the same phenomenon occurs in laboratory animals. Under the influence of marijuana smoke, rats show impairments when they have to respond at certain time intervals. They respond too quickly, as if 10 seconds felt like 20 seconds (Han & Robinson, 2001).

concept check

10. An overdose of opiates produces a life-threatening decrease in breathing and heart rate. Large doses of marijuana do not produce those effects. Why not?

Answer

10. Opiate receptors are abundant in the medulla, which controls heart rate and breathing. The medulla has few receptors sensitive to marijuana.

Figure 3.12 diagrams the effects of several drugs. Table 3.2 summarizes the drugs we have been considering. The list of risks is incomplete because of space. Large or repeated doses of any drug can be life-threatening.

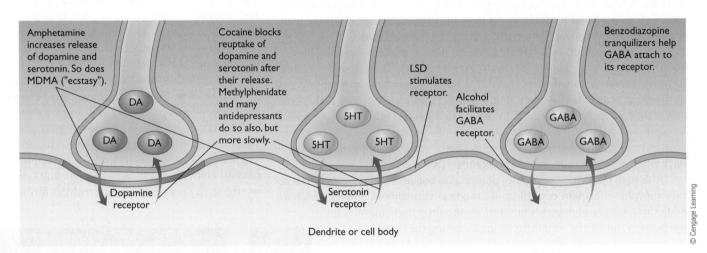

Figure 3.12 Both legal and illegal drugs operate at the synapses. Drugs can increase the release of neurotransmitters, block their reuptake, or directly stimulate or block their receptors.

© Cengage Learning

Table 3.2 Commonly Abused Drugs and Their Effects

Drug Category	Effects on the Nervous System	Short-Term Effects	Risks (partial list)
Stimulants			
Amphetamine	Increases release of dopamine and decreases reuptake, prolonging effects	Increases energy and alertness	Psychotic reaction, agitation, heart problems, sleeplessness, stroke
Cocaine	Decreases reuptake of dopamine, prolonging effects	Increases energy and alertness	Psychotic reaction, heart problems, crime to pay for drugs, death
Methylphenidate (Ritalin)	Decreases reuptake of dopamine but with slower onset and offset than cocaine	Increases alertness; much milder withdrawal effects than cocaine	Increased blood pressure
Caffeine	Blocks a chemical that inhibits arousal	Increases energy and alertness	Sleeplessness
Nicotine	Stimulates some acetylcholine synapses; stimulates some neurons that release dopamine	Increases arousal; abstention by a habitual smoker produces tension and depression	Lung cancer from the tars in cigarettes
Depressants			
Alcohol	Facilitates effects of GABA, an inhibitory neurotransmitter	Relaxation, reduced inhibitions, impaired memory and judgment	Automobile accidents, loss of job
Benzodiazepines	Facilitate effects of GABA, an inhibitory neurotransmitter	Relaxation, decreased anxiety, sleepiness	Dependence. Life-threatening if combined with alcohol or opiates
Narcotics			
Morphine, heroin, other opiates	Stimulate endorphin synapses	Decrease pain; withdrawal from interest in real world; unpleasant withdrawal effects during abstention	Heart stoppage; crime to pay for drugs
Marijuana			
Marijuana	Excites negative feedback receptors of both excitatory and inhibitory transmitters	Decreases pain and nausea; distorted sense of time	Impaired memory; lung diseases; impaired immune response
Hallucinogens			
LSD	Stimulates serotonin type 2 receptors at inappropriate times	Hallucinations, sensory distortions	Psychotic reaction, accidents, panic attacks, flashbacks
MDMA ("ecstasy")	Stimulates neurons that release dopamine; at higher doses also stimulates neurons that release serotonin	At low doses increases arousal; at higher doses hallucinations	Dehydration, fever, lasting damage to serotonin synapses
Rohypnol and GHB	Facilitate action at GABA synapses (which are inhibitory)	Relaxation, decreased inhibitions	Impaired muscle coordination and memory
Phencyclidine (PCP or "angel dust")	Inhibits one type of glutamate receptor	Intoxication, slurred speech; at higher doses hallucinations, thought disorder, impaired memory and emotions	Psychotic reaction

module 3.2

Drugs and Synapses

Except for Novocain and related drugs (which block action potentials), every drug with psychological effects acts at synapses. That statement includes the abused drugs that this module has emphasized as well as antidepressant drugs, antianxiety drugs, drugs to combat schizophrenia, and so forth. Many drugs have medical uses as well as potential for abuse. Examples include opiates, stimulants, and marijuana. Much of the difference between "good" psychiatric drugs and "bad" abused drugs is a matter of how much someone uses, and when, and why.

Summary

- *Stimulants.* Stimulant drugs such as amphetamines and cocaine increase activity levels and pleasure by increasing the release, and decreasing reuptake, of dopamine and certain other neurotransmitters. Compared to other forms of cocaine, crack enters the brain faster and therefore produces more intense effects. (page 68)
- *Hallucinogens.* Hallucinogens induce sensory distortions. LSD acts at one type of serotonin synapse. MDMA produces stimulant effects at low doses and hallucinogenic effects at higher doses. (page 69)
- *Alcohol.* Alcohol, the most widely abused drug in our society, relaxes people and relieves their inhibitions. It can also impair judgment and reasoning. (page 70)
- *Anxiolytics.* Benzodiazepines, widely used to relieve anxiety, can also relax muscles and promote sleep. Anxiolytics and alcohol act by facilitating inhibitory synapses. (page 70)
- *Opiates.* Opiate drugs bind to endorphin receptors in the nervous system. The immediate effect of opiates is pleasure and relief from pain. (page 71)
- *Marijuana.* Marijuana's active compound, THC, acts on abundant receptors. Marijuana acts on receptors on the presynaptic neuron, putting the brakes on release of both excitatory and inhibitory transmitters. (page 71)

Key Terms

alcohol (page 70)
anxiolytic drugs (tranquilizers) (page 70)
depressant (page 70)
endorphins (page 71)
hallucinogens (page 69)

narcotics (page 71)
opiates (page 71)
psychoactive drugs (page 68)
stimulants (page 68)

module 3.3

Brain and Behavior

* If you lose part of your brain, do you also lose part of your mind?

When studying the brain, you can easily get bogged down in memorizing the names and functions of brain areas. Before we get into all those facts, let's start with two points that are important to remember.

The first is that you use all of your brain. You may have heard that "they say" we use only 10% of our brains. No one is sure where this idea originated, but people have been telling it to one another for at least a century. What does it mean? Does anyone believe you could lose 90% of your brain and still do as well as you are doing now? Presumably not. Some people say, "Surely we could do so much more with our brains!" Well, yes, but that has nothing to do with using 10%. A poor athlete uses all of his or her muscles, but just not very skillfully. Similarly, someone who uses the brain poorly nevertheless uses all of it. A slightly better idea is that at any moment some brain areas are more active than usual and others are less active. That's true, but it is wrong to assume that you would be smarter if you increased activity in all of your brain. Simultaneous contraction of every muscle in your body wouldn't give you great athletic performance; it would give you spasms. Similarly, simultaneous activation of every neuron wouldn't give you great thoughts; it would give you convulsions. Useful brain activity requires a pattern of activating some neurons while inhibiting others, and the inhibition is just as important as the excitation.

The second point to remember is the concept of monism, *the idea that mental activity and brain activity are inseparable.* I (your author) remember as a young college student taking it for granted that I had a mind and a brain and that the two were separate. And then I learned not only that many people question that idea (dualism), but also that nearly all scientists and philosophers reject it. You should at least know not to take dualism for granted. So far as we can tell, you can't have mental activity without brain activity, and you can't have certain kinds of brain activity without mental activity. If you lose part of your brain, you lose part of your mind.

The central nervous system, consisting of *the brain and the spinal cord*, communicates with the rest of the body by the peripheral nervous system, consisting of *nerves connecting the spinal cord with the rest of the body.* Within the peripheral nervous system, we distinguish the *somatic nervous system*, which connects to the skin and muscles, and the *autonomic nervous system*, which connects to the heart, stomach, and other organs. Sensory nerves bring information from other body areas to the spinal cord, and motor nerves take information from the spinal cord to the muscles, where they cause contractions. Figure 3.13 summarizes these major divisions of the nervous system.

The Cerebral Cortex

The vertebrate brain has three major divisions—hindbrain, midbrain, and forebrain—as shown in Figure 3.13. In fish, amphibians, reptiles, and birds, the midbrain constitutes a large portion of the brain. In mammals including humans, the forebrain is by far the largest area. It consists of two hemispheres,

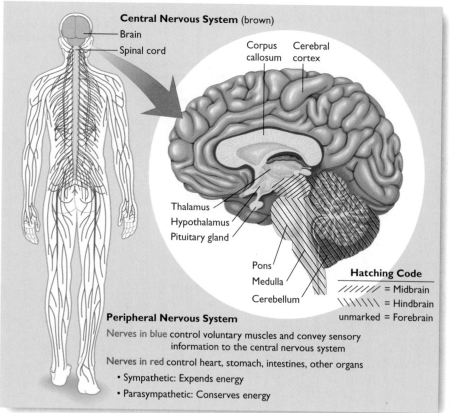

Central Nervous System (brown)
- Brain
- Spinal cord

Corpus callosum Cerebral cortex

Thalamus
Hypothalamus
Pituitary gland

Pons
Medulla
Cerebellum

Hatching Code
/////// = Midbrain
\\\\\\\ = Hindbrain
unmarked = Forebrain

Peripheral Nervous System
Nerves in blue control voluntary muscles and convey sensory information to the central nervous system
Nerves in red control heart, stomach, intestines, other organs
- Sympathetic: Expends energy
- Parasympathetic: Conserves energy

© Cengage Learning

Figure 3.13 The major components of the nervous system are the central nervous system and the peripheral nervous system, which includes the somatic nervous system and the autonomic nervous system.

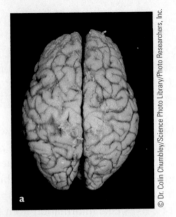

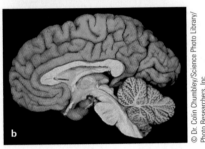

Figure 3.14 The human cerebral cortex: **(a)** left and right hemispheres; **(b)** a view from inside. The folds greatly extend the brain's surface area.

left and right (Figure 3.14). Each hemisphere controls sensation and movement on the opposite side of the body. (Why does it control the opposite side instead of its own side? No one knows, but the same is true for all vertebrates and many invertebrates.) We consider the differences between the left and right hemispheres later in this module. The *outer covering of the forebrain,* known as the cerebral cortex, is especially prominent in humans.

The Occipital Lobe of the Cortex

Researchers describe the cerebral cortex in terms of four *lobes*: occipital, parietal, temporal, and frontal, as shown in Figure 3.15. The occipital lobe, *at the rear of the head, is specialized for vision.* People with damage in this area have *cortical blindness.* Cortical blindness differs from the usual kind of blindness resulting from eye damage. Someone who used to have normal vision and then suffered eye damage can imagine visual scenes and continues (for years, if not necessarily forever) to have visual dreams. People with cortical blindness have no visual imagery, even in dreams. However, the intact eyes continue sending messages to other brain areas, including one that controls wakefulness and sleep. Therefore, someone with cortical blindness continues feeling wakeful during the day and sleepy at night.

Some (not all) people with cortical blindness experience blindsight, *the ability to point to or otherwise indicate the direction to a visual stimulus, without conscious perception of seeing anything at all* (Weiskrantz, Warrington, Sanders, & Marshall, 1974; Striemer, Chapman, & Goodale, 2009). Some can correctly state an object's color, direction of movement, or approximate shape, again insisting that they are just guessing (Radoeva, Prasad, Brainard, & Aguirre, 2008). Some respond to the emotional expression of a face that they do not see consciously (Gonzalez Andino, de Peralta Menendez, Khateb, Landis, & Pegna, 2009; Tamietto et al., 2009).

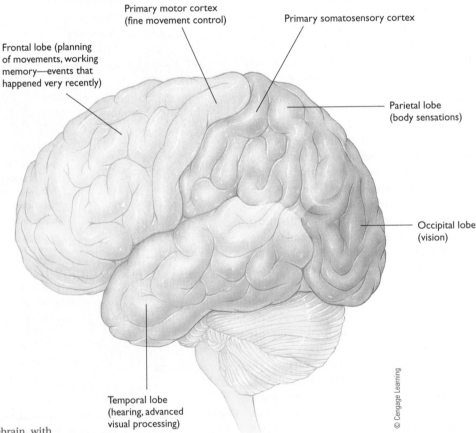

Figure 3.15 The four lobes of the human forebrain, with some of their functions.

What is the explanation? In some cases, small islands of healthy tissue remaining in the damaged visual cortex are large enough for certain functions, though not for conscious perception (Fendrich, Wessinger, & Gazzaniga, 1992; Radoeva et al., 2008). Also, several areas outside the primary visual cortex continue to receive visual information—again, enough to control certain functions but not enough for conscious perception (Schmid et al., 2010). Blindsight demonstrates that many functions occur without consciousness. It also shows what specific kinds of gains and losses can occur after brain damage.

concept check

11. How does cortical blindness differ from blindness caused by eye damage?

Answer

11. Someone with cortical blindness loses visual imagery, even in dreams. However, sunlight continues to regulate the person's wake-sleep cycle. Also, some people with cortical blindness have blindsight, in which they can indicate the location of a stimulus or other properties of the stimulus without conscious perception of it.

The Temporal Lobe of the Cortex

The **temporal lobe** of each hemisphere, *located toward the left and right sides of the head, is the main area for hearing and certain aspects of vision*. People with damage in the auditory parts of the temporal lobe do not become deaf, but they are impaired at recognizing sequences of sounds, as in music or speech. Language comprehension depends on part of the temporal lobe, in the left hemisphere for most people. People with damage in that area have trouble understanding speech and remembering the names of objects. Their own speech, grammatical but lacking most nouns, is hard to understand.

In other parts of the temporal lobe, damage produces visual deficits. One area in the temporal lobe, called the *fusiform gyrus,* responds mainly to the sight of faces (Kanwisher & Yovel, 2006). People with damage in that area no longer recognize faces, although they see well in other regards and recognize people by their voices (Tarr & Gauthier, 2000). Among people without brain damage, the development of that brain area varies from one person to another. People with extensive connections to the fusiform gyrus learn to recognize faces easily, and those with few connections have difficulty recognizing even familiar people (Grueter et al., 2007;

C. Thomas et al., 2009). So, if you have much difficulty recognizing faces, it's probably not that you just aren't trying hard enough. The explanation may relate to your brain anatomy.

People with damage to another part of the temporal lobe become motion blind: Although they see the size, shape, and color of objects, they do not track speed or direction of movement (Zihl, von Cramon, & Mai, 1983). They eventually notice that someone who used to be one place is now in another, and therefore must have moved, but they don't see the movement moment by moment. Crossing a street is hazardous, because the cars seem stationary. Pouring coffee is difficult, as the person can't monitor the rising level.

It is hard to imagine vision without motion perception, but here's how to demonstrate a small sample of the experience. Look at yourself in the mirror and focus on your left eye. Then move your focus to the right eye. Do you see your eyes moving in the mirror? (Go ahead; try it.) People agree that they do not see their eyes move.

try it ▶ yourself

"Oh, but wait," you say. "That movement in the mirror was simply too quick and too small to see." Wrong. Get someone else to look at your left eye and then shift gaze to your right eye. You *do* see the other person's eye movement. You see someone else's eyes move, but you do not see your own eyes move in the mirror.

Why not? During voluntary eye movements, called *saccades*, and in fact beginning 75 milliseconds before such movements, your brain suppresses activity in the part of the temporal cortex responsible for motion perception (Bremmer, Kubischik, Hoffmann, & Krekelberg, 2009; Burr, Morrone, & Ross, 1994; Paus, Marrett, Worsley, & Evans, 1995; Vallines & Greenlee, 2006). That is, you become temporarily motion blind. Now, try to imagine what it would be like to have this condition all the time.

Other parts of the temporal lobe are critical for certain aspects of emotion. The **amygdala** (Figure 3.16), *a structure in the temporal lobe, responds strongly to emotional situations*. People with damage to the amygdala are slow to process emotional information, such as facial expressions and descriptions of emotional situations (Baxter & Murray, 2002). In contrast, people with an easily aroused amygdala tend to be shy and fearful (Hariri et al., 2002; Rhodes et al., 2007).

A simple way to gauge amygdala arousal is to make a sudden, loud sound and measure the startle response. Everyone except the deaf shows some startle response, but some respond more than others, and some *habituate* (decline in response) faster than others. People with a highly reactive amygdala respond strongly and habituate slowly to a loud noise, indicating anxiety. That response correlates with political attitudes: People who favor vigorous military and police action to protect against potentially dangerous people tend to show strong amygdala responses, whereas those who are more relaxed about such dangers show weaker amygdala responses (Oxley et al., 2008). Figure 3.17 shows the results of one study. This research says nothing about which group is correct on the political issues, but it indicates that even our political leanings relate to our brain activities.

12. Under what condition does an intact person experience temporary motion blindness?

Answer

12. During and slightly before a voluntary eye movement.

The Parietal Lobe of the Cortex

The parietal lobe, just anterior (forward) from the occipital lobe, is specialized for the body senses, including touch, pain, temperature, and awareness of the location of body parts in space. The primary somatosensory (so-ma-toh-SEN-so-ree, meaning body-sensory) cortex, a strip in the anterior portion of the parietal lobe, has cells sensitive to touch in different body areas, as shown in Figure 3.18. In that figure, note that the largest areas are devoted to touch in the most sensitive areas, such as the lips and hands. Damage to any part of the somatosensory cortex impairs sensation from the corresponding body part.

Although the somatosensory cortex is the primary site for touch sensations, touch also activates areas that are important for emotional responses. Consider someone who has lost input to the somatosensory cortex. You gently stroke her arm, and she smiles without knowing why. She has the pleasant emotional experience despite no touch sensation (Olausson et al., 2002). You see again that brain damage produces surprisingly specialized changes in behavior and experience.

Parietal lobe damage also interferes with spatial attention. People with such damage see what an object is but not where it is. They have trouble reaching toward it, walking around it, or shifting attention from one object to another. When walking, they can describe what they see, but they bump into objects

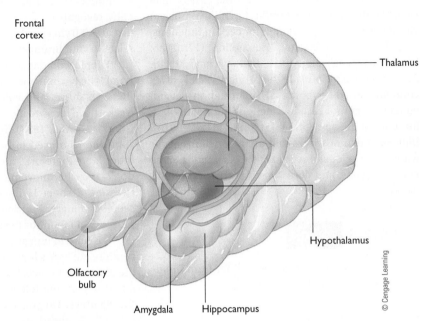

Figure 3.16 A view of the forebrain, showing internal structures as though the outer structures were transparent.

instead of walking around them. They can describe their furniture from memory but not how it is arranged in the house. Sometimes they have trouble finding various parts of their body (Schenk, 2006).

13. Parietal lobe damage interferes with which aspect of vision?

Answer

13. It interferes with identifying the object's location.

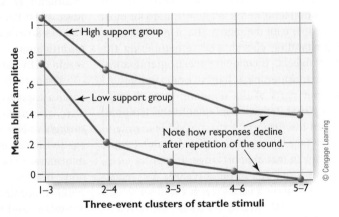

Figure 3.17 People with high support for military action, capital punishment, and immigration control show enhanced eye-blink responses to a sudden loud noise relative to those with low support for these positions. Those with low support show a more rapid decline in response as the noise is repeated.

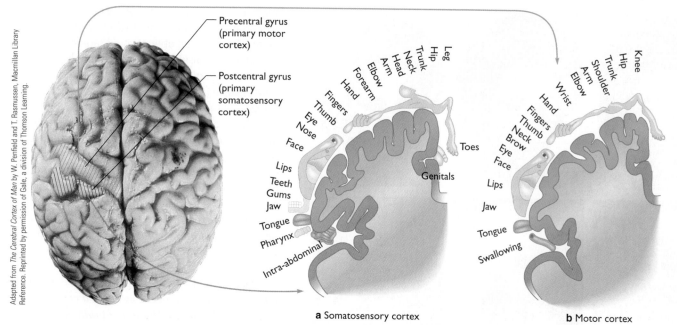

Adapted from *The Cerebral Cortex of Man* by W. Penfield and T. Rasmussen, Macmillan Library Reference. Reprinted by permission of Gale, a division of Thomson Learning.

Precentral gyrus (primary motor cortex)

Postcentral gyrus (primary somatosensory cortex)

Leg Hip Trunk Neck Head Arm Elbow Forearm Hand Fingers Thumb Eye Nose Face Lips Teeth Gums Jaw Tongue Pharynx Intra-abdominal Toes Genitals

a Somatosensory cortex

Knee Hip Trunk Shoulder Arm Elbow Wrist Hand Fingers Thumb Neck Brow Eye Face Lips Jaw Tongue Swallowing

b Motor cortex

Figure 3.18 **(a)** The primary somatosensory cortex and **(b)** the primary motor cortex, illustrating which part of the body each brain area controls. Larger areas of the cortex are devoted to body parts that need to be controlled with great precision, such as the face and hands. (Parts a and b after Penfield & Rasmussen, 1950.)

The Frontal Lobe of the Cortex

The frontal lobe, *at the anterior (forward) pole of the brain*, includes the primary motor cortex, *important for controlling fine movements,* such as moving a finger or wiggling a toe. Each area of the primary motor cortex controls a different part of the body, and larger areas are devoted to the tongue and fingers than, say, the shoulder and elbow muscles. The *anterior sections of the frontal lobe*, called the prefrontal cortex, are important for memory of what has just happened and what you are planning to do next. The prefrontal cortex is also critical for decision making, especially for bypassing a current pleasure in favor of a greater pleasure later. Suppose you have a choice between going to a movie tonight and finishing a paper that is due tomorrow, which will have a big effect on your grade at the end of the semester. That decision depends on your prefrontal cortex (Frank & Claus, 2006). People with impairments of the prefrontal cortex often make impulsive decisions because they have trouble imagining how good they might feel after one outcome and how sad or guilty they might feel after another (S. W. Anderson, Bechara, Damasio, Tranel, & Damasio, 1999; Damasio, 1999).

Since the late 1990s, psychologists have become excited about mirror neurons, found in several brain areas but especially the frontal cortex. Mirror neurons *are active when you make a movement and also when you watch someone else make a similar movement* (Dinstein, Hasson, Rubin, & Heeger, 2007). Do mirror neurons enable you to copy other people's actions? Do they enable you to identify with other people and understand them better? Autistic children, who show little activity in their "mirror neurons" of the frontal cortex while they watch other people, seldom imitate others or even show much interest in them (Dapretto et al., 2006). You can see how psychologists would speculate that mirror neurons are the basis for human civilization.

However, before we speculate too far, researchers need to address some important questions. In particular, were you born with mirror neurons that helped you learn to copy other people? Or did you learn to copy other people,

and thereby develop mirror neurons? That is, perhaps after you have learned the parallels between what you see and what you can do, seeing someone do something reminds you of your own ability to do the same thing and therefore activates neurons responsible for those actions.

We probably have several kinds of mirror neurons. Sometimes infants imitate a few facial movements, as shown in Figure 3.19. That result implies built-in mirror neurons that connect the sight of a movement to the movement itself (Meltzoff & Moore, 1977). However, other mirror neurons develop their properties by learning. For example, expert dancers show activity in certain brain areas when they perform certain well-practiced movements or watch others perform the same movements. They don't show such activity when they watch movements that they themselves don't perform (Calvo-Merino, Grèzes, Glaser, Passingham, & Haggard, 2006).

If you consistently watch someone else move the little finger every time you move your index finger, certain cells in your frontal cortex come to respond whenever you move your *index* finger or see someone else move the *little* finger (Catmur, Walsh, & Heyes, 2007). In other words, at least some—probably many—neurons develop their mirror quality (or in this case an anti-mirror quality) by learning.

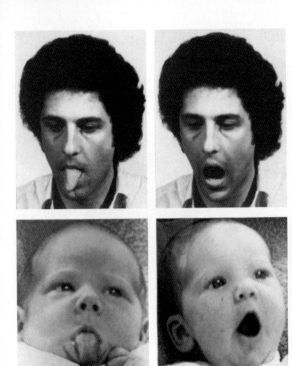

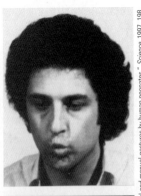

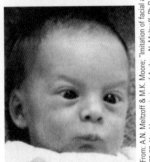

Figure 3.19 Newborn infants sometimes imitate facial expressions. Because they have not had an opportunity to learn to imitate, their behavior implies built-in mirror neurons. (From Meltzoff & Moore, 1977.)

From: A.N. Meltzoff & M.K. Moore; "Imitation of facial and manual gestures by human neonates." *Science*, 1997, 198, 75-78. Used by permission of Andrew N. Meltzoff, Ph.D.

concept check

14. What evidence suggests that imitation produces mirror neurons as opposed to the idea that mirror neurons produce imitation?

Answer

14. It is possible to train neurons to respond to one kind of movement the person produces and a different movement the person watches. If people can learn to develop these "anti-mirror" neurons, then presumably, they also learn to develop mirror neurons.

The Two Hemispheres and Their Connections

Let's focus on a type of brain damage that produces results of widespread interest. Each hemisphere of the brain gets sensory input mostly from the opposite side of the body and controls muscles on the opposite side. The hemispheres differ in other ways, too. For almost all right-handed people and more than 60% of left-handed people, parts of the left hemisphere control speech. For most other left-handers, both hemispheres control speech. Few people have complete right-hemisphere control of

speech. The right hemisphere is more important for certain other functions, including the ability to imagine what an object would look like after it rotated and the ability to understand the emotional connotations of facial expressions and tone of voice (Stone, Nisenson, Eliassen, & Gazzaniga, 1996).

The two hemispheres constantly exchange information. If you feel something with the left hand and something else with the right hand, you can tell whether they are made of the same material because the hemispheres pass information back and forth through the corpus callosum, *a set of axons that connect the left and right hemispheres of the cerebral cortex* (Figure 3.20). What would happen if the corpus callosum were cut?

Occasionally, brain surgeons have cut the corpus callosum to relieve epilepsy, *a condition in which cells somewhere in the brain emit abnormal rhythmic, spontaneous impulses.* Most people with epilepsy respond well to antiepileptic drugs and live normal lives, but a few continue having frequent major seizures. When all else fails, surgeons sometimes sever the corpus callosum. The original idea was that this surgery would limit epileptic seizures to one hemisphere and therefore make the epilepsy less incapacitating.

The operation was more successful than expected. Not only did it limit seizures to one side of the body, but it decreased their frequency. The operation interrupts a feedback loop that lets an epileptic seizure echo back and forth between the hemispheres. However, although these split-brain patients resume a normal life, they show some fascinating behavioral effects.

If you have left-hemisphere control of speech, like most people, the information that enters your right hemisphere passes quickly across the corpus callosum to your left (speaking) hemisphere, enabling you to describe an object, for example, in words. However, when a split-brain patient (whose corpus callosum has been cut) feels something with the left hand, the information goes only to the right (nonspeaking) hemisphere (Nebes, 1974; Sperry, 1967). If asked to point to the object, the person points correctly with the left hand (controlled by the right hemisphere) while saying, "I have no idea what it was. I didn't feel anything."

Now consider what happens when a split-brain patient sees something (Figure 3.21). The person in Figure 3.21 focuses on a point in the middle of the screen. The investigator flashes *hatband* on the screen for a split second, too briefly for an eye movement, and asks for the word. The person replies, "band," which is what the left hemisphere saw. (The left hemisphere sees the right side of the world.) However, the left hand (controlled by the right hemisphere) points to a hat (which the right hemisphere saw).

A split-brain person says he or she feels the same as before the operation and still has just one consciousness. Of course, it is the left hemisphere that is talking, and it doesn't know about the experiences of the right hemisphere! The left hemisphere continues trying to make sense of everything the body does. Consider this study: While the person stares straight ahead, two pictures flash briefly on a screen so that the left hemisphere sees one and the right hemisphere sees the other. Then, from a set of pictures on cards, the two hemispheres, using different hands, select items related to what they saw. In one case, the left hemisphere saw a chicken claw and pointed with the right hand to

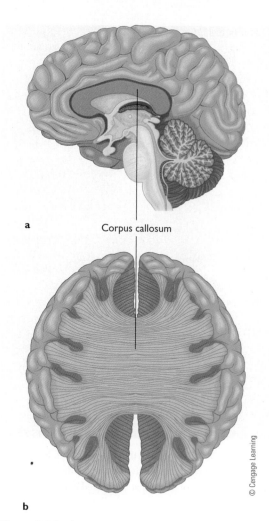

a

Corpus callosum

b

Figure 3.20 The corpus callosum is a large set of fibers that convey information between the two hemispheres of the cerebral cortex. **(a)** A midline view showing the location of the corpus callosum. **(b)** A horizontal section showing how each axon of the corpus callosum links one spot in the left hemisphere to a corresponding spot in the right hemisphere.

a chicken. The right hemisphere saw a snow scene and pointed to a snow shovel (Figure 3.22). When asked to explain the choices, the left (talking) hemisphere said the chicken claw goes with the chicken, and you need a shovel to clean out the chicken shed. Gazzaniga (2000) infers that the left hemisphere has a function that he calls the "interpreter." It makes up a story to explain what happened, even if the behaviors actually happened for a different reason. We shall encounter this point again in later chapters: We often don't know all the reasons for our own behavior, and we make up reasons that may or may not be correct.

Split-brain surgery is rare. We study such patients not because you are likely to meet one but because they teach us something about brain organization and raise important questions about what it means to be conscious.

concept check

15. After damage to the corpus callosum, a person can describe some, but not all, of what he or she feels. With which hand must the person feel an object before speaking about it?

Answer

15. The person must feel something with the right hand, the hand that the left hemisphere feels.

a

b

c

Figure 3.21 **(a)** When the word *hatband* flashes on a screen, a split-brain patient reports only what the left hemisphere saw, *band*, and **(b)** writes *band* with the right hand. However, **(c)** the left hand (controlled by the right hemisphere) points to a hat, which is what the right hemisphere saw.

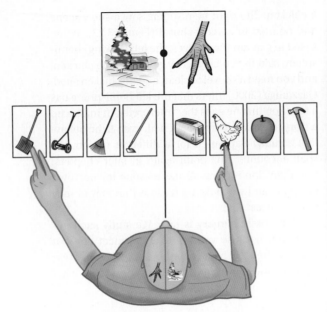

Figure 3.22 After the two hemispheres see a snow scene and a chicken claw, the two hands point to a chicken and a shovel as the related items. However, the left (talking) hemisphere tries to explain both choices in terms of what it saw, the chicken claw. (From Gazzaniga, M. S., "Cerebral specialization and interhemispheric communication: Does the corpus callosum enable the human condition?" *Brain, 123,* 1293-1326 (fig 19a, p. 1318). Copyright © 2000 Oxford University Press. Reprinted by permission.)

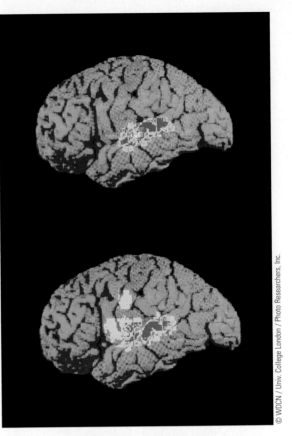

Figure 3.23 A PET scan of the human brain. Red shows areas of most-increased activity during some task; yellow shows areas of next most-increased activity.

Measuring Brain Activity

How did researchers discover the functions of various brain areas? For decades, most research concerned patients with brain damage, and much of it still does. However, researchers now also have techniques to examine brain activity in healthy people.

An electroencephalograph (EEG) *uses electrodes on the scalp to record rapid changes in brain electrical activity.* A similar method is a magnetoencephalograph (MEG), *which records magnetic changes.* Both methods provide data on a millisecond-by-millisecond basis, measuring the brain's reactions to lights, sounds, and other events. However, because they record from the surface of the scalp, they provide little precision about the location of the activity.

Another method offers better anatomical localization but less information about timing: Positron-emission tomography (PET) *records radioactivity of various brain areas emitted from injected chemicals* (Phelps & Mazziotta, 1985). First, someone receives an injection of a radioactively labeled compound such as glucose. The most active brain areas rapidly absorb glucose, a sugar that is the brain's main fuel. Therefore, the labeled glucose emits radioactivity primarily from the most active areas. Detectors around the head record the radioactivity and send results to a computer that generates an image such as the one in Figure 3.23. Red indicates areas of greatest activity, followed by yellow, green, and blue. Unfortunately, PET scans require exposing the brain to radioactivity.

Another technique, functional magnetic resonance imaging (fMRI), *uses magnetic detectors outside the head to compare the amounts of hemoglobin with and without oxygen in different brain areas* (J. D. Cohen, Noll, & Schneider, 1993). (Adding or removing oxygen changes the response of hemoglobin to a magnetic field.) The most active brain areas use the most oxygen and therefore decrease the oxygen bound to the blood's hemoglobin. The fMRI technique indicates relative amounts of brain activity on a second-by-second basis, as shown in Figure 3.24.

If we want to use a PET or fMRI scan to measure the brain activity during some task, the data tell us nothing except by comparison to the activity that occurs otherwise. Suppose we want to find the brain areas important for memory. We record activity while someone is engaged in a memory task and compare that activity to times when the person is doing . . . what? Doing nothing? That comparison wouldn't work; the memory task presumably includes sensory stimuli, motor responses, attention, and other processes. Besides that, "doing nothing" (mind wandering) activates certain brain areas, too (Mason et al., 2007). Researchers must design a comparison task that requires attention to the same sensory stimuli, the same hand movements, and so forth as the memory task. Then they set a computer to subtract the activity in the comparison task from the activity in the memory task. The areas with the largest difference between the tasks are presumably important for some aspect of memory.

Brain scans sometimes lead to important insights about behavior (Gonsalves & Cohen, 2010). However, the impressive pictures sometimes lure people to careless interpretations. After one study reported that the sight of chocolate excites certain brain areas in "chocolate cravers" (Rolls & McCabe, 2007), some people in the media exclaimed, "Wow, now we understand *why* they craved chocolate!" Do we? Knowing which brain areas become excited tells us nothing about why they became more excited in some people than in others.

Another issue: Suppose researchers find that a particular brain area becomes more active when you are angry. Later, when that area becomes active again, can they conclude that you are angry again? No, not unless research shows that the area is active *only* when you are angry. Perhaps that area also becomes active when you are frightened, excited, paying attention to nearby people, or something else. A good test of understanding is this: Can we take fMRI measures at one time, while we know what you are doing, and then use measures at a later time to infer what you are seeing, hearing, or planning to do? A few such studies have reported success (Haynes et al., 2007; Kay, Naselaris, Prenger, & Gallant, 2008). However, in most cases it is less clear that we know what the fMRI data mean.

concept check

16. What is an advantage of fMRI in comparison to PET scans?

Answer

16. An fMRI scan does not expose anyone to radiation.

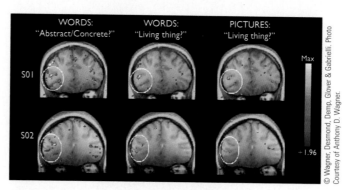

Figure 3.24 This brain scan was made with functional magnetic resonance imaging (fMRI). Participants looked at words or pictures and judged whether each item was abstract or concrete, living or nonliving. Yellow shows the areas most activated by this judgment; red shows areas less strongly activated. (From Wagner, Desmond, Demb, Glover, & Gabrieli, 1997. Photo courtesy of Anthony D. Wagner.)

© Wagner, Desmond, Demp, Glover & Gabrielli. Photo Courtesy of Anthony D. Wagner.

Subcortical Areas

Figure 3.16 shows some of the structures in the interior of the forebrain. At the center is the *thalamus*, the last stop for almost all sensory information on the way to the cerebral cortex. Surrounding the thalamus are areas called the *limbic system*. (A limbus is a margin or border.) The hippocampus, important for memory, will appear again in chapter 7. The hypothalamus, *located just below the thalamus, is important for hunger, thirst, temperature regulation, sex, and other motivated behaviors.*

The cerebral cortex does not directly control the muscles. It sends output to the pons and medulla, *which control the muscles of the head* (e.g., for chewing, swallowing, breathing, and talking), and to the spinal cord, *which controls the muscles from the neck down* (Figures 3.13 and 3.25). The spinal cord also controls many reflexes, such as the knee-jerk reflex. A reflex is a *rapid, automatic response to a stimulus,* such as unconscious adjustments of your legs while you are walking or quickly jerking your hand away from something hot.

The cerebellum (Latin for "little brain"), *part of the hindbrain,* is important for any behavior that requires aim or timing, such as tapping out a rhythm, judging which of two visual stimuli is moving faster, and judging whether one musical tempo is faster or slower than another (Ivry & Diener, 1991; Keele & Ivry, 1990). It is also essential to learned responses that require precise timing (Krupa, Thompson, & Thompson, 1993). People with damage to the cerebellum show motor problems like those of alcoholic intoxication, including slurred speech, staggering, and inaccurate eye movements. The reason for the similarity is that alcohol suppresses activity in the cerebellum.

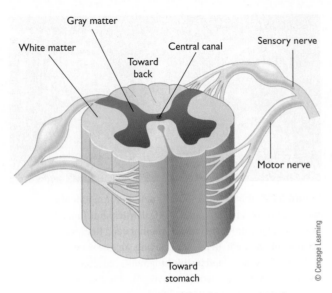

Gray matter
White matter
Toward back
Central canal
Sensory nerve
Motor nerve
Toward stomach

© Cengage Learning

Figure 3.25 The spinal cord receives sensory information from all body parts except the head. Motor nerves in the spinal cord control the muscles and glands.

concept check

17. Someone with a cut through the upper spinal cord still shows many reflexive movements but no voluntary movements of the arms or legs. Why not?

Answer

17. The spinal cord controls many reflexes by itself. However, voluntary control of muscles depends on messages from the brain to the spinal cord, and a cut through the upper spinal cord interrupts those messages.

The Autonomic Nervous System and Endocrine System

The autonomic nervous system, closely associated with the spinal cord, *controls the heart, digestive system, and other organs.* The term *autonomic* means involuntary, or automatic. A sudden loud noise increases your heart rate, but you can't decide to increase your heart rate in the same way that you could decide to wave your hand. Brain activity does, however, influence the autonomic nervous system. For example, your autonomic nervous system reacts more strongly when you are nervous than when you are relaxed.

The autonomic nervous system has two parts: (a) The *sympathetic nervous system*, controlled by a chain of cells lying just outside the spinal cord, increases heart rate, breathing rate, sweating, and other processes that are important for vigorous fight-or-flight activities. It inhibits digestion and sexual arousal,

which can wait until the emergency is over. (b) The *parasympathetic nervous system*, controlled by cells at the top and bottom levels of the spinal cord, decreases heart rate, increases digestive activities, and in general, promotes body activities that take place during rest and relaxation (Figure 3.26). If you are driving and you see a police car wailing its siren behind you, your sympathetic nervous system arouses. Your heart starts racing, you breathe heavily, and you start sweating. When the police car passes and you see that it is chasing someone else, your parasympathetic nervous system kicks in, and you suddenly relax.

The autonomic nervous system influences the endocrine system, *glands that produce hormones and release them into the blood.* Hormones controlled by the hypothalamus and *pituitary gland* regulate the other endocrine organs. Figure 3.27 shows some of the endocrine glands. Hormones are *chemicals released by glands and conveyed by the blood to alter activity in various organs.* Some hormonal effects are brief, such as changes in heart rate or blood pressure. Other hormonal effects prepare a body for pregnancy, migration, hibernation, or other long-lasting activities. Within the brain, hormones produce temporary changes in the excitability of cells, and they also influence the survival, growth, and connections of cells. The sex hormones (*androgens* and *estrogens*) have strong effects during early development, when they produce differences between male and female anatomies, in certain brain areas as well as the rest of the body (Cahill, 2006).

concept check

18. While someone is trying to escape danger, the heart rate and breathing rate increase. After the danger passes, heart rate and breathing rate fall below normal. Which part of the autonomic nervous system is more active during the danger, and which is more active after the danger has passed?

Answer

18. The sympathetic nervous system predominates during the danger, and the parasympathetic system predominates afterward.

Experience and Brain Plasticity

When we talk about brain anatomy, it is easy to get the impression that the structures are fixed. In fact, brain structure shows considerable plasticity—that is, *change as a result of experience.*

Sympathetic system	Parasympathetic system
Preparation for vigorous activity	**Body at rest**
• Pupils open	• Pupils constrict
• Saliva decreases	• Saliva flows
• Pulse quickens	• Pulse slows
• Sweat increases	• Stomach churns
• Stomach less active	
• Epinephrine (adrenaline) secreted	

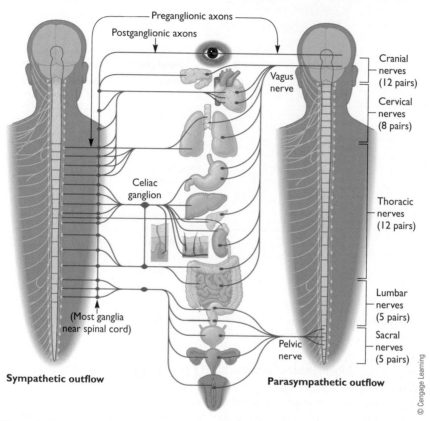

Figure 3.26 The sympathetic nervous system prepares the organs for a brief bout of vigorous activity. The parasympathetic nervous system puts the brakes on vigorous activity and prepares the body for rest and digestion.

Early researchers believed that the nervous system produced no new neurons after early infancy. Later researchers found that *undifferentiated cells called* **stem cells** develop into new neurons in certain brain areas and not others (Gage, 2000; Graziadei & deHan, 1973; Song, Stevens, & Gage, 2002). In the brains of humans and other mammals, new neurons develop in the olfactory bulb (essential for the sense of smell) and in the hippocampus, which is important for memory formation (Kee, Teixeira, Wang, & Frankland, 2007; Meshi et al., 2006; Ramirez-Amaya, Marrone, Gage, Worley, & Barnes, 2006).

New experiences stimulate various axons and dendrites to expand and withdraw their branches. These changes, which occur more rapidly in young people but continue throughout life, enable the brain to adapt to changing circumstances (Boyke, Driemeyer, Gaser, Büchel, & May, 2008). For example, one man lost his hand in an accident at age 19. Thirty-five years later, surgeons grafted a new hand onto his arm. Within a few months, axons connected the new hand to his brain, and he regained partial sensation from the hand (Frey, Bogdanov, Smith, Watrous, & Breidenbach, 2008).

Substantial brain changes also occur after people learn to read, even if they learn in adulthood (Carreiras et al., 2009; Dehaene et al., 2010). Many studies have examined what happens after people learn to play music. One brain area devoted to hearing is 30% larger than average in professional musicians (Schneider et al., 2002), and an area responsive to finger sensations is larger than average in people who

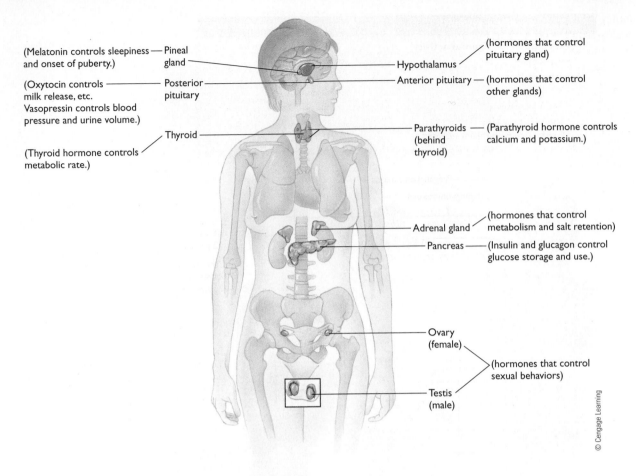

(Melatonin controls sleepiness and onset of puberty.) — Pineal gland

(Oxytocin controls milk release, etc. Vasopressin controls blood pressure and urine volume.) — Posterior pituitary

Thyroid

(Thyroid hormone controls metabolic rate.)

Hypothalamus — (hormones that control pituitary gland)

Anterior pituitary — (hormones that control other glands)

Parathyroids (behind thyroid) — (Parathyroid hormone controls calcium and potassium.)

Adrenal gland — (hormones that control metabolism and salt retention)

Pancreas — (Insulin and glucagon control glucose storage and use.)

Ovary (female)

(hormones that control sexual behaviors)

Testis (male)

© Cengage Learning

Figure 3.27 Glands in the endocrine system produce hormones and release them into the bloodstream.

play stringed instruments (Elbert, Pantev, Wienbruch, Rockstroh, & Taub, 1995). We might wonder whether musical training caused those changes, or whether people with certain kinds of brains are more likely than others to become musicians. However, one study found measurable changes in children's brains as a result of 15 months of music training, as compared to similar children who did not undergo such training (Hyde et al., 2009). The implication is that music training alters the brain. We must await later research to see how long these changes last.

concept check

19. In the study showing changes in children's brains as they learn to play music, why was it necessary to have a control group of untrained children?

Answer

19. It was important to separate the effects of music from the effects of growing 15 months older.

The Binding Problem

We end this module with a theoretical problem that researchers first began to notice around 1990: Vision takes place in one part of your brain, hearing in another, and touch in still another. Those areas do not share much information with one another, nor do they send information to any one central location. Few cells in the brain get information from more than one sense. That is, there is no "little person in the head" who puts it all together. So, when you play a piano, how do you know that the piano you see is also what you hear and feel? *The question of how separate brain areas combine forces to produce a unified perception of a single object* is the binding problem (Treisman, 1999). (The binding problem relates to the mind–brain problem mentioned in chapter 1.)

Part of the answer lies with the parietal cortex, important for spatial perception. Consider the piano: If you identify the location of the hand that you feel, the piano you see, and the sound you hear, and all those locations are the same, you link the sensations together. The parietal cortex is important for localizing sensations. If, like someone with parietal cortex damage, you cannot locate anything in space, you probably won't bind sensations into a single experience. You might look at a yellow lemon and a red tomato and report seeing a yellow tomato and no lemon at all (L. C. Robertson, 2003).

We also know that binding occurs only for precisely simultaneous events. Have you ever watched a film or television show in which the soundtrack is noticeably ahead of or behind the picture? If so, you knew that the sound wasn't coming from the performers on screen. You get the same experience watching a poorly dubbed foreign-language film. However, when you watch a ventriloquist, the motion of the dummy's mouth simultaneous with the sound lets you perceive the sound as coming from the dummy. Even young infants figure out who is talking based on whose lip movements synchronize with the sounds (Lickliter & Bahrick, 2000).

You can experience a demonstration of binding with an Online Try It Yourself activity. Go to your Psychology CourseMate at CengageBrain.com. Navigate to the student website, then to the Online Try It Yourself section, and click Illustration of Binding.

You can also try the following (I. H. Robertson, 2005): Stand or sit by a large mirror as in Figure 3.28, watching both your right hand and its reflection in the mirror. Hold your left hand out of sight. Then repeatedly clench and unclench both hands, and touch each thumb to your fingers and palm, in unison. You will feel your left hand doing the same thing that you see the hand in the mirror doing. After a couple of minutes, you may start to experience the hand in the mirror as your own left hand. You are binding your touch and visual experiences because they occur at the same time, apparently in the same location. For most people, this procedure is just an amusing demonstration, but it is valuable in certain cases. For someone who has had an arm amputated, this procedure helps the person feel an artificial arm as being part of the body.

People with parietal lobe damage have trouble binding aspects of a stimulus, such as color and shape, because they do not perceive visual locations accurately (Treisman, 1999; Wheeler & Treisman, 2002).

When you watch a movie, the sound seems to come from the actors' mouths. You bind the sound and the action because they are simultaneous.

People with intact brains experience the same problem if they see something very briefly while distracted (Holcombe & Cavanagh, 2001). What would it be like to see objects without binding them? You can get some feel for this experience with an Online Try It

Figure 3.28 Move your left and right hands in synchrony while watching the image of one hand in a mirror. Within minutes, you may experience the one in the mirror as being your own hand. This demonstration illustrates how binding occurs.

Yourself activity. Go to your Psychology CourseMate at CengageBrain.com. Navigate to the student website, then to the Online Try It Yourself section, and click Possible Failure of Binding.

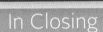

concept check

20. What is the binding problem?
21. What two elements must take place for binding to occur?

Answers

20. The binding problem is the theoretical question of how the brain creates a unified experience, given that different brain areas differ.

21. For binding to occur, the brain must be able to identify that different aspects of the stimulus come from the same location. Also, the different aspects must occur simultaneously.

module 3.3 >

In Closing

Brain and Experience

The main point of this module is that mind and brain activity are tightly linked—indeed, apparently synonymous. If you lose part of your brain, you lose part of your mind. If you have some mental experience, you simultaneously increase activity in some brain area. If two people's behaviors differ, their brains differ too, in some way.

Another major point is that although different brain areas handle different functions without feeding into a central processor, they still manage to function as an organized whole. When we perceive two events simultaneously in the same location, we bind them together as a single object. Brain areas act separately and nevertheless produce a single experience.

Research on brain functioning is challenging because the brain itself is so complex. Just think about all that goes on within this 1.3 kg mass of tissue composed mostly of water. It is an amazing structure.

Summary

- *Two main points to remember.* You use all of your brain, not some percentage of it. Although most people take for granted that their mind is separate from the brain, the evidence points to the contrary: Mind activity and brain activity are the same thing. To lose part of one is to lose part of the other. (page 75)

- *Central and peripheral nervous systems.* The central nervous system consists of the brain and the spinal cord. The peripheral nervous system consists of nerves that communicate between the central nervous system and the rest of the body. (page 75)

- *The cerebral cortex.* The cerebral cortex has four lobes: occipital lobe (vision), temporal lobe (hearing and some aspects of vision), parietal lobe (body sensations), and the frontal lobe (preparation for movement). Damage in the ce-

rebral cortex produces specialized behavioral deficits. (page 75)

- *Hemispheres of the brain.* Each brain hemisphere controls the opposite side of the body. The left hemisphere of the human brain is specialized for language in most people. The right hemisphere is important for understanding spatial relationships and for interpreting emotional expressions. (page 80)

- *Corpus callosum.* The corpus callosum enables the left and right hemispheres of the cortex to communicate with each other. If the corpus callosum is damaged, the two hemispheres cannot share information. (page 80)

- *Split-brain patients.* After damage to the corpus callosum, people can describe information only if it enters the left hemisphere. In some ways such people act as if they have separate fields of consciousness, and in some ways they act as if they are unified. (page 80)

- *Learning about brain functions.* Modern technology enables researchers to develop images showing the structure and activity of various brain areas in living, waking people. Such methods are powerful, but the results should be interpreted with caution. (page 82)
- *Communication between the cerebral cortex and the rest of the body.* Information from the cerebral cortex passes to the medulla and then into the spinal cord. The medulla and spinal cord receive sensory input from the periphery and send output to the muscles and glands. (page 83)
- *Autonomic nervous system and endocrine system.* The autonomic nervous system controls the body's organs, preparing them for emergency activities or for relaxed activities. The endocrine system consists of organs that release hormones into the blood. (page 84)
- *Brain plasticity.* Experiences alter brain connections. Prolonged unusual experiences—such as in musicians who practice many hours per day—change the brain in profound ways. (page 84)
- *The binding problem.* Theoretically, it is problematic to understand how one brain area responsible for vision, another area responsible for hearing, and another area responsible for touch combine forces to yield a unified perception of an object. Binding different senses into one experience requires perceiving the various aspects as occurring in the same place at the same time. (page 86)

Key Terms

amygdala (page 77)

autonomic nervous system (page 84)

binding problem (page 86)

blindsight (page 76)

central nervous system (page 75)

cerebellum (page 83)

cerebral cortex (page 76)

corpus callosum (page 80)

electroencephalograph (EEG) (page 82)

endocrine system (page 84)

epilepsy (page 80)

frontal lobe (page 79)

functional magnetic resonance imaging (fMRI) (page 82)

hemisphere (page 75)

hormone (page 84)

hypothalamus (page 83)

magnetoencephalograph (MEG) (page 82)

medulla (page 83)

mirror neurons (page 79)

monism (page 75)

occipital lobe (page 76)

parietal lobe (page 78)

peripheral nervous system (page 75)

plasticity (page 84)

pons (page 83)

positron-emission tomography (PET) (page 82)

prefrontal cortex (page 79)

primary motor cortex (page 79)

primary somatosensory cortex (page 78)

reflex (page 83)

spinal cord (page 83)

stem cells (page 85)

temporal lobe (page 77)

module 3.4

Genetics and Evolutionary Psychology

- **How do genes influence behavior?**
- **What can we infer about the evolution of behavior?**

Everyone has tens of thousands of genes that control development. If we could go back in time and change just one of the genes you were born with, how would your experience and personality be different?

Obviously, it depends! *Which* gene? Hundreds of your genes control olfactory receptors. A mutation in one of them would decrease your sensitivity to a few smells, and you might not even notice your deficiency. Mutations in certain other genes would change your life drastically or end it.

The effect of changing a gene also depends on your environment. Suppose you have a gene that magnifies your reactions to stressful experiences. That gene would make a big difference if you live under highly stressful conditions, but hardly at all if you live in calmer circumstances.

It makes no sense to ask whether your behavior depends mainly on heredity or environment. Without either heredity or environment, you could not exist. However, if your behavior differs from someone else's we can ask whether that difference depends more on differences in heredity or environment. For example, the difference between having color vision and lacking it depends almost entirely on genetics, whereas the difference between speaking English and speaking Chinese depends on where you were reared. Most behavioral differences depend on differences in both heredity and environment.

The study of genetics has become increasingly important for citizens of the twenty-first century. Let's first review some basic points about genetics and then explore their application to human behavior.

Genetic Principles

Except for your red blood cells, all of your cells contain a nucleus that includes *strands of hereditary material* called chromosomes (Figure 3.29). Each human nucleus has 23 pairs of chromosomes, except that egg and sperm cells have 23 unpaired chromosomes. At fertilization, the 23 chromosomes from an egg cell combine with the 23 of a sperm cell to form 23 pairs for the new person (Figure 3.30).

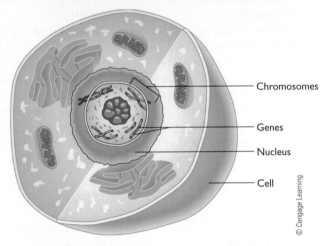

Figure 3.29 Genes are sections of chromosomes in the nuclei of cells. (Scale is exaggerated for illustration purposes.)

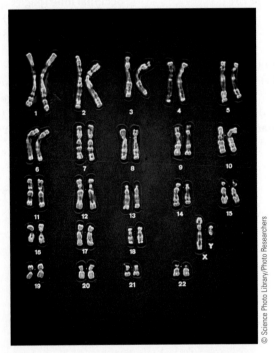

Figure 3.30 The nucleus of each human cell contains 46 chromosomes, 23 from the sperm and 23 from the ovum, united in pairs.

Sections along each chromosome, known as genes, *control the chemical reactions that direct development*—for example, controlling height or hair color. Genes are composed of the chemical DNA, which controls the production of another chemical called RNA, which among other functions controls

Albinos occur in many species, always because of a recessive gene. **(a)** Striped skunk.
(b) American alligator. **(c)** Mockingbird.

the production of proteins. The proteins either become part of the body's structure or control the rates of chemical reactions in the body. To explain the concept of genes, educators often use an example such as eye color. If you have either one or two genes for brown eyes, you will have brown eyes because the brown-eye gene is dominant—*that is, a single copy of the gene is sufficient to produce its effect.* The gene for blue eyes is recessive—*its effects appear only if the dominant gene is absent.* You have blue eyes only if you have two genes for blue eyes.

Sex-Linked and Sex-Limited Genes

Because chromosomes come in pairs (one from the mother and one from the father), you have two of almost all genes. The exceptions are those on the chromosomes that determine whether you developed as a male or as a female. Mammals' sex chromosomes are known as X and Y (Figure 3.31). *A female has two* X *chromosomes in each cell. A male has one X chromosome and one* Y *chromosome.* The mother contributes an X chromosome to each child, and the father contributes either an X or a Y. Because men have one X chromosome and one Y chromosome, they have unpaired genes on these chromosomes. Women have two X chromosomes, but in each cell, one of the X chromosomes is activated and the other is silenced, apparently at random.

Genes located on the X or Y chromosome are known as sex-linked genes. A recessive gene on the X chromosome shows its effects more in men than in women. For example, red-green color deficiency depends on an X-linked recessive gene. A man with that gene on his X chromosome will be red-green deficient because he has no other X chromosome. A woman with that gene probably has a gene for normal color vision on her other X chromosome. Consequently, far more men than women have red-green deficiency (Figure 3.32).

A **sex-limited gene** *occurs equally in both sexes but exerts its effects mainly or entirely in one or the*

Figure 3.31 An electron micrograph shows that the X chromosome is longer than the Y chromosome. (From Ruch, 1984.)

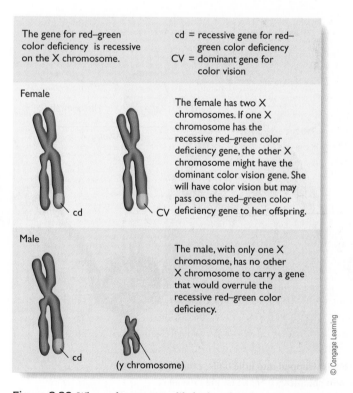

Figure 3.32 Why males are more likely than females to be red-green color deficient.

other. For example, both men and women have the genes for facial hair, but men's hormones activate those genes. Both men and women have the genes for breast development, but women's hormones activate those genes.

concept check

22. Suppose a father is red-green deficient and a mother has two genes for normal color vision. What sort of color vision will their children have?

Answer

22. The sons receive a gene for normal color vision from the mother, and a Y chromosome (irrelevant to color vision) from the father. They will have normal color vision. The daughters receive a gene for normal color vision from the mother and a gene for red-green color deficiency from the father. They will also have normal color vision, but they will be carriers who can pass the red-green deficiency gene to some of their children.

A More Complex View of Genes

To talk about "the gene for" something is convenient at times, but also misleading. Even for the supposedly simple case of eye color, researchers have found at least 10 genes with a significant influence (Liu et al., 2010). Variations in height depend on at least 180 genes as well as the effects of diet and other environmental influences (Allen et al., 2010). We can barely imagine all the influences on behavior. Furthermore, each gene affects many outcomes, not just eye color or height.

Furthermore, the nature of a gene is more complicated than we once thought. In some cases, part of one gene overlaps part of another one, or parts of a gene are located in different places. The newly emerging field of epigenetics *deals with changes in gene expression as a result of environmental influences, without modification of the DNA sequence* (Tsankova, Renthal, Kumar, & Nestler, 2007). Proteins called *histones* wrap the DNA of a chromosome into little balls, as shown in Figure 3.33. When certain chemicals (called *acetyl* groups) attach to a histone, they loosen the ball and increase the expression of genes in that ball. Other chemicals (called *methyl* groups) can attach to a gene and inactivate it. Various experiences produce epigenetic changes. For example, if a rat is malnourished during her pregnancy, certain genes become activated in her offspring, preparing them for a world in which food is presumably scarce. Throughout life, they eat whenever possible, expend no more energy than necessary, and—if food is in fact plentiful—become obese (Godfrey, Lillycrop, Burdge, Gluckman, & Hanson, 2007). If a mother rat neglects her pups during their early life, they alter gene expression to become more vulnerable in stressful situations (Weaver et al., 2004; Zhang et al., 2010). Most of the research to date concerns laboratory animals, but it is likely that the same processes occur in humans. Epigenetics may play an increasingly important role in psychology.

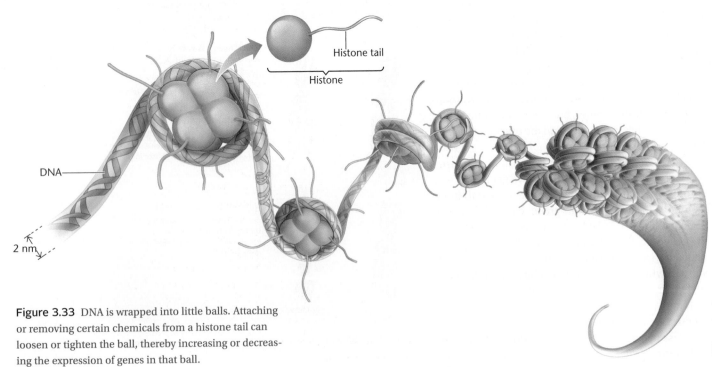

Figure 3.33 DNA is wrapped into little balls. Attaching or removing certain chemicals from a histone tail can loosen or tighten the ball, thereby increasing or decreasing the expression of genes in that ball.

Histone tail

Histone

DNA

2 nm

© Cengage Learning

23. Why is it misleading to talk about "the gene" for some behavior or ability?

24. In what way does the field of epigenetics blur the distinction between hereditary effects and environmental effects?

Answers

23. Almost every aspect of behavior depends on the combined influence of many genes and environmental influences. Also, any gene affects more than one outcome.

24. Epigenetic changes are alterations in gene expression caused by environmental influences.

Estimating Heritability in Humans

All behavior depends on both heredity and environment, but *variations* might depend more on the variation in genes or variations in the environment. Suppose we want to estimate how much of the variation in some behavior depends on differences in genes. The answer is summarized by the term heritability, *an estimate of the variance within a population that is due to heredity.* Heritability ranges from 1, indicating that heredity controls all the variance, to 0, indicating that it controls none of it. For example, red-green color vision deficiency has a heritability of almost 1. Note that the definition of heritability includes the phrase "within a population." The results for one population can be much different from another, depending on how much genetic variation that population has, and how much environmental variation. To estimate the heritability of a behavior, researchers have traditionally relied on evidence from twins and adopted children.

25. If our society changed so that it provided an equally good environment for all children, would the heritability of behaviors increase or decrease?

Answer

25. If all children had equally supportive environments, the total amount of variation in behavior would decrease, but whatever variation remained would have to depend largely on heredity (because differences in the environment have been minimized). Therefore, heritability would *increase*.

Twin Studies

Monozygotic (mon-oh-zie-GOT-ik) twins *develop from a single fertilized egg (zygote) and therefore have identical genes.* Most people call them "identical" twins, but that term is misleading. Some monozygotic twins are mirror images—one right-handed and the other left-handed. It is also possible for a gene to be activated in one twin and suppressed in the other. Dizygotic (DIE-zie-GOT-ik) twins *develop from two eggs and share only half their genes* (Figure 3.34). They are often called "fraternal" twins because they are only as closely related as brother and sister. If dizygotic twins resemble each other almost as much as monozygotic twins do in some trait, then the heritability of that trait is low because genetic similarity did not have much influence. If monozygotic twins resemble each other more strongly than dizygotic twins do, then the heritability is probably high. An alternative explanation, valid in some cases, is that monozygotic twins resemble each other so strongly because people treat them the same way.

Researchers also examine pairs of monozygotic twins who grew up in separate environments. Today's adoption agencies place twins in the same family, but in previous times, many twins were adopted separately. One pair of monozygotic twins, reunited in adulthood after being reared separately, quickly discovered that they had much in common (Figure 3.35). Both had been named Jim by their adoptive parents. Each liked carpentry and drafting, had built a bench around a tree in his yard, and worked as a deputy sheriff. Both chewed their fingernails, gained weight at the same age, smoked the same brand of cigarettes, drove Chevrolets, and took their vacations in western Florida. Each married a woman named Linda, divorced her, and married a woman named Betty. One had a son named James Alan and the other had a son named James Allen, and each had a pet dog named Toy. It is, of course, difficult to know how many of these similarities are mere coincidences. However, many other sets of twins reunited in adulthood also reported detailed similarities (Lykken, McGue, Tellegen, & Bouchard, 1992).

Researchers examined about 100 pairs of twins, some monozygotic and others dizygotic, who were reared separately and reunited as adults. On the average, the monozygotic twins resembled each other more strongly with regard to hobbies, vocational interests, answers on personality tests, tendency to trust other people, political beliefs, probability of voting, job satisfaction, life satisfaction, probability of mental illness, consumption of coffee and fruit juices, and preference for awakening early in the morning or staying up late at night (Bouchard & McGue, 2003; Cesarini et al., 2008; DiLalla, Carey, Gottesman, & Bouchard, 1996; Fowler, Baker, & Dawes, 2008; Hur,

Figure 3.34 Monozygotic twins develop from the same fertilized egg. Dizygotic twins grow from two eggs fertilized by different sperm.

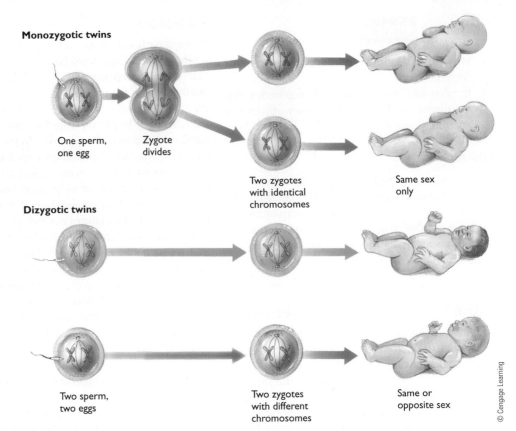

Monozygotic twins

One sperm, one egg

Zygote divides

Two zygotes with identical chromosomes

Same sex only

Dizygotic twins

Two sperm, two eggs

Two zygotes with different chromosomes

Same or opposite sex

© Cengage Learning

Bouchard, & Eckert, 1998; Hur, Bouchard, & Lykken, 1998; Lykken, Bouchard, McGue, & Tellegen, 1993; McCourt, Bouchard, Lykken, Tellegen, & Keyes, 1999). The implication is that genes influence a wide variety of behaviors.

Studies of Adopted Children

Another kind of evidence for heritability comes from studies of adopted children. Resemblance to their adopting parents implies an environmental influence. Resemblance to their biological parents implies a genetic influence.

However, the results are sometimes hard to interpret. For example, consider the evidence that many adopted children with an arrest record had biological mothers with a criminal history (Mason & Frick, 1994). The resemblance could indicate a genetic influence, but the mothers also provided the prenatal environment. Chances are, many of the mothers with a criminal record smoked, drank alcohol, perhaps used other drugs, and in other ways endangered the fetus's brain development. Prenatal environment is an important influence on development.

concept check

26. Suppose someone studies adopted children who developed severe depression and finds that many of their biological parents had depression, whereas few of their adopting parents did. One possible interpretation is that genetic factors influence depression more than family environment does. What is another interpretation?

Answer

26. Perhaps biological mothers who are becoming depressed eat less healthy foods, drink more alcohol, or in some other way impair the prenatal environment of their babies.

Figure 3.35 Monozygotic twins Jim Lewis and Jim Springer were separated at birth, reared in separate cities of western Ohio, and reunited in adulthood. They discovered many detailed similarities in their behaviors.

© Enrico Ferorelli

Examination of Chromosomes

A third type of evidence for heritability: Now that biologists have mapped the human genome (the set of all genes on our chromosomes), it is possible to examine the chromosomes and identify genes that are linked to a particular condition. One gene is strongly linked to Huntington's disease. Several genes are linked to increased risk of certain types of cancer.

Researchers have spent enormous efforts seeking a gene that might explain schizophrenia, depression, alcoholism, or other behavioral conditions. They have found many genes that increase the probability of one condition or another, but so far it appears that none of these conditions is strongly related to variations in any single gene. That is, nearly every behavioral variation depends on many genes as well as variations in the environment.

How Genes Influence Behavior

Based on studies of twins and adopted children, researchers have found at least moderate heritability for almost every behavior they have examined, including loneliness (McGuire & Clifford, 2000), neuroticism (Lake, Eaves, Maes, Heath, & Martin, 2000), time spent watching television (Plomin, Corley, DeFries, & Fulker, 1990), and religious devoutness (Waller, Kojetin, Bouchard, Lykken, & Tellegen, 1990). About the only behavior for which researchers have reported zero heritability is choice of religious denomination (Eaves, Martin, & Heath, 1990). That is, genes apparently influence how often you attend religious services but not which services you attend (or don't). How could genes influence this range of behaviors?

Direct and Indirect Influences

In some cases genes influence behavior by altering development of the brain or sensory receptors. For example, one influence on people's food preferences is the number of taste buds they have on the tongue. In other cases, genes influence behavior in an indirect manner by altering something outside the nervous system. Consider dietary choices: Almost all infants can digest *lactose*, the sugar in milk. Within a few years, nearly all Asian children and many others lose the ability to digest it. (The loss depends on genes, not on how often people drink milk.) People who cannot digest lactose enjoy a little milk and more readily enjoy cheese and yogurt, which are easier to digest, but they get gas and cramps if they consume much milk or ice cream (Flatz, 1987; Rozin & Pelchat, 1988).

Figure 3.36 shows how the ability to digest dairy products varies among ethnic groups. The point is that a gene can affect behavior—in this case, preference for dairy products—by altering chemical reactions outside the brain.

Genes also influence behaviors by altering body anatomy. Consider genes that make you unusually good-looking. Because many people smile at you, invite you to parties, and try to become your friend, you develop increased self-confidence and social skills. The genes changed your behavior by changing how other people treated you.

The Multiplier Effect

Imagine you have a gene that makes you tall, and another gene that helps you develop fast running skills. At first you have a slight natural advantage in basketball playing, compared to others your age. Therefore, you get to be on basketball teams, you receive coaching, and your skills improve. As your skills improve, you experience more success and receive further encouragement. What started as a small natural advantage develops into a huge advantage that reflects environmental influences as well as genetics. Researchers call this tendency a multiplier effect: *A small initial advantage in some behavior, possibly genetic in origin, alters the environment and magnifies that advantage* (Dickens & Flynn, 2001). The same could occur for almost any aspect of behavior. For example, someone who is inclined to be active and vigorous tends to choose outgoing friends and stimulating social situations. Someone with a more reserved temperament gravitates toward quiet activities and smaller social groups. The initial behavioral tendency increases by altering the environment. Thus, it is often difficult to separate the contributions of heredity and environment.

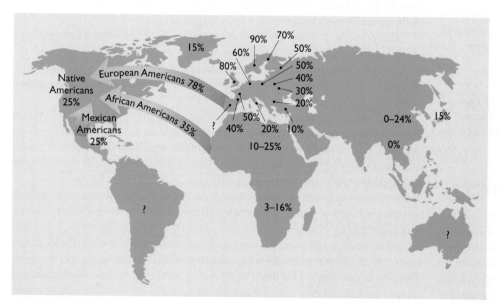

Figure 3.36 Adult humans vary in their ability to digest lactose, the main sugar in milk. The numbers refer to the percentage of each population's adults that can easily digest lactose. (Based on Flatz, 1987; Rozin & Pelchat, 1988.)

27. Because of the multiplier effect, should we expect estimates of heritability to be higher for children or for adults?

Answer

27. In most cases, heritability estimates should be higher for adults. As people grow older, their behavior tendencies alter their environment in ways that increase or exaggerate the initial differences.

Environmental Modification of Genetic Effects

Some people assume that if a gene has a strong influence on some behavior, then we can do nothing about it, short of genetic modification. One example that illustrates that this assumption is not necessarily true is phenylketonuria (PKU), *an inherited condition that, if untreated, leads to mental retardation.* About 2% of people with European or Asian ancestry, and almost no Africans, have the recessive gene that leads to PKU, but because the gene is recessive, one copy is nearly harmless. People with copies from both parents cannot metabolize *phenylalanine*, a common constituent of proteins. On an ordinary diet, an affected child accumulates phenylalanine in the brain and becomes mentally retarded. However, a diet low in phenylalanine protects the brain. Thus, a special diet prevents a disorder that would otherwise show high heritability.

28. Some people assume that if something is under genetic control, we can't do anything about it. Cite an example that contradicts this idea.

Answer

28. Phenylketonuria is a genetic condition that would cause mental retardation, but a special diet minimizes the problem.

Evolutionary Psychology

Since ancient times, people have practiced selective breeding. Farmers use the best egg-laying chickens and best milk-producing cows to breed the next generation. People have selectively bred friendly lap dogs, reliable guard dogs, and dutiful sheep-herding dogs. We have improved crops by selecting seeds of the best-yielding plants. Maize (American corn) is the product of intense selective breeding by Native Americans, and its precursor in nature is barely recognizable as related (Gallavotti et al., 2005; Figure 3.37). Charles Darwin's insight was that nature also acts as a selective breeder. If certain kinds of individuals are more successful than others at surviving and reproducing—especially reproducing—then they pass on their genes, and the next generation resembles them more than it does the less successful individuals. Over time, the species as a whole can change. Darwin's preferred term was *descent with modification*, but the concept quickly became known as evolution, defined as *a gradual change in the frequency of various genes from one generation to the next.* Why do you have the genes that you do? Simply, your parents had those genes and survived long enough to reproduce. So did your parents' parents and so on. Any gene that is common in a large population presumably had benefits in the past, though not necessarily today.

Natural selection acts on brain and behavior, just as it does on the rest of the body. For example, the dodo was a large bird in the pigeon/dove family that adapted to life on an island with no mammals. Living without needing to escape enemies, it gradually lost the ability to fly. (Non-flying dodos evidently had an advantage by saving energy.) The dodo also lost all fear. When humans eventually came to the island, they hunted the flightless, fearless dodos for meat or for sport, and exterminated them.

Kittiwakes, unlike other members of the gull family, usually breed on the narrow ledges of steep cliffs. Many of their behaviors are adapted to this setting, including the fact that their chicks stay in place until they are old enough to fly (Tinbergen, 1958). Even if they are placed on a safe, flat surface, they remain motionless. In contrast, the chicks of other gull species start walking around at an early age—even if they are placed on a narrow ledge, like the ones where kittiwakes nest. (They of course fall off.) The stationary behavior that is so clearly adaptive for kittiwake chicks is a product of evolution, not thinking or trial-and-error learning.

It would be easy to cite other examples of animal behavior that have evolved to special circumstances, but what about humans? Have we evolved specializations in our behavior? Some aspects of human behavior make no sense except in the context of evolution. For example, consider the "goose bumps" you get when you are cold. What good do they do for you? None. However, other mammals, with hairier skin, gain an advantage by erecting their hairs when they are cold. Their raised hairs provide extra insulation. Hair erection in a cold environment was useful to your ancient ancestors, and you continue to show that reaction, even though your body hairs are short, usually covered with clothing, and generally useless.

Also consider a human infant's grasp reflex: An infant's hand tightly grasps anything placed into the palm, such as a finger or pencil. This behavior serves no function today, but for our ancient ancestors, it helped an infant hold onto the mother as she traveled (Figure 3.38). Again, in humans this behavior makes sense only as an evolutionary carry-over.

Evolutionary psychologists try to infer the benefits that favored certain genes. Some of the most controversial interpretations pertain to human sexual behavior. For example, in many species throughout the animal kingdom, males seek mating opportunities with multiple partners more vigorously than females seek multiple partners. When we see this tendency in frogs, birds, or lions, an evolutionary explanation seems clear: A male can spread his genes by mating with many females, whereas a female cannot produce more babies by mating with more males. (She gains some advantage by additional partners, especially if the first male is infertile, but her potential gain is less than a male's.) In humans, too, as shown in Figure 3.39, more men than women are eager for more than one sexual partner (Schmitt et al., 2003). Many men will accept almost any partner for a short-term sexual relationship, whereas most women either refuse

Figure 3.37 Many centuries ago, Native Americans selectively bred *teosinte*, a plant with barely edible hard kernels, until they developed what we now know as maize (American corn).

a short-term sexual relationship or accept only a very appealing partner. The proposed evolutionary explanation parallels that for other species (Bjorklund & Shackelford, 1999; Buss, 2000; Gangestad, 2000; Geary, 2000): A man can spread his genes by either of two strategies: He can devote full efforts to helping one woman rear his children, or have sex with many women and hope they can rear the children without his help (Gangestad & Simpson, 2000). Women can gain possible advantages from multiple partners (Hrdy, 2000), but they cannot multiply their number of children by multiplying their number of sex partners.

This interpretation has been controversial. One objection is that it seems to give men an excuse for sexual infidelity. Evolutionary psychologists respond that explaining what *is* does not equal saying what *ought to be*. Pain is also a product of evolution, for example, but we try to restrain it. Another objection is that even if the evolutionary explanation applies to other animal species, it does not necessarily have the same force in humans. With humans, it is harder to separate our presumably innate tendencies from what we have learned (Eagly & Wood, 1999).

Here is another example of a possible evolutionary explanation of a male–female difference: Whom would you prefer for a long-term mating relationship, someone who is more physically attrac-

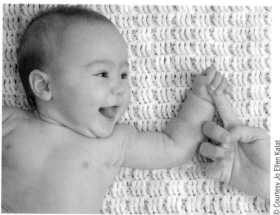

Figure 3.38 Human infants tightly grasp anything in the palm of their hands. In our remote monkey-like ancestors, this reflex helped infants hold onto their mothers.

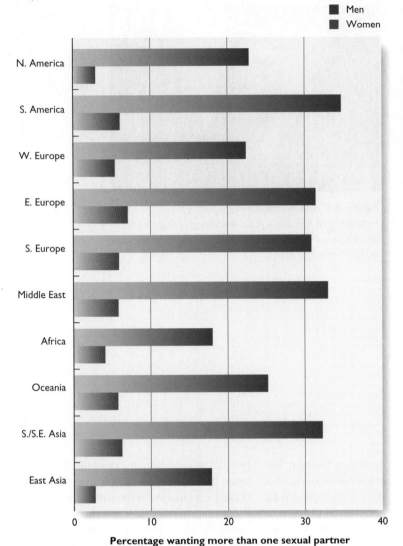

Men
Women

N. America

S. America

W. Europe

E. Europe

S. Europe

Middle East

Africa

Oceania

S./S.E. Asia

East Asia

0   10   20   30   40

Percentage wanting more than one sexual partner

Figure 3.39 In all 52 countries that were surveyed, more men than women hoped for more than one sexual partner within the next month. (Based on data of Schmitt et al., 2003.)

tive, or someone who is more financially successful? Women are more likely than men to prefer the financially successful partner (Buss, 2000). An evolutionary interpretation is that a woman needs a good provider during her time of pregnancy and infant care, when she is limited in her ability to find food and supplies. Therefore, perhaps women evolved to prefer a mate who has this ability. Although this explanation is plausible, it is not convincing. First, as you might guess, women's preference for a successful partner is strongest in countries where women have low economic status, and weakest in countries where economic opportunities are nearly equal (Kasser & Sharma, 1999). Second, this tendency is far from universal even among other mammals. In many mammalian species, the male separates from the female after mating and contributes nothing to caring for her or her babies. So if this is an evolved tendency, it had to evolve specifically in humans.

In short, it is important to distinguish between the most convincing evolutionary explanations (such as for goose bumps and infant grasp reflex) and the more speculative interpretations (de Waal, 2002). In many cases it is easy to propose an evolutionary explanation and more difficult to test it.

concept check

29. What explanation do evolutionary psychologists offer for the human infant's grasp reflex?

Answer

29. Although the reflex is useless for humans, it was important to ancestral species in which infants had to cling to their mothers while the mothers were walking.

module 3.4

Genes and Experience

Physicists say that the development of the universe depended on its "initial conditions"—the array of matter and energy a fraction of a second after the "big bang." The outcome of any experiment in physics or chemistry depends on the initial conditions—the type of matter, its temperature and pressure, and so forth. You had initial conditions, too—your genes. Understanding your genes is important for under-standing why you developed differently from some-one else, but it would not be enough. Your genes influence how you react to your environment, and your environment activates certain genes and inac-tivates others. In this module we have explored just a little of the complex ways in which genes interact with experiences.

Summary

- *Genes.* Genes control heredity. A recessive gene exerts its effects only in someone with two cop-ies of the gene per cell. A dominant gene exerts its effects even if one has only a single copy per cell. (page 90)
- *Sex-linked and sex-limited genes.* Genes on the X or Y chromosome are sex linked. An X-linked re-cessive gene will show its effects more fre-quently in males than in females. A sex-limited gene is present in both sexes, but it affects one sex more than the other. (page 91)
- *Epigenetics.* Various experiences can modify the expression of genes. (page 92)
- *Heritability.* Researchers estimate heritability by comparing monozygotic and dizygotic twins, by comparing twins reared in separate environ-ments, by examining how adopted children re-semble their biological parents, and by finding associations between particular genes and ob-served outcomes. (page 93)
- *How genes affect behavior.* Genes affect behav-iors by altering the chemistry of the brain. They also exert indirect effects by influencing other organs that in turn influence behavior. (page 95)

- *Multiplier effect.* If a gene promotes an advan-tage in some aspect of behavior, the individual may practice that behavior in ways that multiply the initial slight advantage. (page 95)
- *Environmental modification of genetic effects.* A change in the environment can alter or cancel what would otherwise be a major genetic effect. The phenylketonuria gene would lead to mental retardation, but a special diet minimizes its ef-fects. (page 96)
- *Evolution.* Genes that increase the probability of survival and reproduction become more com-mon in the next generation. (page 96)
- *Evolution of behavior.* Many examples of animal behavior can be explained as evolutionary ad-aptations to a particular environment or way of life. (page 96)
- *Evolution of human behavior.* Certain aspects of human behavior, such as the infant grasp reflex, make no sense except as an evolutionary carry-over from ancestors for whom the behavior was useful. However, it is important to distinguish between convincing evolutionary explanations and speculative explanations that await further research. (page 96)

Key Terms

chromosome (page 90)
dizygotic twins (page 93)
dominant (page 91)
epigenetics (page 92)
evolution (page 96)
gene (page 90)
heritability (page 93)
monozygotic twins (page 93)

multiplier effect (page 95)
phenylketonuria (PKU) (page 96)
recessive (page 91)
sex-limited gene (page 91)
sex-linked gene (page 91)
X chromosome (page 91)
Y chromosome (page 91)

exploration and study

Access an interactive eBook and chapter-specific learning tools, including
- **flashcards**
- **quizzes**
- **videos**

and more, in your Psychology CourseMate. Go to **CengageBrain.com.**

If your professor has assigned Aplia:
1. Sign in to your account.
2. Complete the corresponding exercises as required by your professor.
3. When finished, click "Grade It Now" to see which areas you have mastered, which areas need more work, and detailed explanations of every answer.

Meaning and the Temporal Lobes: Is God in the Amygdala?

Alan J. Fridlund, Ph.D.

June 2007, Revised November, 2009

How do we decide the meaning of the everyday things we encounter in our lives? What makes a family heirloom so valuable to us? Why do we like to wear our partner's shirt or keep a lock of her hair? And why do certain sights, smells, and tastes sometimes propel us back in time and make us remember things from our childhoods?

A good deal of brain research suggests that an important part of what links our experiences with their meanings lies in a walnut-sized structure in our brain, the amygdala (actually, the *amygdalae*, since there's one on the left side and one on the right). The amygdala lies deep within the brain, and has connections to the neocortex of the frontal and temporal lobes and many parts of the "old cortex" known as the limbic system. This positions it as a gateway among the sites that are heavily involved in decision-making, memory and motivation. In other chapters, this textbook discusses the amydala's role in fear and anxiety, depression and other disorders.

The first clues that there was something special about the amygdala came from monkey research in the 1930's by Heinrich Klüver and Paul Bucy. They destroyed the amygdalar areas in their monkeys (under anesthesia, to be sure), and after surgery the monkeys acted very peculiarly. They could see well, but didn't react to things appropriately. They would play with snakes as though they were toys (monkeys usually *freak* at snakes), put blocks of wood in their mouth as they were food, and seemed to rub themselves sexually on nearly everything. It seemed as though the monkeys had lost their appreciation for what objects were *for*.

The so-called *Klüver-Bucy Syndrome* is sometimes seen in humans, too, although in humans it is usually caused by head trauma or brain diseases like herpes encephalitis. Much like the monkeys, humans with amygdalar destruction tend to show an inability to recognize objects, a desire to put everything in their mouths, and indiscriminate sexual behavior. And also like the monkeys, humans with Klüver-Bucy Syndrome show an odd emotional indifference to events, remaining especially calm when provoked or threatened – as if they just don't *get* it.

If animals and people appear to lose the meanings of emotional events with destruction of the amygdala, what would happen if the amygdala instead became *hyperactive*? Would people begin to attach too much meaning to events, and maybe even manufacture meaning to what appears trivial and meaningless? It appears that they do, and the evidence comes from people suffering from a certain kind of epilepsy that particularly affects the amygdala. This disorder is known as *temporal lobe epilepsy* (TLE).

In all kinds of epilepsy, damaged neurons in the brain (whether from injury, illness with high fevers, or an inborn defect in brain structure) lose their natural firing rhythm. They begin firing haphazardly and recruit other nearby neurons to join them. Regardless of where the *focus* (the starting point) of the seizure activity lies, the out-of-control firing soon ricochets throughout larger and larger areas of the brain, sometimes even traveling across the corpus callosum and starting seizure activity in the other hemisphere. In the more familiar *psychomotor epilepsy*, the seizures are generalized. They spread throughout the brain and often produce stiffening of the limb muscles followed by convulsive jerking movements.

In TLE, however, the seizures are subtler, and so they're called "partial" seizures. If the seizures are confined to just the amygdala (or an adjacent structure known as the hippocampus), they usually just produce short-lived "spells," known technically as *simple partial seizures*. Simple partial seizures usually last less than a minute, and don't impair consciousness; they just produce weird sensory experiences that may include odd tastes (e.g., something metallic in the mouth), pungent smells (e.g., burning rubber), or "out-of-body" and other bodily sensations. Simple partial seizures can also include cognitive glitches such as *déjà vu* (French for "already seen"), as when we go to a new place yet we feel a strong, odd sense of familiarity about it. Less frequently, we may experience the opposite, *jamais vu* (for "never seen"), when we go to a familiar place but it seems eerily alien and strange (see Brown, 2004). Patients with TLE may have prolonged periods of intense *déjà vu* or *jamais vu* that outlast the seizures.

If the seizures spread more widely within the temporal lobe, they then become known as *complex partial seizures*, which do impair consciousness. People with complex partial seizures may "blank out" for a minute or two, and be completely unresponsive throughout, and when the seizure ends they will likely appear dazed and disoriented. During the seizure itself they may be frozen like a statue, or they may make odd repetitive movements like clucking their tongues, blinking forcefully, or buttoning and unbuttoning their shirt.

What appears to happen in TLE is that the amygdala gets "recruited" with each successive seizure. But unlike most other parts of the brain, which drop back to normal after a seizure, the amygdala shows a phenomenon called "kindling" – when it's stimulated during a seizure, it stays slightly more active than it was before the seizure. With each successive seizure, the amygdala ratchets up its baseline activity level higher and higher. It now stays overactive even between seizures, when the person is supposedly functioning normally.

So in people with TLE, who have a chronically overactive amygdala, the mechanism that attaches meaning to objects and events (let's call it the "Meaning Machinery," or MM) goes into overdrive. This can change the ways they see the world and act in it. About 30-40 years ago, in fact, researchers began to notice that many people with TLE began to show personality changes that are now understandable with our current knowledge (Bear & Fedio, 1977; Benson, 1991; Waxman & Geschwind, 1975).

One change that was noted early was a tendency toward defensive aggression: people with TLE sometimes feel extra-threatened by everyday events, and may be assaultive or damage property all out of proportion to the provocation. This stereotype of the "out-of-control" violent TLE patient was the basis for the popular Michael Crichton sci-fi novel *Terminal Man* (Crichton, 1972), made into a movie two years later. Such episodic violence among TLE patients is rare, though (van Elst, Woermann, Lemieux, Thompson & Trimble, 2000). Much more common in TLE are global personality changes. These include:

Obsession with detail and meaningfulness of trivia. People with TLE are often struck by the "meaningfulness" of the tiniest things. Everything is significant; nothing is accidental. There were *three* people in the checkout line at the grocery this morning, and this evening there were *three* phone calls. A best friend was wearing a *red* sweater the day before another driver ran a *red* light.

Talkativeness and hypergraphia (excessive writing). So much is fraught with meaning that the TLE patient is often bursting with the desire to tell about it, or record it for posterity. One TLE patient kept lengthy, coded diaries consisting of his every daily activity, including exactly what and how much he ate at each meal, and what time he made each trip to the bathroom (as well as what he produced on each trip).

Another TLE patient apologized for being late for an appointment, and began a 15-minute story about how the bus was late, that it was the #43 bus which usually shows up at 10:15 but showed up instead at 10:22, that it was a different bus than the usual #43, that it had blue seats instead of gray, that the seat fabric was ribbed rather than checkered, and so on. Every detail was related with the utmost seriousness.

Interpersonal viscosity. Viscosity means "stickiness." Ever know a person who made it hard to end a conversation? You put on your coat to get ready to go, tell them how nice it was to get together, and they start a new story? People with TLE are sometimes sticky like this. It's not because they don't get the cues, it's because they have so much to tell that they can't let go of you. There's always "Just one more thing …"

Hypermorality and diminished sense of humor. With everything being so meaningful, so important, nothing can – or should – be taken lightly. It's *wrong* to separate the salt and pepper shakers by more than a few inches; it's *wrong* to brush your teeth before you brush your hair; it's *wrong* to keep your checkbook in the left drawer, but then put it in the right drawer willy-nilly. And if you try to joke the person out of his solemn attitude, he may look at you stony-faced and wonder why you don't get how *important* it is to do things right.

Hyperreligiosity w/ expanded sense of personal destiny. As they enter the beginning or "aura" phase of their seizures, TLE patients sometimes experience "rising," "soaring" or spiritual feelings, and even see things like brilliant white lights. Perpetually besieged with meanings, patients with TLE may begin to feel special, as if they were clued into things on a deeper level than others. Through their auras, they were privileged to feel God's immediate presence! Perhaps, they may tell themselves, they received a divine gift, to understand the connectedness in the world, to see the Hand of God. There were *three* people in the grocery checkout line and *three* cell phone calls later that afternoon – two revelations of the Holy Trinity! Indeed, perhaps they have been placed on Earth for a special purpose, to be special witness to God's Earthly work. Neuroscientists expert in TLE have, in fact, argued that many of the world's most celebrated religious visionaries may have had TLE: Moses, Paul on the road to Damascus, Muhammad (the founder of Islam), Joan of Arc, Ellen White (founder of the Seventh-Day Adventist Church).

Fetishism and sexual disinterest Imbued with a special knowledge of the world and the belief that they have a *mission*, the dissipation of one's energies in sexual pleasures seems less and less meaningful and justifiable. Occasionally, the person's sexual interests aren't suppressed but diverted onto objects or body parts (these are known as *fetishes*). One famous TLE patient lost interest in his wife and began to be aroused by paper clips. Another TLE patient in his 20's managed to combine hyperreligiosity, hypermorality, and fetishism in a nightly ritual. Brought up Catholic, he had a crucifix above his headboard. He did not use it as an object of prayer, though. He masturbated nightly while watching it, believing that Jesus would send him to Hell if he did not.

Not all people with TLE show dramatic personality changes, but when they do, these are the kinds they show, and they tend to reflect the hyper-attachment of objects and experiences to *emotions*. According to some observers, the deepened emotional life that comes with TLE may have fueled the creativity of many celebrated writers, with the candidates including Dostoyevsky (who featured an epileptic character in *The Idiot*), Flaubert, Lewis Carroll, Eugene O'Neill, and Carl Jung (LaPlante, 1993).

If malfunctioning MM can produce hyperreligiosity, then does our normal MM produce *normal* religiosity? Many neuroscientists have suggested precisely that. The neurologist Vilayanur Ramachandran, among others, contends that the MM circuits, in which the amygdala is central, are responsible for the feelings of transcendence, spirituality, and contact with God that so many people experience in prayer and meditation. This linking of brain function to spirituality has been termed *neurotheology*, a term first used in the 1960's by *Brave New World* author Aldous Huxley.

Of course, such a "God spot" in the brain does not imply anything about the existence of God or the value of religion. For the neurological reductionist, religion is the natural result of a biological process, the effort of our MM to make sense of an often illogical world (see, for example, Dennett, 2006). For the more spiritually inclined, our MM is the gateway – perhaps a God-given one, at that – by which we can see, and feel, and know, the presence of God.

References

Bear, D. M., & Fedio, P. (1977). Quantitative analysis of interictal behavior in temporal lobe epilepsy. *Archives of Neurology, 34,* 454-467

Benson, D. F. (1991). The Geschwind Syndrome. *Advances in Neurology*, 55, 411-421.

Brown, A. S. The *déjà vu* experience. New York: Psychology Press.

Crichton, M. (1972). *Terminal Man*. New York: Knopf.

Dennett, D. (2006) *Breaking the Spell: Religion as a Natural Phenomenon*. New York: Viking Adult.

Klüver, H. & Bucy, P. (1939) Preliminary analysis of functioning of the temporal lobes in monkeys. Archives of Neurology and Psychiatry, 42, 979-1000.

LaPlante, E. (1993). *Seized: Temporal Lobe Epilepsy as a Medical, Historical, and Artistic Phenomenon.* New York: HarperCollins.

Ramachandran, V. S., & Blakeslee, S. (1998). *Phantoms in the brain: Probing the mysteries of the human mind*. New York: William Morrow.

Van Elst, L. T., Woermann, F. G., Lemieux, L., Thompson, P.J., & Trimble, M. R. (2000). Affective aggression in patients with temporal lobe epilepsy. *Brain, 123*, 234-243.

Waxman, S. G., & Geschwind, N. (1975). The interictal behavior syndrome in temporal lobe epilepsy. *Archives of General Psychiatry, 32*, 1580-1586

n and Donna Rogers

Sensation and Perception

When my son Sam was 8 years old, he asked me, "If we went to some other planet, would we see different colors?" He meant colors that were as different from familiar colors as yellow is from red or blue. I told him that would be impossible, and I tried to explain why. No matter where we go in outer space, we could never experience a color, sound, or other sensation that would be fundamentally different from what we experience on Earth. Different combinations, perhaps, but not fundamentally different sensory experiences.

Three years later, Sam told me he wondered whether people who look at the same thing are all having the same experience: When different people look at something and call it "green," how can we know whether they are having the same experience? I agreed that there is no way to be sure.

Why am I certain that colors on a different planet would look the same as on Earth but uncertain whether colors look the same to different people here? If the answer isn't clear to you now, perhaps it will be after you read this chapter.

Sensation is the *conversion of energy from the environment into a pattern of response by the nervous system*. It is the registration of information. **Perception** is *the interpretation of that information*. For example, light rays striking your eyes produce sensation. Your experience of recognizing your roommate is a perception. In practice, the distinction between sensation and perception is often difficult to make.

No matter how exotic some other planet might be, it could not have colors we do not have here. The reason is that our eyes can see only certain wavelengths of light, and color is the experience our brains create from those wavelengths.

Vision

- How do our eyes convert light into something we can experience?
- How do we perceive colors?

In the late 1980s, someone at the University of Michigan asked every academic department to offer one question that they thought every student should be able to answer before graduation. That is, it was so important that if you can't answer it, you shouldn't get your diploma.

One of the most impressive questions came from the chemistry department: Suppose in the middle of a well-insulated, airtight room, you plug in a refrigerator with its door wide open. Will the result be to cool the room, heat the room, or have no effect on room temperature? (Think about it and answer before you read further.)

To answer, you have to know that a refrigerator doesn't create coldness; it moves heat from its inside to the outside. Then compare the heat added on the outside to the heat removed from the inside. For the two to break even, the refrigerator would have to operate at 100% efficiency, and to cool the room, it would have to operate at more than 100% efficiency. One of the most important physical principles is that every machine wastes some energy. Therefore, the refrigerator will heat the room. Another way to think about it: The refrigerator uses electricity. Using electricity always generates some heat.

That question requires an application of the principles of entropy, or the second law of thermodynamics, an important concept even if you don't know the term itself. By contrast to chemistry's clever question, the psychology department asked, "What is the current definition of psychology?" How embarrassing. After all the research we have done, we have nothing better to offer the world than a definition of ourselves?

Here is a better question. It doesn't represent all of psychology, and it may seem simple-minded, but it's a question that certainly every educated person should be able to answer: What enables you to see something? Do you see because light enters your eyes, or do you send out sight rays?

The correct answer is that light enters your eyes. When you see a tree, your perception of the tree is in your head, not in the tree. If you *did* send sight rays that struck an object, you wouldn't know about it, unless those rays bounced back into your eyes. However, a survey found that 33% of college students believed they sent out sight rays (Winer & Cottrell, 1996; Winer, Cottrell, Gregg, Fournier, & Bica, 2002).

The discovery of how vision works was the first scientific discovery in psychology (Steffens, 2007). About a thousand years ago, the Islamic scholar Ibn al-Haytham reasoned that people see the stars as soon as they open their eyes, and it is implausible that sight rays would travel that fast to something so distant. Further, he demonstrated that when light strikes an object, a viewer sees only the light rays that reflect directly to the viewer's eyes.

In addition to the idea of sight rays, people have other misconceptions about vision. We are often led astray because we imagine that what we see is a copy of the outside world. It is not. Just as a computer translates a sight or sound into a series of 1's and 0's, your brain *translates* stimuli into very different representations.

concept check

1. You may have heard people say that cats can see in total darkness. Is that possible?
2. How far can an ant see?

Answers

1. Like people, cats adapt to dim light. However, cats, like all other animals, see only when light strikes the eyes. In total darkness, vision is impossible.
2. Ants, like any other animal, see as far as the light travels! (Presumably they can see the sun at a distance of 93 million miles or 150 million kilometers.) How *far* any person or animal can see has nothing to do with the eyes, if the eyes work at all.

Detecting Light

Sensation is the detection of stimuli—*energies from the world around us that affect us in some way.* Our eyes, ears, and other sensory organs are packed with receptors—*specialized cells that convert environmental energies into signals for the nervous system.*

What we call *light* is part of the electromagnetic spectrum, *the continuum of all frequencies of radiated energy* from gamma rays and x-rays with very short wavelengths, through ultraviolet, visible light, and infrared, to radio and TV transmissions with very long wavelengths (Figure 4.1). Light is visible only because our receptors respond to wavelengths from 400 to 700 nanometers (nm). With different receptors, we would see a different range of wavelengths. Many insects and birds, in fact, see ultraviolet wavelengths that we do not.

The Structures of the Eye

When we see something, light reflected from the object passes through the pupil, an *adjustable opening* that widens and narrows to control the amount of light entering the eye. The iris, the *colored structure on the surface of the eye surrounding the pupil,* is what we describe when we say someone has brown, green, or blue eyes.

Light passing through the pupil travels through the *vitreous humor* (a clear jellylike substance) to strike the retina, a *layer of visual receptors covering the back surface of the eyeball*. The cornea and the lens focus the light on the retina, as shown in Figure 4.2. The cornea, *a rigid transparent structure on the surface of the eyeball*, always focuses light in the same way. The lens, *a flexible structure that varies its thickness*, enables the eye to accommodate—that is, *to adjust its focus for objects at different distances*. When you focus on a distant object, your eye muscles relax and let the lens become thinner and flatter, as shown in Figure 4.3a. When you focus on a close object, your eye muscles tighten and make the lens thicker and rounder (Figure 4.3b).

The fovea (FOE-vee-uh), *the central area of the human retina*, is adapted for detailed vision (see Figure 4.2). Of all retinal areas, the fovea has the greatest density of receptors. Also, more of the cerebral cortex is devoted to analyzing input from the fovea than input from other areas.

Hawks, owls, and other predatory birds have a greater density of receptors on the top of the retina (for looking down) than on the bottom of the retina (for looking up). When they fly, this arrangement lets them see the ground beneath them in detail. When on the ground, however, they have trouble seeing above themselves (Figure 4.4).

Some common disorders of vision are described in Table 4.1.

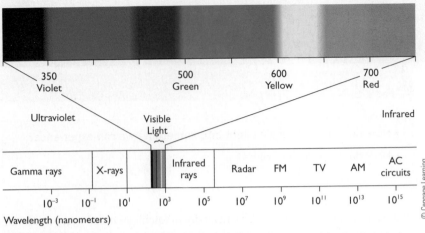

Wavelength (nanometers)

Figure 4.1 Visible light is a small part of the electromagnetic spectrum. We see these wavelengths because our receptors respond to them.

3. As people grow older, the lens becomes more rigid. How would that rigidity affect vision?

Answer

3. Because the lens is more rigid, older people are less able to change their focus for objects at different distances. In particular, they find it difficult to focus on nearby objects.

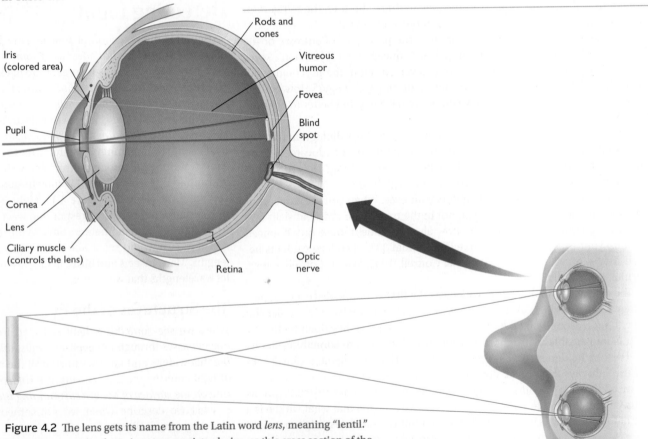

Figure 4.2 The lens gets its name from the Latin word *lens*, meaning "lentil." This reference to its shape is an appropriate choice, as this cross section of the eye shows. The names of other parts of the eye also refer to their appearance.

a

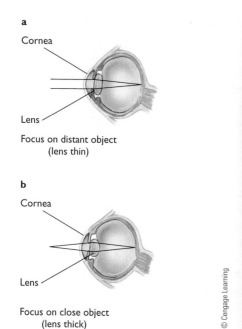

Cornea

Lens

Focus on distant object
(lens thin)

b

Cornea

Lens

Focus on close object
(lens thick)

© Cengage Learning

Figure 4.3 The flexible, transparent lens changes shape so that objects **(a)** far and **(b)** near can come into focus. The lens bends entering light rays so that they fall on the retina.

© Chase Swift Photography

Figure 4.4 Birds of prey, such as these owlets, can see down much more clearly than up. In flight that arrangement is helpful. On the ground, they have to turn their heads almost upside down to look up.

Table 4.1 Common Disorders of Vision

Disorder	Description
Presbyopia	Impaired ability to focus on nearby objects because of decreased flexibility of the lens.
Myopia	Nearsightedness—impaired ability to focus on distant objects.
Hyperopia	Farsightedness—impaired ability to focus on close objects.
Glaucoma	Damage to the optic nerve, usually caused by increased pressure in the eyeball.
Cataract	A disorder in which the lens becomes cloudy.

© Cengage Learning

The Visual Receptors

The retina's two types of visual receptors, cones and rods, differ in function and appearance, as Figure 4.5 shows. The cones are *adapted for color vision, daytime vision, and detailed vision.* The rods are *adapted for vision in dim light.*

Of the visual receptors in the human retina, about 5% are cones. Although 5% may not sound like much, the cone-rich parts of the retina send more axons to the brain than do the rod-rich areas, and cone responses dominate the human visual cortex. Most birds also have many cones and good color vision. Species that are active at night—rats and mice, for example—have mostly rods.

The proportion of cones rises toward the center of the retina. The fovea consists solely of cones (see Figure 4.2). Toward the periphery, the proportion of rods increases sharply, and color vision becomes weaker.

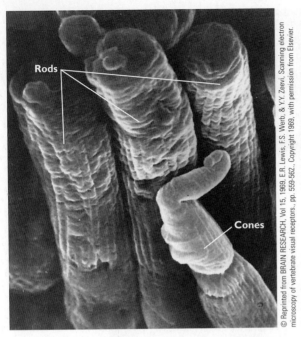

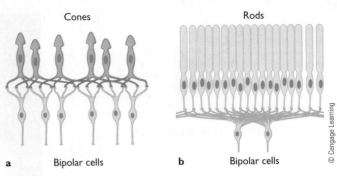

Figure 4.6 Because so many rods converge their input into the next layer of the visual system, known as bipolar cells, even a little light falling on the rods stimulates a bipolar cell. Thus, the periphery of the retina, with many rods, readily detects faint light. However, because bipolars in the periphery get input from so many receptors, they have only imprecise information about the location and shape of objects.

Figure 4.5 Rods and cones seen through a scanning electron micrograph. The rods, numbering more than 120 million in humans, enable vision in dim light. The 6 million cones in the retina distinguish gradations of color in bright light. (Reprinted from *Brain Research,* Vol. 15, 1969, E. R. Lewis, F. S. Werb, & Y. Y. Zeevi. Scanning electron microscopy of vertebrate visual receptors, pp. 559–562. Copyright 1969, with permission from Elsevier.)

concept check

4. Why is it easier to see a faint star in the sky if you look slightly to the side of the star instead of straight at it?

Answer

4. The center of the retina has only cones. If you look slightly to the side, light falls on a retinal area with more rods, which respond to faint light.

try it ▶ yourself

Try this experiment: Hold several pens or pencils of different colors behind your back. (Any objects will work if they are similar in size, shape, and brightness.) Pick one without looking at it. Hold it behind your head and bring it slowly into your field of vision. When you begin to see it, you will probably not see its color. You can also try an Online Try It Yourself activity. Go to your Psychology CourseMate at CengageBrain. com. Navigate to the Online Try It Yourself section, and click Color Blindness in Visual Periphery.

online
try it ▶ yourself

Rods are more effective than cones for detecting dim light for two reasons: First, a rod responds to faint stimulation more than a cone does. Second, the rods pool their resources. Only one or a few cones converge messages onto the next cell, called a *bipolar cell,* whereas many rods converge their messages. In the far periphery of the retina, more than 100 rods send messages to a bipolar cell (Figure 4.6). Table 4.2 summarizes differences between rods and cones.

Table 4.2 Differences Between Rods and Cones

	Rods	Cones
Shape	Nearly cylindrical	Tapered at one end
Prevalence in human retina	90–95%	5–10%
Abundant in	All vertebrate species	Species active during the day
Area of the retina	Toward the periphery	Toward the fovea
Important for color vision?	No	Yes
Important for detail?	No	Yes
Important in dim light?	Yes	No
Number of types	Just one	Three

© Cengage Learning

Dark Adaptation

Suppose you go into a basement at night looking for a flashlight. The only lightbulb is burned out. Just a little moonlight comes through the basement windows. At first, you hardly see anything, but as time passes, your vision gradually improves. *Gradual improvement in the ability to see in dim light* is called dark adaptation.

Here is the mechanism: Exposure to light chemically alters molecules called *retinaldehydes*, thereby stimulating the visual receptors. (Retinaldehydes are derived from vitamin A.) Under moderate light the receptors *regenerate* (rebuild) the molecules no faster than the light keeps breaking them down. In dim light, receptors regenerate their molecules without competition, improving detection of faint light.

Cones and rods adapt at different rates. When you enter a dark place, your cones regenerate their retinaldehydes first, but by the time the rods finish, they are more sensitive to faint light than the cones are. At that point, you see mostly with rods.

Here is how a psychologist demonstrates dark adaptation (E. B. Goldstein, 2007): You enter a room that is completely dark except for a tiny flashing light. You use a knob to adjust the light so that you barely see it. Over 3 or 4 minutes, you gradually decrease the intensity of the light, as shown in Figure 4.7a. Note that a decrease in the intensity of the light indicates increased sensitivity of your eyes. If you stare straight at the point of light, your results demonstrate the adaptation of your cones to the dim light. (You are focusing the light on your fovea, which has no rods.)

Now the psychologist repeats the study with a change in procedure: You stare at a faint light while another light flashes to the side, where it stimulates rods as well as cones. You adjust a knob until the flashing light in the periphery is barely visible (Figure 4.7b.) During the first 7 to 10 minutes, the results are the same as before. But then your rods become more sensitive than your cones, and you begin to see even fainter lights. Your rods continue to adapt over the next 20 minutes or so.

try it ▶ yourself

To demonstrate dark adaptation without any apparatus, try this: At night, turn on one light in your room. Close one eye and cover it tightly with your hand for a minute or more. Your covered eye will adapt to the dark while your opened eye remains adapted to the light. Then turn off the light and open both eyes. You will see better with your dark-adapted eye than with the light-adapted eye. (This instruction assumes you still have some faint light coming through a window. In a *completely* dark room, of course, you see nothing.)

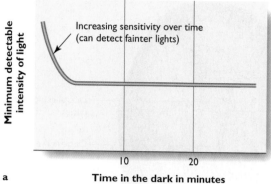

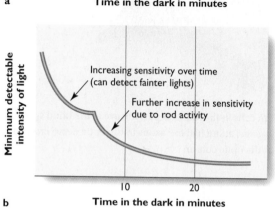

Figure 4.7 These graphs show dark adaptation to **(a)** a light you stare at directly, using only cones, and **(b)** a light in your peripheral vision, which you see with both cones and rods. (Based on E. B. Goldstein, 1989.)

concept check

5. After you have thoroughly adapted to extremely dim light, will you see more objects in your fovea or in the periphery of your eye?

Answer

5. You will see more objects in the periphery of your eye. The fovea contains only cones, which do not become as sensitive as the rods in the periphery.

The Visual Pathway

If you or I were designing an eye, we would probably run connections from the receptors directly back to the brain. Although that route might make logical sense to us, it's not how your eyes actually work. The visual receptors send their impulses *away from* the brain, toward the center of the eye, where they contact neurons called bipolar cells. *The bipolar cells contact still other neurons*, the ganglion cells. The *axons from the ganglion cells join to form* the optic nerve, *which turns around and exits the eye*, as Figures 4.2 and 4.8 show. Half of each optic nerve

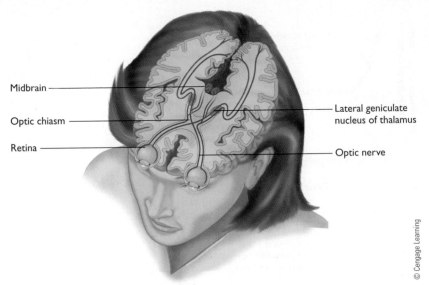

Midbrain

Optic chiasm

Retina

Lateral geniculate
nucleus of thalamus

Optic nerve

© Cengage Learning

Figure 4.8 Axons from ganglion cells in the retina depart the eye at the blind spot and form the optic nerve. In humans, about half the axons in the optic nerve cross to the opposite side of the brain at the optic chiasm.

crosses to the opposite side of the brain at the optic chiasm (KI-az-m). Most of the optic nerve goes to the thalamus, which sends information to the primary visual cortex in the occipital lobe. Some people have up to three times as many axons in their optic nerve as others have. Those with thicker optic nerves are better at detecting faint lights and tiny movements (Andrews, Halpern, & Purves, 1997; Halpern, Andrews, & Purves, 1999).

The *retinal area where the optic nerve exits* is called the blind spot. That part of the retina has no room for receptors because the exiting axons take up all the space. Also, blood vessels enter the eye at this point. Ordinarily, you are unaware of your blind spot.

try it ▶ yourself

To illustrate, close your left eye and stare at the center of Figure 4.9; then slowly move the page forward and backward. When your eye is about 25 to 30 cm (10 to 12 inches) away from the page, the lion disappears because it falls into your blind spot. In its place you perceive a continuation of the circle. Also, go to your Psychology CourseMate at CengageBrain.com. Navigate to the Online Try It Yourself section, and click Filling in the Blind Spot.

online
try it ▶ yourself

Color Vision

How does the visual system convert different wavelengths into a perception of color? The process begins with three kinds of cones. Later, cells in the visual path code this wavelength information in terms of pairs of opposites—red versus green, yellow versus blue, and white versus black. Finally, cells in the cerebral cortex compare the input from various parts of the visual field to synthesize a color experience. Let's examine these stages in turn.

The Trichromatic Theory

Thomas Young was an English physician of the 1700s who, among other accomplishments, helped to decode the Rosetta stone (making it possible to understand Egyptian hieroglyphics), introduced the modern concept of energy, revived and popularized the wave theory of light, showed how to calculate annuities for insurance, and offered the first theory about how people perceive color (Martindale, 2001). His theory, elaborated and modified by Hermann von Helmholtz in the 1800s, came to be known as the Young-Helmholtz theory, or the trichromatic theory. (*Trichromatic* means "three colors.") Phrased in modern terms, it says that *color vision depends on the response rates of three types of cones* (Figure 4.10). One type is most sensitive to short wavelengths (which we generally see as blue), another to medium wavelengths (green), and another to long wavelengths (red). Every wavelength of light produces its own distinct ratio of responses by the three kinds of cones. White light excites all three kinds equally. From the ratio among the three types of cones, the brain determines color.

Young and Helmholtz proposed their theory long before anatomists confirmed the existence of three types of cones (Wald, 1968). Helmholtz found that observers could mix various amounts of three wavelengths of light to match all other colors. (Mixing lights is different from mixing paints. Mixing yellow and blue *paints* produces green; mixing yellow and blue *lights* produces white.)

try it ▶ yourself

The short-wavelength cones, which respond most strongly to blue, are the least numerous. For the retina to detect blueness, the blue must extend over a moderately large area. Figure 4.11 illustrates this effect.

concept check

6. According to the trichromatic theory, how does our nervous system tell the difference between bright yellow-green and dim yellow-green light?

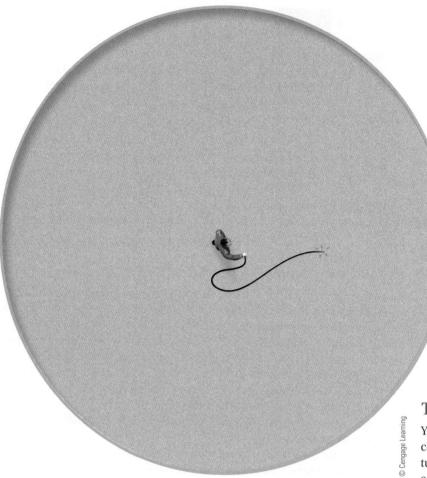

Figure 4.9 Close your left eye and focus your right eye on the animal trainer. Move the page toward your eyes and away from them until the lion on the right disappears. At that point, the lion is focused on the blind spot of your retina, where you have no receptors.

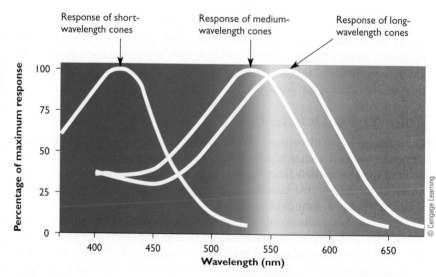

Figure 4.1O Sensitivity of three types of cones to different wavelengths of light. (Based on data of Bowmaker & Dartnall, 1980.)

Figure 4.11 Blue dots look black unless they cover a sizable area. Count the red dots; then count the blue dots. Try again while standing farther from the page. You will probably count as many red dots as before but fewer blue dots.

Answer

6. Although bright yellow and dim yellow-green light evoke the same ratio of activity by the three cone types, the brighter light evokes more total activity.

The Opponent-Process Theory

Young and Helmholtz were right about how many cones we have, but our perception of color has features that the trichromatic theory does not handle easily. For example, if you stare for a minute or so at something red and look away, you see a green afterimage. If you stare at something green, yellow, or blue, you see a red, blue, or yellow afterimage. To account for these afterimages, a nineteenth-century scientist, Ewald Hering, proposed the opponent-process theory of color vision: *We perceive color in terms of paired opposites—red versus green, yellow versus blue, and white versus black.* To illustrate, please follow the instructions in Figure 4.12.

try it ▶ yourself

When you looked away, you saw the cartoon in its normal coloration. After staring at an image, you replace blue with yellow, yellow with blue, red with green, green with red, white with black, and black with white. *Experiences of one color after the removal of another* are called negative afterimages.

Presumably, the explanation depends on cells somewhere in the nervous system that increase their activity in the presence of, say, blue, and decrease it in the presence of yellow. Then after you have stared at something blue, these cells become fatigued and decrease their response. Your brain then interprets the decrease as the color yellow. We could imagine such cells in the retina itself, but here

© AP Photo/U.S. Postal Service

© USPS 1998

Figure 4.12 Stare at one of Daffy's pupils for a minute or more under a bright light without moving your eyes. Then look at a plain white background. You will see a negative afterimage.

is an observation that argues against that interpretation: Stare at the center of Figure 4.13 for a minute or more, and then look at a white surface. The afterimage you see is red on the outside, as expected. But you see *green*, not gray or black, for the inside circle. Your perception of the inside depends on the surrounding context. That result strongly implies that the negative afterimage, and indeed color perception in general, depends on the cerebral cortex, not just interactions within the retina.

 yourself

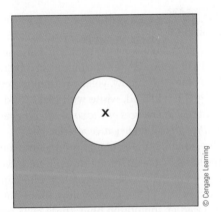

© Cengage Learning

Figure 4.13 Stare at the center for a minute or more and then look at a white surface. What color do you see in the center?

The Retinex Theory

Suppose you look at a large white screen illuminated with green light in an otherwise dark room. How would you know whether this is a white screen illuminated with green light or a green screen illuminated with white light? Or a blue screen illuminated with yellow light? You wouldn't know. Now someone wearing a brown shirt and blue jeans stands in front of the screen. Suddenly, you see the shirt as brown, the jeans as blue, and the screen as white, even though all the objects are reflecting mostly green light. You perceive color by comparing the light one object reflects to the light that other objects reflect. This *tendency of an object to appear nearly the same color under a variety of lighting conditions* is called color constancy (Figure 4.14).

In response to such observations, Edwin Land (the inventor of the Polaroid Land camera) proposed the retinex theory. According to this theory, *the cerebral cortex compares the patterns of light coming from different parts of the retina and synthesizes a color perception for each area* (Land, Hubel, Livingstone, Perry, & Burns, 1983; Land & McCann, 1971). (*Retinex* is a combination of the words *retina* and *cortex*.)

As Figure 4.14 emphasizes, we should not call short-wavelength light "blue" or long-wavelength light "red." A gray square can look blue in one context and yellow in another (Lotto & Purves, 2002; Purves & Lotto, 2003). Color is something our brain constructs, not a property of the light itself.

Vision researchers consider the trichromatic, opponent-process, and retinex theories correct with regard to different aspects of vision. The trichromatic theory states that human color vision starts with three kinds of cones. The opponent-process theory explains how later cells organize color information. The retinex theory notes that the cerebral cortex compares color information from various parts of the visual field.

Color Vision Deficiency

Centuries ago, people assumed that anyone who was not blind could see and recognize colors (Fletcher & Voke, 1985). Then during the 1600s, the phenomenon of color vision deficiency (or colorblindness) was unambiguously recognized. Here was the first clue that color vision is a function of our eyes and brains and not just of the light itself.

The older term color*blindness* is misleading because hardly anyone is totally unable to distinguish colors. About 8% of men and less than 1% of women have difficulty distinguishing red from green (Bowmaker, 1998). The cause is a recessive gene on the X chromosome. Because men have only one X chromosome, they need just one gene to become red-green color deficient. Women, with two X chromosomes, need two such genes to develop the condition. Red-

a

b

c

Figure 4.14 **(a)** When the block is under yellow light (left) or blue light (right), you still recognize the colors of individual squares. Parts **b** and **c** show what happens if we remove the context: The "blue" squares in the left half of part **a** and the "yellow" squares in the right half are actually grayish. (*Why We See What We Do*, by D. Purves and R. B. Lotto, (fig 6.10, p. 134). Copyright © 2003 Sinauer Associates, Inc. Reprinted by permission.)

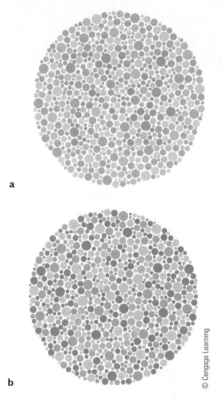

a

b

© Cengage Learning

Figure 4.15 These items provide an informal test for red-green color vision deficiency. What do you see? Compare your answers to answer A on page 112.

green color-deficient people have only the short-wavelength cone and either the long-wavelength or the medium-wavelength cone (Fletcher & Voke, 1985).

Figure 4.15 gives a crude but usually satisfactory test for red-green color vision deficiency. What do you see in each part of the figure?

try it ▶ yourself

How does the world look to people with color vision deficiency? They describe the world with the usual color words: Roses are red, bananas are yellow, and grass is green. But their answers do not mean that they perceive colors the same as other people do. Certain rare individuals are red-green color deficient in one eye but have normal vision in the other eye. Because they know what the color

words really mean (from experience with their normal eye), they can describe what their deficient eye sees. They say that objects that look red or green to the normal eye look yellow or yellow-gray to the other eye (Marriott, 1976).

try it ▶ yourself

If you have normal color vision, Figure 4.16 will show you what it is like to be color deficient. First, cover part b, a typical item from a color deficiency test, and stare at part a, a red field, under a bright light for about a minute. (The brighter the light and the longer you stare, the greater the effect will be.) Then look at part b. Staring at the red field fatigued your long-wavelength cones, weakening your red sensation.

Now stare at part c, a green field, for about a minute and look at part b again. Because you have fatigued your green cones, the figure in b will stand out even more strongly than usual. In fact certain people with red-green color deficiency may be able to see the number in b only after staring at c.

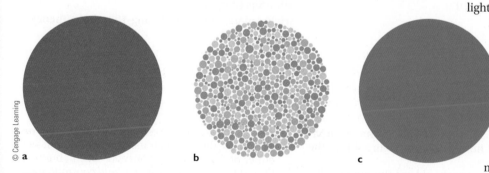

© Cengage Learning

a　　　　**b**　　　　**c**

Figure 4.16 First, stare at pattern **(a)** under bright light for about a minute and then look at **(b)**. What do you see? Next stare at **(c)** for a minute and look at **(b)** again. Now what do you see? See answer B on page 112.

Vision as an Active Process

Before the existence of people or other color-sighted animals on Earth, was there any color? *No.* Light was present, to be sure, and different objects reflected different wavelengths of light, but color exists only in brains.

Your brain does an enormous amount of processing to determine what you are seeing. Imagine build-ing a robot with vision. Light strikes the robot's visual sensors, and then . . . what? How will the robot know what objects it sees or what to do about them? All those processes—which are so difficult to mimic in a robot—happen in your brain in a fraction of a second.

Summary

- *How vision works.* Vision occurs when light rays strike the retina at the back of the eye, causing cells to send messages to the brain. We do not send sight rays out of the eyes. (page 103)
- *Light.* Light is the part of the electromagnetic spectrum that excites receptors in the eyes. If we had different types of receptors, we would de-fine other wavelengths as light. (page 103)
- *Focus.* The cornea and lens focus light onto the retina. (page 104)
- *Cones and rods.* Cones, found mainly in and near the fovea, are essential for color vision. Rods, more numerous toward the periphery, detect dim light. (page 105)

- *Blind spot.* The blind spot is the area of the retina through which the optic nerve exits. (page 108)
- *Color vision.* Color vision depends on three types of cones, each sensitive to a particular range of light wavelengths. Cones transmit mes-sages so that later cells in the visual system indi-cate one color (e.g., blue) by an increase in ac-tivity, and another color (e.g., yellow) by a decrease. The cerebral cortex compares re-sponses from different parts of the retina to de-termine color experiences. (page 108)
- *Color vision deficiency.* Complete colorblindness is rare. Certain people have difficulty distin-guishing reds from greens for genetic reasons. (page 110)

Key Terms

accommodation of the lens (page 104)
blind spot (page 108)
color constancy (page 110)
cone (page 105)
cornea (page 104)
dark adaptation (page 107)
electromagnetic spectrum (page 103)
fovea (page 104)
ganglion cells (page 107)
iris (page 103)
lens (page 104)
negative afterimage (page 109)
opponent-process theory (page 109)

optic nerve (page 107)
perception (page 102)
pupil (page 103)
receptor (page 103)
retina (page 104)
retinex theory (page 110)
rod (page 105)
sensation (page 102)
stimulus (page 103)
trichromatic theory (or Young-Helmholtz theory) (page 108)

Answers to Other Questions in the Module

A. In Figure 4.15a, a person with normal color vi-sion sees the numeral 74; in Figure 4.15b, the numeral 8.

B. In Figure 4.16b, you should see the numeral 29. After you have stared at the red circle in part a, the 29 in part b may look less distinct than usual, as though you were red-green color deficient. After staring at the green circle, the 29 may be even *more* distinct than usual. If you do not see either of these effects at once, try again, but this time stare at part a or c longer *and* continue star-ing at part b a little longer. The effect does not appear immediately.

- How do hearing, the vestibular sense, skin senses, pain, taste, and smell work?

Consider these common expressions:

- I *see* what you mean.
- I *feel* your pain.
- I am deeply *touched* by everyone's support and concern.
- She is a person of fine *taste*.
- He was *dizzy* with success.
- The policies of this company *stink*.
- That *sounds* like a good job offer.

The metaphorical use of sensation terms is no accident. Our thinking and brain activity deal mostly or entirely with sensory stimuli. Perhaps you doubt that assertion: "What about abstract concepts?" you might object. "Sometimes, I think about numbers, time, love, justice, and all sorts of other nonsensory concepts." Yes, but how did you learn those concepts? Didn't you learn numbers by counting objects you could see or touch? Didn't you learn about time by observing changes in sensations? Didn't you learn about love and justice from events that you saw, heard, and felt? Could you explain any abstract concept without referring to something you detected with your senses? In this module we consider sensations from sounds, head tilt, skin stimulation, and chemicals.

Hearing

What we familiarly call the "ear" is a fleshy structure technically known as the *pinna*. It funnels sounds to the inner ear, where the receptors lie. The mammalian ear converts sound waves into mechanical displacements along a row of receptor cells. Sound waves are *vibrations of the air, water, or other medium.* They vary in frequency and amplitude (Figure 4.17). The frequency of a sound wave is the number of *cycles (vibrations) per second,* designated hertz (Hz). Pitch is a *perception closely related to frequency.* We perceive a high-frequency sound wave as high pitched and a low-frequency sound as low pitched.

Loudness is a *perception that depends on the amplitude of sound waves*—that is, their intensity. Other things being equal, the greater the amplitude of a sound, the louder it sounds. Because loudness is a psychological experience, however, other factors influence it also. For example, someone who speaks rapidly seems louder than someone speaking slowly at the same amplitude.

The ear converts relatively weak sound waves into more intense waves of pressure in the *fluid-filled canals of the snail-shaped organ* called the cochlea (KOCK-lee-uh), *which contains the receptors for hearing* (Figure 4.18). When sound waves strike the eardrum, they cause it to vibrate. The eardrum connects to three tiny bones—the hammer, anvil, and stirrup (also known by their Latin names malleus, incus, and stapes). As the weak vibrations of the large eardrum travel through these bones, they transform into stronger vibrations of the much smaller stirrup. The stirrup in turn transmits the vibrations to the fluid-filled cochlea, where the vibrations displace hair cells along the basilar (BASS-uh-ler) membrane in the cochlea. These hair cells, which act like touch receptors on the skin, connect to neurons whose axons form the auditory nerve. The auditory nerve transmits impulses to the brain areas responsible for hearing.

Understanding the mechanisms of hearing helps us explain hearing loss. One kind of hearing loss is conduction deafness, which *results when the bones connected to the eardrum fail to transmit sound waves properly to the cochlea.* Surgery can correct conduction deafness by removing whatever is obstructing the bones' movement. People with conduction deafness still hear their own voice because it is conducted through the skull bones to the cochlea, bypassing the eardrum altogether. The other type of hearing loss is nerve deafness, *resulting from damage to the cochlea, hair cells, or auditory nerve.* Disease, heredity, and exposure to loud noises are common causes of nerve deafness.

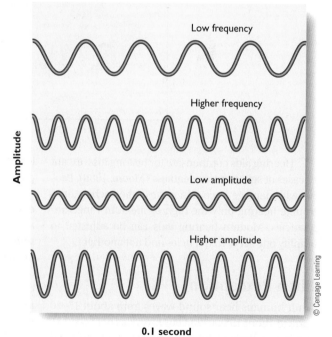

Figure 4.17 The time between the peaks of a sound wave determines the frequency of a sound. We experience frequencies as different pitches. The vertical range, or amplitude, of a wave determines the sound's intensity.

Figure 4.18 Sound waves vibrate the eardrum **(a)**. Three tiny bones convert the eardrum's vibrations into vibrations in the fluid-filled cochlea **(b)**. These vibrations displace hair cells along the basilar membrane in the cochlea, aptly named after the Greek word for *snail*. Here, the dimensions of the cochlea have been changed to make the principles clear.

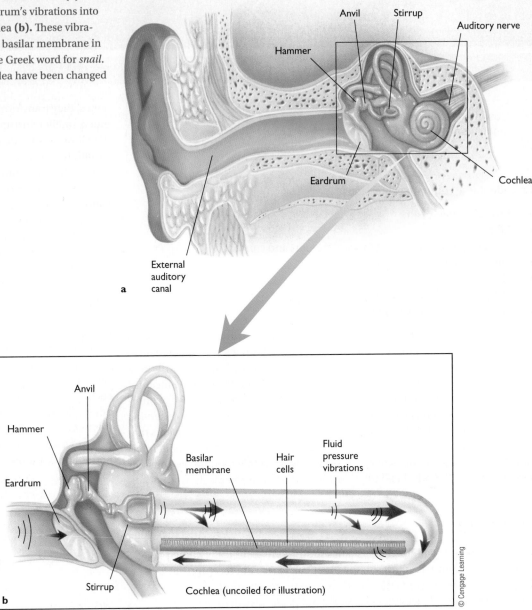

Pitch Perception

Adult humans hear sound waves from about 15–20 hertz to about 15,000–20,000 Hz (cycles per second). The upper limit of hearing declines with age and also after exposure to loud noises. Thus, children hear higher frequencies than adults do. Low frequencies are perceived as low pitch, and high frequencies are perceived as high pitch, but frequency

Hearing aids compensate for hearing loss, except in cases of severe nerve deafness (Moore, 1989). People with damage to certain parts of the cochlea have trouble hearing only the high or medium-range frequencies. Modern hearing aids can be adjusted to amplify one set of frequencies and not another.

is not the same as pitch. For example, doubling the frequency doesn't make the pitch seem twice as high; it makes it one octave higher.

We hear pitch by different mechanisms at different frequencies. At low frequencies (up to about 100 Hz), *a sound wave through the fluid of the cochlea vibrates all the hair cells, which produce action potentials in synchrony with the sound waves.* This is the frequency principle. For example, a sound at a frequency of 50 Hz makes each hair cell send the brain 50 impulses per second.

Beyond about 100 Hz, hair cells cannot keep pace. Still, each sound wave excites at least a few hair cells, and *"volleys" of them (groups) respond to each vibration with an action potential* (Rose, Brugge, Anderson, & Hind, 1967). This is known as the volley principle. Thus, a tone at 1,000 Hz might produce 1,000 impulses per second, even though no neuron fires that rapidly. Volleys keep pace with sounds up to about 4,000 Hz, good enough for almost all speech and music. (The highest note on a piano is 4,224 Hz.)

At still higher frequencies, we rely on a different mechanism. At each point along the cochlea, the hair cells are tuned resonators that vibrate only for sound

Hearing is the sensing of vibrations. Sean Forbes, profoundly deaf since childhood, experienced music by reading lips and holding his leg against a speaker to feel the vibrations. He has become a famous musician. The rapper Eminem helped produce his EP, titled *I'm Deaf.*

concept check

9. Suppose a mouse emits a soft high-frequency squeak in a room full of people. Which kinds of people are least likely to hear the squeak?
10. When hair cells at one point along the basilar membrane become active, we hear a tone at 5,000 Hz. What do we hear when the same hair cells double their rate of activity?

Answers

9. Obviously, the people farthest from the mouse are least likely to hear it. In addition, older people would be less likely to hear the squeak because of declining ability to hear high frequencies. Another group unlikely to hear the squeak are those who had damaged their hearing by repeated exposure to loud noises, including loud music.
10. We still hear a tone at 5,000 Hz, but it is louder than before. For high-frequency tones, the pitch we hear depends on which hair cells are most active, not how many impulses per second they fire.

waves of a particular frequency. *The highest frequency sounds vibrate hair cells near the stirrup end, and lower frequency sounds (down to about 100–200 Hz) vibrate hair cells at points farther along the membrane* (Warren, 1999). This is the place principle. Tones less than 100 Hz excite all hair cells equally, and we hear them by the frequency principle. We identify tones from 100 to 4,000 Hz by a combination of the volley principle and the place principle. Beyond 4,000 Hz, we identify tones only by the place principle. Figure 4.19 summarizes the three principles of pitch perception.

You have probably heard of people who can listen to a note and identify its pitch by name: "Oh, that's a C-sharp." People either name pitches well or not at all. Hardly anyone is intermediate. The main influence on this ability is early music training. Not everyone with musical training develops absolute pitch, but almost everyone with absolute pitch had musical training (Athos et al., 2007). The ability is more widespread among people who speak tonal languages, such as Vietnamese and Mandarin Chinese, in which children learn from the start to pay close attention to the pitch of a word (Deutsch, Henthorn, Marvin, & Xu, 2006). For example, in

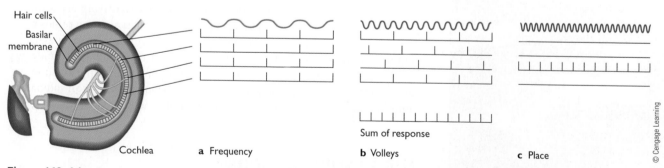

Figure 4.19 **(a)** At low frequencies, hair cells along the basilar membrane produce impulses in synchrony with the sound waves. **(b)** At medium frequencies, different cells produce impulses in synchrony with different sound waves, but a volley (group) produces one or more impulses for each wave. **(c)** At high frequencies, only one point along the basilar membrane vibrates.

Mandarin Chinese, dá (with a rising tone) means dozen, and dà (with a falling tone) means big. You can test yourself for absolute pitch at this website: http://perfectpitch.ucsf.edu.

If you are amazed by people with absolute pitch, your own ability to recognize (though not name) a specific pitch might surprise you. In one study, 48 college students with no special talent or training listened to 5-second segments from television theme songs, played in their normal key or a slightly higher or lower key. The students usually chose the correct version, but only of programs they had watched (Schellenberg & Trehub, 2003). That is, they remembered the familiar pitches.

People who are said to be "tone-deaf" are not *completely* tone-deaf, because if they were, they could not understand speech. However, they are impaired at detecting changes in sound frequency smaller than 10%, whereas most people detect changes smaller than 1% (Hyde & Peretz, 2004; Loui, Alsop, & Schlaug, 2009). Tone-deaf people don't detect when someone is singing off-key, and they don't detect a wrong note in a melody. Many of them have relatives with the same condition, so it probably has a genetic basis (Peretz, Cummings, & Dube, 2007). You can test yourself for tone-deafness at this website: www.brams. umontreal.ca/amusia-demo.

Figure 4.20 The ear located closest to the sound receives the sound waves first. That cue is important for localizing low-frequency sounds.

Localizing Sounds

When you hear, the activity is in your ear, but you experience the sound as "out there," and you can generally estimate its place of origin. What cues do you use?

The auditory system determines the direction of a sound source by comparing the messages from the two ears. When a sound comes from the front, the messages reach the two ears simultaneously at equal intensity. When it comes from the left, it reaches the left ear first and is more intense there (Figure 4.20). The timing is important for localizing low-frequency sounds. Intensity helps us localize high-frequency sounds.

You also detect the approximate distance of sound sources. If a sound grows louder, you interpret it as coming closer. If two sounds differ in pitch, you assume the higher frequency tone is closer. (Low-frequency tones carry better over distance, so if you hear a high-frequency tone, its source is probably close.) However, loudness and frequency tell you only the *relative* distances, not *absolute* distances. The only cue for absolute distance is the amount of reverberation (Mershon & King, 1975). In a closed room, you first hear the sound waves coming directly from the source and then the waves that reflected off the walls, floor, ceiling, or other objects. If you hear many echoes, you judge the source of the sound to be far away. It is hard to localize sound sources in a noisy room where echoes are hard to hear (McMurtry & Mershon, 1985).

concept check

11. Why is it difficult to tell whether a sound is coming from directly in front of or directly behind you?
12. If someone who needs hearing aids in both ears wears one in only the left ear, what will be the effect on sound localization?
13. Suppose you are listening to a monaural (nonstereo) radio. Can the station play sounds that you will localize as coming from different directions, such as left and right? Can it play sounds that you will localize as coming from different distances? Why or why not?

Answers

11. We localize sounds by comparing the input into the two ears. If a sound comes from straight ahead or from directly behind (or from straight above or below), the input into the left and right ears is identical.
12. Sounds will be louder in the left ear than in the right, and therefore, they may seem to be coming from the left side even when they aren't. (However, a sound from the right will still strike the right ear before the left, so time of arrival at the two ears will compete against the relative loudness.)
13. Various sounds from the radio cannot seem to come from different directions because your localization of a sound depends on comparing the responses of the two ears. However, the radio can play sounds that seem to come from different distances because distance localization depends on the amount of reverberation, loudness, and high-frequency tones, all of which can vary with a single speaker. Consequently, the radio can easily give an impression of people walking toward you or away, but not of people walking from side to side.

The Vestibular Sense

Imagine yourself riding a roller coaster with your eyes closed. The up and down, back and forth sensations you feel come from structures called *vestibules* in the inner ear on each side of your head. The vestibular sense detects *the tilt and ac-*

celeration of the head, and the orientation of the head with respect to gravity. It plays a key role in posture and balance. Intense vestibular sensations are responsible for motion sickness.

The vestibular sense also enables you to keep your eyes fixated on a target as your head moves. When you walk down the street, you can keep your eyes fixated on a street sign, even though your head is bobbing up and down. The vestibular sense detects head movements and compensates with eye movements.

try it ▶ yourself

To illustrate, try to read this page while you jiggle the book up and down or side to side, keeping your head steady. Then hold the book steady and move your head up and down and from side to side. You find it much easier to read when you are moving your head than when you are jiggling the book. The reason is that your vestibular sense keeps your eyes fixated on the print during head movements. After damage to the vestibular sense, people report blurry vision while they are walking. To read street signs, they must come to a stop.

The vestibular sense plays a key role in posture and balance as it reports the position of the head.

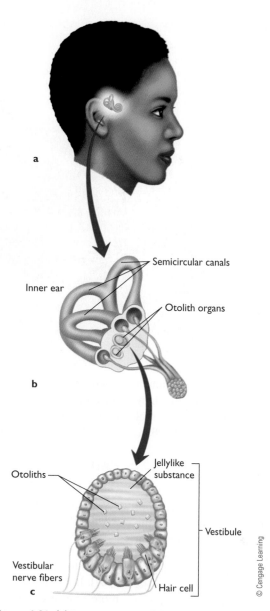

Figure 4.21 **(a)** Location of and **(b)** structures of the vestibule. **(c)** Moving your head or body displaces hair cells that report the tilt of your head and the direction and acceleration of movement.

The vestibular system consists of three semicircular canals oriented in different directions, and two otolith organs (Figure 4.21b). The *semicircular canals* are lined with hair cells and filled with a jellylike substance. When the body accelerates in any direction, the jellylike substance in the corresponding semicircular canal pushes against the hair cells, which send messages to the brain. The *otolith organs* shown in Figure 4.21b also contain hair cells (Figure 4.21c), which lie next to the *otoliths* (calcium carbonate particles). Depending on which way the head tilts, the particles excite different sets of hair cells. The otolith organs report the direction of gravity and therefore which way is up.

Figure 4.22 Cutaneous sensation is the product of many kinds of receptors, each sensitive to a particular kind of information.

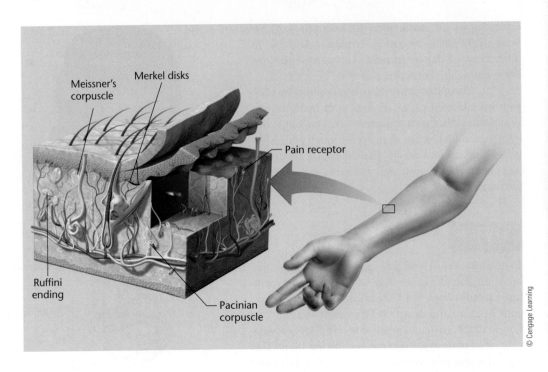

Meissner's corpuscle

Merkel disks

Pain receptor

Ruffini ending

Pacinian corpuscle

© Cengage Learning

For astronauts in the zero-gravity environment of outer space, the vestibular sense cannot identify up or down. Instead, astronauts learn to rely on visual signals, such as the walls of the ship (Lackner, 1993).

The Cutaneous Senses

What we commonly think of as touch consists of several partly independent senses: pressure on the skin, warmth, cold, pain, itch, vibration, movement across the skin, and stretch of the skin. These sensations depend on several kinds of receptors, as Figure 4.22 shows (Iggo & Andres, 1982). A pinprick on the skin feels different from a light touch, and both feel different from a burn because each excites different receptors. Collectively, these sensations are known as the cutaneous senses, meaning the *skin senses.* They are also known as the *somatosensory system,* meaning *body-sensory system.*

Have you ever wondered about the sensation of itch? Is it a kind of touch, pain, or what? Itch depends on a special type of receptor that sends messages through a special path in the spinal cord (Y.-G. Sun et al., 2009). Itch is unlike pain. In fact, pain inhibits itch (Andrew & Craig, 2001). For example, if a dentist anesthetizes your mouth for dental surgery, as the anesthesia wears off, the itch receptors recover before the pain and touch receptors. If you scratch the itchy spot, you don't feel the scratch and it does not relieve the itch.

Tickle is another kind of cutaneous sensation. Have you ever wondered why you can't tickle yourself? Some people can, a little, especially when they are just starting to wake up, but it's not the same as

when someone else tickles them. The reason is that tickle requires surprise. When you are about to touch yourself, certain parts of your brain build up an anticipation response that is similar to the actual stimulation (Carlsson, Petrovic, Skare, Petersson, & Ingvar, 2000). When you try to tickle yourself, the sensation is no surprise.

Pain

Pain is important for its own sake and because of its relation to depression and anxiety. The experience of pain is a mixture of body sensation and emotional reaction. The sensory and emotional qualities depend on different brain areas (Craig, Bushnell, Zhang, & Blomqvist, 1994; Fernandez & Turk, 1992). The brain area responsive to the emotional aspect—the *anterior cingulate cortex*—also responds to the emotional pain of watching someone else get hurt (Singer et al., 2004). Physical pain can be very intense at the moment, but emotional pain is more enduring. Try to remember how you felt during a painful injury. Then try to remember how you felt when someone insulted you in public. Most people relive the emotional pain more intensely (Chen, Williams, Fitness, & Newton, 2008).

People often talk of "hurt feelings." Is that just a saying, or is social distress really like pain? It is like pain in a couple of ways. First, when someone feels rejected by others, activity increases in the anterior cingulate gyrus, just as it does for physical pain (Eisenberger, Lieberman, & Williams, 2003). Second, you can, believe it or not, relieve hurt feelings by taking acetaminophen (Tylenol)! College students kept a daily log of hurt feelings while taking either acetaminophen or a placebo. Those taking acetaminophen reported fewer hurt feelings, and the frequency declined as they continued taking the drug (De Wall et al., 2010). (So, the next time you hurt people's feelings, don't apologize. Just hand them a pill.)

The Gate Theory of Pain

You visit a physician because of severe pain, but as soon as the physician tells you the problem is nothing to worry about, the pain starts to subside. Have you ever had such an experience?

Recall the term *placebo* from chapter 2: A placebo is a drug or other procedure with no important effects beyond those that result from people's expectations. Placebos have little effect on most medical conditions, but they often relieve pain, at least its emotional aspect (Hróbjartsson & Gøtzsche, 2001; Wager et al.,

2004). In one experiment, college students had a smelly brownish liquid rubbed onto one finger. It was in fact a placebo, but they were told it was a painkiller. Then they were painfully pinched on that finger and a finger of the other hand. They consistently reported less pain on the finger with the placebo (Montgomery & Kirsch, 1996). How placebos work is unclear, but these results eliminate mere relaxation as an explanation because relaxation would affect both hands equally.

Because of observations such as these, Ronald Melzack and P. D. Wall (1965) proposed the gate theory of pain, the idea that *pain messages must pass through a gate, presumably in the spinal cord, that can block the messages.* That is, other kinds of input close the gate, preventing pain messages from reaching the brain. If you injure yourself, rubbing the surrounding skin sends inhibitory messages to the spinal cord, closing the pain gates. Pleasant or distracting events also send inhibitory messages. Other stimuli enhance the pain messages. In particular, a barrage of painful stimuli cause pain at the time and increase response to similar stimuli in the future (Walters, 2009). You could say the brain learns how to feel pain and gets better at it (Figure 4.23).

Ways to Decrease Pain

Some people are completely insensitive to pain. Before you start to envy them, consider: They often burn themselves by picking up hot objects, scald their tongues on hot coffee, cut themselves without realizing it, or bite off the tip of the tongue. They don't learn to avoid danger, and many die young (Cox et al., 2006).

Although we shouldn't rid ourselves of pain altogether, we would like to limit it. Distraction is one way. Post-surgery patients in a room with a pleasant view complain less about pain, take less painkilling medicine, and recover faster than do patients in a windowless room (Ulrich, 1984).

Several medications also reduce pain. Endorphins are *neurotransmitters that weaken pain sensations* (Pert & Snyder, 1973; Figure 4.24). The term *endorphin* is a combination of the terms *endogenous* (self-produced) and *morphine.* Morphine, which stimulates endorphin synapses, has long been known for its ability to inhibit dull, lingering pains. Pleasant experiences, such as sexual activity or thrilling music, also release endorphins (A. Goldstein, 1980).

Paradoxically, another method of decreasing pain begins by inducing it. The *chemical* capsaicin *stimulates receptors that respond to painful heat* (Caterina, Rosen, Tominaga, Brake, & Julius, 1999). Capsaicin is what makes jalapeños and similar peppers taste hot. Rubbing capsaicin on the skin produces a temporary burning sensation (Yarsh, Farb, Leeman, & Jessell, 1979). As it subsides, the skin loses some of its pain sensitivity. Several skin creams with capsaicin are used to relieve aching muscles. Capsaicin decreases pain because it releases pain transmitters faster than the neurons can resynthesize them. Also, high doses of capsaicin damage pain receptors.

concept check

14. Naloxone, a drug used as an antidote for an overdose of morphine, is known to block the endorphin synapses. How could we use naloxone to determine whether a pleasant stimulus releases endorphins?
15. Psychologist Linda Bartoshuk recommends candies containing moderate amounts of jalapeño peppers as a treatment for pain in the mouth. Why?

Answers

14. Determine how much the pleasant stimulus decreases pain for several people. Then give half of them naloxone and half of them a placebo. Again measure how much the pleasant stimulus decreases the pain. If the pleasant stimulus decreases pain by releasing endorphins, then naloxone should impair the stimulus's painkilling effects.
15. The capsaicin in the jalapeño peppers will release pain transmitters faster than neurons resynthesize them, thus decreasing the later sensitivity to pain in the mouth. Jalapeños also damage pain receptors.

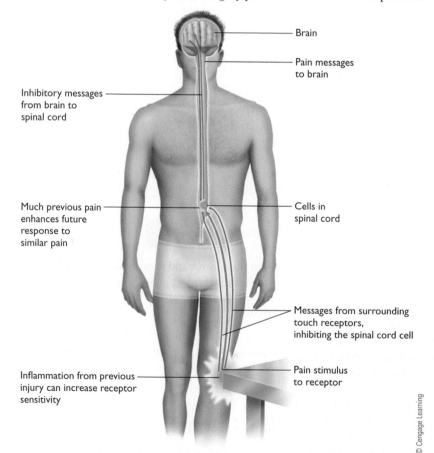

Figure 4.23 Pain messages from the skin are relayed from the spinal cord to the brain. According to the gate theory of pain, spinal cord cells can block or enhance the signal. Green lines indicate axons with excitatory inputs; red lines indicate axons with inhibitory inputs.

Brain

Pain messages to brain

Inhibitory messages from brain to spinal cord

Much previous pain enhances future response to similar pain

Cells in spinal cord

Messages from surrounding touch receptors, inhibiting the spinal cord cell

Pain stimulus to receptor

Inflammation from previous injury can increase receptor sensitivity

© Cengage Learning

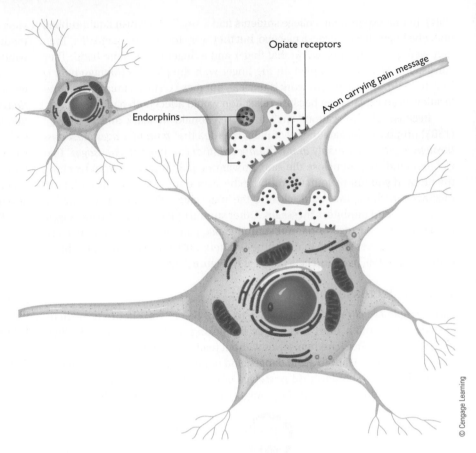

Figure 4.24 Endorphins block the release of a transmitter conveying pain sensations. Opiates imitate the effects of endorphins.

Phantom Limbs

Some people report *continuing sensations, including pain, in a limb long after it has been amputated.* This phenomenon, known as a phantom limb, might last days, weeks, or years after the amputation (Ramachandran & Hirstein, 1998). Physicians and psychologists have long wondered about the cause. Research in the 1990s found the problem within the brain.

Figure 3.18 showed the input from various body areas to the somatosensory cortex. Figure 4.25a repeats part of that illustration. Part b shows what happens immediately after a hand amputation: The hand area of the cortex becomes inactive because the axons from the hand are inactive. (You might think of the neurons in the hand area of the cortex as "widows" that lost their partners.) As time passes, axons from the face, which ordinarily excite only the face area of the cortex, strengthen connections to the nearby hand area of the cortex. From then on, stimulation of the face continues to excite the face area but now also excites the hand area. When the axons from the face area stimulate the hand area, they produce a hand experience—that is, a phantom limb (Flor et al., 1995; Ramachandran & Blakeslee, 1998).

It is possible to relieve phantom sensations: People who learn to use an artificial hand or limb lose their phantoms (Lotze et al., 1999). The relevant areas of the cortex start reacting to the artificial limb, and this sensation displaces the abnormal sensations (Di Pino, Guglielmelli, & Rossini, 2009).

concept check

16. A phantom hand sensation would be strongest after touch to what body part?

Answer

16. The phantom hand sensation would be strongest when something touches the face.

The Chemical Senses

Humans' heavy reliance on vision and hearing is unusual in the animal kingdom. Most animals depend mainly on taste and smell to find food and mates. We humans often overlook the importance of these sensations.

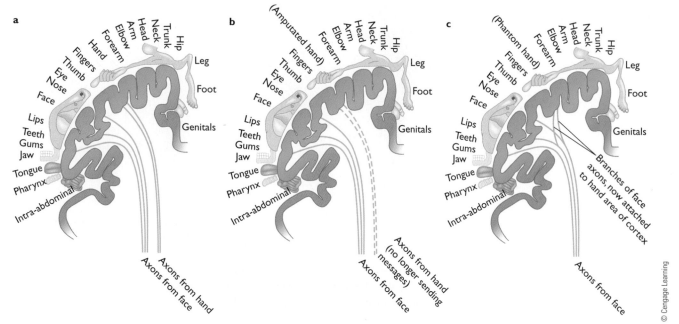

Figure 4.25 **(a)** Each area of the somatosensory cortex gets input from a different body area. **(b)** If one body part, such as the hand, is amputated, its area of the cortex no longer gets its normal input. **(c)** Axons from a neighboring area branch out to excite the vacated area. Now, stimulation of the face excites both the face area and the hand area, producing both a facial sensation and a phantom hand sensation.

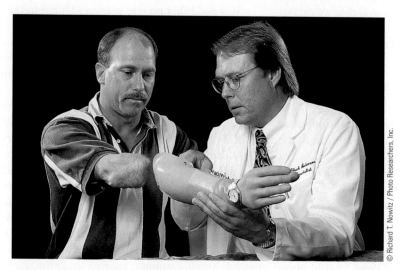

After someone with an amputation gains experience using an artificial limb, phantom limb sensations fade or disappear.

Taste

The sense of taste, which *detects chemicals on the tongue*, serves just one function: It governs eating and drinking. The *taste receptors are in the* taste buds, *located in the folds on the surface of the tongue*, almost exclusively along the outside edge of the tongue in adults (Figure 4.26). (Children's taste buds are more widely distributed.)

try it ▶ yourself

Try this demonstration (based on Bartoshuk, 1991): Soak something small (a cotton swab will do) in sugar water, salt water, or vinegar. Touch it to the center of your tongue, not too far back. You will feel it but taste nothing. Slowly move the soaked substance toward the side or front of your tongue. Suddenly, you taste it. If you go in the other direction (first touching the side of the tongue and then moving toward the center), you will continue to taste the substance even at the center of your tongue. The explanation is that your taste buds do not tell you *where* you taste something. When you stimulate touch receptors on your tongue, your brain interprets the taste perception as coming from wherever it feels touch.

Types of Taste Receptors

Traditionally, Western cultures have talked about four primary tastes: sweet, sour, salty, and bitter. However, the taste of monosodium glutamate (MSG), common in Asian cuisines, cannot be described in these terms (Kurihara & Kashiwayanagi, 1998; Schiffman & Erickson, 1971), and researchers found a taste receptor specific to MSG (Chaudhari, Landin, & Roper, 2000). English had no word for the taste of MSG (similar to the taste of unsalted chicken soup), so researchers adopted the Japanese word *umami*.

Bitter taste is puzzling because such diverse chemicals taste bitter. The only thing they have in common is being poisonous or at least harmful in large amounts. How could such diverse chemicals all excite the same receptor? The answer is, they don't. We have 25 or more kinds of bitter receptors, each sensitive to different chemicals (Adler et al., 2000; Behrens, Foerster, Staehler, Raguse, & Meyerhof, 2007; Matsunami, Montmayeur, & Buck, 2000).

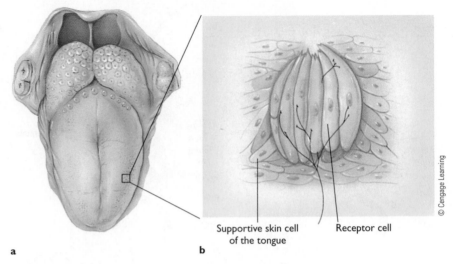

Supportive skin cell
of the tongue

Receptor cell

© Cengage Learning

a   b

Figure 4.26 **(a)** Taste buds, which react to chemicals dissolved in saliva, are located along the edge of the tongue in adult humans. **(b)** A cross section through part of the surface of the tongue showing taste buds.

Any chemical that excites any of these receptors produces the same bitter sensation. One consequence is that a wide variety of harmful chemicals taste bitter. Another consequence is that we do not detect low concentrations of bitter chemicals, because we do not have many of any one type of bitter receptor.

Smell

The *sense of smell* is known as olfaction. The olfactory receptors, located on the mucous membrane in the rear air passages of the nose (Figure 4.27), detect airborne molecules. The axons of the olfactory receptors form the olfactory tract, which extends to the olfactory bulbs at the base of the brain.

The human sense of smell is not as good as that of dogs or many other species, but it is better than we might guess. We watch a dog track someone through the woods and think, "Wow, I could never do that." Well, of course not, if you stand up with your nose far above the ground. Experimenters asked young adults to get down on all fours, touch their nose to the ground, and try to follow a scent trail, blindfolded. Most succeeded, as shown in Figure 4.28 (J. Porter et al., 2007).

How many kinds of olfactory receptors do we have? Until 1991, researchers did not know. In contrast, researchers in the 1800s established that people have three kinds of color receptors. They used behavioral methods, showing that people can mix three colors of light in various amounts to match any other color. Regarding olfaction, however, no one reported comparable studies. Can people match all possible odors by mixing appropriate amounts of three, four, seven, ten, or some other number of odors?

It is good that no one spent a lifetime trying to find out. Linda Buck and Richard Axel (1991), using modern biochemical technology, demonstrated that humans have hundreds of types of olfactory receptors. Rats and mice have about a thousand (Zhang & Firestein, 2002; Figure 4.29).

Many odors produce strong emotional responses. People who lose the sense of smell lose much of their joy in life and in many cases become depressed (Herz, 2007). Our emotional reactions to odors are not built-in, however. Americans experience wintergreen odor only in association with candy. In Britain, wintergreen is often included in rub-on pain medications. Guess what: Most Americans like the odor, and British people do not. One woman reported hating the smell of roses because she first smelled them at her mother's funeral. Another woman reported liking the smell of skunk (from a distance) because it reminded her of a joyful trip through the country when she was a child (Herz, 2007).

Suppose I ask you to smell something labeled "odor of Parmesan cheese." You say you like it. Then I say, "Oops, I'm sorry, that was mislabeled. It's actually the smell of vomit." Oh, no! Now you hate the smell—the same smell! "Wait, my mistake. I was right the first time. It really is Parmesan." Now do you like it or not? Your emotional reaction to an odor depends on what you think it is (Herz & von Clef, 2001).

Olfaction serves important social functions in most nonhuman mammals. In many species, indi-

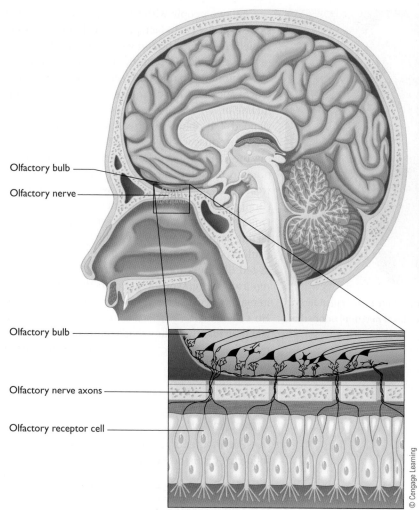

Figure 4.27 The olfactory receptor cells lining the nasal cavity send information to the olfactory bulb in the brain.

Olfactory bulb
Olfactory nerve
Olfactory bulb
Olfactory nerve axons
Olfactory receptor cell

Reprinted by permission from Macmillan Publishers Ltd. From: Nature Neuroscience, 10, 27-29, Mechanisms of scent-tracking in humans; J. Porter et. al, 2007.

Figure 4.28 The yellow line shows a path of chocolate odor. The red line is the path traced by a person trying to follow the odor. (From Porter, J., Craven, B., Khan, R. M., Chang, S.-J., Kang, I., Judkewicz, B., et al. [2007]. Mechanisms of scent-tracking in humans. *Nature Neuroscience, 10,* 27–29.)

viduals use olfaction to recognize one another and to identify when a female is sexually receptive. Most humans *prefer not* to recognize one another by smell. The deodorant and perfume industries exist for the sole purpose of removing and covering up human odors. But olfaction is more important to our social behavior than we generally acknowledge. The smell of a sweaty woman—especially a woman near her time of ovulation—causes a man to increase his testosterone secretion (Miller & Maner, 2010). Something in his brain says, "Ooh. I smell a sweaty woman. I bet she is *hot*!" It's different for women (Wyart et al., 2007). The smell of a sweaty man causes a woman to increase her secretion of stress hormones! Something in her brain says, "I smell a sweaty man. Uh, oh."

Imagine you are exposed to just the smells of several people, and you are to rate each one's desirability as a potential romantic partner. Most people give a low rating to anyone who smells too much like their own relatives (Havlicek & Roberts, 2009).

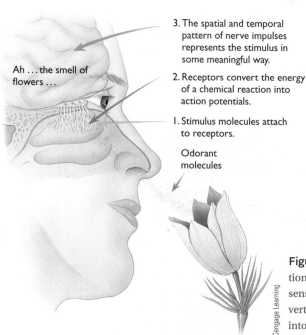

Ah . . . the smell of flowers . . .

3. The spatial and temporal pattern of nerve impulses represents the stimulus in some meaningful way.

2. Receptors convert the energy of a chemical reaction into action potentials.

1. Stimulus molecules attach to receptors.

Odorant molecules

Figure 4.29 Olfaction, like any other sensory system, converts physical energy into a complex pattern of brain activity.

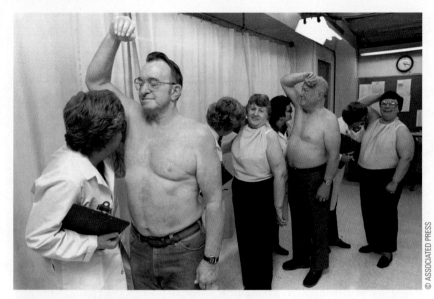

Professional deodorant tester: That's a career option you probably never considered. U.S. industries spend millions of dollars to eliminate the kinds of personal odors that are essential to other mammalian species.

Women show this tendency more strongly if they are capable of becoming pregnant, and less if they are taking contraceptive pills (Roberts, Gosling, Carter, & Petrie, 2008). Avoiding a potential mate who smells like your relatives is a good way to avoid inbreeding, and to provide one's child with a diversity of genes for immunities.

concept check

17. Why are people more sensitive to a weak sugar or salt taste than they are to a weak bitter taste?
18. What accounts for people's emotional responses to smells?

Answers

18. Emotional responses to smells are mostly learned by association with other events.

17. People have many types of bitter receptors, but not a huge number of any one type.

Synesthesia

We end our tour of the senses with synesthesia, a *condition in which a stimulus of one type, such as sound, also elicits another experience, such as color.* Researchers estimate that one person in 500 has synesthesia, but the actual number may be higher because some people try to hide an experience that others do not understand (Day, 2005).

No two people with synesthesia have quite the same experience. In fact, people with this condition sometimes argue about the color of Tuesday or the taste of a melody. A synesthetic perception is quick and automatic. In one study, people listened to sentences such as, "The clear lake was the most beautiful hue of 7." For people with synesthesia who experienced 7 as "blue," this sentence evoked a strong brain response within a tenth of a second after hearing the 7. For those who experienced 7 as yellow, orange, or some other color, the response was weaker, as it is for people without synesthesia (Brang, Edwards, Ramachandran, & Coulson, 2008). One person with a word-taste synesthesia reported tasting a word before he could think of it. He said he couldn't quite remember what the word was, but it tasted like tuna (Simner & Ward, 2006). One man reported seeing synesthetic colors that he never saw in real life because he was red-green color deficient. He called them "Martian colors" (Ramachandran, 2003). Evidently, although his retina could not send messages for those colors, the brain was organized to perceive them.

try it ▶ yourself

For another example, find the 2's and A's in the following displays as quickly as possible.

```
555555555555  555555555555  555555555555  5555555525555
555555555555  555555555525  555555555555  5555555555555
555555555555  555555555555  555255555555  5555555555555
552555555555  555555555555  555555555555  5555555555555
555555555555  555555555555  555555555555  5555555555555

44444444444  44444444444  44444444444  44444444444
44444444444  44A44444444  44444444444  44444444444
44444A444444  44444444444  44444444444  4444444A44444
44444444444  44444444444  44444444444  44444444444
44444444444  44444444444  44444444A44  44444444444
```

One person with synesthesia found it just as hard as anyone else to find the A's among 4's because both looked red to her. However, because 2's look violet and 5's look yellow to her, she was quicker than average to find the 2's, almost as if—but not quite as if—the displays had been printed like this (Laeng, Svartdal, & Oelmann, 2004):

These results are surprising. The colors helped her find the 2's, but somehow her brain had to know the 2's from the 5's *before* it could produce the color experiences. At this point, synesthesia remains a fascinating mystery. In most cases it develops gradually during childhood. Many 6- and 7-year-old children show some degree of synesthesia. By the time they are a few years older, some have lost it, whereas others have developed a stronger, more consistent experience (Simner, Harrold, Creed, Monro, & Foulkes, 2009).

Synesthesia varies greatly from one person to another. Some describe it as a weak, though consistent, internal experience, and others say they strongly perceive the color (or whatever) as really being "out there" in the real world (Rogowska, 2011). Given this diversity, we probably need to look for more than one explanation.

module 4.2 >

In Closing

Sensory Systems

The world as experienced by a bat (which hears frequencies up to 100,000 Hz) or a mouse (which depends on its whiskers to explore the world) is in many ways a different world from the one that you experience. The function of the senses is not to tell you about everything in the world but to alert you to the information you are most likely to use, given the human way of life.

Summary

- *Pitch.* At low frequencies of sound, we identify pitch by the frequency of vibrations of hair cells in our ears. At intermediate frequencies, we identify pitch by volleys of responses from many neurons. At high frequencies, we identify pitch by the location where the hair cells vibrate. (page 114)
- *Localizing sounds.* We localize a sound source by detecting differences in the time and loudness of the sounds in the two ears. We localize the distance of a sound source primarily by the amount of reverberation following the main sound. (page 116)
- *Vestibular system.* The vestibular system tells us about the movement of the head and its position with respect to gravity. It enables us to keep our eyes fixated on an object while the rest of the body is in motion. (page 116)
- *Cutaneous receptors.* We experience many types of sensation on the skin, each dependent on different receptors. Itch is a sensation based on tissue irritation, inhibited by pain. Tickle depends on the unpredictability of the stimulus. (page 118)
- *Pain.* The experience of pain can be greatly inhibited or enhanced by other simultaneous ex-

periences, including touch to surrounding skin. Hurt feelings resemble physical pain, especially in their emotional aspect. (page 118)
- *Phantom limbs.* After an amputation, the corresponding portion of the somatosensory cortex stops receiving its normal input. Axons from neighboring cortical areas form branches that excite the silenced areas of cortex. When these cortical areas receive the new input, they react in the old way, producing a phantom sensation. (page 120)
- *Taste receptors.* People have receptors sensitive to sweet, sour, salty, bitter, and umami (MSG) tastes. We have many kinds of bitter receptors, but not many of any one kind. (page 121)
- *Olfactory receptors.* The olfactory system—the sense of smell—depends on hundreds of types of receptors. We have strong emotional reactions to many odors based on previous experiences. Olfaction influences our social responses more than most people realize. (page 122)
- *Synesthesia.* Some people have consistent experiences of one sensation evoked by another. For example, they might experience particular letters or numbers as having a color. (page 124)

Key Terms

module 4.3 >

Interpreting Sensory Information

- What is the relationship between the world and our perceptions of it?
- Why are we sometimes wrong about what we think we see?

According to a popular expression, "a picture is worth a thousand words." If so, what is a thousandth of a picture worth? One word? Perhaps not even that.

Printed photographs, such as the one below, are composed of a great many dots, which you can see if you magnify the photo, as in Figure 4.30. Although one dot by itself tells us nothing, the pattern of many dots becomes a meaningful picture.

Our vision is like this all the time. Your retina includes more than a hundred million rods and cones, each of which sees one dot of the visual field. What you perceive is not dots but lines, curves, and objects. Your nervous system starts with a vast amount of information and extracts the important patterns.

Perceiving Minimal Stimuli

Some of the earliest psychological researchers tried to determine the weakest sounds, lights, and touches that people could detect. They also measured the smallest difference that people could detect between one stimulus and another—the *just noticeable difference* (JND). Although these questions seemed easy, the answers were more complicated. First, the answer depends on what someone had been doing just before the test. If you had spent the last hour on the beach on a sunny day, you will be poor at detecting faint lights. If you spent the last hour listening to loud music, you will be poor at hearing soft sounds. But even if you spent the last hour in a quiet, dark room, your responses can be hard to interpret.

Sensory Thresholds and Signal Detection

Imagine a typical experiment to determine your threshold of hearing—that is, the minimum intensity that you can hear: On each trial, the experimenter presents either no tone or one of various faint tones, and you report hearing or not hearing something. Figure 4.31 presents typical results. Notice that no sharp line separates sounds that people hear from sounds they do not. Researchers therefore define an absolute sensory threshold as the *intensity at which a given individual detects a stimulus 50% of the time.* However, people sometimes report hearing a tone when none was present. We should not be surprised. Throughout the study, they have been listening to faint tones and saying "yes" when they heard almost nothing. The difference between nothing and almost nothing is slim. Still, if someone reports a tone when none was present, we have to be cautious in interpreting the other responses. How often were they really hearing something, and how often were they just guessing?

Figure 4.30 From a photograph composed of dots, we see objects and patterns.

© ASSOCIATED PRESS

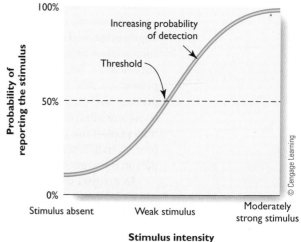

Figure 4.31 Typical results of an experiment to measure an absolute sensory threshold. No sharp boundary separates stimuli that you perceive from those you do not.

© Cengage Learning

Report stimulus present

	Stimulus actually present	Stimulus actually absent
Report stimulus present	**Hit**	**False alarm**
Report stimulus absent	**Miss**	**Correct rejection**

© Cengage Learning

Figure 4.32 People make two kinds of correct judgments (green backgrounds) and two kinds of errors (red backgrounds). If you tend to say the stimulus is present when you are in doubt, you will get many hits but also many false alarms.

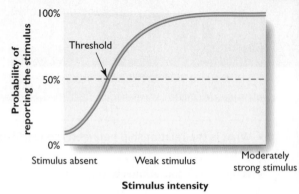

Instructions: You will receive a 10-cent reward for correctly reporting that a light is present. You will be penalized 1 cent for reporting that a light is present when it is not.

a

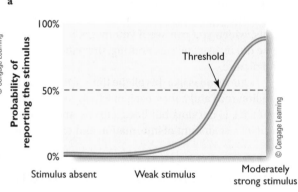

© Cengage Learning

Instructions: You will receive a 1-cent reward for correctly reporting that a light is present. You will be penalized 10 cents *and* subjected to an electric shock for reporting that a light is present when it is not.

b

Figure 4.33 Results of measuring a sensory threshold with different instructions.

When people try to detect weak stimuli, they can be correct in two ways: reporting the presence of a stimulus (a "hit") and reporting its absence (a "correct rejection"). They can also be wrong in two ways: failing to detect a stimulus (a "miss") and reporting it present when it was absent (a "false alarm"). Figure 4.32 outlines these possibilities.

Signal-detection theory is the *study of people's tendencies to make hits, correct rejections, misses, and false alarms* (D. M. Green & Swets, 1966). The theory originated in engineering, where it applies to such matters as detecting radio signals in the presence of noise. Suppose someone reports a stimulus present on 80% of the trials when the stimulus is present. That statistic is meaningless unless we also know how often the person said it was present when it was not. If the person also reported the stimulus present on 80% of trials when it was absent, then the person is just guessing.

In a signal-detection experiment, people's responses depend on their willingness to risk misses or false alarms. (When in doubt, you have to risk one or the other.) Suppose you are the participant and you are told that you will receive a 10-cent reward whenever you correctly report that a light is present, but you will be fined 1 cent if you say "yes" when it is absent. When you are in doubt, you guess "yes," with results like those in Figure 4.33a. Then the rules change: You receive a 1-cent reward for correctly

reporting the presence of a light, but you suffer a 10-cent penalty and an electrical shock if you report a light when it was absent. Now you say "yes" only when certain, with results like those in Figure 4.33b.

People become cautious about false alarms for other reasons, too. In one experiment, participants were asked to read words that flashed briefly on a screen. They performed well with ordinary words such as *river* or *peach*. For emotionally loaded words such as *penis* or *bitch*, however, they generally said they were not sure what they saw. Several explanations are possible (e.g., G. S. Blum & Barbour, 1979). One is that participants hesitate to blurt out an emotionally charged word unless they are certain they are right.

The signal-detection approach is important in many settings remote from the laboratory. For example, the legal system is also a signal-detection situation. A jury can be right in two ways and wrong in two ways:

	Defendant is guilty	Defendant is innocent
Jury votes "guilty"	Hit	False alarm
Jury votes "not guilty"	Miss	Correct rejection

Judges instruct juries to vote "not guilty" when in doubt. A miss, setting a guilty person free, is more acceptable than a false alarm that convicts an innocent person.

Another example is screening baggage at an airport. Screeners can err by "seeing" a weapon that is not present, or missing one that is there. A special problem in this case is that extremely few air travelers actually pack weapons. Researchers find that when items are rare, people often overlook them (Wolfe, Horowitz, & Kenner, 2005). That is, screeners get accustomed to saying, "no weapons found." Forcing people to slow down doesn't help much in cases like this. Giving them an opportunity to correct their errors reduces the errors somewhat, but doesn't eliminate them (Kunar, Rich, & Wolfe, 2010).

concept check

19. Suppose a particular chemical is present in 90% of people with a particular kind of cancer. Can we use that chemical to diagnose the cancer? Think about this problem in terms of signal detection.

Answer

19. We have been told the hit rate, but we cannot evaluate it unless we also know the false alarm rate. That is, how many people without cancer also have this chemical? If that percentage is large, the test is useless.

Subliminal Perception

Subliminal perception is the idea that *stimuli sometimes influence our behavior even when they are presented so faintly or briefly that we do not perceive them consciously.* (*Limen* is Latin for "threshold." Thus, subliminal means "below the threshold.") Is subliminal perception powerful, impossible, or something in between?

What Subliminal Perception Doesn't Do

Many years ago, claims were made that subliminal messages could control people's buying habits. For example, a theater owner might insert a single frame, "EAT POPCORN," in the middle of a film. Viewers, unaware of the message, supposedly would flock to the concession stand to buy popcorn. Many tests of this hypothesis found little or no effect (Cooper & Cooper, 2002), and the advertiser eventually admitted he had no evidence (Pratkanis, 1992).

Another claim is that certain rock-'n'-roll recordings contain "satanic" messages that were recorded backward and superimposed on the songs. Some people allege that listeners unconsciously perceive these messages and then follow the evil advice. Whether or not some rock band may have inserted a backward message is not the question. The issue is, if people hear a backward message, does it influence their behavior? Researchers find that people listening to backward messages cannot determine what they would sound like forward, and the messages have no detectable influence on behavior (Kreiner, Altis, & Voss, 2003; Vokey & Read, 1985).

A third unsupported claim: "Subliminal audiotapes" with faint, inaudible messages can help you improve your memory, quit smoking, lose weight, raise your self-esteem, and so forth. In one study, psychologists asked more than 200 volunteers to listen to a popular brand of audiotape. However, they intentionally mislabeled some of the self-esteem tapes as "memory tapes" and some of the memory tapes as "self-esteem tapes." After a month of listening, most people who *thought* they were listening to self-esteem tapes said they had improved their self-esteem, and those who *thought* they were listening to memory tapes said they had improved their memory. The actual content made no difference. The improvement depended on people's expectations, not the tapes (Greenwald, Spangenberg, Pratkanis, & Eskanazi, 1991).

What Subliminal Perception Can Do

Subliminal messages do produce effects, although most are brief or subtle. For example, people in one study viewed a happy, neutral, or angry face flashed on a screen for less than one thirtieth of a second, followed immediately by a neutral face. Under these conditions, no one reports seeing a happy or angry face, and even if asked to guess, people do no better than chance. However, when they see a happy face, they slightly and briefly move their facial muscles in the direction of a smile. After seeing an angry face, they tense their muscles slightly and briefly in the direction of a frown (Dimberg, Thunberg, & Elmehed, 2000). In another study, people saw a face very briefly with masking patterns to prevent conscious detection. Shortly after it, they saw a different face, which they had to categorize as male or female. On average, they were faster at this task if the first, subliminal face was the same sex as the second one (Finkbeiner & Palermo, 2009).

Subliminal perception effects emerge only as small changes in average performance. However, the fact that such effects occur at all demonstrates the possibility of unconscious influences (Greenwald & Draine, 1997).

concept check

20. Suppose someone claims that broadcasting the subliminal words "Don't shoplift," intermixed with music at a store, decreases shoplifting. What would be the best way to test that claim?

Answer

20. Play that message on half of all days, randomly chosen, for a period of weeks. On other days, play no subliminal message or an irrelevant one. See whether the frequency of shoplifting decreases on days with the message.

Perceiving and Recognizing Patterns

How do you know what you're seeing? Let's start with an apparently simple example: When you look at a light, how does your brain decide how bright it is? We might guess that the more intense the light, the brighter the appearance.

However, perceived brightness depends on comparison to the surrounding objects. **Brightness contrast** *is the increase or decrease in an object's apparent brightness by comparison to objects around it.* Consider Figure 4.34. Compare the pink bars in the middle left section to those in the middle right. The ones on the right probably look darker, but in fact, they are the same. Also go to your Psychology CourseMate at CengageBrain.com. Navigate to the Online Try It Yourself section, and click Brightness Contrast.

If two spots on the page reflect light equally, why don't they look the same? When the brain sees something, it uses its past experience to calculate how that pattern of light probably was generated, taking into account all the contextual information (Purves, Williams, Nundy, & Lotto, 2004). In Figure 4.34, you see what appears to be a partly clear white bar covering the center of the left half of the grid, and the pink bars look light. In the corresponding section to the right, the pink bars appear to be under the red bars and on top of a white background. Here the pink looks darker because you contrast the pink against the white background above and below it.

Figure 4.34 The pink bars in the left center area are in fact the same as the pink bars in the right center area, but those on the left seem lighter.

Figure 4.35 Who is this? We recognize people by hair as well as facial features. If you're not sure who it is, check answer C, page 143.

If perceiving brightness is that complicated, you can imagine how hard it is to explain face recognition. People are amazingly good at recognizing familiar faces, even after not seeing someone in years (Bruck, Cavanagh, & Ceci, 1991). For a demonstration, go to your Psychology CourseMate at CengageBrain.com. Navigate to the Online Try It Yourself section, and click Matching High School Photos. Although we recognize people mostly by facial features, we attend to the hair also. Can you identify the person in Figure 4.35?

The Feature-Detector Approach

How do we recognize patterns? According to one explanation, we begin by breaking a stimulus into its parts. For example, when we look at a letter of the alphabet, *specialized neurons in the visual cortex, called* **feature detectors,** *respond to the presence of simple features, such as lines and angles.* One neuron might detect the feature "horizontal line," while another detects a vertical line, and so forth.

critical check

What's the Evidence?

Feature Detectors

What evidence do we have for feature detectors in the brain? The evidence includes studies of laboratory animals and humans.

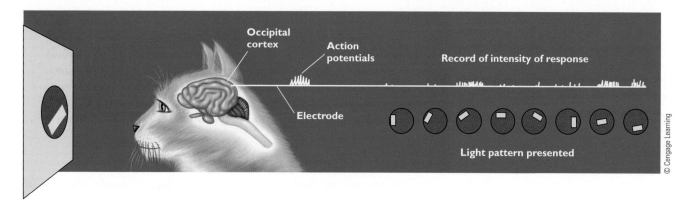

Figure 4.36 Hubel and Wiesel recorded the activity of neurons in the visual cortex. Most neurons responded vigorously only when a portion of the retina saw a bar of light oriented at a particular angle.

First Study

Hypothesis Neurons in the visual cortex of cats and monkeys respond only when light strikes the retina in a particular pattern.

Method Two pioneers in the study of the visual cortex, David Hubel and Torsten Wiesel (1981 Nobel Prize winners in physiology and medicine), inserted thin electrodes into cells of the occipital cortex of cats and monkeys and recorded the cells' activity as various light patterns struck the animals' retinas. At first, they used mere points of light that produced little response. Later they tried lines (Figure 4.36).

Results They found that each cell responds best in the presence of a particular stimulus (Hubel & Wiesel, 1968). Some cells become active only at the sight of a vertical bar of light. Others become active only for a horizontal bar. In other words, the cells appear to be feature detectors. Later investigators found cells that respond to other features, such as movement in a particular direction.

Interpretation Hubel and Wiesel reported feature-detector neurons in cats and monkeys. If the organization of the visual cortex is similar in species as distantly related as cats and monkeys, it is likely (though not certain) to be similar in humans as well.

A second line of evidence follows this reasoning: If the human cortex has feature-detector cells, overstimulation of certain cells should fatigue them. Afterward, someone should see an aftereffect based on the inactivity of those cells. (Recall negative color afterimages, as in Figure 4.12.) An example is the **waterfall illusion**: *If you stare at a waterfall for a minute or more and then turn your eyes to nearby cliffs, the cliffs appear to flow upward.* Staring at the waterfall fatigues neurons that respond to downward motion. When they fatigue they become inactive, while neurons responding to upward motion remain active. The result is an illusion of upward motion. To observe a similar illusion, try the Online Try It Yourself activity. Go to

your Psychology CourseMate at CengageBrain. com. Navigate to the Online Try It Yourself section, and click Motion Aftereffect.

Here is another demonstration:

Second Study

Hypothesis After you stare at vertical lines, you fatigue feature detectors responding to lines of that width. If you then look at wider or narrower lines, they will appear to be even wider or narrower than they really are.

Method Cover the right half of Figure 4.37 and stare at the little rectangle in the middle of the left

Figure 4.37
To fatigue your feature detectors and create an afterimage, follow the directions for the second study. (From Blakemore & Sutton, 1969.)

half for a minute or more. Do not stare at one point, but move your focus around within the rectangle. Then look at the square in the center of the right part of the figure and compare the spacing between the lines of the top and bottom gratings (Blakemore & Sutton, 1969).

Results What did you perceive in the right half? People generally report that the top lines look narrower and the bottom lines look wider.

Interpretation Staring at the left part of the figure fatigues neurons sensitive to wide lines in the top part of the figure and neurons sensitive to narrow lines in the bottom part. Then, when you look at lines of medium width, the fatigued cells are inactive. Cells sensitive to narrower lines dominate your perception in the top part, and those sensitive to wider lines dominate in the bottom part.

To summarize, two types of evidence support the existence of visual feature detectors: (a) The brains of other species contain cells with the properties of feature detectors, and (b) after staring at certain patterns, we see aftereffects that imply fatigue of feature-detector cells in the brain.

The research just described started an enormous amount of activity by laboratories throughout the world. Later results revised our views of what the earlier results mean. For example, even though certain neurons respond well to a single vertical line:

most respond even more strongly to a sine-wave grating of lines:

Thus, the feature that cells detect is probably more complex than just a line. Furthermore, because each cell responds to a range of stimuli, no cell provides an unambiguous message about what you see at any moment.

An important point about scientific advances: A single line of evidence—even Nobel Prize–winning evidence—seldom provides the final answer to a question. We look for multiple ways to test a hypothesis.

> **concept** check

21. What is a feature detector, and what evidence supports the idea of feature detectors?

Answer

21. A feature detector is a neuron that responds mostly to a particular visual feature, such as a straight horizontal line. One kind of evidence is that recordings from neurons in laboratory animals show that each cell responds mainly to a particular kind of stimulus. Another line of evidence is that people who have stared at a stimulus become temporarily less sensitive to that kind of stimulus, implying fatigue of the feature detectors.

Do Feature Detectors Explain Perception?

The neurons just described are active in the early stages of visual processing. Do we simply add up the responses from various feature detectors to perceive a face?

No, feature detectors cannot completely explain how we perceive letters, much less faces. For example, we perceive the words in Figure 4.38a as CAT and HAT, even though the H and A symbols are identical. Likewise, the character in the center of Figure 4.38b can be read as either B or 13. Perceiving a pattern depends on context, not just adding up feature detectors.

Gestalt Psychology

Your ability to perceive something in more than one way, as in Figure 4.38, is the basis of Gestalt psychology, *a field that emphasizes perception of overall patterns. Gestalt* (geh-SHTALT) is a German word meaning pattern or configuration. The founders of Gestalt psychology rejected the idea of breaking down a perception into its component parts. A melody broken into individual notes is no longer a melody. Their slogan was, "The whole is different from the sum of its parts."

Gestalt psychology does not deny the importance of feature detectors. It merely insists that feature detectors are not enough. Feature detectors represent a bottom-up process, *in which tiny elements combine to produce larger items.* However, perception also includes a top-down process, *in which you apply your experience and expectations to interpret each item in context.* Here are some examples.

In either the top or bottom part of Figure 4.39, you might see only meaningless black and white patches for a while and then suddenly you might see an animal. To perceive the animals, you separate figure and ground—that is, you distinguish the *object from the background.* Ordinarily, you make that distinction almost instantly. You become aware of the process only when it is difficult (as it is here).

Figure 4.40 shows five reversible figures *that can be perceived in more than one way.* In effect, we test hypotheses: "Is this the front of the object or is that the front? Is this section the foreground or the background?" The longer you look at a reversible figure, the more frequently you alternate between one perception and another (Long & Toppine, 2004). Part a is called the *Necker cube,* after the psychologist who first called attention to it. Which is the front face of the cube? You can see it either

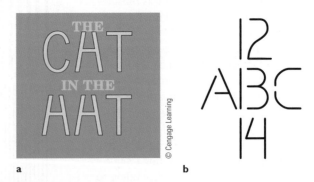

Figure 4.38 Context determines our perception. In (**a**) you see the same item as A or H depending on context. In (**b**) the central character can appear as B or the number 13 depending on whether you read horizontally or vertically. (Part b from Kim, 1989.)

a

b

Figure 4.39 Do you see an animal in each picture? If not, check answer D on page 143. (From "A Puzzle Picture with A New Principle of Concealment," by K.M. Dallenbach, *American Journal of Psychology* vol. 54, (pp. 431–433). Copyright © 1951 by the Board of Trustees of the University of Illinois. Used by permission of the author and the University of Illinois Press.)

way. Part b is either a vase or two profiles. Does part c show an old woman or a young woman? Almost everyone sees one or the other immediately, but many people lock into one perception so tightly that they do not see the other one. The 8-year-old girl who drew part d intended it as a face. Can you find another possibility? If you have trouble with parts c or d, check answers E and F on page 143. The point of the reversible figures is that we perceive by imposing order (top-down), not just by adding up lines and points (bottom-up).

concept check

22. In what way does the phenomenon of reversible figures conflict with the idea that feature detectors fully explain vision?

Answer

22. If vision were simply a matter of stimulating feature detectors and adding up their responses, then a given display would always produce the same perception.

The Gestalt psychologists described principles of how we organize perceptions into meaningful wholes, as illustrated in Figure 4.41. Proximity is the *tendency to perceive objects that are close together as belonging to a group.* The objects in Figure 4.41a form two groups because of their proximity. The *tendency to perceive similar as being a group* is, quite reasonably, called similarity. In Figure 4.41b, we group the X's together and the •'s together because of similarity.

When lines are interrupted, as in Figure 4.41c, we perceive continuation, *a filling in of the gaps.* You probably perceive this illustration as a rectangle covering the center of a very long hot dog.

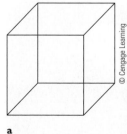

a

b

c

d

Sara Nadaer and Faces or Vace from MIND SIGHTS, © 1990 by Roger N. Shepard. Reprinted by permission of Henry Holt and Company, LLC.

Figure 4.40 Reversible figures: **(a)** The Necker cube. Which is the front face? **(b)** Faces or a vase. **(c)** An old woman or a young woman. **(d)** A face or what? (Part b: Faces or vase from MIND SIGHTS by Roger Shepard. Copyright © 1990 by Roger N. Shepard. Reprinted by arrangement with Henry Holt and Company, LLC; part c: From Boring, "A new ambiguous figure," *American Journal of Psychology* vol. 42 (pp. 444–445). Copyright © 1930 by the Board of Trustees of the University of Illinois. Used by permission of the author and the University of Illinois Press.

a

b

c

d   e

Figure 4.41 Gestalt principles of **(a)** proximity, **(b)** similarity, **(c)** continuation, **(d)** closure, and **(e)** good figure.

When a familiar figure is interrupted, as in Figure 4.41d, we perceive a closure of the figure; that is, *we imagine the rest of the figure* to see something that is simple, symmetrical, or consistent with our past experience (Shimaya, 1997). For example, you probably see the following as an orange rectangle overlapping a blue diamond, although you don't really know what, if anything, is behind the rectangle:

The principle of closure resembles continuation. With a complicated pattern, however, closure deals with more information. For example, in Figure 4.41c, you fill in the gaps to perceive one long hot dog. With additional context, you might perceive the same pattern as two shorter hot dogs:

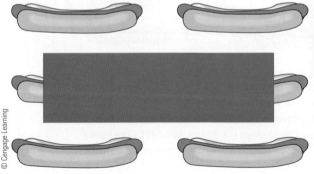

Another Gestalt principle is common fate: *We perceive objects as part of the same group if they change or move in similar ways at the same time.* If you see two objects move in the same direction and speed, you see them as parts of the same thing, as in Figure 4.42. Also, if they grow brighter or darker together, you see them as related (Sekuler & Bennett, 2001).

Finally, when possible, we tend to perceive a good figure—*a simple, familiar, symmetrical figure.* Many familiar objects are geometrically simple or close to it: The sun and moon are round, tree trunks meet the ground at almost a right angle, faces and animals are nearly symmetrical, and so forth. If we

a

b

c

Figure 4.42 From part **a** to part **b**, the head and tail move the same way, and it appears to be one lizard. From part **a** to part **c**, the head moves and the tail doesn't, so it must be two lizards.

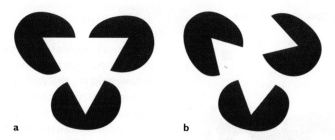

Figure 4.43 In (a) we see a triangle overlapping three irregular ovals. We see it because triangles are "good figures" and symmetrical. If we tilt the ovals, as in (b), the illusory triangle disappears. (From M. Singh, D.D. Hoffman, and M.K. Albert, "Contour Completion and Relative Depth: Petter's Rule and Support Ratio," Psychological Science vol. 10 (pp. 423–428). Copyright © 1999 Sage Publications, Inc. Reproduced with permission.)

can interpret something as a circle, square, or straight line, we do. In Figure 4.41e, the part on the left could represent a red square overlapping a green one or a green backward L overlapping a red object of almost any shape. We are powerfully drawn to the first interpretation because it includes "good," regular, symmetrical objects.

In Figure 4.43a, we perceive a white triangle overlapping three ovals (Singh, Hoffman, & Albert, 1999). However, if we tilt the blue objects, as in Figure 4.43b, the illusion of something on top of them disappears. We "see" the overlapping object only if it is a symmetrical, good figure.

Does the principle of good figure apply only in Westernized societies, where people become familiar with squares, triangles, and so forth from an early age? Apparently not. Researchers studied the Himba, a southwest African culture with no manufactured products and few words for shapes. Even they noticed the difference between squares and almost-square shapes, about as well as U.S. college students did (Biederman, Yue, & Davidoff, 2009).

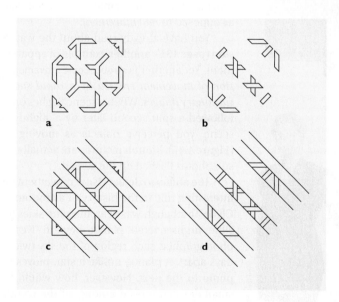

Figure 4.44 (a) and (b) appear to be arrays of flat objects. Introducing a context of overlapping lines causes a cube to emerge in (c) and (d). (From ORGANIZATION IN VISION: ESSAYS ON GESTALT PERCEPTION by Gaetano Kanizsa, p. 7–9. Copyright © 1979 by Gaetano Kaniza. Reproduced with permission of ABC-CLIO, LLC.)

Similarities Between Vision and Hearing

The perceptual organization principles of Gestalt psychology apply to hearing also. Like reversible figures, some sounds can be heard in more than one way. You can hear a clock going "tick, tock, tick, tock" or "tock, tick, tock, tick." You can hear your windshield wipers going "dunga, dunga" or "gadung, gadung."

The Gestalt principles of continuation and closure work best when one item interrupts something else. In Figure 4.44, the context in parts c and d suggests objects partly blocking our view of a three-dimensional cube. In parts a and b, we are much less likely to see a cube, as nothing suggests something occluding the view. Similarly, in Figure 4.45a, we see a series of meaningless patches. In Figure 4.45b, the addition of some black glop helps us see these patches as the word *psychology* (Bregman, 1981).

The same is true in hearing. If a speech or song is broken up by periods of silence, we do not fill in the gaps and we find the utterance hard to understand. However, if the same gaps are filled with noise, we "hear" what probably occurred during the gaps. That is, we apply continuation and closure (C. T. Miller, Dibble, & Hauser, 2001; Warren, 1970).

Perceiving Movement and Depth

As an automobile moves away from us, its image on the retina grows smaller, but we perceive it as moving, not shrinking. That perception illustrates visual constancy—our *tendency to perceive objects as keeping their shape, size, and color, despite distortions in the actual pattern reaching the retina.* Figure 4.46 shows examples of shape constancy and size constancy. Constancies depend on our familiarity with objects and on our ability to estimate distances and angles of view. For example, we know that a door is still rectangular even when we view it from an odd angle. But to recognize that an object keeps its shape and size, we have to perceive movement or changes in distance. How do we do so?

Perception of Movement

Moving objects capture attention for a good reason. Throughout our evolutionary history, moving objects have been more likely than stationary objects to require action. A moving object might be another person. It might be something you could catch and eat, or something that wants to eat you. People are particularly adept at perceiving a body in motion.

a

b

Figure 4.45 Why is the word *psychology* easier to read in (**b**) than in (**a**)? (After Bregman, 1981.)

try it ▶ yourself

Try this simple demonstration: Hold an object in front of your eyes and then move it to the right. Now hold the object in front of your eyes and move your eyes to the left. The image of the object moves across your retina in the same way when you move the object as when you move your eyes. Yet you perceive the object as moving in one case but not in the other. Why?

The object looks stationary when you move your eyes for two reasons. One is that the vestibular system informs the visual areas of the brain about your head and eye movements. When your brain knows that your eyes have moved to the left, it interprets what you see as being a result of the movement. One man with a rare kind of brain damage could not connect his eye movements with his perceptions. Whenever he moved his head or eyes, the world appeared to be moving. Frequently, he became dizzy and nauseated (Haarmeier, Thier, Repnow, & Petersen, 1997).

The other reason is that you perceive motion when an object moves *relative to the background* (Gibson, 1968). When you walk, stationary objects move across your retina but do not move relative to the background.

What do you perceive when an object is stationary and the background moves? In that unusual case, you *incorrectly perceive the object as moving*, a phenomenon called induced movement. When you watch clouds moving across the moon, you might perceive the clouds as stationary and the moon as moving. Induced movement is *apparent movement*, as opposed to *real movement*.

You have already read about the waterfall illusion (page 131), another example of apparent movement. Yet another is stroboscopic movement, an *illusion of movement created by a rapid succession of stationary images*. When a scene flashes on a screen, followed a split second later by a slightly different scene, you perceive objects as moving smoothly (Figure 4.47). Motion pictures are actually a series of still photos flashed on the screen.

The ability to detect visual movement played an interesting role in the history of astronomy. In 1930 Clyde Tombaugh was searching the skies for a possible undiscovered planet beyond Neptune. He photographed each region of the sky twice, several days apart. A planet, unlike a star, moves from one photo to the next. However, how would he find a small dot that moved among all the countless unmoving dots in the sky? He put each pair of photos on a machine that would flip back and forth between one photo and the other. When he came to one pair of photos, he immediately noticed one dot

Suppose we attach small lights to someone's shoulders, elbows, hands, hips, knees, and ankles. Then we turn out all other lights so that you see just the lights on this person. As soon as the person starts to walk, you see the lights as a person in motion. In fact, you have a brain area specialized for just this task (Grossman & Blake, 2001). You can see this fascinating phenomenon at this website: www.biomotionlab.ca/Demos/BMLwalker.html.

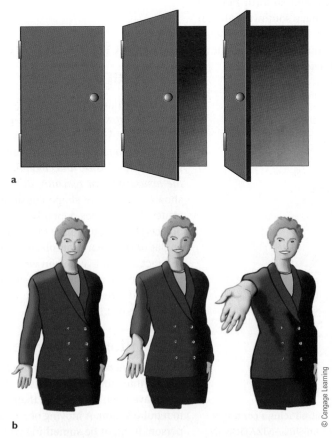

a

b

© Cengage Learning

Figure 4.46 (a) Shape constancy: We perceive all three doors as rectangles. (b) Size constancy: We perceive all three hands as equal in size.

Figure 4.47 ▶ A movie consists of a series of still photographs flickering at 86,400 per hour. Here you see a series of stills spread out in space instead of time.

moving as the machine flipped back and forth (Tombaugh, 1980). He identified that dot as Pluto, which astronomers now list as a dwarf planet (Figure 4.48).

Perception of Depth

Although we live in a world of three dimensions, our retinas are in effect two-dimensional surfaces. Depth perception, the *perception of distance*, enables us to experience the world in three dimensions. This perception depends on several factors.

try it ▶ yourself

One factor is retinal disparity—*the difference in the apparent position of an object as seen by the left and right retinas*. Try this: Hold a finger at arm's length. Focus on it with one eye and then the other. Note that the apparent position of your finger shifts with respect to the background. Now hold your finger closer to your face and repeat. The apparent position of your finger shifts even more. The amount of discrepancy between the two eyes is one way to gauge distance.

A second cue for depth perception is the convergence of the eyes—that is, the *degree to which they turn in to focus on a close object*. When you focus on something close, your eyes turn in, and you sense the tension of your eye muscles. The more the muscles pull, the closer the object must be.

Retinal disparity and convergence are called binocular cues because they *depend on both eyes*. Monocular cues enable you to *judge depth and distance with just one eye* or when both eyes see the same image, as when you look at a picture, such as Figure 4.49. The ability to interpret depth in a picture depends on experience. For example, in Figure 4.50 does it appear to you that the hunter is aiming his spear at the antelope? When this drawing was

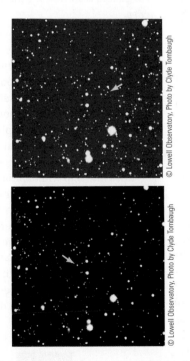

Figure 4.48 Clyde Tombaugh photographed each area of the sky twice, several days apart. Then he used a machine to flip back and forth between the two photos of each pair. When he came to one part of the sky, he noticed a dot moving between the two photos. That dot was Pluto.

Figure 4.49 We judge depth and distance in a photograph using monocular cues (those that would work even with just one eye). Closer objects occupy more space on the retina (or in the photograph) than do distant objects of the same type. Nearer objects show more detail. Closer objects overlap distant objects. Objects in the foreground look sharper than objects on the horizon.

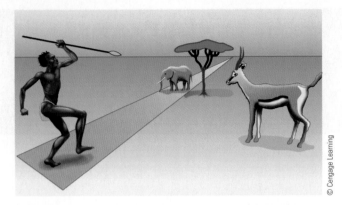

Figure 4.50 Which animal is the hunter attacking? Many people unfamiliar with drawings and photographs said he was attacking a baby elephant. (From Hudson, 1960.)

If you were a passenger on this train looking toward the horizon, the ground beside the tracks would appear to pass by more quickly than more distant parts of the landscape. In this photo's version of motion parallax, the ground is blurred and more distant objects are crisp.

shown to African people who had seldom or never seen drawings, many said the hunter was aiming at a baby elephant (Hudson, 1960).

Let's consider some of the monocular cues we use to perceive depth:

Object size: Other things being equal, a nearby object produces a larger image than a distant one. This cue helps only for objects of known size. For example, the jogger in Figure 4.49 produces a larger image than do any of the houses, which we know are larger. So we see the jogger as closer. However, the mountains in the background differ in actual as well as apparent size, so we cannot assume the ones that look bigger are closer.

Linear perspective: As parallel lines stretch out toward the horizon, they come closer together. Examine the road in Figure 4.49. At the bottom of the photo (close to the viewer), the edges of the road are far apart. At greater distances they come together.

Detail: We see nearby objects, such as the jogger, in more detail than distant objects.

Interposition: A nearby object interrupts our view of a more distant object. For example, the closest telephone pole (on the right) interrupts our view of the closest tree, so we see that the telephone pole is closer than the tree.

Texture gradient: Notice the distance between one telephone pole and the next. At greater distances, the poles come closer and closer together. The "packed together" appearance of objects gives us another cue to their approximate distance.

Shadows: Shadows help us gauge sizes as well as locations of objects.

Accommodation: The lens of the eye *accommodates*—that is, it changes shape—to focus on nearby objects, and your brain detects that change and thereby infers the distance to an object. Accommodation could help tell you how far away the photograph itself is, although it provides no information about the relative distances of objects in the photograph.

Motion parallax. Another monocular cue helps us perceive depth while we are moving, although it does not help with a photograph. If you are walking or riding in a car and fixating at the horizon, nearby objects move rapidly across the retina, while those farther away move less. The *difference in speed of movement of images across the retina as you travel* is the principle of motion parallax. Television and film crews use this principle. If the camera moves slowly, you see closer objects move more than distant ones and get a sense of depth.

23. Which monocular cues to depth are available in Figure 4.50?

24. With three-dimensional photography, cameras take two views of the same scene from different locations through lenses with different color filters or with different polarized-light filters. The two views are then superimposed. The viewer looks at the composite view through special glasses so that one eye sees the view taken with one camera and the other eye sees the view taken with the other camera. Which depth cue is at work here?

Answers

Optical Illusions

Vision is well adapted to understanding what we see, but special situations can fool it. An optical illusion is a *misinterpretation of a visual stimulus.* Figure 4.51 shows a few examples. For many more, visit this site: www.michaelbach.de/ot/index.html.

Psychologists would like to explain the optical illusions as simply and parsimoniously as possible. One approach that applies to many illusions but not all, pertains to mistakes of depth perception.

Depth Perception and Size Perception

As you see in Figure 4.52, an image on the retina may represent either a small, close object or a large, distant object. If you know the size or the distance, you can estimate the other one. However, if you misjudge size or distance, you will be wrong about the other also.

Watch what happens when you take a single image and change its apparent distance: Stare at Figure 4.12 again to form a negative afterimage. Examine the afterimage while looking at a sheet of paper. As you move the paper backward and forward, you can change the apparent size.

The real world provides many cues about the size and distance of objects, but not always for objects in the sky. When people see an unfamiliar object in the sky, they often misjudge its distance, and if so, they also overestimate its size and speed. This illusion may account for reports of UFOs traveling at incredible speeds.

Many optical illusions occur based on misjudging distance. Figure 4.53a shows people in the Ames room (named for its designer, Adelbert Ames). The room looks like a normal rectangular room, although one corner is actually much closer than the other. The two young women are actually the same height. If we eliminated all the background cues, we would correctly perceive the women as being the same size but at different distances. However, the apparently rectangular room provides such misleading cues to distance that the women appear to differ greatly in height.

Many two-dimensional drawings offer misleading depth cues. Because of your long experience

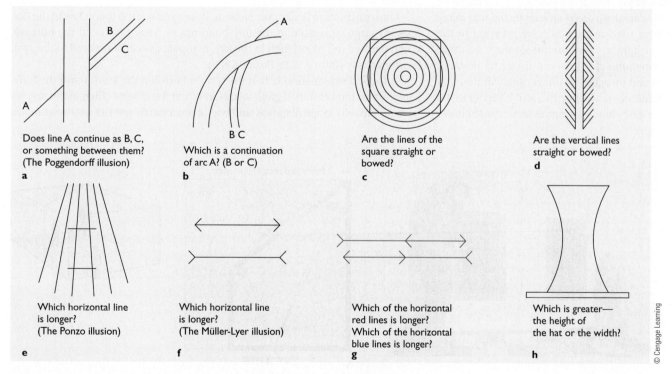

Figure 4.51 These geometric figures illustrate optical illusions. Answers (which you are invited to check with ruler and compass): **(a)** B, **(b)** B, **(c)** straight, **(d)** straight, **(e)** equal, **(f)** equal, **(g)** equal, **(h)** equal.

with photos and drawings, you interpret most drawings as representations of three-dimensional scenes. Figure 4.54 shows a bewildering two-prong/three-prong device and a round staircase that seems to run uphill all the way clockwise or downhill all the way counterclockwise. Both drawings puzzle us when we try to see them as three-dimensional objects.

In Figure 4.55, linear perspective suggests that the right of the picture is farther away than the left. We therefore see the cylinder on the right as being the farthest away. If it is the farthest and still produces the same size image on the retina as the other two, then it would have to be the largest. When we are misled by the cues that ordinarily ensure constancy in size and shape, we experience an optical illusion (Day, 1972).

Figure 4.56 shows the tabletop illusion (Shepard, 1990). Here, almost unbelievably, the vertical dimension of the blue table equals the horizontal dimension of the yellow table, and the horizontal dimension of the blue table equals the vertical dimension of the yellow table. The blue table appears long and thin compared to the yellow one because we interpret it in depth. In effect, your brain constructs what each table would have to really *be* to look this way (Purves & Lotto, 2003).

The Moon Illusion

To most people, the *moon at the horizon appears about 30% larger than it appears when it is higher in the sky*. This moon illusion is so convincing that many people have tried to explain it by referring to the bending of light rays by the atmosphere or other physical phenomena. However, if you photograph the moon and measure its image, you will find that it is the same size at the horizon as it is higher in the sky. Figure 4.57 shows the moon at two positions in

Figure 4.52 No, it's not a bird on steroids. This night heron was close to the camera. If you misjudge the distance to something, you misjudge its size.

the sky. You can measure the two images to demonstrate that they are really the same size. (The atmosphere's bending of light rays makes the moon look orange near the horizon, but it does not increase the size of the image.) However, photographs do not capture the strength of the moon illusion as we see it in real life. In Figure 4.57 or any similar pair of photos, the moon looks almost the same at each position. In the actual night sky, the moon looks enormous at the horizon.

One explanation is size comparison. When you see the moon low in the sky, it seems large compared to the tiny buildings or trees you see at the horizon. When you see the moon high in the sky, it appears small compared to the vast, featureless sky (Baird, 1982; Restle, 1970).

A second explanation is that the terrain between the viewer and the horizon gives an impression of great distance. When the moon is high in the sky, we have no basis to judge distance, and we unconsciously see the overhead moon

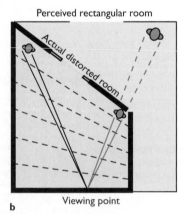

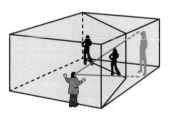

Figure 4.53 The Ames room is designed to view through a peephole with one eye. (a) Both people are the same height, although they appear very different. (b) This diagram shows how the shape of the room distorts the viewer's perception of distance. (Part b from J. R. Wilson et al., 1964.)

as closer. Because we see the horizon moon as more distant, we perceive it as larger (Kaufman & Rock, 1989; Rock & Kaufman, 1962). This explanation is appealing because it relates the moon illusion to perception of distance, a factor already accepted as important for other illusions.

Many psychologists are not satisfied with this explanation, however, because they are not convinced that the horizon moon looks farther away than the overhead moon. If we ask which looks farther away, many people say they are not sure. If we insist on an answer, most say the horizon moon looks *closer*, contradicting the theory. Some psychologists reply that the situation is complicated: We unconsciously perceive the horizon as farther away. Consequently, we perceive the horizon moon as very large. Then, because of the perceived large size of the horizon moon, we consciously say it looks closer, while continuing unconsciously to perceive it as farther (Rock & Kaufman, 1962).

Studies of optical illusions confirm what other phenomena already indicated: What we perceive is not the same as what is "out there." Our visual system does an amazing job of providing us with useful information about the world around us, but under unusual circumstances, we have distorted perceptions.

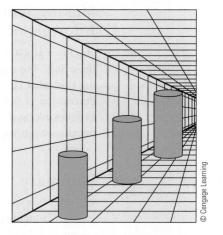

Figure 4.55 The cylinder on the right seems larger because the context makes it appear farther away.

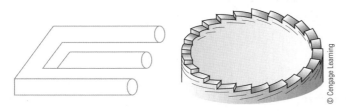

Figure 4.54 These two-dimensional drawings puzzle us because we try to interpret them as three-dimensional objects.

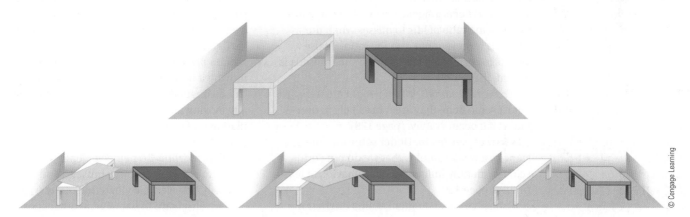

Figure 4.56 The tabletop illusion. The blue table is as wide as the yellow table is long, and as long as the yellow table is wide. The parts below show rotation of the yellow table to overlap the blue one.

Figure 4.57 Ordinarily, the moon looks much larger at the horizon than it does overhead. In photographs this illusion disappears almost completely, but the photographs demonstrate that the physical image of the moon is the same in both cases. The moon illusion requires a psychological explanation, not a physical one.

module 4.3 >

Making Sense of Sensory Information

You have probably heard the expression, "Seeing is believing." The saying is true in many ways, including that what you believe influences what you see. Perception is not just a matter of adding up the events striking the retina. We look for what we expect to see, we impose order on haphazard patterns, we see three dimensions in two-dimensional drawings, and we see optical illusions. The brain does not compute what light is striking the retina but tries to learn what the objects really are and what they are doing.

Summary

- *Perception of minimal stimuli.* No sharp dividing line distinguishes sensory stimuli that can be perceived and sensory stimuli that cannot be perceived. (page 127)
- *Signal detection.* To determine how accurately someone detects a signal, we need to consider not only the ratio of hits to misses when the stimulus is present but also the ratio of false alarms to correct rejections when the stimulus is absent. (page 128)
- *Detecting rare stimuli.* When people are trying to detect some item, they are more likely to overlook it if it occurs rarely. (page 129)
- *Subliminal perception.* Under some circumstances, a weak stimulus that we do not consciously identify influences our behavior, at least briefly. (page 129)
- *Brightness contrast.* An item seems brighter if it contrasts with something darker. (page 130)
- *Feature detectors.* In the first stages of the process of perception, feature-detector neurons identify lines, points, and simple movement. Visual aftereffects can be interpreted in terms of fatiguing certain feature detectors. (page 130)
- *Perception of organized wholes.* According to Gestalt psychologists, we perceive an organized whole by identifying patterns in a top-down manner. (page 132)
- *Visual constancies.* We ordinarily perceive the shape, size, and color of objects as constant, even when the pattern of light striking the retina varies. (page 135)
- *Motion perception.* We perceive an object as moving if it moves relative to its background. We can distinguish between an object that is actually moving and a similar pattern of retinal stimulation that results from our own movement. (page 135)
- *Depth perception.* To perceive depth, we use the accommodation of the eye muscles and retinal disparity between the views that our two eyes see. We also learn to use several other cues that are just as effective with one eye as with two. (page 137)
- *Optical illusions.* Some optical illusions occur because we misperceive the relative distances of objects. We perceive displays by comparing them to our previous experiences with similar objects. (page 139)

Key Terms

absolute sensory threshold (page 127)
binocular cues (page 137)
bottom-up process (page 132)
brightness contrast (page 130)
closure (page 134)
common fate (page 134)
continuation (page 133)
convergence (page 137)
depth perception (page 137)
feature detector (page 130)
figure and ground (page 132)
Gestalt psychology (page 132)
good figure (page 134)
induced movement (page 136)

monocular cues (page 137)
moon illusion (page 140)
motion parallax (page 138)
optical illusion (page 139)
proximity (page 133)
retinal disparity (page 137)
reversible figure (page 132)
signal-detection theory (page 128)
similarity (page 133)
stroboscopic movement (page 136)
subliminal perception (page 129)
top-down process (page 132)
visual constancy (page 135)
waterfall illusion (page 131)

Answers to Other Questions in the Module

C.

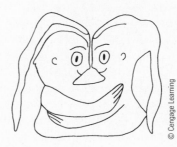

© The Exploratorium,
www.exploratorium.edu

D.

© Steve McCurry/Magnum Photos

E.

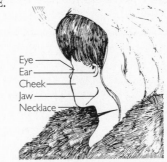

Eye
Ear
Cheek
Jaw
Necklace

Young woman

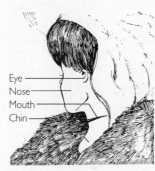

Eye
Nose
Mouth
Chin

Old woman

From American Journal of Psychology. Copyright 1930 by the Board of Trustees of the University of Illinois. Used by permission of the author and the University of Illinois Press.

F.

© Cengage Learning

exploration and study

Access an interactive eBook and chapter-specific learning tools, including
- **flashcards**
- **quizzes**
- **videos**

and more, in your Psychology CourseMate. Go to **CengageBrain.com.**

If your professor has assigned Aplia:
1. Sign in to your account.
2. Complete the corresponding exercises as required by your professor.
3. When finished, click "Grade It Now" to see which areas you have mastered, which areas need more work, and detailed explanations of every answer.

5

ur Tilley/Gettyimages.com

Development

Suppose you buy a robot.

When you get home, you discover that it does nothing useful. It cannot even maintain its balance. It makes irritating, high-pitched noises, moves its limbs haphazardly, and leaks. The store you bought it from refuses to take it back. And you're not allowed to turn it off. So you are stuck with this useless machine.

A few years later, your robot walks and talks, reads and writes, draws pictures, and does arithmetic. It follows your directions (usually) and sometimes does useful things without being told. It beats you at memory games.

How did all this happen? After all, you knew nothing about how to program a robot. Did your robot have some sort of built-in programming that simply took a long time to phase in? Or was it programmed to learn all these skills?

Children are like that robot. Parents wonder, "How did my children get to be the way they are? And why did my two children turn out so different?" Developmental psychology seeks to understand how nature and nurture combine to produce human behavior "from womb to tomb."

As we grow older, our behavior changes in many ways. Developmental psychologists seek to describe and understand these changes.

Cognitive Development in Infancy and Childhood

- How can we know about an infant's abilities and experiences?
- How do children's thought processes differ from adults'?

Young children's artwork is amazingly inventive and revealing. One toddler, 1½ years old, proudly showed off a drawing that consisted only of dots. Adults were puzzled. It is a rabbit, the child explained, while making more dots: "Look: hop, hop, hop . . . " (Winner, 1986). When my daughter, Robin, was 6 years old, she drew a picture of a boy and a girl wearing Halloween costumes and drawing pictures (Figure 5.1). For the little girl's drawing, Robin pasted on some wildlife photos that, she insisted, were the little girl's drawings. The little boy's drawing was just a scribble. When I asked why the little girl's drawing was so much better than the little boy's, Robin replied, "Don't make fun of him, Daddy. He's doing the best he can."

Figure 5.1 A drawing of two children drawing pictures, courtesy of 6-year-old Robin Kalat.

Often, as in this case, a drawing expresses the child's worldview. As children grow older, their art becomes more skillful, but often less expressive. As we grow older, we gain many new abilities and skills, but we lose something, too.

Studying the abilities of young children is challenging. They misunderstand our questions and we misunderstand their answers. Our estimate of children has progressed enormously as developmental psychologists have developed clever new ways to test children. One theme you will encounter repeatedly in this module is that we reach different conclusions about children depending on how we measure some ability.

Research Designs for Studying Development

Studying psychological development poses a special problem. Should a researcher study younger and older people at the same time, or study one group of people repeatedly as they advance from one age to another? Each method has strengths and limitations.

Cross-Sectional and Longitudinal Designs

A **cross-sectional study** *compares groups of individuals of different ages at the same time.* For example, we could compare drawings by 6-year-olds, 8-year-olds, and 10-year-olds. Cross-sectional studies are acceptable for many pur-

As we grow older, we mature, but we revert to childlike behaviors when such behavior is acceptable.

Table 5.1 Cross-Sectional and Longitudinal Studies

	Description	Advantages	Disadvantages	Example
Cross-sectional	Several groups of subjects of various ages studied at one time	1. Quick 2. No risk of confusing age effects with effects of changes in society	1. Risk of sampling error by getting different kinds of people at different ages 2. Risk of cohort effects	Compare memory abilities of 3-, 5-, and 7-year-olds
Longitudinal	One group of subjects studied repeatedly as the members grow older	1. No risk of sampling differences 2. Can study effects of one experience on later development 3. Can study consistency within individuals over time	1. Takes a long time 2. Some participants quit 3. Sometimes hard to separate effects of age from changes in society	Study memory abilities of 3-year-olds, and of the same children again 2 and 4 years later

© Cengage Learning

poses, but they are often problematical when studying adults. For example, if you compared a random sample of 55-year-olds with a random sample of 85-year-olds, you would find that the 85-year-olds have less interest in sports. You would also find that, on average, 85-year-olds are shorter and have smaller heads. Why? The explanation is that, on average, women live longer than men. Women tend to be smaller, have smaller heads, and show less interest in sports. The sample of 55-year-olds you studied was not comparable to the 85-year-olds.

A longitudinal study *follows a single group of individuals as they develop.* For example, we could study a group of children from, say, age 6 to age 12. Table 5.1 contrasts the two kinds of studies. A longitudinal study necessarily takes years to complete. Also, not everyone who participates the first time is willing and available later. Selective attrition is *the tendency for certain kinds of people to drop out of a study* for many reasons, including health, moving far away, or loss of interest. The kind of people who stay in the study may differ in many ways from those who quit. Psychologists can compensate for selective attrition by discarding the data for people who left the study.

Certain questions logically require a longitudinal study. For example, to study the effects of divorce on children, researchers compare how each child reacts at first with how that same child reacts later. To study whether happy children become happy adults, researchers follow a single group over time.

A sequential (or "cross-sequential") design combines cross-sectional and longitudinal designs. In a sequential design, a researcher starts with people of different ages and studies them again at later times. For example, one might study 6-year-olds and 8-year-olds and then examine the same children 2 years later:

First study	2 years later
Group A, age 6 years	Group A, now 8 years old
Group B, age 8 years	Group B, now 10 years old

concept check

1. At Santa Enigma College, the average first-year student has a C-minus average, and the average senior has a B-plus average. An observer concludes that, as students progress through college, they improve their study habits. Based on the idea of selective attrition, propose another possible explanation.

Cohort Effects

If you had been born in 1940, your childhood and adolescence would have been very different from today: no Internet, computers, iPods, cell phones, air conditioners, dishwashers, or appliances for washing and drying clothes. You would have listened to radio instead of watching television. Telephone calls to someone outside your hometown were a luxury. Few women or minorities went to college, and they had limited job opportunities afterward. If you had lived then, how would you have been different?

People of different generations differ in many ways, called *cohort effects* (Figure 5.2). A cohort is *a group of people born at a particular time or a group of people who enter an organization at a particular time.* (We could talk about the cohort of students entering a college in a given year, or the cohort of workers a corporation hires in a given year.)

The era in which you grew up is a powerful influence on your psychological development. For example, Americans whose youth spanned the Great Depression and World War II learned to save money and to sacrifice for the needs of the country. Even after the war was over and prosperity reigned, most remained thrifty and cautious (Rogler, 2002). In contrast, young people of today have much more leisure time (Larson, 2001).

In America long ago, as in many countries today, it was customary for most people to spend their lives in or near the neighborhood where they were born. Today many people move great distances, perhaps repeatedly, in search of a better job. The results include less identification with their community, few lasting friendships, and less feeling of obligation to help their neighbors (Oishi, 2010). According to Jean Twenge (2006), cohort effects are similar to cultural differences. Much of today's technology is so unfamiliar to many older people that they feel like immigrants to this culture.

concept check

2. Suppose you want to study the effect of age on choice of clothing. Would cohort effects have greater influence on a longitudinal study or a cross-sectional study?

Answer

Figure 5.2 People born at different times grow up with different experiences. In an earlier era, bathing suit inspectors prohibited "overly revealing" outfits that would seem extremely modest today.

The Fetus and the Newborn

Let's begin at the beginning. During prenatal development, everyone starts as a *fertilized egg cell*, or zygote, which develops through its first few stages until the stage of fetus *about 8 weeks after conception.* As soon as 6 weeks after conception, the brain is mature enough to produce a few movements. The first movements are spontaneous—that is, not elicited by any stimulus. Contrary to what we might have guessed, the muscles and the nerves controlling these movements mature before the sense organs. Those spontaneous movements are essential, and without them the spinal cord does not develop properly. Later, but still before birth, the sense organs appear, the head and eyes turn toward sounds, and the brain alternates between waking and sleeping (Joseph, 2000). The fetus does a good bit of yawning and hiccupping. Presumably these behaviors serve some function, although that function remains unclear (Provine, 2012).

The growing body receives nutrition from the mother. Undernourished mothers generally give birth to small babies (Figure 5.3). Premature birth and very low birth weight correlate with later deficits in learning, cognitive ability, and emotional self-control (Clark, Woodward, Horwood, & Moor, 2008; Shenkin, Starr, & Deary, 2004). These facts are clear, but their meaning is not.

Before we assume that being born very small or premature impairs brain development, consider: *Why* was the baby born so small or premature? In some cases, the mother was ill nourished or unhealthy. One way to study the effect of birth weight

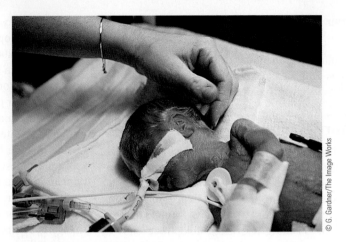

Figure 5.3 Babies with low birth weight are susceptible to physical and behavioral difficulties, but we cannot be sure that low birth weight causes the problems.

separately from other influences is to examine pairs of twins where one twin is born heavier than the other. In most cases, the one with lower birth weight develops about as well as the heavier one (R. S. Wilson, 1987).

A developing fetus is vulnerable to harm from any of a wide variety of *teratogens* (literally, monster-makers, although that term is much too strong). Those influences include many drugs and medications the mother might take, infections she might have, and environmental chemicals she encounters. Any drug that a mother takes reaches the fetus's developing brain (Hubbs-Tait, Nation, Krebs, & Bellinger, 2005). *If the mother drinks too much alcohol during pregnancy*, the infant may develop fetal alcohol syndrome, *a condition marked by malformations of the face, heart, and ears; and nervous system damage, including seizures, hyperactivity, and impairments of learning, memory, problem solving, attention, and motor coordination* (Mattson, Crocker, & Nguyen, 2011). The symptoms range from none to severe, depending on the amount and timing of the mother's drinking (Figure 5.4).

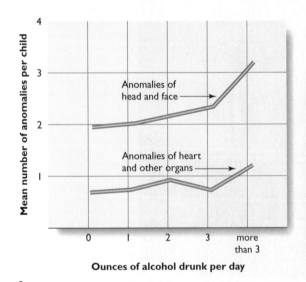

Ounces of alcohol drunk per day

a

b

Figure 5.4 **(a)** The more alcohol a woman drinks per day during pregnancy, the more likely her baby is to have anomalies of the head, face, and organs. (Based on data of Ernhart et al., 1987.) **(b)** A child with fetal alcohol syndrome: Note the wide separation between the eyes, a common feature of this syndrome.

The reason for the nervous system damage is now understood: Developing neurons require persistent excitation to survive. Without it, they activate a self-destruct program. Alcohol interferes with the brain's main excitatory neurotransmitter (glutamate) and facilitates the main inhibitory neurotransmitter (GABA). It therefore decreases neurons' arousal and makes them self-destruct (Ikonomidou et al., 2000).

Still, it is remarkable that an occasional "high-risk" child—small at birth, exposed to alcohol or other drugs before birth, from a disadvantaged family, a victim of prejudice, and so forth—overcomes all obstacles to become healthy and successful. Resilience (the ability to overcome obstacles) is poorly understood, but it relates partly to genetic influences, education, and supportive relatives and friends (Bonanno & Mancini, 2008).

concept check

3. How does drinking too much alcohol during pregnancy harm the brain of the woman's developing fetus?

Answer

3. Alcohol increases inhibition and impairs excitation. Developing neurons that fail to receive enough excitation undergo a self-destruct program.

Infancy

Research progress depends on good measurement. How can we measure psychological processes in infants, who can't talk, and can't even do much? A researcher monitors the few responses available to infants, drawing inferences about their growing understanding of the world.

Infants' Vision

William James, the founder of American psychology, said that as far as an infant can tell, the world is a "buzzing confusion," full of meaningless sights and sounds. Since James's time, psychologists have substantially increased their estimates of infants' vision.

We can start by recording an infant's eye movements. Even 2-day-old infants spend more time looking at drawings of human faces than at other patterns with similar areas of light and dark (Fantz, 1963; Figure 5.5). However, infants do not have the same concept of "face" that adults do. As shown in Figure 5.6, newborns gaze equally at distorted and normal faces. However, they gaze longer at right-side-up faces than upside-down faces regardless of distortion. Evidently, the newborn's concept of face is simply an oval with most of its content toward the top (Cassia, Turati, & Simion, 2004).

The ability to recognize faces continues developing for years. Parents in one study repeatedly read a storybook with photographs of two children's faces from many angles and with many expressions. After 2 weeks, 4-year-old children easily recognized pictures of the two children. However, when they had to choose between a normal picture and one with altered spacing among the features, they guessed randomly (Mondloch, Leis, & Maurer, 2006). By age 6, a child easily sees the difference between the photos in Figure 5.7, but 4-year-olds evidently do not.

The gradual improvement of face recognition depends on experience, and infants, like all of us, become best at recognizing the kinds of faces they

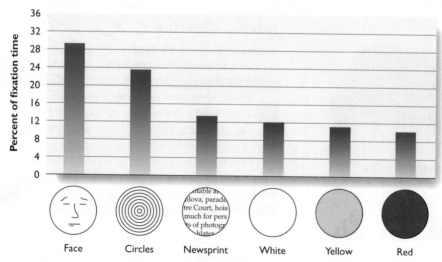

Figure 5.5 Infants pay more attention to faces than to other patterns. These results suggest that infants are born with certain visual preferences. (Based on Fantz, 1963.)

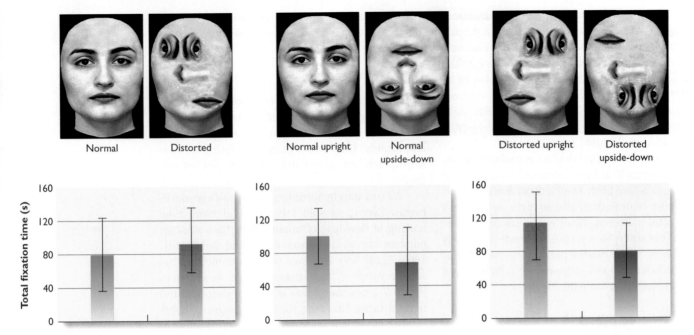

| | Normal | Distorted | | Normal upright | Normal upside-down | | Distorted upright | Distorted upside-down |

Figure 5.6 Infants gaze about equally at normal and distorted faces, but they stare longer at upright than upside-down faces. (From Cassia, V. M., Turati, C., & Simion, F., "Can a nonspecific bias toward top-heavy patterns explain newborns' face preferences?" *Psychological Science, 15*, 379-383. Copyright © 2004 Sage Publications, Inc. Reprinted with permission)

frequently see. At age 6 months, infants are about as good at recognizing monkey faces as human faces. (The test is to show one monkey or human face for 30 seconds, and then that face and another one. If the infant looks more at the new face, we infer that it recognized the old face.) Over the next 3 months, infants' ability to recognize monkey faces declines, unless they have had special training in which each monkey face is assigned a special name (Scott & Monesson, 2009).

Older children and adults are better able to recognize faces of their own ethnic group, or at least ethnic groups familiar to them, than those they see less often. The main reason is that certain brain areas become highly sensitive to small deviations

from the "average" face (Leopold, Bondar, & Giese, 2006). A second reason is that most people pay more attention to their in-group. In one study, college students viewed a series of faces, while being told (incorrectly) that the faces on a red background were from their own college, and those on a green background were from a different college. In fact, the backgrounds were random. On average, students were then better at recognizing the faces they had thought were from their own college (Bernstein, Young, & Hugenberg, 2007).

By age 5 months, infants have had much visual experience but almost no experience at crawling or reaching. Over the next several months, as they increase their control of arm and leg movements, they learn to pick up toys, crawl around objects, and in other ways coordinate what they see with what they do. Apparently, that experience helps them learn a fear of heights (Adolph, 2000). Those who crawl early develop a fear of heights early, and those who are late to crawl are also slow to develop a fear of heights (Campos, Bertenthal, & Kermoian, 1992).

Infants' Hearing

Infants don't do much, but one thing they do is suck. Researchers use that response to measure hearing, because infants suck more vigorously when certain kinds of sounds arouse them.

In one study, the experimenters played a brief sound and noted how it affected infants' sucking rate (Figure 5.8). On the first few occasions, the sound increased the sucking rate. A repeated sound produced less and less effect. We say that the infant became *habituated* to the sound. Habituation is *decreased response to a repeated stimulus*. When the experimenters substituted a new sound, the sucking rate increased. Evidently, the infant was aroused by the unfamiliar sound. *When a change in a stimulus increases a previously habituated response*, we say that the stimulus produced dishabituation.

Monitoring dishabituation tells us whether infants hear a difference between two sounds. For example, infants who have become habituated to the sound *ba* will increase their sucking

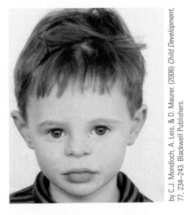

Figure 5.7 These faces differ only in the positions of the eyes, nose, and mouth. Four-year-olds do not recognize which face is familiar. (Source: Mondloch, Leis, & Maurer, 2006)

by C.J. Mondloch, A. Leis, & D. Maurer. (2006) *Child Development, 77*, 234–243. Blackwell Publishers.

rate when they hear the sound *pa* (Eimas, Siqueland, Jusczyk, & Vigorito, 1971). Apparently, even month-old infants notice the difference between *ba* and *pa*, an important distinction for later language comprehension.

Similar studies have shown that infants who have habituated to hearing one language, such as Dutch, dishabituate when they hear a different language, such as Japanese. At first, they show no response to a shift between Dutch and English, presumably because the sounds and rhythms are similar. By age 5 months, however, they dishabituate even to a change from a British to an American accent (Jusczyk, 2002). Studies of this sort show that children attend to language sounds long before they know what the words mean.

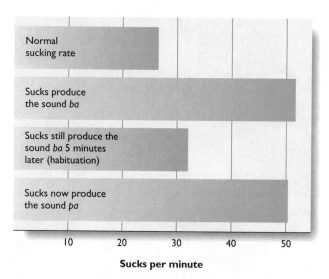

Figure 5.8 After repeatedly hearing a *ba* sound, the infant's sucking habituates. When a new sound, *pa*, follows, the sucking rate increases. (Based on results of Eimas, Siqueland, Jusczyk, & Vigorito, 1971.)

concept check

4. Suppose an infant habituates to the sound *ba*, but when we substitute the sound *bla*, the infant fails to increase his or her sucking rate. What interpretation would be likely?

Answer

4. Evidently, the infant does not hear a difference between *ba* and *bla*. (This is a hypothetical result; the study has not been done.)

Infants' Learning and Memory

How could we measure learning and memory in infants who cannot speak? Many studies have used the fact that infants learn to suck harder on a nipple if their sucking turns on a sound. Investigators then determined whether infants suck harder for some sounds than for others. In one study, babies younger than 3 days old could turn on a tape recording of a woman's voice by sucking on a nipple. The results: They sucked more frequently to turn on recordings of their own mother's voice than another woman's voice (DeCasper & Fifer, 1980). Apparently, they preferred their own mother's voice. Because they showed this preference as early as the day of birth, psychologists believe that the infants learned the sound of the mother's voice before birth.

In a follow-up study, newborns could suck to turn on a recording of an unfamiliar adult speaking either English or Tagalog (a language used in the Philippines). Children of English-speaking mothers sucked more to turn on the English recording. Children of English-Tagalog bilingual mothers sucked equally for both (Byers-Heinlein, Burns, & Werker, 2010). Evidently newborns have learned not only the sound of the mother's voice, but also something about the cadence of her language or languages.

One can also examine heart rate as a measure of learning or memory. Researchers played a simple piano melody for fetuses to hear twice daily for the last three weeks before birth. Six weeks later, those infants (and not other infants) showed a larger heart rate response to the familiar melody than to a different melody (Granier-Deferre, Bassereau, Ribeiro, Jacquet, & deCasper, 2011). This study shows memory of prenatal experiences lasting at least six weeks.

concept check

5. Suppose a newborn sucks to turn on a tape recording of its father's voice. Eventually, the baby habituates and the sucking frequency decreases. Now the experimenters substitute the recording of a different man's voice. What would you conclude if the sucking frequency increased? What if it remained the same? What if it decreased?

Answer

5. If the frequency increased, we would conclude that the infant recognizes the difference between the father's voice and the other voice. If the frequency remained the same, we would conclude that the infant did not notice a difference. If the sucking frequency decreased, we would assume that the infant preferred the sound of the father's voice.

Carolyn Rovee-Collier (1997, 1999) demonstrated that infants can learn a response and remember it. She attached a ribbon to an ankle so that an infant could activate a mobile by kicking with one leg (Figure 5.9). Two-month-old infants quickly

Figure 5.9 Two-month-old infants rapidly learn to kick to activate a mobile attached to their ankles with a ribbon. They remember how to activate the mobile when tested days later. (From Hildreth, Sweeney, & Rovee-Collier, 2003.)

Jean Piaget (on the left) demonstrated that children with different levels of maturity react differently to the same experience.

learned this response and generally kept the mobile going nonstop for a full 45-minute session. (Infants have little control over their leg muscles, but they don't need much control to keep the mobile going.) They remembered what to do when the ribbon was reattached several days later—to the infants' evident delight. Six-month-old infants remembered the response for 2 weeks. Even after they forgot it, they quickly relearned it and retained it for an additional month or more (Hildreth, Sweeney, & Rovee-Collier, 2003).

Jean Piaget's View of Cognitive Development

Somewhat older children are much easier to test, and one quickly discovers that their thinking differs from that of adults. The theorist who made this point most influentially was Jean Piaget (pee-ah-ZHAY; 1896–1980).

Early in his career, while administering IQ tests to French-speaking children in Switzerland, Piaget was fascinated that so many children of a given age gave the *same* incorrect answer to a given question. He concluded that children have qualitatively different thought processes from adults. According to Piaget, as children develop intellectually, they do more than accumulate facts. They construct new mental processes.

In Piaget's terminology, behavior is based on schemata (the plural of *schema*). A schema is *an organized way of interacting with objects.* For instance, infants have a grasping schema and a sucking schema. Older infants gradually add new schemata and adapt their old ones through the processes of assimilation and accommodation. Assimilation means *applying an old schema to new objects or problems.* For example, when a child sees animals move and then sees the sun and moon move, the child may assume that the sun and moon are alive, like animals. Accommodation means *modifying an old schema to fit a new object or problem.* A child may learn that "only living things move on their own" is a rule with exceptions and that the sun and moon are not alive.

Infants shift back and forth between assimilation and accommodation. Equilibration is *the establishment of harmony or balance between assimilation and accommodation*, and according to Piaget, equilibration is the key to intellectual growth. A discrepancy occurs between the child's current understanding and some evidence to the contrary. The child accommodates to that discrepancy and achieves an equilibration at a higher level.

Similar processes occur in adults. When you see a new mathematical problem, you try several familiar methods until you find one that works. That is, you assimilate the new problem to an old schema. However, if the new problem is sufficiently different, you modify (accommodate) your schema to find a solution. In this way, said Piaget, intellectual growth occurs.

Piaget contended that children progress through four stages of intellectual development:

1. *The sensorimotor stage* (from birth to almost 2 years)
2. *The preoperational stage* (from just before 2 to 7 years)
3. *The concrete operations stage* (from about 7 to 11 years)
4. *The formal operations stage* (from about 11 years onward)

The ages are variable, and not everyone reaches the formal operations stage. However, all people progress through the stages in the same order. Let's consider each of Piaget's stages.

Piaget's Sensorimotor Stage

Piaget called the first stage of intellectual development the sensorimotor stage because *at this early age (the first 1½ to 2 years) behavior is mostly simple motor responses to sensory stimuli*—for example, the grasp reflex and the sucking reflex. According to Piaget, infants respond only to what they see and hear at the moment. In particular, he believed that children during this period fail to respond to objects they remember seeing even a few seconds ago. What evidence could he have for this view?

What's the Evidence?

The Infant's Concept of Object Permanence

Piaget argued that infants in the first few months of life lack the concept of **object permanence**, *the idea that objects continue to exist even when we do not see or hear them.* That is, for an infant, "Out of sight, out of existence."

Piaget drew his inferences from observations like this: Place a toy in front of a 6-month-old infant, who reaches out for it. Later, place a toy in the same place, but before the infant has a chance to grab it, cover it with a clear glass. The infant removes the glass and takes the toy. Now repeat that procedure but use an opaque (nonclear) glass. The infant, who watched you place the glass over the toy, makes no effort to remove the glass and obtain the toy. Next, place a thin barrier between the infant and the toy. An infant who cannot see the toy does not reach for it (Piaget, 1937/1954; Figure 5.10).

According to Piaget, the infant does not know that the hidden toy continues to exist. However, the results vary depending on circumstances. For example, if you show a toy and then turn out the lights, a 7-month-old infant reaches out toward the unseen toy if it was a familiar toy but not if it was unfamiliar (Shinskey & Munakata, 2005). A study by Renee Baillargeon (1986) also suggests that infants show signs of understanding object permanence when they are tested differently.

Hypothesis An infant who sees an event that would be impossible (if objects are permanent) will be surprised and therefore will stare longer than will an infant who sees a similar but possible event.

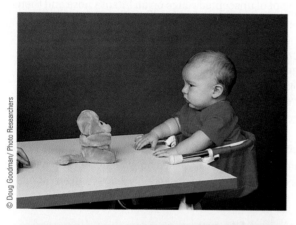

Figure 5.10 (a) A 6- to 9-month-old child reaches for a visible toy but not one that is hidden behind a barrier (b) even if the child sees someone hide the toy. According to Piaget, this observation indicates that the child hasn't yet grasped the concept of object permanence.

Method Infants aged 6 or 8 months watched a series of events. The infant watched the experimenter raise a screen to show the track and then watched a toy car go down a slope and emerge on the other side of the screen, as shown here. This was called a "possible" event.

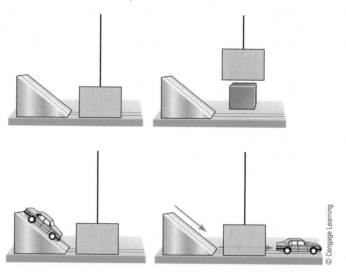

Possible event. The box is behind the track, and the car passes by the box.

The researchers measured how long the child stared after the car passed by. They repeated the procedure until the child's staring time decreased for three trials in a row (showing habituation). Then the experimenters presented a series of "possible" events, as just described, and "impossible" events like this:

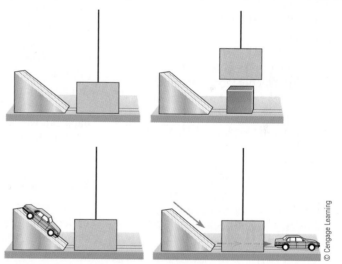

Impossible event. The raised screen shows a box on the track where the car would pass. After the screen lowers, the car goes down the slope and emerges on the other side.

In an impossible event, the raised screen showed a box on the track where the car would pass. After the screen lowered, the car went down the slope and emerged on the other side. (The experimenters pulled the box off the track after lowering the screen.) The experimenters measured each child's staring times after both kinds of events. They repeated both events two more times, randomizing the order of events.

Results As shown in Figure 5.11, infants stared longer after seeing an impossible event. They also stared longer after the first pair of events than after the second and third pairs (Baillargeon, 1986).

Interpretation Why did the infants stare longer at the impossible event? The inference—admittedly only an inference—is that the infants found the impossible event surprising. To be surprised, infants had to expect that the box would continue to exist. If so, even 6-month-old infants have some understanding of object permanence, as well as elementary physics. A later study with a slightly different method demonstrated object permanence in infants as young as 3½ months (Baillargeon, 1987).

Still, remember that 9-month-olds failed Piaget's object permanence task of reaching out to pick up a hidden object. Do infants understand object permanence or not? Evidently, it is not a good question. Infants use a concept in some situations and not others. The same is true for all of us. Did you ever learn a grammatical rule in English class and then violate it in your own speech? Did you ever learn a math formula and then fail to apply it to a new problem?

Other psychologists modified this procedure to test many other infant concepts. Researchers put five objects behind a screen, added five more, and removed the screen. Nine-month-olds stared longer when they saw just five objects than when they saw ten, suggesting some understanding of addition (McCrink & Wynn, 2004). Researchers buried a ball in the sand and then retrieved apparently the same ball from the same or a different location. Infants stared longer when the ball emerged from the new location (Newcombe, Sluzenski, & Huttenlocher, 2005). When infants watched an animated display in which a larger figure and a smaller figure crossed paths, 10-month-olds stared longer if the larger one bowed and stepped aside to let the smaller one pass (Thomsen, Frankenhuis, Ingold-Smith, & Carey, 2011). If we assume that staring means surprise, then infants apparently understand something about social dominance. Related studies suggest that 5-month-olds understand that liquids can pass through a barrier, but solids cannot (Hespos, Ferry, & Rips, 2009). However, infants as old as 12 months show no surprise if you place a toy into a container and then pull out a toy of different shape or color (Baillargeon, Li, Ng, & Yuan, 2009). Evidently, infants imagine that objects can magically change shape or color.

Here are two conclusions: First, we should be cautious about inferring what infants or anyone else can or cannot do, as the results vary with the procedures. Second, concepts develop gradually. An infant may show a concept in one situation and not another.

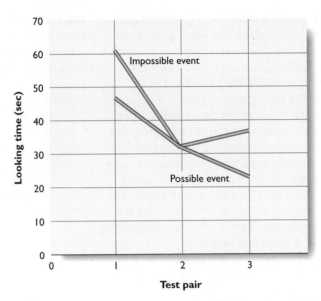

Figure 5.11 Mean looking times of 6- and 8-month-old infants after they had watched either possible or impossible events. (From Baillargeon, 1986.)

Sense of Self

Do young children have a concept of "self"? How would we know? Here is the evidence: Someone puts a spot of unscented rouge on an infant's nose and then puts the infant in front of a mirror. Infants younger than 1½ years old either ignore the red spot on the baby in the mirror or reach out to touch the mirror. At some point after age 1½ years, infants instead touch themselves on the nose, indicating that they recognize themselves in the mirror (Figure 5.12). Infants show this sign of self-recognition at varying ages; the age when they first show self-recognition is about the same as when they begin to act embarrassed (M. Lewis, Sullivan, Stanger, & Weiss, 1991). They show a sense of self in both situations or neither.

Before this time, do infants fail to distinguish between self and other? Perhaps, but we cannot be sure. Before age 1½, we see no evidence for a sense of self, but absence of evidence is not evidence of absence. Perhaps younger infants would show a sense of self in some other test that we have not yet devised.

Piaget's Preoperational Stage

By age 1½ to 2, children begin speaking. A child who asks for a toy obviously understands object permanence. Nevertheless, young children still misunderstand much. They do not understand how a mother can be someone else's daughter. A boy with one brother will assert that his brother has no brother. Piaget refers to this period as the preoperational stage because *the child lacks operations, which are reversible mental processes.* For a boy to understand that his brother has a brother, he must be able to reverse the concept of "having a brother." According to Piaget, three typical aspects of preoperational thought are egocentrism, difficulty distinguishing appearance from reality, and lack of the concept of conservation.

Egocentrism: Failing to Understand Other People's Perspective

According to Piaget, young children's thought is egocentric. Piaget did *not* mean selfish. Instead, he meant that *a child sees the world as centered around himself or herself and cannot easily take another person's perspective.* If you sit opposite

Figure 5.12 If someone places a bit of unscented rouge on a child's nose, a 2-year-old looking at a mirror shows self-recognition by touching his or her own nose.

a preschooler, the child can describe how the blocks on the table look from the child's side but not how they would look from your side.

Another example: Young children hear a story about Lucy, who wants her old pair of red shoes. Lucy's brother Linus enters the room, and she asks him to bring her red shoes. He goes and brings back her new red shoes, and she is angry because she wanted the old red shoes. Young children hearing the story are surprised that he brought the wrong shoes because *they* knew which shoes she wanted (Keysar, Barr, & Horton, 1998).

However, young children do sometimes understand another person's perspective. In one study, 5- and 6-year-old children had to tell an adult to pick up a particular glass. If a child saw that the adult could see two glasses, the child usually said to pick up the "big" or "little" glass to identify the right one. If the child saw that the adult could see only one glass, the child often said just "the glass" (Nadig & Sedivy, 2002; Figure 5.13).

concept check

6. Which of the following is the clearest example of egocentric thinking?
   a. a writer who uses someone else's words without giving credit
   b. a politician who blames others for everything that goes wrong
   c. a professor who gives the same complicated lecture to a freshman class as to a convention of professionals

Answer

6. **c** is a case of egocentric thought, a failure to recognize another person's point of view.

Figure 5.13 Sometimes, a child saw that the adult could see two glasses. At other times, it was clear that the adult could see only one. If two glasses were visible, the child usually told the adult which glass to pick up, instead of saying, "pick up the glass." (From Nadig & Sedivy, 2002.)

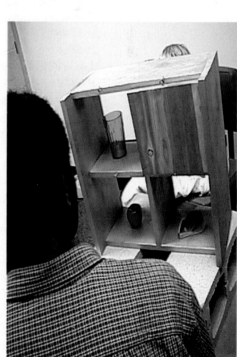

Nadig, A. & Sedivy, J. (2002). Evidence of perspective-taking constraints in children's online reference resolution. *Psychological Science*, 13(4), pp. 329–336. Used by permission of the author.

Theory of Mind: Understanding That Different People Know Different Things

To say that a child is egocentric means that he or she does not understand what other people know and don't know. Psychologists say that a young child lacks, but gradually develops, **theory of mind**, which is *an understanding that other people have a mind, too, and that each person knows some things that other people don't know.* How can we know whether a child has this understanding? Here is one example of a research effort to explore this question.

critical check

What's the Evidence?

Children's Understanding of Other People's Knowledge and Beliefs

How and when do children first understand that other people have minds and knowledge? Researchers have devised some clever experiments to address this question.

Hypothesis A child who understands that other people have minds knows that someone else could have a false belief.

Method A child watches and listens as an adult acts out this story: Maxi sees his mother put chocolate into the blue cupboard. He plans to return later and get some. However, while he is absent, his mother moves the chocolate to the green cupboard. Now, the questions are: Where will Maxi look for the chocolate? The child who has been observing can answer or point. If his grandfather is available to help, where will Maxi tell him to look? If an older brother wants to take the chocolate, and Maxi wants to prevent the brother from finding the chocolate, where will he point? (Figure 5.14).

Results Older children answer correctly: Maxi looks in the blue cupboard and tells his grandfather to get chocolate from the blue cupboard, but tells his brother to look in the green cupboard. Younger children answer incorrectly, as if they thought Maxi had all the correct information that the observers themselves had. Depending on details of procedure, the results vary as to how old a child must be to understand Maxi's false belief. The percentage of children answering correctly increases from age 3 to age 6, and most children beyond about 4½ answer correctly (Wellman, Cross, & Watson, 2001; Wimmer & Penner, 1983).

Interpretation Evidently, children gradually develop in their ability to understand other people's thoughts, beliefs, and knowledge. However, explaining the change is more difficult. For example, it is likely that many 3-year-olds don't fully understand the questions.

Figure 5.14 Maxi watches his mother place chocolate in one place. While he is absent, she moves it. Where will Maxi look for it? Younger children point to the new location, suggesting they do not understand that Maxi will have an incorrect belief.

Furthermore, gaining an understanding of "theory of mind" is not a sudden transition from not understanding to perfectly understanding. Even when adults face a similar situation, they are quicker to answer where some object *is* than where someone else incorrectly *thinks* it is (Apperly, Riggs, Simpson, Chiavarino, & Samson, 2006). Also, very young children show some indication of theory of mind, if tested in certain ways. After some 18-month-olds had some experience wearing blindfolds, they watched an adult put on a similar blindfold after seeing a puppet in one location. While the blindfold was in place, the puppet moved to a different location. Then the adult removed the blindfold and got ready to look for the puppet. The 18-month-olds looked toward the original location, suggesting that they expected the adult to look there (Senju, Southgate, Snape, Leonard, & Csibra, 2011). You see how difficult it is to determine whether someone understands other people's false beliefs. A child can show indications of understanding in some ways or situations and not in others.

concept check

7. If the chocolate is now in the green cupboard, what does it mean if a child says Maxi will look in the blue cupboard?

Answer

7. It means that the child has "theory of mind." The child understands that Maxi, who was absent while the mother moved the chocolate, will have a false belief.

Distinguishing Appearance From Reality

During Piaget's preoperational stage, children apparently do not distinguish clearly between appearance and reality. For example, a child who sees you put a white ball behind a blue filter will say that the ball is blue. When you ask, "Yes, I know the ball *looks* blue, but what color is it *really*?" the child replies that it really *is* blue (Flavell, 1986). Similarly, a 3-year-old who encounters a sponge that looks like a rock will say that it really is a rock, but a child who says it is a sponge will also insist that it *looks like* a sponge.

However, the results depend on exactly how we ask the question. Psychologists showed 3-year-olds a sponge that looked like a rock and let them touch it. When the investigators asked what it looked like and what it was *really*, most of the children said "rock" both times or "sponge" both times. However, if the investigators asked, "Bring me something so I can wipe up some spilled water," the children brought the sponge. And when the investigators asked, "Bring me something so I can take a picture of a teddy bear with something that looks like a rock," they brought the same object. So evidently, the children did understand that something could be a sponge and look like a rock, even if they didn't say so (Sapp, Lee, & Muir, 2000).

Also consider this experiment: A psychologist shows a child a playhouse room that is a scale model of a full-size room. The psychologist hides a tiny toy in the small room and explains that a bigger toy just like it is "in the same place" in the bigger room. (For example, if the little toy is behind the sofa in the little room, the big toy is behind the sofa in the big room.) Then the psychologist asks the child to find the big toy in the big room. Most 3-year-olds go to the correct place at once (DeLoache, 1989). Most 2½-year-old children, however, search haphazardly (Figure 5.15a).

a A 2¹/₂-year-old is shown a small room where a stuffed animal is hidden.

Child is unable to find the stuffed animal in the larger room.

Child is told that the machine expands the room. Child stands out of the way during some noises and then returns.

b Child is shown a small room where a stuffed animal is hidden.

Child is able to find the stuffed animal in the "blown-up" room.

© Cengage Learning

Figure 5.15 If an experimenter hides a small toy in a small room and asks a child to find a larger toy "in the same place" in the larger room, most 2½-year-olds search haphazardly **(a)**. However, the same children know where to look if the experimenter says this is the same room as before, but a machine has expanded it **(b)**.

Once again, the results depend on how we ask the question. As before, a psychologist hides a toy in the small room while the child watches. Then the psychologist shows the child a "machine that can make things bigger." The psychologist aims a beam from the machine at the room and takes the child out of the way. They hear some chunkata-chunkata sounds, and then the psychologist shows the full-size "blown-up" room and asks the child to find the hidden toy. Even 2½-year-olds go immediately to the correct location (DeLoache, Miller, & Rosengren, 1997; Figure 5.15b). (Incidentally, the children had no doubt that the machine had expanded the room. Many continued to believe it even after the psychologist explained what happened!)

Developing the Concept of Conservation

According to Piaget, preoperational children lack the concept of conservation. They fail to *understand that objects conserve such properties as number, length, volume, area, and mass after changes in the shape or arrangement of the objects.* They cannot perform the mental operations necessary to understand the transformations. Table 5.2 shows typical conservation tasks. For example, if we show two equal glasses with the same amount of water and then pour the contents of one glass into a third glass that is taller and thinner, preoperational children say that the third glass contains more water (Figure 5.16).

I once thought perhaps the phrasing of the questions tricks children into saying something they do not believe. If you have the same doubts, find a 6-year-old child and try it yourself with your own wording. Here's my experience: Once when I was discussing Piaget in my introductory psychology class, I invited my son Sam, then 5½ years old, to take part in a class demonstration. I started with two glasses of water, which he agreed contained equal amounts of water. Then I poured the water from one glass into a wider glass, lowering the water level. When I asked which glass contained more water, Sam confidently pointed to the tall, thin one. After class he complained, "Daddy, why did you ask me such an easy question? Everyone could see that there was more water in that glass! You should have asked me something harder to show how smart I am!" The following year, I brought Sam, now 6½ years old, to class for the same demonstration. I poured the water from one of the tall glasses into a wider one and asked him which glass contained more water. He looked and paused. His face turned red. Finally, he whispered, "Daddy, I don't know!" After class he complained, "Why did you ask me such a hard question? I'm never coming back to any of your classes again!" The question that used to be embarrassingly easy had become embarrassingly difficult.

Table 5.2 Typical Tasks Used to Measure Conservation

Conservation of number
Preoperational children say that these two rows contain the same number of pennies.

Preoperational children say that the second row has more pennies.

Conservation of volume
Preoperational children say that the two same-size containers have the same amount of water.

250 cc   250 cc

Preoperational children say that the taller, thinner container has more water.

250 cc   250 cc

Conservation of mass
Preoperational children say that the two same-size balls of clay have the same amount of clay.
Preoperational children say that a squashed ball of clay contains a different amount of clay than the same-size round ball of clay.

© Cengage Learning

Figure 5.16 Preoperational children don't understand that the volume of water remains constant despite changes in its appearance. During the transition to concrete operations, a child finds conservation tasks difficult and confusing.

The next year, when he was 7½, I tried again (at home). This time he answered confidently, "Both glasses have the same amount of water, of course. Why? Is this some sort of trick question?"

Piaget's Stages of Concrete Operations and Formal Operations

At about age 7, children enter the stage of concrete operations and begin to understand the conservation of physical properties. The transition is gradual, however. A 6-year-old may understand that squashing a ball of clay does not change its weight but still think that squashing it changes how much water it displaces when dropped into a glass.

According to Piaget, during the stage of concrete operations, *children perform mental operations on concrete objects but still have trouble with abstract or hypothetical ideas.* For example, ask this question: "How could you move a mountain of whipped cream from one side of the city to the other?" Older children enjoy devising imaginative answers, but children in the concrete operations stage complain that the question is silly.

Or ask, "If you could have a third eye anywhere on your body, where would you put it?" Children in this stage generally respond immediately that they would put it right between the other two, on their foreheads. Older children suggest more imaginative ideas such as on the back of their head, in the stomach (so they could watch food digesting), or on the tip of a finger (so they could peek around corners).

Finally, in Piaget's stage of formal operations, adolescents develop *logical, deductive reasoning and systematic planning.* According to Piaget, children reach the stage of formal operations at about age 11. Later researchers found that many people reach this stage later or not at all. Thinking with formal operations demonstrates planning. For example, we set up five bottles of clear liquid and explain that it is possible to mix some combination to produce a yellow liquid. The task is to find that combination. Children in the concrete operations stage plunge right in with no plan. They try combining bottles A and B, then C and D, then perhaps A, C, and E. Soon they have forgotten which combinations they've already tried. Adolescents in the formal operations stage approach the problem more systematically. They may first try all the two-bottle combinations: AB, AC, AD, AE, BC, and so forth. If those fail, they try three-bottle combinations: ABC, ABD, ABE, ACD, and so on. By trying every possible combination only once, they are sure to succeed. Table 5.3 summarizes Piaget's four stages.

Are Piaget's Stages Distinct?

Piaget regarded the four stages of intellectual development as distinct. He believed a transition from one stage to the next required a major reorganization of thinking, like a caterpillar metamorphosing into a chrysalis and a chrysalis metamorphosing into a butterfly. That is, intellectual growth has periods of revolutionary reorganization.

Later research casts doubt on this conclusion. If it were true, then a child in a given stage of development—say, the preoperational stage—should perform consistently at that level. In fact, children fluctuate as a task is made more or less difficult. For example, consider the conservation-of-number task, in which an investigator presents two rows of

Table 5.3 Summary of Piaget's Stages of Cognitive Development

Stage and Approximate Age	Achievements and Activities	Limitations
Sensorimotor (birth to 1½ years)	Reacts to sensory stimuli through reflexes and other responses	Little use of language; seems not to understand object permanence in the early part of this stage
Preoperational (1½ to 7 years)	Develops language; can represent objects mentally by words and other symbols; can respond to objects that are remembered but not present	Lacks operations (reversible mental processes); lacks concept of conservation; focuses on one property at a time (such as length or width), not on both at once; still has trouble distinguishing appearance from reality
Concrete operations (7 to 11 years)	Understands conservation of mass, number, and volume; can reason logically with regard to concrete objects that can be seen or touched	Has trouble reasoning about abstract concepts and hypothetical situations
Formal operations (11 years onward)	Can reason logically about abstract and hypothetical concepts; develops strategies; plans actions in advance	None beyond the occasional irrationalities of all human thought

© Cengage Learning

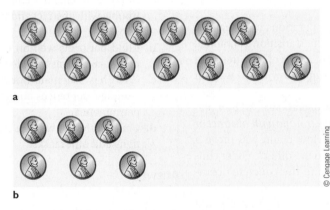

Figure 5.17 (a) With the standard conservation-of-number task, preoperational children answer that the spread-out row has more items. (b) With a simplified task, the same children say that both rows have the same number of items.

seven or more objects, spreads out one row, and asks which row has more. Preoperational children reply that the spread-out row has more. However, when Rochel Gelman (1982) presented two rows of only three objects each (Figure 5.17) and then spread out one of the rows, even 3- and 4-year-old children usually answered that the rows had the same number of items.

Whereas Piaget believed children made distinct jumps from one stage to another, most psychologists today see development as gradual and continuous (Courage & Howe, 2002). That is, the difference between older children and younger children is not so

much a matter of gaining a new ability. It is a matter of using their abilities in more and more situations.

Differing Views: Piaget and Vygotsky

One implication of Piaget's view is that children must discover certain concepts, such as the concept of conservation, mainly on their own. Teaching a concept means directing children's attention to the key aspects and letting them discover the concept. In contrast, Russian psychologist Lev Vygotsky (1978) argued that educators should not wait for children to rediscover the principles of physics and mathematics. Indeed, the value of language is that it lets us profit from the experience of previous generations.

Vygotsky certainly did not mean that adults should ignore a child's developmental level. Rather, every child has a zone of proximal development, *the distance between what a child can do alone and what is possible with help.* Instruction should remain within that zone. For example, one should not try to teach a 4-year-old the concept of conservation of volume. However, a 6-year-old who does not yet understand the concept might learn it with help and guidance. Similarly, children improve their recall of lists or stories if adults help them understand and organize the information (Larkina, Güler, Kleinknecht, & Bauer, 2008). Vygotsky compared this help to *scaffolding,* the temporary supports that builders use during construction: After a building is complete, the scaffolding is removed. Good advice for educators is to be sensitive to a child's zone of proximal development and pursue how much further they can push a child.

concept check

9. What would Piaget and Vygotsky think about the feasibility of teaching the concept of conservation?

Answer

9. Piaget recommended waiting for a child to discover the concept by himself or herself. For Vygotsky, the answer depends on the child's zone of proximal development. An adult can help a child at the right age.

The zone of proximal development is the gap between what a child does alone and what the child can do with help.

How Grown Up Are We?

Both Piaget and Vygotsky implied that we start with infant cognition and eventually attain adult thinking, which we practice from then on. Are they right, or do we sometimes slip into childish ways of thought?

Consider egocentric thinking. Young children seem to assume that whatever they know or understand, other people will know or understand also. Sometimes adults make the same mistake. Suppose you say, "The daughter of the man and the woman arrived." Did one person arrive (who is the daughter of the man and the woman) or two people (the man's daughter and some other woman)? You know what you meant, but you might overestimate how well other people understand you (Keysar & Henly, 2002).

Another example: According to Piaget, after about age 7, we all understand conservation of number, volume, and so forth. If we show two equally tall, thin containers of water and pour the water from one of them into a wider container, older children and adults confidently say that the two containers have equal amounts of water. However, let's test in a different way: We give people a tall, thin glass or a short, wide glass and invite them to add as much juice as they want. Adults as well as children usually put more juice into the short, wide glass, while thinking that they are getting less juice than usual. Even professional bartenders generally pour more liquor into a short, wide glass than into a tall, thin one (Wansink & van Ittersum, 2003). Evidently, even adults don't fully understand conservation of volume if they are tested in this way. In short, as we grow older, we suppress our childlike ways of thinking, but we don't lose them completely. We still have a child's mind hidden inside us.

concept check

10. How could you get someone to pour you a larger than average drink?

Answer

10. Ask to have the drink in a short, wide glass.

Understanding Children

You were once a small child, but you probably don't remember the experience clearly. Jean Piaget called attention to the ways in which children differ from adults. They are not just slower or less well informed; they process information differently. Everything that we do develops over age. But as you can see, it takes much work to pin down exactly what infants and small children understand, and what they misunderstand.

Furthermore, the changes are gradual and incomplete. Even adults revert to childlike thinking at times. Development is not a matter of suddenly gaining cognitive skills. It is a matter of applying skills more consistently and under a wider variety of conditions.

Summary

- *Cross-sectional and longitudinal studies.* Cross-sectional studies examine people of different ages at the same time. Longitudinal studies monitor a group of people as they grow older. A sequential design combines both methods. (page 147)
- *Cohort effects.* Many differences between young people and old people are not due to age but to the era in which they grew up. (page 149)
- *Prenatal development.* The brain begins to mature long before birth. Exposure to drugs such as alcohol decreases brain activity and releases neurons' self-destruct programs. Some people manage to do well in life despite unpromising circumstances. (page 150)
- *Inferring infant capacities.* We easily underestimate newborns' capacities because they have so little control over their muscles. Careful testing demonstrates greater abilities than we might have supposed. (page 151)
- *Infant vision and hearing.* Newborns stare at some visual patterns longer than others. They habituate to a repeated sound but dishabituate to a slightly different sound, indicating that they hear a difference. (page 151)
- *Infant memory.* Newborns suck more vigorously to turn on a recording of their own mother's voice than some other woman's voice, indicating that they recognize the sound of the mother's voice. Infants just 2 months old learn to kick and move a mobile, and they remember how to do it several days later. (page 153)
- *Piaget's view of children's thinking.* According to Jean Piaget, children's thought differs qualitatively from adults' thought. He believed children grow intellectually through accommodation and assimilation. (page 154)
- *Piaget's stages of development.* Children in the sensorimotor stage respond to what they see, hear, or feel at the moment. In the preoperational stage, they lack reversible operations. In the concrete operations stage, children reason about concrete problems but not abstractions. Adults and older children are in the formal operations stage, in which they plan strategies and deal with hypothetical or abstract questions. (page 154)
- *Egocentric thinking.* Young children often fail to understand other people's point of view. (page 156)
- *Theory of mind.* Children gradually develop their ability to assess other people's knowledge and beliefs, including false beliefs. (page 158)
- *Appearance and reality.* Young children sometimes seem not to distinguish between appearance and reality. However, with a simpler task, they do distinguish. Children may show a concept under some conditions and not others. (page 159)
- *Vygotsky.* According to Lev Vygotsky, children must learn new abilities from adults or older children, but only within their zone of proximal development. (page 162)
- *Adults.* Adults revert to childlike reasoning in certain situations. (page 163)

Key Terms

accommodation (page 154)

assimilation (page 154)

cohort (page 149)

conservation (page 160)

cross-sectional study (page 147)

dishabituation (page 152)

egocentric (page 156)

equilibration (page 154)

fetal alcohol syndrome (page 150)

fetus (page 150)

habituation (page 152)

longitudinal study (page 148)

object permanence (page 154)

operation (page 156)

preoperational stage (page 156)

schema (pl. schemata) (page 154)

selective attrition (page 148)

sensorimotor stage (page 154)

sequential design (page 148)

stage of concrete operations (page 161)

stage of formal operations (page 161)

theory of mind (page 158)

zone of proximal development (page 162)

zygote (page 150)

Social and Emotional Development

- How does our social and emotional behavior change as we grow older?

You are a contestant on a new TV game show, *What's My Worry?* Behind the curtain is someone you can't see, who has an overriding concern. You are to identify that concern by questioning a psychologist who knows this person well, asking only questions that can be answered with a single word or phrase. Here's the catch: The more questions you ask, the smaller the prize. If you guess correctly after the first question, you win a million dollars. After two questions, you win half a million and so on. Your best strategy is to ask as few questions as possible and then make an educated guess.

What would your first question be? A good one would be: "How old is this person?" The worries of teenagers differ from those of 20-year-olds, which differ from those of older adults. Each age has its own concerns, opportunities, and pleasures.

Erik Erikson emphasized that each age has special conflicts.

Erikson's Description of Human Development

Erik Erikson divided the human life span into eight periods that he called ages or stages. At each stage, he said, people have specific tasks to master, and each stage generates its own social and emotional conflicts. Table 5.4 summarizes Erikson's stages.

According to Erikson, failure to master the task of any stage generally leads to unfortunate consequences that carry over to later stages. For example, an infant deals with basic trust versus mistrust. An infant with a supportive environment forms strong attachments that positively influence future relationships with other people (Erikson, 1963). A mistreated infant fails to form a trusting

Table 5.4 Erikson's Stages of Human Development

Stages	Main Conflict	Typical Question
Infant	Basic trust versus mistrust	Is my social world predictable and supportive?
Toddler (ages 1–3)	Autonomy versus shame and doubt	Can I do things by myself or must I always rely on others?
Preschool child (ages 3–6)	Initiative versus guilt	Am I good or bad?
Preadolescent (ages 6–12)	Industry versus inferiority	Am I successful or worthless?
Adolescent (early teens)	Identity versus role confusion	Who am I?
Young adult (late teens and early 20s)	Intimacy versus isolation	Shall I share my life with another person or live alone?
Middle adult (late 20s to retirement)	Generativity versus stagnation	Will I succeed in my life, both as a parent and as a worker?
Older adult (after retirement)	Ego integrity versus despair	Have I lived a full life or have I failed?

© Cengage Learning

relationship and has trouble developing close ties with people later. We consider some relevant research later in this module.

In adolescence, the key issue is identity. Most adolescents in Western societies consider many options of how they will spend the rest of their lives. They entertain alternative identities and consider many possible futures.

According to Erikson, the key decision of young adulthood is intimacy or isolation—that is, sharing your life with someone else or living alone. The quality of that relationship, if any, has enormous impact on the rest of one's life.

If you live a full life span, you will spend about half your life in middle adulthood, where the issue is generativity (producing something important, e.g., children or work) versus stagnation (not producing). If all goes well, you take pride in your success. If not, then your difficulties and disappointments continue into old age.

You might describe the main concerns of certain ages differently from what Erikson said. Nevertheless, two of his general points seem valid: Each stage has its own special difficulties, and an unsatisfactory resolution to the problems of one age produces extra difficulty in later life. Let's examine in more detail some of the major social and emotional issues of particular ages.

Infancy and Childhood

An important aspect of human life is attachment—*a feeling of closeness toward another person*. Attachments begin in infancy. John Bowlby (1973) proposed that infants who develop good attachments have a sense of security and safety, and those without strong attachments have trouble developing close relations later as well. Later research confirms this idea. A longitudinal study found that toddlers who received lower quality care developed into young adults who had trouble forming strong romantic attachments. They erupted into verbal hostility with their partners significantly more often than most other people do (Oriña et al., 2011).

Most research on attachment has measured it in the Strange Situation (usually capitalized), pioneered by Mary Ainsworth (1979). In this procedure, *a mother and her infant* (typically 12 to 18 months old) *come into a room with many toys. Then a stranger enters the room. The mother leaves and then returns. A few minutes later, both the stranger and the mother leave. Then the stranger returns, and finally, the mother returns.* Through a one-way mirror, a psychologist observes the infant's reactions to each coming and going. Observers classify infants' responses in the following categories:

- *Securely attached.* The infant uses the mother as a base of exploration, cooing at her, showing her toys, and making eye contact with her. The infant shows some distress when the mother leaves but cries only briefly if at all. When she returns, the infant goes to her with apparent delight, cuddles for a while, and then returns to the toys.
- *Anxious (or resistant).* Responses toward the mother fluctuate between happy and angry. The infant clings to the mother and cries profusely when she leaves, as if worried that she might not return. When she does return, the infant clings to her again but does not use her as a base to explore the toys. A child with an anxious attachment typically shows many fears, including a strong fear of strangers.
- *Avoidant.* While the mother is present, the infant does not stay near her and seldom interacts with her. The infant may or may not cry when she leaves and does not go to her when she returns.
- *Disorganized.* The infant seems not even to notice the mother or looks away while approaching her or covers his or her face or lies on the floor. The infant alternates between approach and avoidance and shows more fear than affection.

The prevalence of the various attachment styles differs from one country to another, but the secure pattern is usually the most common (Ainsworth, Blehar, Waters, & Wall, 1978). Of course, many children do not fit neatly into one category or another, and some who are classified as "secure" or "avoidant" are more secure or avoidant than others. Most children remain stable in their classification from one time to another (Moss, Cyr, Bureau, Tarabulsy, & Dubois-Comtois, 2005).

The Strange Situation also can be used to evaluate the relationship between child and father (Belsky, 1996), child and grandparent, or other relationships. As a rule, the quality of one relationship correlates with the quality of others. For example, most children who have a secure relationship with the mother also have a secure relationship with the father, and chances are the parents are happy with each other as well (Elicker, Englund, & Sroufe, 1992; Erel & Burman, 1995). Most infants who have a secure relationship with their parents at age 12 months continue to have a close relationship with them decades later (Waters, Merrick, Treboux, Crowell, & Albersheim, 2000). Those who show a secure attachment in infancy are more likely than others to form high-quality romantic attachments in adulthood (Roisman, Collins, Sroufe, & Egeland, 2005). They are quick to resolve conflicts with romantic partners and other people (Salvatore, Kuo, Steele, Simpson, & Collins, 2011).

Why do some children develop more secure attachments than others? One reason is that children differ genetically in their temperament—the *tendency to respond vigorously, nervously, or quietly to new experiences* (Bouchard, Lykken, McGue, Segal, & Tellegen, 1990; Matheny, 1989). Temperament is fairly consistent over the years for most people (Durbin, Hayden, Klein, & Olino, 2007). Those with a "difficult" temperament are frightened more easily than others from infancy through adulthood (Kagan, Reznick, & Snidman, 1988; Kagan & Snidman, 1991; Schwartz, Wright, Shin, Kagan, & Rauch, 2003).

Attachment style also relates strongly to how responsive the parents are to the infants' needs, including holding and touching. Gentle touch can be very reassuring (Hertenstein, 2002). Programs that teach parents to be more responsive produce increases in secure attachments (Bakermans-Kranenburg, van Ijzendoorn, & Juffer, 2003).

Patterns of attachment are largely the same across cultures, with a few apparent exceptions. However, what appears to be a difference in attachment sometimes reflects difficulties in measurement. In one study, Western psychologists observing Black children in South Africa found low consistency between measurements of attachment in one situation and another. When they enlisted local people as coinvestigators, the local observers, who understood the local customs, reported data with much greater consistency (Minde, Minde, & Vogel, 2006). One study reported an unusually high prevalence of "anxious attachment" among Japanese infants. However, Japanese mothers customarily stay with their babies almost constantly, including bathing with them and sleeping in the same bed. When the Japanese mothers were persuaded to leave their infants alone with a stranger, it was in many cases a new experience for the infant, who reacted with horror. The same reaction by a U.S. child would have a different meaning (Rothbaum, Weisz, Pott, Miyake, & Morelli, 2000).

Children learn social skills by interacting with brothers, sisters, and friends close to their own age.

concept check

11. If a child in the Strange Situation clings tightly to the mother and cries furiously when she leaves, which kind of attachment does the child have?

12. What attachment style is likely in a child with strong anxieties?

Answers

12. A child with strong anxieties would probably show an anxious (or resistant) attachment style, clinging to the mother and being distressed when she leaves.

11. In the United States, this pattern would indicate an anxious or insecure attachment. In Japan, however, it is an understandable reaction to a surprising experience.

Social Development in Childhood and Adolescence

Social development takes effort. Parents and teachers tell children to share their toys or share their cookies with another child, but before age 6 or 7, most children strongly resist. One notable exception occurs when children work together to obtain some reward. Then they share the reward equally without conflict (Warneken, Lohse, Melis, & Tomasello, 2011).

Social development becomes especially important during adolescence and *puberty*, the onset of sexual maturation. Adolescents begin spending more time with age-mates and less time with their parents. The status of adolescents varies among cultures. In most nontechnological societies, most teenagers are married and working. They move almost directly from childhood into adulthood. The same was true in Europe and America in the 1800s. In Western societies today, improved health and nutrition have resulted in earlier onset of puberty (Okasha, McCarron, McEwen, & Smith, 2001), but the economic situation encourages young people to stay in school and postpone marriage, family, and career. The result is a long period of physical maturity without adult status.

Adolescence is often described as a time of "storm and stress," although that description is inappropriate or exaggerated in most cases. Most adolescents report occasional periods of moodiness and conflict with their parents in early adolescence, but the conflicts decrease in later adolescence (Laursen, Coy, & Collins, 1998). It is reported that adolescents who receive sympathetic support and understanding experience less conflict with their parents (R. A. Lee, Su, & Yoshida, 2005). Of course, we need to ask what caused what. Did the sympathetic parents cause the adolescents to feel less conflict, or did calm, well-behaved adolescents bring out the best in their parents?

Adolescence is also a time of risk-taking behaviors, not only in humans but in other species, too (Spear, 2000). Adolescents are certainly aware of the dangers. If asked about the advisability of drunk driving, unprotected sex, and so forth, they describe the dangers as well as adults do. Why, then, don't they behave like adults? Well, most of the time they do, at least when they take time to consider their decisions. They make risky decisions when they decide quickly, especially under peer pressure (Luna, Padmanabhan, & O'Hearn, 2010).

In a study demonstrating peer pressure, researchers asked people to play the video game Chicken, in which they guide a car on the screen. When a traffic light turns yellow, a participant can earn extra points by getting through the light but at the risk of a game-ending crash if the light turns red before the car gets through the light. Adolescents are more likely than adults to race through yellow lights, and if several of their friends were watching, that tendency increases (Gardner & Steinberg, 2005).

Most adults dismiss risky options almost at once. Suppose you are asked questions like these:

Swimming with alligators: Good idea or bad idea?
Eating salads: Good idea or bad idea?
Setting your hair on fire: Good idea or bad idea?

Nearly all adolescents and adults make the same decisions, but adults decide more quickly. Adults' emotions scream, "No, of course I don't want to swim with alligators!" Adolescents think about it first (Reyna & Farley, 2006). In short, the problem is not that adolescents don't think about consequences. The problem,

(a) American teenagers are financially dependent on their parents but have the opportunity to spend much time in whatever way they choose. (b) In many nontechnological societies, teenagers are expected to do adult work and accept adult responsibilities.

when there is one, is that adolescents don't make good decisions automatically and habitually.

Identity Development

As Erikson pointed out, adolescence is a time of "finding yourself," determining "who am I?" or "who will I be?" It is when most people first construct a coherent "life story" of how they got to be the way they are (Habermas & Bluck, 2000).

An adolescent's *concern with decisions about the future and the quest for self-understanding* has been called an identity crisis. The term *crisis* implies more emotional turbulence than is typical. Identity development has two major elements: whether one is actively exploring the issue and whether one has made any decisions (Marcia, 1980). We can diagram the possibilities using the following grid:

	Has explored or is exploring the issues	**Has not explored the issues**
Decisions already made	Identity achievement	Identity foreclosure
Decisions not yet made	Identity moratorium	Identity diffusion

© Cengage Learning

Those who have not yet given any serious thought to making decisions and who have no clear sense of identity are said to have identity diffusion. They are not actively concerned with their identity at the moment. Identity diffusion is more common among people with low self-esteem and a hopeless, pessimistic attitude toward life (Phillips & Pittman, 2007). People in identity moratorium are *considering the issues but not yet making decisions*. They experiment with various possibilities and imagine themselves in different roles before making a choice. Researchers distinguish between two kinds of moratorium—simply delaying a decision and actively searching for a decision (Crocetti, Rubini, Luyckx, & Meeus, 2008).

Identity foreclosure is a state of *reaching firm decisions without much thought*. For example, a young man might be told that he is expected to go into the family business with his father, or a young woman might be told that she is expected to marry and raise children. Decrees of that sort were once common in North America and Europe, and they are still common in other societies today. In some societies it is still common for parents to choose their children's marriage partners. Someone living in such circumstances has little reason to explore alternative possibilities.

Finally, identity achievement is *the outcome of having explored various possible identities and then making one's own decisions*. Identity achievement does not come all at once. For example, you might decide about your career but not about marriage. You might also reach identity achievement and then rethink a decision years later.

The "Personal Fable" of Teenagers

Answer the following items true or false:

- Other people may fail to realize their life ambitions, but I will realize mine.
- I understand love and sex in a way that my parents never did.
- Tragedy may strike other people but probably not me.
- Almost everyone notices how I look and how I dress.

According to David Elkind (1984), teenagers are particularly likely to harbor such beliefs. Taken

According to David Elkind, one reason for risky behavior is the "personal fable," which includes the secret belief that "nothing bad can happen to me."

together, he calls them the "personal fable," the conviction that "I am special—what is true for everyone else is not true for me." Up to a point, this fable supports an optimistic outlook on life, but it becomes dangerous if it leads people to take foolish risks.

This attitude is hardly unique to teenagers, however. Most middle-aged adults regard themselves as more likely than other people to succeed on the job and as less likely than average to have a serious illness (Quadrel, Fischhoff, & Davis, 1993). They also overestimate their own chances of winning a lottery, especially if they get to choose their own lottery ticket (Langer, 1975). That is, few people fully outgrow the personal fable.

Adulthood

From early adulthood until retirement, the main concern of most adults is, as Erikson noted, "What will I achieve and contribute to society and my family? Will I be successful?"

Adulthood extends from one's first full-time job until retirement. We lump so many years together because it seems that little is changing. During your childhood and adolescence, you grew taller each year. During adulthood, the changes in your appearance are slow and subtle. From infancy until early adulthood, each new age brought new privileges, such as permission to stay out late, your first driver's license, the right to vote, and the opportunity to go to college. After early adulthood, one year blends into the next. Children and teenagers know exactly how old they are, but adults sometimes have to

think about it. Important changes do occur during adulthood, but most of them are self-initiated, such as getting married, having children, changing jobs, or moving to a new location (Rönkä, Oravala, & Pulkkinen, 2003).

Daniel Levinson (1986) describes adult development in terms of a series of overlapping eras. After the transition into adulthood at about age 20, give or take a couple of years, comes early adulthood, which lasts until about age 40. During early adulthood, people make big decisions about career, marriage, and having children. Once people have chosen a career, they usually stay with it or something closely related (Low, Yoon, Roberts, & Rounds, 2005). During early adulthood, people devote maximum energy to pursuing their goals. However, buying a house and raising a family on a young person's salary are difficult and stressful.

During middle adulthood, extending from about age 40 to 65, physical strength and health begin to decline but probably not enough to interfere with an active personal and professional life. At this point, people have already achieved success at work or have come to accept whatever status they have. Many people become more accepting of themselves and others at this time and feel less tyrannized by the stress of the job. In most cases, they also face less day-to-day stress of caring for small children.

In middle adulthood, according to Levinson (1986), people go through a midlife transition, *a period of reassessing goals, setting new ones, and preparing for the rest of life*. This transition often occurs in response to a divorce, illness, death in the family, a career change, or some other event that causes the person to question past decisions and current goals (Wethington, Kessler, & Pixley, 2004). Just as the adolescent identity crisis is a bigger issue in cultures that offer many choices, the same is true for the midlife transition. If you lived in a society that offered no choices, you would not worry about the paths not taken! In Western society, however, you enter adulthood with high hopes. You hope to earn an advanced degree, excel at an outstanding job, marry a wonderful person, have marvelous children, become a leader in your community, run for political office, write a great novel, compose great music, travel the world . . . You know you are not working on all of your goals right now, but you tell yourself, "I'll do it later." As you grow older, you realize that you are running out of "later." Some of your early ambitions have become unrealistic, and others will be, too, if you don't start on them soon.

People deal with their midlife transitions in many ways. Most of them abandon unrealistic goals and set new goals consistent with the direction their lives have taken. Others decide that they have been ignoring dreams that they are not willing to abandon. They go back to school, set up a new business, or try something else they have always wanted to do. The least satisfactory outcome is to decide, "I can't abandon my dreams, but I can't do anything about them either. I can't take the risk of changing my life, even though I am dissatisfied with it." People with that attitude become discouraged and depressed.

The advice is clear: To increase your chances of feeling good in middle age and beyond, make good decisions when you are young. If you care about something, don't wait for a midlife transition. Get started on it now.

concept check

13. How does a midlife transition resemble an adolescent identity crisis?

Answer

13. In both cases, people examine their lives, goals, and possible directions for the future.

Old Age

Finally, people reach late adulthood, beginning around age 65. According to Erikson, those who feel satisfied with their lives experience "ego integrity," and those who are not satisfied feel "despair." How you feel in old age depends on what happened long before.

People age in different ways. Some deteriorate in intellect, coordination, and ability to care for themselves, while others remain alert and active. Memory remains reasonably intact among most healthy, active older people. Programs that increase older people's physical exercise improve their memory and cognition (Colombe & Kramer, 2003; Mattson & Magnus, 2006).

Memory in old age differs across situations. Everyone remembers interesting material better than something that seems unimportant, but the difference is larger for older people, who tend to focus their attention and resources more narrowly on topics likely to bring them pleasure or topics of practical importance to them. Thus, they overlook details that a younger person would remember. When older people can't remember a detail, they often fill in the gap with an educated guess of what "must have happened" (Hess, 2005). As you will see in the memory chapter, all people fill in their memory gaps with inferences. The difference is that older people face memory gaps more frequently.

As we shall see in chapter 12 (emotion), several kinds of evidence indicate that healthy older people are, on average, happier and more satisfied with life than middle-age or younger people are. That result may seem surprising. However, young people face many pressures from work and raising children, whereas older people have more leisure. Furthermore, older people deliberately focus their attention on family, friends, and other events that bring them pleasure (Carstensen, Mikels, & Mather, 2006).

Your satisfaction in old age will depend largely on how you live while younger. Some older people say, "I hope to live many more years, but even if I don't, I have lived my life well. I did everything that I really cared about." Others say, "I wanted to do so much that I never did." Feeling dignity in old age also depends on how people's families, communities, and societies treat them. Some cultures, such as Korea, observe a special ceremony to celebrate a person's retirement or 70th birthday (Damron-Rodriguez, 1991). African American and Native American families traditionally honor their elders, giving them a position of status in the family and calling on them for advice. Japanese families follow a similar tradition, at least publicly (Koyano, 1991).

Retirement is another transition, analogous to an adolescent identity crisis or a midlife transition. Retirement decreases stress, but also brings a sense of loss to those whose lives had focused on their work (Kim & Moen, 2001). Loss of control is a serious issue when health begins to fail. Consider someone who spent half a century running a business and now lives in a nursing home where staff members make all the decisions. Leaving even a few of the choices and responsibilities to the residents improves their self-respect, health, alertness, and memory (Rodin, 1986; Rowe & Kahn, 1987).

In Tibet and many other cultures, children are taught to treat old people with respect and honor.

The Psychology of Facing Death

A man who has not found something he is willing to die for is not fit to live.
—Martin Luther King Jr. (1964)

This is perhaps the greatest lesson we learned from our patients: LIVE, so you do not have to look back and say, "God, how I have wasted my life!"
—Elisabeth Kübler Ross (1975, p. xix)

The worst thing about death is the fact that when a man is dead it's impossible any longer to undo the harm you have done him, or to do the good you haven't done him. They say: live in such a way as to be always ready to die. I would say: live in such a way that anyone can die without you having anything to regret.
—Leo Tolstoy (1865/1978, p. 192)

Have you ever heard the advice, "Live each day as if it were going to be your last"? The point is to appreciate every moment, but the advice would be terrible if you took it seriously. If you really believed you would die today, you wouldn't plan for the future. You wouldn't save money or worry about the long-term health consequences of your actions. You probably wouldn't study this textbook.

Just thinking about the fact of eventual death evokes distress. To go on with life effectively, we try to shield ourselves from thinking too much about dying. According to terror-management theory, *we cope with our fear of death by avoiding thoughts about death and by affirming a worldview that provides self-esteem, hope, and value in life* (Pyszczynski, Greenberg, & Solomon, 2000). When something reminds you of your mortality, you do whatever you can to reduce your anxiety. You reassure yourself that you still have many years to live. "My health is good, I don't smoke, I don't drink too much, and I'm not overweight." If that isn't true, you tell yourself that you plan to quit smoking, you are going to cut down on your drinking, and any day now you are going to start losing weight. You also think about the good job you have (or hope to have), the high salary you earn (or expect to earn), and the exciting things you will do during the rest of your life (Kasser & Sheldon, 2000).

Still, even excellent health merely postpones death, so a reminder of death redoubles your efforts to defend a belief that life is important. You reaffirm your religious beliefs, your patriotism, or other views that help you find meaning in life (Greenberg et al., 2003). You become more dutiful than usual in upholding the customs of your society (Gailliot, Stillman, Schmeichel, Maner, & Plant, 2008). You also take pride in how you have contributed to your family, your profession, or something else that will continue after you are gone (Pyszczynski et al., 2000). How people react to awareness of death varies somewhat as a function of culture. In Western cultures, people primed to think about death distance themselves from victims of violence or other misfortune, saying, "I'm not like that, so it won't happen to me." In Eastern cultures, people become more likely to identify with others, even the unfortunate, saying, "the welfare of the collective society is what matters" (Ma-Kellams & Blascovich, 2011).

Advances in modern medicine raise new ethical issues with regard to dying. We can now keep people alive after their physical and mental capacities have badly deteriorated. Should we? If someone is bedridden and in pain, with little hope of recovery, is it acceptable to help the person hasten death? A growing number of people have to face these difficult decisions for themselves and family members.

module 5.2 >

In Closing

Social and Emotional Issues Through the Life Span

Let's close by reemphasizing a key point of Erik Erikson's theory: Each age or stage builds on the previous ones. The quality of your early attachments to parents and others correlates with your ability to form close, trusting relationships later. How well you handle the identity issues of adolescence affects your adult life. Your productivity as an adult determines how satisfied you will feel in old age. Life is a continuum, and the choices you make at any age link with those you make before and after.

Summary

- *Erikson's view of development.* Erik Erikson described the human life span as a series of eight ages or stages, each with its own social and emotional conflicts. (page 166)
- *Infant attachment.* Infants develop attachments to significant people in their lives, as measured in the Strange Situation. Those with strong early attachments are likely to develop good social and romantic attachments as adults. (page 167)
- *Adolescent identity crisis.* Adolescents deal with the question "Who am I?" (page 169)

- *Adults' concerns.* A major concern of adults is productivity in family and career. Many adults undergo a midlife transition when they reevaluate their goals. (page 170)
- *Old age.* Dignity and independence are key concerns of old age. (page 171)
- *Facing death.* People at all ages face the anxieties associated with the inevitability of death. A reminder of death influences people to defend their worldviews. (page 171)

Key Terms

attachment (page 167)
identity achievement (page 169)
identity crisis (page 169)
identity diffusion (page 169)
identity foreclosure (page 169)

identity moratorium (page 169)
midlife transition (page 170)
Strange Situation (page 167)
temperament (page 167)
terror-management theory (page 172)

module 5.3

Diversity: Gender, Culture, and Family

> • What factors influence development of personality and social behavior?

Suppose we changed you from male to female or female to male. Or suppose we changed your ethnicity or culture. Perhaps we trade you to a different family. How would you be different? With such drastic changes, it is not clear that it would still be *you*! Gender, culture, and family are integral parts of anyone's development and identity.

Gender Influences

Males and females differ biologically in many ways that influence behavior. Some brain areas are proportionately larger in men and other areas proportionately larger in women (Cahill, 2006). Certain genes are more active in male brains, and other genes are more active in female brains, on average (Reinius et al., 2008).

How do men and women differ behaviorally? In most regards the differences are small to negligible, but a few differences are reasonably consistent. Men, being generally larger and stronger, throw harder and get into fights more often (Hyde, 2005). On average, boys are more active, whereas girls have better self-control (Else-Quest, Hyde, Goldsmith, & Van Hulle, 2006). Men are more likely to help a stranger change a flat tire, but women are more likely to provide long-term nurturing support (Eagly & Crowley, 1986). The more pairs of shoes you own, the higher is the probability that you are female. Men and women tend to carry books in different ways, as shown in Figure 5.18.

On average, females are better than males at detecting emotional signals (Chen & Haviland-Jones, 2000; Hall & Matsumoto, 2004). People have long noted how often men misinterpret a woman's smile, mistaking friendliness for sexual interest. Psychologists used to interpret this trend as wishful thinking until they discovered that the opposite is also true: When a woman is trying to signal sexual interest, many men misinterpret her expression as mere friendliness (Farris, Treat, Viken, & McFall, 2008). Evidently, men are just less accurate at recognizing emotional expressions.

When giving directions, men are more likely to use directions and distances—such as "go four blocks east . . ."—whereas women are more likely to use landmarks—such as "go until you see the library . . ." (Saucier et al., 2002). Figure 5.19 compares men's and women's ways of giving directions (Rahman, Andersson, & Govier, 2005). Similarly, in monkeys, mice, and several other species, males perform better than females in mazes without landmarks, whereas females re-

member the landmarks better (C. M. Jones, Braithwaite, & Healy, 2003; C. L. Williams, Barnett, & Meck, 1990). However, if forced to rely on either landmarks or distances, both men and women get along fine (Spelke, 2005).

Another difference: Women apologize more than men do. Why? In one study, men and women kept a diary of how often they did something for which they should have apologized, how often they did apologize, how often they thought someone else should have apologized, and how often that person did. Men reported fewer occasions when they should apologize, and fewer occasions when someone else should apologize (Schumann & Ross, 2010). That is,

© Blend Images / Getty Images

Figure 5.18 Men usually carry books and similar objects at their sides. Women beyond the age of puberty usually carry them at their chest.

Men often fail to read other people's emotions.
(© *ZITS PARTNERSHIP*, King Features Syndicate. Reprinted by permission.)

men often shrug something off as unimportant, when women expect to say or hear, "I'm sorry." You see how this difference can be a source of friction between men and women. However, this is the kind of behavior that is likely to vary among cultures, and we should await cross-cultural studies before drawing a broad conclusion. (P.S. A great quote from a man: "If I have done anything for which I should apologize, I am ready to be forgiven.")

Okay, so men and women differ in miscellaneous behavioral ways. To what extent do males and females differ in intellectual abilities? So far as we can tell, not at all (Halpern et al., 2007; Hyde, 2005; Levine, Vasilyeva, Lourenco, Newcombe, & Huttenlocher, 2005; Spelke, 2005). Most people believe that men are better in mathematics. Males outperform females in math in countries where men have greater economic and political status than women. In countries where men and women have nearly equal status, the difference in average math performance disappears (Guiso, Monte, Sapienza, & Zingales, 2008). In the United States, on average, females do as well as or better than males on standardized math test scores and grades in nearly all math courses from elementary school through

college (Hyde, Lindberg, Linn, Ellis, & Williams, 2008; Spelke, 2005).

An exception to this rule is that males do better on geometrical tasks, such as those in Figure 5.20. With much simpler tasks, we see a hint of a male advantage even among infants (Moore & Johnson, 2008; Quinn & Liben, 2008). However, these results do not necessarily indicate a difference in inborn ability. Boys usually spend more time on activities that require attention to angles and directions, providing the opportunity to learn relevant skills. Young women who spent 10 hours playing action video games significantly narrowed the male–female gap on visuospatial tasks (Feng, Spence, & Pratt, 2007). Thus, it appears that men and women differ more in interests than in abilities.

Vastly more men than women become grand masters in chess. However, a study found that boys and girls start at an equal level in chess and progress at equal rates. The main reason more men than women reached the highest level was that vastly more boys than girls *started* playing chess (Chabris & Glickman, 2006).

Males and females do show differences in interests, from childhood through adulthood. The way

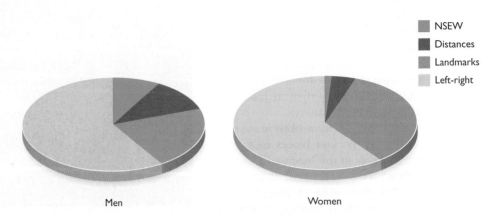

Figure 5.19 When giving directions, men refer to distances and north-south-east-west more often than women do. Women describe more landmarks. (Based on data of Rahman, Andersson, & Govier, 2005.)

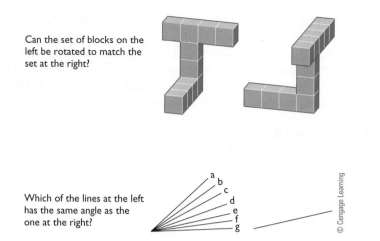

Can the set of blocks on the left be rotated to match the set at the right?

Which of the lines at the left has the same angle as the one at the right?

a
b
c
d
e
f
g

© Cengage Learning

Figure 5.20 On average, men perform slightly better than women on visual-spatial tasks like these. (The answers are given below.)

Answer

No, the set on the left cannot be rotated to match the one on the right. For the second question, line e matches the model to its right.

people rear children certainly contributes to those differences. For example, children who watch a television commercial showing just boys playing with a particular toy say that this is a toy "just for boys" (Pike & Jennings, 2005). However, biological tendencies may contribute also. Male monkeys prefer to play with what people consider "boys' toys," such as a ball and a toy car, and female monkeys prefer to play with "girls' toys," such as a soft doll (Alexander & Hines, 2002; Hassett, Siebert, & Wallen, 2008). Among human infants 3–8 months old (too young to have much experience with toys), girls look more at dolls than at toy trucks, whereas boys look at both about equally (Alexander, Wilcox, & Woods, 2009).

More importantly, researchers have found that girls who were exposed to higher than average levels of the male hormone testosterone during prenatal development tend to play with boys' toys more than the average for other girls (Berenbaum, Duck, & Bryk, 2000; Nordenström, Servin, Bohlin, Larsson, & Wedell, 2002; Pasterski et al., 2005). (Some mothers produce more testosterone, and some of it enters the developing fetus.) Conversely, when pregnant women are exposed to chemicals that interfere with testosterone, their sons show less than average interest in boys' toys at ages 3 to 6 (Swan et al., 2010). These results suggest that males' and females' interests differ for biological as well as socially acquired reasons.

concept check

14. Describe a study showing a social or cultural influence on interest in boys' or girls' toys. Describe a study suggesting a biological influence.

Answer

14. Children who watch a commercial showing just boys playing with a toy assume the toy is just for boys. Levels of testosterone during a woman's pregnancy influence her children's later interest in boys' or girls' toys.

Sex Roles

People's behaviors depend partly on sex roles, *the different activities that society expects of males and females.* Sex roles sometimes constrain people's choices. For example, traditional sex roles discourage some women from pursuing interests or career opportunities that are considered too masculine. Sex roles can be a problem for men, too. In many cultures, young men are required to kill a large animal or withstand great pain to prove their manhood. In the United States, some men feel a need to get into fights or engage in other risky behaviors to prove their manhood (Vandello, Bosson, Cohen, Burnaford, & Weaver, 2008). Many men also feel it is "unmanly" to express intimate emotional feelings.

Biology influences a few aspects of sex roles: For example, only women can nurse babies, and men generally have an edge in physical strength. However, many sex roles are customs set by our society. Do you regard building a fire as mostly men's work or women's? What about basket weaving? Planting crops? Milking cows? The answers vary from one society to another (Wood & Eagly, 2002). Cultures also determine the relative status of men and women. Generally, if a culture lives in conditions that require hunting, fighting, or other use of physical strength, men have greater status than women. When food is abundant and enemies are few, men and women have more equal status.

Reasons Behind Gender Differences

Gender differences reflect several influences. Biological influences include the greater size and strength of males, on average, as well as the apparent influence of prenatal hormones on a child's later interests.

Social influences include the expectations that parents convey to their children. Even with 6- and 9-month-old infants, mothers talk to their daughters in a more conversational way and give more instructions to their sons (Clearfield & Nelson, 2006). At this age, the infants themselves are neither walking nor talking, so the difference demonstrates the mother's behavior, not her reaction to the infants' behavior.

In one fascinating study, researchers set up cameras and microphones to eavesdrop on families in a science museum. Boys and girls spent about equal time looking at each exhibit, and the parents spent about equal time telling boys and girls how to use each exhibit, but on average, the parents provided about three times as much scientific explanation to the boys as to the girls, regardless of how many questions the children themselves asked (Crowley, Callanen, Tenenbaum, & Allen, 2001).

Cultural and Ethnic Influences

Some behaviors are remarkably similar across cultures. Did you know that the average hug lasts 3 seconds? The duration is the same for people from all parts of the world (Nagy, 2011). In contrast, many other customs vary enormously across cultures. In Europe and North America, parents put their newborn in a crib, encouraging independence from the start. In Asia, infants sleep in the parents' bed. Europeans and Americans consider the Asian custom strange, and Asians consider the European/American custom cruel.

If you grew up in the United States or a similar country, you spent most of your playtime with other children close to your own age, including few if any of your relatives. If you grew up in parts of Africa or South America, you played in mixed-age groups that almost certainly included your brothers, sisters, and cousins (Rogoff, Morelli, & Chavajay, 2010).

When complaining about some product or service, would you express anger to try to get your way? In Europe or the United States, moderate expressions of anger are generally effective. In Asia, they usually backfire, unless the circumstances clearly and obviously justify the anger (Adam, Shirako, & Maddux, 2010). American business people or government leaders sometimes make the error of approaching their Asian counterparts with angry demands, when a gentler, politer approach would be more effective.

Describing the effects of culture is difficult and often prone to overgeneralizations. One popular generalization is that Western culture, such as the United States, Canada, and most of Europe, is "individualistic." People value independence, strive for individual achievements, and take pride in personal accomplishments. In "collectivist" cultures such as China, people strive for group advancement, emphasize dependence on one another, and take pride in their family's or group's accomplishments more than their own. This generalization is useful in some ways, but overstated (Brewer & Chen, 2007). In many ways, Americans care about group success as much as Chinese people do, and Chinese people often compete individually like Americans. We don't need to abandon the individualistic versus collectivist distinction, but we need to recognize its limitations.

Consider this example of the difficulty of interpreting a cultural difference: Suppose you fill out a questionnaire. As a reward, the interviewer offers you a choice of five pens. Four of them are the same color and one is different. Americans are more likely to pick the unusual color, whereas Japanese choose the common color. But why? The initial interpreta-

tion was that Japanese want to be the same as everyone else. Can you imagine another explanation? Another possibility is that the Japanese were being polite: "If I take the last pen of this color, then the next person, who might really like it, can't have it!" If researchers say, "all the others have already chosen and you are the last one to choose," then Japanese are as likely as Americans to choose the unusual color (Yamagishi, Hashimoto, & Schug, 2008).

Ethnic Minorities

Growing up as a member of an ethnic minority poses special issues. Achieving ethnic identity is comparable to the process adolescents go through in finding an individual identity. In most cases, minority-group members who achieve a strong, favorable ethnic identity have high self-esteem (Phinney, 1990). Many people enhance their group evaluation during adolescence and thereby solidify their self-esteem (French, Seidman, Allen, & Aber, 2006). However, the outcome depends on the status of one's group. In Miami, Florida, researchers found that Cuban Americans with a strong ethnic identification had high self-esteem, but Nicaraguan Americans with a strong ethnic identification had low self-esteem (Cislo, 2008). Cuban Americans dominate Miami politics and culture, so it is easy to see how ethnic identification would work differently for the Cuban and Nicaraguan Americans.

It is possible to identify with both one's own group and the nation as a whole, and some people maintain double identifications more strongly than others do (Gong, 2007). Muslim Americans faced a special problem in this regard after the terrorist attacks in September 2001: Suddenly, they became targets of hostility and prejudice, and many found it more difficult to feel both Muslim and American (Sirin & Fine, 2007).

Acculturation

Ethnic identity is especially salient for immigrants to a country. In addition to language problems, many immigrants face prejudices and questions about whether they have entered the country legally. They also have to deal with an unfamiliar culture. Immigrants, their children, and sometimes further generations experience biculturalism, *partial identification with two cultures*. For example, Mexican immigrants to the United States speak Spanish and follow Mexican customs at home but switch to the English language and U.S. customs in other places. In most cases, immigrants with this type of bicultural attachment are better adjusted than those who either reject the old ways completely or decline to participate in the surrounding society (Sam & Berry, 2010). Bicultural youth tend to have low rates of substance use, delinquency, and depression (Coatsworth, Moldonado-Molina, Pantin, & Szapocznik, 2005). One reason is that their parents maintain close supervision (Fuligni, 1998). Another reason is that by not feeling fully part of U.S. youth culture, bicultural adolescents are less subject to its peer pressures.

Just as people master a foreign language better if they start young, people who immigrate at a younger age tend to accept the new culture more readily (Cheung, Chudek, & Heine, 2011). People maintain some parts of their original culture longer than others. For example, most immigrants to the United States maintain their ethnic food preferences long after they have switched to American customs of dress and entertainment (Ying, Han, & Wong, 2008).

Many children immigrating to the United States report difficulty understanding U.S. culture, problems of not fitting in with others at school, and difficulties in school because of poor English (Romero & Roberts, 2003). An unfortunate side effect of this difficulty is that many try to prove they belong by imitating superficial aspects of American society. Asian American youth often make a point of publicly eating hamburgers or other typical American foods to show that they are "real Americans" (Guendelman, Cheryan, & Monin, 2011).

Many immigrants are bicultural, being familiar with two sets of customs. These immigrant children attend middle school in Michigan.

Many biracial people have achieved great success. Barack Obama is a prominent example.

At least to a small extent, nearly all of us learn to function in multiple subcultures. Unless you live in a small town where everyone has the same background, religion, and customs, you learn to adjust what you say and do in different settings and with different groups of people. The transitions are more noticeable and more intense for ethnic minorities.

Analogous to biculturalism is biracialism. A growing percentage of people in the United States have parents from different origins, such as African and European, European and Hispanic, or Asian and Native American. People of mixed ancestry are especially common in Hawaii, California, and Puerto Rico. Decades ago, psychologists believed that biracial children and adolescents were at a disadvantage, rejected by both groups. Today, however, most biracial people say they are pleased with their mixed background that enables them to see the best in all cultures and overcome prejudice. Most biracial youth say they feel reasonably well accepted by both groups. The one problem biracial youth often mention is how to label themselves. If a form asks for a racial/ethnic identity, they don't want to check just one identity because that would deny the other part of themselves (Shih & Sanchez, 2005). Many give one answer at one time and a different answer at a different time (Doyle & Kao, 2007). The U.S. Census form now permits people to indicate mixed ancestry.

concept check

15. In what way is biracialism similar to biculturalism?

Answer

15. A bicultural person identifies to some extent with two cultures. A biracial person identifies to some extent with two ethnic origins.

The Family

In early childhood, parents and other relatives are the most important people in a child's life. How do those early family experiences mold personality and social behavior?

Birth Order and Family Size

You have no doubt heard people say that firstborn children are more successful and ambitious than later-borns. Firstborns also rate themselves as more honest and conscientious (e.g., Paulhus, Trapnell, & Chen, 1999). On the other hand, later-born children are said to be more popular, more independent, less conforming, less neurotic, and possibly more creative.

Most of the studies supporting these generalizations used flawed research methods (Ernst & Angst, 1983; Schooler, 1972). A common way to do the research is this: Ask people to tell you their birth order and something else about themselves, such as their grade point average in school. Then measure the correlation between the measurements. Do you see a possible problem here?

The problem is that many firstborns come from families with only one child, whereas later-born children necessarily come from larger families. Many highly educated and ambitious parents have only one child and provide that child with many advantages. Therefore, what appears to be a difference between first- and later-born children could be a difference between small and large families (Rodgers, 2001).

A better method is to compare first- and second-born children in families with at least two children, first- and third-born children in families with at least three children, and so forth. Figure 5.21 shows the results of one study. The average IQ was higher in small families than in large families. However, within a family of a given size, birth order made little difference (Rodgers, Cleveland, van den Oord, & Rowe, 2000).

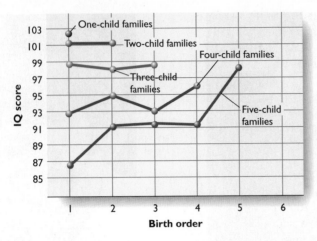

Figure 5.21 Children from small families tend to score higher on IQ tests than children from large families. However, within a family of a given size, birth order is not related to IQ. (Adapted from "Resolving the Debate Over Birth Order, Family Size, and Intelligence" by J. L. Rogers, *American Psychologist*, 55(6), 2000, 599-612. Copyright © 2000 by the American Psychological Association. Reprinted with permission.)

Many other studies also found that apparent differences between firstborn and later-born children are really differences between small and large families (Wichman, Rodgers, & MacCallum, 2006). However, a large Norwegian study found that firstborn children scored slightly higher on IQ tests than later-born children, even within the same family (Bjerkedal, Kristensen, Skjeret, & Brevik, 2007). Contrast the results in Figure 5.22 to those in Figure 5.21. Given this contradiction in results, the true relationship between birth order and IQ is still uncertain, as is the relation-

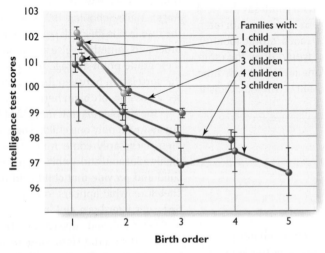

Figure 5.22 In a Norwegian study, children from small families scored higher than those from larger families. In addition, earlier-born children scored higher than later-born children, even when considering family size. (Modified from Figure 1 from Bjerkedal, T., Kristensen, P., Skjeret, G. A., & Brevik, J. I., "Intelligence test scores and birth order among young Norwegian men (conscripts) analyzed within and between families," *Intelligence* vol. 35 (pp. 503-514). Copyright © 2007 Elsevier. Reprinted with permission.)

ship between birth order and personality. However, these points are clear: First, the effect of birth order is small. Second, research must carefully separate the effects of birth order from those of family size.

16. Why is it improper to compare all the firstborns in your class to all the later-borns?

Answer

16. Many firstborns come from one-child families. Small families differ from large families in various ways.

Effects of Parenting Styles

If you have children of your own, will you be loving and kind or strict and distant? Will you give your children everything they want or make them work for rewards? Will you encourage their independence or enforce restrictions? Moreover, how much does your behavior matter?

Psychologists have done a great deal of research comparing parenting styles to the behavior and personality of the children. Much of this research is based on four parenting styles described by Diana Baumrind (1971):

Authoritative parents: These parents *set high standards and impose controls, but they are also warm and responsive to the child's communications.* They set limits but adjust them when appropriate. They encourage their children to strive toward their own goals.

Authoritarian parents: Like the authoritative parents, authoritarian parents set firm controls, but they tend to be *emotionally more distant from the child. They set rules without explaining the reasons behind them.*

Permissive parents: Permissive parents are *warm and loving but undemanding.*

Indifferent or uninvolved parents: These parents *spend little time with their children and do little more than provide them with food and shelter.*

Of course, not everyone fits neatly into one pattern or another, but most parents are reasonably consistent over time and from one child to another. For example, most parents who are permissive with one child are permissive with the others, too (Holden & Miller, 1999). The research has found small but reasonably consistent links between parenting style and children's behavior. For example, most children of authoritative parents are self-reliant, cooperative, and successful in school. Children of authoritarian parents tend to be law-abiding but distrustful and not very independent. Children of permissive parents are often socially irresponsible. Children of indifferent parents tend to be impulsive and undisciplined.

However, the "best" style of parenting depends on the child. Children with a somewhat fearful temperament respond well to mild discipline, developing a strong conscience. Children with a fearless temperament respond poorly to any kind of discipline and respond better to rewards (Kochanska, Aksan, & Joy, 2007). If you become a parent, use some trial and error to find what works best with your children rather than relying on what some authority says is the "right" way to rear children.

Furthermore, interpreting the results about parenting is not as easy as it may appear. For years, psychologists assumed that parental indifference *leads to* impulsive, out-of-control children. However, as Judith Rich Harris (1998) pointed out, other explanations are possible. Maybe impulsive, hard-to-control children cause their parents to withdraw into indifference. Or maybe the parents and children share genes that lead to uncooperative behaviors. Similarly, the kindly behaviors of authoritative parents could encourage well-mannered behaviors in their children, but it is also likely that children who are well behaved from the start elicit kindly, understanding behaviors in their parents.

A better approach to exploring parenting styles is to study adopted children, who are genetically unrelated to the parents rearing them. One study of adult twins who had been adopted by separate families found that the parenting style described by one twin correlated significantly with the parenting style described by the other twin, especially for monozygotic twins (Krueger, Markon, & Bouchard, 2003). That is, if one twin reported being reared by kindly, understanding adoptive parents, the other usually did also, even though they were reared in separate families. The twins' personalities had evidently affected their adopting parents, as well as how the twins perceived their environments.

If we examine long-term personality traits of adopted children and their adopting parents, the results surprise most people: The children's personalities correlate almost zero with the parents' personalities (Heath, Neale, Kessler, Eaves, & Kendler, 1992; Loehlin, 1992; Viken, Rose, Kaprio, & Koskenvuo, 1994). For this reason, Harris (1995, 1998) argued that parenting style has little influence on most aspects of personality. Much personality variation depends on genetic differences, and the rest of the variation, she argued, depends mostly on the influence of other children.

As you can imagine, not everyone happily accepted Harris's conclusion. Psychologists who had spent a career studying parenting styles were not pleased to be told that their results were inconclusive. Parents were not pleased to be told that they had little influence on their children's personalities. Harris (2000), however, chose her words carefully. She did not say that it makes no difference how you treat your children. For one thing, obviously, if you treat your children badly, they won't like you!

Also, parents control where the children live and therefore influence their choice of peers, and parents influence choices that most peers don't care about, such as religion and music lessons. Psychologists using improved research methods have shown real, though not huge, effects of parenting style (Collins, Maccoby, Steinberg, Hetherington, & Bornstein, 2000). The controversy has led to greater appreciation of the mutual influences of parents on their children and children on their parents (Kiff, Lengua, & Zalewski, 2011).

concept check

17. Why is a correlation between parents' behavior and children's behavior inconclusive concerning how parents influence their children? Why does a correlation between adoptive parents' behavior and that of their adopted children provide more useful information?

Answer

17. Children can resemble their parents' behavior because of either genetics or social influences. Adopted children do not necessarily resemble their adoptive parents genetically, so any similarity in behavior would reflect environmental influences. Of course, the question would remain as to whether the parents influenced the children or the children influenced the parents.

Parental Employment and Child Care

What is the normal way to rear infants and young children? The customs vary so widely across cultures and historical eras that "normal" has no clear meaning. In subsistence cultures, a mother returns to her tasks of gathering food and so forth shortly after giving birth, leaving her infant most of the day with other women and older children (McGurk, Caplan, Hennessy, & Moss, 1993). Within the first few months, the infant establishes strong attachments to several adults and children (Tronick, Morelli, & Ivey, 1992).

Still, many psychologists in Europe and North America maintained that healthy emotional development required an infant to establish a strong attachment to a single caregiver—ordinarily, the mother. When more and more families began placing infants in day care so that both parents could return to work shortly after their infant's birth, a

In many cultures, a mother leaves her infant for much of the day with friends, relatives, and other children.

Many children today are reared by a single parent or by gay parents. The research indicates that who rears the child has less influence than whether the caregivers are loving and dependable.

question arose about the psychological effects on those children.

Many studies compared children who stayed with their mothers and those who entered day care within their first year or two of life. The studies examined attachment (as measured by the Strange Situation or in other ways), adjustment and well-being, play with other children, social relations with adults, and intellectual development. The results were that most children develop satisfactorily if they receive adequate day care (Scarr, 1998). Later studies have confirmed that children in dual-income families do just as well academically as those with a parent at home (Goldberg, Prause, Lucas-Thompson, & Himsel, 2008). An exception to this rule is that if both parents return to work full time within the first year of an infant's life, the child later shows a slightly increased probability of problem behaviors toward both children and adults (Hill, Waldfogel, Brooks-Gunn, & Han, 2005; NICHD Early Child Care Research Network, 2006). Also, a child who is surrounded by other children who spent much of their early life in day care becomes more aggressive too (Dmitrieva, Steinberg, & Belsky, 2007). That is, aggressive behavior is contagious. All of these effects, of course, depend on many factors, including the quality of the day care.

Older children are less affected, and perhaps positively affected, by having both parents employed. A longitudinal study of 2,402 low-income families examined preschoolers and older children before and after their mothers took jobs. The preschoolers showed no behavioral changes, and the

older children showed slight benefits in some aspects of adjustment (Chase-Lansdale et al., 2003).

Nontraditional Families

Western society has considered a traditional family to be a mother, a father, and their children. A nontraditional family is, therefore, anything else. In general, two parents are better than one, partly for financial reasons. We might guess that a child whose mother dies early would be more harmed than one whose father died, simply because on average mothers spend more time with their children. However, children whose father died seem to be at more risk, at least as measured by the probability of eventually becoming depressed (Jacobs & Bovasso, 2009). The apparent explanation is that death of a father is (or has been) a greater financial setback, on average. Children reared by a single mother generally do about as well as children in two-parent homes if the single mother has a good income (MacCallum & Golombok, 2004; Weissman, Leaf, & Bruce, 1987).

Children reared by gay and lesbian parents develop about the same as those reared by heterosexuals in terms of social and emotional development, mental health, and romantic relationships (Bos, van Balen, & van den Boom, 2007; Golombok et al., 2003; Wainwright, Russell, & Patterson, 2004). The children's main difficulties relate to the prejudices that their classmates may have against single-sex couples (Bos & Gartrell, 2010).

However, we should be cautious about our conclusions. It is difficult to demonstrate conclusively the *absence* of any difference, and many studies comparing traditional and nontraditional families examined only a limited range of behaviors or had other limitations (Redding, 2001; Schumm, 2008). At most, we can say that being reared by a single parent or by gays or lesbians does not produce a big effect. We are not in a position to dismiss the possibility of any effect at all.

Parental Conflict and Divorce

In an earlier era, people in the United States considered divorce shameful. Political commentators attributed Adlai Stevenson's defeat in the presidential campaign of 1952 to the fact that he was divorced. Americans would never vote

Many sons of divorced parents go through a period when they act out their frustrations by starting fights.

school, and maintain good relationships with both parents (Hetherington, Stanley-Hagan, & Anderson, 1989).

Research results show that divorce's effects vary somewhat among cultures and ethnic groups. Divorce is more common in Black families, but in most regards, divorced Black women adjust better than White women do (McKelvey & McKenry, 2000). Many Black families ease the burden of single parenthood by having a grandmother or other relative help with child care.

None of the research implies that parents must stay together for their children's benefit. Children do not fare well if their parents are constantly fighting. Children who observe much conflict between their parents tend to be nervous, unable to sleep through the night (El-Sheikh, Buckhalt, Mize, & Acebo, 2006), and prone to violent and disruptive behaviors (Sternberg, Baradaran, Abbott, Lamb, & Guterman, 2006).

concept check

18. You may hear someone say that the right way to rear children is with both a mother and a father. Based on the research evidence, what would be a good reply?

Answer

18. According to the evidence so far, children reared by a single parent, gay couple, or divorced parents develop about normally.

for a divorced candidate, the commentators said. "Never" didn't last very long. By 1980, when Ronald Reagan was elected president, voters hardly noticed his divorce and remarriage.

The effects of divorce on children are highly variable. On average, the children show at least temporary setbacks in academic performance and social relationships. Many pout and seek extra attention, especially in the first year after a divorce (Hetherington, 1989). In the long term, many children reared by a divorced mother have difficulties, partly because of the emotional trauma of the divorce and partly because of financial difficulties. Divorce has the strongest effect on elementary schoolchildren's emotions but impairs academic performance more strongly for teenagers (Lansford et al., 2006). However, the effects are much greater in some cases than others (Lansford, 2009). Some children remain distressed for years, whereas others recover quickly. A few seem to do well at first but become more distressed later. Others are resilient throughout their parents' divorce and afterward. They keep their friends, do all right in

module 5.3 >

In Closing

Many Ways of Life

This module began with the question of how you would have been different if you had been born into a different gender, ethnic group, or family. In some ways, it is obvious that the differences would have been drastic. You would have had different friends, different activities, and different experiences. However, many aspects of your intellect and personality might have been about the same. Our group identities affect us enormously in some regards and less in others.

Summary

- *Gender influences.* Men and women differ on average in various aspects of behavior, including interests. However, researchers have found no clear evidence of differences in intellectual abilities. (page 173)
- *Sex roles.* Parents and others convey certain expectations of how boys and girls will act. These expectations substantially influence behavioral development. (page 175)
- *Cultural and ethnic differences.* Being a member of an ethnic minority raises special issues for identity development. Immigrant children have special difficulties as they try to participate in two cultures. Most bicultural and biracial children develop well. (page 176)
- *Birth order.* Many studies comparing firstborn versus later-born children have failed to separate the effects of birth order from the effects of family size. Much of the apparent difference between firstborns and later-borns is really a difference between children of small versus large families. (page 177)
- *Parenting styles.* Parenting style correlates with the behavior of the children. For example, caring, understanding parents tend to have well-behaved children. However, children affect the parents as much as parents affect the children. (page 178)
- *Nontraditional child care.* A child's normal personality and social development require at least one caring adult, but the number of caregivers and their gender and sexual orientation apparently matter little. (page 180)
- *Effects of divorce.* Children of divorced parents often show signs of distress, but the results vary across individuals. (page 180)

Key Terms

authoritarian parents (page 178)

authoritative parents (page 178)

biculturalism (page 176)

indifferent or uninvolved parents (page 178)

permissive parents (page 178)

sex roles (page 175)

exploration and study

Access an interactive eBook and chapter-specific learning tools, including
- **flashcards**
- **quizzes**
- **videos**

and more, in your Psychology CourseMate. Go to **CengageBrain.com.**

If your professor has assigned Aplia:
1. Sign in to your account.
2. Complete the corresponding exercises as required by your professor.
3. When finished, click "Grade It Now" to see which areas you have mastered, which areas need more work, and detailed explanations of every answer.

Photo by Greg Trott/Getty Images

Learning

Newborn humans have almost no control of their muscles, except for their eyes and mouth. Imagine a baby born with complete control of all muscles, including arms, hands, legs, and feet. Would that be a good thing?

After the parents stopped bragging about their precocious youngster, they would discover what a nightmare they had. An infant with extreme mobility but no experience would get into every imaginable danger. From the start, people need to learn what is safe to touch and what isn't, where we can go and where we shouldn't. Just about everything we do requires constant learning and relearning.

Psychologists have devoted an enormous amount of research to learning, and in the process, they developed and refined research methods that they now routinely apply in other areas of psychological investigation. This chapter is about the procedures that change behavior—why you lick your lips at the sight of tasty food, why you turn away from a food that once made you sick, why you handle sharp knives cautiously, and why you shudder if you see someone charging toward you with a bat.

© Andrea Chu /Getty Images

module 6.1 >

- What is the behaviorist viewpoint and how did it arise?
- When we learn to respond to a stimulus, what happens?

During a period in the middle of the twentieth century, most of the leading researchers in experimental psychology focused on animal learning. To understand how this topic seemed so fascinating, we have to understand something of the history. The interest in animal learning arose from both scientific and philosophical roots.

The Behaviorist View in Relation to Learning

As discussed in chapter 1, some of the early psychologists, the structuralists, explored mental events by asking people to describe their sensations, experiences, and so forth. Other psychologists wanted to get as far away from that approach as possible, viewing statements about mental states as explaining nothing:

Q: Why did she yell at him?

A: She yelled because she was angry.

Q: How do you know she was angry?

A: We know she was angry because she was yelling.

Those who objected to discussions of mental states advocated behaviorism, *the position that psychology should concern itself only with what people and other animals do, and the circumstances in which they do it.* According to behaviorists, all that matters is action. Thoughts, ideas, emotions, or other internal processes are important only if they affect action. Furthermore, where did those thoughts, ideas, and so forth come from? They must have arisen from previous events and current stimuli, and therefore those events and stimuli are the real causes of the actions. Behaviorists view discussions of mental events as just sloppy language. As B. F. Skinner (1990) argued, when you say, "I *intend* to . . . ," what you really mean is "I am about to . . ." or "In situations like this, I usually . . ." or "This behavior is in the preliminary stages of happening." Any statement about mental experiences can be converted into a description of behavior.

The same insistence on description is central to the British and American legal systems: A witness is asked, "What did you see and hear?" An acceptable answer might be, "The defendant was sweating and trembling, and his voice was wavering." A witness should not say, "The defendant was nervous and worried," because that statement requires an inference that the witness is not entitled to make. (Of course, the jury might draw an inference.)

You might be tempted to dismiss behaviorism because, at least at first glance, it seems so ridiculous: "What do you *mean*, my thoughts and beliefs and emotions don't cause my behavior?!" The behaviorists' reply is, "Exactly right. Your thoughts and other internal states do not cause your behavior because events in your environment caused your thoughts. Those events are the real causes of your behavior." Just contemplate this: If you believe that your thoughts or other internal states cause behaviors *independently* of your previous experiences, what evidence could you provide to support your claim?

Behaviorists seek the simplest possible explanation for behaviors. You will recognize this idea as the principle of parsimony from chapter 2. Jacques Loeb was one of the earliest, most extreme advocates of this viewpoint. Loeb analyzed the behavior of invertebrate animals in the simplest possible terms. In his words, "Motions caused by light or other agencies appear to the layman as expressions of will and purpose on the part of the animal, whereas in reality the animal is forced to go where carried by its legs" (Loeb, 1918/1973, p. 14). Why do certain caterpillars approach light? It is not, according to Loeb, because they are "fond" of

© Jim Occi - FUNDAMENTAL PHOTOGRAPHS, NYC

Figure 6.1 Jacques Loeb, an early student of animal behavior, argued that much or all of invertebrate behavior could be described as responses to simple stimuli, such as approaching light or moving opposite to the direction of gravity.

light. It is because light in front of them increases their rate of locomotion. If light strikes mainly from the left or right side, the caterpillar turns toward the light, not because it "wants to," but because light from the side causes greater muscle tension on one side of the body and therefore causes the animal to move one set of legs more than the other. Loeb applied similar explanations to why certain animals tend to move toward heat or cold, toward or away from water, up (away from gravity) or down, and so forth (Figure 6.1). Built-in mechanisms caused animals to move in adaptive ways, without the animals necessarily having any thoughts, desires, intentions, or other internal processes. Loeb's view was an example of stimulus–response psychology, *the attempt to explain behavior in terms of how each stimulus triggers a response.*

Although the term *stimulus–response psychology* was appropriate for Loeb, it is a misleading description of today's behaviorists. Behaviorists believe that behavior is a product of not only the current stimuli but also the individual's history of experiences, plus such factors as wakefulness or sleepiness (Staddon, 1999).

Was Loeb's account sufficient to explain all behaviors of caterpillars or other invertebrates? Well, no one had any evidence that it *wasn't* sufficient. The question then was, how far could that approach apply? Could we explain some, much, or all of vertebrate behavior in equally simple terms?

The greatest challenge was to explain learning. Behaviorists' goal was ambitious and optimistic. Their goal was to find basic laws of behavior, especially learning, that would be analogous to the laws of physics. But could they explain learning in simple terms, without reference to understanding, ideas, or other internal processes?

concept check

1. Why do behaviorists reject explanations in terms of thoughts?
2. How did Loeb explain why certain animals turn toward the light?

Answers

1. Previous events and current stimuli are responsible for thoughts, and therefore the events and stimuli are the real causes of behavior.
2. According to Loeb, light from the side caused greater muscle tension on one side of the body. Therefore, muscles on one side or the other moved more vigorously than those on the other side. This imbalance of movement continued until the light stimulation on both sides was equal.

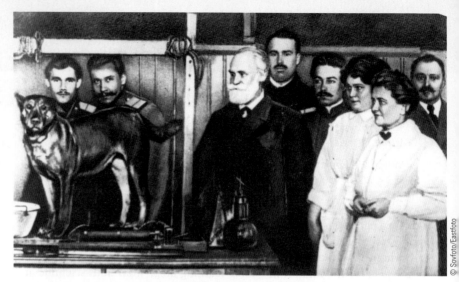

Ivan P. Pavlov (with the white beard) with students and a dog. Pavlov devised simple principles to describe learned changes in a dog's behavior.

Pavlov and Classical Conditioning

In the early 1900s, Ivan P. Pavlov, a Russian physiologist who had won a Nobel Prize in physiology for his research on digestion, stumbled upon an example of animal learning that suggested a possibility for simple explanation. Given the rise of behaviorism, the mood of the time was ripe for Pavlov's ideas.

One day as Pavlov was continuing his digestion research, he noticed that a dog secreted digestive juices as soon as it saw the lab worker who customarily fed the dogs. Because this secretion clearly depended on the dog's previous experiences, Pavlov called it a "psychological" secretion. He enlisted the help of other specialists, who discovered that "teasing" a dog with the sight of food produced salivation that was predictable and automatic. This acquired response is a *conditioned reflex*. The term *conditioned* indicates that it arose from previous conditions, not from genetics.

Pavlov's Procedures

Pavlov assumed that animals are born with *automatic connections*—called unconditioned reflexes—*between a stimulus such as food and a response such as secreting digestive juices.* He conjectured that animals acquire new reflexes by transferring a response from one stimulus to another. For example, if a particular sound always precedes food, an animal would salivate to the sound as if it were food.

The *process by which an organism learns a new association between two stimuli—a neutral stimulus and one that already evokes a reflexive response—*is known as classical conditioning, or Pavlovian conditioning. It is called classical because it has been known and studied for a long time.

Pavlov selected dogs with a moderate degree of arousal. (Highly excitable dogs would not hold still long enough, and highly inhibited dogs would fall asleep.) Then he attached a tube to one of the salivary ducts in a dog's mouth to measure salivation, as shown in Figure 6.2.

Whenever Pavlov gave a dog food, the dog salivated. The food → salivation connection was automatic, requiring no training. Pavlov called food the unconditioned stimulus, and he called salivation the unconditioned response. The unconditioned stimulus (UCS) is *an event that automatically elicits an unconditioned response.* The unconditioned response (UCR) is *the action that the unconditioned stimulus elicits.*

Next Pavlov introduced a new stimulus, such as a metronome (a device that makes rhythmic sounds). Upon hearing the metronome, the dog lifted its ears and looked around but did not salivate, so the metronome was a neutral stimulus with regard to salivation. Pavlov sounded the metronome a couple of seconds before giving food to the dog. After a few pairings of the metronome with food, the dog began to salivate as soon as it heard the metronome (Pavlov, 1927/1960).

We call the metronome the conditioned stimulus (CS) because a dog's *response to it depends on the preceding conditions*—that is, pairing the CS with the UCS. The salivation that follows the metronome is the conditioned response (CR). The conditioned response is *whatever response the conditioned stimulus elicits as a result of the conditioning (training) procedure.* At the start, the conditioned stimulus elicits no significant response. After conditioning, it elicits a conditioned response.

In Pavlov's experiment, the conditioned response was salivation and so was the unconditioned response. However, in some cases, the conditioned response differs from the unconditioned response. For example, the unconditioned response to an electric shock includes shrieking and jumping. The conditioned response to a stimulus paired with shock (i.e., a warning signal for shock) is a tensing of the muscles and cessation of activity (e.g., Pezze, Bast, & Feldon, 2003).

To review, the *unconditioned stimulus* (UCS), such as food, automatically elicits the *unconditioned response* (UCR), such as salivating. A neutral stimulus, such as a sound, that is paired with the UCS becomes a *conditioned stimulus* (CS). At first, it elicits no response or an irrelevant response, such as looking around. After some number of pairings of the CS with the UCS, the conditioned stimulus elicits the *conditioned response* (CR), which usually resembles the UCR. Figure 6.2 diagrams these relationships.

As a rule, conditioning occurs more rapidly if the conditioned stimulus is unfamiliar. If you have heard a tone many times (followed by nothing) and now start hearing the tone followed by some strong stimulus, you will be slow to show signs of conditioning. Similarly, imagine two people who are bit-

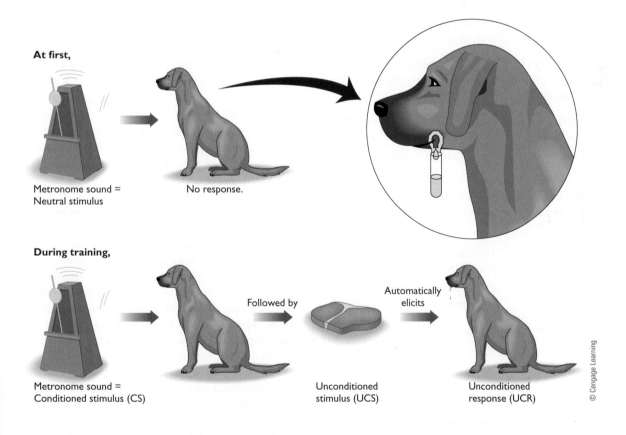

At first,

Metronome sound =
Neutral stimulus

No response.

During training,

Metronome sound =
Conditioned stimulus (CS)

Followed by

Unconditioned
stimulus (UCS)

Automatically
elicits

Unconditioned
response (UCR)

© Cengage Learning

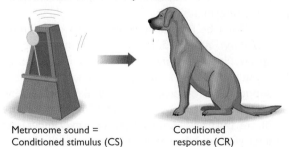

After some number of repetitions,

Metronome sound =
Conditioned stimulus (CS)

Conditioned
response (CR)

Figure 6.2 A conditioned stimulus precedes an unconditioned stimulus. At first, the conditioned stimulus elicits no response, and the unconditioned stimulus elicits the unconditioned response. After sufficient pairings, the conditioned stimulus elicits the conditioned response, which can resemble the unconditioned response.

ten by a snake. One has never been near a snake before, and the other has spent years tending snakes at the zoo. You can guess which one will learn a greater fear.

More Examples of Classical Conditioning

Here are more examples of classical conditioning:

- Your alarm clock makes a faint clicking sound a couple of seconds before the alarm goes off. At first, the click by itself does not awaken you, but the alarm does. After a week or so, you awaken when you hear the click.

| Unconditioned stimulus | = | alarm | → | Unconditioned response | = | awakening |
| Conditioned stimulus | = | click | → | Conditioned response | = | awakening |

- You hear the sound of a dentist's drill shortly before the unpleasant experience of the drill on your teeth. From then on, the sound of a dentist's drill arouses anxiety.

| Unconditioned stimulus | = | drilling | → | Unconditioned response | = | tension |
| Conditioned stimulus | = | sound of the drill | → | Conditioned response | = | tension |

- A nursing mother responds to her baby's cries by putting the baby to her breast, stimulating the flow of milk. After a few days of repetitions, the sound of the baby's cry is enough to start the milk flowing.

| Unconditioned stimulus | = | baby sucking | → | Unconditioned response | = | milk flow |
| Conditioned stimulus | = | baby's cry | → | Conditioned response | = | milk flow |

- Whenever your roommate flicks a switch on the stereo, it starts blasting sounds at deafening level. You flinch as soon as you hear the flick of the switch.

| Unconditioned stimulus | = | very loud music | → | Unconditioned response | = | flinching |
| Conditioned stimulus | = | flick of the switch | → | Conditioned response | = | flinching |

Note the usefulness of classical conditioning. It prepares the body for likely events.

try it ▶ yourself

One more example: Form an image in your mind of a lemon, a nice fresh juicy one. You cut it into slices and then suck on a slice. Imagine that sour taste. As you imagine the lemon, do you notice yourself salivating? If so, your imagination produced enough resemblance to the actual sight and taste of a lemon to serve as a conditioned stimulus.

concept check

3. At the start of training, the CS elicits ___ and the UCS elicits ___. After many repetitions of the CS followed by the UCS, the CS elicits ___ and the UCS elicits ___.

4. In this example, identify the CS, UCS, CR, and UCR: Every time an army drill sergeant calls out "Ready, aim, fire," the artillery shoots, making a painfully loud sound that causes you to flinch. After a few repetitions, you tense your muscles after the word "fire," before the shot itself.

Answers

3. No response (or at least nothing of interest)... the UCR... the CR... the UCR.

4. The conditioned stimulus is the sound "Ready, aim, fire." The unconditioned stimulus is the artillery shot. The unconditioned response is flinching; the conditioned response is tensing.

Additional Phenomena of Classical Conditioning

The *process that establishes or strengthens a conditioned response* is known as acquisition. After discovering classical conditioning, Pavlov and others varied the procedures to produce other outcomes. Here are some of the main phenomena.

Extinction

Suppose someone sounds a buzzer and then blows a puff of air into your eyes. After a few repetitions, you start to close your eyes as soon as you hear the buzzer (Figure 6.3). Now the buzzer sounds repeatedly without the puff of air. What do you do?

You blink your eyes the first time and perhaps the second and third times, but before long, you stop. This decrease of the conditioned response is called extinction. *To extinguish a classically conditioned response, repeatedly present the conditioned stimulus (CS) without the unconditioned stimulus (UCS).* That is, acquisition of a response (CR) occurs when the CS predicts the UCS, and extinction occurs when the CS no longer predicts the UCS.

Extinction is not the same as forgetting. Both weaken a learned response, but they arise in different ways. You forget during a long period without reminders or practice. Extinction occurs because of a specific experience—perceiving the conditioned stimulus without the unconditioned stimulus. If acquisition is learning to make a response, extinction is learning to inhibit it.

Don't be misled by connotations of the term *extinction*. After extinction of an animal or plant species, it is gone forever. In classical conditioning, extinction does *not* mean obliteration. Extinction suppresses a response. Think of it like extinguishing a fire: Pouring water on a huge fire puts out the blazes, but a few smoldering embers may linger long afterward, and they might easily reignite the fire.

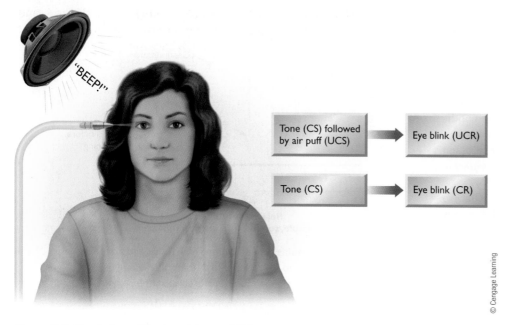

Figure 6.3 Classical conditioning of the eye-blink response.

Spontaneous Recovery

Suppose you are in a classical-conditioning experiment. At first, you repeatedly hear a buzzer (CS) that precedes a puff of air to your eyes (UCS). Then the buzzer stops predicting an air puff. After a few trials, your response to the buzzer extinguishes. Next you sit for a long time with nothing happening until suddenly you hear the buzzer again. What will you do? Chances are, you blink your eyes at least slightly. *Spontaneous recovery* is *a temporary return of an extinguished response after a delay* (Figure 6.4).

Why does spontaneous recovery occur? Think of it this way: At first, the buzzer predicted a puff of air to your eyes, and then it didn't. You behaved in accordance with the more recent experiences. Hours later, neither experience is much more recent than the other, and the effects of acquisition and extinction are about equally strong.

concept check

5. In Pavlov's experiment on conditioned salivation in response to a buzzer, what procedure produces extinction? What procedure produces spontaneous recovery?

Answer

5. To bring about extinction, present the buzzer repeatedly without presenting food. To bring about spontaneous recovery, first bring about extinction. Then wait and present the buzzer again.

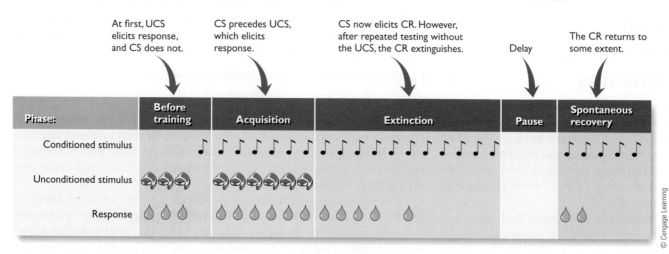

Figure 6.4 If the conditioned stimulus regularly precedes the unconditioned stimulus, acquisition occurs. If the conditioned stimulus is presented by itself, extinction occurs. A pause after extinction yields a brief spontaneous recovery.

Stimulus Generalization

Suppose a bee stings you, and you learn to fear bees. Now you see a wasp or hornet. Will you fear that, too?

You probably will, but you probably will not fear butterflies or other insects that don't resemble bees. The more similar a new stimulus is to the conditioned stimulus, the more likely you are to show a similar response (Figure 6.5). Stimulus generalization is the *extension of a conditioned response from the training stimulus to similar stimuli.*

However, it is often difficult to specify what we mean by "similar" (Pearce, 1994). After a bee stings you, you might fear the sound of buzzing bees when you are walking through a forest but not when you hear the same sounds in a nature documentary on television. Your response depends on the total configuration of stimuli.

Discrimination

You are walking through a wilderness area carrying a baby. At some point the baby shakes a rattle. You hear the sound and smile. A minute later you hear a slightly different rattle—the sound of a rattlesnake. You react very differently because you have learned to discriminate—*to respond differently to stimuli that predict different outcomes.* Similarly, you discriminate between a bell that signals time for class to start and a different bell that signals a fire alarm.

Discrimination training enhances sensitivity to sensory cues. In one study, people sniffed two chemicals that seemed virtually the same. However, one chemical always preceded an electric shock, and the other always preceded a safe interval without shock. As training proceeded, people got better at detecting the difference, and they reacted to the smell that predicted shock (Li, Howard, Parrish, & Gottfried, 2008).

Drug Tolerance as an Example of Classical Conditioning

Classical conditioning shows up in ways you might not expect. One example is drug tolerance: *Users of certain drugs experience progressively weaker effects after taking the drugs repeatedly.* Some longtime users inject themselves with more heroin than it would take to kill an average person, while experiencing relatively mild effects.

Drug tolerance results partly from automatic chemical changes that occur in cells throughout the body. It also depends partly on classical conditioning. Consider: When drug users inject themselves with morphine or heroin, the drug injection proce-

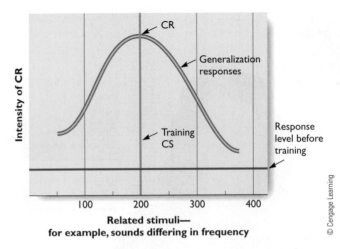

Figure 6.5 Stimulus generalization is the process of extending a learned response to new stimuli that resemble the one used in training. A less similar stimulus elicits a weaker response.

dure is a complex stimulus that includes the time and place as well as the needle injection. This total stimulus predicts a second stimulus, the drug's entry into the brain. When the drug reaches the brain it triggers a variety of body defenses—including changes in hormone secretions, heart rate, and breathing rate—that counteract the effects of the drug itself.

First stimulus	→	**Second stimulus**	→	**Automatic response**
(Injection procedure)		(Drug enters brain)		(Body's defenses)

Whenever one stimulus predicts a second stimulus that produces an automatic response, classical conditioning can occur. The first stimulus is the CS, the second is the UCS, and the response is the UCR. Let's relabel as follows:

Conditioned stimulus	→	**Unconditioned stimulus**	→	**Unconditioned response**
(Injection procedure)		(Drug enters brain)		(Body's defenses)

If conditioning occurs here, what would happen? Suppose the CS (drug injection) produces a CR that resembles the UCR (the body's defenses against the drug). In that case, as soon as the injection starts, before the drug enters the body, the body starts mobilizing its defenses against the drug. Therefore, the drug has less effect, and we say that the body developed tolerance. Shepard Siegel (1977, 1983) conducted several experiments to confirm that classical conditioning occurs during drug injections:

Conditioned stimulus	→	**Conditioned response**
(Injection procedure)		(Body's defenses)

The research tested several predictions. One prediction was this: If the injection procedure serves as a conditioned stimulus, then the body's defense reactions should be strongest if the drug is administered in the usual way, in the usual location, with as many familiar stimuli as possible. (The entire experience constitutes the conditioned stimulus.)

The evidence supports this prediction for a variety of drugs (Siegel & Ramos, 2002). Much of the research deals with laboratory animals, but observations of people confirm the same conclusion. Many drug users suffer "overdose" reactions after taking their usual dose, if they take it in an unusual place or under unusual circumstances. Without the stimuli previously associated with the drug, their learned tolerance weakens or disappears.

A second prediction: If tolerance is classically conditioned, researchers should be able to extinguish it. To produce extinction, present the CS without the UCS. Given the difficulties of working with human drug users, researchers studied rats. Many drug effects are difficult to measure in nonhumans, but one is easy—the ability of morphine to decrease pain. Researchers first measured the smallest pain necessary to make rats flinch. Then they gave the rats morphine and ran the test again, finding that the drug greatly decreased the pain response. The next step was to produce tolerance by daily drug injections, testing the pain response each time. When the pain response increased, showing tolerance to the drug, researchers went to the final step. They gave the rats daily injections of salt water. If we think of the injection procedure as the CS and the drug itself as the UCS, then injecting salt water is presenting the CS without the UCS. After a few repetitions, tolerance partly extinguished. Now an injection of morphine substantially decreased the pain response (Siegel, 1977). In short, drug tolerance shows the properties we would expect it to have if tolerance depends on classical conditioning. Figure 6.6 summarizes this experiment.

Research on the classical conditioning of drug tolerance eventually led to applications to help people quit their addictions. People with a history of addiction experience cravings in the presence of sights, sounds, and smells that remind them of their drug experiences. When psychologists present those stimuli under conditions where the person is able to resist the temptation, the result is partial extinction of the cravings (Loeber, Croissant, Heinz, Mann, & Flor, 2006).

concept check

6. When someone develops tolerance to the effects of a drug injection, what are the conditioned stimulus, the unconditioned stimulus, the conditioned response, and the unconditioned response?

7. How did researchers measure drug tolerance in rats?

Answers

7. They first measured the ability of morphine to decrease rats' pain responses. Then they administered morphine daily for a few days and tested the rats' pain responses each day. After repeated injections, the rats showed increased pain responses, and therefore tolerance to the effects of the drug.

6. The conditioned stimulus is the injection procedure. The unconditioned stimulus is the entry of the drug into the brain. Both the conditioned response and the unconditioned response are the body's defenses against the drug.

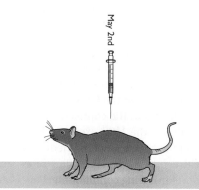

1. Initial response to painful heat: Rat licks its paw.

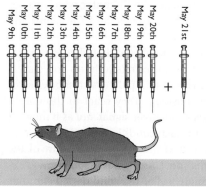

2. First test under morphine: No response unless heat is turned up much higher.

3. After six morphine injections: Rat has tolerance and shows response to pain despite morphine.

4. After 12 saltwater injections, another morphine injection reduces pain. Tolerance is partly extinguished.

© Cengage Learning

Figure 6.6 Morphine decreases pain, but after a few repetitions, a rat develops tolerance to this effect. Repeated injections of salt water produce extinction of the learned tolerance.

Explanations of Classical Conditioning

What is classical conditioning, really? As is often the case, the process appeared simple at first, but later investigation found it to be more complex and more interesting. Pavlov noted that conditioning depended on the timing between CS and UCS, as shown here:

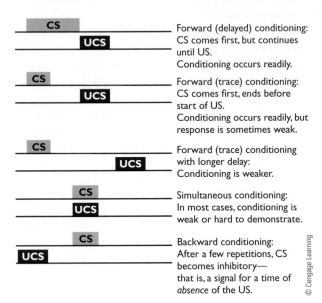

Forward (delayed) conditioning: CS comes first, but continues until US.
Conditioning occurs readily.

Forward (trace) conditioning: CS comes first, ends before start of US.
Conditioning occurs readily, but response is sometimes weak.

Forward (trace) conditioning with longer delay:
Conditioning is weaker.

Simultaneous conditioning: In most cases, conditioning is weak or hard to demonstrate.

Backward conditioning: After a few repetitions, CS becomes inhibitory— that is, a signal for a time of *absence* of the US.

© Cengage Learning

In these displays, read time left to right. Pavlov surmised that presenting the CS and UCS at nearly the same time caused a connection to grow in the brain so that the animal treated the CS as if it were the UCS. Figure 6.7a illustrates the connections before the start of training: The UCS excites a UCS center somewhere in the brain, which immediately stimulates the UCR center. Figure 6.7b illustrates connections that develop during conditioning: Pairing the CS and UCS develops a connection between their brain representations. After this connection develops, the CS excites the CS center, which excites the UCS center, which excites the UCR center and produces a response.

Later studies contradicted that idea. For example, a shock (UCS) causes rats to jump and shriek, but a conditioned stimulus paired with shock makes them freeze in position. They react to the conditioned stimulus as a danger signal, not as if they felt a shock. Also, in trace conditioning, where a delay separates the end of the CS from the start of the UCS, the animal does not make a conditioned response immediately after the conditioned stimulus but instead waits until almost the end of the usual delay between CS and UCS. Again, it is not treating the CS as if it were the UCS; it is using it as a predictor, a way to prepare for the UCS (Gallistel & Gibbon, 2000).

It is true, as Pavlov suggested, that the longer the delay between the CS and the UCS, the weaker the conditioning, other things being equal. However, just having the CS and UCS close together in time is not enough. It is essential that they occur more often together than they occur apart. That is, the CS must be a good predictor of the UCS. Consider this experiment: For rats in both Group 1 and Group 2, every presentation of a CS is followed by a UCS, as shown in Figure 6.8. For Group 2, the UCS also appears at many other times without the CS. In other words, for this group, the UCS happens frequently anyway, and no more with the CS than without it. Group 1 learns a strong response to the CS, and Group 2 does not (Rescorla, 1968, 1988).

concept check

8. If classical conditioning depended *entirely* on presenting the CS and UCS at nearly the same time, what result should the experimenters have obtained in Rescorla's experiment?

Answer

8. If classical conditioning depended entirely on presenting the CS and UCS at nearly the same time, the rats in both groups would have responded equally to the conditioned stimulus, regardless of how often they received the unconditioned stimulus at other times.

Now consider this experiment: Rats are shown a light (CS) followed by shock (UCS) until they respond consistently to the light. The conditioned response is to freeze in place. Then they get a series of trials with both a light and a tone, again followed by shock. Let's test the rats' response to the tone alone. Do they show a conditioned response? No. The same pattern occurs with the reverse order: First, rats learn a response to the tone, and then they get light–tone combinations before the shock. They show a conditioned response to the tone but not to the light (Kamin, 1969; Figure 6.9). These results demonstrate the blocking effect: *The previously established association to one stimulus blocks the formation of an association to the added stimulus.* Research supports two explanations: First, if the first stimulus predicts the outcome, the second stimulus adds no new information. Second, the rat attends strongly to the stimulus that already predicts the outcome and therefore pays less attention to the new stimulus.

The same principle holds in human reasoning. Suppose you have several experiences when you eat something with peppers and have an allergic

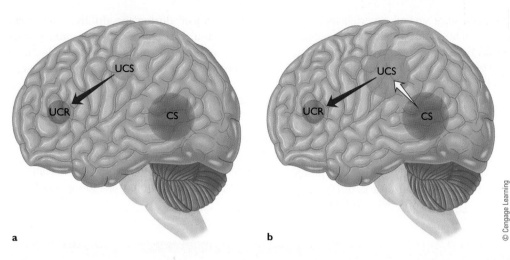

Figure 6.7 According to Pavlov, **(a)** at the start of conditioning, activity in a UCS center automatically activates the UCR center. **(b)** After sufficient pairings of the CS and UCS, a connection develops between the CS and UCS centers. Afterward, activity in the CS center flows to the UCS center and therefore excites the UCR center.

a

b

© Cengage Learning

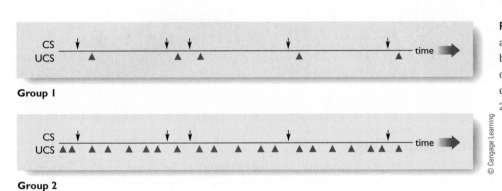

Group 1

Group 2

Figure 6.8 In Rescorla's experiment, the CS always preceded the UCS in both groups, but Group 2 received the UCS frequently at other times also. Group 1 developed a strong conditioned response to the CS, and Group 2 did not.

© Cengage Learning

Group 1

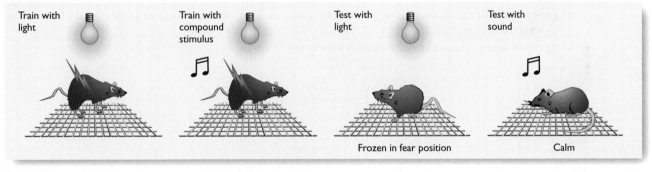

Group 2

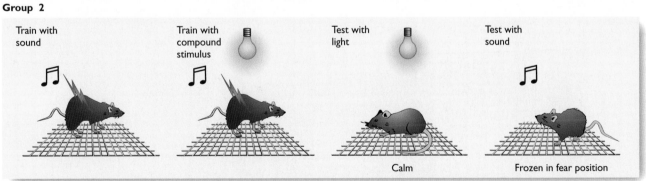

© Cengage Learning

Figure 6.9 Each rat first learned to associate either light or sound with shock. Then it received a compound of both light and sound followed by shock. Each rat continued to show a strong response to the old stimulus (which already predicted shock) but little to the new stimulus.

reaction. Then you have several experiences when you eat peppers and nuts and have the same reaction. You have already decided to try to avoid peppers. Do you now avoid nuts as strongly as the peppers? Probably not (Melchers, Ungor, & Lachnit, 2005).

concept check

9. Suppose you have already learned to flinch when you hear the sound of a dentist's drill. Now your dentist turns on some soothing background music during the drilling. The background music is paired with the pain just as much as the drill sound is. Will you learn to flinch at the sound of that background music?

Answer

9. You will not learn to flinch at the sound of the background music. Because the drill sound already predicted the pain, the new stimulus is uninformative and will not be strongly associated with the pain.

module 6.1

In Closing

It's More Than Drooling Dogs

When you decided to study psychology, if someone had asked you to describe what you hoped to learn, you probably would not have replied, "I want to learn how to make dogs salivate!" I hope you see that the research on conditioned salivation is just a way to explore fundamental mechanisms, much as genetics researchers have studied the fruit fly *Drosophila* or neurophysiologists have studied the nerves of squid. Classical conditioning is important for many important behaviors, ranging from emotional responses to drug tolerance.

People sometimes use the term "Pavlovian" to mean simple, mechanical, robotlike behavior. Pavlovian or classical conditioning is not a mark of stupidity. It is a way of responding to relationships among events, a way of preparing us for what is likely to happen.

Summary

- *Behaviorism.* Behaviorists insist that psychologists should study behaviors and not internal states such as intentions or expectations. Previous events led to the internal states, and therefore those events are the real causes of behavior. (page 187)
- *Behaviorists' interest in learning.* Behaviorists' goal is to explain behavior without relying on terms such as idea or understanding. Much of invertebrate behavior can be described in simple terms, but the greater challenge was to explain learning. (page 188)
- *Classical conditioning.* Ivan Pavlov discovered classical conditioning, the process by which an association forms between a neutral stimulus (the conditioned stimulus) and one that initially evokes a reflexive response (the unconditioned stimulus). The result is a new response (the conditioned response) to the conditioned stimulus. (page 188)
- *Extinction.* A conditioned response can be extinguished by repeatedly presenting the conditioned stimulus by itself. (page 190)
- *Spontaneous recovery.* If the conditioned stimulus is not presented at all for some time after extinction and is then presented again, the conditioned response may return. The return is called spontaneous recovery. (page 191)
- *Stimulus generalization.* A conditioned response to a stimulus will extend to other stimuli to the extent that they resemble the trained stimulus. (page 192)
- *Discrimination.* Animals (including people) learn to respond differently to stimuli that predict different outcomes. (page 192)
- *Drug tolerance.* Drug tolerance results in part from classical conditioning. The drug administration procedure comes to evoke defensive responses. (page 192)
- *Basis for classical conditioning.* Pavlov believed that conditioning occurred because presenting two stimuli close to each other in time developed a connection between their brain representations. Later research showed that animals do not treat the conditioned stimulus as if it were the unconditioned stimulus. Also, being close in time is not enough. Learning requires that the first stimulus predict the second stimulus. (page 194)

Key Terms

acquisition (page 190)

behaviorism (page 187)

blocking effect (page 194)

classical conditioning (or Pavlovian conditioning) (page 188)

conditioned response (CR) (page 189)

conditioned stimulus (CS) (page 189)

discrimination (page 192)

drug tolerance (page 192)

extinction (page 190)

spontaneous recovery (page 191)

stimulus generalization (page 192)

stimulus–response psychology (page 188)

unconditioned reflex (page 188)

unconditioned response (UCR) (page 188)

unconditioned stimulus (UCS) (page 188)

Operant Conditioning

- How do the consequences of our behaviors affect future behaviors?

Suppose a family in another country adopted you at birth. You then lived in a land with different language, customs, food, religion, and so forth. As mentioned in chapter 5, undoubtedly you would be different in many ways. But would that alternative "you" have anything in common with the current "you"? Or does your culture and environment mold your behavior completely? The most extreme statement of environmental determinism came from John B. Watson, one of the founders of behaviorism, who said,

> Give me a dozen healthy infants, well-formed, and my own specified world to bring them up in and I'll guarantee to take any one at random and train him to become any type of specialist I might select—doctor, lawyer, artist, merchant-chief, and yes, even beggar-man thief—regardless of his talents, penchants, tendencies, abilities, vocations, and race of his ancestors. I am going beyond my facts and I admit it, but so have the advocates of the contrary. (1925, p. 82)

Needless to say, Watson never had a chance to demonstrate his point. No one gave him a child and gave him complete control of the environment. If he or anyone else really did have complete control of the environment, how much could someone control a child's fate? We may never know, . . . ethics being what they are, after all. Still, one of the goals of researchers studying learning is to see the ways in which changes in the environment control our behavior.

Thorndike and Operant Conditioning

Shortly before Pavlov's research, Edward L. Thorndike (1911/1970), a Harvard graduate student, began training cats in a basement. Saying that earlier experiments had dealt only with animal intelligence, not animal stupidity, he sought a simple behaviorist explanation of learning. He put cats into puzzle boxes (Figure 6.10) from which they could

Growing up in a different environment would change your behavior, but would it completely determine your behavioral development? How much can the environment control, and how much can it not control?

escape by pressing a lever, pulling a string, or tilting a pole. Sometimes, he placed food outside the box, but usually, cats worked just to escape from the box. The cats learned to make whatever response opened the box, especially if the box opened quickly.

They learned by trial and error. When a cat had to tilt a pole to escape from the box, it might at first paw or gnaw at the door, scratch the walls, or pace back and forth. Eventually, it bumped against the pole and the door opened. The next time, the cat went through a similar repertoire of behaviors but might bump against the pole a little sooner. Over many trials, the cat gradually but inconsistently improved its speed of escape. Figure 6.11 shows a learning curve to represent this behavior. A learning curve is *a graph of the changes in behavior that occur over the course of learning.*

Did the cat understand the connection between bumping against the pole and opening the door? No, said Thorndike. If the cat gained a new insight at some point, its escape should have been quick from that point on. The graph of the cat's escape times shows no sharp break that we could identify as the time of an insight.

Thorndike concluded that learning occurs because certain behaviors are strengthened at the expense of others. An animal enters a situation with a repertoire of responses such as pawing the door, scratching the walls, pacing, and so forth (labeled R_1, R_2, R_3, etc., in Figure 6.12). It starts with its most probable response (R_1). If nothing special happens, it proceeds to other responses, eventually reaching one that opens the door—for example, bumping against the pole (R_7 in this example). Opening the door reinforces the preceding behavior.

Figure 6.10 Each of Thorndike's puzzle boxes had a device that could open it. Here, tilting the pole will open the door. (Based on Thorndike, 1911/1970.)

A reinforcement is *the process of increasing the future probability of the most recent response.* Thorndike said that reinforcement "stamps in," or strengthens, the response. The next time the cat is in the puzzle box, it has a slightly higher probability of the effective response. If it receives reinforcement again, the probability goes up another notch (Figure 6.12). You see how this view fit with behaviorists' hope for an explanation that did not rely on thoughts, understanding, or other mental processes.

Thorndike summarized his views in the law of effect (Thorndike, 1911/1970, p. 244):

> Of several responses made to the same situation, those which are accompanied or closely followed by satisfaction to the animal will, other things being equal, be more firmly connected with the

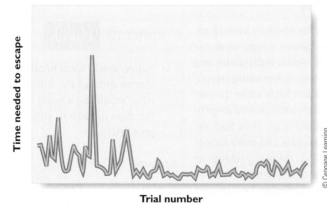

Figure 6.11 As the data from one of Thorndike's experiments show, a cat's time to escape from a box decreases gradually but sporadically. Thorndike concluded that the cat did not at any point "get an idea." Instead, reinforcement gradually increased the probability of the successful behavior.

situation, so that, when it recurs, they will be more likely to recur.

In other words, the most successful responses become more likely in the future. Those responses become more frequent, and the animal does not need to understand why. Similarly, a machine could be programmed to produce random responses and repeat the ones that led to reinforcement.

Was Thorndike's interpretation correct? Another way of putting this question: When an animal learns to make a response that produces some outcome, does it "expect" that outcome, or does it simply register, "This is the response to make in this situation"? That question is harder to answer than it might sound (Burke, Franz, Miller, & Schoenbaum, 2008).

Thorndike revolutionized the study of animal learning, substituting experimentation for collections of anecdotes. He also demonstrated the possibility of simple explanations for apparently complex behaviors (Dewsbury, 1998). On the negative side, his example of studying animals in contrived laboratory situations led researchers to ignore much about how animals learn in nature (Galef, 1998).

The kind of learning that Thorndike studied is called operant conditioning (because the subject *operates* on the environment to produce an outcome) or *instrumental conditioning* (because the subject's behavior is instrumental in producing the outcome). Operant or instrumental conditioning is *the process of changing behavior by providing a reinforcement after a response.* The defining difference between operant conditioning and classical conditioning is the procedure: *In operant conditioning, the subject's behavior produces an outcome that affects future behavior. In classical conditioning, the subject's behavior has no effect on the outcome (the presentation of either the CS or the UCS).* For example, in classical conditioning, the experimenter (or the world) presents two stimuli at particular times, regardless of what the subject does or doesn't do. Those stimuli change future behaviors, but the behaviors do not change the outcomes. In operant conditioning, the subject has to make some response before it receives reinforcement.

In general, the two kinds of conditioning also affect different behaviors. Classical conditioning applies mainly to visceral responses (i.e., *responses of the internal organs*), such as salivation and digestion, whereas operant conditioning applies mainly to skeletal responses (i.e., *movements of leg muscles, arm muscles, etc.*). However, this distinction sometimes breaks down. For example, if a tone predicts an electric shock (a classical-conditioning procedure), the tone makes the animal freeze in position (a skeletal response) as well as increase its heart rate (a visceral response).

© Cengage Learning

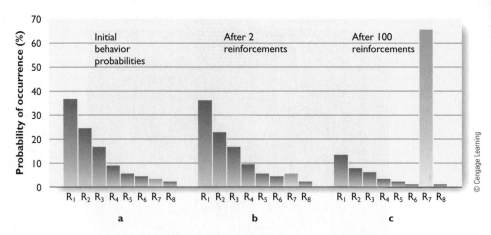

Figure 6.12 According to Thorndike, a cat starts with many potential behaviors in a given situation. When one of the behaviors leads to reinforcement, the future probability of that behavior increases. We need not assume that the cat understands what it is doing or why.

concept check

10. When a bell rings, an animal sits up on its hind legs and drools; then it receives food. Is the animal's behavior an example of classical conditioning or operant conditioning? So far, you do not have enough information to answer the question. What else do you need to know before you can answer?

Answer

10. You need to know whether the bell always predicts food (classical conditioning) or whether the animal receives food only when it sits up (operant conditioning).

Reinforcement and Punishment

Food is an effective reinforcer for a hungry individual, and water for a thirsty one. Some things work extremely well as reinforcers for some individuals and not others. Consider how many hours some people will play a video game just for a high score. In one quirky experiment, mother rats could press a lever to deliver extra baby rats into their cage. They kept on pressing and pressing, adding more and more babies (Lee, Clancy, & Fleming, 1999). Is there any pattern as to what is a good reinforcer and what isn't?

We might guess that reinforcers are biologically useful to the individual, but many are not. For example, saccharin, a sweet but biologically useless chemical, can be a reinforcer. For many people, alcohol and tobacco are stronger reinforcers than vitamin-rich vegetables. So biological usefulness doesn't define reinforcement.

A proposal that works reasonably well toward defining reinforcement relies on the concept of equilibrium. If you could spend your day any way you wanted, how would you divide your time, on average? You might spend 30% of your day sleeping, 10% eating, 5% exercising, 11% reading, 9% talking with friends, 2% grooming, 2% playing the piano, and so forth. Now suppose something kept you away from one of these activities for the last day or two. An opportunity to do that activity would get you back toward equilibrium. According to the disequilibrium principle of reinforcement, *anything that prevents an activity produces disequilibrium, and an opportunity to return to equilibrium will be reinforcing* (Farmer-Dougan, 1998; Timberlake & Farmer-Dougan, 1991).

Of course, some activities are more insistent than others. If you have been deprived of oxygen, the opportunity to breathe will be extremely reinforcing. If you have been deprived of reading time or phone time, the reinforcement value will be less.

concept check

11. Suppose you want to reinforce a child for doing chores around the house, and you don't know what would be a good reinforcer. According to the disequilibrium principle, how should you proceed?

Answer

11. Begin by determining how the child ordinarily spends his or her time when given unlimited opportunities. Then find which of these activities the child has been deprived of recently. The opportunity to do one of those activities should be reinforcing.

What serves as a reinforcer for one person might not for another. Lucy Pearson (left) has collected more than 110,000 hubcaps. Jim Hambrick (right) collects Superman items.

Primary and Secondary Reinforcers

Psychologists distinguish between primary reinforcers (or *unconditioned reinforcers*) *that are reinforcing because of their own properties*, and secondary reinforcers (or *conditioned reinforcers*) *that became reinforcing by association with something else*. Food and water are primary reinforcers. Money (a secondary reinforcer) becomes reinforcing because we can exchange it for food or other primary reinforcers. A student learns that a good grade wins approval, and an employee learns that increased productivity wins the employer's praise. In these cases, *secondary* means "learned." It does not mean unimportant. We spend most of our time working for secondary reinforcers.

Punishment

In contrast to a *reinforcer*, a punishment *decreases the probability of a response*. A reinforcer can be either a presentation (e.g., receiving food) or a removal (e.g., stopping pain). Similarly, punishment can be either a presentation (e.g., receiving pain) or a removal (e.g., withholding food). Punishment is most effective when it is quick and predictable. An uncertain or delayed punishment is less effective. For example, the burn you feel from touching a hot stove is highly effective in teaching you something to avoid. The threat that smoking cigarettes might give you cancer many years from now is also effective, but less so.

Punishments are not always effective. If the threat of punishment were always effective, the crime rate would be zero. B. F. Skinner (1938) tested punishment in a famous laboratory study. He first trained food-deprived rats to press a bar to get food and then he stopped reinforcing their presses. For the first 10 minutes, some rats not only failed to get food, but also received a slap on their paws every time they pressed the bar. (The bar slapped their paws.) The punished rats temporarily suppressed their pressing, but in the long run, they pressed as many times as did the unpunished rats. Skinner concluded that punishment produces no long-term effects.

That conclusion, however, is an overstatement (Staddon, 1993). A better conclusion would be that punishment does not greatly weaken a response when no other response is available. Skinner's food-deprived rats had no other way to seek food. (If someone punished you for breathing, you would continue breathing nevertheless.)

Is physical punishment of children, such as spanking, a good or bad idea? Spanking is widespread in the United States, but illegal in many other countries,

Many secondary reinforcers are surprisingly powerful. Consider how hard children work for a little gold star that the teacher pastes on an assignment.

mostly in Europe (Zolotor & Puzia, 2010). Many psychologists strongly discourage spanking, recommending that parents simply reason with the child or use nonphysical methods of discipline, such as time out or loss of television or other privileges. What evidence backs this recommendation?

All the research presents correlations between physical punishment and later behavior. (It's impossible to randomly assign some parents to spank their children and other parents not to.) The results say that children who are frequently spanked tend to be ill behaved. You should see the problem in interpreting this result: It might mean that spanking causes misbehavior, or it might mean that ill-behaved children provoke their parents to spank them. It could also mean that spanking is more common for families in stressful conditions, families with much parental conflict, or families with other factors that might lead to misbehaviors (Morris & Gibson, 2011). A better type of research compares children who were frequently spanked to children from similar backgrounds who were frequently subjected to nonphysical punishment, such as time out. That type of research shows no difference between those spanked and those given other types of punishment (Larzelere, Cox, & Smith, 2010). So it appears that misbehavior leads to punishment (of whatever type) more than punishment leads to misbehavior.

The conclusions are different with regard to severe punishment bordering on child abuse. Likely outcomes then include antisocial behavior, low self-esteem, and hostility toward the parents (Larzelere & Kuhn, 2005).

concept check

12. Frequently spanked children are likely to misbehave. Why can't we conclude that spanking leads to misbehavior?

Answer

12. It is equally possible that misbehavior leads to spankings. Also, many families that rely on spankings are also families with parental conflict or other factors that might predispose children to misbehavior.

Categories of Reinforcement and Punishment

As mentioned, a reinforcer can be either presenting something like food or avoiding something like pain. A punishment also can be either presenting or avoiding something. Psychologists use different terms to distinguish these possibilities, as shown in Table 6.1.

The upper left and lower right of the table both show reinforcement. Reinforcement *always increases* the probability of a behavior. Reinforcement can be either positive reinforcement—*presenting something such as food*, or negative reinforcement—*avoiding something such as pain.* Many people find the term negative reinforcement confusing or misleading (Baron & Galizio, 2005; Kimble, 1993), and instead of it most researchers use the terms escape learning or avoidance learning. (The individual is reinforced by an opportunity to escape or avoid a danger.)

Table 6.1 Four Categories of Operant Conditioning

	Event Such as Food	Event Such as Pain
Behavior leads to the event	**Positive Reinforcement** *Result:* Increase in the behavior, reinforced by presentation of food. *Example:* "If you clean your room, I'll get you a pizza tonight." 	**Punishment** *Result:* Decrease in the behavior, and therefore a decrease in pain. *Example:* "If you insult me, I'll slap you." 
Behavior avoids the event	**Punishment** *Result:* Decrease in the behavior, and therefore food continues to be available. *Example:* "If you hit your little brother again, you'll get no dessert." 	**Negative Reinforcement = Escape or Avoidance Learning** *Result:* Increase in the behavior, and therefore a decrease in pain. *Example:* "If you go into the office over there, the doctor will remove the thorn from your leg." 

© Cengage Learning

Punishment *always decreases* the probability of some behavior. In Table 6.1, the upper right and lower left items show two types of punishment. Punishment can be either presenting something, such as pain (spanking), or omitting something, such as food (a snack before bed). Punishment by omitting something is occasionally known as negative punishment.

To classify some procedure, attend to the wording. If the procedure increases a behavior, it is reinforcement. If it decreases a behavior, it is punishment. If the reinforcement is the presence of something, it is positive reinforcement. If it is the absence of something it is negative reinforcement, also known as escape or avoidance learning.

concept check

13. Identify each of the following examples using the terms in Table 6.1:
    a. Your employer gives you bonus pay for working overtime.
    b. You learn to stop playing your accordion at 5 A.M. because your roommate threatens to kill you if you do it again.
    c. You put on sunscreen to decrease the risk of skin cancer.
    d. You turn off a dripping faucet, ending the "drip drip drip" sound.
    e. You learn to avoid undercooked seafood because you have felt sick after eating it.
    f. Your swimming coach says you cannot go to the next swim meet (which you are looking forward to) if you break a training rule.
    g. If you get a speeding ticket, you will temporarily lose the privilege of driving the family car.
    h. You learn to come inside when a storm is brewing to avoid getting wet.

Answers

13. **a.** positive reinforcement; **b.** punishment; **c.** avoidance learning or negative reinforcement; **d.** escape learning or negative reinforcement; **e.** punishment; **f.** punishment; **g.** punishment; **h.** avoidance learning or negative reinforcement.

Additional Phenomena

Recall the concepts of extinction, generalization, and discrimination in classical conditioning. The same concepts apply to operant conditioning, with different procedures.

Table 6.2 Classical Conditioning and Operant Conditioning

	Classical Conditioning	Operant Conditioning
Terminology	CS, UCS, CR, UCR	Response, reinforcement
Behavior	Does not control UCS	Controls reinforcement
Paired during acquisition	Two stimuli (CS and UCS)	Response and reinforcement (in the presence of certain stimuli)
Responses	Mostly visceral (internal organs)	Mostly skeletal muscles
Extinction procedure	CS without UCS	Response without reinforcement

© Cengage Learning

Extinction

No doubt you have heard the saying, "If at first you don't succeed, try, try again." The comedian W. C. Fields said, "If at first you don't succeed, try, try again. Then quit. There's no point in being a damn fool about it."

In operant conditioning, extinction *occurs if responses stop producing reinforcements.* For example, you were once in the habit of asking your roommate to join you for supper. The last few times you asked, your roommate said no, so you stop asking. In classical conditioning, extinction is achieved by presenting the CS without the UCS. In operant conditioning, the procedure is response without reinforcement. Table 6.2 compares classical and operant conditioning.

Generalization

Someone who receives reinforcement for a response in the presence of one stimulus will probably make the same response in the presence of a similar stimulus. *The more similar a new stimulus is to the original reinforced stimulus, the more likely is the same response.* This phenomenon is known as stimulus generalization. For example, you might reach for the turn signal of a rented car in the same place you would find it in your own car.

Many animals have evolved an appearance that takes advantage of their predators' stimulus generalization (Darst & Cummings, 2006). A predatory bird that learns to avoid a poisonous snake probably also avoids a harmless look-alike snake. A bird that learns to avoid a bad-tasting butterfly will also avoid other butterflies of similar appearance. Figure 6.13 shows one example.

Poisonous   Harmless

Figure 6.13 The harmless frog evolved an appearance that resembles a poisonous species, taking advantage of the way birds generalize their learned avoidance responses. (Source: C. R. Darst & M. E. Cummings, 2006)

Discrimination and Discriminative Stimuli

If reinforcement occurs for responding to one stimulus and not another, the result is discrimination between them, yielding *a response to one stimulus and not the other.* For example, you smile and greet someone you think you know, but then you realize it is someone else. After several such experiences, you learn to recognize the difference between the two people.

A *stimulus that indicates which response is appropriate or inappropriate* is called a discriminative stimulus. Much of our behavior depends on discriminative stimuli. For example, you learn ordinarily to be quiet during a lecture but to talk when the professor encourages discussion. You learn to drive fast on some streets and slowly on others. Throughout your day, one stimulus after another signals which behaviors will yield reinforcement, punishment, or neither. *The ability of a stimulus to encourage some responses and discourage others* is known as stimulus control.

B. F. Skinner and the Shaping of Responses

One of the most famous psychological researchers, B. F. Skinner (1904–1990), demonstrated many uses of operant conditioning. Skinner was a devoted behaviorist who always sought simple explanations in terms of reinforcement histories rather than complex mental processes.

One problem confronting any behavior researcher is how to define a response. Imagine watching children and trying to count "aggressive behaviors." What is an aggressive act and what isn't? Skinner simplified the measurement by simplifying the situation (Zuriff, 1995): He set up a box, called an *operant-conditioning chamber* (or *Skinner box*, a

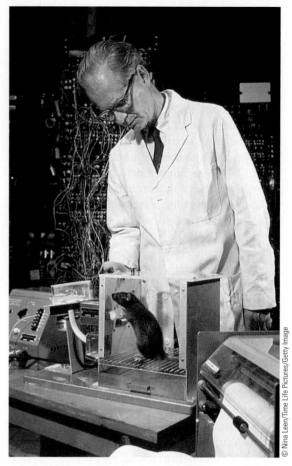

Figure 6.14 B. F. Skinner examines a rat in an operant-conditioning chamber. When the light above the bar is on, pressing the bar is reinforced. A food pellet rolls out of the storage device (left) and down the tube into the cage.

term that Skinner himself never used), in which a rat presses a lever or a pigeon pecks an illuminated "key" to receive food (Figure 6.14). He operationally defined the response as anything that the animal did to depress the lever or key. So if the rat pressed the lever with its snout instead of its paw, the response still counted. If the pigeon batted the key with its wing instead of pecking it with its beak, it still counted. The behavior was defined by its outcome, not by muscle movements.

Does that definition make sense? Skinner's reply was that it did because it led to consistent results. When deciding how to define a behavior—any behavior—the best definition is the one that produces the clearest results.

Shaping Behavior

When Thorndike wanted to train a cat to push a pole or pull a string, he simply put the cat in a puzzle box and waited. Skinner wanted to train rats to push levers and pigeons to peck at keys. These behaviors

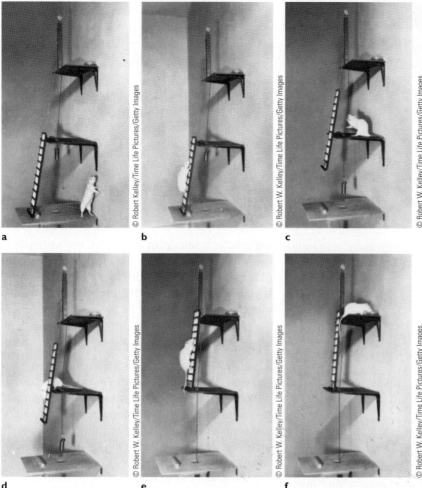

a   b   c

d   e   f

Figure 6.15 In chaining, each behavior is reinforced by the opportunity to engage in the next behavior. To reach food on the top platform, this rat must climb a ladder and pull a string to raise the ladder so that it can climb again.

Chaining Behavior

Ordinarily, you don't do just one action and then stop. You do a long sequence of actions. To produce a sequence, psychologists use a procedure called chaining. Assume you want to train a show horse to go through a sequence of actions. You could *chain* the behaviors, *reinforcing each one with the opportunity to engage in the next one.* The animal starts by learning the final behavior. Then it learns the next to last behavior, which is reinforced by the opportunity to perform the final behavior. And so on.

For example, a rat might be placed on the top platform, as in Figure 6.15f, where it eats. Then it is put on the intermediate platform with a ladder leading to the top platform. The rat learns to climb the ladder. Then it is placed again on the intermediate platform but without the ladder. It must learn to pull a string to raise the ladder so that it can climb to the top platform. Then the rat is placed on the bottom platform (Figure 6.15a). It now learns to climb the ladder to the intermediate platform, pull a string to raise the ladder, and then climb the ladder again. A chain like this can go on and on. Each behavior is reinforced with the opportunity for the next behavior, until the final behavior is reinforced with food.

People learn chains of responses, too. You learn to eat with a fork and spoon. Then you learn to put your own food on the plate before eating. Eventually, you learn to plan a menu, go to the store, buy the ingredients, cook the meal, put it on the plate, and then eat it. Each behavior is reinforced by the opportunity to engage in the next behavior.

To show the effectiveness of shaping and chaining, Skinner performed a demonstration: First, he trained a rat to go to the center of a cage. Then he trained it to do so only when he played a certain piece of music. Next he trained it to wait for the music, go to the center of the cage, and sit up on its hind legs. Step by step, he eventually trained the rat to wait for the music (the "Star-Spangled Banner"), move to the center of the cage, sit up on its hind legs, put its claws on a string next to a pole, pull the string to hoist the U.S. flag, and then stand back and salute. Only then did the rat get its reinforcement. Needless to say, patriotism is not part of a rat's usual repertoire. The point is, chaining can produce complex behaviors.

Schedules of Reinforcement

The simplest procedure in operant conditioning is to *provide reinforcement for every correct response*, a procedure known as continuous reinforcement. However, in the real world, continuous reinforcement is not common.

are not part of the animals' normal routine. If he simply put an animal into a box and waited, he might be in for a very long wait. To speed the process, Skinner introduced a powerful technique, called shaping, for *establishing a new response by reinforcing successive approximations to it.*

To *shape* a rat to press a lever, you might begin by reinforcing the rat for standing up, a common behavior in rats. After a few reinforcements, the rat stands up more frequently. Now you change the rules, giving food only when the rat stands up while facing the lever. Soon it spends more time standing up and facing the lever. It extinguishes its behavior of standing and facing in other directions because those responses are not reinforced.

Next you provide reinforcement only when the rat stands facing the correct direction while in the half of the cage nearer the lever. You gradually move the boundary, and the rat moves closer to the lever. Then the rat must touch the lever and, finally, apply weight to it. Through a series of short, easy steps, you shape the rat to press a lever.

Shaping works with humans, too, of course. Consider education: First, your parents or teachers praise you for counting your fingers. Later, you must add and subtract to earn their congratulations. Step by step, your tasks become more complex until you are doing advanced mathematics.

Table 6.3 Some Schedules of Reinforcement

Type	Description
Continuous	Reinforcement for every response of the correct type
Fixed ratio	Reinforcement following completion of a specific number of responses
Variable ratio	Reinforcement for an unpredictable number of responses that varies around a mean value
Fixed interval	Reinforcement for the first response that follows a given delay since the previous reinforcement
Variable interval	Reinforcement for the first response that follows an unpredictable delay (varying around a mean value) since the previous reinforcement

© Cengage Learning

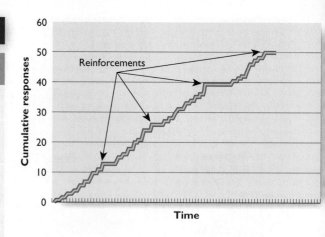

ing greater numbers of responses. For example, if you have just completed 10 math problems, you pause briefly before starting your next assignment. If you had to complete 100 problems, you pause longer.

Variable-Ratio Schedule

A **variable-ratio schedule** is similar to a fixed-ratio schedule, except that *reinforcement occurs after a variable number of correct responses.* For example, reinforcement might sometimes occur after one or two responses, sometimes after five, sometimes after ten, and so on. Variable-ratio schedules generate steady response rates.

Variable-ratio schedules, or approximations of them, occur whenever each response has about an equal probability of success. For example, when you apply for a job, you might or might not be hired. The more times you apply, the better your chances, but you cannot predict how many applications you need to submit before receiving a job offer. Gambling pays off on a variable ratio. If you enter a lottery, each time you enter you have some chance of winning, but you can't predict how many times you must enter before winning (if ever).

Fixed-Interval Schedule

A **fixed-interval schedule** *provides reinforcement for the first response after a specific time interval.* For instance, an animal might get food for its first response after a 15-second interval. Then it would have to wait another 15 seconds before another response is effective. Animals (including humans) on such a schedule learn to pause after reinforcement and begin to respond again toward the end of the time interval. As the time of the next reinforcement approaches, the rate of responding accelerates. The cumulative record is on the next page. Note that the delay from one reinforcement to the next is constant, but the number of responses is variable.

Reinforcement for some responses and not for others is known as intermittent reinforcement or partial reinforcement. We behave differently when we learn that only some of our responses will be reinforced. Psychologists have investigated the effects of many schedules of reinforcement, which are *rules for the delivery of reinforcement.* Four schedules for the delivery of intermittent reinforcement are fixed ratio, fixed interval, variable ratio, and variable interval (see Table 6.3). A ratio schedule provides reinforcements depending on the number of responses. An interval schedule provides reinforcements depending on the timing of responses.

Fixed-Ratio Schedule

A **fixed-ratio schedule** *provides reinforcement only after a certain (fixed) number of correct responses.* Examples include farms that pay fruit pickers by the bushel and bakeries that offer one free bagel for every ten you buy.

A fixed-ratio schedule requiring a small number of responses, such as two or three, produces a steady rate of response. However, if the schedule requires many responses before reinforcement, the typical result is a pause after each reinforcement, and then resumption of steady responding. Researchers sometimes graph the results with a *cumulative record*, in which the line is flat when the individual does not respond, and it moves up with each response. For a fixed-ratio schedule requiring 10 responses, a typical result would look as shown above. Note that the number of responses per reinforcement is constant, but the time between one reinforcement and the next can vary. On average, pauses are longer in schedules requir-

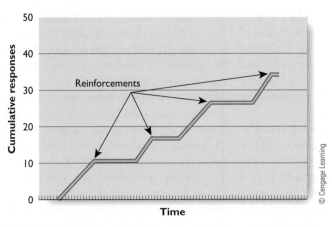

Checking your mailbox is an example of behavior on a fixed-interval schedule. If your mail is delivered at about 3 P.M. and you are eagerly awaiting an important package, you might begin to check around 2:30 and continue checking every few minutes until it arrives.

Variable-Interval Schedule

With a **variable-interval schedule**, *reinforcement is available after a variable amount of time.* For example, reinforcement may come for the first response after 2 minutes, then for the first response after the next 7 seconds, then after 3 minutes 20 seconds, and so forth. You cannot know how long before your next response is reinforced. Consequently, responses on a variable-interval schedule are slow but steady. Checking Facebook is an example: friends can post status updates at any time, so you check occasionally.

Extinction of Responses Reinforced on Different Schedules

Suppose you have two friends, Beth and Becky. Beth has been highly reliable. When she says she will do something, she does it. Becky, however, sometimes keeps her word and sometimes doesn't. Now both of them go through a period of untrustworthy behavior. With whom will you lose patience sooner? It's Beth. One explanation is that you notice the change more quickly. Because Becky has been unreliable in the past, a new stretch of similar behavior is hardly noteworthy.

Another example: You and a friend go to a gambling casino and bet on the roulette wheel. Amazingly, your first 10 bets are all winners. Your friend wins some and loses some. Then both of you go into a prolonged losing streak. Presuming both of you have the same amount of money, which of you will probably continue betting longer?

Your friend will, even though you had a more favorable early experience. Responses extinguish more slowly after intermittent reinforcement (either a ratio schedule or an interval schedule) than after continuous reinforcement. Someone who has received intermittent reinforcement is accustomed to playing without winning, and the behavior persists longer.

concept check

14. Identify which schedule of reinforcement applies to each of the following examples:
    a. You attend every new movie that appears at your local theater, although you enjoy about one fourth of them.
    b. You are told that a company will soon announce a job opportunity, and you want to be one of the first to apply. You don't know when they will post the announcement, so you keep checking every hour or two.

c. You tune your television set to an all-news cable channel, and you look up from your studies to check the sports scores every 30 minutes.

15. Amateur astronomers check the sky in hope of spotting a comet. Are the rewards on a variable-interval schedule or a variable-ratio schedule?

16. A novice gambler and a longtime gambler both lose 20 bets in a row. Which one is more likely to continue betting? Why?

Answers

14. **a. Variable ratio.** (You will be reinforced for about one fourth of your entries to the theater but on an irregular basis.) **b.** variable interval. (Checking will be effective after some interval of time, but the length of that time is unpredictable.) **c.** fixed interval.
15. This is a variable-interval schedule. In a variable-ratio schedule, the number of responses matters, but the timing does not. If you have already checked the stars tonight and found no comets, checking three more times tonight will probably be fruitless. Checking at a later date gives you a better chance.
16. The longtime gambler will continue longer because he or she has a history of being reinforced for gambling on a variable-ratio schedule, which retards extinction. For the same reason, an alcoholic who has had both good experiences and bad experiences while drunk is likely to keep on drinking after several bad experiences.

Applications

Although operant conditioning arose from theoretical concerns, it has a long history of applications. Here are two examples.

Persuasion

How could you persuade someone to do something objectionable? For an extreme example, could a captor convince a prisoner of war to cooperate?

An application of shaping is to start by reinforcing a slight degree of cooperation and then working up to the goal little by little. This principle was applied by people who probably never heard of B. F. Skinner or positive reinforcement. During the Korean War, the Chinese Communists forwarded some of the letters written home by American prisoners of war but intercepted others. (The prisoners could tell from the replies which letters had been forwarded.)

The prisoners suspected that they could get their letters through if they wrote something mildly favorable about their captors. So they began including occasional remarks that the Communists were not really so bad, that certain aspects of the Chinese system seemed to work pretty well, or that they hoped the war would end soon.

After a while, the Chinese started essay contests, offering extra food or other privileges to the soldier who wrote the best essay in the captors' opinion. Most of the winning essays contained a statement or two that offered a minor compliment to the Communists or a minor criticism of the United States. Gradually, more and more soldiers started including such statements. Then the Chinese might ask, "You said the United States is not perfect. Could you tell us some of the ways in which it is not perfect, so that we can better understand your system?" As time passed, without torture and with only modest reinforcements, the Chinese induced prisoners to denounce the United States, make false confessions, inform on fellow prisoners, and reveal military secrets (Cialdini, 1993).

The point is clear: Whether we want to get rats to salute the flag or soldiers to denounce it, the most effective training technique is to start with easy behaviors, reinforce those behaviors, and then gradually shape more complex behaviors.

Applied Behavior Analysis/ Behavior Modification

In one way or another, people almost constantly try to influence other people's behavior. Psychologists have applied operant conditioning to enhance that influence.

In applied behavior analysis, also known as behavior modification, a *psychologist removes reinforcement for unwanted behaviors and provides reinforcement for more acceptable behaviors.* For example, school psychologists instituted a program to encourage children with attention-deficit disor-der to complete more school assignments. In addition to verbal praise, children received points for each assignment completed and additional points for completing it accurately. They lost points for any rule violation, such as being out of the seat. At the end of each week, those who had accumulated enough points could go to a party or take a field trip. The result of this program was a significant increase in completion of assignments and better in-class behavior (Fabiano et al., 2007).

Another example: Many children hurt themselves on playgrounds by using equipment improperly, such as going down the slide head first. The reinforcer for this risky behavior is simply the thrill of it. To stop such behavior, a safety officer talked to elementary school classes about playground safety and offered rewards to the whole class if everyone shifted to safer playground behaviors. College students observed the children in the playground and reported instances of risky behavior. The reinforcers here were trivial, such as a colorful poster for the door of each class with students who played safely. Nevertheless, the result was decreased risky behaviors, and the improvement persisted for weeks afterward (Heck, Collins, & Peterson, 2001).

concept check

17. Of the procedures characterized in Table 6.1, which one applies to giving more attention to someone's appropriate speech? Which one applies to decreasing attention to inappropriate speech?

Answer

17. Increasing attention for appropriate speech is positive reinforcement. Decreasing attention for inappropriate speech is punishment.

module 6.2

Operant Conditioning and Human Behavior

Suppose one of your instructors announces that everyone in the class will receive the same grade at the end of the course, regardless of performance on tests and papers. Will you study hard in that course? Probably not. Or suppose your employer said that all raises and promotions would be made at ran-

dom, with no regard to how well you do your job. Would you work as hard as possible? Not likely. Our behavior depends on its consequences, just like that of a rat or pigeon. That is the main point of operant conditioning.

Summary

- *Reinforcement.* Edward Thorndike defined reinforcement as the process of increasing the future probability of the preceding response. (page 198)
- *Operant conditioning.* Operant conditioning is the process of controlling the rate of a behavior through its consequences. (page 199)
- *The nature of reinforcement.* If someone has been deprived of the opportunity to engage in a behavior, then the opportunity to return to that behavior is reinforcing. Also, something that an individual can exchange for a reinforcer becomes a reinforcer itself. (page 200)
- *Reinforcement and punishment.* Behaviors are reinforced by presenting favorable events or omitting unfavorable events. Behaviors are punished by presenting unfavorable events or omitting favorable events. (page 201)

- *Extinction.* In operant conditioning, a response is extinguished if it is no longer followed by reinforcement. (page 203)
- *Shaping.* Shaping is a technique for training subjects to perform acts by reinforcing them for successive approximations to the desired behavior. (page 204)
- *Schedules of reinforcement.* The frequency and timing of a response depend on the schedule of reinforcement. In a ratio schedule of reinforcement, an individual is given reinforcement after a fixed or variable number of responses. In an interval schedule of reinforcement, an individual is given reinforcement after a fixed or variable period of time. (page 205)
- *Applications.* People have applied operant conditioning to fields such as persuasion and applied behavior analysis. (page 207)

Key Terms

applied behavior analysis (or behavior modification) (page 208)

chaining (page 205)

continuous reinforcement (page 205)

discrimination (page 204)

discriminative stimulus (page 204)

disequilibrium principle (page 200)

extinction (page 203)

fixed-interval schedule (page 206)

fixed-ratio schedule (page 206)

intermittent reinforcement (page 206)

law of effect (page 199)

learning curve (page 198)

negative reinforcement (page 202)

operant conditioning (page 199)

positive reinforcement (page 202)

primary reinforcer (page 201)

punishment (page 201)

reinforcement (page 199)

schedule of reinforcement (page 206)

secondary reinforcer (page 201)

shaping (page 205)

skeletal responses (page 199)

stimulus control (page 204)

stimulus generalization (page 203)

variable-interval schedule (page 207)

variable-ratio schedule (page 206)

visceral responses (page 199)

module 6.3 >

Variations of Learning

- In what way is learning specialized for particular needs?
- How do we learn from the successes and failures of others without trying every response ourselves?

Thorndike, Pavlov, and the other pioneers of research on learning assumed that learning was the same wherever and whenever it occurred. If so, researchers could study any convenient example, such as salivary conditioning or the responses of pigeons in a Skinner box, and discover all the principles of learning.

However, from the start, researchers encountered results that challenge this assumption. At a minimum, some things are easier to learn than others. For example, Thorndike's cats learned to push and pull various devices in their efforts to escape from his puzzle boxes. But when Thorndike tried to teach them to scratch or lick themselves for the same reinforcement, they learned slowly and performed inconsistently (Thorndike, 1911/1970). Why?

One explanation is preparedness, the *concept that evolution has prepared us to learn some associations more easily than others* (Seligman, 1970). Presumably, cats and their ancestors since ancient times have encountered many situations in which pushing or pulling something produced a useful outcome. It makes sense for them to have evolved predispositions to facilitate this type of learning. However, when in nature would licking or scratching yourself move an obstacle and get you out of confinement? We should not expect cats to be prepared for this kind of learning.

Similarly, dogs readily learn to raise one leg or the other depending on the direction of a sound, but they are slow to learn that a ticking sound means raise one leg and a buzzer means raise the other (Dobrzecka, Szwejkowska, & Konorski, 1966). These results make sense if we assume that animals are evolutionarily prepared to learn what is useful in their natural habitat. In this example, it is unlikely in nature that one sound would mean "turn to the left" (regardless of where the sound came from) and a different sound would mean "turn to the right."

The idea of preparedness has many practical applications. People learn easily to turn a wheel

clockwise to move something to the right and counterclockwise to move it to the left (as when turning the steering wheel of a car). If the controls work the opposite way, people often get confused. Many engineers who design machines consult with human-factors psychologists about how to set up the controls so that people can easily learn to use them. In the chapter on abnormal behavior, we consider the hypothesis that people are prepared to learn fears of objects that have been dangerous throughout human existence, such as snakes and spiders.

Conditioned Taste Aversions

If a sound (CS) predicts food (UCS), learning proceeds most quickly if the CS precedes the UCS by about half a second. If a rat receives food after pressing a bar, learning is fastest if the reinforcement occurs within a second or two after the response. Based on research of this type, psychologists were at one time convinced that learning occurs only between events happening within seconds of each other (Kimble, 1961).

However, that generalization fails in certain situations. Consider what happens if you eat something and get sick to your stomach later. Despite a substantial delay between eating and feeling sick, you learn an aversion to that food. If you try eating it again, you find it repulsive. *Associating a food with illness* is conditioned taste aversion, first documented by John Garcia and his colleagues (Garcia, Ervin, & Koelling, 1966). One of its special features is that it occurs reliably after a single pairing of food with illness, even with a long delay between them. An animal drinks something it would ordinarily prefer, such as sweetened water, and receives a treatment to produce nausea minutes or hours later. The experimenter waits days for the animal to recover and then offers it a choice between sweetened and unflavored water. The animal strongly prefers the unflavored water (Garcia et al., 1966).

You would learn an aversion regardless of whether the food itself made you sick or you got sick from something else, such as riding a roller coaster. Some part of your brain reacts, "I don't care about that roller coaster. I feel sick, and I'm not taking any chances. From now on, that food is taboo."

You can learn taste aversions to a familiar food, but you acquire much stronger aversions if you had no previous safe experience with the food. If you eat several foods before becoming ill, you learn aversions mainly to the unfamiliar ones, even if you ate familiar foods closer in time to the illness. A further specialization is that you associate illness with something you ate, and not with other types of events. Let's consider the evidence.

What's the Evidence?

Predisposition in Learning

In nature, the food you eat determines whether you will feel full or hungry, healthy or sick. It doesn't predict pain on your skin. In contrast, what you see or hear might predict pain, but it seldom has anything to do with feeling nauseated.

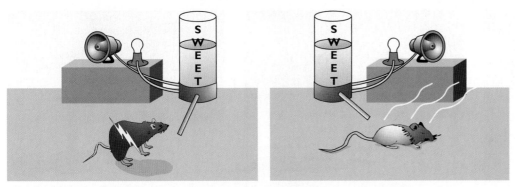

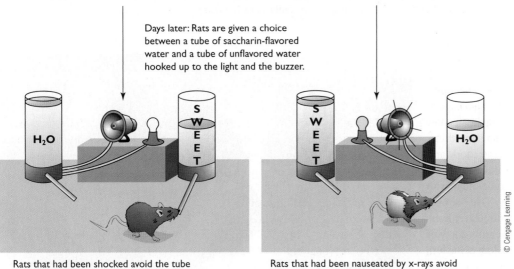

When rats drink, they taste the saccharin-flavored water and turn on a bright light and a clicking sound. Some rats receive electric shock to their feet two seconds after they start drinking. Other rats receive x-rays that produce nausea.

Days later: Rats are given a choice between a tube of saccharin-flavored water and a tube of unflavored water hooked up to the light and the buzzer.

Rats that had been shocked avoid the tube with the lights and noises.

Rats that had been nauseated by x-rays avoid the saccharin-flavored water.

Figure 6.16 An experiment by Garcia and Koelling (1966): Rats associate illness with what they ate. They associate pain with what they saw or heard.

Hypothesis Rats that experience foot shock will learn to avoid visual or auditory signals associated with the shock. Rats that experience nausea will learn to avoid foods that they recently ate.

Method Water-deprived rats were offered a tube of saccharin-flavored water. The tube was set up such that when a rat licked the spout of the tube, it turned on a bright light and a clicking sound, as shown in Figure 6.16. Thus, each rat experienced the taste, light, and noise simultaneously. Half the rats received a mild foot shock two seconds after they started licking the tube. The other half received x-rays, which produce mild nausea. After two days to allow rats to recover from the x-rays, the procedure was repeated, and after another two days it was repeated again. In the final test, rats could drink from a tube containing saccharin-flavored water, or from a separate tube containing unflavored water but connected to the light and clicking sound.

Results Rats that had received shock avoided the tube connected to lights and sounds, but drank normally from the tube with saccharin-flavored water. Rats that had received x-rays avoided the saccharin water but drank normally from the tube connected to lights and sounds.

Interpretation When a rat (or almost any other animal) receives shock to its feet, it learns to avoid the lights, sounds, or other signals that it detects at the time. When it becomes nauseated, it learns to avoid something that it ate. Animals evidently come with predispositions to learn some connections more than others. This tendency is an excellent example of preparedness.

Conditioned taste aversions have several practical applications. Ranchers have taught coyotes to avoid sheep by giving the coyotes sheep meat laced with chemicals that cause nausea (Figure 6.17). This procedure saves the ranchers' sheep without killing the coyotes (Gustavson, Kelly, Sweeney, & Garcia, 1976). One way of treating alcoholism is to follow an alcoholic drink with a drug that causes nausea. This treatment is not widely used, but when it has been

© Stuart Ellins

Figure 6.17 This coyote previously fell ill after eating sheep meat containing lithium salts. Now it reacts with revulsion toward both live and dead sheep.

used, it has been quicker and more effective than other treatments for alcoholism (Revusky, 2009). Most pregnant women experience food aversions, mainly to meats and eggs. Most of them also experience nausea ("morning sickness") during the first few weeks of pregnancy. Apparently they eat something, feel nausea for reasons unrelated to the food, and develop an aversion to the food. Women with the most nausea during pregnancy tend to be those with the strongest food aversions (Bayley, Dye, & Hill, 2009). Similarly, many cancer patients learn aversions to foods they ate just prior to chemotherapy or radiation therapy (Bernstein, 1991; Scalera & Bavieri, 2009). A good strategy is to pick one "scapegoat" food and eat it prior to each treatment. In that way, people learn a strong aversion to just one food instead of losing their appetite for more and more foods.

concept check

18. Which kind of learning takes place despite a long delay between the events to be associated?
19. What evidence indicates that conditioned taste aversion is different from other kinds of learning?

Answers

18. Conditioned taste aversions develop despite a long delay between food and illness.
19. In addition to the fact that conditioned taste aversion occurs over long delays, animals are predisposed to associate foods and not other events with illnesses.

Birdsong Learning

Birdsongs brighten the day for people who hear them, but they are earnest business for the birds themselves. For most species, song is limited to

© Heiko Wolfram/Corbis

Some people drink enough alcohol to produce nausea and vomiting. They may or may not learn an aversion to alcohol, depending on how familiar it was, how quickly they became nauseated, and other factors. Therapists have sometimes used drugs to induce nausea quickly after an alcoholic drink. After a few repetitions, an alcoholic can learn to avoid alcohol.

males during the mating season. As a rule, a song indicates, "Here I am. I am a male of species ___. If you're a female of my species, please come closer. If you're a male of my species, go away." Some species have a built-in song, but others have to learn it. The male *learns his song most readily during a* sensitive period *early in his first year of life.* (Similarly, human children learn language most easily when they are young.)

Song learning is unlike standard examples of classical and operant conditioning. During the sensitive period, the infant bird listens, makes no response, and receives no reinforcement. The following spring, when the bird starts to sing, we see a trial-and-error process. At first, his song is a mixture of sounds, like a babbling human infant, but it gradually changes until he matches the songs he heard the previous summer (Marler & Peters, 1981, 1982). His only reinforcer is recognizing that he has sung correctly.

Later in life, he may modify his song depending on competing noises. Many birds now live in suburban neighborhoods with cars, trucks, other machinery,

A male white-crowned sparrow learns his song in the first months of life but does not begin to sing it until the next year.

Social Learning

Just as many birds learn their song from other birds, humans obviously learn much from each other. You might improve your skills by trial and error, but you get started by watching what other people do, and trying to copy them.

According to the social-learning approach (Bandura, 1977, 1986), *we learn about many behaviors by observing the behaviors of others.* For example, if you want to learn to drive a car, you start by watching people who are already skilled. When you try to drive, you receive reinforcement for driving well and punishments (possible injuries) if you drive badly, but your observations of others facilitate your progress.

Social learning is a type of operant conditioning, and the underlying mechanisms are similar. If your task is to determine whether the green cards or the blue cards are more valuable, you can try choosing cards and see which one usually produces more reinforcement. Or you can take advice from another person who claims to know. Your own experience and the other person's advice produce similar outcomes, and they activate some of the same brain areas (Behrens, Hunt, Woolrich, & Rushworth, 2008). However, in many circumstances, social in-

children at play, and so forth. Humans are a noisy species. How is a little bird to make itself heard? Compared to birds away from people, those near people spend more time singing (Diaz, Parra, & Gallardo, 2011), they sing more at night when the neighborhood tends to be quieter (Fuller, Warren, & Gaston, 2007), and they sing higher-pitched songs, omitting the sounds that car and truck sounds would mask (Slabbekoorn & den Boer-Visser, 2006). Individual birds adjust their calls depending on the noise levels, so the results indicate learning, not changes in their genetics. The point is that the principles of learning vary among situations in a way that makes sense based on the animal's way of life (Rozin & Kalat, 1971).

concept check

20. What aspects of birdsong learning set it apart from classical and operant conditioning?

Answer

20. The most distinctive feature is that birdsong learning occurs when the learner makes no apparent response and receives no apparent reinforcement. Also, birdsong learning occurs most readily during an early sensitive period.

A Japanese toilet is a hole in the ground with no seat. Western visitors usually have to ask how to use it. (You squat.)

formation is much quicker and more efficient than trying to learn something on your own.

Modeling and Imitation

If you visit another country with customs unlike your own, you find much that seems bewildering. Even the way to order food in a restaurant may be unfamiliar. A hand gesture such as

is considered friendly in some countries but rude and vulgar in others. Many visitors to Japan find the toilets confusing. With effort, you learn foreign customs either because someone explains them to you or because you watch and copy. You *model* your behavior after others or *imitate* others.

In high school, what made certain students popular? No doubt you could cite many reasons, but once they became popular, simply being the center of attention increased their popularity. In fact, whenever a friend showed interest in some boy or girl, you started to notice that person, too. You modeled or imitated your friend's interest. The same is true in nonhumans. If one female shows an interest in mating with a particular male, other females increase their interest in him also (Dubois, 2007).

Other people's behavior often provides information. Did you ever have this experience? You tell your parents you want to do something because "everyone else" is doing it. They scream, "If everyone else were jumping off a cliff, would you do it, too?" Well, let's think about it. If literally *everyone* were jumping off a cliff, maybe they have a reason! Maybe you're in great danger where you are, and it would be safer to jump. Maybe if you jump, you won't fall very far, and you'll land on something soft. If everyone is doing it, you should at least consider the possibility that they know something you don't.

Another reason for imitation is that other people's behavior establishes a norm or rule. For example, you wear casual clothing where others dress casually and formalwear where others dress formally. You drive on the right side of the road in America or on the left side in Britain. Copying other people helps in many situations.

You also imitate automatically in some cases. If someone yawns, you become more likely to yawn yourself. Even seeing a photo of an animal yawning may have the same result (Figure 6.18). You are not intentionally copying, and you haven't received any

According to the social-learning approach, we learn by imitating behaviors that are reinforced and avoiding behaviors that are punished. This girl is being blessed by the temple elephant. Others who are watching may later imitate her example.

new information. You imitate because seeing a yawn suggested the idea of yawning.

You automatically imitate many other actions that you see, often with no apparent motivation (Dijksterhuis & Bargh, 2001). If you see someone smile or frown, you briefly start to smile or frown. Your expression may be a quick, involuntary twitch that is hard to notice, but it does occur. Spectators at an athletic event sometimes move their arms or legs slightly in synchrony with what some athlete is doing. When expert pianists listen to a composition they have practiced, they start involuntarily tapping their fingers as if they were playing the music (Haueisen & Knösche, 2001). People also copy the hand gestures they see (Bertenthal, Longo, & Kosobud, 2006). You can demonstrate by telling someone, "Please wave your hands" while you clap your hands. Many people copy your actions instead of following your instructions.

try it ▶ yourself

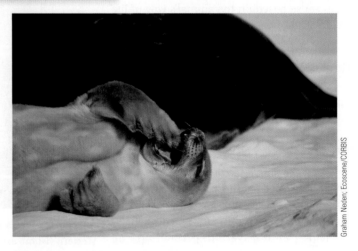

Figure 6.18 Does looking at this photo make you want to yawn?

Figure 6.19 This girl attacks a doll after seeing a film of a woman hitting it. Witnessing violence increases the probability of violent behavior.

Albert Bandura, Dorothea Ross, and Sheila Ross (1963) studied the role of imitation for learning aggressive behavior. They asked two groups of children to watch films in which an adult or a cartoon character violently attacked an inflated "Bobo" doll. Another group watched a different film. They then left the children in a room with a Bobo doll. Only the children who had watched films with attacks on the doll attacked the doll themselves, using many of the same movements they had just seen (Figure 6.19). The clear implication is that children copy the aggressive behavior they have seen in others.

concept check

21. Many American politicians campaign with similar styles and take similar stands on the issues. Explain this observation in terms of social learning.

Politicians consistently run negative ads against their opponents because these kinds of ads have proven to be effective in previous campaigns. Hence the use of negative campaigning is an example of vicarious reinforcement.

Answer

21. One reason that most American politicians run similar campaigns and take similar stands is that they all tend to copy the same models—candidates who have won recent elections. Another reason is that they all pay attention to the same public opinion polls.

Vicarious Reinforcement and Punishment

Six months ago, your best friend quit a job with Consolidated Generic Products to open a restaurant. Now you are considering quitting your job and opening your own restaurant. How do you decide what to do?

You probably start by asking how successful your friend has been. You imitate behavior that has been reinforcing to someone else, especially someone that you like (Mobbs et al., 2009). That is, you learn by vicarious reinforcement or vicarious punishment—by *substituting someone else's experience for your own.*

Whenever a new business venture succeeds, other companies copy it. For example, the first few successful Internet companies were followed by a horde of imitators. When a sports team wins consistently, other teams copy its style of play. When a television program wins high ratings, other producers are sure to present look-alikes the following year. Politicians imitate the campaign tactics of candidates who were previously elected.

Advertisers depend heavily on vicarious reinforcement. They show happy, successful people using their product, with the implication that if you use their product, you too will be happy and successful. The people promoting state lotteries show the ecstatic winners—never the losers!—suggesting that if you play the lottery, you too can win.

Vicarious punishment is generally less effective (Kuroshima, Kuwahata, & Fujita, 2008). If you see someone succeed, you copy the technique as well as you can. If you see people fail, you don't know why they failed or what would work better. Furthermore, people who are optimistic about their own future do not identify with people who have failed. Others suffer because of heavy drinking, cigarette smoking, obesity, risky sex, lack of exercise, or failure to wear seat belts, but we tell ourselves, "It won't happen to me."

Self-Efficacy in Social Learning

We primarily imitate successful people. So, when you watch an Olympic diver win a gold medal, why do you (presumably) *not* try to imitate those dives? You imitate someone else's behavior only if you

We tend to imitate the actions of successful people but only if we feel self-efficacy, a belief that we could perform the task well.

have a sense of self-efficacy—*the belief of being able to perform the task successfully.* You consider your strengths and weaknesses, compare yourself to the successful person, and estimate your chance of success.

This effect is clear in children's life aspirations. Nearly anyone would like a high-paying, high-prestige profession, but many think they could never rise to that level, so they don't try (Bandura, Barbaranelli, Caprara, & Pastorelli, 2001). One value of getting women and minorities into high-visibility leadership jobs is that they provide role models, showing others that the opportunity is available. Athletic teams and other groups also differ in their feeling of efficacy. A group confident of its abilities accomplishes much more than a group with doubts.

We acquire a sense of self-efficacy mainly through our own successes but also partly by watching and identifying with role models.

Self-Reinforcement and Self-Punishment

If your sense of self-efficacy is strong enough, you try to imitate the behavior of a successful person. But actually succeeding may require prolonged efforts. People typically set a goal for themselves and monitor their progress toward that goal. Sometimes people reinforce or punish themselves, just as if they were training someone else. They say, "If I finish this math assignment on time, I'll treat myself to a movie. If I don't finish on time, I'll make myself clean my room." (Nice threat, but people usually forgive themselves without imposing the punishment.)

Some therapists teach clients to use self-reinforcement. One 10-year-old boy had a habit of biting his fingernails, sometimes down to the skin and even drawing blood. He learned to keep records of how much nail-biting he did at various times of day, and then he set goals for himself. If he met the goals of reducing his nail-biting, he wrote compliments such as "I'm great! I did wonderful!" The penalty for doing worse was that he would return his weekly allowance to his parents. An additional reinforcement was that his father promised that if the son made enough progress, he would let the son be the "therapist" to help the father quit smoking. Over several weeks, the boy quit nail-biting altogether (Ronen & Rosenbaum, 2001).

One amusing anecdote shows how self-reinforcement and self-punishment can fail: To try to quit smoking cigarettes, psychologist Ron Ash (1986) vowed to smoke only while he was reading *Psychological Bulletin* and other highly respected but tedious journals. He hoped to associate smoking with boredom. Two months later, he was smoking as much as ever, but he was starting to *enjoy* reading *Psychological Bulletin*!

module 6.3 >

In Closing

All Learning Is Not the Same

When investigators examine how synapses change during learning, they find similar mechanisms in all species and a wide variety of situations. Nevertheless, we find multiple variations on the theme. The ways we learn are adapted to different situations, such as food choice and birdsong. We use social mechanisms to facilitate and hasten learning. The outcome of these specializations is learning that is highly efficient for many purposes.

Summary

- *Preparedness.* Evolution has prepared us (and other animals) to learn some associations more readily than others. (page 210)
- *Conditioned taste aversions.* Animals, including people, learn to avoid foods, especially unfamiliar ones, if they become ill afterward. This type of learning occurs reliably after a single pairing, even with a long delay between the food and the illness. Illness is associated much more strongly with foods than with other stimuli. (page 210)
- *Birdsong learning.* Infant birds of some species must hear their songs during a sensitive period early in life if they are to develop a fully normal song the following spring. During the early learning, the bird makes no response and receives no reinforcement. (page 212)
- *Imitation.* We learn much by observing other people's actions and their consequences. (page 214)
- *Vicarious reinforcement and punishment.* We tend to imitate behaviors that lead to reinforcement for other people. We are less consistent in avoiding behaviors that are unsuccessful for others. (page 215)
- *Self-efficacy.* Whether we imitate a behavior depends on whether we believe we are capable of duplicating it. (page 215)
- *Self-reinforcement and self-punishment.* Once people have decided to try to imitate a certain behavior, they set goals for themselves and may even provide their own reinforcements. (page 216)

Key Terms

conditioned taste aversion (page 210)
preparedness (page 210)
self-efficacy (page 216)
sensitive period (page 212)

social-learning approach (page 213)
vicarious reinforcement (or vicarious punishment) (page 215)

exploration and study

Access an interactive eBook and chapter-specific learning tools, including
- **flashcards**
- **quizzes**
- **videos**

and more, in your Psychology CourseMate. Go to **CengageBrain.com.**

If your professor has assigned Aplia:

1. Sign in to your account.
2. Complete the corresponding exercises as required by your professor.
3. When finished, click "Grade It Now" to see which areas you have mastered, which areas need more work, and detailed explanations of every answer.

Whatever Happened to "Little Albert"?

Alan J. Fridlund, Ph.D.

June 2010

For psychologists, the question in the title is as mythic as "Who Killed JFK?" - one full of history, rumors and falsehoods, and until recently, few facts. Little Albert is a tale of psychological history, too be sure, but it's also a tale of unbridled ego, seedy romance, historical distortion, and child abuse. Who was Little Albert, and why do we care?

"Little Albert" was merely a 9-month-old boy, a boy who was the subject in one of the most famous psychological experiments of all time. The experimenter was John Broadus Watson, a larger-than-life figure known as "Big John" to his family, a famous psychologist who had by 1915 become the President of the American Psychological Association. He was a professor at The Johns Hopkins University in Baltimore, and the founder and editor of the premier psychological journal, the *Journal of Experimental Psychology*.

But by 1920, only five years later, he had to flee Johns Hopkins, his marriage in shambles and his career gone down in flames. But we're getting ahead of the story.

The Theory

Just a few years earlier, Watson had read several Russian "reflexologists," men like Pavlov and Bekhterev, who contended that our brains were simply reflex machines that "built" all we know and do from chains of stimulus-response associations. Watson soon declared himself a "behaviorist," which was an amalgam of a mechanistic reflexology with a dose of can-do liberal American utopianism. For Watson, behaviorism was an antidote to both introspectionism's obsession with thinking, and Freud's emphasis on early childhood sexual conflicts. It was for him a liberating view, because human nature, he argued, was primarily the simple product of "conditioned reflexes." What we thought, how we felt, how we reacted, all were malleable. And through correct training beginning in childhood, we could create a society of just the people we wanted. Here's the most famous Watson quote, taken from a later book:

> Give me a dozen healthy infants, well-formed, and my own specified world to bring them up in and I'll guarantee to take any one at random and train him to become any type of specialist I might select – doctor, lawyer, artist, merchant-chief and, yes, even beggar-man and thief, regardless of his talents, penchants, tendencies, abilities, vocations, and race of his ancestors. (Watson, 1930, p. 82)

Watson began a campaign of evangelical articles, books and speeches promoting his behaviorist agenda. He just needed a little evidence. He hoped to find it with Little Albert.

At part of his grand theory, Watson had argued that our emotional reactions to the people and events in our lives were largely conditioned. Although he believed that the infant arrived in the world with a few innate, primitive reactions (love, fear, and rage), they were essentially unanchored and free-floating. Whom does the infant come to love? What does he come to fear? When does he throw a tantrum? Those things were the product of conditioning, as well as the more refined emotions that arise later in life (Watson & Morgan, 1917). To prove this, Watson hoped to show, via Pavlovian conditioning procedures, that he could create new emotional reactions in a child. Of all the emotions he might have conditioned, Watson picked *fear*.

The "Little Albert" Study

The details of the attempt are contained in the 1920 research article he and his graduate student Rosalie Rayner published on their experiment (Watson & Rayner, 1920, and available at the Web site *http://psychclassics.yorku.ca/Watson/emotion.htm*). First they needed a child, and they found one in the infant they presented as "Albert B.," a 9-month-old Caucasian boy they located at an "invalid children" home on the Johns Hopkins campus, where his mother was employed as a wet nurse. Albert was an ideal subject, because he was "on the whole stolid and unemotional … No one had ever seen him in a state of fear and rage. The infant practically never cried." Watson and Rayner averred that "we felt that we could do him relatively little harm by carrying out such experiments" (p. 2).

As in all basic fear-conditioning experiments, Watson and Rayner had to do 3 things: (1) show Albert did not fear the experimental stimuli at the outset, (2) expose Albert to the experimental stimuli while he was fearful, and (3) test whether that exposure produced a new, conditioned fear to the previously neutral stimuli.

To "pre-test" their stimuli, Watson and Rayner took Albert to a small darkroom outfitted with a table and a mattress. They seated him and proceeded to confront Albert suddenly, and without warning, with an array of stimuli that might be suitable for later testing: "a white rat, a rabbit, a dog, a monkey, with masks with and without hair, cotton wool, burning newspapers, etc." Albert typically reached out to touch whatever was presented him, and as the authors placed in italics type, *"At no time did this infant ever show fear in any situation"* (p.2).

Watson and Rayner with Albert B. ("Little Albert")

Watson and Rayner then had to ensure that they could elicit fear sufficient to produce conditioning. Without warning, one of the experimenters distracted Albert while the other stood behind him and banged a hammer onto a 4-foot steel bar. It worked.

The child started violently, his breathing was checked and the arms were raised in a characteristic manner. On the second stimulation the same thing occurred, and in addition the lips began to pucker and tremble. On the third stimulation the child broke into a sudden crying fit. (Watson & Rayner, 1920, p. 2).

Now knowing that they could induce fear in Albert, and having established that their experimental stimuli were "neutral," Watson and Rayner then went about trying to make Albert afraid of their stimuli. The experimenters admitted to a moment of circumspection:

At first there was considerable hesitation upon our part in making the attempt to set up fear reactions experimentally. A certain responsibility attaches to such a procedure. We decided finally to make the attempt, comforting ourselves by the reflection that such attachments would arise anyway as soon as the child left the sheltered environment of the nursery for the rough and tumble of the home. (Watson & Rayner, 1920, p. 3).

But proceed they did. When Albert had reached 11 months of age, they began a number of conditioning trials in which Albert was exposed to the stimuli while the bar was banged with the hammer behind his head. The results? After seven conditioning trials with the rat and the bar-clang, Albert would begin to cry and turn away just at the sight of the white rat. About 5 days later, Albert continued to show fear toward the rat, but also appeared to generalize this fear toward the rabbit, the dog, and a sealskin coat. He didn't appear fearful toward the Santa Claus mask or a package of white cotton, and he played freely with wooden blocks (see Harris, 1979, for details, as well as the original report by Watson and Rayner, 1920).

Five days later, Watson and Rayner tried to "freshen" Albert's fear of the rat with another conditioning trial, and also attempted to condition Albert directly to the dog and the rabbit by banging the bar with the hammer while presenting each. Unfortunately, the testing occurred in a lecture hall under a skylight with a small audience present. Under these conditions, Albert showed very little reaction to any of the animals. Only after yet another "freshening" of fear to the rat with another bar-banging trial did Albert react much to the rat alone, and at this point, Albert reacted strongly even to the rabbit. But what really terrified Albert was the dog, who until then had been silent, and toward whom Albert had been showing no fear. As Watson and Rayner described the scene:

Just at this moment the dog, which had not barked before, barked three times loudly when only about six inches from the baby's face. Albert immediately fell over and broke into a wail that continued until the dog was removed (Watson & Rayner, 1920, p. 9).

After Albert had been so traumatized, Watson and Raynor struck a bizarre note of levity: "The sudden barking of the hitherto quiet dog produced a marked fear response in the adult observers!" (p. 9)

In a final set of tests, conduced about one month after this last set, Albert showed fear reactions to most of the experimental stimuli, although he reached out ambivalently for the sealskin coat and the rabbit.

What did Watson and Rayner make of these findings? They crowed grandly:

These experiments would seem to show conclusively that directly conditioned emotional responses as well as those conditioned by transfer persist, although with a certain loss in the intensity of the reaction, for a longer period than one month. Our view is that they persist and modify personality throughout life.

Our own view …is that these responses in the home environment are likely to persist indefinitely, unless an accidental method for removing them is hit upon. The importance of establishing some method must be apparent to all. (Watson & Rayner, 1920, p. 12).

Did Watson and Rayner have any compunction about inducing fears in Albert but not removing them? Here, Watson and Rayner portrayed themselves not as trailblazers but as victims of circumstance:

Unfortunately Albert was taken from the hospital the day the above tests were made. Hence the opportunity of building up an experimental technique by means of which we could remove the conditioned emotional responses was denied us. (Watson & Rayner, 1920, p. 12).

Watson would later get the chance to demonstrate that conditioning procedures could be used to remove an existing fear. In 1919-1020, he supervised a Columbia University graduate named Mary Cover (later, Mary Cover *Jones*), who reduced a young boy's fear of a white rabbit by presenting the rabbit along with the boy's favorite food. Her research (Jones, 1924) described the first example of what much later became known as "behavior therapy."

The Study's Influence

For Watson, the Little Albert experiment was proof of his theory of emotion. He went on to use it as the basis for a whole philosophy of child-rearing, which he outlined in his book *Psychological care of infant and child* (Watson, 1928). In his philosophy, emotional reactions are trained, and emotional training should be conducted to maximize independence and not out of sentimentality. Children should not be hugged gratuitously, or necessarily fed when they were hungry, because this might "spoil" them. Instead, they should be hugged only after some success, and should be fed strictly on schedule (Watson, 1928). Watson wrote:

Children should be awakened at 6:30 A.M. for orange juice and a pee. Play 'till 7:30. Breakfast should be at 7:30 sharp; at 8:00 they should be placed on the toilet for twenty minutes or less 'til bowel movement is complete. Then follow up with a verbal report. The child would then play indoors 'till 10:00 A.M., after 10:00 outside, a short nap after lunch, then "social play" with others. In the evening a bath, quiet play until bedtime at 8:00 sharp (Watson, 1928)

Children, he thought, should be taken from their mothers during their third or fourth week, lest the infants become too dependent:

In conclusion won't you then remember when you are tempted to pet your child that mother love is a dangerous instrument? An instrument which … may wreck your adult son or daughter's vocational future and their chances for marital happiness. (Watson, 1928, p. 87).

Excessive touching was always to be discouraged; Watson believed that the Boy Scouts and the YMCA would encourage male homosexuality, while pajama parties and sleepovers could turn young girls into lesbians (Hartley & Commire, 1990).

By the 1930's, Watson's child-rearing nostrums were widely accepted, and his book became a best seller. His unsparing views on discipline and affection held sway until the late 1940's, when pediatrician Dr. Benjamin Spock published *Baby and Child Care*, which advocated close, nurturant bonds between parent and child (see Buckley, 1989).

Did the Little Albert study actually support any of Watson's views? Psychologist Ben Harris (1979) described how, over the years, the findings have been misreported, misinterpreted, and exaggerated, first by Watson himself, and then by later experts in the field – even despite persistent severe criticisms that: (1)the study provided little evidence for any kind of lasting conditioning, much less a phobia; (2) whatever kind of conditioning it did achieve was debatable: the bar was typically struck when Albert reached out to touch the stimulus, making the procedure one of operant punishment more than classical conditioning; (3) the experiment was done only with one participant, and an atypical one at that: a stoical infant who "practically never cried" ; (4) several later investigators were unable to replicate Watson's results; (5) the measurements of Albert's fear were entirely subjective.

Despite its flaws, many of which were widely acknowledged in its day, the "Little Albert" experiment became one of the most-cited experiments in introductory psychology textbooks. It was also cited widely in advanced texts dealing with phobias and behavior therapy, a set of psychotherapy techniques derived from conditioning principles. Even though the study's findings were weak and inconsistent, they were still interpreted as evidence for how emotions are acquired, and how phobias are produced. Still, Mary Cover's later treatment of a rabbit phobia was a hopeful sign, and it led to the modern de-conditioning therapy procedure known as "systematic desensitization" (Wolpe & Lazarus, 1966).

Today, thankfully, the experiment by Watson and Rayner would never be permitted. No research on "Albert," a minor child, would be allowed without the mother's explicitly consenting to the procedures and their risks. The wanton induction of terror in a baby would be considered child abuse, and the failure to act to ameliorate any damage to a research participant would be professionally negligent. In today's research and legal climate, Watson and Rayner would be most likely be dismissed, civilly sued for damages, and criminally tried and imprisoned.

L'*Affaire* Rosalie, and Watson's Fate

Did I mention that Watson was married? Watson's wife was Mary Ickes, of the politically influential Ickes family. Mary's brother was Harold Ickes, who later became Secretary of the Interior under Franklin D. Roosevelt. Harold's son Harold Ickes, Jr., was a lawyer who became a "fixer" during the Clinton scandals of the 1990's, and was chief campaign adviser during Hillary Clinton's successful 2000 run for the New York Senate seat (see Grove, 1997).

Mary had been Watson's undergraduate student at the University of Chicago (he was 26, she was 19), and they began dating after she revealed her crush on her "Professor Watson." They were married secretly in late 1903, and had their daughter Polly in 1905; their son John, Jr. ("Little John"), was born a few years later. The marriage was always troubled, and Watson, who was reputedly always a heavy drinker and a womanizer, did not act to respect it.

By 1919, Watson was becoming a psychology "star," and an ambitious one at that. He was already good friends with Rayner's parents in Baltimore, and became their daughter Rosalie's supervisor when she entered Johns Hopkins as a new psychology grad student. He also began a secret affair with her under their noses (he was 42, she was 19 and only 4 years older than Watson's daughter). By all accounts, Rosalie was a beautiful, wealthy woman who drove to campus in a Stutz Bearcat convertible.

She was also the niece of Senator Isidor Rayner, who spearheaded the official U. S. Senate inquest on the sinking of the Titanic.

Rosalie's affair with Watson was under wraps at first: they worked together during the week but had secret trysts in New York on the weekends. The arrangement blew up when Mary discovered some of the passionate love letters Watson had written Rosalie. The letters found their way (probably via Mary's brother) to the *Baltimore Sun*, which made them front-page news and created a massive P.R. problem for Johns Hopkins. By late 1920, Johns Hopkins asked a shamed Watson to leave. After having endured many such humiliations as the wife of "Big John," Mary Ickes Watson gave a long, revelatory interview to the *New York Herald*, filed for divorce and took him for everything he had (Buckley, 1989).

Nearly penniless, and with the aid of his friend, psychologist Edward Titchener, Watson found his way to New York and a job at the prestigious J. Walter Thompson ad agency, where he was expected to act as a showpiece, bringing scientific principles to advertising (Kneshel, 1990). He consulted with executives at Macy's, monitored sales of Yuban Coffee, and managed the account for Johnson & Johnson's Baby Powder, becoming a vice president within four years. While at "Thompson," he helped develop: (1) the "blindfold" test for telling brands apart; (2) the concept of brand loyalty and how to build it via emotional associations; (3) the notion of "timed obsolescence," in which slight revisions of old products were introduced as "brand new" and thus made more desirable; (4) the "impulse counter," which located guilty purchases like candy and tabloid magazines next to the cash register; and (5) the tradition of the "coffee break," part of an ad campaign for Maxwell House Coffee.

And Watson and Rosalie? They married only 10 days after the ink was dry on his divorce from Mary. They had two sons, and ever Watson's acolyte, she wrote an article for *Parents* magazine entitled, "I am the mother of the behaviorist's sons," about being a "behaviorist's wife" and on using behaviorism to rear her children. The article was revealing. In it, she disclosed that she and Watson were unable to condition their sons' bowels. She also admitted to personal weakness: at times she just couldn't help hugging and kissing her children, and she all too often took their side in the family (Hartley & Commire, 1990). As Rosalie confessed:

> In some respects I bow to the great wisdom in the science of behaviorism, and in others I am rebellious … I secretly wish that on the score of [the children's] affections they will be a little weak when they grow up, that they will have a tear in their eyes for the poetry and drama of life and a throb for romance … I like being merry and gay and having the giggles. The behaviorists think giggling is a sign of maladjustment." (cited in Boakes, 1984, p. 227).

Nonetheless, Rosalie and Watson remained happily married until she died of pneumonia in 1935. Watson's children, the children of the behaviorist, did not fare well. Of his two children with Mary, Polly left school after 10th grade, was alcoholic and repeatedly depressed and suicidal (see below); and "Little John" remained rootless and dependent financially upon his father.

His two sons with Rosalie ("William" and "James", a psychology in-joke) fared little better. The older son Billy renounced his father's behaviorism, became a successful but tormented Freudian psychoanalyst, and committed suicide at age 40. The younger son Jimmy, who always considered his father unable to express emotion or caretaking, suffered from depression, chronic stomach problems and headaches, but after psychoanalysis became a successful corporate executive until he died of bleeding ulcers in the early 1950's.

After Watson left advertising, he retired to a 40-acre Connecticut farm and lived with a female companion until he died in 1958 at age 80. Just one year before, he had been awarded a lifetime achievement award from the American Psychological Association. His research inspired later researchers like B.F. Skinner, and Watson is considered the "Father of Behaviorism." Still, according to one historian, Watson was a bitter recluse, and before he died, he burned all his letters and personal papers (Burnham, 1994).

Watson's life and legacy came in for re-examination in 1990 when TV actress Mariette Hartley published a testimonial book called *Breaking the Silence*, about her life as "Big John's" granddaughter (she was Polly's daughter). In trying to understand her own struggles with alcoholism, depression and suicidality (and those of her mother and uncles), she blamed Watson's behaviorism, and related how her "grandfather's theories infected my mother's life, my life, and the lives of millions" (Hartley & Commire, 1990). In recent years, Hartley has become a spokesperson for suicide prevention. She has also revealed her struggle with bipolar disorder, which is partly hereditary, and which may help explain the always larger-than-life John Broadus Watson.

The Boy

In the years following the experiment, generations of psychologists (and Psych 1 students) have asked, " Whatever happened to Little Albert?" Who was he, what was his real name, how was he affected by the famous experiment? For nearly 90 years, no one was sure. There were many rumors. Some rued that he might have ended up in a therapist's office trying to undo his white-fur phobia, whose origins would surely have been mysterious to him.

The mystery appears to have seen resolved. In 2009, psychologists Hall Beck, Sharman Levinson and Gary Irons reported the results of their seven-year quest to find "Little Albert" (Beck, Levinson, & Irons, 2009). In order to solve this "90-year-old cold case" (p. 605), they had to rifle through U.S. Census data, Maryland birth records, and Johns Hopkins employment data. They sought out FBI photo ID experts, and undertook a painstaking reconstruction of the timeline of the Little Albert study, down to the exact days that Watson and Rayner tested "Albert."

Their investigation reads like a *CSI* episode, and it points to "Albert" as being one Douglas Merritte, the son of unmarried Arvilla Merritte, employed as a wet nurse at the Harriet Lane Home for unwed mothers on the Johns Hopkins University campus. Surviving members of the Merritte family were located and interviewed as to Douglas's fate.

Did he live well? Did he come to realize his fame? Was he scarred by his early traumatization at the hands of Watson and Rayner? Did he require psychotherapy to undo his phobias? It appears that none of this happened. Douglas died at age 6 of a brain condition called hydrocephalus, the accumulation of fluid in the brain, treated these days by a simple shunt. Untreated infant hydrocephalus sometimes presents with signs that include lethargy and indifference, raising the possibility that the stoical temperament exhibited by "Little Albert" was due to his brain disorder.

As Beck et al. concluded with some poignancy:

> None of the folktales we encountered during our inquiry had a factual basis. There is no evidence that the baby's mother was "outraged" at her son's treatment or that Douglas's phobia proved resistant to extinction. Douglas was never deconditioned, and he was not adopted by a family north of Baltimore.
>
> Nor was he ever an old man. Our search of seven years was longer than the little boy's life. I laid flowers on the grave of my longtime "companion," turned, and simultaneously felt a great peace and profound loneliness.

Douglas Merritte is buried in a child's grave in the Locust Grove Church of the Brethren cemetery in Mt. Airy, Maryland.

References

Beck, H. P., Levinson, S., & Irons, G. (2009). Finding Little Albert: A journey to John B. Watson's infant laboratory. *American Psychologist, 64,* 7. pp. 605-614.

Boakes, Robert. (1984). *From Darwin to behaviourism: Psychology and the minds of animals.* Cambridge: Cambridge University Press.

Buckley, K. W. (1989). *Mechanical man: John Broadus Watson and the beginnings of behaviorism.* New York: Guilford.

Burnham, J. C. (1994). "John B. Watson: Interviewee, Professional Figure, Symbol." In J. T. Todd & E. K. Morris (Eds), *Modern Perspectives on John B. Watson and Classical Behaviorism.* Greenwood Press, 1994.

Grove,L. (1997). Harold Ickes, Insider Out. *The Washington Post,* July 18.

Harris, B. (1979). Whatever Happened to Little Albert? *American Psychologist, 34,* 151-160.

Hartley, M. & Commire, A. (1990). *Breaking the Silence.* New York : G.P. Putnam's Sons.

Jones, M. C. (1924). A laboratory study of fear: The case of Peter. *Pedagogical Seminary, 31,* 308-315.

Kreshel, P. J. (1990). John B. Watson at J. Walter Thompson: The legitimation of "science in advertising. *Journal of Advertising, 19,* 49-59.

Watson, J. B. (1930). *Behaviorism* (Rev. Ed.). Chicago: University of Chicago Press.

Watson, J. B. (1928). *Psychological care of infant and child.* New York: Norton.

Watson, J. B., & Morgan, J. J. B. (1917). Emotional Reactions and Psychological Experimentation. *American Journal of Psychology, 28,* 163-174.

Watson, J. B., & Rayner, R. (1920). Conditioned emotional reactions. *Journal of Experimental Psychology, 3,* 1–14.

Wolpe, J., & Lazarus, A. (1966). *Behavior Therapy Techniques.* Oxford: Pergamon.

d Woolley / Getty Images

Memory

Suppose I offer you—for a price—an opportunity to do absolutely anything you want for a day. You will not be limited by the usual physical constraints. You can travel in a flash and visit as many places as you wish, even outer space. You can travel forward and backward through time, finding out what the future holds and witnessing the great events of the past. (You will not be able to alter history.) Anything you want to do—just name it and it is yours. Furthermore, I guarantee your safety: No matter where you choose to go or what you choose to do, you will not get hurt.

With a suitable reminder, you remember some events distinctly, even after a long delay. Other memories are lost or distorted.

How much would you pay for this amazing opportunity?

Oh, yes, I should mention, there is one catch. When the day is over, you will completely forget everything that happened. Any notes or photos will vanish. And anyone else who takes part in your special day will forget it, too.

Now how much would you be willing to pay? Much less, no doubt, and perhaps nothing. Living without remembering is hardly living at all: Our memories are almost the same as our selves.

module 7.1

Types of Memory

- Do we have different types of memory?
- If so, what is the best way to describe those differences?

Every year, people compete in the World Memory Championship in Britain. (You can read about it at www.worldmemorychampionship.com.) One event is speed of memorizing a shuffled deck of 52 cards. The all-time record is 21.9 seconds. Another is memorizing a long number within 1 hour. The record is a 2,280-digit number. People also compete at memorizing dates of fictional events, names of unfamiliar faces in photos, and so forth. Dominic O'Brien, eight-time world champion, gives speeches and writes books about how to train your memory. However, he admits that one time while he was practicing card memorization, an irate friend called from an airport to complain that O'Brien had forgotten to pick him up. O'Brien apologized and drove to London's Gatwick Airport, practicing card memorization along the way. When he arrived, he remembered that his friend was at Heathrow, London's other major airport (Johnstone, 1994).

Anyone—you, me, or Dominic O'Brien—remembers some information and forgets the rest. Memory is *the retention of information.* It includes skills such as riding a bicycle or eating with chopsticks. It also includes facts that never change (your birthday), facts that seldom change (your mailing address), and facts that frequently change (where you left your keys). You remember your most important experiences and some of your unimportant ones, many useful facts and much trivia that you can't imagine ever using.

Some advice: This chapter includes many Try It Yourself activities. You will gain much more from this chapter if you take the time to try them.

Ebbinghaus's Pioneering Studies of Memory

Suppose you wanted to study memory, but no one had ever done memory research before. Where would you start? If you asked people to describe their mem-

Figure 7.1 Hermann Ebbinghaus pioneered the scientific study of memory by observing his own capacity for memorizing lists of nonsense syllables.

Dominic O'Brien, eight-time winner of the World Memory Championship and author of several books on training your memory, admits he sometimes forgets practical information, such as promising to meet a friend at Heathrow Airport.

ories, you would not know when the memories formed, how often people had rehearsed them, or even whether the memories were correct. German psychologist Hermann Ebbinghaus (1850–1909) avoided these problems by an approach that we now take for granted: He taught new material so that he knew exactly what someone had learned and when. Then he measured memory after various delays. To be sure the material was new, he used lists of nonsense syllables, such as *GAK* or *JEK*. He wrote out 2,300 syllables, assembled them randomly into lists (Figure 7.1), and then set out to study memory. He had no cooperative introductory psychology students or friends eager to memorize nonsense syllables, so he ran all the tests on himself. For 6 years, he memorized thousands of lists of nonsense syllables. (He was either very dedicated to his science or uncommonly tolerant of boredom.)

Many of his findings were hardly surprising. For example, as shown in Figure 7.2, he took longer to memorize longer lists than shorter lists. "Of course!" you might scoff. But Ebbinghaus was not just demonstrating the obvious. He measured *how much* longer it took to memorize a longer list. You might similarly object to the law of gravity: "Of course the farther something falls, the longer it takes to hit the ground!" However, measuring the acceleration of gravity was essential to progress in physics, and measuring how long it takes to learn a list enables psychologists to compare conditions: Do adults learn faster than children? Do we learn some kinds of lists faster than other lists? Ebbinghaus's approach led to all the later research on memory.

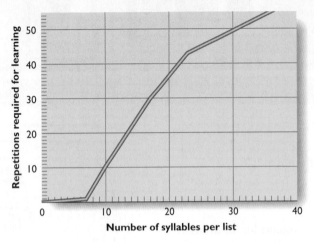

Figure 7.2 Ebbinghaus counted how many times he had to read a list of nonsense syllables before he could recite it once correctly. For a list of seven or fewer, one reading was usually enough. Beyond seven, the longer the list, the more repetitions he needed. (From Ebbinghaus, 1885/1913.)

Methods of Testing Memory

Nearly everyone occasionally has a tip-of-the-tongue experience (Brown & McNeill, 1966). You want to remember someone's name, and all you can think of is a similar name that you know isn't right. You will probably think of the correct name later, and you are sure you would recognize it if you heard it.

In other words, memory is not an all-or-none thing. You might or might not remember something depending on how someone tests you. Let's survey the main methods of testing memory. Along the way, we begin to distinguish among different types of memory.

Free Recall

A simple method for the researcher (though not for the person tested) is to ask for free recall. To recall something is *to produce a response, as you do on essay tests or short-answer tests*. For instance, "Please name all the children in your second-grade class." You probably will not name many, partly because you confuse the names of the children in your second-grade class with those you knew in other grades.

Cued Recall

You will do better with cued recall, in which you *receive significant hints about the material*. For example, a photograph of the children in your second-grade class (Figure 7.3) or a list of their initials will help you remember. Try this: Cover the right side of Table 7.1 with a piece of paper and try to identify the authors of each book on the left. Then uncover the right side, revealing each author's initials, and try again. (This method is cued recall.) Note how much better you do with these hints.

Recognition

With recognition, a third method of testing memory, someone *chooses the correct item among several options*. People usually recognize more items than they recall. For example, I might give you a list of 60 names and ask you to check off the correct names of children in your second-grade class. Multiple-choice tests use the recognition method.

Figure 7.3 Can you recall the names of the students in your second-grade class? Trying to remember without any hints is *free recall*. Using a photo or a list of initials is *cued recall*.

Table 7.1 The Difference Between Free Recall and Cued Recall

Book	Author

Instructions: First try to identify the author of each book listed in the left column while covering the right column. Then expose the right column, which gives each author's initials, and try again (cued recall).

Book	Author
Moby Dick	H. M.
Emma and *Pride* and *Prejudice*	J. A.
Uncle Tom's Cabin	H. B. S.
Sherlock Holmes stories	A. C. D.
The Bluest Eye and *Beloved*	T. M.
War and Peace	L. T.
This textbook	J. K.
The Canterbury Tales	G. C.
The Origin of Species	C. D.
Gone with the Wind	M. M.
Les Miserables	V. H.

© Cengage Learning

(For answers, see page 231, answer A.)

try it ▶ yourself

Here is a demonstration of implicit memories. For each of the following three-letter combinations, fill in additional letters to make any English word:

CON___

SUP___

DIS___

PRO___

You could have thought of any number of words—the dictionary lists well over 100 familiar CON___ words alone. Did you happen to write any of the following: *conversation, suppose, discussion,* or *probably?* Each of these words appeared in the preceding paragraph. *Reading or hearing a word temporarily* primes *that word and increases the chance that you will use it yourself,* even if you are not aware of the influence (Graf & Mandler, 1984; Schacter, 1987). This demonstration works better if you listen to spoken words than if you read them. To get a better sense of priming, try an Online Try It Yourself activity. Go to CengageBrain.com. Navigate to the student website, then to the Online Try It Yourself section, and click Implicit Memories.

online

try it ▶ yourself

Table 7.2 contrasts some memory tests.

Savings

A fourth method, the savings method (also known as the relearning method), detects weak memories *by comparing the speed of original learning to the speed of relearning.* Suppose you cannot name the children in your second-grade class and cannot even pick out their names from a list of choices. You would nevertheless learn a correct list of names faster than a list of people you had never met. That is, you save time when you relearn something. The amount of time saved (time needed for original learning minus the time for relearning) is a measure of memory.

Implicit Memory

Free recall, cued recall, recognition, and savings are tests of explicit (or direct) memory. That is, *someone who states an answer regards it as a product of memory.* In implicit memory (or indirect memory), *an experience influences what you say or do even though you might not be aware of the influence.* If you find that definition unsatisfactory, you are not alone (Frensch & Rünger, 2003). Defining something in terms of a vague concept like "awareness" is not a good practice. This definition is tentative until we develop a better one.

The best way to explain implicit memory is by examples: Suppose you are in a conversation while other people nearby are discussing something else. You ignore the other discussion, but a few words from that background conversation probably creep into your own. You do not even notice the influence, although an observer might.

Procedural Memories and Probabilistic Learning

Procedural memories, *memories of how to do something,* such as walking or eating with chopsticks, are a special kind of implicit memories. Psychologists distinguish procedural memories from declarative memories, *memories we can readily state in words.* For example, if you type, you know the locations of the letters well enough to press the right key at the right time, but can you state that knowledge explicitly? For example, which letter is directly to the right of C? Which is directly to the left of P?

Procedural memory, or habit learning, differs from declarative memory in several ways. First, the two types of memory depend on different brain areas, and brain damage can impair one without impairing the other. Second, procedural memory or habit learning develops gradually. In contrast, you often form a declarative memory all at once. For example, "the men's room is on the left and the women's room is on the right," or "we will have a special event instead of our usual class on Friday." Habit learning is better suited for learning some-

Table 7.2 Several Ways to Test Memory

Title	Description	Example
Recall	You are asked to say what you remember.	Name the Seven Dwarfs.
Cued recall	You are given significant hints to help you remember.	Name the Seven Dwarfs. Hint: One was always smiling, one was smart, one never talked, one always seemed to have a cold . . .
Recognition	You are asked to choose the correct item from among several items.	Which of the following were among the Seven Dwarfs: Sneezy, Sleazy, Dopey, Dippy, Hippy, Happy?
Savings (relearning)	You are asked to relearn something: If it takes you less time than when you first learned that material, some memory has persisted.	Try memorizing this list: Sleepy, Sneezy, Doc, Dopey, Grumpy, Happy, Bashful. Can you memorize it faster than this list: Sleazy, Snoopy, Duke, Dippy, Gripey, Hippy, Blushy?
Implicit memory	You are asked to generate words, without necessarily regarding them as memories.	You hear the story "Snow White and the Seven Dwarfs." Later you are asked to fill in these blanks to make any words that come to mind: _ L _ _ P _ _ N _ _ Z _ _ _ C _ O _ EY _ R _ _ P _ _ _ P P _ _ A _ H _ U _

© Cengage Learning

thing that is usually true or true only under certain circumstances (Shohamy, Myers, Kalanithi, & Gluck, 2008). For example, you might notice that a particular pattern of wind, clouds, and barometric pressure predicts rain, although no one of these cues is reliable by itself. Or you might notice that certain dogs are unfriendly when they hold their head, ears, and tail in certain postures. People sometimes learn to pick up on a variety of cues without realizing that they are doing so.

concept check

1. For each of these examples, identify the type of memory test—free recall, cued recall, recognition, savings, or implicit.
   a. Although you thought you had forgotten your high school French, you do better in your college French course than your roommate, who never studied French before.
   b. You are trying to remember the phone number of the local pizza parlor without looking it up in the phone directory.
   c. You hear a song on the radio without paying much attention to it. Later, you find yourself humming a melody, but you don't know what it is or where you heard it.
   d. You forget where you parked your car, so you scan the parking lot hoping to find your car among all the others.
   e. Your friend asks, "What's the name of our chemistry lab instructor? I think her name starts with an S."

2. What is a major difference between procedural memory and declarative memory?

Answers

1. **a.** savings; **b.** free recall; **c.** implicit; **d.** recognition; **e.** cued recall.
2. Procedural memory develops gradually and is sensitive to information that is usually but not always correct. Also, it depends on different brain areas.

Application: Suspect Lineups as Recognition Memory

Suppose you witness a crime, and now the police want you to identify the guilty person. They ask you to look at suspects in a lineup or examine a book of photos. Your task is an example of recognition memory, as you try to identify the correct item among distracters.

The task raises a problem, familiar from your own experience. When you take a multiple-choice test—also an example of recognition memory—perhaps none of the choices seems exactly right, but you select the best one available. What happens if you do the same with a book of photos? You look through the choices and pick the one who looks most like the perpetrator of the crime. You tell the police you think suspect 42 is the guilty person. "Think?" the police ask. "Your testimony won't be worth much in court unless you're sure." You look

Poole

Cotton

In 1985, Ronald Cotton (right) was convicted of rape, based on a victim's identification from a set of photos. Ten years later, DNA evidence demonstrated that Cotton was innocent and that the real culprit was Bobby Poole (left). Eyewitness testimony has in many cases led to the conviction of innocent people.

again, eager to cooperate. Finally, you say yes, you're sure. The police say, "Good, that's the person we thought did it." Getting that feedback strengthens your confidence in that choice. You testify in court, and the suspect is convicted. But is justice done? Many people have been convicted of crimes because of eyewitness testimony and later exonerated by DNA evidence.

Psychologists have proposed ways to improve suspect lineups. One is for the officer supervising the lineup to be what's known as a "blind" observer (see chapter 2). An officer who knows who is the main suspect might unintentionally bias the witness. Second, if the witness mentioned that the culprit had some distinctive feature, such as a scar above the left eye, all the suspects in the lineup should have that feature (Zarkadi, Wade, & Stewart, 2009). Otherwise the witness just picks the one with a scar, who may or may not be guilty.

A third recommendation is to postpone as long as possible any feedback about whether the witness chose someone the police suspected (Wells, Olson, & Charman, 2003; Zaragoza, Payment, Ackil, Drivdahl, & Beck, 2001). Any sign of agreement adds to a witness's confidence, even if the witness was wrong (Hasel & Kassin, 2009; Semmler, Brewer, & Wells, 2004; Wright & Skagerberg, 2007). Judges and juries generally put much trust in confident statements, although research shows that confidence is only loosely associated with accuracy (Odinot, Wolters, & van Koppen, 2009).

A more controversial recommendation is to present the lineup sequentially (Wells et al., 2000; Wells, Memon, & Penrod, 2006). In a sequential lineup, the witness says "yes" or "no" to each suspect, one at a time. If the witness says yes, the procedure is finished. After all, there is no point in looking at additional suspects if the witness has already decided. Also, the witness has no opportunity to go back and reexamine photos after rejecting them. The witness should make a definite identification or none at all, rather than choose the best suspect available. A sequential lineup greatly decreases the number of false identifications. When witnesses view a simultaneous lineup that does not include the guilty person, most witnesses identify someone anyway (the one who looks closest to the culprit).

With a sequential lineup, witnesses less often choose an innocent person. However, the cost is that witnesses also frequently fail to identify guilty people. That is, with a sequential lineup, witnesses become cautious and frequently fail to choose anyone (Malpass, 2006). The advantages and disadvantages of the two types of lineup depend on how we weigh the risk of setting a guilty person free versus the risk of imprisoning an innocent person.

AP Photo/HO/Burlington Police Department

concept check

3. How does a sequential lineup avoid one of the problems inherent in a multiple-choice test?

Answer

3. With a multiple-choice test, a person chooses the best available answer, even if it is not exactly correct. The same is often true in a simultaneous lineup. With a sequential lineup, a person chooses only when confident.

Children as Eyewitnesses

While on the topic of eyewitness memory, let's consider young children. How much should we trust their reports when they are witnesses or victims of a crime? How could we measure their accuracy?

One research approach is to ask a child to recall a medical or dental examination. How well can the child report those events? In such studies, researchers find that children as young as 3 years old report with reasonable accuracy even 6 weeks later (Baker-Ward, Gordon, Ornstein, Larus, & Clubb, 1993).

Several factors influence the accuracy of young children's reports:

- **Delay of questioning.** After a traumatic experience such as an injury, a child's memory is best at first and becomes less accurate over a long delay. The same is true for people at any age, of course. However, with very young children, a delayed report is sometimes more elaborate and more detailed, presumably because the child has become more articulate in the use of language (Peterson, 2011).
- **Type of question.** To an open-ended question such as, "Tell me what happened," a young child's answer is usually short but accurate. After a suggestive question such as, "Did he touch you under your clothing?" children's accuracy is less dependable (Lamb, Orbach, Hershkowitz, Horowitz, & Abbott, 2007). A suggestive question is especially dangerous after a delay, when the memory has weakened (Quas et al., 2007).

- **Hearing other children.** A child who hears other children reporting something is likely to say the same thing, even if it is wrong (Principe, Kanaya, Ceci, & Singh, 2006).
- **Repeating the question.** If someone asks a child the same question two or three times within a session, the child sometimes changes answers, apparently assuming that the first answer must have been wrong (Krähenbühl & Blades, 2006; Poole & White, 1993). However, repeated open-ended questioning by different interviewers, or by the same interviewer on different days, helps remind the child and sometimes elicits new information (Hershkowitz & Terner, 2007).
- **Using physical representations.** To investigate suspicions of sexual abuse, some psychologists try to prod a child's memory by providing anatomically detailed dolls and asking the child to act out some event. However, children sometimes act out fantasies instead of memories. When researchers ask children to act out a doctor's exam (where they know what happened), children act out many events that did not happen (Greenhoot, Ornstein, Gordon, & Baker-Ward, 1999). Although dolls apparently don't help, drawings do. If a child is asked to draw an event as well as describe it, the result is usually a more detailed description, with no loss of accuracy (Patterson & Hayne, 2011).
- **Understanding a question.** Have you ever seen anyone imbosk a lecythus? You probably answer either "I don't know," or "What do you mean?" A 3-year-old child who doesn't understand a question usually answers "yes" (Imhoff & Baker-Ward, 1999).

Adults easily overestimate a child's understanding. A couple took their 3-year-old daughter on a trip and said they would stop at a barbecue restaurant for dinner. She was so excited that she could hardly wait. She spent most of the trip asking, "Now how long till barbecue?" As they finally approached the restaurant, she asked, "Will other children be there too, with their Barbies?" Suddenly it dawned on the parents, "Ah, that's what she thought 'barbie-cue' meant!"

Can we trust a child's testimony? In short, it depends. With proper questioning, even a 3-year-old provides accurate information. With delayed or biased questioning, the accuracy declines.

The Information-Processing View of Memory

Over the years, psychologists have repeatedly tried to explain the mechanisms of behavior by analogy to the technologies of their time. In the 1600s, René Descartes compared animal behavior to the actions of a hydraulic pump. Psychologists of the early 1900s suggested that learning worked like a telephone switchboard. In the early days of radio, some researchers compared the nervous system to a radio. The information-processing model compares human memory to that of a computer: *Information that enters the system is processed, coded, and stored*, as in Figure 7.4. When you type something on the keyboard, the computer stores it in a temporary memory. When you store something on the hard drive, you set up a stable, long-lasting representation. According to the information-processing model, information first enters short-term memory (a temporary store), and some short-term memory transfers into long-term memory (like a hard disk). Eventually, a cue from the environment prompts the system to retrieve stored information (Atkinson & Shiffrin, 1968). Let's examine this model.

concept check

4. In what ways is the analogy between computer memory and human memory imperfect? (You can't look this one up. Think about it.)

Answer

4. A computer reports its memory exactly, even after not opening a file in years. Human memory becomes less detailed and less accurate over time. It is possible to delete memories from the hard drive of a computer but not easy to delete human memories. You can probably think of other differences.

Short-Term and Long-Term Memory

Information-processing theory distinguishes between short-term memory, *temporary storage of recent events*, and long-term memory, *a relatively permanent store*. For example, while you are playing a game, the current score is in your short-term memory, and the rules of the game are in your long-term memory.

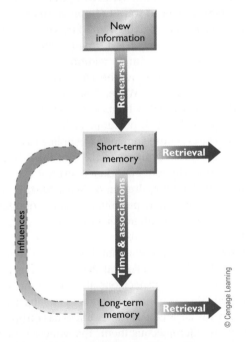

Figure 7.4 The information-processing model of memory resembles a computer's memory system, including temporary and permanent memory.

Psychologists distinguish two types of long-term memory, semantic and episodic. **Semantic memory** is *memory of principles and facts*, like nearly everything you learn in school. **Episodic memory** is *memory for specific events in your life* (Tulving, 1989). For example, your memory of the law of gravity is a semantic memory, whereas remembering the time you dropped your grandmother's vase is an episodic memory. Remembering who is the mayor of your city is a semantic memory, and remembering the time you met the mayor is an episodic memory.

Episodic memories are more fragile than semantic memories. If you don't play tennis for a few years, you will still remember the rules, but your memory of a particular tennis game will fade. Older people are especially likely to forget specific episodes, despite retaining semantic memories (Piolino, Desgranges, Benali, & Eustache, 2002). People with certain kinds of brain damage lose most of their episodic memories but keep their semantic memories.

concept check

5. Classify each of these as semantic memory or episodic memory: **(a)** Naming the first president of the United States. **(b)** Defining "classical conditioning." **(c)** Describing your trip to Disney World. **(d)** Remembering where you had dinner last night, who ate with you, and what you ate.

Answer

5. **(a)** semantic; **(b)** semantic; **(c)** episodic; **(d)** episodic.

You might remember something, a semantic memory, but forget when it occurred, an episodic memory (Friedman, Reese, & Dai, 2011). If you read or hear about something, you may forget where you learned it. If you tell about something, you are likely to forget whom you have told (Gopie & MacLeod, 2009). *Forgetting where or how you learned something* is **source amnesia**. Suppose you hear a rumor that you dismiss because you know it came from an unreliable source. Later, you forget the source and start to take the statement seriously (M. K. Johnson, Hashtroudi, & Lindsay, 1993; Riccio, 1994).

In one study, students read fictional stories that included such facts as "a sextant is a tool used at sea to navigate by the stars." Later, they were asked such questions as, "what tool is used at sea to navigate by the stars?" People who had just read that fact were more likely than other people to answer correctly. Most remembered seeing it in the story, but many said they had already known the fact before reading the story. Another group of students read stories with misinformation such as "a compass is a tool used at sea to navigate by the stars." Many of these students later answered the question incorrectly, saying that a compass is a tool to navigate by the stars. Although most said they remembered seeing this fact in the story, many insisted that they too had "already" known this fact before reading the story! This example illustrates another type of source amnesia—attributing falsely implanted memory to previous experience (Marsh, Meade, & Roediger, 2003).

Psychologists have traditionally drawn several distinctions between short-term and long-term memory. Two of the differences are capacity and decay over time.

Differences in Capacity

Long-term memory has a vast, hard-to-measure capacity. Asking how much information long-term memory can store is like asking how many books a library can hold. The answer depends on the size of the books and how you arrange them. Short-term memory, in contrast, has a limited capacity. Read each of the following letter sequences and then try to repeat them from memory. Or read each aloud and ask a friend to repeat it.

try it ▶ yourself

E H G P H

J R O Z N Q

S R B W R C N

M P D I W F B S

Z Y B P I A F M O

Copyright Frans Lanting/www.lanting.com

Kutbidin Atamkulov travels from one Central Asian village to another singing from memory the tale of the Kirghiz hero, Manas. The song, which lasts 3 hours, has been passed from master to student for centuries.

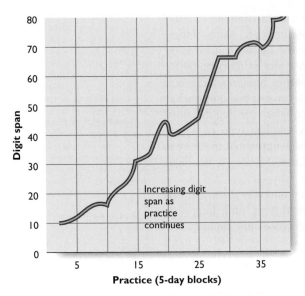

Figure 7.5 A college student gradually increased his ability to repeat a list of numbers. (From Ericsson, Chase, & Faloon, 1980.)

Most normal adults can repeat a list of about seven letters, numbers, or words. Some remember eight or nine; others, only five or six. George Miller (1956) referred to short-term memory capacity as "the magical number seven, plus or minus two." When people try to repeat a longer list, they may fail to remember even the first seven items. It is like trying to hold objects in one hand: if you try to hold too many, you drop them all.

You can store more information in short-term memory by chunking—*grouping items into meaningful sequences or clusters.* For example, the sequence "ventysi" has seven letters, at the limit of most people's capacity. However, "seventysix" with three additional letters can be easily remembered as "76," a two-digit number. "Seventeenseventysix" is even longer, but if you think of it as 1776, an important date in U.S. history, it is a single item to store. Because people are so good at chunking, sometimes without realizing that they are doing it, psychologists are not certain that short-term memory really does hold seven items. When you remembered S R B W R C N, did you really remember it as seven items? Or did you group them, such as SR . . . B . . . WR . . . CN? More recent research indicates that the true limit of short-term memory is three to five chunks rather than seven items (Cowan, 2010).

One college student in a lengthy experiment initially could repeat about seven digits at a time (Ericsson, Chase, & Faloon, 1980). Over a year and a half, working 3 to 5 hours per week, he gradually improved until he could repeat 80 digits, as shown in Figure 7.5, by using elaborate strategies for chunking. He was a competitive runner, so he might store

the sequence "3492 . . ." as "3 minutes, 49.2 seconds," a near world-record time for running a mile. He might store the next set of numbers as a good time for running a kilometer, a mediocre marathon time, or a date in history. With practice, he started recognizing larger and larger chunks of numbers. However, when he was tested on his ability to remember a list of letters, his performance was only average, because he had not developed any chunking strategies for letters.

A cautionary point: We talk about storing a memory as if you were holding objects in your hand. This is only a loose analogy. Memory depends on changes in synapses spread out over a huge population of cells. It is not like something you put in one place.

Decay of Memories Over Time

A short-term memory, by definition, lasts only a short time unless the person continues rehearsing it. Here is the classic demonstration: Lloyd Peterson and Margaret Peterson (1959) presented meaningless sequences of letters, like HOXDF, and then tested people's memory after various delays. If you were in this study, knowing that the experimenter was going to ask you to repeat the letters, you would spend the delay rehearsing, "HOXDF, HOXDF, . . ." To prevent rehearsal, the experimenters used a second task. When they presented the letters, they also presented a number, such as 231. The instruction was to start with that number and count backward by 3s, such as "231, 228, 225, 222, 219, . . ." until the experimenter signaled the end of the delay. At that point, the participant was to say the letters.

Figure 7.6 shows the results. On average, only about 10% of the participants could recall the letters after 18 seconds. In other words, a short-term memory fades rapidly. You can demonstrate this phenomenon yourself with the Online Try It Yourself activity called Decay of Short-Term Memory.

Peterson and Peterson were dealing with nonsense information, such as HOXDF, however. With more meaningful material, people store much informa-

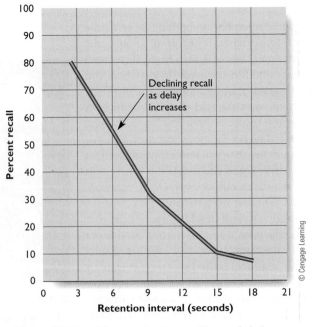

Figure 7.6 People's memory of a set of letters faded quickly if they were prevented from rehearsing.

tion quickly. If someone told you to leave the building by the west exit instead of the east exit because a venomous snake is lurking at the east exit, you don't need to worry that you will forget this advice in the next 18 seconds.

Why do short-term memories fade? The simplest hypothesis is that the brain representation decays over time. Neuroscientists have identified a protein that the brain makes after an experience that weakens the memory trace, presumably to avoid permanently storing unimportant information (Genoux et al., 2002). Another hypothesis is that short-term memories fade because we confuse one with another. If you read a series of letters and then count backward by 3s, your memory of the letters does not fade rapidly on the first trial. On later trials, you confuse one set of letters with another and the interference increases your rate of forgetting (Keppel & Underwood, 1962). You can decrease that interference by taking a rest and then returning to the task (Unsworth, Heitz, & Parks, 2008).

How long does a long-term memory last? It depends (Altmann & Gray, 2002). If you are playing basketball, you remember the score, approximately how much time is left in the game, what defense your team is using, what offense, how many fouls you have committed, and so forth. You won't (and wouldn't want to) remember that information for the rest of your life, but you also don't need to rehearse it constantly to prevent it from fading. Similarly, right now you probably remember approximately how much money is in your wallet, where and when you plan to meet someone for dinner, what you plan to do next weekend, how long until your next psychology test, and much other information you need to store until you update it with new information.

Many long-term memories last a lifetime. Old people can describe events that happened in their childhood. Harry Bahrick (1984) found that people who had studied Spanish 1 or 2 years ago remembered more than those who had studied it 3 to 6 years ago, but beyond 6 years, the retention appeared to be stable (Figure 7.7).

concept check

6. What are two differences between short-term memory and long-term memory?
7. Studies in the 1950s indicated that short-term memories, unless rehearsed, decay within seconds. Why is that conclusion no longer certain?

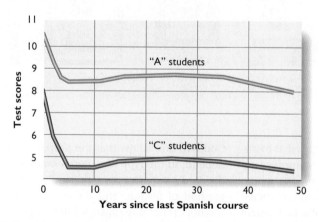

Figure 7.7 Spanish vocabulary as measured by a recognition test declines in the first few years but then becomes stable. The students who received an "A" performed better, but each group showed similar rates of forgetting. (From H. P. Bahrick "Semantic Memory Content in Permastore: Fifty Years of Memory for Spanish Learned in School," Journal of Experimental Psychology 113:1 (pp. 1-29). Copyright ©1984 American Psychological Association. Reprinted with permission.)

Answers

6. Short-term memory has a small capacity, whereas long-term memory has a huge capacity. Also, of course, short-term memory doesn't last as long!
7. It has been found that if interference from previous trials is minimized, short-term memory lasts longer.

Working Memory

"Clarence Birdseye patented a method for selling frozen fish." You probably didn't know that. It is now in your short-term memory, and it may or may not become a long-term memory. "Read the first three paragraphs on page 42 and summarize the main points." That instruction is also in short-term memory, but it is of a different kind. Whereas you might want to remember the fact about Clarence Birdseye, you have no reason to remember forever the instruction about turning to page 42.

Originally, psychologists thought of short-term memory as the way to store something while moving it into long-term storage. That is, you gradually **consolidate** your memory by *converting a short-term memory into a long-term memory*. One problem for this idea is that *how long* information remains in short-term memory is a poor predictor of whether it becomes a long-term memory. You might watch a hockey game in which the score remains 1-0 for 2 hours, but you don't store that score permanently. In contrast, if someone tells you, "Your sister just had a baby," you form a lasting memory quickly.

Today, most researchers emphasize temporary memory storage as the information you are using at the moment. To emphasize this different perspective, they speak of *working* memory instead of short-term memory. Working memory doesn't have to be on the way to permanent memory. It includes information you use and then forget, like "summarize the material on page 42" or "go to the first intersection and turn right." Working memory is *a system for working with current information*. It is almost synonymous with one's current sphere of attention (Baddeley, 2001; Baddeley & Hitch, 1994; Repovš & Baddeley, 2006).

One aspect of working memory is the executive functioning that *governs shifts of attention*. The hallmark of good working memory is the ability to shift attention as needed among different tasks. A hospital nurse has to keep track of the needs of several patients, sometimes interrupting the treatment of one patient to take care of an emergency and then returning to complete work with the first patient. People with good executive functioning manage to minimize distractions. When something does distract them, they recover quickly and get back to the important task (Fukuda & Vogel, 2011).

try it ▶ yourself

Here is a simple way to measure how long it takes your executive functioning to shift attention: Recite aloud a poem, song, or other passage that you know well. (If you can't think of a more interesting example, recite the alphabet.) Time how long it takes. Then measure how long it takes you to say the same thing silently. Finally, time how long it takes you to alternate—the first word aloud, the second silent, the third aloud, and so forth. Alternating takes longer because you keep shifting attention.

Here is another way to measure executive processes: You hear a list of words such as *maple, elm, oak, hemlock, chestnut, birch, sycamore, pine, redwood, walnut, dogwood, hickory.* After each word, you are supposed to say the *previous* word. So after "maple, elm," you should say "maple." After "oak" you reply "elm." If you do well on that task, proceed to a more difficult version: You should repeat what you heard *two* words ago. So you wait for "maple, elm, oak" and reply "maple." Then you hear "hemlock" and reply "elm." You shift back and forth between listening to a new word and repeating something from memory.

People who do well on tasks like these have a high capacity of working memory and good executive functioning. They generally do well on many other tasks, including school performance (Rose, Feldman, & Jankowitz, 2011), understanding other people's point of view (Barrett, Tugade, & Engle, 2004), and resisting impulses to heavy drinking (Houben, Wiers, & Jansen, 2011). They have less than average "mind wandering" while they need to concentrate on a difficult task but more than average mind wandering when performing easy tasks (Kane et al., 2007).

Interestingly, if people working on one memory task have to perform an additional constantly distracting task, such as tapping a rhythm with their fingers, everyone's performance suffers, but those with the best working memory suffer the most (Kane & Engle, 2000; Rosen & Engle, 1997). They still perform better than people with less working memory but not by as much as usual. Of course, one reason is that those with poor working memory weren't doing well anyway, so they had less room to get worse. Another reason is that people with good working memory usually do well by attending to the most important information. When they are distracted, they lose that advantage.

concept check

8. Some students listen to music while studying. Is the music likely to help or impair their study? (What might the answer depend on?)

Answer

8. If the music attracts attention or evokes any response, such as singing along or tapping a foot, it will impair attention. The best students will notice the biggest difference. Background music with no words and no tendency to evoke responses might provide a slight benefit if it prevents the student from noticing other more distracting sounds.

module 7.1 ▶

In Closing

Varieties of Memory

Although researchers cannot clearly say what memory is, they agree about what it is *not*: Memory is not a single store into which we simply dump things and later take them out. When Ebbinghaus conducted his studies of memory in the late 1800s, he thought he was measuring the properties of memory, period. We now know that the properties of memory depend on the type of material memorized, the individual's experience with similar materials, the method of testing, and the recency of the event. Memory is not one process, but many.

Summary

- *Ebbinghaus's approach.* Hermann Ebbinghaus pioneered the experimental study of memory by testing his own ability to memorize and retain lists of nonsense syllables. (page 221)
- *Methods of testing memory.* The free recall method reveals only relatively strong memories. Progressively weaker memories can be demonstrated by the cued recall, recognition, and savings methods. Implicit memories are changes in behavior under conditions in which the person cannot verbalize the memory or is unaware of the influence. (page 222)
- *Procedural memory.* Procedural memory, or habit learning, develops gradually, unlike declarative memory. Procedural memory is well suited to remembering information that is usually true under certain circumstances, as opposed to remembering a single event. (page 223)
- *Suspect lineups.* Suspect lineups are an example of the recognition method of testing memory. Unfortunately, witnesses sometimes choose the best available choice and then decide they are sure. Psychologists have recommended ways to decrease inaccurate identifications. (page 224)
- *Children as eyewitnesses.* Even young children can provide accurate eyewitness reports if they are asked unbiased questions soon after the event. (page 225)
- *The information-processing model.* According to the information-processing model, information progresses from short-term memory to long-term memory. (page 226)
- *Short-term and long-term memory.* Short-term memory has a capacity of only a few items in normal adults, although chunking can enable us to store much information in each item. Long-term memory has a huge capacity. Short-term memories fade over time if not rehearsed, partly because of interference from similar memories. Long-term memories last varying periods, up to a lifetime. (page 226)
- *Working memory.* Working memory is a system for dealing with current information, including the ability to shift attention back and forth among tasks as necessary. (page 229)

Key Terms

chunking (page 228)

consolidation (page 229)

cued recall (page 222)

declarative memory (page 223)

episodic memory (page 227)

executive functioning (page 229)

explicit memory (or direct memory) (page 223)

free recall (page 222)

implicit memory (or indirect memory) (page 223)

information-processing model (page 226)

long-term memory (page 226)

memory (page 221)

priming (page 223)

procedural memory (page 223)

recognition (page 222)

savings method (or relearning method) (page 223)

semantic memory (page 227)

short-term memory (page 226)

source amnesia (page 227)

working memory (page 229)

Answer to Other Question in the Module

A. Herman Melville, Jane Austen, Harriet Beecher Stowe, Arthur Conan Doyle, Toni Morrison, Leo Tolstoy, James Kalat, Geoffrey Chaucer, Charles Darwin, Margaret Mitchell, Victor Hugo. (page 223)

Encoding, Storage, and Retrieval

- **How can we improve our memories?**

Have you ever felt distressed because you can't remember some experience? One woman reports feeling distressed because she can't stop remembering! When she sees or hears a date—such as April 27, 1994—a flood of episodic memories descends on her. "That was Wednesday. . . . I was down in Florida. I was summoned to come down and to say goodbye to my grandmother who they all thought was dying but she ended up living. My Dad and my Mom went to New York for a wedding. Then my Mom went to Baltimore to see her family. I went to Florida on the 25th, which was a Monday. This was also the weekend that Nixon died. And then I flew to Florida and my Dad flew to Florida the next day. Then I flew home and my Dad flew to Baltimore to be with my Mom" (Parker, Cahill, & McGaugh, 2006, p. 40). Tell her another date, and she might describe where she went to dinner and with whom, as well as the major news event of that day. The researchers studying her checked her reports against her extensive diaries and a book of news events. She was almost always correct for any date since she was 11 years old. For one test, they asked her to give the date (e.g., April 7) for every Easter between 1980 and 2003. She was right on all but one and later corrected herself on that one. What makes this feat even more impressive is that she is Jewish and therefore doesn't celebrate Easter (Parker et al., 2006).

You might not want to have the detailed episodic memory of this woman, who says her memories so occupy her that she can hardly focus on the present. Still, you might want to improve your memory of items you want to remember. Memory consists of three aspects—encoding, storage, and retrieval. The main point of this module is simple: When you want to retrieve a memory, it's too late if you didn't encode it well in the first place. To improve your memory, improve the way you study.

Encoding

If you want to memorize a definition, would you repeat it over and over? Repetition by itself is a poor study method, especially if you do it all at one time.

try it ▶ yourself

Most actors preparing for a play spend much time thinking about the meaning of what they will say (a deep level of processing) instead of just repeating the words.

To illustrate the shortcomings of mere repetition, examine Figure 7.8, which shows a real U.S. penny and 14 fakes. If you live in the United States, you have seen pennies countless times, but can you now identify the real one? Most U.S. citizens guess wrong (Nickerson & Adams, 1979). (If you do not have a penny in your pocket, check answer B on page 243. If you are not from the United States, try draw-

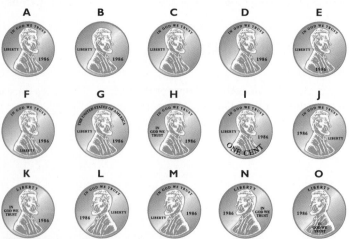

Figure 7.8 Can you spot the genuine penny among 14 fakes? (From R. S. Nickerson and M. J. Adams, "Long-Term Memory for a Common Object," Cognitive Psychology vol 11 (pp. 287-307). Copyright © 1979 Elsevier. Reprinted with permission.)

ing the front or back of a common coin in your own country.) In short, mere repetition, such as looking at a coin many times, does not guarantee a strong memory.

Meaningfulness and Other Influences on Encoding

One influence on how well you remember something is whether you consider it worth remembering. For example, if you know you can easily find something on the Internet, you put less effort into remembering it (Sparrow, Liu, & Wegner, 2011).

Another major influence is whether you consider something interesting. At one high school, students in science courses were randomly assigned to write periodic summaries of what they had learned, or summaries of how the material was relevant to their lives. Those who wrote about relevance to themselves became more interested, remembered the material better, and achieved higher grades (Hulleman & Harackiewicz, 2009).

Because people from different cultures have different needs and interests, they differ in what they remember, even when they have similar experiences (Ross & Wang, 2010). Australian Aborigines, whose lives put them deeply in touch with nature, have an extraordinary memory for where things are in relationship to one another. Americans, with a long history of encouraging individual achievement, report more autobiographical memories than most others do. When Americans describe something they saw, they often focus narrowly on the central object, whereas Asians put more emphasis on the background.

Emotional arousal also enhances memory encoding. Chances are you vividly remember your first day of college, your first kiss, the time your team won the big game, and times you were frightened. Extreme panic interferes with memory, but moderate emotion provides benefits, largely by increasing the release of the hormones cortisol and epinephrine (adrenaline) from the adrenal gland. Those hormones stimulate brain areas that enhance memory storage (Andreano & Cahill, 2006).

The effects of arousal on memory have been known for centuries. In England in the early 1600s, when people sold land, they did not yet have the custom of recording the sale on paper. Paper was expensive and few people could read anyway. Instead, local residents would gather while someone announced the sale and instructed everyone to remember it. Of all those present, whose memory of the sale was most important? The children, because they would live the longest. And of all those present, who were least interested? Right, again, it's the children. To increase the chances that the children would remember, the adults would kick them while telling them about the business deal. The same idea persisted in the custom, still common in the early 1900s, of slapping schoolchildren's hands with a stick to make them pay attention.

Many people report intense, detailed "flashbulb" memories of hearing highly emotional news, in which they remember who told them, where they were, what they were doing, and even the weather and other irrelevant details. When researchers have interviewed people both at the time and years later, they have found that most flashbulb memories remain consistent over time, but occasionally people's later reports are confident and vivid but incorrect. One person originally reported hearing about the terrorist attacks of September 11, 2001, on a car radio, and 2 years later reported having heard about it while standing in line at an airport (Kvavilashvili, Mirani, Schlagman, Foley, & Kornbrot, 2009). Confident, vivid memories aren't always correct.

concept check

9. Most people with post-traumatic stress disorder have lower than normal levels of cortisol. What would you predict about their memory?

Answer

9. Because of the lower cortisol levels, they should have trouble storing memories and therefore report frequent memory lapses.

In addition to attention and emotion, many other factors influence how well you store your memories. To illustrate, read the following list, close the book, and write as many of the words as you can. The demonstration would work better if you saw the words one at a time on a screen. You can approximate that procedure by covering the list with a sheet of paper and pulling it down to reveal one word at a time.

try it ▶ yourself

LEMON
GRAPE
POTATO
COCONUT
CUCUMBER
TOMATO
BROCCOLI
APPLE
SPINACH
TOMATO
ORANGE
LETTUCE
CARROT
STRAWBERRY
BANANA
TOMATO
PEACH
NAKED
LIME
PINEAPPLE
TURNIP
MANGO
TOMATO
BLUEBERRY
TOMATO
APRICOT
WATERMELON

I hope you tried the demonstration. If so, TOMATO was probably one of the words you remembered because it occurred five times instead of just once. Other things being equal, repetition helps, especially if the repetitions are spread out. You probably also remembered LEMON and WATERMELON because they were the first and last items on the list. The primacy effect *is the tendency to remember well the first items.* The recency effect *is the tendency to remember the final items.* The primacy

© Bettmann/CORBIS

© Remi Benali

D-Day, a major event in World War II, occurred on June 6, 1944 (top photo). Bob Williams (bottom photo), a paratrooper on D-Day, was one of 40 who reenacted the jump on its 50th anniversary. We forget most events from long ago but remember the most distinctive ones.

to remember unusual people. If you meet several men of ordinary appearance with similar names, like John Stevens, Steve Johnson, and Joe Stevenson, you will have trouble remembering their names. You will more quickly remember a 7-foot-tall, red-headed man named Stinky Rockefeller.

You might not have remembered MANGO if you didn't grow up eating mangoes in childhood. People find it easier to remember words they learned in early childhood (e.g., APPLE, ORANGE, and BANANA) than words they learned later (Juhasz, 2005). Similarly, if you grew up watching *Sesame Street*, you can probably name Bert, Ernie, and Oscar the Grouch more quickly than most of the characters you have watched on television more recently.

Did you remember the word LIME? Probably not, because it came right after the word NAKED. When people see an unexpected sex-related word, it grabs attention so strongly that they pay less attention to the next word and sometimes up to the next four or five words (Arnell, Killman, & Fijavz, 2007). The effect would be even stronger if you were watching a series of slides, and one of them had a photo of naked people. Some people also forget the word that came *before* a highly emotional word or image (Strange, Kroes, Roiser, Yan, & Dolan, 2008).

concept check

10. What are some factors that increase or decrease your probability of remembering a word on a list?

Answer

10. Moderate emotion enhances memory and distraction impairs it. Memory is enhanced by repetition, distinctiveness, and being either first or last on a list. We also tend to remember those we learned early in life more easily than words we learned later. We tend to forget an item that came right after something unusually arousing.

and recency effects are robust for almost any type of memory. If you try to list all the vacations you have ever taken or all the sporting events you have ever watched, you will probably include the earliest ones and the most recent.

You probably also remembered CARROT and NAKED. The word CARROT was distinctive because of its size, color, and font. NAKED stood out as the only item on the list that was neither a fruit nor a vegetable. In a list of mostly similar items, the distinctive ones are easier to remember. We also tend

try it ▶ yourself

Let's try another demonstration. Below are two lists. As you read through one of the lists—it doesn't matter which one—repeat each word for a couple of seconds. So, if the word were "insect," you would say, "Insect, insect, insect . . ." and then proceed to the next word. For the other list, imagine yourself stranded in the middle of a vast grassland in some foreign country, where you need to find food and water and protect yourself from snakes, lions, and other dangers. As you go through the list, again spend a couple of seconds on each word, thinking about how useful this item would be for survival under these conditions. Give it a rating from 1 (useless) to 5 (extremely valuable). You choose whether to do the repetition list first or the rating-for-survival list first. At the end, pause awhile and then try to recall the items you read.

List A	List B
toothbrush	firecracker
thermometer	rollerblades
marionette	umbrella
jewelry	hammock
tuxedo	binoculars
washcloth	encyclopedia
bandage	saxophone
trampoline	camera
metronome	mirror
flashlight	scissors
chain	string
knife	bottle
balloon	radio
carpet	envelope
overcoat	candy
matches	pencil

Most people remember more words from the survival list than from the repetition list (Nairne, Pandeirada, & Thompson, 2008; Nairne, Thompson, & Pandeirada, 2007). If, instead of rating the words for survival relevance, you rated them for pleasantness, that procedure would help, too, but not as much as rating words for survival. Evidently, thinking about survival engages attention and memory better than anything else does. Certainly, it makes sense for our brains to have evolved this way. In a follow-up study, people read words while rating their value for a hunting contest, or for hunting food for your tribe. Even though it was the same act in both cases—hunting—people remembered more words if they thought of hunting in terms of survival instead of a contest (Nairne, Pandeirada, Gregory, & Van Arsdall, 2009).

Moreover, simply repeating the words is one of the least effective ways to study. According to the depth-of-processing principle (Craik & Lockhart, 1972), *how easily you retrieve a memory depends on the number and types of associations you form.* When you read a list or read a chapter, simply reading the words without much thought is "shallow processing," which produces only weak, fleeting memories. Alternatively, you might stop and consider various points that you read, relate them to your own experiences, and think of your own examples to illustrate each principle. The more ways

Table 7.3 Depth-of-Processing Model of Memory

Superficial processing	Simply repeat the material to be remembered: "Hawk, Oriole, Tiger, Timberwolf, Blue Jay, Bull."
Deeper processing	Think about each item. Note that two start with T and two with B.
Still deeper processing	Note that three are birds and three are mammals. Also, three are major league baseball teams and three are NBA basketball teams. Use whichever associations mean the most to you.

© Cengage Learning

you think about the material, the deeper is your processing and the more easily you will remember later. The difference isn't apparent at once. Immediately after you read something, you may remember it just as well after shallow processing as after deep processing. But after a longer delay, you will remember significantly more after deep processing (Rose, Myerson, Roediger, & Hale, 2010). Table 7.3 summarizes the depth-of-processing model.

concept check

11. Many students who get the best grades in a course read the assigned text chapters more slowly than average. Why?

Answer

11. Students who pause to think about the meaning are engaging in deep processing. They will remember the material better than those who read a chapter quickly.

Encoding Specificity

When you encode something, you form associations. If you form many associations, many possible *reminders*—called retrieval cues—will stimulate your memory later. According to the encoding specificity principle (Tulving & Thomson, 1973), *the associations you form at the time of learning will be the most effective retrieval cues later* (Figure 7.9). Here is an example (modified from Thieman, 1984). First, read the pairs of words (which psychologists call *paired associates*) in Table 7.4a. Then turn to Table 7.4b on page 238. For each of the words on Table 7.4b's list, try to recall a related word on the

Figure 7.9 If you think of the word *queen* as *queen bee*, then the cue *playing card* will not remind you of the word later. If you think of the *queen of England*, then *chess piece* will not be a good reminder.

Table 7.4a	
Clergyman—Cardinal	Geometry—Plane
Trinket—Charm	Tennis—Racket
Type of wine—Port	Music—Rock
U.S. politician—Bush	Magic—Spell
Inch—Foot	Envelope—Seal
Computer—Apple	Graduation—Degree

© Cengage Learning

Table 7.4a list. *Please do this now.* (The answers are on page 243, answer C.)

Most people find this task difficult. If they initially coded the word *cardinal* as a type of clergyman, the retrieval cue *bird* doesn't remind them of it. If they had thought of it as a bird, then *clergyman* would not have been a good reminder.

The principle of encoding specificity extends to other aspects of experience at the time of storage. In one study, college students who were fluent in both English and Russian were given a list of words such as *summer*, *birthday*, and *doctor*, some in English and some in Russian. For each word, they were asked to describe any related event they remembered. In response to Russian words, they recalled mostly events that happened when they were speaking Russian. In response to English words, they recalled mostly events that happened when they were speaking English (Marian & Neisser, 2000).

Some police interviewers use encoding specificity when questioning crime witnesses. They start by asking the witnesses to imagine the original conditions as closely as possible—the location, the weather, the time of day, how they were feeling at the time. Getting back to the original event, at least in imagination, helps people remember more details of what they saw (Fisher, Geiselman, & Amador, 1989).

The encoding specificity principle has this implication: If you want to remember something at a particular time and place, study under the same conditions where you will try to remember. However, if you want to remember something always, you should vary your study habits so that your memory does *not* become too specific to one setting.

© Cengage Learning

concept check

12. Suppose someone cannot remember what happened at a party last night. What steps might help improve the memory?

Answer

12. Often, someone who claims not to remember simply does not want to talk about it. Presuming the person really wants to remember, it would help to return to the place of the party with the same people present, perhaps even at the same time of day. The more similar the conditions of original learning and later recall, the better the probability of remembering.

How to Organize Your Studying

Did you ever have this experience? You read something over and over. You are sure you have studied it hard and know it well. Then you take a test and you don't remember it nearly as well as you had expected. What went wrong?

Studying All at Once or Spread Out

Should you study a little at a time or wait until shortly before the test? You know that waiting until just before the test is risky. An unexpected interruption might prevent you from studying at all. Let's change the question to make the answer less obvious: You don't wait until just before the test, but you nevertheless study all at once. Will your result be better, worse, or the same as if you studied a little at a time over several days?

The answer is that studying all at once is worse for every kind of material that researchers have tested (Cepeda, Pashler, Vul, Wixted, & Rohrer, 2006; Kornell & Bjork, 2008). Suppose you are trying to learn a foreign language. You study a list of words until you know their meanings. Now, you spend another 10 minutes going over the same list again and again. How much do you gain? The research says that the extra 10 minutes is almost completely wasted (Rohrer & Pashler, 2007). You would do much better to stop now and study another 10 minutes tomorrow.

If you are going to wait to study again, how long should you wait? It depends. To remember something next week, you get the best results if you review tomorrow. To remember something next month, you should wait a week and a half before you review. To remember next year, wait about 3 weeks. In each case, it is better to wait a little longer than a little less (Cepeda, Vul, Rohrer, Wixted, & Pashler, 2008). Better yet, review several times.

When you study something all at once, it *seems* that you are learning well because the material is so fresh in your memory at the time. However, people almost always underestimate how much they are going to forget (Koriat, Bjork, Sheffer, & Bar, 2004). To remember something well, you need to practice retrieving the memory—that is, finding it. While you are reading something over and over, it is so fresh in your memory that you gain no practice at retrieving it. If you

If you study all at once, you overestimate how well you will remember the material later. Study is more effective if you review the material at different times and places.

go away and come back later, you need effort to refresh the ideas, and that effort strengthens the memory.

Advantages of Varied Study

Even within a session, you gain by adding variety, although it won't seem that way. Suppose you are trying to learn the artistic styles of several painters so that you can identify new paintings by the same artists. Would you learn better by seeing many paintings by artist A, then many by artist B, many by C, and so forth? Or would it be better to see one by each, and then another by each, and so forth? Most people assume the first way is better, seeing many examples by a given artist all at one time. However, the results show that spacing them out works substantially better (Kornell, Castel, Eich, & Bjork, 2010).

Varying the conditions of learning makes a task seem more difficult, but in the long run, it helps. In one experiment, a group of 8-year-old children practiced throwing a beanbag at a target 3 feet away. Another group practiced with a target sometimes 2 feet away and sometimes 4 feet away but never 3 feet away. Then both groups were tested with the target 3 feet away. The children who had practiced with the 3-foot target missed it by a mean of 8.3 inches. The children who had been practicing with 2-foot and 4-foot targets missed by only 5.4 inches, even though they were aiming at the 3-foot target for the first time (Kerr & Booth, 1978). In another experiment, young adults practiced a technique for mentally squaring two-digit numbers—for example, $23 \times 23 = 529$. Those who practiced with a small range of numbers learned the technique quickly but forgot it quickly. Those who practiced with a wider range of numbers learned more slowly but remembered better later (Sanders, Gonzalez, Murphy, Pesta, & Bucur, 2002).

What You Learn During Testing

In addition to what you gain from varied study, you also gain by alternating between reading and testing. Most people assume that they learn while reading something and not while recalling it. In fact, to strengthen a memory, it is essential to practice recalling it. In several studies, one group of students spent their time reading and rereading. Another group alternated between reading and either answering questions or trying to describe what they had read. At the end of the study session, both groups did equally well, but when tested later, a difference was clear: The students who alternated between reading and testing or describing did best, for many types of material (Karpicke & Blunt, 2011; McDaniel, Howard, & Einstein, 2009; Roediger & Karpicke, 2006). The advantage is greatest with difficult material or difficult delayed tests (Halamish & Bjork, 2011).

A test forces you to generate the material instead of passively reading it. Also, it shows what you don't know, encouraging you to pay more attention to that material or study it in a different way (Karpicke & Roediger, 2008; Pyc & Rawson, 2010). Here is a related finding: Suppose your instructor starts a lecture by asking a question, such as, "What is meant by depth of processing?" You don't know, so either you say you don't know or you offer a guess that's wrong. Then the instructor gives the correct information. Research shows that you will remember the information better than if the instructor had merely stated it without asking the question (Kornell, Hays, & Bjork, 2009). Asking the question builds your curiosity and increases your attention to the answer.

The conclusions: (a) It is hard to judge how well you have learned something if you haven't waited long enough to see how much you will forget. (b) Studying once is seldom effective, no matter how hard you study that one time. (c) Varying the conditions of studying improves long-term memory. (d) You remember better if you test yourself.

concept check

13. So, why is it a good idea to answer Concept Checks like this one?

14. If you want to do well on the final exam in this course, what should you do now—review this chapter or review the first three chapters in the book?

15. How does the advice to spread out your study over a long time instead of doing it all at one sitting fit or contrast with the encoding specificity principle?

15. The ideas are compatible. If you study all at one sitting, you encode the memory to what you are thinking about at that time. If you study at several times, the memory attaches to a greater variety of retrieval cues.

14. To prepare well for the final exam, you should review all the material at irregular intervals. You might profit by skimming chapters 1, 2, and 3 right now. Of course, if you have a test on chapter 7 in a day or two, your goal and your strategy are different.

13. Practicing the retrieval of a memory strengthens it. Students who spent part of their study time answering test questions did better than those who spent the whole time reading.

Table 7.4b

Instructions: For each of these words, write one of the second of the paired terms from the list in Table 7.4a.

Animal—	Stone—
Part of body—	Personality—
Transportation—	Write—
Temperature—	Bird—
Crime—	Harbor—
Shrubbery—	Fruit—

© Cengage Learning

Mnemonic Devices

If you needed to memorize a long, not very exciting list—for example, a list of all the bones in the body—how would you do it? One effective strategy is to attach systematic retrieval cues to each term so that you can remind yourself of the terms when you need them. A mnemonic device is *any memory aid based on encoding items in a special way*. The word *mnemonic* (nee-MAHN-ik) comes from a Greek root meaning "memory." The same root appears in the word *amnesia*, "lack of memory." Some mnemonic devices are simple, such as "Every Good Boy Does Fine" to remember the notes EGBDF on the treble clef in music. To remember the functions of the parasympathetic and sympathetic nervous systems, you might try making connections like those described in Figure 7.10 (Carney & Levin, 1998).

A parachute lets you coast down slowly, like the parasympathetic nervous system.

If the symphony excites you, it arouses your sympathetic nervous system.

© Horizon International Images Limited / Alamy

© Ryan McVay / Stone / Getty Images

Figure 7.10 One mnemonic device is to think of an image that will remind you of what you need to remember.

Suppose you have to memorize a list of Nobel Peace Prize winners (Figure 7.11). You might make up a little story: "Dun (Dunant) passed (Passy) the Duke (Ducommun) of Gob (Gobat) some cream (Cremer). That made him internally ILL (Institute of International Law). He suited (von Suttner) up with some roses (Roosevelt) and spent some money (Moneta) on a Renault (Renault) . . ." You still have to study the names, but your story helps.

Another mnemonic device is the method of loci (method of places). *First, you memorize a series of places, and then you use a vivid image to associate each location with something you want to remember*. For example, you might start by

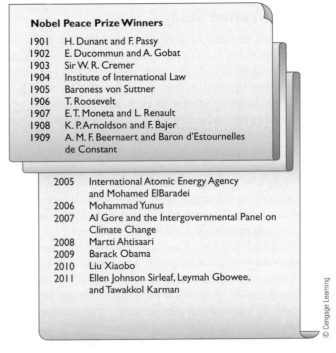

Nobel Peace Prize Winners

1901	H. Dunant and F. Passy
1902	E. Ducommun and A. Gobat
1903	Sir W. R. Cremer
1904	Institute of International Law
1905	Baroness von Suttner
1906	T. Roosevelt
1907	E. T. Moneta and L. Renault
1908	K. P. Arnoldson and F. Bajer
1909	A. M. F. Beernaert and Baron d'Estournelles de Constant

2005	International Atomic Energy Agency and Mohamed ElBaradei
2006	Mohammad Yunus
2007	Al Gore and the Intergovernmental Panel on Climate Change
2008	Martti Ahtisaari
2009	Barack Obama
2010	Liu Xiaobo
2011	Ellen Johnson Sirleaf, Leymah Gbowee, and Tawakkol Karman

© Cengage Learning

Figure 7.11 A list of Nobel Peace Prize winners: Mnemonic devices can be useful when people try to memorize long lists like this one.

Figure 7.12 With the method of loci, you first learn a list of places, such as "my desk, the door of my room, the corridor, . . ." Then you link each place to an item on a list.

memorizing every location along the route from your dormitory room to your psychology classroom. Then you link the locations, in order, to the names.

Suppose the first three locations you pass are the desk in your room, the door to your room, and the corridor. To link the first Nobel Peace Prize winners, Dunant and Passy, to your desk, you might imagine a Monopoly game board on your desk with a big sign "DO NOT (Dunant) PASS (Passy) GO." Then you link the second pair of names to the second location, your door: A DUKE student (as in Ducommun) is standing at the door, giving confusing signals. He says "DO COME IN (Ducommun)" and "GO BACK (Gobat)." Then you link the corridor to Cremer, perhaps by imagining someone has spilled CREAM (Cremer) all over the floor (Figure 7.12). You continue in this manner until you have linked every name to a location. Now, if you can remember all those locations in order and if you have good visual images for each one, you can recite the list of Nobel Peace Prize winners.

Simpler mnemonic devices often help, such as those you can use to remember people's names. You might remember someone named Harry Moore by picturing him as "more hairy." To memorize a traditional wedding vow, you might remember "BRISTLE" to remind you of "**B**etter or worse, **R**icher or poorer, **I**n **S**ickness and health, **T**o **L**ove and to cherish."

Storage

Most of the work of forming a memory pertains to encoding. Storing or maintaining a memory sounds like a passive process, but important things happen here, too. As time passes after initial learning, some memories change in ways that make them available much later, perhaps forever. This process is called consolidation.

Decades ago, psychologists imagined consolidation as a simple process that took a fixed amount of time. Gradually, researchers discovered it to be a diverse and complicated process (Meeter & Murre, 2004). Some memories consolidate much more easily than others. When you hear, "Jakarta is the capital of Indonesia," you might have to work at it to form a lasting memory. If someone

says, "Yes, I will go with you to the dance on Friday," you store the memory almost immediately. If you have a strong interest and background in some topic, you learn new information on that topic quickly compared to a topic that is new to you. You probably remember the important games that your favorite team won better than the big games that it lost (Breslin & Safer, 2011).

How long does consolidation continue? Certain kinds of evidence suggest that it continues for decades, but the interpretation of that evidence is ambiguous. Several studies found that people in their 60s and 70s remember events from their adolescence and early adulthood better than more recent events (Haist, Gore, & Mao, 2001; Maguire & Frith, 2003; Niki & Luo, 2002). For example, older adults generally remember the music, movies, and politicians from their youth better than they remember comparable items from recent years. One interpretation is that the memories continued to consolidate, year after year. Another is that memories in young adulthood formed more strongly in the first place (Berntsen & Rubin, 2002). To most people, the teenage and young adult years are especially interesting and important. Most movies, television shows, and novels focus on that era of life. When children describe their future lives, they describe more events from their teenage and young adult lives than from any other period (Bohn & Berntsen, 2011). Thus, the enhanced recall of events from that age range may be a matter of heightened interest, rather than consolidation of memory.

concept check

16. Which kinds of memory consolidate fastest?
17. Old people remember events from young adulthood better than those from middle adulthood. What are two explanations?

Answers

16. If you already know a topic well, or if something is highly interesting and important to you, you consolidate that material rapidly.
17. Perhaps memories continue to consolidate year after year. Or perhaps memories from young adulthood, being highly interesting, formed more strongly.

Retrieval

People sometimes imagine that memory is like playing back a recording of an event. Memory differs from a recording in many ways. Here is one: Suppose you try to recall something you saw or experienced, or you try to list all the cities you have ever visited. You describe all you can, and then you come back a few days later and try again. On your second try, you will probably recall *more* than you did the first time (Erdelyi, 2010). Whereas loss of memory is called amnesia, this *gain of memory over time* is called hypermnesia. On the second try, you recall most or all of what you said the first time, plus in the meantime something may have reminded you of something you left out the first time. It is for this reason that police sometimes interview a witness several times. It is possible to remember something later that one omitted the first time.

Here is another difference between memory and a recording: Suppose you have some experience, and someone asks you to describe a particular part of the experience—perhaps, "Tell me about the meals you had on your beach trip." Then someone else asks you to describe the beach trip in general. Answering the first question about meals weakens your memory of everything else about the trip (Bäuml & Samenieh, 2010). Furthermore, someone who accompanied you on the beach trip and heard you describing the meals will also tend to forget the events other than meals (Coman, Manier, & Hirst, 2009). Focusing on one part of a memory weakens the rest of it, at least temporarily.

Here is a third, and perhaps the biggest difference between memory and a recording: When you try to remember an experience, you start with the details you remember clearly and reconstruct the rest to fill in the gaps: *During an experience, you construct a memory. When you try to retrieve that memory, you reconstruct an account based partly on surviving memories and partly on your expectations of what must have happened.* For example, you might recall studying in the library three nights ago. With a little effort, you might remember where you sat, what you were reading, who sat next to you, and where you went for a snack afterward. If you aren't quite sure, you fill in the gaps with what usually happens during an evening at the library. Within weeks, you gradually forget that evening, and if you try to remember it, you will rely more and more on "what must have happened," omitting more and more details (Schmolck, Buffalo, & Squire, 2000). If you happen to fall in love with the person who sat next to you that evening, the evening is important enough to become a lifetime memory. Still, when you try to recall it, you reconstruct the details. You remember where you went for a snack and some of what the two of you said, but if you want to recall the book you were reading in the library, you have to reason it out: "Let's see, that semester I was taking a chemistry course that took a lot of study, so maybe I was reading a chemistry book. No, wait, I remember.

When we went out to eat, we talked about politics. So maybe I was reading my political science text."

Reconstruction and Inference in List Memory

Try this demonstration: Read the words in list A once; then turn away from the list, pause for a few seconds, and write as many of the words as you can remember. Repeat the same procedure for list B. *Please do this now, before reading the following paragraph.*

List A	List B
bed	candy
rest	sour
weep	sugar
tired	dessert
dream	salty
wake	taste
snooze	flavor
keep	bitter
doze	cookies
steep	fruits
snore	chocolate
nap	yummy

After you have written your lists, check how many of the words you got right. If you omitted many, you are normal. The point of this demonstration is not how many you got right but whether you included *sleep* on the first list or *sweet* on the second. Many people include one of these words (which are not on the lists), and some do so with confidence (Deese, 1959; Roediger & McDermott, 1995; Watson, Balota, & Roediger, 2003). In list B, *sweet* is related to the other words in meaning. In list A, *sleep* is related to most of the words in meaning, and the list also includes three words that rhyme with sleep (*weep, keep,* and *steep*). This combined influence produces false recall in a higher percentage of people. Apparently, while learning the individual words, people also learn the gist of what they are all about. When they try to retrieve the list later, they reconstruct a memory of what "must have" been on the list (Seamon et al., 2002).

If you did not include *sleep* or *sweet*, try the Online Try It Yourself activity called False Memory. Hearing a list (as you can with the online demonstration) produces a bigger effect than reading a list. Of course, the effect will also be weaker because now you have been warned about what to expect (Roediger & McDermott, 2000; Westerberg & Marsolek, 2006).

This effect occurs mainly if you have a memory of intermediate strength. If a list is short or if you learn it well, you probably won't add an extra word that's not on the list. If you remember few or none of the words on the list, you cannot use them to infer another word (Schacter, Verfaellie, Anes, & Racine, 1998).

18. If you studied a list such as "candy, sour, sugar, dessert, salty, taste, . . ." thoroughly instead of hearing it just once, would you be more likely or less likely to include "sweet," which isn't on the list? Why?

Reconstructing Stories

Suppose you listen to a story about a teenager's day, including both normal events (watching television) and oddities (parking a bicycle in the kitchen). Which would you remember better—the normal events or the oddities? It depends. If you are tested immediately, while your memory is still strong, you remember the unusual and distinctive events best. However, as you start forgetting the story, you begin to omit the unlikely events, reconstructing a more typical day for the teenager, including some that the story omitted, such as "the teenager went to school in the morning." In short, the less certain your memory is, the more you rely on your expectations (Heit, 1993; Maki, 1990). If you retell something repeatedly—either a story you heard or an event from your own experience—the retellings gradually become more coherent (Ackil, Van Abbema, & Bauer, 2003; Bartlett, 1932). They make more sense because you rely more on the gist, keeping the details that fit the overall theme and omitting or modifying the others.

In a study that highlights the role of expectations, U.S. and Mexican adults tried to recall three stories. Some heard U.S. versions of the stories, and others heard Mexican versions. (For example, in the "going on a date" story, the Mexican version had the man's sister go along as a chaperone.) On the average, U.S. participants remembered the U.S. versions better, whereas Mexicans remembered the Mexican versions better (R. J. Harris, Schoen, & Hensley, 1992).

concept check

19. In books about history, it seems that one event led to another in a logical order, but in everyday life, events seem illogical, unconnected, and unpredictable. Why?

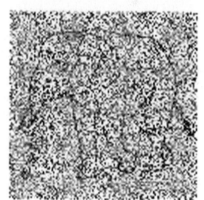

Answer

19. Long after the fact, a historian puts together a coherent story based on the gist of events, emphasizing details that fit the pattern and omitting others. In your everyday life, you are aware of all the facts, including those that do not fit any pattern.

Hindsight Bias

Three weeks before the impeachment trial of U.S. President Clinton in 1999, college students were asked to predict the outcome. On the average, they estimated the probability of a conviction at 50.5%. A week and a half after Clinton was not convicted, they were asked, "What would you have said 4½ weeks ago was the chance [of a conviction]?" On the average, they reported a 42.8% estimate (Bryant & Guilbault, 2002). Their behavior illustrates hindsight bias, *the tendency to mold our recollection of the past to fit how events later turned out.* Something happens and we then say, "I *knew* that was going to happen!"

Another example: As you can see in Figure 7.13, an image gradually morphs from a blur to an elephant. At what point do you think the average person would identify it as an elephant? It is hard to imagine not knowing it will be an elephant. On this and similar sequences, most people overestimate how soon people will recognize the image (Bernstein, Atance, Loftus, & Meltzoff, 2004).

Figure 7.13 At what point in this sequence do you think the average person would recognize it as an elephant? (Source: From Bernstein, Atance, Loftus, & Meltzoff, 2004.)

© Daniel Bernstein

That is, they show hindsight bias. Chapter 5 discussed the fact that children have trouble taking someone else's point of view, or understanding that someone else might not know everything they know. Hindsight bias is similar: In both cases someone assumes that "other people would know what I know" (Birch & Bernstein, 2007).

Hindsight bias affects judgments in legal cases. In one study, people were told about the possible hazards of a train going around a mountain track.

Some participants were asked whether the company should cease operations for safety reasons. One third said "yes." The other participants were told, in addition, that a train had derailed, spilling toxic chemicals into a river. They were asked whether the company should pay punitive damages for irresponsibly continuing operations in spite of foreseeable dangers. Two thirds said "yes" (Hastie, Schkade, & Payne, 1999). That is, after people knew about the accident, they thought it was foreseeable.

module 7.2

In Closing

Improving Your Memory

If you want to improve your memory for something that happened years ago, what can you do? Not much. You might try returning to where the event happened or finding some other reminder. If you remember little at first, you might try again a few days later. Still, your prospects for finding a lost memory are limited. To improve your memory, by far the best strategy is to improve your storage. Think carefully about anything you want to remember, study it under a variety of conditions, and review frequently.

Summary

- *Influences on memory encoding.* High interest enhances memory coding, as does moderate emotion. Distraction impairs it. Memory is best for the first and last items of a list, anything that is unusual, and items familiar since childhood. (page 233)
- *Depth of processing.* A memory becomes stronger if you think about the meaning of the material and relate it to other material. A memory is particularly enhanced if you think about how it could pertain to your survival. (page 235)
- *Encoding specificity.* When you form a memory, you link it to the way you thought about it at the time. When you try to recall the memory, a cue is most effective if it resembles the links you formed at the time of storage. (page 235)
- *Timing of study.* Spreading out your study is more effective than studying in a single session. During a single session, you underestimate how much you will forget later, and you do not practice retrieving a memory, because it is still fresh. (page 236)

- *Variation in learning.* Long-term memory is best if you study under varying conditions. Spreading out examples is better than studying many examples of the same thing at one time. (page 237)
- *Advantages of testing.* Alternating between reading and testing enhances long-term memory better than spending the same amount of time just reading. (page 237)
- *Mnemonics.* Specialized techniques for using systematic retrieval cues help people remember lists of items. (page 238)
- *Storage and consolidation.* Whereas some memories are lost, others gradually strengthen over time. (page 239)
- *Retrieval.* Memory is unlike a recording. Something that you forget at first, you may recall later. Focusing on one aspect of a memory weakens other aspects. (page 239)
- *Reconstructing memories.* Few memories are recalled intact. Ordinarily, we recall parts of an event and fill in the rest with logical reconstructions. (page 240)

- *Reconstructions from a word list.* If people read or hear a list of related words and try to recall them, they often include related words that were not on the list. They remember the gist and reconstruct what must have been on the list. (page 240)

- *Story memory.* Someone whose memory of a story has faded relies on the gist, omits details that seemed irrelevant, and adds or changes other facts to fit the logic of the story. (page 241)
- *Hindsight bias.* People often revise their memories, saying that how an event turned out was what they expected all along. (page 241)

Key Terms

depth-of-processing principle (page 235)
encoding specificity principle (page 235)
hindsight bias (page 241)
hypermnesia (page 240)
method of loci (page 238)

mnemonic device (page 238)
primacy effect (page 233)
recency effect (page 233)
reconstruction (page 240)
retrieval cue (page 235)

Answers to Other Questions in the Module

B. The correct coin is A. (page 232)
C. Animal—Seal; Part of body—Foot; Transportation—Plane; Temperature—Degree; Crime—Racket; Shrubbery—Bush; Stone—Rock; Personality—Charm; Write—Spell; Bird—Cardinal; Harbor—Port; Fruit—Apple. (page 236)

Forgetting

- Why do we forget?
- Why do we sometimes report confident but inaccurate memories?
- Why do some people have severe memory problems?

We all forget, and forgetting doesn't surprise us. A little more surprising is the fact that sometimes we think we remember something clearly, though we are wrong. Here we explore why memory sometimes fails.

Retrieval and Interference

When you try to remember something, you might confuse it with something else you have learned. Remember Hermann Ebbinghaus, who pioneered memory research. Ebbinghaus measured how long he could remember various lists of 13 nonsense syllables. The results appear as the green line on Figure 7.14. On average, he forgot more than half of each list within the first hour (Ebbinghaus, 1885/1913). What a discouraging graph! If people typically forget that fast, then education would be pointless. However, most college students remember nearly 90% of a list of nonsense syllables 24 hours later, as shown in the purple line of Figure 7.14 (Koppenaal, 1963).

Why do you suppose college students remember a list so much better than Ebbinghaus did? You may be tempted to say that college students are very intelligent. Well, yes, but Ebbinghaus was too. Or you might suggest that college students "have had so much practice at memorizing nonsense." (Sorry if you think so.) The explanation is the opposite: Ebbinghaus had memorized *too much* nonsense—thousands of lists of syllables. After you memorize many similar lists, your memory is like a cluttered room: The clutter doesn't prevent you from bringing in still more clutter, but it interferes with finding what you want. Ebbinghaus quickly forgot new lists because of interference from older lists.

If you learn several sets of related materials, they interfere with each other. The *old materials increase forgetting of new materials* by proactive interference (acting forward in time). The *new materials*

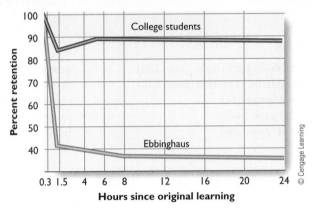

Figure 7.14 Recall of lists of syllables by Ebbinghaus (1885/1913) and by college students after delays of various lengths (based on Koppenaal, 1963). Ebbinghaus learned as fast as other people but forgot faster.

increase forgetting of old materials by retroactive interference (acting backward). Figure 7.15 contrasts the two kinds of interference.

Interference is a major cause of forgetting. You forget where you parked your car today because of proactive interference from the previous times you parked your car. You forget last week's French vocabulary list because of retroactive interference from this week's list.

Ebbinghaus quickly forgot new lists of nonsense syllables because of interference from the previous lists he had learned.

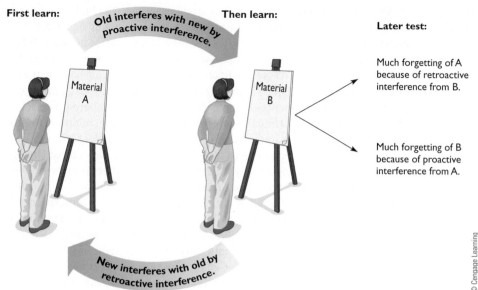

First learn: Old interferes with new by proactive interference.

Material A

Then learn:

Material B

Later test:

Much forgetting of A because of retroactive interference from B.

Much forgetting of B because of proactive interference from A.

New interferes with old by retroactive interference.

© Cengage Learning

Figure 7.15 If you learn similar materials, each interferes with retrieval of the other.

concept check

20. Professor Tryhard learns the names of his students every semester. After several years, he learns them as quickly as ever but forgets them faster. Does he forget because of retroactive or proactive interference?
21. Remember the concept of spontaneous recovery from chapter 6? Can you explain it in terms of proactive interference? (Hint: Original learning comes first and extinction comes second. What would happen if the first interfered with the second?)
22. How does interference explain the primacy effect and recency effect in list learning?

Answers

20. It is due to proactive interference—interference from memories learned earlier.
21. First, someone learns the response; the second learning is the extinction of the response. If the first learning proactively interferes with the later extinction, spontaneous recovery will result.
22. The first item on a list is spared from proactive interference. The last is spared from retroactive interference. However, low interference is just one of many explanations for these effects.

A Controversy: "Recovered Memories" or "False Memories"?

Is it possible to recover forgotten memories? Suppose someone tells a therapist about vague distress, and the therapist replies, "Symptoms like yours are common among people who were sexually abused in childhood. Do you think you were?" In some cases, the client says "no," but the therapist persists: "The fact that you don't remember doesn't mean that it didn't happen. Perhaps it was so painful that you repressed the memory." The therapist recommends hypnosis, repeated attempts to remember, or trying to imagine how it would have happened if it did. (This procedure reflects the assumption that reliving painful old memories is beneficial—an assumption for which there is much reason to doubt.) A few sessions later, the client says, "It's starting to come back. . . . I think I do remember. . . ." Most therapists would not use such aggressive techniques to recover old memories, but some do. *Reports of long-lost memories, prompted by clinical techniques,* are known as recovered memories.

When people claim to recover long-forgotten memories, has the therapist uncovered the truth, distorted the truth, or convinced someone to believe an imagined event? This issue became one of the most heated debates in psychology.

Some reports are bizarre. In one case, two sisters accused their father of repeatedly raping them both vaginally and anally, bringing his friends over on Friday nights to rape them, and forcing them to participate in satanic rituals that included cannibalism and the slaughter of babies (Wright, 1994). The sisters had not remembered any of these events until repeated sessions with a therapist. In another case, 3- and 4-year-old children, after repeated urgings from a therapist, accused their Sunday school teacher of sexually abusing them with a curling iron, forcing them to drink blood and urine, hanging them upside down from a chandelier, dunking them in toilets, and killing an elephant and a giraffe during Sunday school class (M. Gardner, 1994). No one found any physical evidence to support the claims, such as scarred tissues or giraffe bones.

Even when recovered-memory claims are much less bizarre, their accuracy is uncertain. Researchers studied two groups of adults—some who spontaneously remembered an episode of childhood sexual abuse that they hadn't thought about in years, and others who recovered a memory during therapy. In most cases, when someone spontaneously reported a long-lost memory, investigators found supporting evidence, such as other people who reported being abused by the same perpetrator. For the people who reported recovering a memory only as a result of therapy, investigators did not find supporting evidence in a single case (Geraerts et al., 2007).

When people have abusive experiences, are they likely to forget them for years? And can repeated suggestions get someone to recall an event that never happened?

Memory for Traumatic Events

Sigmund Freud, whom we consider more fully in chapter 14, introduced the term repression as *the process of moving an unbearably unacceptable memory or impulse from the conscious mind to the unconscious mind.* Many clinicians now prefer the term dissociation, referring to *memory that one has stored but cannot retrieve* (Alpert, Brown, & Courtois, 1998). However, researchers have found no clear evidence that either process occurs (Holmes, 1990).

Do people ever forget highly emotional events? It depends on what we mean by "forget." Let's start with a relatively minor experience. Students in one experiment viewed 24 lists of words, each from a distinct category, such as tools. Most of the lists were normal sorts of categories, but one was a list of "dirty" words. I won't give you examples, but you can probably guess. If you went through this procedure, and then the researcher asked you to name the categories, wouldn't you be sure to remember that one list was a bunch of dirty words? Ordinarily, yes, but after reading through all 24 lists once, the students had a distractor task and then examined 21 of the lists again—not including the dirty words. Then when they were asked to name all the categories of words, most of them forgot to mention "dirty words." So, had the students forgotten this presumably emotional experience? Not exactly. When they were reminded that they had read a list of dirty words, most said, "Oh, yeah," and then recited most of the words on that list (S. M. Smith & Moynan, 2008). This study illustrates why it is difficult to be sure whether or not someone has forgotten something.

What about traumatic events? One study examined 16 children who had witnessed the murder of one of their parents. All had recurring nightmares and haunting thoughts of the experience, and none had forgotten (Malmquist, 1986). Other studies examined prisoners of war who had been severely mistreated (Merckelbach, Dekkers, Wessel, & Roefs, 2003), children who had been kidnapped or forced to participate in pornographic movies (Terr, 1988), and people with other horrible experiences. People almost always remembered the events, or they forgot only about as much as one might expect for early childhood events. If repression doesn't occur under these circumstances, when does it?

Whether someone remembers a traumatic experience depends on the age at the time of the event, its severity, and the reaction of other family members. Several studies examined young adult women who had been victims of childhood sexual abuse, documented by either hospital records or criminal proceedings. In each study, those who were older at the time of the offense remembered it better than those who were younger. Memory was better among those who had more severe or repeated abuse and those who received more family support and encouragement (Alexander et al., 2005; Goodman et al., 2003; L. M. Williams, 1994). In these regards early traumatic memories are similar to any other memories.

23. Based on material earlier in this chapter, why should we expect traumatic events to be remembered better than most other events?

Answer

23. Emotionally arousing memories are usually more memorable than other events. Any emotionally arousing event stimulates cortisol release and in other ways activates brain areas that help store memories.

Influence of Suggestion

For those skeptical of claims that therapy recovers repressed memories, what is the alternative? Much research indicates that memory recall is a process of reconstruction. Perhaps repeated suggestions to recall a memory of childhood abuse (or anything else, for that matter) can implant a false memory (or false report), *an inaccurate report that someone believes to be a memory* (Lindsay & Read, 1994; Loftus, 1993). Early research found that asking misleading questions about a video, such as "Did you see the children getting on the school bus?" caused many people falsely to report having seen a school bus (Loftus, 1975). Could an experimenter mislead people into reporting false memories about their own lives? Let's examine two experiments.

critical check

What's the Evidence?

Suggestions and False Memories

First Study

Hypothesis In some cases, people who are told about a childhood event will come to believe it happened, even if in fact it did not.

Method Participants were told that the study concerned their childhood memories. Each participant was given paragraphs describing four events. Three of the events had actually happened. (The experimenters had contacted parents to get descriptions of childhood events.) A fourth event was a plausible but false story about getting lost. An example for one Vietnamese woman: "You, your Mom, Tien, and Tuan, all went to the Bremerton Kmart. You must have been 5 years old at the time. Your Mom gave each of you some money to get a blueberry ICEE. You ran ahead to get into the line first, and somehow lost your way in the store. Tien found you crying to an elderly Chinese woman. You three then went together to get an ICEE." After reading the four paragraphs, each participant was asked to write whatever additional details he or she could remember of the event. Participants were asked to try again a week later and then again after another week (Loftus, Feldman, & Dashiell, 1995).

Results Of 24 participants, 6 reported remembering the suggested false event, and some of them elaborated with additional details. The woman in the foregoing example said, "I vaguely remember walking around Kmart crying and looking for Tien and Tuan. I thought I was lost forever. I went to the shoe department, because we always spent a lot of time there. I went to the handkerchief place because we were there last. I circled all over the store it seemed 10 times. I just remember walking around crying. I do not remember the Chinese woman, or the ICEE (but it would be raspberry ICEE if I was getting an ICEE) part. I don't even remember being found."

Interpretation A suggestion can provoke some people to report a personal experience in moderate detail, even though the event never happened. Granted, the suggestion influenced only a quarter of the people tested, and most of them reported only vague memories. Still, the researchers achieved this effect after just a single brief suggestion. In a similar study, 13 of 47 participants reported detailed false memories of getting lost or getting attacked by an animal or another child, and 18 more participants reported partial recollection (Porter, Birt, Yuille, & Lehman, 2000). After being told of getting sick after eating an egg in childhood, many people avoided eggs, and after being told of liking asparagus the first time they tried it, many increased their preference for asparagus (Bernstein & Loftus, 2009).

One objection is that perhaps these false memories were not entirely false. Maybe the young woman *was* lost at some point—if not in a Kmart at age 5, then somewhere else at some other age. Maybe some of these people did get sick after eating something in childhood, even if it wasn't an egg. In other studies, researchers suggested virtually impossible events. For example, college students read fake advertisements for Disneyland that depicted people meeting and shaking hands with Bugs Bunny, a Warner Brothers character who would never appear at Disneyland. About 30% of those who read this ad later reported that they too had met Bugs Bunny at Disneyland. Some reported touching his ears or tail (Loftus, 2003). In another study, British students who were asked to imagine certain experiences later reported that they remembered them, including "having a nurse remove a skin sample from my little finger"—a procedure that British physicians never use (Mazzoni & Memon, 2003). In short, suggestions can lead people to report memories of events that never happened.

Second Study

Some therapists ask their clients to examine childhood photographs to help evoke old memories. They are certainly right that photographs bring back memories. However, might old photographs also facilitate false memories?

Hypothesis A false suggestion about a childhood event will evoke more memory reports if people have examined photographs from that time period.

Method The researchers contacted the parents of 45 college students and asked each to provide a report of an event that happened while these stu-

dents were in third or fourth grade and another that happened in fifth or sixth grade. Both were supposed to be events that the student might or might not remember rather than events the family had repeatedly discussed. The researchers also asked the parents to confirm that the following event—the one they planned to suggest—had *not* happened: In the first grade, the child took a "Slime" toy to school, and then she and another child slid it into the teacher's desk and received a mild punishment later. The researchers also asked the parents for copies of class photographs from first grade, third or fourth grade, and fifth or sixth grade.

After these preparations, they brought in the students and briefly described for each student the three events (two provided by the parents and the one false event). They asked the students to provide whatever additional information they remembered about each event. Half of them (randomly selected) were shown their class photographs and half were not. At the end of the session, they were asked to think about the first-grade event for the next week and try to remember more about it. Those in the photograph group took the photo with them. A week later, the students returned and again reported whatever they thought they remembered (Lindsay, Hagen, Read, Wade, & Garry, 2004).

Results Most students reported clear memories of the two real events. For the false event of first grade, Figure 7.16 shows the percentage of students who reported the event in the first and second sessions. Memories increased from the first to the second session, and students who saw the photographs reported more memories than those who did not see photographs. By the second session, almost two thirds of the students who saw a class photograph reported some memory of the false event.

At the end of the study, the researchers explained that the first-grade event did not really happen. Many of the students expressed surprise, such as, "No way! I remember it! That is so weird!" (Lindsay et al., 2004, p. 153).

Interpretation Examining an old photograph evokes old memories and also increases suggestibility for false memories. Why? When you are trying to decide whether you remember something, you try to call up related thoughts and images. If you can recall extra details, it is probably a real memory. A photo makes it easier for you to recall details and think the event is real (Henkel, 2011; Strange, Garry, Bernstein, & Lindsay, 2011). If you are trying to remember when you and a friend pulled a prank on the teacher, the visual image becomes more vivid and more convincing.

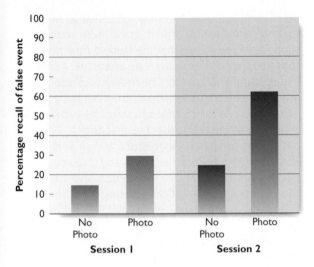

Figure 7.16 More students who saw a first-grade class photograph reported remembering the suggested (false) event. (D. S. Lindsay, L. Hagen, J. D. Read, K. A. Wada, and M. Garry. "True photographs and false memories," *Psychological Science* 9:6. Copyright © 2004 Sage Publications," Inc. Reprinted with permission.)

Figure 7.17 In 1989, a man blocked the path of Chinese tanks in Tiananmen Square in Beijing. People who saw the altered photo (below) reported remembering a large crowd at the event (Sacchi, D. L. M., Agnoli, F., & Loftus, E. F. [2007]. Changing history: Doctored photographs affect memory for past public events. *Applied Cognitive Psychology, 21,* 1005–1022).

In related studies, researchers manipulated photos by computers, showing childhood pictures of people having tea with Prince Charles of England or riding with their families in a hot-air balloon—false events in each case. Many of the participants claimed to remember the events and provided additional details (Strange, Sutherland, & Garry, 2004; Wade, Garry, Read, & Lindsay, 2002). People who viewed doctored photos of historical events misremembered the events to match the photos (Sacchi, Agnoli, & Loftus, 2007; Figure 7.17). The effect of photos relates to source amnesia, as described earlier. Source amnesia occurs if you remember something but don't remember where you learned it. In the case of photos, you see something in the photo and think you remember it from an experience long ago.

Areas of Agreement and Disagreement

What should we conclude about the possibility of recovering lost memories of early trauma? Many clinicians object that the kinds of false memories implanted in research settings (being lost in a mall, first-grade mischief, etc.) differ from emotionally intense memories of sexual abuse. To this criticism researchers reply that ethical concerns prevent them from suggesting memories of traumatic abuse.

If someone reports remembering an event after many years of not remembering it, the memory might be correct. Even psychologists who are skeptical of repression agree that someone might have an experience in childhood and then not think about it again until many years later (McNally & Geraerts, 2009). In many cases it is best to withhold judgment unless independent evidence supports the report. A further recommendation is to avoid using repeated suggestions, photographs, or other techniques that increase the probability of a false memory report.

24. In what way is hindsight bias similar to an implanted "false memory"?

Answer

24. In a case of hindsight bias, something that you later learn operates like a suggestion, so that when you try to remember what you previously thought, you are influenced by that suggestion and change your reported memory to fit it.

Amnesia

Imagine you defied the advice given to computer owners and passed your computer through a powerful magnetic field. Suppose this process erased only the text files and not the graphics files. Or suppose the old memories were intact but you could no longer store new ones. From the damage, you would gain hints about how your computer's memory works.

The same is true of human memory. Various kinds of brain damage impair one kind of memory but not another, enabling us to draw inferences about how memory is organized.

Amnesia After Damage to the Hippocampus

Amnesia is a *loss of memory*. Even in the most severe cases of amnesia, people don't forget everything they ever learned. They don't forget how to walk, talk, or eat. (If they did, we would call it *dementia*, not amnesia.) In many cases they remember most of their factual knowledge. What they most often forget is their personal experiences. Amnesia results from many kinds of brain damage, including damage to the hippocampus.

In 1953 Henry Molaison, known in the research literature by his initials H. M., was suffering from many small daily epileptic seizures and about one major seizure per week. He did not respond to any antiepileptic drugs, and in desperation, surgeons removed most of his hippocampus, *a large forebrain structure in the interior of the temporal lobe* (Figure 7.18), based on a few previous cases in which hippocampal damage reduced the frequency of epileptic seizures. At the time, researchers knew little about what to expect after damage to the hippocampus. Since then, animal research has established that the hippocampus is important for encoding and retrieving memories. It is the brain area where researchers most easily demonstrate changes in synapses during learning.

The surgery greatly decreased the frequency and severity of H. M.'s seizures. (Although it worked in his case, it is not generally effective for treating epilepsy.) His personality remained the same, except that he became more passive (Eichenbaum, 2002). His IQ score increased slightly, presumably because he had fewer epileptic seizures. However, he suffered severe memory problems (Corkin, 1984; Milner, 1959). H. M. suffered massive anterograde (ANT-eh-ro-grade) amnesia, *inability to store new long-term memories*. For years after the operation, he cited the year as 1953 and his own age as 27. Later, he took wild guesses (Corkin, 1984). He would read the same issue of a magazine repeatedly with-

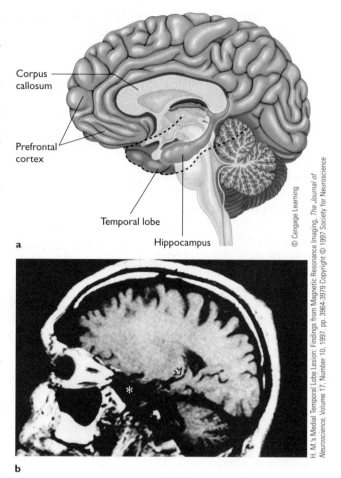

Corpus callosum

Prefrontal cortex

Temporal lobe

Hippocampus

a

H. M.'s Medial Temporal Lobe Lesion: Findings from Magnetic Resonance Imaging, *The Journal of Neuroscience*, Volume 17, Number 10, 1997, pp. 3964-3979 Copyright © 1997 Society for Neuroscience

b

Figure 7.18 (a) The hippocampus is a large subcortical brain structure. (b) The photo shows an MRI scan of H. M.'s brain. The asterisk indicates the area from which the hippocampus is missing. The arrow indicates a portion of the hippocampus that is preserved. (Photo courtesy of Suzanne Corkin and David Amaral.)

out recognizing it. He could not remember where he lived. He also suffered a moderate retrograde amnesia, *loss of memory for events that occurred shortly before the brain damage* (Figure 7.19). Initial reports said that H. M.'s retrograde amnesia was limited to the last couple of years before the surgery. Later reports said it extended much further, especially for episodic (autobiographical) memories. Another person with amnesia following injury to his hippo-

Difficulty retrieving old memories = **Retrograde amnesia**

Time of damage

Difficulty learning new information = **Anterograde amnesia**

Figure 7.19 Brain damage induces retrograde amnesia (loss of old memories) and anterograde amnesia (difficulty storing new memories).

campus and other brain areas suffered a complete loss of his episodic memory. When he looks at old family photos, he names the people, but he cannot describe the event in the photo or any other event including those people (Rosenbaum et al., 2005).

H. M. had normal short-term memory and working memory, as do most other patients with amnesia (Shrager, Levy, Hopkins, & Squire, 2008). If someone told him to remember a number, he could recall it minutes later, if nothing distracted him. However, after any distraction he forgot the number, and forgot that he had tried to remember a number. He often told the same person the same story several times within a few minutes, forgetting that he had told it before (Eichenbaum, 2002).

Like Rip van Winkle, the story character who slept for 20 years and awakened to a vastly changed world, H. M. became more and more out of date with each passing year (Gabrieli, Cohen, & Corkin, 1988; M. L. Smith, 1988). He did not recognize people who became famous after the mid-1950s, although when given a famous person's name, he sometimes provided a bit of correct information (O'Kane, Kensinger, & Corkin, 2004). He did not understand the words and phrases that entered the English language after his surgery, such as *jacuzzi* and *granola* (Corkin, 2002). He guessed that *soul food* meant "forgiveness" and that a *closet queen* might be "a moth" (Gabrieli et al., 1988).

In spite of H. M.'s massive memory difficulties, he could still acquire and retain new skills. Recall the distinction between declarative (factual) memory and procedural memory (skills and habits). H. M. learned to read material written in mirror fashion (N. J. Cohen & Squire, 1980), such as shown below. However, he did not remember having learned this or any other new skill and always expressed surprise at his success.

He could read sentences written backwards, like this.

The results for H. M. led researchers to study both people and laboratory animals with similar damage. The following points have emerged:

- Storing declarative memory requires the hippocampus. Procedural memories depend on a different brain area, the basal ganglia.
- The hippocampus is especially important for episodic memories—memories of specific events in one's life. Episodic memories form all at once, unlike procedural memories that develop gradually.
- The hippocampus is more important for explicit memory than for implicit memory, and more important for difficult tasks than for easy tasks (Reed & Squire, 1999; J. D. Ryan, Althoff, Whitlow, & Cohen, 2000).

- The hippocampus is especially important for spatial memories—remembering where something is (Kumaran & Maguire, 2005).
- Patients with hippocampal damage have trouble imagining the future, just as they have trouble recalling the past. When you imagine a future event, such as a trip to the beach or a visit to a museum, you rearrange and modify your recollections of similar events in the past. If you can't remember your past, you can't put much detail into your imagined future (Hassabis, Kumaran, Vann, & Maguire, 2007). A patient with amnesia truly lives in the present moment, without a past or a future.

Exactly what is the role of the hippocampus in memory? According to one influential theory, the hippocampus is critical for remembering the details and context of a memory. When you recall something you did yesterday, your memory is rich in details, including who, what, where, and when. Those details depend on the hippocampus. As time passes, your memory consolidates, but as it consolidates, it changes. You remember the "gist" of what happened but fewer details (Winocur, Moscovitch, & Sekeres, 2007).

concept check

25. Which kinds of memory were most impaired in H. M.? Which kinds were least impaired?

Answers

25. H. M. was greatly impaired at forming new declarative memories. His short-term memory was intact, as was his memory for facts learned long before the operation and his ability to form new procedural memories.

Amnesia After Damage to the Prefrontal Cortex

Damage to the prefrontal cortex also produces amnesia (see Figure 7.18). Because the prefrontal cortex receives extensive input from the hippocampus, the symptoms of prefrontal cortex damage overlap those of hippocampal damage. However, some special deficits also arise.

Prefrontal cortex damage can be the result of a stroke, head trauma, or Korsakoff's syndrome, *a condition caused by a prolonged deficiency of vitamin B₁ (thiamine), usually as a result of chronic alcoholism.* This deficiency leads to widespread loss or shrinkage of neurons, especially in the prefrontal cortex. Patients suffer apathy, confusion, and amnesia (Squire, Haist, & Shimamura, 1989). If given a list of words to remember, they forget those at the beginning of the list before they reach the end and soon forget those at the end also (Stuss et al., 1994).

Patients with prefrontal cortex damage answer many questions with confabulations, *which are attempts to fill in the gaps in their memory.* Most often they answer a question about what's happening today by describing something from their past (Borsutzky, Fujiwara, Brand, & Markowitsch, 2008; Schnider, 2003). For example, an aged hospitalized woman might insist that she had to go home to feed her baby. Confabulations are not exactly attempts to hide an inability to answer a question, as Korsakoff's patients almost never confabulate on a question such as "Where is Premola?" or "Who is Princess Lolita?" (Schnider, 2003). That is, people who never knew the answer freely admit not knowing. The following interview is a typical example (Moscovitch, 1989, pp. 135–136). Note the mixture of correct information, confabulations that were correct at some time in the past, and imaginative attempts to explain the discrepancies between one answer and another:

Psychologist: How old are you?

Patient: I'm 40, 42, pardon me, 62.

Psychologist: Are you married or single?

Patient: Married.

Psychologist: How long have you been married?

Patient: About 4 months.

Psychologist: What's your wife's name?

Patient: Martha.

Psychologist: How many children do you have?

Patient: Four. (He laughs.) Not bad for 4 months.

Psychologist: How old are your children?

Patient: The eldest is 32; his name is Bob. And the youngest is 22; his name is Joe.

Psychologist: How did you get these children in 4 months?

Patient: They're adopted.

Psychologist: Who adopted them?

Patient: Martha and I.

Psychologist: Immediately after you got married you wanted to adopt these older children?

Patient: Before we were married we adopted one of them, two of them. The eldest girl Brenda and Bob, and Joe and Dina since we were married.

Psychologist: Does it all sound a little strange to you, what you are saying?

Patient: I think it is a little strange.

Psychologist: I think when I looked at your record it said that you've been married for over 30 years. Does that sound more reasonable to you if I told you that?

Patient: No.

Psychologist: Do you really believe that you have been married for 4 months?

Patient: Yes.

Patients with prefrontal cortex damage confidently defend their confabulations and often maintain the same confabulation from one time to the next. Actually, the same is true of normal people who learn something poorly. In one study, college students listened to complicated 2-minute descriptions of topics they knew little about and then answered detailed questions. Once a week for the next 4 weeks, they heard the same description and answered the same questions. Most people repeated the same incorrect guesses from one week to the next (Fritz, Morris, Bjork, Gelman, & Wickens, 2000).

Why do people with prefrontal damage confabulate so much more than the rest of us? According to Morris Moscovitch (1992), the prefrontal cortex is necessary for *working with memory*, the strategies we use to reconstruct memories that we cannot immediately recall. If you are asked what is the farthest north that you have ever traveled or how many salads you ate last week, you reason out your answer. People with prefrontal cortex damage have difficulty making reasonable inferences.

Despite their impoverished memory in other regards, people with brain damage perform well on most tests of implicit memory. For example, after hearing a list of words, a patient may not be able to say any of the words on the list and may not even remember that there was a list. However, when given a set of three-letter stems such as CON—, the patient completes them to make words that were on the list (Hamann & Squire, 1997).

Another example: After patients repeatedly practiced playing the video game Tetris, they said they did not remember playing the game before, although

they did improve from one session to the next. When they closed their eyes to go to sleep at night, they said they saw little images of blocks and wondered what they were (Stickgold, Malia, Maguire, Roddenberry, & O'Connor, 2000).

One important conclusion emerges from all the studies of brain damage and amnesia: We have several different types of memory. It is possible to impair one type without equally damaging another.

concept check

26. Although confabulation is a kind of false memory, how does it differ from the suggested false memories discussed earlier in this module?

Answer

26. Most confabulated statements were true at one time, though not now. They seldom represent new information.

Memory Impairments in Alzheimer's Disease

A more common disorder is Alzheimer's disease, *a condition occurring mostly in old age, characterized by increasingly severe memory loss, confusion, depression, disordered thinking, and impaired attention.* Although several genes have been linked to an onset of Alzheimer's disease before age 60, more than 99% of the people with Alzheimer's disease have a later onset, and most cases of the late-onset form are not linked with any identified gene. Moreover, the genes' effects are not inevitable. The Yoruba people of Nigeria almost never get Alzheimer's disease, even if they have the genes that predispose Americans to this disease (Hendrie, 2001). Which aspect of their culture shields them from Alzheimer's is uncertain, although diet is a likely candidate.

Alzheimer's disease is marked by an accumulation of harmful proteins in the brain and deterioration of brain cells, impairing arousal and attention. The memory problems include both anterograde and retrograde amnesia. Performance may vary from one time to another, depending on someone's alertness (Palop, Chin, & Mucke, 2006). Sometimes a patient does a little better after a cup of coffee or a brisk walk to increase blood flow.

Because the areas of damage include the hippocampus and the prefrontal cortex, memory deficits of people with Alzheimer's overlap those of H. M. and patients with Korsakoff's syndrome. For example, like Korsakoff's patients, they often confabulate (Nedjam, Dalla Barba, & Pillon, 2000). Their mixture of memory problems is hardly surprising, given the overall decrease of arousal and attention. Weak arousal and impaired attention impair almost any aspect of memory. However, like H. M., as a rule they can learn new skills, such as how to use a cell phone (Lekeu, Wojtasik, Van der Linden, & Salmon, 2002).

27. What kinds of memory are impaired in patients with Alzheimer's disease?

Answer

27. Patients with Alzheimer's disease have weaknesses in almost all types of memory, although they can learn new skills (procedural memory).

Infant Amnesia

Let's end with a type of amnesia we all experience. How much do you remember from when you were 6 years old? How about age 4? Age 2? Most adults report at most a few fragmentary memories of early childhood (Bauer, Wenner, & Kroupina, 2002; K. Nelson & Fivush, 2004). The *scarcity of early episodic memories* is known as infant amnesia, or childhood amnesia. Although psychologists have proposed many theories of infant amnesia, none are fully persuasive.

In probably the earliest proposal on this issue, Sigmund Freud suggested that children go through emotionally difficult experiences at ages 4 to 5 that are so disturbing that a child represses everything experienced at that time or before. However, neither Freud nor anyone else has provided persuasive evidence for this idea.

A more modern proposal is that the hippocampus, known to be important for episodic memory, is slow to mature, so memories from the first few years are not stored well (Moscovitch, 1985). Furthermore, most of the memories that we can readily demonstrate in infants are either procedural memories (how to do something) or semantic memories (such as what acts are safe and unsafe).

However, the problem is not that infants don't form memories. It is that the memories don't last very long. Three- and four-year-olds clearly remember their last birthday party and other events from months ago, although they don't remember them a few years later. One very articulate 2-year-old re-

portedly answered detailed questions about his three-day hospitalization at age 5 months, although his parents and grandparents had not talked about the experience since then (Solter, 2008). However, a year later he had forgotten about it. Patricia Bauer (2005) provided novel experiences to preschool children of various ages and tested their recollections later. Although all the children learned well enough, the youngest children forgot fastest.

Another proposal is that a permanent memory of an experience requires a "sense of self" that develops between ages 3 and 4 (Howe & Courage, 1993). However, rats, pigeons, and other nonhuman species develop long-lasting memories. If we want to avoid saying that rats have more sense of self than 3-year-old children, we could argue that rats' memories aren't the same as the kind of memory we are discussing for adult humans. At best, this idea is not convincing.

Another possibility is that as we come to rely on language, we lose access to memories encoded earlier. That idea will not explain why a 4-year-old can describe what happened at age 3, whereas a 7-year-old cannot. Still, some interesting research supports the onset of language as one factor in infant amnesia: Psychologists let 3-year-olds play with a "magic shrinking machine." A child could place a large toy into a slot, crank a handle, and then see a smaller version of the same toy come out, as if the machine had shrunk the toy. When the children returned 6 months or a year later, they clearly remembered the machine and how to work it. However, when they were asked to describe how the machine worked or to name the toys that it shrank, the children described their experience using only the words they had known at the time they originally played with the machine (Simcock & Hayne, 2002). For example, a child who knew the word "teddy bear" at age 3 would use it later, but a child who did not know the term at age 3 would not, even after learning it in the meantime. In a similar study, 2-year-old children learned that only one color of fluid would operate a "magic bubble machine." Of those who did not know the name of that color at the time but who learned it within the next 2 months, 30% could then name the color that operated the machine (Morris & Baker-Ward, 2007). So it appears that children sometimes apply newly learned words to old memories, but not always.

One more possibility is that infant amnesia relates to encoding specificity. If we learn something in one time, place, physiological condition, or state of mind, we remember it more easily under the same or similar conditions. Maybe we forget our early years just because we don't have enough of the right retrieval cues to find those infant memories.

At this point, none of these hypotheses is well established. Infant amnesia may have several explanations, not just one.

28. What evidence indicates that infant amnesia is not due to a failure to establish long-term memories?

Answer

28. Young children remember events that happened months or even years ago. However, over time they lose those memories.

module 7.3

In Closing

Memory Loss and Distortion

The first part of this module presented evidence that when we try to recall something from long ago, we often find that the details have faded and we need to infer or reconstruct much of the information. The fact that we are built this way is not really a failing.

Computers store every detail that we give them indefinitely, but our brains don't need to. The older some experience is, the less likely we are to need all the details. If we do need the details, we can usually reason them out well enough for most purposes.

Summary

- *Interference.* When someone learns several similar sets of material, the earlier ones interfere with retrieval of later ones by proactive interference. The later ones interfere with earlier ones by retroactive interference. Interference is a major cause of forgetting. (page 244)
- *The "recovered memory" versus "false memory" debate.* Some therapists have used hypnosis or suggestions to try to help people remember painful experiences. Many researchers doubt the accuracy of those recovered memories. Suggestions can induce people to distort memories or report events that did not happen. (page 245)
- *Amnesia after damage to the hippocampus.* H. M. and other patients with damage to the hippocampus have great difficulty storing new long-term declarative memories, especially episodic memories, although they form normal short-term, procedural, and implicit memories. (page 249)
- *Role of the hippocampus.* The hippocampus serves many functions in memory. One is to bind together all the details and context of an event. In the absence of a healthy hippocampus or after the information in the hippocampus weakens, one is left with only the "gist" of the event. (page 250)
- *Damage to the prefrontal cortex.* Patients with damage to the prefrontal cortex give confident wrong answers, known as confabulations. Most confabulations were correct information earlier in the person's life. (page 250)
- *Alzheimer's disease.* People with Alzheimer's disease, a condition that occurs mostly after age 60 to 65, have a variety of memory problems, although procedural memory is more intact than explicit, declarative memory. Their problems stem largely from impairments of arousal and attention. (page 251)
- *Infant amnesia.* Most people remember little from early childhood, even though preschoolers have clear recollections of experiences that happened months or even years ago. No explanation is fully convincing. (page 252)

Key Terms

Alzheimer's disease (page 251)
amnesia (page 249)
anterograde amnesia (page 249)
confabulations (page 250)
dissociation (page 246)
false memory (page 246)
hippocampus (page 249)

infant amnesia (or childhood amnesia) (page 252)
Korsakoff's syndrome (page 250)
proactive interference (page 244)
recovered memory (page 245)
repression (page 246)
retroactive interference (page 244)
retrograde amnesia (page 249)

exploration and study

Access an interactive eBook and chapter-specific learning tools, including
- **flashcards**
- **quizzes**
- **videos**

and more, in your Psychology CourseMate. Go to **CengageBrain.com.**

If your professor has assigned Aplia:
1. Sign in to your account.
2. Complete the corresponding exercises as required by your professor.
3. When finished, click "Grade It Now" to see which areas you have mastered, which areas need more work, and detailed explanations of every answer.

eters/CORBIS

Cognition and Language

Consider the statement, "This sentence is false." Is the statement itself true or false? Declaring the statement true agrees with its own assessment that it is false. But declaring it false would make its assessment correct. A sentence about itself, called a *self-referential* sentence, can be confusing. It can be true (like this one!). It can be false ("Anyone who reads this sentence will be transported suddenly to the planet Neptune"), untestable ("Whenever no one is reading this sentence, it changes its font"), or amusing ("This sentence no verb").

In this chapter, you will be asked to think about thinking. Doing so is self-referential, and if you try to "think about what you are thinking now," you can go into a confusing loop like the one in "This sentence is false." Thus, psychological researchers focus as much as possible on results obtained from carefully controlled experiments, not just on what people say that they think about their thought processes.

© Owen Franken/CORBIS

Cognitive psychology studies how people think and what they know.

module 8.1

Attention and Categorization

- What is attention?
- How can we study concepts?

Cognition means *thinking and using knowledge*. Cognitive psychologists also deal with how people organize their thoughts into language. Cognition begins with attending to something and categorizing what it is. How can researchers learn about cognitive processes? Since about 1970, psychologists have developed many ways to infer what they cannot observe.

Research in Cognitive Psychology

You might think cognitive psychology should be simple. "If you want to find out what people think or know, why not ask them?" Sometimes, psychologists do ask, but people don't always know their own thought processes. Consider this experiment: The experimenter presents two cards at a time, each showing a female face, and asks which one looks more attractive. Sometimes the experimenter also asks for an explanation. Occasionally, the experimenter surreptitiously switches cards, asking why someone chose a particular face, when it was in fact, the face *not* chosen, as shown in Figure 8.1. People usually don't notice

a b c d

Fig 1. From Johansson, Hall, Sikström, & Olsson, 2005. *Science*, 310, 116-119. Used by permission of the author

Figure 8.1 The participant identified the face considered more attractive. Then the experimenter switched cards and asked why this face seemed more attractive. (From Johansson, Hall, Sikström, & Olsson, 2005.)

the switch, and on average, their explanations are as long, as specific, and as confident for the switched cards as for the originally chosen cards (Johansson, Hall, Sikström, & Olsson, 2005). Clearly, people are stating reasons that they made up afterward, not at the time of the original choice. Therefore, we suspect that even on the trials without a switch, people choose without knowing a reason and then make up a reasonable-sounding explanation afterward.

If we can't always find out people's thought processes just by asking, how can we discover them? Let's consider one of the first experiments that showed how to measure a mental process.

critical check

What's the Evidence?

Mental Imagery

If you look at something and try to describe how it would look from a different angle, you probably say you imagined rotating the object. Roger Shepard and Jacqueline Metzler (1971) reasoned that if people use mental images, then the time it takes to rotate a mental image should be similar to the time needed to rotate a real object.

Hypothesis When people have to rotate a mental image to answer a question, the farther they have to rotate it, the longer it will take to answer the question.

Method Participants examined pairs of drawings of three-dimensional objects, like those in Figure 8.2, and indicated whether it would be possible to rotate one object to match the other. (Try to answer this question yourself before reading further.)

try it ▶ yourself

People pulled one lever to indicate *same* and another lever to indicate *different*. When the correct answer was *same*, someone might determine that answer by rotating a mental image of the first picture until it matched the second. If so, the delay should depend on how far the image had to be rotated.

Results Participants answered nearly all items correctly. As predicted, their reaction time when they responded *same* depended on the angular

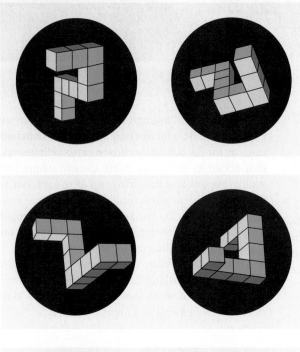

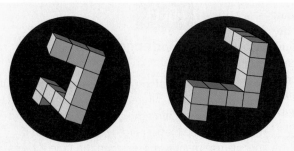

Figure 8.2 Examples of pairs of drawings used in an experiment by Shepard and Metzler (1971). Do the drawings for each pair represent the same object being rotated, or are they different objects? (See answer A on page 267.) (From R. N. Shepard and J. N. Metzler, "Mental Rotation of Three-Dimensional Objects," *Science* Vol. 171 (pp. 701-703). Copyright © 1971 AAAS. Reprinted with permission.)

difference in orientation between the two views, as Figure 8.3 shows. For every additional 20 degrees of rotation, the time to respond increased by a constant amount. That is, people reacted as if they were watching an object rotate at a constant speed.

Interpretation Viewing a mental image is partly like vision. In this case, common sense appears to be correct. However, the main point is that researchers can infer thought processes from people's delay in answering a question. Much research in cognitive psychology leads to inferences from the timing of responses.

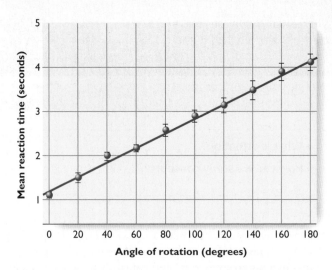

Figure 8.3 Mean times for correctly saying "same" depending on the required degree of rotation. (From R. N. Shepard and J. N. Metzler, "Mental Rotation of Three-Dimensional Objects," *Science* Vol. 171 (pp. 701-703). Copyright © 1971 AAAS. Reprinted with permission.)

Attention

You are constantly bombarded with more sights, sounds, smells, and other stimuli than you can process. **Attention** is *the tendency to respond to and to remember some stimuli more than others.*

Sometimes, something (e.g., a loud noise) suddenly grabs your attention. Psychologists call this a "bottom-up" process because the peripheral stimuli control it. Magicians use this tendency. A magician pulls a rabbit or a dove out of a hat, and the surprised viewers automatically watch the rabbit hop away or the dove fly away. During the brief time that their attention is occupied, the magician sets up the next trick, unnoticed (Macknik et al., 2008).

In contrast to a bottom-up process, you can deliberately decide to shift your attention in a "top-down" process. To illustrate, fixate your eyes on the x in the center and then, without moving your eyes, read the letters in the circle around it clockwise:

As you see, it is possible to control your attention without moving your eyes. When you increase your attention to something in your visual field, the part of your visual cortex sensitive to that area becomes more active and receives more blood flow (Müller, Malinowski, Gruber, & Hillyard, 2003). If you focus on a word, such as **THIS**, and attend to the letters, you increase activity in the language areas of the brain, but if you attend to the color, you shift activity to the color-detecting areas (Polk, Drake, Jonides, Smith, & Smith, 2008).

Let's go back to bottom-up processes, in which a stimulus automatically grabs your attention. Hearing your name or seeing your photograph is almost sure to attract your attention (Brédart, Delchambre, & Laureys, 2006; K. L. Shapiro, Caldwell, & Sorensen, 1997). An angry face in a crowd is easy to spot (Schmidt-Duffy, 2011). A moving object in an otherwise stationary scene grabs attention, especially if it is moving irregularly, like a meandering animal, or moving directly toward you, posing a possible threat (Lin, Franconeri, & Enns, 2008; Pratt, Radulescu, Guo, & Abrams, 2010).

Your attention also flows to anything unusual. I once watched a costume contest in which people were told to dress so distinctively that someone could find them quickly in a crowd. The winner was a young man who came onto the stage naked. Although he certainly earned the prize, the contest had a problem: The most distinctive clothing (or lack of it) depends on what everyone else is wearing. A naked man is easy to spot in most places, but at a nudist beach, you would more quickly notice a man in a coat and tie. What is unusual depends on the context.

© Michael Forsberg/www.michaelforsberg.com

Figure 8.4 Demonstration of preattentive processes: You find the one whooping crane immediately, regardless of how many sandhill cranes are present.

concept check

1. Suppose you are in a field of brownish bushes and one motionless brown rabbit. Will you find the rabbit by attentive or preattentive processes? If the rabbit starts hopping, will you find it by attentive or preattentive processes?

Answer

1. Finding a motionless brown rabbit in a field of brown objects requires attentive processes, but you could use preattentive processes to find a hopping rabbit. (For this reason, animals in danger of predation stay motionless when they can.)

try it ▶ yourself

To illustrate how an unusual object draws attention, find the one whooping crane in Figure 8.4 within the flock of sandhill cranes. That was easy, wasn't it? When anything differs drastically from items around it in size, shape, color, or movement, we find it by a **preattentive process**, meaning that it *stands out immediately*. You would find that whooping crane just as fast in a larger flock or smaller flock.

Contrast that task with Figure 8.5. Here, all the birds are marbled godwits. Your task is to find the one that faces to the right. Here, you have to check each bird separately. The more birds present, the longer you will probably need to find the unusual one. (You might find it quickly if you luckily start your search in the correct corner of the photograph.) You had to rely on an **attentive process**—*one that requires searching through the items in series* (Enns & Rensink, 1990; Treisman & Souther, 1985). The *Where's Waldo* books are an excellent example of a task requiring an attentive process.

The distinction between attentive and preattentive processes has practical applications. Imagine yourself as a human factors psychologist designing a machine with many gauges. Ideally, the first gauge should read about 70, the second 40, the third 30, and the fourth 10. If you arrange the gauges as in the top row of Figure 8.6, then people must check each gauge separately to find anything dangerous. In the bottom row, the gauges are arranged so that all the safe ranges are on the right. Now someone glances at the display and quickly (preattentively) notices anything out of position.

© Wendy Shattil and Bob Rozinski

Figure 8.5 Demonstration of attentive processes: Find the marbled godwit that is facing to the right. In this case, you need to check the birds one at a time.

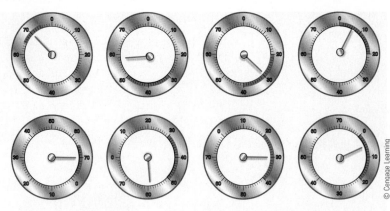

Figure 8.6 Each gauge measures something a machine does. The green area of the dial is the safe zone. In the top row, an operator must check gauges one at a time. In the bottom row, all the safe ranges are in the same place, and an unsafe reading stands out.

The Attention Bottleneck

Much evidence indicates that attention is limited, as if various items were trying to get through a bottleneck that permits very little to pass through at a time. If two or three objects flash briefly on a screen, you can identify their colors. If six objects flash on a screen, you still know the colors of only two or three (Zhang & Luck, 2008). To test your own attention bottleneck, visit this website: http://dualtask.org.

Attending to a warning signal is especially important at a nuclear power plant. In 1979, a nearly disastrous accident occurred at the Three Mile Island nuclear power plant in Pennsylvania. The accident released radioactive gases and incited panic. Figure 8.7 shows a small portion of the room as it appeared then, with an enormous number of knobs and gauges. (Since then, the controls have been redesigned to simplify the task.) A poorly designed control system overwhelms someone's ability to pay attention. Let's consider examples of the limits of human attention.

Conflict in Attention

Can you do two things at once? Sometimes you can easily, such as walking and chewing gum. In fact, when two activities are highly compatible, it is easy to do both at once (Hemond, Brown, & Robertson, 2010). However, people who try to "multi-task," doing two or more tasks at once, are often more impaired than they realize. Many students bring laptop computers to class, ostensibly to take notes, although most of them also use their computers for email and other activities. On average students who bring laptops to class get lower grades than other students (Fried, 2008).

Even when you are doing only one task, your attention level varies. While "your mind wanders," you are thinking about something unrelated to the task, and your ability to process the relevant information decreases (Barron, Riley, Greer, & Smallwood, 2011). Mind wandering interferes especially with performance on difficult tasks (Cohen & Maunsell, 2011).

Many years ago when automobile radios were introduced, people worried that listening to the radio would distract drivers and cause accidents. We no longer worry about radio, but we do worry about drivers using cell phones. A cell-phone conversation is more distracting than a conversation with a passenger in the car, because most passengers pause a conversation when driving conditions are difficult. Someone on a cell phone does not know what difficulty the driver might be facing (Drews, Pasupathi, & Strayer, 2008; Kunar, Carter, Cohen, & Horowitz, 2008). What if a passenger in the car is talking on a cell phone to someone else? In that case, the driver hears a "halfalogue," half of a conversation, which is more distracting than a full conversation (Emberson, Lupyan, Goldstein, & Spivey, 2010). A half-conversation has unpredictable starts and stops. Also, a nonparticipant who overhears it tends to fill in the blanks with imagined content, and doing so takes mental effort.

The Stroop Effect

try it ▶ yourself

Read the following instructions and then examine Figure 8.8: Notice the blocks of color at the top of the figure. Scanning from left to right, name each color as fast as you can. Then notice the nonsense syllables in the center of the figure. Again, say the color of each one as fast as possible. Then turn to the real words at the bottom. Instead of reading them, quickly state each one's color.

Most people read the colors quickly for the first two parts, but they slow down greatly for the colored words (which happen to be the names of colors). After all of your years of reading, you can hardly bring yourself to look at **RED** and say "green." Reading the words distracts from your attention to the colors. *The tendency to read the words instead of saying the color of ink* is known as the Stroop effect, after the psychologist who discovered it. People do better on this task if they blur their vision, say the colors in a different language, or manage to regard the color words as meaningless (Raz, Kirsch, Pollard, & Nitkin-Kaner, 2006).

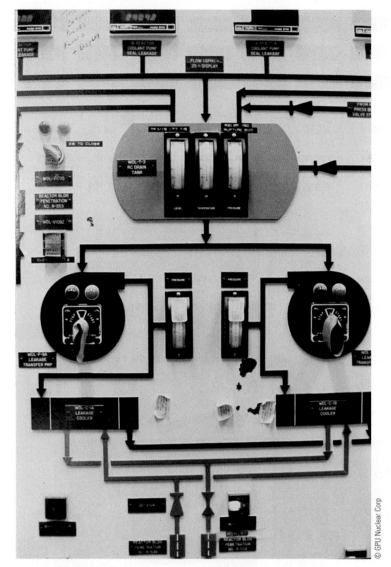

Figure 8.7 The Three Mile Island TMI-2 nuclear power plant had a confusing control system, a small portion of which is shown here. Some of the important gauges were not easily visible, some were poorly labeled, and many alarm signals had ambiguous meanings. After the accident in 1979, the system was redesigned.

try it ▶ yourself

Do words always take priority over colors? Not necessarily. Try the following: Go back to Figure 8.8 and notice the colored patches at the four corners. This time, instead of saying anything, point to the correct color patch. When you come to **RED**, point to the blue patch in the lower left. Then try this demonstration again but point to the color corresponding to the *meaning* of the word. That is, when you come to **RED**, point to the red patch in the upper left. Try it now.

You probably found it easy to point to the patch that matches the color of the ink and harder to point to the color matching the word meaning (Durgin, 2000). When you are speaking, you are primed to read the words you see, but when you are pointing, you are more primed to attend to nonverbal cues, such as ink color.

Change Blindness

Movie directors discovered long ago that if they shot different parts of a scene on different days, few viewers noticed the changes in the cloud pattern, the background props, or the actors' clothes (Simons & Levin, 2003). Why is that? Most people believe they see a whole scene at once. In one sense you do: In one study, people viewed nearly 3,000 complex scenes for 3 seconds each. Occasionally, one of the scenes was repeated, and when that happened, the viewer was to press a key to report recognition. On average, people correctly noted more than 75% of the repeated scenes (Konkle, Brady, Alvarez, & Oliva, 2010).

However, seeing the gist of the scene is different from noticing every detail. When you look at a complex scene, your eyes dart around from one fixation point to another, fixating about three times per second (Henderson, 2007). During each fixation you attend to only a few details (Franconeri, Alvarez, & Enns, 2007). If one of those details changed while you were fixating it, you would notice. A big, sudden change somewhere else might also grab your attention. But you cannot attend to every detail at once, and you can easily overlook something that changes (Cohen, Alvarez, & Nakayama, 2011).

Psychologists call this phenomenon change blindness—*the failure to detect changes in parts of a scene.* If anything moves or changes its appearance suddenly, it automatically draws your attention, but you seldom notice changes that occur slowly or between one view and another (Henderson & Hollingworth, 2003). You are especially unlikely to notice changes if your working memory is occupied with other matters, such as the plot of a movie (Todd, Fougnie, & Marois, 2005). Figure 8.9 shows two pairs of photos. In each pair, one differs from the other in a single regard. How quickly can you find those differences? Most people need 10 seconds or longer (Rensink, O'Regan, & Clark, 1997). For an Online Try It Yourself activity, go to Cengage-Brain.com. Navigate to the student website, then to the Online Try It Yourself section, and click Change Blindness.

online
try it ▶ yourself

concept check

2. Did you find the changes in Figure 8.8 by a preattentive or an attentive mechanism?

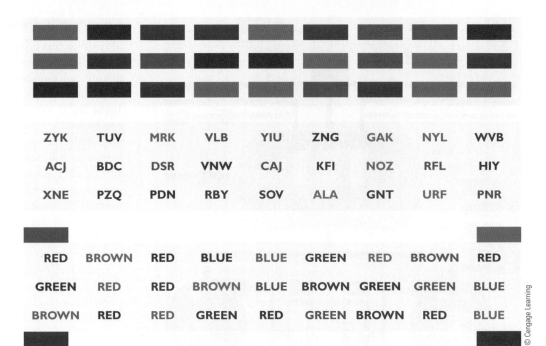

Figure 8.8 Read (left to right) the color of the ink in each part. Try to ignore the words themselves.

© Cengage Learning

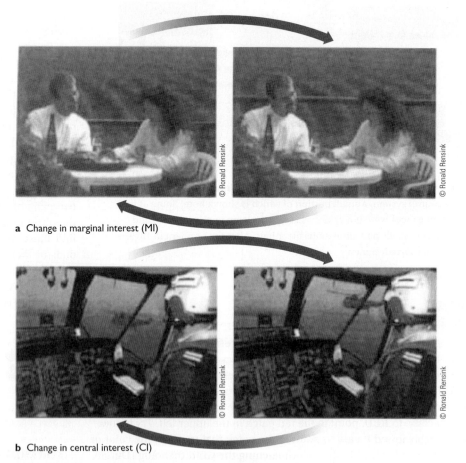

a Change in marginal interest (MI)

© Ronald Rensink

b Change in central interest (CI)

Figure 8.9 How quickly can you find the difference in each pair of pictures? If you need help, check answer B, page 267.

Answer

The conclusion is that you do not maintain a detailed representation of what you see or hear. You hold a few details, but you can't notice everything. An implication is that eyewitness reports are invariably incomplete. Much may have happened that a witness overlooked. Magicians exploit change blindness (Macknik et al., 2008). A magician throws a ball into the air and catches it a few times and then pretends to throw it again, "watching" it go up. Many viewers do not immediately notice the change. They "see" the ball going up . . . and then disappearing!

Attention Deficit Disorder

People vary in their ability to maintain attention, as in anything else. **Attention deficit disorder (ADD)** is characterized by *easy distraction, impulsiveness, moodiness, and failure to follow through on plans* (Wender, Wolf, & Wasserstein, 2001). **Attention-deficit hyperactivity disorder (ADHD)** is *the same except with excessive activity and "fidgetiness."* The symptoms vary considerably in type and intensity. Some people have problems mostly with attention, some mainly with impulsivity, and some with both. Symptoms grow substantially worse when children don't get enough sleep (Gruber et al., 2011). Several studies show behavioral improvements after physical exercise (Gapin, Labban, & Etnier, 2011).

The underlying causes almost certainly vary. Several genetic factors contribute to the risk, but the effect of the genes depends on the environment. One study found a gene that increases the probability of ADHD in children from families of low socioeconomic status, but doesn't affect children in middle-class or wealthier families (Nobile et al., 2010). In some cases, ADHD results from fetal alcohol exposure, lead poisoning, epilepsy, or emotional stress (Pearl, Weiss, & Stein, 2001). In most cases, the cause is unknown. Many people with ADHD show mild abnormalities in certain brain areas, but none of the abnormalities are consistent enough to aid in a diagnosis (Seidman et al., 2011). Many psychologists doubt that ADHD is a single disorder (Furman, 2008).

What exactly do we mean by "attention deficit"? The problem is not an inability to pay attention. People with ADHD easily pay attention to anything they care about. The problem relates to shifting attention quickly and appropriately. Here are two more tasks sensitive to attention deficit disorder:

- **The Choice-Delay Task** Would you prefer a small reward now or a bigger reward later? Obviously, it depends on *how much* bigger and *how much* later. On average, people with ADHD are more likely than other people their age to opt for the immediate reward (Solanto et al., 2001).
- **The Stop-Signal Task** Suppose your task is to press the X key whenever you see an X on the screen and the O key whenever you see an O. However, if you hear a "beep" shortly after either letter, then you should not press. If the letter and beep occur simultaneously, you easily inhibit your urge to press the button. If the beep occurs after you have already started to press, it's too late. The interesting results are with short delays: After how long a delay could you still manage to stop your finger from pressing the button? Most people with ADD or ADHD have trouble inhibiting their response, even af-

ter short delays (Lipszyc & Schachar, 2010). Try the Online Try It Yourself exercise called Stop-Signal Task to get an idea of this task. However, remember that you should try to press the X or O as quickly as possible after you see a letter. Some people wait a second or two to find out whether a beep is coming. If you *always* inhibit your responses, even with long delays between a letter and a beep, then you are "cheating." Try to press as fast as you can.

online
try it ▶ yourself

The choice-delay task and stop-signal task measure different types of attentional problems. Some children show impairments on one task but not the other (Solanto et al., 2001; Sonuga-Barke, 2004).

concept check

3. Describe one of the behavioral tests used to measure deficits of attention or impulse control.

Answer

The most common treatment for ADD or ADHD is stimulant drugs such as methylphenidate (Ritalin) (Elia, Ambrosini, & Rapoport, 1999). Stimulant drugs improve school performance and everyday behaviors (de Wit, Crean, & Richards, 2000; Jerome & Segal, 2001). However, the fact that stimulant drugs appear to help a given child does not confirm a diagnosis of ADD or ADHD. Stimulant drugs also increase the attention span of normal children (R. Elliott et al., 1997; Zahn, Rapoport, & Thompson, 1980).

Behavioral methods are also helpful in dealing with ADD/ADHD, either in addition to the drugs or instead of them (Pelham & Fabiano, 2008). Those methods include classroom use of rewards for good behavior and time outs for inappropriate behavior, as well as techniques that parents learn to use. People who play action video games for many hours also improve their ability to focus attention (Boot,

Kramer, Simons, Fabiani, & Gratton, 2008). Another way to enhance attention is by interacting with nature (Berman, Jonides, & Kaplan, 2008). Along a city street, you are surrounded by traffic and other items that demand your attention and leave you mentally exhausted. If you walk through a forest, you replenish your resources, enhancing your later ability to control your attention.

Categorizing

When you attend to something, you want to know what it is. You put it into a category of some type, such as *building*, *tree*, or *river*. Forming categories or concepts is a major step in cognition.

Ways to Describe a Category

Do we look up our concepts in a mental dictionary to determine their meaning? A few words have simple, unambiguous definitions. For example, a *line* is the shortest distance between two points.

Many concepts are hard to define, however. You can probably recognize country music, but can you define it? What's the border between being bald and not bald? Is a man who loses one hair bald? Of course not. Then he loses one more hair, then another, and another. Eventually, he *is* bald. At what point did losing one more hair make him bald?

Eleanor Rosch (1978; Rosch & Mervis, 1975) argued that many categories are best described by *familiar or typical examples* called **prototypes**. After we identify good prototypes of country music or bald person, we compare other items to them. Depending on how closely something matches, we call it a member of the category, a nonmember, or a borderline case. For example, cars and trucks are members of the category "vehicle." Flowers are nonmembers. Escalators and water skis are borderline cases.

However, some categories are harder to describe by prototypes (Fodor, 1998). We can think about "pigs that fly" or "bug-eyed monsters from outer space" without ever encountering a prototype of that category.

Conceptual Networks and Priming

Try to think about one word and nothing else. It's impossible. Whenever you think about something you relate it to something else. For example, when you think about *bird*, you link it to more specific terms, such as *sparrow*, more general terms, such as *animals*, and related terms, such as *flight* and *eggs*.

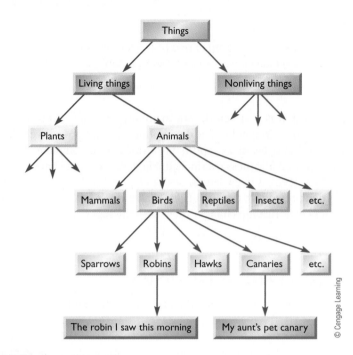

© Cengage Learning

 try it ▶ yourself

We organize items into hierarchies, such as *animal* as a higher level category, *bird* as intermediate, and *sparrow* as a lower level category. Researchers demonstrate the reality of this kind of hierarchy by measuring the delay for people to answer various questions (A. M. Collins & Quillian, 1969, 1970). Answer the following true–false questions as quickly as possible:

- Canaries are yellow.
- Canaries sing.
- Canaries lay eggs.
- Canaries have feathers.
- Canaries have skin.

All five items are true, but most people answer fastest on the *yellow* and *sing* items, slightly slower on the *eggs* and *feathers* items, and still slower on the *skin* item. Why? Yellowness and singing are distinctive of canaries. Because you do not think of eggs or feathers specifically as canary features, you reason, "Canaries are birds, and birds lay eggs. So canaries must lay eggs." For skin, you have to reason, "Canaries are birds and birds are animals. Animals have skin, so canaries must have skin." This way of categorizing things saves you enormous effort overall. When you learn some new fact about birds or animals in general, you don't have to learn it again separately for every species.

 concept check

4. Which would people answer faster: whether politicians give speeches or whether they sometimes eat spaghetti? Why?

Answer

4. It would take longer to answer whether politicians eat spaghetti. Giving speeches is a distinctive feature of politicians. Eating spaghetti is not. To answer the second question, you have to reason that politicians are people, and most people eat spaghetti.

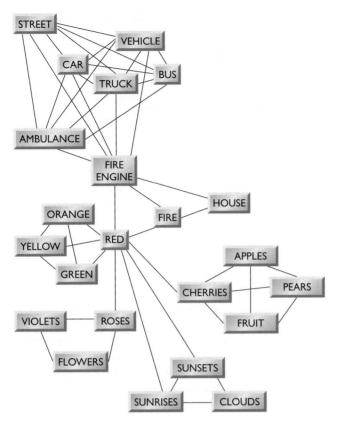

Figure 8.10 We link each concept to a variety of other related concepts. Any stimulus that activates one of these concepts will also partly activate (or prime) the ones that are linked to it. (From A. M. Collins and E. F. Loftus, "A Spreading-Activation Theory of Semantic Processing," *Psychological Review* Vol. 82(6) (pp. 407-428). Reprinted by permission of Elizabeth Loftus.)

We also link a word or concept to related concepts. Figure 8.10 shows a possible network of conceptual links that someone might have at a particular moment (A. M. Collins & Loftus, 1975). Suppose this network describes your own concepts. *Thinking about one of the concepts shown in this figure will activate, or prime, the concepts linked to it* through a process called spreading activation (A. M. Collins & Loftus, 1975). For example, if you hear *flower*, you are primed to think of *rose*, *violet*, and other flowers. If you also hear *red*, the combination of *flower* and *red* primes you to think of *rose*. You would recognize that word more easily than usual if it were flashed briefly on a screen or spoken very softly.

The idea of priming a concept is analogous to priming a pump: If you put some water in the pump to get it started, you can continue using the pump to draw water from a well. Similarly, priming *a concept gets it started. Reading or hearing one word makes it easier to think of or recognize a related word. Seeing something makes it easier to recognize a related object.* Priming is important during reading. When you come to a word that you barely know, you find it easier to understand if the preceding sentences were about closely related concepts (Plaut & Booth, 2000). They provide hints about the meaning of the new word.

Priming occurs in many situations. If you were asked what you plan to do tomorrow, the odor of cleaning fluid in the room would prime you to think of cleaning your room, even if you were not conscious of the odor (Holland, Hendriks, & Aarts, 2005). Viewing the logos for McDonalds, KFC, and other fast-food restaurants primes you to be impatient, to prefer immediate rewards to slightly greater rewards later (Zhong & DeVoe, 2010). If you interview a job candidate whose application is attached to a heavy clipboard, the heaviness primes you to think of this person as important (Ackerman, Nocera, & Bargh, 2010). If you look at pictures and try to identify the people or objects in the foreground, you will find the task easier if the background primes the same answer as the object in the foreground (Davenport & Potter, 2004; Figure 8.11).

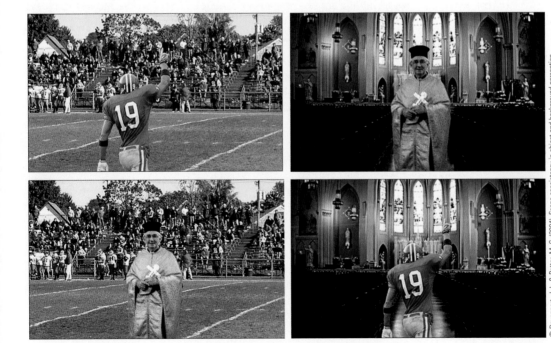

© Davenport, J. L. & Potter, M. C. (2004). Scene consistency in object and background perception. *Psychological Science, 15,* 559-564.

Figure 8.11 A football stadium background primes identification of "football player," and a church primes identification of "priest/ clergyman." When the people are placed in the opposite settings, they are harder to identify. (From Davenport & Potter, 2004.)

Here is an illustration that can be explained in terms of spreading activation. Quickly answer each of the following questions (or ask someone else):

1. How many animals of each kind did Moses take on the ark?
2. What was the famous saying uttered by Louis Armstrong when he first set foot on the moon?
3. Some people pronounce St. Louis "saint loo-iss" and some pronounce it "saint loo-ee." How would you pronounce the capital city of Kentucky?

You can check answer C at the end of this module, page 267. Why do so many people miss these questions? Figure 8.12 offers an explanation in terms of spreading activation (Shafto & MacKay, 2000): The question about Louis Armstrong activates a series of sounds and concepts that are linked to one another and to other items. The sound *Armstrong* and the ideas *first astronaut on the moon* and *famous sayings* are all linked to "One small step for a man . . ." Even the name *Louis Armstrong* is loosely linked to *Neil Armstrong* because both are famous people. The combined effect of all these influences automatically triggers the answer, "One small step for a man . . ."

concept check

5. Suppose someone says "cardinal" and then briefly flashes the word *bird* on a screen. Some viewers identify the word correctly, suggesting priming, and some do not. Considering both priming and the encoding specificity idea from chapter 7, how might you explain why some people and not others identified the word *bird*?

Answer

5. People who heard "cardinal" and thought of it as a bird would have spreading activation to prime the word *bird*. However, other people who thought of "cardinal" as an officer in the Catholic church would have spreading activation to prime a very different set of words and not *bird*.

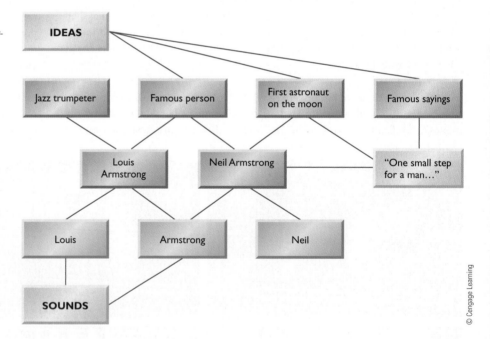

Figure 8.12 According to one explanation, the word *Armstrong* and the ideas *astronaut, first person on the moon*, and *famous sayings* all activate the linked saying "One small step for a man . . ."

module 8.1 >

Thinking About Attention and Concepts

Behaviorists traditionally avoided the topic of cognition because thinking and knowledge are unobservable. Although this module has demonstrated the possibilities for research on cognition, you should also see that the behaviorists' objections were not frivolous. Research on cognition is difficult, and each advance requires many studies to check and recheck conclusions and compare alternative explanations. The results have practical as well as theoretical benefits. For example, the better we can specify what we mean by "attention," the better we can help people with attention deficits.

Summary

- *Research methods in cognitive psychology.* Researchers infer mental processes from measurements of speed and accuracy. (page 257)
- *Mental imagery.* Mental images resemble vision in certain respects. The time required to answer questions about a rotating object depends on how far the object would actually rotate between one position and another. (page 257)
- *Top-down and bottom-up processes.* Some stimuli grab our attention automatically. We also control our attention, deliberately shifting it from one item to another. (page 258)
- *Attentive and preattentive processes.* We quickly notice items that are unusual in certain salient ways, regardless of potential distracters. Noticing less distinct items requires attention to one target after another. (page 259)
- *Attention bottleneck.* Attention is limited, and items compete for it. (page 260)
- *Distraction.* Directing attention to one item means subtracting it from another. For example, talking on a cell phone distracts from attention to driving. (page 260)
- *The Stroop effect.* When we are speaking, written words grab attention, making it difficult to attend to the color of the letters. (page 260)
- *Change blindness.* We often fail to detect changes in a scene if they occur slowly or during an eye movement. (page 261)
- *Attention deficit disorder.* People with attention deficit disorder have trouble shifting attention. Two tests of attention problems are the choice-delay task and the stop-signal task. (page 263)
- *Categorization.* People use many categories that are hard to define. Many items are marginal examples of a category, so we cannot insist on a yes–no decision. (page 264)
- *Conceptual networks and priming.* We represent words or concepts with links to related concepts. Thinking about a concept primes one to think of related concepts. (page 264)

Key Terms

attention (page 258)
attention deficit disorder (ADD) (page 263)
attention-deficit hyperactivity disorder (ADHD) (page 263)
attentive process (page 259)
change blindness (page 261)
choice-delay task (page 263)

cognition (page 257)
preattentive process (page 259)
priming (page 265)
prototype (page 264)
spreading activation (page 265)
stop-signal task (page 263)
Stroop effect (page 260)

Answers to Other Questions in the Module

A. The objects in pair a are the same; in b they are the same; and in c they are different. (page 258)

B. In the top scene, a horizontal bar along the wall has changed position. In the lower scene, the location of the helicopter has changed. (page 262)

C. 1. None. Noah had an ark, not Moses. 2. Neil Armstrong, not Louis Armstrong, set foot on the moon. 3. The correct pronunciation of Kentucky's capital is "frank-furt." (Not "loo-ee-ville"!) (page 266)

- How do we solve problems?
- What are some common errors of thinking?

Figure 8.13 shows an object that was made by cutting and bending an ordinary piece of cardboard (M. Gardner, 1978). How was it made? Take a piece of paper and try to make it yourself. (The solution is on page 278, answer D.)

try it ▶ yourself

This is an "insight" or "aha!" problem. If you solve it, you probably can't explain how you found the answer. You say, "It just came to me."

Here is another example of creative problem solving: A college physics exam asked how to use a barometer to determine the height of a building. One student answered that he would tie a long string to the barometer, go to the top of the building, and lower the barometer to the ground. Then he would cut the string and measure its length.

When the professor marked this answer incorrect, the student asked why. "Well," said the professor, "your method would work, but it's not the method I wanted you to use." When the student objected, the professor offered to let him try again.

"All right," the student said. "Take the barometer to the top of the building, drop it, and measure the time it takes to hit the ground. Then, from the formula for the speed of a falling object, using the gravitational constant, calculate the height of the building."

"Hmmm," replied the professor. "That too would work. And it does make use of physical principles. But it still isn't what I had in mind. Can you think of another way?"

"Another way? Sure," he replied. "Place the barometer next to the building on a sunny day. Measure the height of the barometer and the length of its shadow. Also measure the length of the building's shadow. Then use this formula":

height of barometer ÷ height of building =
length of barometer's shadow ÷
length of building's shadow

The professor was impressed but still reluctant to give credit, so the student persisted with another method: "Measure the barometer's height. Then walk up the stairs of the building, marking it off in units of the barometer's height. At the top, take the number of barometer units and multiply by the height of the barometer to get the height of the building."

The professor sighed: "Give me one more way—any other way—and I'll give you credit, even if it's not the answer I wanted."

"Really?" asked the student with a smile. "*Any other way?*"

"Yes, any other way."

"All right," said the student. "Go to the man who owns the building and say, 'Hey, buddy, if you tell me how tall the building is, I'll give you this cool barometer!'" Sometimes, people develop creative, imaginative solutions like the ones that the physics student proposed. At other times, they suggest a creative idea that couldn't possibly work. Figure 8.14 shows an example. Psychologists study problem-solving behavior and decision making partly to understand the thought processes and partly to look for ways to help people reason more effectively.

How would you carry 98 water bottles—all at once, with no vehicle? When faced with a new problem, people sometimes find a novel and effective solution.

© David Burnett/Contact Press Images

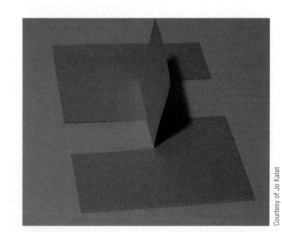

Courtesy of Jo Kalat

Figure 8.13 This object was made by cutting and folding an ordinary piece of cardboard with nothing left over. How was it done?

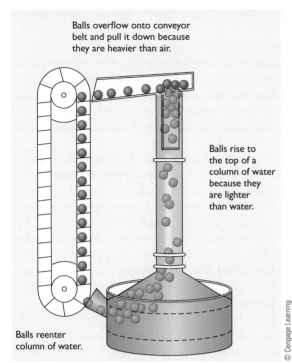

Balls overflow onto conveyor belt and pull it down because they are heavier than air.

Balls rise to the top of a column of water because they are lighter than water.

Balls reenter column of water.

Figure 8.14 An inventor applied for a patent on this "perpetual motion machine." Rubber balls, lighter than water, rise in a column of water and flow over the top. They are heavier than air, so they fall, moving a belt and generating energy. At the bottom, they reenter the water column. Why couldn't this system work? (Check answer E on page 278.)

Two Types of Thinking and Problem Solving

Daniel Kahneman (2011) described human thinking in terms of two systems. We use System 1 *for quick, automatic processes* (such as recognizing familiar faces and routine actions) *and for questions we think are easy.* System 1 often proceeds unconsciously, or at least without much effort. We use System 2 *for mathematical calculations, evaluating evidence, and anything else that requires attention.* Because System 1 saves time and energy, we rely on it whenever we can. Answer the following:

 yourself

A bat and a ball together cost $1.10. The bat costs $1 more than the ball. What does the ball cost?

The intuitive answer, based on System 1, is that the ball costs $0.10. But that is wrong. If the ball costs $0.10 and the bat costs $1 more than the ball, the bat costs $1.10, and the total is $1.20. With a little effort, you can calculate that the ball must cost $0.05. But you might jump to a conclusion without realizing that you

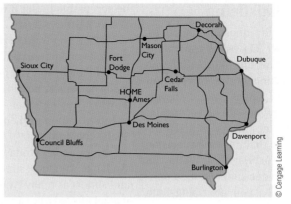

Figure 8.15 In the traveling salesperson task, you want to find the shortest route connecting all the points you need to visit.

need to do some calculations, using your System 2. If the question had been printed in small, blurry print, so that you had to exert some effort just to read it, you would be more likely to think about it and answer correctly (Alter, Oppenheimer, Epley, & Eyre, 2007). Yes, you actually do better if you have trouble reading the question! Anything that gets you to slow down and think about it improves your performance.

In many cases, System 2 solves problems by an algorithm, *an explicit procedure for calculating an answer or testing every hypothesis.* Suppose you are a traveling salesperson in Ames, Iowa (Figure 8.15). You want to visit 10 cities and return home by the shortest route. You might list all possible routes, measure them, and determine which one is shortest.

However, it would take a long time to calculate all those routes, and if you had to visit hundreds of cities instead of 10, you couldn't possibly consider every possibility. You would turn to a heuristic, *a strategy for simplifying a problem and generating a satisfactory guess.* Heuristics provide quick guidance when you are willing or forced to accept some possibility of error, and they work well most of the time (Gigerenzer, 2008). System 1 relies heavily on heuristics. One heuristic: If you want to guess which child is oldest, choose the tallest. Another: If you want to guess which of two cities has a larger population, choose the one you have heard of more often (D. G. Goldstein & Gigerenzer, 2002). Another: If the instructions for a task are difficult to understand, the task itself is probably difficult to do. But if something is difficult to understand, you also assume it is probably important (Labroo et al., 2009). Each heuristic works most of the time but not always. For example, *if the instructions are written in an unfamiliar or unclear font,* people find them difficult to read and therefore overestimate the difficulty of the task (Song & Schwarz, 2008). If a medicine or food additive has a name that is difficult to pronounce, people assume it is unsafe (Song & Schwarz, 2009).

Maximizing and Satisficing

You also use heuristics for questions such as, "Which job shall I take?" or "How shall I spend my money?" You don't have all the information you need, and you are not looking for the "correct" answer, because there is no single correct answer. Instead, you generate a few possibilities, consider them, simplify the problem, and try to make the best choice you can. (Note that not every decision falls neatly into System 1 or System 2. When you use heuristics to simplify a decision and then ponder your decision carefully, you are using both types of thinking.)

Before making a decision, how many possibilities do you consider and how thoroughly do you investigate them? One strategy, maximizing, is *thoroughly considering as many choices as possible to find the best one.* Satisficing is *searching only until you find something satisfactory.* If you have a choice with much at stake—for example, what is the safest design for a new bridge over this river—you should carefully consider every reasonable possibility. However, most of our daily decisions have much less at stake, and it is more important to make a satisfactory choice quickly than to find the very best one (Keys & Schwartz, 2007). Some people habitually follow the maximizing strategy and others prefer satisficing for most of their decisions, big or small. Researchers classify people as mainly maximizers or satisficers based on questions like the following (Schwartz et al., 2002). Rate yourself from 1 (not at all true) to 7 (definitely true):

- When I listen to the car radio, I frequently check other stations.
- I frequently channel-surf to find the best show.
- I shop at many stores before deciding which clothes to buy.
- I expect to interview for many jobs before I accept one.

The higher your score, the more you are a maximizer. Researchers find that high maximizers usually make better choices, according to objective criteria. They get jobs with higher starting pay than do satisficers, in spite of being no better in their college grades. However, they have more difficulty making a choice (Paivandy, Bullock, Reardon, & Kelly, 2008), and they are usually *less satisfied* with their choices. Satisficers look for something "good enough" and find it. Maximizers look for "the best" and continue to wonder whether they were right (Iyengar, Wells, & Schwartz, 2006). Maximizing can backfire in another way, too: What seems the best job offer or best way to invest your money might be outstanding if all goes well, but disastrous if certain events go wrong. You might be wiser to choose something that would be acceptable under a wide variety of circumstances (Schwartz, Ben-Haim, & Dacso, 2010).

When you want to make a choice, how many options do you want to consider? If you know exactly what you want—such as you want the cheapest motel room in town, and you don't care about anything else—then you want to see as many options as possible. However, if you are considering many criteria—such as when buying a car—you probably prefer to limit yourself to five, ten, or twenty possibilities (Lenton, Fasolo, & Todd, 2008; Reed, Mikels, & Simon, 2008; Shah & Wolford, 2007).

Many choices today are difficult just because of the huge number of options available. Your local supermarket may offer 50 or more types of breakfast cereals and almost as many types of potato chips. In one study, researchers at a supermarket offered free samples of jams. If they offered 6 types of jam, 12% of people bought one. If they offered 24 types, a larger number of people stopped to sample a few, but almost no one bought anything (Iyengar & Lepper, 2000). Too many choices inhibit people from making any decision at all (Schwartz, 2004). Similarly, retired people in the United States can choose from about 50 prescription drug plans under Medicare Part D. Research shows that it is hard to make a good choice among so many (Wood et al., 2011).

Let's apply this principle to the problem of dating. At your college, how many potential romantic partners do you meet? Hundreds? Thousands? Would it be feasible to find out enough about each person to choose the best one for you? Researchers studied speed-dating situations, in which each person gets a 3-minute interview with various potential partners. In smaller sessions, people made selections based on education, occupation, and important personality aspects. In sessions of 24 or more candidates, they relied almost entirely on superficial characteristics such as appearance (Lenton & Francesconi, 2010). It is good to have choices, but it is a problem if you have too many choices.

concept check

6. Who would have more trouble choosing a meal from a 6-page menu, maximizers or satisficers?

Answer

6. Maximizers would have more trouble, because they want to consider every choice. A satisficer might find an acceptable choice quickly.

The Representativeness Heuristic and Base-Rate Information

Although heuristic thinking is often helpful, it leads us astray when we rely on it inappropriately. In 2002 Daniel Kahneman won the Nobel Prize in economics for research showing examples of inappropriate use of heuristics. For example, consider the saying: "If something looks like a duck, waddles like a duck, and quacks like a duck, chances are it's a duck." This saying is an example of the representativeness heuristic, *the assumption that an item that resembles members of a category is probably also in that category.* This heuristic is usually correct, except when we deal with uncommon categories. If you see something that looks like a rare bird, you should check carefully to make sure it isn't a similar, more common species. In general, to decide whether something belongs in one category or another, you should consider the base-rate information—that is, *how common the two categories are.*

When people apply the representativeness heuristic, they frequently overlook base-rate information. For example, consider the following question (modified from Kahneman & Tversky, 1973):

Psychologists interviewed 30 engineers and 70 lawyers. One of them, Jack, is a 45-year-old married man with four children. He is generally conservative, cautious, and ambitious. He shows no interest in political and social issues and spends most of his free time on home carpentry, sailing, and solving mathematical puzzles. What is the probability that Jack is one of the 30 engineers in the sample of 100?

Most people estimate a rather high probability—perhaps 80 or 90%—because the description sounds more like engineers than lawyers. That estimate isn't wrong, as we can't know the true probability. The key point is that if some people hear that the sample included 30 engineers and 70 lawyers, and others hear it included 70 engineers and 30 lawyers, both groups make about the same estimate for Jack (Kahneman & Tversky, 1973). Certainly, the base-rate information (the number of engineers in the sample) should have some influence.

Here is another example of misusing the representativeness heuristic:

Linda was a philosophy major. She is 31, bright, outspoken, and concerned about issues of discrimination and social justice.

What would you estimate is the probability that Linda is a bank teller? What is the probability that she is a feminist bank teller? (Answer before you read on.)

The true probabilities are not the point. The interesting result is that many people estimate a higher probability that Linda is a *feminist* bank teller than that she is a bank teller (Tversky & Kahneman, 1983). She couldn't be a feminist bank teller without being a bank teller. Apparently, the word "feminist" triggers people's representativeness heuristic to say, "Yes, that would fit" (Shafir, Smith, & Osherson, 1990).

7. A device was built to protect airplanes by detecting explosives in people's luggage. It detects 95% of bombs. When luggage has no explosives, it has a false alarm (falsely detecting a bomb) 5% of the time. Is this device good enough to use? (Hint: Think about the base-rate probability of the presence of a bomb.)

Answer

7. A false-alarm rate of 5% is far too high. Imagine a plane with 100 innocent passengers, each checking two bags. Of the 200 innocent bags, this device will identify 5%—that is, 10 bags—as containing a bomb! Speer (1989) estimated that this device (which the Federal Aviation Administration considered using) would have 5 million false alarms for every bomb it found.

In 2002 Princeton psychologist Daniel Kahneman (left) won the Nobel Prize in economics. Although others have won Nobel Prizes for research related to psychology, Kahneman was the first winner who had a PhD in psychology.

© AP Photo/Jonas Ekstromer/Pool

mon in summer. The availability heuristic is *the tendency to assume that if we easily think of examples of a category, then that category must be common.* However, this heuristic leads us astray when uncommon events are highly memorable. During the months after the terrorist attacks of September 11, 2001, most Americans thought frequently about airplane disasters, therefore considered such disasters common, and avoided air travel. They traveled by car instead, although the risk of a fatal crash is far greater in cars than in airplanes (Gigerenzer, 2004).

Another example: How would you feel if your favorite team wins its next game? How would you feel if you missed your bus? Most people overestimate how good they would feel after good events and how bad they would feel after bad events. One reason is that you try to remember how you felt after similar experiences in the past, and memories of your most extreme experiences are easily available (Gilbert & Wilson, 2009). Because they are easily available, you assume they are typical.

Also, consider the widespread belief that "you should stick with your first impulse on a multiple-choice test." Researchers have consistently found this claim to be wrong (J. J. Johnston, 1975; Kruger, Wirtz, & Miller, 2005). Changing an answer helps for several reasons. You sometimes discover that you

The Availability Heuristic

When you estimate how common something is, you usually start by thinking of examples. If you remember enjoying your astronomy class more times than you remember enjoying any other class, probably that astronomy class really was interesting. If you remember many summer days when mosquitoes bit you and no winter days when they bit you, you conclude that mosquitoes are more com-

Table 8.1 The Representativeness Heuristic and the Availability Heuristic

	A Tendency to Assume That	Leads Us Astray When	Example of Error
Representativeness Heuristic	An item that resembles members of a category probably belongs to that category.	Something resembles members of a rare category.	Something looks like it might be a UFO, so you decide it is.
Availability Heuristic	The more easily we can think of members of a category, the more common the category is.	One category gets more publicity than another or is more memorable.	You remember more reports of airplane crashes than car crashes, so you think air travel is more dangerous.

© Cengage Learning

misread a question the first time. Sometimes, a question later in the test reminds you of the correct answer to an earlier item. Why, then, do most students believe that their first impulse is correct? When you get your test back, you check the questions you got wrong. You notice the three you changed from right to wrong, but you overlook the five you changed from wrong to right. Your availability heuristic leads you to believe that changing an answer hurts you.

Other Common Errors in Human Cognition

In addition to relying inappropriately on the representativeness heuristic and availability heuristic, people consistently make several other errors. For decades, college professors have emphasized critical thinking, *the careful evaluation of evidence for and against any conclusion.* However, even those who teach critical thinking sometimes find themselves accepting nonsense that they should have questioned. Why do intelligent people sometimes make major mistakes? Here are a few of the reasons.

Overconfidence

How long is the Nile River? You probably don't know, but guess an approximate range, such as "between X and Y" in miles or kilometers. Then state your confidence in your answer. If you say "0%," you mean that you *know* your range is wrong. If so, widen the range until you are fairly confident you must be right.

On difficult questions like this, most people are overconfident of their answers. When they say they are 90% confident, they are actually correct far less

than 90% (Plous, 1993). On easy questions, the trend is reversed and people tend to be underconfident (Erev, Wallsten, & Budescu, 1994; Juslin, Winman, & Olsson, 2000). You can try additional items with the Online Try It Yourself exercise Overconfidence. (Incidentally, the Nile River is 4,187 miles long, or 6,738 kilometers.)

Philip Tetlock (1992) studied government officials and consultants, foreign policy professors, newspaper columnists, and others who make their living by analyzing and predicting world events. He asked them to predict world events over the next 1 to 10 years—what would happen in Korea, the Middle East, and so forth. Later, he compared predictions to actual results and found very low accuracy, especially among those who were the most confident.

Overconfidence is sometimes helpful (Johnson & Fowler, 2011). Highly confident people tend to get good job offers and promotions. Highly confident politicians win elections. If you act certain of winning a fight, a stronger opponent may back down. However, overconfidence can be harmful, too. Overconfident leaders often blunder into costly mistakes. If the stronger opponent doesn't back down, you could find yourself in an unwinnable fight.

Confirmation Bias

We often err by *accepting a hypothesis and then looking for evidence to support it instead of considering other possibilities.* This tendency, the confirmation bias, occurs in all walks of life. People listen mostly to others who agree with them on matters of science, politics, or religion—and then they accuse their opponents of being biased.

Once we have made a decision, we look for reasons to stick with it. Peter Wason (1960) asked students to discover a certain rule he had in mind for generating sequences of numbers. One example of the numbers the rule might generate, he explained, was "2, 4, 6." He told the students that they could ask about other sequences, and he would tell them whether or not those sequences fit his rule. They should tell him as soon as they thought they knew the rule.

Most students started by asking, "8, 10, 12?" When told "yes," they proceeded with "14, 16, 18?" Each time, they were told, "Yes, that sequence fits the rule." Soon most of them guessed, "The rule is three consecutive even numbers." "No," came the reply. "That is not the rule." Many students persisted, trying "20, 22, 24?" "26, 28, 30?" "250, 252, 254?" They continued testing sequences that fit their rule, ignoring other possibilities. The rule Wason had in mind was, "Any three positive numbers of increasing magnitude." For instance, 1, 2, 3 would be acceptable, and so would 21, 25, 601.

A special case of confirmation bias is functional fixedness, *the tendency to adhere to a single approach or a single way of using an item*. Here are three examples:

 yourself

1. You are provided with a candle, a box of matches, some thumbtacks, and a tiny piece of string, as shown in Figure 8.16. Using no other equipment, find a way to mount the candle to the wall so that it can be lit.

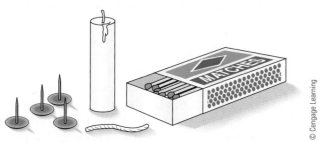

Figure 8.16 Given only these materials, what is the best way to attach the candle to a wall so that it can be lit?

2. Consider an array of nine dots:

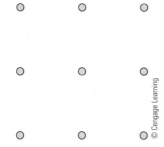

Connect all nine dots with a series of connected straight lines, such that the end of one line is the start of the next. For example, one way would be:

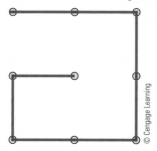

But use the fewest lines possible.

3. There are some students in a room. All but two of them are psychology majors, all but two are chemistry majors, and all but two are history majors. How many students are present? (If your System 1 blurts out, "two of each," try out your answer: It doesn't work.) Now here's the interesting part: There are two possible solutions. After you have found one solution, discard it and find another. After you have either found solutions or given up, check answer F on page 278. (Solve these problems before reading further.)

Question 1 was difficult because most people think of the matchbox as a container for matches, not as a tool on its own. The box is "functionally fixed" for one way of using it. A similar question was put to people in a subsistence society with few tools. They were given a set of objects and asked how they could use them to build a tower to reach a person in distress. If the objects included an empty box, they used it, but if the box contained other objects, they didn't quickly think of emptying the box and using it (German & Barrett, 2005).

Question 2 was difficult because most people assume that the lines must remain within the area defined by the nine dots. On question 3, it is difficult to think of even one solution, and after thinking of it, it is hard to abandon it to think of a different approach.

Framing Questions

A logical person should give the same answer no matter how a question is worded, right? However, most people change their answers depending on the wording of the questions, as you may recall from the discussion of surveys in chapter 2.

 yourself

Which would you rather receive, $5 now or $6.20 four weeks from now? Many people choose $5 now. Let's rephrase: Which would you prefer, $5 today and $0 a month from now, or $0 today and $6.20 a month from now? The second phrasing increases the percentage of people who choose the delayed reward (Magen, Dweck, & Gross, 2008).

Another example: You have been appointed head of the Public Health Service, and you need to choose a plan to deal with a disease that endangers the lives of 600 people. Plan A will save the lives of 200 people. Plan B has a 33% chance to save all 600 and a 67% chance to save no one. *Choose plan A or B before reading further.*

Now another disease breaks out, and again, you must choose between two plans. If you adopt plan C, 400 people will die. If you adopt plan D, there is a 33% chance that no one will die and a 67% chance that 600 will die. *Choose plan C or D now.*

Figure 8.17 shows the results for how a large group of people responded when given these choices. Most chose A over B and D over C. However, plan A is exactly the same as C (200 live, 400 die), and plan B is exactly the same as D. Why then did so many people choose both A and D? As Tversky and Kahneman (1981) demonstrated, most people avoid taking a risk to gain something (e.g., saving lives), because we know that even a small gain will feel good. However, we willingly take a risk to avoid loss (e.g., not letting people die), because any loss will feel bad. *The tendency to answer a question differently when it is framed differently* is called the framing effect. See the Online Try It Yourself activity Framing Effect.

online
 yourself

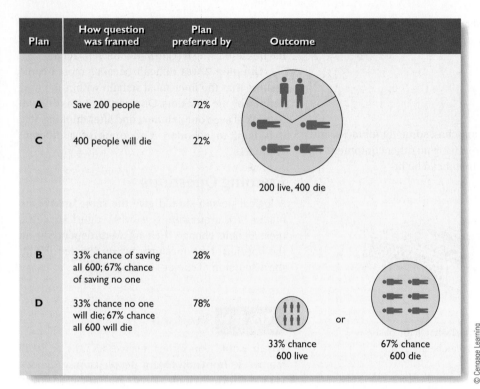

Plan	How question was framed	Plan preferred by	Outcome
A	Save 200 people	72%	200 live, 400 die
C	400 people will die	22%	
B	33% chance of saving all 600; 67% chance of saving no one	28%	33% chance 600 live or 67% chance 600 die
D	33% chance no one will die; 67% chance all 600 will die	78%	

Figure 8.17 Most people chose plan A over B, and D over C, although A produces the same result as C, and B produces the same result as D. Amos Tversky and Daniel Kahneman (1981) proposed that most people play it safe to gain something but accept a risk to avoid a loss.

concept check

8. When students estimate their grades for the coming semester or athletic coaches estimate their teams' success for the coming year, what mistake is likely?
9. Someone says, "More than 90% of all college students like to watch late-night television, but only 20% of adults over 50 do. Therefore, most watchers of late-night television are college students." What error in thinking has this person made?
10. Someone tells me that if I say "abracadabra" every morning, I will stay healthy. I say it daily, and sure enough, I stay healthy. I conclude that this magic word ensures health. What error in thinking have I made?
11. Which of the following claims would probably persuade more customers to pay for new windows? **(a)** "You could save money by replacing your windows." **(b)** "You are losing money by not replacing your windows."

Answers

8. Both are likely to be overconfident.
9. Failure to consider the base rate: 20% of all older adults is a larger number than 90% of all college students.
10. Premature commitment to one hypothesis without testing the hypothesis that one could stay healthy without the magic word.
11. Probably **(b)**. People are generally more willing to do something to avoid a loss than to gain something.

Framing also influences ethical decisions. If you want to sell something, would you lie to make the sale? Would you lie to avoid losing the sale? The actions are the same and the outcomes are the same, but more people say they are willing to lie when the question is phrased in terms of avoiding the loss of a sale (Kern & Chugh, 2009).

The Sunk Cost Effect

The sunk cost effect is a special case of the framing effect. Suppose that months ago you bought an expensive ticket for today's football game, but the weather is miserably cold. You wish you hadn't bought the ticket. Do you go to the game?

Many people suffer through the game in the bad weather because they don't want to waste the money. This example illustrates the sunk cost effect, *the willingness to do something because of money or effort already spent* (Arkes & Ayton, 1999). This tendency arises in many situations. A company continues investing money in an unsuccessful project because it doesn't want to admit that the money already spent was wasted. A professional sports team is disappointed with a high-salaried player's performance, but keeps using that player to avoid wasting the money.

Expertise

Although all of us make mistakes in our reasoning, some develop expertise within a given field that enables them to solve problems quickly with a minimum of error. They apply the appropriate algorithms quickly, and they recognize which heuristics do or do not work in a particular situation. Reaching that point requires enormous effort.

Practice Makes (Nearly) Perfect

Expert performance is extremely impressive. Some people complete the most difficult crossword puzzles rapidly. Some physicians look at an x-ray and immediately notice a dot that indicates a major illness. Someone might see a bird for a split second and identify its species, sex, and age. It is tempting to assume that experts were born with special talent or amazing intelligence. Not so, say psychologists who have studied expertise. Most people who develop expertise in a field are not unusually impressive in other ways. Indeed, extremely brilliant people—the top 1% of the top 1%—seldom become experts at anything, because they get bored.

In fields ranging from chess to sports to violin playing, the rule is that expertise requires about 10 years of intense practice (Ericsson & Charness, 1994; Ericsson, Krampe, & Tesch-Römer, 1993). The top violin players practice 3 to 4 hours every day beginning in early childhood. A world-class tennis player spends hours at a time working on backhand shots, and a golfer spends similar efforts on chip shots. Hungarian author Laszlo Polgar set out to demonstrate that almost anyone can achieve expertise with sufficient effort. He devoted enormous efforts to nurturing his three daughters' chess skills. All three became outstanding, and one, Judit, became the first woman and the youngest person ever to reach grand master status.

Although some have argued that expertise depends entirely on total hours of practice, the research says otherwise. Two people who practice a skill such as piano or chess for the same number of hours are not necessarily equal at the end. Those who learn faster in school tend also to develop expertise faster (Campitelli & Gobet, 2011; Meinz & Hambrick, 2010). Still, most of the difference between outstanding and average performers in any field depends on practice.

In addition to practice, one needs feedback based on the practice (Kahneman & Klein, 2009). For example, athletes see at once whether their performance was better or worse than a previous attempt, and how they compared to other competitors. Computer programmers get excellent feedback: If they program something correctly, it works. If they make a mistake, the computer crashes or does something it wasn't supposed to do. People who get good feedback have a good chance to improve with practice.

On the other end, psychotherapists get relatively weak feedback. Some depressed patients improve in a few weeks even without treatment, and some are slow to improve regardless of treatment. The quality of therapy makes a dif- ference for certain patients, but as a rule it is hard to know how much of the success or failure in a particular case depended on treatment. Consequently, therapists can't improve with practice as effectively as, say, athletes do.

What about politicians? Do they improve with practice? Certainly they improve at their ability to win elections—a task on which they get good feedback. However, experience in office doesn't greatly improve their ability to make the right decisions on public policy. (If it did, then we should expect experienced legislators to agree with one another.) The problem is a lack of feedback: When the government enacts a policy, we seldom know how much better or worse things might have been under some other policy.

Expert Pattern Recognition

What exactly do experts do that sets them apart from others? Primarily, they can look at a pattern and recognize its important features quickly.

In a typical experiment (de Groot, 1966), chess experts and novices briefly examined pieces on a chessboard, as in Figure 8.18, and tried to recall the positions. When the pieces were arranged as might

Figure 8.18 Master chess players quickly recognize and memorize chess pieces arranged as they might occur in a normal game (**a**). However, they are no better than average at memorizing a random pattern (**b**).

Judit Polgar confirmed her father's confidence that prolonged effort could make her a grand master chess player.

occur in a normal game, expert players recalled 91% of the positions correctly, whereas novices recalled only 41%. When the pieces were arranged randomly, however, experts and novices did about the same at recalling the positions. That is, experts do not have a superior memory overall, but they have learned to recognize common chessboard patterns. (Recall the concept of chunking from chapter 7—the process of recognizing a large cluster of items and then remembering them as a unit.)

Another example comes from basketball. Imagine you watch a video clip of someone shooting a free throw, but the clip is interrupted before the ball reaches the net. How much would you have to see before you could guess whether the ball will go through the hoop? Most people aren't sure until the ball is near the basket. Professional basketball players usually know the answer well before the ball leaves the shooter's hands (Aglioti, Cesari, Romani, & Urgesi, 2008; Figure 8.19). In other areas from bird identification to reading x-rays to judging gymnastic competitions, experts recognize important patterns almost immediately (Murphy & Medin, 1985; Ste-Marie, 1999; Tanaka, Curran, & Sheinberg, 2005).

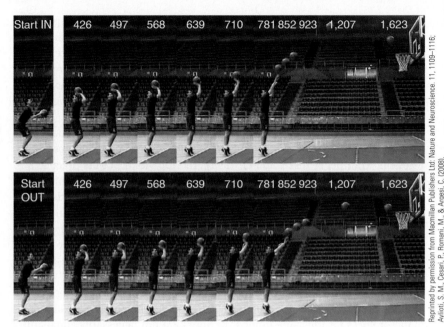

Reprinted by permission from Macmillan Publishers Ltd: Nature and Neuroscience. 11, 1109–1116; Aylioti, S. M. Cesari, P., Romani, M., & Argesi, C. (2008).

Figure 8.19 The lines indicate the point at which people give the correct answer ("in" or "out") more often than they say "uncertain" or an incorrect answer. (From Aglioti, S. M., Cesari, P., Romani, M., & Urgesi, C. [2008]. Action anticipation and motor resonance in elite basketball players. *Nature Neuroscience, 11,* 1109–1116.)

concept check

12. The introduction to module 7.1 mentioned the World Memory Championship, in which contestants compete at memorizing long lists of words, numbers, or cards. How would practice enable them to develop this kind of expertise? That is, what must they do differently from other people?

Answer

12. As with other kinds of expertise, experts at memorizing learn to recognize patterns. Whereas most people would see "king of hearts," two of spades, three of clubs, seven of clubs, ace of diamonds" as five items, someone who has practiced memorizing cards might see this as a single familiar pattern or as a part of an even larger pattern.

Near Transfer and Far Transfer

If you develop expertise in one area, will it help you with anything else? The assumption that it will is an old one. Long ago, college education in Britain and the United States focused on studying Latin and Greek, based on the assumption that students would gain mental discipline that helps in all aspects of life. Today, the premedical curriculum requires cal-

culus. Do you suppose medical doctors use much calculus? Hardly. The hope is to strengthen overall intellectual ability, just by concentrating on something difficult. Similarly, many people recommend that old people do crossword puzzles and Sudoku puzzles to exercise their brains. However, the research finds that when older adults work crossword puzzles, they get better at crossword puzzles. They don't get better at remembering where they left their keys (Salthouse, 2006).

Psychologists distinguish between near transfer and far transfer (Barnett & Ceci, 2002). **Near transfer**, *benefit to a new skill based on practice of a similar skill*, is easy to demonstrate. **Far transfer**, *benefit from practicing something less similar*, is more difficult. Suppose you learn to solve problems like this in a physics course: A train going 25 meters per second (m/s) increases its velocity by 2 m/s each second. How fast will it be going 10 seconds from now? To solve, you multiply 2 m/s times 10 seconds (yielding an increase of 20 m/s) and add it to the original 25 m/s, for an answer of 45 m/s. Now if you face new problems about cars that increase their velocity by a certain amount per second, you should solve them easily. (That's near transfer.) But then you get this problem: Tom receives an allowance of $2 per month beginning on his sixth birthday. The allowance increases by $0.20 each month. How much will he receive on his seventh birthday? This is an example of far transfer, and most people find it difficult to solve (Bassok & Holyoak, 1989). You, of course, see how to solve it, because it was in the same paragraph with the train problem and therefore you recognize its similarity: You multiply $0.20/month times 12 months (yielding $2.40) and add it to the original $2, for a total of $4.40.

Far transfer does occur, but it usually requires extensive practice of the first skill, and even then far transfer is usually a small effect (Herzog, Kramer, Wilson, & Lindenberger, 2009). No known task improves all types of intellectual performance.

One of the best examples of far transfer is the benefit from responding to constantly changing instructions. First you examine pictures, deciding for each one whether it shows a fruit or a vegetable. After a few trials, the instruction changes: You say whether each fruit or vegetable is large or small. Then you might say the color, and then you might go back to saying fruit or vegetable. After enough practice at rapidly switching tasks, you improve your ability to control attention and perform tests of "central executive function," as described in chapter 7 (Karbach & Kray, 2009). Children who grow up speaking two or more languages also show superior performance on tests of controlling attention, presumably because of their experience at shifting from one language to another (Bialystok, Craik, Green, & Gollan, 2009). Certain computer games that require constant attention improve children's executive functions, as do physical exercise, music training, martial arts training, and play acting (Diamond & Lee, 2011; Moreno et al., 2011).

concept check

13. What is one documented example of far transfer?

Answer

13. Practice at switching tasks, including switching from one language to another, aids attention and central executive functions. (However, even this kind of practice aids only attention, not other types of intellectual function.)

module 8.2

In Closing

Successful and Unsuccessful Problem Solving

In this module, we have considered thinking at its best and worst—expertise and error. Experts polish their skills through extensive practice. Of course, we all have to make decisions about topics in which we are not experts. Without insisting on perfection, we can at least hold ourselves to the standard of not doing anything foolish. Perhaps if we become more aware of common errors, we can be more alert to avoid them.

Summary

- *Two types of thinking.* We often make decisions quickly and automatically, using System 1. When we recognize a problem as being more difficult, we do calculations, ponder the evidence, or in other ways engage effortful processes, using System 2. (page 269)
- *Algorithm and heuristics.* People solve problems by algorithms (ways of checking every possibility) and heuristics (ways of simplifying a problem). (page 269)
- *Maximizing and satisficing.* The maximizing strategy is to consider thoroughly every possible choice to find the best one. The satisficing strategy is to accept the first choice one finds that is good enough. People using the maximizing strategy usually make good choices but are often not fully pleased with them. That strategy is especially problematic when many choices are available. (page 270)
- *Representativeness heuristic and base-rate information.* If something resembles members of some category, we usually assume it too belongs to that category. However, that assumption is risky if the category is a rare one. (page 270)
- *Availability heuristic.* We generally assume that the more easily we can think of examples of some category, the more common that category is. However, this heuristic misleads us when items in rare categories get much publicity. (page 271)
- *Some reasons for errors.* People tend to be overconfident about their judgments on difficult

questions. They tend to look for evidence that confirms their hypothesis instead of evidence that might reject it. They answer the same question differently when it is framed differently. They sometimes take unpleasant actions to avoid admitting that previous actions were a waste of time or money. (page 272)

- *Expertise.* Becoming an expert requires years of practice and effort. Experts recognize and mem-orize familiar and meaningful patterns more rapidly than less experienced people do. (page 274)

- *Near and far transfer.* Developing skill at a task aids performance of a similar task. It seldom helps much with a dissimilar task. (page 276)

Key Terms

algorithm (page 269)
availability heuristic (page 271)
base-rate information (page 270)
confirmation bias (page 272)
critical thinking (page 272)
far transfer (page 270)
framing effect (page 273)
functional fixedness (page 273)

heuristics (page 269)
maximizing (page 270)
near transfer (page 276)
representativeness heuristic (page 270)
satisficing (page 270)
sunk cost effect (page 274)
System 1 (page 269)
System 2 (page 269)

Answers to Other Questions in the Module

D. This illustration shows how to cut and fold an ordinary piece of paper or cardboard to match the figure with nothing left over. (page 268)

Step 1. Cut

Step 2. Fold

Step 3. Twist

© Cengage Learning

E. A membrane heavy enough to keep the water in would also keep the rubber balls out. (page 269)

F. (1) The best way to attach the candle to the wall is to dump the matches from the box and thumbtack the side of the box to the wall, as shown in this picture. The tiny piece of string is irrelevant.

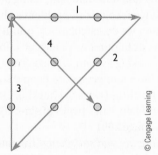

© Cengage Learning

(2) The dots can be connected with four lines:

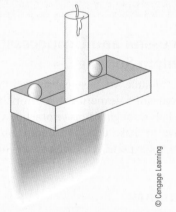

© Cengage Learning

(3) One answer is three students: one psychology major, one chemistry major, and one history major. The other possibility is two students who are majoring in something else—music, for example. (If there are two music majors, all but two of them are indeed majoring in psychology, etc.) (page 273)

Language

- To what extent can other species learn language?
- What specializations enable humans to learn language?
- How do we understand words and sentences?
- What do we do when we read?

Every species of animal has ways of communicating, but only human language has the property of productivity, *the ability to combine words into new sentences that express an unlimited variety of ideas* (Deacon, 1997). Every day, you invent new sentences that no one has ever said before.

You might ask, "How do you know that no one has ever said that sentence before?!" Well, of course, no one can be certain that a particular sentence is new, but we can be confident that many sentences are new (without specifying which ones) because of the vast number of possible ways to rearrange words. Imagine this exercise (but don't really try it unless you have nothing else to do with your life): Pick a sentence of more than 10 words from any book you choose. How long would you need to keep reading, in that book or any other, until you found the exact same sentence again?

In short, we do not memorize all the sentences we use. Instead, we learn rules for making and understanding sentences. The famous linguist Noam Chomsky (1980) described those rules as a transformational grammar, *a system for converting a deep structure into a surface structure*. The deep structure is the underlying logic or meaning of a sentence. The surface structure is the sequence of words as they are actually spoken or written (Figure 8.20). According to this theory, whenever we speak, we transform the deep structure of the language into a surface structure.

Two surface structures can resemble each other without representing the same deep structure, or they can represent the same deep structure without resembling each other. For example, "John is easy to please" has the same deep structure as "Pleasing John is easy" and "It is easy to please John." These sentences represent the same idea. In contrast, consider the sentence "Never threaten someone with a chain saw." The surface structure of that sentence maps into two deep structures, as shown in Figure 8.21.

Nonhuman Precursors to Language

Researcher Terrence Deacon once presented a talk about language to his 8-year-old's elementary school class. One child asked whether other animals have their own languages. Deacon explained that other species communicate but without the productivity of human language. The child persisted, asking whether other animals had at least a simple language with a few words and short sentences. No, he replied, they don't.

Then another child asked, "Why not?" (Deacon, 1997, p. 12). Deacon paused. Why not, indeed? If language is so useful to humans, why haven't other species evolved at least a little of it? And what makes humans so good at learning language?

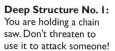

Deep Structure No. 1:
You are holding a chain saw. Don't threaten to use it to attack someone!

Deep Structure No. 2:
Some deranged person is holding a chain saw. Don't threaten him!

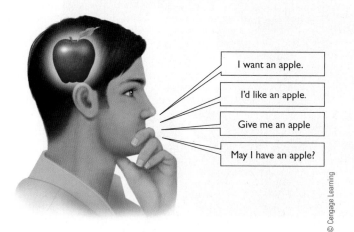

I want an apple.

I'd like an apple.

Give me an apple

May I have an apple?

© Cengage Learning

Figure 8.20 According to transformational grammar, we transform a given deep structure into any of several sentences with different surface structures.

© Cengage Learning

Figure 8.21 The sentence "Never threaten someone with a chain saw" has one surface structure but two deep structures, corresponding to different meanings.

One way to examine humans' language specialization is to ask how far another species could progress toward language. Beginning in the 1920s, several psychologists reared chimpanzees in their homes and tried to teach them to talk. The chimpanzees learned many human habits but understood only a few words.

Part of the problem is that chimpanzees make their sounds while inhaling, whereas humans speak while exhaling. (Just try to make human sounds while inhaling!) However, chimpanzees do make hand gestures in nature. R. Allen Gardner and Beatrice Gardner (1969) taught a chimpanzee named Washoe to use the sign language of the American deaf (Ameslan). Washoe eventually learned the symbols for about 100 words, and other chimps learned to communicate with other visual symbols (Figure 8.22).

How much do these gestures resemble language? Washoe and other chimpanzees trained in this way used their symbols almost exclusively to make requests, not to describe, and rarely in original combinations (Pate & Rumbaugh, 1983; Terrace, Petitto, Sanders, & Bever, 1979; C. R. Thompson & Church, 1980). By contrast, a human child with a vocabulary of 100 words or so links them into short sentences and frequently uses words to describe. However, Washoe did show some understanding. She usually answered "Who" questions with names, "What" questions with objects, and "Where" questions with places, even when she specified the wrong name, object, or place (Van Cantfort, Gardner, & Gardner, 1989).

More impressive results have been reported for another species, the bonobo chimpanzee, *Pan paniscus*. Bonobos' social behavior resembles that of humans in several regards: Males and females form strong attachments, females are sexually responsive outside their fertile period, males contribute to infant care, and adults often share food. Like humans, they stand comfortably on their hind legs, and they often copulate face-to-face. Several bonobos have learned to press keys on a board to make short sentences, as in Figure 8.22c and Figure 8.23. Unlike Washoe and other common chimpanzees, bonobos sometimes use symbols to describe events, without requesting anything. One with a cut on his hand explained that his mother had bitten him. However, unlike children, bonobos almost never use expressions of possession, such as "mine!" (Lyn, Greenfield, Savage-Rumbaugh, Gillespie-Lynch, & Hopkins, 2011).

a

b

c

d

Figure 8.22 Psychologists have tried to teach chimpanzees to communicate with gestures or symbols. **(a)** A chimp arranges plastic chips to request food. **(b)** Another chimp in her human home. She learned to make a few sounds similar to English words. **(c)** Kanzi, a bonobo, presses symbols to indicate words. **(d)** A chimp signing *toothbrush*.

Figure 8.23 Kanzi, a bonobo, points to answers on a board in response to questions he hears through earphones. Experimenter Rose Sevcik does not hear the questions, so she cannot signal the correct answer.

The most proficient bonobos seem to comprehend symbols about as well as a 2- to 2½-year-old child understands language (Savage-Rumbaugh et al., 1993). They also show considerable understanding of spoken English, following such odd commands as "bite your ball" and "take the vacuum cleaner outside" (Savage-Rumbaugh, 1990; Savage-Rumbaugh, Sevcik, Brakke, & Rumbaugh, 1992). They passed a test of responding to commands issued over earphones, eliminating the possibility of "Clever Hans"-type signals, as discussed in chapter 2 (Figure 8.23).

Why have bonobos been more successful with language than common chimpanzees? Apparently, bonobos have a greater predisposition for this type of learning. Also, they learned by observation and imitation, which promote better understanding than the formal training methods that previous studies used (Savage-Rumbaugh et al., 1992). Finally, the bonobos began their language experience early in life.

concept check

14. Based on the studies with bonobos, can you offer advice about how to teach language to children with impaired language learning?

Answer

14. Start language learning when a child is young. Rely on imitation as much as possible instead of providing direct reinforcements for correct responses.

Human Specializations for Learning Language

Humans are clearly more adapted for language than any other species, including bonobos. Why do we learn language so easily?

Language and General Intelligence

Did we evolve language as an accidental byproduct of evolving big brains? Several observations argue strongly against this idea. Dolphins and whales have even larger brains but do not develop a flexible communication system resembling human language. Some people with brain damage have less total brain mass than a chimpanzee but continue to speak and understand language.

Also, some children, up to 7% by some estimates, have normal intelligence in other ways but noticeable limitations in language. For example, they don't understand the difference between "Who was the girl pushing?" and "Who was pushing the girl?" (Leonard, 2007). People in one family whose members have a particular gene have even greater language impairments despite otherwise normal intelligence (Fisher, Vargha-Khadem, Watkins, Monaco, & Pembrey, 1998; Lai, Fisher, Hurst, Vargha-Khadem, & Monaco, 2001). They do not fully master even simple rules, such as how to form plurals of nouns.

At the opposite extreme, consider Williams syndrome, *a genetic condition characterized by mental retardation in most regards but surprisingly good use of language relative to their other abilities* (Meyer-Lindenberg, Mervis, & Berman, 2006). One child, when asked to name as many animals as he could, started with "ibex, whale, bull, yak, zebra, puppy, kitten, tiger, koala, dragon . . ." Another child could sing more than 1,000 songs in 22 languages (Bellugi & St. George, 2000). However, these children prefer 50 pennies to 5 dollars and, when asked to estimate the length of a bus, give answers such as "3 inches or 100 inches, maybe" (Bellugi, Lichtenberger, Jones, Lai, & St. George, 2000). Evidently, language ability is not the same as overall intelligence.

Language Learning as a Specialized Capacity

Susan Carey (1978) calculated that children between the ages of 1½ and 6 learn an average of nine new words per day. But how do they infer the meanings of all those words? A parent points at a frog and says "frog." How does the child guess that the word means *frog* rather than *small thing, green thing,* or *this particular frog*? Indeed, how does the child know the sound means anything at all?

Noam Chomsky has argued that people learn language so easily that children must begin with preconceptions. Chomsky and his followers suggest that people are born with a language acquisition device, *a built-in mechanism for acquiring language* (Pinker, 1994). One line of evidence for this theory is that deaf children who are not taught a sign language invent one of their own and try to teach it to their parents or to other deaf children (Goldin-Meadow, McNeill, & Singleton, 1996; Goldin-Meadow & Mylander, 1998). Further evidence is that children learn to use complex grammatical structures, such as "Is the boy who is unhappy watching Mickey Mouse?" even though they don't hear that kind of expression very often. To pick up that kind of grammar so quickly, children must have predispositions to guide them.

Other psychologists counter that we underestimate children's opportunity to learn. Parents throughout the world simplify the language-learning task by speaking to their infants in *parentese*—a pattern of speech that prolongs the vowels, making clearer than usual the difference between words such as *cat* and *cot* (Kuhl et al., 1997). Even infants less than 1 year old detect regularities in the language they hear (Marcus, Vijayan, Rao, & Vishton, 1999; Saffran, 2003). For example, adults usually run their words together without pausing: "Lookat-theprettybaby." The infant detects which sounds go together as words by statistical relations. For example, the infant frequently hears the two-syllable combination "pre-tty" and frequently hears "ba-by" but less often hears the combination "ty-ba" and concludes that the word break comes between *pretty* and *baby*. We can infer that infants draw this conclusion because infants react to "ty-ba" as a new, attention-getting sound and don't react the same way to "pretty" or "baby" (Saffran, Aslin, & Newport, 1996). In short, infants learn the basics of language from regularities in what they hear.

concept check

15. Suppose biotechnologists manipulate some genes to create a new breed of raccoons with brains as large as humans'. Should we expect these raccoons to develop language?

Answer

15. Probably not. Several species already have brains larger than those of humans without showing language. Some humans have normal intelligence with limited language, and others have nearly normal language despite low overall intelligence. Brain size, intelligence, and language are not the same thing.

Language and the Human Brain

What aspect of the human brain enables us to learn language so easily? Studies of people with brain damage have long pointed to two brain areas as particularly important for language. People with damage in the frontal cortex, including *Broca's area* (Figure 8.24), develop Broca's aphasia, *a condition characterized by difficulties in language production*. Serious language impairment occurs only if the damage extends well outside Broca's area, but that area seems to be central. The person speaks slowly and inarticulately and is no better with writing or typing. Someone with Broca's aphasia is especially impaired with using and understanding grammatical devices such as prepositions, conjunctions, and word endings. For example, one person who was asked about a dental appointment slowly mumbled, "Yes . . . Monday . . . Dad and Dick . . . Wednesday nine o'clock . . . 10 o'clock . . . doctors . . . and . . . teeth" (Geschwind, 1979, p. 186).

People with damage in the temporal cortex, including *Wernicke's area* (Figure 8.24), develop Wernicke's aphasia, *a condition marked by impaired recall of nouns and impaired language comprehension, despite fluent and grammatical speech.* Difficulty with nouns and impaired comprehension fit together: If you can't remember what something is called, you will have trouble processing a sentence based on that word. Because these people omit most nouns, their speech is hard to understand. For example, one patient responded to a question about his health, "I felt worse because I can no longer keep in mind from the mind of the minds to keep me from mind and up to the ear which can be to find among ourselves" (J. Brown, 1977, p. 29).

Our language areas of the brain evolved from precursors in other species. Areas approximately corresponding to Wernicke's area and Broca's area in monkeys respond to monkey vocalizations (Gil-da-Costa et al., 2006; Petkov et al., 2008). However, the structure of those areas evolved considerably from monkeys to apes to humans (Rilling et al., 2008). Furthermore, language depends on far more than just these two areas. When you read or hear an action verb such as *throw*, the brain area responsible for that kind of action increases its activity (Willems, Labruna, D'Esposito, Ivry, & Casasanto, 2011). That is, you understand something by imagining yourself doing it. Reading other words activates brain areas responsible for color perception, facial recognition, emotion, and so forth. It is fair to say that the whole human brain is organized to make language possible.

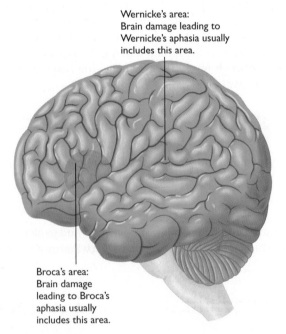

Wernicke's area:
Brain damage leading to Wernicke's aphasia usually includes this area.

Broca's area:
Brain damage leading to Broca's aphasia usually includes this area.

© Cengage Learning

Figure 8.24 Brain damage that produces major deficits in language usually includes the left-hemisphere areas shown here. However, the deficits are severe only if the damage includes these areas and extends beyond them.

Table 8.2 Stages of Language Development

Age	Typical Language Abilities (Much Individual Variation)
3 months	Random vocalizations.
6 months	More distinct babbling.
1 year	Babbling that resembles the typical sounds of the family's language; probably one or more words including "mama"; language comprehension much better than production.
1 1/2 years	Can say some words (mean about 50), mostly nouns; few or no phrases.
2 years	Speaks in two-word phrases.
2 1/2 years	Longer phrases and short sentences with some errors and unusual constructions. Can understand much more.
3 years	Vocabulary near 1,000 words; longer sentences with fewer errors.
4 years	Close to adult speech competence.

© Cengage Learning

concept check

16. Brain-damaged patient A speaks fluently but is hard to understand, and she has trouble understanding other people's speech. Patient B understands most speech, but he speaks slowly and inarticulately, and he leaves out nearly all prepositions, conjunctions, and word endings. Which kind of aphasia does each patient have?

Answer

16. Patient A has Wernicke's aphasia. Patient B has Broca's aphasia.

Language Development

Brain specializations facilitate language learning, but we still have to learn. Children's language learning is amazing. Virtually every child learns language, even if the parents know nothing about how to teach it.

Language in Early Childhood

Table 8.2 lists the average ages at which children reach various stages of language ability (Lenneberg, 1969; Moskowitz, 1978). Remember, these are averages, and children vary considerably. Progression through these stages depends largely on maturation (Lenneberg, 1967, 1969). Parents who expose their children to as much language as possible increase the children's vocabulary, but they hardly affect the rate of progression through language stages. Hearing children of deaf parents are exposed to much less spoken language, but they too progress almost on schedule.

Deaf infants babble as much as hearing infants do for the first 6 months and then start to decline. At first, hearing infants babble only haphazard sounds, but soon they start repeating the sounds they have been hearing. If a parent re-sponds to an infant's sounds by replying, the infant approximately copies the type of reply, such as consonant-vowel (Goldstein & Schwade, 2008). By age 1 year, an infant babbles mostly sounds that resemble the language the family speaks (Locke, 1994).

One of an infant's first sounds is *muh*, and that sound or something similar has been adopted by many of the world's languages to mean "mother." Infants also make the sounds *duh*, *puh*, and *buh*. In many languages, the word for father is similar to *dada* or *papa*. *Baba* is the word for father in Chinese and for grandmother in several other languages. In effect, infants tell their parents what words to use for important concepts.

By age 1½, most toddlers have a vocabulary of about 50 words, but they seldom link words together. A toddler says "Daddy" and "bye-bye" but not "Bye-bye, Daddy." In context, parents can usually discern considerable meaning in these single-word utterances. *Mama* might mean, "That's a picture of Mama," "Take me to Mama," "Mama went away and left me here," or "Mama, I'm hungry." Toddlers do, however, combine a word with a gesture, such as pointing at something while saying "mine" (Iverson & Goldin-Meadow, 2005). The word and gesture constitute a primitive kind of sentence.

By age 2, children start producing telegraphic phrases of two or more words, such as "more page" (read some more), "allgone sticky" (my hands are now clean), and "allgone outside" (someone has closed the door). Note the originality of such phrases. It is unlikely that the parents ever said "allgone sticky"!

By age 2½ to 3 years, most children generate sentences but with some idiosyncrasies. Many young children have their own rules for negative sentences. A common one is to add *no* or *not* to the beginning or end of a sentence, such as, "No I want to go to bed!" One little girl formed her negatives just by saying something louder and at a higher pitch. If she shrieked, "I want to share my toys!" she meant, "I do *not* want to share my toys." She had learned this rule by noting that people screamed when they told her not to do something. My son Sam made negatives for a while by adding the word *either* to the end of a sentence: "I want to eat lima beans either." He had heard people say, "I don't want to do that either."

When young children speak, they apply grammatical rules, although of course they cannot state those rules. For example, they apply the rules of English to produce such sentences as "the womans goed and doed something," or "the mans getted their foots wet." We say that children *overregularize* or *overgeneralize* the rules. My son David invented the word *shis* to mean "belonging to a female." (He apparently generalized the rule "He–his, she–shis.") Clearly, children are not just repeating what they have heard.

Apparently, we have an "optimal period" for learning language in early childhood (Werker & Tees, 2005). Much of the evidence for this conclusion comes from people who learn a second language. Adults learn the vocabulary of a second language faster than children do, but children learn the pronunciation better, as well as difficult aspects of the grammar. To master a language, one must start early, and those who start after age 12 almost never approach the level of a native speaker. Even those who start after the first couple years of life are at a disadvantage (Abrahamsson & Hyltenstam, 2009). However, researchers find no sharp age cutoff when language suddenly becomes more difficult. Learning a second language is easier for 2-year-olds than 4-year-olds but also easier for 13-year-olds than 16-year-olds (Hakuta, Bialystok, & Wiley, 2003; Harley & Wang, 1997).

concept check

17. At what age do children begin to string words into combinations they have never heard before? Why do psychologists believe that even very young children learn rules of grammar?

Answer

17. Children begin to string words into novel combinations as soon as they begin to speak two words at a time. Children show that they learn rules of grammar when they overgeneralize those rules, creating such words as *womans* and *goed*.

Children Exposed to No Language or Two Languages

Would children who were exposed to no language make up a new one? In rare cases, an infant who was accidentally separated from other people grew up in a forest without human contact until discovered years later. Such children not only fail to show a language of their own but also fail to learn much language after they are given the chance (Pinker, 1994). However, their development is so abnormal and their early life so unknown that we should hesitate to draw conclusions.

Better evidence comes from studies of children who are deaf. Children who cannot hear well enough to learn speech and who are not taught sign language invent their own sign language (Senghas, Kita, & Özyürek, 2004). Observations in Nicaragua found that sign language evolved over the decades. Deaf people learned sign language and taught it to the next generation, who, having learned it from

early childhood, elaborated on it, made it more expressive, taught the enhanced sign language to the next generation, and so on (Senghas & Coppola, 2001).

If a deaf child starts to invent a sign language and no one responds to it, because the child meets no other deaf children and the adults fail to learn, the child gradually abandons it. A child who is finally exposed to sign language at age 12 or so struggles to develop signing skills and never catches up with those who started earlier (Harley & Wang, 1997; Mayberry, Lock, & Kazmi, 2002). This observation is our best evidence for the importance of early development in language learning: A child who doesn't learn a language while young is permanently impaired at learning one.

Some children grow up in a bilingual environment, *learning two languages.* Many people guess that a bilingual person might represent the languages in different brain areas. However, the research shows that both languages activate the same areas (Perani & Abutalebi, 2005). Those who are bilingual from early infancy devote more brain areas to language, including parts of both left and right hemispheres, and they develop wider connections in the brain, but the same brain areas participate in both languages (Hull & Vaid, 2007; Luk, Bialystock, Craik, & Grady, 2011; Mechelli et al., 2004; Perani & Abutalebi, 2005). If the brain represents two languages in the same places, how do bilingual people keep their languages separate? They don't, at least not completely (Thierry & Wu, 2007). They often get confused when they switch between languages (Levy, McVeigh, Marful, & Anderson, 2007; Linck, Kroll, & Sunderman, 2009).

Bilingualism has two disadvantages: Children take longer to master two languages than one, and their vocabulary lags behind that of someone who speaks only one language. Bilingual people often take longer than average to think of a word (Bialystok, Craik, & Luk, 2008). The primary advantage of bilingualism is obvious: People who know another language can communicate with more people (Figure 8.25). A second advantage is that bilingual people gain practice in controlling their attention, shifting from one language frame to another. In the process, they improve their ability to control attention, inhibit distraction, and hold information in working memory. On average, they do better than one-language people on many nonverbal tasks (Bialystok, Craik, Green, & Gollan, 2009).

Figure 8.25 Children who grow up in a bilingual or multilingual environment gain in their ability to control their attention, as well as in their ability to communicate with more people.

18. What is the most convincing evidence that early exposure to language is necessary for language development?
19. What are the advantages and disadvantages of bilingualism?

Answers

18. Deaf children who cannot learn spoken language and who have no opportunity to communicate with signs early in life are permanently disadvantaged in learning sign language.
19. Advantages: It becomes possible to speak with more people, and the ability to control attention improves. Disadvantages: It takes longer to learn languages than one, and it is difficult to master either language as well as a person who is learning only one.

Understanding Language

The English language has many words with ambiguous meanings. For instance, *peck* can mean one fourth of a bushel or to strike with a beak. *Rose* can mean a flower or the past tense of the verb *to rise*. *Desert* can mean a dry stretch of land or to abandon someone. In context, however, listeners usually understand the meaning.

We become even more aware of context when we compare languages. Mandarin Chinese draws no distinctions for noun number or verb tense, and it lacks words for *a* and *the*. Thus, the sentence for "A man is buying an apple" is also the sentence for "The men bought apples," "A man will buy apples," and so forth. Despite this ambiguity, listeners ordinarily understand the meaning in context. If the context is insufficient, a speaker adds a word such as *tomorrow* or *yesterday*. The Malay language has one word for "you and I" and a different word for "someone else and I." English translates both words as "we." The Malaysians wonder how listeners understand this ambiguous word, just as English speakers wonder how the Chinese get by without indications of number or tense.

Understanding a Word

Context not only determines how we interpret a word, but also primes us to hear an ambiguous sound one way or another. For example, a computer generated a sound halfway between a normal *s* sound and a normal *sh* sound. When this intermediate sound replaced the *s* sound at the end of the word *embarrass*, people heard it as an *s* sound. When the same sound replaced *sh* at the end of *abolish*, people heard the same sound as *sh* (Samuel, 2001).

We also use lip-reading more than we realize to understand what we hear. If lip movements do not match the sound, we strike a compromise between what we see and what we hear (McGurk & MacDonald, 1976). To experience this phenomenon, go to the Online Try It Yourself activity McGurk Effect.

online try it ▶ yourself

In one study, students listened to a tape recording of a sentence with a sound missing (Warren, 1970). The sentence was, "The state governors met with their respective legislatures convening in the capital city." However, the sound of the first *s* in the word *legislatures*, along with part of the adjacent *i* and *l*, had been replaced by a cough or a tone. The students were asked to listen to the recording and try to identify the location of the cough or tone. None of the 20 students identified the location correctly, and half thought the cough or tone interrupted one of the other words on the tape. Even those who were told that the *s* sound was missing insisted that they clearly heard the sound *s*. The brain uses the context to fill in the missing sound.

Just as we hear the word *legislatures* as a whole, not as a string of separate letters, we interpret a sequence of words as a whole, not one at a time. Suppose you hear a tape-recorded word that is carefully engineered to sound halfway between *dent* and *tent*. The way you perceive it depends on the context:

1. When the *ent in the fender was well camouflaged, we sold the car.
2. When the *ent in the forest was well camouflaged, we began our hike.

Most people who hear sentence 1 report the word *dent*. Most who hear sentence 2 report *tent*. Now consider two more sentences:

3. When the *ent was noticed in the fender, we sold the car.
4. When the *ent was noticed in the forest, we stopped to rest.

For sentences 3 and 4, the context comes too late to help. People are as likely to report hearing *dent* in one sentence as in the other (Connine, Blasko, & Hall, 1991). Consider what this means: In the first two sentences, the fender or forest showed up three syllables after *ent. In the second pair, the fender or forest appeared six syllables later. Evidently, when you hear an ambiguous sound, you hold it in an "undecided" state for about three syllables for the context to clarify it. Beyond that point, it is too late.

Although a long-delayed context cannot help you hear an ambiguous word correctly, it does help you understand its meaning. Consider the following sentence (Lashley, 1951):

Rapid righting with his uninjured hand saved from loss the contents of the capsized canoe.

If you hear this sentence spoken aloud so that spelling provides no clues, you are likely at first to interpret the second word as *writing*, until you reach the final two words of the sentence. Suddenly, *capsized canoe* tells you that *righting* meant "pushing with a paddle." Only the immediate context can influence what you hear, but a delayed context can change the word's meaning.

Understanding Sentences

Making sense of language requires knowledge about the world. For example, consider the following sentences (from Just & Carpenter, 1987):

That store sells horse shoes.
That store sells alligator shoes.

You interpret *horse shoes* to mean "shoes for horses to wear," but you interpret *alligator shoes* as "shoes made from alligator hide." Your understanding of the sentences depends on your knowledge of the world, not just the syntax of the sentences.

Here is another example:

I'm going to buy a pet hamster at the store, if it's open.
I'm going to buy a pet hamster at the store, if it's healthy.

Nothing about the sentence structure told you that *it* refers to the store in the first sentence and a hamster in the second sentence. You understood because you know that stores but not hamsters can be open, whereas hamsters but not stores can be healthy.

In short, understanding a sentence depends on your knowledge of the world and all the assumptions that you share with the speaker or writer of the sentence. Sometimes, you even have to remember where you are because the meaning of a word differs from one place to another (Figure 8.26).

try it ▶ yourself

Now consider this sentence: *While Anna dressed the baby played in the crib.* Quickly: Whom did Anna dress? And who played in the crib? The addition of a comma would simplify the sentence, but even without it, English grammar prohibits "baby" from being both the object of *dressed* and the subject of *played.* If the baby played in the crib (as you no doubt answered), Anna must have dressed herself. Neverthe-

Figure 8.26 In England, a *football coach* is a bus full of soccer fans. In the United States, it's the person who directs a team of American football players.

less, many people think Anna dressed the baby (Ferreira, Bailey, & Ferraro, 2002). When speaking or writing, it is important to try to imagine ways in which people might misunderstand you.

Limits to Our Language Understanding

Some sentences are grammatical but almost incomprehensible. One example is a doubly embedded sentence—a sentence within a sentence within a sentence. A singly embedded sentence is understandable, though not simple:

The dog the cat saw chased a squirrel.
The squirrel the dog chased climbed the tree.

In the first sentence, "the cat saw the dog" is embedded within "the dog chased a squirrel." In the second, "the dog chased the squirrel" is embedded within "the squirrel climbed the tree." So far, so good, but now consider a doubly embedded sentence:

The squirrel the dog the cat saw chased climbed the tree.

Doubly embedded sentences overburden our memory. In fact, if your memory is already burdened with other matters, you may have trouble understanding a singly embedded sentence (Gordon, Hendrick, & Levine, 2002).

Double negatives are also difficult to understand. "I would not deny that . . ." means that I agree. "It is not false that . . ." means that something is true. People often misunderstand such sentences. Have you ever seen a multiple-choice test item that asks "Which of the following is not true . . ." and then one of the choices has a *not* in it? With such items, confusion is almost certain.

Triple negatives are still worse. Consider the following sentence, which includes *four* negatives (emphasis added): "If you do *not* unanimously find from your consideration of all the evidence that there are *no* mitigating factors sufficient to *preclude* the imposition of a death sentence, then you should sign the verdict requiring the court to impose a sentence *other than* death." In Illinois some years ago, judges used to read those instructions to a jury to explain how to decide between a death penalty and life in prison. Do you think many jurors understood?

With a single negative, people often don't fully accept the meaning of the word *not*. Suppose a packaged food says, "Contains no rat pieces!" Does that notice encourage you to buy the product? Hardly! I was once on an airplane that turned around shortly after departure because one of its two engines failed. The attendant told the passengers what was happening, but until she said, "Please don't panic," we didn't realize there might be a reason to panic. If you ask someone for a favor and the person responds, "No problem," how do you react? The expression "no problem" implies there was almost a problem, or maybe there is a bit of a problem.

In one clever experiment, students watched an experimenter pour sugar into two jars. The students were then told to label one jar "sucrose, table sugar" and the other "not sodium cyanide, not poison." Then the experimenter made two cups of Kool-Aid, one from each jar of sugar, and asked the students to choose one to drink (Figure 8.27). Of the 44 who expressed a preference, 35 wanted Kool-Aid made from the jar that they had marked "sucrose," not from the one that they had marked as not having poison (Rozin, Markwith, & Ross, 1990).

Reading

Students of language distinguish between phonemes and morphemes. A phoneme is *a unit of sound*, such as *f* or *sh*. A morpheme is *a unit of meaning.* For example, the noun *thrills* has two morphemes (*thrill* and *s*). The final *s* is a unit

Figure 8.27 Most students preferred Kool-Aid made with sugar labeled "sugar" instead of sugar labeled "not cyanide," even though they had placed the labels themselves. People don't always trust the word *not*. (Based on results of Rozin, Markwith, & Ross, 1990.)

of meaning because it indicates that the noun is plural (Figure 8.28). *Harp* has one morpheme, and *harping* has two, but *harpoon* has just one, as it is not derived from *harp*. Morphemes help us break an unfamiliar word into meaningful parts. For example, we can see *reinvigoration* as *re-in-vigor-ation*, meaning the process of increasing vigor again.

Readers of English and other European languages are accustomed to the idea that a letter or combination of letters represents a phoneme. However, in the Japanese *hiragana* style of writing, each character represents a syllable. In Chinese, each character represents a morpheme and ordinarily a whole word.

Phonemes (units of sound):

Morphemes (units of meaning):

Figure 8.28 The word *shamelessness* has nine phonemes (units of sound) and three morphemes (units of meaning).

whether a briefly flashed word was *fish* or *fist* as they were to recognize whether it was *sung* or *lung* (Adelman, Marquis, & Sabatos-DeVito, 2010). That result implies that we read a word as a whole—we see the last letter of the word just as fast as the first letter.

Consider the following experiment: The investigator flashes a letter on a screen for less than a quarter-second, shows an interfering pattern, and asks, "Was it *C* or *J*?" Then the experimenter flashes an entire word on the screen under the same conditions and asks, "Was the first letter of the word *C* or *J*?" (Figure 8.29). Which question is easier? Most

---

concept check

20. How many phonemes are in the word *thoughtfully*? How many morphemes?

Answer

20. It has seven phonemes: th-ough-t-f-u-ll-y. It has three morphemes: thought-ful-ly.

Word Recognition

As you will recall, expertise develops from many years of practice, enabling someone to recognize complex patterns at a glance. Because you have been reading for hours a day, almost every day since childhood, you have developed expertise at reading. You may not think of yourself as an expert because we usually reserve that term for someone who is far more skilled than others. Nevertheless, you recognize words instantaneously, like an expert who recognizes chess patterns at a glance. In one study, people were just as quick and accurate to recognize

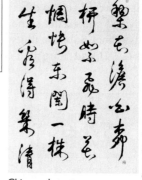

Japanese hiragana

Chinese characters

Illustration of Japanese *hiragana* writing and Chinese writing.

Figure 8.29 Either a word or a single letter flashed on a screen and then an interfering pattern. The observers were asked, "Which was presented, *C* or *J*?" More of them identified the letter correctly when it was part of a word.

people *identify the letter more accurately when it is part of a word than when it is presented by itself* (Reicher, 1969; Wheeler, 1970). This is known as the word-superiority effect. You can experience it yourself with the Online Try It Yourself activity Word-Superiority Effect.

In further research, James Johnston and James McClelland (1974) briefly flashed words on the screen and asked students to identify one letter at a marked position in each word (Figure 8.30). On some trials, the experimenters told the students to try to see the whole word. On other trials, they showed the students exactly where the critical letter would appear on the screen and told them to focus on that spot and ignore the rest of the screen. Most students identified the critical letter more successfully when they looked at the whole word than when they focused on just the letter itself. This benefit occurs only with a real word, like *COIN*, not with a nonsense combination, like *CXQF* (Rumelhart & McClelland, 1982).

You may have experienced the word-superiority effect yourself. To pass time on long car trips, people sometimes try to find every letter of the alphabet on the billboards. It is easier to spot a letter by reading words than by checking letter by letter.

What accounts for the word-superiority effect? According to one model (McClelland, 1988; Rumelhart, McClelland, & the PDP Research Group, 1986), our perceptions and memories are represented by connections among "units" corresponding to sets of neurons. Each unit connects to other units (Figure 8.31). Any activated unit excites some of its neighbors and inhibits others. Suppose units corresponding to the letters *C, O, I,* and *N* are mod-

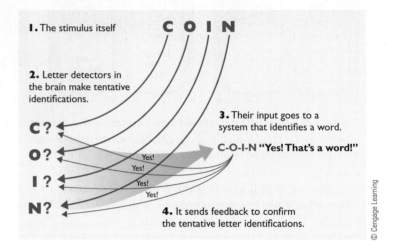

Figure 8.31 According to one model, a visual stimulus activates certain letter units, some more strongly than others. Those letter units then activate a word unit, which in turn strengthens the letter units that compose it. For this reason, we recognize a whole word more easily than a single letter.

erately active. They excite a higher order unit corresponding to the word *COIN*. Although none of the four letter units sends a strong message by itself, the collective impact is strong (McClelland & Rumelhart, 1981). The perception *COIN* then feeds excitation back to the individual letter-identifying units and confirms their tentative identifications.

This model helps explain our perception of Figure 8.32. Why do you see the top word in that figure as *RED* instead of *PFB*? After all, in the other words, those letters do look like *P, F,* and *B*. In the top word, one ambiguous figure activates *P* units and *R* units; the next figure activates *E* and *F* units, and the third figure activates *D* and *B* units. All of those units in turn activate other units corresponding to *RFB, PFB, PFD,* and *RED*. As you tentatively perceive the word as *RED* (the only English word among the choices), the feedback strengthens the

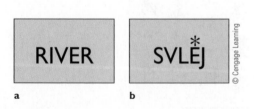

Figure 8.30 Students identified an indicated letter better when they focused on an entire word (**a**) than on a single letter in a designated spot (**b**).

Figure 8.32 The combination of possible letters enables us to identify a word. Word recognition in turn helps to confirm the letter identifications. (From Rumelhart, David E., James L. McClelland, and PDP Research Group, PARALLEL DISTRIBUTED PROCESSING, VOLUME 1: EXPECTATIONS IN THE MICROSTRUCTURE OF COGNITION: FOUNDATIONS. Copyright © 1986 Massachusetts Institute of Technology, by permission of the MIT Press.)

activity of the *R*, *E*, and *D* units. Word recognition can become more complex. Consider the following sentence:

> The boy cuold not slove the porblem so he aksed for help.

Most readers "recognize" the words *could*, *solve*, *problem*, and *asked*, although of course they read faster if all words are spelled correctly (Rayner, White, Johnson, & Liversedge, 2006; White, Johnson, Liversedge, & Rayner, 2008). When we read, we process the context so that even out-of-place letters activate identification of the correct words. (This tendency can pose a probelm for prooofreaders, who sometimes fail to notice a misspelling!)

concept check

21. What evidence indicates that we do *not* read a word one letter at a time?

Answer

21. Ambiguous letters, such as those in Figure 8.32, appear to be one letter in one context and another letter in a different context. Also, a reader sometimes "recognizes" a misspelled word even when certain letters are out of order.

Reading and Eye Movements

Reading requires eye movements, of course. When psychologists monitored eye movements, they discovered that a reader's eyes move in a jerky fashion. You move your eyes steadily to follow a moving object, but when scanning a stationary object, such as a page of print, you alternate between fixations, *when your eyes are stationary*, and saccades (sa-KAHDS), *quick eye movements from one fixation point to another*. You read during fixations, not during saccades. Someone who monitors your eye movements can tell when your attention is wandering. Your fixations become longer, more erratic, and less sensitive to the difficulty of the text (Reichle, Reineberg, & Schooler, 2010). Also you blink your eyes more often (Smilek, Carriere, & Cheyne, 2010).

For an average adult reader, most fixations last about 200 to 250 milliseconds (ms). Fixations are briefer on familiar words like *legal* than on harder words like *luau* or words with more than one meaning like *lead* (Rodd, Gaskell, & Marslen-Wilson, 2002). Because saccades last only 25 to 50 ms, a normal reading pace is about four fixations per second (Rayner, 1998).

How much can someone read during a fixation? The typical limit is about 11 characters at a time. To demonstrate, focus on the letter *i* marked by an arrow (↓) in these sentences:

↓

1. This is a sentence with no misspelled words.

↓

2. Xboc tx zjg rxunce with no mijvgab zucn.

If you permit your eyes to wander back and forth, you notice the gibberish in sentence 2. But as long as you dutifully keep your eyes on the fixation point, the sentence looks all right. You read the letter on which you fixated plus about three or four characters (including spaces) to the left and about seven to the right. The rest is too blurry to make it out. Therefore, you see—*ce with no m*—or possibly—*nce with no mi*—.

This limit of about 11 letters depends partly on the lighting. In faint light, your span decreases to as little as 1 or 2 letters, and your reading ability suffers accordingly (Legge, Ahn, Klitz, & Luebker, 1997). Within a large range, the limit

does not depend on the size of the print (Miellet, O'Donnell, & Sereno, 2009). In the following display, again focus on the letter *i* in each sentence and check how many letters you can read to its left and right:

↓

This is a sentence with no misspelled words.

↓

This is a sentence with no misspelled words.

↓

is a sentence with no misspelled

If your reading span were limited by how many letters can fit into the fovea of your retina, you would read fewer letters as the print gets larger. In fact, you do at least as well, maybe even better, with larger print (up to a point).

The results vary from one language to another. In Japanese and Chinese, where each character conveys more information than English letters do, readers see fewer letters per fixation (Rayner, 1998). That is, the limit depends on how much meaning one can attend to at once. In Hebrew and Farsi, which are written right to left, readers read more letters to the left of fixation and fewer to the right (Brysbaert, Vitu, & Schroyens, 1996; Faust, Kravetz, & Babkoff, 1993; Malamed & Zaidel, 1993).

You might wonder how speed-readers differ from normal readers. An average adult reader has about four or five fixations per second with occasional backtracks, for an overall rate of about 200 words per minute. Speed-readers have briefer fixations with fewer backtracks, and some increase in the number of letters read per fixation (Calef, Pieper, & Coffey, 1999). With practice, they double or triple their reading speed with normal comprehension of most material. However, understanding difficult material requires a reader to slow down and think about it. When speed-readers read college textbooks, they either slow their reading (Just & Carpenter, 1987) or fail the tests (Homa, 1983).

concept check

22. If a word is longer than 11 letters, will a reader need more than one fixation to read it?

Answer

22. Sometimes, but not always. Suppose your eyes fixate on the fourth letter of *memorization*. You should be able to see the three letters to its left and the seven to its right—that is, all except the final letter. Because there is only one English word that starts *memorizatio-*, you already know the word.

module 8.3 >

Language and Humanity

At the start of this module, we considered the question, "If language is so useful to humans, why haven't other species evolved at least a little of it?" None of the research answers this question, but we can speculate.

Many adaptations are much more useful on a large scale than on a small scale. For example, stinkiness is extremely useful to skunks. Being slightly stinky wouldn't help much. Porcupines survive be- cause of their long quills. Having a few short quills could be slightly helpful, but not very. Similarly, a little bit of language development is probably an unstable condition, evolutionarily speaking. Once a species such as humans had evolved a little language, those individuals with still better language abilities would have a huge selective advantage over the others.

Summary

- *Language productivity.* Human languages enable us to create new words and phrases to express new ideas. (page 279)
- *Language training in nonhumans.* Bonobos, and to a smaller extent other species, have learned certain aspects of language. Human evolution evidently elaborated on potentials found in our apelike ancestors but developed that potential further. (page 279)
- *Language and intelligence.* It is possible to have intelligence without language or language without other aspects of intelligence. Therefore, many psychologists regard language as a specialized capacity, not just a byproduct of overall intelligence. (page 281)
- *Predisposition to learn language.* Noam Chomsky and others have argued that the ease with which children acquire language indicates that they are born with a predisposition that facilitates language. (page 281)
- *Brain organization and aphasia.* Brain damage, especially in the left hemisphere, impairs people's ability to understand or use language. Many brain areas contribute to language in varied ways. (page 282)
- *Stages of language development.* Children advance through several stages of language devel- opment, reflecting maturation of brain structures. From the start, children's language is creative, using the rules of language to make new word combinations and sentences. (page 283)
- *Children exposed to no language or two.* If deaf children are not exposed to language, they invent a sign language of their own. However, a deaf child who learns neither spoken language nor sign language in childhood is impaired in learning any language later. Children in a bilingual environment sometimes have trouble keeping the two languages separate but gain increased ability to control and shift attention. (page 284)
- *Understanding language.* We understand ambiguous words and sentences in context by applying the knowledge we have about the world in general. (page 285)
- *Limits to our language understanding.* Many sentences are difficult to understand, especially those with embedded clauses or more than one negative. (page 286)
- *Reading.* When we read, we alternate between fixation periods and saccadic eye movements. An average adult reads about 11 letters per fixation. (page 286)

Key Terms

bilingual (page 284)

Broca's aphasia (page 282)

fixation (page 289)

language acquisition device (page 281)

morpheme (page 286)

phoneme (page 286)

productivity (page 279)

saccade (page 289)

transformational grammar (page 279)

Wernicke's aphasia (page 282)

Williams syndrome (page 281)

word-superiority effect (page 288)

exploration and study

Access an interactive eBook and chapter-specific learning tools, including
- **flashcards**
- **quizzes**
- **videos**

and more, in your Psychology CourseMate. Go to **CengageBrain.com.**

If your professor has assigned Aplia:
1. Sign in to your account.
2. Complete the corresponding exercises as required by your professor.
3. When finished, click "Grade It Now" to see which areas you have mastered, which areas need more work, and detailed explanations of every answer.

Brakefield / The Image Works

nio Mo/Jupiter Images

Intelligence

Alan Turing, a famous mathematician and pioneer in computer science, bicycled to and from work each day. Occasionally, the chain fell off his bicycle, and he had to replace it. Turing kept records and noticed that the chain fell off at regular intervals, after exactly a certain number of turns of the front wheel. He calculated that this number was the product of the number of spokes in the front wheel times the number of links in the chain times the number of cogs in the pedal. He deduced that the chain came loose whenever a particular link in the chain came in contact with a particular bent spoke on the wheel. He identified that spoke, repaired it, and had no more trouble with his bicycle (I. Stewart, 1987).

To repair a bicycle, you could use general problem-solving skills or specific expertise about bicycles. Either approach shows a kind of intelligence.

Turing's solution to his problem is impressive, but hold your applause. Your local bicycle mechanic could have solved the problem without using mathematics at all. So, you might ask, what's the point? Was Turing unintelligent? Of course not. The point is that intelligence includes both the ability to solve unfamiliar problems, as Turing showed, and practiced skills, such as those of a bicycle mechanic.

The goal of the last three chapters was to understand learning, memory, and cognition. The emphasis was on theoretical concerns first and practical applications second. Here, the emphasis shifts. Although the study of intelligence certainly raises important theoretical issues, the study of intelligence traditionally has been guided by the practical concern of measuring individual differences and predicting outcomes in school.

Intelligence and Intelligence Tests

- What do we mean by "intelligence"?
- Is there more than one kind of intelligence?

Is there intelligent life in outer space? For decades, people have pointed huge arrays of dishes toward the stars, hoping to detect signals from alien civilizations. If we did intercept signals, would we make any sense of them? The enterprise assumes that intelligent life in outer space would resemble us enough to let us communicate with them. It is a remarkable assumption, considering that our communication with dolphins here on Earth is limited to such superficialities as "take the ball to the hoop."

Defining Intelligence

What is intelligence? Let's analyze that question before we try to answer it. If we ask what is gravity or what is magnetism, there can be only one correct answer. But if we ask what is beauty, that's different. Beauty is in the eye of the beholder, and if you think something is beautiful, no one can say you are wrong. Is intelligence a "real" thing like gravity, with only one correct definition, or is it a subjective evaluation, like beauty? Or is it something in between?

Precisely defining intelligence is not easy. Here are some attempts (Kanazawa, 2004; Sternberg, 1997; Wolman, 1989):

- The mental abilities that enable one to adapt to, shape, or select one's environment.
- The ability to deal with novel situations.
- The ability to judge, comprehend, and reason.
- The ability to understand and deal with people, objects, and symbols.
- The ability to act purposefully, think rationally, and deal effectively with the environment.

None of these definitions is fully satisfactory. Note the use of ill-defined terms such as *judge, comprehend, understand,* and *think rationally.*

It would be nice if we could say that psychologists first analyzed learning, memory, and cognition and then built upon that knowledge to understand intelligence. In fact, psychological researchers began with tests of intellectual abilities, defined as the ability to do well in school. Then they conducted research to find out what the tests measure. It may strike you as odd to try to measure something before being sure what it is. However, to learn what something is, one needs research, and any good research starts with measurement.

Spearman's Psychometric Approach and the g Factor

One of the earliest research programs in psychology was Charles Spearman's (1904) **psychometric approach** to intelligence, based on *the measurement of individual differences in performance.* Spearman measured how well many people performed tasks such as following directions, judging musical pitch, matching colors, and doing arithmetic. He found that performance on any of his tasks correlated positively with performance on any of the others. Spearman therefore inferred that all the tasks have something in common. To perform well on any test of mental ability, Spearman argued, people need a *"general" ability,* which he called g. The symbol g is always italicized and lowercase, like the mathematical terms e (the base of natural logarithms) and i (the square root of –1).

To account for the fact that performances on various tasks do not correlate perfectly, Spearman suggested that each task also requires a *"specific" ability,* s (Figure 9.1). Thus, intelligence consists of a general ability plus an unknown number of specific abilities, such as mechanical, musical, arithmetical, logical, and spatial abilities. Spearman called his theory a "monarchic" theory of intelligence because it included a dominant ability, or monarch (g), that ruled over the lesser abilities.

Later researchers confirmed that scores on virtually all kinds of cognitive tests correlate positively with one another within almost any popula-

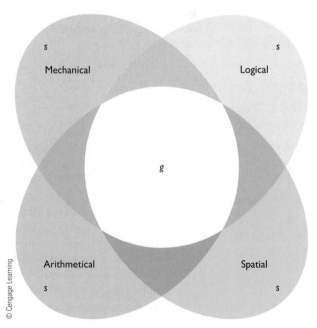

© Cengage Learning

Figure 9.1 According to Spearman (1904), all intelligent abilities have an area of overlap, which he called g (for "general"). Each ability also depends on an s (for "specific") factor.

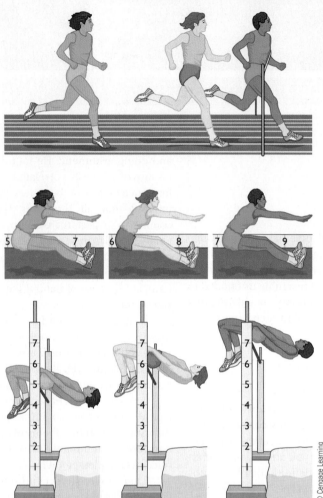

Figure 9.2 Measurements of sprinting, high jumping, and long jumping correlate with one another because they all depend on the same leg muscles. Similarly, the *g* factor that emerges in IQ testing could reflect a single ability.

© Cengage Learning

Possible Explanations for *g*

Why do people who perform well on one type of test perform well on others also? The simplest interpretation is that all the tasks measure a single underlying ability. Consider an analogy with the tasks shown in Figure 9.2: Most people who excel at running a 100-meter race also do well at the high jump and the long jump. They have to, because all three events depend on the same leg muscles.

Similarly, people might perform well on a variety of intellectual tests because all the tests depend on one underlying skill. If so, what might that skill be? One possibility is working memory (e.g., Martínez & Colom, 2009). For almost any intellectual task, holding information in memory is important, as is the ability to shift attention. Another possibility is speed of processing information (Coyle, Pillow, Snyder, & Kochunov, 2011). For people as for computers, processing information quickly makes it possible to complete more complicated tasks.

An alternative explanation for *g* is that several types of intelligence correlate because they grow in the same ways (Petrill, Luo, Thompson, & Detterman, 1996). By analogy, consider the lengths of three body parts—the left leg, the right arm, and the left index finger: As a rule, most people with a long left leg also have a long right arm and a long left index finger, because the factors that increase the growth of one also help the others grow—factors such as genes, health, and nutrition. Similarly, all forms of intelligence depend on genes, health, nutrition, and education. Most people who have good support for developing one intellectual skill also have good support for developing others.

Which of these examples applies to intelligence? Do the various intellectual skills correlate with one another because they all measure a single underlying ability (as do running and jumping, which require good leg muscles) or because they all grow together (as do your arms, legs, and fingers)? To some extent, both hypotheses are probably correct. Most intellectual tasks require attention, working memory, and speed. Also, independent brain functions correlate with one another because factors that promote good development of one area promote good development of all.

tion (W. Johnson, Bouchard, Krueger, McGue, & Gottesman, 2004; W. Johnson, te Nijenhuis, & Bouchard, 2008). You have probably noticed this trend yourself: A student who does well in one course generally does well in others also. Only under special conditions do most of the individuals who perform well on one test score below average on another. For example, in one study, rural Kenyan children who did well on an academic test did poorly on a test of knowledge about traditional herbal medicines, and those who did well on the test of herbal medicines did poorly on the academic test (Sternberg et al., 2001). Presumably, the two groups of children had been exposed to different experiences.

concept check

1. What evidence did Spearman have in favor of the concept of *g*?

2. You read about two explanations for *g*. What would each of them predict about whether something could impair intelligence in one way and spare it in another?

1. Scores on many different kinds of tests correlate positively with one another.

2. If all intelligent abilities depend on a single underlying factor, then it is hard to imagine impairing one but sparing another. For analogy, an injury that impairs running would also impair jumping. However, if intelligent abilities correlate because they usually grow together, we can imagine something that impairs one much more than others—as in the case of Williams syndrome (discussed in chapter 8). For analogy, amputating a finger does not harm the legs.

3. Turing's solution reflected fluid intelligence, a generalized ability that could apply to any topic. The solution provided by a bicycle mechanic reflected crystallized intelligence, an ability developed in a particular area of experience.

Hierarchical Models of Intelligence

Although Spearman and most later researchers have regarded *g* as the key to intelligence, it does not account for everything. Spearman suggested the existence of specific (*s*) factors, but the task fell on other psychologists to try to describe these *s* factors.

Raymond Cattell (1987) drew a distinction between fluid intelligence and crystallized intelligence. The analogy is to water: Fluid water fits into any shape of container, but an ice crystal has a fixed shape. Fluid intelligence is *the power of reasoning and using information.* It includes the ability to perceive relationships, solve unfamiliar problems, and gain new knowledge. Crystallized intelligence consists of *acquired skills and knowledge and the ability to apply that knowledge in specific situations.* Fluid intelligence enables you to learn new skills in a new job, whereas crystallized intelligence includes the job skills you have already acquired. The ability to learn new words is an example of fluid intelligence, and the words already learned are part of your crystallized intelligence. Expertise, as discussed in chapter 8, is crystallized intelligence.

Fluid intelligence reaches its peak before age 20, remains nearly steady for decades, and declines on average in old age, more in some people than others (Horn, 1968). Crystallized intelligence, however, increases over age (Cattell, 1987; Horn & Donaldson, 1976). A 20-year-old may be more successful at solving a new, unfamiliar problem, but a 65-year-old excels on problems in his or her area of specialization. The distinction between fluid and crystallized intelligence is sharper in theory than in practice. Any task taps both crystallized and fluid intelligence to some extent.

Other researchers have described intelligence in terms of a hierarchy with three major aspects: verbal processing (language), perceptual processing (dealing with vision and hearing), and image rotation (spatial relationships). Each of these major abilities could be subdivided further (W. Johnson & Bouchard, 2005).

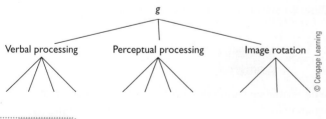

concept check

3. Was Alan Turing's solution to the slipping bicycle chain, from the introduction to this chapter, an example of fluid or crystallized intelligence? Was the solution provided by a bicycle mechanic fluid or crystallized intelligence?

Gardner's Theory of Multiple Intelligences

Certain critics propose to dispense with, or at least deemphasize, the concept of *g*. According to Howard Gardner (1985, 1999), if we could test intellectual abilities in pure form, we might find multiple intelligences—*unrelated forms of intelligence*, consisting of language, musical abilities, logical and mathematical reasoning, spatial reasoning, ability to recognize and classify objects, body movement skills, self-control and self-understanding, and sensitivity to other people's social signals. Gardner argues that people can be outstanding in one type of intelligence but not others. For example, an athlete can excel at body movement skills but lack musical abilities. Someone who seems intelligent in one way may be mediocre or worse in another because different skills require not only different kinds of practice but also, perhaps, different brain specializations.

Gardner makes the important point that each person has different skills. The question is whether those skills represent different types of intelligence. To defend Gardner's position, someone would have to demonstrate that the various intellectual skills are not strongly correlated with one another. However, each of Gardner's proposed types of intelligence correlates positively with the others, except for body movement skills and possibly music (Visser, Ashton, & Vernon, 2006). Therefore, it would seem that language, logic, spatial reasoning, and all the others are simply different manifestations of *g*. Gardner's idea is that these abilities would stop correlating so strongly if we could measure them in pure form, without the contribution of language. Perhaps so, but no one knows how to measure these abilities in pure form. Gardner's theory is an appealing idea without solid evidence to support it.

Parallel to the claim of multiple intelligences, many educators have embraced the concept that people vary in their learning styles. According to this view, some people are visual learners, others are verbal learners, and others learn in other ways. If so, in a classroom using a highly visual style of instruction, one group of students would learn best, and in a classroom with a highly verbal style of instruction, a different group of students would learn best. In fact, almost no evidence supports this prediction,

According to Howard Gardner, we have many intelligences, including mathematical ability, artistic skill, muscle skills, and musical abilities.

and much evidence opposes it (Pashler, McDaniel, Rohrer, & Bjork, 2008)—with the obvious exception that blind children don't learn from visual presentations and deaf children don't learn from spoken presentations. The idea of learning styles became popular without any research basis.

4. What evidence would we need to determine whether music, mathematics, social sensitivity, and so forth are really different kinds of intelligence or just different aspects of a single type of intelligence?

Answer

4. We would need to determine whether ability at each kind of intelligence correlates highly with each others. If they correlate highly, they are simply different aspects of *g*. If they do not, and if the differences reflect more than just different amounts of practice at different skills, then they are separate kinds of intelligence.

Sternberg's Triarchic Theory of Intelligence

Spearman's concept of intelligence has been called "monarchic" because it proposes *g* as a "monarch" that rules over the more specialized abilities. Robert Sternberg (1985) attempted to go beyond this view by proposing a triarchic theory that deals with *three aspects of intelligence: (a) cognitive processes, (b) identifying situations that require intelligence, and (c) using intelligence in practical ways.* He sug-

gested that when solving problems we go through stages that include encoding the information, drawing inferences, mapping relationships, and applying the knowledge. If so, it might make sense for intelligence tests to measure each process separately. However, when Sternberg tried to develop tests of encoding, inferring, and mapping, all his measures correlated fairly highly with one another (Deary, 2002). In other words, he rediscovered *g*.

Sternberg then explored possible distinctions among types of intelligence. He argued that we have at least three types of intelligence: *analytical* (thinking critically), *creative* (developing new ideas), and *practical* (doing something). Sternberg tried to develop new tests that tap all three aspects. He and his colleagues argued that their tests of creative and practical intelligence are better predictors of intelligence in everyday life than are standard IQ tests (Sternberg, 2002). However, many other researchers remain unconvinced, arguing as follows (Brody, 2003; Gottfredson, 2003; Koke & Vernon, 2003):

- Sternberg has overstated the success of his tests at predicting performance.
- The tests that claim to measure analytical, creative, and practical intelligence produce scores that correlate highly with one another, and with the scores on more standard IQ tests, so it is not clear that they are measuring different processes. Sternberg apparently rediscovered *g* one more time.
- The analytical scores (similar to standard IQ tests) predict people's creative and practical behaviors about as well as scores on the creative and practical tests do. Evidently, what are claimed to be three different kinds of tests seem to be measuring the same processes.

Table 9.1 summarizes four theories of intelligence.

5. What evidence would demonstrate the existence of an intellectual ability separate from *g*?

Answer

5. Measurements of this ability would predict some type of intelligent behavior, but would have a low correlation with all the tests that measure *g*.

Table 9.1 Four Theories of Intelligence

Theory	Theorist	Key Ideas and Terms
Psychometric approach	Charles Spearman	g factor: general reasoning ability s factor: specific ability required for a given task
Fluid and crystallized intelligence	Raymond Cattell	Fluid intelligence: solving unfamiliar problems Crystallized intelligence: highly practiced skills
Multiple intelligences	Howard Gardner	Music, social attentiveness, dancing, mathematics, and all other skills that society values
Triarchic theory	Robert Sternberg	Analytical, creative, and practical intelligence

© Cengage Learning

IQ Tests

We have been discussing intelligence and IQ tests in general, and the idea of IQ tests is no doubt familiar to you. However, the time has come to consider examples in more detail.

Let's start with this analogy: You have just been put in charge of choosing the members of your country's next Olympic team. However, the Olympic rules have been changed: Each country will send only 30 men and 30 women, and each athlete must compete in every event. The Olympic committee will not describe those events until all the athletes have been chosen. Clearly, you cannot hold the usual kind of tryouts, but neither will you choose people at random. How will you proceed?

Your best bet would be to devise a test of "general athletic ability." You might measure the abilities of applicants to run, jump, change direction, maintain balance, throw and catch, kick, lift weights, respond rapidly to signals, and perform other athletic feats. You would choose the applicants with the best scores.

No doubt, your test would be imperfect. But if you want your team to do well, you need some way to measure athletic ability. Later, other people begin to use your test also. Does its wide acceptance mean that athletic ability is a single quantity? Of course not. You found it useful to act as if it were a single quantity, but you know that most great basketball players are not great swimmers or gymnasts.

Intelligence tests resemble this imaginary test of athletic ability. If you were in charge of choosing which applicants a college should admit, you would want to select those who will be the best students. Because students will study subjects that they have not studied before, it makes sense to measure a range of academic skills, not knowledge of a single topic. That is, you want a test of aptitude (*ability to learn, or fluid intelligence*) rather than achievement (*what someone has already learned, or crystallized intelligence*). Aptitude and achievement are hard to separate. Aptitude leads to achievement, and past achievement increases future ability to learn. Still, we make an effort to separate the two.

The original goal of intelligence tests was to identify the *least* capable children, who could not learn from ordinary schooling. Later tests were also used to identify the best students, who would profit from accelerated classes. Similar tests are used for selecting among applicants to colleges and professional schools. Grades are useful, too, but grading standards vary from one school to another and from one teacher to another. Objective tests help compare students from different schools and classes.

Intelligence quotient (IQ) tests try to *predict someone's performance in school and similar settings.* The term *quotient* dates from when IQ was determined by dividing mental age by chronological age and then multiplying by 100. Mental age is *the average age of children who perform as well as this child.* Chronological age is time since birth. For example, an 8-year-old who performs like an average 10-year-old has a mental age of 10, a chronological age of 8, and an IQ of $10 \div 8 \times 100 = 125$. That method is now obsolete, but the term remains.

Two French psychologists, Alfred Binet and Theophile Simon (1905), devised the first IQ tests. The French Ministry of Public Instruction wanted a fair way to identify children who had such serious intellectual deficiencies that they should not be placed in the same classes with other students. The school system wanted an impartial test instead of leaving the decision to someone's opinion. Binet and Simon's test measured the skills that children need for success in school, such as counting, remembering, following instructions, and understanding language.

Their test and others like it make reasonably accurate predictions. But suppose a test correctly predicts that one student will perform better than another in school. Can we then say that the first student did better because of a higher IQ score? No, an IQ is a measurement, not an explanation. A child doesn't do poorly *because of* a low IQ score any more than a basketball player misses a shot because of a low shooting average.

The Stanford-Binet Test

The test that Binet and Simon designed was later modified for English speakers by Stanford psychologists and published as the Stanford-Binet IQ test. The test's items are designated by age (Table 9.2). An item designated as "age 8," for example, will be answered correctly by 60 to 90% of 8-year-olds. (A higher percentage of older children answer it correctly and a lower percentage of younger children.) A child who answers correctly most of the age 8 items, but not the age 9 items, has a mental age of 8.

School psychologists are carefully trained on how to administer the test items and score the answers. A psychologist testing an 8-year-old might start with the items designated for 7-year-olds. Unless the child misses many of the 7-year-old items, the psychologist gives credit for all the 6-year-old items without testing them. If the child answers most of the 7-year-old items correctly, the psychologist proceeds to the items for 8-year-olds, 9-year-olds, and so forth, until the child begins to miss most items. At that point, the psychologist ends the test. This method is known as *adaptive testing*. Individuals proceed at their own pace, usually finishing in somewhat over an hour (V. W. McCall, Yates, Hendricks, Turner, & McNabb, 1989).

Stanford-Binet IQ scores are computed from tables set up to ensure that a given IQ score means the same at different ages. The mean IQ at each age is 100. A 6-year-old with an IQ score of, say, 116 has performed better on the test than 84% of other 6-year-olds. Similarly, an adult with an IQ score of 116 has performed better than 84% of other adults. The Stanford-Binet provides subscores reflecting visual reasoning, short-term memory, and other specialized skills (Daniel, 1997; V. W. McCall et al., 1989).

The Wechsler Tests

IQ tests originally devised by David Wechsler, and later modified by others, known as the Wechsler Adult Intelligence Scale–Fourth Edition (WAIS–IV) and the Wechsler Intelligence Scale for Children–Fourth Edition (WISC–IV), produce the same average, 100, and almost the same distribution of scores as the Stanford-Binet. The WISC is for children up to age 16, and the WAIS is for everyone older. As with the Stanford-Binet, the Wechsler tests are administered to one person at a time. The Stanford-Binet and Wechsler tests are the most widely used IQ tests.

A Wechsler test provides an overall score and four major subscores. One is the Verbal Comprehension Index, based on such items as "Define the word *letter*" and "How are a peach and a plum similar?" A second part, the Perceptual Reasoning Index, calls for nonverbal answers, such as arranging blocks to match a pattern (Figure 9.3).

A third part of the Wechsler tests, the Working Memory Index, includes such items as "Listen to these numbers and then repeat them: 3 6 2 5" and "Listen to these numbers and repeat them in reverse order: 4 7 6." In the fourth part, Processing Speed, an example is "Put a slash (/) through all the circles on this page and an X through all the squares, as quickly as possible."

$$\triangle \quad \bigcirc \quad \square \quad \square \quad \bigcirc \quad \triangle \quad \square \quad \square \quad \bigcirc$$

Each part of the WISC–IV or the WAIS–III begins with simple questions and progresses to more difficult ones. The subscores call attention to someone's strengths and weaknesses. For example, a child who learned English as a second language might do poorly on the Verbal Comprehension Index but much better on Perceptual Reasoning and Processing Speed, which call for nonverbal answers. People with certain disabilities perform slowly on the Processing Speed tasks but do well on other parts of the test.

Culture-Reduced Testing

If you learned English as a second language, or if you are hearing impaired, your score on the Stanford-Binet or Wechsler IQ test might badly underestimate your abilities. "Why not translate the tests into other languages, including sign language?" you might ask. Psychologists do, but a translated item may be easier or

---

Table 9.2 Examples of the Types of Items on the Stanford-Binet Test

Age	Sample Test Item
2	Test administrator points at pictures of everyday objects and asks, "What is this?" "Here are some pegs of different sizes and shapes. See whether you can put each one into the correct hole."
4	"Why do people live in houses?" "Birds fly in the air; fish swim in the ___."
6	"Here is a picture of a horse. Do you see what part of the horse is missing?" "Here are some candies. Can you count how many there are?"
8	"What should you do if you find a lost puppy?" "Stephanie can't write today because she twisted her ankle. What is wrong with that?"
10	"Why should people be quiet in a library?" "Repeat after me: 4 8 3 7 1 4."
12	"What does regret mean?" "Here is a picture. Can you tell me what is wrong with it?"
14	"What is the similarity between high and low?" "Watch me fold this paper and cut it. Now, when I unfold it, how many holes will there be?"
Adult	"Make up a sentence using the words *celebrate*, *reverse*, and *appointment*." "What do people mean when they say, 'People who live in glass houses should not throw stones'"?

Source: Modified from Nietzel and Bernstein, 1987.

Figure 9.3 Most IQ tests are administered individually. Here, a psychologist (left) records the responses by a participant (right).

harder than the original. For example, one part of the Stanford-Binet presents words and asks for other words that rhyme with them. Generating rhymes is moderately easy in English, easier in Italian, but almost impossible in Zulu (M. W. Smith, 1974). Other items may refer to information that is familiar in one culture and unfamiliar in another.

Psychologists have tried to devise a culture-fair or culture-reduced test. Although no task is free of cultural influences, some tests are fairer than others. *The most widely used culture-reduced test* is the **Progressive Matrices** test devised by John C. Raven. These matrices, which *progress* gradually from easy to difficult items, attempt to measure abstract reasoning (fluid intelligence) without any use of language or reference to factual information. To answer questions on the Progressive Matrices, someone must generate hypotheses, test them, and infer rules. Figure 9.4 presents three matrices similar to those on this test. The first is relatively easy, the second is harder, and the third is harder still.

How culture-fair is the Progressive Matrices test? It requires less information than the Wechsler or Stanford-Binet tests, but it does assume familiarity with pencil-and-paper, multiple-choice tests. No test can be totally free from cultural influences, but this comes closer than most. A disadvantage is that this

test provides only a single score instead of identifying someone's strengths and weaknesses.

concept check

6. What is one advantage of the Wechsler IQ tests over Raven's Progressive Matrices? What is an advantage of the Progressive Matrices?

Answer

6. The Wechsler tests provide separate scores for different tasks and therefore identify someone's strengths and weaknesses. Raven's Progressive Matrices are fairer for someone who is not a native speaker of English.

Individual Differences in IQ Scores

Why do some people score higher than others on IQ tests? The British scholar Francis Galton (1869/1978)[1] was the first to argue for the importance of heredity.

[1] Remember, a slash like this indicates original publication date and the date of a revised printing. It does not represent Galton's birth and death dates, which were 1822–1911.

Most first-generation immigrants do not score highly on English-language intelligence tests. As a rule, their children and grandchildren get higher scores.

Figure 9.4 Items similar to those on Raven's Progressive Matrices test. Select the item that completes the pattern both going across and going down. (You can check your answers against answer A on page 305.)

His evidence was that politicians, judges, and other eminent and distinguished people generally had distinguished relatives. You can quickly see why this evidence does not justify a conclusion about genetics. Let's consider the better evidence we have today.

Family Resemblances

Table 9.3, based on an extensive literature review (Plomin, DeFries, McClearn, & McGuffin, 2001), shows the correlations of IQ scores for people with various degrees of genetic relationship. These data are based mostly on European or American families.

The scores of monozygotic ("identical") twins correlate with each other about .85, significantly higher than dizygotic twins or nontwin siblings (Bishop et al., 2003; McGue & Bouchard, 1998). Monozygotic twins also closely resemble each other in brain volume (Posthuma et al., 2002) and in specific skills such as working memory, attention, reading, mathematics, and foreign language learning (Dale, Harlaar, Haworth, & Plomin, 2010; Koten et al., 2009; Kovas, Haworth, Dale, & Plomin, 2007; Luciano et al., 2001). The greater similarity between monozygotic than dizygotic twins implies a genetic basis. In Table 9.3, note the high correlation between monozygotic twins reared apart. That is, they strongly resemble each other on IQ tests even if they are adopted by separate sets of parents (Bouchard & McGue, 1981; Farber, 1981).

Monozygotic twins continue to resemble each other throughout life, even beyond age 80 (Petrill et al., 1998). In fact, the difference between monozygotic and dizygotic twins increases with age, indicating that the influence of genes is greater in older than in younger individuals (Davis, Haworth, & Plomin, 2009; Lyons et al., 2009). Why might that be? One reason is that older individuals have more control of their environment. Those who start with an intellectual advantage gravitate toward activities that sustain and increase that advantage. This is an example of the multiplier effect from chapter 3: Slightly better than average performance early in life, perhaps genetically based, leads to encouragement and support that leads to still better performance (Dickens & Flynn, 2001).

A limitation in all this research is that most twin studies rely on data from middle-class families. Studies of impoverished families find much less evidence for a genetic influence. That is, monozygotic twins in those families resemble each other only a little more than dizygotic twins do (Tucker-Drob, Rhemtulla, Harden, Turkheimer, & Fask, 2011; Turkheimer, Haley, Waldron, D'Onofrio, & Gottesman, 2003). The probable meaning is this: For children living in a terrible environment, the chance for intellectual development is limited, regardless of their genes. For

Table 9.3 Mean correlations for the IQs of children with various degrees of genetic and environmental similarity

Degree of Genetic or Environmental Similarity	Correlation of IQ Scores
Parent and child	0.41
Sibling	0.47
Parent & biological child who is adopted by another family	0.23
Biological siblings who are adopted in separate families	0.23
Adoptive parent & adopted child	0.19
Unrelated children adopted in the same family	0.31
Monozygotic twins adopted in separate families	0.78
Monozygotic twins reared together	0.85
Dizygotic twins reared together	0.6

(Adapted from Plomin et al., 2001.)

those in a satisfactory environment, genetic differences have more impact. Similarly, the influence of genetics is weak if the quality of teaching is poor. None of the children do well when the teaching is poor, regardless of genetics. With better teaching, some children advance faster than others (Taylor, Roehrig, Hensler, Connor, & Schatschneider, 2010).

Twins and Single Births

Notice in Table 9.3 that dizygotic twins resemble each other more closely than single-birth siblings do. This finding suggests an influence from being born at the same time and therefore sharing more of the environment. In support of this conclusion, researchers have found a higher correlation between the IQs of brothers born within a couple of years of each other than those born further apart (Sundet, Eriksen, & Tambs, 2008).

Adopted Children

In Table 9.3, note the correlation between unrelated children adopted into the same family, indicating an influence from shared environment (Plomin et al., 2001; Segal, 2000). However, this correlation is lower than the correlation between biological brothers or sisters. The IQs of young adopted children correlate moderately with those of their adoptive parents. As the children grow older, their IQ scores gradually correlate more with those of their biological parents and less with those of their adoptive parents (Loehlin, Horn, & Willerman, 1989; Plomin et al., 2001; Figure 9.5).

These results imply a genetic influence from the biological parents, but another interpretation is possible. Some low-IQ parents who put their children up for adoption are impoverished and probably do not provide good prenatal care. The mother may have poor nutrition, may smoke and drink, or may in other ways put her infant at risk for reasons other than genetics. Poor prenatal care correlates with decreased IQ for the offspring throughout life (Breslau, Dickens, Flynn, Peterson, & Lucia, 2006). In short, adopted children can resemble their biological parents for nongenetic reasons.

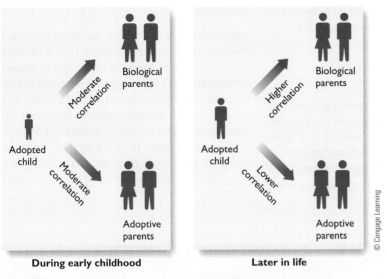

During early childhood   **Later in life**

Figure 9.5 As adopted children grow older, their IQs begin to correlate more strongly with those of their biological parents.

Gene Identification

The Human Genome Project and related research now make it possible to identify particular genes that promote intelligence. The strategy is to locate genes that are more common among those with higher IQ scores than those with lower scores. Similar research has been done with laboratory animals, comparing fast learners to slow learners. Dozens of genes have been found to correlate with human performance, and dozens have been found in mice, some of them the same genes that were identified in humans. However, the research so far suggests a great many genes with small effects rather than one or two with large effects (Deary, Penke, & Johnson, 2010). The task now is to learn more about *how* various genes contribute.

The heritability of variations in IQ scores does not mean that genes dictate people's intellectual accomplishments. Certainly, if we gave every child either an extremely good or extremely bad environment, we could raise or lower ev-

eryone's IQ scores. Genes have an influence, but it is possible to modify that influence to a large extent.

Environmental Influences and Interventions

When we think about environmental influences on intelligence, we might think first about how often parents read to their children, take them to museums, and so forth. Those factors can certainly be important, but other environmental influences deserve attention. In particular, much research emphasizes the role of physical health early in life. Researchers have compared mean IQ scores across countries and across states within the United States. We need to be cautious here, as scores are not always comparable among countries speaking different languages. Still, the finding is that mean IQ is consistently lowest in the countries and states where children have the highest exposure to infectious diseases, such as tetanus, malaria, tuberculosis, hepatitis, cholera, and measles (Eppig, Fincher, & Thornhill, 2010, 2011). Fighting disease takes much of the body's energy, and building a brain does also. IQ scores correlate more strongly with infectious disease than with family wealth or quality of education. However, these results come from correlations, and as always we should beware of assuming cause and effect. Figure 9.6 shows the results across countries.

To what extent can we help low-performing children? A variety of programs have attempted to take children from extremely deprived homes and give them special interventions to foster their intellectual development. People who hoped that brief interventions might lead to long-term gains have been disappointed. Just as no one gene produces a huge effect, no single environmental intervention does either. However, intensive programs occupying many hours per week for several years do produce significant, lasting benefits (Barnett, 2011; Reynolds, Temple, Ou, Arteaga, & White, 2011).

An interesting intervention is music lessons. In one study, 6-year-olds who were randomly assigned to receive music lessons showed a gain of 1 to 2 IQ points, on average, compared to other children (Schellenberg, 2004). Additional research indicates that children with music training show IQ advantages beyond what we can explain in terms of parental income and education (Schellenberg, 2006).

Interventions work best if they start early. Some orphanages provide a particularly deprived environment, including poor nutrition and minimal intellectual stimulation. Most children who remain in the orphanages perform poorly on tests and in school. Those who leave the orphanages and enter adoptive families show clear improvement, with the greatest improvement evident among children adopted be-

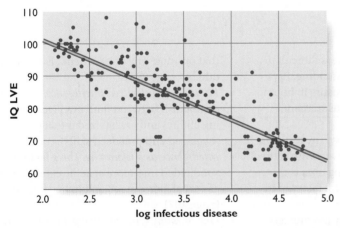

Figure 9.6 Each dot represents the results for one country. Along the *x*-axis is the degree of exposure to infectious disease. Along the *y*-axis is the mean IQ score. The correlation was –.82. (Figure 1 part (a) from Eppig, C., Fincher, C. L., & Thornhill, R., "Parasite prevalence and the worldwide distribution of cognitive ability," *Proceedings of the Royal Society B*, 277, 3801-3808. Copyright © 2010 by the Royal Society. Reprinted with permission.)

fore age 6 months (Beckett et al., 2006; Nelson et al., 2007; van IJzendoorn, Juffer, & Poelhuis, 2005).

concept check

7. What types of evidence support a genetic contribution to individual differences in IQ scores?

8. What evidence suggests an influence of infectious diseases on intellectual development?

9. Under what circumstances do environmental interventions most strongly influence intellectual development?

Answers

7. One type of evidence is that monozygotic twins resemble each other in IQ more than dizygotic twins do. A second type of evidence is that IQs of adopted children correlate significantly with those of their biological parents.

8. The mean IQ score is lowest in those countries and states where children have the highest exposure to infectious diseases.

9. Environmental interventions are most effective if they start early, preferably before age 6 months.

module 9.1

In Closing

Measuring Something We Don't Fully Understand

The standard IQ tests were devised by trial and error long before most of the discoveries about memory and cognition that we discussed in the last two chapters. We still do not understand intelligence very well. Can we measure intelligence without understanding it? Possibly so; physicists measured gravity and magnetism long before they understood them theoretically. Maybe psychologists can do the same with intelligence.

Or maybe not. Measuring a poorly understood phenomenon is risky. Many psychologists who are dissatisfied with the current tests are striving toward better ones. Producing an improved IQ test is not as easy as it may sound.

In the meantime, the current tests have both strengths and weaknesses. An IQ test, like any other tool, can be used in constructive or destructive ways. The next module explores ways of evaluating IQ tests.

Summary

- *Defining intelligence.* Intelligence is difficult to define, given our current understanding. Psychological researchers try to measure it, hoping to learn something from the measurements. (page 295)
- *g factor.* People's scores on almost any test of intelligent abilities correlate positively with scores on other tests. The overlap among tests is referred to as *g*, meaning the general factor in intelligence. (page 295)
- *Possible explanations for* g. Many psychologists believe the *g* factor corresponds to an ability that underlies all kinds of intelligence, such as mental speed or working memory. Another possibility is that different abilities correlate with one another because the same growth factors

that promote any one of them also support the others. (page 296)
- *Fluid and crystallized intelligence.* Psychologists distinguish between fluid intelligence (reasoning ability) and crystallized intelligence (acquired and practiced skills). (page 297)
- *Intelligence as a hierarchy.* The *g* factor can be subdivided into more specific categories, such as verbal, perceptual, and image rotation. (page 297)
- *One or many types of intelligence?* Howard Gardner argued that people have many independent types of intelligence, including social attentiveness, musical abilities, and motor skills. However, so far, no one has demonstrated that different types of intelligence are independent of one another. (page 297)

- *Triarchic theory.* According to Sternberg's triarchic theory, intelligence consists of analytical, creative, and practical abilities. Again, the issue is whether these constitute independent abilities or whether they are different manifestations of a single process, *g.* (page 298)
- *IQ tests.* The Stanford-Binet, Wechsler, and other IQ tests were devised to predict the level of performance in school. Culture-reduced tests such as Raven's Progressive Matrices can be used to test people who are unfamiliar with English. (page 299)
- *Hereditary influences.* Studies of twins and adopted children suggest hereditary influences on individual differences in IQ performance, although no one gene has a major effect. (page 301)
- *Environmental influences.* Intellectual development depends on many aspects of the environment, including physical health in early childhood. Extensive interventions can help children's intellectual development, if started early in life and continued for years. (page 303)

Key Terms

aptitude (page 299)

achievement (page 299)

crystallized intelligence (page 297)

fluid intelligence (page 297)

g (page 295)

intelligence quotient (IQ) tests (page 299)

mental age (page 299)

multiple intelligences (page 297)

Progressive Matrices (page 301)

psychometric approach (page 295)

s (page 295)

Stanford-Binet IQ test (page 299)

triarchic theory (page 298)

Wechsler Adult Intelligence Scale–Fourth Edition (WAIS–IV) (page 300)

Wechsler Intelligence Scale for Children–Fourth Edition (WISC–IV) (page 300)

Answers to Other Questions in the Module (page 301)

A. 1. (8); 2. (2); 3. (4) For item 3, going either across or down, add any parts that are different and subtract any parts that are the same.

Evaluation of Intelligence Tests

- How accurate, useful, and fair are IQ tests?
- Why do some people score higher than others?

Whatever exists at all exists in some amount.
—E. L. Thorndike (1918, p. 16)

Anything that exists in amount can be measured.
—W. A. McCall (1939, p. 15)

Anything which exists can be measured incorrectly.
—D. Detterman (1979, p. 167)

All three of these quotes apply to intelligence: If intelligence exists, it must exist in some amount. It must be measurable, but it can be measured incorrectly. Exactly how accurate, useful, and fair are the IQ tests? Because much is at stake here, the conclusions are often controversial.

The Standardization of IQ Tests

In the first module, we considered examples of IQ tests. To evaluate them or any other test, we need to rely on objective evidence. The evaluation begins with standardization, *the process of evaluating the questions, establishing rules for administering a test, and interpreting the scores.* One step in this process is to find the norms, *descriptions of how frequently various scores occur.* Psychologists try to standardize a test on a large sample of people who are as representative as possible of the population.

You may sometimes hear someone use the term *standardized test* in a way that makes it sound threatening. The opposite of a standardized test is an unstandardized test, like nearly all the ones that professors give in class. Some of the questions might be confusing, and the test might be easier or harder than the professor intended. Standardizing a test improves it.

The Distribution of IQ Scores

Binet, Wechsler, and the others who devised IQ tests chose items and arranged the scoring method to establish a mean score of 100. The standard devia-

tion is 15 for the Wechsler test, and 16 for the Stanford-Binet. (As discussed in chapter 2, the standard deviation measures variance among individuals. The standard deviation is small if most scores are close to the mean and large if scores vary widely.) The scores for a large population approximate a *normal distribution*, or bell-shaped curve, as shown in Figure 9.7.

In a normal distribution, 68% of all people fall within 1 standard deviation above or below the mean, and about 95% are within 2 standard deviations. Someone with a score of 115 on the Wechsler test exceeds the scores of people within 1 standard deviation from the mean plus all of those more than 1 standard deviation below the mean—a total of 84%, as shown in Figure 9.7. We say that such a person is "in the 84th percentile." Someone with an IQ score of 130 is in the 98th percentile, with a score higher than those of 98% of others.

In fact, however, the actual distribution of IQ scores isn't as symmetrical as the theoretical normal distribution. The mode (most common score) is about 105 instead of 100, and more people have scores well below the mean than equally far above it, as shown in Figure 9.8 (W. Johnson, Carothers, & Deary, 2008).

The bulge at the lower end represents people with disabilities, described as mentally challenged. For example, people with Down syndrome *have a variety of physical and medical impairments as a result of having an extra copy of chromosome #21.* They have impairments in speech development, motor skills, memory, and cognition. However, some fare considerably better than others (Carr, 2008).

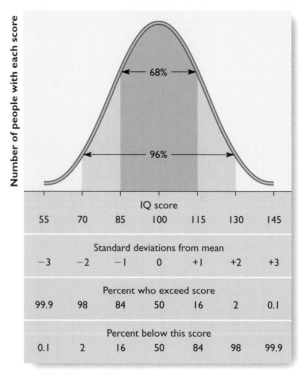

Figure 9.7 The curve shown here represents scores on the Wechsler IQ test, with a standard deviation of 15 (15 points above and below the mean, which is 100).

The term *mentally challenged* or *mentally disabled* refers to people more than two standard deviations below average, corresponding to an IQ score of 68 or 70, depending on the test. This cutoff is arbitrary, and a psychologist considers other observations of the person's level of functioning before making a diagnosis. In the United States, the Individuals with Disabilities Education Act requires public schools to provide "free and appropriate" education for all children regardless of their limitations. Children with mild physical or intellectual disabilities are mainstreamed as much as possible—that is, placed in the same classes as other children but with special consideration. On the plus side, children in mainstream classes develop better language abilities than those in classes limited to children with disabilities (Laws, Byrne, & Buckley, 2000). However, most children with disabilities have few friends, especially as they advance to the later grades (Hall & McGregor, 2000).

An IQ score of 130 or more is the "gifted" range. As with a diagnosis of disabled, a label of gifted requires a judgment based on other behaviors, not just a test score. Gifted children learn rapidly without much help, seek to master knowledge, ask deep questions, and develop new ideas (Winner, 2000). Many have trouble finding friends their own age with similar interests, and they spend much of their time alone.

Since the first IQ tests, psychologists have found that girls tend to do better than boys on certain kinds of language tasks, especially relating to verbal fluency, as well as certain memory tests. Boys tend to do better than girls on visuospatial rotations. On attention tasks, males more often focus on one item at a time whereas females spread their attention more broadly (W. Johnson & Bouchard, 2007). None of these differences are huge. However, by loading IQ tests with one type of item or another, test authors could have produced results favoring one gender or the other. Instead, they balanced various types of items to ensure that the mean scores of both females and males would be the same (Colom, Juan-Espinosa, Abad, & Garciá, 2000).

Males show greater individual variability. On several intellectual measures, more males than females appear at the extreme top and bottom of the range (Arden & Plomin, 2006; Hedges & Nowell, 1995). A study

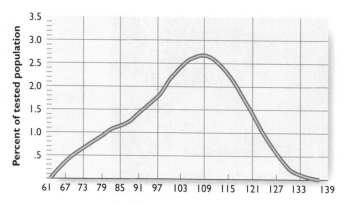

Figure 9.8 The actual distribution of scores is not quite symmetrical. The mode (most common score) is a bit higher than the mean, and more scores lie far below the mean than equally far above it. (From: Johnson, W., Carothers, A., & Deary, I. J., 2008. "Sex differences in variability in general intelligence." *Perspectives on Psychological Science* Vol. 3 (pp. 518-531). Copyright © 2008 Sage Publication, Inc. Reprinted with permission.)

of 41 countries found that males showed more variability than females in 35 countries on verbal scores and in 37 countries on math scores (Machin & Pekkarinen, 2008). However, this tendency is not huge. *Why* males are more variable we do not know.

The Flynn Effect

In 1920 the question "What is Mars?" was considered difficult, because most people knew little about the planets. Today, that question is easy. Researchers periodically restandardize tests to keep the overall difficulty about the same.

A person with Down syndrome.

Many children with low IQ scores can be mainstreamed in regular classes. Those with more severe disabilities are taught in special classes.

Those who restandardized the IQ tests eventually realized that they were consistently making the tests more difficult to keep the mean score from rising. That is, *decade by decade, generation by generation, people's raw scores on IQ tests have gradually increased, and test makers have had to make the tests harder to keep the mean score at 100.* This tendency is known as the Flynn effect, after James Flynn, who called attention to it (Flynn, 1984, 1999). The results vary across countries, tests, and periods of time, but a typical figure is about 3 IQ points per 10 years. If you took the same IQ test that your parents took at your age, then your score probably would be higher than theirs. If you took an IQ test from your grandparents' era, your score would be still higher.

One consequence of the Flynn effect is that if you take an IQ test and later take a restandardized form, your score will drop! You did not deteriorate, but you are being compared to a higher standard. For most people, a few points' change makes little difference, but for people at the low end of the distribution, the loss of a few points might qualify them for special services (Kanaya, Scullin, & Ceci, 2003).

The Flynn effect—increase in IQ scores over generations—has occurred across all ethnic groups (Raven, 2000), over many decades, and in every country for which we have data, including the United States, Canada, Europe, Australia, New Zealand, Israel, Turkey, Japan, Brazil, China, and rural Kenya (Daley, Whaley, Sigman, Espinosa, & Neumann, 2003; Flynn, 1998; Kagitcibasi & Biricik, 2011; Must, te Nijenhuis, Must, & van Vianen, 2009). However, the effect has been stronger at some times

than at others (Sundet, Eriksen, Borren, & Tambs, 2010). It was strong in the early and middle 1900s but it may have slowed or stopped since about 1990, at least in parts of Europe (Sundet, Barlaug, & Torjussen, 2004; Teasdale & Owen, 2005, 2008). The increase is greatest on reasoning tasks, such as Raven's Progressive Matrices, and weak or absent on tests of knowledge (Flynn, 1999; Rodgers & Wänström, 2007) and speed of responding (Nettelbeck & Wilson, 2004).

What accounts for the Flynn effect? Here are some hypotheses:

- Improved education and test-taking skills. Education is important, but it can't account for much of the Flynn effect. The IQ improvement is evident in 6-year-old children, who have just started school, and in rural Kenyan children, who have little schooling (Daley et al., 2003). Also, the gains are greatest on reasoning tests (such as Raven's Progressive Matrices) and least on factual knowledge of the type taught in school.
- An increased tendency for people to marry outside their own neighborhood (Mingroni, 2004). Plant breeders have long noticed *hybrid vigor*, the improvement from crossing two genetic strains of a plant. For people, too, children have an advantage if their parents' genes are not too similar. However, the Flynn effect occurs in countries where people still stay mostly in their home village. Also, one study found that the size of the Flynn effect within a family depends on the difference in ages between one child and another (Sundet et al., 2010). That trend could not be related to their parents' genes.
- Decreases in mental retardation. Advances in medicine have decreased several types of mental retardation. However, over the decades we see an increase in the highest test scores, not just a decrease in low scores (Wai & Putallaz, 2011).
- Increased cognitive stimulation. People have been exposed to more and more stimulation over the years, beginning with radio, and then movies, television, video games, and the Internet. These experiences stimulate skills related to performance on Raven's Progressive Matrices and similar tests (Neisser, 1997). Even in rural Kenya, some homes now have television (Daley et al., 2003).
- Improved health and nutrition (Sigman & Whaley, 1998). People have been getting taller over the years also, presumably because of advances in health and nutrition. Also, infants today on average hold their head up earlier than in past generations. They also sit up, stand, walk, say their first word, and so forth at a younger age (Lynn, 2009). Age of holding the head up has nothing to do with education or exposure to technology, but it has much to do with early health and nutrition. Vitamin and mineral deficiencies were common in the early 1900s, but not now, and women today are less likely to smoke and drink during pregnancy than in the past.

It is possible to argue that young adults today are somewhat smarter than those of previous generations (Cocodia et al., 2003; R. W. Howard, 1999; Schooler, 1998), but do we really believe that today's young people deserve IQ scores 15 to 20 points higher than their grandparents? Flynn (1998) argued that we have seen an increase in IQ scores, but not intelligence, over time. If so, we have to wonder exactly what IQ scores mean.

concept check

10. Why is it unlikely that improved education accounts for much of the Flynn effect?

Evaluation of Tests

Have you ever complained about a test in school that seemed unfair? *Seeming* unfair doesn't necessarily make it unfair—and seeming fair doesn't make it fair. When psychologists want to evaluate the accuracy or fairness of a test, they examine specific kinds of evidence related to its reliability and validity.

Reliability

The *reliability* of a test is defined as *the repeatability of its scores* (T. B. Rogers, 1995). If a test is reliable, it produces nearly the same results every time. To determine the reliability of a test, psychologists calculate a correlation coefficient. (Recall from chapter 2 that a correlation coefficient measures how accurately we can use one measurement to predict another.) Psychologists may test the same people twice with the same test or with equivalent versions of the test and compare the two sets of scores. Or they may compare the scores on the first and second halves of the test or the scores on the test's odd-numbered and even-numbered items. If all items measure approximately the same thing, one set of scores should correlate highly with the other. Correlation coefficients theoretically range from +1 to –1. In the real world, however, a reliability coefficient is always either zero or positive. A negative reliability would mean that most people who score high the first time they take a test do worse than average the second time. That pattern simply never happens. Figure 9.9 illustrates test–retest reliability, *the correlation between scores on a first test and a retest.*

If a test's reliability is perfect (+1), the person with the highest score on the first test also scores highest on the retest, the person who scores second highest on the first test scores second highest on the retest, and so forth. If the reliability is 0, scores vary randomly from one test to another. The WISC, Stanford-Binet, Progressive Matrices, and other commonly used intelligence tests all have reliabilities above .9.

IQ scores are reasonably stable over time for most individuals. Many studies have found correlations near .9 for people taking the same test at times 10 to 20 years apart (Larsen, Hartmann, & Nyborg, 2008), and one study found that IQ scores at age 11 correlated .66 with scores at age 80 (Deary, Whiteman, Starr, Whalley, & Fox, 2004). Figure 9.10 shows the results.

concept check

11. Someone has just devised a new "intelligence test." It measures your intelligence by dividing the length of your head by its width and then multiplying by 100. Will the scores on this test be reliable?

12. Most students find that their scores on any standardized test increase the second time they take it. Does the improvement indicate that the test is unreliable?

Answers

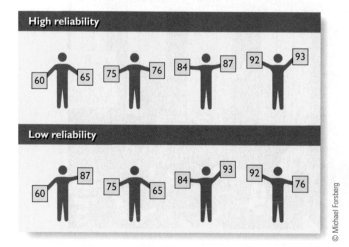

Figure 9.9 On a test with high reliability, people get similar scores each time they take the test. On a test with low reliability, scores fluctuate randomly.

© Michael Forsberg

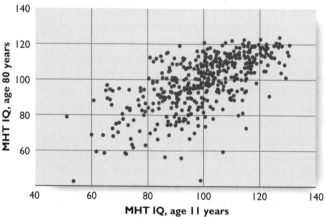

Figure 9.10 In this scatter plot, each point represents one person. The x-axis shows the IQ score at age 11, and the y-axis shows the IQ score at age 80. (MHT = the Moray House Test, a type of IQ test.) (From: Deary, I. J., Whiteman, M. C., Starr, J. M., Whalley, L. J., & Fox, H. C., "The impact of childhood intelligence on later life: Following up the Scottish mental surveys of 1932 and 1947." *Journal of Personality and Social Psychology* Vol. 86 (pp. 130-147). Copyright (2004) American Psychological Association. Reprinted with permission.)

Validity

A test's validity is defined as *the degree to which evidence and theory support the interpretations of test scores for the intended purposes* (Joint Committee on Standards, 1999). In simpler terms, validity indicates how well the test measures what it claims to measure. To determine the validity of a test, researchers examine five types of evidence:

Content. The content of a test should match its purposes. A test given to job applicants should include only tasks that are important for the job. An end-of-grade test for fifth grade should correspond to the fifth-grade curriculum.

Response processes. If a test claims to measure a certain skill, then the test-takers should need to use that skill to answer the questions instead of using shortcuts. For example, tests of reading comprehension include something to read, followed by questions. If people with previous knowledge can guess the answers without reading the passage, then the test isn't really measuring reading comprehension (Katz, Lautenschlager, Blackburn, & Harris, 1990).

Internal structure. If a test claims to measure a single skill, such as working memory, then all the items should correlate with one another. That is, people who answer one item correctly should be more likely than average to answer the other items correctly.

Relation to other variables. If a test is valid, the scores predict important kinds of performance. Scores on an interest inventory should predict which jobs or activities someone would enjoy. Results of a personality test should predict which people might develop anxiety problems or depression. Scores on an IQ test should predict grades in school. In fact, they do correlate positively with grades and achievement tests in all academic subjects (Deary, Strand, Smith, & Fernandes, 2007).

IQ tests were designed to predict school performance. Later results showed that they predicted other outcomes as well, to the surprise of almost everyone. On average, people with higher IQ scores get better jobs than most other people and earn higher salaries (Strenze, 2007). They have fewer automobile accidents than others do (O'Toole, 1990) and are less likely to suffer post-traumatic stress disorder (Vasterling et al., 2002). They do better than others at reading maps, understanding order forms, reading bus schedules, understanding nutrition labels on foods, and taking their medicines correctly (Gottfredson, 2002a; Murray, Johnson, Wolf, & Deary, 2011). They are more likely than average to

forego a smaller pleasure now in favor of a larger one later (Shamosh et al., 2008). They are more likely than average to hold attitudes that are anti-racist and favorable to women's causes (Deary, Batty, & Gale, 2008). Health and life span are greater than average among people with high IQ, especially those who are also high in conscientiousness (Deary, Batty, Pattie, & Gale, 2008; Gottfredson, 2004). Although some of these correlations are small, they indicate that IQ scores relate to real-world outcomes outside the classroom.

As you might expect, high scores predict success in scientific fields. Even among those with a master's or PhD degree, those with higher scores usually have more patents and scientific publications (Park, Lubinski, & Benbow, 2008). IQ scores also predict success on a wide variety of other jobs, especially if combined with other information (Schmidt & Hunter, 1998). According to Linda Gottfredson (2002b, pp. 25, 27), "The general mental ability factor—*g*—is the best single predictor of job performance . . . [It] enhances performance in all domains of work." According to Frank Schmidt and John Hunter (1981, p. 1128), "Professionally developed cognitive ability tests are valid predictors of performance on the job . . . for all jobs . . . in all settings." That is probably an overstatement. (It could hardly be an understatement!) For example, IQ scores are probably not useful predictors of success for singers or professional athletes. Still, for many jobs, using some type of cognitive test score to select employees increases the chances that those who are hired will learn their jobs quickly and succeed at them.

Do IQ tests measure everything that we care about intellectually? Of course not. One study found that eighth graders' performance in school correlated highly with questionnaire measurements of their self-discipline (Duckworth & Seligman, 2005). College grades correlate highly with measures of effort (Credé & Kuncel, 2008) and curiosity (von Stumm, Hell, & Chamorro-Premuzic, 2011). People also vary in initiative, creativity, and other variables that are important but hard to measure.

Consequences of testing. Tests produce benefits, but also some unintended consequences. For example, in the U.S. public school system, students' scores on end-of-grade tests determine whether they advance to the next grade. The scores also influence the teachers' salaries for the next year and the amount of government support that a school receives. As a result, the best qualified teachers don't want to work at schools with low-performing students (Tuerk, 2005).

In some countries, test scores determine a student's future almost irrevocably. Students who perform well are almost assured future success, and those who perform poorly have limited opportunities.

Many students and teachers concentrate heavily on preparing for the tests at the expense of other educational goals. Do the tests accomplish enough good to outweigh these costs? Although opinions are strong, good research on these issues is rare (Braden & Niebling, 2005).

Special Problems in Measuring Validity

Measuring the validity of a test can be difficult. Scores on the SAT or ACT correlate only modestly with college grades. One reason is that college students take different courses. A student with a B average in hard courses may have done better work than a student with all A's in easy courses. If we examine data for only students taking the same courses, the test scores predict success relatively well (Berry & Sackett, 2009).

Another problem arises if we compare grades for students who have nearly the same test scores. Consider data for the Graduate Record Examination (GRE), a test taken by graduate school applicants. According to one large study, grades for first-year graduate students in physics correlated more highly with their GRE verbal scores than with their quantitative scores. For first-year students in English, the pattern was reversed. Their grades correlated more strongly with their quantitative scores than with their verbal scores (Educational Testing Service, 1994). These results seem surprising because physics is such a quantitative field and English is such a verbal field.

The explanation is simple. Almost all graduate students in physics have nearly the same (very high) score on the quantitative test, and almost all English graduate students have nearly the same (very high) score on the verbal test. If almost all the students in a department have nearly the same score, their scores cannot predict who will do better than others. A test predicts performance only when scores vary over a substantial range.

concept check

13. Can a test have high reliability and low validity? Can a test have low reliability and high validity?
14. If physics graduate departments tried admitting some students with low quantitative scores on the GRE and English departments tried admitting some students with low verbal scores, what would happen to the predictive validity of the tests?
15. Would you expect the SAT scores to show higher predictive validity at a college with extremely competitive admissions standards or at a college that admits almost every applicant?

Answers

13. Yes, a test can have high reliability and low validity. A measure of intelligence determined by dividing head length by head width has high reliability (repeatability) but presumably no validity. A test with low reliability cannot have high validity, however. Low reliability means that the scores fluctuate randomly. If the test scores cannot even predict a later score on the same test, then they can hardly predict anything else.
14. The predictive validity of the tests would increase. The predictive validity is low when most students have nearly the same score. It is higher when students' scores are highly variable.
15. The predictive validity of SAT scores will be higher at the university that admits almost anyone. At the university with extremely competitive admissions standards, almost all students have nearly the same SAT scores, and the slight variation in scores cannot predict who will get the best grades.

Interpreting Fluctuations in Scores

Suppose on the first test in some course you get 94% correct. On the second test, which was equally difficult, your score is only 88%. Does that score indicate that you studied harder for the first test? Not necessarily. When tests are not perfectly reliable, your scores fluctuate. The lower the reliability, the greater the fluctuation.

When people lose sight of this fact, they sometimes draw unwarranted conclusions. In one study, Harold Skeels (1966) tested infants in an orphanage and identified those with the lowest IQ scores. He transferred those infants to an institution that provided more attention. Several years later, most of them showed major increases in their IQ scores. Should we conclude, as many psychologists did, that the extra attention improved the children's IQ performances? Not necessarily (Longstreth, 1981). IQ tests for infants have low reliability. The scores fluctuate widely, even from one day to the next. If someone selects infants with low scores and retests them later, their mean IQ score is almost certain to improve simply because the scores had nowhere to go but up.

Similarly, suppose we examine people who had a perfect score on the first test in some class. What scores should we expect on the second test? On average, their scores will go down. It is not because they got overconfident and failed to study. It is because the tests are not perfectly reliable, and a certain amount of fluctuation is inevitable.

Are IQ Tests Biased?

In addition to being reliable and valid, a test should also be unbiased—that is, equally fair and accurate for all groups. A biased test *overstates or understates the true performance of one or more groups.* If one group does better than another on a test, that difference by itself does not necessarily indicate bias. To take an extreme example, students who study hard in a course get better grades than those who don't study. Does that result mean the test is biased against students who don't study? No. (If you do think it is biased, then your idea of an unbiased test is one on which everyone gets the same score.) If groups really do differ in some kind of performance, the test should report that fact accurately. Driver's license examinations include vision tests. Are they biased against people who are blind? Again, no. The results accurately predict that blind people will be poor drivers. However, if someone were selecting applicants to be a school guidance counselor, a vision test *would* be biased against the blind, because it would understate their ability to do the job. The point is that bias means unfairness for a particular

Women who return to school after age 25 usually get better grades than their SAT scores predict. The tests are "biased" against them in the sense of underpredicting their performance.

purpose. Researchers need to determine the bias, or lack of it, for any potential use of any test.

The question of bias is an empirical question—that is, one to be decided by the evidence. For what groups, if any, are IQ tests or other tests biased? Women who enter college or graduate school after age 25 generally receive better grades than their SAT scores predict (Swinton, 1987). Therefore, the tests are biased against them, even though in fact most of them have good test scores. The tests are biased in the sense that a given SAT score means something different for a woman over 25 than for a 20-year-old. Why do older women get better grades than their test scores predict? Here are three hypotheses:

(a) Because they have been away from school for a while, their test-taking skills are rusty. (b) Anyone who returns to school at that point must have strong motivation. (c) A few extra years of experiences give them some advantages.

To determine whether a test is biased against groups, psychologists conduct several kinds of research. They try to identify bias both in individual test items and in the test as a whole.

Evaluating Possible Bias in Single Test Items

Suppose on a test with 100 items, one item is the 10th easiest for group A but only the 42nd easiest for group B. This pattern suggests that the item taps information or skills that are more available to group A than group B. If so, the item is biased (Schmitt & Dorans, 1990). For example, Figure 9.11, an item that once appeared on the SAT, diagrams an American football field and asks for the ratio of the distance between the goal lines to the distance between the sidelines. For men, this was one of the easiest items on the test. Many women missed it, including some of the brightest women who missed almost no other questions.

The reason was that some women had so little interest in football that they did not know which were the goal lines and which were the sidelines. The publishers of the SAT saw that this item was biased and removed it from the test.

Evaluating Possible Bias in a Test as a Whole

By definition, a biased test systematically misestimates the performance by members of some group. For example, if an IQ test is biased against Black students, then Black students who score, say, 100 will do *better* in school than White students with the same score.

However, the evidence indicates that Black students with a given IQ score generally do about the same in school as do White students with the same score and sometimes worse (Pesta & Poznanski, 2008; Sackett, Borneman, & Connelly, 2008). The same is true for SAT scores (McCornack, 1983). The unpleasant fact is that over many years White students have usually had better grades in school than Black students. The difference in IQ scores approximately matches the difference in performance. The tests simply report that difference. Presumably

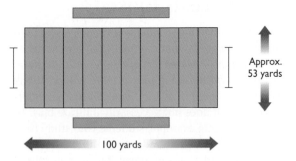

The diagram above represents a football field. What is the ratio of the distance between the goal lines to the distance between the sidelines?

a. 1.89
b. 1.53
c. 0.53
d. 5.3
e. 53

Figure 9.11 This item was eliminated from the SAT when researchers determined that it was biased against women. Some women who did very well on the rest of the test did not know which were the goal lines and which were the sidelines. (In case you are curious, the correct answer is a.)

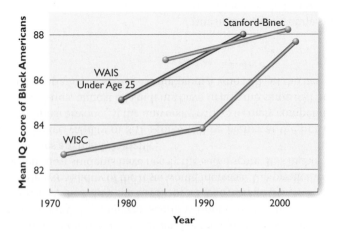

Figure 9.12 The mean IQ scores of Black students increased relative to White students from 1970 to 2000, according to the results of the two most widely used IQ tests. (Modified from Dickens & Flynn, 2006.)

whatever is impairing performance in school is also impairing performance on the tests.

The gap between Black and White students has decreased over the years. In comparison to the mean of 100 for White children, the mean for Black students increased from about 83 in 1970 to about 88 in 2000, according to the Stanford-Binet and Wechsler tests, as shown in Figure 9.12 (Dickens & Flynn, 2006). Other studies suggest an increase in scores until about 1990 and a leveling off since then (Magnuson & Duncan, 2006; Murray, 2007). On average, Black students also increased their grades in school (Grissmer, Williamson, Kirby, & Berends, 1998). The fact that grades and test scores improved simultaneously supports the idea that the tests predict performance validly. The improvement of Black students' IQ scores and grades presumably relates to improved health, education, and occupational opportunities for most Black families.

If IQ and SAT scores predict school performance as accurately for Blacks as for Whites, then the tests are not biased, according to the definition of test bias. However, another possibility remains: Many Black students may be performing at a lower level than they could, in *both* school and the tests.

If so, why? Poverty (which leads to poor prenatal health and nutrition, as well as high levels of stress) is one hypothesis (Evans & Schamberg, 2009), but probably not the whole explanation. If we compare Blacks and Whites of the same socioeconomic status, a difference in scores remains, although it is smaller than usual (Magnuson & Duncan, 2006). A related hypothesis is that growing up in a White family gives a child more familiarity with the skills and content that the tests (and schools) measure. One study found that Black children adopted by White families performed higher on IQ tests than did Black children adopted by Black families (Moore, 1986). Another possibility is impairment by low expectations and aspirations. If you think you don't have a chance anyway, maybe you don't try. On average, Black women score higher than Black men, and Black women are significantly more likely to attend college, strongly suggesting that many Black men are not giving a full effort academically (McKinnon & Bennett, 2005). We explore this possibility more thoroughly in the next section.

concept check

16. A company hiring salespeople proposes to test applicants on their ability to speak Spanish. Is this policy biased against people who don't speak Spanish?

17. Suppose on some new IQ test tall people generally get higher scores than short people. How could we determine whether this test is biased against short people?

Answers

16. It depends. If the salespeople will be working in a neighborhood with many Spanish-speaking customers, this test will accurately predict success on the job, and it would therefore be unbiased. However, if the sales staff works in a neighborhood with no need to use Spanish, the test is biased.

17. We would need to determine whether the test accurately predicts the school performances of both short and tall people. If short people with, say, an IQ score of 100 perform better in school than tall people with the same score, then the test underpredicts the short people's performances, and inaccurate prediction means bias. (The fact that tall people do better on this test does not *by itself* demonstrate bias.)

critical check

What's the Evidence?

Stereotype Threat

Possible test bias depends not only on the test itself but also on how the test is administered and the expectations of those being tested. Imagine you are about to take some test when you are told that "people like you"—left-handers, redheads, people who live in small towns, whatever it might be—usually don't do well on this kind of test. How will that statement affect you? You might become discouraged. Even if you don't believe the statement, it's a distraction. You worry that if you perform poorly, you confirm this hurtful expectation.

Claude Steele termed this idea **stereotype threat**—*people's perceived risk of performing poorly and thereby supporting an unfavorable stereotype about their group.* In particular, Black students who take an IQ test may fear that a poor score would support prejudices about Blacks. They may become distracted or discouraged. Let's examine Steele's study and its results.

Hypothesis If Black students believe they are taking the kind of test on which Black students in general do not perform well, then they worry that their own performance may reflect poorly on their group. They may also lose confidence. As a result, they fail to perform up to their abilities. If they are freed from this kind of concern, their performance may improve.

Method Participants were 20 Black and 20 White undergraduate students at Stanford University, a prestigious, highly selective institution. They were given a set of 27 difficult verbal questions from the Graduate Record Exam, a test intended for college seniors applying to graduate schools. Before the test, two groups (randomly assigned) received different instructions. Those in the "nondiagnostic" group were told that the researchers were studying how people solve difficult verbal problems. In contrast, participants in the "diagnostic" group were told that the research was an attempt to find each participant's strengths and weaknesses in solving verbal problems. This latter instruction was an attempt to increase students' nervousness about being evaluated.

Results Instead of simply presenting the number of correct answers for each group, the researchers adjusted the scores based on participants' SAT scores. The results in Figure 9.13 show the number of correct answers for each group *relative to the scores predicted by their SAT scores.* The mean for these Black students on the SAT was 603, and the mean for these White students was 655. So, if the Black and White students both did as well as their

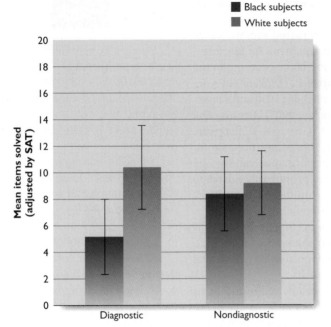

Legend:
■ Black subjects
■ White subjects

Figure 9.13 Black students who believed the test would identify their strengths and weaknesses failed to live up to their abilities. (From Claude M. Steele & Joshua Aronson, "Stereotype threat and the intellectual test performance of African Americans." *Journal of Personality and Social Psychology* Vol. 69 (pp. 797-811). Copyright © 1995 American Psychological Association. Reprinted with permission.)

SAT scores predicted, the graph would show equal performances on the test, even though the White students answered a slightly higher percentage correctly.

The results for the "nondiagnostic" group do in fact show this pattern. However, for students who were given the "diagnostic" instructions, Black students had lower scores than their SAT scores predicted. They answered fewer questions overall, and answered fewer correctly, than Black students given the "nondiagnostic" instructions. The type of instructions did not significantly affect the White students.

When interviewed afterward, the Black students who received the "diagnostic" instructions said that they felt strongly aware of the stereotype about Black students taking ability tests. They also said they felt self-doubts about possibly conforming to this stereotype (Steele & Aronson, 1995). Another study by the same researchers found that simply asking participants to indicate their race prior to the test impaired Black students' scores (Steele & Aronson, 1995).

Interpretation The results confirmed that many Black students are sensitive to a suggestion that they are taking a test on which Black students do not excel. Presumably, the worry distracts from their ability to concentrate on the problems.

Further Research on Stereotype Threat

Many further studies have been conducted on stereotype threat, and most replicate the general finding (Nguyen & Ryan, 2008; Steele, 2010). Stereotype threat also applies to other groups, such as the Turkish minority in Germany (Walton & Spencer, 2009).

Another stereotype is that Blacks have more athletic ability than Whites. In one study, White and Black college students were asked to perform a task similar to miniature golf. When the researchers said it was a measure of athletic ability, the Black students did better than the Whites, who reported more anxiety. When they said it was a measure of strategic thinking, the Whites did better than the Blacks, who then reported more anxiety (Stone, Lynch, Sjomeling, & Darley, 1999).

When anyone highlights the stereotype that women don't do well at math, women's performance on a math test deteriorates, on average. Their anxiety increases and concentration decreases (Krendl, Richeson, Kelley, & Heatherton, 2008). However, women do better if they don't believe the stereotype about women doing poorly at math or if they don't believe it applies to them personally (Dar-Nimrod & Heine, 2006; Kiefer & Sekaquaptewa, 2007; Lesko & Corpus, 2006).

Three fascinating studies presented math problems to Asian women. For some of the women, the researchers primed their attention to being female by first giving a questionnaire about being female. Those women did less well than usual on the test. For other women, the researchers primed their attention to being Asian. (The stereotype is that Asians are especially good at math.) Focusing their attention on being Asian improved their math performance in two of the three studies (Ambady, Shih, Kim, & Pittinsky, 2001; Cheryan & Bodenhausen, 2000; Shih, Pittinsky, & Ambady, 1999).

Given the goal of helping all people live up to their abilities, how can we combat stereotype threat? One approach is simply to tell people about stereotype threat! In one study, researchers described math problems as diagnostic of abilities that differ between men and women. But then they told some of the women (randomly assigned) about stereotype threat and urged them not to let the stereotype bother them. Those women performed as well as men did on average (Johns, Schmader, & Martens, 2005). In several other studies, researchers asked students lacking confidence about their test performance to write about their most important values, their most valuable characteristics, or how it would feel to be highly successful. The result was enhanced test performance (Lang & Lang, 2010; Martens, Johns, Greenberg, & Schimel, 2006; Miyake et al.,

2010). Writing about worries helped also, perhaps by getting them out in the open and then dismissing them (Ramirez & Beilock, 2011). The idea is that worrying about your performance leads to "choking under pressure," just as it does for athletes (Beilock, Jellison, Rydell, McConnell, & Carr, 2006).

Benefits of writing interventions can last surprisingly long. One group of Black seventh-grade students completed a series of self-affirming writing assignments about their family, friendships, interests, and values. The result was improved grades in school for at least the next 2 years (Cohen, Garcia, Purdie-Vaughns, Apfel, & Brzustoski, 2009).

Stereotype threat is a consistent effect, but not a huge one. In most studies, the effect size is the equivalent of about 3 IQ points. However, what we don't know is the cumulative effect over years. Students who are told they aren't likely to do well in school or on tests may be discouraged from the start. Early discouragement could compound into greater discouragement later. How large might the overall effect be?

concept check

18. How does stereotype threat affect the validity of a test?

Answer

18. Stereotype threat leads some people to perform at a lower level than they would otherwise. It therefore decreases the validity of the test.

module 9.2 >

In Closing

Consequences of Testing

Regardless of what we say about intelligence theoretically, testing continues for practical reasons. Just as a coach tries to choose the best players for an athletic team, colleges and employers try to choose the applicants who will learn the fastest. If people are going to make those judgments—as they no doubt will—we want them to use the best available methods and evaluate the results accurately.

Testing has consequences for the individuals who take the tests and the institutions that evaluate the scores, but it can also have another kind of consequence: If we begin to better understand the factors that influence intelligence, we may be able to do something about these factors. As a society, we would like to intervene early to help children develop as well as possible, but to make those interventions work, we need research. How important are prenatal health and early childhood nutrition? Which kinds of environmental stimulation are most effective? Are different kinds of stimulation better for different kinds of children? To answer these questions, we need good measurements—measurements that can come only from testing of some kind.

Summary

- *Standardization.* To determine the meaning of a test's scores, the authors of a test determine the mean and the distribution of scores for a random or representative sample of the population. IQ tests are revised periodically. (page 306)
- *Distribution of IQ scores.* IQ tests have a mean of 100 and a standard deviation of about 15 or 16, depending on the test. However, the mode (most frequent score) is higher than 100, and a bulge of lower scores exists. (page 306)

- *The Flynn effect.* To keep the mean score at 100, authors of IQ tests have had to revise the tests periodically, always making them more difficult. That is, raw performance has been increasing steadily. The reasons for this trend are unknown. (page 307)
- *Reliability and validity.* Tests are evaluated in terms of reliability and validity. Reliability is a measure of the repeatability of a test's scores. Validity is a determination of how well a test measures what it claims to measure. (page 309)

- *Measuring validity.* To evaluate a test's validity for a given purpose, researchers examine its content, the response processes people use while taking the test, the internal structure of the test, the scores' relationship to other variables, and the consequences of using the test. (page 310)
- *Test bias.* Bias means inaccuracy of measurement. Psychologists try to remove from a test any item that tends to be easy for one group of people to answer but difficult for another group. They also try to evaluate whether the test as a whole makes equally accurate predictions for all groups. (page 311)
- *Test anxiety and stereotype threat.* Many Black students perform worse on tests after any reminder of the stereotype of Black students scoring poorly on such tests. However, some simple procedures can weaken this threat. (page 313)

Key Terms

bias (page 311)

Down syndrome (page 306)

Flynn effect (page 308)

norms (page 306)

reliability (page 309)

standardization (page 306)

stereotype threat (page 313)

test–retest reliability (page 309)

validity (page 310)

exploration and study

Access an interactive eBook and chapter-specific learning tools, including
- **flashcards**
- **quizzes**
- **videos**

and more, in your Psychology CourseMate. Go to **CengageBrain.com.**

aplia™

If your professor has assigned Aplia:
1. Sign in to your account.
2. Complete the corresponding exercises as required by your professor.
3. When finished, click "Grade It Now" to see which areas you have mastered, which areas need more work, and detailed explanations of every answer.

Goldman/Getty Images

Consciousness

Of all the questions that humans ask, two are the most profound and the most difficult. One is why there is a universe at all. As the philosopher Gottfried Leibniz (1714) put it, "Why is there something rather than nothing?" A second profound question is why, in a universe of matter and energy, does consciousness exist? Why does the motion of atoms in your brain produce conscious experiences?

So far, no one has any idea how to answer these questions. Indeed, consciousness, being unobservable, is so difficult to study that many psychologists and philosophers have despaired of our ever finding anything useful to say about it (Churchland, 1986; Lashley, 1923). Are nonhuman animals conscious? If so, which ones? How would you know?

Many questions about consciousness are unanswerable, at least by present methods. But that doesn't stop us from dealing with some simpler but related questions. What aspects of brain activity are necessary for consciousness? How does your conscious experience change when you are sleeping, dreaming, or under hypnosis? These questions, too, are fascinating.

Sleep and dreams are alterations of consciousness.

- What brain activity is necessary for consciousness?
- How does consciousness relate to action?

What is consciousness, anyway? As William James (1892/1961) said, "Its meaning we know so long as no one asks us to define it" (p. 19). People use the term in different ways, and it is important to make clear how one is using it. For example, we might call sleeping people unconscious, in the sense that they are unaware of what is happening around them, but they may be conscious of what is happening in their dreams. One definition of consciousness is *the subjective experience of perceiving oneself and one's surroundings.* However, that definition relies on the phrase "subjective experience," which is no better defined than consciousness itself. For practical purposes, many researchers use the operational definition that *you are conscious of something if you can report it in words.* This definition works only for people who speak. We don't assume that infants remain unconscious until they learn to talk. Similarly, nonhuman animals do not talk, nor do people with certain types of brain damage, but we don't necessarily assume they are unconscious.

Levels of Consciousness

Physicians distinguish various gradations of brain activity that relate to arousal, responsiveness, and presumed consciousness. In brain death, *the brain shows no activity and no response to any stimulus.* Most people consider it ethical to remove life support for someone who remains steadily in this condition. In a coma (KOH-muh), *caused by traumatic brain damage, the brain shows a steady but low level of activity and no response to any stimulus*, including potentially painful stimuli. Within a few weeks, someone in a coma usually either dies or begins to recover. Long-term comas are rare.

Someone starting to emerge from a coma enters a vegetative state, *marked by limited responsiveness, such as increased heart rate in response to pain.* Responsiveness varies between a sleeping state and a waking state, but even in the waking state, brain activity is well below normal, and the person shows no purposeful behaviors. The next step up is a minimally conscious state, *in which people have brief periods of purposeful actions and speech comprehension.* A vegetative or minimally conscious state can last for months or years.

Can Someone in a Vegetative State Be Conscious?

Because people in a vegetative state do nothing, it is easy to assume that they are unconscious. However, new research methods challenge that assumption in certain cases. Researchers used fMRI to record the brain activity of a young woman who was in a persistent vegetative state following a traffic accident. When they instructed her to imagine playing tennis, activity increased in the same motor areas of her cortex as in a group of uninjured people. An instruction to imagine walking through her house activated brain areas responsible for spatial navigation, again as it does for uninjured people (Owen et al., 2006). Figure 10.1 shows the results.

A follow-up study of 53 other patients in a vegetative state found results similar to this in 4 of them. One of those was then asked questions such as "Do

you have a brother?" and instructed to imagine playing tennis if the answer was yes, and imagine walking through his house if the answer was no. His brain responses indicated the correct answers to the first five questions. His brain showed no response at all to the sixth question, suggesting that he had fallen asleep (Monti et al., 2010).

Here is another way to infer consciousness for someone in a vegetative state: Researchers presented sequences of tones and monitored brain responses. Let's call two tones A and B. To the sequence AAAAB, the final B produces a somewhat enhanced brain response in both normal and vegetative people, just because the B is different. But now suppose people hear the following:

AAAAB . . . AAAAB . . . AAAAB . . . AAAAB . . . AAAAB . . . AAAAA

Healthy, conscious people show an enhanced response to the final A because they learned the pattern, and the A violates their expectations. Most vegetative patients show no such enhancement, but in one study, two did, of the 22 who were tested. Those two patients advanced from a vegetative state to a minimally conscious state just three or four days later (Faugeras et al., 2011).

The results of all these studies imply that at least a few patients in a vegetative state are sufficiently conscious to understand speech and recognize repeated sound patterns. It is an encouraging result, but also a somewhat scary one. How many times have people said something about a patient, in the patient's presence, assuming that he or she didn't hear?

concept check

1. What evidence suggests that some people in a vegetative state are conscious?

Answer

1. One woman in a vegetative state responded to instructions with brain activity that resembled that of uninjured people who heard the same instructions. Another patient answered yes–no questions by imagining one activity for yes and imagining another activity for no. Some patients learn what to expect from a pattern of tones, and show an enhanced brain response to a violation of the expectation.

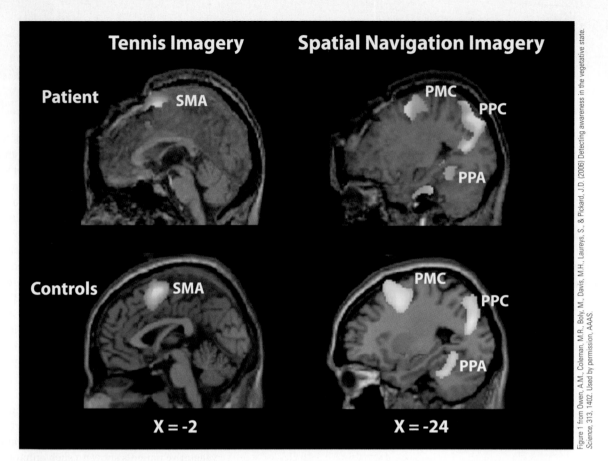

Tennis Imagery   Spatial Navigation Imagery

Patient   SMA

PMC

PPC

PPA

Controls   SMA

PMC

PPC

PPA

X = -2   X = -24

Figure 1 from Owen, A.M., Coleman, M.R., Boly, M., Davis, M.H., Laureys, S., & Pickard, J.D. (2006) Detecting awareness in the vegetative state. *Science*, 313, 1402. Used by permission, AAAS.

Figure 10.1 The brain areas marked in red and yellow showed increased activity after instructions to imagine playing tennis or imagine walking through the house. Note the similarities between a patient in a persistent vegetative state and uninjured people. SMA = supplementary motor cortex, an area important for planning complex movements. PMC, PPC, and PPA = three areas responsible for spatial imagery and memory. (From Owen et al., 2006.)

Spatial Neglect

After damage to parts of the right hemisphere, people are still conscious, but sometimes they are apparently conscious of only half of the information they receive. They show spatial neglect—*a tendency to be unconscious of the left side of the body, the left side of the world, or the left side of objects* (Buxbaum, 2006). This tendency is severest shortly after a right-hemisphere stroke, and then the person begins to recover (Farnè et al., 2006). (Damage in the left hemisphere seldom yields neglect of the right side.)

Many people with spatial neglect eat food from only the right side of the plate and read only the right side of the page. They draw only the right side of an object (Driver & Mattingley, 1998). If asked to point "straight ahead," they point to the right (Richard, Honoré, Bernati, & Rousseaux, 2004). Although some patients have a partial loss of sensation from the left side, the problem usually relates to attention. Even when describing something from memory, they describe only the right side.

 **try it ▶** yourself

You can demonstrate a related experience for yourself. Stare straight ahead and describe what you see *without moving your eyes.* Then hold a napkin or card a finger's length in front of your eyes so that it covers the center of your vision. Again describe what you see without moving your eyes. You will find yourself including more of the objects in the periphery of your view. You saw them before, but you were attending so much to the objects in the center that you ignored those around the sides. Similarly, people showing spatial neglect are capable of responding to objects on the left, if they make a special effort or if someone calls attention to the left.

 **concept** check

2. What evidence indicates that people with spatial neglect have a deficit in attention and not just sensation?

Answer

2. They neglect the left side of objects when describing them from memory. Also, it is possible to increase their attention to the left side in various ways.

Brain Mechanisms Necessary for Consciousness

Not all nervous system activity is conscious, even in normal, waking people. Your spinal cord controls reflexes, your hypothalamus regulates body temperature, and many other processes occur without awareness. Among the stimuli striking your receptors at any moment, you are conscious of only a few. Right now, do you smell or taste anything? What do you feel in your left leg? The back of your neck? As you turn your attention to one sensation after another, you become aware of much that had been present but unconscious until then (Lambie & Marcel, 2002).

In terms of brain activity, how does a stimulus that becomes conscious differ from one that remains unconscious? A good research design is to present the same stimulus under conditions where people report it (conscious) and under conditions where they cannot report it (unconscious). Brain scans then measure how brain activity differs for the two conditions. Participants in one study watched words flash on a screen for just 29 milliseconds (ms) each. On some trials, a blank screen preceded and followed the word:

GROVE

© Cengage Learning

Under those conditions, people usually identified the word, even though it flashed so briefly. On other trials, a masking pattern preceded and followed the word:

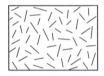 

SALTY

© Cengage Learning

Under those conditions, people almost never saw the word. Under both conditions, the light struck the retina for 29 ms, so we can ask what happened to that information. Brain recordings indicate that the stimuli activated the same areas of the visual cortex in both conditions but produced greater activation on trials when people became conscious of the word. On those trials, the activation spread from the visual cortex to more of the rest of the brain, as shown in Figure 10.2 (Dehaene et al., 2001). Later studies found that the brain responses to a stimulus are about the same for at least the first two-tenths of a second. The responses begin to diverge a bit later. On trials that result in conscious perception, the activity spreads to other areas including the prefrontal cortex, and then echoes back to posterior regions, resulting in synchronized activity in widespread brain areas (Gaillard et al., 2009). That echo amplifies the conscious perception. People with an impaired prefrontal cortex are less likely than average to notice relatively weak stimuli (Del Cul, Dehaene, Reyes, Bravo, & Slachevsky, 2009; Rounis, Maniscalco, Rothwell, Passingham, & Lau, 2010). One explanation for impaired consciousness in a vegetative state is that activity feeds forward to the prefrontal cortex but the prefrontal cortex fails to feed it back to the originating areas (Boly et al., 2011).

Let's consider another example. Ordinarily, your two retinas see almost the same thing. Examine Figure 10.3 to see what happens when the images conflict.

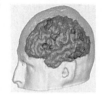

Visible words   Masked words

Figure 10.2 When people were conscious of a briefly flashed word, it activated the areas colored in the brain on the left. When masking prevented consciousness, the word activated only the areas colored on the right. (From Dehaene, S., et al., "Cerebral mechanisms of word masking and unconscious repetition priming," *Nature Neuroscience, 4* (pp. 752-758). Copyright © 2001 Nature Publishing Group. Reprinted with permission.)

try it ▶ yourself

Find or make tubes like those in a roll of paper towels, so your left eye can look at Figure 10.3 through one roll and your right eye can look through the other. For a quick shortcut, you could cup your two hands to form viewing tubes, or touch your nose to the page so that your two eyes are right in front of the two images. Adjust your focus until the two circles appear to overlap. First, you will be conscious of what one eye sees—such as red and black lines. Soon, that perception fades and you start seeing green and black lines. Because you can't see both images at the same time in the same place, your brain alternates between the two perceptions (Blake & Logothetis, 2002). The *alternation between seeing the pattern in the left retina and the pattern in the right retina* is known as binocular rivalry. (If you see well from one eye and poorly from the other eye, you might see one image almost exclusively.)

At any moment during binocular rivalry, parts of your brain continue processing information from both eyes. Suppose your two eyes view different

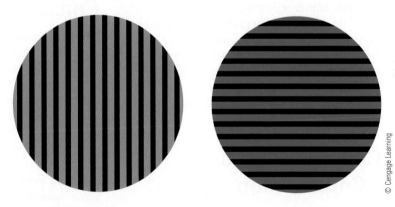

© Cengage Learning

Figure 10.3 To produce binocular rivalry, look through tubes and alter the focus of your eyes until the two circles seem to merge. You will alternate between seeing red lines and seeing green lines.

scenes on a computer screen. While you are conscious of one eye, the experimenter gradually changes the scene in the other eye to show a face. Your attention will shift to that eye faster if the face is right-side-up rather than upside-down. A face with an emotional expression captures your attention faster than a neutral face does (Alpers & Gerdes, 2007). If a word emerges on one side, it captures your attention faster if it is in a language you read than one you don't (Jiang, Costello, & He, 2007). That is, unconscious processes notice something important, and direct your conscious attention to it.

Researchers use fMRI and similar devices, as described in chapter 3, to measure brain activity. To label the activity patterns during binocular rivalry, researchers might make one stimulus flash a few times per second while the other stimulus remains constant. Then they look for patterns of brain activity that pulsate at the same frequency as the flashing stimulus. When research participants say they see the flashing stimulus, researchers see that rhythm of activity over a large portion of the brain (Cosmelli et al., 2004; S. H. Lee, Blake, & Heeger, 2005). As that perception fades and the other replaces it, the rhythmic activity subsides, and a steadier pattern spreads over the brain. In short, a conscious perception controls the activity over a large portion of the brain. We begin to understand why it is hard to be conscious of several things at the same time: When you are conscious of something, it occupies much of your brain.

concept check

3. How did researchers arrange for a stimulus to be conscious on some trials and not others?
4. What do most people perceive during binocular rivalry?

Answers

4. Most people perceive one stimulus and then the other, alternating.

3. Researchers presented a word for a small fraction of a second. When they simply presented the word, most people identified it. In other cases, researchers put interfering patterns before and after the word. In those cases, people were not conscious of it.

Consciousness as a Construction

When we see or hear something, we assume that we see or hear it *as it happens*. However, various studies cast doubt on that assumption. Suppose a word flashes on a screen for 29 ms followed by a masking stimulus, so that you are not conscious of the word. Then the experimenter repeats the procedure but extends the duration to 50 ms. With this longer presentation, you do see the word. More important, you don't have 29 ms of unconscious perception and 21 ms of conscious perception. Rather, the final part of that 50-ms presentation enabled you to become conscious of the first part retroactively. In some way, your brain constructed an experience of a 50-ms stimulus, even though it had to wait until the later part of the stimulus to perceive the first part at all.

Here is a related phenomenon. Suppose you see a display of two vertical lines:

After a delay of one or two tenths of a second, you see a display of circles like this:

When you report the appearance of the lines, you describe something like this:

That is, the lines appear to be displaced partly in the same direction that the circles were displaced (Ono & Watanabe, 2011). The later stimulus changed your perception of the earlier stimulus. Evidently, consciousness does not occur at exactly the same time as the events. You construct a conscious perception of events that already happened.

concept check

5. What evidence suggests that we construct a conscious perception of a stimulus afterward instead of simultaneously with it?

Answer

5. A brief masked stimulus is not perceived consciously, but a slightly longer one is perceived as lasting the entire duration. Also, the perception of a first stimulus can be altered by a stimulus that follows it.

Consciousness and Action

What does consciousness do? A great deal happens unconsciously. Recall subliminal perception from chapter 4: A brief, faint stimulus that you do not detect primes you to detect something similar. Also recall implicit memory from chapter 7: You might not remember seeing or hearing some word, but you become more likely than usual to think of it and use it. What about decisions? We all have the impression that our conscious decisions control our actions. Are we right? At least some of the time, we fool ourselves about how much control we have. Psychologist Daniel Wegner (2002) described a time when he was manipulating a joystick at a video game display, making a monkey jump over barrels . . . or at least so it seemed. Then the notice "Start game" appeared, and he realized that he hadn't been controlling anything after all. You may have had similar experiences yourself. Let's consider a famous experiment that poses a serious challenge to the idea of conscious control.

critical check

What's the Evidence?
Consciousness and Action

In a scientifically and philosophically important study, Benjamin Libet and his associates measured the time when people made a conscious decision to act, the time when brain activity preparing for the movement started, and the time of the act itself. What would you guess was the order of the three events in time?

Hypothesis The researchers considered three hypotheses, any one of which would be interesting: (a) Someone becomes aware of a decision to act before relevant brain activity begins, (b) awareness starts at the same time as the brain activity, and (c) the brain activity responsible for a movement starts before a conscious decision.

Method People were instructed to make a simple movement, to flex the wrist. Although they had no choice of movement, they had complete freedom for the timing. The instruction was to flex the wrist whenever they decided to, but spontaneously, with no planning. While waiting for that spontaneous urge to occur, they were to watch a special clock like the one in Figure 10.4, on which a spot of light moved around the edge every 2.56 seconds. When they suddenly decided to flex the wrist, they were to note the position of the light at that moment, so they could report it later. In this way, the study measured, as well as anyone knows how, the time of the conscious decision. Meanwhile, researchers used electrodes on the scalp to detect increased activity in the motor cortex, the brain area responsible for initiating muscle movements. *The increased motor cortex activity prior to the start of the movement* is known as the **readiness potential**. Researchers also measured when the wrist muscles began to flex. On certain trials, the participants were told to report when they felt the wrist flex instead of the time they felt the intention to move it.

Results Figure 10.5 shows the means for a large sample. On average, people reported forming an intention of movement 200–300 ms before the movement (Libet, Gleason, Wright, & Pearl, 1983). (They noted the time on the clock then and reported it later.) For example, someone might report forming an intention when the light was at location 25 on the clock, 200 ms before the movement began at location 30. (Remember, the light zooms around the circle in 2.56 seconds.) In contrast, the readiness potential in the brain began 300–800 ms before the reported intention. Several other laboratories replicated this finding with varying procedures, confirming that the readiness po-

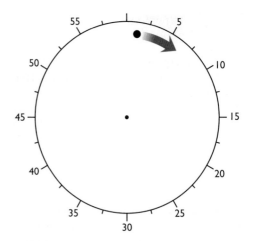

Figure 10.4 A spot of light rotated around the clock once every 2.56 seconds. Participants made a spontaneous decision to flex the wrist and noted the location of the light at the time of the decision. They remembered that time and reported it later. (From Libet, Gleason, Wright, & Pearl, 1983.)

tential comes before the conscious intention (Haggard & Eimer, 1999; Lau, Rogers, Haggard, & Passingham, 2004; Pockett & Miller, 2007; Trevena & Miller, 2002).

Can people report these times accurately? Recall that on certain trials the participants reported the time of the wrist motion. On these trials, people usually reported the movement within 100 ms of the actual time (Lau et al., 2004; Libet et al., 1983). From this finding, the researchers concluded that people report the time of an experience with moderate accuracy.

Interpretation These results indicate that your brain starts producing a voluntary movement before you are conscious of it. If so, your consciousness does not cause your action.

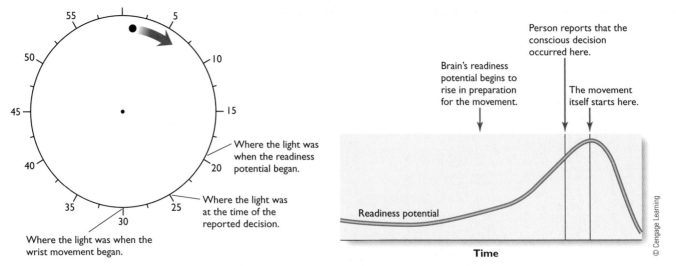

Figure 10.5 On average, the brain's readiness potential began 300 ms or more prior to the reported decision, which occurred 200–300 ms before the movement.

6. In the experiment described in the What's the Evidence? section, what did participants report, and when did they report it?

7. What was the order of these events: Conscious decision to move, brain activity relevant to movement, and the movement itself?

Answers

6. Participants watched a special fast clock and noted the time when they made a spontaneous decision to flex the wrist. They reported it a few seconds later.

7. Measurable brain activity came first, then the perception of the conscious decision, and then the movement.

Imagine yourself in this follow-up study: You watch a screen that displays a different letter of the alphabet every half-second. You choose not only when to act but which of two acts to do. At some point you spontaneously decide whether to press a button on the left or one on the right. As soon as you decide, you press the button, and you remember what letter is on the screen when you decided which button to press. Researchers record your brain activity. The result: You usually report a letter you saw within 1 second of making the response. The letters changed only twice per second, so the researchers could not determine the time of decision with greater accuracy. However, it wasn't necessary, because areas in the frontal and parietal cortex showed activity related to the left or right hand 7 to 10 seconds before your response (Soon, Brass, Heinze, & Haynes, 2008). That is, someone monitoring your cortex could predict your choice a few seconds before you were aware of your decision.

Still, serious objections remain. One is that watching a clock or other device may interfere with the decision process (Miller, Shepherdson, & Trevena, 2011). A second objection is that reporting the time of a voluntary decision may be more difficult than reporting the time of a stimulus or an action. Perhaps people notice when they make a movement and merely guess that the decision came shortly before it. Researchers found that if they sounded a beep shortly after someone's movement, the person guessed the time of the movement later than it really was, and also guessed the time of the decision later than people usually do (Banks & Isham, 2009). That result supports the idea that reported decision times are little more than guesses.

A third, closely related objection is this: A spontaneous, voluntary decision is never a sudden event at a discrete time. If you asked a loving couple when they fell in love, they might tell you the time when they were sure of it, but an astute observer could have seen it developing long before. Similarly, when you state the time of a voluntary decision, you tell when you were sure of it, not the time when it started. In short, investigating conscious processes is difficult, indeed.

What Is the Purpose of Consciousness?

Given that the role of consciousness in decisions remains unclear at best, why do we have consciousness at all? Some theorists have argued that consciousness is merely an observer that does nothing at all. But if it does serve a purpose, what might that purpose be?

A hypothesis worth considering is that conscious thought is a way of rehearsing possibilities for future actions (Baumeister & Masicampo, 2010; Baumeister, Masicampo, & Vohs, 2011). After you do something, you might ponder, "That didn't go well. What could I have done differently? Then what would have happened? Ah, I see. The next time I'm in a situation like this, here is what I'll do . . ." In that way your conscious thinking modifies your behavior on some future occasion.

That sort of process occurs only when we think about something consciously. Still, the question remains, why does it depend on consciousness? Could someone build a robot (presumably unconscious) that calculated possible outcomes of its future actions? If so, why do humans need to be conscious? And what, if anything, is the function of simple awareness, such as the experience you have when you see a flower or hear a melody—the kind of consciousness we probably share with many other animal species? Certainly, many difficult questions remain.

In Closing

The Role of Consciousness

Since the dawn of psychology, most researchers have considered consciousness an impossible topic to research. As you have read in this module, it is a very difficult topic, but it no longer seems impossible. We can do research on some aspects of consciousness, and if we can't answer all the questions, at least we clarify them.

What outcomes can result from research? If we better understand what brain activity is associated with consciousness, we will be in a better position to infer consciousness, or lack of it, in brain-damaged people and in infants, fetuses, and nonhuman animals. We may also be in a position to improve our speculations on the age-old question of the relationship between mind and brain.

Summary

- Why consciousness exists at all is one of the most difficult and profound questions that people ask. We can, however, deal with related questions such as what aspects of brain activity are necessary for consciousness. (page 320)
- Levels of consciousness range from none, in cases of brain death, through coma, vegetative state, minimal consciousness, spatial neglect, and full awareness. (page 321)
- Brain scans provide suggestions of consciousness in some patients who seem unresponsive to their environment. (page 321)
- People with damage in parts of the right hemisphere are conscious, but their consciousness is sometimes limited to the left side of their world. It is possible to direct their attention to information on the left and make it conscious. (page 322)
- A stimulus presented under different conditions may become conscious in some cases and not others. When it becomes conscious, it activates neurons more strongly, and their activity reverberates through other brain areas, establishing synchronized activity in distant brain areas. (page 323)
- In binocular rivalry, we see how two stimuli compete for conscious awareness and for dominance of brain activity. (page 323)
- Conscious experience of a stimulus is a construction that occurs slightly after the stimulus itself. (page 324)
- People's reports of the time of a conscious decision to move indicates that the decision occurs later than the onset of brain activity in preparation for the movement. These results suggest that the first part of a decision process is unconscious. (page 324)
- Some research promotes skepticism that people can report their decision times accurately. Voluntary decisions are gradual, not sudden. (page 326)
- A possible function of conscious thought is to prepare for future action when a similar situation arises. (page 326)

Key Terms

binocular rivalry (page 323)
brain death (page 321)
coma (page 321)
consciousness (page 321)

minimally conscious state (page 321)
readiness potential (page 325)
spatial neglect (page 322)
vegetative state (page 321)

module 10.2

- Why do we sleep?
- What accounts for the content of our dreams?

Consciousness and alertness cycle daily between wakefulness and sleep. During sleep, we become less aware of our surroundings. Dreams take us to a fantasy world where impossible events seem possible. Why do we have these periods of altered consciousness?

Our Circadian Rhythms

Animal life follows cycles. Consider hibernation. Ground squirrels hibernate in winter, when they would have trouble finding food. The females awaken in spring as soon as food is available. The males also need to eat, but they have a reason to awaken earlier: The females are ready to mate as soon as they come out of their winter burrows, and each female mates only once a year. A male who awakens after the females pays for his extra rest by missing his only mating opportunity of the *entire year*. To avoid that risk, males awaken a week before the females do. They spend that week waiting—with no females, nothing to eat, and little to do except fight with one another (French, 1988).

The point is that animals have evolved internal timing mechanisms to prepare them for predictable needs. Male ground squirrels awaken not in response to their current situation but in preparation for what will happen a few days later. Similarly, birds start migrating south in the fall long before their northern homes become inhospitable.

Humans have mechanisms that prepare us for activity during the day and sleep at night. Like other animals, we generate a circadian rhythm, a *rhythm of activity and inactivity lasting about a day*. (The term *circadian* comes from the Latin roots *circa* and *dies*, meaning "about a day.") The rising and setting of the sun provide cues to reset our rhythm, but we generate the rhythm ourselves. In an environment with no cues for time, such as near-polar regions in summer or winter, most people generate a waking–sleeping rhythm a little longer than 24 hours, which gradually drifts out of phase with the clock (Palinkas, 2003).

Your circadian rhythm controls more than sleeping and waking. Over the course of a day, you vary in your hunger, thirst, and urine production. Your body temperature varies from 37.2° C (98.9° F) in late afternoon to 36.7° C (98.1° F) in the middle of the night (Morris, Lack, and Dawson, 1990). Most young people's mood varies over the day, reaching a peak of happiness in late afternoon (Murray et al., 2009).

Certain mice have genes that alter their circadian rhythms (Siepka et al., 2007), and so do some people. People with a faster than average rhythm go to sleep earlier than other people and wake up earlier (Toh et al., 2001). Whereas most people enjoy weekends and vacations as an opportunity to stay up late, people with fast-running rhythms enjoy the opportunity to go to bed even earlier than usual!

Sleepiness and alertness depend on the circadian rhythm, and not just on how long one has gone without sleep. If you have ever gone all night without sleep—as most college students do on occasion—you probably grew very sleepy between 2 and 6 A.M. But in the morning, you began feeling less sleepy, not more. You became more alert because of your circadian rhythm, even though your sleep deprivation continued.

In one study, volunteers went without sleep for three nights. Their body temperature and performance on reasoning tasks declined during the first night and then increased the next morning. During the second and third nights, their temperature and reasoning decreased more than on the first night, but they rebounded somewhat in the day (Figure 10.6). Thus, sleep deprivation produces a pattern of progressive deterioration superimposed on the normal circadian cycle of rising and falling body temperature and alertness (Babkoff, Caspy, Mikulincer, & Sing, 1991).

© Jeff Greenberg/The Image Works

The rising and setting of the sun do not produce our daily rhythm of wakefulness and sleepiness, but they synchronize the rhythm. We adjust our internally generated cycles so that we feel alert during the day and sleepy at night.

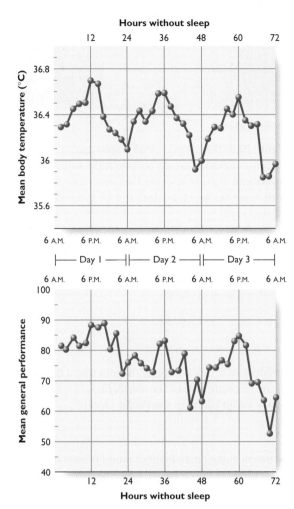

Figure 10.6 Cumulative effects of three nights without sleep: Body temperature and reasoning decrease each night and increase the next morning. They also deteriorate from one day to the next. (From Babkoff, Caspy, Mikulincer, & Sing, 1991.)

concept check

8. If you were on a submarine deep in the ocean with only artificial light that was the same at all times, what would happen to your rhythm of wakefulness and sleepiness?

Answer

8. You would continue to produce a 24-hour circadian rhythm. The sun resets the rhythm, but you generate it within your own body.

Morning People and Evening People

People vary in their circadian rhythms. "Morning people" awaken easily, become alert quickly, and do their best work early. "Evening people" take longer

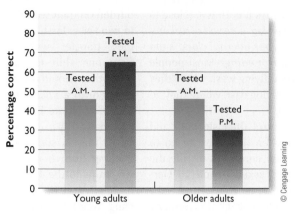

Figure 10.7 Early in the morning, older people perform as well as younger people on memory tasks. Later in the day, young people improve and older people deteriorate.

to warm up in the morning (literally as well as figuratively) and do their best work in the afternoon or evening (Horne, Brass, & Pettitt, 1980). You can probably classify yourself as a morning person, evening person, or intermediate.

Most young adults are either evening people or intermediate, whereas most people over age 65 are morning people. If you ask people at what time they like to go to bed when they have no obligations, their mean answer shifts later and later during the teenage years, reaches 1–2 A.M. at age 20, and then starts reversing, slowly and steadily over decades (Roenneberg et al., 2004). If the shift toward earlier bedtimes after age 20 were a reaction to job requirements, we might expect a sudden change, and we should predict the trend to reverse at retirement. The fact that the trend continues gradually over a lifetime suggests a biological basis. Furthermore, the same pattern occurs in other species. Older rats wake up promptly, whereas younger rats awaken more slowly and improve their performance later (Winocur & Hasher, 1999, 2004).

Age differences in circadian rhythms affect behavior in many ways. Researchers in one study compared the memories of young adults (18–22 years old) and older adults (66–78 years old). Early in the morning, the older adults did about as well as the younger ones. Later in the day, the younger adults remained steady or improved, whereas the older adults deteriorated (May, Hasher, & Stoltzfus, 1993). Figure 10.7 shows the results.

Shifting Sleep Schedules

Ordinarily, the light of early morning resets the body's clock each day to keep it in synchrony with the outside world. If you travel across time zones, your internal rhythm is temporarily out of phase with your new environment. For example, if you travel from California to France, it is 7 A.M. (time to wake up) when your body says it is 10 P.M. (close to bedtime). You experience jet lag, *a period of discomfort and inefficiency while your internal clock is out of phase with your new surroundings.* Most people find it easier to adjust when flying west, where they go to bed later, than when flying east, where they go to bed earlier (Figure 10.8).

People voluntarily control their sleeping and waking times based on when they have to go to school or work, but the sun continues to rule the internal clock. Researchers asked people in Germany the times they prefer to go to bed and wake up. On business days, people throughout Germany awaken at the same time because they are all in the same time zone. However, on weekends and holidays, people in eastern Germany prefer to go to bed and wake up about half an hour earlier than those in western Germany, corresponding to the fact that the sun rises half an hour earlier in eastern Germany (Roenneberg, Kumar, & Merrow, 2007).

People in most parts of the United States have to shift their clock ahead an hour on a Sunday in March because of daylight savings time. On Monday, they awaken when the room clock tells them to, even though their internal clock thinks it is an hour earlier. Waking up while the sky is still dark doesn't effectively reset the internal clock. During the week or two after shifting to daylight savings time, people perform less efficiently than usual (Lahti et al., 2006; Monk & Aplin, 1980). That tendency is strongest for people who were already sleep deprived, including most college students.

Some businesses run three work shifts, such as midnight–8 A.M., 8 A.M.–4 P.M., and 4 P.M.–midnight. Because few people want to work regularly on the midnight–8 A.M. shift, many companies rotate their workers among the three shifts. Long-term shift work has been linked to many problems, including weight gain (Suwazono et al., 2008). Employers can ease the burden on their workers in two ways: First, when they transfer workers from one shift to another, they should transfer them to a *later* shift (Czeisler, Moore-Ede, & Coleman, 1982; Figure 10.9). That is, someone working from 8 A.M.–4 P.M. shifts to the 4 P.M.–midnight time (like traveling west) instead of midnight–8 A.M. (like traveling east). Second, employers can help workers on the night shift by providing bright lights that resemble sunlight. In one study, young people exposed to very bright lights at night adjusted their circadian rhythms to the new schedule within six days. A group who worked under dimmer lights failed to alter their circadian rhythms (Czeisler et al., 1990).

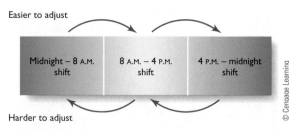

Figure 10.9 The graveyard shift is aptly named: Serious industrial accidents usually occur at night, when workers are least alert. As in jet lag, the direction of change is critical. Moving forward—clockwise—is easier than going backward.

9. Suppose you are the president of a U.S. company, negotiating a business deal with someone from the opposite side of the world. Should you prefer a meeting place in Europe or on an island in the Pacific Ocean?

Answer

9. You should prefer to meet on a Pacific island so that you will travel west.

Brain Mechanisms of Circadian Rhythms

The circadian rhythm of sleep and wakefulness is generated by a tiny structure at the base of the brain known as the *suprachiasmatic nucleus*. If it is damaged, the body's activity cycles become erratic (Rusak, 1977). If cells from that area are kept alive outside the body, they generate a 24-hour rhythm on their own (Earnest, Liang, Ratcliff, & Cassone, 1999; Inouye & Kawamura, 1979). Cells in other areas also produce daily rhythms, but the suprachiasmatic nucleus is the body's main clock (Figure 10.10).

The suprachiasmatic nucleus exerts its control partly by regulating the pineal gland's secretions of the hormone *melatonin*, which is important for both circadian rhythms and many species' annual rhythms of reproduction, hibernation, and so forth (Butler et al., 2010). Ordinarily, the human pineal gland starts releasing melatonin 2 or 3 hours before bedtime. Taking a melatonin pill in the evening has little effect because you are already producing melatonin. However, if you have just flown a few time zones east and want to get to bed before you feel sleepy, then a melatonin pill can help (Deacon & Arendt, 1996).

10. What role does sunlight play in the circadian rhythm?

Answer

10. It resets the rhythm, like resetting the time on your watch.

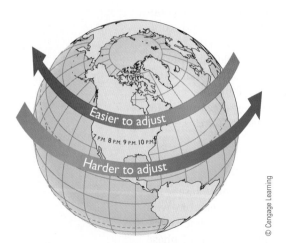

Figure 10.8 People traveling east suffer more serious jet lag than people traveling west.

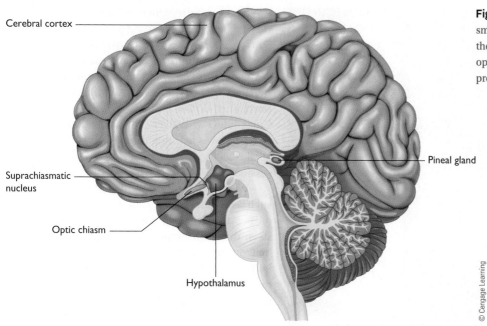

Figure 10.10 The suprachiasmatic nucleus, a small area at the base of the brain, produces the circadian rhythm. Information from the optic nerves resets the timing but doesn't produce it.

Cerebral cortex

Suprachiasmatic nucleus

Optic chiasm

Hypothalamus

Pineal gland

© Cengage Learning

Why We Sleep

We would not have evolved a mechanism that forces us to spend one third of our lives sleeping unless sleep did us some good. But what good does it do? Scientists have identified several benefits.

The simplest is that sleep saves energy. When NASA sent a robot to explore Mars, they programmed it to shut down at night, when exploration would waste energy. Presumably, our ancient ancestors evolved sleep for the same reason. Sleeping mammals and birds lower their body temperatures, and all animals decrease muscle activity, saving energy. When food is scarce, people conserve energy by sleeping longer and at a lower body temperature (Berger & Phillips, 1995).

Various animal species differ in their sleep per day in ways that make sense based on their way of life (Campbell & Tobler, 1984; Siegel, 2005). Predatory animals, including cats and bats, sleep most of the day. They get the nutrition they need from brief, energy-rich meals, and they face little danger of attack during their sleep. In contrast, horses need to spend many hours grazing, and their survival depends on running away from attackers, even at night (Figure 10.11). They sleep little and rouse easily. Woody Allen once wrote, "The lion and the calf shall lie down together, but the calf won't get much sleep."

Some people need less sleep than others (Meddis, Pearson, & Langford, 1973). As a rule, "evening people," who waken late and stay up late, tolerate sleep deprivation better than morning people—partly because evening people tend to be younger and more energetic (Caldwell et al., 2005). Also, some individuals tolerate sleep deprivation better than others. In 1965 a San Diego high school student, Randy

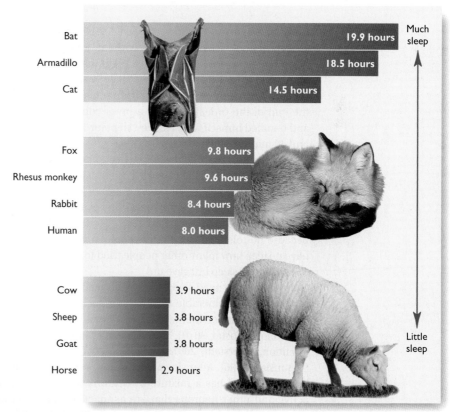

Bat	19.9 hours
Armadillo	18.5 hours
Cat	14.5 hours
Fox	9.8 hours
Rhesus monkey	9.6 hours
Rabbit	8.4 hours
Human	8.0 hours
Cow	3.9 hours
Sheep	3.8 hours
Goat	3.8 hours
Horse	2.9 hours

Much sleep

Little sleep

Figure 10.11 Predatory mammals sleep more than prey animals. Predators are seldom attacked during their sleep, but prey species need to arouse quickly from sleep to avoid being attacked. (Based on data from Zepelin & Rechtschaffen, 1974.)

Figure 10.12 Even near the end of Randy Gardner's 264 consecutive sleepless hours, he remained alert and coordinated. Observers dutifully recorded his every move.

Gardner (Figure 10.12), stayed awake for 11 days as a high school science project without apparent harm (Dement, 1972). On the last night, he played about 100 arcade games against sleep researcher William Dement and won every game. Just before the end of the ordeal, he held a press conference and handled himself well. He then slept for 14 hours and 40 minutes and awoke refreshed.

If a torturer prevented you from sleeping for the next 11 days, would you do as well as Randy Gardner? Probably not, for two reasons: First, Gardner knew he could quit. A sense of control makes any experience less stressful. Second, we heard about Gardner only because he tolerated sleep deprivation so well. We have no idea how many other people tried to deprive themselves of sleep but gave up.

Still, people need sleep. Sleep-deprived people become more vulnerable to illness, especially depression and other mental illnesses (Wulff, Gatti, Wettstein, & Foster, 2010). They also suffer lapses of attention (Åkerstedt, 2007; Gvilia, Xu, McGinty, & Szymusiak, 2006). After sleep deprivation, someone who is "awake" has a mixture of neurons that are active and other neurons that are as inactive as if the person were asleep (Vyazovskiy et al., 2011). As a result, a sleep-deprived driver is as dangerous as a drunk driver (Falleti, Maruff, Collie, Darby, & McStephen, 2003).

Sleep also strengthens learning and memory to varying degrees, depending on the type of learning (Doyon et al., 2009). When you learn something, your memory improves if you go to sleep within the next 3 hours (even a nap), and it deteriorates after a sleepless night (Hu, Stylos-Allan, & Walker, 2006; Korman et al., 2007; Rasch & Born, 2008; Yoo, Hu, Gujar, Jolesz, & Walker, 2007). A good night's sleep also improves learning the next day (Van der Werf et al., 2009). So beware of those all-night study sessions.

When people learn a difficult new motor task, such as a video game skill, the brain areas active during the learning become reactivated during sleep that night, replaying the same patterns they had during the day, only faster (and sometimes backward). The amount of activity in those areas during sleep predicts the amount of improvement the next day (Euston, Tatsuno, & McNaughton, 2007; Huber, Ghilardi, Massimini, & Tononi, 2004; Maquet et al., 2000; Peigneux et al., 2004). Wakefulness and sleep play complementary roles in learning. Animal researchers have demonstrated that learning strengthens the appropriate synapses during wakefulness and weakens other synapses during sleep (Vyazovskiy, Cirelli, Pfister-Genskow, Faraguna, & Tononi, 2008).

concept check

11. Name two important functions of sleep.

Answer

11. Sleep conserves energy, and memories strengthen during sleep.

Stages of Sleep

In the mid-1950s, French and American researchers independently discovered a stage of sleep called *paradoxical sleep*, or rapid eye movement (REM) sleep (Dement & Kleitman, 1957a, 1957b; Jouvet, Michel, & Courjon, 1959). *During this stage of sleep, the sleeper's eyes move rapidly back and forth under the closed lids.* (The other stages of sleep are known as non-REM, or NREM, sleep.) A paradox is an apparent contradiction. REM sleep is paradoxical because it is light in some ways and deep in others. It is light because the brain is active and the body's heart rate, breathing rate, and temperature fluctuate substantially (Parmeggiani, 1982). It is deep because the large muscles of the body that control posture and locomotion are deeply relaxed. Indeed, the nerves to those muscles are virtually paralyzed at this time. REM also has features that are hard to classify as deep or light, such as penis erections and vaginal lubrication.

William Dement's early research indicated that people who were awakened during REM sleep usually reported dreaming, but people who were awakened during other periods seldom reported dreaming. Later research weakened that link, however. Adults who are awakened during REM sleep report dreams about 85 to 90% of the time, whereas those awakened during NREM (non-REM) sleep report dreams on 50 to 60% of occasions (Foulkes, 1999). REM dreams are on average longer, more complicated, and more visual, with more action by the dreamer, but not always (McNamara, McLaren, Smith, Brown, & Stickgold, 2005). Furthermore, some people with brain damage have REM sleep but no dreams, and others have dreams but no REM sleep (Solms, 1997). Thus, REM is not synonymous with dreaming (Domhoff, 1999).

Nevertheless, because vivid dreams are most common during REM sleep and because the postural muscles are paralyzed during REM sleep, people typically do not act out their dreams. A small number of people, with a condition called *REM behavior disorder*, fail to inhibit their muscular activity during REM, and as a result, they sometimes walk around flailing their arms.

Sleep Cycles During the Night

The brain is more active than you might guess during sleep. Neurons' metabolic rate, spontaneous activity, and responsiveness to stimuli decrease by less than 20% (Hobson, 2005). The main characteristic of sleep is an increase of inhibitory messages, preventing brain messages from reverberating widely (Massimini et al., 2005). Activity in one brain area becomes less likely to excite other areas (Esser, Hill, & Tononi, 2009). As noted in the first module of this chapter, a spread of messages through the brain is central to conscious experience, so blocking that spread decreases consciousness.

Sleep researchers distinguish among sleep stages by recording brain waves with electrodes attached to the scalp (Figure 10.13). An electroencephalograph (EEG) *measures and amplifies tiny electrical changes on the scalp that reflect patterns of brain activity.* Sleep researchers *combine an EEG measure with a simultaneous measure of eye movements to produce a* polysomnograph (literally, "many-sleep measure"), as shown in Figure 10.14. A sleeper first enters stage 1, when the eyes are nearly motionless and the EEG shows many short, choppy waves (Figure 10.14a) that indicate a fair amount of brain activity. Because brain cells fire

Figure 10.13 Electrodes monitor the activity in a sleeper's brain, and an EEG records and displays brain-wave patterns.

out of synchrony, their activities nearly cancel each other out, like the sound of many people talking at the same time.

As sleep continues, a person progresses into stages 2, 3, and 4, as shown in Figure 10.14b–e. These stages differ in the number of long, slow waves. Stage 2 has the fewest and stage 4 has the most. These waves indicate synchrony among neurons, related to *decreased* brain activity. The waves grow larger because the little brain activity that does occur drives many neurons in synchrony. Stage 2 is also marked by sleep spindles, *waves of activity at about 12–14 per second* that result from an exchange of information between the cerebral cortex and the underlying thalamus. Sleep spindles are important for storing memory (Eschenko, Mölle, Born, & Sara, 2006), and counts of people's spindles per night correlate surprisingly highly (.7) with their IQ scores (Fogel, Nader, Cote, & Smith, 2007).

A sleeper progresses through stages 2, 3, and 4 then gradually back through stages 3 and 2, and then to REM sleep. In Figure 10.14f, the EEG in REM sleep resembles that of stage 1, but the eyes move steadily. At the end of REM sleep, the sleeper cycles again through stages 2, 3, 4 and then back to 3, 2, and REM. In a healthy young adult, each cycle lasts 90 to 100 minutes on average. As shown in Figure 10.15, over the course of the night, stages 3 and 4 become shorter while REM and stage 2 increase in duration.

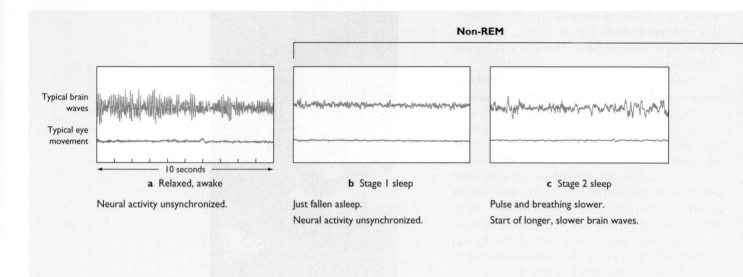

Figure 10.14 During sleep, people progress through stages of varying brain activity. The blue line indicates brain waves, as shown by an EEG. The red li◾ shows eye movements. REM sleep resembles stage 1 sleep, except for the addition of rapid eye movements. (Courtesy of T. E. Le Vere.)

Figure 10.15 This sleeper had five cycles of REM and non-REM sleep and awakened (A) briefly three times during the night. Stage 4 occupies more time◾ earlier in the night than later. REM and stage 2 become more prevalent as the night progresses. (From Dement, 1972.)

concept check

12. During which sleep stage is the brain least active? During which stage are the muscles least active?

Answer

12. The brain is least active during stage 4 sleep. The muscles are least active during REM sleep.

Abnormalities of Sleep

Comedian Steven Wright says that someone asked him, "Did you sleep well last night?" He replied, "No, I made a few mistakes."

We laugh because sleep isn't the kind of activity on which people make mistakes. Sometimes, however, we fail to sleep, feel poorly rested, or have bad dreams. These experiences are not "mistakes," but our sleep is not what we wanted it to be.

Insomnia

Insomnia means "lack of sleep." More specifically, insomnia is *not enough sleep for the person to feel rested the next day.* Six hours sleep could be in-somnia for one person and not another. Insomnia results from causes includ-ing noise, worries, indigestion, uncomfortable temperatures, use of alcohol or caffeine, and medical or psychological disorders (Ohayon, 1997). If you have persistent insomnia, consult a physician, but for occasional or minor insomnia, you can try a few things yourself (Hauri, 1982; Lilie & Rosenberg, 1990):

- Keep a regular time schedule for going to bed and waking up each day.
- Avoid caffeine, nicotine, and other stimulants, especially in the evening.
- Don't rely on alcohol or tranquilizers to fall asleep. After repeated use, you may be unable to sleep without them.
- Keep your bedroom cool and quiet.
- Exercise daily but not shortly before bedtime.

Sleep Apnea

Apnea (AP-nee-uh) means "no breathing." Many people have occasional brief periods without breathing while asleep. People with sleep apnea, however, *fail to breathe for a minute or more and then wake up gasping for breath.* They may lie in bed for 8 to 10 hours but sleep less than half that time. Sleep apnea is most common in overweight middle-aged men whose breathing passages become narrower than usual. While awake, they compensate by breathing frequently and vigorously, but they can't keep up this pattern while they are asleep (Mezzanotte, Tangel, & White, 1992).

Non-REM

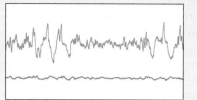

d Stage 3 sleep

Pulse, breathing, and brain activity slower yet.

Neural activity more synchronized.

Stages 3 and 4 dominate first half of night.

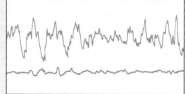

e Stage 4 sleep

Pulse, breathing, and brain activity slowest.

Brain waves highly synchronized, indicating low overall neuron activity.

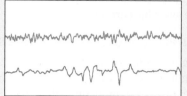

Typical brain waves

Typical eye movement

f REM (paradoxical) sleep

Eyes move back and forth.

Dreams more frequent, vivid, complex.

Brain waves desynchronized.

Postural muscles most relaxed.

Duration gets longer toward morning.

| 3 A.M. | | | 4 A.M. | | | 5 A.M. | | | 6 A.M. | | | 7 A.M. |

2 3 2 REM 1 2 3 2 A 1 REM A A 2 REM

Insomnia is identified by how sleepy the person is the following day.

Treatment includes recommendations to lose weight and to avoid alcohol and tranquilizers before bedtime. Surgeons can remove tissue to widen the airways. Some people with sleep apnea use a device that pumps air into a mask covering the nose and mouth during sleep, forcing the person to breathe.

Narcolepsy

People with narcolepsy experience *sudden attacks of sleepiness during the day*. They also experience sudden attacks of muscle weakness or paralysis and occasional dreamlike experiences while awake. These symptoms represent intrusions of REM sleep into the waking period (Guilleminault, Heinzer, Mignot, & Black, 1998).

Dogs with a particular gene also develop narcolepsy. This gene impairs the brain receptors for a transmitter called *orexin*, also known as *hypocretin* (Lin et al., 1999). Other researchers found that preventing the production of orexin causes narcolepsy in mice (Chemelli et al., 1999). People with narcolepsy have fewer than the normal number of orexin-producing neurons (Thanickal et al., 2000). Orexin does not wake people up, but helps them stay awake (M. G. Lee, Hassani, & Jones, 2005). People lacking orexin alternate between wakefulness and sleepiness repeatedly over a day instead of remaining awake during the day and asleep at night (Mochizuki et al., 2004).

A combination of stimulant and antidepressant drugs maintains wakefulness during the day and blocks the attacks of muscle weakness. Future research may develop medications based on orexin, but none are available currently.

Miscellaneous Sleep Experiences

Sleep talking is a common experience that ranges from a grunted word to a clear paragraph. Many people talk in their sleep more often than they realize because they do not remember sleep talking and usually no one else hears them. Sleep talking is most common during stage 2 sleep, but it occurs in all stages (Moorcroft, 2003). Sleep talkers sometimes pause between utterances, as if they were carrying on a conversation. In fact, it is possible to engage some sleep talkers in a dialogue. Sleep talking is not related to mental or emotional disorders, and sleep talkers rarely say anything embarrassing. So if you talk in your sleep, don't worry about it.

Have you ever had the experience of waking up and finding yourself unable to move? If so, don't be alarmed. When you awaken, various brain areas don't necessarily all awaken at once (Krueger et al., 2008; Silva & Duffy, 2008). Occasionally, most of your cortex awakens but one part of your medulla continues sending inhibitory messages to the spinal cord, just as it does during REM sleep. You then find yourself alert, with your eyes open, but temporarily unable to move your arms or legs.

Sleepwalking tends to run (walk?) in families, mostly in children and mainly during stage 4 sleep (Dement, 1972). Some adults sleepwalk also, mostly during the first half of the night's sleep. They have clumsy, apparently purposeless movements with only limited responsiveness to their surroundings. Contrary to what you may have heard, wakening a sleepwalker is not dangerous, although it is not particularly helpful either (Moorcroft, 2003). A better idea is to guide the person gently back to bed. In addition to walking during sleep, some people have been known to eat, rearrange furniture, drive cars, and engage in sex (either by masturbation or with a partner) during sleep (Mangan, 2004). You might wonder, is the person really asleep? The answer is "sort of." As mentioned, the entire brain doesn't necessarily wake up or go to sleep all at once. Sleep can be localized to one brain area more than another. Sleepwalking occurs when certain brain areas are awake while others are asleep.

Lucid dreaming is another example in which part of the brain is awake and another part asleep. Someone having a lucid dream *is aware that it is a dream*. Evidently part of the brain, probably the prefrontal cortex, is more awake than usual during such a dream, and capable of noticing that the brain is dreaming.

Do you ever lie in bed, trying to fall asleep, when suddenly a leg kicks? An occasional leg jerk while trying to fall asleep is common and no cause for concern. However, some people have *prolonged "creepy-crawly" sensations in their legs, accompanied by repetitive leg movements strong enough to awaken the person, especially during the first half of the night* (Moorcroft, 1993). This condition, known as periodic limb movement disorder (or more informally as restless leg syndrome), interrupts sleep in many people, mostly over age 50. The causes are unknown, and the best advice is to avoid factors that make the condition worse, such as caffeine, stress, or fatigue. Tranquilizers sometimes suppress these leg movements (Schenck & Mahowald, 1996).

Nightmares are merely unpleasant dreams. A night terror, however, *causes someone to awaken screaming and sweating with a racing heart rate, sometimes flailing with the arms*. Night terrors occur during stage 3 or stage 4 sleep, not REM sleep, and their dream content, if any, is usually simple, such as a single image. Comforting or reassuring people during a night terror is futile, and the terror simply has to run its course. Many children have night terrors, as do nearly 3% of adults (Mahowald & Schenck, 2005). Treatments include psychotherapy, antidepressant and antianxiety drugs, and advice to minimize stress.

concept check

13. What experience reflects the fact that part of the brain can be awake while another is asleep?

Answer

13. Any of the following: waking up but finding oneself unable to move, sleepwalking, or lucid dreaming.

Dreams

Even a saint is not responsible for what happens in his dreams.
 —St. Thomas Aquinas

In ancient times, people believed that dreams foretold the future. Occasionally, of course, they do, either by coincidence or because the dreamer had a reason to expect some outcome. Today, scientists do not believe dreams tell us about the future, although many other people do. If you dream about a plane crash tonight, will you hesitate to take a plane trip tomorrow? If you dream your friend treats you badly or your lover is unfaithful, will you become suspicious in real life? If so, you have plenty of company (Morewedge & Norton, 2009).

If dreams do not tell us the future, what do they tell us? Can we explain or interpret dreams? Let's consider dream content.

Descriptive Studies of Dreaming

To determine dream content, some studies ask people to keep dream diaries. Another approach is to awaken people in the laboratory and ask for immediate dream reports (Domhoff, 2003). Table 10.1 lists common dream themes of college students in three countries at two times. Note the similarity across the samples.

Dreams differ from one culture to another in predictable ways (Domhoff & Schneider, 2008). For example, people in hunter-gatherer societies have many dreams about animals and people in dangerous societies have dreams about being victims of violent aggression. Still, the cross-cultural similarities in dream content are striking.

Common usage implies that dreams are happy. In the Disney movie, Cinderella sings, "A dream is a wish your heart makes." Martin Luther King Jr.'s famous "I Have a Dream" speech described a wonderful future. Calling your boy-

Table 10.1 Percentages of College Students Who Reported Certain Dream Topics

Dream Topic	U.S. 1958	Japan 1958	Canada 2003
Falling	83%	74%	74%
Being attacked or pursued	77%	91%	82%
Trying to do something again and again	71%	87%	54%
Schoolwork	71%	86%	67%
Sex	66%	68%	76%
Arriving too late	64%	49%	60%
Eating delicious food	62%	68%	31%
Frozen with fright	58%	87%	41%
Loved one dying	57%	42%	54%

Based on Griffith, Miyagi, & Tago (1958); Nielsen et al. (2003).
© Cengage Learning

friend or girlfriend "dreamy" would be a compliment. Sigmund Freud claimed that all dreams are based on wish fulfillment. However, Table 10.1 shows that much or most of dream content is unpleasant, such as falling, being chased, or being unable to do something. When college students recorded their dreams and their daytime experiences, 73% of their dreams included something threatening, as opposed to only 15% of their daytime activity reports (Valli, Strandholm, Sillanmäki, & Revonsuo, 2008). Curiously, 11- to 13-year-olds have the happiest dreams on average (Foulkes, 1999). From then on, dreams get worse and worse. Sorry about that.

Although some dreams are bizarre, most are similar to what we think about in everyday life (Domhoff, 1996; Hall & Van de Castle, 1966). For example, preteens seldom dream about the opposite sex, but teenagers do (Strauch & Lederbogen, 1999). Blind people frequently dream about difficulties in locomotion or transportation (Hurovitz, Dunn, Domhoff, & Fiss, 1999). In one study, young adults checked off from a list of topics those that were concerns to them and others that were matters of indifference. Then they reported their dreams over three nights. They frequently dreamed of the concerns and rarely of the indifferent topics (Nikles, Brecht, Klinger, & Bursell, 1998). However, we do not dream about everything we do in daily life. People seldom dream about reading, writing,

using a computer, or watching television (Schredl, 2000). They do dream about sexual and other fantasies that they don't act on in real life. For the best research on dream content, visit this website: http://www2.ucsc.edu/dreams.

Many questions about dreaming are difficult to answer. For example, "How accurately do we remember our dreams?" Well, how would we find out? With real events, we compare people's memories to what actually happened, but we have no way to compare reported dreams to the originals. Or consider this apparently simple question: "Do we dream in color?" People ask because they do not remember. But how could an investigator answer the question except by asking people to remember? The best evidence we have is that, when people are awakened and asked immediately, they report color at least half of the time (Herman, Roffwarg, & Tauber, 1968; Padgham, 1975). This result does not mean that other dreams are in black and white. Perhaps the colors in those dreams are not memorable.

Do blind people have visual dreams? It depends. People who become blind because of damage to the visual cortex lose visual dreaming as well as visual imagery. People who experience eye damage after about age 5 to 7 continue to have visual dreams, although their frequency of visual dreams declines over time. People who were born blind or who became blind in early childhood have no visual imagery in their dreams. Instead, they dream of sounds, touch, smells, and tastes (Hurovitz et al., 1999).

concept check

14. How is the content of dreams similar to waking thoughts, and how is it different?

Answer

14. We mostly dream about the same topics we think about, but dreams usually feature less happy emotions.

SLOW WAVE

This comic strip represents an actual dream as described to the artist. Dreams often mix possible with impossible events and frequently explore the theme of "things that could go wrong." (Reprinted with permission of Jesse Reklaw.)

Freud's Theory of Dreams

The Austrian physician Sigmund Freud, founder of psychoanalysis, maintained that dreams reveal the dreamer's unconscious thoughts and motivations. To understand a dream, he said, one must probe for hidden meanings. Each dream has a manifest content—*the content that appears on the surface*—and a latent content—*the hidden ideas that the dream experience represents symbolically.*

For example, Freud (1900/1955) once dreamed that one of his friends was his uncle. He worked out these associations: Two of his friends had been recommended for an appointment as professor, but both had been rejected, probably because they were Jews. Freud himself had been recommended for the same appointment, and he feared that he too would be rejected because he was Jewish. How did the friends relate to the uncle? One of the friends was in Freud's judgment a bit simpleminded, like Freud's uncle. The other had once been accused of misconduct, and Freud's uncle had been convicted of business misdealing. By linking these friends to his uncle, Freud interpreted the dream as meaning, "Maybe they didn't get the university appointment because one was a simpleton (like my uncle) and the other was regarded as a criminal (like my uncle). If so, my being Jewish might not stop me from getting the appointment."

Curiously, whenever Freud described one of his own dreams, as in the case above, his interpretation had nothing to do with sex. When he described anyone else's dream, invariably the interpretation centered on sexual symbolism. In one example, a man described a dream of seeing six or seven white dogs with large tails, sitting motionless. Freud claimed the dream related to a childhood experience of seeing his parents have sex, doggy style. Even the patient himself regarded this interpretation as implausible and far-fetched (Esterson, 1993).

Many therapists offer dream interpretations that their clients find meaningful. However, there is no way to check which interpretations are accurate and which ones are not. Freud's approach to dream analysis has been on the decline (Domhoff, 2003).

15. Are Freud's ideas on dreaming falsifiable in the sense described in chapter 2?

Answer

15. No. A falsifiable theory makes specific predictions so that we could imagine evidence that would contradict it. Freud's dream theories make no clear predictions.

Modern Theories of Dreaming

According to the activation-synthesis theory of dreams, *dreams occur because the cortex takes the haphazard activity that occurs during REM sleep plus whatever stimuli strike the sense organs and does its best to make sense of this activity* (Hobson & McCarley, 1977). Some aspects of dreams do appear to relate to spontaneous brain activity and various stimuli. For example, input from the pons activates the visual areas of the brain, especially during the first minutes of an REM period, and nearly all dreams include visual content (Amzica & Steriade, 1996). Also, when people dream of using a toilet or trying to find a toilet, they often awake and discover that they really do need to use a toilet. Do you ever dream that you are trying to walk or run, but you cannot move? One explanation is that the major postural muscles are really paralyzed during REM sleep. Your brain sends messages telling your muscles to move but receives sensory feedback indicating they have not moved.

One problem is that the activation-synthesis theory makes no clear, testable predictions. For example, the muscles are always paralyzed during REM sleep. Why don't we always dream that we can't move? Also, a dream only occasionally incorporates sounds or other stimuli in the room (Nir & Tononi, 2010). Perhaps a more serious problem for this theory is that dream experiences, while strange, do not appear to be random or haphazard.

An alternative view is that dreaming is a special kind of thinking that occurs under special conditions (Domhoff, 2011; Foulkes, 1999; Solms, 2000), including these:

- reduced sensory stimulation, especially in the brain's primary sensory areas
- reduced activity in the prefrontal cortex, important for planning and working memory
- loss of voluntary control of thinking
- persisting activity of much of the rest of the cortex, including areas responsible for face recognition and certain aspects of motivation and emotion

William Domhoff (2011) compares dreaming to activity of the brain's "default network," the system active during mind wandering and daydreaming. The default network drifts from thought to thought without plan or control, much as a dream does. Because the primary visual and auditory areas of the brain are doing little during sleep, the rest of the brain constructs images without interference, usually focusing on something the dreamer has seen, heard, or thought about in the last several days. Occasionally a dream deals with something that was a worry long ago. For example, an older person might dream about forgetting a high-school locker combination. Because of low activity in the prefrontal cortex, an area important for planning and working memory, the dream story jumps from one event to another without much continuity and without much sense of intention.

Dreams do reveal something about the dreamer's interests and personality. That is, you dream about issues that interest or worry you. However, that kind of interpretation is different from finding hidden symbolic meanings, as Freud and his followers have done.

16. How does dreaming differ from other thinking?

Answer

16. Dreaming resembles other thinking, but it occurs during a time of decreased sensory input and loss of voluntary control of thinking.

module 10.2

The Mysteries of Sleep and Dreams

Sleep and dreams are not a state of unconsciousness but a state of reduced or altered consciousness. For example, a parent will awaken at the sound of a child softly crying. A healthy brain is never completely off duty, never completely relaxed.

Although our understanding of sleep and dreams continues to grow, major questions remain. Even such basic issues as the function of REM sleep remain in doubt. People have long found their dreams a source of wonder, and researchers continue to find much of interest and mystery.

Summary

- *Circadian rhythms.* Even in an unchanging environment, people become sleepy in cycles of approximately 24 hours. (page 328)
- *Morning and evening people.* Some people arouse quickly and reach their peak alertness early. Others increase alertness more slowly and reach their peak in late afternoon or early evening. (page 329)
- *Brain mechanisms of circadian rhythms.* An area of the brain generates an approximately 24-hour rhythm. Sunlight does not generate this rhythm, but it does reset it. It is difficult to maintain a wake–sleep schedule that is out of synchrony with sun time. (page 330)
- *The need for sleep.* Sleep serves several functions, including conservation of energy and an opportunity to strengthen memories. Sleep-deprived people have difficulty maintaining attention. (page 331)
- *Sleep stages.* During sleep, people cycle through sleep stages 1 through 4 and back through stages 3 and 2 to 1 again. The cycle beginning and ending with stage 1 lasts about 90 to 100 minutes. (page 332)
- *REM sleep.* A special stage known as REM sleep replaces the stage 1 periods after the first one. REM sleep is characterized by rapid eye movements, a high level of brain activity, and relaxed muscles. Dreams are common in this stage but not limited to it. (page 332)
- *Insomnia.* Insomnia—subjectively unsatisfactory sleep—results from many influences. Sleep abnormalities include sleep apnea and narcolepsy. (page 334)
- *Dream content.* More dreams are more threatening than pleasant. Freud proposed that dreams are the product of unconscious motivations. Modern theorists describe dreaming as a kind of thinking that occurs under conditions of low sensory input and no voluntary control of thinking. (page 336)

Key Terms

activation-synthesis theory of dreams (page 338)
circadian rhythm (page 328)
electroencephalograph (EEG) (page 333)
insomnia (page 334)
jet lag (page 330)
latent content (page 338)
lucid dreaming (page 336)
manifest content (page 338)

narcolepsy (page 335)
night terror (page 336)
periodic limb movement disorder (page 336)
polysomnograph (page 333)
rapid eye movement (REM) sleep (page 332)
sleep apnea (page 334)
sleep spindles (page 333)

- What can hypnosis do?
- What are its limitations?

Truth is nothing but a path traced between errors.[1]

—Franz Anton Mesmer

If a hypnotist told you that you were 4 years old and you starting acting like a 4-year-old, we would say that you are a good hypnotic subject. If the hypnotist said your cousin was sitting in the empty chair in front of you and you agreed that you see her, then again, we would remark on the depth of your hypnotism.

But what if you had *not* been hypnotized and you suddenly started acting like a 4-year-old or insisted that you saw someone in an empty chair? Then psychologists would suspect that you were suffering from a serious psychological disorder. Hypnosis induces a temporary state that is sometimes bizarre. No wonder we find it so fascinating.

Hypnosis is *a condition of increased suggestibility that occurs in the context of a special hypnotist–subject relationship.* The term *hypnosis* comes from Hypnos, the Greek god of sleep, although the similarity between hypnosis and sleep is superficial. People in both states lose initiative, and hypnotized people, like dreamers, accept contradictory information without protest. Hypnotized people, however, walk around and respond to objects in the real world. Also, their brain activity is like that of a relaxed wakeful person, not a sleeper (Rainville, Hofbauer, Bushnell, Duncan, & Price, 2002).

Hypnosis was introduced by Franz Anton Mesmer (1734–1815), an Austrian physician. Mesmer sometimes treated illnesses by passing a magnet back and forth across a patient's body to redirect the flow of blood, nerve activity, and undefined "fluids." Some patients reported dramatic benefits. Later, Mesmer discovered that he could dispense with the magnet and use only his hand. From this observation, most people would conclude that the phenomenon related to the power of suggestion. Mesmer, however, drew the quirky conclusion that

he did not need a magnet because *he himself* was a magnet. With that claim, he gave us the term *animal magnetism.*

After his death, others studied "animal magnetism" or "Mesmerism," eventually calling it "hypnotism." By that time, many physicians and scientists had already associated hypnosis with charlatans and hocus-pocus. Still today, some stage performers use hypnosis for entertainment. We should carefully distinguish the exaggerated claims from the legitimate use of hypnosis by licensed therapists.

Ways of Inducing Hypnosis

Mesmer thought hypnosis was a power emanating from his body. If so, only special people could hypnotize others. Today, we find that successful hypnotists need practice but no unusual powers.

The first step toward being hypnotized is agreeing to give it a try. Contrary to what you may have heard, no one can hypnotize an uncooperative person. A hypnotist tells you to sit down and relax, and you do so because you would like to experience hypnosis. The whole point of hypnosis is following the hypnotist's suggestions, and when you sit down and relax, you are already following a suggestion.

Although Mesmer is often depicted as being able to control people irresistibly, hypnosis depends on the person's willingness.

[1]Does this seem profound? Or is it nonsense? Many statements sound profound until we try to figure out exactly what they mean.

A hypnotist induces hypnosis by repeating suggestions, relying on the hypnotized person's cooperation and willingness to accept suggestions.

A hypnotist might then monotonously repeat something like, "You are starting to fall asleep. Your eyelids are getting heavy. Your eyelids are getting very heavy. They are starting to close. You are falling into a deep, deep sleep." In another technique (Udolf, 1981), the hypnotist suggests, "After you go under hypnosis, your arm will begin to rise automatically." (Some people, eager for the hypnosis to succeed, shoot their arm up immediately and have to be told, "No, not yet. Just relax. That will happen later.") Then the hypnotist encourages you to relax and suggests that your arm is starting to feel lighter, as if it were tied to a helium balloon.

The hypnotist might suggest that your arm is beginning to feel strange and is beginning to twitch. The timing of this suggestion is important because when you stand or sit in one position long enough, your limbs really do feel strange and twitch. If the hypnotist's suggestion comes at just the right moment, you think, "Wow, that's right. My arm does feel strange. This is starting to work!" Believing that you are being hypnotized is a big step toward actually being hypnotized.

The Uses and Limitations of Hypnosis

Hypnosis resembles ordinary suggestibility. If someone asked you to imagine a bright, sunny day, you almost certainly would, without being hypnotized. If you were asked to please stand and put your hands on your head, you probably would, again without being hypnotized. Then someone asks you to stand, flap your arms, and cluck like a chicken. You might or might not. People vary in how far they will follow suggestions, and the people who follow the most suggestions under hypnosis are the same as those who follow the most suggestions without hypnosis.

Hypnosis enhances suggestibility a little, but only a little (J. Kirsch & Braffman, 2001). If you are easily hypnotizable, you probably also respond strongly to books and movies, reacting almost as if the events were really happening.

What Hypnosis Can Do

One well-established effect of hypnosis is to inhibit pain. Some people undergo medical or dental surgery with only hypnosis and no anesthesia. The benefits of hypnosis are most easily demonstrated for acute (sudden) pains, but hypnosis helps with chronic pains, too (Patterson, 2004). Hypnosis is particularly helpful for people who react unfavorably to anesthetic drugs and those who have developed a tolerance to pain-killing opiates.

Recall from chapter 4 that pain has both sensory and emotional components. Hypnosis alters mostly the emotional components. Even when a hypnotized person says that he or she feels no pain, the heart rate and blood pressure still increase (Hilgard, 1973). Under hypnotic suggestion to feel no unpleasantness, a person subjected to painful stimuli shows high arousal

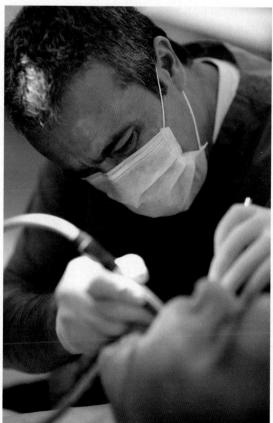

Some dentists use hypnosis to relieve pain, even for tooth extractions and root canal surgery.

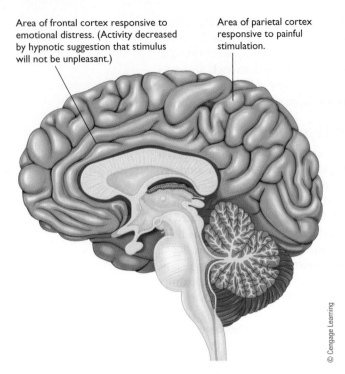

Area of frontal cortex responsive to emotional distress. (Activity decreased by hypnotic suggestion that stimulus will not be unpleasant.)

Area of parietal cortex responsive to painful stimulation.

© Cengage Learning

Figure 10.16 A hypnotic suggestion to experience less pain decreases activity in the frontal cortex areas associated with emotional distress but has little effect on the sensory areas in the parietal cortex.

in the parietal cortex areas responsive to body sensations but not in the frontal cortex areas responsive to unpleasant emotions (Rainville, Duncan, Price, Carrier, & Bushnell, 1997; Figure 10.16).

Another use of hypnosis is posthypnotic suggestion, *a suggestion to do or experience something after coming out of hypnosis.* Suppose you receive a suggestion under hypnosis that whenever you see the number 1, it will look red, and when you see the number 2, it will look yellow. After you emerge from hypnosis, the researcher shows you black numbers on various backgrounds and asks you to press a key as soon as you see a number. You will have no trouble seeing 1 or 2, but you will usually fail to see 1 or 2 (Cohen Kadosh, Henik, Catena, Walsh, & Fuentes, 2009). Until the hypnotist cancels the suggestion or it wears off, you will be like the people with synesthesia, as discussed in chapter 4.

In one study, adults known to be easily hypnotized were randomly assigned to two groups. One group was handed a stack of 120 addressed stamped postcards and asked (without being hypnotized) to mail one back each day until they exhausted the stack. Another group was given a posthypnotic suggestion to mail one card per day. The nonhypnotized group actually mailed back more cards, but they reported that they had to remind themselves each day to mail a card. Those given the posthypnotic suggestion said they never made a deliberate

effort. The idea of mailing a card just "popped into mind," providing a sudden compulsion to mail one (Barnier & McConkey, 1998).

Many therapists have given cigarette smokers a posthypnotic suggestion that they will not want to smoke. The results are mixed. Some studies report significant benefits, but placebo treatments also produce benefits (Elkins, Marcus, Bates, Rajab, & Cook, 2006; J. P. Green, Lynn, & Montgomery, 2008). That is, much of the improvement depends on expectations.

What Hypnosis Does Not Do

Many of the spectacular claims about the power of hypnosis become less impressive on closer scrutiny. For instance, as in Figure 10.17, people under hypnosis can balance their head and neck on one chair and their feet on another chair and even allow someone to stand on their body! Amazing? Not really. It's easier than it looks, with or without hypnosis. Give it a try. (But don't invite someone to stand on you. Someone who does not balance correctly could injure you.)

Many people have attempted to use hypnosis to enhance memory. For example, a distressed person tells a psychotherapist, "I don't know why I have such troubles. Maybe I had a bad experience when I was younger. I just can't remember." Or a witness to a crime says, "I saw the culprit for a second or two, but now I can't give you a good description." Therapists and police officers have sometimes turned to hypnosis in the hope of uncovering lost memories. However, hypnotized people are highly suggestible. When given a suggestion such as "you will remember more than you told us before," hypnotized people report more information, some of it correct and most of it incorrect (Fligstein, Barabasz, Barabasz, Trevisan, & Warner, 1998; J. P. Green & Lynn, 2005; Wagstaff et al., 2004). If nonhypnotized people are asked to "guess" additional information that they can't remember, their additional information is about the same as what hypnosis yields—a few more correct facts, and a great deal of incorrect information. The main difference is that people under hypnosis report their incorrect information with more confidence (Dinges et al., 1992). Let's consider a typical study.

critical check

What's the Evidence?

Hypnosis and Memory

The design of this study and many like it is simple: The experimenter presents material, tests people's memory of it, hypnotizes them, and tests their memory again (Dywan & Bowers, 1983).

Hypothesis People will remember some of the material without hypnosis and more of it after hypnosis.

Method Fifty-four people looked at 60 drawings of simple objects (e.g., pencil, hammer, or bicycle), one every 3.5 seconds. Then they were given a sheet with 60 blank spaces and asked to recall as many of the items as possible. They viewed the drawings a second and third time, and after each session, they had another chance to recall items. Each day for the next week, they again wrote a list of all the items they could remember without seeing the

Figure 10.17 The U.S. Supreme Court ruled in 1987 that criminal defendants may testify about details they recalled under hypnosis. Its decision sparked this protest by the magician known as The Amazing Kreskin, who borrowed a stunt commonly used to demonstrate the power of hypnosis—standing on a person suspended between two chairs.

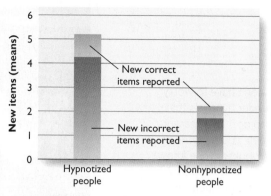

Figure 10.18 Hypnosis increased people's recall of items they had not recalled before. However, most of the new "memories" they confidently reported were incorrect. (From J. Dywan and K. Bowers, "The Use of Hypnosis to Aid Recall," *Science*, vol 222 (pp 184-185). Copyright © 1983 American Association for the Advancement of Science. Reprinted with permission.)

slides again. Finally, a week after the original slide sessions, they returned to the laboratory. Half of them, chosen at random, were hypnotized and the others were just told to relax. All were asked to recall as many of the drawings as possible.

Results Figure 10.18 shows the means for the two groups. The hypnotized people reported some items that they had not recalled before and more than the nonhypnotized group did. However, the hypnotized group also reported more incorrect items than the nonhypnotized group did.

Interpretation These results show no evidence that hypnosis improves memory. Rather, it decreases people's usual hesitance about reporting uncertain or doubtful memories. It may also cause people to confuse imagination with reality.

This study is an example of the signal-detection issue discussed in chapter 4: A reported new memory is a "hit," but the number of hits, by itself, is useless information unless we also know the number of "false alarms"—reported memories that are incorrect.

In response to these results and similar ones, the American Medical Association (1986) recommended that courts of law should refuse to admit any testimony that was elicited under hypnosis, although hypnosis might be used as an investigative tool if all else fails. For example, if a hypnotized witness reports a license plate number and the police track down the car and find blood on it, the blood is certainly admissible evidence, even if the hypnotized report is not. Success stories of that type are rare.

You may encounter the astonishing claim that hypnosis enables people to recall memories from a previous life. Hypnotized young people who claim to be recollecting a previous life most often describe the life of someone similar to themselves, married to someone remarkably similar to the current boyfriend or girlfriend. They often tell good stories, but if they are asked facts about their previous life such as whether their country is at war or what kind of money it uses, their guesses are seldom correct (Spanos, 1987–1988).

concept check

17. Name two practical applications of hypnosis.
18. Does hypnosis improve memory?

Answer

17. Hypnosis can relieve pain, and posthypnotic suggestions help some people break unwanted habits, such as smoking.
18. No. People under hypnosis confidently report more details, but most of the details are wrong.

What's the Evidence?

Hypnosis and Risky Acts

Most hypnotists agree, "You don't have to worry. People will not do anything under hypnosis that they would ordinarily refuse to do." That reassurance is important for persuading you to agree to hypnosis. But is it true? How would anyone know? Do you suppose hypnotists ask clients to perform immoral acts, meet with refusals, and then report the results of these unethical experiments? Not likely. Furthermore, on the rare occasions when investigators have asked hypnotized people to perform dangerous acts, the results have been hard to interpret. Here is an example.

Hypothesis Hypnotized people will sometimes perform acts that people would refuse to do otherwise.

Method Eighteen college students were randomly assigned to three groups. The investigator hypnotized those in one group, instructed the second group to pretend they were hypnotized, and simply asked the third group to participate in the study, without mentioning hypnosis. Each student was then asked to perform three acts: First, pick up a venomous snake from a box. Anyone who got too close was restrained at the last moment. Second, reach into a vat of fuming nitric acid to retrieve a coin (which was already starting to dissolve). Here, there was no last-second restraint. People who followed the instructions were told to wash their hands in warm soapy water immediately afterward. (Today's ethical procedures would prevent this study.) Third, throw the nitric acid into the face of the hypnotist's assistant. While the participant was washing hands, the researcher had replaced the nitric acid with water, but the participant had no way of knowing that.

Results Five of the six hypnotized students followed all three directions (Orne & Evans, 1965). Moreover, so did all six of those who were pretending to be hypnotized! So did two of the six who were just told to take these actions as part of an experiment with no mention of hypnosis. (Nonhypnotized subjects did, however, hesitate longer than the hypnotized subjects.)

Why would people do such extraordinary things? They explained that they trusted the experimenter: "If he tells me to do something, it can't really be dangerous."

Interpretation We do not have adequate evidence to decide whether people under hypnosis will do anything that they would refuse to do otherwise, because it is difficult to find anything that people will refuse to do!

Will hypnotized people do anything that they would otherwise refuse to do? The problem is that nonhypnotized people will sometimes perform some strange and dangerous acts either because an experimenter asked them to or on their own.

Notice the importance of control groups: We cannot simply assume what people would do without hypnosis. We need to test them.

Is Hypnosis an Altered State of Consciousness?

If a hypnotist tells you, "Your hand is rising; you can do nothing to stop it," your hand might indeed rise. If you were later asked why, you might reply that you lost control of your own behavior. Still, you were not a puppet. Was the act voluntary or not? To put the question differently, is hypnosis really different from normal wakefulness?

At one extreme, some psychologists regard hypnosis as a special state of consciousness characterized by increased suggestibility. At the other extreme, some psychologists emphasize the similarities between hypnosis and normal wakeful consciousness. Most psychologists regard hypnosis as a special state in some ways but not others (I. Kirsch & Lynn, 1998). One way to determine whether hypnosis is a special state of consciousness is to find out whether nonhypnotized people can do everything that hypnotized people do. How convincingly could you act like a hypnotized person?

How Well Can Someone Pretend to Be Hypnotized?

In several experiments, some college students were hypnotized and others pretended they were hypnotized. An experienced hypnotist then examined them and tried to determine which ones were really hypnotized.

Fooling the hypnotist was easier than expected. The pretenders tolerated sharp pain without flinching and pretended to recall old memories. When they were told to sit down, they did so immediately (as hypnotized people do) without first checking to make sure they had a chair behind them (Orne, 1959, 1979). When told to experience anger, they exhibited physiological changes such as increased heart rate and sweating, just as hypnotized people do (Damaser, Shor, & Orne, 1963). Even experienced hypnotists could not identify the pretenders.

A few differences between the hypnotized people and pretenders emerged, because the pretenders did not always know how a hypnotized subject would act (Orne, 1979). For instance, when the hypnotist suggested, "You see Professor Schmaltz sitting in that chair," some of the hypnotized subjects asked with puzzlement, "How is it that I see the professor there, but I also see the chair?" Pretenders never reported seeing this double reality. At that point in the experiment, Professor Schmaltz walked into the room. "Who is that?" asked the hypnotist. The pretenders would either say they saw no one, or they would identify Schmaltz as someone else. The hypnotized subjects would say, "That's Professor Schmaltz." Some then said that they were confused about seeing the same person in two places. For some of them, the hallucinated professor faded at that moment. Others continued to accept the double image.

One study reported a way to distinguish hypnotized people from pretenders more than 90% of the time. But it might not be the way you would expect. Simply ask people how deeply hypnotized they thought they were, how relaxed they were, and whether they were aware of their surroundings while hypnotized. People who rate themselves as "extremely" hypnotized, "extremely" relaxed, and "totally unaware" of their surroundings are almost always pretenders. Those who were really hypnotized rate themselves as only mildly influenced (Martin & Lynn, 1996).

So, what is our conclusion? Apparently, people pretending to be hypnotized can mimic almost any effect of hypnosis that they know about. However, hypnosis is ordinarily not just role-playing. The effects that role-players learn to imitate happen spontaneously for the hypnotized people.

concept check

19. Does hypnosis cause people to do anything they would be unwilling to do otherwise?

Answer

19. The evidence is unclear. In certain experiments, hypnotized people have done some strange things, but so have nonhypnotized people.

Meditation excludes the worries and concerns of the day and thereby induces a calm, relaxed state.

Other Altered States of Consciousness

Meditation, *a systematic procedure for inducing a calm, relaxed state through the use of special techniques,* follows traditions that have been practiced in much of the world for thousands of years, especially in India. One variety of meditation seeks "mindfulness" or thoughtless awareness, in which the person is aware of the sensations of the moment but otherwise passive. While seeking this state, the person might concentrate on a single image, or repeat a sound or a short religious statement (e.g., "om" or "God is good"). Meditators may observe their own thoughts, attempt to modify them, or distance themselves from certain thoughts. Goals of meditation vary from the development of wisdom to general well-being (Walsh & Shapiro, 2006).

Many studies document that meditation increases relaxation, decreases pain, decreases anxiety, and improves health in several ways (Hölzel et al., 2011; Wachholtz & Pargament, 2008; Yunesian, Aslani, Vash, & Yazdi, 2008). It is particularly useful for increasing people's ability to control their attention (MacLean et al., 2010).

The déjà vu experience, a *feeling that an event is uncannily familiar,* is fairly common in young adults and less so as people grow older (A. S. Brown, 2003). Because it takes several forms, a single explanation may not suffice. Occasionally, someone is somewhere for the first time and sees it as familiar, as if he or she had been there before. Perhaps the person really had seen something similar, possibly in a movie or photo.

More commonly, people report déjà vu in a familiar setting. You might be sitting in your room, walking down a familiar road, or having an everyday conversation, when you suddenly feel, "This has happened before!" In a sense, of course it has happened before, but your sense is not that it's just similar to a past experience. Instead, it seems *this particular* event happened before. As people talk, you feel, "I knew they were going to say that!" You could not really predict the words, but after you hear them, you feel that you had been *about to* predict them. Apparently, something is triggering the brain to signal "familiar."

One man with epilepsy originating in his temporal cortex had a special feeling, an *aura,* before each of his seizures. Each aura included a strong sense of déjà vu that lasted long enough for him to move around and shift his attention from one item to another. During the aura, *whatever* he looked at seemed strangely familiar (O'Connor & Moulin, 2008). In a case like this, we can discard the hypothesis that what he saw was actually familiar. Many other people with abnormalities in the temporal lobe also experience intense feelings of déjà vu (Moulin, Conway, Thompson, James, & Jones, 2005).

WENDELL HAS A STRANGE FEELING THAT HE HAS SEEN THIS WORD BEFORE.

 concept check

20. What evidence shows that déjà vu does not always indicate that an experience was actually familiar?

Answer

20. A person with temporal lobe epilepsy reported an intense déjà vu experience immediately before his seizures, regardless of where he was or what he was seeing at the time.

module 10.3 >

In Closing

What Hypnosis Is and Isn't

Researchers agree on a few general points: Hypnosis is not faking or pretending to be hypnotized, and it does not give people mental or physical powers that they otherwise lack. Hypnosis enables people to relax, concentrate, and follow suggestions better than they usually do. Meditation also improves concentration, but in a more lasting way.

Summary

- *Nature of hypnosis.* Hypnosis is a condition of increased suggestibility that occurs in the context of a special hypnotist–subject relationship. Psychologists distinguish the genuine phenomenon, which deserves serious study, from exaggerated claims. (page 340)

- *Hypnosis induction.* To induce hypnosis, a hypnotist asks a person to concentrate and then makes repetitive suggestions. The first steps toward being hypnotized are the willingness to be hypnotized and the belief that one is becoming hypnotized. (page 340)

- *Uses.* Hypnosis can alleviate pain, and through posthypnotic suggestion, it sometimes helps people combat bad habits. (page 341)
- *Non-uses.* Hypnosis does not give people special strength or unusual powers. When asked to report their memories under hypnosis, people report a mixture of correct and incorrect information with much confidence. (page 342)
- *Uncertain limits.* Although many hypnotists insist that hypnotized people will not do anything that they would refuse to do when not hypnotized, little evidence is available to support this claim. (page 344)

- *Hypnosis as an altered state.* Hypnosis is not greatly different from normal wakefulness, but it is also not just something that people pretend. (page 344)
- *Meditation.* Meditation increases relaxation, decreases anxiety, and enhances attention. (page 345)
- *Déjà vu.* People sometimes feel that the current experience is uncannily familiar. The phenomenon may need more than one explanation. (page 345)

Key Terms

déjà vu experience (page 345)
hypnosis (page 340)

meditation (page 345)
posthypnotic suggestion (page 342)

exploration and study

Access an interactive eBook and chapter-specific learning tools, including

- **flashcards**
- **quizzes**
- **videos**

and more, in your Psychology CourseMate. Go to **CengageBrain.com.**

aplia™

If your professor has assigned Aplia:

1. Sign in to your account.
2. Complete the corresponding exercises as required by your professor.
3. When finished, click "Grade It Now" to see which areas you have mastered, which areas need more work, and detailed explanations of every answer.

Reproductive Behaviors

11

CHAPTER OUTLINE

MAIN IDEAS

1. Sex chromosomes influence development mainly, but not entirely, by controlling production of sex hormones such as testosterone and estradiol.

2. Sex hormones exert organizing and activating effects on the genitals and the brain. Organizing effects occur during a sensitive period and last indefinitely. Activating effects are temporary.

3. In mammals, organizing effects of hormones influence the external genitals and the hypothalamus. The difference between masculine and feminine appearance of the external genitals depends on the amount of testosterone during an early sensitive period.

4. Parental behavior depends on both hormones and experience.

5. Much about men's and women's sexual behavior, including mate choice, could be the product of evolutionary selection. However, current data do not enable us to determine how much is built-in and how much is determined by our experiences.

6. Hormones contribute to the development of sexual identity and orientation.

OPPOSITE: Humans may be the only species that plans parenthood, but all species have a strong biological drive that leads to parenthood.

What good is sex? Well, yes, of course: We enjoy it. Presumably we evolved to enjoy it because sexual activity sometimes leads to reproduction, which passes on the genes. You evolved from a long line of ancestors who engaged in sexual activity at least once.

But why did we evolve to reproduce sexually instead of individually? In some species of reptiles, a female sometimes has offspring by herself, using only her own genes and none from a male (Booth, Johnson, Moore, Schal, & Vargo, 2011). In many ways, reproduction would be easier without sex. What advantage does sex provide?

You might suggest the advantage of having a partner while you rear children. In humans, that kind of cooperation is usually helpful. However, many species reproduce sexually even though the male doesn't help at all with the young, and in some fish species, *neither* sex cares for the young—they just release their sperm and eggs in the same place and then depart.

Biologists' explanation is that sexual reproduction increases variation and thereby enables quick evolutionary adaptations to changes in the environment. Certain invertebrates reproduce sexually when they live in a complex and changing environment, but reproduce nonsexually when they live in a constant environment (Becks & Agrawal, 2010). Sex also corrects errors: If you have a disadvantageous mutation in one gene and your mate has a disadvantageous mutation in a different gene, your children could have a normal copy of both genes.

In this chapter, we consider many questions about sexual reproduction that we often ignore or take for granted. We also consider some of the ways in which being biologically male or female influences our behavior.

Sex and Hormones

Being male or female influences many aspects of your life. For humans and other mammals, it all begins with your genes. Females have two X chromosomes, whereas males have an X and a Y chromosome. Biologists used to believe that the chromosomes determine sexual differentiation entirely through hormones. Let's examine that story, and then see how it is incomplete.

Male and female mammals start with the same anatomy during an early stage of prenatal development. Both have a set of **Müllerian ducts** (precursors to female internal structures) and a set of Wolffian ducts (precursors to male internal structures), as well as undifferentiated gonads that are on their way to becoming either testes or ovaries. The male's Y chromosome includes the **SRY** (sex-determining region on the Y chromosome) **gene**, which causes those primitive gonads to develop into **testes**, the sperm-producing organs. The developing testes produce **androgens** (hormones that

are more abundant in males) that increase the growth of the testes, causing them to produce more androgens and so forth. That positive feedback cannot go on forever, but it lasts for a period of early development. Androgens also cause the primitive **Wolffian ducts**, precursors for other male reproductive structures, to develop into *seminal vesicles* (saclike structures that store semen) and the *vas deferens* (a duct from the testis into the penis). The testes also produce *Müllerian inhibiting hormone (MIH)*, which causes the Müllerian ducts to degenerate. The final result is the development of a penis and scrotum. Because females do not have the SRY gene, their gonads develop into **ovaries** instead of testes, and their Wolffian ducts degenerate. Because their ovaries do not produce MIH, females' Müllerian ducts develop and mature into oviducts, uterus, and the upper vagina. Figure 11.1 shows how the primitive unisex structures develop into male or female external genitals.

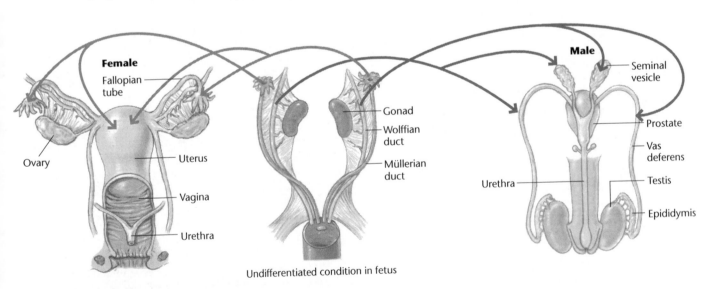

FIGURE 11.1 Differentiation of human genitals
We begin life with undifferentiated structures, as shown in the center. The gonad shown in blue for the fetus develops into either the ovaries, as shown on the left, or the testes, as shown on the right. The Müllerian ducts of the fetus develop into a female's uterus, oviducts, and the upper part of the vagina. The Wolffian ducts of the fetus develop into a male's seminal vesicles (which store semen) and vas deferens, a duct from the testis into the penis. The Müllerian ducts degenerate in males, and the Wolffian ducts degenerate in females.
(Based on Netter, 1983)

From then on, the male's testes produce more androgens than **estrogens** (hormones that are more abundant in females). The female's ovaries produce more estrogens than androgens. Androgens and estrogens are **steroid hormones**, containing four carbon rings, derived from cholesterol, as in Figure 11.2. We are often warned about the risks of excessive cholesterol, but a moderate amount is necessary for generating these important hormones. Steroids exert their effects in three ways (Nadal, Díaz, & Valverde, 2001). First, they bind to membrane receptors, like neurotransmitters, exerting rapid effects. Second, they enter cells and activate certain kinds of proteins in the cytoplasm. Third, they bind to receptors that bind to chromosomes, where they activate or inactivate certain genes (Figure 11.3).

Androgens and estrogens are categories of chemicals; neither androgen nor estrogen is a specific chemical itself. The most widely known androgen is **testosterone**. The most prominent type of estrogen is **estradiol**. **Progesterone**, another predominantly female hormone, prepares the uterus for the implantation of a fertilized ovum and promotes the maintenance of pregnancy.

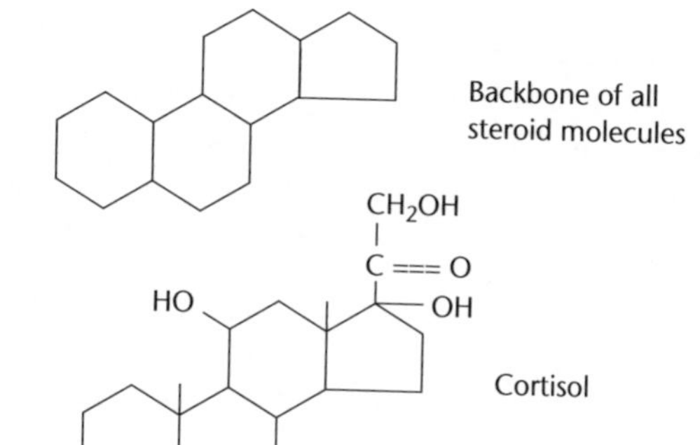

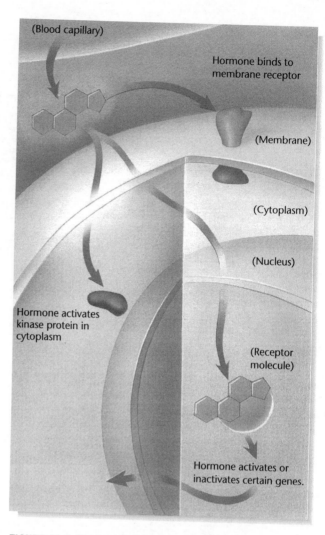

FIGURE 11.3 **Routes of action for steroid hormones**
Steroid hormones such as estrogens and androgens bind to membrane receptors, activate proteins in the cytoplasm, and activate or inactivate certain genes. *(Revised from Starr & Taggart, 1989)*

FIGURE 11.2 **Steroid hormones**
Note the similarity between testosterone and estradiol.
(© Cengage Learning 2013)

Androgens promote the development of typically masculine features, such as facial hair. Estrogens promote typically female features, such as breast development. Androgens and estrogens also influence activity in many brain areas and alter the pattern of which neurons survive during early development (Forger et al., 2004; Morris, Jordan, & Breedlove, 2004). Certain brain areas are relatively larger in men, on average, and others relatively larger in women, as Figure 11.4 shows (Cahill, 2006; J. M. Goldstein et al., 2001). These differences relate to gender and not to brain size. When researchers compare men and women who have the same overall brain volume, many of the patterns shown in Figure 11.4 still emerge (Luders, Gaser, Narr, & Toga, 2009). However, remember that these are averages. Most individuals show male-typical patterns in some ways and female-typical patterns in others.

For many years, biologists assumed that hormones account for all the biological differences between males and

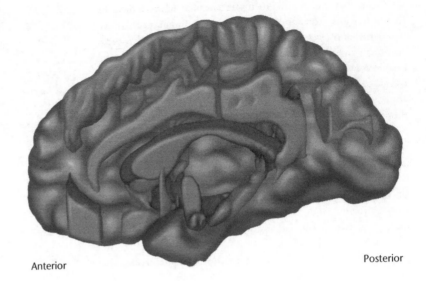

FIGURE 11.4 Men's and women's brains
Areas in red are, on average, larger in women relative to the total mass of the brain. Areas in blue are, on average, larger in men relative to the total mass. *(Nature Reviews Neuroscience, 7, 477–484, from Cahill, L. (2006). Reprinted by permission of Macmillan Publishing Ltd.)*

Anterior   Posterior

females. Later research demonstrated that some differences depend directly on control by the X and Y chromosomes independently of hormones (Arnold, 2009). At least three genes on the Y chromosome (found only in men) are active in specific brain areas, and at least one gene on the X chromosome is active only in the female brain (Arnold, 2004; Carruth, Reisert, & Arnold, 2002; Vawter et al., 2004). In both humans and nonhumans, the Y chromosome has many sites that alter the expression of genes on other chromosomes (Lemos, Araripe, & Hartl, 2008). In short, genes on the X and Y chromosomes produce sex differences in addition to those that we can trace to androgens and estrogens.

STOP & CHECK

1. What does the SRY gene do?

2. How do sex hormones affect neurons?

ANSWERS

1. The SRY gene (sex-determining region on the Y chromosome) causes the undifferentiated gonad of a mammal to develop into a testis, which then produces testosterone and MIH to direct development toward the male pattern. 2. Sex hormones, which are steroids, bind to receptors on the membrane, activate certain proteins in the cell's cytoplasm, and activate or inactivate particular genes.

Organizing Effects of Sex Hormones

If we injected estrogens into adult males and androgens into adult females, could we make males act like females or females act like males? Researchers of the mid-1900s, working with a

variety of mammals and birds, were surprised to find that the answer was almost always *no*. But hormones injected early in life have much stronger effects.

Biologists distinguish between the organizing and activating effects of sex hormones (Arnold, 2009). **Organizing effects** produce long-lasting structural effects. The most prominent organizing effects occur during a sensitive stage of early development—shortly before and after birth in rats and well before birth in humans—determining whether the body develops female or male anatomy. The surge of hormones at puberty also produces long-lasting effects, such as breast development in women, facial hair in men, and male–female differences in the anatomy of certain parts of the hypothalamus (Ahmed et al., 2008). **Activating effects** are more temporary, when a hormone increases some activity that lasts only while the hormone is present. Activating effects occur at any time in life. The distinction between the two kinds of effects is not absolute, as a hormone can produce a combination of temporary and longer-lasting effects (Arnold & Breedlove, 1985; C. L. Williams, 1986). Still, the distinction is often useful.

Let's consider organizing effects during an early **sensitive period**, when hormones determine whether an embryo develops a male or female anatomy. You might imagine that testosterone produces male anatomy and estradiol produces female anatomy. No. Differentiation of the external genitals and several aspects of brain development depend mainly on the level of testosterone. A high level of testosterone causes the external genitals to develop the male pattern, and a low level leads to the female pattern. Estradiol produces important effects on the internal organs, but it has little effect on the external genitals.

The human sensitive period for genital formation is about the third and fourth months of pregnancy (Money & Ehrhardt, 1972). In rats, testosterone begins masculinizing the external genitals during the last several days of pregnancy and first few days after birth and then continues masculinizing them at a declining rate for the next month (Bloch & Mills, 1995; Bloch, Mills, & Gale, 1995; E. C. Davis, Shryne, & Gorski, 1995; Rhees, Shryne, & Gorski, 1990). A female rat that is injected with testosterone shortly before or after birth is partly masculinized, just as if her own body had produced the testosterone (I. L. Ward & Ward, 1985). Her clitoris grows larger than normal, and her behavior is partly masculinized. She approaches sexually receptive females (Woodson & Balleine, 2002), mounts them, and makes copulatory thrusting movements rather than arching her back and allowing males to mount her. In short, early testosterone promotes the male pattern and inhibits the female pattern (Gorski, 1985; J. D. Wilson, George, & Griffin, 1981).

Injecting a genetic male with estrogens produces little effect on his external anatomy. However, he develops the female-typical pattern of anatomy and behavior if he genetically lacks androgen receptors, if he is castrated (deprived of his testes), or if he is exposed to substances that block testosterone effects. Drugs that tend to feminize or demasculinize early development include alcohol, marijuana, haloperidol (an antipsychotic drug), phthalates (chemicals common in many manufactured products), and cocaine (Ahmed, Shryne, Gorski, Branch, & Taylor, 1991; Dalterio & Bartke, 1979; Hull, Nishita, Bitran, & Dalterio, 1984; Raum, McGivern, Peterson, Shryne, & Gorski, 1990; Swan et al., 2010). To a slight extent, even aspirin interferes with the male pattern of development (Amateau & McCarthy, 2004). Although estradiol does not significantly alter a male's external anatomy, estradiol and several related compounds do produce abnormalities of the prostate gland—the gland that stores sperm and releases it during intercourse. Some of those estradiol-like compounds are now prevalent in the linings of plastic bottles and cans, so almost everyone is exposed to them (Timms, Howdeshell, Barton, Richter, & vom Saal, 2005). In short, male development is vulnerable to many sources of interference.

The overall mechanism of early sexual differentiation has been described by saying that nature's "default setting" is to make every mammal a female. Add early testosterone and the individual becomes a male; without testosterone, it develops as a female, regardless of the amount of estradiol or other estrogens. That generalization is an overstatement. A genetic female that lacks estradiol during the early sensitive period develops approximately normal female external anatomy but does not develop normal sexual behavior. Even if she is given estradiol injections as an adult, she shows little sexual response toward either male or female partners (Bakker, Honda, Harada, & Balthazart, 2002). So estradiol contributes to female development, including certain aspects of brain differentiation, even if it is not important for external anatomy.

3. What would be the genital appearance of a mammal exposed to high levels of both androgens and estrogens during early development? What if it were exposed to low levels of both?

4. From the standpoint of protecting a male fetus's sexual development, what are some drugs that a pregnant woman should avoid?

ANSWERS

3. A mammal exposed to high levels of both male and female hormones will appear male. One exposed to low levels of both will appear female. Genital development depends mostly on the presence or absence of androgens and is nearly independent of estradiol levels. **4.** Pregnant women should avoid alcohol, marijuana, haloperidol, phthalates, and cocaine because these drugs interfere with male sexual development. Even aspirin and the chemicals lining bottles and cans produce mild abnormalities. Obviously, the results depend on both quantities and timing of exposure to these chemicals.

Sex Differences in the Hypothalamus

In addition to controlling differences in the external genitals, sex hormones early in life influence development in parts of the hypothalamus, amygdala, and other brain areas (Shah et al., 2004). For example, one area in the anterior hypothalamus, known as the **sexually dimorphic nucleus**, is larger in males than in females and contributes to control of male sexual behavior. Parts of the female hypothalamus generate a cyclic pattern of hormone release, as in the human menstrual cycle. The male hypothalamus cannot, and neither can the hypothalamus of a female who was exposed to extra testosterone early in life. Typical female rats have a characteristic way of holding food and dodging from other rats that might try to take it away. A female rat that was either deprived of estrogens or exposed to extra testosterone in infancy pivots around the midpoint of her trunk, like males, instead of around her pelvis, like other females (Field, Whishaw, Forgie, & Pellis, 2004).

In rodents, testosterone exerts much of its organizing effect through a surprising route: After it enters a neuron in early development, it is converted to estradiol! Testosterone and estradiol are chemically very similar, as you can see in Figure 11.2. In organic chemistry, a ring of six carbon atoms containing three double bonds is an *aromatic* compound. An enzyme found in the brain can *aromatize* testosterone into estradiol. Other androgens that cannot be aromatized into estrogens are less effective in masculinizing the hypothalamus. Drugs that prevent testosterone from being aromatized to estradiol block the organizing effects of testosterone on sexual development and thereby impair male sexual behavior and fertility (Gerardin & Pereira, 2002; Rochira et al., 2001).

Why, then, does a female rodent's own estradiol fail to masculinize her hypothalamus? During the early sensitive period, immature mammals have a protein called **alpha-fetoprotein**, which is not present in adults (Gorski, 1980; MacLusky & Naftolin, 1981). Alpha-fetoprotein in rodents binds with estradiol and prevents it from entering cells, where it could produce masculinizing effects. Because testosterone does not bind to alpha-fetoprotein, it can enter neurons, where enzymes convert it into estradiol. That is, testosterone is a way of getting estradiol to its receptors when estradiol circulating in the blood is inactivated.

This explanation of testosterone's effects makes sense of an otherwise puzzling fact: Injecting a large amount of estradiol actually masculinizes a female rodent's development. The reason is that normal amounts are bound to alpha-fetoprotein, but a larger amount exceeds the capacity of alpha-fetoprotein and therefore enters the cells and masculinizes them.

STOP & CHECK

5. How would the external genitals appear on a genetic female rat that lacked alpha-fetoprotein?

ANSWER

5. A female that lacked alpha-fetoprotein would be masculinized by her own estradiol, as researchers have in fact demonstrated (Bakker et al., 2006).

Sex Differences in Childhood Behavior

As prenatal hormones influence the structure of the male or female brain, do they also contribute to differences in behavior? In the second module of this chapter we shall consider influences on sexual behavior and sexual orientation, but at this point let's consider possible influences on childhood behavior.

Typically, most boys play mostly with "boys' toys" such as balls and toy cars, whereas most girls play mostly with "girls' toys"

such as dolls and toy tea sets. Some children have a stronger preference for boys' or girls' toys than others do, and their preferences tend to be consistent over time. Those who show the greatest preference for boys' toys and activities at age 3½ usually show the greatest amount of typical boys' activities at age 8, and they tend to be the most physically active at age 12. Similarly, those with the greatest preference for girls' toys and activities at 3½ usually show the greatest preference for typical girls' activities at later ages (Golombok et al., 2008; Mattocks et al., 2010).

Much of this pattern results from socialization, as most parents give their sons and daughters different sets of toys. However, socialization need not be the whole story. Indeed, it may be that parents give those toys because previous generations found that boys and girls typically differ in their interests from the start. In one study, infants 3–8 months old (too young to walk, crawl, or do much with a toy) sat in front of pairs of toys, where researchers could monitor eye movements. The girls looked at dolls more than they looked at toy trucks. The boys looked at both about equally (Alexander, Wilcox, & Woods, 2009). (Note that the children had not seen the trucks move, so at this point the trucks were simply unknown objects.) This study suggests a predisposition for boys and girls to prefer different types of toys, although we should consider an alternative explanation: Girls mature faster than boys, and perhaps it was harder for boys at this age to show a preference, whatever that preference may have been.

In two studies male monkeys played with balls and toy cars more than female monkeys did, whereas the females played more with dolls (Alexander & Hines, 2002; Hassett, Siebert, & Wallen, 2008). Figure 11.5 summarizes the results from one of those studies. Monkeys' preferences were not as strong as most children's, but it is noteworthy that the sexes differed at all in their first encounters with these toys. Other studies found that prenatal injections of testosterone into female monkey fetuses led to increased masculine-type play after they were born. In those cases the focus was on spontaneous, rough-and-tumble play rather than playing with toys, but the idea is similar (Wallen, 2005).

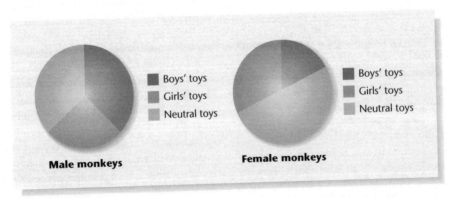

FIGURE 11.5 Toy choices by male and female monkeys
Male monkeys spent more time than female monkeys did with "boys' toys" and the females spent more time than the males with "girls' toys." *(Based on data from G. M. Alexander & M. Hines (2002). "Sex differences in response to children's toys in nonhuman primates" (Cercopithecus aethiops sabaeus). Evolution and Human Behavior, 23, 467–479.)*

Finally, two studies correlated chemicals in the mother's blood during pregnancy with their children's choices of toys years later. Researchers took blood samples from pregnant women, measuring testosterone (some of which would enter the fetus). When the daughters reached age 3½, researchers observed their toy play. The girls who had been exposed to higher testosterone levels in prenatal life showed slightly elevated preferences for boys' toys (Hines et al., 2002). These girls were anatomically normal, and we have no reason to believe that the parents treated girls differently based on how much testosterone had been present in prenatal life. In another study, researchers measured phthalate levels in pregnant women. Phthalates inhibit testosterone production. U.S. law bans phthalates from children's toys, but pregnant women are exposed to phthalates from other sources, including perfumes, hair spray, and food packaging. Researchers measured phthalate levels in pregnant women's urine samples and compared results to the sons' toy use at ages 3 to 6. On average, sons of women with high phthalate levels showed less interest in typical boys' toys and more interest in typical girls' toys (Swan et al., 2010). In summary, these studies suggest that prenatal hormones, especially testosterone, alter the brain in ways that influence differences between boys and girls in their activities and interests.

Do these studies imply that prenatal hormones determine toy preferences, regardless of rearing? No. Prenatal hormones combine forces with rearing experiences. When a child shows a preference for a certain kind of toy, even if it is just a small preference, parents tend to provide more of that kind of toy and more opportunities to strengthen that preference. Psychologists call this a "multiplier effect" (Dickens & Flynn, 2001). Furthermore, if most boys in the past have preferred one kind of toy and most girls preferred another, parents start with this presupposition and provide those toys from the start.

STOP & CHECK

6. What evidence most directly links children's toy play to prenatal hormones?

ANSWER

6. Girls whose mothers had higher testosterone levels during pregnancy tend to play with boys' toys more than the average for other girls. Boys whose mothers had higher phthalate exposure tend to play with boys' toys less than the average for other boys.

Activating Effects of Sex Hormones

At any time in life, not just during a sensitive period, current levels of testosterone or estradiol exert activating effects, temporarily modifying behavior. Changes in hormonal secretions influence sexual behavior within 15 minutes (Taziaux, Keller, Bakker, & Balthazart, 2007). Behaviors can also influence hormonal secretions. For example, when doves court each other, each stage of their behavior initiates hormonal changes that alter the birds' readiness for the next sequence of behaviors (C. Erickson & Lehrman, 1964; Lehrman, 1964; Martinez-Vargas & Erickson, 1973).

Rodents

For rodents, as for other mammals, sex hormones facilitate sexual activity. Testosterone is essential for male sexual arousal (Hull & Dominguez, 2007). A combination of estradiol and progesterone is the most effective combination for females (Matuszewich, Lorrain, & Hull, 2000). Arousal also depends on previous experience. Sexually experienced rats are aroused more easily because the effects of previous experience sensitize the response to future stimuli (Dominguez, Brann, Gil, & Hull, 2006).

Sex hormones activate sexual behavior partly by enhancing sensations. Estrogens increase the sensitivity of the *pudendal nerve*, which transmits tactile stimulation from the vagina and cervix to the brain (Komisaruk, Adler, & Hutchison, 1972). Testosterone increases sensitivity in the penis (Etgen, Chu, Fiber, Karkanias, & Morales, 1999). Sex hormones also bind to receptors that increase responses in parts of the hypothalamus, including the ventromedial nucleus, the medial preoptic area (MPOA), and the anterior hypothalamus.

Erection depends partly on the fact that testosterone increases the release of nitric oxide (NO), which increases blood flow to the penis. (As mentioned in Chapter 3, nitric oxide also increases blood flow in the brain.) The drug sildenafil (Viagra) increases male sexual ability by prolonging the effects of nitric oxide (Rowland & Burnett, 2000).

Testosterone and estradiol prime the MPOA and several other brain areas to release dopamine. MPOA neurons release dopamine strongly during sexual activity, and the more dopamine they release, the more likely the male is to copulate (Putnam, Du, Sato, & Hull, 2001). Castrated male rats produce normal amounts of dopamine in the MPOA, but they do not release it in the presence of a receptive female, and they do not attempt to copulate (Hull, Du, Lorrain, & Matuszewich, 1997).

In moderate concentrations, dopamine stimulates mostly type D_1 and D_5 receptors, which facilitate erection of the penis in the male (Hull et al., 1992) and sexually receptive postures in the female (Apostolakis et al., 1996). In higher concentrations, dopamine stimulates type D_2 receptors, which leads to orgasm (Giuliani & Ferrari, 1996; Hull et al., 1992). The sudden burst of dopamine in several brain areas at the time of orgasm resembles the "rush" that addictive drugs produce (Holstege et al., 2003). Whereas dopamine stimulates sexual activity, the neurotransmitter serotonin inhibits it, in part by blocking dopamine release (Hull et al., 1999). Many popular antidepressant drugs increase serotonin activity, and one of their side effects is to decrease sexual arousal and orgasm.

Researchers found what appeared to be a major difference between male and female rats in their sexual motivation: After rats have had sexual relations in a particular cage, males work hard to return to that cage, but females generally do not. Then the researchers varied the procedure. A male rat was confined to that cage, but the female was free to enter or leave at any time. She could therefore control the timing of when their sexual activity started and stopped. Under these conditions, females developed a clear preference for that cage (Paredes & Vazquez, 1999). Evidently, female rats find sex reinforcing only if they get to decide when it occurs. (The rumor is that the same trend may be true for other species as well.)

> **STOP & CHECK**
>
> 7. By what mechanism do testosterone and estradiol affect the hypothalamic areas responsible for sexual behavior?

ANSWER

7. Testosterone and estradiol prime hypothalamic cells to be ready to release dopamine. They also increase sensitivity in the genital area.

Humans

Although humans are less dependent on current sex hormone levels than other species are, hormones do alter people's sexual arousal. They also affect brain systems with functions not directly related to sex. For example, testosterone decreases pain and anxiety, and estrogens probably do, too (Edinger & Frye, 2004). Decreases of sex hormones—for example, in men being treated for prostate cancer—lead to impairments of memory (Bussiere, Beer, Neiss, & Janowsky, 2005). Estrogens directly stimulate parts of the prefrontal cortex that are important for working memory—that is, memory for what one is doing at the moment (Wang, Hara, Janssen, Rapp, & Morrison, 2010). In short, sex hormones serve functions that go beyond sexual behavior itself.

Testosterone

Among men, levels of testosterone correlate positively with sexual arousal and the drive to seek sexual partners. Researchers found that, on average, married men and men living with a woman in a committed relationship have lower testosterone levels than single, unpaired men of the same age (M. McIntyre et al., 2006). The apparently obvious interpretation was that once a man established a lasting relationship, he no longer needed to work so hard to seek a sexual partner, and his testosterone levels dropped. However, that study did not tell us which came first, the committed relationship or the lower testosterone level. Another study found that men's testosterone levels did not change after marriage. Instead, men with lower testosterone levels were more likely to marry than were men with high testosterone levels (van Anders & Watson, 2006). Similar studies found that single women had higher testosterone levels than women with a long-term partner, either homosexual or heterosexual (van Anders & Goldey, 2010; van

Anders & Watson, 2006). Also, both men and women with high testosterone levels are more likely than average to seek additional sex partners, even after they marry or establish a long-term relationship (M. McIntyre et al., 2006; van Anders, Hamilton, & Watson, 2007).

Overall, these results say that high testosterone levels are associated with seeking multiple partners, to some extent for both men and women. It is tempting to assume that testosterone causes the drive for multiple partners, but the data are correlational, and we should hesitate about a cause and effect conclusion. The alternative interpretation is that some other influence leads to an interest in multiple partners, and the variety of partners increases testosterone production. It has been shown that when women think about sex or anticipate having sex, their testosterone levels increase temporarily (van Anders, Brotto, Farrell, & Yule, 2009; van Anders, Hamilton, Schmidt, & Watson, 2007). So, the relationship between testosterone and sexual interest may go both directions.

Decreases in testosterone levels generally decrease male sexual activity. For example, castration (removal of the testes) generally decreases a man's sexual interest and activity (Carter, 1992). However, low testosterone is not the usual basis for **impotence**, the inability to have an erection. The most common cause is impaired blood circulation, especially in older men. Other common causes include neurological problems, reactions to drugs, and psychological tension (Andersson, 2001).

Testosterone reduction has sometimes been tried as a means of controlling sex offenders, including exhibitionists, rapists, child molesters, and those who commit incest. One major practical problem is getting sex offenders to continue taking drugs that block testosterone (Hughes, 2007). Another drawback is the side effects of testosterone deprivation, including weight gain, diabetes, and depression (Giltay & Gooren, 2009).

> **STOP & CHECK**
>
> 8. What is the explanation for why married men tend to have lower testosterone levels than single men of the same age?

ANSWER

8. Men with lower testosterone levels are more likely to get married than men with higher testosterone levels.

Estradiol and Related Hormones

A woman's hypothalamus and pituitary interact with the ovaries to produce the **menstrual cycle**, a periodic variation in hormones and fertility over the course of about 28 days (Figure 11.6). After the end of a menstrual period, the anterior pituitary releases **follicle-stimulating hormone (FSH)**, which promotes the growth of a follicle in the ovary. The follicle nurtures the *ovum* (egg cell) and produces several types of estrogen, including estradiol. Toward the middle of the menstrual cycle, the follicle builds up more and more receptors to FSH, so even though the actual concentration of FSH in the blood is decreasing, its effects on the follicle increase. As a result, the follicle produces increasing amounts of estradiol. The increased release of estradiol causes an increased release of FSH as well as a sudden surge in the release of **luteinizing hormone (LH)** from the anterior pituitary (see the top graph in Figure 11.6). FSH and LH combine to cause the follicle to release an ovum.

The remnant of the follicle (now called the *corpus luteum*) releases the hormone progesterone, which prepares the uterus for the implantation of a fertilized ovum. Progesterone also inhibits the further release of LH. Toward the end of the menstrual cycle, the levels of LH, FSH, estradiol, and progesterone all decline. If the ovum is not fertilized, the lining of the uterus is cast off (menstruation), and the cycle begins again. If the ovum is fertilized, the levels of estradiol and progesterone increase gradually during pregnancy. One consequence of high estradiol and progesterone levels is fluctuating activity at the serotonin 3 (5HT$_3$) receptor, which is responsible for nausea (Rupprecht et al., 2001). Pregnant women often experience nausea because of the heightened activity of that receptor. Figure 11.7 summarizes the interactions between the pituitary and the ovary. Increased sensitivity to nausea may be an evolved adaptation to minimize the risk of eating something harmful to the fetus.

Birth-control pills prevent pregnancy by interfering with the usual feedback cycle between the ovaries and the pituitary.

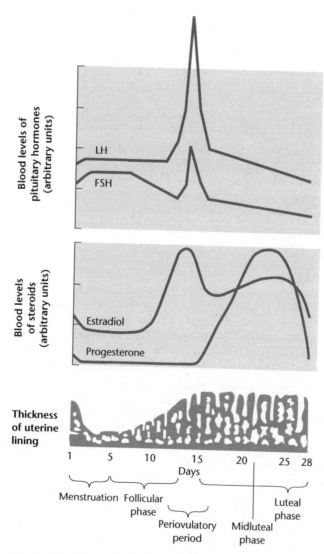

FIGURE 11.6 Blood levels of four hormones during the human menstrual cycle
Note that estrogen and progesterone are both at high levels during the midluteal phase but drop sharply at menstruation. *(© Cengage Learning 2013)*

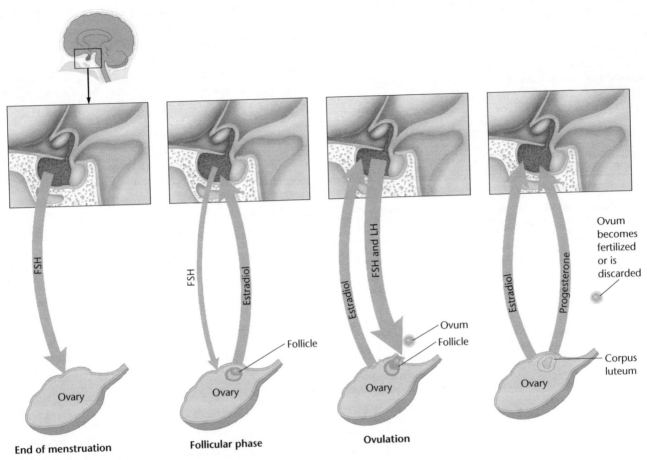

FSH

FSH   Estradiol

Estradiol   FSH and LH

Estradiol   Progesterone

Follicle

Ovum
Follicle

Ovum
becomes
fertilized
or is
discarded

Corpus
luteum

Ovary   Ovary   Ovary   Ovary

End of menstruation   **Follicular phase**   **Ovulation**

FIGURE 11.7 **Interactions between the pituitary and the ovary**
FSH from the pituitary stimulates a follicle of the ovary to develop and produce estradiol, releasing a burst of FSH and LH from the
pituitary. Those hormones cause the follicle to release its ovum and become a corpus luteum. The corpus luteum releases progesterone
while the ovary releases estradiol. *(© Cengage Learning 2013)*

The most widely used birth-control pill, the *combination pill*, containing estrogen and progesterone, prevents the surge of FSH and LH that would otherwise release an ovum. The estrogen–progesterone combination also thickens the mucus of the cervix, making it harder for a sperm to reach the egg, and prevents an ovum, if released, from implanting in the uterus. Thus, the pill prevents pregnancy in many ways. Note, however, that it does not protect against sexually transmitted diseases such as AIDS or syphilis. "Safe sex" must go beyond the prevention of pregnancy.

Changes in hormones over the menstrual cycle also alter women's sexual interest. The **periovulatory period**, consisting of the days around the middle of the menstrual cycle, is the time of maximum fertility and high estrogen levels. According to two studies, women not taking birth-control pills initiate more sexual activity (either with a partner or by masturbation) during the periovulatory period than at other times of the month (D. B. Adams, Gold, & Burt, 1978; Udry & Morris, 1968) (Figure 11.8). According to another study, women rate an erotic video as more pleasant and arousing if they watch it during the

periovulatory period than if they watch it at other times (Slob, Bax, Hop, Rowland, & van der Werff ten Bosch, 1996).

Another study used a method that is, shall we say, not common among laboratory researchers. The researchers studied erotic lap dancers, who earn tips by dancing between a man's legs, rubbing up against his groin, while wearing, in most cases, just a bikini bottom. Lap dancers recorded the times of their menstrual periods and the amount of tip income they received each night. Lap dancers who were taking contraceptive pills (which keep hormone levels about constant through the month) earned about the same amount from one day to another. Those not taking contraceptive pills received the largest tips 9 to 15 days after menstruation, which is a time of increasing estrogen levels (G. Miller, Tybur, & Jordan, 2007). A likely hypothesis is that the women felt and acted sexier at this time.

Sex hormones also influence women's attention to sex-related stimuli. Women in one study were asked to look at facial photos on a screen and classify each as male or female as quickly as possible. They made the classifications more quickly when they were in their periovulatory period than at

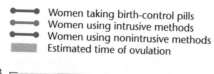

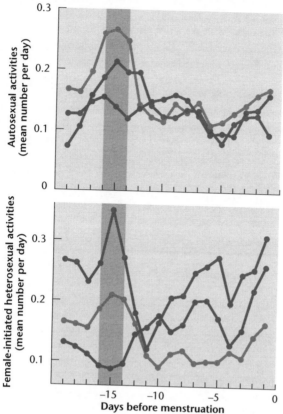

FIGURE 11.8 Female-initiated sexual activities
The top graph shows autosexual activities (masturbation and sexual fantasies); the bottom graph shows female-initiated activities with a male partner. "Intrusive" birth-control methods are diaphragm, foam, and condom; "nonintrusive" methods are IUD and vasectomy. Women other than pill users initiate sex more often when their estrogen levels peak. *(Adams, Gold, & Burt, 1978)*

other times of the cycle (Macrae, Alnwick, Milne, & Schloerscheidt, 2002). In another study, women were presented with a computer that enabled them to modify pictures of men's faces to make each one look more feminine or more masculine. When they were asked specifically to show the face of the man they would prefer for a "short-term sexual relationship," women preferred more masculine-looking faces around the time of ovulation than they did at other times (Penton-Voak et al., 1999). When women were asked to view videotapes of two men and choose one for a short-term relationship, women around the time of ovulation were more likely to choose a man who seemed athletic, competitive, and assertive and who did *not* describe himself as having a "nice personality" (Gangestad, Simpson, Cousins, Garver-Apgar, & Christensen, 2004). In short, the hormones associated

with fertility move women's mate preferences toward men who look and act more masculine.

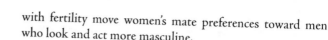

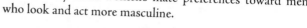

9. At what time in a woman's menstrual cycle do her estradiol levels increase? When are they lowest?

ANSWER

9. Estrogen levels increase during the days leading up to the middle of the menstrual cycle. They are lowest during and just after menstruation.

Oxytocin

In addition to the sex hormones, the pituitary hormone **oxytocin** is also important for reproductive behavior. Oxytocin stimulates contractions of the uterus during delivery of a baby, and it stimulates the mammary gland to release milk.

Sexual pleasure also releases oxytocin, especially at orgasm (M. R. Murphy, Checkley, Seckl, & Lightman, 1990). People typically experience a state of relaxation shortly after orgasm as a result of oxytocin release. In animal studies, rats show increased exploration of potentially dangerous places—that is, decreased anxiety—after orgasm. Blocking the release of oxytocin prevents that effect, so oxytocin is apparently responsible for the calmness and lack of anxiety after orgasm (Waldherr & Neumann, 2007). Strong release of oxytocin facilitates formation of pair bonds between mating partners (Kosfeld, Heinrichs, Zak, Fischbacher, & Fehr, 2005). It is also apparently related to the formation of a pair bond between mother and infant. A study found that women who had the highest oxytocin levels during pregnancy spent the most time gazing at, vocalizing to, touching, and pleasurably interacting with their infants after delivery (Feldman, Welle, Zagoory-Sharon, & Levine, 2007).

Oxytocin also facilitates other social behaviors. When people inhale a nasal spray containing oxytocin, as compared to a placebo, they become more accurate at recognizing familiar faces (Rimmele, Hediger, Heinrichs, & Klaver, 2009). They are also quicker to recognize blurry words on a screen, if those words refer to pleasant social relationship words, such as *love* or *kissing* (Unkelbach, Guastella, & Forgas, 2008).

Also consider effects on the "Trust Game." If you are playing this game, someone hands you some money. You can give some or all of it to another person, and if so the amount you give triples in value. That person can then return to you whatever amount he or she chooses. So you have to decide how much you trust that person. What effect would you expect from oxytocin? It depends. People who are given oxytocin give more money to people who seem trustworthy, but not to people who seem competitive and aggressive (Mikolajczak et al., 2010). People sometimes call oxytocin a "love hormone," but as you can see, that term is misleading. It might enhance your attraction toward someone you already love, but it doesn't make you love or trust everyone. Testosterone, incidentally, *decreases* trust (Bos, Terburg, & van Honk, 2010).

10. What behavioral change occurs after orgasm, and which young?

ANSWER

10. Anxiety decreases after orgasm because of release of the pituitary hormone oxytocin.

Parental Behavior

A female mammal's behavior changes in many ways when she becomes a mother. In addition to nursing and caring for the young, she eats and drinks more than usual, and becomes less fearful and more aggressive, especially in defense of her young. Although the role of hormones is less central for humans, it is critical for maternal behavior in other species. After a mother rat delivers her babies, she increases her secretion of estradiol and prolactin, while decreasing production of progesterone (Numan & Woodside, 2010). Prolactin is necessary for milk production and certain aspects of maternal behavior, such as retrieving the young when they wander away from the nest (Lucas, Ormandy, Binart, Bridges, & Kelly, 1998). It also inhibits sensitivity to leptin, enabling the mother to eat far more than usual.

In addition to secreting hormones, the female changes her pattern of hormone receptors. Late in pregnancy, her brain increases its sensitivity to estradiol in the areas responsible for maternal behavior (Rosenblatt, Olufowobi, & Siegel, 1998). The hormonal changes increase the mothers' attention to their young after delivery. Hormones increase activity in the medial preoptic area and anterior hypothalamus (Featherstone, Fleming, & Ivy, 2000), areas that are necessary for rats' maternal behavior (J. R. Brown, Ye, Bronson, Dikkes, & Greenberg, 1996) (Figure 11.9). We have already encountered the preoptic area/anterior hypothalamus, or POA/AH, because of its importance for temperature regulation, thirst, and sexual behavior. It's a busy little area.

Another key hormone is vasopressin, synthesized by the hypothalamus and secreted by the posterior pituitary gland. Vaso-pressin is important for social behavior in many species, partly by facilitating olfactory recognition of other individuals (Tobin et al., 2010). Male prairie voles, which secrete much vasopressin, establish long-term pair bonds with females and help rear their young. A male meadow vole, with much lower vasopressin levels, mates with a female and then virtually ignores her (Figure 11.10). Imagine a male meadow vole in a long, narrow cage. At one end, he can sit next to a female with which he has just mated. (She is confined there.) At the other end, he can sit next to a different female. Will he choose his recent mate (showing loyalty) or the new female (seeking variety)? The answer: neither. He sits right in the middle, by himself, as far away as he can get from both females. However, these little social isolates changed their behavior after researchers found a way to increase activity of the genes responsible for vasopressin in the voles' hypothalamus. Suddenly, they showed a strong preference for a recent mate and, if placed into the same cage, they even helped her take care of her babies (M. M. Lim et al., 2004). Whether the female was surprised, we don't know. This result is a strong example of altering social behavior by manipulating the activity of a single gene.

Although rodent maternal behavior depends on hormones for the first few days, it becomes less dependent later. If a female that has never been pregnant is left with some baby rats, she ignores them at first but gradually becomes more attentive. (Because the babies cannot survive without parental care, the experimenter must periodically replace them with new, healthy babies.) After about 6 days, the adoptive mother builds a nest, assembles the babies in the nest, licks them, and does everything else that normal mothers do, except nurse them. This experience-dependent behavior does not require hormonal changes and occurs even in rats that had their ovaries removed (Mayer & Rosenblatt, 1979; Rosenblatt, 1967). That is, humans are not the only species in which a mother can adopt young without first going through pregnancy.

An important influence from being with babies is that the mother becomes accustomed to their odors. Infant rats release chemicals that stimulate the mother's vomeronasal organ, which responds to pheromones (see Chapter 7). We might imagine that

FIGURE 11.9 Brain development and maternal behavior in mice
The mouse on the left shows normal maternal behavior. The one on the right has a genetic mutation that impairs the development of the preoptic area and anterior hypothalamus. *(Reprinted from Cell, 86/2, Brown, J. R., Ye, H., Bronson, R. T., Dikkes, P., & Greenberg, M. E., "A defect in nurturing in mice lacking the immediate early gene fosB," 297–309, 1996, with permission of Elsevier.)*

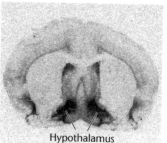

(a)

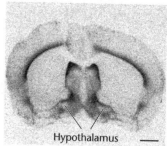

Hypothalamus

Hypothalamus

(b)

FIGURE 11.10 Effects of vasopressin on social and mating behaviors
Prairie voles (top) form long-term pair bonds. Staining of their brain shows much expression of the hormone vasopressin in the hypothalamus. A closely related species, meadow voles (bottom), show no social attachments. Their brains have lower vasopressin levels, as indicated by less staining in the hypothalamus. *(Reprinted by permission from "Enhanced partner preference in a promiscuous species by manipulating the expression of a single gene," by Lim, M. M., Wang, Z., Olazabal, D. E., Ren, X., Terwilliger, E. F., & Young, L. J., Nature, 429, 754–757. Copyright 2004 Nature Publishing Group/Macmillan Magazines Ltd.)*

evolution would have equipped infants with pheromones that elicit maternal behavior, but actually, their pheromones stimulate aggressive behaviors that *interfere* with maternal behavior (Sheehan, Cirrito, Numan, & Numan, 2000). For a mother that has just gone through pregnancy, this interference does not matter because her hormones primed her medial preoptic area so strongly that it overrides competing impulses. A female without hormonal priming, however, rejects the young until she has become familiar with their smell (Del Cerro et al., 1995).

Why do mammals need two mechanisms for maternal behavior—one hormone-dependent and one not? In the early phase, hormones compensate for the mother's lack of familiarity with the young. In the later phase, experience maintains the maternal behavior even though the hormones start to decline (Rosenblatt, 1970).

Are hormones important for human parental behavior? Hormonal changes are necessary for a woman to nurse a baby, and oxytocin levels correlate with several aspects of motherly attention to an infant. However, hormonal changes are not necessary for human parental behavior. After all, many people adopt children and become excellent parents.

STOP & CHECK

11. What factors are responsible for maternal behavior shortly after rats give birth? What factors become more important in later days?

ANSWER

11. The early stage of rats' maternal behavior depends on a surge in the release of the hormones prolactin and estradiol. A few days later, her experience with the young decreases the vomeronasal responses that would tend to make her reject them. Experience with the young maintains maternal behavior after the hormone levels begin to drop.

MODULE 11.1 ■ IN CLOSING

Reproductive Behaviors and Motivations

A mother rat licks her babies all over shortly after their birth, and that stimulation is essential for their survival. Why does she do it? Presumably, she does not understand that licking will help them. She licks because they are covered with a salty fluid that tastes good to her. If she has access to other salty fluids, she stops licking her young (Gubernick & Alberts, 1983). Analo-

gously, sexual behavior in general serves the function of passing on our genes, but we engage in sexual behavior just because it feels good. We evolved a tendency to enjoy the sex act. The same principle holds for hunger, thirst, and other motivations: We evolved tendencies to enjoy acts that have, in general, increased our ancestors' probability of surviving and reproducing.

SUMMARY

1. Male and female behaviors differ because of sex hormones that activate particular genes. Also, certain genes on the X and Y chromosomes exert direct effects on brain development. **328**

2. Organizing effects of a hormone, exerted during a sensitive period, produce relatively permanent alterations in anatomy and physiology. **330**

3. In the absence of sex hormones, an infant mammal develops female-looking external genitals. The addition of testosterone shifts development toward the male pattern. Extra estradiol, within normal limits, does not determine whether the individual looks male or female. However, estradiol and other estrogens modify development of the brain and internal sexual organs. **330**

4. During early development in rodents, testosterone is converted within certain brain cells to estradiol, which actually masculinizes their development. Estradiol in the blood does not masculinize development because it is bound to proteins in the blood. **331**

5. In adulthood, sex hormones activate sex behaviors, partly by facilitating activity in the medial preoptic area and anterior hypothalamus. The hormones prime cells to release dopamine in response to sexual arousal. **333**

6. A woman's menstrual cycle depends on a feedback cycle that increases and then decreases the release of several hormones. Although women can respond sexually at any time in their cycle, on average, they show increased sexual interest when estrogen levels are increasing. **334**

7. The pituitary hormone oxytocin is important for sexual pleasure, delivery of a baby, and milk production. Its release after orgasm decreases anxiety. It also increases attention to anything associated with favorable social or sexual relationships. **337**

8. Hormones released around the time of giving birth facilitate maternal behavior in females of many mammalian species. Prolonged exposure to young also induces parental behavior. Hormonal facilitation is not necessary for human parental behavior. **338**

KEY TERMS

Terms are defined in the module on the page number indicated. They're also presented in alphabetical order with definitions in the book's Subject Index/Glossary, which begins on page 561. Interactive flashcards and crossword puzzles are among the online resources available to help you learn these terms and the concepts they represent.

activating effects **330**
alpha-fetoprotein **332**
androgens **328**
estradiol **329**
estrogens **329**
follicle-stimulating hormone (FSH) **335**
impotence **334**

luteinizing hormone (LH) **335**
menstrual cycle **334**
Müllerian ducts **328**
organizing effects **330**
ovaries **328**
oxytocin **337**
periovulatory period **336**
progesterone **329**

sensitive period **330**
sexually dimorphic nucleus **331**
SRY gene **328**
steroid hormones **329**
testis **328**
testosterone **329**
Wolffian ducts **328**

THOUGHT QUESTIONS

1. The pill RU-486 produces abortions by blocking the effects of progesterone. Why would blocking progesterone interfere with pregnancy?

2. The presence or absence of testosterone determines whether a mammal will differentiate as a male or a female. In birds, the story is the opposite: The presence or absence of estrogen is critical (Adkins & Adler, 1972). What problems would sex determination by estrogen create if that were the mechanism for mammals? Why do those problems not arise in birds? (Hint: Think about the difference between live birth and hatching from an egg.)

3. Antipsychotic drugs, such as haloperidol and chlorpromazine, block activity at dopamine synapses. What side effects might they have on sexual behavior?

Variations in Sexual Behavior

People vary considerably in their frequency of sexual activity, preferred types of sexual activity, and sexual orientation. In this module, we explore some of that diversity, but first we consider a few differences between men and women in general. Do men's and women's mating behaviors make biological sense? If so, should we interpret these behaviors as products of evolution? These questions have proved to be difficult and controversial.

Evolutionary Interpretations of Mating Behavior

Part of Charles Darwin's theory of evolution by natural selection was that individuals whose genes help them survive will produce more offspring, and therefore the next generation will resemble those with these favorable genes. A second part of his theory, not so widely accepted at first, was **sexual selection**: Genes that make an individual more appealing to the other sex will increase the probability of reproduction, and therefore the next generation will resemble those who had these favorable genes.

Sexual selection can go only so far, however, if it starts to interfere with survival. A male deer with large antlers attracts females, but being impressive wouldn't help if the weight became so great that it interfered with the deer's movement. A bird's bright colors attract potential mates, but they also run the risk of attracting a predator's attention. In many bird species, the male is brightly colored, but the female is not, presumably because she sits on the nest and needs to be less conspicuous. In a few species, such as phalaropes, the female is more brightly colored, but in those species, the female lays the egg and deserts it, leaving the dull-colored male to sit on the nest. In species where the male and female share the nesting duties, such as pigeons and doves, the male and female look alike, and neither is especially gaudy.

In humans, too, some of the differences between men and women may be results of sexual selection. That is, to some extent women evolved based on what appeals to men, and men evolved based on what appeals to women. Certain aspects of behavior may also reflect different evolutionary pressures for men and women. Evolutionary psychologists cite several pos-

Phalaropes are shore birds, in which the female is brilliantly colored and the male is drabber. The female lays eggs and deserts the nest, leaving the male to attend to it.

sible examples, although each has been controversial (Buss, 2000). Let's examine the evidence and reasoning.

Interest in Multiple Mates

More men than women seek opportunities for casual sexual relationships with many partners. Why? From the evolutionary standpoint of spreading one's genes, men can succeed by either of two strategies (Gangestad & Simpson, 2000): Be loyal to one woman and devote your energies to helping her and her babies, or mate with many women and hope that some of them can raise your babies without your help. No one needs to be conscious of these strategies, of course. The idea is that men who acted these ways in the past propagated their genes, and today's men might have inherited genes that promote these behaviors. In contrast, a woman can have no more than one pregnancy per 9 months, regardless of her number of sex partners. So evolution may have predisposed men, or at least some men, to be more interested in multiple mates than women are.

341

One objection is that a woman does sometimes gain from having multiple sex partners (Hrdy, 2000). If her husband is infertile, mating with another man could be her only way of reproducing. Also, another sexual partner may provide aid of various sorts to her and her children. In addition, she has the possibility of "trading up," abandoning her first mate for a better one. So the prospect of multiple mates may be more appealing to men, but it has advantages for women, too. Human cultures vary substantially in how well they tolerate women having multiple sexual partners.

Another objection is that researchers have no direct evidence that genes influence people's preferences for one mate or many. We shall return to this issue later.

What Men and Women Seek in a Mate

Almost all people seeking a romantic partner prefer someone who is healthy, intelligent, honest, and physically attractive. Typically, women have some additional interests that are less common for men. In particular, women are more likely than men are to prefer a mate who is likely to be a good provider (Buss, 2000). As you might guess, that tendency is strongest in societies where women have no income of their own. According to evolutionary theorists, the reason is this: While a woman is pregnant or taking care of a small child, she needs help getting food and other requirements. Evolution would have favored any gene that caused women to seek good providers. Related to this tendency, most women tend to be cautious during courtship. Even if a man seems interested in her, a woman waits before concluding that he has a strong commitment to her (Buss, 2001). She would not want a man who acts interested briefly and then leaves when she needs him.

A woman is also much more likely to reject a man because of his smell than a man is to reject a woman because of her smell (Herz & Inzlicht, 2002). One possible reason is that body odor relates to some of the same genes that control the immune system, known as the *major histocompatibility complex*. Research has found that a woman tends to be less sexually responsive to a man whose immune genes, and therefore body odor, are too similar to her own (Garver-Apgar, Gangestad, Thornhill, Miller, & Olp, 2006). Avoiding a man of similar odor may be a way to avoid inbreeding.

Men tend to have a stronger preference for a young partner. An evolutionary explanation is that young women are likely to remain fertile longer than older women are, so a man can have more children by pairing with a young woman. Curiously, male chimpanzees show no preference for young females, perhaps because chimpanzee mating does not entail a long-term commitment. In fact, male chimps usually prefer older (but still fertile) females, who tend to have a higher social rank than younger females do (Muller, Thompson, & Wrangham, 2006).

Men remain fertile into old age, so a woman has less need to insist on youth. Women do prefer young partners when possible, but in many societies, only older men have enough financial resources to get married.

Differences in Jealousy

Traditionally, in most cultures, men have been more jealous of women's infidelities than women have been of men's infidelities. From an evolutionary standpoint, why might men be more jealous than women? If a man is to pass on his genes—the key point in evolution—he needs to be sure that the children he supports are his own. An unfaithful wife threatens that certainty. A woman knows that any children she bears are her own, so she does not have the same worry.

One way to test this interpretation of jealousy is to compare cultures. Some cultures consider sexual infidelity acceptable for both husband and wife; some prohibit it completely for both; and some consider it more acceptable for the husband than for the wife. However, no known society considers it more acceptable for the wife. Should we be more impressed that jealousy is always at least as strong for men as for women, and usually more, or should we be more impressed that jealousy varies among cultures? The answer is not obvious.

Which would upset you more: if your partner had a brief sexual affair with someone else, or if he or she became emotionally close to someone else? According to several studies, men say they would be more upset by the sexual infidelity, whereas women would be more upset by the emotional infidelity (Shakelford, Buss, & Bennett, 2002). However, those studies dealt with hypothetical situations. Most men and women who have actually dealt with an unfaithful partner say they were more upset by their partner's becoming emotionally close to someone else than by the sexual affair (C. H. Harris, 2002).

Evolved or Learned?

If a behavior has clear advantages for survival or reproduction and is similar across most or all cultures, can we conclude that it developed by evolution? Not necessarily. Of course, the brain evolved, just like any other organ, and of course, our behavioral tendencies are a product of evolution. But the key question is whether evolution has micromanaged our behavior down to such details as whether to look for a mate with high earning potential or how jealous to be of an unfaithful mate.

Cross-cultural similarity is not necessarily good evidence for an evolved tendency. For example, people throughout the world agree that $2 + 2 = 4$, but we don't assume that they have a gene for that belief. To establish that we evolved a tendency to act in some way, the most decisive evidence would be to demonstrate genes that affect the relevant behaviors. For example, if most men have genes influencing them to prefer young women, then presumably, we should be able to find some men with a mutation in that gene causing them to lose that preference. Although this example may not be the best, the point is that we need to be cautious about inferring what is a product of our evolution and what is learned.

Conclusions

Discussing these issues is difficult. Ideally, we would like to consider the evidence and logical arguments entirely on their scientific merits. However, when someone describes how evolutionary selection may have led men to be interested in multiple sex partners or to be more jealous than women are, it sometimes sounds like a justification for men to act that way. No gene forces men or women to behave in any particular way.

Even leaving aside the social implications as far as we can, no firm scientific consensus emerges. We need more data, especially about the effects of particular genes, before we draw a firm conclusion.

STOP & CHECK

12. What evolutionary advantage is suggested for why women are more interested in men's wealth and success than men are interested in women's wealth?

ANSWER

12. During pregnancy and early child care, a female is limited in her ability to get food and therefore prefers a male partner who can provide for her. A healthy male is not similarly dependent on a female.

Gender Identity and Gender-Differentiated Behaviors

The coral goby is a species of fish in which the male and female tend their eggs and young together. If one of them dies, the survivor looks for a new partner. But it does not look far. This is a very stay-at-home kind of fish. If it cannot easily find a partner of the opposite sex but does find an unmated member of its own sex—oh, well—it simply changes sex and mates with the neighbor. Male-to-female and female-to-male switches are equally common (Nakashima, Kuwamura, & Yogo, 1995).

People do not have the same flexibility as coral gobies, but we do have variations in sexual development. Sexual development is a sensitive issue, so let us specify from the start: "Different" does not mean "wrong." People differ naturally in their sexual development just as they do in anything else.

Gender identity is how we identify sexually and what we call ourselves. The biological differences between males and females are *sex differences*, whereas the differences that result from people's thinking about themselves as male or female are *gender differences*. To maintain this useful distinction, we should resist the trend to speak of the "gender" of dogs, fruit flies, and so forth. Gender identity is a human characteristic.

In most cases people accept the gender identity that matches their external appearance, which matches the way they were reared. However, some are dissatisfied with their assigned gender, and many would describe

themselves as being masculine in some ways and feminine in others. Psychologists have long assumed that gender depends mainly or entirely on the way people rear their children. However, several kinds of evidence suggest that biological factors, especially prenatal hormones, are important also.

Intersexes

Some people have anatomies intermediate between male and female (Haqq & Donahoe, 1998). Individuals who appear to be a mixture of male and female are referred to as **hermaphrodites** (from Hermes and Aphrodite in Greek mythology). For example, some people are born with an XX chromosome pattern but an SRY gene that translocated from the father's Y chromosome onto another chromosome. Despite their XX chromosomes, they have either an ovary and a testis, or two testes, or a mixture of testis and ovary tissue on each side.

Others develop an intermediate appearance because of an atypical hormone pattern. Recall that testosterone masculinizes the genitals and the hypothalamus during early development. A genetic male with low levels of testosterone or a deficiency of testosterone receptors may develop a female or intermediate appearance (Misrahi et al., 1997). A genetic female who is exposed to more testosterone than the average female can be partly masculinized.

The most common cause of this condition is **congenital adrenal hyperplasia (CAH)**, meaning overdevelopment of the adrenal glands from birth. Ordinarily, the adrenal gland has a negative feedback relationship with the pituitary gland. The pituitary secretes adrenocorticotropic hormone (ACTH), which stimulates the adrenal gland. Cortisol, one of the hormones from the adrenal gland, feeds back to decrease the release of ACTH.

Accord Alliance

This group of intersexed people gathered to provide mutual support and to protest against the early surgical treatments they received. They requested that their names be used to emphasize that their intersexuality should not be considered shameful. From left to right: Martha Coventry, Max Beck, David Vandertie, Kristi Bruce, and Angela Moreno.

Some people have a genetic limitation in their ability to produce cortisol. Because the pituitary fails to receive much cortisol as a feedback signal, it continues secreting more ACTH, causing the adrenal gland to secrete larger amounts of its other hormones, including testosterone. In a genetic male, the extra testosterone causes no apparent difficulty. However, genetic females with this condition develop various degrees of masculinization of their external genitals. (The ovaries and other internal organs are less affected.) Figure 11.11 shows a structure that appears intermediate between clitoris and penis and swellings that appear intermediate between labia and scrotum. After birth, these children are given medical treatments to bring their adrenal hormones within normal levels. Some are also given surgery to alter their external genital appearance, as we shall discuss later.

People whose sexual development is intermediate, as in Figure 11.11, are called **intersexes**. How common are intersexes? An estimated 1 child in 100 in the United States is born with some degree of genital ambiguity, and 1 in 2,000 has enough ambiguity to make its male or female status uncertain (Blackless et al., 2000). However, the accuracy of these estimates is doubtful, as hospitals and families keep the information private. Maintaining confidentiality is of course important, but an unfortunate consequence is that intersexed people have trouble finding others like themselves. For more information, consult the website of the Intersex Society of North America (ISNA): http://www.isna.org/.

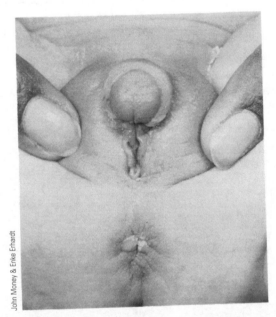

John Money & Anke Ehrhardt

FIGURE 11.11 External genitals of a genetic female, age 3 months
The genitals were masculinized by excess androgens from the adrenal gland before birth. *(From Money, John and Ehrhardt, Anke A., Man and Woman, Boy and Girl: Differentiation and Dimorphism of Gender Identity from Conception to Maturity, p. 115, Figure 6.2. © 1972 The Johns Hopkins University Press. Reprinted by permission of The Johns Hopkins University Press.)*

13. What is a common cause for a genetic female (XX) to develop a partly masculinized anatomy?

ANSWER 13. If a genetic female is genetically deficient in her ability to produce cortisol, the pituitary gland does not receive negative feedback signals and therefore continues stimulating the adrenal gland. The adrenal gland then produces large amounts of other hormones, including testosterone, which masculinizes development.

Interests and Preferences of CAH Girls

For many years, the policy was to raise most intersexed people as girls, on the assumption that surgery could make them look like normal girls, and they would develop behaviors corresponding to the way they were reared. However, their brains were exposed to higher than normal testosterone levels during prenatal and early postnatal life compared to other girls. Was their behavior masculinized? As discussed in the first module of this chapter, prenatal levels of testosterone correlate with girls' toy choices. The same idea applies here. In several studies, girls with CAH were observed in a room full of toys—including some that were girl typical (dolls, plates and dishes, cosmetics kits), some that were boy typical (toy car, tool set, gun), and some that were neutral (puzzles, crayons, board games). Figure 11.12 shows the results from one such study (Pasterski et al., 2005). Note how girls with CAH were intermediate between the preferences of boys and girls without CAH. When the children tested with a parent present, again the girls with CAH were intermediate between the other two groups.

Other studies have reported similar results and have found that the girls exposed to the largest amount of testosterone in early development showed the largest preference for boys' toys (Berenbaum, Duck, & Bryk, 2000; Nordenström, Servin, Bohlin, Larsson, & Wedell, 2002). You might wonder whether the parents, knowing that these girls had been partly masculinized in appearance, might have encouraged "tomboyish" activities. Psychologists' observations suggest the opposite: The parents encouraged the girls with CAH any time they played with girl-typical toys (Pasterski et al., 2005). A study of CAH girls in adolescence found that, on average, their interests are intermediate between those of typical male and female adolescents. For example, they read more sports magazines and fewer style and glamour magazines than the average for other teenage girls (Berenbaum, 1999). In adulthood, they show more physical aggression than most other women do, and less interest in infants (Mathews, Fane, Conway, Brook, & Hines, 2009). They are more interested in rough sports and more likely than average to be in heavily male-dominated occupations such as auto mechanic and truck driver (Frisén et al., 2009).

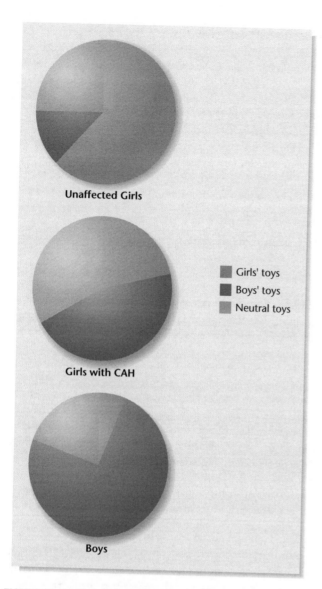

FIGURE 11.12 Toy preferences by CAH girls, unaffected girls, and unaffected boys
CAH girls were intermediate between unaffected girls and boys. These data show results when the children played alone. Results changed slightly when the mother or father was present, but in each case, the CAH girls were intermediate between the other groups. *(Based on data of Byne et al., 2001)*

[legend: Girls' toys / Boys' toys / Neutral toys]

14. If a genetic female is exposed to extra testosterone during prenatal development, what behavioral effect is likely?

ANSWER

14. A girl who is exposed to extra testosterone during prenatal development is more likely than most other girls to prefer boy-typical toys.

Testicular Feminization

Certain individuals with an XY chromosome pattern have the genital appearance of a female. This condition is known as **androgen insensitivity**, or **testicular feminization**. Although such individuals produce normal amounts of androgens (including testosterone), they lack the receptor that enables androgen to activate genes in a cell's nucleus. Consequently, the cells are insensitive to androgens, and development proceeds as if the level of testosterone and similar hormones was low. This condition occurs in various degrees, resulting in anatomy that ranges from a smaller than average penis to genitals like those of a normal female. In some cases, no one has any reason to suspect the person is anything other than a normal female, until puberty. Then, in spite of breast development and broadening of the hips, menstruation does not begin because the body has internal testes instead of ovaries and a uterus. (The vagina is short and leads to nothing but skin.) Also, pubic hair is sparse or absent, because it depends on androgens in females as well as males.

15. What would cause a genetic male (XY) to develop a partly feminized external anatomy?

ANSWER

15. A genetic male with a gene that prevents testosterone from binding to its receptors will develop an appearance that partly or completely resembles a female.

Issues of Gender Assignment and Rearing

Many girls with CAH and related conditions are born with a nearly normal appearance, but some look as much male as female and presumably were exposed to high levels of prenatal testosterone. Some genetic males are born with a very small penis because of a condition called *cloacal exstrophy*, a defect of pelvis development (Reiner & Gearhart, 2004). Despite their genital anatomy, they had typical male levels of testosterone in prenatal development.

How should children with either of these conditions be reared? Beginning in the 1950s, medical doctors began recommending that all intersexed people be reared as girls, using surgery if necessary to make their genitals look more feminine (Dreger, 1998). The reason was that it is easier to reduce an enlarged clitoris to normal size than expand it to penis size. If necessary, surgeons can build an artificial vagina or lengthen a short one. After the surgery, the child looks female. Physicians and psychologists assumed that any child who was consistently reared as a girl would fully accept that identity.

And she lives happily ever after, right? Not necessarily. Of those with cloacal exstrophy who are reared as girls, all develop typical male interests, many or most eventually demand reassignment as males, and nearly all develop sexual attraction toward women, not men (Reiner & Gearhart, 2004).

Girls with the CAH history also have a difficult adjustment, especially if they were subjected to clitoris-reduction surgery. A surgically created or lengthened vagina may be satisfactory to a male partner, but it provides no sensation to the woman and requires almost daily attention to prevent it from scarring over. Nearly all women with a history of CAH have significant sexual difficulties, including lack of orgasm. Many report no sexual partner ever, little or no interest in sex, and little or no romantic attraction to men (Frisén et al., 2009; Meyer-Bahlburg, Dolezal, Baker, & New, 2008; Minto, Liao, Woodhouse, Ransley, & Creighton, 2003; Nordenström et al., 2010; Zucker et al., 1996).

Many intersexes wish they had their original "abnormal" enlarged clitoris instead of the mutilated, insensitive structure left to them by a surgeon. Moreover, intersexes resent being deceived. Historian Alice Dreger (1998) describes the case of one intersex:

> As a young person, [she] was told she had "twisted ovaries" that had to be removed; in fact, her testes were removed. At the age of twenty, "alone and scared in the stacks of a [medical] library," she discovered the truth of her condition. Then "the pieces finally fit together. But what fell apart was my relationship with both my family and physicians. It was not learning about chromosomes or testes that caused enduring trauma, it was discovering that I had been told lies. I avoided all medical care for the next 18 years. . . . [The] greatest source of anxiety is not our gonads or karyotype. It is shame and fear resulting from an environment in which our condition is so unacceptable that caretakers lie." (p. 192)

How should such a child be reared? A growing number of specialists follow these recommendations (Diamond & Sigmundson, 1997):

- Be completely honest with the intersexed person and the family, and do nothing without their informed consent.
- Identify the child as male or female based mainly on the predominant external appearance. That is, there should be no bias toward calling every intersex a female. Those born with masculinized external genitals seldom make a successful adaptation to a female gender assignment (Houk & Lee, 2010).
- Rear the child as consistently as possible, but be prepared that the person might later be sexually oriented toward males, females, both, or neither.
- Do not perform surgery to reduce the ambiguous penis/clitoris to the size of a normal clitoris. Such surgery impairs the person's erotic sensation and is at best premature, as no one knows how the child's sexual orientation will develop. If the intersexed person makes an informed request for such surgery in adulthood, then it is appropriate, but otherwise it should be avoided.

Discrepancies of Sexual Appearance

The evidence from intersexes does not indisputably resolve the roles of rearing and hormones in determining gender identity. From a scientific viewpoint, the most decisive way to settle the issue would be to raise a normal male baby as a female or to raise a normal female baby as a male. If the process succeeded in producing an adult who was fully satisfied in the assigned role, we would know that upbringing determines gender identity. Although no one would perform such an experiment intentionally, we can learn from accidental events. In some cases, someone was exposed to a more-or-less normal pattern of male hormones before and shortly after birth but then reared as a girl.

One kind of case was reported first in the Dominican Republic and then in other places, usually in communities with much inbreeding. In each case, certain genetic males fail to produce 5α-reductase 2, an enzyme that converts testosterone to dihydrotestosterone. Dihydrotestosterone is an androgen that is more effective than testosterone for masculinizing the external genitals. At birth, some of these individuals look almost like a typical female, while others have a swollen clitoris and somewhat "lumpy" labia. Nearly all are considered girls and reared as such. However, their brains had been exposed to male levels of testosterone during early development. At puberty, the testosterone levels increase sharply, the body makes increased amounts of a different enzyme that converts testosterone to dihydrotestosterone, and the result is the growth of a penis and scrotum.

Women: Imagine that at about age 12 years, your external genitals suddenly changed from female to male. Would you say, "Yep, okay, I guess I'm a boy now"? Most (but not all) of these people reacted exactly that way. The girl-turned-boy developed a male gender identity and directed his sexual interest toward females (Cohen-Kettenis, 2005; Imperato-McGinley, Guerrero, Gautier, & Peterson, 1974). Remember, these were not typical girls. Their brains had been exposed to male levels of testosterone from prenatal life onward.

A particularly upsetting case is that of one infant boy whose penis foreskin would not retract enough for easy urination. His parents took him to a physician to circumcise the foreskin, but the physician, using an electrical procedure, set the current too high and accidentally burned off the entire penis. On the advice of respected and well-meaning authorities, the parents elected to rear the child as a female, with the appropriate surgery. What makes this case especially interesting is that the child had a twin brother (whom the parents did not let the physician try to circumcise). If both twins developed satisfactory gender identities, one as a girl and the other as a boy, the results would say that rearing was decisive in gender identity.

Initial reports claimed that the child reared as a girl had a female gender identity, though she also had strong tomboyish tendencies (Money & Schwartz, 1978). However, by about age 10, she had figured out that something was wrong and that "she" was really a boy. She had preferred boys' activities and played only with boys' toys. She even tried urinating in a standing position, despite always making a mess. By age 14, she insisted that she wanted to live as a boy. At that time, her (now his) father tearfully explained the earlier events. The child changed names and became known as a boy. At age 25, he married a somewhat older woman and adopted her children. Clearly, a biological predisposition had won out over the family's attempts to rear the child as a girl (Colapinto, 1997; Diamond & Sigmundson, 1997). Some years later, the story ended tragically with this man's suicide.

We should not draw universal conclusions from a single case. However, the point is that it was a mistake to impose surgery and hormonal treatments to try to force this child to become female. When the prenatal hormone pattern of the brain is in conflict with a child's appearance, no one can be sure how that child will develop psychologically. Hormones don't have complete control, but rearing patterns don't, either.

> **STOP & CHECK**

16. When "girls" reached puberty and grew a penis and scrotum, what happened to their gender identity?

ANSWER

16. Most changed their gender identity from female to male.

Sexual Orientation

Contrary to what biologists once assumed, homosexual behavior occurs in many animal species, and not just in captive animals, those that cannot find a member of the opposite sex, or those with hormonal abnormalities (Bagemihl, 1999). If "natural" means "occurs in nature," then homosexuality is natural.

What accounts for differences in sexual orientation? Many influences appear to be important, including genetics, prenatal environment, and as-yet unidentified aspects of experience. The explanations will probably be different for different people, and in general different for men than for women. Whereas most men discover their sexual orientation early, many women are slower. Feminine-type behaviors in childhood and adolescence correlate strongly with homosexual orientation in adulthood for men (Cardoso, 2009; Alanko et al., 2010), but early masculine-type behaviors are poor predictors of sexual orientation in women (Udry & Chantala, 2006). A higher percentage of women than men experience at least some physical attraction to both males and females (Chivers, Rieger, Latty, & Bailey, 2004; Lippa, 2006), and some women switch—once or more—between homosexual and heterosexual orientations (Diamond, 2007). Switches in sexual orientation are rare in men. Although we shall note certain biological correlates of female homosexuality, the case for a biological predisposition seems stronger for men.

Behavioral and Anatomical Differences

On average, homosexual and heterosexual people differ anatomically in several ways. On average, heterosexual men are slightly taller and heavier than homosexual men (Bogaert, 2010). However, let's emphasize that term "slightly": The difference on average is only 1.5 cm (about half an inch). Despite the stereotype, a fair number of homosexual men are tall, athletic, and masculine in appearance.

On average, people who differ in sexual orientation also differ in several behaviors that are not directly related to sex. More men than women give directions in terms of distances and north, south, east, or west. Women are more likely to describe landmarks. Gay men also tend to use landmarks and are better than heterosexual men at remembering landmarks (Hassan & Rahman, 2007). Consider this task: Experimenters repeatedly present a loud noise and measure the startle response. On some trials, they present a weaker noise just before the loud noise; the first noise decreases the startle response to the louder one. The decrease is called "prepulse inhibition." Prepulse inhibition is ordinarily stronger in men than in women. In this regard, homosexual women are slightly shifted in the male direction compared to heterosexual women (Rahman, Kumari, & Wilson, 2003).

Genetics

Studies of the genetics of sexual orientation have focused mainly on twins. Early studies of the genetics of human sexual orientation began by advertising in gay or lesbian publications for homosexual people with twins. Then they contacted the other twin to fill out a questionnaire. The questionnaire included diverse items to conceal the fact that the real interest was sexual orientation. The results showed a stronger concordance for monozygotic than dizygotic twins (Bailey & Pillard, 1991; Bailey, Pillard, Neale, & Agyei, 1993). That is, if one twin is homosexual, the probability for the other to be homosexual is fairly high for a monozygotic twin, and less high for a dizygotic twin. However, the kind of person who answers an ad in a gay or lesbian magazine may not be representative of others. A later study examined the data from all the twins in Sweden between ages 20 and 47 (Långström, Rahman, Carlström, & Lichtenstein, 2010). The Swedish study differed not only in the breadth of the sample but also in the behavioral criterion. Instead of asking about sexual orientation, the researchers asked whether someone had ever had a same-sex partner. Figure 11.13 compares the data from the two studies. The results do not indicate total number of people with homosexual activity or orientation. Rather, they indicate concordance—the probability of homosexual activity or orientation in one twin, given that the other twin had already indicated such activity. Although both sets of results show a higher concordance for monozygotic than dizygotic twins, note the huge difference between the studies. From these data it is reasonable to infer a genetic contribution to sexual orientation, but we can't be sure about the size of that contribution.

Several studies reported a higher incidence of homosexuality among the maternal than paternal relatives of homosexual men (Camperio-Ciani, Corna, & Capiluppi, 2004; Hamer, Hu, Magnuson, Hu, & Pattatucci, 1993). For example, uncles and cousins on the mother's side were more likely to be homosexual than uncles and cousins on the father's side. These results suggest a gene on the X chromosome, which a man necessarily receives from his mother. However, other studies have not replicated these results, and the current status is inconclusive (Bailey et al., 1999; Rice, Anderson, Risch, & Ebers, 1999).

An Evolutionary Question

If certain genes promote a homosexual orientation, why hasn't evolution selected strongly against those genes, which de-

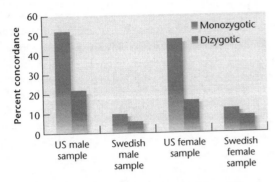

FIGURE 11.13 Twin concordance for homosexuality
The concordance for homosexual orientation (U.S. study) or homosexual activity (Swedish study) was higher for monozygotic twins than for dizygotic twins. *(Based on the data of Bailey & Pillard, 1991; Bailey, Pillard, Neale, & Agyei, 1993; Långström, Rahman, Carlström, & Lichtenstein, 2010)*

crease the probability of reproduction? Several possibilities are worth considering (Gavrilets & Rice, 2006). One is that genes for homosexuality are maintained by kin selection, as discussed in Chapter 1. That is, even if homosexual people do not have children themselves, they might do a wonderful job of helping their brothers and sisters rear children. Survey data in the United States indicate that homosexual men are no more likely than heterosexuals, and perhaps less likely, to help support their relatives (Bobrow & Bailey, 2001). However, observations in Samoa found that homosexual men are more helpful than average toward their nephews and nieces (Vasey & VanderLaan, 2010). It is difficult to know what might have been the usual pattern through human existence.

According to a second hypothesis, genes that produce homosexuality in males produce advantageous effects in their sisters and other female relatives, increasing their probability of reproducing and spreading the genes. The results of one study support this hypothesis. Homosexual men's mothers and aunts had a greater than average number of children (Camperio-Ciani et al., 2004). However, a common estimate is that the average homosexual man has one fifth as many children as the average heterosexual man. Could his female relatives have enough children to compensate for this decrease? It seems unlikely.

A third hypothesis is that certain genes lead to homosexuality in men homozygous for the gene but produce reproductive advantages in men heterozygous for the gene (Rahman & Wilson, 2003). A closely related idea is that several genes produce advantages for survival or reproduction, but a combination of them leads to homosexuality.

A fourth idea is that homosexuality relates to the activation or inactivation of genes (Bocklandt, Horvath, Vilain, & Hamer, 2006). As mentioned in Chapter 1, it is possible for environmental events to attach a methyl group (CH_3) to a gene and inactivate it. A parent can pass the inactivation of a gene to the next generation. Conceivably, this mechanism might produce a significant amount of homosexuality without relying on the spread of a gene that promotes homosexuality.

17. For which kind of twin pair is the concordance for sexual orientation greatest?

18. It seems difficult to explain how a gene could remain at a moderately high frequency in the population if most men with the gene do not reproduce. How would the hypothesis about inactivation by a methyl group help with the explanation?

ANSWERS

17. Monozygotic twins have higher concordance than dizygotic twins. Note the importance of stating this point correctly: Do *not* say that homosexuality is more common in monozygotic than dizygotic twins. It is the concordance that is greater—that is, the probability that both twins have the same sexual orientation. **18.** According to this hypothesis, some unknown event in the environment can attach a methyl group to some unidentified gene, inactivating the gene. That gene could be passed to the next generation, producing evidence for a hereditary effect, even though there is no "gene for homosexuality." If this event of attaching a methyl group to that gene happens often enough, the result could be a moderately high prevalence of homosexuality, even if men with the inactivated gene seldom reproduce.

Prenatal Influences

Adult hormone levels do *not* explain sexual orientation. On average, homosexual and heterosexual men have nearly the same hormone levels, and most lesbian women have about the same hormone levels as heterosexual women. However, it is possible that sexual orientation depends on testosterone levels during a sensitive period of brain development (Ellis & Ames, 1987). Animal studies have shown that prenatal or early postnatal hormones can produce organizing effects on both anatomy and sexual behavior. External anatomy develops at a different time from brain anatomy, and so it is possible for hormones to alter one differently from the other.

The mother's immune system may exert prenatal effects. Several studies (though not all) report that the probability of a homosexual orientation is slightly higher among men who have older brothers. Younger brothers make no difference, nor do younger or older sisters (Bogaert, 2003b; Purcell, Blanchard, & Zucker, 2000). Furthermore, what matters is the number of *biological* older brothers. Growing up with older stepbrothers or adopted brothers has no apparent influence. Having a biological older brother has an influence, even if the brothers were reared separately (Bogaert, 2006). In short, the influence does not stem from social experiences. The key is how many previous times the mother gave birth to a son. The most prominent hypothesis is that a mother's immune system sometimes reacts against a protein in a son and then attacks subsequent sons enough to alter their development. That hypothesis fits with the observation that later-born homosexual men tend to be shorter than average (Bogaert, 2003a).

Another aspect of prenatal environment relates to stress on the mother during pregnancy. Research has shown that prenatal stress alters sexual development in laboratory animals. In several experiments, rats in the final week of pregnancy had the stressful experience of confinement in tight Plexiglas tubes for more than 2 hours each day under bright lights. In some cases, they were given alcohol as well. These rats' daughters looked and acted approximately normal. The sons, however, had normal male anatomy but in adulthood often responded to the presence of another male by arching their backs in the typical rat female posture for sex (I. L. Ward, Ward, Winn, & Bielawski, 1994). Most males that were subjected to either prenatal stress or alcohol developed male sexual behavior in addition to these female sexual behaviors, but those that were subjected to both stress and alcohol had decreased male sexual behaviors (I. L. Ward, Bennett, Ward, Hendricks, & French, 1999).

Prenatal stress and alcohol may alter brain development through several routes. Stress releases endorphins, which can antagonize the effects of testosterone on the hypothalamus (O. B. Ward, Monaghan, & Ward, 1986). Stress also elevates levels of the adrenal hormone corticosterone, which decreases testosterone release (O. B. Ward, Ward, Denning, French, & Hendricks, 2002; M. T. Williams, Davis, McCrea, Long, & Hennessy, 1999). The long-term effects of either prenatal stress or alcohol include several changes in the structure of the nervous system, making the affected males' anatomy closer to that of females (Nosenko & Reznikov, 2001; I. L. Ward, Romeo, Denning, & Ward, 1999).

Although the relevance of these results to humans is uncertain, they prompted investigators to examine possible effects of prenatal stress on humans. One approach is to ask the mothers of homosexual men whether they experienced any unusual stress during pregnancy. Three surveys compared mothers of homosexual sons to mothers of heterosexual sons. In two of the three, the mothers of homosexual sons recalled more than average stressful experiences during their pregnancies (Bailey, Willerman, & Parks, 1991; Ellis, Ames, Peckham, & Burke, 1988; Ellis & Cole-Harding, 2001). However, these studies relied on women's memories of pregnancies more than 20 years earlier. A better but more difficult procedure would be to measure stress during pregnancy and examine the sexual orientation of the sons many years later.

STOP & CHECK

19. By what route might having an older brother increase the probability of male homosexuality?

20. How might stress to a pregnant rat alter the sexual orientation of her male offspring?

ANSWERS **19.** Having an older brother might increase the probability of male homosexuality by altering the mother's immune system in the prenatal environment. The effect of the older brother does not depend on growing up in the same home. **20.** Evidently, stress increases the release of endorphins in the hypothalamus, and very high endorphin levels can block the effects of testosterone.

Brain Anatomy

Do brains also differ as a function of sexual orientation? The results are complex. On average, homosexual men are shifted partly in the female-typical direction for some brain structures but not others. Similarly, on average, homosexual women's brains are slightly shifted in the male direction in some ways but not others (Rahman & Wilson, 2003). Several of the reported differences have no clear relationship to sexuality itself, although they may relate to other behavioral differences between heterosexual and homosexual people.

On average, the left and right hemispheres of the cerebral cortex are of nearly equal size in heterosexual females, whereas the right hemisphere is a few percent larger in heterosexual males. Homosexual males resemble heterosexual females in this regard, and homosexual females are intermediate between heterosexual females and males. Also, in heterosexual females the left amygdala has more widespread connections than the right amygdala, whereas in heterosexual males the right amygdala has more widespread connections. Again, homosexual males resemble heterosexual females in this regard, and homosexual females are intermediate (Savic & Lindström, 2008). The anterior commissure (Figures 4.13 and 14.5) is, on average, larger in heterosexual women than in heterosexual men. In homosexual men, it is at least as large as in women, perhaps even slightly larger (Gorski & Allen, 1992). The suprachiasmatic nucleus (SCN) is also larger in homosexual men than in heterosexual men (Swaab & Hofman, 1990). However, when interpreting these and other reported differences, we should remember two cautions (Kaiser, Haller, Schmitz, & Nitsch, 2009): First, we don't know whether these brain differences are causes or effects of sexual orientation. Brain differences can predispose to different behaviors, but it is also true, as discussed in Chapter 5, that persistent behaviors can change brain anatomy. Second, it is relatively easy to publish results showing a difference between two groups, such as homosexual and heterosexual people, even if the difference was unpredicted, small, and hard to explain. It is less easy to publish results showing no difference. Thus it is possible that the published papers overstate certain anatomical differences.

The most widely cited research concerns the third interstitial nucleus of the anterior hypothalamus (INAH-3), which is generally more than twice as large in heterosexual men as in women. This area has more cells with androgen receptors in men than in women (Shah et al., 2004) and probably plays a role in sexual behavior, although the exact role is uncertain. Simon LeVay (1991) examined INAH-3 in 41 people who had died between the ages of 26 and 59. Of these, 16 were heterosexual men, 6 were heterosexual women, and 19 were homosexual men. All of the homosexual men, 6 of the 16 heterosexual men, and 1 of the 6 women had died of AIDS. LeVay found that the mean volume of INAH-3 was larger in heterosexual men than in heterosexual women or homosexual men, who were about equal in this regard. Figure 11.14 shows typical cross-sections for a heterosexual man and a homosexual man. Figure 11.15 shows the distribution of volumes for the three

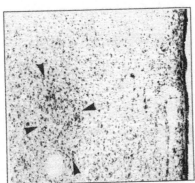
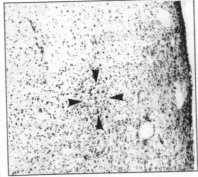

FIGURE 11.14 Typical sizes of interstitial nucleus 3 of the anterior hypothalamus
On average, the volume of this structure was more than twice as large in a sample of heterosexual men (left) than in a sample of homosexual men (right), for whom it was about the same size as in women. *(From "A difference in hypothalamic structure between heterosexual and homosexual men," S. LeVay, Science, 253, pp. 1034–1037. Copyright 1991. Reprinted by permission from AAAS.)*

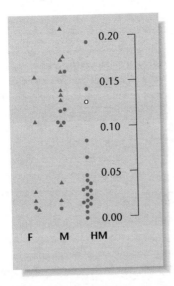

FIGURE 11.15 Volumes of the interstitial nucleus 3 of the anterior hypothalamus (INAH-3)
Samples are females (F), heterosexual males (M), and homosexual males (HM). Each filled circle represents a person who died of AIDS, and each triangle represents a person who died from other causes. The one open circle represents a bisexual man who died of AIDS. *(Reprinted by permission from "A difference in hypothalamic structure between heterosexual and homosexual men," by S. LeVay, Science, 253, pp. 1034–1037. Copyright © 1991 American Association for the Advancement of Science.)*

man's INAH-3, you could make a reasonable guess about sexual orientation, but you could not be confident.

A later study partly replicated these trends. Researchers found that the INAH-3 nucleus was slightly larger in heterosexual than homosexual men, although in this study the homosexual men's INAH-3 nucleus was larger than that of heterosexual women (Byne et al., 2001). Among heterosexual men or women, the INAH-3 nucleus was larger in those who were HIV negative than those who were HIV positive, but even if we look only at HIV+ men, we still find a difference in the hypothalamus between heterosexual and homosexual men. Figure 11.16 displays the means for the five groups. On microscopic examination of the INAH-3, researchers found that heterosexual men had larger neurons than homosexual men but about the same number. (Neither this study nor LeVay's earlier study included homosexual females.) Still another study found INAH-3 to be larger in heterosexual males than in male-to-female transsexuals—that is, people

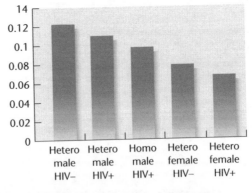

FIGURE 11.16 Another comparison of INAH-3
In this study, the mean volume for homosexual men was larger than that of women but smaller than that of heterosexual men. *(Based on data of Byne et al., 2001)*

groups. Note that the difference between heterosexual men and the other two groups is fairly large, on average, and that the cause of death (AIDS versus other) has no clear relationship to the results. LeVay (1993) later examined the hypothalamus of a homosexual man who died of lung cancer; he had a small INAH-3, like the homosexual men who died of AIDS. In Figure 11.15, note also the substantial amount of difference among individuals. If you could examine some

born as males who changed their identities to female (Garcia-Falgueras & Swaab, 2008).

The meaning of these results is not clear. Do differences in the hypothalamus influence sexual orientation, or does sexual activity influence the size of hypothalamic neurons? Some brain areas do grow or shrink in adults because of hormones or behavioral activities (Cooke, Tabibnia, & Breedlove, 1999). Studies of nonhumans offer suggestive results. About 8% of rams (male sheep) direct their sexual behavior toward other males. One area of the anterior hypothalamus was larger in female-oriented rams than in male-oriented rams and larger in them than in females (Roselli, Larkin, Resko, Stellflug, & Stormshak, 2004). (Whether this area corresponds to human INAH-3 is uncertain.) This area becomes larger in male than female sheep before birth as a result of prenatal testosterone levels (Roselli, Stadelman, Reeve, Bishop, & Stormshak, 2007). In sheep, at least, an anatomical difference appears before any sexual behavior, and so it is more likely a cause than a result. The same may or may not be true in humans.

STOP & CHECK

21. In LeVay's study, what evidence argues against the idea that INAH-3 volume depends on AIDS rather than sexual orientation?

ANSWER

21. The average size of INAH-3 was about the same for heterosexual men who died of AIDS and those who died of other causes. One homosexual man who died of other causes had about the same size INAH-3 as heterosexual men who died of AIDS.

MODULE 11.2 ■ IN CLOSING

We Are Not All the Same

When Alfred Kinsey conducted the first massive surveys of human sexual behavior, he found that most of the people he interviewed considered their own behavior "normal," whatever it was. Many believed that sexual activity much more frequent than their own was excessive and abnormal and might even lead to insanity (Kinsey, Pomeroy, & Martin, 1948; Kinsey, Pomeroy, Martin, & Gebhard, 1953).

How far have we come since then? People today are more aware of sexual diversity than they were in Kinsey's time and generally more accepting. Still, intolerance remains common. Biological research will not tell us how to treat one another, but it can help us understand how we come to be so different.

SUMMARY

1. In many species, males and females evolve different appearances and behaviors because of sexual selection. That is, they evolve in ways that make them more appealing to the other sex.   **341**

2. Many of the mating habits of people can be interpreted in terms of increasing the probability of passing on our genes. However, it is hard to know how many of the differences between men and women are evolutionary adaptations and how many are learned.   **341**

3. People can develop ambiguous genitals or genitals that don't match their chromosomal sex for several reasons. One is congenital adrenal hyperplasia, in which a genetic defect in cortisol production leads to overstimulation of the adrenal gland and therefore extra testosterone production. When that condition occurs in a female fetus, she becomes partly masculinized.   **343**

4. On average, girls with a history of congenital adrenal hyperplasia show more interest in boy-typical toys than other girls do, and during adolescence and young adulthood, they continue to show partly masculinized interests.   **344**

5. Testicular feminization, or androgen insensitivity, is a condition in which someone with an XY chromosome pattern is partly or fully insensitive to androgens and therefore develops a female external appearance.   **345**

6. People born with intermediate or ambiguous genitals are called intersexes. For many years, physicians recommended surgery to make these people look more feminine. However, many intersexed people do not develop an unambiguous female identity, and many protest against the imposed surgery.   **345**

7. Some children have a gene that decreases their early production of dihydrotestosterone. Such a child looks female at birth and is considered a girl but develops a penis at adolescence. Most of these people then accept a male gender identity.   **346**

8. On average, homosexual people differ from heterosexual people in several anatomical and physiological regards, although the averages do not apply to every individual.   **347**

9. Plausible biological explanations for homosexual orientation include genetics, prenatal hormones, and (in males)

reactions to the mother's immune system. Hormone levels in adulthood are within the normal range. **347**

10. Several hypotheses have been offered for how genes promoting homosexuality could remain at moderate frequencies in the population when most homosexual people do not have children. **347**

11. On average, certain aspects of brain anatomy differ between homosexual and heterosexual men, although it is not certain whether these differences are causes or effects of the behavior. **349**

KEY TERMS

Terms are defined in the module on the page number indicated. They're also presented in alphabetical order with definitions in the book's Subject Index/Glossary, which begins on page 561. Interactive flashcards and crossword puzzles are among the online resources available to help you learn these terms and the concepts they represent.

androgen insensitivity **345**

congenital adrenal
   hyperplasia **343**

gender identity **343**

hermaphrodite **343**

intersex **344**

sexual selection **341**

testicular feminization **345**

THOUGHT QUESTION

1. On average, intersexes have IQ scores in the 110 to 125 range, well above the mean for the population (Dalton, 1968; Ehrhardt & Money, 1967; Lewis, Money, & Epstein, 1968). One possible interpretation is that a hormonal pattern intermediate between male and female promotes great intellectual development. Another possibility is that intersexuality may be more common in intelligent families than in less intelligent ones or that the more intelligent families are more likely to bring their intersexed children to an investi-

gator's attention. What kind of study would be best for deciding among these hypotheses? (For one answer, see Money & Lewis, 1966.)

2. Recall LeVay's study of brain anatomy in heterosexual and homosexual men. Certain critics have suggested that one or more of the men classified as "heterosexual" might actually have been homosexual or bisexual. If so, would that fact strengthen or weaken the overall conclusions?

CHAPTER 11 Interactive Exploration and Study

The **Psychology CourseMate** for this text brings chapter topics to life with interactive learning, study, and exam preparation tools, including quizzes and flashcards for the Key Concepts that appear throughout each module, as well as an interactive media-rich eBook version of the text that is fully searchable and includes highlighting and note taking capabilities and interactive versions of the book's **Stop & Check** quizzes and **Try It Yourself Online** activities. The site also features **Virtual Biological Psychology Labs, videos,** and **animations** to help you better understand concepts—logon and learn more at **www.cengagebrain.com**, which is your gateway to all of this text's complimentary and premium resources, including the following:

Virtual Biological Psychology Labs

Explore the experiments that led to modern-day understanding of biopsychology with the Virtual Biological Psychology Labs, featuring a realistic lab environment that allows you to conduct experiments and evaluate data to better understand how scientists came to the conclusions presented in your text. The labs cover a range of topics, including perception, motivation, cognition, and more. You may purchase access at **www.cengagebrain.com**, or login at **login.cengagebrain.com** if an access card was included with your text.

Videos

Erectile Dysfunction

Animations

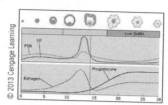

Menstrual Cycle

Suggestions for Further Exploration

Books

Colapinto, J. (2000). *As nature made him: The boy who was raised as a girl.* New York: HarperCollins. Describes the boy whose penis was accidentally removed.

Diamond, J. (1997). *Why is sex fun?* New York: Basic Books. Human sexual behavior differs from that of other species in many ways and therefore raises many evolutionary issues, which this book addresses. For example, why do humans have sex at times when the woman cannot become pregnant? Why do women have menopause? Why don't men breast-feed their babies? And what good are men, anyway? If you haven't thought about such questions before, you should read this book.

LeVay, S. (2011). *Gay, straight, and the reason why.* New York: Oxford University Press. A scientific discussion of the research concerning the factors that influence sexual orientation.

Websites

The Psychology CourseMate for this text provides regularly updated links to relevant online resources for this chapter, such as **The Endocrine Society** and the **Intersex Society of America**.

Kimball

12

Emotions, Stress, and Health

Suppose your romantic partner asks,

"How much do you love me?" You reply, "Oh, compared to other loving couples, probably about average." "What?" your partner screams. "Average? Average!" You are in deep trouble, even though your answer was probably true. (It is for most people. That's what "average" means!)

If that was the wrong answer, what would be better? "Forty-two cubic meters per second"? No, we don't measure love in physical units. So instead, you say, "I love you more than you can possibly imagine. More than any other person has ever loved." That was a good answer, and your partner is happy, even though the answer is almost certainly false. You get away with that answer because there is no way to check whether it is true.

When we are talking about emotions, measurement is a serious problem. Psychologists make reasonably good measurements of sensation, perception, learning, memory, and cognition. As we now move to emotion, social behavior, and personality, the measurement problems become greater, and consequently, the research progress has been slower. In this chapter, we consider what psychologists have learned so far about emotions despite the difficulties.

© Getty Images

Would you make more intelligent decisions if you could suppress your emotions, like the fictional character Spock? After brain damage that impairs emotion, people make worse-than-average decisions.

The Nature of Emotion

- How does arousal relate to emotion?
- Do people have a countable number of "basic" emotions?
- How do emotions influence our thinking?

Imagine trying to list all the emotions you feel during a day. You might include frightened, angry, sad, joyful, disgusted, worried, bored, ashamed, frustrated, contemptuous, embarrassed, surprised, proud, and confused. But which of those states are really emotions? And how many are *different* emotions instead of overlapping or synonymous conditions?

Defining the term *emotion* is difficult. Psychologists usually define it in terms of a combination of cognitions, physiology, feelings, and actions (Keltner & Shiota, 2003; Plutchik, 1982). For example, you might have the *cognition* "he was unfair to me," *physiological* changes that include increased heart rate, a *feeling* you call anger, and *behaviors* such as a clenched fist. However, that definition implies that the four components always occur together. Do they? Don't you sometimes feel fear, anger, or other emotions without knowing why?

For the way most people use the term *emotion*, the key component is the feeling. If you say you feel frightened but don't know why, most people would agree that you are experiencing an emotion. If you say, "I recognize that this is a dangerous situation," but you feel nothing, your experience is unemotional.

Measuring Emotions

Research progress depends on good measurement. Psychologists measure emotions by self-reports, behavioral observations, and physiological measures. Each method has its strengths and weaknesses.

Self-Reports

Psychologists most often measure emotions by asking people how happy they are, how nervous, and so forth. Self-reports are quick and easy, but their accuracy is limited. If you rated your happiness 4 yesterday and 7 today, it seems clear that you have become happier. But if your friend rates her happiness 6, are you happier today than she is? Maybe, maybe not.

Behavioral Observations

We infer emotion from people's behavior and its context. If we see someone shriek and run away, we infer fear. When you were an infant, your parents must have inferred your emotions before you could report them verbally. They had to, in order to teach you the words for emotions! At some point, you screamed and someone said you were "afraid." At another time, you smiled and someone said you were "happy."

We especially watch facial expressions. People sometimes control their expressions voluntarily. However, *very brief, sudden emotional expressions*, called microexpressions, are harder to control. For example, someone who is pretending to be calm or happy may show occasional brief signs of anger, fear, or sadness (Ekman, 2001). With practice (or a videotape that can be played slowly), psychologists observe emotions that people would like to hide. However, microexpressions are infrequent, and we cannot rely on them for much information (Porter & ten Brinke, 2008).

Physiological Measures

Originally, the term *emotion* referred to turbulent motion. Centuries ago, people described thunder as an "emotion of the atmosphere." Eventually, people limited the term to body motions and their associated feelings, but the idea still includes turbulent arousal.

Any stimulus that arouses emotion alters the activity of the autonomic nervous system, *the section of the nervous system that controls the organs* such as the heart and intestines. The word *autonomic* means "independent" (autonomous). Biologists once believed that the autonomic nervous system was independent of the brain and spinal cord. We now know that the brain and spinal cord regulate the autonomic nervous system, but the term *autonomic* remains.

Rex Features via AP Images

Ordinarily, an emotional state elicits a tendency toward vigorous action, even if we suppress that tendency. Here, a soldier disarms a mine.

Figure 12.1 The autonomic nervous system consists of the sympathetic and parasympathetic nervous systems, which sometimes act in opposing ways and sometimes cooperate. The sympathetic nervous system readies the body for emergency action. The parasympathetic nervous system supports digestive and other nonemergency functions.

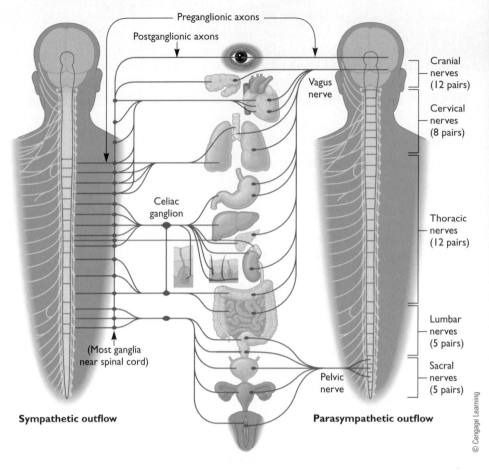

Preganglionic axons

Postganglionic axons

Vagus nerve

Celiac ganglion

(Most ganglia near spinal cord)

Pelvic nerve

Sympathetic outflow

Parasympathetic outflow

Cranial nerves (12 pairs)

Cervical nerves (8 pairs)

Thoracic nerves (12 pairs)

Lumbar nerves (5 pairs)

Sacral nerves (5 pairs)

© Cengage Learning

The autonomic nervous system consists of the sympathetic and the parasympathetic nervous systems (Figure 12.1). *Chains of neuron clusters just to the left and right of the spinal cord* comprise the sympathetic nervous system, *which arouses the body for vigorous action.* It is often called the "fight-or-flight" system because it increases your heart rate, breathing rate, sweating, and flow of epinephrine (EP-i-NEF-rin; also known as adrenaline), thereby prepar-

ing you for vigorous activity. Different situations activate different parts of the sympathetic nervous system to facilitate different kinds of activity.

The parasympathetic nervous system consists of *neurons whose axons extend from the medulla* (see Figure 12.1) *and the lower part of the spinal cord to neuron clusters near the organs. The parasympathetic nervous system decreases the heart rate and promotes digestion and other nonemergency functions.* Both the sympathetic and parasympathetic systems send axons to the heart, the digestive system, and most other organs. A few organs, such as the adrenal gland, receive only sympathetic input.

© Tom Brakefield/CORBIS

© Phil Schermeister/CORBIS

The sympathetic nervous system prepares the body for a vigorous burst of activity.

Both systems are constantly active, although one system can temporarily dominate. If you spot danger at a distance (in either time or space), you pay attention to it with mainly parasympathetic activity. If the danger is close enough to require action, you shift to vigorous sympathetic activity (Löw, Lang, Smith, & Bradley, 2008). Many situations activate parts of both systems (Berntson, Cacioppo, & Quigley, 1993). Some emergency situations increase your heart rate and sweating (sympathetic responses) and also promote bowel and bladder evacuation (parasympathetic responses). Have you ever been so frightened that you thought you might lose your bladder control?

Researchers measure sympathetic nervous system arousal as an indicator of strong emotion. For example, moment-by-moment changes in the electrical conductivity across the skin indicate instantaneous changes in the amount of sweating, a sympathetic nervous system response. Strong emotions also make people breathe faster (Gomez, Zimmermann, Guttormsen-Schär, & Danuser, 2005). However, remember that the sympathetic nervous system is the fight-*or*-flight system, so its responses could indicate either anger or fear (which are physiologically similar), or any other intense emotion. Physiological measurements do not tell us *which* emotion someone is feeling.

Brain measurements also fail to identify which emotion someone feels. Figure 12.2 summarizes the results of many studies using PET and fMRI brain scans (see chapter 3) to measure brain activity when different emotions were aroused in various ways (Phan, Wager, Taylor, & Liberzon, 2002). As you can see, the areas aroused by any emotion largely overlap those aroused by other emotions.

concept check

1. Why should we not insist on verbal reports to infer or measure emotions?
2. Why are physiological measurements more helpful for determining the intensity of an emotion than for identifying which emotion is present?

Answers

1. It would be impossible to teach a child (or anyone else) the words for emotions unless we had already inferred the emotions from the individual's behavior.
2. The sympathetic nervous system is aroused by either anger or fear (fight or flight), and therefore, its arousal indicates the strength of one or the other response but does not identify which one. Also, different emotions activate overlapping brain areas.

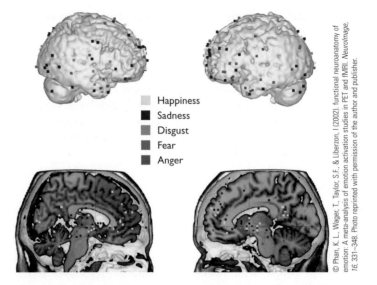

© Phan, K. L., Wager, T., Taylor, S.F., & Liberzon, I (2002). functional neuroanatomy of emotion: A meta-analysis of emotion activation studies in PET and fMRI. *Neurolmage*. 16, 331–348. Photo reprinted with permission of the author and publisher.

- Happiness
- Sadness
- Disgust
- Fear
- Anger

Figure 12.2 Researchers aroused emotions in various ways and then used PET or fMRI scans to identify which brain areas became aroused. No brain area appears specific to one type of emotion. (Source: Phan, Wager, Taylor, & Liberzon, 2002)

Emotion, Arousal, and Action

How do emotional cognitions, feelings, behavior, and arousal relate to one another? William James, the founder of American psychology, proposed one of psychology's first theories.

The James-Lange Theory of Emotions

According to common sense, you feel sad and therefore you cry. You become afraid and therefore you tremble. You feel angry and therefore your face turns red. In 1884 William James and Carl Lange independently proposed the opposite. According to the James-Lange theory, *your interpretation of a stimulus evokes autonomic changes and sometimes muscle actions. Your perception of those changes is the feeling aspect of your emotion.* In James's original article, he said simply that the situation (e.g., the sight of a bear) gives rise to an action (e.g., running away), and your perception of the action is the emotion. That is, you don't run away because you are afraid; you feel afraid because you perceive yourself running away. In response to his critics, he clarified his view (James, 1894): Obviously, the sight of a bear doesn't automatically cause you to run away. You first appraise the situation. If it is a caged bear or a circus bear, you do not run. If it appears dangerous, you do run. Your appraisal of the situation is the cognitive aspect of the emotion. Your perception of yourself running away, with soaring heart rate and breathing rate, is what you *feel* as the emotion. That is,

Situation →	Appraisal →	Actions →	Perception of the actions
	= cognitive aspect of the emotion	= physiological and behavioral aspects	= feeling aspect of the emotion

Given this interpretation, the James-Lange theory seems reasonable. Indeed, where else would the feeling aspect come from if the body didn't react in some way? Furthermore, much evidence supports the theory. The main types of evidence are that decreases in body reaction decrease emotional feelings, and increases in body reaction increase emotional feelings.

Decreased Body Reaction

According to the James-Lange theory, people with weak physiological responses still identify emotional situations cognitively, but they should have little emotional feeling. People with paralyzed muscles because of spinal cord injuries report normal or nearly normal emotions (Cobos, Sánchez, García, Vera, & Vila, 2002). However, people with weakened autonomic responses report weaker emotional feelings. In people with pure autonomic failure, *the autonomic nervous system stops regulating the organs.* That is, nothing in the nervous system influences heart rate, breathing rate, and so forth. One effect is that someone who stands up quickly faints because none of the usual reflexes kick in to prevent gravity from drawing blood from the head. With regard to emotions, affected people still recognize that some situation calls for anger, fear, or sadness, but they report that their emotions feel less intense than before (Critchley, Mathias, & Dolan, 2001). The cognitive aspect of emotion remains, but the feeling is weak, exactly as the James-Lange theory predicts.

Related evidence comes from a study of people with Botox (Botulinum toxin) injections that temporarily paralyzed all their facial muscles. While unable to smile or frown, they reported weaker than usual emotional feelings while watching short videos (Davis, Senghas, Brandt, & Ochsner, 2010).

Increased Body Reaction

Suppose researchers mold your posture and breathing pattern into the pattern typical of an emotion. Will you then feel that emotion? Have someone read these instructions to you, or read them to someone else and check what happens:

try it ▶ yourself

Lower your eyebrows toward your cheeks. Sigh. Close your mouth and push your lower lip slightly upward. Sigh again. Sit back in your chair and draw your feet under the chair. Be sure you feel no tension in your legs or feet. Sigh again. Fold your hands in your lap, cupping one in the other. Drop your head, letting your rib cage fall, letting most of your body go limp, except for a little tension in the back of your neck and across your shoulder blades. Sigh again.

Most people who follow these directions report starting to feel sad (Flack, Laird, & Cavallaro, 1999; Philippot, Chapelle, & Blairy, 2002). Instructions to hold the posture and breathing pattern characteristic of happiness, anger, or fear induce those emotions, too, although the instructions for fear sometimes induce anger and those for anger sometimes induce fear. Fear and anger are physiologically similar.

With studies like this, one worry is that the participants guess what the experimenter is trying to demonstrate. (Recall the idea of "demand characteristics" from chapter 2.) To conceal the purpose of the study, researchers told participants they were studying how people with paralyzed arms learn to write. They told participants to hold a pen either with their teeth or with their pro-

a

© Anne Dowie

b

© Anne Dowie

Figure 12.3 Facial expression can influence mood. When people hold a pen with their teeth **(a)**, they rate cartoons as funnier than when they hold it with their lips **(b)**.

truded lips, as in Figure 12.3, and then to make check marks to rate the funniness of cartoons.

try it ▶ yourself

When they held the pen with their teeth, their faces were forced into a near smile, and they rated the cartoons as very funny. When they held the pen with their lips, they could not smile, and they rated the cartoons as less funny (Strack, Martin, & Stepper, 1988). Try holding a pen one way and then the other while reading newspaper cartoons. Do you notice a difference? However, although a smile slightly facilitates happiness or amusement, you don't need to smile to feel happy. Children with a facial paralysis that prevents smiling can still experience joy and humor (G. Miller, 2007b).

concept check

3. According to the James-Lange theory, do you run away from something because you are afraid of it?
4. What happens to emotions in people with conditions that weaken their autonomic responses? What happens when people adopt postures and breathing patterns characteristic of a particular emotion? How do these results relate to the James-Lange theory?

Answers

3. No. According to the James-Lange theory, you feel fear because you are running away.
4. People with pure autonomic failure have no systematic autonomic changes, and their emotions feel weak. People who adopt postures and breathing patterns characteristic of a certain emotion become slightly more likely to feel that emotion. These results confirm the predictions of the James-Lange theory.

Schachter and Singer's Theory of Emotions

All right, once you get your body into a hunched-over posture with tension only in your neck and you are constantly sighing, you feel sad. But how did you get into that posture in the first place? Ordinarily, your appraisal of the situation entered into the process.

Furthermore, how do you know whether you are angry or frightened? Anger and fear produce very similar physiological responses. Your autonomic changes don't tell you which emotion you are experiencing (Lang, 1994).

Because of such considerations, Stanley Schachter and Jerome Singer (1962) proposed a theory of how we identify one emotion from another. According to Schachter and Singer's theory of emotions (Figure 12.4), *the intensity of the physiological state—that is, the degree of sympathetic nervous system arousal—determines the intensity of the emotion, but a cognitive appraisal of the situation identifies the type of emotion.* A given type of arousal might produce an experience of fear, anger, joy, or none of these depending on the situation. Schachter and Singer saw their theory as an alternative to the James-Lange theory, but it really addresses a different question.

The ideal test of Schachter and Singer's theory would be to wire you to someone else so that whenever the other person's heart rate, breathing rate, and so forth changed, yours would, too, at the same time and to the same degree. Then, when the other person felt an emotion, researchers would ask whether you feel it, too. That procedure is impossible with current technology, so Schachter and Singer (1962) tried a simpler procedure.

critical check

What's the Evidence?

The Cognitive Aspect of Emotion
Stimulant drugs induce body changes similar to those of emotions. Might you label that arousal as one emotion or another, depending on the situation?

Hypothesis A drug that increases arousal will enhance whatever emotion a situation arouses, but the type of emotion will depend on the situation.

Method The experimenters put college students into different situations but gave some of them injections of epinephrine to induce (they hoped) the same physiological condition regardless of the situation. (Epinephrine mimics the effects of the sympathetic nervous system.) They tried to influence some participants to attribute their increased arousal to the situation and others to attribute it to the injection.

Specifically, the experimenters told some participants that the injections would produce no important side effects. These participants would presumably notice their arousal and attribute it to the situation, feeling intense emotions. Others were told to expect side effects such as increased heart rate and butterflies in the stomach. When they felt the changes, they would presumably attribute them to the injections and not consider them emotional experiences. Additional participants were given one set of instructions or the other but injected with a placebo instead of epinephrine.

Participants were then placed in situations to elicit euphoria or anger. Each student in the euphoria situation waited in a room with a playful young man who flipped paper wads into a trash can, sailed paper airplanes, built a tower with manila folders, shot paper wads at the tower with a

Figure 12.4 According to Schachter and Singer's theory, physiological arousal determines the intensity of an emotion, but a cognitive appraisal determines which emotion one feels.

rubber band, played with a hula hoop, and tried to get the other student to join his play. Each participant in the anger situation was asked to answer a questionnaire full of such insulting items as these:

Which member of your immediate family does not bathe or wash regularly?

With how many men (other than your father) has your mother had extramarital relationships?

4 or fewer   5–9   10 or more

Results Many students in the euphoria situation joined the playful partner (Figure 12.5). One jumped up and down on the desk, and another opened a window and threw paper wads at passersby. The anger situation was less effective than expected, although a few students muttered angry comments or refused to complete the questionnaire.

Recall that some of the participants had been informed beforehand that the injections would produce certain autonomic effects. No matter which situation they were in, they showed only slight emotional responses. When they felt themselves sweating and their hands trembling, they said to themselves, "Aha! I'm getting the side effects, just as they said I would."

Interpretation Unfortunately, this experiment has problems that limit the conclusions. Recall that some participants were injected with a placebo instead of epinephrine. These participants showed about as much euphoria in the euphoria situation and as much anger in the anger situation as did the participants injected with epinephrine. Therefore, the epinephrine injections apparently had nothing to do with the results. If so, we are left with this unexciting summary of the results: People in a situation designed to induce euphoria act happy, and those in an anger situation act angry (Plutchik & Ax, 1967). However, if they attribute their arousal to an injection, their response is more restrained.

Despite the problems in Schachter and Singer's experiment, the idea behind it is reasonable, and other research since then has supported it in many, though not all, cases (Reisenzein, 1983). That idea, to reiterate, is that feeling more highly aroused increases the intensity of your emotion, but you evaluate the situation to determine which emotion you feel. Consider this example: A young woman inter-

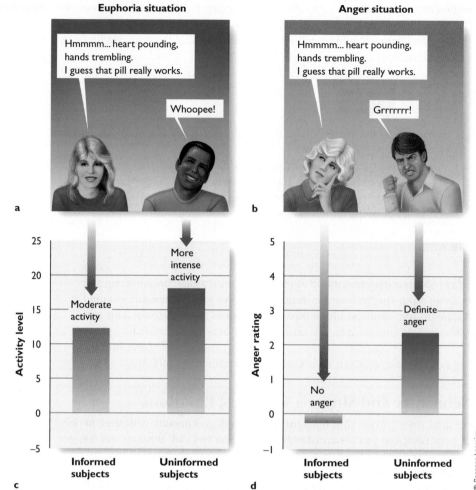

Figure 12.5 (**a** and **b**) In Schachter and Singer's experiment, people who were uninformed about the effects of epinephrine reported strong emotions appropriate to the situation. (**c** and **d**) According to Schachter and Singer, autonomic arousal controls the strength of an emotion, but cognitive factors tell us which emotion we are experiencing.

viewed young men, either on a wide, sturdy bridge, or on the wobbly Capilano Canyon suspension bridge (Figure 12.6). After the interview, she gave each man a card with her phone number in case he wanted to ask further questions about the study. Of those interviewed on the suspension bridge, 39% called her, as opposed to 9% from the sturdy, low bridge (Dutton & Aron, 1974). The interpretation was that men on the suspension bridge experienced high arousal from the situation itself, but attributed it to the woman. ("Wow, what an exciting woman! My heart is racing!") There is, however, a problem with this study. Might the woman herself have been more excited on the suspension bridge than on the low bridge? Maybe the men were responding to her excitement, not just their own. You can begin to perceive the difficulty of doing research on emotion.

concept check

5. You are going on a first date with someone you hope will find you exciting. According to Schachter and Singer's theory, should you plan a date walking through an art gallery or riding on roller coasters?

Figure 12.6 How much arousal might you feel while crossing the Capilano Canyon suspension bridge? If you met an attractive person on this bridge, might you think that person was exciting?

Answer

5. According to Schachter and Singer's theory, you should plan a date riding on roller coasters. If your date gets emotionally excited, he or she may attribute the arousal to you. (However, if you are dating someone who gets nauseated on roller coasters, you should change your strategy!)

Figure 12.7 A disgust expression (left) decreases your exposure to something foul. A fear expression (right) increases your readiness to see dangers and take necessary actions.

Do We Have a Few "Basic" Emotions?

How many emotions do humans experience? Do we have a few "basic" emotions that combine to form other experiences, like the elements of chemistry? These questions have a long history. Charles Darwin (1872/1965), noting that a few facial expressions of emotion occur throughout the world, favored the idea of a few basic emotions. Wilhelm Wundt, who started the first psychology laboratory, and William James, founder of American psychology, both argued against the idea of distinct categories, favoring instead the idea that one emotion grades into another.

Some psychologists have proposed a short list of emotions, such as happiness, sadness, anger, fear, disgust, and surprise. Others add more candidates, such as contempt, shame, guilt, interest, hope, pride, relief, frustration, love, awe, boredom, jealousy, regret, and embarrassment (Keltner & Buswell, 1997). Japanese people include *amae*, translated as "the pleasant feeling of depending on someone else" or "the feeling of comfort in another person's acceptance" (Doi, 1981; Niiya, Ellsworth, & Yamaguchi, 2006). Japanese are also more likely than Americans to list loneliness as an emotion (Kobayashi, Schallert, & Ogren, 2003). Hindus include heroism, amusement, peace, and wonder (Hejmadi, Davidson, & Rozin, 2000).

How can we decide what is a basic emotion (if there is such a thing)? Psychologists generally consider the following criteria:

- Basic emotions should emerge early in life without requiring much experience. For example, nostalgia and pride emerge slowly and seem less basic than fear, anger, or joy (M. Lewis, 1995). The problem with this criterion is that all emotional expressions emerge gradually. Infants' expressions at first do not distinguish among distress, anger, and fear (Messinger, 2002).
- Basic emotions should be similar across cultures. Because most emotions look similar throughout human cultures, this criterion does not eliminate much.
- Each basic emotion should have its own facial expression and characteristic physiology. Most of the research has focused on this last criterion.

Producing Facial Expressions

Does each emotion have its own special expression? And why do we have facial expressions of emotions anyway?

Emotional expressions are not altogether arbitrary, as shown in Figure 12.7. When you are frightened, you open your eyes wide, increasing your ability to see dangers, and you inhale deeply, preparing for possible action. If you see something disgusting, you partly close your eyes and turn your nose away from the offending object, decreasing your exposure to it (Susskind et al., 2008).

In addition, emotional expressions are specialized for communication in a social context. For example, Olympic medal winners generally smile if they are waiting for the awards ceremony with others but not if they are waiting alone (Fernández-Dols & Ruiz-Belda, 1997). Even 10-month-old infants smile more when their mothers are watching than when they are not (S. S. Jones, Collins, & Hong, 1991). Robert Provine (2000) spent many hours in shopping malls and elsewhere recording and observing laughter. He found that people laughed almost entirely when they were with friends and that the speakers laughed more than the listeners. People laughed mostly while saying something that wasn't even funny, such as, "Can I join you?" or "It was nice meeting you too." Laughter expresses friendliness.

Intentional emotional expressions seldom exactly match the spontaneous expressions. For example, the smile of a truly happy person includes movements of the mouth muscles and the muscles surrounding the eyes (Figure 12.8a). Voluntary smiles (Figure 12.8b) generally do not include the muscles around the eyes (Ekman & Davidson, 1993). *The full expression including the muscles around the eyes* is called the Duchenne smile, named after Duchenne de Boulogne, the first person to describe it.

Because the Duchenne smile is hard to produce voluntarily, it is a good indicator of someone's true feelings. Researchers have found that women with a Duchenne smile in their college yearbooks are more likely than other women to have happy, long-lasting marriages and to report feeling happy and competent long after their college years (Harker & Keltner, 2001). Major league baseball players with a Duchenne smile in their photos lived longer than those with less smile or no smile (Abel & Kruger, 2010).

Do we learn to make appropriate facial expressions, or are they part of our biological heritage? Irenäus Eibl-Eibesfeldt (1973, 1974) photographed people in various world cultures, documenting smiling, frowning, laughing, and crying, even in children who were born deaf and blind (Figure 12.9). He also found that people throughout the world express a friendly greeting by briefly raising their eyebrows (Figure 12.10). That expression has the same meaning in all cultures and the same duration—one third of a second.

Understanding Facial Expressions

The similarity of facial expressions across cultures implies that they are unlearned, but do they always have the same meanings? Researchers asked people

Figure 12.8 A spontaneous, happy smile **(a)** uses both the mouth muscles and the muscles surrounding the eyes. This expression is sometimes called the *Duchenne smile*. A voluntary smile **(b)** ordinarily includes only the mouth muscles. Most people cannot voluntarily activate the eye muscles associated with the Duchenne smile.

in different cultures to interpret six facial expressions like those in Figure 12.11. Look at each face and try to name its expression. (Please try now.) Also try the online activity Universal Emotions.

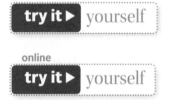

After researchers translated the emotion-naming labels into other languages, people in other cultures also identified the emotions, though somewhat less accurately (Ekman, 1992; Ekman & Friesen, 1984; Russell, 1994). Evidently,

Figure 12.9 Even children born deaf and blind show the typical facial expressions of emotion, including laughter.

Figure 12.10 Throughout the world, people raise their eyebrows as a friendly greeting, indicating "I am glad to see you." The usual duration of the expression is 1/3 second, in all known cultures.

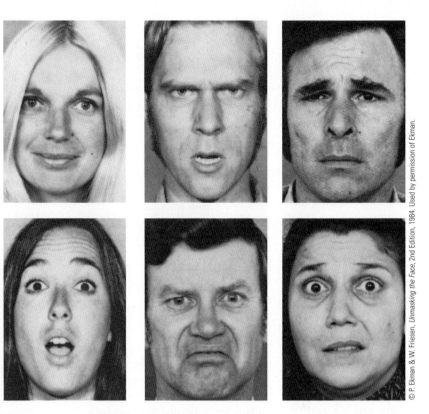

Figure 12.11 Paul Ekman has used these faces in experiments testing people's ability to recognize emotional expressions. Can you identify them? Check answer A on page 400. (From Ekman & Friesen, 1984.)

these facial expressions have similar meanings throughout the world, but with regional "accents." Just as you understand the speech from your own region better than that from elsewhere, you recognize facial expressions a bit more accurately among people from your own culture (Elfenbein, Beaupré, Lévesque, & Hess, 2007). People examined photos of Japanese people expressing anger and disgust. Of Japanese people, 82% correctly recognized the first one, and 66% the second one. Only 34% of Americans recognized the first, and 18% the second (Dailey et al., 2010).

However, the ability of people throughout the world to classify these facial expressions is not strong evidence for the idea of six "basic" emotions (Barrett, Mesquita, & Gendron, 2011). First, researchers typically list six emotion names and ask which face goes with which label. Without those suggestions, people name the expressions less accurately. Second, we identify someone's emotion by context, posture, tone of voice, gestures, and sometimes even smell—not just by facial expression (K. Edwards, 1998; Leppänen & Hietanen,

2003; Zhou & Chen, 2009). Consider Figure 12.13. Out of context, most people would call the expression sadness. The posture on the left confirms that judgment. However, given the posture on the right, most people call the expression fear (Aviezer et al., 2008).

Another issue: The faces in Figure 12.11 are all posed looking at the viewer. From the standpoint of experimental design, putting all the faces in the same position seems right. However, sad people almost always look down and make eye contact with you only briefly, if at all. Frightened people look at what frightens them. They make eye contact with you only if they are afraid of *you*. Examine the photos in Figure 12.13. Which expression is easier to identify? Most observers identify sad or frightened expressions faster when they see someone looking away (Adams & Kleck, 2003). In contrast, happy and angry expressions are easier to identify if the person is looking directly forward (Adams & Kleck, 2005). Even 7-month-old infants respond more strongly to an angry face looking at them rather than to the side (Hoehl & Striano, 2008).

a

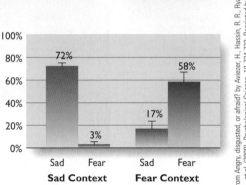

b

From Angry, disgusted, or afraid? by Aviezar, H., Hassin, R. R., Ryan, J., Grady, C., Susskind, J., Anderson, A., et al. (2008). Psychological Science, 19, 724-732. Reprinted by permission of SAGE Publications.

Figure 12.12 The same facial expression can look like sadness or fear depending on someone's posture. (From Aviezar, H. et al., "Angry, disgusted, or afraid?" *Psychological Science 19*, 724-732. Copyright © 2008 Sage Publications, Inc. Reprinted with permission.)

try it ▶ yourself

Sad people not only look down, but also they cry. If you see someone with a sad face and tears, you immediately identify the expression as sadness, as in Figure 12.14. Take away the tears, and you are often less certain what the expression means. You may describe it as awe, puzzlement, or concern (Provine, Krosnowski, & Brocato, 2009). If someone's eyes are red, they add to the impression of sadness (Provine, Cabrera, Brocato, & Krosnowski, 2011).

Figure 12.14 Tears make a face look much sadder than it would be without them.

concept check

6. Researchers often show a set of photographs and ask observers to identify the emotions. In what way might this procedure underestimate the accuracy of recognizing emotions?

Answer

6. We ordinarily have many other cues, including gestures, posture, tone of voice, and context. Also, it is easier to recognize expressions of sadness and fear when someone looks down or to the side.

Do Facial Expressions Indicate Basic Emotions?

The question is whether we have a few basic emotions. The research shows that people throughout the world recognize facial expressions of joy, sadness, fear, anger, disgust, and surprise. However, the

Fear

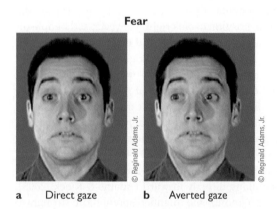

a   Direct gaze   b   Averted gaze

Figure 12.13 Most people identify fearful expressions more easily when the person is looking away.

photos in Figure 12.11 were carefully posed to be the best possible examples so that people could recognize them accurately. In everyday life, most expressions show a mixture of emotions. If we take photographs of spontaneous everyday expressions, observers show poor agreement when they try to label one emotion per face (Naab & Russell, 2007).

Furthermore, the ability of people to recognize expressions of six emotions could not tell us whether people have precisely six basic emotions. People can, with a little less accuracy, also identify an expression of contempt, which is a little different from disgust. People also readily identify expressions of pride from facial expression and posture (Tracy & Robins, 2004; Tracy, Robins, & Lagattuta, 2005). From videotapes, though not from still photographs, most people can identify expressions of peace and heroism, which Hindu people generally list as emotions (Hejmadi et al., 2000). So if the ability to identify an expression is evidence for a basic emotion, our list should grow.

Also, we readily identify the facial expressions of sleepiness and confusion, although we probably would not classify either of them as an emotion (Keltner & Shiota, 2003; Rozin & Cohen, 2003). So the fact that we recognize facial expressions of surprise and disgust is not convincing evidence to regard them as emotions.

concept check

7. Why is the ability to recognize the expressions of six emotions not convincing evidence that these are basic emotions?

Answer

7. Most everyday expressions do not neatly fit into those six categories. Also, we can identify facial expressions of other conditions that may or may not be emotions.

An Alternative to Basic Emotions

Many psychologists doubt that it makes sense to talk about basic emotions at all (Barrett, 2006). If fear, anger, or anything else is a basic emotion, we should expect that when people show its expression, they should also show the gestures, postures, vocal intonation, and everything else that goes along with it. However, people frequently show part of one emotional expression, part of another, and a posture or gesture that doesn't fit either one (Scherer & Ellgring, 2007).

Instead of considering an emotional expression as a unit, we might think of it as a compound of parts that can occur separately. As shown in Figure 12.15, you widen your eyes for a novel, surprising event. You turn down the corners of your mouth to indicate displeasure and furrow your eyebrows to indicate a desire to change something. You compress your lips when you feel in control of a situation. The expression we call anger is the sum of these components, but any of the components can occur on its own (Ortony & Turner, 1990; Scherer, 1992).

Instead of basic emotions, we might regard emotion as a series of dimensions. According to the "circumplex" model, emotions range on a continuum from pleasure to misery and along another continuum from arousal to sleepiness (Russell, 1980). Figure 12.16 shows this idea. Note that this model deals with the feeling aspect of emotion, not the cognitive aspects. For example, both anger and fear would fit near "distress" on this graph, even though we associate anger and fear with different cognitions. Other psychologists have proposed different descriptions but maintain the idea that emotions range along continuous dimensions (D. Watson, Wiese, Vaidya, & Tellegen, 1999; Yik, Russell, & Steiger, 2011).

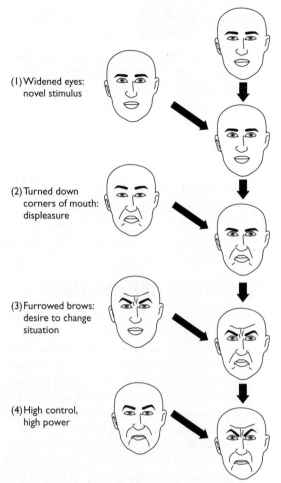

(1) Widened eyes: novel stimulus

(2) Turned down corners of mouth: displeasure

(3) Furrowed brows: desire to change situation

(4) High control, high power

Figure 12.15 What we usually regard as a single expression—in this case, anger—may be analyzed as a compound of independent parts. (From Scherer, K. R., "What does facial expression express?" In K. T. Strongman (Ed.), *International Review of Studies of Emotion* Vol. 2 (pp. 139-165). Copyright © 1992 John Wiley & Sons, Inc. Reprinted with permission.)

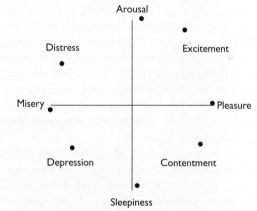

Figure 12.16 According to the circumplex model of emotion, emotional feelings occur along a continuum of arousal and another continuum of pleasure. (From Russell, J. A., "A circumplex model of affect," *Journal of Personality and Social Psychology 39* (pp. 1161-1178). Copyright © 1980 American Psychological Association. Reprinted with permission.)

8. In what way does research on facial expressions support the idea of basic emotions?

9. How could we explain facial expressions without the idea of basic emotions?

Answers

8. Because people throughout the world can recognize the meaning of a few facial expressions, they appear to be universal among humans.

9. A facial expression, such as that for anger, can be described as a combination of independent components.

Usefulness of Emotions

Presumably, emotions must be useful for something, or we would not have evolved the capacity to feel them. One function is that emotions focus our attention on important information. Your eyes and your attention turn at once toward strongly pleasant or unpleasant images, even if you are trying to pay attention to something else (Schupp et al., 2007; Yoon, Hong, Joormann, & Kang, 2009).

Emotions or moods also adjust our priorities. If you see something frightening, you concentrate on the danger, as if you saw hardly anything else (Adolphs, Denburg, & Tranel, 2001; Mathews & Mackintosh, 2004). If you are running away from a mad attacker with a chainsaw, you don't stop to smell the roses. When you are in a happy mood, you expand your focus. According to Barbara Fredrickson's (2001) broaden-and-build hypothesis of positive emotions, *a happy mood increases your readiness to explore new ideas and opportunities*. You think creatively, notice the details in the background that you ordinarily overlook, and increase your pursuit of new experiences that will help maintain your happy mood (Fredrickson & Losada, 2005). That tendency relates to the fact that happiness is usually a low-intensity emotion. Very intense emotions of any type tend to narrow one's focus of attention (Gable & Harmon-Jones, 2010).

Although major depression impairs reasoning, a mildly sad mood aids reasoning under some conditions. As discussed in chapter 11, most people overestimate their own abilities and underestimate how long a task will take. People in a happy mood are especially prone to that error. Sad people cautiously examine the evidence before making a decision. In one study, students listened to a weaker and a stronger argument concerning possible increases in student fees at their university. Students in a sad mood were more persuaded by the stronger argu-

ment, whereas students in a happy mood found both arguments about equally persuasive (Bless, Bohner, Schwarz, & Strack, 1990).

10. What is one apparent advantage of feeling sad?

Answer

10. In some regards, sad people are more realistic and more likely to consider evidence slowly and carefully before making a decision.

Emotions and Moral Reasoning

People often advise us not to let our emotions get in the way of our decisions. Emotions sometimes impair decisions, but they often provide a guide when we have to make a quick decision about right and wrong (Beer, Knight, & D'Esposito, 2006). Let's begin with two moral dilemmas on which well-meaning people disagree.

The Trolley Dilemma. A trolley car with defective brakes is coasting downhill toward five people standing on the tracks. You could throw a switch to divert the trolley onto a different track, where one person is standing. If you flip the switch, the trolley will kill one instead of five. Should you do it?

The Footbridge Dilemma. Another trolley with defective brakes is coasting downhill and about to kill five people. This time you are standing on a footbridge over the track. You see a way to save those five people: Someone is beside you, leaning over. If you push him off the bridge, he will land on the track and block the trolley. (Let's assume your path is obstructed such that you couldn't jump over in time yourself. Or perhaps you aren't heavy enough to block the trolley.) Again your action would kill one to save five. Should you do it (Figure 12.17)?

Most people say "yes" to flipping the switch in the first dilemma, although they might find it difficult. We hesitate to do something that harms someone, even when doing nothing harms a greater number (DeScioli, Christner, & Kurzban, 2011). Fewer people say they would push someone off the bridge in the second dilemma (Greene, Sommerville, Nystrom, Darley, & Cohen, 2001). Logically, the answers should be the same because the act kills one person to save five. Of course, the situations are not quite comparable. What if you pushed someone to his death and the trolley killed the others anyway? Or what if they jumped out of the way, so that killing him was unnecessary? However, even if you were fully confident that pushing someone off a bridge would save five others, it would still be emotionally repulsive.

After people make moral decisions in cases like these, they often have trouble stating a reason for their decisions (Haidt, 2012). They make their decisions quickly and emotionally and then look for an explanation afterward. The emotional guidance usually works. As a rule, pushing someone off a bridge is a horrendously bad idea. Your emotional reaction is a quick guide to making a decision that is almost always right.

Decisions by People with Impaired Emotions

Antonio Damasio (1994) described patients who suffered impoverished or inappropriate emotions following brain damage. One was the famous patient Phineas Gage, who in 1848 survived an accident in which an iron bar shot through his head. Nearly one-and-a-half centuries later, researchers examined his skull (which is still on display in a Boston museum) and reconstructed the route that the bar must have taken through his brain (H. Damasio, Grabowski, a

b

© Cengage Learning

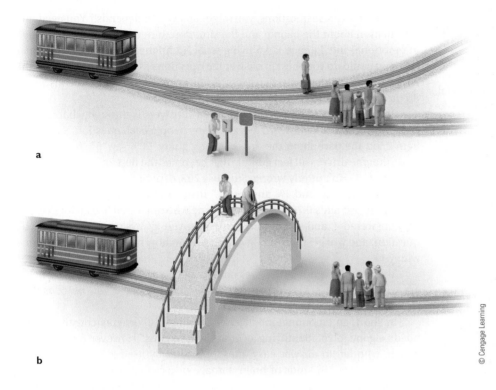

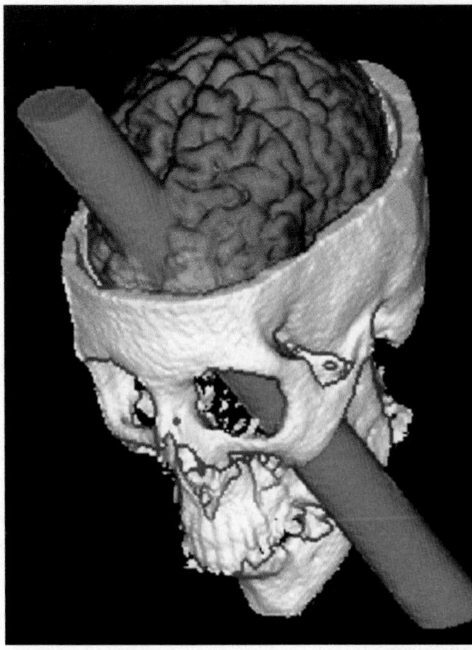

Figure 12.17 **(a)** Should you flip a switch so the trolley goes down a track with one person instead of five? **(b)** Should you push someone off a bridge to save five people?

Frank, Galaburda, & Damasio, 1994). As you can see in Figure 12.18, the accident damaged part of his prefrontal cortex. During the months after this accident, Gage often showed little emotion, and he made poor, impulsive decisions. However, the reports at the time provided little detail. Over the years, people retold this story and elaborated on it. If you have read about this case before, you may have read some exaggerations (Kotowicz, 2007).

A patient known to us as "Elliot" provides a more recent example (A. R. Damasio, 1994). Elliot suffered damage to his prefrontal cortex during surgery to remove a brain tumor. After the operation, he showed almost no emotional expression, no impatience, no frustration, no joy from music or art, and almost no anger. He described his brain surgery and the resulting deterioration of his life with calm detachment, as if describing events that happened to a stranger. Besides his impaired emotions, he had trouble making or following reasonable plans. He could discuss the probable outcome of each possible choice but still had trouble deciding. As a result, he could not keep a job, invest his money intelligently, or maintain normal friendships.

Other people with damage to the frontal and temporal cortex also make impulsive decisions and process emotional information slowly (Levenson & Miller, 2007). We see this effect especially with moral decisions. For example, they quickly and calmly decide it is okay to kill one person to save five, such as pushing a stranger off a bridge to save five others. They also fail to show guilt after being unfair to someone or embarrassment after doing something silly. It is as if they don't care about other people's opinions or outcomes (Krajbich, Adolphs, Tranel, Denburg, & Camerer, 2009; Sturm, Ascher, Miller, & Levenson, 2008).

According to Damasio (1994), impaired decision-making stems from weak emotions. Ordinarily, when you consider possible decisions, you contemplate the possible outcomes and imagine how each outcome might feel. If you consider a job offer from a company that fired your best friend, you imagine the unpleasant scene when you face your friend. People with temporal or frontal lobe damage don't easily imagine the emotional outcomes. As Damasio (1999, p. 55) said, "Emotions are inseparable from the idea of good and evil." If you cannot imagine feeling good or bad, proud or guilty, you make bad decisions.

concept check

11. In what way does damage to the prefrontal cortex interfere with decision making?

Answer

11. People with damage to the prefrontal cortex cannot imagine feeling good or bad after various outcomes; therefore, they see little reason to prefer one outcome to another.

© H. Damasio, T. Grabowski, R. Frank, A. M. Galaburda & A. R. Damasio, The Return of Phineas Gage: Clues about the Brain from the Skull of a Famous Patient, *Science 264*, 1994.

Figure 12.18 Researchers reconstructed the path that an iron bar must have made through the brain of Phineas Gage, who survived this injury in 1848. The damage impaired Gage's judgment and decision-making ability.

Emotional Intelligence

Is reasoning about emotional issues different from reasoning about anything else? The observations on patient Elliot imply a difference, because he answers questions normally as long as they have nothing to do with emotional consequences. Casual observations in everyday life also suggest that reasoning about emotional topics might be special. Some people know the right thing to say to make someone else feel better. They notice subtle signals in people's facial expressions that indicate who needs reassurance or a pat on the back. They know when a smile is sincere or fake. They foresee whether their romantic attachments are going well or about to break up. And other people, smart in their own way, seem clueless in all these emotional situations. Psychologists therefore speak of emotional intelligence, *the ability to perceive, imagine, and understand emotions and to use that information in making decisions* (Mayer & Salovey, 1995, 1997).

The idea of emotional intelligence quickly became popular, but the evidence behind the idea is still not strong. If the concept is going to be useful, emotional intelligence must have enough in common with other kinds of intelligence to deserve being called intelligence. However, it should not overlap too heavily with academic intelligence, or we would have no reason to talk about it separately. Most important, it should predict some outcome that we can't already predict using other measures.

First, we need a way to measure emotional intelligence. Several psychologists have devised pencil-and-paper tests. Here are two example questions, reworded slightly (Mayer, Caruso, & Salovey, 2000):

1. A man has been so busy at work that he spends little time with his wife and daughter. He feels guilty for spending so little time with them, and they feel hurt. Recently, a relative who lost her job moved in with them. A few weeks later, they told her she had to leave because they needed their privacy.
   On a scale from 1 to 5, where 5 is highest, rate how much this man feels:
   Depressed _____
   Frustrated _____
   Guilty _____
   Energetic _____
   Happy _____

2. A driver hit a dog that ran into the street. The driver and the dog's owner hurried to check on the dog.
   On a scale from 1 to 5, where 5 means "extremely likely" and 1 means "extremely unlikely," how would the people probably feel?
   The owner would feel angry at the driver. _____

The owner would feel embarrassed at not training the dog better. _____
The driver would feel guilty for not driving more carefully. _____
The driver would feel relieved that it was a dog and not a child. _____

To each of these questions, you might answer, "It depends!" You need more information about the people and the situation. Indeed, one of the key aspects of emotional intelligence is knowing what additional information to request. Still, you could do your best to answer the questions as stated. The problem then is, gulp, what are the correct answers? In fact, are there any correct answers, or do they vary depending on culture and circumstances?

The usual way to determine the "right" answers is through what is known as consensus scoring: Researchers ask many people each question. Suppose on item 2, on the part about the driver feeling guilty, 70% say "5" (it is extremely likely that the driver will feel guilty). That becomes the best answer. However, an answer of "4" isn't utterly wrong. Suppose 20% of people answer "4," 5% answer "3," 4% answer "2," and 1% answer "1." Instead of counting anything right or wrong, the test adds 0.70 point for everyone who answered 5, 0.20 for everyone who answered 4, and so on. In other words, you always get part credit on any question, and you get more credit depending on how many other people agreed with you.

The main objection is that we could imagine an item on which most people are wrong. Because the correct answer is uncommon, it will be considered wrong.

In short, an emotional intelligence question as currently constituted does not do a good job of identifying an emotional "genius." However, it does identify people who fail to answer easy questions. That by itself is worth something. People with certain kinds of brain damage or psychiatric disorders do poorly even on easy questions about emotional situations (Adolphs, Baron-Cohen, & Tranel, 2002; Blair et al., 2004; J. Edwards, Jackson, & Pattison, 2002; Townshend & Duka, 2003). So the test identifies "emotional stupidity," even if it doesn't identify exceptional emotional intelligence.

The key criteria for any test are reliability and validity, as discussed in chapter 9. The authors of the current tests of emotional intelligence claim that the tests have high reliability (Mayer, Salovey, Caruso, & Sitarenios, 2001), but other researchers find problems with many of the test items and report much lower reliability (Føllesdal & Hagtvet, 2009). With regard to validity, high emotional intelligence scores are associated with high quality of friendships (Lopes et al., 2004), ability to detect the emotional content of someone's voice (Trimmer & Cuddy, 2008), and avoidance of illegal drugs (Brackett, Mayer, & Warner, 2004).

However, emotional intelligence is a useful concept only if it predicts such outcomes better than we already could with other tests. We can predict people's friendships, happiness, and life satisfaction moderately well from tests of academic intelligence and personality factors. What do emotional intelligence scores add to those predictions? Several studies have concluded "not much" (Amelang & Steinmayr, 2006; Gannon & Ranzijn, 2005; Karim & Weisz, 2010). So either emotional intelligence is not a useful concept, or we need to improve our measurements of it.

concept check

12. What is the main objection to "consensus" scoring?

Answer

12. A test based on consensus scoring can't easily identify the truly outstanding individuals because it doesn't give much credit on difficult items.

module 12.1

Research on Emotions

Research on emotions is fascinating but difficult. Of the various components of emotion, the cognitive and feeling aspects are the hardest to measure. Behavioral and physiological measures are more objective, but they have their own problems. The best solution is to approach any question in multiple ways. Any study has limitations, but if several different kinds of research point to the same conclusion, we gain confidence in the overall idea. That principle is, indeed, important throughout psychology: Seldom is any study fully decisive, so we strive for independent lines of research that converge on the same conclusion.

Summary

- *Measuring emotions.* Emotions are inferred, not observed directly. Researchers rely on self-reports, observations of behavior, and measurements of physiological changes. (page 385)
- *Emotions and autonomic arousal.* Many emotional states are associated with increased arousal of the sympathetic nervous system, which readies the body for emergency action. (page 385)
- *James-Lange theory.* According to the James-Lange theory of emotions, the feeling aspect of an emotion is the perception of a change in the body's physiological state. (page 387)
- *Evidence supporting the James-Lange theory.* People who lose control of their autonomic responses generally report weakened emotional feelings. Molding someone's posture and breathing pattern into the pattern typical for some emotion facilitates that emotion. (page 388)
- *Schachter and Singer's theory.* According to Schachter and Singer's theory, autonomic arousal determines the intensity of an emotion but does not determine which emotion occurs. We identify an emotion on the basis of how we perceive the situation. (page 389)
- *Do we have basic emotions?* Certain psychologists propose that we have a few basic emotions. The main evidence is that people throughout the world can recognize the same emotional expressions. However, interpreting a facial expression out of context is sometimes difficult, and most everyday expressions do not fit neatly into a few categories. The fact that we recognize expressions of disgust and surprise is not decisive for calling them emotions, because we also recognize expressions of sleepiness and confusion, which most people do not regard as emotions. (page 391)
- *Facial expressions.* People produce facial expressions of emotion as a means of communicating their probable social behaviors. Many human facial expressions have similar meanings in cultures throughout the world. However, we rely on posture, context, tone of voice, and other signals to infer an emotion. (page 391)
- *Alternative views.* Instead of speaking of a list of basic emotions, an alternative is to consider emotions as varying along continuous dimensions. (page 395)
- *Usefulness of emotions.* Emotions call our attention to important information and adjust our priorities to our situation in life. (page 396)
- *Emotions and moral decisions.* When we face a moral decision, we often react emotionally. Those quick emotional feelings may be an evolved mechanism to steer our behavior toward what is usually the right choice. (page 396)
- *Effects of brain damage.* People with brain damage that impairs their emotions have trouble making good decisions. (page 396)
- *Emotional intelligence.* People need skills to judge other people's emotions and the probable emotional outcomes of their own actions. The ability to handle such issues may constitute an "emotional intelligence." However, it is not clear that current measurements of emotional intelligence predict much that we could not already predict based on academic intelligence and certain aspects of personality. (page 398)

Key Terms

autonomic nervous system (page 385)
broaden-and-build hypothesis (page 396)
Duchenne smile (page 392)
emotional intelligence (page 398)
James-Lange theory (page 387)
microexpressions (page 385)

parasympathetic nervous system (page 386)
pure autonomic failure (page 388)
Schachter and Singer's theory of emotions
  (page 389)
sympathetic nervous system (page 386)

Answer to Other Question in the Module (page 393)

A. The faces express (a) happiness, (b) anger, (c) sadness, (d) surprise, (e) disgust, and (f) fear.

A Survey of Emotions

- What makes people frightened, angry, happy, or sad?

Let's proceed to issues of practical importance to almost everyone, especially clinical psychologists, such as controlling fear and increasing happiness. The emphasis will be on fear and happiness, because chapter 13 discusses anger and aggressive behavior in more detail, and chapter 15 includes sadness and depression.

Fear and Anxiety

Fear is a response to an immediate danger, whereas *anxiety* is a vague sense that "something bad might happen." The "right" level of anxiety depends on the situation. We readjust our anxiety based on our experiences.

Measuring Anxiety

Most emotion research relies on self-reports, but anxiety researchers also use an operational definition based on behavior: Anxiety is *an increase in the startle reflex*. The startle reflex is the quick, automatic response that follows a sudden loud noise. Within a fifth of a second after the noise, you tense your muscles,

especially your neck muscles, close your eyes, and mobilize your sympathetic nervous system to prepare for escape if necessary. The startle reflex itself is automatic, but experiences and context modify its intensity.

Imagine yourself sitting with friends in a familiar place on a nice, sunny day when you hear a sudden loud noise. You startle, but just a bit. Now imagine yourself walking alone at night through a graveyard when you notice someone following you . . . and then you hear the same loud noise. Your startle response will be greater. The increase in the startle reflex is an objective measurement of anxiety. As you would expect, the startle reflex is enhanced for people with anxiety disorders, including post-traumatic stress disorder (Bakker, Tijssen, van der Meer, Koelman, & Boer, 2009; Pole, Neylan, Best, Orr, & Marmar, 2003). Happiness and anger decrease the startle reflex (Amodio & Harmon-Jones, 2011).

Learned associations also alter the startle reflex in laboratory animals. Suppose a rat frequently sees a "danger" stimulus—say, a light—before receiving a shock. Now that danger stimulus enhances the startle reflex to a loud noise. The increase in the startle reflex, reflecting anxiety, depends on activity of the amygdala (uh-MIG-duh-luh), shown in Figure 12.19 (Antoniadis, Winslow, Davis, & Amaral, 2007; Wilensky, Schafe, Kristensen, & LeDoux, 2006). The figure shows a human brain, although much of the research has been conducted with laboratory animals.

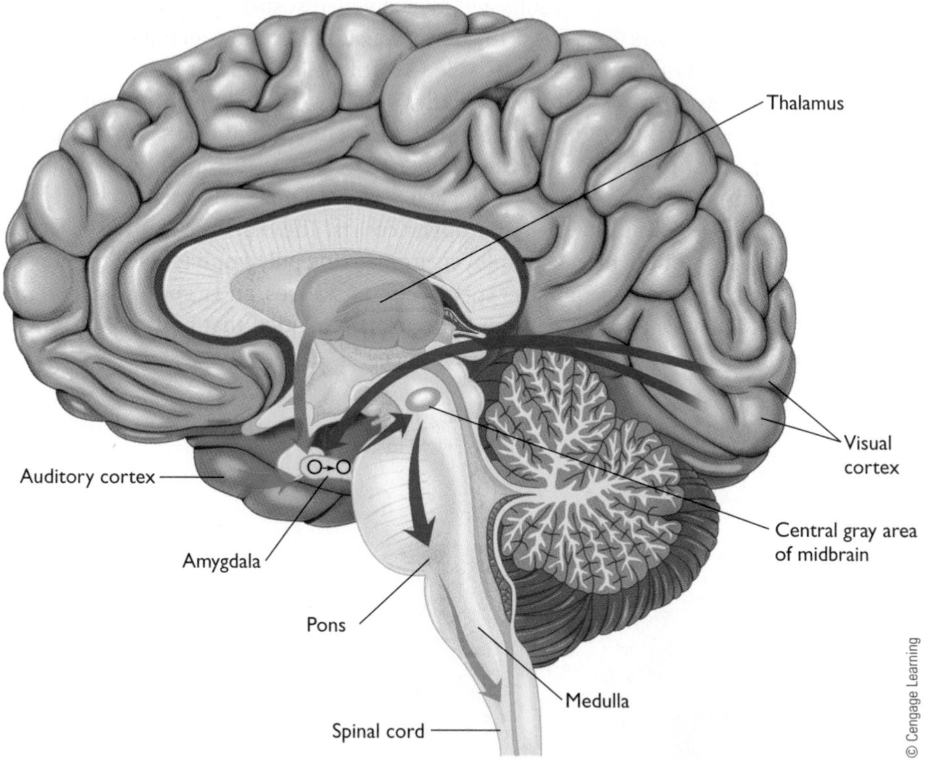

Back to humans: When someone sees a frightening picture, the amygdala increases activity, and the amount of activity correlates with other behaviors. People with a highly responsive amygdala are more likely than others to report many emotionally unpleasant experiences (Barrett, Bliss-Moreau, Duncan, Rauch, & Wright, 2007). Soldiers with strong amygdala responses at the start of their service are more likely than others to report severe combat stress (Admon et al., 2009). Although soldiers experiencing a head wound leading to brain damage have a high probability of post-traumatic stress disorder (PTSD), those whose damage includes the amygdala apparently never experience PTSD (Koenigs et al., 2008). All

Figure 12.19 Structures in the pons and medulla control the startle response. The amygdala sends information that modifies activity in the pons and medulla. This drawing shows a human brain, although much of the research has used rats.

© Cengage Learning

these studies indicate that amygdala activity is related to intense fear responses, and perhaps necessary for them.

People with amygdala damage no longer respond quickly the way other people do to complex emotional signals (Baxter & Murray, 2002; Whalen, 1998). For example, they are impaired at recognizing emotions from facial expressions (A. Anderson & Phelps, 2000) or tone of voice (Scott et al., 1997). Most people remember emotionally disturbing pictures better than emotionally neutral ones, but people with amygdala damage remember both kinds of photos about equally (LaBar & Phelps, 1998). A woman with damage to her amygdala in both brain hemispheres describes herself as fearless. When she watches horror movies, she experiences excitement but no fear. At an exotic pet store, people had to restrain her from trying to touch the venomous snakes and spiders. In everyday life, she enters dangerous situations without the caution other people would show. As a result, she has been robbed and assaulted several times. When she describes these events, she recalls feeling angry, but not frightened (Feinstein, Adolphs, Damasio, & Tranel, 2011).

concept check

13. How could we measure anxiety levels of nonhuman animals, preverbal children, or others who cannot answer in words?
14. What brain area is especially important for experiencing fear and anxiety?

Answers

14. The amygdala.
13. Measure the strength of the startle reflex.

Anxiety, Arousal, and Lie Detection

Let's consider an attempt to use physiological measurement of anxiety for a practical purpose, lie detection. It is, in fact, difficult to tell when someone is lying, even though many people think they can do so. People watch for averted gaze, hand twitches, and so forth, but most of these signals are worthless. Could a machine do better than we do?

The polygraph, or "lie-detector test," records sympathetic nervous system arousal, as measured by blood pressure, heart rate, breathing rate, and electrical conduction of the skin (Figure 12.20). (Slight sweating increases electrical conduction of the skin.) The assumption is that when people lie, they feel nervous and therefore increase their sympathetic nervous system arousal.

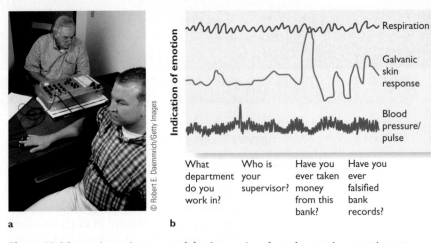

a   b

Figure 12.20 A polygraph operator (a) asks a series of nonthreatening questions to establish baseline readings of the subject's autonomic responses (b) and then asks questions relevant to an investigation.

(A bit of trivia: William Marston, the inventor of the polygraph, was also the originator of the *Wonder Woman* cartoons. Wonder Woman used a "lasso of truth" to force people to stop lying.)

The polygraph sometimes accomplishes its goal simply because an accused person hooked up to a polygraph confesses, "Oh, what's the use. You're going to figure it out now anyway, so I may as well tell you. . . ." But if people do not confess, how effectively does a polygraph detect lying?

In one study, investigators selected 50 criminal cases where two suspects took a polygraph test and one of the suspects later confessed to the crime (Kleinmuntz & Szucko, 1984). Thus, they had data from 100 suspects, of whom 50 were later shown to be guilty and 50 shown to be innocent. Six professional polygraph administrators examined the polygraph results and judged which suspects appeared to be lying. Figure 12.21 shows the results. The polygraph administrators identified 76% of the guilty suspects as liars but also classified 37% of the innocent suspects as liars.

The few other well-designed studies that have been done produced equally unimpressive results. Although many police officers still believe in polygraph testing, most researchers regard the accuracy as too uncertain for important decisions (Fiedler, Schmid, & Stahl, 2002). Polygraph results are only rarely admissible as evidence in U.S. or European courts. The U.S. Congress passed a law in 1988 prohibiting private employers from giving polygraph tests to employees or job applicants, except under special circumstances, and a commission of the U.S. National Academy of Sciences in 2002 concluded that polygraphs should not be used for national security clearances.

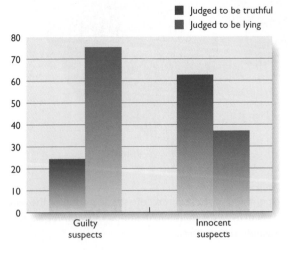

Figure 12.21 Polygraph examiners correctly identified 76% of guilty suspects as lying. However, they also identified 37% of innocent suspects as lying. (Based on data of Kleinmuntz & Szucko, 1984.)

Alternative Methods of Detecting Lies

The guilty-knowledge test, *a modified version of the polygraph test*, produces more accurate results by *asking questions that should be threatening only to someone who knows the facts of a crime* (Lykken, 1979). Instead of asking, "Did you rob the gas station?" the interrogator asks, "Was the gas station robbed at 8 p.m.? At 10:30? At midnight? Did the robber carry a gun? A knife? A club? Was the getaway car green? Red? Blue?" Someone who shows arousal only in response to the correct details is presumed to have "guilty knowledge" that only the guilty person or someone who had talked to the guilty person would possess. The guilty-knowledge test, when properly administered, rarely classifies an innocent person as guilty (Iacono & Patrick, 1999).

Another approach for detecting lies is to ask better questions. For example, if you ask, "What were you doing at the time of the crime?" someone can repeat a rehearsed lie. However, if you ask the person to describe the event backward, liars often falter, because it is easier to remember the truth than to remember a made-up story. Also, if you ask someone detailed, unexpected questions, or ask someone to draw a picture of where they were, innocent people generally do better than those who are lying (Vrij, Granhag, & Porter, 2010). Researchers also report that when people lie, they tend to provide few details, perhaps to avoid saying something that could be shown to be wrong (DePaolo et al., 2003). These techniques help, but the point remains that we have no way to identify lying with high confidence.

concept check

15. What does a polygraph measure?
16. What is the main objection to polygraph tests?

Answers

16. A polygraph too often identifies an innocent person as lying.

15. The polygraph measures several aspects of sympathetic nervous system activity, such as heart rate, breathing rate, and electrical conduction of the skin (an indicator of sweating).

Anger and Related Emotions

Anger is associated with a desire to harm people or drive them away, usually in response to a feeling that someone has done harm without good reason. Participants in one study kept an "anger diary" for a week (Averill, 1983). A typical entry was, "My roommate locked me out of the room when I went to the shower." They also described how they reacted, such as, "I talked to my roommate about it," or "I did nothing about it."

Surveys across a variety of cultures find that people experience anger frequently but seldom even consider resorting to violence (Ramirez, Santisteban, Fujihara, & Van Goozen, 2002). Chapter 13 has more to say about aggressive behavior.

Anger, disgust, and contempt are reactions to different types of offense. Anger occurs when someone interferes with your rights or expectations. Disgust is literally *dis* (bad) + *gust* (taste). In the English language, we use the term loosely to refer to almost anything displeasing (Royzman & Sabini, 2001), but narrowly speaking, disgust refers to *a reaction to something that would make you feel contaminated if it got into your mouth* (Rozin, Lowery, et al., 1999*)*. Most people find the idea of eating feces or insects highly disgusting. We also react with disgust to moral offenses, such as when one person cheats another (Chapman, Kim, Susskind, & Anderson, 2009; Danovitch & Bloom, 2009). In general, disgust is a

feeling that something or someone is unclean (S. Schnall, Benton, & Harvey, 2008). Contempt is *a reaction to a violation of community standards*, such as when someone fails to do a fair share of the work or claims credit for something another person did (Rozin, Lowery, et al., 1999).

Happiness, Joy, and Positive Psychology

"What makes people happy?" is a more complicated question than it sounds. If we ask, "What *would* make you happy?" people often ask for more money, a better job, or other tangibles. If we ask, "What *does* make you happy?" people are more likely to cite family, friends, nature, a sense of accomplishment, and perhaps music or religious faith.

Another way to measure happiness is to ask people to record what they are doing at various moments (in response to an unpredictable beeper) and how much they enjoy their activity. Although that method seems reasonable, it fails with regard to the joy of parenthood (Lybomirsky & Boehm, 2010). Parenting activities include changing diapers, comforting a crying child, caring for pain or illness, and other unpleasant chores. Nevertheless, parenthood is one of the greatest joys in life for many if not most people. Measuring "happiness at this moment" doesn't capture a sense of meaning in life (White & Dolan, 2009). Also, the occasional moments when a child gives a parent a hug and a smile outweigh a long series of tedious tasks.

Positive psychology *studies the features that enrich life, such as happiness, hope, creativity, courage, spirituality, and responsibility* (Seligman & Csikszentmihalyi, 2000). It includes not only momentary happiness, but also subjective well-being, *a self-evaluation of one's life as pleasant, interesting, satisfying, and meaningful* (Diener, 2000).

Influence of Wealth

How important is money for happiness? As you might guess, people who have just won a lottery call themselves very happy. As you might not guess, people who won a lottery a few months ago no longer rate themselves happier than average (Diener, Suh, Lucas, & Smith, 1999; Myers, 2000). One explanation is that lottery winners get used to their new level of happiness, so a given rating doesn't mean what it used to. Also, rich people get used to the fine things that money can buy, so that they get less joy from some of the ordinary pleasures of life (Quoidbach, Dunn, Petrides, & Mikolajczak, 2010). Besides that, many people are never satisfied. According to a newspaper survey, people earning

$25,000 a year thought $50,000 a year would make them happy, but those earning $50,000 a year said they would need $100,000 a year, and those earning $100,000 a year wanted $200,000 (Csikszentmihalyi, 1999).

Are rich people happier than poor people? It depends on *how* poor. Beyond a certain level of wealth, additional money doesn't add much happiness, but on average, poor people are less happy (Lucas & Schimmack, 2009). Impoverished people are particularly unhappy if their friends and relatives are doing better (Fliessbach et al., 2007). That is, people evaluate their wealth compared to how well they would expect to be doing, based on those around them (Boyce, Brown, & Moore, 2010). Health also enters into the equation. It is possible to be poor and happy, or sick and happy, but it is hard to be poor and sick and happy (D. M. Smith, Langa, Kabeto, & Ubel, 2005).

Cross-cultural research on happiness is difficult, because it relies entirely on self-reports. Does "above average happiness" mean the same thing to Venezuelans as it does to Bulgarians? Probably not, but for what it's worth, here are the results: In general, people in richer countries rate themselves happier than those in poorer countries, as shown in Figure 12.22 (Oishi & Schimmack, 2010). Another factor is wealth inequality. Remember that people's happiness relates to how wealthy they are *compared to others*. When the gap between the wealthiest people and everyone else increases—as it has in the United States since the late 1960s—most people report declining happiness (Oishi, Kesebir, & Diener, 2011).

In addition to wealth, the mean level of happiness of various countries correlates positively with individual freedoms, social equality, education, good opportunities for women, and a government with little corruption (Basabe et al., 2002; Oishi & Schimmack, 2010). Happiness also correlates with tolerance for minority groups (Inglehart et al., 2008). It is likely that a tolerant attitude leads to happiness, but it is also true that feeling happy makes people more tolerant (Ashton-James, Maddux, Galinsky, & Chartrand, 2009).

concept check

17. Under what circumstances are poor people most likely to be unhappy?

Answer

17. Poor people are unhappiest if they have friends and relatives who are wealthier and also if they are sick as well as poor.

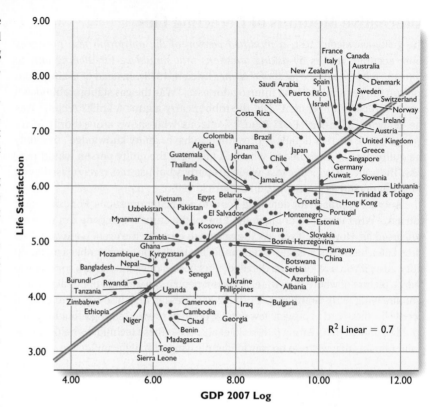

Figure 12.22 For each country, gross domestic product (GDP), a measure of wealth, is represented on the *x*-axis and an index of life satisfaction is on the *y*-axis. (From Oishi, S., & Schimmack, U., "Culture and well-being: A new inquiry into the psychological wealth of nations," *Perspectives on Psychological Science* vol 5 (pp. 463-471). Copyright © 2010 Sage Publications, Inc. Reprinted with permission.)

More Influences on Happiness

One of the strongest influences on happiness is people's temperament or personality. In one study, most pairs of identical twins reported almost the same level of happiness, even if they differed in their wealth, education, and job prestige (Lykken & Tellegen, 1996). Most people fluctuate around a particular level of happiness for most of their lives (Diener, Lucas, & Scollon, 2006). (Abraham Lincoln said, "Most people are about as happy as they make up their minds to be.")

Several factors influence happiness less than we might expect. Wouldn't you guess that especially good-looking people would be happier than average? If you are good-looking, more people smile at you, want to be your friend, and so forth. However, researchers have found only a small correlation between attractiveness and happiness among college students—except that highly attractive people are generally happier with their romantic life (Diener, Wolsic, & Fujita, 1995).

Weather also makes less difference than we might guess. People rate themselves slightly happier on sunny days than on cloudy days (Denissen, Butalid, Penke, & van Aken, 2008), but on a given day, happy people rate today's weather more pleasant than unhappy people do (Messner & Wänke, 2011). That is, most of happiness comes from inside, not from outside. On average, people in a cold state like Michigan rate themselves about as happy as those in sunny southern California (Schkade & Kahneman, 1998). Either people in a cold climate get used to it, or they mean something different when they rate themselves "happy."

Certain life events produce long-term decreases in life satisfaction. People who get divorced show a gradual decrease in happiness in the years leading up to the divorce. They recover slowly and incompletely over the next few years (Diener & Seligman, 2004; Lucas, 2005; Figure 12.23). People who lose a spouse through death also have decreased happiness leading up to the event (because of the spouse's failing health) and they recover slowly and incompletely. Naturally, the results vary from one person to another. Losing a job is a similar blow to life satisfaction, and many people do not fully recover (Lucas, Clark, Georgellis, & Diener, 2004).

Many aspects of life correlate with happiness or subjective well-being. In the following list, remember that correlations do not demonstrate causation, so alternative explanations are possible.

- Married people tend to be happier than unmarried people (DeNeve, 1999; Myers, 2000), and college students with close friendships and romantic attachments are usually happier than those without such attachments (Diener & Seligman, 2002). One explanation is that close social contacts are helpful in many ways (Cacioppo, Hawkley, & Berntson, 2003). Another is that happy people are more likely than sad people to get married or develop friendships (Lyubomirsky, King, & Diener, 2005). (Would you want to marry or become close friends with someone who was mostly sad?)
- Happy people are more likely than average to have goals in life other than the goal of making money (Csikszentmihalyi, 1999; Diener et al., 1999). One reason the money goal does not lead to happiness is that most people who strive to be rich do not succeed (Nickerson, Schwarz, Diener, & Kahneman, 2003). Also, as mentioned before, people who gain wealth set their sights at still more wealth.
- Health and happiness go together, to no one's surprise (DeNeve, 1999; Myers, 2000). Health improves happiness, and a happy disposition improves habits that lead to health.
- People who have many conversations that exchange important information tend to be happier than those who engage only in small talk (Mehl, Vazire, Holleran, & Clark, 2010).
- Religious people tend to be happier than nonreligious people (Myers, 2000). Faith supports hopeful attitudes. Also, unhappy people tend to be more critical of religious teachings.
- People who have happy friends tend also to be happy. A massive longitudinal study suggests a cause-and-effect relationship: If your friends or other people with whom you have frequent contact become happier, then within a few months, you will probably become happier also, and a few months later, your other friends will start becoming happier (Fowler & Christakis, 2008). Evidently, happiness is contagious!

Ways to Improve Happiness

If you want to improve your happiness, your best strategy is to change your activities. A nature walk improves mood far more than most people guess (Nisbet & Zelenski, 2011). For students, joining a club or starting better study habits yields long-term improvements in mood and satisfaction (Sheldon & Lyubomirsky, 2006).

More advice: Take out time once a week—not more, or you won't take it seriously—to list a few things about which you feel grateful. People who write about feeling grateful improve their life satisfaction (Emmons & McCullough, 2003; Lyubomirsky, Dickerhoof, Boehm, & Sheldon, 2011). Also, perform an occasional act of kindness for someone you hardly know (Sheldon & Lyubomirsky, 2004). In one study, experimenters asked people to rate their happiness in the morning and then gave them money, instructing them to spend it by evening. Some (chosen randomly) were told to spend it on themselves. Others were told to buy a gift for someone else. When they were questioned that evening, those who gave presents were happier, on average, than those who spent the money on themselves (Dunn, Aknin, & Norton, 2008). In the words of a Chinese prov-

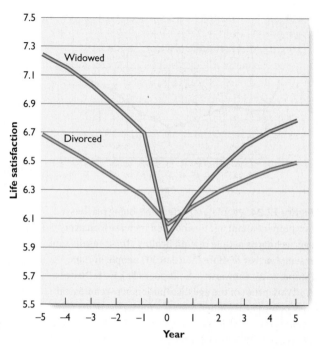

Figure 12.23 For each person, 0 marks the year of loss of a spouse through divorce or death. On average, life satisfaction declines until the loss and gradually but incompletely recovers afterward. (From E. Diener and M. E. P. Seligman "Beyond money: Toward an economy of well-being," *Psychological Science in the Public Interest* vol 5 (pp. 1-31). Copyright © Sage Publications, Inc. Reprinted by permission.)

erb, if you want happiness for an hour, take a nap. If you want happiness for a day, go fishing. If you want happiness for a year, inherit a fortune. If you want happiness for a lifetime, help somebody.

Age

Other things being equal, would you expect old people to be happier than young people, less happy, or about the same? Figure 12.24 shows the trend over age, according to a survey of more than 340,000 people in the United States (Stone, Schwartz, Broderick, & Deaton, 2010). Overall well-being declines from early adulthood until about age 50, on average, and then begins a steady increase as long as people remain healthy.

What explains the reported happiness of older people? One explanation is decreased stress (Stone et al., 2010). Beyond a certain age, people can stop worrying about becoming a success, paying the bills, rearing a family, and so forth. They already know how successful they are, or aren't, and there is little need to continue worrying about it. Also, older people deliberately regulate their mood. They attend to happy events and turn away from unpleasant ones, especially if they are already in an unhappy mood (Isaacowitz, Toner, Goren, & Wilson, 2008). Support for this view comes from evidence

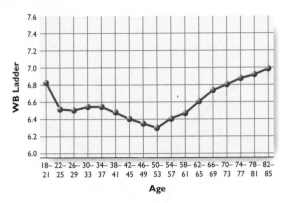

Figure 12.24 People's reported well-being reaches a low point at about age 50 and then increases, on average, as long as people remain healthy. These results represent a survey of more than 340,000 people in 2008. (Stone, A. A., Schwartz, J. E., Broderick, J. E., & Deaton, A., "A snapshot of the age distribution of psychological well-being in the United States," *Proceedings of the National Academy of Sciences, USA* vol 107 (pp. 9985-9990). Copyright 2010 National Academy of Sciences. Reprinted with permission.)

that although older people usually direct their gaze away from emotionally negative photos, distraction (which weakens voluntary control) causes them to reverse that trend and stare at the negative photos (Knight et al., 2007).

concept check

18. List some factors that correlate with happiness.

Answer

18. Happiness correlates positively (though not in all cases strongly) with wealth, health, living in a country that tolerates minority groups and gives high status to women, having close personal relationships, having goals in life, having happy conversations, having happy friends, expressing gratitude, and helping others. It also increases in old age.

Sadness

If you ask people what makes them happy, you get many answers, but if you ask what makes them sad, most answers fit a pattern: People feel sad from a sense of loss. It could be death of a loved one, breakup of a romantic relationship, failure of health, or financial setbacks, but whatever someone lost, they see little hope of recovering it.

Crying

Sad people often react by crying. Just as cultures differ in their attitudes toward loud public laughter, they also differ in attitudes about adult crying. Adults in the United States cry far more often than those in China. Women reported crying more than men in each of 30 cultures in one survey (Becht & Vingerhoets, 2002).

Many people say that crying relieves tension and makes them feel better, but the evidence says otherwise. While people are crying, sympathetic nervous system arousal and other signs of tension visibly increase. Relaxation occurs when people *stop* crying (Gross, Fredrickson, & Levenson, 1994). Even then, they may be no more relaxed than if they had not cried at all. In one experiment, one group was encouraged to cry and another was instructed to hold back their tears while watching a sad film. Contrary to the idea that crying relieves tension, the two groups had equal tension at the end, and those who cried reported more depression (Kraemer & Hastrup, 1988). The function of crying may be to elicit sympathy and social support (Provine et al., 2009). It produces no demonstrable health benefits (Rottenberg, Bylsma, & Vingerhoets, 2008).

concept check

19. What evidence conflicts with the idea that crying relieves tension?

Answer

19. People who cried during a sad movie had no less tension than people who restrained their crying, and they reported feeling more depressed.

Other Emotions

Many psychologists consider surprise an emotion. It occurs when events do not match expectations. When people are surprised, they become more sensitive to dangers and turn their attention toward anything that suggests a threat (Schützwohl & Borgstedt, 2005). They also tend to remember previous events that were surprising (Parzuchowski & Szymkow-Sudziarska, 2008).

Embarrassment, shame, guilt, and pride are the "self-conscious" emotions. They occur when you think about how other people regard you or might regard you if they knew what you had done. People who feel guilty want to pay back the person they wronged, and if they can't rectify the situation, they feel as if they deserve punishment (Nelissen & Zeelenberg, 2009). The distinctions among embarrassment, shame, and guilt are not sharp, and different cultures draw the distinctions in different ways. For example, the Japanese use a word translated as *shame* far more often than the word translated into English as *embarrassment* (Imahori & Cupach, 1994). For English speakers, most causes of embarrassment fall into three categories (Sabini, Siepmann, Stein, & Meyerowitz, 2000):

- *mistakes,* such as thinking someone was flirting with you when in fact they were flirting with the person behind you
- *being the center of attention,* such as having people sing "Happy Birthday" to you
- *sticky situations,* such as having to ask someone for a major favor

Sometimes, people also feel embarrassed out of sympathy for someone else who is in an embarrassing situation (Shearn, Spellman, Straley, Meirick, & Stryker, 1999). Imagining how the other person feels causes you embarrassment, too.

module 12.2

Emotions and the Richness of Life

We try to feel happy as much as possible and try to avoid feeling sad, angry, or frightened, right? Well, usually but not always. People voluntarily go to movies that they know will make them sad or frightened. They ride roller coasters that advertise how scary they are. Some people seem to enjoy being angry. Alcoholics and drug abusers experience wild swings of emotion, and many who quit say that although life is better since they quit, they miss the emotional swings. All of our emotions, within limits, provide richness to our experiences.

Summary

- *Fear and anxiety.* Anxiety can be measured objectively by variations in the startle reflex after a loud noise. (page 401)
- *Anxiety and the amygdala.* Variations in anxiety relate to activity of the amygdala. People with damage to the amygdala have weakened feelings of anxiety. (page 401)
- *Polygraph.* The polygraph measures the activity of the sympathetic nervous system. The polygraph is sometimes used as a "lie detector." However, because the responses of honest people overlap those of liars, the polygraph makes many mistakes. (page 402)
- *Anger.* Anger arises when we perceive that someone has done something intentionally that blocks our intended actions. (page 403)
- *Positive psychology.* Positive psychology is the study of features that enrich life. (page 403)
- *Happiness and joy.* Happiness level is usually fairly stable over time. However, it decreases for years, sometimes permanently, after the death of a close loved one, divorce, or loss of a job. (page 403)
- *Increasing happiness.* Happiness increases from changes in activities, such as listing things to feel grateful about and helping other people. (page 405)
- *Sadness.* Sadness is a reaction to a loss. Crying is a way of communicating sadness or distress to others. (page 406)
- *Other emotions.* Embarrassment, shame, guilt, and pride depend on how we believe others will react to our actions. (page 406)

Key Terms

anxiety (page 401)
contempt (page 403)
disgust (page 403)
embarrassment (page 406)

guilty-knowledge test (page 403)
polygraph (page 402)
positive psychology (page 403)
subjective well-being (page 403)

module 12.3

Stress, Health, and Coping

- What is stress and how does it affect health?

- How can we deal more effectively with stress?

Imagine you meet a man suffering from multiple sclerosis. Would you say, "It's his own fault. He's being punished for his sins"? Many people in previous times believed just that. We congratulate ourselves today on having learned not to blame the victim.

Or have we? We think that cigarette smokers are at least partly at fault if they develop lung cancer. We note that AIDS is most common among people with a history of intravenous drug use or unsafe sex. If women drink alcohol during pregnancy, we hold them partly to blame if their infants have deformities or mental retardation. As we learn more and more about the causes of various illnesses, we expect people to accept more responsibility for their own health, although it is also easy to overstate the effect of behavior on health. Even if you are careful about your diet, exercise regularly, and avoid known risks, you could become ill anyway.

Health psychology *addresses how people's behavior influences health,* including such issues as why people smoke, why they sometimes ignore their physician's advice, and how they can reduce pain. In this module, we focus on stress, the effects of stress on health, and means of coping with stress.

Stress

Have you ever gone without sleep several nights in a row trying to meet a deadline? Or waited in a dangerous area for someone who was supposed to pick you up? Or had a close friend suddenly not want to see you anymore? Or tried to explain why you no longer want to date someone? These experiences and countless others cause stress.

Selye's Concept of Stress

Hans Selye, an Austrian-born physician who worked at McGill University in Montreal, noticed that a wide variety of illnesses produce the same symptoms— fever, inactivity, sleepiness, and loss of appetite. He noted that stressful experiences sometimes produce

Our emotions affect physiological processes and thereby influence health.

those symptoms, too. He inferred that these symptoms were the body's response to an illness or challenge, its way of fighting the difficulty. According to Selye (1979), stress is *the nonspecific response of the body to any demand made upon it.* All demands on the body evoke responses that prepare for fighting some kind of threat.

Selye's concept of stress included any experience that changes a person's life. Getting married and being promoted are presumably pleasant experiences, but they also require changes in your life, so in Selye's sense, they produce stress. However, Selye's definition does not include the effects of poverty, racism, a lifelong disability, or anything else that is unchanging. An alternative definition of stress is *"an event or events that are interpreted as threatening to an individual and which elicit physiological and behavioral responses"* (McEwen, 2000, p. 173). Because this definition highlights what an individual interprets as threatening, it recognizes that some event might be stressful to you and not someone else, or to you at one time and not at another. For example, seeing a snake in your backyard could terrify you but not bother someone who recognizes it as harmless. A critical word from your boss ordinarily disturbs you but not as much if you know why your boss is in a bad mood.

Measuring Stress

To do research on stress, we need to measure it. One approach is to give people a checklist of stressful experiences. For example, the Social Readjustment Rating Scale lists 43 life-change events (Holmes & Rahe, 1967). The authors of this test asked people to rate how stressful each event would be, and on that basis, they

The stressfulness of an event depends on how we interpret it. Most people would be delighted to finish second in an Olympic event, but someone who hoped to finish first may consider it a defeat.

assigned each event a certain number of points, such as 100 for death of a spouse and 11 for a traffic ticket. On this questionnaire, you check the events you experienced recently, and a psychologist totals your points to measure your stress.

Table 12.1 Ten Common Hassles and Uplifts	
Hassles	**Uplifts**
1. Concerns about weight	1. Relating well with your spouse or lover
2. Health of a family member	2. Relating well with friends
3. Rising prices of common goods	3. Completing task
4. Home maintenance	4. Feeling healthy
5. Too many things to do	5. Getting enough sleep
6. Misplacing or losing things	6. Eating out
7. Yard work or outside home maintenance	7. Meeting your responsibilities
8. Property, investment, or taxes	8. Visiting, phoning, or writing someone
9. Crime	9. Spending time with family
10. Physical appearance	10. Home (inside) pleasing to you

Adapted from A. D. Kanner, J. C. Coyne, C. Schaefer, and R. S. Lazarus, "Comparison of Two Modes of Stress Measurement: Daily Hassles and Uplifts Versus Major Life Events," *Journal of Behavioral Medicine* vol 4 (p. 14). Copyright © 1981 Springer. Reprinted by permission.

Checklists of this sort have serious problems. One is the assumption that many small stressors add to the same as one large stressor. For example, graduating from college, getting unexpected money, moving to a new address, and starting a new job are all considered stressors. According to the checklist, this combination rates almost twice as many points as you would get from a divorce. Another problem is the ambiguity of many items. You get 44 points for "change in health of a family member." You would certainly check that item if you discover that your 5-year-old son or daughter has diabetes. Should you also check it if your aunt, whom you seldom see, recovers nicely from a bout of influenza? Apparently, you get to decide what counts and what doesn't.

Moreover, a given event has different meanings depending on how people interpret the event and what they can do about it (Lazarus, 1977). Becoming pregnant is not the same for a 27-year-old married woman as for an unmarried 16-year-old. Losing a job is devastating for a 50-year-old, disappointing to a 17-year-old, and trivial for an actor who works in many plays each year and never expects any of them to last long. How would you feel about winning a silver medal in the Olympics? Most of us would feel great, but many silver medal winners are disappointed that they didn't win the gold (Medver, Madey, & Gilovich, 1995). The bronze medal winner is generally happy to have won anything at all. What matters is not the event itself but what it means to you.

The effects of stress depend not only on the unpleasant events ("hassles") that we have to deal with but also the pleasant events ("uplifts") that brighten our day (Kanner, Coyne, Schaefer, & Lazarus, 1981). Table 12.1 presents one example of this approach. Given that the stressfulness of an event depends on our interpretation of the event, the best way to measure someone's stress is through a careful, well-structured interview that evaluates all the pluses and minuses in someone's life (G. W. Brown, 1989).

concept check

20. According to Selye's definition of stress, is getting married stressful? Would constant quarreling with your family be stressful?
21. Why are checklists an unsatisfactory way to measure stress?

Answers

20. By Selye's definition, getting married produces stress because it requires a change in one's life. However, constant quarreling would not be stressful because it is not a change. 21. Items on stress checklists are often ambiguous. Also, an event can be more stressful for one person than another.

How Stress Affects Health

People who have recently endured severe stress, such as the death of a husband or wife, have an increased risk of medical problems, ranging from life-threatening illnesses to tooth decay (Hugoson, Ljungquist, & Breivik, 2002; Lillberg et al., 2003; Manor & Eisenbach, 2003). How does stress lead to health problems?

Indirect Effects

Stress can influence health by altering people's behavior. For example, people who have just lost a husband or wife lose their appetite (Shahar, Schultz, Shahar, & Wing, 2001). They don't sleep well, they forget to take their medications, and some—especially men—increase their alcohol intake (Byrne, Raphael, & Arnold, 1999). One study found that people who had endured serious stress during childhood, such as physical or sexual abuse, were more likely than others to engage in health-risking behaviors in adulthood, such as smoking, drinking excessively, using illegal drugs, overeating, and having unsafe sex (Felitti et al., 1998).

Stress also impairs health in roundabout ways. Back in the 1940s, a midwife who delivered three female babies on a Friday the 13th announced that all three were hexed and would die before their 23rd birthday. The first two did die young. As the third woman approached her 23rd birthday, she checked into a hospital and informed the staff of her fears. The staff noted that she dealt with her anxiety by extreme hyperventilation (rapid breathing). Shortly before her birthday, she hyperventilated to death.

How did this happen? Ordinarily, when people do not breathe voluntarily, the carbon dioxide in their blood triggers reflexive breathing. By extreme hyperventilation, this woman exhaled so much carbon dioxide that she did not have enough left to trigger reflexive breathing. When she stopped breathing voluntarily, she stopped breathing altogether (Clinicopathologic Conference, 1967). This is a clear example of an indirect effect of emotions on health: The fact that she believed the hex caused its fulfillment.

Direct Effects

Stress also affects health more directly. Your sympathetic nervous system readies your body for brief vigorous activity, but your body reacts differently to a prolonged stressor. Perhaps you have a miserable job, you live in a war zone, or you live with someone who is often abusive. If you face a constant threat, you activate your adrenal glands to release the *hormone* cortisol, *which enhances metabolism and increases the supply of sugar and other fuels to the cells.* The increased fuel enables cells to sustain a high, steady

level of activity to combat stress. A moderate, brief increase in cortisol improves attention and memory (Krugers, Hoogenraad, & Groc, 2010). However, extreme or prolonged cortisol leads to problems. Stress activates parts of your immune system, preparing it to fight anything from infections to tumors (Benschop et al., 1995; Connor & Leonard, 1998). Presumably, the reason is that throughout our evolutionary history, stressful situations often led to injury, so the immune system must be ready to fight infections. That effect made more sense when injuries were people's main source of stress. Today, the immune system reacts to the stress of such things as feeling socially rejected (Moor, Crone, & van der Molen, 2010) or giving a public lecture (Dickerson, Gable, Irwin, Aziz, & Kemeny, 2009). Your immune system fights infections by producing a fever, because most bacteria do not reproduce well at elevated temperatures (Kluger, 1991). It also conserves energy by increasing sleepiness and decreasing overall activity levels. Note the result: Prolonged stress *by itself*, acting through the immune system, leads to fever, fatigue, and sleepiness (Maier & Watkins, 1998). You may feel ill and look ill, even if you are not.

Still more prolonged stress leads to exhaustion. You feel withdrawn, your performance declines, and you complain about low quality of life (Evans, Bullinger, & Hygge, 1998). Prolonged high release of cortisol damages the hippocampus, a key brain area for memory (deQuervain, Roozendaal, Nitsch, McGaugh, & Hock, 2000; Kleen, Sitomer, Killeen, & Conrad, 2006; Kuhlmann, Piel, & Wolf, 2005). Eventually, the immune system weakens, and you become more vulnerable to illness (S. Cohen et al., 1998).

concept check

22. How do the short-term effects of cortisol differ from the effects of prolonged cortisol?

Answer

22. Short-term, moderate increases in cortisol enhance memory and increase immune responses. (For example, many college students have increased immune system activity during the stressful time of taking final exams.) Prolonged cortisol damages the hippocampus, impairs memory, and exhausts the immune system.

Heart Disease

An upholsterer repairing the chairs in a physician's waiting room once noticed that the fronts of the seats wore out before the backs. To figure out why, the physician began watching patients in the waiting room. He noticed that his heart patients habitually sat on the front edges of their seats, waiting impatiently to be called in for their appointments. This observation led to a hypothesis linking heart disease to an impatient, success-driven personality, now known as type A personality (M. Friedman & Rosenman, 1974).

People with type A personality are *highly competitive, insisting on always winning. They are impatient and often hostile.* By contrast, people with a type B personality are *more easygoing, less hurried, and less hostile.* Heart disease correlates with type A behavior, especially with hostility, but only weakly (Eaker, Sullivan, Kelly-Hayes, D'Agostino, & Benjamin, 2004). The best way to conduct the research is to measure hostility now and heart problems later. (We want to know how hostility affects heart problems, not how heart problems affect hostility.) A study of that kind found a correlation of only .08 (Rutledge & Hogan, 2002). Even that weak effect may not indicate an emotional influence. Many people with high hostility also smoke, drink excessively, and eat a high-fat diet. Each of those behaviors increases the risk of heart problems (Krantz, Sheps, Carney, & Natelson, 2000).

People in some cultures (a) live at a frantic pace. In other cultures (b), no one cares what time it is. Heart disease is more common in cultures with a hectic pace.

The strongest known psychological influence on heart disease is social support. People with strong friendships and family ties usually take better care of themselves and keep their heart rate and blood pressure under control (Uchino, Cacioppo, & Kiecolt-Glaser, 1996). Also, people who learn techniques for managing stress lower their blood pressure and decrease their risk of heart disease (Linden, Lenz, & Con, 2001).

Variations in the prevalence of heart disease across cultures may depend on behavior (R. V. Levine, 1990). In some cultures, people walk fast, talk fast, wear watches, and tend to do everything in a hurry. In other, more relaxed cultures, people are seldom in a rush. Almost nothing happens on schedule, but no one seems to care. As you might guess, heart disease is more common in countries with a hurried pace.

concept check

23. People with a type A personality have an increased risk of stress-related heart disease. Yet, when they fill out the Social Readjustment Rating Scale, their scores are often low. Why might that scale understate the stress levels of type A people?

Answer

23. The Social Readjustment Rating Scale measures life changes but not constant sources of stress such as the pressures of work.

Post-Traumatic Stress Disorder

A profound result of severe stress is post-traumatic stress disorder (PTSD), *marked by prolonged anxiety and depression.* This condition has been recognized in postwar periods throughout history under such terms as "battle fatigue" and "shell shock." It also occurs in rape or assault victims, torture victims, survivors of life-threatening accidents, and witnesses to a murder. People with PTSD suffer from frequent nightmares, outbursts of anger, unhappiness, and guilt. A brief reminder of the tragic experience triggers a flashback that borders on panic. Mild problems seem unduly stressful, even years after the event (Solomon, Mikulincer, & Flum, 1988).

However, most people who endure traumatic events do not develop PTSD. Most suffer for a few weeks and then begin to recover (McFarlane, 1997). Many psychologists have assumed that people with an intense initial reaction to a stressful event are likely to develop PTSD. If so, an immediate intervention such as talking to a therapist, might be helpful. Although this idea sounds reasonable, the evidence does not support it. The intensity of someone's initial response to a trauma is a poor predictor of PTSD (Harvey & Bryant, 2002), and most studies find that talking to a therapist right after a traumatic event has little benefit (McNally, Bryant, & Ehlers, 2003), and often makes people feel even worse (Bootzin & Bailey, 2005; Lilienfeld, 2007).

Perhaps some people are simply more vulnerable than others. Most PTSD victims have a smaller than average hippocampus, and their brains differ from the average in several other ways (Stein, Hanna, Koverola, Torchia, & McClarty, 1997; Yehuda, 1997). Given that stress releases cortisol and that high levels of cortisol damage the hippocampus, it would seem likely that high stress caused the smaller hippocampus. However, one study compared identical twins in which one twin developed PTSD after wartime experiences and the other was not in battle and did not develop PTSD. The results: *Both* twins had a smaller than average hippocampus (Gilbertson et al., 2002). These results imply that the hippocampus was already small before the trauma, perhaps for genetic reasons, and having a small hippocampus increases the risk of PTSD.

concept check

24. What conclusion would follow if researchers had found that the twin without PTSD had a normal size hippocampus?

Coping With Stress

How you react to an event depends not only on the event itself but also on how you interpret it (Frijda, 1988; Lazarus, Averill, & Opton, 1970). Was it better or worse than you had expected? Was it a one-time event or the start of a trend? Your reaction also depends on your personality. Some people keep their spirits high in the face of tragedy, whereas others are devastated by minor setbacks. Coping with stress is the process of developing ways to get through difficult times.

People cope with stress in many ways, grouped into three categories. One is problem-focused coping, *doing something to improve the situation.* Problem-focused methods are usually the most effective, whenever possible (Gross, 2001). Another category is reappraisal, *or reinterpreting a situation to make it seem less threatening.* The third category is emotion-focused coping, *regulating one's emotional reaction.* Suppose you are nervous about an upcoming test. Studying harder is a problem-focused method of coping. Deciding that you don't care about your grade is a reappraisal. Deep breathing exercises are an emotion-focused method. When problem-focused coping is not available, people usually react to low-level stress by reappraising the situation. With intense stress, reappraisal is less effective, and people usually try to distract themselves or use other types of emotion-focused coping (Sheppes, Scheibe, Suri, & Gross, 2011).

The distinctions among the various stress-coping strategies are not clear-cut, however (E. A. Skinner, Edge, Altman, & Sherwood, 2003). For example, one way of coping is to seek help and support from friends. Their support helps calm emotions (emotion-focused) but also may help deal with the problem itself (problem-focused).

Problem-Focused Coping

The best way to handle stress is to do something about the problem. In one experiment, college students in one group spent half an hour per day for 3 to 5 days writing about a deeply upsetting experience, while participants in the control group wrote about unemotional topics. All the writings were confidential, so no one received any feedback or advice. Follow-up studies found that during the succeeding months, those who had written about their upsetting experiences showed better health, better grades, and less alcohol use than those in the control group, mainly because writing about the problem helped students plan what to do the next time they faced a similar problem (Pennebaker, 1997; Pennebaker & Graybeal, 2001).

Gaining a sense of control over a situation makes it less stressful. Suppose a snowstorm has trapped you in a small cabin. You have food and fuel, but you have no idea how long you will be stuck. The snow melts 5 days later, enabling you to leave. Contrast that with a case where you decide to isolate yourself in a cabin for 5 days so you can finish a painting. In both cases, you spend 5 days in a cabin, but when you do it voluntarily, you know what to expect, you feel in control, and you have less stress. Hospital patients who are told exactly what to expect show less anxiety and recover more quickly than average (Van Der Zee, Huet, Cazemier, & Evers, 2002).

How does a sense of prediction or control reduce stress? First, we fear an unpredictable event may grow so intense that it might become unbearable. Second, when an event is predictable, we prepare for it at the appropriate time and relax at other times.

When people feel they are out of control, they look for a way to gain control (Whitson & Galinsky, 2008). Thinking that you have control is calming, even if you really don't. In one study, people received painfully hot stimuli to their arms while playing a video game. Participants in one group knew they had no control over the pain. Those in the other group were told (incorrectly) that they could decrease the painful stimuli if they made the correct joystick response quickly enough. In fact, the painful stimuli varied randomly, but whenever it decreased, these people assumed they were responding "quickly enough." Those who *thought* they were in control reported less pain, and brain scans confirmed that the pain-sensitive areas of the brain responded less strongly (Salomons, Johnstone, Backonja, & Davidson, 2004).

Sometimes a good way to reduce stress is to get a small-scale preview of an upcoming experience. You inoculate yourself against stressful events by *exposing*

People who devote a short time each day to relaxation report diminished stress. Exercise works off excess energy, allowing greater relaxation.

Practicing self-defense serves as an inoculation against fear. The thought of being attacked is less frightening if you know how to handle a situation.

yourself to small amounts of the events (Janis, 1983; Meichenbaum, 1985; Meichenbaum & Cameron, 1983). Armies have soldiers practice combat skills under realistic conditions. A police trainee might pretend to intervene while two people enact a violent quarrel. If you are nervous about going to your landlord with a complaint, you might practice what you plan to say while your friend plays the part of the landlord. Inoculation has helped young people suffering from "dating anxiety." Some people are so nervous about saying or doing the wrong thing that they avoid dating opportunities. By role-playing, they practice dating behaviors with assigned partners and reduce their apprehension (Jaremko, 1983).

concept check

25. Which would disrupt your studying more, your own radio or your roommate's radio? Why?
26. Suppose you are nervous about giving a speech before a group of 200 strangers. How could you inoculate yourself to reduce the stress?

Answers

26. Practice giving your speech to a small group of friends, preferably in the room where you will deliver it.
25. Your roommate's radio would be more disruptive. You can turn your own radio on or off, switch stations, or reduce the volume. You have no such control over your roommate's radio.

Coping by Reappraisal

Suppose you are in a situation that offers no control. You applied for admission to graduate schools, and now you are waiting for the replies. You underwent medical tests, and you are nervously waiting for the results. While waiting, what can you do?

You might reappraise the situation: "Even if the news is bad, I can handle it. It's an opportunity for me to rise to the occasion, to show how strong I can be." People who recover well from tragedies and defeats say that they try to see the positive side of any event (Tugade & Fredrickson, 2004). Most people say they want to maintain a moderately optimistic outlook even when it is not completely accurate (Armor, Massey, & Sackett, 2008).

Here is an example of reappraisal: Students were asked to restrain their emotions by whatever means they chose while examining pictures that included some disturbing images, such as injured people and crying children. Those who restrained their emotions most successfully relied on reinterpreting the pictures. For example, they might regard a picture of an injured person as "someone about to receive good medical care" (Jackson, Malmstadt, Larson, & Davidson, 2000).

Emotion-Focused Coping

Emotion-focused strategies do not solve an underlying problem, but they help you manage your reaction to it. If you feel an unpleasant emotion—fear, anger, sadness, or disgust—would it help to simply suppress your emotion and act as if you are doing okay? It might, but the more effort you put into suppressing your emotional expressions, the less energy you'll have available for something else (Segerstrom & Nes, 2007). Most Europeans and North Americans find it difficult and unpleasant to suppress their emotions. However, people in Asian cultures routinely practice emotional suppression and find it much less burdensome (Butler, Lee, & Gross, 2007). In addition to actively suppressing emotions, other ways of handling your emotions include social support, relaxation, exercise, and distraction.

Social Support

When you feel bad, do you turn to others for support? This tendency varies across cultures. An American might discuss personal problems with a friend without necessarily expecting the friend to help. In Asian cultures, anyone who knows about your problem feels obligated to help. Many Asians therefore avoid telling people about their difficulties for fear of burdening them with an obligation (Kim, Sherman, & Taylor, 2008).

Social support is helpful in many situations. A study found that people who had recently fallen in love reacted less strongly than usual to the stress of watching an unpleasant film, even if the loved one wasn't present (Schneiderman, Zilberstein-Kra, Leckman, & Feldman, 2011). Close contact with a loved one helps even more. Researchers recorded women's reactions while they watched for signals

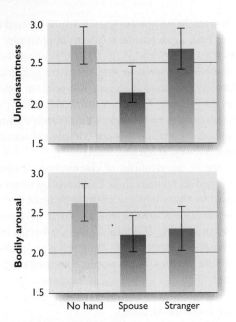

Figure 12.25 On average, a woman exposed to the threat of an upcoming shock reported less distress while holding her husband's hand. (From Coan, J. A., Schaefer, H. S., Davidson, R. J., "Lending a hand: Social regulation of the neural response to a threat," *Psychological Science* vol 17 (pp. 1032-1039). Copyright © 2006 Sage Publications, Inc. Reprinted with permission.)

that indicated that they might be about to receive an electric shock. At various times, each woman held her husband's hand, an unfamiliar man's hand, or no hand. As shown in Figure 12.25, on average, a woman reported less unpleasantness and lower arousal while holding her husband's hand. Holding the hand of an unfamiliar man helped less. Women who reported a highly satisfactory marriage received more benefit from holding their husband's hand than did women reporting a less satisfactory marriage (Coan, Schaefer, & Davidson, 2006).

Relaxation

Relaxation is an excellent way to reduce unnecessary anxiety. Here are some suggestions (Benson, 1985):

- Find a quiet place, or at least a spot where the noise is not too disturbing.
- Adopt a comfortable position, relaxing your muscles. If you are not sure how to do so, start with the opposite: *Tense* all your muscles so you notice how they feel. Then relax them one by one, starting from your toes and working toward your head.
- Reduce sources of stimulation, including your own thoughts. Focus your eyes on a simple, unexciting object. Or repeat something—a word, a

phrase, a prayer, perhaps the Hindu syllable *om*—whatever feels comfortable to you.
- Don't worry about anything, not even about relaxing. If worrisome thoughts pop into your head, dismiss them with "oh, well."

People who practice this technique, a form of meditation, report that they feel less stress. Many improve their overall health (Benson, 1977, 1985). One study found that people who went through a 12-week meditation program had a long-lasting decrease in anxiety and depression compared with a control group who spent the same amount of time listening to lectures on how to reduce stress (Sheppard, Staggers, & John, 1997).

Exercise

Exercise also reduces stress. It may seem contradictory to say that both relaxation and exercise reduce stress, but exercise helps people relax. If you are tense about something that you have to do tomorrow, your best approach may be to put your energy to use: Exercise and relax afterward.

People in good physical condition react less strongly than average to stressful events (Crews & Landers, 1987). An event that would elevate heart rate enormously in other people elevates it only moderately in someone who has been exercising regularly. The exercise should be consistent, almost daily, but it does not need to be vigorous. In fact, strenuous activity often worsens someone's mood (Salmon, 2001).

Part of the effect of exercise depends on expectations. Researchers studied the female room attendants at seven hotels. They randomly chose certain hotels to inform these women (correctly) that their daily activities constitute good exercise that meets recommendations for a healthy, active lifestyle. When the researchers followed up 4 weeks later, they found that the women who were told that they were getting good exercise had in fact lost weight, and their blood pressure had decreased, even though they reported no actual change in their activities (Crum & Langer, 2007). Activity is more helpful if you think of it as healthy exercise than if you think of it as dull work.

Distraction

Another emotion-focused strategy is to distract yourself. Many people reduce dental or postsurgical pain by playing video games or by watching comedies on television. The Lamaze method teaches pregnant women to suppress the pain of childbirth by concentrating on breathing exercises. Hospitalized patients handle their pain better if they distract themselves with a view or pleasant music (Fauerbach, Lawrence, Haythornthwaite, & Richter, 2002). Many people distract themselves from stressful or sad events by going shopping and buying themselves presents (Cryder, Lerner, Gross, & Dahl, 2008; Hama, 2001). If you find yourself brooding about some disappointment, you might feel better after reminding yourself of pleasant or successful experiences in your past (DeWall et al., 2011).

The effectiveness of distraction depends partly on people's expectations. In one study, college students were asked to hold their fingers in ice water until the sensation became too painful to endure (Melzack, Weisz, & Sprague, 1963). Some of them listened to music of their own choice and were told that listening to music would reduce the pain. Others also listened to music but were given no suggestion that it would ease the pain. Still others heard nothing but were told that a special "ultrasonic sound" was being transmitted that would lessen the pain. The group that heard music and expected it to reduce the pain tolerated the pain better than either of the other two groups did. Evidently, neither the music nor the suggestion of reduced pain is as effective as both are together.

27. Some people control anxiety with tranquilizers. In which of the three categories of coping strategy do these drugs belong?

Answer

27. Using tranquilizers is an example of emotion-focused coping.

Individual Differences

All of us can learn to handle stress better by using some of the techniques just described. In addition, some people seem to handle stress better naturally (Haas, Omura, Constable, & Canli, 2007). They also remain happy and productive most of the time. Psychologists paid little attention to this phenomenon until the late 1990s, but now it has emerged as an important research topic.

Happy, optimistic people have many advantages. One is that they bounce back from painful experiences. However, if an investigator measures optimism and health at the same time, we have no way of knowing which one influenced the other. (Being healthy could make people optimistic just as easily as being optimistic could improve health.) A better design is to measure optimism first and health years later. In one study, investigators measured optimism for more than 5,000 city employees. Three years later, they examined work records to see how many sick-leave days each person took shortly after stressful or traumatic events, such as death of a loved one. They found that the more optimistic people took fewer sick days and returned more quickly to their normal activities (Kivimäki et al., 2005). They were less devastated.

module 12.3 >

In Closing

Health Is Mental as Well as Medical

We have considered the ways people try to deal with stressful situations. How well do these strategies work? The answer is that they work well for many people but at a cost. The cost is that coping with serious stressors requires energy. Many people who have had to cope with long-lasting stressors break their diets, resume smoking and drinking habits that they had abandoned long ago, and find it difficult to concentrate on challenging cognitive tasks (Muraven & Baumeister, 2000).

Still, in spite of the costs, an amazing number of people say that the experience of battling a chronic illness, tending to a loved one with a severe illness, or dealing with other painful experiences has brought them personal strength and an enhanced feeling of meaning in life (Folkman & Moskowitz, 2000). They found positive moments even in the midst of fear and loss. Not everyone rises to the occasion, but many do.

Summary

- *Selye's concept of stress.* According to Hans Selye, stress is "the nonspecific response of the body to any demand made upon it." Any event, pleasant or unpleasant, that brings about change in a person's life produces some measure of stress. However, this definition omits lifelong problems, such as coping with racism. By an alternative definition, stress is an event that someone interprets as threatening. (page 408)
- *Difficulties of measuring stress.* Stress checklists are problematic because many items are ambiguous. Also, the stressfulness of an event depends on the person's interpretation of the event and ability to cope with it. (page 408)
- *Indirect effects on health.* Stress affects health indirectly because people exposed to stressful events often change their eating, sleeping, and drinking habits. (page 410)
- *Direct effects on health.* Stress causes increased secretion of the hormone cortisol. Brief, moderate elevations of cortisol enhance memory and immune system responses. However, prolonged cortisol damages health by impairing the hippocampus and by exhausting the immune system. (page 410)

- *Heart disease.* Research has found only a small link between emotional responses and the onset of heart disease. (page 410)
- *Post-traumatic stress disorder.* After severe traumatic experiences, some people (not all) have long-lasting changes in their emotional reactions. (page 411)
- *Coping styles.* Most strategies for dealing with stress fall into three major categories: trying to fix the problem, reappraisal, and trying to control emotions. (page 412)
- *Prediction and control.* Events are generally less stressful when people think they can predict or control them. (page 412)
- *Reappraisal.* Interpreting a situation in a new, less threatening way reduces tension. (page 413)
- *Emotion-focused coping.* Relaxation, exercise, and distraction reduce excess anxiety. (page 413)
- *Individual differences.* Optimistic people tend to handle stress more effectively than others. (page 415)

Key Terms

cortisol (page 410)
emotion-focused coping (page 412)
health psychology (page 408)
inoculation (page 412)
post-traumatic stress disorder (PTSD) (page 411)

problem-focused coping (page 412)
reappraisal (page 412)
stress (page 408)
type A personality (page 410)
type B personality (page 410)

exploration and study

Access an interactive eBook and chapter-specific learning tools, including
- **flashcards**
- **quizzes**
- **videos**

and more, in your Psychology CourseMate. Go to **CengageBrain.com.**

If your professor has assigned Aplia:
1. Sign in to your account.
2. Complete the corresponding exercises as required by your professor.
3. When finished, click "Grade It Now" to see which areas you have mastered, which areas need more work, and detailed explanations of every answer.

campo/Getty Images

Social Psychology

In the *Communist Manifesto*, Karl Marx and Friedrich Engels wrote, "Mankind are more disposed to suffer, while evils are sufferable, than to right themselves by abolishing the forms to which they are accustomed. But when a long train of abuses and usurpations, pursuing invariably the same object, evinces a design to reduce them under absolute despotism, it is their right, it is their duty, to throw off such government." Fidel Castro wrote, "A little rebellion, now and then, is a good thing."

Do you agree with those statements? Why or why not? Can you think of anything that would change your mind?

What if I told you that the first statement is not from the *Communist Manifesto*, but from the United States' Declaration of Independence? And what if I told you that the second quotation is from Thomas Jefferson, not Castro? Would you agree more with these statements if they came from democratic revolutionaries instead of communist revolutionaries?

Well, those quotes did in fact come from the Declaration of Independence and Thomas Jefferson, so you can now start trying to negotiate one of the fundamental questions in social psychology: What influences your opinions?

Social psychology includes the study of attitudes, persuasion, self-understanding, and almost all everyday behaviors of relatively normal people in their relationships with others. **Social psychologists** *study social behavior and how people influence one another.*

Influence depends not only on what someone says but also on what the listeners think of the speaker.

- What determines whether we cooperate or compete with others?
- What accounts for acts of violence?

Young people, especially in the United States, look forward to becoming adults and being "independent." Americans have a long history of praising "rugged individualism." But how independent are any of us, really? Do you make your own clothing? Do you expect to build your own home? How much of your food do you grow or hunt? Do you perform your own medical care? Will you build your own car or pave your own roads? Of all the acts you need for survival, do you do *any* of them by yourself, other than breathe? (Even for that, you count on the government to prevent excessive air pollution.) Humans are extremely *inter*dependent. Our survival depends on cooperation.

Furthermore, most of us at least occasionally give to charity, volunteer time for worthy projects, offer directions to a stranger who appears lost, and in other ways help people who will never pay us back. Why do people behave in cooperative, moral ways?

Morality: Logical or Emotional?

Psychologists once regarded morality as a set of arbitrary rules, like learning to stop at a red light and go at a green light. Lawrence Kohlberg (1969; Kohlberg & Hersh, 1977) proposed instead that moral reasoning is a process that matures through a series of stages, similar to Piaget's stages of cognitive development. For example, children younger than about 6 years old say that accidentally breaking a valuable object is worse than intentionally breaking a less valuable object. Older children and adults care about intentions and not just results. The change is a natural unfolding, according to Kohlberg, not a matter of memorizing rules. As the reasoning ability matures, one moves toward making decisions based on justice and avoiding harm to others.

According to Kohlberg, to evaluate people's moral reasoning, we should ask about the reasons for their decisions, not just about the decisions themselves. In George Bernard Shaw's (1911) play *The Doctor's Dilemma*, two men are dying. The only doctor in town has enough medicine to save one of them but not both. One man is an artistic genius but dishonest, rude, and disagreeable. The other will make no great accomplishments, but he is honest and decent. The doctor, forced to choose between them, saves the honest but untalented man. Did he make the right choice? According to Kohlberg, this is the wrong question. The right question is *why* he made that choice. In the play, the doctor chose this man because he hoped to marry the wife of the artistic genius after letting him die. (What do you think about the quality of the doctor's moral reasoning?)

Kohlberg focused psychologists' attention on the reasoning processes behind moral decisions, but people don't always think logically about issues of right and wrong before they act. More often, they make a quick decision and then look for reasons afterward. In the terminology of cognitive psychology (chapter 8), we use System 1 for the initial decision, and we call upon System 2 mostly to generate logical-sounding explanations for what System 1 already decided. Consider the following: Mark and his sister Julie are college students. During one summer, they traveled together and one night they stayed at a cabin in the woods. They decided it would be fun to have sex together, so they did. Julie was taking birth-control pills, but Mark used a condom anyway just to be sure. Both enjoyed the experience, and neither felt hurt in any way. They decided not to do it again but to keep it as their little secret. They feel closer than ever as brother and sister. Was their action okay?

Almost everyone reacts immediately, "No! No! No!" Why? Mark and Julie used two reliable methods of birth control, and both said they enjoyed the experience and did not feel hurt. If their act was wrong, why was it wrong? When you (presumably) said that they were wrong, did you carefully reason it out? You probably decided at once, intuitively and emotionally, and then looked for a justification (Haidt, 2001, 2007).

In addition to the fact that most moral decisions are intuitive and emotional rather than coldly logical, Kohlberg's analysis falls short in another way. According to Kohlberg, our only bases for morality are seeking justice and avoiding harm to others. That description works for most highly educated Americans and Europeans, especially political liberals, but it leaves out a great deal, so far as most of the rest of the world's people are concerned. Most people also base their moral decisions on loyalty to their group, respect for authority, and spiritual purity. For example, they would insist that incest between Mark and Julie was an impure act that defiles them spiritually, regardless of how much they say they enjoyed it (Haidt, 2012). If we care about moral thinking by all people, and not just certain types of people, we need to consider more than Kohlberg did.

concept check

1. How did Kohlberg evaluate moral reasoning?
2. What are some limitations of Kohlberg's approach?

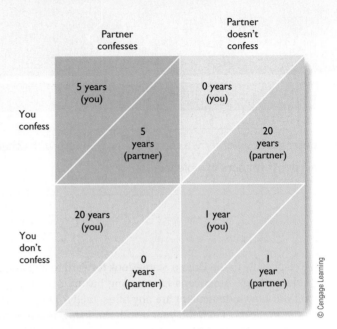

Figure 13.1 In the prisoner's dilemma, each person has an incentive to confess. But if both people confess, they suffer worse penalties than if both had refused to confess.

Altruistic Behavior

Why do we sometimes engage in altruistic behavior—*helping others despite a cost to ourselves?* It seems so natural that we take it for granted, but altruism is uncommon in other animal species. Let's qualify that: In almost every species, animals devote great energies and risk their lives to help their babies or other relatives. But they seldom do much to help unrelated individuals.

In one study, each chimpanzee could pull either of two ropes. Sometimes, it could pull one rope to get food or pull another to get nothing. It almost always chose the rope with food. At other times, one rope brought food, and the other rope brought food to *both* itself and a chimp it saw in another cage. The chimp in control seemed indifferent to the other chimp, even when the other chimp made begging gestures. Usually, the chimp pulled whichever rope was on the right regardless of whether it fed the other chimp or not (Silk et al., 2005).

Given that altruism is uncommon in the rest of the animal kingdom, why do people do so much to help one another? You may reply that we help others because it feels good. Yes, but why does it feel good? Did we evolve genes that make altruistic behavior feel good? If so, why? No one has found such a gene, and if someone did, a theoretical mystery would remain about how natural selection could favor such a gene. You may reply that an altruistic gene helps the species. Yes, but if a gene helps those who *don't* have the gene as much as or more than those who do, the gene won't spread in the population. If we consider the issue in nongenetic terms, the same problem arises: If you learn a habit of helping others, including people who are not altruistic themselves, they profit and you do not. Why would you learn to act that way? Researchers have used game situations to explore these issues.

The Prisoner's Dilemma

To investigate cooperation and competition, many researchers have used the prisoner's dilemma, *a situation where people choose between a cooperative act and a competitive act that benefits themselves but hurts others.* Imagine that you and a partner are arrested and charged with armed robbery. The police take you into separate rooms and urge each of you to confess. If neither of you confesses, the police do not have enough evidence to convict you of armed robbery, but they can convict you of a lesser offense with a sentence of 1 year in prison. If either confesses and testifies against the other, the confessor goes free and the other gets 20 years in prison. If both confess, you each get 5 years in prison. Each of you knows that the other person has the same options. Figure 13.1 illustrates the choices.

If your partner does not confess, you can confess and go free. (Let's assume you care only about yourself and not about your partner.) If your partner confesses, you still gain by confessing because you will get only 5 years in prison instead of 20. So you confess. Your partner, reasoning the same way, also confesses, so you both get 5 years in prison. If you had both kept quiet, you would have served only 1 year in prison. The situation trapped both people into uncooperative behavior.

The two of you are most likely to cooperate if you stay in constant communication (Nemeth, 1972). If you overhear each other, you know that, if one confesses, the other will retaliate. This kind of situation occurs in real life among nations as well as individuals. During the arms race between the United States and the Soviet Union, both sides wanted a treaty to stop building nuclear weapons. However, if one country kept the agreement while the other made additional weapons, the cheater could build a military advantage. The only way to keep an agreement was to allow each side to inspect the other. Eventually, spy satellites made it possible to monitor the agreement.

The prisoner's dilemma can also be stated in terms of gains. Suppose you and another person have a choice between two moves, which we call *cooperate* and *compete*. Depending on your choices, here are the payoffs:

Here are the payoffs:

	Other person cooperates	Other person competes
You cooperate	Both win $1	Other person gains $2; you lose $2
You compete	You gain $2; other person loses $2	Both lose $1

© Cengage Learning

Suppose you play this game only once with someone you will never meet. Both of you will reveal your answers by telephone to a third person. Which move do you choose? If the other person cooperates, your winning choice is *compete* because you will get $2 instead of $1. If the other person competes, again you gain by competing because you will lose just $1 instead of $2. Logically, you should compete, as should the other person, and you both lose $1. In situations like this, not everyone chooses to compete. Some people and some cultures are more trusting than others are (Henrich et al., 2010). Still, the situation tends to foster uncooperative behavior. You can explore the prisoner's dilemma at this website, where you compete against a computer opponent: http://serendip.brynmawr.edu/bb/pd.html.

In real life, people do cooperate most of the time. What is the difference between real-life situations and the prisoner's dilemma? One big difference is that we deal with people repeatedly, not just once. If you play the prisoner's dilemma many times with the same partner, the two of you will probably learn to cooperate, especially if real rewards are at stake. Furthermore, in real life it is important to develop a reputation for cooperating, if you want people to continue doing business with you (Nowak & Sigmund, 2005; D. S. Wilson, Near, & Miller, 1996). Thus, here is one explanation for altruistic behavior: *People want a reputation for being fair and helpful* (McNamara, Barta, Fromhage, & Houston, 2008).

A second reason for cooperation is that *people who do cooperate punish those who don't.* In some cases, people will pay for the opportunity to punish an uncooperative person (Gächter, Renner, & Sefton, 2008). However, punishment is effective only if most people can combine efforts to punish the few who don't cooperate. If too many people become uncooperative, it is difficult or ineffective to try punishing them all (Dreber, Rand, Fudenberg, & Nowak, 2008; Herrmann, Thöni, & Gächter, 2008).

concept check

3. Theoretically, how can we explain why people sometimes act altruistically toward people they have never met? Why do they tend to be even more cooperative with people they have known for a long time?
4. You have read two explanations for humans' altruistic behavior. Why do both of them require individual recognition?

Answers

3. Even with a stranger, you behave altruistically to develop a reputation for cooperating. With a familiar person who has cooperated in the past, you expect the person to return favors.
4. One explanation for altruistic behavior is that cooperating builds a reputation, and a reputation requires individuals to recognize one another. The other explanation is that people who cooperate will punish those who do not. Again, to retaliate, they need to recognize who has failed to cooperate.

Accepting or Denying Responsibility Toward Others

Other people can encourage us to do something we would not have done on our own. They can also inhibit us from doing something that we would have done on our own. We look around to see what others are doing—or *not* doing—and we say, "Okay, I'll do that, too." Why do people sometimes work together and sometimes ignore the needs of others?

Bystander Helpfulness and Apathy

Suppose while you are waiting at a bus stop, you see me trip and fall down, not far away. I am not screaming in agony, but I don't get up either, so you are not sure whether I need help. Would you come over and offer to help? Or would you stay there and ignore me? Before you answer, try to imagine the situation in two ways: First, you and I are the only people in sight. Second, many other people are nearby, none of them rushing to my aid. Does the presence of those other people make any difference to you? (It doesn't to me. I am in the same pain regardless of how many people ignore me.)

One tragic real-life event will help to illustrate. Late one night in March 1964, Kitty Genovese was stabbed to death near her apartment in Queens, New York. A newspaper article at the time reported that 38 of her neighbors heard her screaming for more than half an hour, but none of them called the police, each of them either declining to get involved or assuming that someone else had already called the police. Later investigations of the crime indicated that this report was greatly exaggerated (Manning, Levine, & Collins, 2007). About six people saw the attack, and at least one or two did call the police. Genovese went into the building on her own, and her attacker returned to attack again half an hour later, out of sight of witnesses, while she was too weak to scream.

Although the original newspaper article was full of errors, it prompted interest in why people often fail to help someone in distress. Are we less likely to act when we know that someone else could act? Bibb Latané and John Darley (1969) proposed that being in a crowd decreases our probability of action because of diffusion of responsibility: *We feel less responsibility to act when other people are equally able to act.*

In an experiment designed to test this hypothesis, a young woman ushered one or two students into a room and asked them to wait for the start of a market research study (Latané & Darley, 1968, 1969). She went into the next room, closing the door behind her. Then she played a tape recording that sounded as though she climbed onto a chair, fell off, and moaned, "Oh . . . my foot . . . I can't move it. Oh . . . my ankle . . ." Of the participants who were waiting alone, 70% went next door and offered to help. Of the participants who were waiting with someone else, only 13% offered to help.

In another study, investigators entered 400 Internet chat groups of different sizes and in each one asked, "Can anyone tell me how to look at someone's profile?" The researchers found that the more people in a chat room at the time, the longer the wait before anyone answered the question. In large groups, the researchers sometimes had to post the same question repeatedly (Markey, 2000).

Diffusion of responsibility is one explanation. Each person thinks, "It's not my responsibility to help any more than someone else's." A second possible explanation is that the presence of other people who are doing nothing provides information (or misinformation). The situation is ambiguous: "Do I need to act or not?" Other people's inaction implies that the situation requires no action. In fact, the others, who are just as uncertain as you are, draw conclusions from *your* inaction. Social psychologists use the term pluralistic ignorance to describe *a situation in which people say nothing, and each person falsely assumes that others have a better-informed opinion.* Other people's inactivity implies that doing nothing is acceptable (a norm) and that the situation is not an emergency (information).

Social Loafing

When you take a test, you work alone, and your success depends on your own effort. Often, however, you are part of a team. If you work for a company that gives workers a share of the profits, your rewards depend on other workers' productivity as well as your own. Do you work as hard as you can when the rewards depend on the group's productivity?

In many cases, you do not. In one experiment, students were told to scream, clap, and make as much noise as possible, like cheerleaders at a sports event. Sometimes, each student screamed and clapped alone; sometimes, students acted in groups; and sometimes, they acted alone but *thought* other people were screaming and clapping, too. (They wore headphones so they could not hear anyone else.) Most of the students who screamed and clapped alone made more noise than those who were or thought they were part of a group (Latané, Williams, & Harkins, 1979). Social psychologists call this phenomenon social loafing—*the tendency to "loaf" (or work less hard) when sharing work with other people.*

Social loafing has been demonstrated in many situations. Suppose you are asked to "name all the uses you can think of for a brick" (e.g., crack nuts,

People watch other people's responses to decide how they should respond. When a group of sidewalk Santas—who had gathered in Manhattan to promote a back-rub business—came to the aid of an injured cyclist, a few Santas made the first move and the others followed.

anchor a boat, use as a doorstop) and write each one on a card. You probably fill out many cards by yourself but fewer if you are tossing cards into a pile along with other people's suggestions (Harkins & Jackson, 1985). You don't bother submitting ideas that you assume other people have already suggested.

At this point, you may be thinking, "Wait a minute. When I'm playing basketball or soccer, I try as hard as I can. I don't think I loaf." You are right; social loafing is rare in team sports because observers, including teammates, watch your performance. People work hard in groups if they expect other people to notice their effort or if they think they can contribute something that other group members cannot (Shepperd, 1993; K. D. Williams & Karau, 1991).

concept check

5. Given what we have learned about social loafing, why are most people unlikely to work hard to clean the environment?
6. In a typical family, one or two members have jobs, but their wages benefit all. Why do those wage earners *not* engage in social loafing?

Answers

5. Social loafing is likely because many one-person contributions, such as picking up litter, would not earn individual credit or recognition. Also, each person thinks, "What good could one person do with such a gigantic problem?"
6. The main reason is that the wage earners see they can make a special contribution that the others (children, injured, or retired) cannot. Also, others can easily observe the wage earners' contributions.

During a catastrophe, people abandon their usual tendencies toward bystander apathy and social loafing.

Violent and Aggressive Behavior

During World War II, nearly all the industrialized nations were at war, the Nazis were exterminating the Jews, and the United States was preparing a nuclear bomb that it later dropped on Japan. Meanwhile, Mohandas K. Gandhi was in jail for leading a nonviolent protest march against British rule in India. The charge against Gandhi was, ironically, "disturbing the peace." Someone asked Gandhi what he thought of Western civilization. He replied that he thought it might be a good idea.

Cruelty and violence have always been part of human experience, just as kindness and altruism have been. But that is not to say that the balance between kindness and cruelty must always remain the same. As Steven Pinker (2011) has argued, since World War II, the worldwide rate of death by war and murder has declined to its lowest level ever. Education is probably a major contributor to the decline, as are travel and communication. (It's harder to hate people after you have visited their country or played Internet games with them.) In short, violence is still a problem, but we can do much about it.

Causes of Anger and Aggression

According to the frustration-aggression hypothesis, *the main cause of anger and aggression is frustration—an obstacle that stands in the way of doing something or obtaining something* (Dollard, Miller, Doob, Mowrer, & Sears, 1939). How-

Does playing games like this make you more prone to violence?

ever, frustration makes you angry only when you believe the other person acted intentionally. You might feel angry if someone ran down the hall and bumped into you, but probably not if someone slipped on a wet spot and bumped into you.

Leonard Berkowitz (1983, 1989) proposed a more comprehensive theory: Any unpleasant event—frustration, pain, heat, foul odors, bad news, whatever—excites both the impulse to fight and the impulse to flee. That is, it excites the sympathetic nervous system and its fight-or-flight response. Your choice to fight or flee depends on the circumstances. If the person who just annoyed you looks weak, you express your anger. If that person looks intimidating, you suppress your anger. And if the one who bumped into you is the loan and scholarship officer at your college, you smile and apologize for getting in the way.

Individual Differences in Aggression

Why are some people aggressive more often than others? One hypothesis has been that low self-esteem leads to violence. According to this idea, people who think little of themselves try to build themselves up by tearing someone else down. The data on this point are mixed. Some studies find a small relationship between aggressive behaviors and low self-esteem, but others find virtually no relationship between the two (Baumeister, Campbell, Krueger, & Vohs, 2003; Donnellan, Trzesniewski, Robins, Moffitt, & Caspi, 2005). A better possibility is that people who are accustomed to feeling powerful and successful become angry and aggressive when they find their self-confidence threatened (Fast & Chen, 2009).

Another hypothesis not consistently supported is a link between violence and mental illness. Drug and alcohol abuse are highly associated with violence, and many mental patients abuse alcohol or other drugs. However, mentally ill people without drug- or alcohol-abuse are no more likely than anyone else to be violent (Hodgins, Mednick, Brennan, Schulsinger, & Engberg, 1996).

If low self-esteem and mental illness do not predict violence, what does? Research has pointed to genetic factors that predispose to violence, but the effect of those genes depends on the environment. People with a genetic predisposition and a history of maltreatment during childhood are more likely to turn to violence than are people who have just the genetic predisposition or just the history of maltreatment (Caspi et al., 2002; Enoch, Steer, Newman, Gibson, & Goldman, 2010).

Several other factors are associated with a tendency toward violent behavior (Bushman & Anderson, 2009; Davidson, Putnam, & Larson, 2000; Hay et al., 2011; D. O. Lewis et al., 1985; Lynam,

1996; Osofsky, 1995; Raine, Lencz, Bihrle, LaCasse, & Colletti, 2000):

- Growing up in a violent neighborhood
- Having parents with a history of antisocial behavior
- Not feeling guilty after hurting someone
- Weaker than normal physiological responses to arousal
- A history of suicide attempts
- Frequently watching violent television programs or playing violent video games

As always, we should beware of drawing cause-and-effect conclusions from these correlational studies. For example, liking violent television and video games could be either the cause of an aggressive tendency or the result of it.

Culture is also a powerful influence. A fascinating study documented the influence of culture on aggressive behavior even in nonhuman primates. Researchers observed one troop of baboons for 25 years. At one point, all the most aggressive males in the troop tried to take food from a neighboring troop. The food happened to be contaminated, and all the aggressive males died. The troop then consisted of females, juveniles, and the least aggressive males. They got along well, stress levels decreased, and health improved. Over the years, new males occasionally entered the troop and adopted this troop's customs. Years later, none of the original males remained there, but the troop continued its nonaggressive tradition (Sapolsky & Share, 2004).

concept check

7. Is genetic predisposition a powerful contributor to aggressive behavior?

Answer

7. It depends. The probability of aggressive behavior is highest among those who have both a genetic predisposition and a history of childhood maltreatment.

Cognitive Influences on Violence

Most people think of themselves as good. Most of the time you treat other people fairly, right? You know it is wrong to hurt or cheat anyone. But at times, you might. If you serve in the police or military, certain situations might require you to shoot someone. In business, you might give in to a temptation to raise profits by doing something unfair to your competitors or risky to your customers. If so, you want to justify your actions, to make them seem acceptable.

People often justify their acts by thinking of themselves as better than the people they are hurting. In war, soldiers give their enemies a derogatory name and think of them as less than human. The same occurs for violence against racial minorities or other groups. Psychologists describe this process as *deindividuation* (perceiving others as anonymous, without any real personality) and *dehumanization* (perceiving others as less than human). The result is greater acceptance of violence and injustice (Reimann & Zimbardo, 2011). Certain brain areas are known to respond strongly when you interact socially with someone, or even when you see someone with whom you would like to interact socially. These brain areas hardly respond at all when you see homeless people, drug addicts, or others for whom you have a low regard (Harris & Fiske, 2006). In effect, you don't see them as human. (That study is one example of *social neuroscience*—the use of brain measurements to shed light on social behavior.)

People also justify their violent behavior by decreasing their own sense of identity. A soldier on duty is no longer acting as an individual making his or her own decisions. A Ku Klux Klansman wearing a hood suppresses a sense of personal identity. A criminal wearing a mask not only decreases the probability of witness identification, but also creates a distance between the "real self" and the perpetrator of the act. Even wearing sunglasses has been found to decrease people's sense of personal responsibility and to increase their probability of dishonest acts (Zhong, Bohns, & Gino, 2010).

concept check

8. How do deindividuation and dehumanization increase aggressive behavior?

Answer

8. Deindividuation and dehumanization enable the perpetrator of a violent act to think that the victim is less worthy of kind treatment.

Sexual Aggression

Most acts of violence occur between people who know each other well, including romantic couples. A review of the extensive research on heterosexual couples reported that women commit *more* acts of violence against men than men do against women (Archer, 2000). Almost everyone finds that result surprising. After all, we hear of battered women's clinics but not battered men's clinics. The explanation is that most researchers defined violence to include slaps, pushes, and other minor acts. Men inflict most of the serious injuries, and women inflict many minor events.

Rape is *sexual activity without the consent of the partner*. In one survey, about 10% of adult women reported that they had been forcibly raped, and another 10% said they had sex while incapacitated by alcohol or other drugs (Testa, Livingston, Vanzile-Tamsen, & Frone, 2003). However, the statistics vary considerably from one study to another. Recall from chapter 2 that slight changes in the wording of a survey question can enormously influence people's answers. Surveys that ask about "unwanted" sex report very high numbers because many people interpret "unwanted" to include times when they weren't in the mood but agreed to sex to please a partner (Hamby & Koss, 2003). Not only most women but also most men say they have sometimes had sex when they did not want to (Struckman-Johnson, Struckman-Johnson, & Anderson, 2003).

Of all sexual assaults that legally qualify as rape, only about half the victims think of the experience as rape, and far fewer report it to the police (Fisher, Daigle, Cullen, & Turner, 2003). Most women who have involuntary sex with a boyfriend or other acquaintance do not call the event rape, especially if alcohol was involved (Kahn, Jackson, Kully, Badger, & Halvorsen, 2003). In some cases, the man does not realize that the woman considered his behavior abusive.

Rapists are not all alike. Many are hostile, distrustful men with a history of other acts of violence and criminality (Hanson, 2000). Sexually aggressive men tend to be high users of pornography (Vega & Malamuth, 2007), and rapists are much more likely than other men to enjoy violent pornography (Donnerstein & Malamuth, 1997). Another element in rape is extreme self-centeredness, or lack of concern for others (Dean & Malamuth, 1997).

module 13.1

In Closing

Is Cooperative Behavior Logical?

Either we have evolved a tendency to help others, or we learn to. The research on the prisoner's dilemma and similar games attempts to demonstrate that cooperation and mutual aid are logical under certain conditions. You cooperate to develop a good reputation so that others will cooperate with you and not penalize you.

Do you find this explanation completely satisfactory? Sometimes, you make an anonymous contribution to a worthy cause with no expectation of personal gain, not even an improvement of your reputation. You simply wanted to help that cause.

You occasionally help someone you'll never see again while no one else is watching. Perhaps these acts require no special explanation. You have developed habits of helping for all the reasons that investigators have identified. Once you developed those habits, you generalize them to other circumstances, even when they do you no good. Yes, perhaps. Or maybe researchers are still overlooking something. Conclusions in psychology are almost never final. You are invited to think about these issues yourself and develop your own hypotheses.

Summary

- *Kohlberg's view of moral reasoning.* Lawrence Kohlberg argued that we should evaluate moral reasoning on the basis of the reasons people give for a decision rather than the decision itself. (page 421)
- *Limits to Kohlberg's views.* Kohlberg concentrated on logical reasoning. In fact, people often or usually act first, based on an emotional urge, and look for a justification later. Also, many people, especially in non-Western cultures, base their moral decisions on factors Kohlberg overlooked, including loyalty, authority, and purity. (page 421)
- *The prisoner's dilemma.* In the prisoner's dilemma, two people can choose to cooperate or compete. The *compete* move seems best from the individual's point of view, but it is harmful to the group. (page 422)
- *Reasons for cooperation.* Studies of the prisoner's dilemma demonstrate two rational reasons for cooperation: A cooperative person enhances

his or her reputation and therefore gains cooperation from others. Also, people who cooperate punish those who do not. (page 423)
- *Bystander apathy.* People are less likely to help someone if other people are in an equally good position to help. (page 423)
- *Social loafing.* Most people work less hard when they are part of a group than when they work alone, except when they think they can make a unique contribution or if they think others are evaluating their contribution. (page 424)
- *Aggressive behavior.* Frustration or discomfort of any kind increases the probability of anger and aggression, especially if one perceives that others have caused the frustration intentionally. (page 425)
- *Cognitive factors in aggression.* People sometimes justify cruel or uncooperative behavior by lowering their opinion of the victims. People also decrease their own sense of personal responsibility. (page 426)

Key Terms

altruistic behavior (page 422)
diffusion of responsibility (page 423)
frustration-aggression hypothesis (page 425)
pluralistic ignorance (page 424)

prisoner's dilemma (page 422)
rape (page 426)
social loafing (page 424)
social psychologists (page 420)

- What factors influence our judgments of others?
- How can we measure stereotypes that people do not want to admit?
- How can we overcome prejudices?
- How do we explain the causes of our own behavior and that of others?

People generally measure their success by comparing themselves to others. You cheer yourself up by noting that you are doing better than some other people you know. You motivate yourself to try harder by comparing yourself to someone more successful (Suls, Martin, & Wheeler, 2002).

To make these comparisons, we need accurate information about other people. We also need that information to form expectations about how others will act and whom we can trust. Social perception and cognition are *the processes for learning about others and making inferences from that information*. Social perception and cognition influence our observations, memory, and thinking.

First Impressions

Other things being equal, *the first information we learn about someone influences us more than later information does* (E. E. Jones & Goethals, 1972). This tendency is known as the primacy effect. (We also encountered this term in chapter 7 on memory, where it refers to the tendency to remember well the first items on a list.) For example, if you hear both favorable and unfavorable reports about a restaurant, the reports you hear first influence you the most (Russo, Carlson, & Meloy, 2006).

We form first impressions quickly and more accurately than we might guess. In one study, college students viewed three 2-second videos of several professors lecturing, without sound, and rated how good they thought these professors were. Their mean rating correlated .6 with the end-of-semester ratings by the students in those classes (Ambady & Rosenthal, 1993). People watching 10-second videos of couples could in most cases guess how much romantic interest they felt (Place, Todd, Penke, & Asendorpf, 2009). People listening to 30-second statements by recently divorced people could generally predict which people would make more successful adjustments over the next 3 months (Mason, Sbarra, & Mehl, 2010). From a brief view of women's faces, or even a view of just the eyes, people could guess with better-than-chance accuracy which women were lesbians and which were heterosexual (Rule, Ambady, & Hallett, 2009). People viewing faces for just 39 milliseconds fairly accurately guessed how aggressive those people were (Carré, McCormick, & Mondloch, 2009). You may have heard the expression, "You only have one chance to make a first impression." The research suggests that you have barely a moment to make that impression!

First impressions can become self-fulfilling prophecies, *expectations that increase the probability of the predicted event*. Suppose a psychologist hands you a cell phone and asks you to talk with someone, while showing you a photo supposedly of that person. Unknown to the person you are talking to, the psychologist might hand you a photo of a very attractive person or a much less attractive photo. Not surprisingly, you act friendlier to someone you regard as attractive. Furthermore, if you think you are talking to someone attractive, that person reacts by becoming more cheerful and talkative. In short, your first impression changes how you act and influences the other person to live up to (or down to) your expectations (M. Snyder, Tanke, & Berscheid, 1977).

© Jupiterimages/Getty Images

What's your first impression of this man—rich or poor? Businessman, professional athlete, or manual laborer? (Yeah, you got it right.)

concept check

9. Why do some professors avoid looking at students' names when they grade essay exams?

Answer

9. They want to avoid being biased by their first impressions of the students.

Stereotypes and Prejudices

A **stereotype** is *a belief or expectation about a group of people*. A **prejudice** is *an unfavorable attitude toward a group of people*. It is usually associated with dis-crimination, which is *unequal treatment of different groups*, such as minority groups, the physically disabled, people who are obese, or gays and lesbians.

Stereotypes affect us in subtle, unconscious ways. Imagine yourself in this experiment: You are given sets of five words to arrange into sentences. Here are three examples:

CAR REPAIRS OLD THIS NEEDS

CLOUDY GRAY SKY THE WAS

OFFER GAMES SMALL BINGO PRIZES

Easy, right? You think the experiment is over, and now you are walking out. The real point of the experiment is to watch you walk out! People in one experi-mental condition—the one you were in—unscrambled sentences that included words associated with the stereotype of old people, such as *old, gray,* and *bingo*. On average, people who have just been thinking about old people tend to walk more slowly than usual, like their stereotype of old people (Bargh, Chen, & Burrows, 1996).

People tend to draw generalizations quickly, and sometimes the result is a false stereotype. Suppose you learn a few things, either mostly good or mostly bad, about one member of a fictitious group called Niffians. Based on this one example, you are likely to form an opinion about other Niffians (Ranganath & Nosek, 2008).

However, stereotypes are not always wrong. Who do you think gets into more fistfights on average—men or women? If you answered "men," you are supporting a stereotype, but you are correct. Similarly, who do you think is more likely to notice the subtle social connotations in conversation—a liberal arts major or an engineering major? Again, if you said "liberal arts major," you are endorsing a stereotype, but the research supports you (Ottati & Lee, 1995). In-deed, whenever we say that culture influences behavior, we imply that members of those cultures behave differently on average, and therefore that a stereotype about them is partly correct. However, even for a mostly correct stereotype, we need to recognize exceptions to the rule.

Implicit Measures of Stereotypes and Prejudice

Decades ago, Americans admitted their prejudices openly. Today, almost all people believe in fair treatment for everyone, or so they say. But are people as unprejudiced as they claim to be? Researchers have sought methods of measur-ing subtle prejudices that people do not want to admit, even to themselves.

One method is the **Implicit Association Test (IAT)**, which *measures reactions to combinations of categories, such as flowers and pleasant*. Imagine this example: You rest your left and right forefingers on a computer keyboard. When you hear a word, you should press with your left finger if it is an unpleasant word, such as *death*, and press with your right finger if it is a pleasant word, such as *joy*. After a while, the instructions change. Now you should press the left key if you hear the name of an insect and the right key if you hear the name of a flower. Next you combine two categories: Press the left key for unpleasant words or insects and the right key for pleasant words or flowers. Then the pairings switch: Press the left key for unpleasant words or flowers and the right key for pleasant words or insects. The procedure continues, alternating between the two instructions.

Most people respond faster to the combination "pleasant or flowers" than to "pleasant or insects." The conclusion is that most people like flowers more than insects. The procedure may seem more trouble than it is worth, as people readily agree that they like flowers more than insects. However, the research established the validity of the method, which researchers then used to measure other prefer-ences (Greenwald, Nosek, & Banaji, 2003).

The stereotype of old people as inactive has many exceptions.

Imagine yourself in this experiment: You view a computer screen that sometimes shows a photo and sometimes a word. If it is a photo of a Black person or a pleasant word, press the left key. If it is a photo of a White person or an unpleasant word, press the right key. After you respond that way for a while, the rule switches to the opposite pairing. Figure 13.2 il-lustrates the procedures and Figure 13.3 summa-rizes the results for a group of White college stu-dents. Most responded faster to the combinations *Black/unpleasant* and *White/pleasant*, even though they claimed to have no racial prejudice (Phelps et al., 2000). Black participants, however, show nearly equal responses to Blacks and Whites on average —that is, little or no prejudice (Stewart, von Hippel, & Radvansky, 2009).

Researchers have also used the IAT to gauge at-titudes toward men and women (Nosek & Banaji, 2001; Rudman & Goodwin, 2004), toward obese people (Agerström & Rooth, 2011), and toward many other groups. Researchers have provided a simplified version of the Implicit Association Test on a website that you can try yourself: https://implicit.harvard.edu/implicit/demo

online

try it ▶ yourself

SET 1: Press left key if   Press right key if

Photo of a   or   Pleasant   Photo of a   or   Unpleasant
Black person   word   White person   word

PEACE   CANCER

SET 2: Press left key if   Press right key if

Photo of a   or   Unpleasant   Photo of a   or   Pleasant
Black person   word   White person   word

BOMB   JOY

Figure 13.2 Procedures for an Implicit Association Test to measure prejudices. (© Cengage Learning).

The results of the Implicit Association Test suggest that even well-meaning people have unrecognized prejudices (Greenwald, Poehlman, Uhlmann, & Banaji, 2009). Those unacknowledged prejudices might affect people's decisions, such as deciding which job applicant to hire. If so, we should counsel people to take deliberate steps to counter their automatic, unconscious discrimination. However, we should be cautious about overstating the policy implications of this research. First, because the Implicit Association Test requires people to pay attention to race, even if they ordinarily don't, the results probably exaggerate people's prejudices (M. A. Olson & Fazio, 2003). Second, only a few studies have examined the relationship between IAT results and important decisions, such as those related to hiring job applicants. Those few studies have found weak effects. Certainly the results of the IAT are not strong enough to predict what any individual will do in a given situation (Blanton et al., 2009).

concept check

10. What is the advantage of the Implicit Association Test over asking people about their racial prejudices?

Answer

10. The Implicit Association Test may reveal prejudices that people don't want to admit, even to themselves.

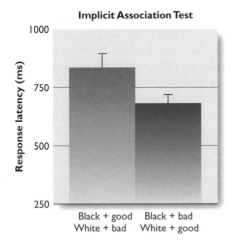

Implicit Association Test

Response latency (ms)

1000

750

500

250

Black + good   Black + bad
White + bad   White + good

Figure 13.3 On average, White students who claimed to have no racial prejudice responded slower if they had to make one response for "Black face or pleasant word" and a different response for "White face or unpleasant word" than if the pairings were reversed—Black and unpleasant, White and pleasant. (From "Performance on Indirect Measures of Race Evaluation Predicts Amygdala Activation" by E. A. Phelps, K. J. O'Connor, W. A. Cunningham, E. S. Funayama, J. C. Gatenby, J. C. Gore, & M. R. Banaji, *Journal of Cognitive Neuroscience* vol 12 (pp. 729-738). Copyright © 2000 MIT Press. Reprinted by permission.)

Overcoming Prejudice

After people form a prejudice, what can overcome it? Increasing contact between groups usually helps. A study of White and Black college students who were assigned to be roommates found that they spent little time together at first, but over the course of a semester, they formed more favorable attitudes and felt less anxiety about interracial interactions (Shook & Fazio, 2008). Another study found that minority students at a mostly White college came to like the college more after developing a friendship with one or more White students (Mendoza-Denton & Page-Gould, 2008). Even an imaginary positive experience helps to increase favorable attitudes toward people from another group (Crisp & Turner, 2009).

A particularly effective technique is to get groups to work toward a common goal (Dovidio & Gaertner, 1999). Long ago, psychologists demonstrated the power of this technique using two arbitrarily chosen groups (Sherif, 1966). At a summer camp at Robbers' Cave, Oklahoma, 11- and 12-year-old boys were divided into two groups in separate cabins. The groups competed for prizes in sports, treasure hunts, and other activities. With each competition, the antagonism between the two groups grew more intense. The boys made threatening posters, shouted insults, and engaged in food fights.

People who work together for a common goal can overcome prejudices that initially divide them.

Up to a point, the "counselors" (experimenters) tolerated the hostility. Then they tried to reverse it. First, they asked the two groups to work together to find and repair a leak in the water pipe that supplied the camp. Then they had the two groups pool their treasuries to rent a movie that both groups wanted to see. Later, they had the boys pull together to get a truck out of a rut. Gradually, hostility turned into friendship—except for a few holdouts who nursed their hatred to the bitter end! The point is that competition breeds hostility, and cooperation leads to friendship.

The media also play a role in strengthening or weakening prejudices. In 1994 Rwanda (in south-central Africa) had a vicious civil war in which the majority Hutus, urged on by their government and Rwanda's primary radio station, killed three fourths of the Tutsi minority. (Televisions and newspapers are rare in Rwanda, and radio is the primary means of communication and entertainment.) Today, the Hutus and surviving Tutsis live in an uneasy truce. A radio soap opera, made available on an experimental basis to some villages and not others, described a fictional place in which one group attacked another group, but leaders spoke out against violence, and people from the two groups formed friendships. The people in villages that heard this soap opera showed increased sympathy, trust, and cooperation, breaking down the barriers between Hutus and Tutsis (Paluck, 2009).

Decreasing Prejudice by Increasing Acceptance

Most people today publicly endorse the goal of treating all people fairly, without prejudice. However, the way of expressing this goal has major effects on the result. Consider the expression "we treat all people the same." Although that goal sounds good, it seems to imply, "We expect all people to act the same." You might *not* be the same as everyone else. You might differ from the others in racial or ethnic background, sexual orientation, education, or interests. You might be older or younger than most, or the only man or only woman in the organization. Your career goals might be different from everyone else's. A policy of treating everyone the same pressures you to act like something you are not, and

pressures other people to ignore the fact that you are different. When people try not to notice skin color, sexual orientation, or anything else, or try to avoid seeming prejudiced, they find the effort unpleasant and tiring. The result is often an *increase* in prejudice (Legault, Gutsell, & Inzlicht, 2011; Trawalter & Richeson, 2006; Wegner, 2009). In some cases this "we're all the same" approach has been carried so far that certain schools tried to teach about Martin Luther King, Jr., without mentioning that he was Black, or that he was fighting against racial prejudice (Apfelbaum, Paulker, Sommers, & Ambady, 2010).

An alternative is multiculturalism—*accepting, recognizing, and enjoying the differences among people and groups.* A multiculturalist approach emphasizes the positive aspects of enjoying others as they are. Research shows advantages of the multiculturalism approach. When a company or other organization endorses a multiculturalist position, prejudices decrease and minorities feel more comfortable (Plaut, Thomas, & Goren, 2009; Richeson & Nussbaum, 2004; Vorauer, Gagnon, & Sasaki, 2009).

concept check

11. What would be an improvement on the advice "try to avoid seeming prejudiced"?

Answer

11. It is better to try to have a positive experience and to enjoy cultural differences. Increased contact helps overcome intergroup tensions, especially if people work together for a common goal.

Attribution

Yesterday, you won the state lottery, and today, classmates who previously ignored you want to be your friends. You draw inferences about their reasons. **Attribution** is *the set of thought processes we use to assign causes to our own behavior and that of others.*

Internal Versus External Causes

Fritz Heider, the founder of attribution theory, emphasized the distinction between internal and external causes of behavior (Heider, 1958). **Internal attributions** are *explanations based on someone's attitudes, personality traits, abilities, or other characteristics.* **External attributions** are *explanations based on the situation, including events that would influence almost anyone.* An example of an internal attribution is saying that your brother walked to work

In the United States, a funeral usually calls for reserved behavior. Many other places expect loud wailing.

Harold Kelley (1967) proposed that three types of information influence us to make an internal or external attribution:

- Consensus information *(how the person's behavior compares with other people's behavior)*. If someone behaves the same way you believe other people would in the same situation, you make an external attribution, recognizing that the situation led to the behavior. When a behavior seems unusual, you look for an internal attribution. (You can be wrong if you misunderstand the situation.)
- Consistency information *(how the person's behavior varies from one time to the next)*. If someone almost always seems friendly, you make an internal attribution ("a friendly person"). If someone's friendliness varies, you make an external attribution, such as an event that elicited a good or bad mood.
- Distinctiveness *(how the person's behavior varies from one situation to another)*. If your friend is pleasant to all but one individual, you assume that person has done something to irritate your friend (an external attribution).

concept check

12. Classify the following as either internal or external attributions:
    a. She contributed money to charity because she is generous.
    b. She contributed money to charity because she wanted to impress her boss, who was watching.
    c. She contributed money to charity because she owed a favor to the man who was asking for contributions.
13. Juanita returns from watching *The Return of the Son of Sequel Strikes Back Again Part 2* and says it was excellent. Most other people disliked the movie. Will you make an internal or external attribution for Juanita's opinion? On what type of information will you base your attribution (distinctiveness, consensus, or consistency)?

Answers

12. **a.** internal; **b.** external; **c.** external. An internal attribution relates to a stable aspect of personality or attitudes; an external attribution relates to the current situation.
13. You probably will make an internal attribution because of *consensus*. When one person's behavior differs from others, we make an internal attribution.

this morning "because he likes the exercise." An external attribution would be that he walked "because his car wouldn't start." Internal attributions are also known as *dispositional* (i.e., relating to the person's disposition). External attributions are also known as *situational* (i.e., relating to the situation).

You make internal attributions when someone's act surprises you. For example, you draw no conclusions about someone who would like to visit Hawaii. (After all, who wouldn't?) However, if someone wants to visit northern Norway in winter, you look for something special about that person. When a man gets angry in public, most people assume he had a reason. When a woman gets equally angry in public, her behavior is more surprising, and people attribute it to her personality (Brescoll & Uhlmann, 2008).

This tendency sometimes leads to misunderstandings between members of different cultures. Each person views the other's behavior as "something I would not have done" and therefore a reason to make an attribution about personality. For example, some cultures expect people to cry loudly at funerals, whereas others expect more restraint. People who are unfamiliar with other cultures may attribute a behavior to personality, when in fact it is a dictate of culture.

The Actor-Observer Effect

If you see someone complaining loudly to a sales clerk, how do you react? You say, "There is an aggressive loudmouth!" When you complain equally loudly, how do you explain it? You say, "I had been treated unfairly!" *People are more likely to make internal attributions for other people's behavior and more likely to make external attributions for their own* (E. E. Jones & Nisbett, 1972). This tendency is called the actor-observer effect. You are an "actor" when you try to explain the causes of your own behavior and an "observer" when you try to explain someone else's behavior.

We can account for this tendency in terms of the three influences just mentioned. First, *consensus*: When you see someone angry with a sales clerk, would you be as angry as the complainer in that situation? You don't know, because you don't know the situation. But usually you are polite to salespeople, so maybe there is something unusual about that other person. Second, *consistency*: Is that other person angry all the time? Could be, so far as you know. But you know you get angry only on rare occasions. Third, *distinctiveness*: Is that other person aggressive in many situations? Could be, so far as you know. Are you aggressive in many situations? You know that you aren't.

Another explanation for the actor-observer effect is perceptual. We see other people as objects in our visual field, and we tend to think that whatever we are watching is the cause of the action. If you watch a videotape of your own behavior, you tend to explain the behavior in terms of personality more than situational factors, just as you do when you watch other people (Storms, 1973).

An application of this idea: Suppose you watch a videotape of two people who participate equally in a conversation. You are randomly given a version of the videotape with the camera focused on one person or the other. You tend to perceive that the person you are watching dominates the conversation. Similarly, if you watch a videotape of an interrogation between a detective and a suspect, you judge the suspect's confession to be more voluntary if the camera focuses on the suspect and more coerced if the camera focuses on the detective (Lassiter, Geers, Munhall, Ploutz-Snyder, & Breitenbecher, 2002).

The Fundamental Attribution Error

A common error is *to make internal attributions for people's behavior even when we see evidence for an external influence on behavior.* This tendency is known as the fundamental attribution error (Ross, 1977). It is also known as the *correspondence bias,* meaning a tendency to assume a strong similarity between someone's current actions and his or her dispositions.

Imagine yourself in a classic study demonstrating this phenomenon. You are told that U.S. college students were randomly assigned to write essays praising or condemning Fidel Castro, then the communist leader of Cuba. You read an essay that praises Castro. What's your guess about the actual attitude of the student who wrote this essay?

|—|—|—|—|—|—|—|—|—|—|
very anti-Castro   neutral   very pro-Castro

Most U.S. students in one study guessed that the student was at least mildly pro-Castro, even though they were informed, as you were, that the author had been required to praise Castro (E. E. Jones & Harris, 1967). In a later study, experimenters explained that one student in a creative writing class had been assigned to write a pro-Castro essay and an anti-Castro essay at different times. When the participants read the two essays, most thought that the writer had changed attitudes between the two essays (Allison, Mackie, Muller, & Worth, 1993). That is, even when people are told of a powerful external reason for someone's behavior, they seem to believe the person probably had internal reasons as well (McClure, 1998).

One more example to illustrate the fundamental attribution error: College #1 and College #2 are similar in admission standards and most other ways, but College #1 has had much grade inflation. The average GPA at College #1 is 3.6, compared to 2.7 at College #2. If you were on a graduate admissions committee, would you favor a student from College #1 with a GPA of 3.6, or one from College #2 with a GPA of 2.7? Most people pick that first student, overlooking the powerful influence of the situation (Moore, Swift, Sharek, & Gino, 2010).

concept check

14. How would the fundamental attribution error affect people's attitudes toward actors and actresses who portrayed likable and contemptible characters?

Answer

14. Because of the fundamental attribution error, people would tend to think that performers who portray likable characters are themselves likable, and those who play contemptible people probably resemble those characters.

Cultural Differences in Attribution and Related Matters

The fundamental attribution error relates to culture. In general, people of Western cultures make more frequent internal (personality) attributions, whereas people in China and other Asian countries tend to make more external (situational) attributions. How would you explain the behavior of the fish designated with an arrow in this drawing? Most Americans say it is leading the others, whereas many Chinese say the other fish are chasing it (Hong, Morris, Chiu, & Benet-Martinez, 2000). That is, the cultures differ in whether they think the fish controls its own behavior or obeys the influence of the others.

try it ▶ yourself

© Cengage Learning

Richard Nisbett and his colleagues noted other cases in which Asian people tend to focus more on the situation and less on personality than do most people in Western cultures (Nisbett, Peng, Choi, & Norenzayan, 2001). As a result, Asians expect more change and less consistency in people's behavior from one situation to another. They are also more likely to accept contradictions and look for compromises instead of viewing one position as correct and another as incorrect. Here are a few examples:

- When given a description of a conflict, such as one between mother and daughter, Chinese students are more likely than Americans to see merit in both arguments (Peng & Nisbett, 1999).
- Far more Chinese than English-language proverbs include apparent self-contradictions, such as "beware of your friends, not your enemies" and "too humble is half proud" (Peng & Nisbett, 1999).
- Chinese people are more likely than Americans to predict that current trends—whatever they might be—will reverse themselves. If life seems to have been getting better lately, most Americans predict that things will continue getting better, whereas Chinese expect them to get worse (Ji, Nisbett, & Su, 2001).

Figure 13.4 On average, Asian cities are more crowded and cluttered than U.S. and European cities.

The reported differences are interesting. Still, an important question remains: To the extent that Asian people respond differently from Western-culture people, is that difference due to ancient traditions or current conditions? Perhaps Asians notice the influence of their environment more just because their environment looks different from that of Western countries. Most Asian cities are more cluttered than American and European cities (Figure 13.4). Researchers found that Japanese students tended to notice the background of photographs more than Americans, who focused heavily on objects in the foreground. However, after Americans viewed a series of pictures of Japanese cities, they too began paying more attention to the backgrounds (Miyamoto, Nisbett, & Masuda, 2006). The question remains whether Asians pay more attention to backgrounds because of the way they build their cities or whether they build their cities that way because of a cultural tendency in their perception and thinking.

Using Attributions to Manage Perceptions of Ourselves

Even if you generally attribute your own behavior largely to external causes, you vary your attributions to try to present yourself in a favorable light. For example, you might credit your good grades to your intelligence and hard work (an internal attribution) but blame your worst grades on unfair tests (an external attribution). *Attributions that we adopt to maximize credit for success and minimize blame for failure* are

called self-serving biases (D. T. Miller & Ross, 1975; van der Pligt & Eiser, 1983). Self-serving biases are robust. Even students who have learned about them usually think the biases apply to other people more than themselves (Pronin, Gilovich, & Ross, 2004). Most Americans rate themselves above average on almost everything. Self-serving biases are, however, less prominent among Asians. One reason is that their culture defines self-worth in terms of fitting into the group rather than outcompeting one's peers (Balcetis, Dunning, & Miller, 2008; Heine & Hamamura, 2007). Another reason is that America today has big disparities between rich and poor, unlike Asian countries, and that income gap tends to foster competition in many aspects of life (Loughnan et al., 2011).

People also protect their images with self-handicapping strategies, in which they *intentionally put themselves at a disadvantage to provide an excuse for failure.* Suppose you fear you will do poorly on a test. You stay out late at a party the night before. Now you can blame your low score on your lack of sleep without admitting that you might have done poorly anyway.

In one study, one group of students worked on solvable problems while others worked on a mixture of solvable and unsolvable problems. (The students did not know that some of the problems were impossible.) The experimenters told all students that they had done well. The students who had been given solvable problems (and solved them) felt good. Those who had worked on unsolvable problems were unsure in what way they had "done well." They had no confidence that they could continue to do well.

Next the experimenters told the participants that the purpose of the experiment was to investigate the effects of drugs on problem solving. Before starting on the next set of problems, each student could choose between taking a drug that supposedly impaired problem-solving abilities and another drug that supposedly improved them. The participants who had worked on unsolvable problems were more likely than the others to choose the drug that supposedly impaired performance. Because they were not sure they could do well anyway, they provided themselves with an excuse (Berglas & Jones, 1978).

15. Who is more likely to make the fundamental attribution error, Americans or Chinese?
16. If instead of watching someone, you close your eyes and imagine yourself in that person's position, will you be more likely to explain the behavior with internal or external attributions? Why?
17. Why would people sometimes intentionally do something likely to harm their own performance?

Answers

15. Americans and others from Western cultures are more likely to make the fundamental attribution error because the Chinese tend to attribute behavior more to situational factors than do Westerners.
16. You will be more likely to give an external attribution because you will become more like an actor and less like an observer.
17. People sometimes do something to harm their own performance, especially if they expected to do poorly anyway.

module 13.2

In Closing

How Social Perceptions Affect Behavior

We are seldom fully aware of the reasons for our own behavior, much less someone else's, but we make our best guesses. If someone you know passes by without saying "hello," you might attribute that person's behavior to absentmindedness, indifference, or hostility. You might attribute someone's friendly response to your own personal charm, the other person's extraverted personality, or that person's devious and manipulative personality. The attributions you make are sure to influence your own social behaviors. And sometimes your attributions about someone tell us more about you than about the other person.

Summary

- *First impressions.* Other things being equal, we pay more attention to the first information we learn about someone than to later information. First impressions form rapidly, and some are more accurate than we might guess. (page 428)
- *Stereotypes and prejudices.* Stereotypes are generalized beliefs about groups of people. A prejudice is an unfavorable stereotype. (page 429)
- *Measuring unconscious prejudice.* The Implicit Association Test finds evidence of subtle prejudice, even among many people who deny having such prejudices. Unconscious prejudices influence behavior, but the strength of that influence is not certain. (page 429)

- *Overcoming prejudice.* Spending time together and working together for a common goal weaken prejudices between groups. (page 430)
- *Enjoying diversity.* A goal of treating everyone the same sometimes backfires by implying that everyone should act the same. A goal of accepting and enjoying the differences among people is generally a better goal. (page 431)
- *Attribution.* Attribution is the set of thought processes by which we assign internal or external causes to behavior. According to Harold Kelley, we are likely to attribute behavior to an internal cause if it is consistent over time, different from most other people's behavior, and directed to-

ward a variety of other people or objects. (page 431)

- *Actor-observer effect.* We are more likely to attribute internal causes to other people's behavior than to our own. (page 432)
- *Fundamental attribution error.* People frequently attribute people's behavior to internal causes, even when they see evidence of external influences. (page 433)
- *Cultural differences.* People in Asian cultures are less likely than those in Western cultures to at-

tribute behavior to consistent personality traits and more likely to attribute it to the situation. (page 433)

- *Self-serving bias and self-handicapping.* People sometimes try to protect their self-esteem by attributing their successes to skill and their failures to outside influences. They sometimes place themselves at a disadvantage to provide an excuse for failure. (page 434)

Key Terms

actor-observer effect (page 432)
attribution (page 431)
consensus information (page 432)
consistency information (page 432)
discrimination (page 429)
distinctiveness (page 432)
external attribution (page 431)
fundamental attribution error (page 433)
Implicit Association Test (IAT) (page 429)

internal attribution (page 431)
multiculturalism (page 431)
prejudice (page 429)
primacy effect (page 428)
self-fulfilling prophecy (page 428)
self-handicapping strategies (page 434)
self-serving biases (page 434)
social perception and cognition (page 428)
stereotypes (page 429)

- What are some effective ways to influence attitudes?

You may have heard people say, "If you want to change people's behavior, you have to change their attitudes first." That sounds reasonable, but let's test it out with these questions: (a) What is your attitude about paying higher taxes? (b) If the government raises taxes, will you pay them?

Most people say their attitude is opposed to higher taxes. However, if the government did raise the taxes, almost everyone would pay them. In this case, it was easier to change behavior than to change attitudes. Also, as we shall see, sometimes changing behavior leads to a change in attitudes. Let's explore the effects attitudes have on behavior, and the influences that change people's attitudes.

Attitudes and Behavior

An attitude is *a like or dislike that influences behavior* (Allport, 1935; Petty & Cacioppo, 1981). Your attitudes include an evaluative or emotional component (how you feel about something), a cognitive component (what you know or believe), and a behavioral component (what you are likely to do). *Persuasion* is an attempt to alter your attitudes or behavior.

Attitude Measurement

Psychologists commonly measure attitudes through attitude scales. On a Likert scale (named after psychologist Rensis Likert), you would check a point along a line from 1, meaning "strongly disagree," to 7, meaning "strongly agree," for each statement, as illustrated in Figure 13.5.

Indicate your level of agreement with the items below, using the following scale:

	Strongly disagree		Neutral			Strongly agree
1. Labor unions are necessary to protect the rights of workers.	1	2	3	4	5	6	7
2. Labor union leaders have too much power.	1	2	3	4	5	6	7
3. If I worked for a company with a union, I would join the union.	1	2	3	4	5	6	7
4. I would never cross a picket line of striking workers.	1	2	3	4	5	6	7
5. Striking workers hurt their company and unfairly raise prices for the consumer.	1	2	3	4	5	6	7
6. Labor unions should not be permitted to engage in political activity.	1	2	3	4	5	6	7
7. America is a better place for today's workers because of the efforts by labor unions in the past.	1	2	3	4	5	6	7

Note: Items 2, 5, and 6 are scored the opposite of 1, 3, 4, and 7.

© Cengage Learning

Figure 13.5 This Likert scale assesses attitudes toward labor unions.

People's reported attitudes do not always match their behaviors. Many people say one thing and do another with regard to cigarettes, alcohol, safe sex, wearing seat belts in a car, and studying hard for tests. Your attitudes are most likely to match your behavior if you have much personal experience with the topic (Glasman & Albarracín, 2006). For example, if you have had extensive experience dealing with mental patients, then you know how you react to them, and you state your attitude accordingly. Someone with less experience states only a hypothetical attitude, which is less certain.

concept check

18. Suppose someone expresses a positive attitude on a Likert scale but you suspect the person really has a negative attitude. Which method from an earlier module of this chapter might confirm your suspicion?

Answer

18. The Implicit Association Test measures attitudes that don't match what people say.

Cognitive Dissonance and Attitude Change

Much research asks whether people's attitudes change their behavior. The theory of cognitive dissonance reverses the direction: It holds that a change in people's behavior alters their attitudes (Festinger, 1957). Cognitive dissonance is *a state of unpleasant tension that people experience when they hold contradictory attitudes or when their behavior contradicts their stated attitudes, especially if the inconsistency distresses them.*

Suppose you pride yourself on honesty but find yourself saying something you do not believe. You feel tension that you can reduce in three ways: You can change what you are saying to match your attitudes, change your attitude to match what you are saying, or

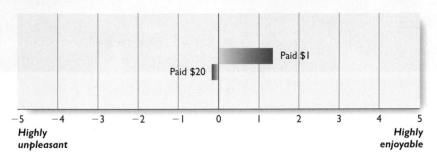

-5 -4 -3 -2 -1 0 1 2 3 4 5
Highly unpleasant   *Highly enjoyable*

Figure 13.6 Participants were paid either $1 or $20 for telling another subject that they enjoyed an experiment (which was actually boring). Later, they were asked for their real opinions. Participants who were paid the smaller amount said that they enjoyed the study. (Based on data from Festinger & Carlsmith, 1959.)

find an explanation that justifies your behavior under the circumstances (Wicklund & Brehm, 1976). Most research focuses on how cognitive dissonance changes people's attitudes.

Imagine yourself as a participant in this classic experiment on cognitive dissonance (Festinger & Carlsmith, 1959). The experimenters say they are studying motor behavior. They show you a board full of pegs. Your task is to take each peg out of the board, rotate it one fourth of a turn, and return it to the board. When you finish all the pegs, you start over, rotating all the pegs again as quickly and accurately as possible for an hour. As you proceed, an experimenter silently takes notes. You find the task immensely tedious. In fact, the researchers chose this task because it was so boring.

At the end of the hour, the experimenter thanks you for participating and "explains" (falsely) that the study's purpose is to determine whether people's performance depends on their attitudes toward the task. You were in the neutral-attitude group, but those in the positive-attitude group are told before they start that they will enjoy the experience.

In fact, the experimenter continues, right now the research assistant is supposed to give that instruction to the next participant, who is waiting in the next room. The experimenter excuses himself to find the research assistant and returns distraught. The assistant is nowhere to be found, he says. He turns to you and asks, "Would you be willing to tell the next participant that you thought this was an interesting, enjoyable experiment? If so, I will pay you." Assume that you consent. After you have told someone that you enjoyed the study, what would you really think of it, assuming the experimenter paid you $1? What if he paid you $20? (This study occurred in the 1950s. In today's money, that $20 would be worth more than $150.)

After you finished describing how much fun the experiment was, you leave and walk down the hall. A representative of the psychology department greets you and explains that the department wants to learn about all the experiments and their educational value.

(The answers to these questions are the real point of the experiment.) Two questions are how much you enjoyed the experiment and whether you would be willing to participate in a similar experiment later.

The students who received $20 said the experiment was boring and they wanted nothing to do with another such experiment. However, contrary to what you might guess, those who received $1 said they enjoyed the experiment and would be willing to participate again (Figure 13.6).

Why did those who were paid less say that they enjoyed the experiment? According to the theory of cognitive dissonance, if you accept $20 to tell a lie, you experience little conflict. You are lying, but you are doing it for $20. However, if you tell a lie for $1, do you want to think you can be bribed so cheaply? You feel cognitive dissonance—unpleasant tension from the conflict between your true attitude and what you had said about the experiment. You reduce your tension by changing your attitude, deciding that the experiment really was interesting after all. ("I learned a lot of interesting things about myself, like . . . uh . . . how good I am at rotating pegs.")

The idea of cognitive dissonance attracted much attention and inspired a great deal of research (Aronson, 1997). Here are two examples:

- An experimenter left a child in a room with toys but forbade the child to play with one particular toy. If the experimenter threatened the child with severe punishment for playing with the toy, the child avoided it but still regarded it as desirable. However, if the experimenter merely said that he or she would be disappointed if the child played with that toy, the child avoided the toy and said (even weeks later) that it was not a good toy (Aronson & Carlsmith, 1963).

- An experimenter asked college students to write an essay defending a position that the experimenter knew, from previous information, contradicted the students' beliefs. For example, college students who favored freer access to alcohol might be asked to write essays on why the college should increase restrictions on alcohol. Those who were told they must write the essays did not change their views significantly, but those who were asked to "please" voluntarily write the essay generally came to agree with what they wrote (Croyle & Cooper, 1983).

The general principle is that, if you entice people to do something by a minimum reward or a tiny threat so that they are acting almost voluntarily, they change their attitudes to support what they are doing. People try to seem consistent. You might be able to use this principle to your advantage: At the start of a job interview, ask why the employer chose to interview you. That question prompts the interviewer to cite something positive about you. Once you get someone to compliment you, that person seeks evidence to support the compliment.

Back to this question: If you want to change people's behavior, do you have to change their attitudes first? The results of cognitive dissonance experiments say quite the opposite: If you change people's behavior first, their attitudes will change, too.

concept check

19. Suppose your parents pay you to get a good grade in a boring course. According to cognitive dissonance theory, are you more likely to develop a positive attitude toward your studies if your parents pay you $10 or $100?

Answer

19. You will come to like your studies more if you are paid $10. If you are paid only $10, you won't be able to tell yourself that you are studying harder only for the money. Instead, you will tell yourself that you must be really interested.

Central and Peripheral Routes of Attitude Change and Persuasion

Some of our attitudes come from careful examination of the evidence, and some have only a superficial basis. Richard Petty and John Cacioppo (1981, 1986) proposed this distinction: *When people take a decision seriously, they invest the necessary time and effort to evaluate the evidence and logic behind each message.* This logical approach, the central route to persuasion, is generally most successful with people who are intelligent enough and motivated enough to evaluate the evidence. In contrast, *when people listen to a message on a topic they consider unimportant, they attend to more superficial factors* such as the speaker's appearance and reputation or the sheer length of someone's speech. This peripheral route to persuasion also influences people who are too tired or distracted to pay careful attention to the argument (Petty & Briñol, 2008). Note the similarity to a distinction from chapter 8: The peripheral route, like System 1, gives a quick, effortless response. The central route, like System 2, devotes enough energy to consider a response carefully.

Suppose someone is trying to convince you that it would be a good idea to institute a special comprehensive examination for all graduating seniors at some other college. The speaker repeats the same weak argument several times and persuades you. However, if you thought it was a proposed requirement at *your* college, you would listen carefully and evaluate the logic more accurately (Moons, Mackie, & Garcia-Marques, 2009).

concept check

20. You listen to a discussion about the best kinds of seafood for people to eat. Later, you hear a discussion about the best kind of cat food. You don't have a cat. In which case will you follow the central route to persuasion?

Answer

20. You will pay more attention to the evidence and logic, following the central route to persuasion, for the discussion about what seafood is best for people to eat.

Special Techniques of Persuasion

Many people will try to persuade you to buy something, contribute to a cause, or do something else that may or may not be in your best interests. Robert Cialdini (1993) has described many techniques in the category of peripheral routes to persuasion. Let's consider a few. The goal here is not to teach you how to persuade others but to help you recognize and resist certain kinds of manipulation.

Liking and Similarity

People persuade you more easily if you like them or see them as similar to yourself. Suppose someone you don't know calls and immediately asks, "How are you today?" You reply, "Okay." The reply: "Oh, I'm so glad to hear that!" Is this caller, who doesn't even know you, really delighted that you are "okay"? Or is this an attempt to seem friendly so that you will buy something? Salespeople, politicians, and others also try to emphasize the ways in which they are similar to you. For example, "I grew up in a small town, much like this one."

To illustrate the influence of similarity, students were asked to read a very unflattering description of Grigory Rasputin, the "mad monk of Russia," and

Grigory Rasputin's unsavory influence on the czar of Russia led to the Communist revolution. However, people who are told Rasputin resembled them, even in trivial ways, soften their criticisms.

then rate Rasputin on several scales. All students read the same description except for Rasputin's birth date: In some cases, Rasputin's birth date had been changed to match the student's own birth date. Students who thought Rasputin had the same birth date as their own were more likely than others to rate him as "strong" and "effective" (Finch & Cialdini, 1989).

Social Norms

We'll consider conformity in more detail later in this chapter, but you already know the idea: People tend to do what others are doing. A powerful influence technique is to show that many other people are doing something. A bartender or singer with a tip jar ordinarily puts a few dollars in at the start to imply that other people have already left tips. A politician publishes photographs showing crowds of enthusiastic supporters. However, if you know that most people do not do something—for example, most people do not undergo a cancer-screening test—you become less likely to do it yourself (Sieverding, Decker, & Zimmermann, 2010).

Many hotels try to influence guests to agree to use towels more than once instead of expecting daily replacements. A typical message in the room points out that reusing towels saves energy, reduces the use of detergents that pollute the water supply, and helps protect the environment. More guests agree to reuse their towels if the message adds that most other guests have agreed to reuse their towels. It works even better to say that most other guests using *this room* have agreed (N. J. Goldstein, Cialdini, & Griskevicius, 2008). You conform to people similar to yourself. Here, appealing to people's desire to save the environment is an example of the central route to persuasion, and asking people to conform to others is the peripheral route.

concept check

21. A salesperson calls at your door and says that several of your neighbors (whom the salesperson names) have bought the product and recommended you as another possible customer. What techniques of persuasion is this salesperson using?

Answer

21. The salesperson is relying on an endorsement by a group that you presumably like and trust. Also, you are likely to be persuaded by people similar to yourself.

Reciprocation

Civilization is based on the concept of reciprocation: If you do me a favor, then I owe you one. However, it is possible to abuse this principle. Many companies hand out free samples, confident that many people who accept the samples will feel obligated to buy something in return.

Here's another version of reciprocation: An alumni organization once called me asking for a contribution. Their representative said that many other alumni were pledging $1,000, and he hoped he could count on me for the same. No, I explained, I wasn't prepared to make that kind of contribution. Oh, he responded, with a tone that implied "too bad you don't have a *good* job like the other alumni." He then said that if I couldn't afford $1,000, how about $500? The suggestion was that we should compromise! He was giving in $500 from his original proposal, so I should give in $500 from my end.

Contrast Effects

An offer can seem good or bad, depending on how it compares to something else. A restaurant menu might list one entrée at such a high price that almost no one orders it. However, sales increase for the second most expensive item, which now seems not too expensive by contrast. A realtor might start by showing you several overpriced houses in bad condition, before showing a nicer house at a more reasonable price. If you had seen that house first, you might not have been impressed, but by contrast it seems like a good deal. Almost anything can seem good by contrast to something worse. (How do politicians use this approach?)

Foot in the Door

Sometimes, someone *starts with a modest request, which you accept, and follows with a larger request.* This procedure is called the foot-in-the-door technique. When Jonathan Freedman and Scott Fraser (1966) asked suburban residents in Palo Alto, California, to put a small "Drive Safely" sign in their windows, most agreed to do so. A couple of weeks later, other researchers asked the same residents to let them set up a large "Drive Safely" billboard in their front yards for 10 days. They also made the request to residents who had not been approached by the first researchers. Of those who had already agreed to display the small sign, 76% agreed to the billboard. Only 17% of the others agreed. Those who agreed to the first request felt they were already committed to the cause, and to be consistent, they agreed to further participation. Another study found that people who agreed to fill out a 20-minute survey became more willing a month later to take a 40-minute survey on the same topic. However, although this tendency was strong for Americans, it was weak for Chinese students. An interpretation was that Chinese culture puts less emphasis on the individual, including less emphasis on individual consistency from one time to another (Petrova, Cialdini, & Sills, 2006).

Bait and Switch

Someone using the bait-and-switch technique *first offers an extremely favorable deal, gets the other person to commit to the deal, and then makes additional demands.* Alternatively, the person might offer a product at a low price to get customers to the store but then claim to be out of the product and try to sell something else. A car dealer might offer you an exceptionally good price on a new car and a generous price for the trade-in of your old car. The deal seems too good to resist. After you have committed yourself to buying, the dealer checks with the boss and returns, saying, "I'm so sorry. I forgot that this car has some special features that raise the value. If we sold it for the price I quoted, we'd lose money." So you agree to a higher price. Then the company's used car specialist looks at your old car and "corrects" the trade-in value to a lower amount. Still, you have committed yourself. You leave with a deal that you would not have accepted at the start.

That's Not All!

In the that's-not-all technique, *someone makes an offer and then improves the offer before you have a chance to reply.* The television announcer says, "Here's your chance to buy this amazing combination paper shredder and coffeemaker for only $39.95. But wait, there's more! We'll throw in a can of dog deodorant! Also this handy windshield wiper cleaner and a solar-powered flashlight and a subscription to *Modern Lobotomist*! If you call now, you get this amazing offer, which usually costs $39.95, for only $19.95! Call now!" People who hear the first offer and then the "improved" offer are more likely to comply than are people who hear the "improved" offer from the start (Burger, 1986).

You may notice a similarity among the foot-in-the-door, bait-and-switch, and that's-not-all techniques: The persuader starts with one proposal and then switches to another. The first proposal changes the listener's state of mind, making him or her more open to the second proposal.

concept check

22. Identify each of the following as an example of reciprocation, the contrast effect, foot-in-the-door technique, the bait-and-switch technique, or the that's-not-all technique.
    a. A credit card company offers you a card with a low introductory rate. After a few months, the interest rate on your balance doubles.
    b. A store marks its prices "25% off," scratches that out and marks them "50% off!"
    c. A friend asks you to help carry some supplies over to the elementary school for an afternoon tutoring program. When you get there, the principal says that one of the tutors is late and asks whether you could take her place until she arrives. You agree and spend the rest of the afternoon tutoring. The principal then talks you into coming back every week as a tutor.

Answer

22. a. bait-and-switch technique; b. either the contrast effect or the that's-not-all technique; c. foot-in-the-door technique.

Fear Messages

Some attempts at persuasion use threats, such as, "If you don't send money to support our cause, our political opponents will gain power and do terrible things." One organization appealed for contributions with a message on the envelope, "Every day an estimated 800 dolphins, porpoises, and whales will die . . . unless you act now!" How effective are fear messages as persuasion?

Fear messages can be effective, but only if they are believable. Do you really believe one person's contribution will save 800 dolphins, porpoises, and whales per day? An extremely frightening message is ineffective for two reasons. First, it is hard to convince people of something that sounds extreme (Wood, Perunovic, & Lee, 2009). Second, people resist a message that is too frightening. If people hear about moderate dangers from global climate change, they listen. If they hear warnings about total disaster, then they don't want to believe climate change is a problem at all (Feinberg & Willer, 2011).

Also, a fear message is effective only if people can easily take effective actions. An extreme fear message carries the unintended implication, "The problem is hopeless" (Cialdini, 2003). Messages about global warming don't motivate many people to conserve energy, because most people doubt that their behavior will make a difference.

Delayed Influence

Some messages have little influence at first but more later. Let's consider two examples.

The Sleeper Effect

Suppose you hear an idea from someone with poor qualifications. Because of what you think of the speaker, you reject the idea. Weeks later, you forget where you heard the idea (*source amnesia*) and remember only the idea itself. At that point, its persuasive impact may increase (Kumkale & Abarracín, 2004). If you completely forget the source, you might even claim it as your own idea! Psychologists use the term sleeper effect to describe *delayed persuasion by an initially rejected message.*

Minority Influence

Delayed influence also occurs when a minority group proposes a worthwhile idea. It could be an ethnic, religious, political, or any other kind of minority. The majority rejects the idea at first but reconsiders it later. If the minority continually repeats a single simple message and its members seem united, it has a good chance of eventually influencing the decision. The minority's influence often increases gradually, even if the majority hesitates to admit that the minority has swayed them (Wood, Lundgren, Ouellette, Busceme, & Blackstone, 1994). By expressing its views and demonstrating the possibility of disagreeing with the majority, the minority also prompts others to offer new ideas (Nemeth, 1986). Suppose you disagree with what everyone else is saying, but you hesitate to speak out. Then someone voices an objection different from what you meant to say, and you feel more comfortable expressing your own idea.

One powerful example of minority influence is that of the Socialist Party of the United States, which ran candidates for elective offices from 1900 through the 1950s. The party never received more than 6% of the vote in any presidential election. No Socialist candidate was elected senator or governor, and only a few were elected to the House of Representatives (Shannon, 1955). Beginning in the 1930s, the party's support dwindled, until eventually it stopped nominating candidates. Had they failed? No! Most of their major proposals had been enacted into law (Table 13.1). Of course, the Democrats and Republicans who voted for these changes claimed credit for the ideas.

Table 13.1 Political Proposals of the U.S. Socialist Party, Around 1900

Proposal	Eventual Fate of Proposal
Women's right to vote	Established by 19th Amendment to U.S. Constitution; ratified in 1920
Old-age pensions	Included in the Social Security Act of 1935
Unemployment insurance	Included in the Social Security Act of 1935; also guaranteed by other state and federal legislation
Health and accident insurance	Included in part in the Social Security Act of 1935 and in the Medicare Act of 1965
Increased wages, including minimum wage	First minimum-wage law passed in 1938; periodically updated since then
Reduction of working hours	Maximum 40-hour workweek (with exceptions) established by the Fair Labor Standards Act of 1938
Public ownership of electric, gas, and other utilities and of the means of transportation and communication	Utilities not owned by government but heavily regulated by federal and state government since the 1930s
Initiative, referendum, and recall (mechanisms for private citizens to push for changes in legislation and for removal of elected officials)	Adopted by most state governments

Sources: Foster, 1968; and Leuchtenburg, 1963

concept check

23. At a meeting of your student government, you suggest a new method of testing and grading students. The other members immediately reject your plan. Should you give up?

Answer

23. The fact that your idea was rejected does not mean that you should give up. If you and a few allies continue to present this plan, showing apparent agreement among yourselves, the majority may eventually adopt a similar plan—probably without giving you credit for it.

Differences in Resistance to Persuasion

You may be more easily influenced at some times than at others. *Simply informing people that they are about to hear a persuasive speech activates their resistance and weakens the persuasion* (Petty & Cacioppo, 1977). This tendency is called the fore-warning effect. Actually, the results are somewhat complex. Suppose you have a strongly unfavorable attitude toward something—increased tuition at your college, for example. Now someone tells you that a well-informed person is going to try to persuade you in favor of higher tuition. At once, before the speech even begins, your attitudes shift slightly in the direction of favoring higher tuition! Exactly why is unclear, but perhaps you are telling yourself, "I guess there must be some good reason for that opinion." Then when you hear the speech itself, it does have some influence, and your attitudes shift still further, but not as much as those of someone who had not been forewarned. The warning alerts you to resist the persuasion, to criticize weak arguments, and to reject weak evidence (Wood & Quinn, 2003).

In the closely related inoculation effect, *people first hear a weak argument and then a stronger argument supporting the same conclusion.* After they have rejected the first argument, they usually reject the second one also. So if you want to convince someone, start with your strong evidence.

concept check

24. If you want your children to preserve the beliefs and attitudes you try to teach them, should you give them only arguments that support those beliefs or should you also expose them to attacks on those beliefs? Why?

Answer

24. You should expose them to weak attacks on their beliefs so that they will learn how to resist such attacks.

Coercive Persuasion

Finally, let's consider the most unfriendly kinds of persuasion. In some places, military or police interrogators have used torture (which they prefer to call "enhanced interrogation techniques") until suspects confessed or revealed information about subversive plots. If you were innocent, might you confess anyway and make up some plausible story about a plot, just to end the torture? Most people underestimate how painful torture can be (Nordgren, McDonnell, & Loewenstein, 2011). Any technique strong enough to get guilty people to confess gets innocent people to confess also.

Similar problems occur with what we might call "psychological torture." Suppose the police want you to confess to some crime. You agree to talk with them. After all, what do you have to lose? You're innocent, so you have nothing to hide. First the police claim your crime is horrendous and you face a stiff sentence. Then they offer sympathy and excuses, implying that if you confess, you can get a much lighter sentence. They claim to have solid evidence of your guilt anyway, so you may as well confess, because they can convict you even if you don't. They tell you that you failed a polygraph test. You stay in isolation, without food or sleep for many hours, with no promise of when, if ever, this ordeal will end. Apparently, confession is the only way you can get them to stop badgering you. Might you confess, even though you are innocent? You think, "Oh, well, eventually they will realize their mistake. They can't really convict me, because they won't have any other evidence."

Many innocent people do confess under these conditions. Unfortunately, juries consider a confession extremely strong evidence, even if they know it was coerced (Kassin & Gudjonsson, 2004). To test the effects of coercive persuasion, researchers set up this experiment: They asked pairs of students to work independently on logic problems. For half of the pairs, one of them (a confederate of the experimenter) asked for help, which the first person usually gave. Later, they were told that offering help was considered cheating. For the other pairs, the confederate did not ask for help and therefore no cheating occurred. After both completed the problems, the experimenter entered the room, accused the par-ticipant of cheating, and threatened to treat this event as harshly as any other case of academic cheating. However, the experimenter suggested they could settle the problem quickly if the student signed a confession. Under these circumstances, 87% of the guilty students and 43% of the innocent ones agreed to confess, as illustrated in Figure 13.7 (Russano, Meissner, Narchet, & Kassin, 2005). The message is that coercive techniques increase confessions by both guilty and innocent people, and therefore make the confessions unreliable evidence.

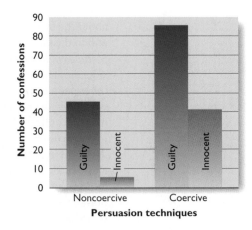

Figure 13.7 Coercive persuasion techniques increased the number of confessions by both guilty and innocent people. (Based on data of Russano, Meissner, Narchet, & Kassin, 2005.)

module 13.3 >

In Closing

Persuasion and Manipulation

Broadly defined, attitudes influence almost everything we do. When you form an attitude about something of little consequence, it is understandable that you follow the peripheral route, paying little attention to the complexities of the evidence. When you deal with important matters, however, you usually follow the central route, examining the facts as carefully as you can. It is important to be alert to some of the influences that might throw you off course. Advertisers, politicians, and others try to polish their techniques of persuasion, and not everyone has your best interest at heart.

Summary

- *Attitudes.* An attitude is a like or dislike that influences behavior. (page 437)
- *Cognitive dissonance.* Cognitive dissonance is a state of unpleasant tension that arises from contradictory attitudes or from a behavior that conflicts with an attitude. When people's behavior does not match their attitudes, they try to eliminate the inconsistency by changing their behavior or their attitudes. (page 437)
- *Two routes to persuasion.* When people consider a topic of little importance to them, they are easily persuaded by the speaker's appearance and other superficial factors. When people care about the topic, they pay more attention to logic and to the quality of the evidence. (page 439)
- *Methods of influence.* Someone you like or consider similar to yourself is more persuasive than other people are. Being told that most people favor some idea or action makes it appealing. You may feel obligated to perform a favor for someone who did a favor for you or gave you something. An item may appear more desirable because of its contrast to something else. In the foot-in-the-door, bait-and-switch, and that's-not-all techniques, a first request makes people more likely to accept a second request. (page 439)
- *Influence of fear.* Messages that appeal to fear are effective if people perceive the danger as real and think they can do something about it. (page 441)
- *Sleeper effect.* When people reject a message because of their low regard for the person who proposed it, they sometimes forget where they heard the idea and later come to accept it. (page 441)
- *Minority influence.* Although a minority may have little influence at first, it can, through persistent repetition of its message, eventually persuade the majority to adopt its position or consider other ideas. (page 441)
- *Forewarning and inoculation effects.* If people have been warned that someone will try to persuade them of something or if they have previously heard a weak version of the persuasive argument, they tend to resist the argument. (page 442)
- *Coercive persuasion.* Techniques designed to pressure a suspect into confessing decrease the reliability of the confession because, under these circumstances, many innocent people confess also. (page 443)

Key Terms

attitude (page 437)

bait-and-switch technique (page 440)

central route to persuasion (page 439)

cognitive dissonance (page 437)

foot-in-the-door technique (page 440)

forewarning effect (page 422)

inoculation effect (page 422)

peripheral route to persuasion (page 439)

sleeper effect (page 441)

that's-not-all technique (page 441)

Interpersonal Attraction

- How do we choose our partners?
- Why do some marriages succeed and others fail?

William Proxmire, a former U.S. senator, used to give Golden Fleece Awards to those who, in his opinion, most flagrantly wasted the taxpayers' money. He once bestowed an award on psychologists who had received a federal grant to study how people fall in love. According to Proxmire, the research was pointless because people do not want to understand love. They prefer, he said, to let such matters remain a mystery.

This module presents the information Senator Proxmire thought you didn't want to know.

Establishing Relationships

Of all the people you meet, how do you choose those who become your friends or romantic attachments? How do they choose you?

Proximity and Familiarity

Proximity means *closeness.* (It comes from the same root as *approximate.*) Not surprisingly, *we are most likely to become friends with people who live or work in proximity to us.* One professor assigned students to seats randomly and followed up on them a year later. Students most often became friends with those who sat in adjacent seats (Back, Schmulkle, & Egloff, 2008). One reason proximity is important is that people who live nearby discover what they have in common. Another reason is the mere exposure effect, the principle that *the more often we come in contact with someone or something, the more we tend to like that person or object* (Saegert, Swap, & Zajonc, 1973; Zajonc, 1968).

However, familiarity does not always increase liking. Researchers contacted people who were about to go on a date arranged by an online dating service. Prior to the date, most people gave moderately high ratings on how much they expected to like the person they were about to date. After the date, more ratings went down than up (Norton, Frost, & Ariely, 2007). Becoming familiar with someone gives you a chance to find out what you have in common, but it also lets you see the other person's flaws.

Physical Attractiveness

What characteristics do you look for in a potential romantic partner? Most people have many of the same preferences regardless of whether they are male or female, homosexual or heterosexual (Holmberg & Blair, 2009). People look for intelligence, honesty, a sense of humor, and of course, physical attractiveness.

In a study long ago, psychologists arranged blind dates for 332 freshman couples for a dance before the start of classes. They asked participants to fill out questionnaires, and then ignored the questionnaires and paired students at random. Midway through the dance, the experimenters separated the men and

women and asked them to rate how much they liked their dates. The only factor that influenced the ratings was physical attractiveness (Walster, Aronson, Abrahams, & Rottman, 1966). Similarities of attitudes, personality, and intelligence counted for almost nothing. Surprising? Hardly. During the brief time they had spent together, the couples had little opportunity to learn much about each other. Intelligence, honesty, and other character values are critical for a lasting relationship but not for the first hour of the first date (Keller, Thiessen, & Young, 1996).

Later studies examined speed-dating situations, in which people briefly met 10 to 25 other people and then reported which potential partners they might like to meet for a more extended date. For both men and women, physical attractiveness was by far the main influence on their choices (Finkel & Eastwick, 2008).

Possible Biological Value of Attractiveness: Birds

Why do we care about physical appearance? Its importance is so much a given that we rarely think about this question. Humans are not the only creatures that care about attractiveness. For a moment let's consider other species.

In many bird species, early in the mating season, females shop around and choose a brilliantly colored male that sings vigorously from the treetops. In several species, females also prefer males with especially long tails (Figure 13.8). From an evolutionary standpoint, aren't these foolish choices? The popular males are those that risk their lives by singing loudly from the treetops, where they call the attention of predators such as hawks and eagles. They waste energy by growing bright feathers. (It takes more energy to produce bright than dull colors.) A long tail may look pretty, but it interferes with flying. Why does the female prefer a mate who wastes energy and endangers his life?

Biologists eventually decided that wasting energy and risking life were precisely the point (Zahavi & Zahavi, 1997). Only a healthy, vigorous male has enough energy to make bright, colorful feathers (Blount, Metcalfe, Birkhead, & Surai, 2003; Faivre, Grégoire, Préault, Cézilly, & Sorci, 2003). Only a strong male can fly despite a long tail, and only a strong male would risk predation by singing from an

Figure 13.8 In some bird species, males with long tails attract more mates. Only a healthy male can afford this trait that impairs his flying ability.

exposed perch. A colorful, singing male is showing off his health, and (perhaps) his good genes. The female presumably does not understand why she is attracted to colorful loudmouths. She just is, because throughout her evolutionary history, most females who chose such partners reproduced more successfully than those who chose dull-colored, quiet, inactive males.

Possible Biological Value of Attractiveness: Humans

Are attractive people more likely than others to be healthy and fertile? Theoretically, they should be. Certainly, many illnesses decrease people's attractiveness. Also, *good-looking* generally means *normal*, and normal appearance probably indicates good genes. Suppose a computer takes photographs of many people and averages their faces. The resulting composite face has about an average nose, average distance between the eyes, and so forth, and most people rate this face "highly attractive"

(Langlois & Roggman, 1990; Langlois, Roggman, & Musselman, 1994; Rhodes, Sumich, & Byatt, 1999; Figure 13.9). That is, a highly attractive person has average features and few irregularities—no crooked teeth, skin blemishes, or asymmetries, and no facial hair on women (Fink & Penton-Voak, 2002). A good smile also increases a woman's attractiveness, although it doesn't work as well for men (Tracy & Beall, 2011).

Why is normal attractive? First, normal implies healthy. Presumably, the genes for an average face spread in the population because of their link to success. Any face far different from the average might indicate an undesirable mutation. Second, we like anything that is familiar. If you have recently seen many faces that are thinner than usual, fatter than usual, or in some other way distorted, your judgment of "attractive" is shifted slightly in the direction of the faces you have just seen (Rhodes, Jeffery, Watson, Clifford, & Nakayama, 2003).

Do attractive people tend to be healthier than others? Researchers obtained photos of hundreds of teenagers from long ago. They asked other people to rate the faces for attractiveness, and then correlated the results with outcomes of health and survival. The results varied among several studies, but overall it appears that attractive people have a slight advantage in health (Henderson & Anglin, 2003; Jokela, 2009; Kalick, Zebrowitz, Langlois, & Johnson, 1998; Weeden & Sabini, 2005). The advantage may have been greater in earlier times when medical care was less effective and less readily available. Still, even if appearance is only a weak indicator of health and good genes, it is better than no information at all. We see how a preference for good appearance might have evolved.

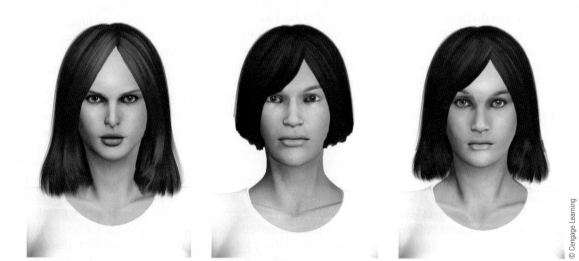

Figure 13.9 Averaging or morphing many faces produces a generalized face that most people consider attractive. In this example, the first two faces were morphed to produce the one on the right.

Would you consider a face similar to your own to be especially attractive? It depends. Suppose we take a photograph of someone's face and let a computer morph it to look somewhat more like your face. If it was the face of someone of your own sex, you will probably regard this face as better looking than the original. If the face was someone of the opposite sex (and you are heterosexual), you will regard the morphed face as trustworthy and likeable, but not sexually attractive (DeBruine, 2004, 2005). That is, you like to associate with someone who looks like you, but you don't want to mate with such a person. Presumably the advantage is to decrease inbreeding.

concept check

25. According to evolutionary theory, attractiveness is a sign of good health. Why would it be difficult for an unhealthy individual to produce "counterfeit" attractiveness?
26. According to evolutionary theory, a face with average features is attractive. Why?

Answers

26. Average features must have been successful for our ancestors for the genes to spread in the population. Therefore, average features are a sign of probable health.

25. Attractive features such as bright feathers in a bird or large muscles in a man require much energy. It would be difficult for an unhealthy individual to devote enough energy to produce such features.

Even when friends differ in some ways, they generally have much in common, such as interests, attitudes, and level of education.

Similarity

The saying "opposites attract" is true for magnets. It doesn't apply to people. Most romantic partners and close friends resemble each other in age, physical attractiveness, political and religious beliefs, intelligence, education, and attitudes (Eastwick, Finkel, Mochon, & Ariely, 2007; Laumann, 1969; L. Lee, Loewenstein, Ariely, Hony, & Young, 2008; Montoya, 2008; Rushton & Bons, 2005). As a relationship matures, people's interests become more and more alike (Anderson, Keltner, & John, 2003). Couples with much in common enjoy the relationship more because they share many activities and agree more often than disagree. The only known point on which similarity doesn't help is smell: Many women (unconsciously) prefer a romantic partner who does not smell too much like herself, her brothers, and other members of her family. That tendency is presumably a way to decrease the chance of mating with a close relative. Curiously, women taking birth-control pills fail to show this tendency (Roberts, Gosling, Carter, & Petrie, 2008).

Members of minority groups face special difficulties. If your ethnic or religious group is greatly outnumbered where you live, your choice of potential friends or romantic partners may be limited to members of your group who do not share your interests or members of other groups who do (Hamm, 2000).

The Equity Principle

According to exchange or equity theories, *social relationships are transactions in which partners exchange goods and services.* As in business, a relationship is most stable if both partners believe the deal is fair. It is easiest to establish a fair deal if the partners are about equally attractive and intelligent, contribute about equally to the finances and the chores, and so forth. For most couples, one partner contributes more in one way, and the other contributes more in another way.

The equity principle applies readily in the early stages of friendships or romances but less so later. You might nurse your spouse or lifelong friend through a long illness without worrying about whether you are still getting a fair deal.

concept check

27. Someone your own age from another country moves next door. Neither of you speaks the other's language. What factors will tend to strengthen the likelihood of your becoming friends? What factors will tend to weaken it?

Answer

27. Proximity and familiarity will strengthen the likelihood of your becoming friends. The similarity principle will weaken it. Because of the difference in languages, you will have little chance to discover similarities in interests or attitudes. In fact, proximity will probably not be as potent a force as usual because it serves largely as a means of enabling people to discover what they have in common.

Dating and Modern Technology

The Internet has added a new dimension to dating. Internet dating services introduce couples who never would have met otherwise. A potential couple can learn each other's background and evaluate what they have in common before deciding whether to meet on a real date. The system is not perfect. Despite all the information available through dating websites, most people, both men and women, react more strongly to the attractiveness of the photographs than to anything else (Sritharan, Heilpern, Wilbur, & Gawronski, 2010). Still, these dating services help many people find good matches (Mahfouz, Philaretou, & Theocharous, 2008).

Analysis of online postings reveals much about men's and women's desires. A study including 14 countries found that men always prefer younger women, whereas women prefer men their own age or older (Dunn, Brinton, & Clark, 2010). One reason is that in general, older men have more money and resources. In countries where women have jobs and resources of their own, the man's wealth becomes less important, and women prefer a partner close to their own age (Moore, Cassidy, & Perret, 2010).

Some people also have Internet contacts with no intention of meeting face to face. They establish an online character (who may or may not look like the real person) who interacts with someone else's online character, sometimes even having on-screen sex. Most people who have this kind of relationship rate their real-life relationships as not very close (Scott, Mottarella, & Lavooy, 2006). Perhaps people who have trouble in their face-to-face relationships turn to online relationships as a substitute. Another possibility is that the online relationships cause their real-life relationships to suffer.

In a mature, lasting relationship, a couple can count on each other for care and affection through both good times and bad times.

Marriage and Long-Term Commitments

Most people hope to have a long-term loving relationship. Although the available research deals mainly with heterosexual marriages, the conclusions probably apply to other types of long-term commitments as well.

Is it possible to predict which marriages will succeed and which will not? To some extent, yes. Psychologists have studied newlywed couples and compared the results to how the marriages developed later. Couples whose arguments escalate to greater and greater anger are likely to consider divorce later. Many people have been told that it is good to express their feelings fully. However, venting anger at your partner makes both of you feel bad. If your partner retaliates by screaming at you, nothing good will come of it (Fincham, 2003). If you have a complaint against your partner—an annoying habit, for example—it is best to state it politely, not angrily. Another bad sign for any couple is a display of contempt, such as rolling the eyes (Gottman, Coan, Carrere, & Swanson, 1998; Gottman & Levenson, 2000; Huston, Niehuis, & Smith, 2001).

However, the goal is not just to avoid divorce, but also to experience satisfaction in the marriage. The best predictor of long-term satisfaction is much display of genuine affection between the newlyweds (Graber, Laurenceau, Miga, Chango, & Coan, 2011). That is, positive expressions are important. If your partner cheers you up when things are going badly, that's good, but often a better sign of affection is if your partner feels genuine pleasure at your successes.

Apparently, other subtle cues, hard to quantify, also distinguish successful from less successful marriages. In one fascinating study, people watched 3-minute videotaped conversations between married couples and estimated how satisfied each couple was. Their estimates were then compared to reports by the couples themselves. People who reported that their own marriages were either highly satisfying or highly unsatisfying were the best at judging the quality of other couples' marriages. Marriage counselors and marriage researchers lagged behind, as did unmarried people (Ebling & Levenson, 2003).

When you hear about how many marriages end in divorce, it is easy to despair, but many marriages remain strong for a lifetime. A romantic relationship changes over the years, just as individual lives do. Dating couples and newlyweds feel the intense excitement of learning about each other and doing new things together. The mere sight of the other person brings a rush of excitement (Bartels & Zeki, 2000;

Kim & Hatfield, 2004). *Sexual desire, romance, and friendship increase in parallel* during the stage called passionate love (Diamond, 2004; Hatfield & Rapson, 1993). As time passes, the relationship develops into companionate love, *marked by sharing, care, and protection* (Gonzaga, Turner, Keltner, Campos, & Altemus, 2006; Hatfield & Rapson, 1993). The couple feels more confident and secure in their relationship. The passion may remain, but it is no longer the main bond holding the couple together. Generally, people with strong companionate love have high satisfaction with life (Kim & Hatfield, 2004).

28. If you have a troubled relationship with a boyfriend or girlfriend, will you have a good chance of working out your problems after you get married?

Answer

28. No. Intense arguments or displays of contempt are strong predictors of a failed marriage.

module 13.4

In Closing

Choosing Your Partners Carefully

Life is like a roller-coaster ride in the dark: It has lots of ups and downs, and you never know what is going to happen next. You want to ride with someone you like and trust. Many people choose their partners poorly. In some regards, forming impressions of romantic partners is especially difficult. A person you date is trying to make a good impression, and you *hope* to like the person. As the relationship progresses, another factor kicks in: Remember from the section on persuasion that anyone you like tends to be highly persuasive. In short, it is easy to form an attachment and later regret it.

Summary

- *Forming relationships.* People generally choose friends and romantic partners who live near them. In the early stage of romantic attraction, physical appearance is the key factor, but similarity of interests and goals becomes more serious later. Relationships are most likely to thrive if each person believes that he or she is getting about as good a deal as the other person is. (page 445)
- *Physical attractiveness.* Theoretically, physical attractiveness should be a cue to someone's health and therefore desirability as a mate.

Someone with approximately average features is attractive, presumably because average features have been associated with successful breeding in the past. (page 445)
- *Marriage.* Marriage and similar relationships often break up because of problems that were present from the start. (page 448)
- *Romantic love.* The early stages of a romantic relationship are marked by passionate love. Later, the relationship develops into companionate love. (page 448)

Key Terms

companionate love (page 449)
exchange (or equity) theories (page 447)
mere exposure effect (page 445)

passionate love (page 449)
proximity (page 445)

module 13.5

Interpersonal Influence

- How are we influenced by other people's actions or inactions?

People influence us constantly. First, they provide us with *information* (or misinformation). For example, if you approach a building and find crowds quickly fleeing from it, they probably know something you don't. Second, people set *norms* that define the expectations of a situation. If you find yourself in a clean, well-kept neighborhood, you do your part to keep things clean. In a neighborhood where graffiti cover the walls, you feel less restraint against littering (Keizer, Lindenberg, & Steg, 2008). Third, people influence us just by suggesting a possible action. Seeing people yawn makes you feel like yawning, too. Why? They haven't given you any new information, and you don't necessarily wish to resemble them. You copy just because seeing a yawn suggested the possibility. In fact, you may find yourself yawning right now!

Conformity

Conformity means *altering one's behavior to match other people's behavior or expectations.* In many situations, conformity is good. When you are driving, it

People conform to one another in their clothing and other customs.

is helpful if everyone going the same direction drives on the same side of the road. If you are having a discussion, it is helpful if everyone speaks the same language. If you go to a meeting, it is helpful if everyone arrives at about the same time.

Don't underestimate the power of conformity. Koversada, Croatia, used to be an officially nudist town. If a first-time visitor walked around the city wearing clothes, other people stopped and stared, shaking their heads with disapproval. The visitor felt as awkward and self-conscious as a naked person would be in a city of clothed people. Most visitors quickly undressed (Newman, 1988).

If you exclaim, "I wouldn't conform," compare your own clothing right now to what others around you are wearing. Professors have sometimes noted the irony of watching a class full of students in blue jeans insisting that they do not conform to other people's style of dress (C. R. Snyder, 2003). Do you think you conform about as much as most other people do, or more, or less? *Most* U.S. students insist that they conform *less* than average. One group of students were asked, "Here is what most students at your college think about this issue . . . Now, what do you think?" Regardless of what they were told the others thought, most students said they agreed with that position . . . while insisting that it was really their own opinion, and they weren't just going along with the crowd (Pronin, Berger, & Molouki, 2007).

Conformity occurs even in your writing. Just after reading something written in scientific style, college students write in a more scientific style. After reading something informal and chatty, students write in an informal, chatty style. After reading something with more than the usual number of pronouns or prepositions, students do the same in their own writing, without realizing what they are doing (Ireland & Pennebaker, 2010). So, before writing your next paper, read something that is well written.

Conformity to an Obviously Wrong Majority

Early research suggested that we conform our opinions mostly when we are unsure of our own judgment (Sherif, 1935). Would we also conform if we knew that everyone else was wrong? To answer that question, Solomon Asch (1951, 1956) conducted a now-famous series of experiments. He asked groups of students to look at a vertical bar, as shown in Figure 13.10, which he defined as the model. He showed them three other vertical bars (right half of Figure 13.10) and asked which bar was the same length as the model. As you can see, the task is simple. Asch asked the students to give their answers aloud. He repeated the procedure with 18 sets of bars.

Figure 13.10 In Asch's conformity studies, a participant was asked which of three lines matched another line. Before answering, the participant heard other people answer incorrectly.

Figure 13.11 Three of the participants in one of Asch's experiments on conformity. The one in the middle looking uncomfortable is the real participant. The others are the experimenter's confederates. (From Asch, 1951.)

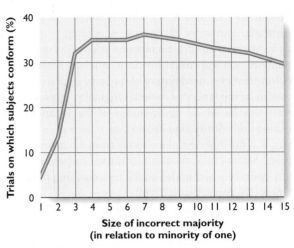

Figure 13.12 Asch found that conformity became more frequent as group size increased to about three, and then it leveled off. (Adapted from "Opinion and Social Pressure" by Solomon Asch, *Scientific American*, November 1955. Copyright © 1955 by Scientific American, Inc. All rights reserved.)

In each group, only one student was a real participant. The others were confederates who had been instructed to give incorrect answers on 12 of the 18 trials. Asch arranged for the real participant to be the next-to-last person in the group to announce his answer so that he would hear most of the confederates' incorrect responses before giving his own (Figure 13.11). Would he go along with the crowd?

To Asch's surprise, 37 of the 50 participants conformed to the majority at least once, and 14 conformed on most of the trials. Asch (1955) was disturbed by these results: "That we have found the tendency to conformity in our society so strong . . . is a matter of concern. It raises questions about our ways of education and about the values that guide our conduct" (p. 34).

Why did people conform so readily? When they were interviewed after the experiment, some said they thought the rest of the group was correct or they guessed that an optical illusion was influencing the appearance of the bars. Others said they knew their conforming answers were wrong but went along with the group for fear of ridicule. The nonconformists were interesting, too. Some were nervous but felt duty bound to say how the bars looked to them. A few seemed socially withdrawn. Still others were supremely self-confident, as if to say, "I'm right and everyone else is wrong. It happens all the time." When Asch (1951, 1955) varied the number of confederates who gave incorrect answers, he found that people conformed to a group of three or four just as readily as to a larger group (Figure 13.12). However, a participant with an ally giving correct answers conformed much less. Being a minority of one is painful, but being in a minority of two is not as bad (Figure 13.13).

Variation in Conformity

Over the years since Asch's experiments, many similar studies have been conducted. In the United States, most studies show a decrease in the amount of conformity since the 1950s. In most Asian countries, the percentage of conforming answers tends to be higher than in the United States, partly because people try to be polite and not embarrass the others by pointing out their error (R. Bond & Smith, 1996). That is, when researchers use the same procedure in different cultures, they may not be testing the same psychological processes.

Are people in certain cultures more prone to conformity as a general rule? The cultures of southern Asia, including China and Japan, are often described as more "collectivist" in contrast to the "in-

concept check

29. Are you more likely to conform to a group when you are outnumbered 5 to 1, 10 to 1, or 10 to 2?

Answer

29. You would be about equally likely to conform when outnumbered 5 to 1 or 10 to 1. Any group of 3 or more produces about the same urge to conform. However, having even 1 ally decreases the pressure, so you would be less likely to conform when outnumbered 10 to 2.

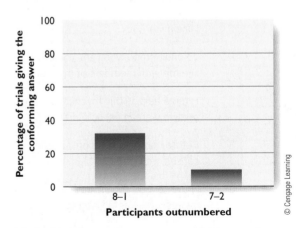

Figure 13.13 In Asch's experiments, participants who were faced with a unanimous incorrect majority conformed on 32% of trials. Participants who had one ally giving the correct answer were less likely to conform.

dividualist" cultures of the United States, Canada, Australia, and most of Europe. According to this view, Western culture encourages originality, competition, and individual freedom, whereas Eastern culture favors subordination of the individual to the welfare of the family or society. Originally, this contrast was based on observations of the Japanese during and shortly after World War II. However, Japan is a far different place today from what it was then. Acting collectively is a common response of any country when under attack or recovering from attack (Takano & Osaka, 1999).

Many studies have contrasted Japanese and U.S. attitudes, mostly using college students and relying on questions like those in Table 13.2. A few investigators have directly observed conformist, cooperative, and competitive behaviors in various countries. The research finds current Japanese culture to be more collectivist than American culture in some ways, but just as individualistic in other ways (Hamamura, 2012; Oyserman, Coon, & Kemmelmeier, 2002).

Some researchers therefore suggest that the "collectivist" notion is wrong, at least for modern-day Japan (Takano & Osaka, 1999). Others point out that each country has multiple subcultures (A. P. Fiske, 2002). People in rural Japan differ from those in Tokyo, just as people in rural American differ from New Yorkers. Also, we need to measure collectivism or individualism more carefully (M. H. Bond, 2002). In any case, we should beware of the generalization that all Asian cultures are collectivist or conformist.

concept check

30. What is one possible explanation for why collectivism may have been a more prominent aspect of Japanese thinking in the past than it is today?

Answer

30. During and shortly after World War II, the people of Japan were under attack or recovering from attack. In that situation, people of any country are motivated to work collectively.

Obedience to Authority

Ordinarily, if someone ordered you to hurt another person, you would refuse. However, certain situations exert powerful pressure.

Decades ago, psychologist Philip Zimbardo and his colleagues paid college students to play the roles of guards and prisoners for 2 weeks during a vacation period. The researchers set up the basement of a university building as a prison but gave the students only minimal instructions on how to conduct themselves. Within 6 days, the researchers had to cancel the study because many of the "guards" were physically and emotionally bullying the "prisoners" (Haney, Banks, & Zimbardo, 1973). Why? None of the students were habitually cruel in everyday life. However, in this situation, they could get away with cruelty without any penalties or retaliation. Also, they perhaps inferred that cruelty was expected. After all, what would be the point of "playing prison" for 2 weeks while behaving politely?

Although we should beware of drawing too broad a conclusion from this study, as the results would differ with changes in instructions or procedure, we can see parallels in real life. In 2003 American soldiers admitted brutally degrading Iraqi prisoners at the Abu Ghraib prison. Early speculation attributed their actions to "a few bad apples" among the soldiers. Later, it became apparent that none of them were habitually cruel. They were ill trained as prison guards, lightly supervised, under constant stress and discomfort, and in almost constant danger. Further, they had the usual military custom of obedience to authority and conformity to their peers. No one can excuse their terrible actions, but the actions probably stemmed more from the evil situation than from inherently evil people (S. T. Fiske, Harris, & Cuddy, 2004). It is hard to know what you would do in a situation you have not faced. One of psychology's most famous studies investigated what normal people would do in a situation they had never before faced.

Table 13.2 Examples of Questions to Measure Collectivist Versus Individualist Attitudes

T	F	I take pride in accomplishing what no one else can accomplish.
T	F	It is important to me that I perform better than others on a task.
T	F	I am unique—different from others in many respects.
T	F	I like my privacy.
T	F	To understand who I am, you must see me with members of my group.
T	F	I would help, within my means, if a relative were in financial difficulty.
T	F	Before making a decision, I always consult with others.
T	F	I have respect for the authority figures with whom I interact.

Note: The first four items measure individualism; the second four measure collectivist attitudes.
Source: From Oyserman, Coon, & Kemmelmeier, 2002.

critical check

What's the Evidence?

The Milgram Experiment

If an experimenter asked you to deliver shocks to another person, starting with weak shocks and progressing to stronger ones, at what point, if any, would you refuse? Research by Stanley Milgram (1974) was inspired by reports of atrocities in the Nazi concentration camps during World War II. People who had committed the atrocities defended themselves by saying they were only obeying orders. International courts rejected that defense, and outraged people throughout the world told themselves, "If I had been there, I would have refused to follow such orders" or "I would have been like the woman in the movie *Schindler's List* who risked her life to save Jewish people from the Nazi Holocaust."

Well, maybe you would have, and maybe not. Milgram suspected that people might yield to pressure.

Hypothesis When an authority figure gives normal people instructions to do something that might hurt another person, some of them will obey.

Method Two adult men at a time arrived at the experiment—a real participant and a confederate of the experimenter pretending to be a participant. The experimenter told them that in this study on learning, one participant would be the "teacher" and the other would be the "learner." The teacher would read lists of words through a microphone to the learner, sitting in another room. The teacher would then test the learner's memory for the words. Whenever the learner made a mistake, the teacher was to deliver an electric shock as punishment.

The experiment was rigged so that the real participant was always the teacher and the confederate was always the learner. The teacher watched as the learner was strapped into an escape-proof shock device (Figure 13.14). The learner never received shocks, but the teacher was led to believe that he did. In fact, before the start of the study, the experimenter had the teacher feel a sample shock from the machine.

Throughout the experiment, the learner made many mistakes. The experimenter instructed the teacher to begin by punishing the learner with the 15-volt switch for his first mistake and increase by 15 volts for each successive mistake, up to the maximum of 450 volts (Figure 13.15).

As the voltage went up, the learner in the next room cried out in pain. If the teacher asked who would take responsibility for any harm to the learner, the experimenter replied that he, the experimenter, would take responsibility but insisted, "while the shocks may be painful, they are not dangerous." When the shocks reached 150 volts, the learner begged to be let out of the experiment, complaining that his heart was bothering him. Beginning at 270 volts, he screamed in agony. At 300 volts, he shouted that he would no longer answer any questions. After 330 volts, he made no response at all. Still, the experimenter ordered the teacher to continue asking questions and delivering shocks. Remember, the learner was not really being shocked. The screams came from a recording.

Results Of 40 participants, 25 delivered shocks all the way to 450 volts. Most of those who quit did so early. Most of those who went beyond 150 volts and everyone who continued beyond 330 persisted all the way to 450. Those who delivered the maximum shock were not sadists but normal adults recruited from the community through newspaper ads. They were paid a few dollars for their services, and if they asked, they were told that they could keep the money even if they quit. (Not many asked.) People from all walks of life obeyed the experimenter's orders, including blue-collar workers, white-collar workers, and professionals. Most became nervous and upset while they were supposedly delivering shocks to the screaming learner.

Interpretation Why did so many people obey orders? One reason was that the experimenter agreed to take responsibility. (Remember the diffusion of responsibility principle.) Also, the experimenter started with a small request, a 15-volt shock, and gradually progressed to stronger shocks. It is easy to agree to the small request, and after you have agreed to that one, it is easy to agree to the next one. Someone who has already delivered many shocks finds it dif-

Irena Sendler, a Polish social worker, saved the lives of more than 2,500 Jewish children from the Nazis, not giving up their whereabouts even under torture. She was later able to reunite many of the children with their families by digging up thousands of jars in which she had buried their identities and information.

ficult to quit, because quitting implies taking responsibility for your actions. That is, if you quit after 300 volts, why didn't you quit earlier? You could no longer say, "I was just following orders."

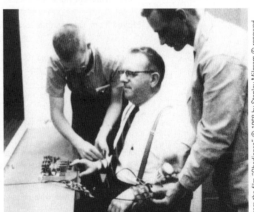

Figure 13.14 In Milgram's experiment, a rigged selection chose a confederate of the experimenter to be the "learner." Here the learner is strapped to a device that supposedly delivers shocks.

Figure 13.15 The "teacher" in Milgram's experiment flipped switches on this box, apparently delivering stronger and stronger shocks for each successive error that the "learner" made. Although the device looked realistic, it did not actually shock the learner.

Figures 13.16 and 13.17 illustrate the results of some variations in procedure. Participants were more obedient to an experimenter who remained in the same room than to one who left. They were less obedient if they needed to force the learner's hand back onto the shock plate. If additional "teachers" divided the task—the other "teachers" being confederates of the experimenter—a participant was likely to obey if the others obeyed but unlikely if the others did not.

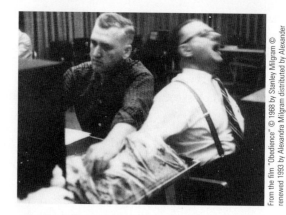

Figure 13.16 In one variation of the procedure, the experimenter asked the teacher to hold the learner's hand on the shock plate. This close contact with the learner decreased obedience to less than half its usual level. (From Milgram's 1965 film *Obedience.*)

Still, the remarkable conclusion remains that many normal people followed orders, even though they thought they might hurt or even kill someone. If people in this experiment felt compelled to obey, just imagine the pressure to obey orders from a government or military leader.

Ethical Issues Milgram's experiment told us something about ourselves that we did not want to hear. No longer could we say, "What happened in Nazi Germany could never happen here." We found that most of us do follow or-

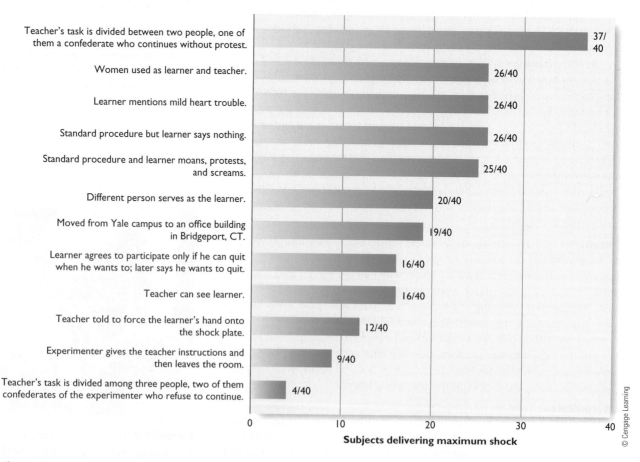

Figure 13.17 Milgram varied his procedure in many ways. Division of responsibility increased obedience. An implication of personal responsibility decreased obedience.

ders, even offensive ones. We are indebted to Milgram's study for this important, if unpleasant, information.

However, although it is good to know about Milgram's results, you would not have enjoyed participating in his experiment. Most people found the experience very upsetting.

A few years after Milgram's studies, the U.S. government established regulations to protect people participating in research. Milgram's studies had little influence on these regulations; they were enacted in response to abusive experiments in medicine (Benjamin & Simpson, 2009). Nevertheless, the rules included psychological research. In addition, psychologists became more sensitive to the ethics of research. Today, before the start of any study—even the simplest and most innocuous—the researcher must submit a plan to an institutional committee that considers the ethics and approves or rejects the study. One of the main rules is *informed consent*. Before you participate, you must understand what is about to happen, and you must agree to it.

Could anyone replicate Milgram's research today? Psychologists long assumed that the ethical restraints would prohibit a replication. However, one researcher found a way to replicate the essential aspect of the research. Milgram reported that most of the people who went beyond 150 volts continued all the way to 450. The teacher's tension and stress accumulated as the learner screamed and protested at the higher voltages. So Burger (2009) repeated the procedure but just until 150 volts. The result was that most people, both men and women, continued as far as 150 volts, as in Milgram's research more than 40 years earlier (Burger, 2009). The level of obedience was a bit lower than in Milgram's era, probably because of societal trends toward greater individualism and assertiveness (Twenge, 2009). Still, the finding remains that most normal people are willing to follow orders that might hurt someone.

It is interesting to speculate about what would have happened under other conditions that Milgram didn't try. Would people quit earlier if they thought they were shocking a child? What if they were told that they would eventually trade places so that the previous learner would start delivering shocks to the teacher? How do you think the teachers would behave then? What other changes in procedure can you imagine that might influence the degree of obedience?

concept check

31. In what way did the obedience in Milgram's experiment resemble the foot-in-the-door procedure? How did it resemble Skinner's shaping procedure?

Answer

31. As with the foot-in-the-door procedure, Milgram started with a small request (give a small shock) and then built up. Skinner's shaping procedure also starts with an easy task and then builds to something more difficult.

Group Decision Making

An organization that needs to reach a decision often sets up a committee to consider the issues and make recommendations. A committee has more time, more information, and fewer peculiarities than any individual has. Group decisions are generally better than individual decisions, but the outcome depends on circumstances. If you and someone else are equally well informed, you probably will make a better decision together than either of you would separately. However, if you are better informed than the other person, you will do better to decide by yourself (Bahrami et al., 2010). Also, some groups work together better than others do. One study compared many groups that were asked to make decisions about moral judgments, visual problems, ways of dividing limited resources, and so forth. Some groups consistently made better decisions than others. In this study, decisions were best in groups that cooperated, letting everyone participate about equally rather than letting one person dominate. Groups with a high percentage of women usually outperformed groups with mostly men, who tended to argue and compete (Wooley, Chabris, Pentland, Hashmi, & Malone, 2010). However, the results would certainly be different for groups making decisions about more technical topics. For a decision relating to nuclear engineering, for example, it would be better to have one expert on nuclear engineering than a friendly group in which everyone participates equally.

Furthermore, groups sometimes interact in unfavorable ways that stifle dissent or rush to a judgment. We'll consider how this happens.

Group Polarization

If nearly all the people who compose a group lean in the same direction on a particular issue, then a group discussion moves the group as a whole even further in that direction. This phenomenon is known as group polarization. Note that it requires a fairly homogeneous group. If the group has several disagreeing factions, the trends are less predictable (Rodrigo & Ato, 2002).

The term *polarization* does not mean that the group breaks up into fragments favoring different positions. Rather, it means that the members of a group move *together* toward one pole (extreme position) or the other. For example, a group of people who are opposed to abortion or in favor of animal rights or opposed to gun regulations will, after discussing the issue among themselves, generally become more extreme in their views than they had been at the start (Lamm & Myers, 1978). During the discussion, if most of the members were already leaning in the same direction, they hear new arguments favoring that side of the issue and few or none for the opposition (Kuhn & Lao, 1996). Also, as the members of the group become aware of the consensus during the discussion, the pressure to conform is powerful, especially for those who do not feel fully accepted by the group (Noel, Wann, & Branscombe, 1995).

Many organizations try to resist the tendency toward groupthink, which stifles dissenting views. During the Renaissance, European kings sometimes called on a "fool" (or court jester) to describe some proposal in a fresh and possibly amusing light. In a court composed largely of yes-men, the fool was the only one who could point out the folly of a proposed action without fear of reprisals.

concept check

32. Is a jury more likely to reach a biased or extreme decision than a single individual would be?

Answer

32. It depends. Group polarization would probably move a nearly unanimous jury toward a unanimous verdict. However, a jury that starts out divided would not experience group polarization. Most research has found that juries and similar groups are no more extreme than the average individual (Kerr, MacCoun, & Kramer, 1996).

Groupthink

An extreme form of group polarization, known as groupthink, occurs when *the members of a group suppress their doubts about a group's decision for fear of making a bad impression or disrupting group harmony* (Janis, 1972, 1985). The main elements leading to groupthink are overconfidence by the leadership, underestimation of the problems, and pressure to conform. Sometimes, dissenters conform on their own, and sometimes, the leadership actively urges them to conform.

A classic example of groupthink led to the Bay of Pigs fiasco of 1962. President John F. Kennedy and his advisers were considering a plan to support a small-scale invasion of Cuba at the Bay of Pigs. They assumed that a small group of Cuban exiles could overwhelm the Cuban army and trigger a spontaneous rebellion of the Cuban people against their government. Most of the advisers who doubted this assumption kept quiet. The only one who expressed doubts was told that he should loyally support the president. Within a few hours after the invasion began, all the invaders were killed or captured. The decision makers then wondered how they could have made such a stupid decision.

Groupthink is not easy to avoid. We generally admire government or business leaders who are decisive and confident. Groupthink occurs when they become *too* decisive and confident, and when other group members hesitate to risk their status by objecting. Occasionally, some people do speak out, especially people who care deeply about the issue under discussion (Packer, 2009). To decrease groupthink, one strategy is for a leader to consult with advisers individually so they are not influenced by what they hear other advisers saying.

Fix the Situation, Not Human Nature

Certain situations bring out the worst in people, even well-educated people with the best intentions. If we want to prevent people from panicking when a fire breaks out in a crowded theater, the best solution is not to remind people what to do. The solution is to build more exits. Similarly, it is difficult to teach people to behave ethically or intelligently when they are under strong pressure to conform or to obey orders. To avoid the temptation to make bad decisions, we need to choose our situations carefully.

Summary

- *Social influence.* People influence our behavior by offering information and by setting norms of expected conduct. We also follow others' examples just because they suggested a possible action. (page 450)
- *Conformity.* Many people conform to the majority view even when they are confident that the majority is wrong. An individual is as likely to conform to a group of three as to a larger group, but an individual with an ally is less likely to conform. (page 450)
- *Cultural differences.* Although some cultures tend to be more collectivist or conforming than others, it is an overgeneralization to regard all Asian cultures as collectivist or to assume that all members of a society are equally collectivist. (page 451)
- *Obedience.* In Milgram's obedience study, many people followed directions in which they thought they were delivering painful shocks to another person. (page 452)
- *Group polarization.* Groups of people who lean mostly in the same direction on a given issue often make more extreme decisions than most people would have made on their own. (page 455)
- *Groupthink.* Groupthink occurs when members of a cohesive group fail to express their opposition to a decision for fear of making a bad impression or harming the cohesive spirit of the group. (page 456)

Key Terms

conformity (page 450)

group polarization (page 455)

groupthink (page 456)

exploration and study

Access an interactive eBook and chapter-specific learning tools, including
- **flashcards**
- **quizzes**
- **videos**

and more, in your Psychology CourseMate. Go to **CengageBrain.com.**

aplia™

If your professor has assigned Aplia:
1. Sign in to your account.
2. Complete the corresponding exercises as required by your professor.
3. When finished, click "Grade It Now" to see which areas you have mastered, which areas need more work, and detailed explanations of every answer.

14

Aoki / AFLO Sport

Personality

Several thousand people have the task of assembling the world's largest jigsaw puzzle, with more than a trillion pieces. Cody Conclusionjumper scrutinizes 20 pieces, stares off into space, and announces, "When the puzzle is fully assembled, it will be a picture of the Sydney Opera House!" Prudence Plodder says, "Well, I don't know what the whole puzzle will look like, but I think I've found two little pieces that fit together."

Which of the two has made the greater contribution to completing the puzzle? We could argue either way. Clearly, the task requires an enormous number of small accomplishments like Prudence's. But if Cody is right, her flash of insight will be extremely valuable for assembling all the pieces. Of course, if the puzzle turns out to be a picture of a sailboat at sunset, then Cody will have misled us and wasted our time.

Some psychologists have offered grand theories about the nature of personality. Others have tried to classify personality types and understand why people act differently in specific situations. In this chapter, we explore several methods of approaching personality. In the first module, we consider some famous personality theorists, including Sigmund Freud. The second module concerns descriptions of personality. Any description is, of course, a theory, but description differs from the kinds of theories in the first module. The final module concerns personality measurements.

This three-dimensional jigsaw puzzle of the ocean liner *Titanic* consists of 26,000 pieces. Understanding personality is an even more complex puzzle.

module 14.1

- How can we best describe the overall structure of personality?

Every individual is virtually an enemy of civilization. . . . Thus civilization has to be defended against the individual. . . . For the masses are lazy and unintelligent . . . and the individuals composing them support one another in giving free rein to their indiscipline.
—Sigmund Freud (1927/1961, pp. 6–8)

It has been my experience that persons have a basically positive direction. In my deepest contacts with individuals in therapy, even those whose troubles are most disturbing, whose behavior has been most anti-social, whose feelings seem most abnormal, I find this to be true.
—Carl Rogers (1961, p. 26)

What is human nature? The seventeenth-century philosopher Thomas Hobbes argued that humans are by nature selfish. Life in a state of nature, he said, is "nasty, brutish, and short." We need the government to protect ourselves from one another. The eighteenth-century political philosopher Jean-Jacques Rousseau disagreed, maintaining that people are naturally good and that governments are the problem, not the solution. Rational people acting freely, he maintained, would advance the welfare of all.

The debate between those two viewpoints survives in theories of personality (Figure 14.1). Sigmund Freud held that people are born with impulses that must be held in check if civilization is to survive. Carl Rogers believed that people seek good and noble goals after they have been freed from unnecessary restraints.

Which point of view is correct? Way down deep, are we good, bad, both, or neither? What is the basic nature of human personality?

The term *personality* comes from the Latin word *persona*, meaning "mask." In the plays of ancient Greece and Rome, actors wore masks to indicate their characters. Unlike a mask, however, the term *personality* implies something stable. **Personality** consists of *all the consistent ways in which the behavior of one*

Sigmund Freud interpreted dreams, slips of the tongue, and so forth to infer unconscious thoughts and motivations.

person differs from that of others, especially in social situations. (Differences in learning, memory, sensation, or muscle control are generally not considered personality.)

Sigmund Freud and the Psychodynamic Approach

Sigmund Freud (1856–1939), an Austrian physician, developed the first psychodynamic theory. *A* **psychodynamic theory** *relates personality to the interplay of conflicting forces, including unconscious ones, within the individual.* That is, internal forces that we do not understand push us and pull us.

Freud's influence extends into sociology, literature, art, religion, and politics. And yet, here we are, about three fourths of the way through this text on psychology, and until now, it has barely mentioned Freud. Why?

The reason is that Freud's influence within psychology has declined substantially. According to one psychologist, Frederick Crews (1996, p. 63), "independent studies have begun to converge toward a verdict that was once considered a sign of extremism or even of neurosis: that there is literally nothing to be said, scientifically or therapeutically, to the advantage of the entire Freudian system or any of its constituent dogmas." Think about that: *nothing* to be said in favor of *any* of Freud's theories. Not everyone agrees with that statement. Still, the decline of Freud's influence is striking.

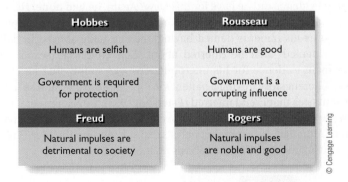

Hobbes	Rousseau
Humans are selfish	Humans are good
Government is required for protection	Government is a corrupting influence

Freud	Rogers
Natural impulses are detrimental to society	Natural impulses are noble and good

Figure 14.1 Sigmund Freud, like the philosopher Thomas Hobbes, stressed the more destructive aspects of human nature. Carl Rogers, like Jean-Jacques Rousseau, emphasized the more favorable aspects.

Freud's Search for the Unconscious

Although Freud was a physician, he admitted in letters to his friends that he was never much interested in medicine. His goal was a theoretical understanding of the human mind. Early in his career, Freud worked with the psychiatrist Josef Breuer, who was treating a young woman with a fluctuating variety of physical complaints. As she talked with Breuer about her past, she described various emotionally traumatic experiences. Breuer, and later Freud, said that remembering these experiences produced ca- tharsis, *a release of pent-up emotional tension,* thereby relieving her illness. However, later scholars who reexamined the medical records found that this woman who was so central to the history of psycho- analysis showed little or no benefit from the treat- ment (Ellenberger, 1972). Further, we should not take it for granted that catharsis is a good thing. Re- living painful experiences is painful. People who are encouraged to cry during sad movies end up feeling worse, not better, than people who restrain their emotions (Kraemer & Hastrup, 1988). Expressing your anger generally makes you more tense after- ward, not less (Verona & Sullivan, 2008). Playing vio- lent video games doesn't "get it out of your system." It increases later aggressive behavior (Anderson et al., 2010).

Regardless of whether catharsis had been suc- cessful in this case, Freud began seeking a "talking cure" with other patients. He referred to *his method of explaining and dealing with personality, based on the interplay of conscious and unconscious forces,* as psychoanalysis. To this day, psychoanalysts remain loyal to some version of Freud's methods and theo- ries, although their views have of course developed over the decades.

Central to Freud's theory was his concept of the unconscious, *a repository of memories, emotions, and thoughts, many of them illogical, that affect our be- havior even though we cannot talk about them.* Ac- cording to this theory, traumatic experiences and unresolved childhood conflicts force thoughts and emotions into the unconscious. The goal of psycho- analysts is to bring those memories back to con- sciousness, producing catharsis and enabling the person to overcome irrational impulses. The psy- choanalyst should listen intently to everything the patient says and help the patient explore possible meanings of each thought and memory. The as- sumption was that simply understanding and bring- ing the unconscious material into consciousness was the key to psychological improvement.

So Freud said, at any rate. Later interviews with his surviving ex-patients revealed that Freud often deviated from the procedure he recommended.

Sometimes he administered morphine or other drugs. In many cases he gave explicit, and often harmful, advice. In one case he urged a client who was having an affair with a married woman to divorce his wife and marry the other woman. He also told the other woman it was essential that she divorce her husband and marry this other man to save him from what Freud claimed was his "latent ho- mosexuality." When they followed his advice, the result was the breakup of two marriages and the substitute of a new one that ended in divorce two years later. Although Freud publicly claimed that his treatment always cured his patients, his private correspondence to friends admitted that many of his cases ended badly, and few if any patients reached a cure (Kramer, 2006).

Changes in Freud's Theory

Initially, Freud attributed neurotic behavior to recent traumatic experiences in his patients' lives. However, the recent events often seemed insufficient expla- nations. For a while in the early 1890s, Freud attributed patients' problems to sexual difficulties and recommended increased sexual activity as a cure (Macmillan, 1997). Then he abandoned that idea and suggested instead that the ultimate problem was traumatic childhood sexual experiences, such as sexual abuse. Freud's patients denied any such memories, but Freud put together parts of the patients' dream reports, slips of the tongue, and so forth and claimed that they pointed to early sexual abuse. He then tried to persuade his patients of these interpretations. Note the similarity to implanted memories or false mem- ories, as discussed in chapter 7.

A few years later, he abandoned the emphasis on childhood sexual abuse. According to Freud, he decided that his patients had "misled" him into believ- ing they were sexually abused in early childhood (Freud, 1925). Why did Freud abandon his early theory? According to one view (Masson, 1984), Freud simply lost the courage to defend his theory. As other scholars insist, however, Freud never had any evidence for it (Esterson, 2001; Powell & Boer, 1994; Schatzman, 1992). Freud had inferred his patients' early sexual abuse despite their denials of such experiences. It was hardly fair, then, to complain that the patients had misled him into believing they had been abused.

Freud replaced the idea about early sexual abuse with theories focusing on children's sexual fantasies. Although he did not fully develop his views of girls' early sexual development, he was explicit about boys: During early childhood, every boy goes through an Oedipus complex, *when he develops a sexual interest in his mother and competitive aggression toward his father.* (Oedipus—EHD- ah-puhs—in the ancient Greek play by Sophocles unknowingly murdered his father and married his mother.) Most boys negotiate through this stage and emerge with a healthy personality, but those who fail to resolve these sexual fantasies develop long-term personality problems.

What evidence did he have for this view? Again, he had none. He reconsid- ered the same statements his patients made to him earlier and reinterpreted them. Just as his patients denied having been sexually abused in childhood, they also denied what he inferred about their childhood sexual fantasies. Freud's main evidence for his interpretations was simply that he could con- struct a coherent story linking a patient's symptoms, dreams, and so forth to the sexual fantasies that Freud inferred (Esterson, 1993). Developmental psycholo- gists report that they virtually never see evidence of an Oedipus complex in children. Although some psychoanalysts still see merit in the idea (Luborsky & Barrett, 2006), most put little emphasis on it.

concept check

1. What was Freud's original view of the cause of personality problems, and what view did he substitute? What evidence did he have for either view?

Stages of Psychosexual Development in Freud's Theory of Personality

Right or wrong, Freud's theory is so widely known that you should understand it. One of his central points was that psychosexual interest and pleasure begin in infancy. He used the term psychosexual pleasure broadly to include *all strong, pleasant excitement arising from body stimulation.* He maintained that how we deal with our psychosexual development influences nearly all aspects of personality.

According to Freud (1905/1925), people have a *psychosexual energy*, which he called libido (lih-BEE-doh), from a Latin word meaning "desire." During infancy, libido is focused in the mouth. As the child grows older, libido flows to other body parts. Children go through five stages of psychosexual development, and each leaves its mark on the adult personality. If normal sexual development is blocked or frustrated at any stage, Freud said, part of the libido becomes fixated at that stage, and the person *continues to be preoccupied with the pleasure area associated with that stage.* Table 14.1 summarizes these stages.

Table 14.1 Freud's Stages of Psychosexual Development

Stage (approximate ages)	Sexual Interests	Effects of Fixation at This Stage
Oral stage (birth to 1½ years)	Sucking, swallowing, biting	Lasting concerns with dependence and independence; pleasure from eating, drinking, and other oral activities
Anal stage (1½ to 3 years)	Expelling feces, retaining feces	Orderliness or sloppiness, stinginess or wastefulness, stubbornness
Phallic stage (3 to 5 or 6 years)	Touching penis or clitoris; Oedipus complex	Difficulty feeling closeness. Males: fear of castration Females: penis envy
Latent period (5 or 6 to puberty)	Sexual interests suppressed	—
Genital stage (puberty onward)	Sexual contact with other people	—

© Cengage Learning

The Oral Stage

In the oral stage, from birth to about age 1½, *the infant derives intense psychosexual pleasure from stimulation of the mouth, particularly while sucking at the mother's breast.* According to Freud, someone fixated at this stage continues to receive great pleasure from eating, drinking, and smoking and may also have lasting concerns with dependence and independence.

The Anal Stage

At about age 1½, children enter the anal stage, when *they get psychosexual pleasure from the sensations of bowel movements.* If toilet training is too strict—or too lenient—the child becomes fixated at this stage. Someone fixated at the anal stage goes through life "holding things back"—being orderly, stingy, and stubborn—or less commonly, goes to the opposite extreme, becoming messy and wasteful. (Remember the concept of "falsifiable" from chapter 2. Can you imagine any evidence that would contradict this aspect of Freud's theory?)

The Phallic Stage

Beginning at about age 3, in the phallic stage, children begin to *play with their genitals* and according to Freud become sexually attracted to the opposite-sex parent. Freud claimed that every boy is afraid of having his penis cut off, whereas girls develop "penis envy." These ideas have always been doubtful, and they have few defenders today.

The Latent Period

From about age 5 or 6 until adolescence, Freud said, most children enter a latent period in which they *suppress their psychosexual interest.* At this time, they play mostly with peers of their own sex. The latent period is evidently a product of European culture and does not appear in all societies.

The Genital Stage

Beginning at puberty, young people *take a strong sexual interest in other people.* This is known as the genital stage. According to Freud, anyone who has fixated a great deal of libido in an earlier stage has little libido left for the genital stage. But people who have successfully negotiated the earlier stages now derive primary satisfaction from sexual intercourse.

Evaluation of Freud's Stages

It is undeniable that infants get pleasure from sucking, that toddlers go through toilet training, that older children begin to notice their genitals, and that adolescents become interested in sexual contact with other people. However, the idea of fixation at various stages, central to much of Freud's thinking, is difficult to test (Grünbaum, 1986; Popper, 1986).

According to Freud, if normal sexual development is blocked at the oral stage, the child seeks pleasure from drinking and eating and later from kissing and smoking. Perhaps this cigarette smoker's mother weaned him too quickly—or let him nurse too long. Like many of Freud's ideas, this one is difficult to test.

© Masterfile

© Jeff Greenberg / Photo Edit

concept check

2. If someone has persistent problems with independence and dependence, Freud would suggest a fixation at which psychosexual stage?

Answer

2. Freud would interpret this behavior as a fixation at the oral stage.

Structure of Personality

Personality, Freud claimed, consists of three aspects: id, ego, and superego. (Actually, he used German words that mean *it*, *I*, and *over-I*. A translator used Latin equivalents instead of English words.) The id consists of *sexual and other biological drives* that demand immediate gratification. The ego is *the rational, decision-making aspect of the personality*. The superego contains *the memory of rules and prohibitions we learned from our parents and others*, such as, "Nice little boys and girls don't do that." If the id produces sexual desires that the superego considers repugnant, the result is guilty feelings. Most psychologists today find it difficult to imagine the mind in terms of three warring factions and therefore regard Freud's description as only a metaphor.

concept check

3. What kind of behavior would Freud expect of someone with a strong id and a weak superego? What behavior would Freud expect of someone with an unusually strong superego?

Answer

3. Someone with a strong id and a weak superego would be expected to give in to a variety of sexual and other impulses that other people would inhibit. Someone with an unusually strong superego would be unusually inhibited and dominated by feelings of guilt.

Defense Mechanisms Against Anxiety

According to Freud, *the ego defends itself against anxieties by relegating unpleasant thoughts and impulses to the unconscious mind*. Among the defense mechanisms that the ego employs are repression, denial, rationalization, displacement, regression, projection, reaction formation, and sublimation. He saw these as normal processes that sometimes went to extremes. His daughter, Anna, developed and elaborated descriptions of these mechanisms.

Repression

The defense mechanism of repression is *motivated removal of something to the unconscious*—rejecting unacceptable thoughts, desires, and memories. For example, someone who has an unacceptable sexual impulse becomes unaware of it. Repressed material is suppressed but not forgotten. Freud once compared a repressed thought to a rowdy person expelled from a polite room who continues banging on the door, trying to get back in.

Is repression real? The evidence for it is shaky. As discussed in chapter 7, most people remember well their most miserable experiences, unless they were very young at the time. Laboratory attempts to demonstrate repression have produced, at best, weak and ambiguous evidence (Holmes, 1990). People can and often do intentionally suppress unwanted thoughts and memories (Erdelyi, 2006). That is, they simply refuse to think about them. However, intentional suppression is not like repression. According to most research, people who intentionally suppress unpleasant memories *improve* their psychological adjustment. They do not experience the distorted perceptions and pathological behaviors Freud saw as linked to repression (Rofé, 2008). The evidence suggests much reason to be skeptical of repression.

Denial

The refusal to believe unpleasant information ("This can't be happening") is denial. Whereas repression is the motivated removal of information from consciousness, denial is an assertion that the information is incorrect. For example, someone with an alcohol problem may insist, "I'm not an alcoholic. I can take it or leave it."

Rationalization

When people *attempt to prove that their actions are justifiable*, they are using rationalization. For example, a student who wants to go to the movies says, "More studying won't do me any good anyway." Someone who misses a deadline to apply for a job says, "I didn't really want that job."

Displacement

By diverting a behavior or thought away from its natural target toward a less threatening target, displacement lets people engage in the behavior with less anxiety. For example, if you are angry with your employer or your professor, you might yell at someone else.

Regression

A *return to a more immature level of functioning*, regression is an effort to avoid the anxiety of the current situation. By adopting a childish role, a person returns to an earlier, more secure, way of life. For example, after a new sibling is born, an older child may cry or pout. An adult who has just gone through a divorce or lost a job may move in with his or her parents.

Projection

Attributing one's own undesirable characteristics to other people is known as projection. If someone tells you to stop being angry, you might reply, "I'm not angry! You're the one who's angry!" Suggesting that other people have your faults might make the faults seem less threatening. For example, someone who secretly enjoys pornography might accuse other people of enjoying it. However, the research finds that people using projection do not ordinarily decrease their anxiety or their awareness of their own faults (Holmes, 1978; Sherwood, 1981).

Reaction Formation

To avoid awareness of some weakness, people sometimes use reaction formation to *present themselves as the opposite of what they really are*. In other words, they go to the opposite extreme. A man troubled by doubts about his religious faith might try to convert others to the faith. Someone with unacceptable aggressive tendencies might join a group dedicated to preventing violence.

Sublimation

The transformation of sexual or aggressive energies into culturally acceptable, even admirable, behaviors is sublimation. According to Freud, sublimation lets someone express an impulse without admitting its existence. For example, painting and sculpture may represent a sublimation of sexual impulses. Someone may sublimate aggressive impulses by becoming a surgeon. Sublimation is the one proposed defense mechanism that is associated with socially constructive behavior. However, if the true motives of a painter are sexual and the true motives of a surgeon are violent, they are well hidden indeed.

concept check

4. Match these Freudian defense mechanisms with the situations that follow: repression, regression, denial, projection, rationalization, reaction formation, displacement, and sublimation.
    a. A man who is angry with his neighbor goes deer hunting.
    b. A smoker insists there is no convincing evidence that smoking impairs health.
    c. Someone who secretly enjoys pornography campaigns to outlaw pornography.
    d. A man who beats his wife writes a book arguing that people have an instinctive need for aggressive behavior.
    e. A man who used to be a criminal seems unaware of his past.
    f. Someone who has difficulty dealing with others resorts to pouting and crying.
    g. A boss takes credit for an employee's idea because "If I get the credit, our department will look good and all employees will benefit."
    h. Someone with an impulse to shout obscenities writes novels.

Answers

4. **a.** displacement; **b.** denial; **c.** reaction formation; **d.** projection **e.** repression; **f.** regression; **g.** rationalization; **h.** sublimation.

Evaluating Freud

How much credit should we give Freud? He was right that people have conflicting impulses, but that idea was hardly original with him. Yes, people have unconscious thoughts and feelings. However, that idea too had been around before Freud (Kramer, 2006). Freud's elaboration on that idea was to say that the unconscious developed mostly from repressed sexual thoughts, such as boys' fear of losing the penis and girls' wish to have a penis. The part original to Freud is the part that is most doubtful. Even the idea of helping mentally troubled people by talking with them was not new.

Freud did introduce a few new ideas that have stood the test of time, such as his recognition of *transference*: You might react to your therapist, or your husband or wife, or other people in a particular way because they remind you of someone else, especially your parents. Still, Freud's main lasting contribution is that he popularized psychotherapy. Others had done psychotherapy before him, but he made it seem *interesting*. Many psychotherapists today, including some who acknowledge no allegiance to Freud, try to help their clients understand where their conflicts and emotional reactions come from. They help their clients think about their developmental history and what it means. In that way, Freud deserves credit, even if most of his specific theories fail to impress.

Karen Horney, a Neo-Freudian

Psychologists known as neo-Freudians *kept parts of Freud's theory while modifying other aspects.* One of the most influential was the German-born physician Karen Horney (HOR-nigh; 1885–1952), who kept the concept of repression but argued that penis envy in women was no more likely than womb envy in men. She also argued that women have the same drive to achievement that men do, and that women feel frustrated when forced into subordinate roles. In that way

The idea behind the psychoanalytic couch is for the client to relax and say everything that comes to mind. This was Freud's couch.

she was a forerunner to later feminist thinkers. Contrary to Freud's idea of an Oedipus complex, Horney emphasized the detrimental effects a child might feel from parental neglect or indifference.

Horney focused on what happens when someone's unrealistic view of the *ideal self* contrasts with a low evaluation of the *real self*. The constant feeling that "I should be better in so many ways" tyrannizes the person, leading to psychological distress. In pronounced cases, the result is the emotional turbulence we call neurosis.

Other theorists, including Carl Jung and Alfred Adler, disagreed more sharply with Freud. Although Jung and Adler were at one time associates of Freud, each broke with Freud's theory in substantial ways and should not be classified as neo-Freudians.

Carl Jung and the Collective Unconscious

Freud gathered around him several others to discuss issues of personality development and abnormal behavior. Two of them, Carl Jung and Alfred Adler, broke with Freud in major ways and proposed theories of their own. Carl G. Jung (YOONG; 1875–1961), was a Swiss physician whom Freud regarded as the "heir

Karen Horney, a neo-Freudian, revised some of Freud's theories and paid greater attention to cultural influences. She pioneered the study of feminine psychology.

Carl G. Jung rejected Freud's concept that dreams hide their meaning from the conscious mind: "To me dreams are a part of nature, which harbors no intention to deceive, but expresses something as best it can" (Jung, 1965, p. 161).

a

c

Figure 14.2 Carl Jung was fascinated that similar images appear in the artworks of different cultures. One recurring image is the circular mandala, a symbol of unity and wholeness. These mandalas are **(a)** a Hindu painting from Bhutan; **(b)** a tie-dye tapestry created in California; and **(c)** a Navajo sand painting from the southwestern United States.

b

apparent" or "crown prince" of the psychoanalytic movement, until their father–son relationship deteriorated (Alexander, 1982).

Jung's theory of personality emphasized people's search for a spiritual meaning in life. In contrast to Freud, who traced much of adult personality to childhood events, Jung stressed the possibility of personality changes in adulthood. Jung was impressed that many of his patients described dreams with no clear relation to anything in their own lives. Rather, they were similar to images that are common in the myths, religions, and artworks of cultures throughout the world. He suggested that these images arise from inborn aspects of human nature. If you dream about a beetle, Jung might relate your dream to the important role beetles have played in human mythology dating back to the ancient Egyptians. If you dream about a baby, he might relate the symbolism to the possibility of psychological rebirth (Lawson, 2008).

According to Jung, people have not only a conscious mind and a "personal unconscious" (equivalent to Freud's unconscious) but also a collective unconscious mind. The collective unconscious, present at birth, relates to *the cumula-*

tive experience of preceding generations. Whereas the conscious mind and the personal unconscious vary from one person to another, the collective unconscious is universal for all people. It contains archetypes, which are *vague images—*or at least the predisposition to form images—*that have always been part of the human experience.* As evidence for this view, Jung pointed out similarities in the art of cultures throughout the world (Figure 14.2) as well as similarities in their myths and folklore.

Exactly how did the collective experiences of our ancestors become part of our unconscious minds? Jung offered little by way of explanation, and our current understanding of biology offers no route by which an experience could get into the genes. A more realistic hypothesis is that ancient people who thought in certain ways had advantages and therefore survived long enough to become our ancestors. As a result, we evolved a tendency to think in those same ways.

Another of Jung's contributions was the idea of psychological types. He believed that people's personalities fell into a few distinct categories, such as extraverted or introverted. Although the results of personality testing do not support this idea, the authors of the Myers-Briggs personality test have revived it, as we shall see in the third module of this chapter.

concept check

5. How does Jung's idea of the collective unconscious differ from Freud's idea of the unconscious?

Answer

5. Jung's collective unconscious is the same for all people and is present at birth. Freud believed the unconscious developed from repressed experiences.

Alfred Adler and Individual Psychology

Alfred Adler (1870–1937), an Austrian physician who, like Jung, was an early associate of Freud, broke away because he believed Freud overemphasized the sex drive and neglected other influences. They parted company in 1911, with Freud insisting that women experience "penis envy" and Adler replying that women were more likely to envy men's status and power.

Adler founded a rival school of thought, which he called individual psychology. Adler did not mean

Alfred Adler emphasized the ways in which personality depended on people's goals, especially their way of striving for a sense of superiority.

"psychology of the individual." Rather, he meant *"indivisible psychology," a psychology of the person as a whole rather than parts* such as id, ego, and superego. Adler emphasized the importance of conscious, goal-directed behavior.

Adler's Description of Personality

Several of Adler's early patients were acrobats who had suffered childhood injuries to an arm or leg. After they worked to overcome their disabilities, they continued until they developed unusual strength and coordination. Perhaps, Adler surmised, people in general try to overcome weaknesses and transform them into strengths (Adler, 1932/1964).

As infants, Adler noted, we are small, dependent, and surrounded by others who seem so superior. We try to overcome that feeling of inferiority. Occasional experiences with failure goad us to try harder. However, persistent failures and excessive criticism produce an inferiority complex, *an exaggerated feeling of weakness, inadequacy, and helplessness.*

According to Adler, everyone has a natural striving for superiority, *a desire to seek personal excellence and fulfillment.* Each person creates a master plan for achieving a sense of superiority. A typical strategy is to seek success in business, sports, or other competitive activities. People also strive for success in other ways. Someone who withdraws from life gains a sense of accomplishment or superiority from being uncommonly self-sacrificing. Someone who constantly complains about illnesses or disabilities wins a measure of control over friends and family. Another person may commit crimes to savor the attention the crimes bring. People also get a feeling of superiority by making excuses. If you marry someone who is likely to thwart your ambitions, perhaps your underlying motivation is to maintain an illusion: "I could have been a great success if my spouse hadn't prevented me." Failure to study can have a similar motivation: "I could have done well on this test, but my friends talked me into partying the night before." According to Adler, people often engage in self-defeating behavior because they are not fully aware of their goals and strategies.

Adler tried to determine people's real motives. For example, he would ask someone who complained of a backache, "How would your life be different if you could get rid of your backache?" Those who eagerly said they would become more active were presumably trying to overcome their ailment. Those who said they could not imagine how their life would change, or said only that they would get less sympathy from others, were presumably exaggerating their discomfort if not imagining it.

concept check

6. According to Adler, what is people's main motivation?
7. How could we explain self-handicapping (from chapter 13) in Adler's theory?

Answers

6. Adler said people's main motivation was striving for superiority.
7. In Adler's theory, people sometimes put themselves at a disadvantage to provide an excuse for failure so that in their imagination they can maintain a sense of superiority.

Adler's View of Psychological Disorders

According to Adler, seeking success or a feeling of superiority for yourself alone is unhealthy (Adler, 1928/1964). The healthiest goal is to seek success for a larger group, such as your family, your community, your nation, or better yet, all of humanity. Adler was ahead of his time, and many psychologists since then have rediscovered this idea (Crocker & Park, 2004).

According to Adler, people's needs for one another require a social interest, *a sense of solidarity and identification with other people*. Note that social interest does not mean a desire to socialize. It means an interest in the welfare of society. People with social interest want to cooperate. In equating mental health with social interest, Adler saw mental health as a positive state, not just a lack of impairments. In Adler's view, people with excessive anxieties are not suffering from an illness. Rather, they set immature goals, follow a faulty style of life, and show little social interest. Their response to new opportunity is, "Yes, but . . ." (Adler, 1932/1964). That is, they find some excuse for not even trying.

Adler's Legacy

Adler's influence exceeds his fame, and he probably would be glad for that. His concept of the inferiority complex has become part of the common culture. He was the first to talk about mental health as a positive state of activity and accomplishment rather than merely the absence of impairments. Many later psychologists have endorsed this idea (Keyes, 2007). Various later forms of therapy drew upon Adler's emphasis on understanding the assumptions that people make and how those assumptions influence behavior. Many psychologists also followed Adler by urging people to take responsibility for their own behavior. According to Adler, the key to a healthy personality was not just freedom from disorders but a desire for the welfare of other people.

The Learning Approach

How did you develop your personality? As discussed in chapter 13, many social situations influence and constrain your behavior. You learn much of what we call personality in terms of what to do in one situation after another (Mischel, 1973, 1981). Because situations vary, so does your behavior. You might be honest about returning a lost wallet to its owner but lie to your professor about why your paper is late. The learning approach to personality emphasizes the ways in which we learn our social behaviors, one situation at a time. As described in the Social Learning section of chapter 6, we learn social behaviors by vicarious reinforcement and punishment. That is, we copy behaviors that were successful for other people and avoid behaviors that failed for others. Also, we imitate the people whom we respect and want to resemble.

Let's consider how this idea applies to masculine and feminine tendencies. Beginning in early childhood, most boys prefer to spend their time with other boys, and most girls prefer to spend their time with other girls. The result is to magnify the differences between boys and girls. Researchers see a slight tendency for girls to prefer dolls and boys to prefer toy cars and trucks beginning even before age 1 year (Alexander, Wilcox, & Woods, 2009), but that tendency grows from year to year, influenced by playmates of the same sex (Golombok et al., 2008). Children also tend to identify more with adults of their own gender. In one experiment, children watched adults choose between an apple and a banana. If all the men chose one fruit and all the women chose the other, the boys wanted what the men had and the girls wanted what the women had (Perry & Bussey, 1979).

As we learn people's expectations for us, we develop a gender role, *the pattern of behavior that a person is expected to follow because of being male or female*. A gender role is the psychological aspect of being male or female, as opposed to sex, which is the biological aspect. We know that gender role is at least partly learned because of the variation among cultures (Figure 14.3). For example, some cultures define cooking as women's work, and others define it as men's work. Men wear their hair short in some cultures and long in others. We also see changes in gender differences over time. For example, in the United States, the prevalence of heart disease has increased among women, and the prevalence of depression has increased for men. Those changes imply changes in gender roles as culture has

Children learn gender roles partly by imitating adults, but they probably learn more from other children.

changed (Dedovic, Wadiwalla, Engert, & Pruessner, 2009). Gender role impacts personality in detailed ways. For example, women tend to be more sensitive to other people's feelings than men are (Bekker & van Assen, 2008). Men, however, tend to be more tolerant of other men's quirky habits—more willing, for example, to stay with an assigned college roommate instead of switching (Benenson et al., 2009).

concept check

8. Suppose someone observes your behavior over a period of time and reports that your personality seems "inconsistent." How does the learning approach to personality explain that inconsistency?

Answer

8. You learn your behaviors one situation at a time. You may have learned to be friendly in one situation and not another or honest in one situation and not another.

Humanistic Psychology

Another perspective on personality, humanistic psychology, *deals with consciousness, values, and abstract beliefs, including spiritual experiences and the beliefs that people live and die for.* According to humanistic psychologists, personality depends on people's beliefs and perceptions of the world. If you *believe* that a particular experience was highly meaningful, then it *was* highly meaningful. A psychologist can understand you only by asking you to interpret and evaluate the events of your life. (In theology, a *humanist* glorifies human potentials, generally denying or de-emphasizing a supreme being. The term *humanistic psychologist* implies nothing about someone's religious beliefs.)

Humanistic psychology emerged in the 1950s and 1960s as a protest against both behaviorism and psychoanalysis, the dominant psychological viewpoints at the time (Berlyne, 1981). Behaviorists and psychoanalysts often emphasize the less noble aspects of people's thoughts and actions, whereas humanistic psychologists see people as essentially good and striving to achieve their potential. Also, behaviorism and psychoanalysis, despite their differences, both assume *determinism* (the belief that every behavior has a cause) and *reductionism* (the attempt to explain behavior in terms of its component elements).

Humanistic psychologists do not try to explain behavior in terms of its parts or hidden causes. They claim that people make deliberate, conscious decisions. For example, people might devote themselves to a great cause, sacrifice their own well-being, or risk their lives. To the humanistic psychologist, ascribing

Figure 14.3 Gender roles vary greatly among cultures and even from one time period to another for a single culture. Here, a Palestinian man (**a**) and a Vietnamese woman (**b**) plow the fields. Men in Bangladesh (**c**) and women in Thailand (**d**) do the wash.

such behavior to past reinforcements or unconscious thought processes misses the point.

Humanistic psychologists generally study the special qualities of a given individual as opposed to studying groups. Their research consists mostly of recording narratives, more like a biographer than like a scientist. Their data are qualitative, not quantitative, and often difficult to evaluate.

Carl Rogers and Unconditional Positive Regard

Carl Rogers, the most influential humanistic psychologist, studied theology before turning to psychology, and the influence of those early studies is apparent in his view of human nature. Rogers (1980) regarded human nature as basically good. According to Rogers, it is as natural for people to strive for excellence as it is for a plant to grow.

Children evaluate themselves and their actions beginning at an early age. They learn that their actions can be good or bad. They develop a self-concept, *an image of what they really are,* and an ideal self, *an image of what they would like to be.* Rogers measured self-concept and ideal self by handing someone a stack of cards containing statements such as "I am honest" and "I am suspicious of others." The person would then sort the statements into piles representing *true of me* and *not true of me* or arrange them in a continuum from *most true of me* to *least true of me.* (This method is known as a *Q-sort.*) Then Rogers would provide an identical stack of cards and ask the person to sort them into two piles: *true of my ideal self* and *not true of my ideal self.* In this manner, he could compare someone's self-concept to his or her ideal self. People who perceive much discrepancy between the two generally feel distress. Humanistic psychologists try to help people overcome their distress by improving their self-concept or by revising their ideal self.

To promote human welfare, Rogers maintained that people should relate to one another with unconditional positive regard, a relationship that Thomas Harris (1967) described as "I'm OK—You're OK." Unconditional positive regard is *the complete, unqualified acceptance of another person as he or she is,* much like the love of a parent for a child. If you feel unconditional positive regard, you might disapprove of someone's actions or intentions, but you would still accept and love the person. (This view resembles the Christian advice to "hate the sin but love the sinner.") The alternative is *conditional positive regard,* the attitude that "I shall like you only if . . . ." People who are treated with conditional positive regard feel restrained about opening themselves to new ideas or activities for fear of losing someone else's support.

Abraham Maslow and the Self-Actualized Personality

Carl Rogers maintained that people naturally strive toward positive goals without special urging. He recommended that people relate to one another with unconditional positive regard.

Abraham Maslow, another humanistic psychologist, complained that most psychologists concentrate on disordered personalities, assuming that personality is either normal or worse than normal. Maslow insisted, as Alfred Adler had, that personality can also be better than normal. He emphasized self-actualization, *the achievement of one's full potential.* The concept of self-actualization is similar to Adler's concept of striving for superiority.

As a first step toward describing the self-actualized personality, Maslow (1962, 1971) made a list of people who in his opinion were approaching their full potential. His list included people he knew personally as well as some from history. He sought to discover what, if anything, they had in common.

Abraham Maslow, one of the founders of humanistic psychology, introduced the concept of a "self-actualized personality," a personality associated with high productivity and enjoyment of life.

According to Maslow (1962, 1971), people with a self-actualized (or self-actualizing) personality show the following characteristics:

- An accurate perception of reality: They perceive the world as it is, not as they would like it to be. They accept uncertainty and ambiguity.

Harriet Tubman, identified by Maslow as having a self-actualized personality, was a leader of the Underground Railroad, a system for helping slaves escape from the southern states before the Civil War. Maslow defined the self-actualized personality by first identifying admirable people, such as Tubman, and then determining what they had in common.

- Independence, creativity, and spontaneity: They make their own decisions, even if others disagree.
- Acceptance of themselves and others: They treat people with unconditional positive regard.
- A problem-centered outlook rather than a self-centered outlook: They think about how to solve problems, not how to make themselves look good. They concentrate on significant philosophical or political issues, not just on getting through the day.
- Enjoyment of life: They are open to positive experiences, including "peak experiences" when they feel truly fulfilled and content.
- A good sense of humor.

Critics have noted that, because Maslow's description is based on his own choice of examples, it may simply reflect the characteristics that he himself admired. That is, his reasoning was circular: He defined certain people as self-actualized and then inquired what they had in common to figure out what "self-actualized" means (Neher, 1991). In any case, Maslow paved the way for other attempts to define a healthy personality as something more than a personality without disorder.

concept check

9. What does humanistic psychology have in common with the ideas of Alfred Adler?

Answer

9. Adler emphasized the importance of people's beliefs and the possibility of a better-than-normal personality. Humanistic psychology is based on Adler's approach.

module 14.1

In Closing

In Search of Human Nature

The three most comprehensive personality theorists—Freud, Jung, and Adler—lived and worked in Austria in the early 1900s. Here we are, a century later, and most specialists in personality research neither accept those theories nor try to replace them with anything better. Recall from chapter 1 that a good research question is interesting and answerable. Fundamental questions about human nature are extraordinarily interesting but not easily answerable. Most researchers today try to answer smaller questions about specific, measurable aspects of behavior, as the next two modules will describe. After researchers answer many of the smaller questions, perhaps they may return to the big questions of "what makes people tick?"

Summary

- *Personality theories as views of human nature.* Personality consists of the stable, consistent ways in which each person's behavior differs from that of others. Theories of personality relate to conceptions of whether people are naturally good or bad. (page 461)
- *Psychodynamic theories.* Several historically influential theories have described personality as the outcome of unconscious internal forces. (page 461)
- *Freud.* Sigmund Freud, the founder of psychoanalysis, proposed that much of what we do and say has hidden meanings. However, most psychologists today doubt most of his interpretations of those hidden meanings. (page 461)
- *Freud's psychosexual stages.* Freud believed that many unconscious thoughts and motives are sexual in nature. He proposed that people progress through stages or periods of psychosexual development—oral, anal, phallic, latent, and genital—and that frustration at any stage fixates the libido at that stage. (page 463)
- *Defense mechanisms.* Freud and his followers argued that people defend themselves against anxiety by such mechanisms as denial, repression, projection, and reaction formation. (page 464)
- *Jung.* Carl Jung believed that all people share a collective unconscious that represents the entire experience of humanity. (page 466)

- *Adler.* Alfred Adler proposed that people's primary motivation is a striving for superiority. Each person adopts his or her own method of striving, and to understand people, we need to understand their goals and beliefs. (page 468)
- *Adler's view of a healthy personality.* According to Adler, the healthiest style of life is one that emphasizes social interest—that is, concern for the welfare of others. (page 468)

- *The learning approach.* Much of what we call personality is learned through individual experience, imitation, or vicarious reinforcement and punishment. (page 469)
- *Humanistic psychology.* Humanistic psychologists emphasize conscious, deliberate decision making. (page 470)

Key Terms

anal stage (page 463)

archetypes (page 467)

catharsis (page 462)

collective unconscious (page 467)

defense mechanism (page 464)

denial (page 465)

displacement (page 465)

ego (page 464)

fixation (page 463)

gender role (page 469)

genital stage (page 463)

humanistic psychology (page 470)

id (page 464)

ideal self (page 471)

individual psychology (page 468)

inferiority complex (page 468)

latent period (page 463)

libido (page 463)

neo-Freudians (page 466)

Oedipus complex (page 462)

oral stage (page 463)

personality (page 461)

phallic stage (page 463)

projection (page 465)

psychoanalysis (page 462)

psychodynamic theory (page 461)

psychosexual pleasure (page 463)

rationalization (page 465)

reaction formation (page 465)

regression (page 465)

repression (page 465)

self-actualization (page 471)

self-concept (page 471)

social interest (page 469)

striving for superiority (page 468)

sublimation (page 465)

superego (page 464)

unconditional positive regard (page 471)

unconscious (page 462)

Personality Traits

- What traits provide the best description of personality?
- Why do people differ in their personalities?

Did you ever wonder *why* people differ in personality? Why don't we all have the "best" personality, whatever that is? If there were such a thing as a best personality, presumably natural selection would have established it for all of us, so the likely conclusion is that there is no best personality for all people (Nettle, 2006). Highly aggressive behavior is sometimes successful, but it also entails a risk of injury. Is fearfulness helpful or harmful? It depends. Is it a good thing to trust other people? Up to a point, yes, but dishonest people take advantage of anyone who is too trusting. Society works best if people have a variety of personalities.

Psychologists study personalities in two ways, called the nomothetic and the idiographic approaches. The word *nomothetic* (NAHM-uh-THEHT-

ick) comes from the Greek *nomothetes*, meaning "legislator." The nomothetic approach *seeks broad, general principles of personality* based on studies of groups of people. For example, we might make the nomothetic statement that more extraverted people are more likely to introduce themselves to a stranger. Most personality research uses the nomothetic approach.

In contrast, the word *idiographic* is based on the root *idio-*, meaning "individual." (The same root appears in the word *idiosyncratic*, meaning *peculiar to some individual*.) The idiographic approach concentrates on *intensive studies of individuals*, looking for what makes someone special (Allport, 1961). For example, a psychologist might study one person's goals, moods, and reactions. The conclusions would apply to this person and perhaps no one else.

Personality Traits and States

Meteorologists distinguish between climate (the usual conditions) and weather (the current conditions). For example, the climate in Scotland is moister and cooler than the climate in Texas, but on a given day, the weather could be warm in Scotland or cool in Texas. Similarly, psychologists distinguish between long-lasting personality conditions and temporary fluctuations.

A consistent tendency in behavior, such as shyness, hostility, or talkativeness, is a trait. In contrast, a state is *a temporary activation of a particular behavior*. For example, being nervous most of the time is a trait, but being afraid right now is a state. Being quiet habitually is a trait, but being quiet in the library is a state. A trait, like a climatic condition, is an average over time. Both traits and states are descriptions of behavior, not explanations. To say that someone is nervous and quiet does not explain anything. It merely describes what we are trying to explain.

concept check

10. Suppose someone becomes nervous as soon as he sits down in a dentist's chair. Is this experience "trait anxiety" or "state anxiety"?

Answer

10. It is state anxiety because the situation evokes it. Trait anxiety, on the other hand, is a tendency to become nervous in many situations.

Like this man playing the role of a woman in Japanese kabuki theater, actors can present personalities that are very different from their private ones. All of us occasionally display temporary personalities that are different from our usual selves.

© Fujifotos/The Image Works

The Search for Broad Personality Traits

According to the trait approach to personality, *people have consistent characteristics in their behavior*. Psychologists have described, studied, and measured many personality traits. Let's consider one example: belief in a just world. People with a strong belief in a just world *maintain that life is fair and people usually get what they deserve* (Lerner, 1980). Here are examples of questions to measure this belief, reworded from a standard questionnaire (Lipkus, 1991). Indicate your degree of agreement from 1 (complete disagreement) to 6 (complete agreement). The higher your score (scores range from 6 to 36), the greater your belief in a just world:

People usually get the rewards and punishments they deserve.

Most people who meet with misfortune did something to bring it on themselves.

Most of the lucky breaks I get are earned.

Promotions go to the people who work hardest.

People who have no job or no money have only themselves to blame.

Only rarely does an innocent person go to prison.

It is comforting to believe that life is fundamentally fair, that good deeds are rewarded and bad deeds punished. People with a strong belief in a just world usually handle stressful situations well, confident that things will turn out favorably after all (Bègue & Muller, 2006; Otto, Boos, Dalbert, Schöps, & Hoyer, 2006). They are more likely than average to offer help to a person in distress or to seek revenge against whoever caused the harm, presumably to restore a sense of justice (Furnham, 2003; Kaiser, Vick, & Major, 2004). However, they are also more likely than average to "blame the victim" for an illness or other disadvantage (Ebneter, Latner, & O'Brien, 2011). (After all, if it is a just world, then people get what they deserve.) The point is that a personality trait—in this case, belief in a just world—manifests itself in many ways.

11. Accident victims often respond, "It could have been worse." How might this reaction relate to a belief in a just world?

Answer

11. It seems unjust for an innocent person to sustain an injury. Minimizing the damage makes the injustice seem less.

Issues in Personality Measurement

In personality as in other areas of psychology, research progress depends on good measurement. The problem in measuring personality is that behavior fluctuates. You might be friendly toward some people and not others. You might be cheerful at some times and not others. You might take risks in one situation and not another (Hanoch, Johnson, & Wilke, 2006). To observe general trends in personality, we would have to watch people in a huge variety of situations. Instead, researchers use questionnaires to ask people how they usually behave.

When people rate their own personality, can we trust them to be accurate? Most Americans rate themselves above average in self-esteem, honesty, friendliness, intelligence, acceptance of minority groups, creativity, sense of humor, and almost everything else. The British tend to be more modest, and Asians are still more modest (Furnham, Hosoe, & Tang, 2002). Americans who call themselves average (possibly an honest answer), are assumed to have a *low* opinion of themselves, just because most other Americans rate themselves tip-top on everything (Baumeister, Campbell, Krueger, & Vohs, 2003).

One way to check the validity of a personality questionnaire is to compare questionnaire results to behaviors recorded in diary form. In several studies, people filled out questionnaires about various personality dimensions. Then they kept daily records of their behaviors. Both kinds of data rely on self-reports, but the daily behavior records are more detailed, closer in time to the actual events, and presumably more accurate. The questionnaire results correlated moderately well with the daily reports, suggesting that the questionnaires are accurate enough for most research (Fleeson & Gallagher, 2009).

An Example of Measurement Problems: Self-Esteem

Let's consider the personality dimension of self-esteem, *the evaluation of one's own abilities, performance, and worth.* People in general, and Americans in particular, like to have high self-esteem. They do what they can to maintain it, including trying to improve their skills, or reminding themselves that they are more successful than other people in certain ways (Nussbaum & Dweck, 2008). Psychologists generally expect that high self-esteem should lead to increased productivity and other good outcomes. However, programs to raise people's self-esteem have often had disappointing results. On the plus side, people who increase their self-esteem are better able to cope with stress (Creswell et al., 2005; Marsh & Craven, 2006). However, raising people's self-esteem generally has little effect on aggressive behavior and sometimes *decreases* school and job performance (Baumeister et al., 2003). (Perhaps people who think they are already wonderful feel little need to prove it.) Psychologists also expect that all successful people should have high self-esteem, but many studies reported that young women, including many who seem bright and accomplished, report somewhat lower self-esteem than comparable men.

Much of the discrepancy between expectations and data depends on how we measure self-esteem (Blascovich & Tomaka, 1991). Here is one set of items from a self-esteem questionnaire:

- I feel that I have a number of good qualities.
- I can do things as well as most other people.
- At times I think I'm no good at all.
- I'm a failure.

An answer of "true" to the first two or "false" to the second two would count toward a high self-esteem score. Contrast those items to another self-esteem questionnaire, on which you are to answer from 1 (rarely or never) to 5 (usually or always):

- I feel that I am a beautiful person.
- I think that I make a good impression on others.
- I think that I have a good sense of humor.
- I feel that people really like me very much.

Do those items measure self-esteem or bragging? Here are some true–false items from a third test of self-esteem:

- There are lots of things about myself I'd change if I could.
- I'm often sorry for the things I do.
- I'm not doing as well in school as I'd like.
- I wish I could change my physical appearance.

Do "true" answers on these items indicate low self-esteem or do they indicate high goals? Someone who says "true" is presumably striving for self-improvement. People who say "false" think they are just about perfect already.

How concerned should we be that many young women report low self-esteem? It depends on how someone measured self-esteem. According to a careful analysis of answers to individual items, women's self-esteem is equal to men's or higher with regard to academics, emotion, social acceptance, moral behavior, and many other regards. They tend to have lower self-esteem only with regard to athletic ability (where, in fact, more men concentrate their efforts) and physical appearance, presumably because women strive for a higher standard than men do (Gentile, Grabe, Dolan-Pascoe, Twenge, & Wells, 2009).

The message, in short, is this: Personality is difficult to measure, and we should look carefully at how it was measured before we draw conclusions.

concept check

12. If someone's questionnaire results indicate "low self-esteem," what else might the results actually mean other than low self-esteem?

Answer

12. Depending on the questionnaire items, what appears to be low self-esteem might indicate high goals and therefore lack of satisfaction with one's current performance.

The Big Five Model of Personality

Psychologists have devised questionnaires to measure belief in a just world, self-esteem, and hundreds of other traits. Are some of these traits more important than others? Remember the principle of parsimony from chapter 2: If we can adequately describe personality with a few traits, we should not measure more.

One way to begin is to examine our language. The English language probably has a word for every important personality trait. Although this assumption is not a necessity, it seems likely considering how much attention people pay to other people's personalities. Gordon Allport and H. S. Odbert (1936) plodded through an English dictionary and found almost 18,000 words that might be used to describe personality. They deleted from this list words that were merely evaluations, such as *nasty*, and terms referring to temporary states, such as *confused*. (At least, we hope that being confused is

temporary.) In the remaining list, they looked for clusters of synonyms, such as *affectionate*, *warm*, and *loving*, and kept only one of the terms. When they found opposites, such as *honest* and *dishonest*, they also kept just one term. After eliminating synonyms and antonyms, Raymond Cattell (1965) narrowed the original list to 35 traits.

Derivation of the Big Five Personality Traits

Although some of the 35 personality traits that Cattell identified are not exactly synonyms or antonyms of one another, many of them overlap. Psychologists looked for clusters of traits that correlate strongly with one another, but don't correlate with the other clusters. Using this approach, researchers found what they call the Big Five personality traits: *neuroticism, extraversion, agreeableness, conscientiousness, and openness to new experience* (McCrae & Costa, 1987). The case for these five traits is that (a) each correlates with many personality dimensions for which our language has a word and (b) none of these traits correlates highly with any of the other four, so they are not measuring the same thing. The Big Five dimensions are described in the following list (Costa, McCrae, & Dye, 1991):

Neuroticism is *a tendency to experience unpleasant emotions frequently.* Some personality researchers prefer to use the term *emotional stability*, the opposite of neuroticism. Neuroticism correlates positively with anxiety, hostility, self-consciousness, frequent conflicts with other people, and many physical and mental illnesses (Lahey, 2009). People high in neuroticism tend to have troubles in their jobs and marriages (Roberts, Kuncel, Shiner, Caspi, & Goldberg, 2007).

Extraversion is *a tendency to seek stimulation and to enjoy the company of other people.* The opposite of extraversion is introversion. Extraversion is associated with warmth, gregariousness, assertiveness, impulsiveness, and a need for excitement. The unpleasant side of extraversion is an increased chance of alcohol abuse and other risky behaviors (Martsh & Miller, 1997). The pleasant side is that extraverts tend to be happy (Francis, Brown, Lester, & Philipchalk, 1998). The relationship goes in both directions: Feeling happy makes people more outgoing, and outgoing behavior makes people feel happy (Lucas, Le, & Dyrenforth, 2008). In one study, people who pretended to be extraverted reported feeling happier afterward (Fleeson, Malanos, & Achille, 2002).

Active, outgoing behavior → Happy feelings

© Cengage Learning

Agreeableness is *a tendency to be compassionate toward others.* It implies a concern for the welfare of other people and is closely related to Adler's concept of social interest. People high in agreeableness trust other people and expect other people to trust them. They are more likely than average to have stable marriages and stable employment (Roberts et al., 2007). They are less likely than average to have prejudices (Akrami, Ekehammar, & Bergh, 2011). They recover better than average from an injury, partly because they have good social support (Boyce & Wood, 2011).

Conscientiousness is *a tendency to show self-discipline, to be dutiful, and to strive for achievement and competence.* People high in conscientiousness work hard and complete their tasks on time (Judge & Ilies, 2002). They exercise and eat a healthy diet. They avoid tobacco, excessive alcohol, and risky sex (Bogg & Roberts, 2004). They have greater than average life expectancy (Roberts et al., 2007), and so do their spouses (Roberts, Smith,

Jackson, & Edmonds, 2009). That is, a conscientious person follows the rules that lead to long life, and makes sure the spouse does, too.

Openness to experience is *a tendency to enjoy new intellectual experiences and new ideas.* People high in this trait enjoy modern art, unusual music, and thought-provoking films and books. They enjoy meeting different kinds of people and exploring new ideas (McCrae, 1996). In one study, young adults listed their favorite songs. Then another person listened to those songs and tried to guess the personality of the person who chose them. From music alone, they guessed people's openness to experience with a correlation above .6 (Rentfrow & Gosling, 2006).

Table 14.2 summarizes the Big Five model.

concept check

13. Some psychologists suggest that we should divide extraversion into two traits—which they call *ambition* and *sociability*—changing the Big Five into the Big Six. How should psychologists determine whether to do so?

14. If you wanted to predict someone's happiness, which personality trait would you measure? What if you wanted to predict how long someone would live?

Answers

13. They should determine whether measures of ambition and sociability correlate strongly with measures of sociability. If so, then ambition and sociability can be considered two aspects of a single trait, extraversion. If not, then they are indeed separate personality traits.

14. Extraversion correlates significantly with happiness. To predict longevity, you could measure someone's conscientiousness. Conscientious people tend to follow recommendations about good diet, exercise, and avoiding risky behaviors.

Cross-cultural studies offer partial support to the Big Five approach. Several studies have found results consistent with the Big Five model for people in other cultures using other languages (McCrae & Costa, 1997; Yamagata et al.,

© Morimura Yasumasa

The Japanese artist Morimura Yasumasa re-creates famous paintings, substituting his own face for the original. People high in "openness to experience" delight in new, unusual artforms such as this.

2006). However, some studies do find cross-cultural differences (Panayiotou, Kokkinos, & Spanoudis, 2004). A study in China identified traits corresponding to extraversion, neuroticism, conscientiousness, and loyalty to Chinese traditions (Cheung et al., 1996).

Limitations

If we want to predict who pays their bills on time, a measure of conscientiousness works well. To predict who will try a new exotic restaurant, we can rely on openness to experience. Similarly, one or another of these Big Five traits correlates well with many other aspects of behavior. But do the Big Five capture everything of importance about human behavior? Many psychologists remain unconvinced. For example, some employees steal from their company, treat coworkers abusively, and frequently arrive late for work or leave early. Their behavior goes beyond mere lack of conscientiousness. A different kind of questionnaire, measuring lack of integrity (honesty and virtue) provides a better measure (O'Neill & Hastings, 2011). Other researchers fault the Big Five approach for overlooking sense of humor, religiousness, sexiness, thriftiness, conservativeness, masculinity–femininity, and snobbishness (Paunonen & Jackson, 2000). In short, the Big Five description accounts for enough of the variability in human behavior to be useful, but for certain purposes we need to explore other aspects of personality.

Table 14.2 The Big Five Model of Personality		
Trait	**Description**	**Typical True–False Question to Measure Trait**
Neuroticism	Prone to unpleasant emotions	I have many worries.
Extraversion	Seeking excitement and social contact	I make friends easily.
Agreeableness	Compassionate and trusting	I believe others have good intentions.
Conscientiousness	Self-disciplined and dutiful	I complete most tasks on time or early.
Openness	Stimulated by new ideas	I believe art is important for its own sake.

© Cengage Learning

The Origins of Personality

A description of personality differences is not an explanation. What makes some people more extraverted, neurotic, agreeable, conscientious, or open to experience than other people are?

Heredity and Environment

If you want evidence that heredity can influence personality, you need look no further than the nearest pet dog. For centuries, people have selectively bred dogs for their personalities, ranging from shy lapdogs to watchdogs that attack intruders.

To measure the influences of heredity and environment on human personality, much research relies on studies of twins and adopted children (Bouchard & McGue, 2003). As Figure 14.4 shows, studies in five locations indicated greater similarities in extraversion between monozygotic pairs than dizygotic pairs (Loehlin, 1992). Similar research shows a hereditary component to neuroticism (Lake, Eaves, Maes, Heath, & Martin, 2000), conscientiousness (Luciano, Wainwright, Wright, & Martin, 2006), and other personality traits. However, careful studies of the genome (all the chromosomes) have found no gene with a major effect on any of these traits (Calboli et al., 2010; Terracciano et al., 2010). Evidently a great many genes influence personality, each in small ways.

Also, researchers have compared personalities of parents, their biological children, and their adopted children. As Figure 14.5 shows, parents' extraversion levels correlate moderately with those of their biological children but hardly at all with their adopted children. Similarly, biologically related brothers or sisters growing up together resemble each other moderately in personality, and unrelated children adopted into the same family do not (Loehlin, 1992). The results shown in Figures 14.4 and 14.5 pertain to extraversion; other studies provide a largely similar pattern for other personality traits (Heath, Neale, Kessler, Eaves, & Kendler, 1992; Loehlin, 1992; Viken, Rose, Kaprio, & Koskenvuo, 1994).

The low correlations between adopted children and adoptive parents imply that children learn rather little of their personalities by imitating their parents. (As mentioned in chapter 5, Judith Harris made this same point.) Many researchers believe that much of the variation among people's personalities relates to the unshared environment, *the aspects of environment that differ from one individual to another, even within a family.* Unshared environment includes the effects of a particular playmate, a particular teacher, an injury or illness, or any other isolated experience. Because of its idiosyncratic nature, unshared environment is difficult to investigate.

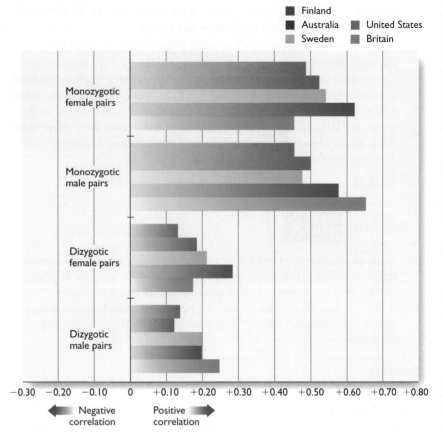

Figure 14.4 The length of each bar indicates the strength of a correlation between pairs of twins in their degree of extraversion. Correlations (similarities) were greater between monozygotic twins (who share all their genes) than between dizygotic twins (who share half their genes). (Based on data summarized by Loehlin, 1992.)

concept check

15. What evidence would indicate an important role of the *shared environment*—the influences that are the same for all children within a family?

Answer

15. If the personalities of adopted children within a family highly correlated with one another, we would conclude that the similarity reflected the shared environment. The weakness of such correlations is the main evidence for the importance of the unshared environment.

Influences of Age, Culture, and Cohort

How much does your personality now resemble what it was in childhood? In one study, investigators followed people's behavior from age 3 to 26. Children who were fearful and easily upset at age 3 were more nervous and inhibited than others at age 26. Those who were impulsive and restless at age 3 tended to have trouble with others from then on and felt alienated from society. Those who were confident, friendly, and eager to explore their environment at 3 tended to be confident adults, eager to take charge of events (Caspi et al., 2003).

How will your personality change in the future? According to the research, the older people get, the more slowly they change. In childhood, answers on a personality questionnaire correlate a modest .34 with a second test given 6 or 7

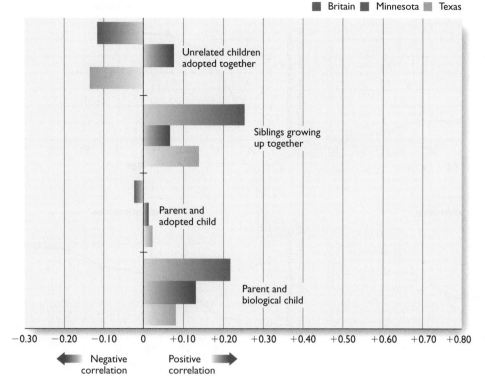

Unrelated children
adopted together

Siblings growing
up together

Parent and
adopted child

Parent and
biological child

−0.30   −0.20   −0.10   0   +0.10   +0.20   +0.30   +0.40   +0.50   +0.60   +0.70   +0.80

◄ Negative   Positive ►
correlation   correlation

Figure 14.5 The length and direction of each bar indicate the correlations between pairs of people in their degree of extraversion. Biological relatives (siblings or parent and child) showed low positive correlations. People related by adoption had close to zero correlations. (Based on data summarized by Loehlin, 1992.)

years later. By college age, the correlation is .54. It increases to .64 at age 30 and to .74 at age 60 (Roberts & DelVecchio, 2000). One reason for personality to become more fixed is that older people usually stay in the same environment, doing the same things year after year. Perhaps you can suggest additional possible explanations.

Although the differences that occur over age are not large, some trends are consistent. One trend, found in cultures throughout the world, is that middle-aged people tend to be more conscientious than teenagers (Donnellan & Lucas, 2008; McCrae et al., 2000). A simple hypothesis (not necessarily the whole explanation) is that adults are forced, whether they like it or not, to hold a job, pay the bills, repair the house, care for children, and take responsibility in other ways.

Most people reach their peak of social vitality and sensation seeking during adolescence or early adulthood and then decline gradually with further age (Roberts, Walton, & Viechtbauer, 2006). Again, this trend occurs across cultures (Donnellan & Lucas, 2008; Labouvie-Vief, Diehl, Tarnowski, & Shen, 2000). Older people also tend to be less neurotic—that is, more emotionally stable—and more agreeable (Cramer, 2003; McCrae et al., 2000). In most countries, young adults score higher on openness to new experience than older people (Donnellan & Lucas, 2008; Roberts et al., 2006). This trend is no surprise, as we see that young people enjoy new types of music, new kinds of food, new styles of clothing, and so forth (Sapolsky, 1998), whereas older people stay with old habits. Figure 14.6 shows mean changes in six aspects of personality over age (Roberts et al., 2006). Note that this research distinguished between two aspects of extraversion—social vitality and social dominance.

Does personality vary among cultures or countries? Here we encounter a research difficulty. Most personality research relies on self-reports. In one study, Mexicans' self-ratings of sociability were lower, on average, than Americans' self-ratings. However, observations found that Mexicans spent more of their time talk-

ing with people face to face than Americans did (Ramírez-Esparza, Mehl, Álvarez-Bermúdez, & Pennebaker, 2009). Similarly, Puerto Ricans rate themselves as only average in extraversion (Terracciano et al., 2005), although most visitors to the island consider Puerto Ricans highly extraverted. The problem is that if you rate your own personality, you of course rate it in comparison to people you know. If you are highly sociable or highly extraverted (by some global standard), but so is everyone else in your community, you rate yourself about average. Self-reports won't help us much in comparing one country to another.

A better approach is to examine actual behavior. Researchers measured conscientiousness from observations of such items as the accuracy of clocks in public places and postal workers' speed and accuracy when selling stamps and making change. These objective measures of conscientiousness correlated significantly with the general reputation of various countries, such as the highly efficient and conscientious Swiss (Heine, Buchtel, & Norenzayan, 2008). That is, personality does differ among cultures after all if we measure it properly.

Within the United States, different geographical areas vary slightly, on average, in personality. "Creative productivity" tends to be highest in the Northeast, Midwest, and West Coast. People in the Southeast are more likely to defend their reputation violently. People in cities tend to be more extraverted than those in rural areas. These are just a few of the differences. One reason for the differences is that the reputation of a place tends to attract like-minded people. If you read about people in Portland, Oregon, and think, "those sound like my kind of people," you might want to move there, too. Another example is that extraverts tend to seek exciting places with many opportunities to socialize, whereas people high in neuroticism tend to seek less threatening places (Rentfrow, Gosling, & Potter, 2008).

Finally, does personality change from one generation to the next? Remember the Flynn effect from chapter 9: Over the years, people's performance on IQ tests has gradually increased so that each generation does better on the tests than the previous generation. Researchers have also found generational differences in personality. For example, over the years, beginning in the 1950s, measurements of anxiety have steadily increased (Twenge, 2000). On the Child Manifest Anxiety Scale, the mean score in the 1950s was 15.1, and the mean for children in mental hospitals was 20.1. By the 1980s, the mean for *all* children was 23.3! Do we

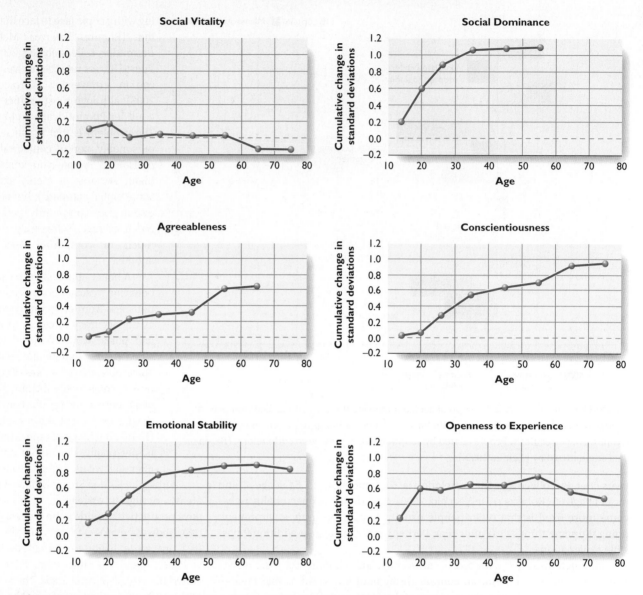

Figure 14.6 Six aspects of personality show different patterns of change over age based on the means of longitudinal research studies. The numbers along the vertical axis represent changes from the earliest age tested, measured in terms of standard deviations. (From Roberts, Walton, & Viechtbauer, 2006.)

really have that much more anxiety than in past generations? Perhaps people's answers do not mean what they used to. The more disturbing possibility is that we really do live in an age of anxiety. Compared to past generations, more children today have to live through their parents' divorce, and fewer live in a neighborhood with many friends and relatives. Might those social changes have raised the average anxiety level? The answer is uncertain, but today's researchers worry about why people worry so much.

Generations also differ in other aspects of personality. From the 1980s to 2006, American college students showed a steady increase in measures of narcissism, self-centeredness (Twenge, Konrath, Foster, Campbell, & Bushman, 2008). Narcissism relates to self-confidence, which is generally a good thing, but it also relates to risk taking, selfishness,

and troubled romantic relationships. The general point here is that the era in which you live exerts a major influence on personality development.

16. Why is it difficult to use self-reports to compare personality trends from one country to another?

Answer

16. When people rate themselves, they compare themselves to others within the country, and therefore, their ratings are not necessarily a good gauge of what the country as a whole does.

The Challenges of Classifying Personality

Personality descriptions refer to averages over time. We don't expect anyone to be equally extraverted at all times, equally neurotic, or anything else. What you do at any moment depends largely on the situation. In a sufficiently novel situation, you may be surprised by the actions of people you know well and even by your own behavior. The variation across situations makes the measurement of general tendencies difficult. Research progress always depends on good measurement, and you can see why progress in understanding personality is difficult.

Summary

- *Nomothetic and idiographic research.* Nomothetic studies examine large numbers of people briefly, whereas idiographic studies examine one or a few individuals intensively. (page 474)
- *Traits and states.* Traits are personality characteristics that persist over time; states are temporary tendencies in response to particular situations. (page 474)
- *Measurement problems.* Personality researchers rely mostly on self-reports, which are not entirely accurate. (page 475)
- *Five major traits.* Much of personality can be explained by these five traits: neuroticism, extraversion, agreeableness, conscientiousness, and openness to new experience. (page 476)
- *Determinants of personality.* Studies of twins and adopted children indicate that heredity contributes to the observed differences in personality. However, no single gene controls much of the variance. Family environment evidently contributes rather little. Much of personality relates to unshared environment, the special experiences that vary from one person to another even within a family. (page 478)
- *Changes over age.* Compared to younger people, older people tend to be higher in conscientiousness and agreeableness. They are somewhat lower in extraversion and neuroticism. Openness to experience decreases with age in most countries. (page 478)
- *Changes over generations.* Measurements of anxiety have gradually increased over the decades so that normal people now report anxiety levels that in earlier times characterized people in mental hospitals. (page 479)

Key Terms

agreeableness (page 476)

belief in a just world (page 474)

Big Five personality traits (page 476)

conscientiousness (page 476)

extraversion (page 476)

idiographic approach (page 474)

neuroticism (page 476)

nomothetic approach (page 474)

openness to experience (page 477)

self-esteem (page 475)

state (page 474)

trait (page 474)

trait approach to personality (page 474)

unshared environment (page 478)

Personality Assessment

- What do the results of a personality test mean?
- What are proper and improper uses of such tests?

A new P. T. Barnum Psychology Clinic that just opened at your local shopping mall is offering a grand opening special on personality tests. You would like to know more about yourself, so you sign up. Here is Barnum's true–false test:

Questionnaire for Universal Assessment of Zealous Youth (QUAZY)

1. I have never met a cannibal I didn't like.	T	F
2. Robbery is the only felony I have ever committed.	T	F
3. I eat "funny mushrooms" less frequently than I used to.	T	F
4. I don't care what people say about my nose-picking habit.	T	F
5. Sex with vegetables no longer disgusts me.	T	F
6. This time I am quitting glue-sniffing for good.	T	F
7. I generally lie on questions like this one.	T	F
8. I spent much of my childhood sucking on computer cables.	T	F
9. I find it impossible to sleep if I think my bed might be clean.	T	F
10. Naked bus drivers make me nervous.	T	F
11. I spend my spare time playing strip solitaire.	T	F

You turn in your answers. A few minutes later, a computer prints out your personality profile:

> You have a need for other people to like and admire you, and yet you tend to be critical of yourself. While you have some personality weaknesses, you are generally able to compensate for them. You have considerable unused capacity that you have not turned to your advantage. Disciplined and self-controlled on the outside, you tend to be worrisome and insecure on the inside. At times, you have serious doubts as to whether you have made the right decision or done the right thing. You prefer a certain amount of change and variety and become dissatisfied when hemmed in by restrictions and limitations. You also pride yourself as an independent thinker and do not accept others' statements without satisfactory proof. But you have found it unwise to be too frank in revealing yourself to others. At times you are extraverted, affable, and sociable, while at other times you are introverted, wary, and reserved. Some of your aspirations tend to be rather unrealistic. (Forer, 1949, p. 120)

Do you agree with this assessment? Did it capture your personality? Several experiments have been conducted along these lines with psychology classes (Forer, 1949; Marks & Kammann, 1980; Ulrich, Stachnik, & Stainton, 1963). Students filled out a questionnaire that looked reasonable, not the ridiculous questions above (which were included just for amusement). Several days later, each student received a sealed envelope containing a personality profile supposedly based on the student's answers to the questionnaire. The students were asked, "How accurately does this profile describe you?" About 90% rated it as good or excellent, and some expressed amazement at its accuracy. They didn't know that everyone had received exactly the same personality profile—the same one you just read.

The students accepted this personality profile partly because it vaguely describes almost everyone and partly because people accept almost *any* statement

People tend to accept almost any personality assessment, especially if it is stated in vague terms that people can interpret to fit themselves.

that a psychologist makes about them (Marks & Kammann, 1980). This *tendency to accept vague descriptions of our personality is known as the* Barnum effect, named after P. T. Barnum, the circus owner who specialized in fooling people out of their money.

The conclusion: Psychological testing must be done carefully. If we want to know whether a test measures personality, we cannot simply ask for people's opinions. Psychologists need to design a test carefully and then determine its reliability and validity.

Standardized Personality Tests

A standardized test is *one that is administered according to rules that specify how to interpret the results.* An important step for standardizing a test is to determine the distribution of scores. We need to know the mean score and the range of scores for a representative sample of the population and how these scores differ for special populations, such as people with severe depression. Given such information, we can determine whether a particular score on a personality test is within the normal range or whether it is more typical of people with a disorder.

Most of the tests published in popular magazines have not been standardized. A magazine may herald an article: "Test Yourself: How Good Is Your Marriage?" or "Test Yourself: How Well Do You Control Stress?" After you compare your answers to the scoring key, the article may tell you that "if your score is greater than 80, you are doing very well . . . if it is below 20, you need to work on improving yourself." Unless the magazine states otherwise, you can assume that the author pulled the scoring norms out of thin air with no supporting research.

Over the years, psychologists have developed an enormous variety of tests to measure normal and abnormal personality. Let's examine a few prominent examples.

An Objective Personality Test: The Minnesota Multiphasic Personality Inventory

A widely used personality test, the Minnesota Multiphasic Personality Inventory (mercifully abbreviated MMPI), consists of *true-false questions intended to measure certain personality dimensions and clinical conditions*. The original MMPI, developed in the 1940s and still in use, has 550 items. *The second edition*, MMPI-2, published in 1990, has 567. Example items are "my mother never loved me" and "I think I would like the work of a pharmacist." (The items stated in this text are rewordings of actual items.)

The MMPI was devised *empirically*—that is, based on evidence rather than theory (Hathaway & McKinley, 1940). The authors wrote hundreds of questions that they thought might relate to personality. They put these questions to people with various psychological disorders and to a group of hospital visitors, who were assumed to be psychologically normal. The researchers selected the items that most people in any clinical group answered differently from most normal people. They assumed, for example, that if your answers resemble those of people with depression, you probably are depressed also. The MMPI includes scales for depression, paranoia, schizophrenia, and others.

Some of the items on the MMPI make sense theoretically, but others do not. For example, some items on the Depression scale ask about feelings of helplessness or worthlessness, an important part of depression. But two other items on the original MMPI are "I attend religious services frequently" and "occasionally I tease animals." If you answer *false* to either of those items, you get a point on the Depression scale! These items were included simply because more depressed people than others answered *false*. The reason is not clear, except that depressed people seldom do anything they don't have to do.

Revision of the Test

The MMPI was standardized in the 1940s. As time passed, the meaning of certain items or their answers changed. For example, how would you respond to the following item?

I believe I am important.   T   F

In the 1940s, fewer than 10% of all people marked *true*. At the time, the word *important* meant about the same as *famous*, and people who called themselves important were thought to have an inflated view of themselves. Today, we stress that every person is important.

What about this item?

I like to play drop the handkerchief.   T   F

Drop the handkerchief, a game similar to tag, fell out of popularity in the 1950s. Most people today have never heard of the game, much less played it.

To bring the MMPI up to date, psychologists eliminated obsolete items and added new ones to deal with drug abuse, suicidal thoughts, and other issues (Butcher, Graham, Williams, & Ben-Porath, 1990). They also removed most of the items that made little sense theoretically, such as the one about teasing animals. Then they standardized the new MMPI-2 on a large representative sample of the U.S. population. The MMPI-2 has 10 clinical scales, as shown in Table 14.3. The items of any type are scattered throughout the test so that people won't see that "oh, this seems to be a set of items about depression." Most people get at

Table 14.3 The 10 MMPI-2 Clinical Scales

Scale	Typical Item
Hypochondria (Hs)	I have chest pains several times a week. (T)
Depression (D)	I am glad that I am alive. (F)
Hysteria (Hy)	My heart frequently pounds so hard I can hear it. (T)
Psychopathic Deviation (Pd)	I get a fair deal from most people. (F)
Masculinity–Femininity (Mf)	I like to arrange flowers. (T = female)
Paranoia (Pa)	There are evil people trying to influence my mind. (T)
Psychasthenia (Obsessive–Compulsive) (Pt)	I save nearly everything I buy, even after I have no use for it. (T)
Schizophrenia (Sc)	I see, hear, and smell things that no one else knows about. (T)
Hypomania (Ma)	When things are dull I try to get some excitement started. (T)
Social Introversion (Si)	I have the time of my life at parties. (F)

© Cengage Learning

least a few points on each scale. A score above a certain level indicates probable difficulty.

Culture and the MMPI

Is the MMPI a fair measure of personality for people of different ethnic and cultural backgrounds? The means and ranges on each scale are close, though not identical, across countries and ethnic groups, even after translation into different languages (Negy, Leal-Puente, Trainor, & Carlson, 1997; Scott & Mamani-Pampa, 2008). However, differences do occur. For example, Mexicans are more likely than U.S. people to say *true* to "Life is a constant strain for me." Presumably, life really is more difficult for many people in Mexico (Lucio, Ampudia, Durán, León, & Butcher, 2001). Consequently, anyone using the test with people from another culture should be cautious about possible meanings of the scores.

Detecting Deception

If you take the MMPI, could you lie to make yourself look mentally healthier than you really are? Yes. Could someone catch your lies? Probably.

The designers of the MMPI and MMPI–2 included items designed to identify lying (Woychyshyn, McElheran, & Romney, 1992). For example, consider the items "I like every person I have ever met" and "Occasionally I get angry at someone." If you answer *true* to the first question and *false* to the second, you are either a saint or a liar. The test authors, convinced that liars outnumber saints, count such answers on a "lie" scale. If you get too many points on that scale, a psychologist distrusts your answers to the other items. Strangely enough, some people lie to try to look bad. For example, a criminal defendant might want to be classified as mentally ill. The MMPI includes items to detect that kind of faking also (Bagby, Nicholson, Bacchiochi, Ryder, & Bury, 2002).

Several other questionnaires also try to detect deception. Suppose an employer's questionnaire asks you how much experience you have had at various skills, including "determining myopic weights for periodic tables." You're not sure what that means, but you want the job. Do you claim to have extensive experience? If so, your claimed expertise will count *against* you because "determining myopic weights for periodic tables" is nonsense. The employer asked about it just to see whether you were exaggerating your qualifications on other items.

concept check

17. Suppose a person thinks "Black is my favorite color" would be a good true–false item for the Depression scale of the MMPI. How would a researcher decide whether to include this item?

18. Why does the MMPI include some items that ask about common flaws, such as, "Sometimes I think more about my own welfare than that of others"?

Answers

The NEO PI-R

A more recent personality test is based on the Big Five personality model. An early version of this test measured neuroticism, extraversion, and openness to experience, abbreviated NEO. A revised test added scales for conscientiousness and agreeableness, but kept the name NEO, which is now considered just the name of the test and not an abbreviation. (It's like the company AT&T, which no longer stands for American Telephone and Telegraph. After all, how many people use telegraphs anymore?) The NEO PI-R (NEO personality inventory-revised) *includes 240 items to measure neuroticism, extraversion, openness, agreeableness, and conscientiousness*. A typical conscientiousness item resembles this:

| Very inaccurate | Moderately inaccurate | Neither | Moderately accurate | Very accurate |

I keep my promises.

Scores on this test have good reliability, about .9. They correlate with observable behaviors, too. For example, students who score high on conscientiousness tend to spend much time studying (Chamorro-Premuzic, & Furnham, 2008). People who score high on extraversion make efforts to meet new people, and people high in openness are more likely than others to visit an art gallery (Church et al., 2008). The test has been translated into several other languages and seems to work reasonably well in other cultures (Wu, Lindsted, Tsai, & Lee, 2007). It is intended mainly to measure normal personality, as contrasted to the MMPI, which is often used to identify clinical problems.

concept check

19. For what purposes might the NEO PI-R be more suitable, and for what purposes might the MMPI be more suitable?

Answer

The Myers-Briggs Type Indicator

The Myers-Briggs Type Indicator (MBTI) is *a test of normal personality, loosely based on Carl Jung's theories*. Jung emphasized the distinction between extraversion, which he defined as attending to the outside world, and introversion, concentrating on one's inner world. He thought each person remained throughout life either extraverted or introverted. Unlike the MMPI, which gives people scores ranging continuously from zero upward on each scale, the MBTI classifies people as types. In addition to being either extraverted or introverted, each person is classed as sensing or intuitive, thinking or feeling, and judging or perceiving. For example, you might be classified as introverted-intuitive-thinking-judging. The test identifies a total of 16 personality types (McCaulley, 2000). The MBTI is more popular with businesses, which use it to describe the personalities of their employees, than with most psychologists, who are skeptical of dividing people into distinct categories. Some counselors also use the MBTI to help students choose a possible career, although other tests are more suitable for that purpose (Pulver & Kelly, 2008). You can take a simplified version of the MBTI at the website www.humanmetrics.com/cgi-win/JTypes2.asp and see how it classifies you. But remember the Barnum effect: The description may be reasonably accurate, but most people are inclined to accept almost any personality report they receive.

Someone said that there are two kinds of people—the kind who believe there are two kinds of people and the kind who don't believe it. It is tempting to divide people into personality types, but is it true that people fall into discrete groups? It would make sense to divide people into extraverted and introverted types if most people's scores were far to one end of the scale or the other. In fact, most people get scores close to the middle. Changing your answer to one question might switch you from one personality type to another according to this test (Pittenger, 2005). Although the MBTI is a reasonable test in many regards, its insistence on putting people into distinct categories is hard to defend.

Projective Techniques

Many people are reluctant to confide embarrassing information, either on a personality test or in an interview. To avoid embarrassment, sometimes people seeking help say, "Let me tell you about my friend's problem and ask what my friend should do." They then describe their own problem. They are "projecting" their problem onto someone else in Freud's sense of the word—that is, attributing it to someone else.

Rather than discouraging projection, psychologists often make use of it with **projective techniques**, which are *designed to encourage people to project their personality characteristics onto ambiguous stimuli*. Let's consider two well-known projective techniques: the Rorschach Inkblots and the Thematic Apperception Test.

concept check

20. Which of the following is a projective technique?
    a. A psychologist gives a child a set of puppets with instructions to act out a story about a family.
    b. A psychologist hands you a stack of cards, each containing one word, and asks you to sort the cards into a stack that applies to you and a stack that does not apply to you.

Answer

20. The puppet activity could be a projective technique if the child projects his or her own concerns onto the puppets. Sorting cards is an objective measure, not a projective test.

The Rorschach Inkblots

The **Rorschach Inkblots**, *a projective technique based on people's interpretations of 10 ambiguous inkblots*, is the most famous and most widely used projective personality technique. It was created by Hermann Rorschach (ROAR-shock), a Swiss psychiatrist, who showed people inkblots and asked them to say whatever came to mind (Pichot, 1984). Other psychiatrists and psychologists gradually developed the Rorschach into the projective technique we know today.

Administering the Rorschach

The Rorschach Inkblot Technique consists of ten cards similar to the one in Figure 14.7, five of them in color. A psychologist hands you a card and asks, "What might this be?" The instructions are intentionally vague on the assumption that you reveal more about your personality in an ill-defined situation.

Sometimes, people's answers are revealing either immediately or in response to a psychologist's probes. Here is an example (Aronow, Reznikoff, & Moreland, 1995):

Client: Some kind of insect; it's not pretty enough to be a butterfly.

Psychologist: Any association to that?

Client: It's an ugly black butterfly, no colors.

Psychologist: What does that make you think of in your own life?

Client: You probably want me to say "myself." Well, that's probably how I thought of myself when I was younger—I never thought of myself as attractive—my sister was the attractive one. I was the ugly duckling—I did get more attractive as I got older.

Evaluation of the Rorschach

When you describe what you see in a picture, your answer undoubtedly relates in some way to your experiences, concerns, and personality. But how accurately can psychologists perceive that relationship? And when they perceive a relationship, did they really get the information from the Rorschach or from something they already knew about you?

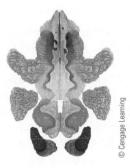
© Cengage Learning

Figure 14.7 In the Rorschach Inkblot Technique, people examine an abstract pattern and say what it looks like.

One man described a particular inkblot as "like a bat that has been squashed on the pavement under the heel of a giant's boot" (Dawes, 1994, p. 149). Psychologist Robyn Dawes initially was impressed with how the Rorschach had revealed this client's sense of being overwhelmed and crushed by powers beyond his control. But then he realized that he had already known the man was depressed. If a client with a history of violence had made the same response, he would have focused on the aggressive nature of the giant's foot stomp. Psychologists often believe the Rorschach gave them an insight, when in fact it just confirmed an opinion they already had (Wood, Nezworski, Lilienfeld, & Garb, 2003).

James Exner (1986) developed methods to standardize the interpretations of Rorschach responses, such as counting the number of times a client mentions aggressive themes. Clinicians using this system achieve a reasonably high level of agreement in their interpretations (Viglione & Taylor, 2003). However, serious problems remain (Garb, Wood, Lilienfeld, & Nezworski, 2005; Lilienfeld, Wood, & Garb, 2000; Wood et al., 2003):

- The test identifies *most* people as psychologically disturbed.
- An evaluation depends on your *total number* of pathological answers, not what percentage of your answers are abnormal. Highly intelligent or talkative people say more than other people do and thus are more likely to say something that seems "disturbed."
- Most important, the Rorschach rarely gives information that could not be obtained more easily in other ways. In most cases, psychologists who are given biographical and MMPI information plus Rorschach results make no better personality judgments than psychologists who are given the biographical and MMPI information alone.

Critics of the Rorschach stop short of calling it completely invalid. Their point is that it is not valid enough to make important decisions about an individual, such as which parent should get custody of a child or which prisoners should get parole (Wood et al., 2003). In spite of the criticisms of the Rorschach, it continues to be in wide use (Musewicz, Marczyk, Knauss, & York, 2009). Its defenders insist that when the Rorschach is used properly, its reliability and validity are comparable to those of other psychological tests (Society for Personality Assessment, 2005). The problem is that many other tests also have validity too low for making important decisions. Personality measurement is, frankly, difficult.

concept check

21. Suppose that research using the Rorschach suggests that highly talkative people are more mentally disturbed than average. What would be a possible explanation?

Answer

21. The psychologist administering the test counts the total number of answers that are considered abnormal or disturbed. The more answers someone gives, the greater the probability of saying something that seems disturbed.

The Thematic Apperception Test

The **Thematic Apperception Test (TAT)** consists of pictures similar to the one shown in Figure 14.8. *The person is asked to make up a story for each picture, describing what events led up to this scene, what is happening now, and what will happen in the future.* Christiana Morgan and Henry Murray devised this test to measure people's needs (Murray, 1943). It includes 31 pictures, including some showing women, some showing men, some with both or neither, and one that is totally blank. A psychologist selects a few cards to use with a given client (Lilienfeld et al., 2000).

The assumption is that when you tell a story about someone in the drawing, you probably identify with that person, and so the story is really about yourself. You might describe events and concerns that you might be reluctant to discuss openly. For example, one young man told the following story about a picture of a man clinging to a rope:

> This man is escaping. Several months ago he was beat up and shanghaied and taken aboard ship. Since then, he has been mistreated and unhappy and has been looking for a way to escape. Now the ship is anchored near a tropical island and he is climbing down a rope to the water. He will get away successfully and swim to shore. When he gets there, he will be met by a group of

© Sanjay Deva/Shutterstock

Figure 14.8 In the Thematic Apperception Test, people tell a story about what is going on in a picture, including what led up to this event, what is happening now, and what will happen in the future.

beautiful native women with whom he will live the rest of his life in luxury and never tell anyone what happened. Sometimes he will feel that he should go back to his old life; but he will never do it. (Kimble & Garmezy, 1968, pp. 582–583).

This young man had entered divinity school to please his parents but was unhappy there. He was wrestling with a secret desire to escape to a new life with greater worldly pleasures. In his story, he described someone doing what he wanted to do.

Psychologists use the TAT in inconsistent ways. Many therapists interpret the results according to their clinical judgment, without any clear rules. If you took the TAT with two psychologists and said the same thing both times, they might reach different conclusions about you (Cramer, 1996).

The TAT is also used to measure people's need for achievement by counting all the times they mention achievement. It is also used to measure power and affiliation needs. These results are useful for research purposes, although not necessarily for making decisions about an individual (Lilienfeld et al., 2000).

Handwriting as a Projective Technique

Based on the theory that your personality affects everything you do, some psychologists (and others) have tried analyzing people's handwriting. For example, perhaps people who dot their i's with a dash—*i*—are especially energetic, or perhaps people who draw large loops above the line—as in *allow*—are highly idealistic. Carefully collected data, however, show no dependable relationship between handwriting and personality (Tett & Palmer, 1997).

Implicit Personality Tests

Although projective tests have debatable usefulness, the motivation behind them remains: Psychologists would like to measure personality aspects that people cannot or will not discuss openly. So the search for another kind of personality test continues.

Chapter 7 distinguished between explicit and implicit memory. If you hear a list of words and try to repeat them, your recall is explicit memory. If you later use words from the list in your conversation, your use of those words constitutes implicit memory. Implicit memory can affect you without your awareness.

Analogous to that, an implicit personality test *measures some aspect of your personality without your awareness.* One example is the Implicit Association Test. Chapter 13 described how this test could be used to measure prejudices that people do not want to admit. It can also detect other emotional reactions. For example, someone who is nervous around other people might pair social words (*party, friend, companion*) more readily with unpleasant words than with pleasant words. Someone who strongly dislikes drug users will pair drug-use words with unpleasant words more strongly than most other people do. In some cases this kind of test provides useful information, such as predicting which nurses will quit a job in which they have to deal with drug users (von Hippel, Brener, & von Hippel, 2008).

Another implicit personality test is the Affective Priming Paradigm. A participant sees first a picture (such as a butterfly or a spider) and then a word (such as *happy* or *awful*). In one version of the task, all the participant has to do is to say the word aloud. The idea is that someone afraid of spiders will be quick to say *awful* after seeing a spider, but slower to say *happy*. The delay of response might measure the strength of someone's dislike of spiders, filthiness, loneliness, or anything else.

Both the Implicit Association Test and the Affective Priming Paradigm can distinguish moderately well between groups, such as people with a severe fear of spiders and people without such fear. The important question is whether such tests can become accurate enough to identify a given individual's concerns or problems. At present, the answer is uncertain (DeHouwer, Teige-Mocigemba, Spruyt, & Moors, 2009; Roefs et al., 2011).

concept check

22. What behavior do both the Implicit Association Test and the Affective Priming Paradigm measure?

Answer

22. They both measure the delay of a person's response after presentation of some stimulus.

Uses and Misuses of Personality Tests

Personality tests serve several functions. Researchers use them to investigate how personality develops. Clinicians use them to help identify disorders and to measure improvement during therapy. Some businesses use them to help select which job applicants to hire. Using personality tests for job selection has positive but low validity. For example, the NEO-PI-R measures conscientiousness (among other factors), and conscientiousness correlates about .15 with job performance and cooperativeness (Hough & Oswald, 2008; Morgeson et al., 2007). Low neuroticism also correlates with good job performance, although less consistently than conscientiousness does (Barrick, Mount, & Judge, 2001). Should businesses or anyone else make important decisions based on tests with such unimpressive validity? It is certainly a reasonable question, although one could argue that even low validity is better than sheer guesswork.

A further problem is that people can fake good scores. If you are taking a personality test and you want to make a good impression, you might pretend to be more conscientious, more agreeable, and less neurotic than you really are. (On a cognitive test, you can't pretend to be smarter than you really are.)

How useful are personality tests for diagnosing psychological disorders? They are useful up to a point, but we need to be aware of their limits. Suppose someone's MMPI personality profile resembles the profile typical for schizophrenia. Identifying schizophrenia or any other unusual condition is a signal-detection problem, as we saw in chapter 4:

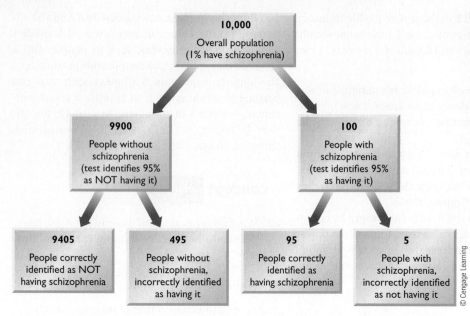

10,000
Overall population
(1% have schizophrenia)

9900
People without
schizophrenia
(test identifies 95%
as NOT having it)

100
People with
schizophrenia
(test identifies 95%
as having it)

9405
People correctly
identified as NOT
having schizophrenia

495
People without
schizophrenia,
incorrectly identified
as having it

95
People correctly
identified as
having schizophrenia

5
People with
schizophrenia,
incorrectly identified
as not having it

© Cengage Learning

Figure 14.9 Assume that a certain profile occurs in 95% of people with schizophrenia and 5% of other people. If we relied entirely on this test, we would correctly identify 95 schizophrenic people and misidentify 495 normal people.

We want to report a stimulus when it is present but not when it is absent. People without schizophrenia outnumber people with schizophrenia by about 100 to 1. Suppose a particular score on some personality test characterizes 95% of people with schizophrenia and 5% of everyone else. As Figure 14.9 shows, 5% of the total population is a larger group than 95% of the people with schizophrenia. Thus, if we label as "schizophrenic" everyone with a high score, we are wrong more often than right. (Recall the representativeness heuristic and the issue of base-rate information discussed in chapter 8: Someone who seems representative of people in a rare category does not necessarily belong to that category.) Therefore, although the personality test provides a helpful clue, a psychologist looks for evidence beyond the test score before drawing a conclusion.

23. Is a personality test more likely to be accurate in identifying common disorders or rare disorders?

Answer

23. It is more likely to be accurate with common disorders, such as depression. If a condition is rare, let's say present in 1% or 0.1% of people, the chance of a false positive (saying that a normal person has the disorder) could easily exceed the probability of correctly identifying someone with the disorder.

Personality Tests in Action: Criminal Profiling

Personality traits are moderately accurate predictors of people's behavior in certain situations. Can we go in the other direction? Can we observe a behavior and infer someone's personality? Consider crime. Although you might not have thought of it this way, psychological profiling of criminals is an application of personality testing. It assumes that people who commit similar crimes have similar personalities or backgrounds, and therefore, an investigator can observe a crime and infer something about the criminal. In 1956 the New York City police asked psychiatrist James Brussel to help them find the "mad bomber" who had planted more than 30 bombs over 16 years. Brussel examined the evidence and told police the mad bomber hated the power company, Con Ed. The bomber was probably unmarried, foreign-born, probably Slavic, 50–60 years old, and living in Bridgeport, Connecticut. Brussel said to look for a man who dresses neatly and wears a buttoned double-breasted suit. That evidence led police directly to a suspect, George Metesky, who was wearing a buttoned double-breasted suit! Metesky confessed, and criminal profiling established itself as a powerful tool.

Well, that's the way James Brussel told the story, anyway. Sometimes people have memory distortions and hindsight bias (chapter 7). Brussel apparently distorted his memory of what he told the police. According to police records, Brussel didn't say the bomber was Slavic; he said German. Metesky in fact was Lithuanian. Brussel didn't say the bomber lived in Bridgeport, Connecticut; he said White Plains, New York, and the police spent much time fruitlessly searching for suspects in White Plains. Metesky in fact lived in Waterbury, Connecticut. Brussel said the bomber was 40–50 years old and revised his memory when Metesky turned out to be a bit older. Brussel also said the bomber had a facial scar, had a night job, and was an expert on civil or military ordnance (none of which was true). And Metesky was not wearing a buttoned double-breasted suit when the police arrested him. He was wearing pajamas. Nothing that Brussel said led the police to the mad bomber. They found Metesky because a clerk from Con Ed patiently went through years of letters the company had received until she found a threatening letter that resembled messages the mad bomber had planted (Foster, 2000).

Many television shows and several movies have featured a criminal profiler who examines the scene of the crime and infers the personality of the perpetrator. This idea makes for a good story, but in fact criminal profiling has much less accuracy.

Brussel's *reported* success in helping the police (which was really no success at all) inspired interest in criminal profiling, and today, FBI profilers consult with police on a thousand or so cases per year. How accurate are their profiles? Researchers examined 21 criminal profiles that various police departments obtained. Most statements in those profiles were useless to investigators, such as, "The offender felt no remorse" (Alison, Smith, Eastman, & Rainbow, 2003). Most of the "evidence" to support profiling consists of lists of correct statements that profilers made (Snook, Cullen, Bennell, Taylor, & Gendreau, 2008). However, the number of correct statements is meaningless unless we also know the number of incorrect statements. We also need to know whether professional profilers' surmises are more accurate than other people's guesses. Only a few studies have investigated these questions. Let's examine one of the best such studies.

critical check

What's the Evidence?

Criminal Profiling

Richard Kocsis and his associates first did a study of profiling in a murder case. They provided extensive details about the murder to five professional profilers and larger numbers of police officers, psychologists, college students, and self-declared psychics. Then each person tried to guess the murderer's sex, height, age, religion, and so forth in 30 multiple-choice questions, with varying numbers of choices per item. Researchers determined the accuracy of these answers, based on facts about the actual murderer, who had in fact been caught. Random guessing would produce 8.1 correct answers for the 30 items, but no one would guess at random. Even without knowing any details, aren't you more likely to guess the murderer was a young man than an 80-year-old woman? If the crime was in the United States, you probably aren't going to guess that the criminal was a Buddhist. And so forth. All groups did better than the random score of 8.1, but none did well. The professional profilers did the best, at 13.8 correct out of 30, and psychics did the worst, at 11.3 (Kocsis, Irwin, Hayes, & Nunn, 2000).

However, it may be hard to profile a criminal from a single crime. Kocsis (2004) therefore did a similar study concerning someone who had committed a series of 13 cases of arson (setting fires).

Hypothesis Professional profilers will guess correctly more facts about the arsonist than other people will.

Method As in Kocsis's first study, most profilers refused to participate, but three were willing. Other groups were police officers with much experience investigating arson, professional fire investigators, and sophomore chemistry majors. Each person examined all the evidence that police had assembled, including photos and descriptions of the crime scenes, statements by witnesses, fingerprints, shoe prints, information about how the fires were set, and so forth. The study also included a group of community college students who received *no* information about the crimes (except that they were arson), but took guesses about the arsonist anyway. Then each participant answered 33 questions about the probable arsonist. All were questions to which the researcher knew the correct answer. Examples (reworded slightly for brevity):

- The offender is: (1) male, (2) female.
- The offender is: (1) thin, (2) average, (3) solid/muscular, (4) fat.
- The offender was: (1) highly familiar with the crime locations, (2) somewhat familiar, (3) unfamiliar.
- The offender is: (1) single, (2) married, (3) living with someone, (4) divorced.
- The offender is: (1) a student, (2) unemployed, (3) employed part time, (4) a blue-collar worker, (5) a semiskilled worker, (6) a skilled or white-collar worker.
- The offender's alcohol use is: (1) none, (2) low, (3) medium, (4) in binges, (5) high.
- The offender: (1) has a previous criminal record, (2) has no previous criminal record.

Results Questions had between 2 and 9 choices each, and random guessing would produce a bit more than 10 correct answers out of 33. Figure 14.10 shows the results. The three professional profilers did the best, but only 3 to 4 items better than the chemistry majors. (Chemistry majors were used to represent people with no relevant experience but high intelligence. Take a bow, chemistry majors.) Police and firefighters, despite their experience, did hardly better than the community college students who had no information about the crimes.

Interpretation This study has clear limitations, especially that it included only three professional pro-

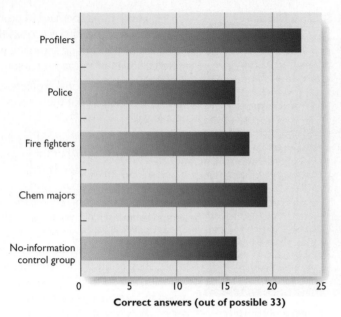

Figure 14.10 Of 33 multiple-choice questions, many of them with only 2 or 3 choices, profilers answered a mean of 23 items correctly. Random guessing would produce 10 correct. People with no information about the crime guessed more than 16 correct. (Source: Based on data from Kocsis, 2004.)

filers, just one criminal, and a set of questions that may not have been ideal. Still, the profilers did better than the other groups, so it appears that the field is not entirely bogus. A few similar studies have yielded similar results: Professional profilers do a bit better than other people, but not by much, and police investigators do no better than inexperienced people. In no case did anyone answer a very high percentage of questions correctly (Snook, Eastwood, Gendreau, Goggin, & Cullen, 2007).

A critical question remains: Did the profilers do well *enough*? On average, they answered 23 questions correctly, which is closer to the scores of people who knew nothing (16+) than to a perfect score (33). If profilers provide the police with a mixture of correct and incorrect information, is the net result to advance the investigation or lead the police astray?

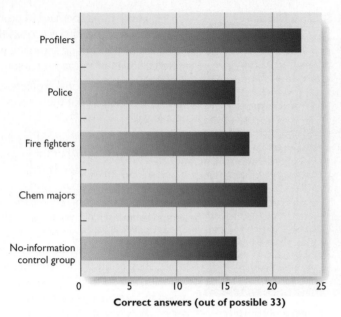

concept **check**

24. Note the use of a control group who knew nothing about the crime. Why was this group necessary? We already knew how many answers someone would get right by random guessing.

Answer

24. No one would guess randomly. Some guesses are more likely than others regardless of the details of the crime.

We should not conclude that criminal profiling is impossible, but as of now, police should beware of putting more confidence in a profile than it merits. At best, a profile is a statement of probabilities, never of certainties. Research under way to improve the quality of criminal profiling begins by identifying the features most common for a given crime, such as arson, rape, or serial murder. Something that occurs in nearly every case of arson tells us little about the individual responsible for a particular case. A focus on the unusual aspects of a particular crime leads to a greater likelihood of reaching a useful conclusion (Canter, 2011). With criminal profiling, as with all the rest of personality research, we need much more research before we can draw confident conclusions.

module 14.3 >

In Closing

Possibilities and Limits of Personality Tests

One of most people's main topics of conversation could be described uncharitably as "gossip" or more kindly as "understanding other people." Knowing about other people is important. You need to know whom to trust and whom to distrust.

Given our focus on personality, most of us tend to believe that personality is highly stable and governs a great deal of behavior. If so, someone should be able to look at a crime scene and infer the personality of the perpetrator. Psychologists should be able to listen to people's answers to the Rorschach Inkblots and discern their innermost secrets. So it might seem, but the research suggests we should be cautious. Personality is somewhat consistent over time and situations, but it is like climate—a trend over a long period of time and not always a good guide to what is happening at the moment. Our actions depend on our situations at least as much as they depend on our personalities.

Summary

- *People's tendency to accept personality test results.* Because most people accept almost any interpretation of their personality based on a personality test, tests must be carefully scrutinized to ensure that they are measuring what they claim to measure. (page 482)
- *Standardized personality tests.* A standardized test is administered according to explicit rules, and its results are interpreted in a prescribed fashion based on the norms for the population. (page 482)
- *The MMPI.* The MMPI, a widely used personality test, consists of a series of true–false questions selected in an effort to distinguish among various personality types. The MMPI–2 is a modern version. (page 483)
- *Detection of lying.* The MMPI and other tests guard against lying by including items about common faults and rare virtues. Anyone who denies common faults or claims rare virtues is probably lying. (page 484)
- *Projective techniques.* A projective technique, such as the Rorschach Inkblots or the Thematic Apperception Test, lets people describe their concerns indirectly while talking about ambiguous stimuli. The results from projective techniques have unimpressive validity for making decisions about any individual. (page 485)
- *Implicit personality tests.* The Implicit Association Test and Affective Priming Paradigm are attempts to measure personality traits that people do not or cannot describe about themselves. So far, such tests are useful for research but not for decisions about an individual. (page 487)
- *Uses and misuses of personality tests.* Personality tests can help assess personality, but their results should be interpreted in conjunction with other evidence. (page 487)
- *Criminal profiling.* Some psychologists try to aid police investigations by constructing personality profiles of the kind of person who would commit a certain crime. Research has been limited, and so far, it suggests low accuracy of personality profiles. (page 488)

Key Terms

Barnum effect (page 482)

implicit personality test (page 487)

Minnesota Multiphasic Personality Inventory (MMPI) (page 483)

Myers-Briggs Type Indicator (MBTI) (page 484)

NEO PI-R (NEO personality inventory-revised) (page 484)

projective techniques (page 485)

Rorschach Inkblots (page 485)

standardized test (page 482)

Thematic Apperception Test (TAT) (page 486)

exploration and study

Access an interactive eBook and chapter-specific learning tools, including
- **flashcards**
- **quizzes**
- **videos**

and more, in your Psychology CourseMate. Go to **CengageBrain.com.**

If your professor has assigned Aplia:
1. Sign in to your account.
2. Complete the corresponding exercises as required by your professor.
3. When finished, click "Grade It Now" to see which areas you have mastered, which areas need more work, and detailed explanations of every answer.

Gettyimages.com

Abnormal Psychology: Disorders and Treatment

Over the past 4 months, George has injured dozens of people whom he hardly knew. Two of them needed hospital treatment. George expresses no guilt, no regrets. He says he would hit every one of them again if he got the chance. What should society do with George?

1. Send him to jail.
2. Commit him to a mental hospital.
3. Give him an award for being the best defensive player in the National Football League.

You cannot answer the question unless you know the context of George's behavior. Behavior that seems normal at a party is bizarre at a business meeting. Behavior expected of a rock star might earn a trip to the mental hospital for a college professor.

Even knowing the context of someone's behavior may not tell us whether the behavior is normal. Suppose your rich aunt Tillie starts passing out money to strangers on a street corner and plans to continue until she has exhausted her fortune. Does that sound crazy? Should you urge her to seek therapy? If so, how is she different from Warren Buffett, one of the richest men in the world, saying he will donate half of his estate, currently valued at approximately $56 billion, to charity?

Assessing abnormal behavior is difficult. What seems abnormal for one person or in one context may be normal for someone else. Deciding what to do about abnormal behavior is often even more difficult.

Pittsburgh Steelers All-Pro linebacker James Harrison has been suspended and fined multiple times for delivering helmet-to-helmet hits to opposing players. Every time he delivers a tackle that way he risks injury not only to the opposing player but also to himself. How does the context of sport impact how we view this behavior? How would we view it outside of the sports arena?

module 15.1

- What do we mean by "abnormal" behavior?
- How should we classify psychological disorders?

Edvard Munch (1864–1944), *Self Portrait, The Night Wanderer,* 1923–1924, Munch Museum, Oslo, Norway. The uncurtained windows and the bare room emphasize the feeling of loneliness and isolation.

Many students in medical school contract what is called "medical students' disease." Imagine reading a medical textbook that describes, say, Cryptic Ruminating Umbilicus Disorder (CRUD): "The symptoms are hardly noticeable until the condition becomes hopeless. The first symptom is a pale tongue." (You go to the mirror. You can't remember what your tongue is supposed to look like, but it *does* look a little pale.) "Later, a hard spot forms in the neck." (You feel your neck. "Wait! I never felt *this* before! I think it's something hard!") "Just before the arms and legs fall off, the person has shortness of breath, increased heart rate, and sweating." (Already distressed, you *do* have shortness of breath, your heart *is* racing, and you *are* sweating profusely.)

Sooner or later, most medical students misunderstand the description of some disease and confuse it with their own normal condition. When my brother was in medical school, he diagnosed himself as having a rare, fatal illness, checked himself into a hospital, and wrote out his will. (He finished medical school and is still doing fine today, decades later.)

Students of psychological disorders are particularly vulnerable to medical students' disease. As you read this chapter, you may decide that you are suffering from one of the disorders you read about. Perhaps you are, but recognizing a little of yourself in the description of a disorder does not mean that you have it. Most people feel nervous occasionally, and most have mood swings and a peculiar behavior or two. A diagnosis of a psychological disorder should be reserved for people whose problems seriously interfere with their lives.

Defining Abnormal Behavior

How should we define abnormal behavior? To try to be objective, we might define it as any behavior significantly different from the average. However, by that definition, unusually happy or successful people are abnormal, and severe depression would be normal if it became common enough.

The American Psychiatric Association (1994) defined abnormal behavior as any act that leads to distress (including distress to others), disability, or an increased risk of death, pain, or loss of freedom. This definition includes too much. When Dr. Martin Luther King Jr. fought for the rights of African Americans, he risked death, pain, and loss of freedom, but we regard his acts as heroic, not abnormal.

Could we define abnormal behavior as actions that are undesirable? If so, who gets to decide what is undesirable? Totalitarian governments have been known to put political dissidents in mental hospitals because the dissidents' behavior was undesirable, from the government's point of view.

In short, every definition of abnormal behavior has problems. It is sometimes easy to agree that someone has a psychological disorder. In other cases, we find room for disagreement.

Traditional Views of Abnormality

Over the years, people have had many views of abnormal behavior and its causes. One recurrent idea is demon possession, an idea that was popular in medieval Europe and still widespread in much of the world today (Cohen & Barrett, 2008). Although the idea conflicts with a scientific worldview, we understand its appeal: When someone's behavior changes drastically, we feel like saying, "That's not the person I knew."

The ancient Greeks explained behavior in terms of four fluids: An excess of blood caused a sanguine (courageous and loving) personality. An excess of phlegm caused a phlegmatic (calm) personality. Too much yellow bile made one choleric (easily angered). Too much black bile made one melancholic (sad). Although the four-fluids theory is obsolete, the terms *sanguine, phlegmatic, choleric,* and *melancholic* persist. This theory was an early attempt at a biological explanation of personality.

Traditional Chinese philosophy held that personality progresses through five states of change, analogous to the seasons: Winter rain helps the trees (wood) grow in spring. The trees burn (fire) in summer, and the ashes return to earth in late summer. The earth can be mined for metal in autumn, and melted metal becomes a liquid, like water, completing the cycle. According to this view, personality also cycles with the season, and an excessive response could cause too much fear, anger, and so forth. Figure 15.1 illustrates the idea.

The Biopsychosocial Model

In Western cultures today, the predominant view is the biopsychosocial model that emphasizes *three aspects of abnormal behavior: biological, psychological, and sociological.* The *biological* roots of abnormal behavior include genetic factors, infectious diseases, poor nutrition, inadequate sleep, drugs, and other influences on brain functioning.

The *psychological* component includes reactions to stressful experiences. For example, people who were physically or sexually abused in childhood are more likely than others to develop psychological problems in adulthood (J. G. Johnson, Cohen, Brown, Smailes, & Bernstein, 1999). Living in poverty increases the risk of conduct disorder (marked by disruptive or law-breaking activity). A study of Cherokees before and after a casino was built on their reservation found that children who moved out of poverty had decreased rates of conduct disorder (Costello, Compton, Keeler, & Angold, 2003). Supportive experiences can decrease the risk of mental illness. For example, although Blacks and Hispanics in the United States have increased rates of heart disease and many other physical ailments, they have lower than average rates of depression and anxiety

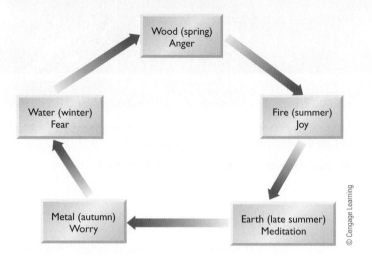

Figure 15.1 In traditional Chinese philosophy, personality cycles through five stages or elements, just as the seasons do. An excessive response could lead to abnormalities.

disorders (Breslau et al., 2006). Although the explanation is not known, likely hypotheses include increased social support within their communities.

Also, behavior must be understood in a *social* and cultural context. Behavior that is considered acceptable in one society might be labeled abnormal in another. For example, loud wailing at a funeral is expected in some societies, but not in others. Public drunkenness is acceptable in some cultures, but strictly forbidden in others.

Cultural Influences on Abnormality

We learn from our culture how to behave normally. We also learn some of the options for behaving abnormally. In part of Sudan some years ago, women had low status and very limited rights. If a woman's husband mistreated her, she had no defense. However, people believed that a woman could be possessed by a demon that caused her to lose control and scream "crazy" things that she "could not possibly believe," including insults against her own husband (!). Her husband could not scold or punish her because, after all, it was not she who was speaking, but a demon. The standard way to remove the demon was to provide

What we consider abnormal depends on the context. (a) People dressed as witches ski down a mountain as part of an annual festival in Belalp, Switzerland, in which dressing as witches is supposed to chase away evil spirits. (b) People parade while dressed as zombies. Unusual behavior is not necessarily a sign of psychological disorder.

Fans sometimes celebrate a major sports victory with a destructive rampage. In some ways, it is like running amok. People copy abnormal behavior from other people's example.

the woman with the best available food, new clothing, an opportunity to spend much time with other women, freedom from work responsibilities, and almost anything else she demanded until the demon departed. You can imagine how common demon possession became (Constantinides, 1977).

More examples: *Koro*, said to be common in China, is a fear that a man's penis will retract into the body, causing death. Some men have been known to hold onto their penis constantly to prevent it from disappearing into the body (Bracha, 2006). You have probably heard the expression "to run amok." *Running amok* occurs in parts of Southeast Asia, where someone (usually a young man) runs around engaging in indiscriminate violent behavior (Berry, Poortinga, Segal, & Dasen, 1992). Such behavior is considered an understandable reaction to psychological stress.

An Australian psychiatrist found that three mental patients in a hospital had cut off one of their ears. Assuming that this behavior must be a common symptom of mental illness, he asked other psychiatrists how often they had seen the same thing. He found that ear removal occurred only at his own hospital. Apparently, after one patient cut off his ear, the other two copied (Alroe & Gunda, 1995).

Culture also influences the expression of more widespread disorders. Depressed people in Europe and North America complain more about how they feel, whereas those in China and similar cultures complain more about their physical symptoms such as fatigue, pain, and sleeplessness (Ryder et al., 2008). Conduct disorder and other conditions marked by antisocial behavior occur throughout the world, but their prevalence depends on cultural influences. Conduct disorder is much more prevalent among Puerto Rican youth in New York, where they feel less comfortable with local culture, than among Puerto Rican youth living in Puerto Rico (Bird et al., 2001; Canino & Alegria, 2008).

Classifying Psychological Disorders

In other medical areas, progress depended on separating one disorder from another so that researchers could find the causes and best treatment for each. Presumably, the same should be true for psychological disorders. If we are going to find the causes of depression, for example, psychologists need to agree on what depression is and how it differs from other disorders.

To standardize their definitions and diagnoses, psychiatrists and psychologists developed a reference book called the *Diagnostic and Statistical Manual of Mental Disorders (DSM) that sets specific criteria for each psychological diagnosis.* The fourth edition of this book, known as *DSM-IV*, was published in 1994 and given a text revision, *DSM-IV-TR*, in 2000 (American Psychiatric Association, 2000). A new edition, *DSM-5*, is scheduled for publication in 2013, a few months after publication of this textbook. Table 15.1 shows the categories of disorder, in the

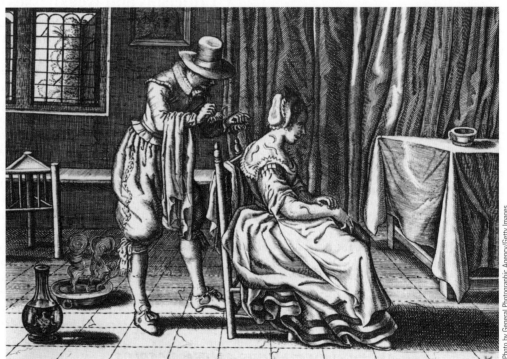
In the early days of medicine, physicians provided the same treatments for all diseases (e.g., applying leeches to draw blood, as shown). Progress depended on differentiating particular disorders and developing individual treatments for each. Can we also find specific treatments for psychological disorders?

Table 15.1 Categories of Psychological Disorders According to *DSM-5*

Neurodevelopmental Disorders

Schizophrenia Spectrum

Bipolar and Related Disorders

Depressive Disorders

Anxiety Disorders

Obsessive-Compulsive Disorders

Trauma-Related Disorders

Dissociative Disorders

Somatic Symptom Disorders

Eating Disorders

Elimination Disorders

Sleep-Wake Disorders

Sexual Dysfunctions

Gender Dysphoria

Impulse Control Disorders

Substance Abuse and Addictions

Neurocognitive Disorders

Personality Disorders

Paraphilias

Others

© Cengage Learning

Inattention	Hyperactivity/Impulsivity
Fails to attend to details	Often fidgets
Difficulty sustaining attention	Restless while others sit quietly
Seems not to listen	Runs about inappropriately
Easily distracted from tasks	Excessively loud during play
Difficulty organizing an activity	Acts as if driven by a motor
Avoids tasks requiring sustained effort	Talks excessively
Frequently loses objects	Blurts out answer before question is complete
Easily distracted	Difficulty waiting his/her turn
Forgetful in daily tasks	Interrupts others
	Acts without thinking
	Impatient
	Rushes through activities
	Difficulty resisting temptation

concept check

1. In what way does *DSM* help psychologists do research?
2. Is it possible for two people to get the same diagnosis without having many symptoms in common?

Answers

1. Carefully classifying disorders helps ensure that psychologists who say they are studying the same disorder, such as depression, really are.
2. Yes. Two people with attention-deficit hyperactivity disorder could differ significantly in their symptoms.

Criticisms and Weaknesses of *DSM*

DSM has helped standardize psychiatric diagnoses so that psychologists use terms like *depression, schizophrenia*, and so forth in consistent ways. However, the system has many limitations.

One criticism is that *DSM* labels too many conditions as "mental illnesses." If you seek help to increase your enjoyment of sex, you have *hypoactive sexual desire disorder*. A woman with premenstrual distress gets a diagnosis of *premenstrual dysphoric disorder*. A child who hates school because of bullying gets a diagnosis of *school phobia*, implying a problem in the child instead of the situation. Surveys have found that almost half of all people in the United States qualify for a *DSM* diagnosis of some type at some time in life (Kessler, Berglund, Demler, Jin, & Walters, 2005; Kessler, Chiu, Demler, & Walters, 2005). The most common disorders are anxiety disorders, mood disorders (e.g., depression), impulse control problems (including attention deficit disorder), and substance abuse, as shown in Figure 15.2.

Another problem is the uncertainty of diagnoses. In the rest of medicine, physicians rely on lab tests. If a patient has a cough, the physician runs tests for pneumonia, bronchitis, tuberculosis, lung cancer, and others. For mental illness, no lab tests are available. Each physical illness has a specific cause and, in many cases, a specific treatment. Not so for mental illness: Various disorders—such as anxiety, depression, and schizophrenia—result from many of the same causes, such as stress (Nolen-Hoeksema & Watkins, 2011), and sometimes respond favorably to the same medications or other treatments (Dean, 2011).

Furthermore, many troubled people fit several diagnoses partly and none of them perfectly (Ahn, Flanagan, Marsh, & Sanislow, 2006; Kupfer, First, & Regier, 2002). Of all people with any psychiatric diagnosis, nearly half qualify for

order planned for *DSM-5*. Previous chapters discussed attention-deficit disorder, eating disorders, and sleep disorders. Later in this chapter we shall consider many more disorders.

For each disorder, *DSM* lists the criteria for making a diagnosis. For example, to qualify for a diagnosis of specific phobia, someone must show extreme anxiety related to a particular object or situation. For a diagnosis of attention-deficit hyperactivity disorder, someone must frequently show at least 6 symptoms (or 4 if over age 17) from either of these columns:

Table 15.2 Six Personality Disorders

Personality Disorder	Description
Antisocial personality disorder	Lack of affection for others, lack of guilt feelings
Avoidant personality disorder	Avoidance of social contact, lack of friends
Borderline personality disorder	Unstable self-image, no lasting relationships or firm decisions, repeated self-endangering behaviors
Narcissistic personality disorder	Exaggerated self-regard, disregard for others
Obsessive-compulsive personality disorder	Excessive preoccupation with details
Schizotypal personality disorder	Cognitive impairments and interpersonal deficits

© Cengage Learning

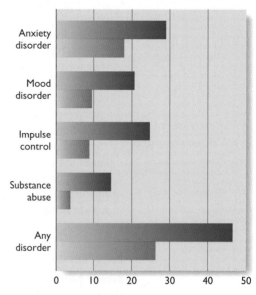

Figure 15.2 In this survey, just over one fourth of U.S. adults suffer a psychological disorder in any given year, and nearly half do at some time in life. (Based on data of Kessler, Berglund, et al., 2005; Kessler, Chiu, et al., 2005.)

at least one additional diagnosis, and people with a serious disorder are especially likely to have additional disorders (Kessler, Chiu, et al., 2005). In particular, most people with depression also have anxiety problems.

Many psychologists who are dissatisfied with the *DSM* approach would prefer to rate each client's problems along several dimensions, such as mood disorder, anxiety, substance abuse, and thought disorder, instead of trying to give each person a label (Watson & Clark, 2006). The authors of *DSM-5* plan to move part way in that direction, but only for personality disorders. A **personality disorder** is *a maladaptive, inflexible way of dealing with the environment and other people*, such as being unusually self-centered. The plan is for *DSM-5* to give clinicians two options. First, they can classify someone in terms of six personality disorders, as briefly described in Table 15.2. Second, they can dispense with labels and rate someone along several dimensions of personality, including impulsivity, suspiciousness, withdrawal, and hostility. It is fair to say that our understanding of personality disorders is in a state of flux, as is the whole concept of mental illness.

concept check

3. What are some criticisms of *DSM*?

Answer

3. One criticism is that *DSM* risks giving too many people the stigma of a mental illness. Also, diagnoses are uncertain, with no lab test to confirm them. Many patients have symptoms that partly fit more than one diagnosis.

module 15.1

In Closing

Is Anyone Normal?

According to the studies described in this module, nearly half of all people in the United States will have a *DSM* disorder at some point in life. If those statistics are even close to accurate, one implication is obvious: Most of the people who qualify for a psychological diagnosis are not a rare group who would stand out immediately from everyone else. At some point in your life, you may have a bout of some kind of psychological distress. If so, remember that you have plenty of company.

Summary

- *Defining abnormal behavior.* The American Psychiatric Association defines behavior as abnormal if it leads to distress, disability, or increased risk of harm. However, any definition of abnormal behavior has difficulties. (page 495)
- *Views of abnormality.* In the past, people have described abnormal behavior in many ways, including spirit possession. The standard view today is that abnormal behavior results from a combination of biological, psychological, and social influences. (page 495)
- *Cultural influences.* A culture provides examples not only of how to behave normally but also of how to behave abnormally. (page 496)

- *The Diagnostic and Statistical Manual.* The *Diagnostic and Statistical Manual of Mental Disorders* lists possible diagnoses and the criteria for identifying each of them. (page 497)
- *Limitations of DSM. DSM* has been criticized for giving psychiatric labels to people with minor difficulties or understandable reactions to stressful situations. Another problem is that many diagnoses are uncertain, with no lab test to verify them. Many clients have problems that don't fit neatly into a single diagnosis. (page 499)

Key Terms

biopsychosocial model (page 496)
Diagnostic and Statistical Manual of Mental Disorders (DSM) (page 497)

personality disorder (page 499)

Anxiety Disorders

- Why do some people develop exaggerated fears?
- Why do some people develop strange habits of thought and action?

You go to the beach, looking forward to an afternoon of swimming and surfing. Will you stay out of the water if someone tells you that a shark attacked a swimmer yesterday? What if the shark attack was a month ago? What if someone saw a small shark that did not attack anyone?

Staying out of the water because you see a large shark is reasonable. Staying out because a small shark was present a few days ago is less sensible. If you refuse to look at ocean photographs that might *remind* you of sharks, you have a serious problem. Excessive fear and anxiety relate to several psychological disorders.

Disorders With Excessive Anxiety

Many psychological disorders are marked by anxiety and attempts to avoid anxiety. Anxiety is similar to fear, except that fear is tied to a specific situation. You might be afraid of a growling dog, but your fear subsides when you get away. Anxiety is a long-lasting apprehensive feeling you cannot easily escape. Figure 15.3 shows the prevalence of anxiety disorders in six countries (Bijl et al., 2003; Murali, 2001). Chapter 12 discussed post-traumatic stress disorder. Here we consider additional anxiety disorders.

Generalized Anxiety Disorder (GAD)

People with generalized anxiety disorder (GAD) have *frequent and exaggerated worries*. They worry that "I might get sick," "My daughter might get sick," "I might lose my job," or "I might not be able to pay my bills." Although they have no more reason for worry than anyone else, they grow so tense, irritable, and fatigued that they have trouble working, maintaining social relationships, or

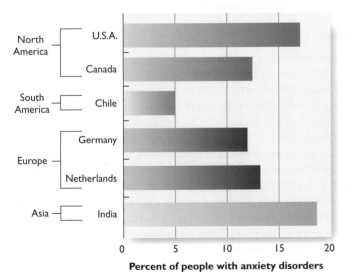

Percent of people with anxiety disorders

enjoying life (Henning, Turk, Mennin, Fresco, & Heimberg, 2007). Many people with depression also have GAD (Bruce, Machan, Dyck, & Keller, 2001).

Panic Disorder (PD)

Suddenly, you feel warm all over. You breathe faster and faster, and your heart is pounding vigorously for no apparent reason. You feel dizzy and nauseated, you sweat profusely, and your hands are shaking. But within a few minutes, the episode is over and you feel normal again. No heart attack would end so quickly. What happened?

This description fits a panic attack. People with panic disorder (PD) *have frequent periods of anxiety and occasional attacks of panic—rapid breathing, increased heart rate, chest pains, sweating, faintness, and trembling.* Panic disorder occurs in 1 to 3% of adults at some time during their lives. For reasons unknown, it is more common in Whites than in Blacks (Himle, Baser, Taylor, Campbell, & Jackson, 2009), and more common in women than in men (Weissman, Warner, Wickramaratne, Moreau, & Olfson, 1997). It is fairly common in adolescents and young adults, and its prevalence declines as people age (Swoboda, Amering, Windhaber, & Katschnig, 2003).

Several studies have indicated a genetic contribution, although no single gene has a strong influence (Hettema, Neale, & Kendler, 2001; Kim, Lee, Yang, Hwang, & Yoon, 2009). A few studies have found that people with *joint laxity* (the ability to bend fingers farther than usual, popularly called "double-jointedness") are more likely than average to develop panic disorder or other anxiety disorders (Bulbena et al., 2011; Gratacòs et al., 2001).

Panic disorder is linked to having strong autonomic responses, such as rapid heartbeat and hyperventilation, *rapid deep breathing*. Almost anything that causes hyperventilation makes the body react as if it were suffocating, thereby triggering other sympathetic nervous system responses such as sweating and increased heart rate (Coplan et al., 1998; Klein, 1993). Fluctuations in heart rate and

Figure 15.3 Percentage of people in six countries who have an anxiety disorder within a given year. (Based on data of Bijl, R. V., de Graaf, R., Hiripi, E., Kessler, R. C., Kohn, R., Offord, D. R., et al., 2003. The prevalence of treated and untreated mental disorders in five countries. *Health Affairs, 22,* 122-133; and Murali, M. S., 2001. Epidemiological study of prevalence of mental disorders in India. *Indian Journal of Community Medicine, 26,* 198.}

breathing usually begin well before the panic attack itself—sometimes half an hour or more—even though the panic attack seems to occur suddenly and spontaneously (Meuret et al., 2011). Panic disorder is more common among cigarette smokers than nonsmokers, perhaps because smoking interferes with lung capacity (Knuts et al., 2010).

Many people with panic disorder also develop agoraphobia (from *agora*, the Greek word for "marketplace"), *an excessive fear of open or public places*, or social phobia, *a severe avoidance of other people and a fear of doing anything in public*. They develop these fears because they are afraid of being incapacitated or embarrassed by a panic attack in a public place. In a sense, they are afraid of their own anxiety (McNally, 1990).

The usual treatment focuses on teaching the patient to control breathing and learning to relax (Marchand et al., 2008). Controlling stress helps also. A stressful experience doesn't trigger an immediate panic attack, but it increases the frequency of attacks over the next 3 months (Moitra et al., 2011). In addition, therapists help the person experience sweating and increased heart rate in a controlled setting, showing that they need not lead to a full-scale panic attack. Over a period of months, most patients can decrease or stop their panic attacks (Butler, Chapman, Forman, & Beck, 2006).

4. Why is agoraphobia common in people with panic disorder?

Answer

4. People with panic disorder avoid public places because they worry about embarrassing themselves by having a panic attack.

Disorders With Exaggerated Avoidance

Sometimes extreme efforts to avoid harm interfere with normal life. Let's begin with avoidance learning, which is relevant to phobias and compulsions. Suppose you learn to press a lever to avoid electric shocks. After you are responding consistently, the experimenter disconnects the shock generator without telling you. What will you do? You continue pressing, of course. As far as you can tell, nothing has changed, and the response still works. *Avoidance behaviors are highly resistant to extinction.*

You can see how this tendency would support superstitions. If you believe that Friday the 13th is dangerous, you are cautious on that day. If nothing goes wrong, you decide that your caution was successful. If a misfortune happens anyway, it confirms your belief that Friday the 13th is dangerous. As long as you continue an avoidance behavior, you never learn whether it is useful or not!

5. Suppose you are an experimenter, and you have trained someone to press a lever to avoid shocks. Now you disconnect the shock generator. Other than telling the person what you have done, how could you facilitate extinction of the lever pressing?

Answer

5. Temporarily prevent the person from pressing the lever. Only by ceasing to press it does the person discover that pressing is not necessary.

Phobias

A phobia is *a fear that interferes with normal living*. It is not necessarily irrational. Many people have phobias of snakes, spiders, lightning, and other items that really are dangerous. What is irrational is the degree of the fear, leading to panic in the presence of the feared object. Most people with phobias are not so much afraid of the object itself but of their own reactions (Beck & Emery, 1985). They fear that they will have a heart attack or that they will embarrass themselves by trembling or fainting. Consequently, they vigorously avoid the object or any reminder of it.

Prevalence

According to a study of U.S. adults, about 11% of people suffer a phobia at some time in life, and 5 to 6% have a phobia at any given time (Magee, Eaton, Wittchen, McGonagle, & Kessler, 1996). However, phobias vary from mild to extreme, so the apparent prevalence depends on how many marginal cases we include. As with other anxiety disorders, phobias are more common in women than in men, and more common in young adults than in older people (Burke, Burke, Regier, & Rae, 1990). Common objects of phobias include public places, public speaking, heights including elevators, air travel and water travel, being observed by strangers, snakes or other dangerous animals, blood, and lightning storms (Cox, McWilliams, Clara, & Stein, 2003).

Acquiring Phobias

Some phobias can be traced to a specific event. For example, one child who was locked in a trunk developed a phobia of closed spaces. Another person developed a phobia of water after finding a corpse in a lake (Kendler et al., 1995). However, many people with phobias do not remember any personal event that started the phobia, and many people who had traumatic experiences do not develop phobias (Field, 2006).

John B. Watson, one of the founders of behaviorism, was the first to demonstrate the possibility of learning fears (Watson & Rayner, 1920). Trying to teach a child an intense fear is ethically dubious, but Watson worked before the day of institutional review boards that oversee research ethics. Watson and Rosalie Rayner studied an 11-month-old child, "Albert B.," who had previously shown no fear of animals (Figure 15.4). They set a white rat in front of him and then struck a large steel bar behind him with a hammer. The sound made Albert whimper and cover his face. After a few repetitions, the presence of the rat made him cry and

Many people who watched the famous shower scene in the movie *Psycho* became afraid to take showers. Actress Janet Leigh, who portrayed the woman killed in that scene, subsequently avoided showers herself.

crawl away. Watson and Rayner declared that they had created a strong fear. Unfortunately, they made no attempt to extinguish it. Later scholars discovered "Albert's" true identity and fate: He was the son of an unmarried woman who worked at the university, and he died at age 6 (Beck, Levinson, & Irons, 2009). Contrary to Watson's assurances that the child was healthy and normal, medical records and family recollections indicate that he had hydrocephalus, meningitis, and severely impaired vision (Fridlund, Beck, Goldie, & Irons, 2012). So, Watson's study was scientifically and ethically even worse than we had thought.

Watson and Rayner's explanation of phobias ignored important questions: Why do many people develop phobias toward objects that have never injured them? Why are some phobias more common than others? And why are phobias so persistent?

concept check

6. In classical conditioning terms, what was the conditioned stimulus (CS) in Watson and Rayner's experiment? The unconditioned stimulus (UCS)? The conditioned response (CR)? The unconditioned response (UCR)?

Answer

6. The CS was the white rat. The UCS was the loud noise. The CR and the UCR were a combination of crying and other fear reactions.

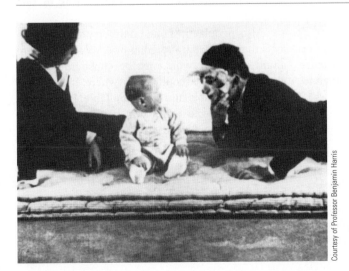

Figure 15.4 John B. Watson first demonstrated that Albert B. showed little fear of small animals. Then Watson paired a white rat with a loud, frightening noise. Albert became afraid of the white rat, as well as other small animals and odd-looking masks.

critical check

What's the Evidence?

Learning Fear by Observation

Given that many people develop phobias without any traumatic experience, maybe they learn their phobias by watching others. Susan Mineka and her colleagues demonstrated that monkeys learn fears by observing other monkeys (Mineka, 1987; Mineka, Davidson, Cook, & Keir, 1984). This animal study sheds light on important human issues.

First Study

Hypothesis Monkeys that have seen other monkeys avoid a snake will develop a similar fear themselves.

Method Nearly all wild-born monkeys show a fear of snakes, but laboratory monkeys do not. Mineka put a laboratory-reared monkey with a wild-born monkey and let them both see a snake (Figure 15.5). The lab monkey watched as the wild monkey shrieked and ran away. Later, Mineka tested the lab monkey's response to a snake.

Results When the lab monkey saw its partner shriek and run away from the snake, it became frightened, too (Figure 15.5b). It continued to fear the snake when tested by itself, even months later.

Interpretation The lab monkey may have learned a fear of snakes because it saw that its partner was afraid of snakes. But Mineka asked a further question: What was the critical experience—seeing the other monkey show fear *of snakes* or seeing the other monkey show fear *of anything*? To find out, Mineka conducted a second experiment.

Second Study

Hypothesis A monkey learns a fear from another monkey only if it sees *what* the other monkey fears.

Method A monkey reared in a lab watched a monkey reared in the wild through a window. The wild monkey saw a snake, and reacted with fear. The lab monkey saw the wild monkey's fear without seeing the snake. Later, the lab monkey was placed with a snake.

Results The lab monkey showed no fear of the snake.

Interpretation To develop a fear of snakes, the observer monkey needed to see that the other monkey was frightened of snakes, not just that it was frightened (Figure 15.5c).

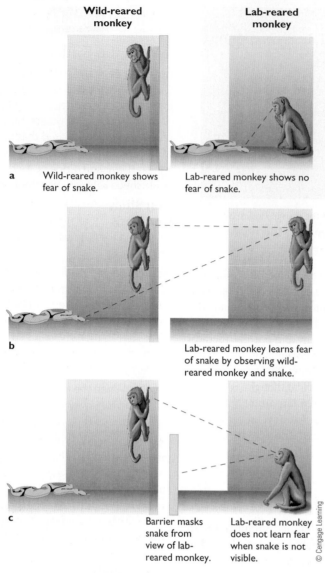

Wild-reared monkey | **Lab-reared monkey**

a
Wild-reared monkey shows fear of snake. | Lab-reared monkey shows no fear of snake.

b
| Lab-reared monkey learns fear of snake by observing wild-reared monkey and snake.

c
Barrier masks snake from view of lab-reared monkey. | Lab-reared monkey does not learn fear when snake is not visible.

© Cengage Learning

Figure 15.5 A lab-reared monkey learns to fear snakes from the reactions of a wild-reared monkey. But if the snake is not visible, the lab-reared monkey learns no fear.

Some Phobias Are More Common Than Others

Imagine that you survey your friends. You can actually survey them, if you wish, but it's easy enough to imagine the results. You ask them:

- Are you afraid of snakes?
- Are you afraid of cars?
- Have you ever been bitten by a snake or seen someone else bitten?
- Have you ever been injured in a car accident or seen someone else injured?

You know what to expect. Far more people have been injured or seen someone injured by cars than by snakes, but far more are afraid of snakes than cars. Few people have phobias of cars, guns, tools, or electricity, even though they produce many injuries. When my son Sam was a toddler, three times that we know about he stuck his finger into an electric outlet. He even had a name for it: "Smoky got me again." But he never developed a fear of electricity or electric devices.

Why do people develop fears of some objects more readily than of other objects? One explanation is that we may be evolutionarily prepared to learn certain fears easily (Öhman & Mineka, 2003; Seligman, 1971). Nearly every infant develops a fear of heights and of strangers, especially unfamiliar men. Heights and unfamiliar adult males have been dangerous throughout mammalian evolution. Less universal but still widespread are the fears of snakes, darkness, and confined spaces, which have been dangerous throughout primate (monkey and ape) evolution. Cars, guns, and electricity became dangerous only within the last few generations. Our predisposition to develop fears and phobias corresponds to how long various items have been dangerous in our evolutionary history (Bracha, 2006). In support of this idea, people who receive electric shocks paired with snake pictures quickly develop a strong conditioned response. People who receive shocks paired with pictures of houses show a much weaker response (Öhman, Eriksson, & Olofsson, 1975).

Evolution is not the only explanation for why snake and spider phobias are more common than car or tool phobias (Mineka & Zinbarg, 2006). Consider safe experiences. Okay, you have hurt yourself with tools and you have been in a car accident or seen others injured in a car accident. But how many times have you had safe experiences with tools and cars? In contrast, how often have you had safe experiences with snakes, spiders, or falling from high places? What matters is not the number of bad experiences but the ratio of bad experiences to safe experiences.

Also, people most often develop phobias of objects that they cannot predict or control. If you are afraid of spiders, you must be constantly on the alert, because they could be anywhere. Lightning is also unpredictable and uncontrollable. In contrast, you don't have to worry that hammers, saws, or electric outlets will take you by surprise.

concept check

7. Give three explanations for why more people develop phobias of snakes and spiders than of cars and guns.

Many people are afraid of extreme heights, partly because the danger is hard to control.

Answer

7. People may be born with a predisposition to learn fears of objects that have been dangerous throughout our evolutionary history. We more readily fear objects with which we have few safe experiences. We more readily fear objects that we cannot predict or control.

Treatment for Phobias

Well-established phobias last many years. Remembering the discussion about avoidance learning, you see why phobias are difficult to extinguish: If you have learned to press a lever to avoid shock, you may not stop pressing long enough to find out that you no longer need to respond. Similarly, if you always avoid snakes, you don't learn that your avoidance is unnecessary.

One common and usually successful type of behavior therapy for phobia is systematic desensitization, *a method of reducing fear by gradually exposing people to the object of their fear* (Wolpe, 1961). Someone with a phobia of snakes, for example, is exposed to pictures of a snake in the reassuring environment of the therapist's office. The therapist might start with a cartoon drawing and gradually work up to a black-and-white photograph, a color photograph, and then a real snake (Figure 15.6). Or the therapist might start with the snake itself (with the client's consent). The client is terrified at first, but the autonomic nervous system is not capable of sustaining a permanent panic. Gradually, the person becomes calmer and learns, "It's not that bad after all. Here I am, not far from that horrid snake, and I'm not having a heart attack."

The process resembles Skinner's shaping procedure (chapter 6). The person masters one step before going on to the next. If the distress becomes too great, the therapist then goes back several steps. Systematic desensitization is often combined with social learning: The person with a phobia watches the therapist or other people display a fearless response to the object.

Most therapists do not keep handy a supply of snakes, spiders, and so forth. Increasingly, they use virtual reality (Coelho,

Waters, Hine, & Wallis, 2009): The client wears a helmet that displays a virtual-reality scene, as shown in Figure 15.7. For example, a client with a phobia of heights can view going up a glass elevator or crossing a narrow bridge over a chasm. This technology provides control of the situation, including the option of quickly turning off the display.

concept check

8. How does systematic desensitization resemble extinction of a learned shock-avoidance response?

Answer

8. To extinguish a learned shock-avoidance response, prevent the response so that the individual learns that a failure to respond is not dangerous. Similarly, in systematic desensitization, the patient is prevented from fleeing the feared stimulus. He or she learns that the danger is not as great as imagined.

Obsessive-Compulsive Disorder

People with obsessive-compulsive disorder have two kinds of problems. An obsession is a *repetitive, unwelcome stream of thought,* such as worrying about doing something shameful. A compulsion is a *repetitive, almost irresistible action.* Obsessions generally lead to compulsions, as an itching sensation leads to scratching. For example, someone obsessed about dirt and

Figure 15.6 In systematic desensitization for phobia, a therapist gradually exposes a client to the object of the phobia. The therapist demonstrates fearlessness in the presence of the object and encourages the client to do the same.

disease develops compulsions of continual cleaning and washing. Someone obsessively worried about doing something shameful develops compulsive rituals that maintain rigorous self-control.

An estimated 2 to 3% of all people in the United States suffer from obsessive-compulsive disorder at some time in life, mostly to a mild degree (Karno, Golding, Sorenson, & Burnam, 1988). The disorder develops most often in perfectionist people of average or above-average intelligence, usually between the ages of 10 and 25. It tends to run in families, but no gene has been identified as being responsible.

People with obsessive-compulsive disorder say they feel guilt and anxiety over persistent impulses—perhaps an impulse to engage in a sexual act that they consider shameful, an impulse to hurt someone, or an impulse to commit suicide. They decide, "Oh, what a terrible thought. I don't want to think that ever again." And so they resolve to avoid that thought or impulse.

However, trying to block out a thought only makes it more intrusive. As a child, the Russian novelist Leo Tolstoy once organized a club with an unusual qualification for membership: A prospective member had to stand alone in a corner *without thinking about a white bear* (Simmons, 1949). If you think that sounds easy, try it. Ordinarily, you go months between thoughts about polar bears, but when you try *not* to think about them, you can think of little else.

try it ▶ yourself

Many kinds of compulsions occur. The most common compulsions are cleaning and checking. Another common one is counting one's steps, counting objects, or counting almost anything. One man with obsessive-compulsive disorder could not go to sleep at night until he had counted the corners of every object in the room to make sure that the total was evenly divisible by 16. Another man collected newspapers under his bed until they raised the bed so high it almost touched the ceiling. Others have odd habits such as touching everything they see, trying to arrange objects in a completely symmetrical manner, or walking back and forth through a doorway nine times before leaving a building.

Distrusting Memory

Many obsessive-compulsive people repeatedly check whether the doors and windows are locked and the water faucets are turned off. But then they worry, "Did I *really* check them all, or did I only imagine it?" Because they distrust their memory, they check again and again.

Figure 15.7 Virtual reality lets a patient with a phobia of heights experience heights without leaving the therapist's office.

Why do people with obsessive-compulsive disorder distrust their memory? One study found that repeated checking makes the memories less distinct! Normal college students were asked to turn on and off the gas rings of a "virtual gas stove" on a computer. One group did it just once, and the other group turned the rings on and off repeatedly. Then all were asked whether the rings were on or off at the end of the procedure. Those who had manipulated the controls repeatedly answered correctly but expressed low confidence in their answers. That is, not trusting your memory leads to checking, and repeated checking dulls the memory (van den Hout & Kindt, 2003).

Therapies

Most people with obsessive-compulsive disorder improve over time with or without treatment (Skoog & Skoog, 1999). Still, no one wants to wait years for recovery. The therapy best supported by the evidence is *exposure therapy with response prevention*: The person is simply prevented from performing the ob-

It's probably a long time since you thought about polar bears. But see what happens if you are trying as hard as possible to *avoid* thinking about them.

OBSESSIVE COMPULSIVE FOUNDATION

EVERY MEMBER COUNTS

This button says it all.

sessive ritual (Rosa-Alcázar, Sánchez-Meca, Gómez-Conesa, & Marín-Martínez, 2008). Someone might be prevented from cleaning the house or checking the doors more than once before going to sleep. The point is to demonstrate that nothing catastrophic occurs if one leaves a little mess in the house or runs a slight risk of leaving a door unlocked.

concept check

9. In what way do people with obsessive-compulsive disorder have an abnormal memory?

10. Suppose someone reports that a long-term therapy, lasting 10 years, cures many people of obsessive-compulsive disorder. Should we be impressed? Why or why not?

module 15.2

In Closing

Emotions and Avoidance

Phobias and obsessive-compulsive disorder illustrate some of the complex links between emotions and cognitions. People with phobias experience emotional attacks associated with a particular thought, image, or situation. People with obsessive-compulsive disorder experience repetitive thoughts that produce emotional distress. In both conditions, most people know that their reactions are exaggerated, but mere awareness of the problem does not correct it. Dealing with such conditions requires attention to emotions and cognitions, and the links between them.

Summary

- *Generalized anxiety disorder and panic disorder.* People with generalized anxiety disorder experience excessive anxiety much of the day, even when actual dangers are low. Panic disorder is characterized by episodes of disabling anxiety, high heart rate, and rapid breathing. (page 501)
- *Persistence of avoidance behaviors.* A learned shock-avoidance response can persist long after the possibility of shock has been removed. As with shock-avoidance responses, phobias and obsessive-compulsive disorder persist because people do not discover that their avoidance behaviors are unnecessary. (page 502)
- *Phobia.* A phobia is a fear so extreme that it interferes with normal living. Phobias are learned through observation as well as through experience. (page 502)

- *Common phobias.* People are more likely to develop phobias of certain objects (e.g., snakes) than of others (e.g., cars). The most common objects of phobias have menaced humans throughout evolutionary history. They pose dangers that are difficult to predict or control, and we generally have few safe experiences with them. (page 504)
- *Systematic desensitization.* A common therapy for phobia is systematic desensitization. The patient relaxes while being gradually exposed to the object of the phobia. (page 505)
- *Obsessive-compulsive disorder.* People with obsessive-compulsive disorder have distressing thoughts or impulses. Many also perform repetitive behaviors. (page 505)

Key Terms

agoraphobia (page 502)
compulsion (page 505)
generalized anxiety disorder (GAD) (page 501)
hyperventilation (page 501)
obsession (page 505)

obsessive-compulsive disorder (page 505)
panic disorder (PD) (page 501)
phobia (page 502)
social phobia (page 502)
systematic desensitization (page 505)

- Why do people abuse alcohol and other drugs?
- Are some people more vulnerable than others?
- What can be done to help people with substance-related disorders?

How would you like to volunteer for an experiment? I want to implant into your brain a little device that will automatically lift your mood. There are still a few kinks in it, but most people who have tried say that it makes them feel good at least some of the time, and some people like it a great deal.

I should tell you about the possible risks. My device will endanger your health and reduce your life expectancy. Some people believe it causes brain damage, but they haven't proved that charge, so I don't think you should worry about it. Your behavior will change a good bit, though. You may have difficulty concentrating, for example. The device affects some people more than others. If you happen to be strongly affected, you will have difficulty completing your education, getting or keeping a job, and carrying on a satisfactory personal life. But if you are lucky, you might avoid all that. Anyway, you can quit the experiment anytime you decide. You should know, though, that the longer the device remains in your brain, the harder it is to remove.

I cannot pay you for taking part in this experiment. In fact, you will have to pay me. But I'll give you a bargain rate: only $10 for the first week and then a little more each week as time passes. One other thing: Technically speaking, this experiment is illegal. We probably won't get caught, but if we do, we could both go to prison.

What do you say? Is it a deal? I presume you will say "no." I get very few volunteers. And yet, if I change the term *brain device* to *drug* and change *experiment* to *drug deal*, it is amazing how many volunteers come forward. Chapter 3 examined the effects of drugs on the brain and behavior. In this module, we focus on addiction.

Substance Dependence (Addiction)

Use and abuse of alcohol and other drugs come in all degrees, from occasional social drinking to ruinous problems. People who *are unable to quit a self-destructive habit* are said to have a dependence on it or an addiction to it. Two major questions are what causes occasional drug use to develop into an overwhelming craving, and why some people are more vulnerable than others.

People who attend Alcoholics Anonymous for the first time often ask, "How can I tell whether I am an alcoholic?" First, just asking is a bad sign. Second, consider two questions: Does alcohol use cause serious trouble in your life? And do you sometimes decide you will quit after a certain amount, and then find yourself unable to stop at that point? The same questions apply to drug abuse and any other addiction.

Either all or nearly all addictive drugs increase the release of dopamine in a small brain area called the *nucleus accumbens*, which is apparently critical for attention and reinforcement. It is reasonable to describe addiction as something that monopolizes someone's attention (Berridge & Robinson, 1998; Koob & LeMoal, 1997; Robinson & Berridge, 2000). Figure 15.8 shows the location of the nucleus accumbens.

However, it is not helpful to say that something becomes addictive *because* it releases dopamine in the nucleus accumbens. For example, compulsive gambling and video game playing have much in common with drug addictions (Gentile, 2009), and these compulsive habits develop the ability to stimulate the

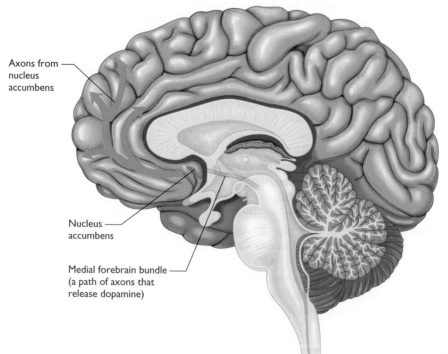

Axons from nucleus accumbens

Nucleus accumbens

Medial forebrain bundle (a path of axons that release dopamine)

© Cengage Learning

Figure 15.8 The nucleus accumbens is a small brain area that is critical for the motivating effects of many experiences, including drugs, food, and sex. Most abused drugs increase the activity of the neurotransmitter dopamine in this area.

nucleus accumbens (Ko et al., 2009; Koepp et al., 1998). People also develop compulsive shopping, binge eating, and other non-drug habits that sometimes qualify as addictions (Olsen, 2011).

It is hard to say what can or cannot be an addictive substance. In a hospital ward where alcoholics were being treated, one patient moved his bed into the men's room (Cummings, 1979). At first, the hospital staff ignored his curious behavior. Then, more and more patients moved their beds into the men's room. Eventually, the staff discovered what was happening. These men, deprived of alcohol, had found that by drinking about 30 liters of water per day and urinating the same amount (which was why they moved into the men's room), they could alter the acid-to-base balance of their blood enough to produce a sensation like drunkenness. (Do *not* try this yourself. Some people have died from an overdose of water!)

concept check

11. Why is it probably pointless to distinguish between substances that are and are not addictive?

Answer

11. There is no reliable way to identify addictive substances chemically. Some people show addictions to gambling or video games, which are not substances at all. Some have managed to abuse water.

What Motivates Addictive Behavior?

Repeated use of a drug leads to tolerance. Most people with addictions say the substance seldom produces much pleasure any more. It releases *less* dopamine to their nucleus accumbens than it does for nonaddicted people. Still, while the drug itself doesn't release much dopamine, cues associated with the drug (such as a picture of someone else taking the drug) release a great amount of dopamine (Volkow, Wang, Fowler, Tomasi, & Telang, 2011). That is, the drug itself doesn't do as much as before, but thoughts about it produce powerful effects. Terry Robinson and Kent Berridge (2000, 2001) distinguish between "liking" and "wanting." Addicted drug users rarely get much pleasure ("liking") from a drug, but they continue to want it anyway. Why do addictive behaviors continue with such intensity, despite reduced pleasure and mounting harm?

Sometimes people really are still seeking pleasure. Even if substance use doesn't produce much pleasure, a little pleasure is better than none. This answer works best for chronic marijuana users, who say that it continues to provide pleasure and a chance to socialize with other users (Hartwell, Back, McRae-Clark, Shaftman, & Brady, 2012).

Another reason for substance use is to escape unpleasant feelings. Abstaining from a drug produces unpleasant withdrawal symptoms. Withdrawal symptoms from prolonged alcoholism include sweating, nausea, sleeplessness, and sometimes hallucinations and seizures. With opiate drugs, withdrawal symptoms include anxiety, restlessness, vomiting, diarrhea, and sweating. A user learns to take the drug to escape these feelings. Using a drug during a withdrawal state produces especially strong effects, and the user learns to return to the substance after any attempt to quit (Hoebel, Rada, Mark, & Pothos, 1999; Hopf et al., 2010; Hutcheson, Everitt, Robbins, & Dickinson, 2001). Someone who *uses a drug to reduce unpleasant withdrawal symptoms* is said to have a physical dependence. In contrast, a psychological dependence is a *strong desire for something without withdrawal symptoms*. For example, habitual gamblers have

a psychological dependence. A psychological dependence can be extremely insistent, and the distinction between physical and psychological dependence is not always helpful.

Also, someone who takes a drug to relieve withdrawal symptoms learns its power to relieve distress, and then begins using it to relieve other kinds of displeasure. People who have quit drugs are most likely to relapse during periods of financial or social difficulties (Baker, Piper, McCarthy, Majeskie, & Fiore, 2004). Even a brief, mild stress, such as seeing unpleasant photos or remembering an unpleasant experience, increases a smoker's urge to smoke (McKee et al., 2010; Vinci, Copeland, & Carrigan, 2011).

The relief-from-distress explanation works, but it seems incomplete. People often use a substance so obsessively that its effect on their lives produces more distress than it relieves. Neuroscientists have demonstrated that when an addictive behavior bombards the nucleus accumbens with massive amounts of dopamine, it stimulates synaptic changes of the same type that occur in learning. When, for example, cocaine leads to these changes, the result is that the synapses learn to respond strongly to almost any reminders of cocaine, but the synapses decrease their response to other reinforcers. The result is a craving for cocaine and a loss of interest in most other activities (Lubman et al., 2009; Mameli & Lüscheer, 2011). Researchers have said that addiction "hijacks" the brain areas that are important for motivation and attention (Kalivas, Volkow, & Seamans, 2005; Liu, Pu, & Poo, 2005; Volkow et al., 2006).

Okay, but one problem with that statement: Saying that an addiction hijacks those brain areas makes it all sound hopeless. True, addiction leads to death or ruin for many people (Degenhardt et al., 2010). Nevertheless, many if not most young people who abuse alcohol or other drugs manage to quit or greatly reduce their use by age 30, even without treatment (Heyman, 2011). Even of those who don't quit early, some quit later (Genberg et al., 2011). Quitting is more likely for marijuana or amphetamine users than for heroin or cocaine users, but even for the most powerful addictions, persistent lifetime addiction is not inevitable (Calabria et al., 2010).

concept check

12. According to one of the hypotheses just described, how do people learn to use drugs when they are feeling bad?

13. What happens in the brain when people repeatedly use cocaine?

12. At first, they learn to use the drug to escape withdrawal symptoms caused by abstention from the drug itself. Later, they learn to use the drug to escape from other kinds of distress.

13. When the nucleus accumbens is bombarded with dopamine, it causes a learned adjustment of synapses so that they respond more strongly to the drug and less strongly to other activities.

Alcoholism

Although most people drink alcohol in moderation, alcohol is ruinous to others. Alcoholism is *the habitual overuse of alcohol.* Treating alcoholism is difficult, and the success rate is not impressive. If we could identify young people who are at high risk for alcoholism, perhaps we could initiate effective prevention. At least, psychologists would like to try.

Genetics and Family Background

Twin studies indicate a strong genetic basis for alcoholism (Liu, Blacker, Xu, Fitzmaurice, Lyons, & Tsuang, 2004; True et al., 1999). Most alcoholics also smoke cigarettes and many abuse other drugs, too, so the genes that predispose to alcoholism evidently predispose to addictive behavior in general. Researchers have identified at least six genes linked to increased probability of addiction (Li & Burmeister, 2009).

A genetic predisposition contributes mainly to early-onset alcoholism. Late-onset or **Type I (or Type A) alcoholism** *develops gradually over the years, affects about as many women as men, is generally less severe, and often occurs in people with no family history of alcoholism.* Early-onset or **Type II (or Type B) alcoholism** *develops rapidly, usually by age 25, occurs more often in men than in women, is usually more severe, and shows a stronger genetic basis* (Devor, Abell, Hoffman, Tabakoff, & Cloninger, 1994; McGue, 1999). Naturally, not everyone with alcoholism fits neatly into one category or the other.

Alcoholism, of course, depends on the environment also. The prevalence of alcoholism and other kinds of substance abuse varies among cultures and subcultures. For example, alcoholism is more prevalent in Irish culture, which tolerates heavy drinking, than among Jews or Italians, who emphasize moderation (Cahalan, 1978; Vaillant & Milofsky, 1982). The incidence of alcoholism is greater than average among people who grew up in families marked by conflict, hostility, and inadequate parental supervision (Schulsinger, Knop, Goodwin, Teasdale, & Mikkelsen, 1986; Zucker & Gomberg, 1986). Women who were sexually abused in childhood are at increased risk for alcoholism (Kendler, et al., 2000).

Alcohol abuse is more common in cultures that tolerate it, such as the Irish, than in cultures that emphasize moderation.

Furthermore, individuals differ. Not all children of alcoholic parents become alcoholics themselves, and not all children who grow up in a culture that tolerates heavy drinking become alcoholics. Can we identify people who are highly vulnerable to alcoholism?

critical check

What's the Evidence?

Predicting Alcoholism

Perhaps people's behavior might indicate who is more likely to develop alcoholism. Several studies found that many alcoholics have difficulty estimating their own degree of intoxication. This study tested whether young drinkers who underestimate their intoxication are more likely than others to become alcoholics later in life (Schuckit & Smith, 1997).

Hypothesis Men who underestimate their intoxication after moderate drinking are more likely than others to develop alcoholism later.

Method This study was limited to 18- to 25-year-old men with a close relative who was alcoholic. Presumably, many of them had a genetic predisposition toward alcoholism. After each of them drank a fixed amount of alcohol, they were asked to walk and to describe how intoxicated they felt. Experimenters measured the stagger or sway when the men walked. Ten years later, the experimenters located as many of these men as possible and interviewed them about their alcohol use.

Results Of the 81 who either did not sway much when walking or stated that they did not feel intoxicated, 51 (63%) became alcoholics within 10 years. Of those who clearly swayed and reported feeling intoxicated, 9 of 52 (17%) became alcoholics (Schuckit & Smith, 1997).

Interpretation Someone who drinks a moderate amount and starts to stagger and feel intoxicated may stop drinking at that point. Someone who shows less effect thinks, "I hold my liquor well," and continues drinking. By the time he begins to stagger, he may have drunk enough to impair his judgment. He also may be less likely to experience the sedation that makes most people slow down and stop drinking (Moreau & Corbin, 2010).

Although the original study examined only men, a later study found similar results for women: Women with a family history of alcoholism are more likely than average to report low intoxication and experience little body sway after drinking a moderate amount (Eng, Schuckit, & Smith, 2005).

Measuring people's body sway as they walk after drinking is a time-consuming process. A later study found it possible to achieve a similar result just by asking people a few questions, such as how many drinks before you feel dizzy, how many before you stumble when walking, and how many before you slur your speech. Those who reported needing more drinks to produce these effects were more likely than average to become heavy drinkers within the next 5 years (Schuckit et al., 2007). Additional research has found several genes that influence people's apparent responses to moderate amounts of alcohol (Joslyn et al., 2008; Roh et al., 2011). That is, genes influence alcohol use partly by influencing how fast people start to feel tipsy.

concept check

14. What is one way to predict which young people will later become heavy drinkers?

Answer

14. Measure the amount of body sway after drinking, or ask people to report how many drinks they need to experience various effects. People who report experiencing little effect from a moderate amount of alcohol are more likely than average to become heavy drinkers.

Treatments

> My mind is a dark place, and I should not be left alone there at night.
> —Participant at Alcoholics Anonymous Meeting

Of all the people who try to quit alcohol or other drugs on their own, an estimated 10 to 20% manage to succeed (S. Cohen et al., 1989), though not necessarily on the first try. Some people quit and relapse many times before eventual success. In many cases, however, people with a substance-abuse problem find that they cannot quit on their own. Eventually, they "hit bottom," discovering that they have damaged their health, their ability to hold a job, and their relationships with friends and family. At that point, they might seek help. Let's consider several options.

Alcoholics Anonymous

The most popular treatment for alcoholism in North America is Alcoholics Anonymous (AA), *a self-help group of people who are trying to abstain from alcohol use and help others do the same.* AA meetings take place in community halls, church basements, and other available spaces. The meeting format varies but often includes study of the book *Alcoholics Anonymous* (Anonymous, 1955) and discussions of participants' individual problems. Some meetings feature an invited speaker. The group has a strong spiritual focus, including a reliance on "a Power greater than ourselves," but no affiliation with any particular religion. Although AA imposes no requirements on its members other than making an effort to quit alcohol, new members are strongly encouraged to attend 90 meetings during the first 90 days. The idea is to make a strong commitment. From then on, members attend as often as they like.

Millions of people have participated in the AA program. One reason for its appeal is that all its members have had similar experiences. If someone makes an excuse for drinking and says, "You just don't understand how I feel," others can retort, "Oh, yes we do!" A member who feels the urge to take a drink can phone a fellow member day or night for support. The only charge is a voluntary contribution toward the cost of renting the meeting place. AA has inspired Narcotics Anonymous (NA) and other "anonymous" self-help groups that help compulsive gamblers, compulsive eaters, and others.

Researchers find that people who regularly attend AA or NA meetings, and who have a strong commitment to the program, are more likely than other addicts to abstain from alcohol and drugs (Gossop, Stewart, & Marsden, 2008; Laffaye, McKellar, Ilgen, & Moos, 2008). However, we cannot draw a cause-and-effect conclusion. Presumably, people who attend regularly differ in many ways from those who decline to participate or who try a few times and then quit.

Antabuse

Many years ago, investigators noticed that the workers in a certain rubber manufacturing plant drank very little alcohol. The investigators eventually linked this behavior to *disulfiram*, a chemical that was used in the manufacturing process. Ordinarily, the liver converts alcohol into a toxic substance, *acetaldehyde* (ASS-eh-TAL-de-HIDE) and then converts acetaldehyde into harmless *acetic acid*. Disulfiram blocks the conversion of acetaldehyde to acetic acid. When the workers exposed to disulfiram drank alcohol, they accumulated acetaldehyde, became ill, and learned to avoid alcohol. (Acetaldehyde is probably responsible for hangovers, although research is sparse on the topic.)

Disulfiram, available under the trade name Antabuse, is sometimes used in treating alcoholism. *Alcoholics who take a daily Antabuse pill become sick if they have a drink.* The threat of sickness is more effective than the sickness itself (Fuller & Roth, 1979). By taking a daily Antabuse pill, a recovering alcoholic renews the decision not to drink. Those who do take a drink in spite of the threat become ill, and then decide either not to drink again or not to take the pill again! Several other medications are also moderately effective in helping people quit alcohol. In each case, the medication is most effective for people who are strongly motivated to quit (Krishnan-Sarin, Krystal, Shi, Pittman, & O'Malley, 2007; Mason, Goodman, Chabac, & Lehert, 2006).

concept check

15. About 50% of Southeast Asians have a gene that makes them unable to convert acetaldehyde to acetic acid. Would such people be more likely or less likely than others to become alcoholics?

Answer

15. They are less likely than others to become alcoholics. This gene is considered the probable reason that relatively few Asians become alcoholics (Harada, Agarwal, Goedde, Tagaki, & Ishikawa, 1982; Reed, 1985).

Contingency Management

Another approach to treating alcoholism and other addictions is *contingency management*. Practitioners monitor alcohol use by a Breathalyzer or other drugs by urine samples. Whenever the test shows no alcohol or drugs, a therapist provides an immediate reinforcement. For example, teenagers might receive a movie pass or a voucher for a pizza (Kaminer, 2000).

The effectiveness of contingency management is surprising, as the rewards are small. That is, people could have abstained from alcohol and drugs and then used the money they saved to give themselves the same or greater rewards. Evidently, there is something powerful about testing negative for drugs and then receiving an immediate reinforcement.

Opiate Dependence

Prior to 1900, opiate drugs such as morphine and heroin were considered less dangerous than alcohol (Siegel, 1987). In fact, many doctors urged patients with alcoholism to switch from alcohol to morphine. Then, around 1900, opiates became illegal in the United States, except by prescription to control pain.

Opiate dependence generally has a more rapid onset than alcohol or tobacco dependence. Like al-

Heroin withdrawal resembles a weeklong bout of severe flu, with aching limbs, intense chills, vomiting, and diarrhea. Unfortunately, even after people have endured withdrawal, they still sometimes crave the drug.

Table 15.3 Comparison of Methadone and Morphine

	Morphine	Methadone by Injection	Methadone Taken Orally
Addictive?	Yes	Yes	Weakly
Onset	Rapid	Rapid	Slow
"Rush"?	Yes	Yes	No
Relieves craving?	Yes	Yes	Yes
Rapid withdrawal symptoms?	Yes	Yes	No

© Cengage Learning

coholism, opiate abuse shows a hereditary tendency. That is, the closer your genetic relationship to an opiate abuser, the higher your probability of developing the same problem (Kendler, Karkowski, Neale, & Prescott, 2000).

Treatments

Some people who are trying to quit heroin or other opiates turn to self-help groups, contingency management, and other treatments. Therapists emphasize the importance of identifying the locations and situations in which someone has the greatest cravings, and then trying to minimize exposure to those situations (Witkiewitz & Marlatt, 2004).

For those who cannot quit, researchers have sought to find a nonaddictive substitute that would satisfy the craving for opiates without harmful side effects. (Heroin was originally introduced as a substitute for morphine before physicians discovered that it is even more troublesome!)

The drug methadone (METH-uh-don) *is sometimes offered as a less dangerous substitute for opiates.* Methadone, chemically similar to morphine and heroin, can itself be addictive. (Table 15.3 compares methadone and morphine.) When methadone is taken as a pill, however, it enters the bloodstream gradually and departs gradually. (If morphine or heroin is taken as a pill, much of it is digested without reaching the brain.) Thus, methadone does not produce the "rush" associated with injected opiates. It satisfies the craving without producing a strong "high" and blocks heroin or morphine from reaching the same receptors. However, methadone does not eliminate the addiction. If the dosage is reduced, the craving returns.

The drugs *buprenorphine* and *levo-α-acetylmethadol acetate* (LAAM) have effects similar to methadone. Most buprenorphine users decrease their use of heroin and other drugs, decrease their criminal activities, and improve their health (Teesson et al., 2006).

concept check

16. Many methadone clinics carefully watch patients while they are taking their pills. Why?

Answer

16. Someone who didn't swallow the pill could dissolve it in water and inject it to get a "high" similar to that of heroin or morphine.

© Ed Kashi/CORBIS

Substances, the Individual, and Society

Substance abuse is a big problem for everyone because of its link to crime, unemployment, drunk driving, and other threats to society. In the 1970s, the United States government declared a "war on drugs." Decades later, it seems unlikely that we shall ever declare victory in that war. Fighting addiction is more like fighting weeds in your garden. You can never expect to eliminate all weeds permanently. Your best hope is to keep the weeds down to a level that doesn't seriously interfere with the plants you are trying to cultivate.

Summary

- *Substance dependence.* People who find it difficult or impossible to stop using a substance are said to be dependent on it or addicted to it. (page 508)
- *Addictive substances.* Addictive substances stimulate dopamine synapses in the nucleus accumbens, a brain area that is associated with attention. After people develop a compulsive habit of gambling, video game playing, or other activities, those activities also elicit dopamine release in the nucleus accumbens. (page 508)
- *Motivations behind addiction.* After repeatedly using a substance, a person develops a tolerance to it, and it releases less dopamine in the nucleus accumbens. Nevertheless, the habit remains strong. Reasons for continued use include seeking pleasure, avoiding withdrawal symptoms, and coping with distress. Also, addictive substances alter the brain's synapses to increase response to substance-related experiences and decrease response to other activities. In spite of all this, some people do manage to quit. (p. 509)
- *Predisposition to alcoholism.* People who have less than average intoxication from moderate drinking are more likely than average to become heavy drinkers. (page 510)
- *Alcoholics Anonymous.* The self-help group Alcoholics Anonymous provides the most common treatment for alcoholism in North America. (page 511)
- *Antabuse.* Some alcoholics are treated with Antabuse, a prescription drug that makes them ill if they drink alcohol. (page 511)
- *Contingency management.* Rewarding people for abstaining from drugs is sometimes effective. (page 512)
- *Opiate abuse.* Some opiate users manage to quit. Others substitute methadone or buprenorphine under medical supervision. (page 512)

Key Terms

Alcoholics Anonymous (AA) (page 511)
alcoholism (page 510)
Antabuse (page 511)
dependence (or addiction) (page 508)
methadone (page 512)

physical dependence (page 509)
psychological dependence (page 509)
Type I (or Type A) alcoholism (page 510)
Type II (or Type B) alcoholism (page 510)

- What causes severe mood swings and what treatments are best?
- What is schizophrenia and what can be done about it?
- What is autism and what can be done about it?

All psychological disorders range from mild to severe, but depression and schizophrenia stand out in their likelihood of becoming severe. When people enter a mental hospital, the usual reasons are depression or schizophrenia. We shall consider both conditions, along with autism, another condition that often produces long-term disability.

Mood Disorders

People who say "I'm depressed," often mean "I'm discouraged." A major depression is a more *extreme condition in which the person experiences little interest, pleasure, or motivation for weeks at a time.* Sadness is characteristic of depression, but lack of happiness is even more characteristic. Many people with depression say they cannot even imagine anything that would make them happy. In one study, people

Treatment for bipolar disorder enables people to lead successful lives. Dr. Alice W. Flaherty is a neurologist who says having the disorder has made her more empathetic to her patients.

had a beeper that alerted them at unpredictable times to make a note of what they were doing and how they felt about it. People with depression reported about an average number of sad experiences but far fewer than average happy experiences (Peters, Nicolson, Berkhof, Delespaul, & deVries, 2003).

Nearly all depressed people experience sleep abnormalities (Carroll, 1980; Healy & Williams, 1988; Figure 15.9). They enter REM sleep much faster than average. They wake up early and cannot get back to sleep. A longitudinal study found that adolescents who had trouble sleeping were more likely than average to become depressed later (Roane & Taylor, 2008).

About 20% of U.S. adults are depressed at some time in life (Kessler, Berglund, Demler, Jin, & Walters, 2005). The reported prevalence varies greatly among countries, but the standards for diagnosis may not be the same everywhere. Women experience depression more than men in all cultures for which we have data (Culberson, 1997; Cyranowski, Frank, Young, & Shear, 2000; Silberg et al., 1999).

The good news is that few people remain permanently depressed. Typically, people have an episode of depression that lasts a few months (less commonly, years) and then recover. The bad news is that depression is likely to return. Later episodes tend to be briefer but more frequent (Solomon et al., 1997). A common pattern is that an intensely stressful event triggers the first episode of depression, but later episodes occur with little or no provocation. It is as if the brain learns how to become depressed (Monroe & Harkness, 2005; Post, 1992). The same is true for epilepsy and migraine headaches: The more episodes one has had, the easier it is to have another one.

In seasonal affective disorder (SAD), *people repeatedly become depressed during a particular season of the year.* It is common in Scandinavia, which has many hours of sunlight in summer and few in winter (Haggarty et al., 2002), and it is almost universal among explorers who spend long times in Antarctica (Palinkas, 2003). Although annual winter depressions receive the most publicity, annual summer depressions also occur (Faedda et al., 1993). The disorder is linked to a gene that affects circadian rhythms (Johansson et al., 2003). The most effective treatment for seasonal affective disorder is exposure to a bright light for a few hours each day (Wirz-Justice, 1998). To find more information about seasonal affective disorder and light therapy, visit the website www.sada.org.uk.

Bipolar disorder, previously known as manic-depressive disorder, is a condition in which someone alternates between mood extremes. In many respects, mania is the *opposite of depression.* In mania, people are *constantly active and uninhibited.* Those with a mild degree of mania ("hypomania") are energetic, life-of-the-party types, but people with more severe mania are dangerous to themselves and others. Some mental hospitals have to disable the fire alarms because manic patients impulsively pull the alarm every time they pass it. In the past, about 1% of all adults in the United States were diagnosed with bipolar disorder (Robins et al., 1984), but the term is applied more loosely today, thus including more people (Bih et al., 2008).

concept check

17. What are the similarities and differences between seasonal affective disorder (SAD) and bipolar disorder?

Normal sleep

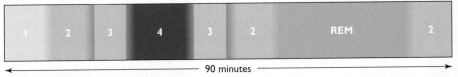

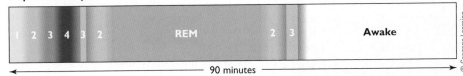

Figure 15.9 Depressed people enter REM sooner than average and awaken frequently during the night.

Answer

17. Both conditions have repetitive cycles. However, people with bipolar disorder swing back and forth between depression and mania, whereas people with seasonal affective disorder alternate between depression and normal mood.

Effective treatments for bipolar disorder include lithium salts (Baldessarini & Tondo, 2000) and anticonvulsant drugs, such as valproate (e.g., trade names Depakene, Depakote) (Hilty, Brady, & Hales, 1999). People usually recover from bipolar disorder faster in Taiwan (China) than in the United States (Strakowski et al., 2007). One reason is that U.S. patients with bipolar disorder are far more likely than the Taiwanese to abuse alcohol or other drugs. Another is that people in Taiwan are more likely to seek help quickly instead of waiting for the symptoms to become severe.

concept check

18. How does major depression differ from sadness or discouragement?
19. What might you observe to determine who is likely to become depressed later?

Answers

18. Major depression is more severe than sadness and lasts months. A person with major depression finds almost no pleasure in anything.
19. Adolescents with sleep problems are more likely than others to develop depression later.

Environmental and Genetic Influences on Depression

As a rule, people become depressed after stressful events that leave them feeling helpless, humiliated, or guilty (Kendler, Hettema, Butera, Gardner, & Prescott, 2003). However, a given experience affects different people in different ways (Monroe & Reid, 2009). Of people living in New York City during the terrorist attack in 2001, about 9% became depressed within the next 6 months, including mostly people with a history of previous traumatic experiences (Person, Tracy, & Galea, 2006). That is, depression seldom results from a single event.

Genetic factors influence people's likelihood of depression, although it is genes plus stressful experiences rather than genes alone that result in depression (Kendler et al., 2011). Several specific genes related to depression have been identified (Kohli et al., 2011; Richardson-Jones et al., 2010). If you become depressed before age 30, you probably have relatives with depression (Kendler, Gardner, & Prescott, 1999; Lyons et al., 1998) and other relatives with substance abuse, antisocial personality disorder, attention deficit disorder, bulimia nervosa, and migraine headaches (Fu et al., 2002; Hudson et al., 2003; Kendler et al., 1995). If you become depressed later in life, you probably have relatives with blood circulation disorders (Kendler, Fiske, Gardner, & Gatz, 2009). These results imply two sets of genes and two ways of becoming depressed—one of them related to brain functioning and the other related to blood flow.

concept check

20. How does early-onset depression differ from late-onset?

Answer

20. People with early-onset depression have relatives with depression and other behavioral problems. People with late-onset depression have relatives with circulatory problems.

Treatments for Major Depression

The common treatments for depression are antidepressant medications and psychotherapy. Much research has addressed the effectiveness of each.

Antidepressant Medications

Three common classes of antidepressants are tricyclics, serotonin reuptake inhibitors, and monoamine oxidase inhibitors. Tricyclic drugs *interfere with the axon's ability to reabsorb the neurotransmitters dopamine, norepinephrine, and serotonin after releasing them* (Figure 15.10b). Thus, tricyclics prolong the effect of these neurotransmitters at the synapses. Selective serotonin reuptake inhibitors (SSRIs) (e.g., fluoxetine, trade name Prozac) have a similar effect, but *block reuptake of only serotonin*. Monoamine (MAHN-oh-ah-MEEN) oxidase inhibitors (MAOIs) *block the metabolic breakdown of dopamine, norepinephrine, and serotonin* by the enzyme monoamine oxidase (MAO) (Figure 15.10c). Thus, MAOIs also increase the effects of these neurotransmitters.

Depression is most common among people who have little social support.

pocampus, expanded dendrites of cells already there, and improved learning (Drzyzga, Marcinowska, & Obuchowicz, 2009; Vetencourt et al., 2008). (These benefits occur only in people with depression, which impairs learning and cell growth in the hippocampus.) Those changes in the hippocampus may be the main reason for how antidepressants help.

concept check

21. Tricyclics and SSRIs block reuptake of neurotransmitters. Which other drugs, discussed in chapter 3, block reuptake also?

Answer

21. Cocaine and Ritalin (methylphenidate) also block reuptake of neurotransmitters.

Based on these descriptions of antidepressants, researchers long assumed that the cause of depression was inadequate release of serotonin or other transmitters. However, antidepressant drugs alter synaptic activity within an hour or so, whereas mood improvement begins 2 to 3 weeks later (Blaine, Prien, & Levine, 1983). Evidently the effect on serotonin and other transmitters is not the whole explanation of how the drugs work. It may not even be relevant. In addition to altering the neurotransmitters, prolonged use of antidepressants increases production of a chemical called BDNF (brain-derived neurotrophic factor) that over a period of weeks leads to the birth of new neurons in the hip-

Depressed Cognition and Cognitive Therapy

Suppose you fail a test. Choose your probable explanation:

- The test was difficult. Probably other students did poorly, too.
- Other students had a better previous background in this topic than I did.
- I didn't get a good chance to study.
- I'm just stupid. I always do badly no matter how hard I try.

The first three explanations attribute your failure to something temporary, specific, or correctable, but the fourth applies always in all situations. If you consistently make that type of attribution, you have

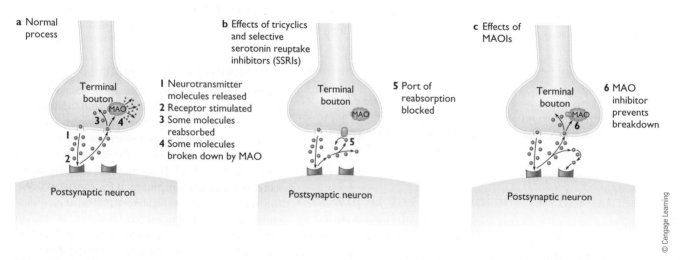

Figure 15.10 **(a)** Ordinarily, after the release of a neurotransmitter, some of the molecules are reabsorbed, and some are broken down by the enzyme monoamine oxidase (MAO). **(b)** Selective serotonin reuptake inhibitors (SSRIs) prevent reabsorption of serotonin. Tricyclic drugs prevent reabsorption of dopamine, norepinephrine, and serotonin. **(c)** MAO inhibitors (MAOIs) block the enzyme monoamine oxidase and thereby increase the availability of the neurotransmitter.

a *pessimistic explanatory style*. People with a pessimistic style are likely to be depressed or to become depressed in the future (Alloy et al., 1999; Haeffel et al., 2005).

Cognitive therapy focuses on changing people's thoughts and encouraging a more active life. According to Aaron Beck, a pioneer in cognitive therapy, depressed people are guided by thoughts that he calls the negative cognitive triad of depression:

- I am deprived or defeated.
- The world is full of obstacles.
- The future is devoid of hope.

People who have these "automatic thoughts" interpret ambiguous situations to their own disadvantage (Beck, 1991). Psychologists today put less emphasis than Beck did on faulty reasoning and more on excessive emotions as the cause of depression (Johnson-Laird, Mancini, & Gangemi, 2006). Therapists also encourage people to become more active—to take part in more activities that might bring pleasure or a sense of accomplishment (Jacobson et al., 1996). Think about a parallel finding in chapter 14: Introverts who pretended to be extraverted (i.e., more outgoing) reported feeling happier. The same applies here: Just getting people to become more active helps relieve depression.

Effectiveness or Ineffectiveness of Treatments

Because depression occurs in episodes, even people without treatment sometimes improve within a few months. Giving a placebo increases the chance of recovery, just by the expectation of improvement. Placebos tend to be especially effective for younger patients (Bridge, Birmaher, Iyengar, Barbe, & Brent, 2009). About a third of depressed patients improve over a few months with a placebo, and about half improve with either antidepressant drugs or psychotherapy (Hollon, Thase, & Markowitz, 2002).

Figure 15.11 summarizes the results of many studies with many antidepressant drugs. People with mild to moderate depression respond about as well to placebos as they do to the drugs. The drugs are better than placebos for people with severe depression, mainly because those people don't respond well to placebos (Kirsch et al., 2008). Other researchers reevaluated the data and came to the same conclusion: Drugs are no better than placebos for people with mild to moderate depression (Fournier et al., 2010).

When patients fail to respond to a drug, psychiatrists sometimes increase the dosage or switch to a different drug, but no solid research supports this strategy. One study took people who failed to respond to a drug or quit it early because of side effects, switched them to another drug, and found that 21% of them improved within the next few weeks (Rush et al., 2006). Do you see a problem with this design? The problem is the lack of a control group that stayed on the first drug. We don't know whether switching drugs was the key, or whether people recovered because of more total time of treatment.

Choosing Between Psychotherapy and Antidepressant Drugs

Psychotherapy helps about the same percentage of patients as antidepressant drugs do—that is, not greatly better than placebos (Bortolotti, Menchetti, Bellini, Montaguti, & Berardi, 2008). Antidepressant drugs usually show benefits a little faster. They are less expensive, and it's easier to take a pill than to drive somewhere and spend an hour with a therapist. However, the drugs produce unpleasant side effects, such as dry mouth, difficulty urinating, or increased blood pressure. Also, many people find that after they stop taking the drugs, their depression returns within a few months. The benefits of psychotherapy

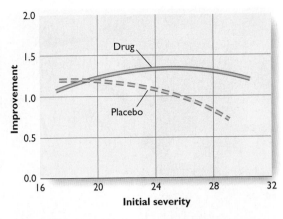

Figure 15.11 For people with mild to moderate depression, antidepressant drugs produce no more benefit than placebos. The drugs show a significant benefit for severely depressed people, who do not respond well to placebos. (From Kirsch et al., 2008.)

usually last longer after the end of therapy (Imel, Malterer, McKay, & Wampold, 2008).

Combining psychotherapy and antidepressant drugs helps, but not as much as you might guess. A combination has the advantages of acting fast and giving a good chance of long-term relief. However, combined treatment doesn't help a much higher percentage of patients than either treatment alone does (Hollon et al., 2005).

Electroconvulsive Shock Therapy

For those who don't respond to either psychotherapy or antidepressant drugs, another option is electroconvulsive therapy (ECT) (Figure 15.12): *A brief electrical shock is administered across the patient's head to induce a convulsion similar to epilepsy.* ECT, widely used in the 1940s and 1950s, fell out of favor because of its history of abuse. Some patients were subjected to ECT hundreds of times without informed consent, and sometimes, ECT was used more as a punishment than a therapy.

Beginning in the 1970s, ECT made a comeback in modified form, mostly for severely depressed people who fail to respond to antidepressant drugs or patients with strong suicidal tendencies (Scovern & Kilmann, 1980). For suicidal patients, ECT has the advantage of rapid effect, often within 1 week. When a life is at stake, rapid relief is important. However, about half of those who respond will relapse into depression within 6 months unless they receive some other therapy to prevent relapse (Riddle & Scott, 1995).

ECT is now used only after patients have given their informed consent. The shock is less intense than what was once used, and the patient is given muscle relaxants to prevent injury and anesthetics to reduce discomfort. The main side effect is temporary mem-

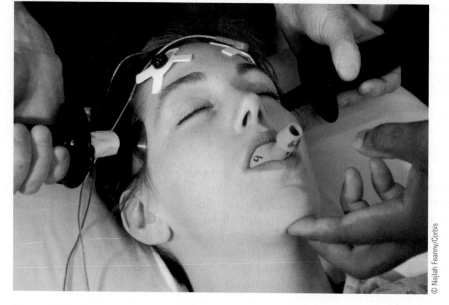

Figure 15.12 Electroconvulsive therapy is administered today only with the patient's informed consent. ECT is given in conjunction with muscle relaxants and anesthetics to minimize discomfort.

ory impairment. How ECT works is uncertain, but it is not by causing people to forget depressing memories. ECT that is administered to just the frontal part of the brain or just the right hemisphere is as effective as whole-brain ECT but without significant memory loss (Lisanby, Maddox, Prudic, Devanand, & Sackeim, 2000; Sackeim et al., 2000).

Other Treatments

Many studies show that people who get frequent exercise, such as jogging or brisk walking, are less likely than others to become depressed (ten Have, de Graaf, & Monshouwer, 2011). However, the evidence is correlational. Perhaps exercise prevents depression, but it is also likely that depression stops people from exercising (De Moor, Boomsma, Stubbe, Willemsen, & de Geus, 2008).

Seafood contains omega-3 fatty acids that are important for brain functioning. People who eat at least a pound (0.45 kg) of seafood per week have a decreased probability of mood disorders (Noaghiul & Hibbeln, 2003). Placebo-controlled studies have confirmed the value of omega-3 fatty acids for relieving depression (Freeman, 2009; Saris, Mischoulon, & Schweitzer, 2012).

concept check

22. What dietary change is recommended for people with depression?

Answer

22. Increased consumption of seafood helps depression, because seafood contains omega-3 fatty acids that help the brain.

Schizophrenia

Many people mistakenly use the term *schizophrenia* when they mean *dissociative identity disorder*, or *multiple personality*, an uncommon condition in which people alternate personalities. The term *schizophrenia* does come from Greek roots meaning "split mind," but the idea was a split between the intellectual and emotional aspects of one personality, as if the intellect were no longer in contact with the emotions. Someone suffering from schizophrenia might express inappropriate emotion or fail to show appropriate emotion. This separation of intellect and emotions is no longer considered a defining feature of schizophrenia, but the term remains.

To be diagnosed with schizophrenia, someone must exhibit a deterioration of daily activities such as work, social relations, and self-care, and some combination of the following: hallucinations, delusions, disorganized speech and thought, movement disorder (Figure 15.13), and loss of normal emotional responses and social behaviors. The symptoms must include at least one of the first three (delusions, hallucinations, and disorganized speech) and at least two of the five overall. As you can see, two people diagnosed with schizophrenia might have no symptoms in common.

Hallucinations, delusions, thought disorder, and movement disorder are considered positive symptoms, in contrast to the negative symptoms of impoverished emotional responses and social behaviors. In this case, *positive* and *negative* mean *present* and *absent*, not *good* and *bad*. Psychologists note a positive symptom by the *presence of some behavior*, and a negative symptom by the *absence of a behavior*.

Hallucinations

Hallucinations are *perceptions that do not correspond to anything in the real world*, such as hearing voices that no one else hears. The voices may speak nonsense, or they may direct the person to do something. People sometimes think the voices are real, sometimes they know the voices are unreal, and sometimes they are not sure (Junginger & Frame, 1985). Spontaneous activity in the auditory cortex accompanies auditory hallucinations (Shergill, Brammer, Williams, Murray, & McGuire, 2000).

Have you ever heard a voice when you knew you were alone? I asked my class this question. At first, just a few people hesitantly raised their hands, and then more and more, until about

Figure 15.13 Some people with schizophrenia alternate between periods of rigidity and periods of frantic activity.

one fourth of the class—and I, too—admitted to hearing a voice at least once. Often, the experience occurred while someone lay in bed, just waking up. Having an occasional auditory hallucination does not mean you are losing your mind.

Delusions

Delusions are *beliefs that are strongly held despite a lack of evidence for them.* Three common types are delusions of persecution, grandeur, and reference. A delusion of persecution is *a belief that enemies are persecuting you.* A delusion of grandeur is *a belief that you are unusually important,* perhaps a special messenger from God. A delusion of reference is *a tendency to take all sorts of messages personally.* For example, someone may interpret a newspaper headline as a coded message of what he or she should do today. People with prominent hallucinations and delusions are classified as having paranoid schizophrenia.

It is hazardous to diagnose someone with schizophrenia if the main symptom is a delusion. Suppose someone constantly sees evidence of government conspiracies in everyday events. Is that belief a delusion or merely an unusual opinion? Might it even be correct? Most people who believe they have been abducted by outer-space aliens do not seem mentally ill, even though they hold implausible beliefs (Clancy, 2005). Probably most of us believe something that someone else might consider ridiculous.

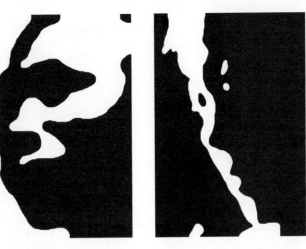

Figure 15.14 Patterns like these are known as Mooney faces. Many people with schizophrenia are slow to see the faces.

Disordered Speech and Thought

Here is a quote that illustrates disordered speech by one person with schizophrenia (Duke & Nowicki, 1979, p. 162):

> Who can tell me the name of my song? I don't know, but it won't be long. It won't be short, tall, none at all. My head hurts, my knees hurt—my nephew, his uncle, my aunt. My God, I'm happy . . . not a care in the world. My hair's been curled, the flag's unfurled. This is my country, land that I love, this is the country, land that I love.

Most but not all people with schizophrenia show intellectual impairments of various types (Wexler et al., 2009). For example, the Wisconsin Card Sorting Task asks people to sort a stack of cards by one rule (e.g., in piles by color) and then shift to a different rule (in piles by number or shape). Most people with schizophrenia have trouble shifting, as do people with frontal cortex damage. People with schizophrenia also have trouble perceiving patterns in ambiguous displays, such as the faces shown in Figure 15.14 (Uhlhaas et al., 2006).

Another characteristic of schizophrenic thought is difficulty using abstract concepts, such as interpreting proverbs literally instead of seeing the intended meaning. Here are examples (Krueger, 1978, pp. 196–197):

Proverb: People who live in glass houses shouldn't throw stones.
Interpretation: "It would break the glass."
Proverb: All that glitters is not gold.
Interpretation: "It might be brass."

23. If someone alternates between one personality and another, is that a case of schizophrenia?
24. What are typical "positive" and "negative" symptoms of schizophrenia?

Answers

23. No. Someone who alternates between personalities has dissociative identity disorder (multiple personality).
24. Positive symptoms of schizophrenia include hallucinations, delusions, and thought disorder. Negative symptoms include lack of speech, lack of emotional expression, and lack of social contact.

Prevalence

Worldwide, about 7–8 people per thousand develop schizophrenia at some point in life (Saha, Chant, Welham, & McGrath, 2005). As well as researchers can reconstruct from historical records, the incidence of schizophrenia and severe mental illness in general increased from the late 1700s until about 1950. Since then, it stopped increasing and apparently started decreasing in some parts of the world (Suvisaari, Haukka, Tanskanen, & Lönnqvist, 1999; Torrey & Miller, 2001).

Schizophrenia occurs in all ethnic groups, but it is less common and usually less severe in Third World countries (El-Islam, 1982; Leff et al., 1987; Saha et al., 2005; Torrey, 1986; Wig et al., 1987). First- and second-generation immigrants to the United States or European countries increase their risk of schizophrenia (Brown, 2011; Dealberto, 2010). Schizophrenia is also less common among people who grew up in rural areas or small towns than in people from big cities (Brown, 2011). For each of these effects, a possible explanation is social support: Social support tends to be greater in Third World countries and small towns than in big cities, and it is least for those who leave one country for another. However, many other explanations are also possible.

Schizophrenia is most frequently diagnosed in young adults in their 20s, occasionally in teenagers. Some studies find it to be more common in men than in women, but other studies find about equal prevalence (Aleman, Kahn, & Selten, 2003; Saha et al., 2005). Once it begins, schizophrenia is usually permanent, but not always. Some people have episodes of schizophrenia, like the episodes of depression, each followed by a period of reasonably normal behavior (Harrow & Jobe, 2007).

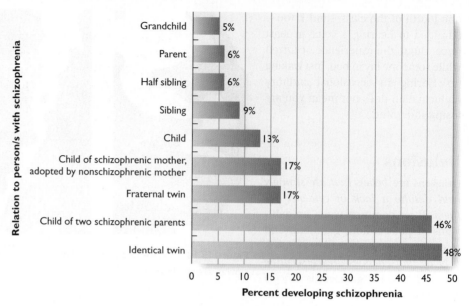

Figure 15.15 The relatives of a person with schizophrenia have an increased probability of developing schizophrenia themselves. (Based on data from Gottesman, 1991.)

Causes

Schizophrenia probably develops from a variety of influences. The prime candidates are genetics and prenatal environment, aggravated by difficulties later in life.

Genetics

The evidence for a genetic basis rests primarily on studies of twins and adopted children. Monozygotic twins have much higher overlap than dizygotic twins, indicating high heritability of schizophrenia (Cardno et al., 1999; Gottesman, 1991; Sullivan, Kendler, & Neale, 2003; Figure 15.15). Adopted children with schizophrenia have more biological relatives than adoptive relatives with schizophrenia (Kety et al., 1994). However, the data on adopted children are subject to another interpretation. Many women with schizophrenia smoke and drink during pregnancy, take poor care of their health, and fail to eat a good diet. That prenatal environment can unfavorably affect the fetus's brain development.

The strongest evidence would be a demonstration linking schizophrenia to a specific gene. Researchers have found links to at least 14 genes, including *DISC1*, meaning *disrupted in schizophrenia-1*, a gene that regulates production of new neurons in the hippocampus (Duan et al., 2007). However, none of these 14 genes shows a consistent link to schizophrenia across all populations (Sanders et al., 2008).

One problem with a genetic explanation is the question of why natural selection has not eliminated a gene responsible for schizophrenia. People with schizophrenia usually die younger than other people (Saha, Chant, & McGrath, 2007), they have only about half as many children as average, and their unaffected brothers and sisters do not compensate by reproducing more than average (Haukka, Suvisaari, & Lönnqvist, 2003).

Currently the most promising genetic hypothesis is that schizophrenia can arise from a mutation in any of a large number of genes (Keller, 2008). Ordinarily, mutation is an uncommon event, but proper brain development depends on many genes (Najmabadi et al., 2011). A mutation of any one of them is a rare event, but if we multiply by the number of relevant genes, the chance grows.

Researchers have found copy number variants (*deletions and duplications of tiny parts of a chromosome*) in about 15% of people with schizophrenia (International Schizophrenia Consortium, 2008; Stefansson et al., 2008). These errors of gene copying sometimes occur for one monozygotic twin and not the other (Bruder et al., 2008). Several of these errors show convincing links to schizophrenia (Vacic et al., 2011). Researchers estimate that copy number variants occur for 1 in about 3,000 to 30,000 people. Even if natural selection removed them from the population within a few generations, new occurrences could replenish the supply as fast as they disappeared, maintaining something like the current prevalence of schizophrenia (Rees, Moskvina, Owen, O'Donovan, & Kirov, 2011).

concept check

25. How do researchers explain how schizophrenia can have a strong genetic basis, even though no single gene is strongly linked with schizophrenia?

Answer

25. Brain development depends on many genes, and a disruption of any of them (including a spontaneous deletion or duplication of part of a gene) can increase the risk of schizophrenia.

The Neurodevelopmental Hypothesis

Some cases of schizophrenia probably don't result from genetic factors at all. According to the neurodevelopmental hypothesis, *schizophrenia originates with nervous system impairments that develop before birth or in early childhood because of either genetics or early environment, especially prenatal environment* (McGrath, Féron, Burne, Mackay-Sim, & Eyles, 2003; Weinberger, 1996). Schizophrenia is known to be more common in any of these cases (Brown, 2011):

- The mother had a difficult pregnancy, labor, or delivery.
- The mother was poorly nourished during pregnancy.
- The mother had influenza, rubella, or other infection during early to mid pregnancy.
- The mother had an extremely stressful experience early in her pregnancy.
- A mother with Rh-negative blood type has given birth to more than one baby with Rh-positive blood.
- The patient was exposed to lead or other toxins in early childhood.
- The patient was infected during childhood with the parasite *Toxoplasma gondii*, which attacks parts of the brain (Niebuhr et al., 2008). The usual route of infection with this parasite is handling cat feces (Leweke et al., 2004; Torrey & Yolken, 2005).

Furthermore, *a person born in the winter or early spring is slightly more likely to develop schizophrenia than a person born at other times* (Bradbury & Miller, 1985; Davies, Welham, Chant, Torrey, & McGrath, 2003). This season-of-birth effect occurs only in northern climates, not near the equator. No other psychological disorder has this characteristic. One possible explanation relates to the fact that influenza and other epidemics are most common in the fall. If a woman catches influenza or another infection during the first or second trimester of pregnancy, her illness impairs the brain development of her fetus. A virus does not cross the placenta into the fetus, but the mother's fever, as well as elevated activity of her immune system, can impair the fetus's brain development.

concept check

26. According to the neurodevelopmental hypothesis, what is one reason why researchers cannot find a single gene responsible for schizophrenia?

Answer

26. In addition to the fact that many genes may contribute, schizophrenia can also result from abnormalities of the prenatal environment.

Brain Abnormalities

Brain scans indicate that the hippocampus and several areas of the cerebral cortex are a few percent smaller, on average, in people with schizophrenia than in the rest of the population (Honea, Crow, Passingham, & Mackay, 2005; Lui et al., 2009). On average, people with schizophrenia have slightly enlarged cerebral ventricles, the fluid-filled cavities in the brain (Wolkin et al., 1998; Wright et al., 2000). Figure 15.16 shows an example of enlarged cerebral ventricles.

Most people with schizophrenia also have smaller than average neurons (Pierri, Volk, Auh, Sampson, & Lewis, 2001; Weinberger, 1999) and fewer than average synapses, especially in the prefrontal cortex (Glantz & Lewis, 1997, 2000). One of the most impaired areas, the dorsolateral prefrontal cortex, controls aspects of working memory that are often weak in schizophrenia (Gur et al., 2000; Pearlson, Petty, Ross, & Tien, 1996; Sowell, Thompson, Holmes, Jernigan, & Toga, 1999).

However, these results must be interpreted cautiously. Many people with schizophrenia abuse alcohol or other drugs that might impair brain functioning, shrink dendrites, and so forth (Rais et al., 2008; Sullivan et al., 2000).

concept check

27. Suppose someone argues that the brain abnormalities in schizophrenia indicate that brain damage causes schizophrenia. What is an alternative explanation?

Answer

27. Perhaps schizophrenia leads to alcohol abuse, which in turn leads to brain abnormalities.

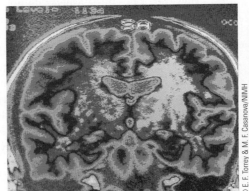 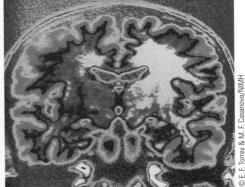

Figure 15.16 The twin on the left has schizophrenia; the twin on the right does not. The fluid-filled ventricles are larger in the twin with schizophrenia. An enlargement of the ventricles implies a loss of brain tissue.

© E. F. Torrey & M. F. Casanova/NIMH

© E. F. Torrey & M. F. Casanova/NIMH

Therapies

Before the discovery of effective drugs to combat schizophrenia, many people spent years or decades in mental hospitals, growing more disoriented. Matters are better now, although hardly ideal. Psychotherapy helps, presumably by controlling the stress that often aggravates schizophrenia (Sensky et al., 2000). However, nearly all patients with schizophrenia receive drugs as part of their treatment.

Medications

During the 1950s, researchers discovered the first effective antipsychotic drug—that is, *a drug that can relieve schizophrenia*. That drug was chlorpromazine (klor-PRAHM-uh-ZEEN; trade name Thorazine). This and other antipsychotic drugs have enabled many people with schizophrenia to live active, productive lives. Although the drugs do not cure the disorder, a daily pill helps control it, much as insulin injections control diabetes. Antipsychotic drugs produce variable degrees of recovery, emerging gradually in a month or more (Szymanski, Simon, & Gutterman, 1983). When affected people stop taking the drugs, the symptoms usually return (Figure 15.17).

Typical antipsychotic drugs block dopamine synapses in the brain (Seeman & Lee, 1975). Furthermore, large doses of amphetamines, cocaine, or other drugs that stimulate dopamine activity produce hallucinations and delusions. These observations led to the dopamine hypothesis of schizophrenia—the idea that *the underlying cause of schizophrenia is excessive stimulation of certain types of dopamine synapses.*

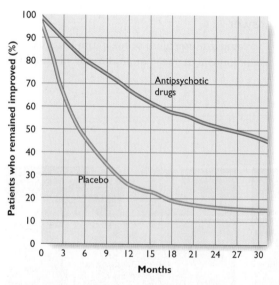

Figure 15.17 After recovery from schizophrenia, the percentage of people who remained improved for the next 2½ years was higher in the group that received continuing drug treatment than in the placebo group. (Based on Baldessarini, 1984.)

People with schizophrenia produce normal amounts of dopamine, but they may have increased dopamine release or increased numbers of dopamine receptors (Hirvonen et al., 2006; Howes et al., 2009).

However, dopamine may not be the entire explanation. The brain's release of dopamine is regulated largely by the neurotransmitter glutamate, and several lines of evidence suggest that people with schizophrenia have deficient glutamate release in the prefrontal cortex (D. A. Lewis & Gonzalez-Burgos, 2006). Prolonged use of *phencyclidine* ("angel dust"), which inhibits glutamate receptors, produces both the positive and the negative symptoms of schizophrenia (Olney & Farger, 1995).

Side Effects and Alternative Drugs

Antipsychotic drugs produce unwelcome side effects, including tardive dyskinesia (TAHRD-eev DIS-ki-NEE-zhuh), *a condition characterized by tremors and involuntary movements* (Kiriakakis, Bhatia, Quinn, & Marsden, 1998). Presumably, tardive dyskinesia relates to the fact that antipsychotic drugs block dopamine synapses, some of which control movement. Researchers have sought new drugs to combat schizophrenia without causing tardive dyskinesia.

Atypical (or *second-generation*) antipsychotic drugs, such as risperidone and clozapine, *relieve schizophrenia without causing tardive dyskinesia*. These drugs alter activity at both dopamine and serotonin synapses. Atypical antipsychotic drugs relieve the negative symptoms of schizophrenia that most antipsychotic drugs fail to address (J. M. Davis, Chen, & Glick, 2003). However, the atypical antipsychotic drugs have side effects of their own, and it is not clear that they improve overall quality of life any better than the older drugs (P. B. Jones et al., 2006).

28. What are the advantages of atypical antipsychotic drugs?

Answer

28. Atypical antipsychotic drugs relieve the negative symptoms of schizophrenia better than the older drugs do, and they do not produce tardive dyskinesia.

Autism

Autism is a lifelong condition characterized by impaired social contact. The main symptoms of autism are (Ritvo, 2006):

- *Impaired social relationships* (little eye contact; little social contact)
- *Impaired communication* (repetitive speech; no sustained conversations)
- *Stereotyped behaviors* (repetitive movements such as flapping fingers)

However, these three aspects do not correlate highly with one another. Many people have severe symptoms in one area and only mild symptoms in another (Happé, Ronald, & Plomin, 2006). As with schizophrenia, what we call autism may represent several disorders with different causes.

In addition to the primary symptoms, most individuals with autism show other symptoms, including fluctuations of temperature regulation, insensitivity to pain, and decreased tendency to become dizzy after spinning with the lights on (Ritvo, 2006). (Interestingly, they show a normal tendency to dizziness with the lights off.) Another characteristic is a tendency to focus attention narrowly on one item to the exclusion of everything else (Bryson, 2005). Many people with autism perform below average on some intellectual tasks and above average, sometimes way above average, on other tasks (Dawson, Soulières, Gernsbacher, & Mottron, 2007).

Parents usually notice autism before age 2 and sometimes within the first weeks of life, as the infant seems not to cuddle like other infants. Twin studies point to a strong genetic basis. One study found 92% concordance for autism or related problems in monozygotic ("identical") twins. That is, if one twin had autism or related problems, the probability was 92% that the other did also. For dizygotic twins, the concordance was only 10% (A. Bailey et al., 1995). To explain this huge discrepancy between monozygotic and dizygotic twins, one possibility is that autism depends on a combination of two or more genes. If autism requires two or three genes, dizygotic twins would have a low probability of getting the same combination.

Researchers have found many brain abnormalities in autism but none that occur consistently. One of the most surprising is that about one fifth of autistic people have large heads and brains—larger than 97% of everyone else (White, O'Reilly, & Frith, 2009). Evidently they have more neurons but abnormal connections among them (Ke et al., 2009). Other abnormalities include decreased number of neurons in the cerebellum and alterations of neuron structure in the cerebral cortex (Bauman & Kemper, 2005; Voineagu et al., 2011).

Given enough patience and special education, some individuals with autism develop well enough to live reasonably normal lives. Many drug therapies have been tried, but so far, the results have not been impressive. Autism remains a fascinating mystery.

concept check

29. Of the most common symptoms of autism, which would be considered *negative symptoms* analogous to the negative symptoms of schizophrenia?

Answer

29. Impaired social relationships and impaired communication.

module 15.4 >

In Closing

Disabling Psychological Disorders

Depression, schizophrenia, and autism have at least three major points in common: First, they seriously impair people for a long time. Second, at present the treatment options are not very satisfactory for any of these conditions. Third, each of them can be a result of various causes. Schizophrenia is probably a family of loosely related disorders rather than a single disorder. The same may be true for autism.

As you have read about these disorders, you could easily become discouraged with how little we know. An antidote to complete discouragement would be to read what the textbooks of the mid-1900s had to say. They blamed schizophrenia and autism on bad parents, who failed to show their children enough love. Those days, mercifully, have passed. We don't yet have all the answers that we seek, but at least we know what the answers are *not*. That progress is worth celebrating.

Summary

- *Symptoms of depression.* People with depression find little interest or pleasure in life, have trouble sleeping, lose interest in sex and food, and have difficulty concentrating. (page 514)
- *Episodes.* Depression occurs in episodes. Although the first episode is usually triggered by a stressful event, later episodes occur more easily. (page 514)
- *Seasonal affective disorder and bipolar disorder.* People with seasonal affective disorder become depressed during one season of the year. Those with bipolar disorder alternate between periods of depression and periods of mania. (page 514)

- *Antidepressant drugs.* Although antidepressants affect the synapses within an hour or so, their behavioral effects begin after 2 or 3 weeks of treatment. They probably produce their benefits by enhancing cell growth in the hippocampus. (page 515)
- *Effectiveness of treatment.* About one third of depressed patients recover without treatment within a few months. Of patients receiving psychotherapy or antidepressant drugs, about one half recover—that is, about 20% more than those receiving placebos or no treatment. Antidepressants are not significantly more helpful than pla-

cebos for people with mild to moderate depression. (page 517)

- *Antidepressants or psychotherapy?* Antidepressants are convenient and less expensive than psychotherapy, but psychotherapy's effects are more likely to produce long-lasting benefits. (page 517)
- *Other treatments.* For the many people who do not respond to drugs or psychotherapy, electroconvulsive therapy (ECT) is another option. (page 517)
- *Symptoms of schizophrenia.* A diagnosis of schizophrenia applies if someone has deteriorated in everyday functioning and shows other symptoms from this list: hallucinations, delusions, disorganized speech and thought, movement disorder, and loss of normal emotional responses and social behaviors. (page 518)
- *Genetic influences.* Much evidence indicates that it is possible to inherit a predisposition toward schizophrenia. A current hypothesis is that schizophrenia can result from changes in any of a large number of genes. (page 520)
- *The neurodevelopmental hypothesis.* Many researchers believe that schizophrenia originates with abnormal brain development before or around the time of birth because of either genetics or prenatal environment. Early abnormal development leaves a person vulnerable to further deterioration in adulthood. (page 521)
- *Brain abnormalities.* Many people with schizophrenia show indications of mild brain abnormalities, especially in the prefrontal cortex. However, some of the damage may be due to alcohol abuse. (page 521)
- *Antipsychotic drugs.* Drugs that alleviate schizophrenia block dopamine synapses. Atypical antipsychotic drugs are less likely to produce movement disorders. (page 522)
- *Autism.* Autism, a condition that begins in early childhood, is characterized by impaired social contact, impaired language, and stereotyped movements. (page 522)

Key Terms

antipsychotic drugs (page 522)
atypical antipsychotic drugs (page 522)
autism (page 514)
bipolar disorder (page 514)
copy number variants (page 520)
delusion (page 519)
delusion of grandeur (page 519)
delusion of persecution (page 519)
delusion of reference (page 519)
DISC1 (page 520)
dopamine hypothesis of schizophrenia (page 522)
electroconvulsive therapy (ECT) (page 517)
hallucinations (page 518)
major depression (page 514)

mania (page 514)
monoamine oxidase inhibitors (MAOIs) (page 515)
negative symptoms (page 518)
neurodevelopmental hypothesis (page 521)
paranoid schizophrenia (page 519)
positive symptoms (page 518)
schizophrenia (page 518)
season-of-birth effect (page 521)
seasonal affective disorder (SAD) (page 514)
selective serotonin reuptake inhibitors (SSRIs) (page 515)
tardive dyskinesia (page 522)
tricyclic drugs (page 515)

Treatment of Mental Illness

- What methods do therapists use to combat psychological disorders?
- How effective are these methods?
- How should society deal with psychological disorders?

Some nearsighted people lost in the woods were trying to find their way home. One of the few who wore glasses said, "I think I know the way. Follow me." The others burst into laughter. "That's ridiculous," said one. "How could anybody who needs glasses be our leader?"

In 1972 the Democratic Party nominated Senator Thomas Eagleton for vice president of the United States. Shortly after his nomination, he revealed that he had once received psychiatric treatment for depression. He was ridiculed mercilessly: "How could anybody who needed a psychiatrist be our leader?"

Many troubled people decline to seek help, partly because of the stigma (Wang et al., 2005). All of us need to consider our reactions toward the idea of therapeutic help. We also need to deal with other issues. Can society as a whole take steps to prevent psychological disorders? Who, if anyone, should receive psychiatric treatment involuntarily? Under what circumstances, if any, should a criminal defendant be acquitted because of "insanity"?

Overview of Psychotherapy

Treatments for psychological disorders are of two types, medications and psychotherapy. We considered antidepressant and antipsychotic medications in the last module. We have also briefly considered psychotherapy, but now it is time to examine it in more detail. **Psychotherapy** is *a treatment of psychological disorders by methods that include a personal relationship between a trained therapist and a client.*

Treatment of mental illness has changed greatly since the mid-1900s, for both scientific and economic reasons (Sanchez & Turner, 2003). If you had sought treatment in the mid-1900s, you probably would have gone to a psychiatrist, because clinical psychology was just getting started. Freud's theories were dominant, and if you went to a Freudian therapist (a psychoanalyst), you would schedule one-hour sessions, four or five days a week, for months or years. You had to pay for it yourself, because few people had health insurance, and if you did have health insurance, it didn't cover psychiatric care. No research had tested the effectiveness of treatments, and so you just had to hope and trust that your treatment was appropriate. Your therapist might give you no diagnosis at all, or a vague diagnosis like "neurotic."

Today, all of that has changed. If you want treatment, you can choose among psychiatrists, clinical psychologists, social workers, and others. Therapists use many methods, not just psychoanalysis. Instead of paying for your treatment, you will probably charge it to your health maintenance organization (HMO) or other insurance program. HMOs and other insurers are unwilling to pay for more treatment than necessary, or for any untested techniques. If you want to crawl naked into a hot tub with your therapist to reenact the moment of birth, you can do it every day for the rest of your life if you pay for it yourself. But if you expect insurance to pay for it, someone needs to demonstrate that this treatment is effective. Consequently, therapists have felt pressure to test their methods and adopt **empirically supported treatments**, *therapies demonstrated to be helpful* (APA Presidential Task Force on Evidence-Based Practice, 2006). Many therapists follow published manuals that specify exactly how to treat various disorders. Because insurers limit the number of sessions they will reimburse for a given client, therapists have worked to develop brief therapies that accomplish as much as possible in a moderate number of sessions. As Figure 15.18 shows, about half of all people who enter psychotherapy show significant improvement within eight sessions (K. I. Howard, Kopta, Krause, & Orlinsky, 1986). Setting a deadline is not a bad idea, although many clients would benefit from more treatment than their insurers will provide (Hamm, Reiss, Paul, & Bursztajn, 2007).

A psychotherapist, like this military psychologist in a Haitian refugee camp, tries to help people overcome problems.

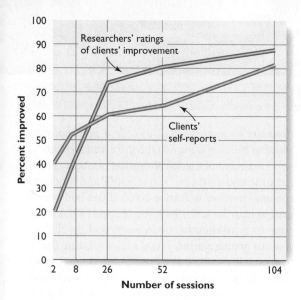

Figure 15.18 The relationship of the number of psychotherapy sessions to the percentage of clients who improved. (From Howard et al., "The Dose-Effect Relationship in Psychotherapy," *American Psychologist*, vol 41 (pp. 159-164). Copyright © 1986 by the American Psychological Association. Reprinted by permission of the author.)

Insurance companies might pay for a session or two if you just feel bad and need to talk to someone, but they pay for more if you have a diagnosed mental disorder. As you might guess, the consequence is that a therapist is almost certain to give you a diagnosis of some sort, no matter what your problem is. Therapists have also become more careful about defining the diagnoses more precisely. Table 15.4 summarizes these changes.

30. How has treatment of psychological disorders changed since the 1950s?

Answer

30. In the 1950s, psychiatrists conducted almost all psychotherapy. Today, clinical psychologists and other specialists also provide treatment. Today's therapists use a variety of empirically supported treatments, with less reliance on Freudian methods. Therapists try to achieve good results in just a few sessions, when possible, instead of proceeding for months or years. Today's therapists provide diagnoses for more disorders and define their diagnoses more carefully.

Types of Psychotherapy

Many types of psychotherapy are available, differing in their procedures and assumptions. The discussion here focuses on psychotherapy as it is practiced in the United States and Europe. Most Chinese consider it shameful to discuss personal or family matters with a stranger (Bond, 1991). Psychologists in India adapt their practice to local customs. For example, to maintain a close relationship with a client, they have to respect beliefs in astrology and other concepts that most Western psychologists dismiss (Clay, 2002).

Psychodynamic Therapies

Psychodynamic therapies *attempt to understand conflicting impulses, including some that the individual does not consciously recognize.* Both Sigmund Freud's procedure (looking for sexual motives) and Alfred Adler's procedure (looking for power and superiority motives) are psychodynamic despite the differences between them.

Psychoanalysis *tries to bring unconscious thoughts and emotions to consciousness.* It is therefore an "insight-oriented therapy." Psychoanalysts offer interpretations of what the client says—that is, they explain the underlying meaning—and sometimes argue with a client about interpretations. They may regard the client's disagreement as resistance. For example, a client who has begun to touch on an extremely anxiety-provoking topic may turn the conversation to something trivial or may simply "forget" to come to the next session.

Table 15.4 Changes in Psychotherapy Between the 1950s and the 21st Century

Aspect of Therapy	1950s	Early 21st Century
Payment	By the patient or family	By health insurance
Types of therapist	Psychiatrists	Psychiatrists, clinical psychologists, others
Types of treatment	Mostly Freudian	Many types; emphasis on evidence-based treatments
Duration of treatment	Usually long, often years	A few sessions if effective; more if necessary
Diagnoses	Usually vague, such as "neurosis" or "psychosis." Often, no diagnosis.	Many diagnoses. Each carefully defined.
Treatment decisions	By the therapist and patient	By the insurer, unless the patient pays for more

© Cengage Learning

One technique used in psychoanalysis is free association, in which *the client says everything that comes to mind*—a word, phrase, or image—without censoring anything or even speaking in complete sentences. The psychoanalyst listens for links that might tie the remarks together. The assumption is that every jump from one thought to another reveals a relationship between them. Another technique is dream analysis, seeking to understand symbolism in reported dreams. Therapists also attend to transference, in which clients *transfer onto the therapist the behaviors and feelings they originally established toward their father, mother, or other important person.*

Psychoanalysts today modify Freud's approach in many ways. The goal is still to bring about a major reorganization of the personality, changing a person from the inside out, by helping people understand the hidden reasons behind their actions.

Figure 15.19 A Potty Pager in a child's underwear vibrates when it becomes moist. This awakens the child, who then learns to awaken when the bladder is full.

31. What methods do psychoanalysts use to try to gain access to the unconscious?

Answer

31. Psychoanalysts use free association, dream analysis, and transference to infer the contents of the unconscious.

Behavior Therapy

Behavior therapists assume that abnormal behavior is learned and can be unlearned. They identify the behavior that needs to be changed, such as a fear or bad habit, and then set about changing it through reinforcement and other principles of learning. They may try to understand the causes of a behavior as a first step toward changing it, but unlike psychoanalysts, they are more interested in changing behaviors than in understanding their hidden meanings.

Behavior therapy *begins with a clear, well-defined goal, such as eliminating test anxiety, and then attempts to achieve it through learning.* Setting a clear goal enables the therapist to judge whether the therapy is succeeding. If the client shows no improvement, the therapist changes the procedure.

One example of behavior therapy is for children who continue wetting the bed after the usual age of toilet training. The most effective procedure uses classical conditioning to train the child to wake up when the bladder is full. A small battery-powered device is attached to the child's underwear at night (Figure 15.19). If the child urinates, the device detects the moisture and produces a vibration that awakens the child. According to one interpretation, the vibration acts as an unconditioned stimulus (UCS) that evokes the unconditioned response (UCR) of waking up. In this instance, the body itself generates the conditioned stimulus (CS): the sensation produced by a full bladder (Figure 15.20). That sensation signals that the vibration is imminent. After a few pairings (or more), the sensation of a full bladder is enough to wake the child.

Actually, the situation is a little more complicated. A child who awakens to go to the toilet gains rewards, as in operant conditioning (Ikeda, Koga, & Minami, 2006). Also, many children begin sleeping through the night, as hormones stop the body from producing so much urine at night (Butler et al., 2007). In any case, the alarm method is an application of behavior therapy, successful for at least two thirds of bed-wetting children, sometimes after as few as one or two nights.

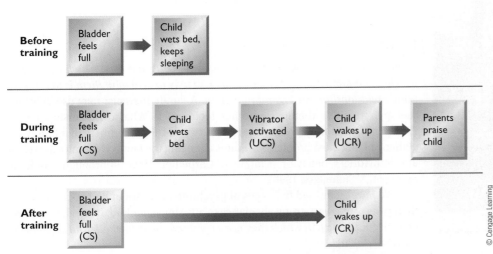

Figure 15.20 At first, the sensation of a full bladder (the CS) produces no response, and the child wets the bed. The moisture causes a vibration (the UCS), and the child wakes up (the UCR). Soon the sensation of a full bladder wakens the child (CR). CS = conditioned stimulus; UCS = unconditioned stimulus; UCR = unconditioned response; CR = conditioned response.

32. In the alarm method to treat bed-wetting, what is the conditioned stimulus? What is the unconditioned stimulus? What is the conditioned response?

Answer

32. The conditioned stimulus is the sensation of a full bladder. The unconditioned stimulus is the alarm. The conditioned response (and unconditioned response) is waking up.

Cognitive Therapies

Suppose someone asks for your opinion and then asks someone else also. You might react, "It's good to get several opinions." Or you might feel hurt that your opinion wasn't good enough. Your emotions depend not only on the events but also on how you interpret them. Cognitive therapy *seeks to improve psychological well-being by changing people's interpretation of events* (Beck, 1976; Hollon & Beck, 1979). A cognitive therapist identifies distressing thoughts (such as "no one likes me") and encour-

An event can be upsetting or not, depending on how we interpret it.

© Don Hammond/Design Pics/Jupiter Images

ages the client to explore the evidence behind them. Usually, the client discovers that the beliefs are unjustified. The therapist helps people identify and abandon unrealistic goals, such as a need to excel all the time. Cognitive therapy also encourages people to find opportunities for activity, pleasure, or a sense of accomplishment.

Many therapists combine features of behavior therapy and cognitive therapy to form cognitive-behavior therapy, in which therapists *set explicit behavioral goals, but also try to change people's interpretation of situations.* For example, they help clients distinguish between serious problems and imagined or exaggerated problems. Then they try to change clients' behavior in handling the more serious problems.

Humanistic Therapy

As we saw in chapter 14, humanistic psychologists believe that people can decide deliberately what kind of person to be. According to humanistic therapists, once people are freed from a feeling of rejection or failure, they can solve their own problems.

In Carl Rogers's version of humanistic therapy, person-centered therapy, also known as *nondirective* or *client-centered* therapy, *the therapist listens to the client with total acceptance and unconditional positive regard.* Most of the time, the therapist paraphrases and clarifies what the client has said, conveying the message, "I'm trying to understand your experience from your point of view." The therapist strives to be genuine, empathic, and caring, seldom if ever offering interpretation or advice. Few therapists today rely entirely on person-centered therapy, but most therapists follow its emphasis on a caring, honest relationship between therapist and client (Hill & Nakayama, 2000).

33. Answer the following questions with reference to psychoanalysis, cognitive therapy, humanistic therapy, and behavior therapy.
   a. Which is least likely to offer advice and interpretations of behavior?
   b. Which is least concerned with people's emotions?
   c. Which focuses more on changing what people do than what they think?
   d. Which two types of therapy try to change what people think?

Answers

33. a. humanistic therapy; **b.** behavior therapy; **c.** behavior therapy; **d.** psychoanalysis and cognitive therapy.

Family Systems Therapy

In family systems therapy, *the guiding assumption is that most people's problems develop in a family setting and that the best way to deal with them is to improve family relationships and communication.* A family therapist may use behavior therapy, cognitive therapy, or other techniques. What distinguishes family therapists is that they prefer to talk with two or more members of a family together. Solving most problems requires changing the family dynamics as well as any individual's behavior (Clarkin & Carpenter, 1995; Rohrbaugh, Shoham, Spungen, & Steinglass, 1995).

We have examined five types of psychotherapy. About half of U.S. psychotherapists profess no strong allegiance to any single method. Instead, they practice eclectic therapy, in which they *use a combination of methods and approaches* (Wachtel, 2000).

Family therapy is especially helpful for those with anorexia (the person fourth from the right). Many who suffer from the disorder have family difficulties, which if addressed can aid in recovery.

Group Therapies

The pioneers of psychotherapy saw their clients individually. Individual treatment has advantages, such as privacy. Group therapy *is administered to several people at once.* It first became popular for economic reasons. (Spreading the costs among several people makes it more affordable.) Soon therapists discovered other advantages to group therapy. Just meeting other people with similar problems is reassuring. Also, group therapy lets people examine how they relate to others, practice social skills, and receive feedback (Ballinger & Yalom, 1995).

A self-help group, such as Alcoholics Anonymous, *operates much like group therapy, except without a therapist.* Each participant both gives and receives help. People who have experienced a problem can offer special insights to others with the same problem. In some places, mental patients or former mental patients have organized self-help centers as an alternative to mental hospitals. These small, homelike environments may or may not include professional therapists. Instead of treating people as patients who need medical help, they expect people to take responsibility for their own actions. These facilities produce results equal to or better than those of mental hospitals, and the clients

certainly like them better (Greenfield, Stoneking, Humphreys, Sundby, & Bond, 2008).

The ultimate in self-help is to deal with your own problems, such as by writing about them. In a series of studies, James Pennebaker and his colleagues randomly assigned participants to two groups. One group wrote about their intense and difficult emotional experiences for 15 minutes on 3 or more days. The other group spent the same time writing about unemotional events. The people writing about their emotions consistently showed improved mental and physical health over the next few months (Campbell & Pennebaker, 2003; Pennebaker & Seagal, 1999). In many cases, the writing experience prompted people to make decisions and change their way of life. Also, after people stated their problems in writing, they spent less time brooding about them (Sloan, Marx, Epstein, & Dobbs, 2008).

a
b

(a) Individual therapy offers complete privacy and the opportunity to pursue individual problems in depth. (b) In group therapy, participants can explore how they relate to other people.

concept check

34. Brief therapy is a goal or policy for many therapists. Why would it be less important in self-help groups such as Alcoholics Anonymous?

Answer

34. One advantage of brief therapy is that it limits the expense. Expense is not an issue for self-help groups because they charge nothing other than a voluntary contribution toward rental of the facilities.

How Effective Is Psychotherapy?

Long ago, Hans Eysenck (1952) pointed out that most psychological crises are temporary, and most people recover with or without therapy. *Improvement without therapy* is called spontaneous remission. Psychotherapy is effective only if its results are better than those of spontaneous remission.

To evaluate psychotherapy, we can't simply compare people who did or did not choose to enter therapy. Those who sought help might differ from the others in the severity of their problems or their motivation for improvement. In the best studies, people who contact a clinic are randomly assigned to receive therapy at once or wait for therapy later. A few months later, the investigators evaluate people's improvement, often by their answers to a standardized questionnaire.

Most experiments have included only a modest number of people, such as 10 or 20 receiving therapy and a similar number on the waiting list. To draw a conclusion, researchers use a method called meta-analysis, *taking the results of many experiments, weighting each one in proportion to the number of participants, and determining the overall average effect.* According to one meta-analysis that pooled the results of 475 experiments, the average person in therapy showed greater improvement than 80% of similarly troubled people who did not receive therapy (M. L. Smith, Glass, & Miller, 1980). Figure 15.21 illustrates this effect.

One could easily complain that investigators invested much effort for little payoff. From 475 experiments, we conclude that therapy is usually better than no therapy for mild disorders. This outcome

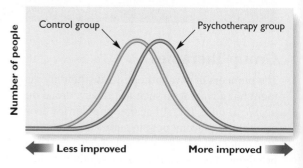

Figure 15.21 According to a review of 475 studies, the average person receiving psychotherapy showed more improvement than 80% of similar, randomly assigned people not in therapy. This comparison lumps together all kinds of therapy and all kinds of disorders. (From The Benefits of Psychotherapy, by M. L. Smith, G. V. Glass and T. I. Miller, Copyright © 1980 The Johns Hopkins University Press. Reprinted by permission.)

a   b

Because everyone's moods and behavior fluctuate over time, an apparent improvement between **(a)** the start of therapy and **(b)** the end is hard to interpret. How much improvement is due to therapy and how much would have occurred without it?

is like saying that medicine is usually better than no medicine. However, the research paved the way for more detailed studies about how therapy produces its benefits and which types of therapy are or are not effective.

concept check

35. Although well-designed experiments on psychotherapy use a blind observer to rate clients' mental health, double-blind studies are difficult or impossible. Why?

Answer

35. A double-blind design requires that neither the observers nor the subjects know which subjects received the experimental treatment and which ones were in the control group. It is not possible to prevent subjects from knowing whether they have received psychotherapy. (It is, however, possible to use a treatment believed to be ineffective and call it psychotherapy.)

Comparing Therapies and Therapists

Next, we would like to know which kinds of therapy are most effective for each disorder. Research has led to a stunningly simple conclusion: For a variety of disorders relating to anxiety or depression, all the mainstream types of therapy appear nearly equal in effectiveness (Benish, Imel, & Wampold, 2008; Cuijpers, van Straten, Andersson, & van Oppen, 2008; Leichsenring & Leibing, 2003; Lipsey & Wilson, 1993; Stiles, Shapiro, & Elliott, 1986; Wampold et al., 1997). The research also shows that more experienced therapists are not necessarily more effective than less experienced therapists, although they do tend to make more accurate diagnoses (Christensen & Jacobson, 1994; Dawes, 1994; Spengler et al., 2009). However, it is not true that literally *all* therapies work. Responsible therapists distinguish between evidence-based treatments and fad treatments that often do more harm than good (Lilienfeld, 2007).

It should be surprising that several forms of psychotherapy seem to be similar in their effectiveness, despite differences in their assumptions, methods, and goals. Evidently, what they have in common is more important than the ways in which they differ. One feature they share is a "therapeutic alliance"—a relationship between therapist and client characterized by acceptance, caring, respect, and attention. Second, in nearly all forms of therapy, clients talk openly and honestly about their beliefs, emotions, and personal difficulties. They examine aspects of themselves that they usually take for granted. Third, the mere fact of entering therapy improves clients' morale. Just doing something—anything—suggests that things will get better.

Finally, every form of therapy requires clients to commit themselves to change their lifestyle. Simply by coming to the therapy session, they reaffirm their commitment to feel less depressed, overcome their fears, or conquer some bad habit. Between sessions, they work to make progress that they can report at the next session. Table 15.5 highlights similarities and differences among four types of therapy.

concept check

36. Name four ways in which nearly all forms of psychotherapy are similar.

Answer

36. Nearly all forms of psychotherapy include a close relationship between client and therapist, an effort to discuss personal difficulties openly, an expectation of improvement, and a commitment to make changes in one's life.

Table 15.5 Similarities and Differences Among Four Types of Psychotherapy

Procedure	Psychoanalysis	Behavior Therapy	Cognitive Therapy	Person-Centered Therapy
Therapeutic alliance	√	√	√	√
Discuss problems openly	√	√	√	√
Expect improvement	√	√	√	√
Commit to make changes	√	√	√	√
Probe unconscious	√			
Specific goals		√	√	
Emphasize new learning		√		
Reinterpret situation			√	
Unconditional positive regard				√
Change thinking	√		√	

© Cengage Learning

Advice for Potential Clients

At some point, you or someone close to you may be interested in seeing a psychotherapist. If so, here are some points to remember:

- Consulting a therapist does not mean that something is wrong with you. Many people simply need to talk with someone during a crisis.
- If you live in the United States, you can look up the telephone number for the Mental Health Association. Call and ask for a recommendation. You can specify how much you can pay, what kind of problem you have, and even what type of therapist you prefer.
- Effective therapy depends on a good relationship between client and therapist. If you feel more comfortable talking with someone from your own culture, ethnic group, or religious background, look for such a therapist (La Roche & Christopher, 2008; Worthington, Kurusu, McCullough, & Sandage, 1996).
- Be skeptical of any therapist who seems overconfident. Clinical experience does not give anyone quick access to your private thoughts.

The Future of Psychotherapy and Prospects for Prevention

Sigmund Freud's procedure featured one therapist and one client for an hour at a time, four or five times a week, month after month. Today's therapists provide briefer treatments, often with a group of people at a time. Still, recall the estimate earlier in this chapter that nearly half of all people have a *DSM* problem of some type at some point in life. Alan Kazdin and his associates have argued that we will never have enough psychologists and psychiatrists to provide individual help to every troubled person (Kazdin & Blase, 2011). So, what should we do instead? Kazdin suggests therapy by telephone or the Internet, good self-help books, and informative movie and television programs. Better yet, the goal should be to prevent disorders as much as possible. Just as our society puts fluoride into drinking water to prevent tooth decay and immunizes people against contagious diseases, it can take action to prevent certain types of psychological disorders (Albee, 1986; Wandersman & Florin, 2003).

Let's distinguish prevention from intervention and maintenance. Prevention is *avoiding a disorder from the start*. Intervention is *identifying a disorder and relieving it*, and maintenance is *taking steps to keep a disorder from becoming more serious*. Prevention takes several forms. A *universal* program targets everyone, such as an antismoking campaign, or ab-

olition of lead-based paints and leaded gasoline. A *selective* program includes only people at risk, such as people with a family history of some disorder. An *indicated* program identifies people in the early stages of a disorder and tries to stop it. An indicated program is closer to intervention than to prevention.

Community psychologists *try to help people change their environment, both to prevent disorders and to promote a positive sense of mental well-being*, analogous to the goals set by Alfred Adler (Trickett, 2009). For example, many schools have instituted Social and Emotional Learning programs (SEL) to teach self-management, social relationship skills, and responsible decision-making. These programs reliably reduce the prevalence of conduct problems and emotional distress, but in addition they improve social skills, emotional control, and academic performance even for students who were already doing reasonably well (Durlak, Weissberg, Dymncki, Taylor, & Schellinger, 2011). Success of this type shows the potential of well-designed universal prevention programs.

Effective prevention programs need careful testing. Many interventions that sound reasonable don't work. For example, prolonged discussions of a stressful experience shortly after the event are more likely to cause than prevent post-traumatic stress disorder. "Scared straight" interventions tend to increase, not decrease, criminal behavior. Group therapy for aggressive teenagers often backfires by introducing them to potential bad influences. Several programs intended to prevent anorexia nervosa or decrease suicide rates have in fact increased the rates (Joiner, 1999; Mann et al., 1997; Moller, 1992; Stice & Shaw, 2004; C. B. Taylor et al., 2006). The point is that we need careful research to identify effective methods of prevention and treatment (Lilienfeld, 2007; Nicholson, Foote, & Gigerick, 2009).

The best programs give participants active practice at specific behaviors, such as resisting peer pressure to risky behaviors. They build up step by step from simpler skills to more complex ones, analogous to Skinner's method of shaping. And they work with people at appropriate times in their lives. For example, AIDS prevention or pregnancy prevention should start at an age when students might begin to be sexually active, not many years earlier or many years later.

Here are examples of effective prevention programs:

- **Early screening.** Most people do not seek a therapist's help until they have struggled with a problem on their own for years. Early detection increases the probability of a good outcome.
- **Ban toxins.** The sale of lead-based paint has been banned because children who eat flakes of it sustain brain damage.
- **Educate pregnant women about prenatal care.** The use of alcohol or other drugs during pregnancy damages the brain of a fetus, and bacterial and viral infections during pregnancy can impair fetal brain development.
- **Outlaw smoking in public places and educate people about the risks of smoking.** Improvements in physical health improve psychological well-being, too.
- **Help people get jobs.** People who lose their jobs lose self-esteem and increase their risk of depression and substance abuse.
- **Provide child care.** Improved, affordable day-care services relieve stress for both parents and children.

concept check

37. Why is it important to do careful research before initiating a new program to prevent a psychological disorder?

Answer

37. Some programs intended for prevention have been ineffective or counter-productive.

Social Issues Related to Mental Illness

Finally, let's consider some public-policy issues you may face as a citizen. First, mental hospitals: Until the 1950s, huge numbers of troubled people were confined in understaffed, overcrowded state mental hospitals supported by the government. Residents included not only mental patients but also Alzheimer's disease patients and people with mental retardation. Most of these hospitals were grim places.

In the 1950s, hospitals moved toward deinstitutionalization, *the removal of patients from mental hospitals*, to give them the least restrictive care possible—an idea that many people had been advocating for 100 years or more (Tuntiya, 2007). The hope was that patients would go home, free to live as normal a life as possible, while receiving outpatient care at community mental health centers, which are usually cheaper and more effective than large mental hospitals (Fenton, Hoch, Herrell, Mosher, & Dixon, 2002; Fenton, Mosher, Herrell, & Blyler, 1998). England and Wales had 130 psychiatric hospitals in 1975 but only 12 in 2000 (Leff, 2002). The United States had almost 200,000 people in mental hospitals in 1967 and fewer than 40,000 in 2007 (Scott, Lakin, & Larson, 2008).

But what happened to people after release from the mental hospitals? Some received the intended treatment at community mental health centers, but many others ended up homeless or in nursing homes or prisons (Nilsson & Lögdberg, 2008; Odell & Commander, 2000). Deinstitutionalization was and is a good idea in principle but only if implemented well, and too often it has not been.

Deinstitutionalization moved people out of mental hospitals, but many received little or no treatment after their release.

Involuntary Commitment and Treatment of Potentially Dangerous Patients

Suppose a family moves into the house next to yours, and their adult son, who lives at home, has a psychiatric disorder. Are you in danger? Swedish researchers examined the whole country's medical and criminal records and found that people with severe mental illnesses, who constituted about 1.4% of the population, committed about 5% of the violent crimes (Fazel & Grann, 2006). However, as illustrated in Figure 15.22, the increased danger is associated only with those mental patients who are also alcohol or substance abusers (Elbogen & Johnson, 2009).

If someone with a history of mental illness appears to be dangerous and refuses to be treated, should it be possible to require treatment? In the United States, the law varies from state to state, but typically, a judge can order involuntary commitment to a mental hospital for people who are either dangerous or incompetent to make their own decisions. That judgment is also difficult. On the one hand, some seriously disordered people fail to recognize their problems. On the other hand, some psychiatrists have given strong medications to people with minor problems, doing more harm than good.

The Duty to Protect

Suppose someone tells his therapist that he plans to kill a woman who refused his attentions. Months later, he really does kill her. Should her family be able to sue the therapist and collect damages?

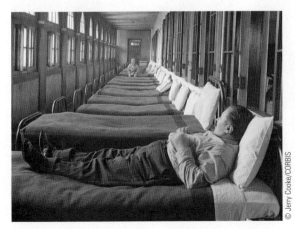

Most mental hospitals of the mid-1900s were unpleasant warehouses that provided minimal care.

In the 1976 *Tarasoff* case, a California court ruled that *a therapist who has reason to believe that a client is dangerous to someone must warn the endangered person or take other steps to prevent harm.* That rule has become widely accepted in the United States and Canada, although its application is sometimes unclear (Quattrocchi & Schopp, 2005). Unfortunately, therapists don't always know who is dangerous. Many people (not only those in therapy) have at some point said, "I'm so angry I could kill," with no intention to carry out the threat. To protect against lawsuits, many therapists now decline to take potentially violent clients, and they sometimes recommend involuntary commitment, even when someone's potential for danger is not clear (Buckner & Firestone, 2000).

The Insanity Defense

Suppose someone slips into your drink a drug that causes you to hallucinate wildly. You see what looks like a hideous giant cockroach, and you kill it. Later, you discover it was not a cockroach but a person. Should you be convicted of murder? Of course not. Now suppose your own brain chemistry causes the same hallucination. You kill what you think is a giant cockroach, but it is actually a human being. Are you guilty of murder?

The tradition since Roman times has been that you are "not guilty by reason of insanity." You had no intention to do harm, and you did not know what you were doing. You should go to a mental hospital, not a prison. Most people agree with that principle in extreme cases. The problem is where to draw the line. Under what conditions is someone legally insane? *Insanity* is a legal term, not a psychological or medical term.

One point of agreement is that the crime itself, no matter how atrocious, does not demonstrate insanity. Jeffrey Dahmer, arrested in 1991 for murdering and cannibalizing several men, was ruled sane and sentenced to prison. Theodore Kaczynski, arrested for mailing bombs for more than two decades, refused to plead insanity and probably would not have been ruled insane anyway. Bizarre crimes do not, in themselves, demonstrate insanity. Each of these murderers knew what he was doing and tried to avoid capture. Trying to avoid capture implies that the person *did* understand what he or she was doing.

Lawyers, physicians, and psychologists have long struggled to establish a clear definition of insanity. The most famous definition, the M'Naghten rule, written in Great Britain in 1843, states:

> To establish a defense on the ground of insanity, it must be clearly proved that, at the time of the committing of the act, the party accused was la-

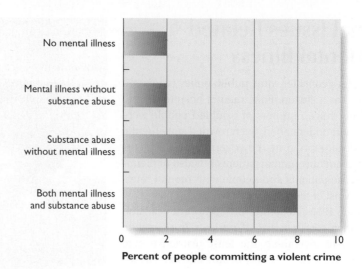

Figure 15.22 People with mental illness who are also substance abusers have an 8% chance of committing a violent crime within 2 to 3 years. Those who are not substance abusers are no more dangerous than the rest of the population. (Based on data from Elbogen, E. B., & Johnson, S. C., 2009. The intricate link between violence and mental disorder. *Archives of General Psychiatry, 66,* 152–161.)

> boring under such a defect of reason, from disease of the mind, as not to know the nature and quality of the act he was doing; or if he did know it, that he did not know he was doing what was wrong (Shapiro, 1985).

In other words, *to be regarded as insane under the M'Naghten rule, people must be so disordered that they do not understand what they are doing.* An insanity verdict requires a difficult judgment about the defendant's state of mind at the time of the act. To help make that judgment, psychologists and psychiatrists are called as expert witnesses. The insanity cases that come to a jury trial are the difficult ones in which the experts disagree. In the United States, fewer than 1% of accused felons plead insanity, and of those, fewer than 25% are found not guilty (Knoll & Resnick, 2008). So, in essence, no more than 0.25% of all defendants are found not guilty by reason of insanity. However, those few cases get enough publicity that many people overestimate how common they are.

Jeffery Dahmer, who murdered and cannibalized several men, was ruled sane. The bizarreness of the crime itself does not demonstrate legal insanity.

Another misconception is that defendants found not guilty by reason of insanity simply go free. In fact, they are almost always committed to a mental hospital, where they usually stay at least as long as they would have in prison (Silver, 1995). When they are released, it is a "conditional release" that requires them to follow certain rules, such as continuing to take their medicine (Vitacco et al., 2008).

For more information about cases using the insanity defense, as well as other legal cases relevant to psychology, visit the Psychiatry & the Law web page at bama.ua.edu/~jhooper/tableofc.html.

concept check

38. Someone who has been involuntarily committed to a mental hospital escapes and commits a murder. Will this person be judged not guilty by reason of insanity?

Answer

38. Not necessarily. A defendant is insane only if the disorder prevented the person from understanding what he or she was doing.

module 15.5

In Closing

The Science and Politics of Mental Illness

Suppose you are a storekeeper. Someone dressed as Batman stands outside your store every day shouting gibberish at anyone who comes by. Your once-thriving business draws fewer and fewer customers each day. The disturbing man outside does not seem to be breaking any laws. He wants nothing to do with psychologists or psychiatrists. Should he nevertheless be forced to accept treatment for his odd behavior? If not, what happens to your rights as a storekeeper?

Similarly, the insanity defense and all the other issues in this module are complicated questions that require political decisions by society as a whole, not just the opinions of psychologists or psychiatrists. Regardless of what career you enter, you will be a voter and potential juror, and you will have a voice in deciding these issues. The decisions deserve serious, informed consideration.

Summary

- *Historical trends.* In the mid-1900s, people seeking psychotherapy paid for it themselves. Today, most people rely on insurance, and the insurance companies urge brief treatment with empirically supported therapies. Because they pay for more treatment if someone has a diagnosis, therapists now apply a greater variety of diagnoses, carefully described. (page 525)
- *Psychoanalysis.* Psychoanalysts try to uncover the unconscious reasons behind self-defeating behaviors. To bring the unconscious to consciousness, they rely on free association, dream analysis, and transference. (page 526)
- *Behavior therapy.* Behavior therapists set specific goals for changing a client's behavior and

use learning techniques to help a client achieve those goals. (page 527)
- *Cognitive therapies.* Cognitive therapists try to get clients to give up their irrational beliefs and unrealistic goals and to replace defeatist thinking with more favorable views of themselves and the world. Many therapists combine features of behavior therapy and cognitive therapy, attempting to change people's behaviors by altering how they interpret the situation. (page 528)
- *Humanistic therapy.* Humanistic therapists, including person-centered therapists, assume that people can solve their own problems. (page 528)
- *Family systems therapy.* In many cases, an individual's problem is part of an overall disorder of

family communications and expectations. Family systems therapists try to work with a whole family. (page 528)

- *Group therapies and self-help groups.* Psychotherapy is sometimes provided to people in groups, often composed of individuals with similar problems. Self-help groups provide sessions similar to group therapy but without a therapist. (page 529)
- *Effectiveness of psychotherapy.* The average troubled person in therapy improves more than at least 80% of the troubled people not in therapy. In general, all mainstream therapies appear about equally effective, although a few "fad" therapies are useless or harmful. Therapists today emphasize empirically supported therapies. (page 530)
- *Similarities among therapies.* A wide variety of therapies share certain features: All rely on a caring relationship between therapist and client. All promote self-understanding. All improve clients' morale. And all require a commitment by clients to try to make changes in their lives. (page 531)

- *Prevention.* Psychologists, especially community psychologists, seek to help people change their environment to promote mental health. (page 532)
- *Deinstitutionalization.* Few patients stay long in mental hospitals, but many patients released from mental hospitals do not receive adequate alternative care. (page 533)
- *Involuntary commitment.* People can be committed to a mental hospital if they are judged to be dangerous or incompetent. It is difficult to frame laws that ensure treatment for those who need it while also protecting those with good reasons to refuse it. (page 533)
- *Duty to warn.* The courts have ruled that a therapist who is convinced that a client is dangerous should warn the endangered person. (page 533)
- *The insanity defense.* Some defendants accused of a crime are acquitted for reasons of insanity, which is a legal rather than a medical or psychological concept. (page 534)

Key Terms

behavior therapy (page 527)

cognitive therapy (page 528)

cognitive-behavior therapy (page 528)

community psychologist (page 532)

deinstitutionalization (page 533)

dream analysis (page 527)

eclectic therapy (page 528)

empirically supported treatments (page 525)

family systems therapy (page 528)

free association (page 527)

group therapy (page 529)

intervention (page 532)

maintenance (page 532)

meta-analysis (page 530)

M'Naghten rule (page 534)

person-centered therapy (page 528)

prevention (page 532)

psychoanalysis (page 526)

psychodynamic therapies (page 526)

psychotherapy (page 525)

self-help group (page 529)

spontaneous remission (page 530)

Tarasoff (page 534)

transference (page 527)

exploration and study

Access an interactive eBook and chapter-specific learning tools, including

- **flashcards**
- **quizzes**
- **videos**

and more, in your Psychology CourseMate. Go to **CengageBrain.com.**

If your professor has assigned Aplia:

1. Sign in to your account.
2. Complete the corresponding exercises as required by your professor.
3. When finished, click "Grade It Now" to see which areas you have mastered, which areas need more work, and detailed explanations of every answer.

we are at the end of the book. As I've been writ-
and revising, I've imagined you sitting there
ing. I've imagined a student much like I was in
ge, reading about psychology for the first time
often growing excited about it. I remember pe-
cally telling a friend or relative, "Guess what I
learned about psychology! Isn't this interest-
" (I still do the same today.) I also remember
sionally thinking, "Hmm. The book says such-
so, but I'm not convinced. I wonder whether
hologists ever considered a different explana-
...." I started thinking about research I might do
ecame a psychologist.

I hope that you've had similar experiences
self. I hope you've occasionally become so ex-
t about something you read that you thought
t it and told other people about it. In fact I hope
old your roommate so much about psychology
you started to become mildly annoying. I also
e you've sometimes doubted a conclusion,
ining a research project that might test it or
ove on it. Psychology is still a work in progress.
Now, as I picture you reaching the end of the
se, I'm not sure how you'll react. You might be
ing, "Wow, I sure have learned a lot!" Or you
t be thinking, "Is that *all*?" Maybe you are react-
oth ways: "Yes, I learned a lot. But it seems like
e should be more. I still don't understand what
cious experience is all about, and I don't under-
d why I react the way I do sometimes. And this
—*wonderful as it is!*—hardly mentioned certain
s. Why do we laugh? How do we sense the pas-
of time? Why do people like to watch sports?
are some people religious and others not?"

I have two good reasons for not answering all of
your questions. One is that this is an introductory
text and it can't go on forever. If you want to learn
more, you should take other psychology courses or
do additional reading. The other reason is that psychologists do not know all the answers.

Perhaps someday you'll become a researcher
yourself and add to our knowledge. If not, you can try
to keep up to date on current developments in psychology by reading good books and magazine articles. The magazine *Scientific American Mind* is an
excellent source. One of my main goals has been to
prepare you to continue learning about psychology.

Try to read critically: Is a conclusion based on
good evidence? If you read about a survey, were the
questions worded clearly? How reliable and valid
were the measurements? Did the investigators obtain a representative or random sample? If someone
draws a cause-and-effect conclusion, was the evidence based on experiments or only correlations?
Even if the evidence looks solid, is the author's explanation the best one?

Above all, remember that *any* conclusion is
tentative. Psychological researchers seldom use the
word *prove;* their conclusions are almost always
tentative. I once suggested to my editor, half seriously, that we should include in the index to this
book the entry "*maybe*—see pages 1–539." We did
not include such an entry, partly because I doubt
anyone would have noticed the humor, and partly
because our understanding of psychology isn't really that bad. Still, be leery of anyone who seems a
little too certain about a great new insight in psychology. It's a long route from *maybe to definitely.*

references

Numbers in parentheses indicate the chapter in which a source is cited.

Abel, E. L., & Kruger, M. L. (2010). Smile intensity in photographs predicts longevity. *Psychological Science, 21*, 542–544. (12)

Abrahamsson, N., & Hyltenstam, K. (2009). Age of onset and nativelikeness in a second language: Listener perception versus linguistic scrutiny. *Language Learning, 59*, 249–306. (8)

Ackerman, J. M., Nocera, C. C., & Bargh, J. A. (2010). Incidental haptic sensations influence social judgments and decisions. *Science, 328*, 1712–1715. (8)

Ackil, J. K., Van Abbema, D. L., & Bauer, P. J. (2003). After the storm: Enduring differences in mother-child recollections of traumatic and nontraumatic events. *Journal of Experimental Child Psychology, 84*, 286–309. (7)

Adam, H., Shirako, A., & Maddux, W. W. (2010). Cultural variance in the interpersonal effects of anger in negotiations. *Psychological Science, 21*, 882–889. (5)

Adams, J. S. (1963). Wage inequities, productivity, and work quality. *Industrial Relations, 3*, 9–16. (11)

Adams, R. B., & Kleck, R. E. (2003). Perceived gaze direction and the processing of facial displays of emotion. *Psychological Science, 14*, 644–647. (12)

Adams, R. B., & Kleck, R. E. (2005). Effects of direct and averted gaze on the perception of facially communicated emotion. *Emotion, 5*, 3–11. (12)

Adelman, J. S., Marquis, S. J., & Sabatos-DeVito, M. G. (2010). Letters in words are read simultaneously, not in left-to-right sequence. *Psychological Science, 21*, 1799–1801. (8)

Adler, A. (1964). Brief comments on reason, intelligence, and feeble-mindedness. In H. L. Ansbacher & R. R. Ansbacher (Eds.), *Superiority and social interest* (pp. 41–49). New York: Viking Press. (Original work published 1928) (14)

Adler, A. (1964). The structure of neurosis. In H. L. Ansbacher & R. R. Ansbacher (Eds.), *Superiority and social interest* (pp. 83–95). New York: Viking Press. (Original work published 1932) (14)

Adler, E., Hoon, M. A., Mueller, K. L., Chandrashekar, J., Ryba, N. J. P., & Zuker, C. S. (2000). A novel family of mammalian taste receptors. *Cell, 100*, 693–702. (4)

Admon, R., Lubin, G., Stern, O., Rosenberg, K., Sela, L., Ben-Ami, H., . . . Hendler, T (2009). Human vulnerability to stress depends on amygdala's predisposition and hippocampal plasticity. *Proceedings of the National Academy of Sciences, U.S.A., 106*, 14120–14125. (12)

Adolph, K. E. (2000). Specificity of learning: Why infants fall over a veritable cliff. *Psychological Science, 11*, 290–295. (5)

Adolphs, R., Baron-Cohen, S., & Tranel, D. (2002). Impaired recognition of social emotions following amygdala damage. *Journal of Cognitive Neuroscience, 14*, 1264–1274. (12)

Adolphs, R., Denburg, N. L., & Tranel, D. (2001). The amygdala's role in long-term declarative memory for gist and detail. *Behavioral Neuroscience, 115*, 983–992. (12)

Agar, W. E., Drummond, F. H., Tiegs, O. W., & Gunson, M. M. (1954). Fourth (final) report on a test of McDougall's Lamarckian experiment on the training of rats. *Journal of Experimental Biology, 31*, 307–321. (2)

Agerström, J., & Rooth, D. O. (2011). The role of automatic obesity stereotypes in real hiring decisions. *Journal of Applied Psychology, 96*, 790–805. (13)

Aglioti, S. M., Cesari, P., Romani, M., & Urgesi, C. (2008). Action anticipation and motor resonance in elite basketball players. *Nature Neuroscience, 11*, 1109–1116. (8)

Ahn, W., Flanagan, E. H., Marsh, J. K., & Sanislow, C. A. (2006). Beliefs about essences and the reality of mental disorders. *Psychological Science, 17*, 759–766. (15)

Ainsworth, M. D. S. (1979). Attachment as related to mother-infant interaction. In J. S. Rosenblatt, R. A. Hinde, C. Beer, & M. Busnel (Eds.), *Advances in the study of behavior* (Vol. 9, pp. 1–51). New York: Academic Press. (5)

Ainsworth, M. D. S., Blehar, M., Waters, E., & Wall, S. (1978). *Patterns of attachment.* Hillsdale, NJ: Erlbaum. (5)

Åkerstedt, T. (2007). Altered sleep/wake patterns and mental performance. *Physiology and Behavior, 90*, 209–218. (10)

Akrami, N., Ekehammar, B., & Bergh, R. (2011). Generalized prejudice: Common and specific components. *Psychological Science, 22*, 57–59. (14)

Albee, G. W. (1986). Toward a just society: Lessons from observations on the primary prevention of psychopathology. *American Psychologist, 41*, 891–898. (15)

Alcock, J. E. (2011, March/April). Back from the future: Parapsychology and the Bem affair. *Skeptical Inquirer, 35*(2), 31–39. (2)

Aleman, A., Kahn, R. S., & Selten, J. P. (2003). Sex differences in the risk of schizophrenia. *Archives of General Psychiatry, 60*, 565–571. (15)

Alexander, G. M., & Hines, M. (2002). Sex differences in response to children's toys in nonhuman primates (*Cercopithecus aethiops sabaeus*). *Evolution and Human Behavior, 23*, 467–479. (5)

Alexander, G. M., Wilcox, T., & Woods, R. (2009). Sex differences in infants' visual interest in toys. *Archives of Sexual Behavior, 38*, 427–433. (5, 14)

Alexander, I. E. (1982). The Freud-Jung relationship—the other side of Oedipus and countertransference. *American Psychologist, 37*, 1009–1018. (14)

Alexander, K. W., Quas, J. A., Goodman, G. S., Ghetti, S., Edelstein, R. S., Redlich, A. D., . . . Jones, D. P. H. (2005). Traumatic impact predicts long-term memory for documented child sexual abuse. *Psychological Science, 16*, 33–40. (7)

Alexander, M. G., & Fisher, T. D. (2003). Truth and consequences: Using the bogus pipeline to examine sex differences in self-reported sexuality. *Journal of Sex Research, 40*, 27–35. (11)

Alison, L. J., Smith, M. D., Eastman, O., & Rainbow, L. (2003). Toulmin's philosophy of argument and its relevance to offender profiling. *Psychology, Crime and Law, 9*, 173–183. (14)

Allen, H. L., Estrada, K., Lettre, G., Berndt, S. I., Weedon, M. N., Rivadeneira, F., . . . Hirschhorn, J. L. (2010). Hundreds of variants clustered in genomic loci and biological pathways affect human height. *Nature, 467*, 832–838. (3)

Allison, S. T., Mackie, D. M., Muller, M. M., & Worth, L. T. (1993). Sequential correspondence biases and perceptions of change: The Castro studies revisited. *Personality and Social Psychology Bulletin, 19*, 151–157. (13)

Alloy, L. B., Abramson, L. Y., Whitehouse, W. G., Hogan, M. E., Tashman, N. A., Steinberg, D. L., . . . Donovan, P. (1999). Depressogenic cognitive styles: Predictive validity, information processing and personality characteristics, and developmental origins. *Behaviour Research and Therapy, 37*, 503–531. (15)

Allport, G. W. (1935). Attitudes. In C. Murchison (Ed.), *A handbook of social psychology* (pp. 798–844). Worcester, MA: Clark University Press. (13)

Allport, G. W. (1961). *Pattern and growth in personality.* New York: Holt, Rinehart & Winston. (14)

Allport, G. W., & Odbert, H. S. (1936). Traitnames: A psycholexical study. *Psychological Monographs, 47*(Whole No. 211). (14)

Alpers, G. W., & Gerdes, A. B. M. (2007). Here is looking at you: Emotional faces predominate in binocular rivalry. *Emotion, 7*, 495–506. (10)

Alpert, J. L., Brown, L. S., & Courtois, C. A. (1998). Symptomatic clients and memories of childhood abuse. *Psychology, Public Policy, and Law, 4*, 941–995. (7)

Alroe, C. J., & Gunda, V. (1995). Self-amputation of the ear. *Australian and New Zealand Journal of Psychiatry, 29*, 508–512. (15)

Alter, A. L., Oppenheimer, D. M., Epley, N., & Eyre, R. N. (2007). Overcoming intuition: Metacognitive difficulty activates analytic reasoning. *Journal of Experimental Psychology: General, 136*, 569–576. (8)

Altmann, E. M., & Gray, W. D. (2002). Forgetting to remember: The functional relationship of decay and interference. *Psychological Science, 13*, 27–33. (7)

Amabile, T. M. (2001). Beyond talent. *American Psychologist, 56*, 333–336. (11)

Ambady, N., & Rosenthal, R. (1993). Half a minute: Predicting teacher evaluations from thin slices of nonverbal behavior and physical attractiveness. *Journal of Personality and Social Psychology, 64*, 431–441. (13)

Ambady, N., Shih, M., Kim, A., & Pittinsky, T. L. (2001). Stereotype susceptibility in children: Effects of identity activation on quantitative performance. *Psychological Science, 12*, 385–390. (9)

Amelang, M., & Steinmayr, R. (2006). Is there a validity increment for tests of emotional intelligence in explaining the variance of performance criteria? *Intelligence, 34*, 459–468. (12)

American Medical Association. (1986). Council report: Scientific status of refreshing recollection by the use of hypnosis. *International Journal of Clinical and Experimental Hypnosis, 34*, 1–12. (10)

American Psychiatric Association. (1994). *Diagnostic and statistical manual of mental disorders* (4th ed.). Washington, DC: Author. (15)

American Psychiatric Association. (2000). *Diagnostic and statistical manual of mental disorders* (4th ed., Text revision.). Washington, DC: Author. (15)

Amodio, D. M., & Harmon-Jones, E. (2011). Trait emotions and affective modulation of the startle eyeblink: On the unique relationship of trait anger. *Emotion, 11*, 47–51. (12)

Amzica, F., & Steriade, M. (1996). Progressive cortical synchronization of pontogeniculo-occipital potentials during rapid eye movement sleep. *Neuroscience, 72*, 309–314. (10)

Anderson, A., & Phelps, E. A. (2000). Expression without recognition: Contributions of the human amygdala to emotional communication. *Psychological Science, 11*, 106–111. (12)

Anderson, C. A., Shibuya, A., Ihori, N., Swing, E. L., Bushman, B. J., . . . Saleem, M. (2010). Violent video game effects on aggression, empathy, and prosocial behavior in Eastern and Western cultures: A meta-analytic review. *Psychological Bulletin, 136*, 151–173. (14)

Anderson, C., Keltner, D., & John, O. P. (2003). Emotional convergence between people over time. *Journal of Personality and Social Psychology, 84*, 1054–1068. (13)

Anderson, S. W., Bechara, A., Damasio, H., Tranel, D., & Damasio, A. R. (1999). Impairment of social and moral behavior related to early damage in human prefrontal cortex. *Nature Neuroscience, 2*, 1032–1037. (3)

Andreano, J. M., & Cahill, L. (2006). Glucocorticoid release and memory consolidation in men and women. *Psychological Science, 17*, 466–470. (7)

Andrew, D., & Craig, A. D. (2001). Spinothalamic lamina I neurons selectively sensitive to histamine: A central neural pathway for itch. *Nature Neuroscience, 4*, 72–77. (4)

Andrews, T. J., Halpern, S. D., & Purves, D. (1997). Correlated size variations in human visual cortex, lateral geniculate nucleus, and optic tract. *Journal of Neuroscience, 17*, 2859–2868. (4)

Anglin, D., Spears, K. L., & Hutson, H. R. (1997). Flunitrazepam and its involvement in date or acquaintance rape. *Academy of Emergency Medicine, 4*, 323–326. (3)

Anonymous. (1955). *Alcoholics anonymous* (2nd ed.). New York: Alcoholics Anonymous World Services. (15)

Antoniadis, E. A., Winslow, J. T., Davis, M., & Amaral, D. G. (2007). Role of the primate amygdala in fear-potentiated startle. *Journal of Neuroscience, 27*, 7386–7396. (12)

APA Presidential Task Force on Evidence-Based Practice. (2006). Evidence-based practice in psychology. *American Psychologist, 61*, 271–285. (15)

Apfelbaum, E. P., Paulker, K., Sommers, S. R., & Ambady, N. (2010). In blind pursuit of racial equality? *Psychological Science, 21*, 1587–1592. (13)

Apperly, I. A., Riggs, K. J., Simpson, A., Chiavarino, C., & Samson, D. (2006). Is belief reasoning automatic? *Psychological Science, 17*, 841–844. (5)

Archer, J. (2000). Sex differences in aggression between heterosexual partners: A meta-analytic review. *Psychological Bulletin, 126*, 651–680. (13)

Arden, R., & Plomin, R. (2006). Sex differences in variance of intelligence across childhood. *Personality and Individual Differences, 41*, 39–48. (9)

Ariely, D., & Wertenbroch, K. (2002). Procrastination, deadlines, and performance: Self-control by precommitment. *Psychological Science, 13*, 219–224. (11)

Arkes, H. R., & Ayton, P. (1999). The sunk cost and Concorde effects: Are humans less rational than lower animals? *Psychological Bulletin, 125*, 591–600. (8)

Armor, D. A., Massey, C., & Sackett, A. M. (2008). Prescribed optimism: Is it right to be wrong about the future? *Psychological Science, 19*, 329–331. (12)

Armstrong, J. B., & Schindler, D. E. (2011). Excess digestive capacity in predators reflects a life of feast and famine. *Nature, 476*, 84–87. (11)

Arnell, K. M., Killman, K. V., & Fijavz, D. (2007). Blinded by emotion: Target misses follow attention capture by arousing distractors in RSVP. *Emotion, 7*, 465–477. (7)

Arnold, H. J., & House, R. J. (1980). Methodological and substantive extensions to the job characteristics model of motivation. *Organizational Behavior and Human Performance, 25*, 161–183. (11)

Aronow, E., Reznikoff, M., & Moreland, K. L. (1995). The Rorschach: Projective technique or psychometric test? *Journal of Personality Assessment, 64*, 213–228. (14)

Aronson, E. (1997). The theory of cognitive dissonance: The evolution and vicissitudes of an idea. In C. McGarty & S. A. Haslam (Eds.), *The message of social psychology* (pp. 20–35). Cambridge, MA: Blackwell. (13)

Aronson, E., & Carlsmith, J. M. (1963). Effect of the severity of threat on the devaluation of forbidden behavior. *Journal of Abnormal and Social Psychology, 66*, 584–588. (13)

Arvey, R. D., McCall, B. P., Bouchard, T. J., Jr., Taubman, P., & Cavanaugh, M. A. (1994). Genetic influences on job satisfaction and work values. *Personality and Individual Differences, 17*, 21–33. (11)

Asch, S. E. (1951). Effects of group pressure upon the modification and distortion of judgments. In H. Guetzkow (Ed.), *Groups, leadership, and men* (pp. 177–190). Pittsburgh, PA: Carnegie Press. (13)

Asch, S. E. (1955, November). Opinions and social pressure. *Scientific American, 193*(5), 31–35. (13)

Asch, S. E. (1956). Studies of independence and conformity: I. A minority of one against a unanimous majority. *Psychological Monographs, 70*(9, Whole No. 416). (13)

Ash, R. (1986, August). An anecdote submitted by Ron Ash. *The Industrial-Organizational Psychologist, 23*(4), 8. (6)

Ashton-James, C. E., Maddux, W. W., Galinsky, A. D., & Chartrand, T. L. (2009). Who I am depends on how I feel. *Psychological Science, 20*, 340–346. (12)

Askum, D., & Ataca, B. (2007). Sexuality related attitudes and behaviors of Turkish university students. *Archives of Sexual Behavior, 36*, 741–752. (11)

Athos, E. A., Levinson, B., Kistler, A., Zemansky, J., Bostrom, A., Freimer, N., . . . Gitschier, J. (2007). Dichotomy and perceptual distortions in absolute pitch ability. *Proceedings of the National Academy of Sciences, USA, 104*, 14795–14800. (4)

Atkinson, R. C., & Shiffrin, R. M. (1968). Human memory: A proposed system and its control. In K. W. Spence & J. T. Spence (Eds.), *The psychology of learning and motivation* (Vol. 2, pp. 89–105). New York: Academic Press. (7)

Auyeung, B., Baron-Cohen, S., Ashwin, E., Knickmeyer, R., Taylor, K., Hackett, G., . . . Hines, M. (2009). Fetal testosterone predicts sexually differentiated childhood behavior in girls and boys. *Psychological Science, 20*, 144–148. (11)

Averill, J. R. (1983). Studies on anger and aggression: Implications for theories of emotion. *American Psychologist, 38*, 1145–1160. (12)

Aviezer, H., Hassin, R. R., Ryan, J., Grady, C., Susskind, J., Anderson, A., . . . Bentin, S. (2008). Angry, disgusted, or afraid? *Psychological Science, 19*, 724–732. (12)

Babkoff, H., Caspy, T., Mikulincer, M., & Sing, H. C. (1991). Monotonic and rhythmic influences: A challenge for sleep deprivation research. *Psychological Bulletin, 109*, 411–428. (10)

Back, M. D., Schmukle, S. C., & Egloff, B. (2008). Becoming friends by chance. *Psychological Science, 19*, 439–440. (13)

Baddeley, A. D. (2001). Is working memory still working? *American Psychologist, 56*, 851–864. (7)

Baddeley, A., & Hitch, G. J. (1994). Developments in the concept of working memory. *Neuropsychology, 8*, 485–493. (7)

Bagby, R. M., Nicholson, R. A., Bacchiochi, J. R., Ryder, A. G., & Bury, A. S. (2002). The predictive capacity of the MMPI-2 and PAI validity scales and indexes to detect coached and uncoached feigning. *Journal of Personality Assessment, 78*, 69–86. (14)

Bagemihl, B. (1999). *Biological exuberance.* New York: St. Martin's Press. (11)

Bahrami, B., Olsen, K., Latham, P. E., Roepstorff, A., Rees, G., & Frith, C. D. (2010). Optimally interacting minds. *Science, 329*, 1081–1085. (13)

Bahrick, H. (1984). Semantic memory content in permastore: 50 years of memory for Spanish learned in school. *Journal of Experimental Psychology: General, 113*, 1–29. (7)

Bailey, A., Le Couteur, A., Gottesman, I., Bolton, P., Simonoff, E., Yuzda, E., . . . Rutter, M. (1995). Autism as a strongly genetic disorder: Evidence from a British twin study. *Psychological Medicine, 25*, 63–78. (15)

Bailey, J. M., & Pillard, R. C. (1991). A genetic study of male sexual orientation. *Archives of General Psychiatry, 48*, 1089–1096. (11)

Bailey, J. M., Pillard, R. C., Neale, M. C., & Agyei, Y. (1993) Heritable factors influence sexual orientation in women. *Archives of General Psychiatry, 50*, 217–223. (11)

Baillargeon, R. (1986). Representing the existence and the location of hidden objects: Object permanence in 6- and 8-month-old infants. *Cognition, 23*, 21–41. (5)

Baillargeon, R. (1987). Object permanence in $3\frac{1}{2}$- and $4\frac{1}{2}$-month-old infants. *Developmental Psychology, 23*, 655–664. (5)

Baillargeon, R., Li, J., Ng, W., & Yuan, S. (2009). An account of infants' physical reasoning. In A. Woodward & A. Needham (Eds.), *Learning and the infant* (pp. 66–116). New York: Oxford University Press. (5)

Baird, J. C. (1982). The moon illusion: A reference theory. *Journal of Experimental Psychology: General, 111,* 304–315. (4)

Baker-Ward, L., Gordon, B. N., Ornstein, P. A., Larus, D. M., & Clubb, P. A. (1993). Young children's long-term retention of a pediatric examination. *Child Development, 64,* 1519–1533. (7)

Baker, T. B., Piper, M. E., McCarthy, D. E., Majeskie, M. R., & Fiore, M. C. (2004). Addiction motivation reformulated: An affective processing model of negative reinforcement. *Psychological Review, 111,* 33–51. (15)

Bakermans-Kranenburg, M. J., van IJzendoorn, M. H., & Juffer, F. (2003). Less is more: Meta-analyses of sensitivity and attachment interventions in early childhood. *Psychological Bulletin, 129,* 195–215. (5)

Bakker, M. J., Tijssen, M. A. J., van der Meer, J. N., Koelman, J. H. T. M., & Boer, F. (2009). Increased whole-body auditory startle reflex and autonomic reactivity in children with anxiety disorders. *Journal of Psychiatry and Neuroscience, 34,* 314–322. (12)

Balcetis, E., Dunning, D., & Miller, R. L. (2008). Do collectivists know themselves better than individualists? Cross-cultural studies of the holier than thou phenomenon. *Journal of Personality and Social Psychology, 95,* 1252–1267. (13)

Baldessarini, R. J. (1984). Antipsychotic drugs. In T. B. Karasu (Ed.), *The psychiatric therapies: I. The somatic therapies* (pp. 119–170). Washington, DC: American Psychiatric Press. (15)

Baldessarini, R. J., & Tondo, L. (2000). Does lithium treatment still work? *Archives of General Psychiatry, 57,* 187–190. (15)

Ballinger, B., & Yalom, I. (1995). Group therapy in practice. In B. Bongar & L. E. Beutler (Eds.), *Comprehensive textbook of psychotherapy: Theory and practice* (pp. 189–204). Oxford, England: Oxford University Press. (15)

Bandura, A. (1977). *Social learning theory.* Upper Saddle River, NJ: Prentice Hall. (6)

Bandura, A. (1986). *Social foundations of thought and action.* Upper Saddle River, NJ: Prentice Hall. (6)

Bandura, A., Barbaranelli, C., Caprara, G. V., & Pastorelli, C. (2001). Self-efficacy beliefs as shapers of children's aspirations and career trajectories. *Child Development, 72,* 187–206. (6)

Bandura, A., Ross, D., & Ross, S. A. (1963). Imitation of film-mediated aggressive models. *Journal of Abnormal and Social Psychology, 66,* 3–11. (6)

Banks, W. P., & Isham, E. A. (2009). We infer rather than perceive the moment we decided to act. *Psychological Science, 20,* 17–21. (10)

Bargh, J. A., Chen, M., & Burrows, L. (1996). The automaticity of social behavior: Direct effects of trait concept and stereotype activation on action. *Journal of Personality and Social Psychology, 71,* 230–244. (13)

Barnett, S. M., & Ceci, S. J. (2002). When and where do we apply what we learn? A taxonomy for far transfer. *Psychological Bulletin, 128,* 612–637. (8)

Barnett, W. S. (2011). Effectiveness of early educational intervention. *Science, 333,* 975–978. (9)

Barnier, A. J., & McConkey, K. M. (1998). Posthypnotic responding away from the hypnotic setting. *Psychological Science, 9,* 256–262. (10)

Baron, A., & Galizio, M. (2005). Positive and negative reinforcement: Should the distinction be preserved? *Behavior Analyst, 28,* 85–98. (6)

Barrett, L. F. (2006). Are emotions natural kinds? *Perspectives on Psychological Science, 1,* 28–58. (12)

Barrett, L. F., Bliss-Moreau, E., Duncan, S. L., Rauch, S. L., & Wright, C. I. (2007). The amygdala and the experience of affect. *Social Cognitive and Affective Neuroscience, 2,* 73–83. (12)

Barrett, L. F., Mesquita, B., & Gendron, M. (2011). Context in emotion perception. *Current Directions in Psychological Science, 20,* 286–290. (12)

Barrett, L. F., Tugade, M. M., & Engle, R. W. (2004). Individual differences in working memory capacity and dual-process theories of the mind. *Psychological Bulletin, 130,* 553–573. (7)

Barrick, M. R., Mount, M. K., & Judge, T. A. (2001). Personality and performance at the beginning of the new millennium: What do we know and where do we go next? *International Journal of Selection and Assessment, 9,* 9–29. (14)

Barron, E., Riley, L. M., Greer, J., & Smallwood, J. (2011). Absorbed in thought: The effect of mind wandering on the processing of relevant and irrelevant events. *Psychological Science, 22,* 596–601. (10)

Bartels, A., & Zeki, S. (2000). The neural basis of romantic love. *NeuroReport, 11,* 3829–3834. (13)

Bartlett, F. C. (1932). *Remembering.* Cambridge, England: Cambridge University Press. (7)

Bartoshuk, L. M. (1991). Taste, smell, and pleasure. In R. C. Bolles (Ed.), *The hedonics of taste* (pp. 5–28). Hillsdale, NJ: Erlbaum. (4)

Bartoshuk, L. M., Duffy, V. B., Lucchina, L. B., Prutkin, J., & Fast, K. (1998). PROP (6-n-propyl-thiouracil) supertasters and the saltiness of NaCl. *Annals of the New York Academy of Sciences, 855,* 793–796. (1)

Basabe, N., Paez, D., Valencia, J., Gonzalez, J. L., Rimé, B., & Diener, E. (2002). Cultural dimensions, socioeconomic development, climate, and emotional hedonic level. *Cognition and Emotion, 16,* 103–125. (12)

Bassok, M., & Holyoak, K. J. (1989). Interdomain transfer between isomorphic topics in algebra and physics. *Journal of Experimental Psychology: Learning, Memory, and Cognition, 15,* 153–166. (8)

Batson, C. D., & Thompson, E. R. (2001). Why don't people act morally? Motivational considerations. *Current Directions in Psychological Science, 10,* 54–57. (11)

Bauer, P. J. (2005). Developments in declarative memory. *Psychological Science, 16,* 41–47. (7)

Bauer, P. J., Wenner, J. A., & Kroupina, M. G. (2002). Making the past present: Later verbal accessibility of early memories. *Journal of Cognition and Development, 3,* 21–47. (7)

Bauman, M. L., & Kemper, T. L. (2005). Structural brain anatomy in autism: What is the evidence? In M. L. Bauman & T. L. Kemper (Eds.), *The neurobiology of autism* (pp. 121–135). Baltimore: Johns Hopkins University Press. (15)

Baumeister, R. F. (2008). Free will in scientific psychology. *Perspectives on Psychological Science, 3,* 14–19. (1)

Baumeister, R. F., & Masicampo, E. J. (2010). Conscious thought is for facilitating social and cultural interactions: How mental simulations serve the animal-culture interface. *Psychological Review, 117,* 945–971. (10)

Baumeister, R. F., Campbell, J. D., Krueger, J. I., & Vohs, K. D. (2003). Does high self-esteem cause better performance, interpersonal success, happiness, or healthier lifestyles? *Psychological Science in the Public Interest, 4,* 1–44. (13, 14)

Baumeister, R. F., Masicampo, E. J., & Vohs, K. D. (2011). Do conscious thoughts cause behavior? *Annual Review of Psychology, 62,* 331–361. (10)

Bäuml, K.-H. T., & Samenieh, A. (2010). The two faces of memory retrieval. *Psychological Science, 21,* 793–795. (7)

Baumrind, D. (1971). Current patterns of parental authority. *Developmental Psychology Monographs, 4*(1, Pt. 2). (5)

Baxter, M. G., & Murray, E. A. (2002). The amygdala and reward. *Nature Reviews Neuroscience, 3,* 563–573. (3, 12)

Bayley, T. M., Dye, L., & Hill, A. J. (2009). Taste aversions in pregnancy. In S. Reilly & T. R. Schachtman (Eds.), *Conditioned taste aversion* (pp. 497–512). New York: Oxford University Press. (6)

Beauchamp, G. K., Cowart, B. J., Mennella, J. A., & Marsh, R. R. (1994). Infant salt taste: Developmental, methodological, and contextual factors. *Developmental Psychobiology, 27,* 353–365. (1)

Becht, M. C., & Vingerhoets, A. J. J. M. (2002). Crying and mood change: A cross-cultural study. *Cognition and Emotion, 16,* 87–101. (12)

Beck, A. T. (1976). *Cognitive therapy and the emotional disorders.* New York: New American Library. (15)

Beck, A. T. (1991). Cognitive therapy: A 30-year retrospective. *American Psychologist, 46,* 368–375. (15)

Beck, A. T., & Emery, G. (1985). *Anxiety disorders and phobias.* New York: Basic Books. (15)

Beck, H. P., Levinson, S., & Irons, G. (2009). Finding Little Albert: A journey to John B. Watson's infant laboratory. *American Psychologist, 64,* 605–614. (15)

Beck, K., & Wilson, C. (2000). Development of affective organizational commitment: A cross-sequential examination of change with tenure. *Journal of Vocational Behavior, 56,* 114–136. (11)

Becker, A. E., Burwell, R. A., Gilman, S. E., Herzog, D. B., & Hamburg, P. (2002). Eating behaviours and attitudes following prolonged exposure to television among ethnic Fijian adolescent girls. *British Journal of Psychiatry, 180,* 509–514. (11)

Becker, A. E., Burwell, R. A., Navara, K., & Gilman, S. E. (2003). Binge eating and binge eating disorder in a small-scale, indigenous society: The view from Fiji. *International Journal of Eating Disorders, 34,* 423–431. (11)

Beckett, C., Maughan, B., Rutter, M., Castle, J., Colvert, E., Groothues, C., . . . Sonuga-Barke, E. J. S. (2006). Do the effects of early severe deprivation on cognition persist into early adolescence? Findings from the English and Romanian adoptees study. *Child Development, 77,* 696–711. (9)

Beer, J. S., Knight, R. T., & D'Esposito, M. (2006). Controlling the integration of emotion and cognition. *Psychological Science, 17,* 448–453. (12)

Bègue, L., & Muller, D. (2006). Belief in a just world as moderator of hostile attributional bias. *British Journal of Social Psychology, 45,* 117–126. (14)

Behrens, M., Foerster, S., Staehler, F., Raguse, J.-D., & Meyerhof, W. (2007). Gustatory expression pattern of the human TAS2R bitter receptor gene family reveals a heterogenous population of bitter responsive taste receptor cells. *Journal of Neuroscience, 27,* 12630–12640. (4)

Behrens, T. E. J., Hunt, L. T., Woolrich, M. W., & Rushworth, M. F. S. (2008). Associative learning of social value. *Nature, 456,* 245–249. (6)

Beilock, S. L., Jelllison, W. A., Rydell, R. J., McConnell, A. R., & Carr, T. H. (2006). On the causal mechanisms of stereotype threat: Can skills that don't rely heavily on working memory still be threatened? *Personality and Social Psychology Bulletin, 32,* 1059–1071. (9)

Bekker, M. H. J., & van Assen, M. A. L. M. (2008). Autonomy-connectedness and gender. *Sex Roles, 59,* 532–544. (14)

Bell, R., & Pliner, P. L. (2003). Time to eat: The relationship between the number of people eating and meal duration in three lunch settings. *Appetite, 41,* 215–218. (11)

Bellugi, U., & St. George, M. (2000). Preface. *Journal of Cognitive Neuroscience, 12*(Suppl.), 1–6. (8)

Bellugi, U., Lichtenberger, L., Jones, W., Lai, Z., & St. George, M. (2000). I. The neurocognitive profile of Williams syndrome: A complex pattern of strengths and weaknesses. *Journal of Cognitive Neuroscience, 12*(Suppl.), 7–29. (8)

Belsky, J. (1996). Parent, infant, and social-contextual antecedents of father-son attachment security. *Developmental Psychology, 32,* 905–913. (5)

Bem, D. J. (2011). Feeling the future: Experimental evidence for anomalous retroactive influences on cognition and affect. *Journal of Personality and Social Psychology, 100,* 407–425. (2)

Bem, D. J., & Honorton, C. (1994). Does psi exist? Replicable evidence for an anomalous process of information transfer. *Psychological Bulletin, 115,* 4–18. (2)

Benenson, J. F., Markovits, H., Fitzgerald, C., Geoffroy, D., Flemming, J., Kahlenberg, S. M., . . . Wrangham, R. W. (2009). Males' greater tolerance of same-sex peers. *Psychological Science, 20,* 184–190. (14)

Benish, S. G., Imel, Z. E., & Wampold, B. E. (2008). The relative efficacy of bona fide psychotherapies for treating post-traumatic stress disorder: A meta-analysis of direct comparisons. *Clinical Psychology Review, 28,* 746–758. (15)

Benjamin, L. T., Jr., & Simpson, J. A. (2009). The power of the situation. *American Psychologist, 64,* 12–19. (13)

Benschop, R. J., Godaert, G. L. R., Geenen, R., Brosschot, J. F., DeSmet, M. B. M., Olff, M., . . . Ballieux, R. E. (1995). Relationships between cardiovascular and immunologic changes in an experimental stress model. *Psychological Medicine, 25,* 323–327. (12)

Benson, H. (1977). Systemic hypertension and the relaxation response. *New England Journal of Medicine, 296,* 1152–1156. (12)

Benson, H. (1985). Stress, health, and the relaxation response. In W. D. Gentry, H. Benson, & C. J. de Wolff (Eds.), *Behavioral medicine: Work, stress and health* (pp. 15–32). Dordrecht, The Netherlands: Martinus Nijhoff. (12)

Berenbaum, S. A. (1999). Effects of early androgens on sex-typed activities and interests in adolescents with congenital adrenal hyperplasia. *Hormones and Behavior, 35,* 102–110. (11)

Berenbaum, S. A., Duck, S. C., & Bryk, K. (2000). Behavioral effects of prenatal versus postnatal androgen excess in children with 21-hydroxylase-deficient congenital adrenal hyperplasia. *Journal of Clinical Endocrinology and Metabolism, 85,* 727–733. (5, 11)

Berger, R. J., & Phillips, N. H. (1995). Energy conservation and sleep. *Behavioural Brain Research, 69,* 65–73. (10)

Berglas, S., & Jones, E. E. (1978). Drug choice as a self-handicapping strategy in response to noncontingent success. *Journal of Personality and Social Psychology, 36,* 405–417. (13)

Berkman, N. D., Lohr, K. N., & Bulik, C. M. (2007). Outcomes of eating disorders: A systematic review of the literature. *International Journal of Eating Disorders, 40,* 293–309. (11)

Berkowitz, L. (1983). Aversively stimulated aggression: Some parallels and differences in research with animals and humans. *American Psychologist, 38,* 1135–1144. (13)

Berkowitz, L. (1989). Frustration-aggression hypothesis: Examination and reformulation. *Psychological Bulletin, 106,* 59–73. (13)

Berlyne, D. E. (1981). Humanistic psychology as a protest movement. In J. R. Royce & L. P. Mos (Eds.), *Humanistic psychology: Concepts and criticisms* (pp. 261–293). New York: Plenum Press. (14)

Berman, M. G., Jonides, J., & Kaplan, S. (2008). The cognitive benefits of interacting with nature. *Psychological Science, 19,* 1207–1212. (8)

Bernstein, D. M., & Loftus, E. F. (2009). The consequences of false memories for food preferences and choices. *Perspectives on Psychological Science, 4,* 135–139. (7)

Bernstein, D. M., Atance, C., Loftus, G. R., & Meltzoff, A. (2004). We saw it all along. *Psychological Science, 15,* 264–267. (7)

Bernstein, I. L. (1991). Aversion conditioning in response to cancer and cancer treatment. *Clinical Psychology Review, 11,* 185–191. (6)

Bernstein, M. J., Young, S. G., & Hugenberg, K. (2007). The cross-category effect. Psychological Science, 18, 706–712. (5)

Berntsen, D., & Rubin, D. C. (2002). Emotionally charged autobiographical memories across the lifespan: The recall of happy, sad, traumatic and involuntary memories. *Psychology and Aging, 17,* 636–652. (7)

Berntson, G. G., Cacioppo, J. T., & Quigley, K. S. (1993). Cardiac psychophysiology and autonomic space in humans: Empirical perspectives and conceptual implications. *Psychological Bulletin, 114,* 296–322. (12)

Berridge, K. C., & Robinson, T. E. (1998). What is the role of dopamine in reward: Hedonic impact, reward learning, or incentive salience? *Brain Research Reviews, 28,* 309–369. (15)

Berry, C. M., & Sackett, P. R. (2009). Individual differences in course choice result in underestimation of the validity of college admission systems. *Psychological Science, 20,* 822–830. (9)

Berry, J. W., Poortinga, Y. H., Segal, H., & Dasen, P. R. (1992). *Cross-cultural psychology.* Cambridge, England: Cambridge University Press. (15)

Bertenthal, B. I., Longo, M. R., & Kosobud, A. (2006). Imitative response tendencies following observation of intransitive actions. *Journal of Experimental Psychology: Human Perception and Performance, 32,* 210–225. (6)

Beuming, T., Kniazeff, J., Bergmann, M. L., Shi, L., Gracia, L., Raniszewska, K., . . . Loland, C. J. (2008). The binding sites for cocaine and dopamine in the dopamine transporter overlap. *Nature Neuroscience, 11,* 780–789. (3)

Bialystok, E., Craik, F. I. M., Green, D. W., & Gollan, T. H. (2009). Bilingual minds. *Psychological Science in the Public Interest, 10,* 89–129. (8)

Bialystok, E., Craik, F., & Luk, G. (2008). Cognitive control and lexical access in younger and older bilinguals. *Journal of Experimental Psychology: Learning, Memory, and Cognition, 34,* 859–873. (8)

Biederman, I., Yue, X., & Davidoff, J. (2009). Representation of shape in individuals from a culture with minimal exposure to regular, simple artifacts. *Psychological Science, 20,* 1437–1442. (4)

Bih, S.-H., Chien, I-C., Chou, Y.-J., Lin, C.-H., Lee, C.-H., & Chou, P. (2008). The treated prevalence and incidence of bipolar disorder among national health insurance enrollees in Taiwan, 1996–2003. *Social Psychiatry and Psychiatric Epidemiology, 43,* 860–865. (15)

Bijl, R. V., de Graaf, R., Hiripi, E., Kessler, R. C., Kohn, R., Offord, D. R., . . . Wittchen, H. U. (2003). The prevalence of treated and untreated mental disorders in five countries. *Health Affairs, 22,* 122–133. (15)

Billy, J. O. G., Tanfer, K., Grady, W. R., & Klepinger, D. H. (1993, March/April). The sexual behavior of men in the United States. *Family Planning Perspectives, 25,* 52–60. (11)

Binet, A., & Simon, T. (1905). Méthodes nouvelles pour le diagnostic du niveau intellectual des anormaux [New methods for the measurement of the intellectual level of the abnormal]. *L'Année Psychologique, 11,* 191–244. (9)

Birch, S. A. J., & Bernstein, D. M. (2007). What can children tell us about hindsight bias: A fundamental constraint on perspective-taking? *Social Cognition, 25,* 98–113. (7)

Bird, H. R., Canino, G. J., Davies, M., Zhang, H., Ramirez, R., & Lahey, B. B. (2001). Prevalence and correlates of antisocial behaviors among three ethnic groups. *Journal of Abnormal Child Psychology, 29,* 465–478. (15)

Bishop, E. G., Cherny, S. S., Corley, R., Plomin, R., DeFries, J. C., & Hewitt, J. K. (2003). Development genetic analysis of general cognitive ability from 1 to 12 years in a sample of adoptees, biological siblings, and twins. *Intelligence, 31,* 31–49. (9)

Bjerkedal, T., Kristensen, P., Skjeret, G. A., & Brevik, J. I. (2007). Intelligence test scores and birth order among young Norwegian men (conscripts) analyzed within and between families. *Intelligence, 35,* 503–514. (5)

Bjorklund, D. F., & Shackelford, T. K. (1999). Differences in parental investment contribute to important differences between men and women. *Current Directions in Psychological Science, 8,* 86–92. (3)

Blackless, M., Charuvastra, A., Derryck, A., Fausto-Sterling, A., Lauzanne, K., & Lee, E. (2000). How sexually dimorphic are we? Review and synthesis. *American Journal of Human Biology, 12,* 151–166. (11)

Blaine, J. D., Prien, R. F., & Levine, J. (1983). The role of antidepressants in the treatment of affective disorders. *American Journal of Psychotherapy, 37,* 502–520. (15)

Blair, R. J. R., Mitchell, D. G. V., Peschardt, K. S., Colledge, E., Leonard, R. A., Shine, J. H., . . . Perrett, D. I. (2004). Reduced sensitivity to others' fearful expressions in psychopathic individuals. *Personality and Individual Differences, 37,* 1111–1122. (12)

Blake, R., & Logothetis, N. K. (2002). Visual competition. *Nature Reviews Neuroscience, 3,* 13–23. (10)

Blakemore, C., & Sutton, P. (1969). Size adaptation: A new aftereffect. *Science, 166,* 245–247. (4)

Blanton, H., Jaccard, J., Klick, J., Mellers, B., Mitchell, G., & Tetlock, P. E. (2009). Strong claims and weak evidence: Reassessing the predictive validity of the IAT. *Journal of Applied Psychology, 94,* 567–582. (13)

Blascovich, J., & Tomaka, J. (1991). Measures of self-esteem. In J. P. Robinson, R. R. Shaver, & L. S. Wrightsman (Eds.), *Measures of personality and social psychological attitudes* (Vol. 1, pp. 115–160). San Diego, CA: Academic Press. (14)

Bless, H., Bohner, G., Schwarz, N., & Strack, F. (1990). Mood and persuasion: A cognitive response analysis. *Personality and Social Psychology Bulletin, 16,* 331–345. (12)

Blount, J. D., Metcalfe, N. B., Birkhead, T. R., & Surai, P. F. (2003). Carotenoid modulation of immune function and sexual attractiveness in zebra finches. *Science, 300,* 125–127. (13)

Blum, D. (1994). *The monkey wars.* New York: Oxford University Press. (2)

Blum, G. S., & Barbour, J. S. (1979). Selective inattention to anxiety-linked stimuli. *Journal of Experimental Psychology: General, 108,* 182–224. (4)

Bobrow, D., & Bailey, J. M. (2001). Is male homosexuality maintained via kin selection? *Evolution and Human Behavior, 22,* 361–368. (11)

Bocklandt, S., Horvath, S., Vilain, E., & Hamer, D. H. (2006). Extreme skewing of X chromosome inactivation in mothers of homosexual men. *Human Genetics, 118,* 691–694. (11)

Bogaert, A. F. (2003). The interaction of fraternal birth order and body size in male sexual orientation. *Behavioral Neuroscience, 117,* 381–384. (11)

Bogaert, A. F. (2006). Biological versus nonbiological older brothers and men's sexual orientation. *Proceedings of the National Academy of Sciences, USA, 103,* 10771–10774. (11)

Bogg, T., & Roberts, B. W. (2004). Conscientiousness and health-related behaviors: A meta-analysis of the leading behavioral contributors to mortality. *Psychological Bulletin, 130,* 887–919. (14)

Bohn, A., & Berntsen, D. (2011). The reminiscence bump reconsidered: Children's prospective life stories show a bump in young adulthood. *Psychological Science, 22,* 197–202. (7)

Boly, M., Garrido, M. I., Gosseries, O., Bruno, M.-A., Boveroux, P., Schnakers, C., . . . Friston, K. (2011). Preserved feedforward but impaired top-down processes in the vegetative state. *Science, 332,* 858–862. (10)

Bonanno, G. A., & Mancini, A. D. (2008). The human capacity to thrive in the face of potential trauma. *Pediatrics, 121,* 369–375. (5)

Bond, M. H. (1991). *Beyond the Chinese face.* New York: Oxford University Press. (15)

Bond, M. H. (2002). Reclaiming the individual from Hofstede's ecological analysis—A 20-year odyssey: Comment on Oyserman et al. (2002). *Psychological Bulletin, 128,* 73–77. (13)

Bond, R., & Smith, P. B. (1996). Culture and conformity: A meta-analysis of studies using Asch's (1952, 1956) line judgment task. *Psychological Bulletin, 119,* 111–137. (13)

Bonnie, R. J. (1997). Research with cognitively impaired subjects: Unfinished business in the regulation of human research. *Archives of General Psychiatry, 54,* 105–111. (1)

Boot, W. R., Kramer, A. F., Simons, D. J., Fabiani, M., & Gratton, G. (2008). The effects of video game playing on attention, memory, and executive control. *Acta Psychologica, 129,* 387–398. (8)

Bootzin, R. R., & Bailey, E. T. (2005). Understanding placebo, nocebo, and iatrogenic treatment effects. *Journal of Clinical Psychology, 61,* 871–880. (12)

Borden, V. M. H., & Rajecki, D. W. (2000). First-year employment outcomes of psychology baccalaureates: Relatedness, preparedness, and prospects. *Teaching of Psychology, 27,* 164–168. (1)

Boring, E. G. (1930). A new ambiguous figure. *American Journal of Psychology, 42,* 444–445. (4)

Boroditsky, L., & Gaby, A. (2010). Remembrances of times east: Absolute spatial representations of time in an Australian aboriginal community. *Psychological Science, 21,* 1635–1639. (2)

Borsutzky, S., Fujiwara, E., Brand, M., & Markowitsch, H. J. (2008). Confabulations in alcoholic Korsakoff patients. *Neuropsychologia, 46,* 3133–3143. (7)

Bortolotti, B., Menchetti, M., Bellini, F., Montaguti, M. B., & Berardi, D. (2008). Psychological interventions for major depression in primary care: A meta-analytic review of randomized controlled trials. *General Hospital Psychiatry, 30,* 293–302. (15)

Bos, H. M. W., van Balen, F., & van den Boom, D. C. (2007). Child adjustment and parenting in planned lesbian-parent families. *American Journal of Orthopsychiatry, 77,* 38–48. (5)

Bos, H., & Gartrell, N. (2010). Adolescents of the USA National Longitudinal Lesbian Family Study: Can family characteristics counteract the negative effects of stigmatization. *Family Process, 49,* 559–572. (5)

Bouchard, T. J., Jr., & McGue, M. (1981). Familial studies of intelligence: A review. *Science, 212,* 1055–1059. (9)

Bouchard, T. J., Jr., & McGue, M. (2003). Genetic and environmental influences on human psychological differences. *Journal of Neurobiology, 54,* 4–45. (5, 14)

Bouchard, T. J., Lykken, D. T., McGue, M., Segal, N. L., & Tellegen, A. (1990). Sources of psychological differences: The Minnesota study of twins reared apart. *Science, 250,* 223–228. (5)

Bowlby, J. (1973). *Attachment and loss: Vol. II. Separation.* New York: Basic Books. (5)

Bowmaker, J. K. (1998). Visual pigments and molecular genetics of color blindness. *News in Physiological Sciences, 13,* 63–69. (4)

Bowmaker, J. K., & Dartnall, H. J. A. (1980). Visual pigments of rods and cones in a human retina. *Journal of Physiology* (London), *298,* 501–511. (4)

Boyce, C. J., & Wood, A. M. (2011). Personality prior to disability determines adaptation: Agreeable individuals recover lost life satisfaction faster and more completely. *Psychological Science, 22,* 1397–1402. (14)

Boyce, C. J., Brown, G. D. A., & Moore, S. C. (2010). Money and happiness: Rank of income, not income, affects life satisfaction. *Psychological Science, 21,* 471–475. (12)

Boyke, J., Driemeyer, J., Gaser, C., Büchel, C., & May, A. (2008). Training-induced brain structure changes in the elderly. *Journal of Neuroscience, 28,* 7031–7035. (3)

Bracha, H. S. (2006). Human brain evolution and the "neuroevolutionary time-depth principle": Implications for the reclassification of fear-circuitry-related traits in *DSM–V* and for studying resilience to warzone-related posttraumatic stress disorder. *Progress in Neuro-Psychopharmacology and Biological Psychiatry, 30,* 827–853. (15)

Brackett, M. A., Mayer, J. D., & Warner, R. M. (2004). Emotional intelligence and its relation to everyday behaviour. *Personality and Individual Differences, 36,* 1387–1402. (12)

Bradbury, T. N., & Miller, G. A. (1985). Season of birth in schizophrenia: A review of evidence, methodology, and etiology. *Psychological Bulletin, 98,* 569–594. (15)

Braden, J. P., & Niebling, B. C. (2005). Using the joint test standards to evaluate the validity evidence for intelligence tests. In D. P. Flanagan & P. L. Harrison (Eds.), *Contemporary intellectual assessment* (pp. 615–630). New York: Guilford Press. (9)

Brang, D., Edwards, L., Ramachandran, V. S., & Coulson, S. (2008). Is the sky 2? Contextual priming in grapheme-color synesthesia. *Psychological Science, 19,* 421–428. (4)

Brédart, S., Delchambre, M., & Laureys, S. (2006). One's own face is hard to ignore. *Quarterly Journal of Experimental Psychology, 59,* 46–52. (8)

Bregman, A. S. (1981). Asking the "what for" question in auditory perception. In M. Kubovy & J. R. Pomerantz (Eds.), *Perceptual organization* (pp. 99–118). Hillsdale, NJ: Erlbaum. (4)

Bremmer, F., Kubischik, M., Hoffmann, K.-P., & Krekelberg, B. (2009). Neural dynamics of saccadic suppression. *Journal of Neuroscience, 29,* 12374–12383. (3)

Brescoll, V. L., & Uhlmann, E. L. (2008). Can an angry woman get ahead? *Psychological Science, 19,* 268–275. (13)

Breslau, J., Aguilar-Gaxiola, S., Kendle, K. S., Su, M., Williams, D., & Kessler, R. C. (2006). Specifying race-ethnic differences in risk for psychiatric disorder in a USA national sample. *Psychological Medicine, 36,* 57–68. (15)

Breslau, N., Dickens, W. T., Flynn, J. R., Peterson, E. L., & Lucia, V. C. (2006). Low birthweight and social disadvantage: Tracking their relationship with children's IQ during the period of school attendance. *Intelligence, 34,* 351–362. (9)

Breslin, C. W., & Safer, M. A. (2011). Effects of event valence on long-term memory for two baseball championship games. *Psychological Science, 22,* 1408–1412. (7)

Brewer, M. B., & Chen, Y.-R. (2007). Where (who) are collectives in collectivism? Toward conceptual clarification of individualism and collectivism. *Psychological Review, 114,* 131–151. (5)

Bridge, J. A., Birmaher, B., Iyengar, S., Barbe, R. P., & Brent, D. A. (2009). Placebo response in randomized controlled trials of antidepressants for pediatric major depressive disorder. *American Journal of Psychiatry, 166,* 42–49. (15)

Brody, N. (2003). Construct validation of the Sternberg Triarchic Abilities Test: Comment and reanalysis. *Intelligence, 31,* 319–329. (9)

Brower, K. J., & Anglin, M. D. (1987). Adolescent cocaine use: Epidemiology, risk factors, and prevention. *Journal of Drug Education, 17,* 163–180. (3)

Brown, A. S. (2003). A review of the déjà vu experience. *Psychological Bulletin, 129,* 394–413. (10)

Brown, A. S. (2011). The environment and susceptibility to schizophrenia. *Progress in Neurobiology, 93,* 23–58. (15)

Brown, G. P., MacLeod, A. K., Tata, P., & Goddard, L. (2002). Worry and the simulation of future outcomes. *Anxiety, Stress and Coping, 15*, 1–17. (12)

Brown, G. W. (1989). Life events and measurement. In G. W. Brown & T. O. Harris (Eds.), *Life events and illness* (pp. 3–45). New York: Guilford Press. (12)

Brown, J. (1977). *Mind, brain, and consciousness.* New York: Academic Press. (8)

Brown, R., & McNeill, D. (1966). The "tip of the tongue." *Journal of Verbal Learning and Verbal Behavior, 5*, 325–337. (7)

Bruce, S. E., Machan, J. T., Dyck, I., & Keller, M. B. (2001). Infrequency of "pure" GAD: Impact of psychiatric comorbidity on clinical course. *Depression and Anxiety, 14*, 219–225. (15)

Bruck, M., Cavanagh, P., & Ceci, S. J. (1991). Fortysomething: Recognizing faces at one's 25th reunion. *Memory and Cognition, 19*, 221–228. (4)

Brüning, J. C., Gautham, D., Burks, D. J., Gillette, J., Schubert, M., Orban, P. C., . . . Kahn, C. R. (2000). Role of brain insulin receptor in control of body weight and reproduction. *Science, 289*, 2122–2125. (11)

Bryant, F. B., & Guilbault, R. L. (2002). "I knew it all along" eventually: The development of hindsight bias in the Clinton impeachment verdict. *Basic and Applied Social Psychology, 24*, 27–41. (7)

Brysbaert, M., Vitu, F., & Schroyens, W. (1996). The right visual field advantage and the optimal viewing position effect: On the relation between foveal and parafoveal word recognition. *Neuropsychology, 10*, 385–395. (8)

Bryson, S. E. (2005). The autistic mind. In M. L. Bauman & T. L. Kemper (Eds.), *The neurobiology of autism* (pp. 34–44). Baltimore: Johns Hopkins University Press. (15)

Buck, L., & Axel, R. (1991). A novel multigene family may encode odorant receptors: A molecular basis for odor recognition. *Cell, 65*, 175–187. (4)

Buckner, F., & Firestone, M. (2000). "Where the public peril begins": 25 years after *Tarasoff. Journal of Legal Medicine, 21*, 187–222. (15)

Buehler, R., Griffin, D., & Ross, M. (1994). Exploring the "planning fallacy": Why people underestimate their task completion times. *Journal of Personality and Social Psychology, 67*, 366–381. (11)

Bulbena, A., Gago, J., Pailhez, G., Sperry, L., Fullana, M. A., & Vilarroya, O. (2011). Joint hypermobility syndrome is a risk factor for anxiety disorder: A 15-year follow-up cohort study. *General Hospital Psychiatry, 33*, 363–370. (15)

Burger, J. M. (1986). Increasing compliance by improving the deal: The that's-not-all technique. *Journal of Personality and Social Psychology, 51*, 277–283. (13)

Burger, J. M. (2009). Replicating Milgram: Would people still obey today? *American Psychologist, 64*, 1–11. (13)

Burke, K. A., Franz, T. M., Miller, D. N., & Schoenbaum, G. (2008). The role of the orbitofrontal cortex in the pursuit of happiness and more specific rewards. *Nature, 454*, 340–344. (6)

Burke, K. C., Burke, J. D., Jr., Regier, D. A., & Rae, D. S. (1990). Age at onset of selected mental disorders in five community populations. *Archives of General Psychiatry, 47*, 511–518. (15)

Burr, D. C., Morrone, M. C., & Ross, J. (1994). Selective suppression of the magnocellular visual pathway during saccadic eye movements. *Nature, 371*, 511–513. (8)

Bushman, B. J., & Anderson, C. A. (2009). Comfortably numb: Desensitizing effects of violent media on helping others. *Psychological Science, 20*, 273–277. (13)

Buss, D. M. (2000). Desires in human mating. *Annals of the New York Academy of Sciences, 907*, 39–49. (13)

Butcher, J. N., Graham, J. R., Williams, C. L., & Ben-Porath, Y. S. (1990). *Development and use of the MMPI-2 content scales.* Minneapolis: University of Minnesota Press. (14)

Butler, A. C., Chapman, J. E., Forman, E. M., & Beck, A. T. (2006). The empirical status of cognitive-behavioral therapy: A review of meta-analyses. *Clinical Psychology Review, 26*, 17–31. (15)

Butler, E. A., Lee, T. L., & Gross, J. J. (2007). Emotion regulation and culture: Are the social consequences of emotion suppression culture-specific? *Emotion, 7*, 30–48. (12)

Butler, L. (2002). A list of published papers is no measure of value. *Nature, 419*, 877. (11)

Butler, M. R., Turner, K. W., Park, J. H., Schoomer, E. E., Zucker, I., & Gorman, M. R. (2010). Seasonal regulation of reproduction: Altered role of melatonin under naturalistic conditions in hamsters. *Proceedings of the Royal Society B, 277*, 2867–2874. (10)

Butler, R. J., Holland, P., Gasson, S., Norfolk, S., Houghton, L., & Penney, M. (2007). Exploring potential mechanisms in alarm treatment for primary nocturnal enuresis. *Scandinavian Journal of Urology and Nephrology, 41*, 407–413. (15)

Buxbaum, L. J. (2006). On the right (and left) track: Twenty years of progress in studying hemispatial neglect. *Cognitive Neuropsychology, 23*, 184–201. (10)

Byers-Heinlein, K., Burns, T. C., & Werker, J. F. (2010). The roots of bilingualism in newborns. *Psychological Science, 21*, 343–348. (5)

Byne, W., Tobet, S., Mattiace, L. A., Lasco, M. S., Kemether, E., Edgar, M. A., . . . Jones, L. B. (2001). The interstitial nuclei of the human anterior hypothalamus: An investigation of variation with sex, sexual orientation, and HIV status. *Hormones and Behavior, 40*, 86–92. (11)

Byrne, G. J. A., Raphael, B., & Arnold, E. (1999). Alcohol consumption and psychological distress in recently widowed older men. *Australian and New Zealand Journal of Psychiatry, 33*, 740–747. (12)

Cacioppo, J. T., Hawkley, L. C., & Berntson, G. G. (2003). The anatomy of loneliness. *Current Directions in Psychological Science, 12*, 71–74. (12)

Cahalan, D. (1978). Subcultural differences in drinking behavior in U.S. national surveys and selected European studies. In P. E. Nathan, G. A. Marlatt, & T. Løberg (Eds.), *Alcoholism: New directions in behavioral research and treatment* (pp. 235–253). New York: Plenum Press. (15)

Cahill, L. (2006). Why sex matters for neuroscience. *Nature Reviews Neuroscience, 7*, 477–484. (3, 5)

Calabria, B., Degenhardt, L., Briegleb, C., Vos, T., Hall, W., . . . McLaren, J. (2010). Systematic review of prospective studies investigating "remission" from amphetamine, cannabis, cocaine or opioid dependence. *Addictive Behaviors, 35*, 741–749. (15)

Calboli, F. C. F., Tozzi, F., Galwey, N. W., Antoniades, A., Mooser, V. . . . Balding, D. J. (2010). A genome-wide association study of neuroticism in a population-based sample. *PLoS One, 5*, e11504. (14)

Caldwell, J. A., Mu, Q., Smith, J. K., Mishory, A., Caldwell, J. L., Peters, G., . . . George, M. S. (2005). Are individual differences in fatigue vulnerability related to baseline differences in cortical activation? *Behavioral Neuroscience, 119*, 694–707. (10)

Calef, T., Pieper, M., & Coffey, B. (1999). Comparisons of eye movements before and after a speed-reading course. *Journal of the American Optometric Association, 70*, 171–181. (8)

Calvo-Merino, B., Grèzesm J., Glaser, D. E., Passingham, R. E., & Haggard, P. (2006). Seeing or doing? Influence of visual and motor familiarity on action observation. *Current Biology, 16*, 1905–1910. (3)

Cameron, P., Proctor, K., Coburn, W., & Forde, N. (1985). Sexual orientation and sexually transmitted disease. *Nebraska Medical Journal, 70*, 292–299. (11)

Campbell, R. S., & Pennebaker, J. W. (2003). The secret life of pronouns: Flexibility in writing style and physical health. *Psychological Science, 14*, 60–65. (15)

Campbell, S. S., & Tobler, I. (1984). Animal sleep: A review of sleep duration across phylogeny. *Neuroscience and Biobehavioral Reviews, 8*, 269–300. (10)

Camperio-Ciani, A., Corna, F., & Capiluppi, C. (2004). Evidence for maternally inherited factors favouring male homosexuality and promoting female fecundity. *Proceedings of the Royal Society of London, B, 271*, 2217–2221. (11)

Campion, M. A., & McClelland, C. L. (1991). Interdisciplinary examination of the costs and benefits of enlarged jobs: A job design quasi-experiment. *Journal of Applied Psychology, 76*, 186–198. (11)

Campion, M. A., & Thayer, P. W. (1985). Development and field evaluation of an interdisciplinary measure of job design. *Journal of Applied Psychology, 70*, 29–43. (11)

Campion, M. A., & Thayer, P. W. (1989). How do you design a job? *Personnel Journal, 68*, 43–46. (1)

Campitelli, G., & Gobet, F. (2011). Deliberate practice: Necessary but not sufficient. *Current Directions in Psychological Science, 20*, 280–285. (8)

Campos, J. J., Bertenthal, B. I., & Kermoian, R. (1992). Early experience and emotional development. *Psychological Science, 3*, 61–64. (5)

Canino, G., & Alegria, M. (2008). Psychiatric diagnosis—Is it universal or relative to culture? *Journal of Child Psychology and Psychiatry, 49*, 237–250. (15)

Cannon, W. B. (1929). Organization for physiological homeostasis. *Physiological Reviews, 9*, 399–431. (11)

Canter, D. V. (2011). Resolving the offender "profiling equations" and the emergence of an investigative psychology. *Current Directions in Psychological Science, 20*, 5–10. (14)

Capela, J. P., Carmo, H., Remiao, F., Bastos, M. L., Meisel, A., & Carvalho, F. (2009). Molecular and cellular mechanisms of ecstasy-induced neurotoxicity: An overview. *Molecular Neurobiology, 39*, 210–271. (3)

Cardno, A. G., Marshall, E. J., Coid, B., Macdonald, A. M., Ribchester, T. R., Davies, N. J., . . . Murray, R. M. (1999). Heritability estimates for psychotic disorders. *Archives of General Psychiatry, 56*, 162–168. (15)

Carey, S. (1978). The child as word learner. In M. Halle, J. Bresnan, & G. A. Miller (Eds.), *Linguistic theory and psychological reality* (pp. 264–293). Cambridge, MA: MIT Press. (8)

Carlsson, K., Petrovic, P., Skare, S., Petersson, K. M., & Ingvar, M. (2000). Tickling expectations: Neural processing in anticipation of a sensory stimulus. *Journal of Cognitive Neuroscience, 12,* 691–703. (4)

Carney, R. N., & Levin, J. R. (1998). Coming to terms with the keyword method in introductory psychology: A "neuromnemonic" example. *Teaching of Psychology, 25,* 132–134. (7)

Carr, J. (2008). The everyday life of adults with Down syndrome. *Journal of Applied Research in Intellectual Disabilities, 21,* 389–397. (9)

Carré, J. M., McCormick, C. M., & Mondloch, C. J. (2009). Facial structure is a reliable cue of aggressive behavior. *Psychological Science, 20,* 1194–1198. (13)

Carreiras, M., Seghier, M. L., Baquero, S., Estévez, A., Lozano, A., Devlin, J. T., . . . Price, C. J. (2009). An anatomical signature for literacy. *Nature, 461,* 983–986. (3)

Carroll, B. J. (1980). Implications of biological research for the diagnosis of depression. In J. Mendlewicz (Ed.), *New advances in the diagnosis and treatment of depressive illness* (pp. 85–107). Amsterdam: Excerpta Medica. (15)

Carstensen, L. L., Mikels, J. A., & Mather, M. (2006). Aging and the intersection of cognition, motivation, and emotion. In J. E. Birren & K. W. Schaie (Eds.), *Handbook of the psychology of aging* (6th ed., pp. 343–362). Burlington, MA: Elsevier. (5)

Caspi, A., McClay, J., Moffitt, T. E., Mill, J., Martin, J., Craig, I. W., . . . Poulton, R. (2002). Role of genotype in the cycle of violence in maltreated children. *Science, 297,* 851–854. (13)

Caspi, A., Sugden, K., Moffit, T. E., Taylor, A., Craig, I. W., Harrington, H. L., . . . Poulton, R. (2003). Influence of life stress on depression: Moderation by a polymorphism in the 5-HTT gene. *Science, 301,* 386–389. (14)

Cassia, V. M., Turati, C., & Simion, F. (2004). Can a nonspecific bias toward top-heavy patterns explain newborns' face preference? *Psychological Science, 15,* 379–383. (5)

Caterina, M. J., Rosen, T. A., Tominaga, M., Brake, A. J., & Julius, D. (1999). A capsaicin-receptor homologue with a high threshold for noxious heat. *Nature, 398,* 436–441. (4)

Catmur, C., Walsh, V., & Heyes, C. (2007). Sensorimotor learning configures the human mirror system. *Current Biology, 17,* 1527–1531. (3)

Cattell, R. B. (1965). *The scientific analysis of personality.* Chicago: Aldine. (14)

Cattell, R. B. (1987). *Intelligence: Its structure, growth and action.* Amsterdam: North-Holland. (9)

Center for Psychology Workforce Analysis and Research. (2007). Doctorate Employment Survey. Washington, DC: American Psychological Association. (1)

Cepeda, N. J., Pashler, H., Vul, E., Wixted, J. T., & Rohrer, D. (2006). Distributed practice in verbal recall tasks: A review and quantitative synthesis. *Psychological Bulletin, 132,* 354–380. (7)

Cepeda, N. J., Vul, E., Rohrer, D., Wixted, J. T., & Pashler, H. (2008). Spacing effects in learning. *Psychological Science, 19,* 1095–1102. (7)

Cesarini, D., Dawes, C. T., Fowler, J. H., Johanesson, M., Lichtenstein, P., & Wallace, B. (2008). Heritability of cooperative behavior in the trust game. *Proceedings of the National Academy of Sciences, USA, 105,* 3721–3726. (5)

Chabris, C. F., & Glickman, M. E. (2006). Sex differences in intellectual performance: Analysis of a large cohort of competitive chess players. *Psychological Science, 17,* 1040–1046. (5)

Chamorro-Premuzic, T., & Furnham, A. (2008). Personality, intelligence and approaches to learning as predictors of academic performance. *Personality and Individual Differences, 44,* 1596–1603. (14)

Changeux, J.-P. (2010). Nicotine addiction and nicotinic receptors: Lessons from genetically modified mice. *Nature Reviews Neuroscience, 11,* 389–401. (3)

Chapman, H. A., Kim, D. A., Susskind, J. M., & Anderson, A. K. (2009). In bad taste: Evidence for the oral origins of moral disgust. *Science, 323,* 1222–1226. (12)

Chase-Lansdale, P., Moffitt, R. A., Lohrman, B. J., Cherlin, A. J., Coley, R. L., Pittman, L. D., . . . Votruba-Drzal, E. (2003). Mothers' transitions from welfare to work and the well-being of preschoolers and adolescents. *Science, 299,* 1548–1552. (5)

Chaudhari, N., Landin, A. M., & Roper, S. D. (2000). A metabotropic glutamate receptor variant functions as a taste receptor. *Nature Neuroscience, 3,* 113–119. (4)

Cheetham, E. (1973). *The prophecies of Nostradamus.* New York: Putnam's. (2)

Chehab, F. F., Mounzih, K., Lu, R., & Lim, M. E. (1997). Early onset of reproductive function in normal female mice treated with leptin. *Science, 275,* 88–90. (11)

Chemelli, R. M., Willie, J. T., Sinton, C. M., Elmquist, J. K., Scammell, T., Lee, C., . . . Yanagisawa, M. (1999). Narcolepsy in orexin knockout mice: Molecular genetics of sleep regulation. *Cell, 98,* 437–451. (10)

Chen, D., & Haviland-Jones, J. (2000). Human olfactory communication of emotion. *Perceptual and Motor Skills, 91,* 771–781. (5)

Chen, Z., Williams, K. D., Fitness, J., & Newton, N. C. (2008). When hurt will not heal. *Psychological Science, 19,* 789–795. (4)

Cheryan, S., & Bodenhausen, G. V. (2000). When positive stereotypes threaten intellectual performance: The psychological hazards of "model minority" status. *Psychological Science, 11,* 399–402. (9)

Cheung, B. Y., Chudek, M., & Heine, S. J. (2011). Evidence for a sensitive period for acculturation: Younger immigrants report acculturating at a faster rate. *Psychological Science, 22,* 147–152. (5)

Cheung, F. M., Leung, K., Fang, R. M., Song, W. Z., Zhang, J. X., & Zhang, J. P. (1996). Development of the Chinese Personality Assessment Inventory (CPAI). *Journal of Cross-Cultural Psychology, 27,* 181–199. (14)

Cheung, F. Y.-L., & Tang, C. S.-K. (2007). The influence of emotional dissonance and resources at work on job burnout among Chinese human sevice employees. *International Journal of Stress Management, 14,* 72–87. (11)

Chivers, M. L., Rieger, G., Latty, E., & Bailey, J. M. (2004). A sex difference in the specificity of sexual arousal. *Psychological Science, 15,* 736–744. (11)

Chomsky, N. (1980). *Rules and representations.* New York: Columbia University Press. (8)

Christensen, A., & Jacobson, N. S. (1994). Who (or what) can do psychotherapy: The status and challenge of nonprofessional therapies. *Psychological Science, 5,* 8–14. (15)

Church, A. T., Katigbak, M. S., Reyes, J. A. S., Salanga, M. G. C., Miramontes, L. A., & Adams, N. B. (2008). Prediction and cross-situational consistency of daily behavior across cultures: Testing trait and cultural psychology perspectives. *Journal of Research in Personality, 42,* 1199–1215. (14)

Churchland, P. S. (1986). *Neurophilosophy.* Cambridge, MA: MIT Press. (10)

Cialdini, R. B. (1993). *Influence: The psychology of persuasion* (Rev. ed.). New York: Morrow. (6, 13)

Cialdini, R. B. (2003). Crafting normative messages to protect the environment. *Current Directions in Psychological Science, 12,* 105–109. (13)

Cimino, K. (2007, June 20). After it blooms, it will smell as bad as a blooming corpse. *News and Observer* (Raleigh, NC), p. 4B. (11)

Cislo, A. M. (2008). Ethnic identity and self-esteem: Contrasting Cuban and Nicaraguan young adults. *Hispanic Journal of Behavioral Sciences, 30,* 230–250. (5)

Clancy, S. A. (2005). *Abducted: How people come to believe they were kidnapped by aliens.* Cambridge, MA: Harvard University Press. (15)

Clark, C. A. C., Woodward, L. J., Horwood, L. J., & Moor, S. (2008). Development of emotional and behavioral regulation in children born extremely preterm and very preterm: Biological and social influences. *Child Development, 79,* 1444–1462. (5)

Clarkin, J. F., & Carpenter, D. (1995). Family therapy in historical perspective. In B. Bongar & L. E. Beutler (Eds.), *Comprehensive textbook of psychotherapy: Theory and practice* (pp. 205–227). Oxford, England: Oxford University Press. (15)

Clay, R. A. (2002, May). An indigenized psychology. *Monitor on Psychology, 33*(5), 58–59. (15)

Clearfield, M. W., & Nelson, N. M. (2006). Sex differences in mothers' speech and play behavior with 6-, 9-, and 14-month-old infants. *Sex Roles, 54,* 127–137. (5)

Clément, K., Vaisse, C., Lahlou, N., Cabrol, S., Pelloux, V., Cassuto, D., . . . Guy-Grand, B. (1998). A mutation in the human leptin receptor gene causes obesity and pituitary dysfunction. *Nature, 392,* 398–401. (11)

Clinicopathologic conference. (1967). *Johns Hopkins Medical Journal, 120,* 186–199. (12)

Coan, J. A., Schaefer, H. S., & Davidson, R. J. (2006). Lending a hand: Social regulation of the neural response to threat. *Psychological Science, 17,* 1032–1039. (12)

Coatsworth, J. D., Maldonado-Molina, M., Pantin, H., & Szapocznik, J. (2005). A person-centered and ecological investigation of acculturation strategies in Hispanic immigrant youth. *Journal of Community Psychology, 33,* 157–174. (5)

Cobos, P., Sánchez, M., García, C., Vera, M. N., & Vila, J. (2002). Revisiting the James versus Cannon debate on emotion: Startle and autonomic modulation in patients with spinal cord injuries. *Biological Psychology, 61,* 251–269. (12)

Cocodia, E. A., Kim, J. S., Shin, H.-S., Kim, J. W., Ee, J., Wee, M. S. W., . . . Howard, R. W. (2003). Evidence that rising population intelligence is impacting in formal education. *Personality and Individual Differences, 35,* 797–810. (9)

Coelho, C. M., Waters, A. M., Hine, T. J., & Wallis, G. (2009). The use of virtual reality in acrophobia research and treatment. *Journal of Anxiety Disorders, 23,* 563–574. (15)

Cohen Kadosh, R., Henik, A., Catena, A., Walsh, V., & Fuentes, L. J. (2009). Induced cross-modal synaesthetic experience without abnormal neuronal connections. *Psychological Science, 20*, 258–265. (10)

Cohen, E., & Barrett, J. L. (2008). Conceptualizing spirit possession: Ethnographic and experimental evidence. *Ethos, 36*, 246–267. (15)

Cohen, G. L., Garcia, J., Purdie-Vaughns, V., Apfel, N., & Brzustoski, P. (2009). Recursive processes in self-affirmation: Intervening to close the minority achievement gap. *Science, 324*, 400–403. (9)

Cohen, J. D., Noll, D. C., & Schneider, W. (1993). Functional magnetic resonance imaging: Overview and methods for psychological research. *Behavior Research Methods, Instruments, and Computers, 25*, 101–113. (3)

Cohen, M. A., Alvarez, G. A., & Nakayama, K. (2011). Natural-scene perception requires attention. *Psychological Science, 22*, 1165–1172. (8)

Cohen, M. R., & Maunsell, J. H. R. (2011). When attention wanders: How uncontrolled fluctuations in attention affect performance. *Journal of Neuroscience, 31*, 15802–15806. (8)

Cohen, N. J., & Squire, L. R. (1980). Preserved learning and retention of pattern-analyzing skill in amnesia: Dissociation of knowing how and knowing that. *Science, 210*, 207–211. (7)

Cohen, S., Frank, E., Doyle, W. J., Skoner, D. P., Rabin, B. S., & Swaltney, J. M., Jr. (1998). Types of stressors that increase susceptibility to the common cold in healthy adults. *Health Psychology, 17*, 214–223. (12)

Cohen, S., Lichtenstein, E., Prochaska, J. O., Rossi, J. S., Gritz, E. R., Carr, C. R., . . . Ossip-Klein, D. (1989). Debunking myths about self-quitting: Evidence from 10 prospective studies of persons who attempt to quit smoking by themselves. *American Psychologist, 44*, 1355–1365. (15)

Colantuoni, C., Rada, P., McCarthy, J., Patten, C., Avena, N. M., Chadcayne, A., . . . Hoebel, B. G. (2002). Evidence that intermittent, excessive sugar intake causes endogenous opioid dependence. *Obesity Research, 10*, 478–488. (11)

Colantuoni, C., Schwenker, J., McCarthy, J., Rada, P., Ladenheim, B., Cadet, J. L., . . . Hoebel, B. G. (2001). Excessive sugar intake alters binding to dopamine and mu-opioid receptors in the brain. *NeuroReport, 12*, 3549–3552. (11)

Colcombe, S., & Kramer, A. F. (2003). Fitness effects on the cognitive function of older adults: A meta-analytic study. *Psychological Science, 14*, 125–130. (5)

Collins, A. M., & Loftus, E. F. (1975). A spreading-activation theory of semantic processing. *Psychological Review, 82*, 407–428. (8)

Collins, A. M., & Quillian, M. R. (1969). Retrieval time from semantic memory. *Journal of Verbal Learning and Verbal Behavior, 8*, 240–247. (8)

Collins, A. M., & Quillian, M. R. (1970). Does category size affect categorization time? *Journal of Verbal Learning and Verbal Behavior, 9*, 432–438. (8)

Collins, W. A., Maccoby, E. E., Steinberg, L., Hetherington, E. M., & Bornstein, M. H. (2000). Contemporary research on parenting: The case for nature and nurture. *American Psychologist, 55*, 218–232. (5)

Colom, R., Juan-Espinosa, M., Abad, F., & Garciá, L. F. (2000). Negligible sex differences in general intelligence. *Intelligence, 28*, 57–68. (9)

Coman, A., Manier, D., & Hirst, W. (2009). Forgetting the unforgettable through conversation. *Psychological Science, 20*, 627–633. (7)

Conley, T. D., Moors, A. C., Matsick, J. L., Ziegler, A., & Valentine, B. A. (2011). Women, men, and the bedroom: Methodological and conceptual insights that narrow, reframe, and eliminate gender differences in sexuality. *Current Directions in Psychological Science, 20*, 296–300. (11)

Connine, C. M., Blasko, D. G., & Hall, M. (1991). Effects of subsequent sentence context in auditory word recognition: Temporal and linguistic constraints. *Journal of Memory and Language, 30*, 234–250. (8)

Connor, T. J., & Leonard, B. E. (1998). Depression, stress and immunological activation: The role of cytokines in depressive disorders. *Life Sciences, 62*, 583–606. (12)

Constantinides, P. (1977). Ill at ease and sick at heart: Symbolic behavior in a Sudanese healing cult. In I. Wilson (Ed.), *Symbols and sentiments* (pp. 61–84). New York: Academic Press. (15)

Cooper, J., & Cooper, G. (2002). Subliminal motivation: A story revisited. *Journal of Applied Social Psychology, 32*, 2213–2227. (4)

Coplan, J. D., Goetz, R., Klein, D. F., Papp, L. A., Fyer, A. J., Leibowitz, M. R., . . . Gorman, J. M. (1998). Plasma cortisol concentrations preceding lactate-induced panic. *Archives of General Psychiatry, 55*, 130–136. (15)

Corkin, S. (1984). Lasting consequences of bilateral medial temporal lobectomy: Clinical course and experimental findings in H. M. *Seminars in Neurology, 4*, 249–259. (7)

Corkin, S. (2002). What's new with the amnesic patient H. M.? *Nature Reviews Neuroscience, 3*, 153–159. (7)

Cosmelli, D., David, O., Lachaux, J.-P., Martinerie, J., Garnero, L., Renault, B., . . . Varela, F. (2004). Waves of consciousness: Ongoing cortical patterns during binocular rivalry. *NeuroImage, 23*, 128–140. (10)

Costa, P. T., Jr., McCrae, R. R., & Dye, D. A. (1991). Facet scales for agreeableness and conscientiousness: A revision of the NEO personality inventory. *Personality and Individual Differences, 12*, 887–898. (14)

Costello, E. J., Compton, S. N., Keeler, G., & Angold, A. (2003). Relationships between poverty and psychopathology: A natural experiment. *Journal of the American Medical Association, 290*, 2023–2029. (15)

Courage, M. L., & Howe, M. L. (2002). From infant to child: The dynamics of cognitive change in the second year of life. *Psychological Bulletin, 128*, 250–277. (5)

Cowan, N. (2010). The magical mystery four: How is working memory capacity limited, and why? *Current Directions in Psychological Science, 19*, 51–57. (7)

Cox, B. J., McWilliams, L. A., Clara, I. P., & Stein, M. B. (2003). The structure of feared situations in a nationally representative sample. *Journal of Anxiety Disorders, 17*, 89–101. (15)

Cox, J. J., Reimann, F., Nicholas, A. K., Thornton, G., Roberts, E., Springell, K., . . . Woods, C. G. (2006). An *SCN9A* channelopathy causes congenital inability to experience pain. *Nature, 444*, 894–898. (4)

Coyle, T. R., Pillow, D. R., Snyder, A. C., & Kochunov, P. (2011). Processing speed mediates the development of general intelligence (*g*) in adolescence. *Psychological Science, 22*, 1265–1269. (9)

Craig, A. D., Bushnell, M. C., Zhang, E. T., & Blomqvist, A. (1994). A thalamic nucleus specific for pain and temperature sensation. *Nature, 372*, 770–773. (4)

Craig, S. B., & Gustafson, S. B. (1998). Perceived leader integrity scale: An instrument for assessing employee perceptions of leader integrity. *Leadership Quarterly, 9*, 127–145. (11)

Craik, F. I. M., & Lockhart, R. S. (1972). Levels of processing: A framework for memory research. *Journal of Verbal Learning and Verbal Behavior, 11*, 671–684. (7)

Cramer, P. (1996). *Storytelling, narrative, and the Thematic Apperception Test.* New York: Guilford Press. (14)

Cramer, P. (2003). Personality change in later adulthood is predicted by defense mechanism use in early adulthood. *Journal of Research in Personality, 37*, 76–104. (14)

Credé, M., & Kuncel, N. R. (2008). Study habits, skills, and attitudes. *Perspectives on Psychological Science, 3*, 425–453. (9)

Creswell, J. D., Welch, W. T., Taylor, S. E., Sherman, D. K., Gruenwald, T. L., & Mann, T. (2005). Affirmation of personal values buffers neuroendocrine and psychological stress responses. *Psychological Science, 16*, 846–851. (14)

Crews, D. J., & Landers, D. M. (1987). A meta-analytic review of aerobic fitness and reactivity to psychosocial stressors. *Medicine and Science in Sports and Exercise, 19*, S114–S120. (12)

Crews, F. (1996). The verdict on Freud. *Psychological Science, 7*, 63–68. (14)

Crisp, R. J., & Turner, R. N. (2009). Can imagined interactions produce positive perceptions? *American Psychologist, 64*, 231–240. (13)

Critchley, H. D., Mathias, C. J., & Dolan, R. J. (2001). Neuroanatomical basis for first- and second-order representations of bodily states. *Nature Neuroscience, 4*, 207–212. (12)

Crocetti, E., Rubini, M., Luyckx, K., & Meeus, W. (2008). Identity formation in early and middle adolescents from various ethnic groups: From three dimensions to five statuses. *Journal of Youth and Adolescence, 37*, 983–996. (5)

Crocker, J., & Park, L. E. (2004). The costly pursuit of self-esteem. *Psychological Bulletin, 130*, 392–414. (14)

Crowley, K., Callanen, M. A., Tenenbaum, H. R., & Allen, E. (2001). Parents explain more often to boys than to girls during shared scientific thinking. *Psychological Science, 12*, 258–261. (5)

Crowther, J. H., Armey, M., Luce, K. H., Dalton, G. R., & Leahey, T. (2008). The point prevalence of bulimic disorders from 1990 to 2004. *International Journal of Eating Disorders, 41*, 491–497. (11)

Croyle, R. T., & Cooper, J. (1983). Dissonance arousal: Physiological evidence. *Journal of Personality and Social Psychology, 45*, 782–791. (13)

Crum, A. J., & Langer, E. J. (2007). Mind-set matters. *Psychological Science, 18*, 165–171. (12)

Cryder, C. E., Lerner, J. S., Gross, J. J., & Dahl, R. E. (2008). Misery is not miserly: Sad and self-focused individuals spend more. *Psychological Science, 19*, 525–530. (12)

Csikszentmihalyi, M. (1999). If we are so rich, why aren't we happy? *American Psychologist, 54*, 821–827. (12)

Cuijpers, P., van Straten, A., Andersson, G., & van Oppen, P. (2008). Psychotherapy for depression in adults: A meta-analysis of comparative outcome studies. *Journal of Consulting and Clinical Psychology, 76*, 909–922. (15)

Culbertson, F. M. (1997). Depression and gender. *American Psychologist, 52,* 25–31. (15)

Cumming, G. (2008). Replication and *p* intervals. *Perspectives on Psychological Science, 3,* 286–300. (2)

Cummings, N. A. (1979). Turning bread into stones: Our modern antimiracle. *American Psychologist, 34,* 1119–1129. (15)

Cynkar, A. (2007, June). The changing gender composition of psychology. *Monitor on Psychology, 38*(6), 46. (1)

Cyranowski, J. M., Frank, E., Young, E., & Shear, K. (2000). Adolescent onset of the gender difference in lifetime rates of major depression. *Archives of General Psychiatry, 57,* 21–27. (15)

Czeisler, C. A., Johnson, M. P., Duffy, J. F., Brown, E. N., Ronda, J. M., & Kronauer, R. E. (1990). Exposure to bright light and darkness to treat physiologic maladaptation to night work. *New England Journal of Medicine, 322,* 1353–1359. (10)

Czeisler, C. A., Moore-Ede, M. C., & Coleman, R. M. (1982). Rotating shift work schedules that disrupt sleep are improved by applying circadian principles. *Science, 217,* 460–463. (10)

Dailey, M. N., Joyce, C., Lyons, M. J., Kamachi, M., Ishi, H., . . . Cottrell, G. W. (2010). Evidence and a computational explanation of cultural differences in facial expression recognition. *Emotion, 10,* 874–893. (12)

Dale, P. S., Harlaar, N., Haworth, C. M. A., & Plomin, R. (2010). Two by two: A twin study of second-language learning. *Psychological Science, 21,* 635–640. (9)

Daley, T. C., Whaley, S. E., Sigman, M. D., Espinosa, M. P., & Neumann, C. (2003). IQ on the rise: The Flynn effect in rural Kenyan children. *Psychological Science, 14,* 215–219. (9)

Dallenbach, K. M. (1951). A puzzle picture with a new principle of concealment. *American Journal of Psychology, 64,* 431–433. (4)

Damaser, E. C., Shor, R. E., & Orne, M. E. (1963). Physiological effects during hypnotically requested emotions. *Psychosomatic Medicine, 25,* 334–343. (10)

Damasio, A. (1999). *The feeling of what happens.* New York: Harcourt Brace. (12)

Damasio, A. R. (1994). *Descartes' error: Emotion, reason, and the human brain.* New York: G. P. Putnam's Sons. (3, 12)

Damasio, H., Grabowski, T., Frank, R., Galaburda, A. M., & Damasio, A. R. (1994). The return of Phineas Gage: The skull of a famous patient yields clues about the brain. *Science, 264,* 1102–1105. (12)

Damron-Rodriguez, J. (1991). Commentary: Multicultural aspects of aging in the U.S.: Implications for health and human services. *Journal of Cross-Cultural Gerontology, 6,* 135–143. (5)

Daniel, M. H. (1997). Intelligence testing: Status and trends. *American Psychologist, 52,* 1038–1045. (9)

Danovitch, J., & Bloom, P. (2009). Children's extension of disgust to physical and moral events. *Emotion, 9,* 107–112. (12)

Dapretto, M., Davies, M. S., Pfeifer, J. H., Scott, A. A., Sigman, M., Bookheimer, S. Y., . . . Iacoboni, M. (2006). Understanding emotions in others: Mirror neuron dysfunction in children with autism spectrum disorders. *Nature Neuroscience, 9,* 28–30. (3)

Dar-Nimrod, I., & Heine, S. J. (2006). Exposure to scientific theories affects women's math performance. *Science, 314,* 435. (9)

Darst, C. R., & Cummings, M. E. (2006). Predator learning favours mimicry of a less-toxic model in poison frogs. *Nature, 440,* 208–211. (6)

Darwin, C. (1859). *On the origin of species by means of natural selection.* New York: D. Appleton. (1)

Darwin, C. (1871). *The descent of man.* New York: D. Appleton. (1)

Darwin, C. (1965). *The expression of emotions in man and animals.* Chicago: University of Chicago Press. (Original work published 1872) (12)

Davenport, J. L., & Potter, M. C. (2004). Scene consistency in object and background perception. *Psychological Science, 15,* 559–564. (8)

Davidson, J. K., Sr., Moore, N. B., Earle, J. R., & Davis, R. (2008). Sexual attitudes and behavior at four universities: Do region, race, and/or religion matter? *Adolescence, 43,* 189–220. (11)

Davidson, R. J., Putnam, K. M., & Larson, C. L. (2000). Dysfunction in the neural circuitry of emotion regulation—A possible prelude to violence. *Science, 289,* 591–594. (12)

Davies, G., Welham, J., Chant, D., Torrey, E. F., & McGrath, J. (2003). A systematic review and meta-analysis of Northern Hemisphere season of birth studies in schizophrenia. *Schizophrenia Bulletin, 29,* 587–593. (15)

Davis, J. L., Senghas, A., Brandt, F., & Ochsner, K. N. (2010). The effects of BOTOX injections on emotional experience. *Emotion, 10,* 433–440. (12)

Davis, J. M., Chen, N., & Glick, I. D. (2003). A meta-analysis of the efficacy of second-generation antipsychotics. *Archives of General Psychiatry, 60,* 553–564. (15)

Davis, O. S. P., Haworth, C. M. A., & Plomin, R. (2009). Dramatic increase in heritability of cognitive development from early to middle childhood. *Psychological Science, 20,* 1301–1308. (9)

Dawes, R. M. (1994). *House of cards: Psychology and psychotherapy.* New York: Free Press. (14, 15)

Dawson, M., Soulières, I., Gernsbacher, M. A., & Mottron, L. (2007). The level and nature of autistic intelligence. *Psychological Science, 18,* 657–662. (15)

Day, R. H. (1972). Visual spatial illusions: A general explanation. *Science, 175,* 1335–1340. (4)

Day, S. (2005). Some demographic and socio-cultural aspects of synesthesia. In L. C. Robertson & N. Sagiv (Eds.), *Synesthesia* (pp. 11–33). Oxford, England: Oxford University Press. (4)

de Castro, J. M. (2000). Eating behavior: Lessons from the real world of humans. *Nutrition, 16,* 800–813. (1, 11)

de Groot, A. D. (1966). Perception and memory versus thought: Some old ideas and recent findings. In B. Kleinmuntz (Ed.), *Problem solving* (pp. 19–50). New York: Wiley. (8).

De Houwer, J., Teige-Mocigemba, S., Spruyt, A., & Moors, A. (2009). Implicit measures: A normative analysis and review. *Psychological Bulletin, 135,* 347–368. (14)

De Moor, M. H. M., Boomsma, D. I., Stubbe, J. H., Willemsen, G., & de Geus, E. J. C. (2008). Testing causality in the association between regular exercise and symptoms of anxiety and depression. *Archives of General Psychiatry, 65,* 897–905. (15)

de Quervain, D. J.-F., Roozendaal, B., Nitsch, R. M., McGaugh, J. L., & Hock, C. (2000). Acute cortisone administration impairs retrieval of long-term declarative memory in humans. *Nature Neuroscience, 3,* 313–314. (12)

de Waal, F. B. M. (2002). Evolutionary psychology: The wheat and the chaff. *Current Directions in Psychological Science, 11,* 187–191. (1, 3)

de Wit, H., Crean, J., & Richards, J. B. (2000). Effects of *d*-amphetamine and ethanol on a measure of behavioral inhibition in humans. *Behavioral Neuroscience, 114,* 830–837. (8)

Deacon, S., & Arendt, J. (1996). Adapting to phase shifts: II. Effects of melatonin and conflicting light treatment. *Physiology and Behavior, 59,* 675–682. (10)

Deacon, T. W. (1997). *The symbolic species.* New York: W. W. Norton. (8)

Dealberto, M.-J. (2010). Ethnic origin and increased risk for schizophrenia in immigrants to countries of recent and longstanding immigration. *Acta Psychiatrica Scandinavica, 121,* 325–339. (15)

Dean, C. E. (2011). Psychopharmacology: A house divided. *Progress in Neuro-Psychopharmacology & Biological Psychiatry, 35,*1–10. (15)

Dean, K. E., & Malamuth, N. M. (1997). Characteristics of men who aggress sexually and of men who imagine aggressing: Risk and moderating variables. *Journal of Personality and Social Psychology, 72,* 449–455. (13)

Deary, I. J. (2002). *g* and cognitive elements of information processing: An agnostic view. In R. J. Sternberg & E. L. Grigorenko (Eds.), *The general intelligence factor: How general is it?* (pp. 151–181). Mahwah, NJ: Erlbaum. (9)

Deary, I. J., Batty, G. D., & Gale, C. R. (2008). Bright children become enlightened adults. *Psychological Science, 19,* 1–6. (9)

Deary, I. J., Batty, G. D., Pattie, A., & Gale, C. R. (2008). More intelligent, more dependable children live longer. *Psychological Science, 19,* 874–880. (9)

Deary, I. J., Penke, L., & Johnson, W. (2010). The neruoscience of human intelligence differences. *Nature Reviews Neuroscience, 11,* 201–211. (9)

Deary, I. J., Strand, S., Smith, P., & Fernandes, C. (2007). Intelligence and educational achievement. *Intelligence, 35,* 13–21. (9)

Deary, I. J., Whiteman, M. C., Starr, J. M., Whalley, L. J., & Fox, H. C. (2004). The impact of childhood intelligence on later life: Following up the Scottish mental surveys of 1932 and 1947. *Journal of Personality and Social Psychology, 86,* 130–147. (9)

DeBruine, L. M. (2004). Facial resemblance increases the attractiveness of same-sex faces more than other-sex faces. *Proceedings of the Royal Society of London, B, 271,* 2085–2090. (13)

DeBruine, L. M. (2005). Trustworthy but not lust-worthy: Context-specific effects of facial resemblance. *Proceedings of the Royal Society of London, B, 272,* 919–922. (13)

DeCasper, A. J., & Fifer, W. P. (1980). Of human bonding: Newborns prefer their mothers' voices. *Science, 208,* 1174–1177. (5)

Dedovic, K., Wadiwalla, M., Engert, V., & Pruessner, J. C. (2009). The role of sex and gender socialization in stress reactivity. *Developmental Psychology, 45,* 49–55. (14)

Deese, J. (1959). On the prediction of occurrence of particular verbal intrusions in immediate recall. *Journal of Experimental Psychology, 58,* 17–22. (7)

Degenhardt, L., Bucello, C., Mathers, B., Briegleb, C., Ali, H., . . . McLaren, J. (2010). Mortality among regular or dependent users of heroi and other opioids: A systematic review and meta-analysis of cohort studies. *Addiction, 106,* 32–51. (15)

Dehaene, S., Naccache, L., Cohen, L., LeBihan, D., Mangin, J.-F., Poline, J. B., . . . Riviere, D. (2001). Cerebral mechanisms of word masking and unconscious repetition priming. *Nature Neuroscience, 4,* 752–758. (10)

Dehaene, S., Pegado, F., Braga, L. W., Ventura, P., Nunez Filho, G., Jobert, A., . . . Cohen, L. (2010). How learning to read changes the cortical networks for vision and language. *Science, 330,* 1359–1364. (3)

Del Cul, A., Dehaene, S., Reyes, P., Bravo, E., & Slachevsky, A. (2009). Causal role of prefrontal cortex in the threshold for access to consciousness. *Brain, 132,* 2531–2540. (10)

DeLoache, J. S. (1989). The development of representation in young children. *Advances in Child Development and Behavior, 22,* 1–39. (5)

DeLoache, J. S., Miller, K. F., & Rosengren, K. S. (1997). The credible shrinking room: Very young children's performance with symbolic and nonsymbolic relations. *Psychological Science, 8,* 308–313. (5)

Dement, W. C. (1972). *Some must watch while some must sleep.* Stanford, CA: Stanford Alumni Association. (10)

Dement, W., & Kleitman, N. (1957a). Cyclic variations in EEG during sleep and their relation to eye movements, body motility, and dreaming. *Electroencephalography and Clinical Neurophysiology, 9,* 673–690. (10)

Dement, W., & Kleitman, N. (1957b). The relation of eye movements during sleep to dream activity: An objective method for the study of dreaming. *Journal of Experimental Psychology, 53,* 339–346. (10)

DeNeve, K. M. (1999). Happy as an extraverted clam? The role of personality for subjective well-being. *Current Directions in Psychological Science, 8,* 141–144. (12)

Denissen, J. J. A., Butalid, L., Penke, L., & van Aken, M. A. G. (2008). The effects of weather on daily mood. A multilevel approach. *Emotion, 8,* 662–667. (12)

DePaolo, B. M., Lindsay, J. J., Malone, B. E., Muhlenbruck, L., Charlton, K., & Cooper, H. (2003). Cues to deception. *Psychological Bulletin, 129,* 74–118. (12)

DeScioli, P., Christner, J., & Kurzban, R. (2011). The omission strategy. *Psychological Science, 22,* 442–446. (12)

Detterman, D. K. (1979). Detterman's laws of individual differences research. In R. J. Sternberg & D. K. Detterman (Eds.), *Human intelligence* (pp. 165–175). Norwood, NJ: Ablex. (9)

Deutsch, D., Henthorn, T., Marvin, E., & Xu, H. S. (2006). Absolute pitch among American and Chinese conservatory students: Prevalence differences, and evidence for a speech-related critical period. *Journal of the Acoustical Society of America, 119,* 719–722. (4)

Deutsch, J. A., & Ahn, S. J. (1986). The splanchnic nerve and food intake regulation. *Behavioral and Neural Biology, 45,* 43–47. (11)

Deutsch, J. A., & Gonzalez, M. F. (1980). Gastric nutrient content signals satiety. *Behavioral and Neural Biology, 30,* 113–116. (11)

Devane, W. A., Hanuš, L., Breuer, A., Pertwee, R. G., Stevenson, L. A., Griffin, G., . . . Mechoulam, R. (1992). Isolation and structure of a brain constituent that binds to the cannabinoid receptor. *Science, 258,* 1946–1949. (3)

DeWall, C. N., MacDonald, G., Webster, G. D., Masten, C. L., Baumeister, R. F., Powell, C., .

. . Eisenberger, N. I. (2010). Acetaminophen reduces social pain: Behavioral and neural evidence. *Psychological Science, 21,* 931–937. (4)

DeWall, C. N., Twenge, J. M., Koole, S. L., Baumeister, R. F., Marquez, A., & Reid, R. W. (2011). Automatic emotion regulation after social exclusion: Turning to positivity. *Emotion, 11,* 623–636. (12)

Dewsbury, D. A. (1998). Celebrating E. L. Thorndike a century after *Animal Intelligence. American Psychologist, 53,* 1121–1124. (6)

Dewsbury, D. A. (2000). Introduction: Snapshots of psychology circa 1900. *American Psychologist, 55,* 255–259. (1)

Dhingra, R., Sullivan, L., Jacques, P. F., Wang, T. J., Fox, C. S., Meigs, J. B., . . . Ramachandran, S. (2007). Soft drink consumption and risk of developing cardiometabolic risk factors and the metabolic syndrome in middle-aged adults in the community. *Circulation, 116,* 480–488. (11)

Di Pino, G., Guglielmelli, E., & Rossini, P. M. (2009). Neuroplasticity in amputees: Main implications on bidirectional interfacing of cybernetic hand prostheses. *Progress in Neurobiology, 88,* 114–126. (4)

Diamond, A., & Lee, K. (2011). Interventions shown to aid executive function development in children 4 to 12 years old. *Science, 333,* 959–964. (8)

Diamond, L. M. (2004). Emerging perspectives on distinctions between romantic love and sexual desire. *Current Directions in Psychological Science, 13,* 116–119. (13)

Diamond, L. M. (2007). A dynamical systems approach to the development and expression of female same-sex sexuality. *Perspectives in Psychological Science, 2,* 142–161. (11)

Diamond, L. M. (2008). Female bisexuality from adolescence to adulthood: Results from a 10-year longitudinal study. *Developmental Psychology, 44,* 5–14. (11)

Diaz, M., Parra, A., & Gallardo, C. (2011). Serins respond to anthropogenic noise by increasing vocal activity. *Behavioral Ecology, 22,* 332–336. (6)

Dickens, W. T., & Flynn, J. R. (2001). Heritability estimates versus large environmental effects: The IQ paradox resolved. *Psychological Review, 108,* 346–369. (3, 9)

Dickens, W. T., & Flynn, J. R. (2006). Black Americans reduce the racial IQ gap. *Psychological Science, 17,* 913–920. (9)

Dickerson, S. S., Gable, S. L., Irwin, M. R., Aziz, N., & Kemeny, M. E. (2009). Social-evaluative threat and proinflammatory cytokine regulation. *Psychological Science, 20,* 1237–1244. (12)

Dickson, N., Paul, C., & Herbison, P. (2003). Same-sex attraction in a birth cohort: Prevalence and persistence in early adulthood. *Social Science and Medicine, 56,* 1607–1615. (11)

Diener, E. (2000). Subjective well-being. *American Psychologist, 55,* 34–43. (12)

Diener, E., Lucas, R. E., & Scollon, C. N. (2006). Beyond the hedonic treadmill. *American Psychologist, 61,* 305–314. (12)

Diener, E., & Seligman, M. E. P. (2002). Very happy people. *Psychological Science, 13,* 81–84. (12)

Diener, E., & Seligman, M. E. P. (2004). Beyond money: Toward an economy of well-being. *Psychological Science in the Public Interest, 5,* 1–31. (12)

Diener, E., Suh, E. M., Lucas, R. E., & Smith, H. L. (1999). Subjective well-being: Three decades of progress. *Psychological Bulletin, 125,* 276–302. (12)

Diener, E., Wolsic, B., & Fujita, F. (1995). Physical attractiveness and subjective well-being. *Journal of Personality and Social Psychology, 69,* 120–129. (12)

Dijksterhuis, A., & Bargh, J. A. (2001). The perception-behavior expressway: Automatic effects of social perception on social behavior. *Advances in Experimental Social Psychology, 33,* 1–40. (6)

DiLalla, D. L., Carey, G., Gottesman, I. I., & Bouchard, T. J., Jr. (1996). Heritability of MMPI personality indicators of psychopathology in twins reared apart. *Journal of Abnormal Psychology, 105,* 491–499. (5)

DiMarzo, V., Goparaju, S. K., Wang, L., Liu, J., Bátkai, S., Járai, Z., . . . Kunos, G. (2001). Leptin-regulated endocannabinoids are involved in maintaining food intake. *Nature, 410,* 822–825. (3)

Dimberg, U., Thunberg, M., & Elmehed, K. (2000). Unconscious facial reactions to emotional facial expressions. *Psychological Science, 11,* 86–89. (4)

Dinges, D. F., Whitehouse, W. G., Orne, E. C., Powell, J. W., Orne, M. T., & Erdelyi, M. H. (1992). Evaluating hypnotic memory enhancement (hypermnesia and reminiscence) using multitrial forced recall. *Journal of Experimental Psychology: Learning, Memory, and Cognition, 18,* 1139–1147. (10)

Dinstein, I., Hasson, U., Rubin, N., & Heeger, D. J. (2007). Brain areas selective for both observed and executed movements. *Journal of Neurophysiology, 98,* 1415–1427. (3)

Dittmar, H., Halliwell, E., & Ive, S. (2006). Does Barbie make girls want to be thin? The effect of experimental exposure to images of dolls on the body image of 5- to 8-year-old girls. *Developmental Psychology, 42,* 283–292. (11)

Dmitrieva, J., Steinberg, L., & Belsky, J. (2007). Child-care history, classroom composition, and children's functioning in kindergarten. *Psychological Science, 18,* 1032–1039. (5)

Dobrzecka, C., Szwejkowska, G., & Konorski, J. (1966). Qualitative versus directional cues in two forms of differentiation. *Science, 153,* 87–89. (6)

Doi, T. (1981). *The anatomy of dependence.* Tokyo: Kodansha International. (12)

Dollard, J., Miller, N. E., Doob, L. W., Mowrer, O. H., & Sears, R. R. (1939). *Frustration and aggression.* New Haven, CT: Yale University Press. (13)

Domhoff, G. W. (1996). *Finding meaning in dreams: A quantitative approach.* New York: Plenum Press. (10)

Domhoff, G. W. (1999). Drawing theoretical implications from descriptive empirical findings on dream content. *Dreaming, 9,* 201–210. (10)

Domhoff, G. W. (2003). *The scientific study of dreams.* Washington, DC: American Psychological Association. (2, 10)

Domhoff, G. W. (2011). The neural substrate for dreaming: Is it a subsystem of the default network? *Consciousness and Cognition, 20,* 1163–1174. (10)

Domhoff, G. W., & Schneider, A. (2008). Similarities and differences in dream content at the cross-cultural, gender, and individual levels. *Consciousness and Cognition, 17,* 1257–1265. (10)

Dompnier, B., Darnon, C., & Butera, F. (2009). Faking the desire to learn. *Psychological Science, 20,* 939–943. (2)

Donnellan, M. B., & Lucas, R. E. (2008). Age differences in the big five across the life span: Evidence from two national samples. *Psychology and Aging, 23,* 558–566. (14)

Donnellan, M. B., Trzesniewski, K. H., Robins, R. W., Moffitt, T. E., & Caspi, A. (2005). Low self-esteem is related to aggression, antisocial behavior, and delinquency. *Psychological Science, 16,* 328–335. (13)

Donnerstein, E., & Malamuth, N. (1997). Pornography: Its consequences on the observer. In L. B. Schlesinger & E. Revitch (Eds.), *Sexual dynamics of antisocial behavior* (2nd ed., pp. 30–49). Springfield, IL: Charles C Thomas. (13)

Dovidio, J. F., & Gaertner, S. L. (1999). Reducing prejudice: Combating intergroup biases. *Current Directions in Psychological Science, 8,* 101–105. (13)

Doyle, J. M., & Kao, G. (2007). Are racial identities of multiracials stable? *Social Psychology Quarterly, 70,* 405–423. (5)

Doyon, J., Korman, M., Morin, A., Dostie, V., Tahar, A. H., Benali, H., . . . Carrier, J. (2009). Contribution of night and day sleep vs. simple passage of time to the consolidation of motor sequence and visuomotor adaptation learning. *Experimental Brain Research, 195,* 15–26. (10)

Dreber, A., Rand, D. G., Fudenberg, D., & Nowak, M. A. (2008). Winners don't punish. *Nature, 452,* 348–351. (13)

Dreger, A. D. (1998). *Hermaphrodites and the medical invention of sex.* Cambridge, MA: Harvard University Press. (11)

Drewnowski, A., Henderson, S. A., Shore, A. B., & Barratt-Fornell, A. (1998). Sensory responses to 6-n-propylthiouracil (PROP) or sucrose solutions and food preferences in young women. *Annals of the New York Academy of Sciences, 855,* 797–801. (1)

Drews, F. A., Pasupathi, M., & Strayer, D. L. (2008). Passenger and cell phone conversations in simulated driving. *Journal of Experimental Psychology: Applied, 14,* 392–400. (8)

Driver, J., & Mattingley, J. B. (1998). Parietal neglect and visual awareness. *Nature Neuroscience, 1,* 17–22. (10)

Drzyzga, L. R., Marcinowska, A., & Obuchowicz, E. (2009). Antiapoptotic and neurotrophic effects of antidepressants: A review of clinical and experimental studies. *Brain Research Bulletin, 79,* 248–257. (15)

Duan, X., Chang, J. H., Ge, S., Faulkner, R. L., Kim, J. Y., Kitabatake, Y., . . . Song, H. (2007). Disrupted-in-schizophrenia 1 regulated integration of newly generated neurons in the adult brain. *Cell, 130,* 1146–1158. (15)

Dubois, F. (2007). Mate choice copying in monogamous species: Should females use public information to choose extrapair males? *Animal Behaviour, 74,* 1785–1793. (6)

Duckworth, A. L., & Seligman, M. E. P. (2005). Self-discipline outdoes IQ in predicting academic performance of adolescents. *Psychological Science, 16,* 939–944. (9)

Duke, M., & Nowicki, S., Jr. (1979). *Abnormal psychology: Perspectives on being different.* Monterey, CA: Brooks/Cole. (15)

Dunn, E. W., Aknin, L. B., & Norton, M. I. (2008). Spending money on others promotes happiness. *Science, 319,* 1687–1688. (12)

Dunn, M. J., Brinton, S., & Clark, L. (2010). Universal sex differences in online advertisers age preferences: Comparing data from 14 countries and 2 religious groups. *Evolution and Human Behavior, 31,* 383–393. (13)

Dunning, D., Heath, C., & Suls, J. M. (2005). Flawed self-assessment: Implications for health, education, and the workplace. *Psychological Science in the Public Interest, 5,* 69–106. (11)

Durbin, C. E., Hayden, E. P., Klein, D. N., & Olino, T. M. (2007). Stability of laboratory-assessed temperamental emotionality traits from ages 3 to 7. *Emotion, 7,* 388–399. (5)

Durgin, F. H. (2000). The reverse Stroop effect. *Psychonomic Bulletin and Review, 7,* 121–125. (8)

Durlak, J. A., Weissberg, R. P., Dymnicki, A. B., Taylor, R. D., & Schellinger, K. B. (2011). The impact of enhancing students' social and emotional learning: A meta-analysis of school-based universal interventions. *Child Development, 82,* 405–432. (15)

Dutton, D. G., & Aron, A. P. (1974). Some evidence for heightened sexual attraction under conditions of high anxiety. *Journal of Personality and Social Psychology, 30,* 510–517. (12)

Dywan, J., & Bowers, K. (1983). The use of hypnosis to enhance recall. *Science, 22,* 184–185. (10)

Eagly, A. H., & Crowley, M. (1986). Gender and helping behavior: A meta-analytic review of the social psychological literature. *Psychological Bulletin, 100,* 283–308. (5)

Eagly, A. H., & Wood, W. (1999). The origins of sex differences in human behavior. *American Psychologist, 54,* 408–423. (3)

Eaker, E. D., Sullivan, L. M., Kelly-Hayes, M., D'Agostino, R. B., Sr., & Benjamin, E. J. (2004). Anger and hostility predict the development of atrial fibrillation in men in the Framingham Offspring Study. *Circulation, 109,* 1267–1271. (12)

Earnest, D. J., Liang, F.-Q., Ratcliff, M., & Cassone, V. M. (1999). Immortal time: Circadian clock properties of rat suprachiasmatic cell lines. *Science, 283,* 693–695. (10)

Eastwick, P. W., Finkel, E. J., Mochon, D., & Ariely, D. (2007). Selective versus unselective romantic desire. *Psychological Science, 18,* 317–319. (13)

Eaves, L. J., Martin, N. G., & Heath, A. C. (1990). Religious affiliation in twins and their parents: Testing a model of cultural inheritance. *Behavior Genetics, 20,* 1–22. (5)

Ebbinghaus, H. (1913). *Memory.* New York: Teachers College Press. (Original work published 1885) (7)

Ebling, R., & Levenson, R. W. (2003). Who are the marital experts? *Journal of Marriage and the Family, 65,* 130–142. (13)

Ebneter, D. S., Latner, J. D., & O'Brien, K. S. (2011). Just world beliefs, causal beliefs, and acquaintance: Associations with stigma toward eating disorders and obesity. *Personality and Individual Differences, 51,* 618–622. (14)

Educational Testing Service. (1994). *GRE 1994–95 guide.* Princeton, NJ: Author. (9)

Edwards, J., Jackson, H. J., & Pattison, P. E. (2002). Emotion recognition via facial expression and affective prosody in schizophrenia: A methodological review. *Clinical Psychology Review, 22,* 789–832. (12)

Edwards, K. (1998). The face of time: Temporal cues in facial expressions of emotion. *Psychological Science, 9,* 270–276. (12)

Eibl-Eibesfeldt, I. (1973). *Der vorprogrammierte Mensch* [The preprogrammed human]. Vienna: Verlag Fritz Molden. (12)

Eibl-Eibesfeldt, I. (1974). *Love and hate.* New York: Schocken Books. (12)

Eichenbaum, H. (2002). *The cognitive neuroscience of memory.* New York: Oxford University Press. (7)

Eimas, P. D., Siqueland, E. R., Jusczyk, P., & Vigorito, J. (1971). Speech perception in infants. *Science, 171,* 303–306. (5)

Eisenberger, N. I., Lieberman, M. D., & Williams, K. D. (2003). Does rejection hurt? An fMRI study of social exclusion. *Science, 302,* 290–292. (4)

Ekman, P. (1992). Facial expressions of emotion: New findings, new questions. *Psychological Science, 3,* 34–38. (12)

Ekman, P. (2001). *Telling lies* (3rd ed.). New York: W. W. Norton. (12)

Ekman, P., & Davidson, R. J. (1993). Voluntary smiling changes regional brain activity. *Psychological Science, 4,* 342–345. (12)

Ekman, P., & Friesen, W. V. (1984). *Unmasking the face* (2nd ed.). Palo Alto, CA: Consulting Psychologists Press. (12)

El-Islam, M. F. (1982). Rehabilitation of schizophrenics by the extended family. *Acta Psychiatrica Scandinavica, 65,* 112–119. (15)

El-Sheikh, M., Buckhalt, J. A., Mize, J., & Acebo, C. (2006). Marital conflict and disruption of children's sleep. *Child Development, 77,* 31–43. (5)

Elbert, T., Pantev, C., Wienbruch, C., Rockstroh, B., & Taub, E. (1995). Increased cortical representation of the fingers of the left hand in string players. *Science, 270,* 305–307. (3)

Elbogen, E. B. & Johnson, S. C. (2009). The intricate link between violence and mental disorder. *Archives of General Psychiatry, 66,* 152–161. (15)

Elfenbein, H. A., Beaupré, M., Lévesque, M., & Hess, U. (2007). Toward a dialect theory: Cultural differences in the expression and recognition of posed facial expressions. *Emotion, 7,* 131–146. (12)

Elia, J., Ambrosini, P. J., & Rapoport, J. L. (1999). Treatment of attention-deficit hyperactivity disorder. *New England Journal of Medicine, 340,* 780–788. (8)

Elicker, J., Englund, M., & Sroufe, L. A. (1992). Predicting peer competence and peer relationships in childhood from early parent-child relationships. In R. D. Parke & G. W. Ladd (Eds.), *Family-peer relationships* (pp. 77–106). Hillsdale, NJ: Erlbaum. (5)

Elkind, D. (1984). *All grown up and no place to go.* Reading, MA: Addison-Wesley. (5)

Elkins, G., Marcus, J., Bates, J., Rajab, M. H., & Cook, T. (2006). Intensive hypnotherapy for smoking cessation: A prospective study. *International Journal of Clinical and Experimental Hypnosis, 54,* 303–315. (10)

Ellenberger, H. F. (1972). The story of "Anna O": A critical review with new data. *Journal of the History of the Behavioral Sciences, 8,* 267–279. (14)

Elliot, A. J., Maier, M. A., Moller, A. C., Friedman, R., & Meinhardt, J. (2007). Color and psychological functioning: The effect of red on performance attainment. *Journal of Experimental Psychology: General, 136,* 154–168. (1)

Elliott, C. (1997). Caring about risks: Are severely depressed patients competent to consent to research? *Archives of General Psychiatry, 54,* 113–116. (2)

Elliott, R., Sahakian, B. J., Matthews, K., Bannerjea, A., Rimmer, J., & Robbins, T. W. (1997). Effects of methylphenidate on spatial working memory and planning in healthy young adults. *Psychopharmacology, 131,* 196–206. (8)

Else-Quest, N. M., Hyde, J. S., Goldsmith, H. H., & Van Hulle, C. A. (2006). Gender differences in temperament: A meta-analysis. *Psychological Bulletin, 132,* 33–72. (5)

Emberson, L. L., Lupyan, G., Goldstein, M. H., & Spivey, M. I. (2010). Overheard cell-phone conversations: When less speech is more distracting. *Psychological Science, 21,* 1383–1388. (8)

Emery, C. E., Jr. (1997, November/December). UFO survey yields conflicting conclusions. *Skeptical Inquirer, 21,* 9. (2)

Emmons, R. A., & McCullough, M. E. (2003). Counting blessings versus burdens: An experimental investigation of gratitude and subjective well-being in daily life. *Journal of Personality and Social Psychology, 84,* 377–389. (12)

Eng, M. Y., Schuckit, M. A., & Smith, T. L. (2005). The level of response to alcohol in daughters of alcoholics and controls. *Drug and Alcohol Dependence, 79,* 83–93. (15)

Enns, J. T., & Rensink, R. A. (1990). Sensitivity to three-dimensional orientation in visual search. *Psychological Science, 1,* 323–326. (8)

Enoch, M.-A., Steer, C. D., Newman, T. K., Gibson, N., & Goldman, D. (2010). Early life stress, *MAOA,* and gene-environment interactions predict behavioral disinhibition in children. *Genes, Brain and Behavior, 9,* 65–74. (13)

Eppig, C., Fincher, C. L., & Thornhill, R. (2010). Parasite prevalence and the worldwide distribution of cognitive ability. *Proceedings of the Royal Society B, 277,* 3801–3808. (9)

Eppig, C., Fincher, C. L., & Thornhill, R. (2011). Parasite prevalence and the distribution of intelligence among the states of the USA. *Intelligence, 39,* 155–160. (9)

Erdelyi, M. H. (2006). The unified theory of repression. *Behavioral and Brain Sciences, 29,* 499–551. (14)

Erdelyi, M. H. (2010). The ups and downs of memory. *American Psychologist, 65,* 623–633. (7)

Erel, O., & Burman, B. (1995). Interrelatedness of marital relations and parent-child relations: A meta-analytic review. *Psychological Bulletin, 118,* 108–132. (5)

Erev, I., Wallsten, T. S., & Budescu, D. V. (1994). Simultaneous over- and underconfidence: The role of error in judgment processes. *Psychological Review, 101,* 519–527. (8)

Ericsson, K. A., & Charness, N. (1994). Expert performance: Its structure and acquisition. *American Psychologist, 49,* 725–747. (8)

Ericsson, K. A., Chase, W. G., & Faloon, S. (1980). Acquisition of a memory skill. *Science, 208,* 1181–1182. (7)

Ericsson, K. A., Krampe, R. T., & Tesch-Römer, C. (1993). The role of deliberate practice in the acquisition of expert performance. *Psychological Review, 100,* 363–406. (8)

Erikson, E. H. (1963). *Childhood and society* (2nd ed.). New York: W. W. Norton. (5)

Ernhart, C. B., Sokol, R. J., Martier, S., Moron, P., Nadler, D., Ager, J. W., . . . Wolf, A. (1987). Alcohol teratogenicity in the human: A detailed assessment of specificity, critical period, and threshold. *American Journal of Obstetrics and Gynecology, 156,* 33–39. (5)

Ernst, C., & Angst, J. (1983). *Birth order: Its influence on personality.* New York: Springer-Verlag. (5)

Eschenko, O., Mölle, M., Born, J., & Sara, S. J. (2006). Elevated sleep spindle density after learning or after retrieval in rats. *Journal of Neurophysiology, 26,* 12914–12920. (10)

Esser, S. K., Hill, S., & Tononi, G. (2009). Breakdown of effective connectivity during slow wave sleep; Investigating the mechanism underlying a cortical gate using large-scale modeling. *Journal of Neurophysiology, 102,* 2096–2111. (10)

Esterson, A. (1993). *Seductive mirage.* Chicago: Open Court. (10, 14)

Esterson, A. (2001). The mythologizing of psychoanalytic history: Deception and self-deception in Freud's accounts of the seduction theory episode. *History of Psychology, 12,* 329–352. (14)

Euston, D. R., Tatsuno, M., & McNaughton, B. L. (2007). Fast-forward playback of recent memory sequences in prefrontal cortex during sleep. *Science, 318,* 1147–1150. (10)

Evans, G. W., Bullinger, M., & Hygge, S. (1998). Chronic noise exposure and physiological response: A prospective study of children living under environmental stress. *Psychological Science, 9,* 75–77. (12)

Evans, G. W., & Schamberg, M. A. (2009). Childhood poverty, chronic stress, and adult working memory. *Proceedings of the National Academy of Sciences, USA, 106,* 6545–6549. (9)

Exner, J. E., Jr. (1986). *The Rorschach: A comprehensive system* (2nd ed.). New York: Wiley. (14)

Eysenck, H. J. (1952). The effects of psychotherapy: An evaluation. *Journal of Consulting Psychology, 16,* 319–324. (15)

Fabiano, G. A., Pelham, W. E., Jr., Gnag, E. M., Burrows-MacLean, L., Coles, E. K., Chaco, A., . . . Robb, J. A. (2007). The single and combined effects of multiple intensities of behavior modification and methylphenidate for children with attention deficit hyperactivity disorder in a classroom setting. *School Psychology Review, 36,* 195–216. (6)

Faedda, G. L., Tondo, L., Teicher, M. H., Baldessarini, R. J., Gelbard, H. A., & Floris, G. F. (1993). Seasonal mood disorders: Patterns of seasonal recurrence in mania and depression. *Archives of General Psychiatry, 50,* 17–23. (15)

Faivre, R., Grégoire, A., Préault, M., Cézilly, F., & Sorci, G. (2003). Immune activation rapidly mirrored in a secondary sexual trait. *Science, 300,* 103. (13)

Falleti, M. G., Maruff, P., Collie, A., Darby, D. G., & McStephen, M. (2003). Qualitative similarities in cognitive impairment associated with 24 h of sustained wakefulness and a blood alcohol concentration of 0.05%. *Journal of Sleep Research, 12,* 265–274. (10)

Fallon, A. E., & Rozin, P. (1985). Sex differences in perceptions of desirable body shape. *Journal of Abnormal Psychology, 94,* 102–105. (11)

Fan, P. (1995). Cannabinoid agonists inhibit the activation of 5-HT3 receptors in rat nodose ganglion neurons. *Journal of Neurophysiology, 73,* 907–910. (3)

Fantz, R. L. (1963). Pattern vision in newborn infants. *Science, 140,* 296–297. (1)

Farber, S. L. (1981). *Identical twins reared apart: A reanalysis.* New York: Basic Books. (9)

Farmer-Dougan, V. (1998). A disequilibrium analysis of incidental teaching. *Behavior Modification, 22,* 78–95. (6)

Farnè, A., Buxbaum. L. J., Ferraro, M., Frassinetti, F., Whyte, J., Veramonti, T., . . . Ladavas, E. (2004). Patterns of spontaneous recovery of neglect and associated disorders in acute right brain-damaged patients. *Journal of*

Neurology, Neurosurgery, and Psychiatry, 75, 1401–1410. (10)

Farooqi, I. S., Keogh, J. M., Kamath, S., Jones, S., Gibson, W. T., Trussell, R., . . . O'Rahilly, S. (2001). Partial leptin deficiency and human adiposity. *Nature, 414,* 34–35. (11)

Farris, C., Treat, T. A., Viken, R. J., & McFall, R. M. (2008). Perceptual mechanisms that characterize gender differences in decoding women's sexual intent. *Psychological Science, 19,* 348–354. (5)

Fast, N. J., & Chen, S. (2009). When the boss feels inadequate. *Psychological Science, 20,* 1406–1413. (13)

Fauerbach, J. A., Lawrence, J. W., Haythornthwaite, J. A., & Richter, L. (2002). Coping with the stress of a painful medical procedure. *Behaviour Research and Therapy, 40,* 1003–1015. (12)

Faugeras, F., Rohaut, B., Weiss, N., Bekinschtein, T., Galanaud, D., Puybasset, L., . . . Naccache, L. (2011). Probing consciousness in clinically defined vegetative patients with event-related potentials. *Neurology, 77,* 264–268. (10)

Faust, M., Kravetz, S., & Babkoff, H. (1993). Hemispheric specialization or reading habits: Evidence from lexical decision research with Hebrew words and sentences. *Brain and Language, 44,* 254–263. (8)

Fay, R. E., Turner, C. F., Klassen, A. D., & Gagnon, J. H. (1989). Prevalence and patterns of same-gender sexual contact among men. *Science, 243,* 338–348. (11)

Fazel, S., & Grann, M. (2006). The population impact of severe mental illness on violent crime. *American Journal of Psychiatry, 163,* 1397–1403. (15)

Feeney, D. M. (1987). Human rights and animal welfare. *American Psychologist, 42,* 593–599. (2)

Feinberg, M., & Willer, R. (2011). Apocalypse soon? Dire messages reduce belief in global warming by contradicting just-world beliefs. *Psychological Science, 22,* 34–38. (13)

Feinstein, J. S., Adolphs, R., Damasio, A., & Tranel, D. (2011). The human amygdala and the induction and experience of fear. *Current Biology, 21,* 34–38. (12)

Felitti, V. J., Anda, R. F., Nordenberg, D., Williamson, D. F., Spitz, A. M., Edwards, V., . . . Marks, J. S. (1998). Relationship of childhood abuse and household dysfunction to many of the leading causes of death in adults. *American Journal of Preventive Medicine, 14,* 245–258. (12)

Fendrich, R., Wessinger, C. M., & Gazzaniga, M. S. (1992). Residual vision in a scotoma: Implications for blindsight. *Science, 258,* 1489–1491. (3)

Feng, J., Spence, I., & Pratt, J. (2007). Playing an action video game reduces gender differences in spatial cognition. *Psychological Science, 18,* 850–855. (5)

Fenton, W. S., Hoch, J. S., Herrell, J. M., Mosher, L., & Dixon, L. (2002). Cost and cost-effectiveness of hospital vs. residential crisis care for patients who have serious mental illness. *Archives of General Psychiatry, 59,* 357–364. (15)

Fenton, W. S., Mosher, L. R., Herrell, J. M., & Blyler, C. R. (1998). Randomized trial of general hospital and residential alternative care for patients with severe and persistent mental illness. *American Journal of Psychiatry, 155,* 516–522. (15)

Ferguson, C. P., & Pigott, T. A. (2000). Anorexia and bulimia nervosa: Neurobiology and pharmacotherapy. *Behavior Therapy, 31,* 237–263. (11)

Fernald, D. (1984). *The Hans legacy: A story of science.* Hillsdale, NJ: Erlbaum. (2)

Fernández-Dols, J. M., & Ruiz-Belda, M. A. (1997). Spontaneous facial behavior during intense emotional episodes: Artistic truth and optical truth. In J. A. Russell & J. M. Fernández-Dols (Eds.), *The psychology of facial expression* (pp. 255–274). Cambridge, England: Cambridge University Press. (12)

Fernandez, E., & Turk, D. C. (1992). Sensory and affective components of pain: Separation and synthesis. *Psychological Bulletin, 112,* 205–217. (4)

Ferreira, F., Bailey, K. G. D., & Ferraro, V. (2002). Good-enough representations in language comprehension. *Current Directions in Psychological Science, 11,* 11–15. (8)

Festinger, L. (1957). *A theory of cognitive dissonance.* Stanford, CA: Stanford University Press. (13)

Festinger, L., & Carlsmith, J. M. (1959). Cognitive consequences of forced compliance. *Journal of Abnormal and Social Psychology, 58,* 203–210. (13)

Fiedler, K., Schmid, J., & Stahl, T. (2002). What is the current truth about polygraph lie detection? *Basic and Applied Social Psychology, 24,* 313–324. (12)

Field, A. P. (2006). Is conditioning a useful framework for understanding the development and treatment of phobias? *Clinical Psychology Review, 26,* 857–875. (15)

Finch, J. F., & Cialdini, R. B. (1989). Another indirect tactic of (self-) image imagement: Boosting. *Personality and Social Psychology Bulletin, 15,* 222–232. (13)

Fincham, F. D. (2003). Marital conflict: Correlates, structure, and context. *Current Directions in Psychological Science, 12,* 23–27. (13)

Fine, I., Wade, A. R., Brewer, A. A., May, M. G., Goodman, D. F., . . . MacLeod, D. I. A. (2003). Long-term deprivation affects visual perception and cortex. *Nature Neuroscience, 6,* 915–916. (4)

Fink, B., & Penton-Voak, I. (2002). Evolutionary psychology of facial attractiveness. *Current Directions in Psychological Science, 11,* 154–158. (13)

Finkbeiner, M., & Palermo, R. (2009). The role of spatial attention in nonconscious processing. *Psychological Science, 20,* 42–51. (4)

Finkel, E. J., & Eastwick, P. W. (2008). Speed-dating. *Current Directions in Psychological Science, 17,* 193–197. (13)

Fisher, B. S., Daigle, L. E., Cullen, F. T., & Turner, M. G. (2003). Acknowledging sexual victimization as rape: Results from a national-level survey. *Justice Quarterly, 20,* 535–574. (13)

Fisher, R. P., Geiselman, R. E., & Amador, M. (1989). Field test of the cognitive interview: Enhancing the recollection of actual victims and witnesses of crime. *Journal of Applied Psychology, 74,* 722–727. (7)

Fisher, S. E., Vargha-Khadem, F., Watkins, K. E., Monaco, A. P., & Pembrey, M. E. (1998). Localisation of a gene implicated in a severe speech and language disorder. *Nature Genetics, 18,* 168–170. (8)

Fiske, A. P. (2002). Using individualism and collectivism to compare cultures—A critique of the validity and measurement of the constructs: Comment on Oyserman et al. (2002). *Psychological Bulletin, 128,* 78–88. (13)

Fiske, S. T., Harris, L. T., & Cuddy, A. J. C. (2004). Why ordinary people torture enemy prisoners. *Science, 306,* 1482–1483. (13)

Flack, W. F., Jr., Laird, J. D., & Cavallaro, L. A. (1999). Separate and combined effects of facial expressions and bodily postures on emotional feelings. *European Journal of Social Psychology, 29,* 203–217. (12)

Flatz, G. (1987). Genetics of lactose digestion in humans. *Advances in Human Genetics, 16,* 1–77. (5)

Flavell, J. (1986). The development of children's knowledge about the appearance–reality distinction. *American Psychologist, 41,* 418–425. (5)

Fleeson, W., & Gallagher, P. (2009). The implications of Big Five standing for the distribution of trait manifestation in behavior: Fifteen experience-sampling studies and meta-analysis. *Journal of Personality and Social Psychology, 97,* 1097–1114. (14)

Fleeson, W., Malanos, A. B., & Achille, N. M. (2002). An intraindividual process approach to the relationship between extraversion and positive affect: Is acting extraverted as "good" as being extraverted? *Journal of Personality and Social Psychology, 83,* 1409–1422. (14)

Fletcher, R., & Voke, J. (1985). *Defective colour vision.* Bristol, England: Hilger. (4)

Fliessbach, K., Weber, B., Trautner, P., Dohmen, T., Sunde, U., Elger, C. E., . . . Falk, A. (2007). Social comparison affects reward-related brain activity in the human ventral striatum. *Science, 318,* 1305–1308. (4)

Fligstein, D., Barabasz, A., Barabasz, M., Trevisan, M. S., & Warner, D. (1998). Hypnosis enhances recall memory: A test of forced and non-forced conditions. *American Journal of Clinical Hypnosis, 40,* 297–305. (10)

Flor, H., Elbert, T., Knecht, S., Wienbruch, C., Pantev, C., Birbaumer, N., . . . Taub, E. (1995). Phantom-limb pain as a perceptual correlate of cortical reorganization following arm amputation. *Nature, 375,* 482–484. (4)

Flynn, J. R. (1984). The mean IQ of Americans: Massive gains 1932 to 1978. *Psychological Bulletin, 95,* 29–51. (9)

Flynn, J. R. (1998). IQ gains over time: Toward finding the causes. In U. Neisser (Ed.), *The rising curve* (pp. 25–66). Washington, DC: American Psychological Association. (9)

Flynn, J. R. (1999). Searching for justice: The discovery of IQ gains over time. *American Psychologist, 54,* 5–20. (9)

Fodor, J. (1998). When is a dog a DOG? *Nature, 396,* 325–327. (8)

Fogel, S. M., Nader, R., Cote, K. A., & Smith, C. T. (2007). Sleep spindles and learning potential. *Behavioral Neuroscience, 121,* 1–10. (10)

Folkman, S., & Moskowitz, J. T. (2000). Positive affect and the other side of coping. *American Psychologist, 55,* 647–654. (12)

Føllesdal, H., & Hagtvet, K. A. (2009). Emotional intelligence: The MSCEIT from the perspective of generalizability theory. *Intelligence, 37,* 94–105. (12)

Forer, B. R. (1949). The fallacy of personal validation: A classroom demonstration of gullibility. *Journal of Abnormal and Social Psychology, 44,* 118–123. (14)

Foster, D. (2000). *Author unknown.* New York: Henry Holt. (14)

Foster, W. Z. (1968). *History of the Communist Party of the United States.* New York: Greenwood Press. (13)

Foulkes, D. (1999). *Children's dreaming and the development of consciousness.* Cambridge, MA: Harvard University Press. (10)

Fournier, J. C., DeRubeis, R. J., Hollon, S. D., Dimidjian, S., Amsterdam, J., . . . Fawcett, J. (2010). Antidepressant drug effects and depression severity. *Journal of the American Medical Association, 303,* 47–53. (15)

Fowler, J. H., Baker, L. A., & Dawes, C. T. (2008). Genetic variation in political participation. *American Political Science Review, 102,* 233–248. (5)

Fowler, J. H., & Christakis, N. A. (2008). Dynamic spread of happiness in a large social network: Longitudinal analysis over 20 years in the Framingham Heart Study. *British Medical Journal, 337,* a2338. (12)

Fox, R. E., DeLeon, P. H., Newman, R., Sammons, M. T., Dunivin, D. L., & Baker, D. C. (2009). Prescriptive authority and psychology. *American Psychologist, 64,* 257–268. (1)

Francis, L. J., Brown, L. B., Lester, D., & Philipchalk, R. (1998). Happiness as stable extraversion: A cross-cultural examination of the reliability and validity of the Oxford Happiness Inventory among students in the U.K., U.S.A., Australia, and Canada. *Personality and Individual Differences, 24,* 167–171. (14)

Franconeri, S. L., Alvarez, G. A., & Enns, J. T. (2007). How many locations can be selected at once? *Journal of Experimental Psychology: Human Perception and Performance, 33,* 1003–1012. (8)

Frank, M. J., & Claus, E. D. (2006). Anatomy of a decision: Striato-orbitofrontal interactions in reinforcement learning, decision making, and reversal. *Psychological Review, 113,* 300–326. (3)

Fredrickson, B. L. (2001). The role of positive emotion in psychology: The broaden-and-build theory of positive emotions. *American Psychologist, 56,* 218–226. (12)

Fredrickson, B. L., & Losada, M. F. (2005). Positive affect and the complex dynamics of human flourishing. *American Psychologist, 60,* 678–686. (12)

Freedman, J. L., & Fraser, S. C. (1966). Compliance without pressure: The foot in the door technique. *Journal of Personality and Social Psychology, 4,* 195–202. (13)

Freeman, M. P. (2009). Omega-3 fatty acids in major depressive disorder. *Journal of Clinical Psychiatry, 70,* 7–11. (15)

French, A. R. (1988). The patterns of mammalian hibernation. *American Scientist, 76,* 568–575. (10)

French, S. E., Seidman, E., Allen, L., & Aber, J. L. (2006). The development of ethnic identity during adolescence. *Developmental Psychology, 42,* 1–10. (5)

Frensch, P. A., & Rünger, D. (2003). Implicit learning. *Current Directions in Psychological Science, 12,* 13–18. (7)

Freud, S. (1925). An autobiographical study. In J. Strachey, A. Freud, A. Strachey, & A. Tyson (Eds.), *The standard edition of the complete psychological works of Sigmund Freud* (Vol. 20, pp. 7–70). London: Hogarth Press and the Institute of Psycho-Analysis. (14)

Freud, S. (1925). *Three contributions to the theory of sex* (A. A. Brill, Trans.). New York: Nervous and Mental Disease Publishing. (Original work published 1905) (14)

Freud, S. (1955). *The interpretation of dreams* (J. Strachey, Trans.). New York: Basic Books. (Original work published 1900) (10)

Freud, S. (1961). *The future of an illusion* (J. Strachey, Trans.). New York: W. W. Norton. (Original work published 1927) (14)

Frey, S. H., Bogdanov, S. Smith, J. C., Watrous, S., & Breidenbach, W. C. (2008). Chronically deafferented sensory cortex recovers a grossly typical organization after allogenic hand transplantation. *Current Biology, 18*, 1530–1534. (3)

Fridlund, A. J., Beck, H. P., Goldie, W. D., & Irons, G. (2012, January 23). Little Albert: A neurologically impaired child. *History of Psychology*, Advance online publication: doi:10.1037/a0026720. (15)

Fried, C. B. (2008). In-class laptop use and its effects on student learning. *Computers & Education, 50*, 906–914. (8)

Friedman, J. M. (2000). Obesity in the new millennium. *Nature, 404*, 632–634. (11)

Friedman, M., & Rosenman, R. H. (1974). *Type-A behavior and your heart.* New York: Knopf. (12)

Friedman, W. J., Reese, E., & Dai, X. (2011). Children's memory for the times of events from the past years. *Applied Cognitive Psychology, 25*, 156–165. (7)

Frijda, N. H. (1988). The laws of emotion. *American Psychologist, 45*, 349–358. (12)

Fritz, C. O., Morris, P. E., Bjork, R. A., Gelman, R., & Wickens, T. D. (2000). When further learning fails: Stability and change following repeated presentation of text. *British Journal of Psychology, 91*, 493–511. (7)

Fritzsche, B. A., Young, B. R., & Hickson, K. C. (2003). Individual differences in academic procrastination tendency and writing success. *Personality and Individual Differences, 35*, 1549–1557. (11)

Fu, Q., Heath, A. C., Bucholz, K. K., Nelson, E., Goldberg, J., Lyons, M. J., . . . Eisen, S. A. (2002). Shared genetic risk of major depression, alcohol dependence, and marijuana dependence. *Archives of General Psychiatry, 59*, 1125–1132. (15)

Fukuda, K., & Vogel, E. K. (2011). Individual differences in recovery time from attentional capture. *Psychological Science, 22*, 361–368. (7)

Fuligni, A. J. (1998). The adjustment of children from immigrant families. *Current Directions in Psychological Science, 7*, 99–103. (5)

Fuller, R. A., Warren, P. H., & Gaston, K. J. (2007). Daytime noise predicts nocturnal singing in urban robins. *Biology Letters, 3*, 368–370. (6)

Fuller, R. K., & Roth, H. P. (1979). Disulfiram for the treatment of alcoholism: An evaluation in 128 men. *Annals of Internal Medicine, 90*, 901–904. (15)

Furman, L. M. (2008). Attention-deficit hyperactivity disorder (ADHD): Does new research support old concepts? *Journal of Child Neurology, 23*, 775–784. (8)

Furnham, A. (2003). Belief in a just world: Research progress over the last decade. *Personality and Individual Differences, 34*, 795–817. (14)

Furnham, A., Hosoe, T., & Tang, T. L.-P. (2002). Male hubris and female humility? A crosscultural study of ratings of self, parental, and sibling multiple intelligence in America, Britain, and Japan. *Intelligence, 30*, 101–115. (14)

Furukawa, T. (1997). Cultural distance and its relationship to psychological adjustment of international exchange students. *Psychiatry and Clinical Neurosciences, 51*, 87–91. (1)

Gable, P., & Harmon-Jones, E. (2010). The blues broaden, but the nasty narrows: Attentional consequences of negative affects low and high in motivational intensity. *Psychological Science, 21*, 211–215. (12)

Gabrieli, J. D. E., Cohen, N. J., & Corkin, S. (1988). The impaired learning of semantic knowledge following bilateral medial temporal-lobe resection. *Brain and Cognition, 7*, 157–177. (7)

Gächter, S., Renner, E., & Sefton, M. (2008). The long-run benefits of punishment. *Science, 322*, 1510. (13)

Gage, F. H. (2000). Mammalian neural stem cells. *Science, 287*, 1433–1438. (3)

Gaillard, R., Dehaene, S., Adam, C., Clémenceau, S., Hasboun, D., Baulac, M., . . . Naccache, L. (2009). Converging intracranial markers of conscious access. *PLoS Biology, 7*, e1000061. (10)

Gailliot, M. T., Stillman, T. F., Schmeichel, B. J., Maner, J. K., & Plant, E. A. (2008). Mortality salience increases adherence to salient norms and values. *Personality and Social Psychology Bulletin, 34*, 993–1003. (5)

Galef, B. G., Jr. (1998). Edward Thorndike: Revolutionary psychologist, ambiguous biologist. *American Psychologist, 53*, 1128–1134. (6)

Gallavotti, A., Zhao, Q., Kyozuka, J., Meeley, R. B., Ritter, M. K., Doebley, J. F., . . . Schmidt, R. J. (2004). The role of *barren stalk1* in the architecture of maize. *Nature, 432*, 630–635. (3)

Gallistel, C. R., & Gibbon, J. (2000). Time, rate, and conditioning. *Psychological Review, 107*, 289–344. (6)

Galton, F. (1978). *Hereditary genius.* New York: St. Martin's Press. (Original work published 1869) (1, 9)

Gangestad, S. W. (2000). Human sexual selection, good genes, and special design. *Annals of the New York Academy of Sciences, 907*, 50–61. (13)

Gangestad, S. W., & Simpson, J. A. (2000). The evolution of human mating: Trade-offs and strategic pluralism. *Behavioral and Brain Sciences, 23*, 573–644. (3)

Gannon, N., & Ranzijn, R. (2005). Does emotional intelligence predict unique variance in life satisfaction beyond IQ and personality? *Personality and Individual Differences, 38*, 1353–1364. (12)

Gapin, J. I., Labban, J. D., & Etnier, J. L. (2011). The effects of physical activity on attention deficit disorder symptoms: The evidence. *Preventive Medicine, 52*, S70–S74. (8)

Garb, H. N., Wood, J. N., Lilienfeld, S. O., & Nezworski, M. T. (2005). Roots of the Rorschach controversy. *Clinical Psychology Review, 25*, 97–118. (14)

Garcia, J., Ervin, F. R., & Koelling, R. A. (1966). Learning with prolonged delay of reinforcement. *Psychonomic Science, 5*, 121–122. (6)

Garcia, J., & Koelling, R. A. (1966). Relation of cue to consequence in avoidance learning. *Psychonomic Science, 4*, 123–124. (6)

Gardner, H. (1985). *Frames of mind.* New York: Basic Books. (9)

Gardner, H. (1999). *Intelligence reframed.* New York: Basic Books. (9)

Gardner, M. (1978). Mathematical games. *Scientific American, 239*(5), 22–32. (8)

Gardner, M. (1994). Notes of a fringe watcher: The tragedies of false memories. *Skeptical Inquirer, 18*, 464–470. (7)

Gardner, M., & Steinberg, L. (2005). Peer influence on risk taking, risk preference, and risky decision making in adolescence and adulthood: An experimental study. *Developmental Psychology, 41*, 625–635. (5)

Gardner, R. A., & Gardner, B. T. (1969). Teaching sign language to a chimpanzee. *Science, 165*, 664–672. (8)

Gazzaniga, M. S. (2000). Cerebral specialization and interhemispheric communication: Does the corpus callosum enable the human condition? *Brain, 123*, 1293–1326. (3)

Geary, D. C. (2000). Evolution and proximate expression of human paternal investment. *Psychological Bulletin, 126*, 55–77. (13)

Gelman, R. (1982). Accessing one-to-one correspondence: Still another paper about conservation. *British Journal of Psychology, 73*, 209–220. (5)

Genberg, B. L., Gange, S. J., Go, V. F., Celentano, D. D., Kirk, G. D., & Mehta, S. H. (2011). Trajectories of injection drug use over 20 years (1988-2008) in Baltimore, Maryland. *American Journal of Epidemiology, 173*, 829–836. (15)

Genoux, D., Haditsch, U., Knobloch, M., Michalon, A., Storm, D., & Mansuy, I. M. (2002). Protein phosphatase 1 is a molecular constraint on learning and memory. *Nature, 418*, 970–975. (7)

Gentile, B., Grabe, S., Dolan-Pascoe, B., Twenge, J. M., & Wells, B. E. (2009). Gender differences in domain-specific self-esteem: A meta-analysis. *Review of General Psychology, 13*, 34–45. (14)

Gentile, D. (2009). Pathological video-game use among youth ages 8 to 18: A national study. *Psychological Science, 20*, 594–602. (15)

Geraerts, E., Schooler, J. W., Merckelbach, H., Jelicic, M., Hauer, B. J. A., & Ambadar, Z. (2007). The reality of recovered memories. *Psychological Science, 18*, 564–568. (7)

German, T. P., & Barrett, H. C. (2005). Functional fixedness in a technologically sparse culture. *Psychological Science, 16*, 1–5. (8)

Gershoff, E. T. (2002). Corporal punishment by parents and associated child behaviors and experiences: A meta-analytic and theoretical review. *Psychological Bulletin, 128*, 539–579. (6)

Geschwind, N. (1979). Specializations of the human brain. In *Scientific American* (Ed.), *The brain: A Scientific American book.* San Francisco: W. H. Freeman. (8)

Gibbs, J., Young, R. C., & Smith, G. P. (1973). Cholecystokinin decreases food intake in rats. *Journal of Comparative and Physiological Psychology, 84*, 488–495. (11)

Gibson, J. J. (1968). What gives rise to the perception of movement? *Psychological Review, 75*, 335–346. (4)

Giebel, H. D. (1958). Visuelles Lernvermögen bei Einhufern [Visual learning capacity in hoofed animals]. *Zoologische Jahrbücher Abteilung für Allgemeine Zoologie, 67*, 487–520. (1)

Gigerenzer, G. (2004). Dread risk, September 11, and fatal traffic accidents. *Psychological Science, 15*, 286–287. (8)

Gigerenzer, G. (2008). Why heuristics work. *Perspectives on Psychological Science, 3*, 20–29. (8)

Gil-da-Costa, R., Martin, A., Lopes, M. A., Muñoz, M., Fritz, J. B., & Braun, A. R. (2006). Species-specific calls activate homologs of Broca's and Wernicke's areas in the macaque. *Nature Neuroscience, 9*, 1064–1070. (8)

Gilbert, D. T., & Wilson, T. D. (2009). Why the brain talks to itself: Sources of error in emotional prediction. *Philosophical Transactions of the Royal Society, B, 364*, 1335–1341. (8)

Gilbertson, M. W., Shenton, M. E., Ciszewski, A., Kasai, K., Lasko, N. B., Orr, S. P., . . . Pitman, R. K. (2002). Smaller hippocampal volume predicts pathological vulnerability to psychological trauma. *Nature Neuroscience, 5*, 1242–1247. (12)

Gilbreth, F. B. (1911). *Motion study.* London: Constable. (11)

Gino, F., Ayal, S., & Ariely, D. (2009). Contagion and differentiation in unethical behavior. *Psychological Science, 20,* 393–398. (11)

Glantz, L. A., & Lewis, D. A. (1997). Reduction of synaptophysin immunoreactivity in the prefrontal cortex of subjects with schizophrenia. *Archives of General Psychiatry, 54,* 660–669. (15)

Glantz, L. A., & Lewis, D. A. (2000). Decreased dendritic spine density on prefrontal cortical pyramidal neurons in schizophrenia. *Archives of General Psychiatry, 57,* 65–73. (15)

Glasman, L. R., & Albarracín, D. (2006). Forming attitudes that predict future behavior: A meta-analysis of the attitude–behavior relation. *Psychological Bulletin, 132,* 778–822. (13)

Glass, M. (2001). The role of cannabinoids in neurodegenerative diseases. *Progress in Neuro-Psychopharmacology and Biological Psychiatry, 25,* 743–765. (3)

Godfrey, K. M., Lillycrop, K. A., Burdge, G. C., Gluckman, P. D., & Hanson, M. A. (2007). Epigenetic mechanisms and the mismatch concept of the developmental origins of health and disease. *Pediatric Research, 61*(5), Part 2, 5R–10R. (3)

Goldberg, W. A., Prause, J., Lucas-Thompson, R., & Himsel, A. (2008). Maternal employment and children's achievement in context: A meta-analysis of four decades of research. *Psychological Bulletin, 134,* 77–108. (5)

Golden, S. M. (2009). Does childhood use of stimulant medication as a treatment for ADHD affect the likelihood of future drug abuse and dependence? A literature reviw. *Journal of Child & Adolescent Substance Abuse, 18,* 343–358. (3)

Goldin-Meadow, S., McNeill, D., & Singleton, J. (1996). Silence is liberating: Removing the handcuffs on grammatical expression in the manual modality. *Psychological Review, 103,* 34–55. (8)

Goldin-Meadow, S., & Mylander, C. (1998). Spontaneous sign systems created by deaf children in two cultures. *Nature, 391,* 279–281. (8)

Goldstein, A. (1980). Thrills in response to music and other stimuli. *Physiological Psychology, 8,* 126–129. (3, 4)

Goldstein, D. G., & Gigerenzer, G. (2002). Models of ecological rationality: The recognition heuristic. *Psychological Review, 109,* 75–90. (8)

Goldstein, E. B. (1989). *Sensation and perception* (3rd ed.). Belmont, CA: Wadsworth. (4)

Goldstein, E. B. (2007). *Sensation and perception* (7th ed.). Belmont, CA: Wadsworth. (4)

Goldstein, M. H., & Schwade, J. A. (2008). Social feedback to infants' babbling facilitates rapid phonological learning. *Psychological Science, 19,* 515–523. (8)

Goldstein, N. J., Cialdini, R. B., & Griskevicius, V. (2008). A room with a viewpoint: Using social norms to motivate environmental conservation in hotels. *Journal of Consumer Research, 35,* 472–482. (13)

Golombok, S., Perry, B., Burston, A., Murray, C., Mooney-Somers, J., Stevens, M., . . . Golding, J. (2003). Children with lesbian parents: A community study. *Developmental Psychology, 39,* 20–33. (5)

Golombok, S., Rust, J., Zervoulis, K., Croudace, T., Golding, J., & Hines, M. (2008). Developmental trajectories of sex-typed behavior in boys and girls: A longitudinal general population study of children aged 2.5–8 years. *Child Development, 79,* 1583–1593. (14)

Gómez-Pinilla, F. (2008). Brain foods: The effects of nutrients on brain function. *Nature Reviews Neuroscience, 9,* 568–578. (2)

Gomez, P., Zimmermann, P., Guttormsen-Schär, S., & Danuser, B. (2005). Respiratory responses associated with affective processing of film stimuli. *Biological Psychology, 68,* 223–235. (12)

Gong, L. (2007). Ethnic identity and identification with the majority group; Relations with national identity and self-esteem. *International Journal of Intercultural Relations, 31,* 503–523. (5)

Gonsalves, B. D., & Cohen, N. J. (2010). Brain imaging, cognitive processes, and brain networks. *Perspectives on Psychological Science, 5,* 744–752. (3)

Gonzaga, G. C., Turner, R. A., Keltner, D., Campos, B., & Altemus, M. (2006). Romantic love and sexual desire in close relationships. *Emotion, 6,* 163–179. (13)

Gonzalez Andino, S. L., de Peralta Menendez, R. G., Khateb, A., Landis, T., & Pegna, A. J. (2009). Electrophysiological correlates of affective blindsight. *NeuroImage, 44,* 581–589. (3)

Goodall, J. (1971). *In the shadow of man.* Boston: Houghton Mifflin. (2)

Goodman, G. S., Ghetti, S., Quas, J. A., Edelstein, R. S., Alexander, K. W., Redlich, A. D., . . . Jones, D. P. H. (2003). A prospective study of memory for child sexual abuse: New findings relevant to the repressed-memory controversy. *Psychological Science, 14,* 113–118. (7)

Gopie, N., & MacLeod, C. M. (2009). Destination memory. *Psychological Science, 20,* 1492–1499. (7)

Gordon, P. C., Hendrick, R., & Levine, W. H. (2002). Memory-load interference in syntactic processing. *Psychological Science, 13,* 425–430. (8)

Gossop, M., Stewart, D., & Marsden, J. (2008). Attendance at Narcotics Anonymous and Alcoholics Anonymous meetings, frequency of attendance and substance use outcomes after residential treatment for drug dependence: A 5-year follow-up study. *Addiction, 103,* 119–125. (15)

Gottesman, I. I. (1991). *Schizophrenia genesis.* New York: W. H. Freeman. (15)

Gottfredson, L. S. (2002a). *g:* Highly general and highly practical. In R. J. Sternberg & E. L. Grigorenko (Eds.), *The general intelligence factor: How general is it?* (pp. 331–380). Mahwah, NJ: Erlbaum. (9)

Gottfredson, L. S. (2002b). Where and why *g* matters: Not a mystery. *Human Performance, 15,* 25–46. (9)

Gottfredson, L. S. (2003). Dissecting practical intelligence theory: Its claims and evidence. *Intelligence, 31,* 343–397. (9)

Gottfredson, L. S. (2004). Intelligence: Is it the epidemiologists' elusive "fundamental cause" of social class inequalities in health? *Journal of Personality and Social Psychology, 86,* 174–199. (9)

Gottman, J. M., Coan, J., Carrere, S., & Swanson, C. (1998). Predicting marital happiness and stability from newlywed interactions. *Journal of Marriage and the Family, 60,* 5–22. (13)

Gottman, J. M., & Levenson, R. W. (2000). The timing of divorce: Predicting when a couple will divorce over a 14-year period. *Journal of Marriage and the Family, 62,* 737–745. (13)

Grabe, S., & Hyde, J. S. (2006). Ethnicity and body dissatisfaction among women in the United States: A meta-analysis. *Psychological Bulletin, 132,* 622–640. (11)

Graber, E. C., Laurenceau, J.-P., Miga, E., Chango, J., & Coan, J. (2011). Conflict and love: Predicting newlywed marital outcomes from two interaction contexts. *Journal of Family Psychology, 25,* 541–550. (13)

Graf, P., & Mandler, G. (1984). Activation makes words more accessible, but not necessarily more retrievable. *Journal of Verbal Learning and Verbal Behavior, 23,* 553–568. (7)

Granier-Deferre, C., Bassereau, S., Ribeiro, A., Jacquet, A.-Y., & DeCasper, A. J. (2011). A melodic contour repeatedly experienced by human near-term fetuses elicits a profound cardiac reaction one month after birth. *PLoS One, 6,* e17304. (5)

Gratacòs, M., Nadalm, M., Martín-Santos, R., Pujana, M. A., Gago, J., Peral, B., . . . Estivill, X. (2001). A polymorphic genomic duplication on human chromosome 15 is a susceptibility factor for panic and phobic disorders. *Cell, 106,* 367–379. (15)

Graziadei, P. P. C., & deHan, R. S. (1973). Neuronal regeneration in the frog olfactory system. *Journal of Cell Biology, 59,* 525–530. (3)

Green, D. M., & Swets, J. A. (1966). *Signal detection theory and psychophysics.* New York: Wiley. (4)

Green, J. P., & Lynn, S. J. (2005). Hypnosis versus relaxation: Accuracy and confidence in dating international news events. *Applied Cognitive Psychology, 19,* 679–691. (10)

Green, J. P., Lynn, S. J., & Montgomery, G. H. (2008). Gender-related differences in hypnosis-based treatments for smoking: A follow-up meta-analysis. *American Journal of Clinical Hypnosis, 50,* 259–271. (10)

Greenberg, J., Martens, A., Jonas, E., Eisenstadt, D., Pyszczynski, T., & Solomon, S. (2003). Psychological defense in anticipation of anxiety. *Psychological Science, 14,* 516–519. (5)

Greene, J. D., Sommerville, R. B., Nystrom, L. E., Darley, J. M., & Cohen, J. D. (2001). An fMRI investigation of emotional engagement in moral judgment. *Science, 293,* 2105–2108. (12)

Greenfield, T. K., Stoneking, B. C., Humphreys, K., Sundby, E., & Bond, J. (2008). A randomized trial of a mental health consumer-managed alternative to civil commitment for acute psychiatric crisis. *American Journal of Community Psychology, 42,* 135–144. (15)

Greenhoot, A. F., Ornstein, P. A., Gordon, B. N., & Baker-Ward, L. (1999). Acting out the details of a pediatric check-up: The impact of interview condition and behavioral style on children's memory reports. *Child Development, 70,* 363–380. (7)

Greeno, C. G., & Wing, R. R. (1994). Stress-induced eating. *Psychological Bulletin, 115,* 444–464. (11)

Greenwald, A. G., & Draine, S. C. (1997). Do subliminal stimuli enter the brain unnoticed? Tests with a new method. In J. D. Cohen & J. W. Schooler (Eds.), *Scientific approaches to consciousness* (pp. 83–108). Mahwah, NJ: Erlbaum. (4)

Greenwald, A. G., Nosek, B. A., & Banaji, M. R. (2003). Understanding and using the Implicit Association Test: I. An improved scoring algorithm. *Journal of Personality and Social Psychology, 85,* 197–216. (13)

Greenwald, A. G., Poehlman, A. T., Uhlmann, E. L., & Banaji, M. R. (2009). Understanding and using the Implicit Association Test: III. Meta-analysis of predictive validity. *Journal of Personality and Social Psychology, 97,* 17–41. (13)

Greenwald, A. G., Spangenberg, E. R., Pratkanis, A. R., & Eskanazi, J. (1991). Double-blind tests of subliminal self-help audiotapes. *Psychological Science, 2,* 119–122. (4)

Griffith, R. M., Miyagi, O., & Tago, A. (1958). The universality of typical dreams: Japanese vs. Americans. *American Anthropologist, 60,* 1173–1179. (10)

Grissmer, D. W., Williamson, S., Kirby, S. N., & Berends, M. (1998). Exploring the rapid rise in the Black achievement scores in the United States (1970–1990). In U. Neisser (Ed.), *The rising curve* (pp. 251–285). Washington, DC: American Psychological Association. (9)

Gross, J. J. (2001). Emotion regulation in adulthood: Timing is everything. *Current Directions in Psychological Science, 10,* 214–219. (12)

Gross, J. J., Fredrickson, B. L., & Levenson, R. W. (1994). The psychophysiology of crying. *Psychophysiology, 31,* 460–468. (12)

Grossman, E. D., & Blake, R. (2001). Brain activity evoked by inverted and imagined biological motion. *Vision Research, 41,* 1475–1482. (4)

Gruber, R., Wiebe, S., Montecalvo, L., Brunetti, B., Amsel, R., & Carrier, J. (2011). Impact of sleep restriction on neurobehavioral functioning of children with attention deficit hyperactivity disorder. *Sleep, 34,* 315–323. (8)

Grueter, M., Grueter, T., Bell, V., Horst, J., Laskowski, W., Sperling, K., . . . Kennerknecht, I. (2007). Hereditary prosopagnosia: The first case series. *Cortex, 43,* 734–749. (3)

Grünbaum, A. (1986). Précis of *The foundations of psychoanalysis:* A philosophical critique. *Behavioral and Brain Sciences, 9,* 217–284. (14)

Guendelman, M. D., Cheryan, S., & Monin, B. (2011). Fitting in but getting fat: Identity threat and dietary choices among U.S. immigrant groups. *Psychological Science, 22,* 959–967. (5)

Guilleminault, C., Heinzer, R., Mignot, E., & Black, J. (1998). Investigations into the neurologic basis of narcolepsy. *Neurology, 50*(Suppl. 1), S8–S15. (10)

Guiso, L., Monte, F., Sapienza, P., & Zingales, L. (2008). Culture, gender, and math. *Science, 320,* 1164–1165. (5)

Gur, R. E., Cowell, P. E., Latshaw, A., Turetsky, B. I., Grossman, R. I., Arnold, S. E., . . . Gur, R. C. (2000). Reduced dorsal and orbital prefrontal gray matter volumes in schizophrenia. *Archives of General Psychiatry, 57,* 761–768. (15)

Gustavson, C. R., Kelly, D. J., Sweeney, M., & Garcia, J. (1976). Prey-lithium aversions: I. Coyotes and wolves. *Behavioral Biology, 17,* 61–72. (6)

Gvilia, I., Xu, F., McGinty, D., & Szymusiak, R. (2006). Homeostatic regulation of sleep: A role for preoptic area neurons. *Journal of Neuroscience, 26,* 9426–9433. (10)

Haarmeier, T., Thier, P., Repnow, M., & Petersen, D. (1997). False perception of motion in a patient who cannot compensate for eye movements. *Nature, 389,* 849–852. (4)

Haas, B. W., Omura, K., Constable, R. T., & Canli, T. (2007). Is automatic emotion regulation associated with agreeableness? *Psychological Science, 18,* 130–132. (12)

Habermas, T., & Bluck, S. (2000). Getting a life: The emergence of the life story in adolescence. *Psychological Bulletin, 126,* 748–769. (5)

Hackman, J. R., & Lawler, E. E., III (1971). Employee reactions to job characteristics. *Journal of Applied Psychology, 55,* 259–286. (11)

Haeffel, G. J., Abramson, L. Y., Metalsky, G. I., Dykman, B. M., Donovan, P., . . . Halberstadt, L. (2005). Negative cognitive styles, dysfunctional attitudes, and the remitted depression paradigm: A search for the elusive cognitive vulnerability to depression factor among remitted depressives. *Emotion, 5,* 343–348. (15)

Haggard, P., & Eimer, M. (1999). On the relation between brain potentials and the awareness of voluntary movements. *Experimental Brain Research, 126,* 128–133. (10)

Haggarty, J. M., Cernovsky, Z., Husni, M., Minor, K., Kermean, P., & Merskey, H. (2002). Seasonal affective disorder in an arctic community. *Acta Psychiatrica Scandinavica, 105,* 378–384. (15)

Haidt, J. (2001). The emotional dog and its rational tail: A social intuitionist approach to moral judgment. *Psychological Review, 108,* 814–834. (13)

Haidt, J. (2007). The new synthesis in moral psychology. *Science, 316,* 998–1002. (13)

Haidt, J. (2012). *The righteous mind.* New York: Pantheon. (13)

Haist, F., Gore, J. B., & Mao, H. (2001). Consolidation of human memory over decades revealed by functional magnetic resonance imaging. *Nature Neuroscience, 4,* 1139–1145. (7)

Hakuta, K., Bialystok, E., & Wiley, E. (2003). Critical evidence: A test of the critical-period hypothesis for second-language acquisition. *Psychological Science, 14,* 31–38. (8)

Halamish, V., & Bjork, R. A. (2011). When does testing enhance retention? A distribution-based interpretation of retrieval as a memory modifier. *Journal of Experimental Psychology: Learning, Memory, and Cognition, 37,* 801–812. (7)

Hall, C. S., & Van de Castle, R. L. (1966). *The content analysis of dreams.* New York: Appleton-Century-Crofts. (10)

Hall, J. A., & Matsumoto, D. (2004). Gender differences in judgments of multiple emotions from facial expressions. *Emotion, 4,* 201–206. (12)

Hall, L. J., & McGregor, J. A. (2000). A follow-up study of the peer relationships of children with disabilities in an inclusive school. *Journal of Special Education, 34,* 114–126. (9)

Halmi, K. A., Sunday, S. R., Strober, M., Kaplan, A., Woodside, D. B., Fichter, M., . . . Kaye, W. H. (2000). Perfectionism in anorexia nervosa: Variation by clinical subtype, obsessionality, and pathological eating behavior. *American Journal of Psychiatry, 157,* 1799–1805. (11)

Halpern, D. F., Benbow, C. P., Geary, D. C., Gur, R. C., Hyde, J. S., & Gernsbacher, M. A. (2007). The science of sex differences in science and mathematics. *Psychological Science in the Public Interest, 8,* 1–51. (5)

Halpern, S. D., Andrews, T. J., & Purves, D. (1999). Interindividual variation in human visual performance. *Journal of Cognitive Neuroscience, 11,* 521–534. (4)

Hama, Y. (2001). Shopping as a coping behavior for stress. *Japanese Psychological Research, 43,* 218–224. (12)

Hamamura, T. (2012). Are cultures becoming individualistic? A cross-temporal comparison of individualism-collectivism in the United States and Japan. *Personality and Social Psychology, 16,* 3–24. (13)

Hamann, S. B., & Squire, L. R. (1997). Intact perceptual memory in the absence of conscious memory. *Behavioral Neuroscience, 111,* 850–854. (7)

Hamby, S. L., & Koss, M. P., (2003). Shades of gray: A qualitative study of terms used in the measurement of sexual victimization. *Psychology of Women Quarterly, 27,* 243–255. (13)

Hamm, J. V. (2000). Do birds of a feather flock together? The variable bases for African American, Asian American, and European American adolescents' selection of similar friends. *Developmental Psychology, 36,* 209–219. (13)

Hamm, R. M., Reiss, D. M., Paul, R. K., & Bursztajn, H. J. (2007). Knocking at the wrong door: Insured workers' inadequate psychiatric care and workers' compensation claims. *Journal of Law and Psychiatry, 30,* 416–426. (15)

Hammock, E. A. D., & Young, L. J. (2005). Microsatellite instability generates diversity in brain and sociobehavioral traits. *Science, 308,* 1630–1634. (5)

Han, C. J., & Robinson, J. K. (2001). Cannabinoid modulation of time estimation in the rat. *Behavioral Neuroscience, 115,* 243–246. (3)

Haney, C., Banks, C., & Zimbardo, P. (1973). Interpersonal dynamics in a simulated prison. *International Journal of Criminology and Penology, 1,* 69–97. (14)

Hanoch, Y., Johnson, J. G., & Wilke, A. (2006). Domain specificity in experimental measures and participant recruitment. *Psychological Science, 17,* 300–304. (14)

Hanson, K. L., & Luciana, M. (2010). Neurocognitive impairments in MDMA and other drug users: MDMA alone may not be a cognitive risk factor. *Journal of Clinical and Experimental Neuropsychology, 32,* 337–349. (3)

Hanson, R. K. (2000). Will they do it again? Predicting sex-offense recidivism. *Current Directions in Psychological Science, 9,* 106–109. (13)

Happé, F., Ronald, A., & Plomin, R. (2006). Time to give up on a single explanation for autism. *Nature Neuroscience, 9,* 1218–1220. (15)

Harada, S., Agarwal, D. P. Goedde, H. W., Tagaki, S., & Ishikawa, B. (1982). Possible protective role against alcoholism for aldehyde dehydrogenase isozyme deficiency in Japan. *Lancet, ii,* 827. (3)

Hariri, A. R., Mattay, V. S., Tessitore, A., Kolachana, B., Fera, F., Goldman, D., . . . Weinberger, D. R. (2002). Serotonin transporter genetic variation and the response of the human amygdala. *Science, 297,* 400–403. (3)

Harker, L. A., & Keltner, D. (2001). Expressions of positive emotion in women's college yearbook pictures and their relationship to personality and life outcomes across adulthood. *Journal of Personality and Social Psychology, 80,* 112–124. (12)

Harkins, S. G., & Jackson, J. M. (1985). The role of evaluation in eliminating social loafing. *Journal of Personality and Social Psychology, 11,* 457–465. (13)

Harley, B., & Wang, W. (1997). The critical period hypothesis: Where are we now? In A. M. B. deGroot & J. F. Knoll (Eds.), *Tutorials in bilingualism* (pp. 19–51). Mahwah, NJ: Erlbaum. (8)

Harris, J. R. (1995). Where is the child's environment? A group socialization theory of development. *Psychological Review, 102,* 458–489. (5)

Harris, J. R. (1998). *The nurture assumption.* New York: Free Press. (5)

Harris, J. R. (2000). Context-specific learning, personality, and birth order. *Current Directions in Psychological Science, 9,* 174–177. (5)

Harris, L. T., & Fiske, S. T. (2006). Dehumanizing the lowest of the low: Neuroimaging responses to extreme out-groups. *Psychological Science, 17,* 847–853. (13)

Harris, R. J., Schoen, L. M., & Hensley, D. L. (1992). A cross-cultural study of story memory. *Journal of Cross-Cultural Psychology, 23,* 133–147. (7)

Harris, T. (1967). *I'm OK—You're OK.* New York: Avon. (14)

Harrow, M., & Jobe, T. H. (2007). Factors involved in outcome and recovery in schizophrenia patients not on antipsychotic medications: A 15-year multifollow-up study. *Journal of Nervous and Mental Disease, 195,* 406–414. (15)

Hartwell, K. J., Back, S. E., McRae-Clark, A. L., Shaftman, S. R., & Brady, K. T. (2012). Motives for using: A comparison of prescription opioid, marijuana and cocaine dependent individuals. *Addictive Behaviors, 37,* 373–378. (15)

Harvey, A. G., & Bryant, R. A. (2002). Acute stress disorder: A synthesis and critique. *Psychological Bulletin, 128,* 886–902. (12)

Hasel, L. E., & Kassin, S. M. (2009). On the presumption of evidentiary independence. *Psychological Science, 20,* 122–126. (7)

Hassabis, D., Kumaran, D., Vann, S. D., & Maguire, E. A. (2007). Patients with hippocampal amnesia cannot imagine new experiences. *Proceedings of the National Academy of Sciences, 104,* 1726–1731. (7)

Hassett, J. M., Siebert, E. R., & Wallen, K. (2008). Sex differences in rhesus monkey toy preferences parallel those of children. *Hormones and Behavior, 54,* 359–364. (5)

Hastie, R., Schkade, D. A., & Payne, J. W. (1999). Juror judgments in civil cases: Hindsight effects on judgments of liability for punitive damages. *Law and Human Behavior, 23,* 597–614. (7)

Hatfield, E., & Rapson, R. L. (1993). *Love, sex, and intimacy.* New York: HarperCollins. (13)

Hathaway, S. R., & McKinley, J. C. (1940). A multiphasic personality schedule (Minnesota): I. Construction of the schedule. *Journal of Psychology, 10,* 249–254. (14)

Haueisen, J., & Knösche, T. R. (2001). Involuntary motor activity in pianists evoked by music perception. *Journal of Cognitive Neuroscience, 13,* 786–792. (6)

Haukka, J., Suvisaari, J., & Lönnqvist, J. (2003). Fertility of patients with schizophrenia, their siblings, and the general population: A cohort study from 1950 to 1959 in Finland. *American Journal of Psychiatry, 160,* 460–463. (15)

Hauri, P. (1982). *The sleep disorders.* Kalamazoo, MI: Upjohn. (10)

Havlicek, J., & Roberts, S. C. (2009). MHC-correlated mate choice in humans: A review. *Psychoneuroendocrinology, 34,* 497–512. (4)

Hay, D. F., Mundy, L., Roberts, S., Carta, R., Waters, C. S., . . . van Goozen, S. (2011). Known risk factors for violence predict 12-month-old infants' aggressiveness with peers. *Psychological Science, 22,* 1205–1211. (13)

Haynes, J.-D., Katsuyuki, S., Rees, G., Gilbert, S., Frith, C., & Passingham, R. E. (2007). Reading hidden intentions in the human brain. *Current Biology, 17,* 323–328. (3)

Healy, D., & Williams, J. M. G. (1988). Dysrhythmia, dysphoria, and depression: The interaction of learned helplessness and circadian dysrhythmia in the pathogenesis of depression. *Psychological Bulletin, 103,* 163–178. (15)

Heath, A. C., Neale, M. C., Kessler, R. C., Eaves, L. J., & Kendler, K. S. (1992). Evidence for genetic influences on personality from self-reports and informant ratings. *Journal of Personality and Social Psychology, 63,* 85–96. (5, 14)

Heatherton, T. G., & Baumeister, R. F. (1991). Binge eating as escape from self-awareness. *Psychological Bulletin, 110,* 86–108. (11)

Heck, A., Collins, J., & Peterson, L. (2001). Decreasing children's risk taking on the playground. *Journal of Applied Behavior Analysis, 34,* 349–352. (6)

Hedges, L. V., & Nowell, A. (1995). Sex differences in mental test scores, variability, and numbers of high-scoring individuals. *Science, 269,* 41–45. (9)

Heider, F. (1958). *The psychology of interpersonal relations.* New York: Wiley. (13)

Heine, S. J., Buchtel, E. E., & Norenzayan, A. (2008). What do cross-national comparisons of personality traits tell us? *Psychological Science, 19,* 309–313. (14)

Heine, S. J., & Hamamura, T. (2007). In search of East Asian self-enhancement. *Personality and Social Psychology Review, 11,* 4–27. (13)

Heit, E. (1993). Modeling the effects of expectations on recognition memory. *Psychological Science, 4,* 244–251. (7)

Hejmadi, A., Davidson, R. J., & Rozin, P. (2000). Exploring Hindu Indian emotion expressions. *Psychological Science, 11,* 183–187. (12)

Hemond, C., Brown, R. M., & Robertson, E. M. (2010). A distraction can impair or enhance motor performance. *Journal of Neuroscience, 30,* 650–654. (8)

Henderson, J. J. A., & Anglin, J. M. (2003). Facial attractiveness predicts longevity. *Evolution and Human Behavior, 24,* 351–356. (13)

Henderson, J. M. (2007). Regarding scenes. *Current Directions in Psychological Science, 16,* 219–222. (8)

Henderson, J. M., & Hollingworth, A. (2003). Global transsaccadic change blindness during scene perception. *Psychological Science, 14,* 493–497. (8)

Hendrie, H. C. (2001). Exploration of environmental and genetic risk factors for Alzheimer's disease: The value of cross-cultural studies. *Current Directions in Psychological Science, 10,* 98–101. (7)

Henkel, L. A. (2011). Photograph-induced memory errors: When photographs make people claim they have done things they have not. *Applied Cognitive Psychology, 25,* 78–86. (7)

Henning, E. R., Turk, C. L., Mennin, D. S., Fresco, D. M., & Heimberg, R. G. (2007). Impairment and quality of life in individuals with generalized anxiety disorder. *Depression and Anxiety, 24,* 342–349. (15)

Henrich, J., Ensminger, J., McElreath, R., Barr, A., Barrett, C., . . . Ziker, J. (2010). Markets, religion, community size, and the evolution of fairness and punishment. *Science, 327,* 1480–1484. (13)

Henrich, J., Heine, S. J., & Norenzayan, A. (2010). Most people are not WEIRD. *Nature, 466,* 29. (2)

Herbenick, D., Reece, M., Schick, V., Sanders, S. A., Dodge, B., & Fortenberry, J. D. (2010). Sexual behavior in the United States: Results from a national probability sample of men and women ages 14–94. *Journal of Sexual Medicine, 7* (suppl 5), 255–265. (11)

Hergenhahn, B. R. (1992). *An introduction to the history of psychology* (2nd ed.). Belmont, CA: Wadsworth. (1)

Herkenham, M., Lynn, A. B., de Costa, B. R., & Richfield, E. K. (1991). Neuronal localization of cannabinoid receptors in the basal ganglia of the rat. *Brain Research, 547,* 267–274. (3)

Herkenham, M., Lynn, A. B., Little, M. D., Johnson, M. R., Melvin, L. S., deCosta, B. R., . . . Rice, K. C. (1990). Cannabinoid receptor localization in brain. *Proceedings of the National Academy of Sciences, USA, 87,* 1932–1936. (3)

Herman, C. P., Roth, D. A., & Polivy, J. (2003). Effects of the presence of others on food intake: A normative interpretation. *Psychological Bulletin, 129,* 873–886. (11)

Herman, J., Roffwarg, H., & Tauber, E. S. (1968). Color and other perceptual qualities of REM and NREM sleep. *Psychophysiology, 5,* 223. (10)

Herrmann, B., Thöni, C., & Gächter, S. (2008). Antisocial punishment across societies. *Science, 319,* 1362–1367. (13)

Hershkowitz, I., & Terner, A. (2007). The effects of repeated interviewing on children's forensic statements of sexual abuse. *Applied Cognitive Psychology, 21,* 1131–1143. (7)

Hertenstein, M. J. (2002). Touch: Its communicative functions in infancy. *Human Development, 45,* 70–94. (5)

Hertzog, C., Kramer, A. F., Wilson, R. S., & Lindenberger, U. (2009). Enrichment effects on adult cognitive development. *Psychological Science in the Public Interest, 9,* 1–65. (8)

Herz, R. (2007). *The scent of desire.* New York: HarperCollins. (4)

Herz, R. S., & von Clef, J. (2001). The influence of verbal labeling on the perception of odors: Evidence for olfactory illusions? *Perception, 30,* 381–391. (4)

Hespos, S. J., Ferry, A. L., & Rips, L. J. (2009). Five-month-old infants have different expectations for solids and liquids. *Psychological Science, 20,* 603–611. (5)

Hess, T. M. (2005). Memory and aging in context. *Psychological Bulletin, 131,* 383–406. (5)

Hetherington, E. M. (1989). Coping with family transitions. Winners, losers, and survivors. *Child Development, 60,* 1–14. (5)

Hetherington, E. M., Stanley-Hagan, M., & Anderson, E. R. (1989). Marital transitions: A child's perspective. *American Psychologist, 44,* 303–312. (5)

Hettema, J. M., Neale, M. C., & Kendler, K. S. (2001). A review and meta-analysis of the genetic epidemiology of anxiety disorders. *American Journal of Psychiatry, 158,* 1568–1578. (15)

Heyman, G. M. (2011). Received wisdom regarding the roles of craving and dopamine in addiction: A response to Lewis's critique of *Addiction: A disorder of choice. Perspectives on Psychological Science, 6,* 156–160. (15)

Hildreth, K., Sweeney, B., & Rovee-Collier, C. (2003). Differential memory-preserving effects of reminders at 6 months. *Journal of Experimental Child Psychology, 84,* 41–62. (5)

Hilgard, E. R. (1973). A neodissociation interpretation of pain reduction in hypnosis. *Psychological Review, 80,* 396–411. (10)

Hill, C. E., & Nakayama, E. Y. (2000). Client-centered therapy: Where has it been and where is it going? A comment on Hathaway (1948). *Journal of Clinical Psychology, 56,* 861–875. (15)

Hill, J. L., Waldfogel, J., Brooks-Gunn, J., & Han, W.-J. (2005). Maternal employment and child development: A fresh look using newer methods. *Developmental Psychology, 41,* 833–850. (5)

Hilty, D. M., Brady, K. T., & Hales, R. E. (1999). A review of bipolar disorder among adults. *Psychiatric Services, 50,* 201–213. (15)

Himle, J. A., Baser, R. E., Taylor, R. J., Campbell, R. D., & Jackson, J. S. (2009). Anxiety disorders among Africans, Blacks of Caribbean descent, and non-Hispanic Whites in the United States. *Journal of Anxiety Disorders, 23,* 578–590. (15)

Hirvonen, J., van Erp, T. G. M., Huttunen, J., Aalto, S., Någren, K., Huttunen, M., . . . Hietala, J. (2006). Brain dopamine D₁ receptors in twins discordant for schizophrenia. *American Journal of Psychiatry, 163,* 1747–1753. (15)

Hobson, J. A. (2005). Sleep is of the brain, by the brain and for the brain. *Nature, 437,* 1254–1256. (10)

Hobson, J. A., & McCarley, R. W. (1977). The brain as a dream state generator: An activation-synthesis hypothesis of the dream process. *American Journal of Psychiatry, 134,* 1335–1348. (10)

Hodgins, S., Mednick, S. A., Brennan, P. A., Schulsinger, F., & Engberg, M. (1996). Mental disorder and crime. *Archives of General Psychiatry, 53,* 489–496. (13)

Hoebel, B. G., Rada, P. V., Mark, G. P., & Pothos, E. (1999). Neural systems for reinforcement and inhibition of behavior: Relevance to eating, addiction, and depression. In D. Kahneman, E. Diener, & N. Schwartz (Eds.), *Well-being: Foundations of hedonic psychology* (pp. 560–574). New York: Russell Sage Foundation. (11, 15)

Hoehl, S., & Striano, T. (2008). Neural processing of eye gaze and threat-related emotional facial expressions in infancy. *Child Development, 79,* 1752–1760. (12)

Hoek, H. W., & van Hoeken, D. (2003). Review of the prevalence and incidence of eating disorders. *International Journal of Eating Disorders, 34,* 383–396. (11)

Holcombe, A. O., & Cavanagh, P. (2001). Early binding of feature pairs for visual perception. *Nature Neuroscience, 4,* 127–128. (3)

Holden, G. W., & Miller, P. C. (1999). Enduring and different: A meta-analysis of the similarity in parents' child rearing. *Psychological Bulletin, 125,* 223–254. (5)

Holland, R. W., Hendriks, M., & Aarts, H. (2005). Smells like clean spirit. *Psychological Science, 16,* 689–693. (8)

Hollon, S. D., & Beck, A. T. (1979). Cognitive therapy of depression. In P. C. Kendall & S. D. Hollon (Eds.), *Cognitive-behavioral interventions* (pp. 153–203). New York: Academic Press. (15)

Holmberg, D., & Blair, K. L. (2009). Sexual desire, communication, satisfaction, and preferences of men and women in same-sex versus mixed-sex relationships. *Journal of Sex Research, 46,* 57–66. (13)

Holmes, D. S. (1978). Projection as a defense mechanism. *Psychological Bulletin, 85,* 677–688. (14)

Holmes, D. S. (1990). The evidence for repression: An examination of sixty years of research. In J. L. Singer (Ed.), *Repression and dissociation* (pp. 85–102). New York: Wiley. (7, 14)

Holmes, T., & Rahe, R. (1967). The social readjustment rating scale. *Journal of Psychosomatic Research, 11,* 213–218. (12)

Hölzel, B. K., Lazar, S. W., Gard, T., Shuman-Olivier, Z., Vago, D. R., & Ott, U. (2011). How does mindfulness meditation work? Proposing mechanisms of action from a conceptual and neural perspective. *Perspectives in Psychological Science, 6,* 537–559. (10)

Homa, D. (1983). An assessment of two extraordinary speed-readers. *Bulletin of the Psychonomic Society, 21,* 123–126. (8)

Honea, R., Crow, T. J., Passingham, D., & Mackay, C. E. (2005). Regional deficits in brain volume in schizophrenia: A meta-analysis of voxel-based morphometry studies. *American Journal of Psychiatry, 162,* 2233–2245. (15)

Hong, Y., Morris, M. W., Chiu, C., & Benet-Martinez, V. (2000). Multicultural minds: A dynamic constructivist approach to culture and cognition. *American Psychologist, 55,* 709–720. (13)

Hoover, D. W., & Milich, R. (1994). Effects of sugar ingestion expectancies on mother-child interactions. *Journal of Abnormal Child Psychology, 22,* 501–515. (2)

Hopf, F. W., Bowers, M. S., Chang, S.-J, Chen, B. T., Martin, M., . . . Bonci, A. (2010). Reduced nucleus accumbens SK channel activity enhances alcohol seeking during abstinence. *Neuron, 65,* 682–694. (15)

Horn, J. L. (1968). Organization of abilities and the development of intelligence. *Psychological Review, 75,* 242–259. (9)

Horn, J. L., & Donaldson, G. (1976). On the myth of intellectual decline in adulthood. *American Psychologist, 31,* 701–719. (9)

Horne, J. A., Brass, C. G., & Pettitt, A. N. (1980). Circadian performance differences between morning and evening "types." *Ergonomics, 23,* 29–36. (10)

Houben, K., Wiers, R. W., & Jansen, A. (2011). Getting a grip on drinking behavior: Training working memory to reduce alcohol abuse. *Psychological Science, 22,* 968–975. (7)

Hough, L. M., & Oswald, F. L. (2008). Personality testing and industrial-organizational psychology: Reflections, progress, and prospects. *Industrial and Organizational Psychology, 1,* 272–290. (14)

Howard, K. I., Kopta, S. M., Krause, M. S., & Orlinsky, D. E. (1986). The dose-effect relationship in psychotherapy. *American Psychologist, 41,* 159–164. (15)

Howard, R. W. (1999). Preliminary real-world evidence that average human intelligence really is rising. *Intelligence, 27,* 235–250. (9)

Howe, M. L., & Courage, M. L. (1993). On resolving the enigma of infantile amnesia. *Psychological Bulletin, 113,* 305–326. (7)

Howes, O. D., Montgomery, A. J., Asselin, M.-C., Murray, R. M., Valli, I., Tabraham, P., . . . Grasby, P. M. (2009). Elevated striatal dopamine function linked to prodromal signs of schizophrenia. *Archives of General Psychiatry, 66,* 13–20. (15)

Hrdy, S. B. (2000). The optimal number of fathers. *Annals of the New York Academy of Sciences, 907,* 75–96. (13)

Hróbjartsson, A., & Gøtzsche, P. C. (2001). Is the placebo powerless? *New England Journal of Medicine, 344,* 1594–1602. (4)

Hu, P., Stylos-Allan, M., & Walker, M. P. (2006). Sleep facilitates consolidation of emotional declarative memory. *Psychological Science, 17,* 891–898. (10)

Hubbs-Tait, L., Nation, J. R., Krebs, N. F., & Bellinger, D. C. (2005). Neurotoxicants, micronutrients, and social environments: Individual and combined effects on children's development. *Psychological Science in the Public Interest, 6,* 57–121. (5)

Hubel, D. H., & Wiesel, T. N. (1968). Receptive fields and functional architecture of monkey striate cortex. *Journal of Physiology* (London), *195,* 215–243. (4)

Huber, R., Ghilardi, M. F., Massimini, M., & Tononi, G. (2004). Local sleep and learning. *Nature, 430,* 78–81. (10)

Hudson, J. I., Hiripi, E., Pope, H. G., Jr., & Kessler, R. C. (2007). The prevalence and correlates of eating disorders in the National Comorbidity Survey Replication. *Biological Psychiatry, 61,* 348–358. (11)

Hudson, J. I., Mangweth, B., Pope, H. G., Jr., De Col, C., Hausmann, A., Gutweniger, S., . . . Tsuang, M. T. (2003). Family study of affective spectrum disorder. *Archives of General Psychiatry, 60,* 170–177. (15)

Hudson, W. (1960). Pictorial depth perception in sub-cultural groups in Africa. *Journal of Social Psychology, 52,* 183–208. (4)

Huff, D. (1954). *How to lie with statistics.* New York: W. W. Norton. (2)

Hughes, J., Smith, T. W., Kosterlitz, H. W., Fothergill, L. A., Morgan, B. A., & Morris, H. R. (1975). Identification of two related pentapeptides from the brain with potent opiate antagonist activity. *Nature, 258,* 577–579. (3)

Hugoson, A., Ljungquist, B., & Breivik, T. (2002). The relationship of some negative events and psychological factors to periodontal disease in an adult Swedish population 50 to 80 years of age. *Journal of Clinical Periodontology, 29,* 247–253. (12)

Hull, C. L. (1932). The goal gradient hypothesis and maze learning. *Psychological Review, 39,* 25–43. (1)

Hull, C. L. (1943). *Principles of behavior: An introduction to behavior theory.* New York: D. Appleton. (11)

Hull, R., & Vaid, J. (2007). Bilingual language lateralization: A meta-analytic tale of two hemispheres. *Neuropsychologia, 45,* 1987–2008. (8)

Hulleman, C. S., & Harackiewicz, J. M. (2009). Promoting interest and performance in high school science classes. *Science, 326,* 1410–1412. (7)

Hunter, J. E. (1997). Needed: A ban on the significance test. *Psychological Science, 8,* 3–7. (2)

Hur, Y.-M., Bouchard, T. J., Jr., & Eckert, E. (1998). Genetic and environmental influences on self-reported diet: A reared-apart twin study. *Physiology and Behavior, 64,* 629–636. (5)

Hur, Y.-M., Bouchard, T. J., Jr., & Lykken, D. T. (1998). Genetic and environmental influence on morningness–eveningness. *Personality and Individual Differences, 25,* 917–925. (5)

Hurovitz, C. S., Dunn, S., Domhoff, G. W., & Fiss, H. (1999). The dreams of blind men and women: A replication and extension of previous findings. *Dreaming, 9,* 183–193. (10)

Huston, T. L., Niehuis, S., & Smith, S. E. (2001). The early marital roots of conjugal distress and divorce. *Current Directions in Psychological Science, 10,* 116–119. (13)

Hutcheson, D. M., Everitt, B. J., Robbins, T. W., & Dickinson, A. (2001). The role of withdrawal in heroin addiction: Enhances reward or promotes avoidance? *Nature Neuroscience, 4,* 943–947. (15)

Hyde, J. (2005). The gender similarities hypothesis. *American Psychologist, 60,* 581–592. (5)

Hyde, J. S., Lindberg, S. M., Linn, M. C., Ellis, A. B., & Williams, C. C. (2008). Gender similarities characterize math performance. *Science, 321,* 494–495. (5)

Hyde, K. L., Lerch, J., Norton, A., Forgeard, M., Winner, E., Evans, A. C., . . . Schlaug, G. (2009). Musical training shapes structural brain development. *Journal of Neuroscience, 29,* 3019–3025. (3)

Hyde, K. L., & Peretz, I. (2004). Brains that are out of tune but in time. *Psychological Science, 15,* 356–360. (4)

Iacono, W. G., & Patrick, C. J. (1999). Polygraph ("lie detector") testing: The state of the art. In A. K. Hess & I. B. Weiner (Eds.), *The handbook of forensic psychology* (pp. 440–473). New York: Wiley. (12)

Iggo, A., & Andres, K. H. (1982). Morphology of cutaneous receptors. *Annual Review of Neuroscience, 5,* 1–31. (4)

Ikeda, K., Koga, A., & Minami, S. (2006). Evaluation of a cure process during alarm treatment for nocturnal enuresis. *Journal of Clinical Psychology, 62,* 1245–1257. (15)

Ikonomidou, C., Bittigau, P., Ishimaru, M. J., Wozniak, D. F., Koch, C., Genz, K., . . . Olney, J. W. (2000). Ethanol-induced apoptotic neurodegeneration and fetal alcohol syndrome. *Science, 287,* 1056–1060. (5)

Ilies, R., & Judge, T. A. (2003). On the heritability of job satisfaction: The mediating role of personality. *Journal of Applied Psychology, 88,* 750–759. (11)

Imahori, T. T., & Cupach, W. R. (1994). A cross-cultural comparison of the interpretation and management of face: U.S. American and Japanese responses to embarrassing predicaments. *International Journal of Intercultural Relations, 18,* 193–219. (12)

Imel, Z. E., Malterer, M. B., McKay, K. M., & Wampold, B. E. (2008). A meta-analysis of psychotherapy and medication in unipolar depression and dysthymia. *Journal of Affective Disorders, 110,* 197–206. (15)

Imhoff, M. C., & Baker-Ward, L. (1999). Preschoolers' suggestibility: Effects of developmentally appropriate language and interviewer supportiveness. *Journal of Applied Developmental Psychology, 20,* 407–429. (7)

Inglehart, R., Foa, R., Peterson, C., & Welzel, C. (2008). Development, freedom, and rising happiness. *Perspectives on Psychological Science, 3,* 264–285. (12)

Inouye, S. T., & Kawamura, H. (1979). Persistence of circadian rhythmicity in a mammalian hypothalamic "island" containing the suprachiasmatic nucleus. *Proceedings of the National Academy of Sciences, USA, 76,* 5962–5966. (10)

International Schizophrenia Consortium. (2008). Rare chromosomal deletions and duplications increase risk of schizophrenia. *Nature, 455,* 237–241. (15)

Ireland, M. E., & Pennebaker, J. W. (2010). Language style matching in writing: Synchrony in essays, correspondence, and poetry. *Journal of Personality and Social Psychology, 99,* 549–571. (13)

Isaacowitz, D. M., Toner, K., Goren, D., & Wilson, H. R. (2008). Looking while unhappy. *Psychological Science, 19,* 848–853. (12)

Iverson, J. M., & Goldin-Meadow, S. (2005). Gesture paves the way for language development. *Psychological Science, 16,* 367–371. (8)

Ivry, R. B., & Diener, H. C. (1991). Impaired velocity perception in patients with lesions of the cerebellum. *Journal of Cognitive Neuroscience, 3,* 355–366. (3)

Iyengar, S. S., & Lepper, M. R. (2000). When choice is demotivating. *Journal of Personality and Social Psychology, 79,* 995–1006. (8)

Iyengar, S. S., Wells, R. E., & Schwartz, B. (2006). Doing better but feeling worse. *Psychological Science, 17,* 143–150. (8)

Izazola-Licea, J. A., Gortmaker, S. L., Tolbert, K., De Gruttola, V., & Mann, J. (2000). Prevalence of same-gender sexual behavior and HIV in a probability household survey of Mexican men. *Journal of Sex Research, 37,* 37–43. (11)

Jackson, D. C., Malmstadt, J. R., Larson, C. L., & Davidson, R. J. (2000). Suppression and enhancement of emotional responses to unpleasant pictures. *Psychophysiology, 37,* 515–522. (12)

Jacobs, B. L. (1987). How hallucinogenic drugs work. *American Scientist, 75,* 386–392. (3)

Jacobs, J. R., & Bovasso, G. B. (2009). Re-examining the long-term effects of experiencing parental death in childhood on adult psychopathology. *Journal of Nervous and Mental Disease, 197,* 24–27. (5)

Jacobs, K. M., Mark, G. P., & Scott, T. R. (1988). Taste responses in the nucleus tractus solitarius of sodium-deprived rats. *Journal of Physiology, 406,* 393–410. (1)

Jacobson, N. S., Dobson, K. S., Truax, P. A., Addis, M. E., Koerner, K., Gollan, J. K., . . . Prince, S. E. (1996). A component analysis of cognitive-behavior therapy for depression. *Journal of Consulting and Clinical Psychology, 64,* 295–304. (15)

James, W. (1890). *The principles of psychology.* New York: Henry Holt. (1)

James, W. (1894). The physical basis of emotion. *Psychological Review, 1,* 516–529. (12)

James, W. (1961). *Psychology: The briefer course.* New York: Harper. (Original work published 1892) (10)

Janis, I. L. (1972). *Victims of groupthink.* Boston: Houghton Mifflin. (13)

Janis, I. L. (1983). Stress inoculation in health care. In D. Meichenbaum & M. E. Jaremko (Eds.), *Stress reduction and prevention* (pp. 67–99). New York: Plenum Press. (12)

Janis, I. L. (1985). Sources of error in strategic decision making. In J. M. Pennings & associates (Eds.), *Organizational strategy and change* (pp. 157–197). San Francisco: Jossey-Bass. (13)

Jaremko, M. E. (1983). Stress inoculation training for social anxiety, with emphasis on dating anxiety. In D. Meichenbaum & M. E. Jaremko (Eds.), *Stress reduction and prevention* (pp. 419–450). New York: Plenum Press. (12)

Jawahar, I. M., Stone, T. H., & Kisamore, J. L. (2007). Role conflict and burnout: The direct and moderating effects of political skill and perceived organizational support on burnout dimensions. *International Journal of Stress Management, 14,* 142–159. (11)

Jerome, L., & Segal, A. (2001). Benefit of long-term stimulants on driving in adults with ADHD. *Journal of Nervous and Mental Disease, 189,* 63–64. (8)

Ji, L-J, Nisbett, R. E., & Su, Y. (2001). Culture, change, and prediction. *Psychological Science, 12,* 450–456. (13)

Jiang, Y., Costello, P., & He, S. (2007). Processing of invisible stimuli. *Psychological Science, 18,* 349–355. (10)

Johansson, C., Willeit, M., Smedh, C., Ekholm, J., Paunio, T., Kieseppä, T., . . . Partonen, T. (2003). Circadian clock-related polymorphisms in seasonal affective disorder and their relevance to diurnal preference. *Neuropsychopharmacology, 28,* 734–739. (15)

Johansson, P., Hall, L., Sikström, S., & Olsson, A. (2005). Failure to detect mismatches between intention and outcome in a simple decision task. *Science, 310,* 116–119. (8)

Johns, M., Schmader, T., & Martens, A. (2005). Knowing is half the battle. *Psychological Science, 16,* 175–179. (9)

Johnson-Laird, P. N., Mancini, F., & Gangemi, A. (2006). A hyper-emotion theory of psychological illnesses. *Psychological Review, 113,* 822–841. (15)

Johnson, D. D. P., & Fowler, J. H. (2011). The evolution of overconfidence. *Nature, 477,* 317–320. (8)

Johnson, J. G., Cohen, P., Brown, J., Smailes, E. M., & Bernstein, D. P. (1999). Childhood maltreatment increases risk for personality disorders during early adulthood. *Archives of General Psychiatry, 56,* 600–606. (15)

Johnson, M. K., Hashtroudi, S., & Lindsay, D. S. (1993). Source monitoring. *Psychological Bulletin, 114,* 3–28. (7)

Johnson, W., & Bouchard, T. J., Jr. (2005). The structure of human intelligence: It is verbal, perceptual, and image rotation (VPR), not fluid and crystallized. *Intelligence, 33,* 393–416. (9)

Johnson, W., & Bouchard, T. J., Jr. (2007). Sex differences in mental abilities: g masks the dimensions on which they lie. *Intelligence, 35,* 23–39. (9)

Johnson, W., Bouchard, T. J., Jr., Krueger, R. F., McGue, M., & Gottesman, I. I. (2004). Just one g: Consistent results from three test batteries. *Intelligence, 32,* 95–107. (9)

Johnson, W., Carothers, A., & Deary, I. J. (2008). Sex differences in variability in general intelligence. *Perspectives on Psychological Science, 3,* 518–531. (9)

Johnson, W., te Nijenhuis, J., & Bouchard, T. J., Jr. (2008). Still just 1 g: Consistent results from five test batteries. *Intelligence, 36,* 81–95. (9)

Johnston, J. C., & McClelland, J. L. (1974). Perception of letters in words: Seek not and ye shall find. *Science, 184,* 1192–1194. (8)

Johnston, J. J. (1975). Sticking with first responses on multiple-choice exams: For better or for worse? *Teaching of Psychology, 2,* 178–179. (8)

Johnstone, H. (1994, August 8). Prince of memory says victory was on the cards. *The Times* (London), p. 2. (7)

Joiner, T. E., Jr. (1999). The clustering and contagion of suicide. *Current Directions in Psychological Science, 8,* 89–92. (15)

Joint Committee on Standards for Educational and Psychological Testing of the American Educational Research Association, the American Psychological Association, and the National Council on Measurement in Education. (1999). *Standards for educational and psychological testing.* Washington, DC: American Educational Research Association. (9)

Jokela, M. (2009). Physical attractiveness and reproductive success: Evidence from the late 20th century United States. *Evolution and Human Behavior, 30,* 342–350. (13)

Jones, C. M., Braithwaite, V. A., & Healy, S. D. (2003). The evolution of sex differences in spatial ability. *Behavioral Neuroscience, 117,* 403–411. (5)

Jones, E. E., & Goethals, G. R. (1972). Order effects in impression formation: Attribution context and the nature of the entity. In E. Jones, D. Kanouse, H. Kelley, R. Nisbett, S. Valins, & B. Wiener (Eds.), *Attribution: Perceiving the causes of behavior* (pp. 27–46). Morristown, NJ: General Learning Press. (13)

Jones, E. E., & Harris, V. A. (1967). The attribution of attitudes. *Journal of Experimental Social Psychology, 13,* 1–24. (13)

Jones, E. E., & Nisbett, R. E. (1972). The actor and the observer: Divergent perception of the causes of behavior. In E. Jones, D. Kanouse, H. Kelley, R. Nisbett, S. Valins, & B. Wiener (Eds.), *Attribution: Perceiving the causes of behavior* (pp. 79–94). Morristown, NJ: General Learning Press. (13)

Jones, P. B., Barnes, T. R. E., Davies, L., Dunn, G., Lloyd, H., Hayhurst, K. P., . . . Lewis, S. W. (2006). Randomized controlled trial of the effect on quality of life of second- vs. first-generation antipsychotic drugs in schizophrenia. *Archives of General Psychiatry, 63,* 1079–1087. (15)

Jones, S. S., Collins, K., & Hong, H. W. (1991). An audience effect on smile production in 10-month-old infants. *Psychological Science, 2,* 45–49. (12)

Joseph, R. (2000). Fetal brain behavior and cognitive development. *Developmental Review, 20,* 81–98. (5)

Joslyn, G., Brush, G., Robertson, M., Smith, T. L., Kalmijn, J., . . . White, R. L. (2008). Chromosome 15q25.1 genetic markers associated with level of response to alcohol in humans. *Proceedings of the National Academy of Sciences (U.S.A.), 105,* 20368–20373. (15)

Jouvet, M., Michel, F., & Courjon, J. (1959). Sur un stade d'activité électrique cérébrale rapide au cours du sommeil physiologique [On a state of rapid electrical cerebral activity during physiological sleep]. *Comptes Rendus des Séances de la Société de Biologie, 153,* 1024–1028. (10)

Judge, T. A., & Ilies, R. (2002). Relationship of personality to performance motivation: A meta-analytic review. *Journal of Applied Psychology, 87,* 797–807. (14)

Judge, T. A., & Larsen, R. J. (2001). Dispositional affect and job satisfaction: A review and theoretical extension. *Organizational Behavior and Human Decision Processes, 86,* 67–98. (11)

Judge, T. A., Thoresen, C. J., Bono, J. E., & Patton, G. K. (2001). The job satisfaction–job performance relationship: A qualitative and quantitative review. *Psychological Bulletin, 127,* 376–407. (11)

Juhasz, B. J. (2005). Age-of-acquisition effects in word and picture identification. *Psychological Bulletin, 131,* 684–712. (7)

Jung, C. G. (1965). *Memories, dreams, reflections* (A. Jaffe, Ed.). New York: Random House. (14)

Junginger, J., & Frame, C. L. (1985). Self-report of the frequency and phenomenology of verbal hallucinations. *Journal of Nervous and Mental Disease, 173,* 149–155. (15)

Jusczyk, P. W. (2002). How infants adapt speech-processing capacities to native-language structure. *Current Directions in Psychological Science, 11,* 15–18. (5)

Juslin, P., Winman, A., & Olsson, H. (2000). Naive empiricism and dogmatism in confidence research: A critical examination of the hard–easy effect. *Psychological Review, 107,* 384–396. (8)

Just, M. A., & Carpenter, P. A. (1987). *The psychology of reading and language comprehension.* Boston: Allyn & Bacon. (8)

Kagan, J., & Snidman, N. (1991). Infant predictors of inhibited and uninhibited profiles. *Psychological Science, 2,* 40–44. (5)

Kagan, J., Reznick, J. S., & Snidman, N. (1988). Biological bases of childhood shyness. *Science, 240,* 167–171. (5)

Kagitcibasi, C., & Biricik, D. (2011). Generational gains on the Draw-a-Person IQ scores: A three-decade comparison from Turkey. *Intelligence, 39,* 351–356. (9)

Kahn, A. S., Jackson, J., Kully, C., Badger, K., & Halvorsen, J. (2003). Calling it rape: Differences in experiences of women who do or do not label their sexual assault as rape. *Psychology of Women Quarterly, 27,* 233–242. (13)

Kahneman, D. (2011). *Thinking, fast and slow.* New York: Farrar, Straus and Giraux. (8)

Kahneman, D., & Klein, G. (2009). Conditions for intuitive expertise: A failure to disagree. *American Psychologist, 64,* 515–526. (8)

Kahneman, D., & Tversky, A. (1973). On the psychology of prediction. *Psychological Review, 80,* 237–251. (8)

Kaiser, C. R., Vick, S. B., & Major, B. (2004). A prospective investigation of the relationship between just-world beliefs and the desire for revenge after September 11, 2001. *Psychological Science, 15,* 503–506. (14)

Kalick, S. M., Zebrowitz, L. A., Langlois, J. H., & Johnson, R. M. (1998). Does human facial attractiveness honestly advertise health? *Psychological Science, 9,* 8–13. (13)

Kalivas, P. W., Volkow, N., & Seamans, J. (2005). Unmanageable motivation in addiction: A pathology in prefrontal-accumbens glutamate transmission. *Neuron, 45,* 647–650. (15)

Kamin, L. J. (1969). Predictability, surprise, attention, and conditioning. In B. A. Campbell & R. M. Church (Eds.), *Punishment and aversive behavior* (pp. 279–296). New York: Appleton-Century-Crofts. (6)

Kaminer, Y. (2000). Contingency management reinforcement procedures for adolescent substance abuse. *Journal of the American Academy of Child and Adolescent Psychiatry, 39,* 1324–1326. (15)

Kanaya, T., Scullin, M. H., & Ceci, S. J. (2003). The Flynn effect and U.S. policies. *American Psychologist, 58,* 778–790. (9)

Kanazawa, S. (2004). General intelligence as a domain-specific adaptation. *Psychological Review, 111,* 512–523. (9)

Kane, M. J., Brown, L. H., McVay, J. C., Silvia, P. J., Myin-Germeys, I., & Kwapil, T. R. (2007). For whom the mind wanders, and when. *Psychological Science, 18,* 614–621. (7)

Kane, M. J., & Engle, R. W. (2000). Working-memory capacity, proactive interference, and divided attention: Limits on long-term memory retrieval. *Journal of Experimental Psychology: Learning, Memory, and Cognition, 26,* 336–358. (7)

Kanizsa, G. (1979). *Organization in vision.* New York: Praeger. (4)

Kanner, A. D., Coyne, J. C., Schaefer, C., & Lazarus, R. S. (1981). Comparison of two modes of stress measurement: Daily hassles and uplifts versus major life events. *Journal of Behavioral Medicine, 4,* 1–39. (12)

Kanwisher, N., & Yovel, G. (2006). The fusiform face area: A cortical region specialized for the perception of faces. *Philosophical Transactions of the Royal Society, B, 361,* 2109–2128. (3)

Karbach, J., & Kray, J. (2009). How useful is executive control training? Age differences in near and far transfer of task-switching training. *Developmental Science, 12,* 978–990. (8)

Karim, J., & Weisz, R. (2010). Cross-cultural research on the reliability and validity of the Mayer-Salovey-Caaruso Emotional Intelligence Test (MSCEIT). *Cross-Cultural Research, 44,* 374–404. (12)

Karno, M., Golding, J. M., Sorenson, S. B., & Burnam, A. (1988). The epidemiology of obsessive-compulsive disorder in five U.S. communities. *Archives of General Psychiatry, 45,* 1094–1099. (15)

Karpicke, J. D., & Blunt, J. R. (2011). Retrieval practice produces more learning than elaborative studying with concept mapping. *Science, 331,* 772–775. (7)

Karpicke, J. D., & Roediger, H. L. III (2008). The critical importance of retrieval for learning. *Science, 319,* 966–968. (7)

Kasser, T., & Sharma, Y. S. (1999). Reproductive freedom, educational equality, and females' preference for resource-acquisition characteristics in mates. *Psychological Science, 10,* 374–377. (3)

Kasser, T., & Sheldon, K. M. (2000). Of wealth and death. Materialism, mortality salience, and consumption behavior. *Psychological Science, 11,* 348–351. (5)

Kassin, S. M., & Gudjonsson, G. H. (2004). The psychology of confessions: A review of the literature and issues. *Psychological Science in the Public Interest, 5,* 33–67. (13)

Katz, S., Lautenschlager, G. J., Blackburn, A. B., & Harris, F. H. (1990). Answering reading comprehension items without passages on the SAT. *Psychological Science, 1,* 122–127. (9)

Kaufman, L., & Rock, I. (1989). The moon illusion thirty years later. In M. Hershenson (Ed.), *The moon illusion* (pp. 193–234). Hillsdale, NJ: Erlbaum. (4)

Kay, K. N., Naselaris, T., Prenger, R. J., & Gallant, J. L. (2008). Identifying natural images from human brain activity. *Nature, 452,* 352–355. (3)

Kazdin, A. E., & Blase, S. L. (2011). Rebooting psychotherapy research and practice to reduce the burden of mental illness. *Perspectives on Psychological Science, 6,* 21–37. (15)

Ke, X., Tang, T., Hong, S., Hang, Y., Zou, B., Zi, H., . . . Liu, Y. (2009). White matter impairments in autism: Evidence from voxel-based morphometry and diffusion tensor imaging. *Brain Research, 1265,* 171–177. (15)

Kee, N., Teixeira, C. M., Wang, A. H., & Frankland, P. W. (2007). Preferential incorporation of adult-generated granule cells into spatial memory networks in the dentate gyrus. *Nature Neuroscience, 10,* 355–362. (3, 7)

Keel, P. K., & Klump, K. L. (2003). Are eating disorders culture-bound syndromes? Implications for conceptualizing their etiology. *Psychological Bulletin, 129,* 747–769. (11)

Keele, S. W., & Ivry, R. B. (1990). Does the cerebellum provide a common computation for diverse tasks? *Annals of the New York Academy of Sciences, 608,* 179–207. (3)

Keizer, K., Lindenberg, S., & Steg, L. (2008). The spreading of disorder. *Science, 322,* 1681–1685. (13)

Keller, M. C. (2008). The evolutionary persistence of genes that increase mental disorders risk. *Current Directions in Psychological Science, 17,* 395–399. (15)

Keller, M. C., Fredrickson, B. L., Ybarra, O., Cote, S., Johnson, K., Mikels, J., . . . Wager, T. (2005). A warm heart and a clear head. *Psychological Science, 16,* 724–731. (2)

Keller, M. C., Thiessen, D., & Young, R. K. (1996). Mate assortment in dating and married couples. *Personality and Individual Differences, 21,* 217–221. (13)

Kelley, H. H. (1967). Attribution theory in social psychology. In D. Levine (Ed.), *Nebraska Symposium on Motivation* (Vol. 15, pp. 192-238). Lincoln: University of Nebraska Press. (13)

Keltner, D., & Buswell, B. N. (1997). Embarrassment: Its distinct form and appeasement functions. *Psychological Bulletin, 122,* 250-270. (12)

Keltner, D., & Shiota, M. N. (2003). New displays and new emotions: A commentary on Rozin and Cohen (2003). *Emotion, 3,* 86-91. (12)

Kendler, K. S., Bulik, C. M., Silberg, J., Hettema, J. M., Myers, J., & Prescott, C. A. (2000). Childhood sexual abuse and adult psychiatric and substance abuse disorders in women. *Archives of General Psychiatry, 57,* 953-959. (15)

Kendler, K. S., Eaves, L. J., Loken, E. K., Pedersen, N. L., Middeldorp, C. M., . . . Gardner, C. O. (2011). The impact of environmental experiences on symptoms of anxiety and depression across the lifespan. *Psychological Science, 22,* 1343-1352. (15)

Kendler, K. S., Fiske, A., Gardner, C. O., & Gatz, M. (2009). Delineation of two genetic pathways to major depression. *Biological Psychiatry, 65,* 808-811. (15)

Kendler, K. S., Gardner, C. O., & Prescott, C. A. (1999). Clinical characteristics of major depression that predict risk of depression in relatives. *Archives of General Psychiatry, 56,* 322-327. (15)

Kendler, K. S., Hettema, J. M., Butera, F., Gardner, C. O., & Prescott, C. A. (2003). Life event dimensions of loss, humiliation, entrapment, and danger in the prediction of onsets of major depression and generalized anxiety. *Archives of General Psychiatry, 60,* 789-796. (15)

Kendler, K. S., Karkowski, L. M., Neale, M. C., & Prescott, C. A. (2000). Illicit psychoactive substance use, heavy use, abuse, and dependence in a US population-based sample of male twins. *Archives of General Psychiatry, 57,* 261-269. (15)

Kendler, K. S., Thornton, L. M., Gilman, S. E., & Kessler, R. C. (2000). Sexual orientation in a U.S. sample of twin and nontwin sibling pairs. *American Journal of Psychiatry, 157,* 1843-1846. (11)

Kendler, K. S., Walters, E. E., Neale, M. C., Kessler, R. C., Heath, A. C., & Eaves, L. J. (1995). The structure of the genetic and environmental risk factors for six major psychiatric disorders in women. *Archives of General Psychiatry, 52,* 374-383. (15)

Kenrick, D. T., Griskevicius, V., Neuberg, S. L., & Schaller, M. (2010). Renovating the pyramid of needs: Contemporary extensions built upon ancient foundation. *Perspectives on Psychological Science, 5,* 292-314. (11)

Keppel, G., & Underwood, B. J. (1962). Proactive inhibition in short-term retention of single items. *Journal of Verbal Learning and Verbal Behavior, 1,* 153-161. (7)

Kern, M. C., & Chugh, D. (2009). Bounded ethicality. *Psychological Science, 20,* 378-384. (8)

Kerr, N. L., MacCoun, R. J., & Kramer, G. P. (1996). Bias in judgment: Comparing individuals and groups. *Psychological Review, 103,* 687-719. (13)

Kerr, R., & Booth, B. (1978). Specific and varied practice of motor skill. *Perceptual and Motor Skills, 46,* 395-401. (7)

Kessler, R. C., Berglund, P., Demler, O., Jin, R., & Walters, E. E. (2005). Lifetime prevalence and age-of-onset distributions of *DSM-IV* disorders in the National Comorbidity Survey Replication. *Archives of General Psychiatry, 62,* 593-602. (15, 16)

Kessler, R. C., Chiu, W. T., Demler, O., & Walters, E. E. (2005). Prevalence, severity, and comorbidity of 12-month *DSM-IV* disorders in the National Comorbidity Survey Replication. *Archives of General Psychiatry, 62,* 617-627. (15, 16)

Kety, S. S., Wendler, P. H., Jacobsen, B., Ingraham, L. J., Jansson, L., Faber, B., . . . Kinney, D. K. (1994). Mental illness in the biological and adoptive relatives of schizophrenic adoptees. *Archives of General Psychiatry, 51,* 442-455. (15)

Keyes, C. L. M. (2007). Promoting and protecting mental health as flourishing. *American Psychologist, 62,* 95-108. (14)

Keys, D. J., & Schwartz, B. (2007). "Leaky" rationality: How research on behavioral decision making challenges normative standards of rationality. *Perspectives on Psychological Science, 2,* 162-180. (8)

Keysar, B., & Henly, A. S. (2002). Speakers' overestimation of their effectiveness. *Psychological Science, 13,* 207-212. (5)

Keysar, B., Barr, D. J., & Horton, W. S. (1998). The egocentric basis of language use: Insights from a processing approach. *Current Directions in Psychological Science, 7,* 46-50. (5)

Kiefer, A. K., & Sekaquaptewa, D. (2007). Implicit stereotypes, gender identification, and math-related outcomes. *Psychological Science, 18,* 13-18. (9)

Kiff, C. J., Lengua, L. J., & Zalewski, M. (2011). Nature and nurturing: Parenting in the conext of child temperament. *Clinical Child and Family Psychology Review, 14,* 251-301. (5)

Kim, H. S., Sherman, D. K., & Taylor, S. E. (2008). Culture and social support. *American Psychologist, 63,* 518-526. (12)

Kim, J., & Hatfield, E. (2004). Love types and subjective well-being: A cross-cultural study. *Social Behavior and Personality, 32,* 173-182. (13)

Kim, J. E., & Moen, P. (2001). Is retirement good or bad for subjective well-being? *Current Directions in Psychological Science, 10,* 83-86. (5)

Kim, S. (1989). *Inversions.* San Francisco: W. H. Freeman. (4)

Kim, Y.-K., Lee, H.-J., Yang, J.-C., Hwang, J.-A., & Yoon, H.-K. (2009). A tryptophan hydroxylase 2 gene polymorphism is associated with panic disorder. *Behavior Genetics, 39,* 170-175. (15)

Kimble, G. A. (1961). *Hilgard and Marquis' conditioning and learning* (2nd ed.). New York: Appleton-Century-Crofts. (6)

Kimble, G. A. (1993). A modest proposal for a minor revolution in the language of psychology. *Psychological Science, 4,* 253-255. (6)

Kimble, G. A., & Garmezy, N. (1968). *Principles of general psychology* (3rd ed.). New York: Ronald Press. (14)

King, M. L., Jr. (1964, November 13). Speech at Duke University, Durham, NC. (5)

Kinsey, A. C., Pomeroy, W. B., & Martin, C. E. (1948). *Sexual behavior in the human male.* Philadelphia: Saunders. (11)

Kinsey, A. C., Pomeroy, W. B., Martin, C. E., & Gebhard, P. H. (1953). *Sexual behavior in the human female.* Philadelphia: Saunders. (11)

Kiriakakis, V., Bhatia, K. P., Quinn, N. P., & Marsden, C. D. (1998). The natural history of tardive dyskinesia: A long-term follow-up of 107 cases. *Brain, 121,* 2053-2066. (15)

Kirsch, I., Deacon, B. J., Huedo-Medina, T. B., Scoboria, A., Moore, T. J., & Johnson, B. T. (2008). Initial severity and antidepressant benefits: A meta-analysis of data submitted to the Food and Drug Administration. *PLoS Medicine, 5*(2), e45. (15)

Kirsch, I., & Lynn, S. J. (1998). Dissociation theories of hypnosis. *Psychological Bulletin, 123,* 100-115. (10)

Kirsch, J., & Braffman, W. (2001). Imaginative suggestibility and hypnotizability. *Current Directions in Psychological Science, 10,* 57-61. (10)

Kivimäki, M., Vahtera, J., Elovainio, M., Helenius, H., Singh-Manoux, A., & Pentti, J. (2005). Optimism and pessimism as predictors of change in health after death or onset of severe illness in family. *Health Psychology, 24,* 413-421. (12)

Kleen, J. K., Sitomer, M. T., Killeen, P. R., & Conrad, C. D. (2006). Chronic stress impairs spatial memory and motivation for reward without disrupting motor ability and motivation to explore. *Behavioral Neuroscience, 120,* 842-851. (12)

Klein, D. F. (1993). False suffocation alarms, spontaneous panics, and related conditions. *Archives of General Psychiatry, 50,* 306-317. (15)

Kleinmuntz, B., & Szucko, J. J. (1984). A field study of the fallibility of polygraphic lie detection. *Nature, 308,* 449-450. (12)

Kluger, M. J. (1991). Fever: Role of pyrogens and cryogens. *Physiological Reviews, 71,* 93-127. (12)

Knight, M., Seymour, T. L., Gaunt, J. T., Baker, C., Nesmith, K., & Mather, M. (2007). Aging and goal-directed emotional attention: Distraction reverses emotional biases. *Emotion, 7,* 705-714. (12)

Knoll, J. L., IV, & Resnick, P. J. (2008). Insanity defense evaluations: Toward a model for evidence-based practice. *Brief Treatment and Crisis Intervention, 8,* 92-110. (15)

Knuts, I. J. E., Cosci, F., Esquivel, G., Goosens, L., van Duinen, M., . . . Schruers, K. R. J. (2010). Cigarette smoking and 35% CO_2 induced panic in panic disorder patients. *Journal of Affective Disorders, 124,* 215-218. (15)

Ko, C.-H., Liu, G.-C., Hsiao, S., Yen, J.-Y., Yan, M.-J., . . . Chen, C.-S. (2009). Brain activities associated with gaming urge of online gaming addiction. *Journal of Psychiatric Research, 43,* 739-747. (15)

Kobayashi, F. (2011). Japanese high school students' television viewing and fast food consumption. *Nutrition & Food Science, 41,* 242-248. (2)

Kobayashi, F., Schallert, D. L., & Ogren, H. A. (2003). Japanese and American folk vocabularies for emotion. *Journal of Social Psychology, 143,* 451-478. (12)

Kochanska, G., Aksan, N., & Joy, M. E. (2007). Children's fearfulness as a moderator of parenting in early socialization: Two longitudinal studies. *Developmental Psychology, 43,* 222-237. (5)

Kocsis, R. N. (2004). Psychological profiling of serial arson offenses: An assessment of skills and accuracy. *Criminal Justice and Behavior, 31,* 341-361. (14)

Kocsis, R. N., Irwin, H. J., Hayes, A. F., & Nunn, R. (2000). Expertise in psychological profiling: A comparative assessment. *Journal of Interpersonal Violence, 15,* 311-331. (14)

Koenigs, M., Huey, E. D., Raymont, V., Cheon, B., Solomon, J., . . . Grafman, J. (2008). Focal brain damage protects against post-traumatic stress disorder in combat veterans. *Nature Neuroscience, 11,* 232-237. (12)

Koepp, M. J., Gunn, R. N., Lawrence, A. D., Cunningham, V. J., Dagher, A., Jones, T., . . . Grasby, P. M. (1998). Evidence for striatal dopamine release during a video game. *Nature, 393,* 266–268. (3, 15)

Kohlberg, L. (1969). Stage and sequence: The cognitive-developmental approach to socialization. In D. A. Goslin (Ed.), *Handbook of socialization theory and research* (pp. 347–480). Chicago: Rand McNally. (13)

Kohlberg, L., & Hersh, R. H. (1977). Moral development: A review of the theory. *Theory into Practice, 16,* 53–59. (13)

Kohli, M. A., Lucae, S., Saemann, P. G., Schmidt, M. V., Demirkan, A., . . . Binder, E. B. (2011). The neuronal transporter gene *SLC6A15* confers risk to major depression. *Neuron, 70,* 252–265. (15)

Koke, L. C., & Vernon, P. A. (2003). The Sternberg Triarchic Abilities Test (STAT) as a measure of academic achievement and general intelligence. *Personality and Individual Differences, 35,* 1803–1807. (9)

Konkle, T., Brady, T. F., Alvarez, G. A., & Oliva, A. (2010). Scene memory is more detailed than you think: The role of categories in visual long-term memory. *Psychological Science, 21,* 1551–1556. (8)

Kontula, O., & Haavio-Mannila, E. (2009). The impact of aging on human sexual activity and sexual desire. *Journal of Sex Research, 46,* 46–56. (11)

Koob, G. F., & LeMoal, M. (1997). Drug abuse: Hedonic homeostatic dysregulation. *Science, 278,* 52–58. (15)

Kopelman, P. G. (2000). Obesity as a medical problem. *Nature, 404,* 635–643. (11)

Koppenaal, R. J. (1963). Time changes in the strengths of A-B, A-C lists: Spontaneous recovery? *Journal of Verbal Learning and Verbal Behavior, 2,* 310–319. (7)

Koriat, A., Bjork, R. A., Sheffer, L., & Bar, S. K. (2004). Predicting one's own forgetting: The role of experience-based and theory-based processes. *Journal of Experimental Psychology: General, 133,* 643–656. (7)

Korman, M., Doyon, J., Doljansky, J., Carrier, J., Dagan, Y., & Karni, A. (2007). Daytime sleep condenses the time course of motor memory consolidation. *Nature Neuroscience, 10,* 1206–1213. (10)

Kornell, N., & Bjork, R. A. (2008). Learning concepts and categories. *Psychological Science, 19,* 585–592. (7)

Kornell, N., Castel, A. D., Eich, T. S., & Bjork, R. A. (2010). Spacing as the friend of both memory and induction in young and older adults. *Psychology and Aging, 25,* 498–503. (7)

Kornell, N., Hays, M. J., & Bjork, R. A. (2009). Unsuccessful retrieval attempts enhance subsequent learning. *Journal of Experimental Psychology: Learning, Memory, and Cognition, 35,* 989–998. (7)

Kosfeld, M., Heinrichs, M., Zak, P. J., Fischbacher, U., & Fehr, E. (2005). Oxytocin increases trust in humans. *Nature, 435,* 673–676. (11)

Koten, J. W. Jr., Wood, G., Hagoort, P., Goebel, R., Propping, P., Willmes, K., . . . Boomsma, D. I. (2009). Genetic contribution to variation in cognitive function: An fMRI study in twins. *Science, 323,* 1737–1740. (9)

Kotowicz, Z. (2007). The strange case of Phineas Gage. *History of the Human Sciences, 20,* 115–131. (12)

Kovas, Y., Haworth, C. M. A., Dale, P. S., & Plomin, R. (2007). The genetic and environmental origins of learning abilities and disabilities in the early preschool years. *Monographs of the Society for Research in Child Development, 72,* 1–144. (9)

Koyano, W. (1991). Japanese attitudes toward the elderly: A review of research findings. *Journal of Cross-Cultural Gerontology, 4,* 335–345. (5)

Kozel, N. J., & Adams, E. H. (1986). Epidemiology of drug abuse: An overview. *Science, 234,* 970–974. (3)

Kraemer, D. L., & Hastrup, J. L. (1988). Crying in adults: Self-control and autonomic correlates. *Journal of Social and Clinical Psychology, 6,* 53–68. (12, 14)

Krähenbühl, S., & Blades, M. (2006). The effect of question repetition within interviews on young children's eyewitness recall. *Journal of Experimental Child Psychology, 94,* 57–67. (7)

Krajbich, I., Adolphs, R., Tranel, D., Denburg, N. L., & Camerer, C. F. (2009). Economic games quantify diminished sense of guilt in patients with damage to the prefrontal cortex. *Journal of Neuroscience, 29,* 2188–2192. (12)

Kramer, P. D. (2006). *Freud: Inventor of the modern mind.* New York: Harper Collins. (14)

Krantz, D. S., Sheps, D. S., Carney, R. M., & Natelson, B. H. (2000). Effects of mental stress in patients with coronary artery disease. *Journal of the American Medical Association, 283,* 1800–1802. (12)

Kreiner, D. S., Altis, N. A., & Voss, C. W. (2003). A test of the effect of reverse speech on priming. *Journal of Psychology, 137,* 224–232. (4)

Kreitzer, A. C., & Regehr, W. G. (2001). Retrograde inhibition of presynaptic calcium influx by endogenous cannabinoids at excitatory synapses onto Purkinje cells. *Neuron, 29,* 717–727. (3)

Krendl, A. C., Richeson, J. A., Kelley, W. M., & Heatherton, T. F. (2008). The negative consequences of threat. *Psychological Science, 19,* 168–175. (9)

Kreskin. (1991). *Secrets of The Amazing Kreskin.* Buffalo, NY: Prometheus. (2)

Kripke, D. F., Garfinkel, L., Wingard, D. L., Klauber, M. R., & Marler, M. R. (2002). Mortality associated with sleep duration and insomnia. *Archives of General Psychiatry, 59,* 131–136. (2)

Krishnan-Sarin, S., Krystal, J. H., Shi, J., Pittman, B., & O'Malley, S. S. (2007). Family history of alcoholism influences naloxone-induced reduction in alcohol drinking. *Biological Psychiatry, 62,* 694–697. (15)

Krueger, D. W. (1978). The differential diagnosis of proverb interpretation. In W. E. Fann, I. Karacan, A. D. Pokorny, & R. L. Williams (Eds.), *Phenomenology and treatment of schizophrenia* (pp. 193–201). New York: Spectrum. (15)

Krueger, J. M., Rector, D. M., Roy, S., Van Dongen, H. P. A., Belenky, G., & Panksepp, J. (2008). Sleep as a fundamental property of neuronal assemblies. *Nature Reviews Neuroscience, 9,* 910–919. (10)

Krueger, R. F., Markon, K. E., & Bouchard, T. J., Jr. (2003). The extended genotype: The heritability of personality accounts for the heritability of recalled family environments in twins reared apart. *Journal of Personality, 71,* 809–833. (5)

Kruger, J., Wirtz, D., & Miller, D. T. (2005). Counterfactual thinking and the first instinct fallacy. *Journal of Personality and Social Psychology, 88,* 725–735. (8)

Krugers, H. J., Hoogenraad, C. C., & Groc. L. (2010). Stress hormones and AMPA receptor trafficking in synaptic plasticity and memory. *Nature Reviews Neuroscience, 11,* 675–681. (12)

Krupa, D. J., Thompson, J. K., & Thompson, R. F. (1993). Localization of a memory trace in the mammalian brain. *Science, 260,* 989–991. (3)

Kübler-Ross, E. (1975). *Death: The final stage of growth.* Englewood Cliffs, NJ: Prentice Hall. (5)

Kuhl, P. K., Andruski, J. E., Chistovich, I. A., Chistovich, L. A., Kozhevnikova, E. V., Ryskina, V. L., . . . Lacerda, F. (1997). Cross-language analysis of phonetic units in language addressed to infants. *Science, 277,* 684–686. (8)

Kuhlmann, S., Piel, M., & Wolf, O. T. (2005). Impaired memory retrieval after psychosocial stress in healthy young men. *Journal of Neuroscience, 25,* 2977–2982. (12)

Kuhn, D., & Lao, J. (1996). Effects of evidence on attitudes: Is polarization the norm? *Psychological Science, 7,* 115–120. (13)

Kumaran, D., & Maguire, E. A. (2005). The human hippocampus: Cognitive maps or relational memory? *Journal of Neuroscience, 25,* 7254–7259. (7)

Kumkale, G. T., & Abarracín, D. (2004). The sleeper effect in persuasion: A meta-analytic review. *Psychological Bulletin, 130,* 143–172. (13)

Kunar, M. A., Carter, R., Cohen, M., & Horowitz, T. S. (2008). Telephone conversation impairs sustained visual attention via a central bottleneck. *Psychonomic Bulletin and Review, 15,* 1135–1140. (8)

Kunar, M. A., Rich, A. N., & Wolfe, J. M. (2010). Spatial and temporal separation fails to counteract the effects of low prevalence in visual search. *Visual Cognition, 18,* 881–897. (4)

Kupfer, D. J., First, M. B., & Regier, D. A. (2002). *A research agenda for DSM–V.* Washington, DC: American Psychiatric Association. (15)

Kurihara, K., & Kashiwayanagi, M. (1998). Introductory remarks on umami taste. *Annals of the New York Academy of Sciences, 855,* 393–397. (4)

Kuroshima, H., Kuwahata, H., & Fujita, K. (2008). Learning from others' mistakes in capuchin monkeys (*Cebus apella*). *Animal Cognition, 11,* 611–623. (6)

Kvavilashvili, L., Mirani, J., Schlagman, S., Foley, K., & Kornbrot, D. E. (2009). Consistency of flashbulb memories of September 11 over long delays: Implications for consolidation and wrong time slice hypotheses. *Journal of Memory and Language, 61,* 556–572. (7)

La Roche, M., & Christopher, M. S. (2008). Culture and empirically supported treatments: On the road to a collision? *Culture and Psychology, 14,* 333–356. (15)

LaBar, K. S., & Phelps, E. A. (1998). Arousal-mediated memory consolidation: Role of the medial temporal lobe in humans. *Psychological Science, 9,* 490–493. (12)

Labouvie-Vief, G., Diehl, M., Tarnowski, A., & Shen, J. (2000). Age differences in adult personality: Findings from the United States and China. *Journal of Gerontology: Psychological Sciences, 55B,* P4–P17. (14)

Labroo, A. A., Lambotte, S., & Zhang, Y. (2009). The "name-ease" effect and its dual impact on importance judgments. *Psychological Science, 20,* 1516–1522. (8)

Lackner, J. R. (1993). Orientation and movement in unusual force environments. *Psychological Science, 4,* 134–142. (4)

Laeng, B., Svartdal, F., & Oelmann, H. (2004). Does color synesthesia pose a paradox for early-selection theories of attention? *Psychological Science, 15*, 277–281. (4)

Laffaye, C., McKellar, J. D., Ilgen, M. A., & Moos, R. H. (2008). Predictors of 4-year outcome of community residential treatment for patients with substance use disorders. *Addiction, 103*, 671–680. (15)

Lahey, B. B. (2009). Public health significance of neuroticism. *American Psychologist, 64*, 241–256. (14)

Lahti, T. A., Leppamäki, S., Ojanen, S.-M., Haukka, J., Tuulio-Henriksson, A., Lönnqvist, J., . . . Partonen, T. (2006). Transition into daylight saving time influences the fragmentation of the rest–activity cycle. *Journal of Circadian Rhythms, 4*, 1. (10)

Lai, C. S. L., Fisher, S. E., Hurst, J. A., Vargha-Khadem, F., & Monaco, A. P. (2001). A forkhead-domain gene is mutated in a severe speech and language disorder. *Nature, 413*, 519–523. (8)

Lake, R. I. E., Eaves, L. J., Maes, H. H. M., Heath, A. C., & Martin, N. G. (2000). Further evidence against the environmental transmission of individual differences in neuroticism from a collaborative study of 45,850 twins and relatives on two continents. *Behavior Genetics, 30*, 223–233. (5, 14)

Lamb, M. E., Orbach, Y., Hershkowitz, I., Horowitz, D., & Abbott, C. B. (2007). Does the type of prompt affect the accuracy of information provided by alleged victims of abuse in forensic interviews? *Applied Cognitive Psychology, 21*, 1117–1130. (7)

Lambie, J. A., & Marcel, A. J. (2002). Consciousness and the varieties of emotion experience: A theoretical framework. *Psychological Review, 109*, 219–259. (10)

Lamm, H., & Myers, D. G. (1978). Group-induced polarization of attitudes and behavior. *Advances in Experimental Social Psychology, 11*, 145–195. (13)

Land, E. H., Hubel, D. H., Livingstone, M. S., Perry, S. H., & Burns, M. M. (1983). Colour-generating interactions across the corpus callosum. *Nature, 303*, 616–618. (4)

Land, E. H., & McCann, J. J. (1971). Lightness and retinex theory. *Journal of the Optical Society of America, 61*, 1–11. (4)

Lang, J. W. B., & Lang, J. (2010). Priming competence diminishes the link between cognitive test anxiety and test performance: Implications for the interpretation of test scores. *Psychological Science, 21*, 811–819. (9)

Lang, P. J. (1994). The varieties of emotional experience: A meditation on James-Lange theory. *Psychological Review, 101*, 211–221. (12)

Langer, E. J. (1975). The illusion of control. *Journal of Personality and Social Psychology, 32*, 311–328. (5)

Langlois, J. H., & Roggman, L. A. (1990). Attractive faces are only average. *Psychological Science, 1*, 115–121. (13)

Langlois, J. H., Roggman, L. A., & Musselman, L. (1994). What is average and what is not average about average faces? *Psychological Science, 5*, 214–220. (13)

Långström, N., Rahman, Q., Carlström, E., & Lichtenstein, P. (2010). Genetic and environmental effects on same-sex sexual behavior: A population study of twins in Sweden. *Archives of Sexual Behavior, 39*, 75–80. (11)

Langworthy, R. A., & Jennings, J. W. (1972). Oddball, abstract olfactory learning in laboratory rats. *Psychological Record, 22*, 487–490. (1)

Lansford, J. E. (2009). Parental divorce and children's adjustment. *Perspectives in Psychological Science, 4*, 140–152. (5)

Lansford, J. E., Malone, P. S., Castellino, D. R., Dodge, K. A., Pettit, G. S., & Bates, J. E. (2006). Trajectories of internalizing, externalizing, and grades for children who have and have not experienced their parents' divorce or separation. *Journal of Family Psychology, 20*, 292–301. (5)

Larkina, M., Güler, O. E., Kleinknecht, E., & Bauer, P. J. (2008). Maternal provision of structure in a deliberate memory task in relation to their preschool children's recall. *Journal of Experimental Child Psychology, 100*, 235–251. (5)

Larsen, L., Hartmann, P., & Nyborg, H. (2008). The stability of general intelligence from early adulthood to middle age. *Intelligence, 36*, 29–34. (9)

Larson, R. W. (2001). How U.S. children and adolescents spend time: What it does (and doesn't) tell us about their development. *Current Directions in Psychological Science, 10*, 160–164. (5)

Larzelere, R. E., Cox, R. B. Jr., & Smith, G. L. (2010). Do nonphysical punishments reduce antisocial behavior more than spanking? A comparison using the strongest previous causal evidence against spanking. *BMC Pediatrics, 10*, article 10. (6)

Larzelere, R. E., & Kuhn, B. R. (2005). Comparing child outcomes of physical punishment and alternative disciplinary tactics: A meta-analysis. *Clinical Child and Family Psychology Review, 8*, 1–37. (6)

Lashley, K. (1923). The behavioristic interpretation of consciousness. *Psychological Bulletin, 30*, 237–272, 329–353. (10)

Lashley, K. S. (1951). The problem of serial order in behavior. In L. A. Jeffress (Ed.), *Cerebral mechanisms in behavior* (pp. 112–146). New York: Wiley. (8)

Lassiter, G. D., Geers, A. L., Munhall, P. J., Ploutz-Snyder, R. J., & Breitenbecher, D. L. (2002). Illusory causation: Why it occurs. *Psychological Science, 13*, 299–305. (13)

Latané, B., & Darley, J. M. (1968). Group inhibition of bystander intervention in emergencies. *Journal of Personality and Social Psychology, 10*, 215–221. (13)

Latané, B., & Darley, J. M. (1969). Bystander "apathy." *American Scientist, 57*, 244–268. (13)

Latané, B., Williams, K., & Harkins, S. (1979). Many hands make light the work: The causes and consequences of social loafing. *Journal of Personality and Social Psychology, 37*, 823–832. (13)

Latner, J. D. (2003). Macronutrient effects on satiety and binge eating in bulimia nervosa and binge eating disorder. *Appetite, 40*, 309–311. (11)

Lau, H. C., Rogers, R. D., Haggard, P., & Passingham, R. E. (2004). Attention to intention. *Science, 303*, 1208–1210. (10)

Laumann, E. O. (1969). Friends of urban men: An assessment of accuracy in reporting their socio-economic attributes, mutual choice, and attitude development. *Sociometry, 32*, 54–69. (13)

Laumann, E. O., Gagnon, J. H., Michael, R. T., & Michaels, S. (1994). *The social organization of sexuality: Sexual practices in the United States.* Chicago: University of Chicago Press. (11)

Laumann, E. O., Nicolosi, A., Glasser, D. B., Paik, A., Buvat, J., Gingell, C., . . . for the GSSAB Investigators' Group. (2003). *Prevalence of sexual problems among men and women aged 40 to 80 years: Results of an international survey.* Paper presented at the second international consultation on erectile and sexual dysfunctions, Paris. (11)

Laumann, E. O., Paik, A., Glassser, D. B., Kang, J.-H., Wang, T., Levinson, G., . . . Gingell, C. (2006). A cross-national study of subjective sexual well-being among older women and men: Findings from the global study of sexual attitudes and behaviors. *Archives of Sexual Behavior, 35*, 145–161. (11)

Laursen, B., Coy, K. C., & Collins, W. A. (1998). Reconsidering changes in parent-child conflict across adolescence: A meta-analysis. *Child Development, 69*, 817–832. (5)

Laws, G., Byrne, A., & Buckley, S. (2000). Language and memory development in children with Down syndrome at mainstream schools and special schools: A comparison. *Educational Psychology, 20*, 447–457. (9)

Lawson, T. T. (2008). *Carl Jung, Darwin of the mind.* London: Karnac. (14)

Lazarus, R. S. (1977). Cognitive and coping processes in emotion. In A. Monat & R. S. Lazarus (Eds.), *Stress and coping* (pp. 145–158). New York: Columbia University Press. (12)

Lazarus, R. S., Averill, J. R., & Opton, E. M., Jr. (1970). Towards a cognitive theory of emotion. In M. B. Arnold (Ed.), *Feelings and emotions* (pp. 207–232). New York: Academic Press. (12)

Lee, A., Clancy, S., & Fleming, A. S. (1999). Mother rats bar-press for pups: Effects of lesions of the MPOA and limbic sites on maternal behavior and operant responding for pup-reinforcement. *Behavioural Brain Research, 100*, 15–31. (6)

Lee, L., Loewenstein, G., Ariely, D., Hong, J., & Young, J. (2008). If I'm not hot, are you hot or not? *Psychological Science, 19*, 669–677. (13)

Lee, M. G., Hassani, O. K., & Jones, B. E. (2005). Discharge of identified orexin/hypocretin neurons across the sleep–waking cycle. *Journal of Neuroscience, 25*, 6716–6720. (10)

Lee, R. A., Su, J., & Yoshida, E. (2005). Coping with intergenerational family conflict among Asian American college students. *Journal of Counseling Psychology, 52*, 389–399. (5)

Lee, S.-H., Blake, R., & Heeger, D. J. (2005). Traveling waves of activity in primary visual cortex during binocular rivalry. *Nature Neuroscience, 8*, 22–23. (10)

Leff, J. (2002). The psychiatric revolution: Care in the community. *Nature Reviews Neuroscience, 3*, 821–824. (15)

Leff, J., Wig, N. N., Ghosh, A., Bedi, H., Menon, D. K., Kuipers, L., . . . Sartorius, N. (1987). Expressed emotion and schizophrenia in North India: III. Influence of relatives' expressed emotion on the course of schizophrenia in Chandigarh. *British Journal of Psychiatry, 151*, 166–173. (15)

Legault, L., Gutsell, J. N., & Inzlicht, M. (2011). Ironic effects of antiprejudice messages: How motivational interventions can reduce (but also increase) prejudice. *Psychological Science, 22*, 1472–1477. (13)

Legge, G. E., Ahn, S. J., Klitz, T. S., & Luebker, A. (1997). Psychophysics of reading: XVI. The visual span in normal and low vision. *Vision Research, 37*, 1999–2010. (8)

Lehrer, J. (2010, Dec. 13). The truth wears off. *New Yorker, 86*, 52–57. (2)

Leibniz, G. (1714). *The Principles of Nature and Grace, Based on Reason.* Retrieved Dec. 1, 2011 from http://www.earlymoderntexts.com/pdf/leibprin.pdf (10)

Leichsenring, F., & Leibing, E. (2003). The effectiveness of psychodynamic therapy and cognitive behavior therapy in the treatment of personality disorders: A meta-analysis. *American Journal of Psychiatry, 160,* 1223-1232. (15)

Lekeu, F., Wojtasik, V., Van der Linden, M., & Salmon, E. (2002). Training early Alzheimer patients to use a mobile phone. *Acta Neurologica Belgica, 102,* 114-121. (7)

LeMagnen, J. (1981). The metabolic basis of dual periodicity of feeding in rats. *Behavioral and Brain Sciences, 4,* 561-607. (11)

Lenneberg, E. H. (1967). *Biological foundations of language.* New York: Wiley. (8)

Lenneberg, E. H. (1969). On explaining language. *Science, 164,* 635-643. (8)

Lenton, A. P., Fasolo, B., & Todd, P. M. (2008). "Shopping" for a mate: Expected versus experienced preferences in online mate choice. *IEEE Transactions on Professional Communication, 51,* 169-182. (8)

Lenton, A. P., & Francesconi, M. (2010). How humans cognitively manage an abundance of mate options. *Psychological Science, 21,* 528-533. (8)

Leonard, L. B. (2007). Processing limitations and the grammatical profile of children with specific language impairment. In R. V. Kail (Ed.), *Advances in child development and behavior* (Vol. 35, pp. 139-171). Oxford, England: Elsevier. (8)

Leopold, D. A., Bondar, I. V., & Giese, M. A. (2006). Norm-based face encoding by single neurons in the monkey inferotemporal cortex. *Nature, 442,* 572-575. (5)

Leppänen, J. M., & Hietanen, J. K. (2003). Affect and face perception: Odors modulate the recognition advantage of happy faces. *Emotion, 3,* 315-326. (12)

Lerner, M. J. (1980). *The belief in a just world: A fundamental delusion.* New York: Plenum Press. (14)

Lesko, A. C., & Corpus, J. H. (2006). Discounting the difficult: How high math-identified women respond to stereotype threat. *Sex Roles, 54,* 113-125. (9)

Leuchtenberg, W. E. (1963). *Franklin D. Roosevelt and the New Deal 1932-1940.* New York: Harper & Row. (13)

Levav, J., & Fitzsimons, G. J. (2006). When questions change behavior. *Psychological Science, 17,* 207-213. (11)

LeVay, S. (1991). A difference in hypothalamic structure between heterosexual and homosexual men. *Science, 253,* 1034-1037. (11)

Levenson, R. W., & Miller, B. L. (2007). Loss of cells—Loss of self. *Current Directions in Psychological Science, 16,* 289-294. (12)

Levine, J. A., Lanningham-Foster, L. M., McCrady, S. K., Krizan, A. C., Olson, L. R., Kane, P. H., . . . Clark, M. M. (2005). Interindividual variation in posture allocation: Possible role in human obesity. *Science, 307,* 584-586. (11)

Levine, R. V. (1990). The pace of life. *American Scientist, 78,* 450-459. (12)

Levine, S. C., Vasilyeva, M., Lourenco, S. F., Newcombe, N. S., & Huttenlocher, J. (2005). Socioeconomic status modifies the sex difference in spatial skill. *Psychological Science, 16,* 841-845. (5)

Levinson, D. J. (1986). A conception of adult development. *American Psychologist, 41,* 3-13. (5)

Levy, B. J., McVeigh, N. D., Marful, A., & Anderson, M. C. (2007). Inhibiting your native language. *Psychological Science, 18,* 29-34. (8)

Leweke, F. M., Gerth, C. W., Koethe, D., Klosterkötter, J., Ruslanova, I., Krivogorsky, B., . . . Yolken, R. H. (2004). Antibodies to infectious agents in individuals with recent onset schizophrenia. *European Archives of Psychiatry and Clinical Neuroscience, 254,* 4-8. (15)

Lewis, D. A., & Gonzalez-Burgos, G. (2006). Pathophysiologically based treatment interventions in schizophrenia. *Nature Medicine, 12,* 1016-1022. (15)

Lewis, D. O., Moy, E., Jackson, L. D., Aaronson, R., Restifo, N., Serra, S., . . . Simos, A. (1985). Biopsychosocial characteristics of children who later murder: A prospective study. *American Journal of Psychiatry, 142,* 1161-1167. (13)

Lewis, M. (1995). Self-conscious emotions. *American Scientist, 83,* 68-78. (12)

Lewis, M., Sullivan, M. W., Stanger, C., & Weiss, M. (1991). Self development and self-conscious emotions. In S. Chess & M. E. Hertzig (Eds.), *Annual progress in child psychiatry and child development 1990* (pp. 34-51). New York: Brunner/Mazel. (5)

Li, M. D., & Burmeister, M. (2009). New insights into the genetics of addiction. *Nature Reviews Neuroscience, 10,* 225-231. (15)

Li, W., Howard, J. D., Parrish, T. B., & Gottfried, J. A. (2008). Aversive learning enhances perceptual and cortical discrimination of indiscriminable odor cues. *Science, 319,* 1842-1845. (6)

Libet, B., Gleason, C. A., Wright, E. W., & Pearl, D. K. (1983). Time of conscious intention to act in relation to onset of cerebral activities (readiness potential): The unconscious initiation of a freely voluntary act. *Brain, 106,* 623-642. (10)

Lickliter, R., & Bahrick, L. E. (2000). The development of infant intersensory perception: Advantages of a comparative convergent-operations approach. *Psychological Bulletin, 126,* 260-280. (3)

Liebman, M., Pelican, S., Moore, S. A., Holmes, B., Wardlaw, M. K., Melcher, L. M., . . . Haynes, G. W. (2006). Dietary intake-, eating behavior-, and physical activity-related determinants of high body mass index in the 2003 Wellness IN the Rockies cross-sectional study. *Nutrition Research, 26,* 111-117. (11)

Lilie, J. K., & Rosenberg, R. P. (1990). Behavioral treatment of insomnia. *Progress in Behavior Modification, 25,* 152-177. (10)

Lilienfeld, S. O. (2007). Psychological treatments that cause harm. *Perspectives on Psychological Science, 2,* 53-70. (12, 15)

Lilienfeld, S. O., Wood, J. M., & Garb, H. N. (2000). The scientific status of projective tests. *Psychological Science in the Public Interest, 1,* 27-66. (14)

Lillberg, K., Verkasalo, P. K., Kaprio, J., Teppo, L., Helenius, H., & Koskenvuo, M. (2003). Stressful life events and risk of breast cancer in 10,808 women: A cohort study. *American Journal of Epidemiology, 157,* 415-423. (12)

Lin, J. Y., Franconeri, S., & Enns, J. T. (2008). Objects on a collision path with the observer demand attention. *Psychological Science, 19,* 686-692. (8)

Lin, L., Faraco, J., Li, R., Kadotani, H., Rogers, W., Lin, X., . . . Nishino, E. M. (1999). The sleep disorder canine narcolepsy is caused by a mutation in the hypocretin (orexin) receptor 2 gene. *Cell, 98,* 365-376. (10)

Linck, J. A., Kroll, J. F., & Sunderman, G. (2009). Losing access to the native language while immersed in a second language. *Psychological Science, 20,* 1507-1515. (8)

Lindberg, L., & Hjern, A. (2003). Risk factors for anorexia nervosa: A national cohort study. *International Journal of Eating Disorders, 34,* 397-408. (11)

Linden, W., Lenz, J. W., & Con, A. H. (2001). Individualized stress management for primary hypertension: A randomized trial. *Archives of Internal Medicine, 161,* 1071-1080. (12)

Lindsay, D. S., Hagen, L., Read, J. D., Wade, K. A., & Garry, M. (2004). True photographs and false memories. *Psychological Science, 15,* 149-154. (7)

Lindsay, D. S., & Read, J. D. (1994). Psychotherapy and memories of childhood sexual abuse: A cognitive perspective. *Applied Cognitive Psychology, 8,* 281-338. (7)

Lipkus, I. (1991). The construction and preliminary validation of a global Belief in a Just World scale and the exploratory analysis of the multidimensional Belief in a Just World scale. *Personality and Individual Differences, 12,* 1171-1178. (14)

Lipsey, M. W., & Wilson, D. B. (1993). The efficacy of psychological, educational, and behavioral treatment. *American Psychologist, 48,* 1181-1209. (15)

Lipszyc, J., & Schachar, R. (2010). Inhibitory control and psychopathology: A meta-analysis of studies using the stop signal task. *Journal of the International Neuropsychological Society, 16,* 1064-1076. (8)

Lisanby, S. H., Maddox, J. H., Prudic, J., Devanand, D. P., & Sackeim, H. A. (2000). The effects of electroconvulsive therapy on memory of autobiographical and public events. *Archives of General Psychiatry, 57,* 581-590. (15)

Liu, F., Wollstein, A., Hysi, P. G., Ankra-Badu, G. A., Spector, T. D., Park, D, . . . Kayser, M. (2010). Digital quantification of human eye color highlights genetic association of three new loci. *PLoS Genetics, 6,* e1000934. (3)

Liu, I.-C., Blacker, D. L., Xu, R., Fitzmaurice, G., Lyons, M. J., & Tsuang, M. T. (2004). Genetic and environmental contributions to the development of alcohol dependence in male twins. *Archives of General Psychiatry, 61,* 897-903. (15)

Liu, Q., Pu, L., & Poo, M. (2005). Repeated cocaine exposure *in vivo* facilitates LTP induction in midbrain dopamine neurons. *Nature, 437,* 1027-1031. (15)

Locke, E. A., & Latham, G. P. (2002). Building a practically useful theory of goal setting and task motivation. *American Psychologist, 57,* 705-717. (11)

Locke, J. L. (1994). Phases in the child's development of language. *American Scientist, 82,* 436-445. (8)

Loeb, J. (1973). *Forced movements, tropisms, and animal conduct.* New York: Dover. (Original work published 1918) (6)

Loeber, S., Croissant, B., Heinz, A., Mann, K., & Flor, H. (2006). Cue exposure in the treatment of alcohol dependence: Effects on drinking outcome, craving and self-efficacy. *British Journal of Clinical Psychology, 45,* 515-529. (6)

Loehlin, J. C. (1992). *Genes and environment in personality development.* Newbury Park, CA: Sage. (5, 14)

Loehlin, J. C., Horn, J. M., & Willerman, L. (1989). Modeling IQ change: Evidence from the Texas adoption project. *Child Development, 60,* 993–1004. (9)

Loewi, O. (1960). An autobiographic sketch. *Perspectives in Biology, 4,* 3–25. (3)

Loftus, E. (2003). Our changeable memories: Legal and practical implications. *Nature Reviews Neuroscience, 4,* 231–234. (7)

Loftus, E. F. (1975). Leading questions and the eyewitness report. *Cognitive Psychology, 7,* 560–572. (7)

Loftus, E. F. (1993). The reality of repressed memories. *American Psychologist, 48,* 518–537. (7)

Loftus, E. F., Feldman, J., & Dashiell, R. (1995). The reality of illusory memories. In D. L. Schacter (Ed.), *Memory distortion* (pp. 47–68). Cambridge, MA: Harvard University Press. (7)

Loftus, G. R. (1996). Psychology will be a much better science when we change the way we analyze data. *Current Directions in Psychological Science, 5,* 161–171. (2)

Long, G. M., & Toppine, T. C. (2004). Enduring interest in perceptual ambiguity: Alternating views of reversible figures. *Psychological Bulletin, 130,* 748–768. (4)

Longstreth, L. E. (1981). Revisiting Skeels' final study: A critique. *Developmental Psychology, 17,* 620–625. (9)

Lopes, P. N., Brackett, M. A., Nezlak, J. B., Schütz, A., Sellin, I., & Salovey, P. (2004). Emotional intelligence and social interaction. *Personality and Social Psychology Bulletin, 30,* 1018–1034. (12)

Lotto, R. B., & Purves, D. (2002). The empirical basis of color perception. *Consciousness and Cognition, 11,* 609–629. (4)

Lotze, M., Grodd, W., Birbaumer, N., Erb, M., Huse, E., & Flor, H. (1999). Does use of a myoelectric prosthesis prevent cortical reorganization and phantom limb pain? *Nature Neuroscience, 2,* 501–502. (4)

Loughnan, S., Kuppens, P., Allik, J., Balazs, K., de Lemus, S., . . . Haslam, N. (2011). Economic inequality is linked to biased self-perception. *Psychological Science, 22,* 1254–1258. (13)

Löw, A., Lang, P. J., Smith, J. C., & Bradley, M. M. (2008). Both predator and prey. *Psychological Science, 19,* 865–873. (12)

Low, K. S. D., Yoon, M. J., Roberts, B. W., & Rounds, J. (2005). The stability of vocational interests from early adolescence to middle adulthood: A quantitative review of longitudinal studies. *Psychological Bulletin, 131,* 713–737. (5)

Lowe, K. B., Kroeck, K. G., & Sivasubramaniam, N. (1996). Effectiveness correlates of transformational and transactional leadership: A meta-analytic review of the MLQ literature. *Leadership Quarterly, 7,* 385–425. (11)

Lubman, D. I., Yücel, M., Kettle, J. W. L., Scaffidi, A., Mackenzie, T., Simmons, J. G., . . . Allen, N. B. (2009). Responsiveness to drug cues and natural rewards in opiate addiction. *Archives of General Psychiatry, 66,* 205–212. (15)

Luborsky, L., & Barrett, M. S. (2006). The history and empirical status of key psychoanalytic concepts. *Annual Review of Clinical Psychology, 2,* 1–19. (14)

Lucas, R. E. (2005). Time does not heal all wounds. *Psychological Science, 16,* 945–950. (12)

Lucas, R. E., Clark, A. E., Georgellis, Y., & Diener, E. (2004). Unemployment alters the set point for life satisfaction. *Psychological Science, 15,* 8–13. (12)

Lucas, R. E., Le, K., & Dyrenforth, P. S. (2008). Explaining the extraversion/positive affect relation: Sociability cannot account for extraverts' greater happiness. *Journal of Personality, 76,* 385–414. (14)

Lucas, R. E., & Schimmack, U. (2009). Income and well-being: How big is the gap between the rich and the poor? *Journal of Research in Personality, 43,* 75–78. (12)

Luciano, M., Wainwright, M. A., Wright, M. J., & Martin, N. G. (2006). The heritability of conscientiousness facets and their relationshp to IQ and academic achievement. *Personality and Individual Differences, 40,* 1189–1199. (14)

Luciano, M., Wright, M. J., Smith, G. A., Geffen, G. M., Geffen, L. B., & Martin, N. G. (2001). Genetic covariance among measures of information processing speed, working memory, and IQ. *Behavior Genetics, 31,* 581–592. (9)

Lucio, E., Ampudia, A., Durán, C., León, I., & Butcher, J. N. (2001). Comparison of the Mexican and American norms of the MMPI-2. *Journal of Clinical Psychology, 57,* 1459–1468. (14)

Lui, S., Deng, W., Huang, X., Jiang, L., Ma, X., Chen, H., . . . Gong, Q. (2009). Association of cerebral deficits with clinical symptoms in antipsychotic-naïve first-episode schizophrenia: An optimized voxel-based morphometry and resting state functional connectivity study. *American Journal of Psychiatry, 166,* 196–205. (15)

Luk, G., Bialystok, E., Craik, F. I. M., & Grady, C. L. (2011). Lifelong bilingualism maintains white matter integrity in older adults. *Journal of Neuroscience, 31,* 16808–16813. (8)

Luna, B., Padmanabhan, A., & O'Hearn, K. (2010). What has fMRI told us about the development of cognitive control through adolescence? *Brain and Cognition, 72,* 101–113. (5)

Luppino, F. S., de Wit, L. M., Bouvy, P. F., Stijnen, T., Cuijpers, P., . . . Zitman, F. G. (2010). Overweight, obesity, and depression. *Archives of General Psychiatry, 67,* 220–229. (11)

Lykken, D., & Tellegan, A. (1996). Happiness is a stochastic phenomenon. *Psychological Science, 7,* 186–189. (12)

Lykken, D. T. (1979). The detection of deception. *Psychological Bulletin, 86,* 47–53. (12)

Lykken, D. T., Bouchard, T. J., Jr., McGue, M., & Tellegen, A. (1993). Heritability of interests: A twin study. *Journal of Applied Psychology, 78,* 649–661. (3)

Lykken, D. T., McGue, M., Tellegen, A., & Bouchard, T. J. (1992). Emergenesis: Genetic traits that may not run in families. *American Psychologist, 47,* 1565–1577. (3)

Lyn, H., Greenfield, P. M., Savage-Rumbaugh, S., Gillespie-Lynch, K., & Hopkins, W. D. (2011). Nonhuman primates do declare! A comparison of declarative symbol and gesture use in two children, two bonobos, and a chimpanzee. *Language & Communication, 31,* 63–74. (8)

Lynam, D. R. (1996). Early identification of chronic offenders: Who is the fledgling psychopath? *Psychological Bulletin, 120,* 209–234. (13)

Lynn, R. (2009). What has caused the Flynn effect? Secular increases in the developmental quotients of infants. *Intelligence, 37,* 16–24. (9)

Lyons, M. J., Eisen, S. A., Goldberg, J., True, W., Lin, N., Meyer, J. M., . . . Tsuang, M. T. (1998). A registry-based twin study of depression in men. *Archives of General Psychiatry, 55,* 468–472. (15)

Lyons, M. J., York, T. P., Franz, C. E., Grant, M. D., Eaves, L. J., Jacobson, K. C., . . . Kremen, W. S. (2009). Genes determine stability and the environment determines change in cognitive ability during 35 years of adulthood. *Psychological Science, 20,* 1146–1152. (9)

Lyubomirsky, S., & Boehm, J. K. (2010). Human motives, happiness, and the puzzle of parenthood: Commentary on Kenrick et al. (2010). *Perspectives on Psychological Science, 5,* 327–334. (12)

Lyubomirsky, S., Dickerhoof, R., Boehm, J. K., & Sheldon, K. M. (2011). Becoming happier takes both a will and a proper way: An experimental longitudinal intervention to boost well-being. *Emotion, 11,* 391–402. (12)

Lyubomirsky, S., King, L., & Diener, E. (2005). The benefits of frequent positive affect: Does happiness lead to success? *Psychological Bulletin, 131,* 803–855. (12)

Ma-Kellams, C., & Blascovich, J. (2011). Culturally divergent responses to mortality salience. *Psychological Science, 22,* 1019–1024. (5)

MacCallum, F., & Golombek, S. (2004). Children raised in fatherless families from infancy: A follow-up of children of lesbian and single heterosexual mothers at early adolescence. *Journal of Child Psychology and Psychiatry, 45,* 1407–1419. (5)

Machin, S., & Pekkarinen, T. (2008). Global sex differences in test score variability. *Science, 322,* 1331–1332. (9)

Macknik, S. L., King, M., Randi, J., Robbins, A., Teller, Thompson, J., & Martinez-Conde, S. (2008). Attention and awareness in stage magic: Turning tricks into research. *Nature Reviews Neuroscience, 9,* 871–879. (8)

MacLean, K. A., Ferrer, E., Aichele, S. R., Bridwell, D. A., Zanesco, A.P., Jacobs, T.L., . . . Saron, C.D. (2010). Intensive meditation training improves perceptual discrimination and sustained attention. *Psychological Science, 21,* 829–839. (10)

Macmillan, M. (1997). *Freud evaluated.* Cambridge, MA: MIT Press. (14)

Madson, L. (2005). Demonstrating the importance of question wording on surveys. *Teaching of Psychology, 32,* 40–43. (2)

Magen, E., Dweck, C. S., & Gross, J. J. (2008). The hidden-zero effect. *Psychological Science, 19,* 648–649. (8)

Magnuson, K. A., & Duncan, G. J. (2006). The role of socioeconomic resources in the Black-White test score gap among young children. *Developmental Review, 26,* 365–399. (9)

Maguire, E. A., & Frith, C. D. (2003). Lateral asymmetry in the hippocampal response to the remoteness of autobiographical memories. *Journal of Neuroscience, 23,* 5302–5307. (7)

Mahfouz, A. Y., Philaretou, A. G., & Theocharous, A. (2008). Virtual social interactions: Evolutionary, social psychological and technological perspectives. *Computers in Human Behavior, 24,* 3014–3026. (13, 14)

Mahowald, M. W., & Schenck, C. H. (2005). Insights from studying human sleep disorders. *Nature, 437,* 1279–1285. (10)

Maier, S. F., & Watkins, L. R. (1998). Cytokines for psychologists: Implications of bidirectional immune-to-brain communication for understanding behavior, mood, and cognition. *Psychological Review, 105,* 83–107. (12)

Maki, R. H. (1990). Memory for script actions: Effects of relevance and detail expectancy. *Memory and Cognition, 18*, 5–14. (7)

Malamed, F., & Zaidel, E. (1993). Language and task effects on lateralized word recognition. *Brain and Language, 45*, 70–85. (8)

Maldonado, R., Saiardi, A., Valverde, O., Samad, T. A., Roques, B. P., & Borrelli, E. (1997). Absence of opiate rewarding effects in mice lacking dopamine D2 receptors. *Nature, 388*, 586–589. (3)

Malmquist, C. P. (1986). Children who witness parental murder: Posttraumatic aspects. *Journal of the American Academy of Child Psychiatry, 25*, 320–325. (7)

Malpass, R. S. (2006). A policy evaluation of simultaneous and sequential lineups. *Psychology, Public Policy, and Law, 12*, 394–418. (7)

Mameli, M., & Lüscher, C. (2011). Synaptic plasticity and addiction: Learning mechanisms gone awry. *Neuropharmacology, 61*, 1052–1059. (15)

Mangan, M. A. (2004). A phenomenology of problematic sexual behavior. *Archives of Sexual Behavior, 33*, 287–293. (10)

Mann, T., Nolen-Hoeksema, S., Huang, K., Burgard, D., Wright, A., & Hanson, K. (1997). Are two interventions worse than none? Joint primary and secondary prevention of eating disorders in college females. *Health Psychology, 16*, 215–225. (15)

Mann, T., Tomiyama, A. J., Westling, E., Lew, A.-M., Samuels, B., & Chatman, J. (2007). Medicare's search for effective obesity treatments. *American Psychologist, 62*, 220–233. (11)

Manning, R., Levine, M., & Collins, A. (2007). The Kitty Genovese murder and the social psychology of helping. *American Psychologist, 62*, 555–562. (13)

Manor, O., & Eisenbach, Z. (2003). Mortality after spousal loss: Are there socio-demographic differences? *Social Science and Medicine, 56*, 405–413. (12)

Maquet, P., Laureys, S., Peigneux, P., Fuchs, S., Petiau, C., Phillips, C., . . . Cleeremans, A. (2000). Experience-dependent changes in cerebral activation during human REM sleep. *Nature Neuroscience, 3*, 831–836. (10)

Marchand, A., Coutu, M.-F., Dupuis, G., Fleet, R., Borgeat, F., Todorov, C., . . . Mainguy, N. (2008). Treatment of panic disorder with agoraphobia: Randomized placebo-controlled trial of four psychosocial treatments combined with imipramine or placebo. *Cognitive Behaviour Therapy, 37*, 146–159. (15)

Marcia, J. E. (1980). Identity in adolescence. In J. Adelson (Ed.), *Handbook of adolescent psychology* (pp. 159–187). New York: Wiley. (5)

Marcus, G. F., Vijayan, S., Rao, S. B., & Vishton, P. M. (1999). Rule learning by seven-month-old infants. *Science, 283*, 77–80. (8)

Marian, V., & Neisser, U. (2000). Language-dependent recall of autobiographical memories. *Journal of Experimental Psychology: General, 129*, 361–368. (7)

Markey, P. M. (2000). Bystander intervention in computer-mediated intervention. *Computers in Human Behavior, 16*, 183–188. (13)

Marks, D., & Kammann, R. (1980). *The psychology of the psychic*. Buffalo, NY: Prometheus. (2, 14)

Marler, P., & Peters, S. (1981). Sparrows learn adult song and more from memory. *Science, 213*, 780–782. (6)

Marler, P., & Peters, S. (1982). Long-term storage of learned birdsongs prior to production. *Animal Behaviour, 30*, 479–482. (6)

Marriott, F. H. C. (1976). Abnormal colour vision. In H. Davson (Ed.), *The eye* (2nd ed., pp. 533–547). New York: Academic Press. (4)

Marsh, E. J., Meade, M. L., & Roediger, H. L., III. (2003). Learning facts from fiction. *Journal of Memory and Language, 49*, 519–536. (7)

Marsh, H. W., & Craven, R. G. (2006). Reciprocal effects of self-concept and performance from a multidimensional perspective. *Perspectives on Psychological Science, 1*, 133–163. (14)

Martens, A., Johns, M., Greenberg, J., & Schimel, J. (2006). Combating stereotype threat: The effect of self-affirmation on women's intellectual performance. *Journal of Experimental Social Psychology, 42*, 236–243. (9)

Martin, D. J., & Lynn, S. J. (1996). The hypnotic simulation index: Successful discrimination of real versus simulating participants. *International Journal of Clinical and Experimental Hypnosis, 44*, 338–353. (10)

Martindale, C. (2001). Oscillations and analogies: Thomas Young, MD, FRS, genius. *American Psychologist, 56*, 342–345. (4)

Martínez, K., & Colom, R. (2009). Working memory capacity and processing efficiency predict fluid but not crystallized and spatial intelligence: Evidence supporting the neural noise hypothesis. *Personality and Individual Differences, 46*, 281–286. (9)

Martsh, C. T., & Miller, W. R. (1997). Extraversion predicts heavy drinking in college students. *Personality and Individual Differences, 23*, 153–155. (14)

Maslow, A. H. (1962). *Toward a psychology of being*. Princeton, NJ: Van Nostrand. (14)

Maslow, A. H. (1970). *Motivation and personality* (2nd ed.). New York: Harper & Row. (11)

Maslow, A. H. (1971). *The farther reaches of human nature*. New York: Viking Press. (14)

Mason, A. E., Sbarra, D. A., & Mehl, M. R. (2010). Thin-slicing divorce: Thirty seconds of information predict changes in psychological adjustment over 90 days. *Psychological Science, 21*, 1420–1422. (13)

Mason, B. J., Goodman, A. M., Chabac, S., & Lehert, P. (2006). Effect of oral acamprosate on abstinence in patients with alcohol dependence in a double-blind, placebo-controlled trial: The role of patient motivation. *Journal of Psychiatric Research, 40*, 383–393. (15)

Mason, D. A., & Frick, P. J. (1994). The heritability of antisocial behavior: A meta-analysis of twin and adoption studies. *Journal of Psychopathology and Behavioral Assessment, 16*, 301–323. (5)

Mason, M. F., Norton, M. I., Van Horn, J. D., Wegner, D. M., Grafton, S. T., & Macrae, C. N. (2007). Wandering minds: The default network and stimulus-independent thought. *Science, 315*, 393–395. (3)

Massimini, M., Ferrarelli, F., Huber, R., Esser, S. K., Singh, H., & Tononi, G. (2005). Breakdown of cortical effective connectivity during sleep. *Science, 309*, 2228–2232. (10)

Masson, J. M. (1984). *The assault on truth*. New York: Farrar, Straus and Giroux. (14)

Masters, W. H., & Johnson, V. E. (1966). *Human sexual response*. Boston: Little, Brown. (11)

Matheny, A. P., Jr. (1989). Children's behavioral inhibition over age and across situations: Genetic similarity for a trait to change. *Journal of Personality, 57*, 215–235. (5)

Mathews, A., & Mackintosh, B. (2004). Take a closer look: Emotion modifies the boundary extension effect. *Emotion, 4*, 36–45. (12)

Matsunami, H., Montmayeur, J.-P., & Buck, L. B. (2000). A family of candidate taste receptors in human and mouse. *Nature, 404*, 601–604. (4)

Mattson, M. P., & Magnus, T. (2006). Ageing and neuronal variability. *Nature Reviews Neuroscience, 7*, 278–294. (5)

Mattson, S. N., Crocker, N., & Nguyen, T. T. (2011). Fetal alcoholism spectrum disorders: Neuropsychological and behavioral features. *Neuropsychology Review, 21*, 8–101. (5)

May, C. P., Hasher, L., & Stoltzfus, E. R. (1993). Optimal time of day and the magnitude of age differences in memory. *Psychological Science, 4*, 326–330. (10)

Mayberry, R. I., Lock, E., & Kazmi, H. (2002). Linguistic ability and early language exposure. *Nature, 415*, 1026–1029. (8)

Mayer, J. D., Caruso, D. R., & Salovey, P. (2000). Emotional intelligence meets traditional standards for an intelligence. *Intelligence, 27*, 267–298. (12)

Mayer, J. D., & Salovey, P. (1995). Emotional intelligence and the construction and regulation of feelings. *Applied and Preventive Psychology, 4*, 197–208. (12)

Mayer, J. D., & Salovey, P. (1997). What is emotional intelligence? In P. Salovey & D. J. Sluyter (Eds.). *Emotional development and emotional intelligence* (pp. 3–34). New York: Basic Books. (12)

Mayer, J. D., Salovey, P., Caruso, D. R., & Sitarenios, G. (2001). Emotional intelligence as a standard intelligence. *Emotion, 1*, 232–242. (12)

Mazar, N., Amir, O., & Ariely, D. (2008). The dishonesty of honest people: A theory of self-concept maintenance. *Journal of Marketing Research, 45*, 633–644. (11)

Mazzoni, G., & Memon, A. (2003). Imagination can create false autobiographical memories. *Psychological Science, 14*, 186–188. (7)

McCall, V. W., Yates, B., Hendricks, S., Turner, K., & McNabb, B. (1989). Comparison between the Stanford-Binet: L-M and the Stanford-Binet: Fourth edition with a group of gifted children. *Contemporary Educational Psychology, 114*, 93–96. (9)

McCall, W. A. (1939). *Measurement*. New York: Macmillan. (9)

McCaulley, M. H. (2000). Myers-Briggs Type Indicator: A bridge between counseling and consulting. *Consulting Psychology Journal: Practice and Research, 52*, 117–132. (14)

McClelland, J. L. (1988). Connectionist models and psychological evidence. *Journal of Memory and Language, 27*, 107–123. (8)

McClelland, J. L., & Rumelhart, D. E. (1981). An interactive activation model of context effects in letter perception: Part 1. An account of basic findings. *Psychological Review, 88*, 375–407. (8)

McClure, J. (1998). Discounting causes of behavior: Are two reasons better than one? *Journal of Personality and Social Psychology, 74*, 7–20. (13)

McCornack, R. L. (1983). Bias in the validity of predicted college grades in four ethnic minority groups. *Educational and Psychological Measurement, 43*, 517–522. (9)

McCourt, K., Bouchard, T. J., Jr., Lykken, D. T., Tellegen, A., & Keyes, M. (1999). Authoritarianism revisited: Genetic and environmental influences examined in twins reared apart and together. *Personality and Individual Differences, 27*, 985–1014. (5)

McCrae, R. R. (1996). Social consequences of experiential openness. *Psychological Bulletin, 120*, 323–337. (14)

McCrae, R. R., & Costa, P. T., Jr. (1987). Validation of the five-factor model of personality across instruments and observers. *Journal of Personality and Social Psychology, 52*, 81–90. (14)

McCrae, R. R., & Costa, P. T., Jr. (1997). Personality trait structure as a human universal. *American Psychologist, 52*, 509–516. (14)

McCrae, R. R., Costa, P. T., Jr., Ostendorf, F., Angleitner, A., Hrebíčková, M., Avia, M. D., . . . Smith, P. B. (2000). Nature over nurture: Temperament, personality, and life span development. *Journal of Personality and Social Psychology, 78*, 173–186. (14)

McCrea, S. M., Liberman, N., Trope, Y., & Sherman, S. J. (2008). Construal level and procrastination. *Psychological Science, 19*, 1308–1314. (11)

McCrink, K., & Wynn, K. (2004). Large-number addition and subtraction by 9-month-old infants. *Psychological Science, 15*, 776–781. (5)

McDaniel, M. A., Howard, D. C., & Einstein, G. O. (2009). The read-recite-review study strategy. *Psychological Science, 20*, 516–522. (7)

McDougall, W. (1938). Fourth report on a Lamarckian experiment. *British Journal of Psychology, 28*, 321–345, 365–395. (2)

McElheny, V. (2004). Three Nobelists ask: Are we ready for the next frontier? *Cerebrum, 5*, 69–81. (1)

McEwen, B. S. (2000). The neurobiology of stress: From serendipity to clinical relevance. *Brain Research, 886*, 172–189. (12)

McFadden, D. (2008). What do sex, twins, spotted hyenas, ADHD, and sexual orientation have in common? *Perspectives on Psychological Science, 3*, 309–323. (11)

McFarlane, A. C. (1997). The prevalence and longitudinal course of PTSD. *Annals of the New York Academy of Sciences, 821*, 10–23. (12)

McGovern, P. E., Glusker, D. L., Exner, L. J., & Voigt, M. M. (1996). Neolithic resinated wine. *Nature, 381*, 480–481. (3)

McGrath, J. J., Féron, F. P., Burne, T. H. J., Mackay-Sim, A., & Eyles, D. W. (2003). The neurodevelopmental hypothesis of schizophrenia: A review of recent developments. *Annals of Medicine, 35*, 86–93. (15)

McGregor, D. M. (1960). *The human side of enterprise.* New York: McGraw-Hill. (11)

McGue, M. (1999). The behavioral genetics of alcoholism. *Current Directions in Psychological Science, 8*, 109–115. (15)

McGue, M., & Bouchard, T. J., Jr. (1998). Genetic and environmental influences on human behavioral differences. *Annual Review of Neuroscience, 21*, 1–24. (9)

McGuire, S., & Clifford, J. (2000). Genetic and environmental contributions to loneliness in children. *Psychological Science, 11*, 487–491. (5)

McGurk, H., Caplan, M., Hennessy, E., & Moss, P. (1993). Controversy, theory, and social context in contemporary day care research. *Journal of Child Psychology, 34*, 3–23. (5)

McGurk, H., & MacDonald, J. (1976). Hearing lips and seeing voices. *Nature, 264*, 746–748. (8)

McIntyre, M., Gangestad, S. W., Gray, P. B., Chapman, J. F., Burnham, T. C., O'Rourke, M. T., . . . Thornhill, R. (2006). Romantic involvement often reduces men's testosterone levels—But not always: The moderating effect of extrapair sexual interest. *Journal of Personality and Social Psychology, 91*, 642–651. (11)

McIntyre, R. S., Konarski, J. Z., Wilkins, K., Soczynska, J. K., & Kennedy, S. H. (2006). Obesity in bipolar disorder and major depressive disorder: Results from a national community health survey on mental health and well-being. *Canadian Journal of Psychiatry, 51*, 274–280. (11)

McKee, S. A., Sinha, R., Weinberger, A. H., Sofuoglu, M., Harrison, E. L. R., . . . Wanzer, J. (2010). Stress decreases the ability to resist smoking and potentiates smoking intensity and reward. *Journal of Psychopharmacology, 25*, 490–502. (15)

McKelvey, M. W., & McKenry, P. C. (2000). The psychosocial well-being of Black and White mothers following marital dissolution. *Psychology of Women Quarterly, 24*, 4–14. (5)

McKinnon, J. D., & Bennett, C. E. (2005). *We the people: Blacks in the United States.* Washington, DC: U.S. Census Bureau. (9)

McMurtry, P. L., & Mershon, D. H. (1985). Auditory distance judgments in noise, with and without hearing protection. *Proceedings of the Human Factors Society* (Baltimore), pp. 811–813. (4)

McNally, R. J. (1990). Psychological approaches to panic disorder: A review. *Psychological Bulletin, 108*, 403–419. (15)

McNally, R. J., Bryant, R. A., & Ehlers, A. (2003). Does early psychological intervention promote recovery from posttraumatic stress? *Psychological Science in the Public Interest, 4*, 45–77. (12)

McNally, R. J., & Geraerts, E. (2009). A new solution to the recovered memory debate. *Perspectives on Psychological Science, 4*, 126–134. (7)

McNamara, J. M., Barta, Z., Fromhage, L., & Houston, A. I. (2008). The coevolution of choosiness and cooperation. *Nature, 451*, 189–192. (13)

McNamara, P., McLaren, D., Smith, D., Brown, A., & Stickgold, R. (2005). A "Jekyll and Hyde" within: Aggressive versus friendly interactions in REM and non-REM dreams. *Psychological Science, 16*, 130–136. (10)

Mechelli, A., Crinion, J. T., Noppeney, U., O'Doherty, J., Ashburner, J., Frackowiak, R. S., . . . Price, C. J. (2004). Structural plasticity in the bilingual brain. *Nature, 431*, 757. (8)

Meddis, R., Pearson, A. J. Z., & Langford, G. (1973). An extreme case of healthy insomnia. *EEG and Clinical Neurophysiology, 35*, 213–214. (10)

Medver, V. H., Madey, S. F., & Gilovich, T. (1995). When less is more: Counterfactual thinking and satisfaction among Olympic athletes. *Journal of Personality and Social Psychology, 69*, 603–610. (12)

Meeter, M., & Murre, J. M. J. (2004). Consolidation of long-term memory: Evidence and alternatives. *Psychological Bulletin, 130*, 843–857. (7)

Mehl, M. R., Vazire, S., Holleran, S. E., & Clark, C. S. (2010). Eavesdropping on happiness: Well-being is related to having less small talk and more substantive conversations. *Psychological Science, 21*, 539–541. (12)

Meichenbaum, D. (1985). *Stress inoculation training.* New York: Pergamon Press. (12)

Meichenbaum, D., & Cameron, R. (1983). Stress inoculation training. In D. Meichenbaum & M. E. Jaremko (Eds.), *Stress reduction and prevention* (pp. 115–154). New York: Plenum Press. (12)

Meinz, E. J., & Hambrick, D. Z. (2010). Deliberate practice is necessary but not sufficient to explain individual differences in piano sight-reading skill: The role of working memory capacity. *Psychological Science, 21*, 914–919. (8)

Melamed, S., Shirom, A., Toker, S., Berliner, S., & Shapira, I. (2006). Burnout and risk of cardiovascular disease: Evidence, possible causal paths, and promising research directions. *Psychological Bulletin, 132*, 327–353. (11)

Melchers, K. G., Ungor, M., & Lachnit, H. (2005). The experimental task influences cue competition in human causal learning. *Journal of Experimental Psychology: Animal Behavior Processes, 31*, 477–483. (6)

Meltzoff, A. N., & Moore, M. K. (1977). Imitation of facial and manual gestures by human neonates. *Science, 198*, 75–78. (3)

Melzack, R., & Wall, P. D. (1965). Pain mechanisms: A new theory. *Science, 150*, 971–979. (4)

Melzack, R., Weisz, A. Z., & Sprague, L. T. (1963). Stratagems for controlling pain: Contributions of auditory stimulation and suggestion. *Experimental Neurology, 8*, 239–247. (12)

Mendieta-Zéron, H., López, M., & Diéguez, C. (2008). Gastrointestinal peptides controlling body weight homeostasis. *General and Comparative Endocrinology, 155*, 481–495. (11)

Mendoza-Denton, R., & Page-Gould, E. (2008). Can cross-group friendships influence minority students' well-being at historically White universities? *Psychological Science, 19*, 933–939. (13)

Merckelbach, H, Dekkers, T., Wessel, I., & Roefs, A. (2003). Dissociative symptoms and amnesia in Dutch concentration camp survivors. *Comprehensive Psychiatry, 44*, 65–69. (7)

Mershon, D. H., & King, L. E. (1975). Intensity and reverberation as factors in the auditory perception of egocentric distance. *Perception and Psychophysics, 18*, 409–415. (4)

Meshi, D., Drew, M. R., Saxe, M., Ansorge, M. S., David, D., Santarelli, L., . . . Hen, R. (2006). Hippocampal neurogenesis is not required for behavioral effects of environmental enrichment. *Nature Neuroscience, 9*, 729–731. (3)

Messinger, D. S. (2002). Positive and negative: Infant facial expressions and emotions. *Current Directions in Psychological Science, 11*, 1–6. (12)

Messner, C., & Wänke, M. (2011). Good weather for Schwarz and Clore. *Emotion, 11*, 436–437. (12)

Meuret, A. E., Rosenfield, D., Wilhelm, F. H., Zhou, E., Conrad, A., . . . Roth, W. T. (2011). Do unexpected panic attacks occur spontaneously? *Biological Psychiatry, 70*, 985–991. (15)

Meyer-Bahlburg, H. F. L., Dolezal, C., Baker, S. W., & New, M. I. (2008). Sexual orientation in women with classical or non-classical congenital adrenal hyperplasia as a function of degree of prenatal androgen excess. *Archives of Sexual Behavior, 37*, 85–99. (11)

Meyer-Lindenberg, A., Mervis, C. B., & Berman, K. F. (2006). Neural mechanisms in Williams syndrome: A unique window to genetic influences on cognition and behaviour. *Nature Reviews Neuroscience, 7*, 380–393. (8)

Meyer, J. P., Becker, T. E., & Vandenberghe, C. (2004). Employee commitment and motivation: A conceptual analysis and integrative model. *Journal of Applied Psychology, 89*, 991–1007. (11)

Mezzanotte, W. S., Tangel, D. J., & White, D. P. (1992). Waking genioglossal electromyogram in sleep apnea patients versus normal controls (a neuromuscular compensatory mechanism).

Journal of Clinical Investigation, 89, 1571–1579. (10)

Miellet, S., O'Donnell, P. J., & Sereno, S. C. (2009). Parafoveal magnification. *Psychological Science, 20,* 721–728. (8)

Milar, K. S. (2000). The first generation of women psychologists and the psychology of women. *American Psychologist, 55,* 616–619. (1)

Milgram, S. (1974). *Obedience to authority.* New York: Harper & Row. (13)

Milich, R., Wolraich, M., & Lindgren, S. (1986). Sugar and hyperactivity: A critical review of empirical findings. *Clinical Psychology Review, 6,* 493–513. (2)

Milkman, K. L., Rogers, T., & Bazerman, M. H. (2008). Harnessing our inner angels and demons. *Perspectives on Psychological Science, 3,* 324–338. (11)

Miller, C. T., Dibble, E., & Hauser, M. D. (2001). Amodal completion of acoustic signals by a nonhuman primate. *Nature Neuroscience, 4,* 783–784. (4)

Miller, D. T., & Ross, M. (1975). Self-serving biases in the attribution of causality: Fact or fiction? *Psychological Bulletin, 82,* 213–225. (13)

Miller, G. (2007a). Animal extremists get personal. *Science, 318,* 1856–1858. (2)

Miller, G. (2007b). The mystery of the missing smile. *Nature, 316,* 826–827. (12)

Miller, G. A. (1956). The magical number seven, plus or minus two: Some limits on our capacity for processing information. *Psychological Review, 63,* 81–97. (7)

Miller, G. E., & Wrosch, C. (2007). You've gotta know when to fold 'em. *Psychological Science, 18,* 773–777. (11)

Miller, J., Shepherdson, P., & Trevena, J. (2011). Effects of clock monitoring on electroencephalographic activity: Is unconscious movement initiation an artifact of the clock? *Psychological Science, 22,* 103–109. (10)

Miller, L. C., & Fishkin, S. A. (1997). On the dynamics of human bonding and reproductive success: Seeking windows on the adapted-for human–environmental interface. In J. A. Simpson & D. T. Kenrick (Eds.), *Evolutionary social psychology* (pp. 197–235). Mahwah, NJ: Erlbaum. (2)

Miller, S. L., & Maner, J. K. (2010). Scent of a woman: Men's testosterone responses to olfactory ovulation cues. *Psychological Science, 21,* 276–283. (4)

Milne, S. E., Orbell, S., & Sheeran, P. (2002). Combining motivational and volitional interventions to promote exercise participation: Protection motivation theory and implementation intentions. *British Journal of Health Psychology, 7,* 163–184. (11)

Milner, B. (1959). The memory defect in bilateral hippocampal lesions. *Psychiatric Research Reports, 11,* 43–52. (7)

Milton, J., & Wiseman, R. (1999). Does psi exist? Lack of replication of an anomalous process of information. *Psychological Bulletin, 125,* 387–391. (2)

Minde, K., Minde, R., & Vogel, W. (2006). Culturally sensitive assessment of attachment in children aged 18–40 months in a South African township. *Infant Mental Health Journal, 27,* 544–558. (5)

Mineka, S. (1987). A primate model of phobic fears. In H. Eysenck & I. Martin (Eds.), *Theoretical foundations of behavior therapy* (pp. 81–111). New York: Plenum Press. (15)

Mineka, S., Davidson, M., Cook, M., & Keir, R. (1984). Observational conditioning of snake fear in rhesus monkeys. *Journal of Abnormal Psychology, 93,* 355–372. (15)

Mineka, S., & Zinbarg, R. (2006). A contemporary learning theory perspective on the etiology of anxiety disorders. *American Psychologist, 61,* 10–26. (15)

Mingroni, M. A. (2004). The secular rise in IA: Giving heterosis a closer look. *Intelligence, 32,* 65–83. (9)

Minto, C. L., Liao, L.-M., Woodhouse, C. R. J., Ransley, P. G., & Creighton, S. M. (2003). The effect of clitoral surgery on sexual outcome in individuals who have intersex conditions with ambiguous genitalia: A cross-sectional study. *Lancet, 361,* 1252–1257. (11)

Mischel, W. (1973). Toward a cognitive social learning reconceptualization of personality. *Psychological Review, 80,* 252–283. (14)

Mischel, W. (1981). Current issues and challenges in personality. In L. T. Benjamin, Jr. (Ed.), *The G. Stanley Hall Lecture Series* (Vol. 1, pp. 81–99). Washington, DC: American Psychological Association. (14)

Misrahi, M., Meduri, G., Pissard, S., Bouvattier, C., Beau, I., Loosfelt, H., . . . Bougneres, P. (1997). Comparison of immunocytochemical and molecular features with the phenotype in a case of incomplete male pseudohermaphroditism associated with a mutation of the luteinizing hormone receptor. *Journal of Clinical Endocrinology and Metabolism, 82,* 2159–2165. (11)

Miyake, A., Kost-Smith, L. E., Finkelstein, N. D., Pollock, S. J., Cohen, G. L., & Ito, T. A. (2010). Reducing the gender achievement gap in college science: A classroom study of values affirmation. *Science, 330,* 1234–1237. (9)

Miyamoto, Y., Nisbett, R. E., & Masuda, T. (2006). Culture and the physical environment. *Psychological Science, 17,* 113–119. (13)

Mobbs, D., Yu, R., Meyer, M., Passamonti, L., Seymour, B., Calder, A. J., . . . Dalgleish, T. (2009). A key role for similarity in vicarious reward. *Science, 324,* 900. (6)

Mochizuki, T., Crocker, A., McCormack, S., Yanagisawa, M., Sakurai, T., & Scammell, T. E. (2004). Behavioral state instability in orexin knock-out mice. *Journal of Neuroscience, 24,* 6291–6300. (10)

Moitra, E., Dyck, I., Beard, C., Bjornsson, A. S., Sibrava, N. J., . . . Keller, M. B. (2011). Impact of stressful life events on the course of panic disorder in adults. *Journal of Affective Disorders, 134,* 373–376. (15)

Mojtabai, R., & Olfson, M. (2008). National trends in psychotherapy by office-based psychiatrists. *Archives of General Psychiatry, 65,* 962–970. (1)

Moller, H. J. (1992). Attempted suicide: Efficacy of different aftercare strategies. *International Clinical Psychopharmacology, 6*(Suppl. 6), 58–59. (15)

Mondloch, C. J., Leis, A., & Maurer, D. (2006). Recognizing the face of Johnny, Suzy, and me: Insensitivity to the spacing among features at 4 years of age. *Child Development, 77,* 234–243. (5)

Money, J., & Ehrhardt, A. A. (1972). *Man & woman, boy & girl.* Baltimore: Johns Hopkins University Press. (11)

Monk, T. H., & Aplin, L. C. (1980). Spring and autumn daylight time changes: Studies of adjustment in sleep timings, mood, and efficiency. *Ergonomics, 23,* 167–178. (10)

Monroe, S. M., & Harkness, K. L. (2005). Life stress, the "kindling" hypothesis, and the recurrence of depression: Considerations from a life stress perspective. *Psychological Review, 112,* 417–445. (15)

Monroe, S. M., & Reid, M. W. (2009). Life stress and major depression. *Current Directions in Psychological Science, 18,* 68–72. (15)

Montgomery, G., & Kirsch, I. (1996). Mechanisms of placebo pain reduction: An empirical investigation. *Psychological Science, 7,* 174–176. (4)

Monti, M. M., Vanhaudenhuyse, A., Coleman, M. R., Boly, M., Pickard, J. D., Tshibanda, L., . . . Laureys, S. (2010). Willful modulation of brain activity in disorders of consciousness. *New England Journal of Medicine, 362,* 579–589. (10)

Montoya, A. G., Sorrentino, R., Lucas, S. E., & Price, B. H. (2002). Long-term neuropsychiatric consequences of "ecstasy" (MDMA): A review. *Harvard Review of Psychiatry, 10,* 212–220. (3)

Montoya, R. M. (2008). I'm hot, so I'd say you're not: The influence of objective physical attractiveness on mate selection. *Personality and Social Psychology Bulletin, 34,* 1315–1331. (13)

Moons, W. G., Mackie, D. M., & Garcia-Marques, T. (2009). The impact of repetition-induced familiarity on agreement with weak and strong arguments. *Journal of Personality and Social Psychology, 96,* 32–44. (13)

Moor, B. G., Crone, E. A., & van der Molen, M. W. (2010). The heartbrake of social rejection: heart rate deceleration in response to unexpected peer rejection. *Psychological Science, 21,* 1326–1333. (12)

Moorcroft, W. (1993). *Sleep, dreaming, and sleep disorders: An introduction* (2nd ed.). Lanham, MD: University Press of America. (10)

Moorcroft, W. H. (2003). *Understanding sleep and dreaming.* New York: Kluwer. (10)

Moore, B. C. J. (1989). *An introduction to the psychology of hearing* (3rd ed.). London: Academic Press. (4)

Moore, D. A., Swift, S. A., Sharek, Z. S., & Gino, F. (2010). Correspondence bias in performance evaluation: Why grade inflation works. *Personality and Social Psychology Bulletin, 36,* 843–852. (13)

Moore, D. S., & Johnson, S. P. (2008). Mental rotation in human infants. *Psychological Science, 19,* 1063–1066. (5)

Moore, E. G. J. (1986). Family socialization and the IQ test performance of traditionally and transracially adopted Black children. *Developmental Psychology, 22,* 317–326. (9)

Moore, F., Cassidy, C., & Perret, D. I. (2010). The effects of control of resources on magnitudes of sex differences in human mate preferences. *Evolutionary Psychology, 8,* 72–735. (13)

Moreau, M. E., & Corbin, W. R. (2010). Subjective response to alcohol: A critical review of the literature. *Alcoholism: Clinical and Experimental Research, 34,* 385–395. (15)

Moreno, S., Bialystok, E., Barac, R., Schellenberg, E. G., Cepeda, N. J., & Chau, T. (2011). Short-term music training enhances verbal intelligence and executive function, *Psychological Science, 22,* 1425–1433. (8)

Morewedge, C. K., & Norton, M. I. (2009). When dreaming is believing: The (motivated) interpretation of dreams. *Journal of Personality and Social Psychology, 96,* 249–264. (10)

Morgeson, F. P., Campion, M. A., Dipboye, R. L., Hollenbeck, J. R., Murphy, K., & Schmitt, N. (2007). Are we getting fooled again? Coming to terms with limitations in the use of personality tests for personnel selection. *Personnel Psychology, 60,* 1029–1049. (14)

Morris, G., & Baker-Ward, L. (2007). Fragile but real: Children's capacity to use newly acquired words to convey preverbal memories. *Child Development, 78*, 448–458. (7)

Morris, M., Lack. L., & Dawson, D. (1990). Sleep-onset insomniacs have delayed temperature rhythms. *Sleep, 13*, 1–14. (10)

Morris, S. Z., & Gibson, C. L. (2011). Corporal punishments influence on children's aggressive and delinquent behavior. *Criminal Justice and Behavior, 38*, 818–839. (6)

Moscovitch, M. (1985). Memory from infancy to old age: Implications for theories of normal and pathological memory. *Annals of the New York Academy of Sciences, 444*, 78–96. (7)

Moscovitch, M. (1989). Confabulation and the frontal systems: Strategic versus associative retrieval in neuropsychological theories of memory. In H. L. Roediger, III, & F. I. M. Craik (Eds.), *Varieties of memory and consciousness: Essays in honour of Endel Tulving* (pp. 133–160). Hillsdale, NJ: Erlbaum. (7)

Moscovitch, M. (1992). Memory and working-with-memory: A component process model based on modules and central systems. *Journal of Cognitive Neuroscience, 4*, 257–267. (7)

Moskowitz, B. A. (1978). The acquisition of language. *Scientific American, 239*(5), 92–108. (8)

Moss, E., Cyr, C., Bureau, J.-F., Tarabulsy, G. M., & Dubois-Comtois, K. (2005). Stability of attachment during the preschool period. *Developmental Psychology, 41*, 773–783. (5)

Moulin, C. J. A., Conway, M. A., Thompson, R. G., James, N., & Jones, R. W. (2005). Disordered memory awareness: Recollective confabulation in two cases of persistent déjà vecu. *Neuropsychologia, 43*, 1362–1378. (10)

Müller, M. M., Malinowski, P., Gruber, T., & Hillyard, S. A. (2003). Sustained division of the attentional spotlight. *Nature, 424*, 309–312. (8)

Murali, M. S. (2001). Epidemiological study of prevalence of mental disorders in India. *Indian Journal of Community Medicine, 26*, 198. (15)

Muraven, M., & Baumeister, R. F. (2000). Self-regulation and depletion of limited resources: Does self-control resemble a muscle? *Psychological Bulletin, 126*, 247–259. (12)

Murphy, G. L., & Medin, D. L. (1985). The role of theories in conceptual coherence. *Psychological Review, 92*, 289–316. (8)

Murphy, M. R., Checkley, S. A., Seckl, J. R., & Lightman, S. L. (1990). Naloxone inhibits oxytocin release at orgasm in man. *Journal of Clinical Endocrinology & Metabolism, 71*, 1056–1058. (11)

Murray, C., (2007). The magnitude and components of change in the black-white IQ difference from 1920 to 1991: A birth cohort analysis of the Woodcock-Johnson standardizations. *Intelligence, 35*, 305–318. (9)

Murray, C., Johnson, W., Wolf, M. S., & Deary, I. J. (2011). The association between cognitive ability across the lifespan and health literacy in old age: The Lothian birth cohort 1936. *Intelligence, 39*, 178–187. (9)

Murray, G., Nicholas, C. L., Kleiman, J., Dwyer, R., Carrington, M. J., Allen, N. B., . . . Trinder, J. (2009). Nature's clocks and human mood: The circadian system modulates reward motivation. *Emotion, 9*, 705–716. (10)

Murray, H. A. (1943). *Thematic Apperception Test manual.* Cambridge, MA: Harvard University Press. (14)

Musewicz, J., Marczyk, G., Knauss, L., & York, D. (2009). Current assessment practice, personality measurement, and Rorschach usage by psychologists. *Journal of Personality Assessment, 91*, 453–461. (14)

Must, O., te Nijenhuis, J., Must, A., & van Vianen, A. E. M. (2009). Comparability of IQ scores over time. *Intelligence, 37*, 25–33. (9)

Myers, D. G. (2000). The funds, friends, and faith of happy people. *American Psychologist, 55*, 56–67. (12)

Naab, P. J., & Russell, J. A. (2007). Judgments of emotion from spontaneous facial expressions of New Guineans. *Emotion, 7*, 736–744. (12)

Nadig, A. S., & Sedivy, J. C. (2002). Evidence of perspective-taking constraints in children's on-line reference resolution. *Psychological Science, 13*, 329–336. (5)

Nagy, E. (2011). Sharing the moment: The duration of embraces in humans. *Journal of Ethology, 29*, 389–393. (5)

Nairne, J. S., Pandeirada, J. N. S., Gregory, K. J., & Van Arsdall, J. E. (2009). Adaptive memory. *Psychological Science, 20*, 740–746. (7)

Nairne, J. S., Pandeirada, J. N. S., & Thompson, S. R. (2008). Adaptive memory: The comparative value of survival processing. *Psychological Science, 19*, 176–180. (7)

Nairne, J. S., Thompson, S. R., & Pandeirada, J. N. S. (2007). Adaptive memory: Survival processing enhances retention. *Journal of Experimental Psychology: Learning, Memory, and Cognition, 33*, 263–273. (7)

Najmabadi, H. Hu, H., Garshasbi, M., Zemojtel, T., Abedini, S. S., . . . Ropers, H. H. (2011). Deep sequencing reveals 50 novel genes for recessive cognitive disorders. *Nature, 478*, 57–63. (15)

Napier, J. L., & Jost, J. T. (2008). Why are conservatives happier than liberals? *Psychological Science, 19*, 565–572. (2)

National Institutes of Health. (2000). *The practical guide: Identification, evaluation, and treatment of overweight and obesity in adults* (NIH Publication No. 00-4084). Washington, DC: Author. (11)

Nebes, R. D. (1974). Hemispheric specialization in commissurotomized man. *Psychological Bulletin, 81*, 1–14. (3)

Nedjam, Z., Dalla Barba, G., & Pillon, B. (2000). Confabulation in a patient with fronto-temporal dementia and a patient with Alzheimer's disease. *Cortex, 36*, 561–577. (7)

Negy, C., Leal-Puente, L., Trainor, D. J., & Carlson, R. (1997). Mexican American adolescents' performance on the MMPIA. *Journal of Personality Assessment, 69*, 205–214. (14)

Neher, A. (1991). Maslow's theory of motivation: A critique. *Journal of Humanistic Psychology, 31*, 89–112. (14)

Neisser, U. (1997). Rising scores on intelligence tests. *American Scientist, 85*, 440–447. (9)

Nelissen, R. M. A., & Zeelenberg, M. (2009). When guilt evokes self-punishment: Evidence for the existence of a *Dobby effect. Emotion, 9*, 118–122. (12)

Nelson, C. A. III, Zeanah, C. H., Fox, N. A., Marshall, P. J., Smyke, A. T., & Guthrie, D. (2007). Cognitive recovery in socially deprived young children: The Bucharest Early Intervention Project. *Science, 318*, 1937–1940 (9)

Nelson, K., & Fivush, R. (2004). The emergence of autobiographical memory: A social cultural developmental theory. *Psychological Review, 111*, 486–511. (7)

Nemeth, C. (1972). A critical analysis of research utilizing the prisoner's dilemma paradigm for the study of bargaining. In L. Berkowitz (Ed.), *Advances in experimental social psychology* (Vol. 6, pp. 203–234). New York: Academic Press. (13)

Nemeth, C. J. (1986). Differential contributions of majority and minority influence. *Psychological Review, 93*, 23–32. (13)

Nettelbeck, T., & Wilson, C. (2004). The Flynn effect: Smarter not faster. *Intelligence, 32*, 85–93. (9)

Nettle, D. (2006). The evolution of personality variation in humans and other animals. *American Psychologist, 61*, 622–631. (14)

Newcombe, N. S., Sluzenski, J., & Huttenlocher, J. (2005). Preexisting knowledge versus on-line learning. *Psychological Science, 16*, 222–227. (5)

Newman, B. (1988, September 9). Dressing for dinner remains an issue in the naked city. *The Wall Street Journal*, p. 1. (13)

Nguyen, H.-H. D., & Ryan, A. M. (2008). Does stereotype threat affect test performance of minorities and women? A meta-analysis of experimental evidence. *Journal of Applied Psychology, 93*, 1314–1334. (9)

NICHD Early Child Care Research Network. (2006). Child-care effect sizes for the NICHD study of early child care and youth development. *American Psychologist, 61*, 99–116. (5)

Nichols, S. (2011). Experimental philosophy and the problem of free will. *Science, 331*, 1401–1403. (1)

Nicholson, H., Foote, C., & Gigerick, S. (2009). Deleterious effects of psychotherapy and counseling in the schools. *Psychology in the Schools, 46*, 232–237. (15)

Nickerson, C., Schwarz, N., Diener, E., & Kahneman, D. (2003). Zeroing in on the dark side of the American Dream: A closer look at the negative consequences of the goal for financial success. *Psychological Science, 14*, 531–536. (12)

Nickerson, D. W., & Rogers, T. (2010). Do you have a voting plan? Implementation intentions, vote turnout, and organic plan making. *Psychological Science, 21*, 194–199. (11)

Nickerson, R. S., & Adams, M. J. (1979). Long-term memory for a common object. *Cognitive Psychology, 11*, 287–307. (7)

Niebuhr, D. W., Millikan, A. M., Cowan, D. N., Yolken, R., Li, Y., & Weber, N. S. (2008). Selected infectious agents and risk of schizophrenia among U.S. military personnel. *American Journal of Psychiatry, 165*, 99–106. (15)

Nielsen, T. A., Zadra, A. L., Simard, V., Saucier, S., Stenstrom, P., Smith, C., . . . Kuiken, D. (2003). The typical dreams of Canadian university students. *Dreaming, 13*, 211–235. (10)

Nietzel, M.T., & Bernstein, D.A. (1987). *Introduction to clinical psychology.* Upper Saddle River, NJ: Prentice Hall. (9)

Niiya, Y., Ellsworth, P. C., & Yamaguchi, S. (2006). Amae in Japan and the United States: An exploration of a "culturally unique" emotion. *Emotion, 6*, 279–295. (12)

Niki, K., & Luo, J. (2002). An fMRI study on the time-limited role of the medial temporal lobe in long-term topographical autobiographic memory. *Journal of Cognitive Neuroscience, 14*, 500–507. (7)

Nikles, C. D., II, Brecht, D. L., Klinger, E., & Bursell, A. L. (1998). The effects of current-concern and nonconcern-related waking suggestions on nocturnal dream content. *Journal of Personality and Social Psychology, 75*, 242–255. (10)

Nilsson, L.-L., & Lögdberg, B. (2008). Dead and forgotten—Postmortem time before discovery as indicator of social isolation and inadequate mental healthcare in schizophrenia. *Schizophrenia Bulletin, 102,* 337-339. (15)

Nir, Y., & Tononi, G. (2010). Dreaming and the brain: From phenomenology to neurophysiology. *Trends in Cognitive Sciences, 14,* 88-100. (10)

Nisbet, E. K., & Zelenski, J. M. (2011). Underestimating nearby nature: Affective forecasting errors obscure the happy path to sustainability. *Psychological Science, 22,* 1101-1106. (12)

Nisbett, R. E., Peng, K., Choi, I., & Norenzayan, A. (2001). Culture and systems of thought: Holistic versus analytic cognition. *Psychological Review, 108,* 291-310. (13)

Noaghiul, S., & Hibbeln, J. R. (2003). Cross-national comparisons of seafood consumption and rates of bipolar disorders. *American Journal of Psychiatry, 160,* 2222-2227. (15)

Nobile, M., Rusconi, M., Bellina, M., Marino, C., Giorda, R., Carlet, O., . . . Battaglia, M. (2010). COMT Val158Met polymorphism and socioeconomic status interact to predict attention deficit/hyperactivity problems in children aged 10-14. *European Child & Adolescent Psychiatry, 19,* 549-557. (8)

Noel, J. G., Wann, D. L., & Branscombe, N. R. (1995). Peripheral ingroup membership status and public negativity toward outgroups. *Journal of Personality and Social Psychology, 68,* 127-137. (13)

Nolen-Hoeksema, S., & Watkins, E. R. (2011). A heuristic for developing transdiagnostic models of psychopathology: Explaining multifinality and divergent trajectories. *Perspectives on Psychological Science, 6,* 589-609. (15)

Norcross, J. C., Kohout, J. L., & Wicherski, M. (2005). Graduate study in psychology: 1971 to 2004. *American Psychologist, 60,* 959-975. (1)

Nordenström, A., Servin, A., Bohlin, G., Larsson, A., & Wedell, A. (2002). Sex-typed toy play behavior correlates with the degree of prenatal androgen exposure assessed by CYP21 genotype in girls with congenital adrenal hyperplasia. *Journal of Clinical Endocrinology and Metabolism, 87,* 5119-5124. (5, 11)

Nordgren, L. F., McDonnell, M.-H. M., & Loewenstein, G. (2011). What constitutes torture? Psychological impediments to an objective evaluation of enhanced interrogation tactics. *Psychological Science, 22,* 689-694. (13)

Nordgren, L. F., van Harreveld, F., & van der Pligt, J. (2009). The restraint bias. *Psychological Science, 20,* 1523-1528. (11)

Norman, R. A., Tataranni, P. A., Pratley, R., Thompson, D. B., Hanson, R. L., Prochazka, M., . . . Ravussin, E. (1998). Autosomal genomic scan for loci linked to obesity and energy metabolism in Pima Indians. *American Journal of Human Genetics, 62,* 659-668. (11)

Norton, M. I., Frost, J. H., & Ariely, D. (2007). Less is more: The lure of ambiguity, or why familiarity breeds contempt. *Journal of Personality and Social Psychology, 92,* 97-105. (13)

Nosek, B. A., & Banaji, M. R. (2001). The go/no-go association task. *Social Cognition, 19,* 625-664. (13)

Nowak, M. A., & Sigmund, K. (2005). Evolution of indirect reciprocity. *Nature, 437,* 1291-1298. (13)

Nussbaum, A. D., & Dweck, C. S. (2008). Defensiveness versus remediation: Self-theories and modes of self-esteem maintenance. *Personality and Social Psychology Bulletin, 34,* 599-612. (14)

O'Connell, K. A., Schwartz, J. E., & Shiffman, S. (2008). Do resisted temptations during smoking cessation deplete or augment self-control resources? *Psychology of Addictive Behaviors, 22,* 486-495. (11)

O'Connor, A. R., & Moulin, C. J. A. (2008). The persistence of erroneous familiarity in an epileptic male: Challenging perceptual theories of déjà vu activation. *Brain and Cognition, 68,* 144-147. (10)

O'Kane, G., Kensinger, E. A., & Corkin, S. (2004). Evidence for semantic learning in profound amnesia: An investigation with patient H. M. *Hippocampus, 14,* 417-425. (7)

O'Neill, T. A., & Hastings, S. E. (2011). Explaining workplace deviance behavior with more than just the "Big Five." *Personality and Individual Differences, 50,* 268-273. (14)

O'Toole, B. I. (1990). Intelligence and behaviour and motor vehicle accident mortality. *Accident Analysis and Prevention, 22,* 211-221. (9)

Odell, S. M., & Commander, M. J. (2000). Risk factors for homelessness among people with psychotic disorders. *Social Psychiatry and Psychiatric Epidemiology, 35,* 396-401. (15)

Odinot, G., Wolters, G., & van Koppen, P. J. (2009). Eyewitness memory of a supermarket robbery: A case study of accuracy and confidence after 3 months. *Law and Human Behavior, 33,* 506-514. (7)

Ohayon, M. M. (1997). Prevalence of *DSM-IV* diagnostic criteria of insomnia: Distinguishing insomnia related to mental disorders from sleep disorders. *Journal of Psychiatric Research, 31,* 333-346. (10)

Öhman, A., Eriksson, A., & Olofsson, C. (1975). One-trial learning and superior resistance to extinction of autonomic responses conditioned to potentially phobic objects. *Journal of Comparative and Physiological Psychology, 88,* 619-627. (15)

Öhman, A., & Mineka, S. (2003). The malicious serpent: Snakes as a prototypical stimulus for an evolved module of fear. *Current Directions in Psychological Science, 12,* 5-9. (15)

Oishi, S. (2010). The psychology of residential mobility: Implications for the self, social relationships, and well-being. *Perspectives on Psychological Science, 5,* 5-21. (5)

Oishi, S., Kesebir, S., & Diener, E. (2011). Income inequality and happiness. *Psychological Science, 22,* 1095-1100. (12)

Oishi, S., & Schimmack, U. (2010). Culture and well-being: A new inquiry into the psychological wealth of nations. *Perspectives on Psychological Science, 5,* 463-471. (12)

Okasha, M., McCarron, P., McEwen, J., & Smith, G. D. (2001). Age at menarche: Secular trends and association with adult anthropometric measures. *Annals of Human Biology, 28,* 68-78. (5)

Olausson, H., Lamarre, Y., Backlund, H., Morin, C., Wallin, B. G., Starck, G., . . . Bushnell, M. C. (2002). Unmyelinated tactile afferents signal touch and project to insular cortex. *Nature Neuroscience, 5,* 900-904. (3)

Oliet, S. H. R., Baimoukhametova, D. V., Piet, R., & Bains, J. S. (2007). Retrograde regulation of GABA transmission by the tonic release of oxytocin and endocannabinoids governs postsynaptic firing. *Journal of Neuroscience, 27,* 1325-1333. (3)

Olney, J. W., & Farger, N. B. (1995). Glutamate receptor dysfunction and schizophrenia. *Archives of General Psychiatry, 52,* 998-1007. (15)

Olsen, C. M. (2011). Natural rewards, neuroplasticity, and non-drug addictions. *Neuropharmacology, 61,* 1109-1122. (15)

Olson, M. A., & Fazio, R. H. (2003). Relations between implicit measures of prejudice: What are we measuring? *Psychological Science, 14,* 636-639. (13)

Ono, F., & Watanabe, K. (2011). Attention can retrospectively distort visual space. *Psychological Science, 22,* 472-477. (10)

Oriña, M. M., Collins, W. A., Simpson, J. A., Salvatore, J. E., Haydon, K. C., & Kim, J. S. (2011). Developmental and dyadic perspectives on commitment in adult romantic relationships. *Psychological Science, 22,* 908-915. (5)

Orne, M. T. (1959). The nature of hypnosis: Artifact and essence. *Journal of Abnormal and Social Psychology, 58,* 277-299. (10)

Orne, M. T. (1969). Demand characteristics and the concept of quasi-controls. In R. Rosenthal & R. L. Rosnow (Eds.), *Artifact in behavioral research* (pp. 143-179). New York: Academic Press. (2)

Orne, M. T. (1979). On the simulating subject as a quasi-control group in hypnosis research: What, why, and how. In E. Fromm & R. E. Shor (Eds.), *Hypnosis: Developments in research and new perspectives* (2nd ed., pp. 519-565). New York: Aldine. (10)

Orne, M. T., & Evans, F. J. (1965). Social control in the psychological experiment: Antisocial behavior and hypnosis. *Journal of Personality and Social Psychology, 1,* 189-200. (10)

Ortony, A., & Turner, T. J. (1990). What's basic about basic emotions? *Psychological Review, 97,* 315-331. (12)

Osofsky, J. D. (1995). The effects of exposure to violence on young children. *American Psychologist, 50,* 782-788. (13)

Ottati, V., & Lee, Y. T. (1995). Accuracy: A neglected component of stereotype research. In Y. T. Lee, L. J. Jussim, & C. R. McCauley (Eds.), *Stereotype accuracy* (pp. 29-59). Washington, DC: American Psychological Association. (13)

Otto, K., Boos, A., Dalbert, C., Schöps, D., & Hoyer, J. (2006). Posttraumatic symptoms, depression, and anxiety of flood victims: The impact of the belief in a just world. *Personality and Individual Differences, 40,* 1075-1084. (14)

Otto, R. K., & Heilbrun, K. (2002). The practice of forensic psychology. *American Psychologist, 57,* 5-18. (1)

Owen, A. M., Coleman, M. R., Boly, M., Davis, M. H., Laureys, S., & Pickard, J. D. (2006). Detecting awareness in the vegetative state. *Science, 313,* 1402. (10)

Oxley, D. R., Smith, K. B., Alford, J. R., Hibbing, M. V., Miller, J. L., Scalora, M., . . . Hibbing, J. R. (2008). Political attitudes vary with physiological traits. *Science, 321,* 1667-1670. (3)

Oyserman, D., Coon, H. M., & Kemmelmeier, M. (2002). Rethinking individualism and collectivism: Evaluation of theoretical assumptions and meta-analyses. *Psychological Bulletin, 128,* 3-72. (13)

Packer, D. J. (2009). Avoiding groupthink: Whereas weakly identified members remain silent, strongly identified members dissent about collective problems. *Psychological Science, 20,* 546-548. (13)

Padgham, C. A. (1975). Colours experienced in dreams. *British Journal of Psychology, 66,* 25-28. (10)

Paiva, V., Aranha, F., & Bastos, F. I. (2008). Opinions and attitudes regarding sexuality: Brazilian national research, 2005. *Revista de Saúde Pública, 42*(Suppl. 1). (11)

Paivandy, S., Bullock, E. E., Reardon, R. C., & Kelly, F. D. (2008). The effects of decision-making style and cognitive thought patterns on negative career thoughts. *Journal of Career Assessment, 16,* 474–488. (8)

Palinkas, L. A. (2003). The psychology of isolated and confined environments. *American Psychologist, 58,* 353–363. (10, 16)

Palop, J. J., Chin, J., & Mucke, L. (2006). A network dysfunction perspective on neurodegenerative diseases. *Nature, 443,* 768–773. (7)

Paluck, E. L. (2009). Reducing intergroup prejudice and conflict using the media: A field experiment in Rwanda. *Journal of Personality and Social Psychology, 96,* 574–587. (13)

Panayiotou, G., Kokkinos, C. M., & Spanoudis, G. (2004). Searching for the "big five" in a Greek context: The NEO-FFI under the microscope. *Personality and Individual Differences, 36,* 1841–1854. (14)

Panikashvili, D., Simeonidou, C., Ben-Shabat, S., Hanuš, L. Breuer, A., Mechoulam, E., . . . Shohami, E. (2001). An endogenous cannabinoid (2-AG) is neuroprotective after brain injury. *Nature, 413,* 527–531. (3)

Parish, W. L., Laumann, E. O., & Mojola, S. A. (2007). Sexual behavior in China: Trends and comparisons. *Population and Development Review, 33,* 729–756. (11)

Park, G., Lubinski, D., & Benbow, C. P. (2008). Ability differences among people who have commensurate degrees matter for scientific creativity. *Psychological Science, 19,* 957–961. (9)

Parke, R. D., Berkowitz, L., Leyens, J. P., West, S. G., & Sebastian, R. J. (1977). Some effects of violent and nonviolent movies on the behavior of juvenile delinquents. In L. Berkowitz (Ed.), *Advances in experimental social psychology* (Vol. 10, pp. 135–172). New York: Academic Press. (2)

Parker, E. S., Cahill, L., & McGaugh, J. L. (2006). A case of unusual autobiographical remembering. *Neurocase, 12,* 35–49. (7)

Parmeggiani, P. L. (1982). Regulation of physiological functions during sleep in mammals. *Experientia, 38,* 1405–1408. (10)

Parrott, A. C. (1999). Does cigarette smoking cause stress? *American Psychologist, 54,* 817–820. (3)

Parzuchowski, M., & Szymkow-Sudziarska, A. (2008). Well, slap my thigh: Expression surprise facilitates memory of surprising material. *Emotion, 8,* 430–434. (12)

Pashler, H., McDaniel, M., Rohrer, D., & Bjork, R. (2008). Learning styles: Concepts and evidence. *Psychological Science in the Public Interest, 9,* 105–119. (9)

Pasterski, V. L., Geffner, M. E., Brain, C., Hindmarsh, P., Brook, C., & Hines, M. (2005). Prenatal hormones and postnatal socialization by parents as determinants of male-typical toy play in girls with congenital adrenal hyperplasia. *Child Development, 76,* 264–278. (5, 11)

Pate, J. L., & Rumbaugh, D. M. (1983). The language-like behavior of Lana chimpanzee: Is it merely discrimination and paired-associate learning? *Animal Learning and Behavior, 11,* 134–138. (8)

Patterson, D. R. (2004). Treating pain with hypnosis. *Current Directions in Psychological Science, 13,* 252–255. (10)

Patterson, T., & Hayne, H. (2011). Does drawing facilitate older chldren's reports of emotionally laden events? *Applied Cognitive Psychology, 25,* 119–126. (7)

Paulhus, D. L., Trapnell, P. D., & Chen, D. (1999). Birth order effects on personality and achievement within families. *Psychological Science, 10,* 482–488. (5)

Paunonen, S. V., & Jackson, D. N. (2000). What is beyond the big five? Plenty! *Journal of Personality, 68,* 821–835. (14)

Paus, T., Marrett, S., Worsley, K. J., & Evans, A. C. (1995). Extraretinal modulation of cerebral blood flow in the human visual cortex: Implications for saccadic suppression. *Journal of Neurophysiology, 74,* 2179–2183. (8)

Pavlov, I. P. (1960). *Conditioned reflexes.* New York: Dover. (Original work published 1927) (6)

Pearce, J. M. (1994). Similarity and discrimination: A selective review and a connectionist model. *Psychological Review, 101,* 587–607. (6)

Pearl, P. L., Weiss, R. E., & Stein, M. A. (2001). Medical mimics. *Annals of the New York Academy of Sciences, 931,* 97–112. (8)

Pearlson, G. D., Petty, R. G., Ross, C. A., & Tien, A. Y. (1996). Schizophrenia—a disease of heteromodal association cortex. *Neuropsychopharmacology, 14,* 1–17. (15)

Peigneux, P., Laureys, S., Fuchs, S., Collette, F., Perrin, F., Reggers, J., . . . Maquet, P. (2004). Are spatial memories strengthened in the human hippocampus during slow wave sleep? *Neuron, 44,* 535–545. (10)

Pelham, W. E., Jr., & Fabiano, G. A. (2008). Evidence-based psychosocial treatments for attention-deficit/hyperactivity disorder. *Journal of Clinical Child and Adolescent Psychology, 37,* 184–214. (8)

Penfield, W., & Rasmussen, T. (1950). *The cerebral cortex of man.* New York: Macmillan. (3)

Peng, K., & Nisbett, R. E. (1999). Culture dialectics, and reasoning about contradiction. *American Psychologist, 54,* 741–754. (13)

Pennebaker, J. W. (1997). Writing about emotional experiences as a therapeutic process. *Psychological Science, 8,* 162–166. (12)

Pennebaker, J. W., & Graybeal, A. (2001). Patterns of natural language use: Disclosure, personality, and social integration. *Current Directions in Psychological Science, 10,* 90–93. (12)

Pennebaker, J. W., & Seagal, J. D. (1999). Forming a story: The health benefits of narrative. *Journal of Clinical Psychology, 55,* 1243–1254. (15)

Perani, D., & Abutalebi, J. (2005). The neural basis of first and second language processing. *Current Opinion in Neurobiology, 15,* 202–206. (8)

Peretz, I., Cummings, S., & Dube, M. P. (2007). The genetics of congenital amusia (tone deafness): A family-aggregation study. *American Journal of Human Genetics, 81,* 582–588. (4)

Perez, E. A. (1995). Review of the preclinical pharmacology and comparative efficacy of 5-hydroxytryptamine-3 receptor antagonists for chemotherapy-induced emesis. *Journal of Clinical Oncology, 13,* 1036–1043. (3)

Perry, D. G., & Bussey, K. (1979). The social learning theory of sex differences: Imitation is alive and well. *Journal of Personality and Social Psychology, 37,* 1699–1712. (14)

Person, C., Tracy, M., & Galea, S. (2006). Risk factors for depression after a disaster. *Journal of Nervous and Mental Disease, 194,* 659–666. (15)

Pert, C. B., & Snyder, S. H. (1973). The opiate receptor: Demonstration in nervous tissue. *Science, 179,* 1011–1014. (3, 4)

Pesta, B. J., & Poznanski, P. J. (2008). Black–White differences on IQ and grades: The mediating role of elementary cognitive tasks. *Intelligence, 36,* 323–329. (9)

Peters, F., Nicolson, N. A., Berkhof, J., Delespaul, P., & deVries, M. (2003). Effects of daily events on mood states in major depressive disorder. *Journal of Abnormal Psychology, 112,* 203–211. (15)

Peterson, C. (2011). Children's memory reports over time: Getting both better and worse. *Journal of Experimental Child Psychology, 109,* 275–293. (7)

Peterson, L. R., & Peterson, M. J. (1959). Short-term retention of individual verbal items. *Journal of Experimental Psychology, 58,* 193–198. (7)

Peterson, Z. D., Janssen, E., & Laan, E. (2010). Women's sexual responses to heterosexual and lesbian erotica: The role of stimulus intensity, affective reaction, and sexual history. *Archives of Sexual Behavior, 39,* 880–897. (11)

Petkov, C. I., Kayser, C., Steudel, T., Whittingstall, K., Augath, M., & Logothetis, N. K. (2008). A voice region in the monkey brain. *Nature Neuroscience, 11,* 367–374. (8)

Petrill, S. A., Luo, D., Thompson, L. A., & Detterman, D. K. (1996). The independent prediction of general intelligence by elementary cognitive tasks: Genetic and environmental influences. *Behavior Genetics, 26,* 135–147. (9)

Petrill, S. A., Plomin, R., Berg, S., Johansson, B., Pedersen, N. L., Ahern, F., . . . McClearn, G. E. (1998). The genetic and environmental relationship between general and specific cognitive abilities in twins age 80 and older. *Psychological Science, 9,* 183–189. (9)

Petrova, P. K., Cialdini, R. B., & Sills, S. J. (2006). Consistency-based compliance across cultures. *Journal of Experimental Psychology, 43,* 104–111. (13)

Petty, R. E., & Briñol, P. (2008). Persuasion: From single to multiple to metacognitive processes. *Perspectives on Psychological Science, 3,* 137–147. (13)

Petty, R. E., & Cacioppo, J. T. (1977). Effects of forewarning of persuasive intent and involvement on cognitive responses and persuasion. *Personality and Social Psychology Bulletin, 5,* 173–176. (13)

Petty, R. E., & Cacioppo, J. T. (1981). *Attitudes and persuasion: Classic and contemporary approaches.* Dubuque, IA: William C. Brown. (13)

Petty, R. E., & Cacioppo, J. T. (1986). *Communication and persuasion: Central and peripheral routes to attitude change.* New York: Springer-Verlag. (13)

Pezze, M. A., Bast, T., & Feldon, J. (2003). Significance of dopamine transmission in the rat medial prefrontal cortex for conditioned fear. *Cerebral Cortex, 13,* 371–380. (6)

Pfungst, O. (1911). *Clever Hans.* New York: Holt. (2)

Phan, K. L., Wager, T., Taylor, S. F., & Liberzon, I. (2002). Functional neuroanatomy of emotion: A meta-analysis of emotion activation studies in PET and fMRI. *NeuroImage, 16,* 331–348. (12)

Phelps, E. A., O'Connor, K. J., Cunningham, W. A., Funayama, E. S., Gatenby, J. C., Gore, J. C., . . . Banaji, M. R. (2000). Performance on indirect measures of race evaluation predicts amygdala activation. *Journal of Cognitive Neuroscience, 12,* 729–738. (13)

Phelps, M. E., & Mazziotta, J. C. (1985). Positron emission tomography: Human brain function and biochemistry. *Science, 228,* 799–809. (1, 3)

Philippot, P., Chapelle, G., & Blairy, S. (2002). Respiratory feedback in the generation of emotions. *Cognition and Emotion, 16,* 605–627. (12)

Phillips, T. M., & Pittman, J. F. (2007). Adolescent psychological well-being by identity style. *Journal of Adolescence, 30,* 1021–1034. (5)

Phinney, J. S. (1990). Ethnic identity in adolescents and adults: Review of research. *Psychological Bulletin, 108,* 499–514. (5)

Piaget, J. (1954). *The construction of reality in the child* (M. Cook, Trans.). New York: Basic Books. (Original work published 1937) (5)

Pichot, P. (1984). Centenary of the birth of Hermann Rorschach. *Journal of Personality Assessment, 48,* 591–596. (14)

Pierri, J. N., Volk, C. L. E., Auh, S., Sampson, A., & Lewis, D. A. (2001). Decreased somal size of deep layer 3 pyramidal neurons in the prefrontal cortex of subjects with schizophrenia. *Archives of General Psychiatry, 58,* 466–473. (15)

Pike, J. J., & Jennings, N. A. (2005). The effects of commercials on children's perceptions of gender appropriate toy use. *Sex Roles, 52,* 83–91. (5)

Pike, K. M., Hilbert, A., Wilfley, D. E., Fairburn, C. G., Dohm, F.-A., Walsh, B. T., . . . Striegel-Moore, R. (2007). Toward an understanding of risk factors for anorexia nervosa: A case-control study. *Psychological Medicine, 38,* 1443–1453. (11)

Pinel, J. P. J., Assanand, S., & Lehman, D. R. (2000). Hunger, eating, and ill health. *American Psychologist, 55,* 1105–1116. (11)

Pinker, S. (1994). *The language instinct.* New York: Morrow. (8)

Pinker, S. (2011). Taming the devil within us. *Naure, 478,* 309–311. (13)

Piolino, P., Desgranges, B., Benali, K., & Eustache, F. (2002). Episodic and semantic remote autobiographical memory in ageing. *Memory, 10,* 239–257. (7)

Pittenger, D. J. (2005). Cautionary comments regarding the Myers-Briggs Type Indicator. *Consulting Psychology Journal: Practice and Research, 57,* 210–221. (14)

Place, S. S., Todd, P. M., Penke, L., & Asendorpf, J. B. (2009). The ability to judge the romantic interest of others. *Psychological Science, 20,* 22–26. (13)

Plaut, D. C., & Booth, J. R. (2000). Individual and developmental differences in semantic priming: Empirical and computational support for a single-mechanism account of lexical priming. *Psychological Review, 107,* 786–823. (8)

Plaut, V. C., Thomas, K. M., & Goren, M. J. (2009). Is multiculturalism or color blindness better for minorities? *Psychological Science, 20,* 444–446. (13)

Plomin, R., Corley, R., DeFries, J. C., & Fulker, D. W. (1990). Individual differences in television viewing in early childhood: Nature as well as nurture. *Psychological Science, 1,* 371–377. (5)

Plomin, R., DeFries, J. C., McClearn, G. E., & McGuffin, P. (Eds.). (2001). *Behavioral genetics* (4th ed.) New York: Worth. (9)

Plomin, R., Fulker, D. W., Corley, R., & DeFries, J. C. (1997). Nature, nurture, and cognitive development from 1 to 16 years: A parent-offspring adoption study. *Psychological Science, 8,* 442–447. (9)

Plous, S. (1993). *The psychology of judgment and decision making.* Philadelphia: Temple University Press. (8)

Plous, S. (1996). Attitudes toward the use of animals in psychological research and education. *American Psychologist, 51,* 1167–1180. (2)

Plutchik, R. (1982). A psychoevolutionary theory of emotions. *Social Science Information, 21,* 529–553. (12)

Plutchik, R., & Ax, A. F. (1967). A critique of "determinants of emotional state" by Schachter and Singer (1962). *Psychophysiology, 4,* 79–82. (12)

Pockett, S., & Miller, A. (2007). The rotating spot method of timing subjective events. *Consciousness and Cognition, 16,* 241–254. (10)

Pole, N., Neylan, T. C., Best, S. R., Orr, S. P., & Marmar, C. R. (2003). Fear-potentiated startle and posttraumatic stress symptoms in urban police officers. *Journal of Traumatic Stress, 16,* 471–479. (12)

Polivy, J., & Herman, C. P. (1985). Dieting and binging: A causal analysis. *American Psychologist, 40,* 193–201. (11)

Polk, T. A., Drake, R. M., Jonides, J. J., Smith, M. R., & Smith, E. E. (2008). Attention enhances the neural processing of relevant features and suppresses the processing of irrelevant features in humans: A functional magnetic resonance imaging study of the Stroop task. *Journal of Neuroscience, 28,* 13786–13792. (8)

Pond, S. B., III, & Geyer, P. D. (1991). Differences in the relation between job satisfaction and perceived work alternatives among older and younger blue-collar workers. *Journal of Vocational Behavior, 39,* 251–262. (11)

Poole, D. A., & White, L. T. (1993). Two years later: Effect of question repetition and retention interval on the eyewitness testimony of children and adults. *Developmental Psychology, 29,* 844–853. (7)

Pope, H. G., Jr., Gruber, A. J., Hudson, J. I., Huestis, M. A., & Yurgelun-Todd, D. (2001). Neuropsychological performance in long-term cannabis users. *Archives of General Psychiatry, 58,* 909–915. (3)

Popper, K. (1986). Predicting overt behavior versus predicting hidden states. *Behavioral and Brain Sciences, 9,* 254–255. (14)

Porter, J., Craven, B., Khan, R. M., Chang, S.-J., Kang, I., Judkewicz, B., . . . Sobel, N. (2007). Mechanisms of scent-tracking in humans. *Nature Neuroscience, 10,* 27–29. (4)

Porter, S., Birt, A. R., Yuille, J. C., & Lehman, D. R. (2000). Negotiating false memories: Interviewer and rememberer characteristics relate to memory distortion. *Psychological Science, 11,* 507–510. (7)

Porter, S., & ten Brinke, L. (2008). Reading between the lies. *Psychological Science, 19,* 508–514. (12)

Post, R. M. (1992). Transduction of psychosocial stress into the neurobiology of recurrent affective disorder. *American Journal of Psychiatry, 149,* 999–1010. (15)

Posthuma, D., De Geus, E. J. C., Baaré, W. F. C., Pol, H. E. H., Kahn, R. S., & Boomsma, D. I. (2002). The association between brain volume and intelligence is of genetic origin. *Nature Neuroscience, 5,* 83–84. (9)

Powell, L. H., Calvin, J. E., III, & Calvin, J. E., Jr. (2007). Effective obesity treatments. *American Psychologist, 62,* 234–246. (11)

Powell, R. A., & Boer, D. P. (1994). Did Freud mislead patients to confabulate memories of abuse? *Psychological Reports, 74,* 1283–1298. (14)

Pratkanis, A. R. (1992, Spring). The cargo-cult science of subliminal perception. *Skeptical Inquirer, 16,* 260–272. (4)

Pratt, J., Radulescu, P. V., Guo, R. M., & Abrams, R. A. (2010). It's alive! Animate motion captures visual attention. *Psychological Science, 21,* 1724–1730. (8)

Principe, G. F., Kanaya, T., Ceci, S. J., & Singh, M. (2006). Believing is seeing. *Psychological Science, 17,* 243–248. (7)

Pronin, E. (2008). How we see ourselves and how we see others. *Science, 320,* 1177–1180. (13)

Pronin, E., Berger, J., & Molouki, S. (2007). Alone in a crowd of sheep: Asymmetric perceptions of conformity and their roots in an introspection error. *Journal of Personality and Social Psychology, 92,* 585–595. (13)

Pronin, E., Gilovich, T., & Ross, L. (2004). Objectivity in the eye of the beholder: Divergent perceptions of bias in self versus others. *Psychological Review, 111,* 781–799. (13)

Pronin, E., & Kugler, M. B. (2010). People believe they have more free will than others. *Proceedings of the National Academy of Sciences, 107,* 22469–22474. (1)

Provine, R. (2000). *Laughter.* New York: Viking Press. (2, 12)

Provine, R. R. (2012). *Quirks: Yawning, Laughing, Crying, Hiccupping, and Beyond.* Boston: Harvard University Press. (5)

Provine, R. R., Cabrera, M. O., Brocato, N. W., & Krosnowski, K. A. (2011). When the whites of the eyes are red: A uniquely human cue. *Ethology, 117,* 1–5. (12)

Provine, R. R., Krosnowski, K. A., & Brocato, N. W. (2009). Tearing: Breakthrough in human emotional signaling. *Evolutionary Psychology, 7,* 52–56. (12)

Public Agenda. (2001). *Medical research: Red flags.* Retrieved February 8, 2007, from http://www.publicagenda.org/charts/support-stem-cell-research-can-vary-dramatically-depending-question-wording-0. (2)

Pulver, C. A., & Kelly, K. R. (2008). Incremental validity of the Myers-Briggs Type Indicator in predicting academic major selection of undecided university students. *Journal of Career Assessment, 16,* 441–455. (14)

Purves, D., & Lotto, R. B. (2003). *Why we see what we do: An empirical theory of vision.* Sunderland, MA: Sinauer Associates. (4)

Purves, D., Williams, S. M., Nundy, S., & Lotto, R. B. (2004). Perceiving the intensity of light. *Psychological Review, 111,* 142–158. (4)

Pyc, M. A., & Rawson, K. A. (2010). Why testing improves memory: Mediator effectiveness hypothesis. *Science, 330,* 335. (7)

Pyszczynski, T., Greenberg, J., & Solomon, S. (2000). Proximal and distal defense: A new perspective on unconscious motivation. *Current Directions in Psychological Science, 9,* 156–160. (5)

Quadrel, M. J., Fischhoff, B., & Davis, W. (1993). Adolescent (in)vulnerability. *American Psychologist, 48,* 102–116. (5)

Quas, J. A., Malloy, L. C., Melinder, A., Goodman, G. S., D'Mello, M., & Schaaf, J. (2007). Developmental differences in the effects of repeated interviews and interview bias on young children's event memory and false reports. *Developmental Psychology, 43,* 823–837. (7)

Quattrocchi, M. R., & Schopp, R. F. (2005). Tarasaurus rex: A standard of care that could not adapt. *Psychology, Public Policy, and Law, 11,* 109–137. (15)

Quinn, P. C., & Liben, L. S. (2008). A sex difference in mental rotation in young infants. *Psychological Science, 19,* 1067–1070. (5)

Quoidbach, J., Dunn, E. W., Petrides, K. V., & Mikolajczak, M. (2010). Money giveth, money taketh away: The dual effect of wealth on happiness. *Psychological Science, 21,* 759–763. (12)

Radoeva, P. D., Prasad, S., Brainard, D. H., & Aguirre, G. K. (2008). Neural activity within area VI reflects unconscious visual performance in a case of blindsight. *Journal of Cognitive Neuroscience, 20,* 1927–1939. (3)

Rahman, Q., Andersson, D., & Govier, E. (2005). A specific sexual orientation-related difference in navigation strategy. *Behavioral Neuroscience, 119,* 311–316. (5)

Raine, A., Lencz, T., Bihrle, S., LaCasse, L., & Colletti, P. (2000). Reduced prefrontal gray matter volume and reduced autonomic activity in antisocial personality disorder. *Archives of General Psychiatry, 57,* 119–127. (13)

Rainville, P., Duncan, G. H., Price, D. D., Carrier, B., & Bushnell, M. C. (1997). Pain affect encoded in human anterior cingulate but not somatosensory cortex. *Science, 277,* 968–971. (10)

Rainville, P., Hofbauer, R. K., Bushnell, M. C., Duncan, G. H., & Price, D. D. (2002). Hypnosis modulates activity in brain structures involved in the regulation of consciousness. *Journal of Cognitive Neuroscience, 14,* 887–901. (10)

Rais, M., Cahn, W., Van Haren, N., Schnack, H., Caspers, E., . . . Kahn, R. (2008). Excessive brain volume loss over time in cannabis-using first-episode schizophrenia patients. *American Journal of Psychiatry, 165,* 490–496. (15)

Raison, C. L., Klein, H. M., & Steckler, M. (1999). The moon and madness reconsidered. *Journal of Affective Disorders, 53,* 99–106. (2)

Ramachandran, V. S. (2003, May). Hearing colors, tasting shapes. *Scientific American, 288*(5), 52–59. (4)

Ramachandran, V. S., & Blakeslee, S. (1998). *Phantoms in the brain.* New York: Morrow. (4)

Ramachandran, V. S., & Hirstein, W. (1998). The perception of phantom limbs: The D. O. Hebb lecture. *Brain, 121,* 1603–1630. (4)

Ramirez-Amaya, V., Marrone, D. F., Gage, F. H., Worley, P. F., & Barnes, C. A. (2006). Integration of new neurons into functional neural networks. *Journal of Neuroscience, 26,* 12237–12241. (3)

Ramírez-Esparza, N., Mehl, M. R., Álvarez-Bermúdez, J., & Pennebaker, J. W. (2009). Are Mexicans more or less sociable than Americans? Insights from a naturalistic observation study. *Journal of Research in Personality, 43,* 1–7. (14)

Ramirez, G., & Beilock, S. L. (2011). Writing about testing worries boosts exam performance in the classroom. *Science, 331,* 211–213. (9)

Ramirez, J. M., Santisteban, C., Fujihara, T., & Van Goozen, S. (2002). Differences between experience of anger and readiness to angry action: A study of Japanese and Spanish students. *Aggressive Behavior, 28,* 429–438. (12)

Ranganath, K. A., & Nosek, B. A. (2008). Implicit attitude generalization occurs immediately; explicit attitude generalization takes time. *Psychological Science, 19,* 249–254. (13)

Ransley, J. K., Donnelly, J. K., Botham, H., Khara, T. N., Greenwood, D. C., & Cade, J. E. (2003). Use of supermarket receipts to estimate energy and fat content of food purchased by lean and overweight families. *Appetite, 41,* 141–148. (11)

Rasch, B., & Born, J. (2008). Reactivation and consolidation of memory during sleep. *Current Directions in Psychological Science, 17,* 188–192. (10)

Raven, J. (2000). The Raven's Progressive Matrices: Change and stability over culture and time. *Cognitive Psychology, 41,* 1–48. (9)

Rayner, K. (1998). Eye movements in reading and information processing: 20 years of research. *Psychological Bulletin, 124,* 372–422. (8)

Rayner, K., White, S. J., Johnson, R. L., & Liversedge, S. P. (2006). Raeding wrods with jumbled lettres. *Psychological Science, 17,* 192–193. (8)

Raz, A., Kirsch, I., Pollard, J., & Nitkin-Kaner, Y. (2006). Suggestion reduces the Stroop effect. *Psychological Science, 17,* 91–95. (8)

Redding, R. E. (2001). Sociopolitical diversity in psychology. *American Psychologist, 56,* 205–215. (5)

Reed, A. E., Mikels, J. A., & Simon, K. I. (2008). Older adults prefer less choice than younger adults. *Psychology and Aging, 23,* 671–675. (8)

Reed, J. M., & Squire, L. R. (1999). Impaired transverse patterning in human amnesia is a special case of impaired memory for two-choice discrimination tasks. *Behavioral Neuroscience, 113,* 3–9. (7)

Reed, T. E. (1985). Ethnic differences in alcohol use, abuse, and sensitivity: A review with genetic interpretation. *Social Biology, 32,* 195–209. (15)

Rees, E., Moskvina, V., Owen, M. J., O'Donovan, M. C., & Kirov, G. (2011). De novo rates and selection of schizophrenia-associated copy number variants. *Biological Psychiatry, 70,* 1109–1114. (15)

Reicher, G. M. (1969). Perceptual recognition as a function of meaningfulness of stimulus material. *Journal of Experimental Psychology, 81,* 275–280. (8)

Reichle, E. D., Reineberg, A. E., & Schooler, J. W. (2010). Eye movements during mindless reading. *Psychological Science, 21,* 1300–1310. (8)

Reimann, M., & Zimbardo, P. G. (2011). The dark side of social encounters: Prospects for a neuroscience of human evil. *Journal of Neuroscience, Psychology, and Economics, 4,* 174–180. (13)

Reinius, B., Saetre, P., Leonard, J. A., Blekhman, R., Merino-Martinez, R., Gilad, Y., . . . Jazin, E. (2008). An evolutionarily conserved sexual signature in the primate brain. *PLoS Genetics, 4,* e1000100. (5)

Reisenzein, R. (1983). The Schachter theory of emotions: Two decades later. *Psychological Bulletin, 94,* 239–264. (12)

Reneman, L., Lavalaye, J., Schmand, B., de Wolff, F. A., van den Brink, W., den Heeten, G. J., . . . Booij, J. (2001). Cortical serotonin transporter density and verbal memory in individuals who stopped using 3,4-methylenedioxymethamphetamine (MDMA or "ecstasy"). *Archives of General Psychiatry, 58,* 901–906. (3)

Rensink, R. A., O'Regan, J. K., & Clark, J. J. (1997). To see or not to see: The need for attention to perceive changes in scenes. *Psychological Science, 8,* 368–373. (8)

Rentfrow, P. J., & Gosling, S. D. (2006). Message in a ballad. *Psychological Science, 17,* 236–242. (14)

Rentfrow, P. J., Gosling, S. D., & Potter, J. (2008). A theory of the emergence, persistence, and expression of geographic variation in psychological characteristics. *Perspectives on Psychological Science, 3,* 339–369. (14)

Repovš, G., & Baddeley, A. (2006). The multi-component model of working memory: Explorations in experimental cognitive psychology. *Neuroscience, 139,* 5–21. (7)

Rescorla, R. A. (1968). Probability of shock in the presence and absence of CS in fear conditioning. *Journal of Comparative and Physiological Psychology, 66,* 1–5. (6)

Rescorla, R. A. (1988). Pavlovian conditioning: It's not what you think it is. *American Psychologist, 43,* 151–160. (6)

Restle, F. (1970). Moon illusion explained on the basis of relative size. *Science, 167,* 1092–1096. (4)

Revusky, S. (2009). Chemical aversion treatment of alcoholism. In S. Reilly & T. R. Schachtman (Eds.), *Conditioned taste aversion* (pp. 445–472). New York: Oxford University Press. (6)

Reyna, V. F., & Farley, F. (2006). Risk and rationality in adolescent decision making: Implications for theory, practice, and public policy. *Psychological Science in the Public Interest, 7,* 1–44. (5)

Reynolds, A. J., Temple, J. A., Ou, S.-R., Arteaga, I. A., & White, B. A. B. (2011). School-based early childhood education and age-28 well-being: Effects by timing, dosage, and subgroups. *Science, 333,* 360–364. (9)

Rhodes, G., Jeffery, L., Watson, T. L, Clifford, C. W. G., & Nakayama, K. (2003). Fitting the mind to the world: Face adaptation and attractiveness aftereffects. *Psychological Science, 14,* 558–566. (13)

Rhodes, G., Sumich, A., & Byatt, G. (1999). Are average facial configurations attractive only because of their symmetry? *Psychological Science, 10,* 52–58. (13)

Rhodes, R. A., Murthy, N. V., Dresner, M. A., Selvaraj, S., Stavrakakis, N., Babar, S., . . . Grasby, P. M. (2007). Human 5-HT transporter availability predicts amygdala reactivity *in vivo. Journal of Neuroscience, 27,* 9233–9237. (3)

Riccio, D. C. (1994). Memory: When less is more. *American Psychologist, 49,* 917–926. (7)

Richard, C., Honoré, J., Bernati, T., & Rousseaux, M. (2004). Straight-ahead pointing correlates with long-line bisection in neglect patients. *Cortex, 40,* 75–83. (10)

Richardson-Jones, J. W., Craige, C. P., Guiard, B. P., Stephen, A., Metzger, K. L., . . . Leonardo, D. (2010). 5HT$_{1A}$ autoreceptor levels determine vulnerability to stress and response to antidepressants. *Neuron, 65,* 40–52. (15)

Richeson, J. A., & Nussbaum, R. J. (2004). The impact of multiculturalism versus color-blindness on racial bias. *Journal of Experimental Social Psychology, 40,* 417–423. (13)

Riddle, W. J. R., & Scott, A. I. F. (1995). Relapse after successful electroconvulsive therapy: The use and impact of continuation antidepressant drug treatment. *Human Psychopharmacology, 10,* 201–205. (15)

Rieger, G., Chivers, M. L., & Bailey, J. M. (2005). Sexual arousal patterns of bisexual men. *Psychological Science, 16,* 579–584. (11)

Rieger, G., Linsenmeier, J. A. W., Gygax, L., & Bailey, J. M. (2008). Sexual orientation and childhood gender nonconformity: Evidence from home videos. *Developmental Psychology, 44,* 46–58. (11)

Rilling, J. K., Glasser, M. F., Preuss, T. M., Ma, X., Zhao, T., Hu, X., . . . Behrens, T. E. (2008). The evolution of the arcuate fasciculus revealed with comparative DTI. *Nature Neuroscience, 11,* 426–428. (8)

Ritchie, S. J., Wiseman, R., & French, C. C. (2012). Failing the future: Three unsuccessful attempts to replicate Bem's 'retroactive facilitation of recall' experiment. *PLoS One, 7,* e33423. (2)

Ritvo, E. R. (2006). *Understanding the nature of autism and Asperger's syndrome.* London: Jessica Kingsley. (15)

Roane, B. M., & Taylor, D. J. (2008). Adolescent insomnia as a risk factor for early adult depression and substance abuse. *Sleep, 31,* 1351–1356. (15)

Roberts, B. W., & DelVecchio, W. F. (2000). The rank-order consistency of personality traits from childhood to old age: A quantitative review of longitudinal studies. *Psychological Bulletin, 126,* 3–25. (14)

Roberts, B. W., Kuncel, N. R., Shiner, R., Caspi, A., & Goldberg, L. R. (2007). The power of personality. *Perspectives on Psychological Science, 2,* 313–345. (14)

Roberts, B. W., Smith, J., Jackson, J. J., & Edmonds, G. (2009). Compensatory conscientiousness and health in older couples. *Psychological Science, 20,* 553–559. (14)

Roberts, B. W., Walton, K. E., & Viechtbauer, W. (2006). Patterns of mean-level change in personality traits across the life course: A meta-analysis of longitudinal studies. *Psychological Bulletin, 132,* 1–25. (14)

Roberts, S. B., Savage, J., Coward, W. A., Chew, B., & Lucas, A. (1988). Energy expenditure and intake in infants born to lean and overweight mothers. *New England Journal of Medicine, 318,* 461–466. (11)

Roberts, S. C., Gosling, L. M., Carter, V., & Petrie, M. (2008). MHC-correlated odour preferences in humans and the use of oral contraceptives. *Proceedings of the Royal Society, B, 275,* 2715–2722. (4, 13)

Robertson, I. H. (2005, Winter). The deceptive world of subjective awareness. *Cerebrum, 7*(1), 74–83. (3)

Robertson, L. C. (2003). Binding, spatial attention and perceptual awareness. *Nature Reviews Neuroscience, 4,* 93–102. (3)

Robins, L. N., Helzer, J. E., Weissman, M. M., Orvaschel, H., Gruenberg, E., Burke, J. D., Jr., . . . Regier, D. A. (1984). Lifetime prevalence of specific psychiatric disorders in three sites. *Archives of General Psychiatry, 41,* 949–958. (15)

Robinson, T. E., & Berridge, K. C. (2000). The psychology and neurobiology of addiction: An incentive-sensitization view. *Addiction, 95*(Suppl. 2), S91–S117. (15)

Robinson, T. E., & Berridge, K. C. (2001). Incentive-sensitization and addiction. *Addiction, 96,* 103–114. (15)

Rock, I., & Kaufman, L. (1962). The moon illusion, II. *Science, 136,* 1023–1031. (4)

Rodd, J., Gaskell, G., & Marslen-Wilson, W. (2002). Making sense of semantic ambiguity: Semantic competition in lexical access. *Journal of Memory and Language, 46,* 245–266. (8)

Rodgers, J. L. (2001). What causes birth order-intelligence patterns? *American Psychologist, 56,* 505–510. (5)

Rodgers, J. L., Cleveland, H. H., van den Oord, E., & Rowe, D. C. (2000). Resolving the debate over birth order, family size, and intelligence. *American Psychologist, 55,* 599–612. (5)

Rodgers, J. L., & Wänström, L. (2007). Identification of a Flynn effect in the NLSY:

Moving from the center to the boundaries. *Intelligence, 35,* 187–196. (9)

Rodin, J. (1986). Aging and health: Effects of the sense of control. *Science, 233,* 1271–1276. (5)

Rodrigo, M. F., & Ato, M. (2002). Testing the group polarization hypothesis by using logit models. *European Journal of Social Psychology, 32,* 3–18. (13)

Roediger, H. L., III, & Karpicke, J. D. (2006). Test-enhanced learning. *Psychological Science, 17,* 249–255. (7)

Roediger, H. L., III, & McDermott, K. B. (1995). Creating false memories: Remembering words not presented in lists. *Journal of Experimental Psychology: Learning, Memory, and Cognition, 21,* 803–814. (7)

Roediger, H. L., III, & McDermott, K. B. (2000). Tricks of memory. *Current Directions in Psychological Science, 9,* 123–127. (7)

Roefs, A., Huijding, J., Smulders, F. T. Y., MacLeod, C. M., de Jong, P. J., . . . Jansen, A. T. M. (2011). Implicit measures of association in psychopathology research. *Psychological Bulletin, 137,* 149–193. (14)

Roenneberg, T., Kuehnle, T., Pramstaller, P. P., Ricken, J., Havel, M., Guth, A., . . . Merrow, M. (2004). A marker for the end of adolescence. *Current Biology, 14,* R1038–R1039. (10)

Roenneberg, T., Kumar, C. J., & Merrow, M. (2007). The human circadian clock entrains to sun time. *Current Biology, 17,* R44–R45. (10)

Rofé, Y. (2008). Does repression exist? Memory, pathogenic, unconscious and clinical evidence. *Review of General Psychology, 12,* 63–85. (14)

Rogers, C. R. (1961). *On becoming a person.* Boston: Houghton Mifflin. (14)

Rogers, C. R. (1980). *A way of being.* Boston: Houghton Mifflin. (14)

Rogers, T. B. (1995). *The psychological testing enterprise: An introduction.* Pacific Grove, CA: Brooks/Cole. (9)

Rogler, L. H. (2002). Historical generations and psychology. *American Psychologist, 57,* 1013–1023. (5)

Rogoff, B., Morelli, G. A., & Chavajay, P. (2010). Children's integration in communities and segregation from people of different ages. *Perspectives on Psychological Science, 5,* 431–440. (5)

Rogowska, A. (2011). Categorization of synesthesia. *Review of General Psychology, 15,* 213–227. (4)

Roh, S., Matsushita, S., Hara, S., Maesato, H., Matsui, T., . . . Higuchi, S. (2011). Role of *GABRA2* in moderating subjective responses to alcohol. *Alcoholism: Clinical and Experimental Research, 35,* 400–407. (15)

Rohrbaugh, M., Shoham, V., Spungen, C., & Steinglass, P. (1995). Family systems therapy in practice: A systemic couples therapy for problem drinking. In B. Bongar & L. E. Beutler (Eds.), *Comprehensive textbook of psychotherapy: Theory and practice* (pp. 228–253). Oxford, England: Oxford University Press. (15)

Rohrer, D., & Pashler, H. (2007). Increasing retention without increasing study time. *Current Directions in Psychological Science, 16,* 183–186. (7)

Roisman, G. I., Collins, W. A., Sroufe, L. A., & Egeland, B. (2005). Predictors of young adults' representations of and behavior in their current romantic relationship: Prospective tests of the prototype hypothesis. *Attachment and Human Development, 7,* 105–121. (5)

Rolls, E. T., & McCabe, C. (2007). Enhanced affective brain representations of chocolate in cravers vs. non-cravers. *European Journal of Neuroscience, 26,* 1067–1076. (3)

Romero, A. J., & Roberts, R. E. (2003). Stress within a bicultural context for adolescents of Mexican descent. *Cultural Diversity and Ethnic Minority Psychology, 9,* 171–184. (5)

Ronen, T., & Rosenbaum, M. (2001). Helping children to help themselves: A case study of enuresis and nail biting. *Research on Social Work Practice, 11,* 338–356. (6)

Rönkä, A., Oravala, S., & Pulkkinen, L. (2003). Turning points in adults' lives: The effects of gender and the amount of choice. *Journal of Adult Development, 10,* 203–215. (5)

Rosa-Alcázar, A. I., Sánchez-Meca, J., Gómez-Conesa, A., & Marín-Martínez, F. (2008). Psychological treatment of obsessive-compulsive disorder: A meta-analysis. *Clinical Psychology Review, 28,* 1310–1325. (15)

Rosch, E. (1978). Principles of categorization. In E. Rosch & B. B. Lloyd (Eds.), *Cognition and categorization* (pp. 27–48). Hillsdale, NJ: Erlbaum. (8)

Rosch, E., & Mervis, C. B. (1975). Family resemblances: Studies in the internal structure of categories. *Cognitive Psychology, 7,* 573–605. (8)

Rose, J. E., Brugge, J. F., Anderson, D. J., & Hind, J. E. (1967). Phase-locked response to low-frequency tones in single auditory nerve fibers of the squirrel monkey. *Journal of Neurophysiology, 30,* 769–793. (4)

Rose, N. S., Myerson, J., Roediger, H. L. III, & Hale, S. (2010). Similarities and differences between working memory and long-term memory: Evidence from the levels-of-processing span task. *Journal of Experimental Psychology: Learning, Memory, and Cognition, 36,* 471–483. (7)

Rose, S. A., Feldman, J. F., & Jankowitz, J. J. (2011). Modeling a cascade of effects: The role of speed and executive functioning in preterm/full-term differences in academic achievement. *Developmental Science, 14,* 1161–1175. (7)

Rosen, V. M., & Engle, R. W. (1997). The role of working memory capacity in retrieval. *Journal of Experimental Psychology: General, 126,* 211–227. (7)

Rosenbaum, R. S., Köhler, S., Schacter, D. L., Moscovitch, M., Westmacott, R., Black, S. E., . . . Tulving, E. (2005). The case of K. C.: Contributions of a memory-impaired person to memory theory. *Neuropsychologia, 43,* 989–1021. (7)

Ross, L. (1977). The intuitive psychologist and his shortcomings: Distortions in the attribution process. In L. Berkowitz (Ed.), *Advances in experimental social psychology* (Vol. 10, pp. 173–220). New York: Academic Press. (13)

Ross, M., & Wang, Q. (2010). Why we remember and what we remember: Culture and autobiographical memory. *Perspectives on Psychological Science, 5,* 401–409. (7)

Roth, B. L., Lopez, E., & Kroeze, W. K. (2000). The multiplicity of serotonin receptors: Uselessly diverse molecules or an embarrassment of riches? *The Neuroscientist, 6,* 252–262. (3)

Rothbaum, F., Weisz, J., Pott, M., Miyake, K., & Morelli, G. (2000). Attachment and culture: Security in the United States and Japan. *American Psychologist, 55,* 1093–1104. (5)

Rottenberg, J., Bylsma, L. M., & Vingerhoets, A. J. J. M. (2008). Is crying beneficial? *Current*

Directions in Psychological Science, 17, 400–404. (12)

Rotton, J., & Kelly, I. W. (1985). Much ado about the full moon: A meta-analysis of lunar-lunacy research. Psychological Bulletin, 97, 286–306. (2)

Rouder, J. N., & Morey, R. D. (2011). A Bayes factor meta-analysis of Bem's ESP claim. Psychonomic Bulletin & Review, 18, 682–689. (2)

Rounis, E., Maniscalco, B., Rothwell, J. C., Passingham, R., & Lau, H. (2010). Theta-burst transcranial magnetic stimulation to the prefrontal cortex impairs metacognitive visual awareness. Cognitive Neuroscience, 1, 165–175. (10)

Routh, D. K. (2000). Clinical psychology training: A history of ideas and practices prior to 1946. American Psychologist, 55, 236–241. (1)

Rovee-Collier, C. (1997). Dissociations in infant memory: Rethinking the development of explicit and implicit memory. Psychological Review, 104, 467–498. (5)

Rovee-Collier, C. (1999). The development of infant memory. Current Directions in Psychological Science, 8, 80–85. (5)

Rowe, J. W., & Kahn, R. L. (1987). Human aging: Usual and successful. Science, 237, 143–149. (5)

Royzman, E. B., & Sabini, J. (2001). Something it takes to be an emotion: The interesting case of disgust. Journal for the Theory of Social Behavior, 31, 29–59. (12)

Rozin, P. (1996). Sociocultural influences on human food selection. In E. D. Capaldi (Ed.), Why we eat what we eat (pp. 233–263). Washington, DC: American Psychological Association. (1)

Rozin, P., & Cohen, A. B. (2003). High frequency of facial expressions corresponding to confusion, concentration, and worry in an analysis of naturally occurring facial expressions of Americans. Emotion, 3, 68–75. (12)

Rozin, P., Fallon, A., & Augustoni-Ziskind, M. L. (1986). The child's conception of food: The development of categories of acceptable and rejected substances. Journal of Nutrition Education, 18, 75–81. (1)

Rozin, P., & Fallon, A. E. (1987). A perspective on disgust. Psychological Review, 94, 23–41. (1)

Rozin, P., Kabnick, K., Pete, E., Fischler, C., & Shields, C. (2003). The ecology of eating: Smaller portion sizes in France than in the United States help explain the French paradox. Psychological Science, 14, 450–454. (11)

Rozin, P., & Kalat, J. W. (1971). Specific hungers and poison avoidance as adaptive specializations of learning. Psychological Review, 78, 459–486. (1, 6)

Rozin, P., Lowery, L., Imada, S., & Haidt, J. (1999). The CAD triad hypothesis: A mapping between three moral emotions (contempt, anger, disgust) and three moral codes (community, autonomy, divinity). Journal of Personality and Social Psychology, 76, 574–586. (12)

Rozin, P., Markwith, M., & Ross, B. (1990). The sympathetic magical law of similarity, nominal realism and neglect of negatives in response to negative labels. Psychological Science, 1, 383–384. (8)

Rozin, P., Markwith, M., & Stoess, C. (1997). Moralization and becoming a vegetarian: The transformation of preferences into values and the recruitment of disgust. Psychological Science, 8, 67–73. (1)

Rozin, P., Millman, L., & Nemeroff, C. (1986). Operation of the laws of sympathetic magic in disgust and other domains. Journal of

Personality and Social Psychology, 50, 703–712. (1)

Rozin, P., & Pelchat, M. L. (1988). Memories of mammaries: Adaptations to weaning from milk. Progress in Psychobiology and Physiological Psychology, 13, 1–29. (5)

Ruch, J. (1984). Psychology: The personal science. Belmont, CA: Wadsworth. (5)

Rudman, L. A., & Goodwin, S. A. (2004). Gender differences in automatic in-group bias: Why do women like women more than men like men? Journal of Personality and Social Psychology, 87, 494–509. (13)

Rule, N. O., Ambady, N., & Hallett, K. C. (2009). Female sexual orientation is perceived accurately, rapidly, and automatically from the face and its features. Journal of Experimental Social Psychology, 45, 1245–1251. (13)

Rumbaugh, D. M., Savage-Rumbaugh, E. S., King, J. E., & Taglialatela, J. P. (2010). The foundations of primate intelligence and language skills. In D. Broadfield, M. Yuan, K. Schick, & N. Toth (Eds.), The human brain evolving (pp. 283–292). Gosport, IN: Stone Age Institute Press. (6)

Rumelhart, D. E., & McClelland, J. L. (1982). An interactive activation model of context effects in letter perception: Part 2. The contextual enhancement effect and some tests and extensions of the model. Psychological Review, 89, 60–94. (8)

Rumelhart, D. E., McClelland, J. L., & the PDP Research Group. (1986). Parallel distributed processing. Cambridge, MA: MIT Press. (8)

Rusak, B. (1977). The role of the suprachiasmatic nuclei in the generation of circadian rhythms in the golden hamster, Mesocricetus auratus. Journal of Comparative Physiology A, 118, 145–164. (10)

Rush, A. J., Trivedi, M. H., Wisniewski, S. R., Stewart, J. W., Nierenberg, A. A., . . . Fava, M. (2006). Bupropion-SR, sertraline, or venlafaxine-XR after failure of SSRIs for depression. New England Journal of Medicine, 354, 1231–1242. (15)

Rushton, J. P., & Bons, T. A. (2005). Mate choice and friendship in twins. Psychological Science, 16, 555–559. (13)

Russano, M. B., Meissner, C. A., Narchet, F. M., & Kassin, S. M. (2005). Investigating true and false confessions within a novel experimental paradigm. Psychological Science, 16, 481–486. (13)

Russell, J. A. (1980). A circumplex model of affect. Journal of Personality and Social Psychology, 39, 1161–1178. (12)

Russell, J. A. (1994). Is there universal recognition of emotion from facial expression? A review of the cross-cultural studies. Psychological Bulletin, 115, 102–141. (12)

Russo, J. E., Carlson, K. A., & Meloy, M. G. (2006). Choosing an inferior alternative. Psychological Science, 17, 899–904. (13)

Rutledge, T., & Hogan, B. E. (2002). A quantitative review of prospective evidence linking psychological factors with hypertension development. Psychosomatic Medicine, 64, 758–766. (12)

Ryan, J. D., Althoff, R. R., Whitlow, S., & Cohen, N. J. (2000). Amnesia is a deficit in relational memory. Psychological Science, 11, 454–461. (7)

Ryder, A. G., Yang, J., Zhu, X., Yao, S., Yi, J., Heine, S. J., & Bagby, R. M. (2008). The cultural shaping of depression: Somatic symptoms in China, psychological symptoms in North

America? Journal of Abnormal Psychology, 117, 300–313. (15)

Sabini, J., Siepmann, M., Stein, J., & Meyerowitz, M. (2000). Who is embarrassed by what? Cognition and Emotion, 14, 213–240. (12)

Sacchi, D. L. M., Agnoli, F., & Loftus, E. F. (2007). Changing history: Doctored photographs affect memory for past public events. Applied Cognitive Psychology, 21, 1005–1022. (7)

Sackeim, H. A., Prudic, J., Devanand, D. P., Nobler, M. S., Lisanby, S. H., Peyser, S., . . . Clark, J. (2000). A prospective, randomized, double-blind comparison of bilateral and right unilateral electroconvulsive therapy at different stimulus intensities. Archives of General Psychiatry, 57, 425–434. (15)

Sackett, P. R., Borneman, M. J., & Connelly, B. S. (2008). High-stakes testing in higher education and employment. American Psychologist, 63, 215–227. (9)

Saegert, S., Swap, W., & Zajonc, R. B. (1973). Exposure, context, and interpersonal attraction. Journal of Personality and Social Psychology, 25, 234–242. (13)

Saffran, J. R. (2003). Statistical language learning: Mechanisms and constraints. Current Directions in Psychological Science, 12, 110–114. (8)

Saffran, J. R., Aslin, R. N., & Newport, E. L. (1996). Statistical learning by 8-month-old infants. Science, 274, 1926–1928. (8)

Saha, S., Chant, D., & McGrath, J. (2007). A systematic review of mortality in schizophrenia. Archives of General Psychiatry, 64, 1123–1131. (15)

Saha, S., Chant, D., Welham, J., & McGrath, J. (2005). A systematic review of the prevalence of schizophrenia. PLoS Medicine, e141. (15)

Sales, B. D., & Folkman, S. (2000). Ethics in research with human participants. Washington, DC: American Psychological Association. (1)

Salmon, P. (2001). Effects of physical exercise on anxiety, depression, and sensitivity to stress: A unifying theory. Clinical Psychology Review, 21, 33–61. (12)

Salomons, T. V., Johnstone, T., Backonja, M.-M., & Davidson, R. J. (2004). Perceived controllability modulates the neural response to pain. Journal of Neuroscience, 24, 7199–7203. (12)

Salthouse, T. A. (2006). Mental exercise and mental aging. Perspectives on Psychological Science, 1, 68–87. (8)

Salvatore, J. E., Kuo, S. I.-C., Steele, R. D., Simpson, J. A., & Collins, W. A. (2011). Recovering from conflict in romantic relationships: A developmental perspective. Psychological Science, 22, 376–383. (5)

Sam, D. L., & Berry, J. W. (2010). Acculturation: When individuals and groups of different cultural backgrounds meet. Perspectives on Psychological Science, 5, 472–481. (5)

Samuel, A. G. (2001). Knowing a word affects the fundamental perception of the sounds within it. Psychological Science, 12, 348–351. (8)

Sanchez, L. M., & Turner, S. M. (2003). Practicing psychology in the era of managed care. American Psychologist, 58, 116–129. (15)

Sanders, A. R., Duan, J., Levinson, D. F., Shi, J., He, D., Hou, C., . . . Gejman, P. V. (2008). No significant association of 14 candidate genes with schizophrenia in a large European ancestry sample: Implications for psychiatric genetics. American Journal of Psychiatry, 165, 497–506. (15)

Sanders, R. E., Gonzalez, D. J., Murphy, M. D., Pesta, B. J., & Bucur, B. (2002). Training content variability and the effectiveness of learning: An adult age assessment. *Aging, Neuropsychology, and Cognition, 9,* 157–174. (7)

Sandfort, T. G. M., de Graaf, R., Bijl, R. V., & Schnabel, P. (2001). Same-sex sexual behavior and psychiatric disorders. *Archives of General Psychiatry, 58,* 85–91. (11)

Sandhya, S. (2009). The social context of marital happiness in urban Indian couples: Interplay of intimacy and conflict. *Journal of Marital and Family Conflict, 35,* 74–96. (11)

Sapolsky, R. M. (1998, March 30). Open season. *The New Yorker, 74*(6), 57–58, 71–72. (14)

Sapolsky, R. M., & Share, L. J. (2004). A pacific culture among wild baboons: Its emergence and transmission. *PLoS Biology, 2,* 534–541. (13)

Sapp, F., Lee, K., & Muir, D. (2000). Three-year-olds' difficulty with the appearance–reality distinction: Is it real or is it apparent? *Developmental Psychology, 36,* 547–560. (5)

Saris, S., Mischoulon, D., & Schweitzer, I. (2012). Omega-3 for bipolar disorder: Meta-analyses of use in mania and bipolar depression. *Journal of Clinical Psychiatry, 73,* 81–86. (15)

Saucier, D. M., Green, S. M., Leason, J., MacFadden, A., Bell, S., & Elias, L. J. (2002). Are sex differences in navigation caused by sexually dimorphic strategies or by differences in the ability to use the strategies? *Behavioral Neuroscience, 116,* 403–410. (5)

Savage-Rumbaugh, E. S. (1990). Language acquisition in a nonhuman species: Implications for the innateness debate. *Developmental Psychology, 23,* 599–620. (8)

Savage-Rumbaugh, E. S., Murphy, J., Sevcik, R. A., Brakke, K. E., Williams, S. L., & Rumbaugh, D. M. (1993). Language comprehension in ape and child. *Monographs of the Society for Research in Child Development, 58*(Serial no. 233). (8)

Savage-Rumbaugh, E. S., Sevcik, R. A., Brakke, K. E., & Rumbaugh, D. M. (1992). Symbols: Their communicative use, communication, and combination by bonobos *(Pan paniscus).* In L. P. Lipsitt & C. Rovee-Collier (Eds.), *Advances in infancy research* (Vol. 7, pp. 221–278). Norwood, NJ: Ablex. (8)

Scalera, G., & Bavieri, M. (2009). Role of conditioned taste aversion on the side effects of chemotherapy in cancer patients. In S. Reilly & T. R. Schachtman (Eds.), *Conditioned taste aversion* (pp. 513–541). New York: Oxford University Press. (6)

Scarborough, E., & Furomoto, L. (1987). *Untold lives: The first generation of American women psychologists.* New York: Columbia University Press. (1)

Scarr, S. (1997). Rules of evidence: A larger context for the statistical debate. *Psychological Science, 8,* 16–17. (2)

Scarr, S. (1998). American child care today. *American Psychologist, 53,* 95–108. (5)

Schachter, D. L. (1987). Implicit memory: History and current status. *Journal of Experimental Psychology: Learning, Memory, and Cognition, 13,* 501–518. (7)

Schachter, S. (1982). Recidivism and self-cure of smoking and obesity. *American Psychologist, 37,* 436–444. (11)

Schachter, S., & Singer, J. (1962). Cognitive, social, and physiological determinants of emotional state. *Psychological Review, 69,* 379–399. (12)

Schacter, D. L., Verfaellie, M., Anes, M. D., & Racine, C. (1998). When true recognition suppresses false recognition: Evidence from amnesic patients. *Journal of Cognitive Neuroscience, 10,* 668–679. (7)

Schatzman, M. (1992, March 21). Freud: Who seduced whom? *New Scientist,* pp. 34–37. (14)

Schellenberg, E. G. (2004). Music lessons enhance IQ. *Psychological Science, 15,* 511–514. (9)

Schellenberg, E. G. (2006). Long-term positive associations between music lessons and IQ. *Journal of Educational Psychology, 98,* 457–468. (9)

Schellenberg, E. G., & Trehub, S. E. (2003). Good pitch memory is widespread. *Psychological Science, 14,* 262–266. (4)

Schenck, C. H., & Mahowald, M. W. (1996). Long-term, nightly benzodiazepine treatment of injurious parasomnias and other disorders of disrupted nocturnal sleep in 170 adults. *American Journal of Medicine, 100,* 333–337. (10)

Schenk, T. (2006). An allocentric rather than perceptual deficit in patient D. F. *Nature Neuroscience, 9,* 1369–1370. (3)

Scherer, K. R. (1992). What does facial expression express? In K. T. Strongman (Ed.), *International review of studies on emotion* (Vol. 2, pp. 139–165). Chichester, England: Wiley. (12)

Scherer, K. R., & Ellgring, H. (2007). Multimodal expression of emotion: Affect programs or componential appraisal patterns? *Emotion, 7,* 158–171. (12)

Schiffman, S. S., & Erickson, R. P. (1971). A psychophysical model for gustatory quality. *Physiology and Behavior, 7,* 617–633. (4)

Schkade, D. A., & Kahneman, D. (1998). Does living in California make people happy? *Psychological Science, 9,* 340–346. (12)

Schlesier-Stropp, B. (1984). Bulimia: A review of the literature. *Psychological Review, 95,* 247–257. (11)

Schmid, M. C., Mrowka, S. W., Turchi, J., Saunders, R. C., Wilke, M., Peters, A. J., . . . Leopold, D. A. (2010). Blindsight depends on the lateral geniculate nucleus. *Nature, 466,* 373–377. (3)

Schmidt-Duffy, M. (2011). Modeling automatic threat detection: Development of a face-in-the-crowd task. *Emotion, 11,* 153–168. (8)

Schmidt, F. L., & Hunter, J. E. (1981). Employment testing: Old theories and new research findings. *American Psychologist, 36,* 1128–1137. (9)

Schmidt, F. L., & Hunter, J. E. (1998). The validity and utility of selection methods in personnel psychology: Practical and theoretical implications of 85 years of research findings. *Psychological Bulletin, 124,* 262–274. (9)

Schmitt, A. P., & Dorans, N. J. (1990). Differential item functioning for minority examinees on the SAT. *Journal of Educational Measurement, 27,* 67–81. (9)

Schmitt, D. P., & 118 members of the International Sexuality Description Project. (2003). Universal sex differences in the desire for sexual variety: Tests from 52 nations, 6 continents, and 13 islands. *Journal of Personality and Social Psychology, 85,* 85–104. (13)

Schmolck, H., Buffalo, E. A., & Squire, L. R. (2000). Memory distortions develop over time. *Psychological Science, 11,* 39–45. (7)

Schnall, S., Benton, J., & Harvey, S. (2008). With a clean conscience. *Psychological Science, 19,* 1219–1222. (12)

Schneider, P., Scherg, M., Dosch, G., Specht, H. J., Gutschalk, A., & Rupp, A. (2002). Morphology of Heschl's gyrus reflects enhanced activation in the auditory cortex of musicians. *Nature Neuroscience, 5,* 688–694. (3, 8)

Schneiderman, I., Zilberstein-Kra, Y., Leckman, J. F., & Feldman, R. (2011). Love alters autonomic reactivity to emotions. *Emotion, 11,* 1314–1321. (12)

Schnider, A. (2003). Spontaneous confabulation and the adaptation of thought to ongoing reality. *Nature Reviews Neuroscience, 4,* 662–671. (7)

Schomacher, M., Müller, H. D., Sommer, C., Schwab, S., & Schäbitz, W.-R. (2008). Endocannabinoids mediate neuroprotection after transient focal cerebral ischemia. *Brain Research, 1240,* 213–220. (3)

Schooler, C. (1972). Birth order effects: Not here, not now! *Psychological Bulletin, 78,* 161–175. (5)

Schooler, C. (1998). Environmental complexity and the Flynn effect. In U. Neisser (Ed.), *The rising curve* (pp. 67–79). Washington, DC: American Psychological Association. (9)

Schredl, M. (2000). Continuity between waking life and dreaming: Are all waking activities reflected equally often in dreams? *Perceptual and Motor Skills, 90,* 844–846. (10)

Schuckit, M. A., & Smith, T. L. (1997). Assessing the risk for alcoholism among sons of alcoholics. *Journal of Studies on Alcohol, 58,* 141–145. (15)

Schuckit, M. A., Smith, T. L., Danko, G. P., Pierson, J., Hesselbrock, V., . . . Chan, G. (2007). The ability of the self-rating of the effects of alcohol (SRE) scale to predict alcohol-related outcomes five years later. *Journal of Studies of Alcohol, 68,* 371–378. (15)

Schulsinger, F., Knop, J., Goodwin, D. W., Teasdale, T. W., & Mikkelsen, U. (1986). A prospective study of young men at high risk for alcoholism. *Archives of General Psychiatry, 43,* 755–760. (15)

Schumann, K., & Ross, M. (2010). Why women apologize more than men: Gender differences in thresholds for perceiving offensive behavior. *Psychological Science, 21,* 1649–1655. (5)

Schumm, W. R. (2008). Re-evaluation of the "no differences" hypothesis concerning gay and lesbian parenting as assessed in eight early (1979–1986) and four later (1997–1998) dissertations. *Psychological Reports, 103,* 275–304. (5)

Schupp, H. T., Stockburger, J., Codispoti, M., Junghöfer, M., Weike, A. I., & Hamm, A. O. (2007). Selective visual attention to emotion. *Journal of Neuroscience, 27,* 1082–1089. (12)

Schützwohl, A., & Borgstedt, K. (2005). The processing of affectively valenced stimuli: The role of surprise. *Cognition and Emotion, 19,* 583–600. (12)

Schwartz, B. (2004). *The paradox of choice.* New York: HarperCollins. (8)

Schwartz, B., Ben-Haim, Y., & Dacso, C. (2010). What makes a good decision? Robust satisficing as a normative standard of rational decision making. *Journal for the Theory of Social Behavior, 41,* 209–227. (8)

Schwartz, B., Ward, A., Monterosso, J., Lyubomirsky, S., White, K., & Lehman, D. R. (2002). Maximizing versus satisficing: Happiness is a matter of choice. *Journal of Personality and Social Psychology, 83,* 1178–1197. (8)

Schwartz, C. E., Wright, C. I., Shin, L. M., Kagan, J., & Rauch, S. L. (2003). Inhibited and uninhibited infants "grown up": Adult amygdalar response to novelty. *Science, 300,* 1952–1953. (5)

Scott, L. S., & Monesson, A. (2009). The origin of biases in face perception. *Psychological Science, 20,* 676–680. (5)

Scott, N., Lakin, K. C., & Larson, S. A. (2008). The 40th anniversary of deinstitutionalization in the United States: Decreasing state institutional populations, 1967–2007. *Intellectual and Developmental Disabilities, 46*, 402–405. (15)

Scott, R. L., & Mamani-Pampa, W. (2008). MMPI-A for Peru: Adaptation and normalization. *International Journal of Clinical and Health Psychology, 8*, 719–732. (14)

Scott, S. K., Young, A. W., Calder, A. J., Hellawell, D. J., Aggleton, J. P., & Johnson, M. (1997). Impaired auditory recognition of fear and anger following bilateral amygdala lesions. *Nature, 385*, 254–257. (12)

Scott, T. R., & Verhagen, J. V. (2000). Taste as a factor in the management of nutrition. *Nutrition, 16*, 874–885. (1)

Scott, V. M., Mottarella, K. E., & Lavooy, M. J. (2006). Does virtual intimacy exist? A brief exploration into reported levels of intimacy in online relationships. *CyberPsychology and Behavior, 9*, 759–761. (13)

Scovern, A. W., & Kilmann, P. R. (1980). Status of electroconvulsive therapy: Review of the outcome literature. *Psychological Bulletin, 87*, 260–303. (15)

Seamon, J. G., Lee, I. A., Toner, S. K., Wheeler, R. H., Goodkind, M. S., & Birch, A. D. (2002). Thinking of critical words during study is unnecessary for false memory in the Deese, Roediger, and McDermott procedure. *Psychological Science, 13*, 526–531. (7)

Seeley, R. J., Kaplan, J. M., & Grill, H. J. (1995). Effect of occluding the pylorus on intraoral intake: A test of the gastric hypothesis of meal termination. *Physiology and Behavior, 58*, 245–249. (11)

Seeman, P., & Lee, T. (1975). Antipsychotic drugs: Direct correlation between clinical potency and presynaptic action on dopamine neurons. *Science, 188*, 1217–1219. (15)

Segal, N. L. (2000). Virtual twins: New findings on within-family environmental influences on intelligence. *Journal of Educational Psychology, 92*, 442–448. (9)

Segerstrom, S. C., & Nes, L. S. (2007). Heart rate variability reflects self-regulatory strength, effort, and fatigue. *Psychological Science, 18*, 275–281. (12)

Seidman, L. J., Biederman, J., Liang, L., Valera, E. M., Monuteaux, M. C., Brown, A., . . . Makris, N. (2011). Gray matter alterations in adults with attention-deficit/hyperactivity disorder identified by voxel based morphometry. *Biological Psychiatry, 69*, 857–866. (8)

Sekuler, A. B., & Bennett, P. J. (2001). Generalized common fate: Grouping by common luminance changes. *Psychological Science, 12*, 437–444. (4)

Seligman, M. E. P. (1970). On the generality of the laws of learning. *Psychological Review, 77*, 406–418. (6)

Seligman, M. E. P. (1971). Phobias and preparedness. *Behavior Therapy, 2*, 307–320. (15)

Seligman, M. E. P., & Csikszentmihalyi, M. (2000). Positive psychology. *American Psychologist, 55*, 5–14. (12)

Selye, H. (1979). Stress, cancer, and the mind. In J. Taché, H. Selye, & S. B. Day (Eds.), *Cancer, stress, and death* (pp. 11–27). New York: Plenum Press. (12)

Semmler, C., Brewer, N., & Wells, G. L. (2004). Effects of postidentification feedback on eyewitness identification and nonidentification

confidence. *Journal of Applied Psychology, 89*, 334–346. (7)

Senghas, A., & Coppola, M. (2001). Children creating language: How Nicaraguan sign language acquired a spatial grammar. *Psychological Science, 12*, 323–328. (8)

Senghas, A., Kita, S., & Özyürek, A. (2004). Children creating core properties of language: Evidence from an emerging sign language in Nicaragua. *Science, 305*, 1779–1782. (8)

Senju, A., Southgate, V., Snape, C., Leonard, M., & Csibra, G. (2011). Do 18-month-olds really attribute mental states to others? A critical test. *Psychological Science, 22*, 878–880. (5)

Sensky, T., Turkington, D., Kingdon, D., Scott, J. L., Scott, J., Siddle, R., . . . Barnes, T. R. (2000). A randomized controlled trial of cognitive-behavioral therapy for persistent symptoms in schizophrenia resistant to medication. *Archives of General Psychiatry, 57*, 165–172. (15)

Seo, M.-G., Barrett, L. F., & Bartunek, J. M. (2004). The role of affective experience in work motivation. *Academy of Management Review, 29*, 423–439. (11)

Shafir, E. (1983). Choosing versus rejecting: Why some options are both better and worse than others. *Memory & Cognition, 21*, 546–556. (2)

Shafir, E. B., Smith, E. E., & Osherson, D. N. (1990). Typicality and reasoning fallacies. *Memory and Cognition, 18*, 229–239. (8)

Shafto, M., & MacKay, D. G. (2000). The Moses, mega-Moses, and Armstrong illusions: Integrating language comprehension and semantic memory. *Psychological Science, 11*, 372–378. (8)

Shah, A. M., & Wolford, G. (2007). Buying behavior as a function of parametric variation of number of choices. *Psychological Science, 18*, 369–370. (8)

Shahar, D. R., Schultz, R., Shahar, A., & Wing, R. R. (2001). The effect of widowhood on weight change, dietary intake, and eating behavior in the elderly population. *Journal of Aging and Health, 13*, 186–199. (12)

Shamosh, N. A., DeYoung, C. G., Green, A. E., Reis, D. L., Johnson, M. R., Conway, A. R. A., . . . Gray, J. R. (2008). Individual differences in delay discounting. *Psychological Science, 19*, 904–911. (9)

Shannon, D. A. (1955). *The Socialist Party of America.* New York: Macmillan. (13)

Shapiro, D. L. (1985). Insanity and the assessment of criminal responsibility. In C. P. Ewing (Ed.), *Psychology, psychiatry, and the law: A clinical and forensic handbook* (pp. 67–94). Sarasota, FL: Professional Resource Exchange. (15)

Shapiro, K. L., Caldwell, J., & Sorensen, R. E. (1997). Personal names and the attentional blink: A visual "cocktail party" effect. *Journal of Experimental Psychology: Human Perception and Performance, 23*, 504–514. (8)

Shaw, G. B. (1911). *The doctor's dilemma.* New York: Brentano's. (13)

Shearn, D., Spellman, L., Straley, B., Meirick, J., & Stryker, K. (1999). Empathic blushing in friends and strangers. *Motivation and Emotion, 23*, 307–316. (12)

Sheldon, K., & Lyubomirsky, S. (2004). Achieving sustainable new happiness: Prospects, practices, and prescriptions. In P. A. Linley & S. Joseph (Eds.), *Positive psychology in practice* (pp. 127–145). Hoboken, NJ: Wiley. (12)

Sheldon, K. M., & Lyubomirsky, S. (2006). Achieving sustainable gains in happiness: Change your actions, not your circumstances. *Journal of Happiness Studies, 7*, 55–86. (12)

Shenkin, S. D., Starr, J. M., & Deary, I. J. (2004). Birth weight and cognitive ability in childhood: A systematic review. *Psychological Bulletin, 130*, 989–1013. (5)

Shepard, R. N. (1990). *Mind sights.* New York: W. H. Freeman. (4)

Shepard, R. N., & Metzler, J. N. (1971). Mental rotation of three-dimensional objects. *Science, 171*, 701–703. (8)

Sheppard, W. D., II, Staggers, F. J., Jr., & John, L. (1997). The effects of a stress management program in a high security government agency. *Anxiety, Stress, and Coping, 10*, 341–350. (12)

Shepperd, J. A. (1993). Productivity loss in performance groups: A motivation analysis. *Psychological Bulletin, 113*, 67–81. (13)

Sheppes, G., Scheibe, S., Suri, G., & Gross, J. J. (2011). Emotion-regulation choice. *Psychological Science, 22*, 1391–1396. (12)

Shergill, S. S., Brammer, M. J., Williams, S. C. R., Murray, R. M., & McGuire, P. K. (2000). Mapping auditory hallucinations in schizophrenia using functional magnetic resonance imaging. *Archives of General Psychiatry, 57*, 1033–1038. (15)

Sherif, M. (1935). A study of some social factors in perception. *Archives of Psychology, 27*, 1–60. (13)

Sherif, M. (1966). *In common predicament.* Boston: Houghton Mifflin. (13)

Sherwood, G. G. (1981). Self-serving biases in person perception: A reexamination of projection as a mechanism of defense. *Psychological Bulletin, 90*, 445–459. (14)

Shih, M., Pittinsky, T. L., & Ambady, N. (1999). Stereotype susceptibility: Identity salience and shifts in quantitative performance. *Psychological Science, 10*, 80–83. (9)

Shih, M., & Sanchez, D. T. (2005). Perspectives and research on the positive and negative implications of having multiple racial identities. *Psychological Bulletin, 131*, 569–591. (5)

Shimaya, A. (1997). Perception of complex line drawings. *Journal of Experimental Psychology: Human Perception and Performance, 23*, 25–50. (4)

Shinskey, J. L., & Munakata, Y. (2005). Familiarity breeds searching. *Psychological Science, 16*, 595–600. (5)

Shoda, Y., Mischel, W., & Peake, P. K. (1990). Predicting adolescent cognitive and self-regulatory competencies from preschool conditions. *Developmental Psychology, 26*, 978–986. (11)

Shogren, E. (1993, June 2). Survey finds 4 in 5 suffer sex harassment at school. *Los Angeles Times*, p. A10. (2)

Shohamy, D., Myers, C. E., Hopkins, R. O., Sage, J., & Gluck, M. A. (2009). Distinct hippocampal and basal ganglia contributions to probabilistic learning and reversal. *Journal of Cognitive Neuroscience, 21*, 1821–1833. (7)

Shohamy, D., Myers, C. E., Kalanithi, J., & Gluck, M. A. (2008). Basal ganglia and dopamine contributions to probabilistic category learning. *Neuroscience and Biobehavioral Reviews, 32*, 219–236. (7)

Shook, N. J., & Fazio, R. H. (2008). Interracial roommate relationships. *Psychological Science, 19*, 717–723. (13)

Shrager, Y., Levy, D. A., Hopkins, R. O., & Squire, L. R. (2008). Working memory and the organization of brain systems. *Journal of Neuroscience, 28*, 4818–4822. (7)

Siegel, J. M. (2005). Clues to the functions of mammalian sleep. *Nature, 437*, 1264–1271. (10)

Siegel, S. (1977). Morphine tolerance as an associative process. *Journal of Experimental Psychology: Animal Behavior Processes, 3,* 1–13. (6)

Siegel, S. (1983). Classical conditioning, drug tolerance, and drug dependence. *Research Advances in Alcohol and Drug Problems, 7,* 207–246. (6)

Siegel, S. (1987). Alcohol and opiate dependence: Reevaluation of the Victorian perspective. *Research Advances in Alcohol and Drug Problems, 9,* 279–314. (15)

Siegel, S., & Ramos, B. M. C. (2002). Applying laboratory research: Drug anticipation and the treatment of drug addiction. *Experimental and Clinical Psychopharmacology, 10,* 162–183. (6)

Siepka, S. M., Yoo, S. H., Park, J., Song, W. M., Kumar, V., Hu, Y. N., . . . Takahashi, J. S. (2007). Circadian mutant overtime reveals F-box protein FBXL3 regulation of cryptochrome and period gene expression. *Cell, 129,* 1011–1023. (10)

Sieverding, M., Decker, S., & Zimmermann, F. (2010). Information about low participation in cancer screening demotivates other people. *Psychological Science, 21,* 941–943. (13)

Sigman, M., & Whaley, S. E. (1998). The role of nutrition in the development of intelligence. In U. Neisser (Ed.), *The rising curve* (pp. 155–182). Washington, DC: American Psychological Association. (9)

Silk, J. B., Brosnan, S. F., Vonk, J., Henrich, J., Povinelli, D. J., Richardson, A. S., . . . Schapiro, S. J. (2005). Chimpanzees are indifferent to the welfare of unrelated group members. *Nature, 437,* 1357–1359. (13)

Silva, E. J., & Duffy, J. F. (2008). Sleep inertia varies with circadian phase and sleep stage in older adults. *Behavioral Neuroscience, 122,* 929–935. (10)

Silver, E. (1995). Punishment or treatment? Comparing the lengths of confinement of successful and unsuccessful insanity defendants. *Law and Human Behavior, 19,* 375–388. (15)

Simcock, G., & Hayne, H. (2002). Breaking the barrier? Children fail to translate their preverbal memories into language. *Psychological Science, 13,* 225–231. (7)

Simmons, E. J. (1949). *Leo Tolstoy.* London: Lehmann. (15)

Simmons, J. P., Nelson, L. D., & Simonsohn, U. (2011). False-positive psychology: Undisclosed flexibility in data collection and analysis allows presenting anything as significant. *Psychological Science, 22,* 1359–1366. (2)

Simner, J., Harrold, J., Creed, H., Monro, L., & Foulkes, L. (2009). Early detection of markers for syaesthesia in childhood populations. *Brain, 132,* 57–64. (4)

Simner, J., & Ward, J. (2006). The taste of words on the tip of the tongue. *Nature, 444,* 438. (4)

Simon, N. W., Mendez, I. A., & Setlow, B. (2007). Cocaine exposure causes long-term increases in impulsive choice. *Behavioral Neuroscience, 121,* 543–549. (3)

Simons, D. J., & Levin, D. T. (2003). What makes change blindness interesting? *The Psychology of Learning and Motivation, 42,* 295–322. (8)

Simons, T., & Roberson, Q. (2003). Why managers should care about fairness: The effects of aggregate justice perceptions on organizational outcomes. *Journal of Applied Psychology, 88,* 432–443. (11)

Singer, T., Seymour, B., O'Doherty, J., Kaube, H., Dolan, R. J., & Frith, C. D. (2004). Empathy for pain involves the affective but not sensory components of pain. *Science, 303,* 1157–1162. (4)

Singh, M., Hoffman, D. D., & Albert, M. K. (1999). Contour completion and relative depth: Petter's rule and support ratio. *Psychological Science, 10,* 423–428. (4)

Sirin, S. R., & Fine, M. (2007). Hyphenated selves: Muslim American youth negotiating identities on the fault lines of global conflict. *Applied Developmental Science, 11,* 151–163. (5)

Skeels, H. M. (1966). Adult status of children with contrasting early life experiences. *Monographs of the Society for Research in Child Development, 31,* 1–65. (9)

Skinner, B. F. (1938). *The behavior of organisms.* New York: D. Appleton-Century. (6)

Skinner, B. F. (1990). Can psychology be a science of mind? *American Psychologist, 45,* 1206–1210. (6)

Skinner, E. A., Edge, K., Altman, J., & Sherwood, H. (2003). Searching for the structure of coping: A review and critique of category systems for classifying ways of coping. *Psychological Bulletin, 129,* 216–269. (12)

Skoog, G., & Skoog, I. (1999). A 40-year follow-up of patients with obsessive-compulsive disorder. *Archives of General Psychiatry, 56,* 121–127. (15)

Slabbekoorn, H., & den Boer-Visser, A. (2006). Cities change the songs of birds. *Current Biology, 16,* 2326–2331. (6)

Sloan, D. M., Marx, B. P., Epstein, E. M., & Dobbs, J. L. (2008). Expressive writing buffers against maladaptive rumination. *Emotion, 8,* 302–306. (15)

Smilek, D., Carriere, J. S. A., & Cheyne, J. A. (2010). Out of mind, out of sight: Eye blinking as indicator and embodiment of mind wandering. *Psychological Science, 21,* 786–789. (8)

Smith, D. M., Langa, K. M., Kabeto, M. U., & Ubel, P. A. (2005). Health, wealth, and happiness. *Psychological Science, 16,* 663–666. (12)

Smith, J. M., Bell, P. A., & Fusco, M. E. (1986). The influence of color and demand characteristics on muscle strength and affective ratings of the environment. *Journal of General Psychology, 113,* 289–297. (2)

Smith, L. T. (1975). The interanimal transfer phenomenon: A review. *Psychological Bulletin, 81,* 1078–1095. (2)

Smith, M. L. (1988). Recall of spatial location by the amnesic patient H. M. *Brain and Cognition, 7,* 178–183. (7)

Smith, M. L., Glass, G. V., & Miller, T. I. (1980). *The benefits of psychotherapy.* Baltimore: Johns Hopkins University Press. (15)

Smith, M. W. (1974). Alfred Binet's remarkable questions: A cross-national and cross-temporal analysis of the cultural biases built into the Stanford-Binet intelligence scale and other Binet tests. *Genetic Psychology Monographs, 89,* 307–334. (9)

Smith, S. M., & Moynan, S. C. (2008). Forgetting and recovering the unforgettable. *Psychological Science, 19,* 462–468. (7)

Snook, B., Cullen, R. M., Bennell, C., Taylor, P. J., & Gendreau, P. (2008). The criminal profiling illusion: What's behind the smoke and mirrors? *Criminal Justice and Behavior, 35,* 1257–1276. (14)

Snook, B., Eastwood, J., Gendreau, P., Goggin, C., & Cullen, R. M. (2007). Taking stock of criminal profiling: A narrative review and meta-analysis. *Criminal Justice and Behavior, 34,* 437–453. (14)

Snyder, C. R. (2003). "Me conform? No way": Classroom demonstrations for sensitizing students to their conformity. *Teaching of Psychology, 30,* 59–61. (13)

Snyder, M., Tanke, E. D., & Berscheid, E. (1977). Social perception and interpersonal behavior: On the self-fulfilling nature of social stereotypes. *Journal of Personality and Social Psychology, 35,* 656–666. (13)

Society for Personality Assessment. (2005). The status of the Rorschach in clinical and forensic practice: An official statement by the Board of Trustees of the Society for Personality Assessment. *Journal of Personality Assessment, 85,* 219–237. (14)

Solanto, M. V., Abikoff, H., Sonuga-Barke, E., Schachar, R., Logan, G. D., Wigal, T., . . . Turkel, E. (2001). The ecological validity of delay aversion and response inhibition as measures of impulsivity in AD/HD: A supplement to the NIMH multimodal treatment study of AD/HD. *Journal of Abnormal Child Psychology, 29,* 215–228. (8)

Solms, M. (1997). *The neuropsychology of dreams.* Mahwah, NJ: Erlbaum. (10)

Solms, M. (2000). Dreaming and REM sleep are controlled by different brain mechanisms. *Behavioral and Brain Sciences, 23,* 843–850. (10)

Solomon, D. A., Keller, M. B., Leon, A. C., Mueller, T. I., Shea, T., Warshaw, M., . . . Endicott, J. (1997). Recovery from major depression. *Archives of General Psychiatry, 54,* 1001–1006. (15)

Solomon, Z., Mikulincer, M., & Flum, H. (1988). Negative life events, coping responses, and combat-related psychopathology: A prospective study. *Journal of Abnormal Psychology, 97,* 302–307. (12)

Solter, A. (2008). A 2-year-old child's memory of hospitalization during early infancy. *Infant and Child Development, 17,* 593–605. (7)

Song, H., & Schwarz, N. (2008). If it's hard to read, it's hard to do. *Psychological Science, 19,* 986–988. (8)

Song, H., & Schwarz, N. (2009). If it's difficult to pronounce, it must be risky. *Psychological Science, 20,* 135–138. (8)

Song, H., Stevens, C. F., & Gage, F. H. (2002). Neural stem cells from adult hippocampus develop essential properties of functional CNS neurons. *Nature Neuroscience, 5,* 438–445. (3)

Sonuga-Barke, E. J. S. (2004). Causal models of attention-deficit/hyperactivity disorder: From common simple deficits to multiple developmental pathways. *Biological Psychology, 57,* 1231–1238. (8)

Soon, C. S., Brass, M., Heinze, H.-J., & Haynes, J.-D. (2008). Unconscious determinants of free decisions in the human brain. *Nature Neuroscience, 11,* 543–545. (10)

Sowell, E. R., Thompson, P. M., Holmes, C. J., Jernigan, T. L., & Toga, A. W. (1999). *In vivo* evidence for post-adolescent brain maturation in frontal and striatal regions. *Nature Neuroscience, 2,* 859–861. (1)

Spanos, N. P. (1987–1988). Past-life hypnotic regression: A critical view. *Skeptical Inquirer, 12,* 174–180. (10)

Sparrow, B., Liu, J., & Wegner, D. M. (2011). Google effects on memory: Cognitive consequences of having information at our fingertips. *Science, 333,* 776–778. (7)

Spear, L. P. (2000). Neurobehavioral changes in adolescence. *Current Directions in Psychological Science, 9,* 111–114. (5)

Spearman, C. (1904). "General intelligence," objectively determined and measured. *American Journal of Psychology, 15,* 201–293. (9)

Speer, J. R. (1989). Detection of plastic explosives. *Science, 243,* 1651. (8)

Spelke, E. S. (2005). Sex differences in intrinsic aptitude for mathematics and science? *American Psychologist, 60,* 950–958. (5)

Spellman, B. (2005, March). Could reality shows become reality experiments? *APS Observer, 18*(3), 34–35. (2)

Spengler, P. M., White, M. J., Ægisdóttir, S., Maugherman, A. S., Anderson, L. A., Cook, R. S., . . . Rush, J. D. (2009). The meta-analysis of clinical judgment project: Effects of experience on judgment accuracy. *The Counseling Psychologist, 37,* 350–399. (15)

Sperry, R. W. (1967). Split-brain approach to learning problems. In G. C. Quarton, T. Melnechuk, & F. O. Schmitt (Eds.), *The neurosciences: A study program* (pp. 714–722). New York: Rockefeller University Press. (3)

Spira, A., & Bajos, N. (1993). *Les comportements sexuels en France* [Sexual behaviors in France]. Paris: La documentation Française. (11)

Squire, L. R., Haist, F., & Shimamura, A. P. (1989). The neurology of memory: Quantitative assessment of retrograde amnesia in two groups of amnesic patients. *Journal of Neuroscience, 9,* 828–839. (7)

Sritharan, R., Heilpern, K., Wilbur, C. J., & Gawronski, B. (2010). I think I like you: Spontaneous and deliberate evaluations of potential romantic partners in an online dating context. *European Journal of Social Psychology, 40,* 1062–1077. (13)

Staddon, J. (1993). *Behaviorism.* London: Duckworth. (6)

Staddon, J. E. R. (1999). Theoretical behaviorism. In W. O'Donohue & R. Kitchener (Eds.), *Handbook of behaviorism* (pp. 217–241). San Diego, CA: Academic Press. (6)

Stalnaker, T. A., Roesch, M. R., Franz, T. M., Calu, D. J., Singh, T., & Schoenbaum, G. (2007). Cocaine-induced decision-making deficits are mediated by miscoding in basolateral amygdala. *Nature Neuroscience, 10,* 949–951. (3)

Starr, C., & Taggart, R. (1992). *Biology: The unity and diversity of life* (6th ed.). Belmont, CA: Wadsworth. (3)

Ste-Marie, D. M. (1999). Expert–novice differences in gymnastic judging: An information-processing perspective. *Applied Cognitive Psychology, 13,* 269–281. (8)

Steele, C. (2010). *Whistling Vivaldi.* New York: W. W. Norton. (9)

Steele, C. M., & Aronson, J. (1995). Stereotype threat and the intellectual test performance of African Americans. *Journal of Personality and Social Psychology, 69,* 797–811. (9)

Stefansson, H., Rujescu, D., Cichon, S., Pietiläinen, O. P. H., Ingason, A., Steinberg, S., . . . Stefansson, K. (2008). Large recurrent microdeletions associated with schizophrenia. *Nature, 455,* 232–236. (15)

Steffens, B. (2007). *Ibn al-Haytham: First Scientist.* Greensboro, NC: Morgan Reynolds Publishing. (4)

Stein, M. B., Hanna, C., Koverola, C., Torchia, M., & McClarty, B. (1997). Structural brain changes in PTSD. *Annals of the New York Academy of Sciences, 821,* 76–82. (12)

Steinberg, L., Graham, S., O'Brien, L., Woolard, J., Cauffman, E., & Banich, M. (2009). Age differences in future orientation and delay discounting. *Child Development, 80,* 28–44. (11)

Steinhausen, H.-C., Grigoroiu-Serbanescu, M., Boyadjieva, S., Neumärker, K.-J., & Metzke, C. W. (2009). The relevance of body weight in the medium-term to long-term course of adolescent anorexia nervosa. Findings from a multisite study. *International Journal of Eating Disorders, 42,* 19–25. (11)

Stella, N., Schweitzer, P., & Piomelli, D. (1997). A second endogenous cannabinoid that modulates long-term potentiation. *Nature, 382,* 677–678. (3)

Sternberg, K. J., Baradaran, L. P., Abbott, C. B., Lamb, M. E., & Guterman, E. (2006). Type of violence, age, and gender differences in the effects of family violence on children's behavior problems: A mega-analysis. *Developmental Review, 26,* 89–112. (5)

Sternberg, R. J. (1985). *Beyond IQ.* Cambridge, England: Cambridge University Press. (9)

Sternberg, R. J. (1997). The concept of intelligence and its role in lifelong learning and success. *American Psychologist, 52,* 1030–1037. (9)

Sternberg, R. J. (2002). Beyond *g*: The theory of successful intelligence. In R. J. Sternberg & E. L. Grigorenko (Eds.), *The general intelligence factor: How general is it?* (pp. 447–479). Mahwah, NJ: Erlbaum. (9)

Sternberg, R. J., Nokes, C., Geissler, P. W., Prince, R., Okatcha, F., Bundy, D. A., . . . Grigorenko, E. L. (2001). The relationship between academic and practical intelligence: A case study in Kenya. *Intelligence, 29,* 401–418. (9)

Stevens, S. S. (1961). To honor Fechner and repeal his law. *Science, 133,* 80–86. (1)

Stewart, B. D., von Hippel, W., & Radvansky, G. A. (2009). Age, race, and implicit prejudice. *Psychological Science, 20,* 164–168. (13)

Stewart, I. (1987). Are mathematicians logical? *Nature, 325,* 386–387. (9)

Stice, E. (2002). Risk and maintenance factors for eating pathology: A meta-analytic review. *Psychological Bulletin, 128,* 825–848. (11)

Stice, E., & Shaw, H. (2004). Eating disorder prevention programs: A meta-analytic review. *Psychological Bulletin, 130,* 206–227. (15)

Stice, E., Shaw, H., & Marti, C. N. (2006). A meta-analytic review of obesity prevention programs for children and adolescents: The skinny on interventions that work. *Psychological Bulletin, 132,* 667–691. (11)

Stickgold, R., Malia, A., Maguire, D., Roddenberry, D., & O'Connor, M. (2000). Replaying the game: Hypnagogic images in normals and amnesics. *Science, 290,* 350–353. (7)

Stiles, W. B., Shapiro, D. A., & Elliott, R. (1986). "Are all psychotherapies equivalent?" *American Psychologist, 41,* 165–180. (15)

Stone, A. A., Schwartz, J. E., Broderick, J. E., & Deaton, A. (2010). A snapshot of the age distribution of psychological well-being in the United States. *Proceedings of the National Academy of Sciences, U.S.A., 107,* 9985–9990. (12)

Stone, J., Lynch, C. I., Sjomeling, M., & Darley, J. M. (1999). Stereotype threat effects on Black and White athletic performance. *Journal of Personality and Social Psychology, 77,* 1213–1227. (9)

Stone, V. E., Nisenson, L., Eliassen, J. C., & Gazzaniga, M. S. (1996). Left hemisphere representations of emotional facial expressions. *Neuropsychologia, 34,* 23–29. (3)

Storms, M. D. (1973). Videotape and the attribution process: Reversing actors' and observers' points of view. *Journal of Personality and Social Psychology, 27,* 165–175. (13)

Strack, F., Martin, L. L., & Stepper, S. (1988). Inhibiting and facilitating conditions of the human smile: A nonobtrusive test of the facial feedback hypothesis. *Journal of Personality and Social Psychology, 54,* 768–777. (12)

Strakowski, S. M., Tsai, S.-Y., DelBello, M. P., Chen, C.-C., Fleck, D. E., Adler, C. M., . . . Amicone, J. (2007). Outcome following a first manic episode: Cross-national US and Taiwan comparison. *Bipolar Disorders, 9,* 820–827. (15)

Strange, B. A., Kroes, M. C. W., Roiser, J. P., Yan, G. C. Y., & Dolan, R. J. (2008). Emotion-induced retrograde amnesia is determined by a 5-HTT genetic polymorphism. *Journal of Neuroscience, 28,* 7036–7039. (7)

Strange, D., Garry, M., Bernstein, D. M., & Lindsay, D. S. (2011). Photographs cause false memories for the news. *Acta Psychologica, 136,* 90–94. (7)

Strange, D., Sutherland, R., & Garry, M. (2004). A photographic memory for false autobiographical events: The role of plausibility in children's false memories. *Australian Journal of Psychology, 56*(Suppl. S), 137. (7)

Strauch, I., & Lederbogen, S. (1999). The home dreams and waking fantasies of boys and girls between ages 9 and 15: A longitudinal study. *Dreaming, 9,* 153–161. (10)

Strenze, T. (2007). Intelligence and socioeconomic success: A meta-analytic review of longitudinal research. *Intelligence, 35,* 401–426. (9)

Striemer, C. L., Chapman, C. S., & Goodale, M. A. (2009). "Real-time" obstacle avoidance in the absence of primary visual cortex. *Proceedings of the National Academy of Sciences, 106,* 15996–16001. (3)

Stroebele, N., de Castro, J. M., Stuht, J., Catenacci, V., Wyatt, H. R., & Hill, J. O. (2008). A small-changes approach reduces energy intake in free-living humans. *Journal of the American College of Nutrition, 28,* 63–68. (11)

Struckman-Johnson, C., Struckman-Johnson, D., & Anderson, P. B. (2003). Tactics of sexual coercion: When men and women won't take no for an answer. *Journal of Sex Research, 40,* 76–86. (13)

Sturm, V. E., Ascher, E. A., Miller, B. L., & Levenson, R. W. (2008). Diminished self-conscious emotional responding in frontotemporal lobar degeneration patients. *Emotion, 8,* 861–869. (12)

Stuss, D. T., Alexander, M. P., Palumbo, C. L., Buckle, L., Sayer, L., & Pogue, J. (1994). Organizational strategies of patients with unilateral or bilateral frontal lobe injury in word list learning tasks. *Neuropsychology, 8,* 355–373. (7)

Sullivan, E. V., Deshmukh, A., Desmond, J. E., Mathalon, D. H., Rosenbloom, M. J., Lim, K. O., & Pfefferbaum, A. (2000). Contribution of alcohol abuse to cerebellar volume deficits in men with schizophrenia. *Archives of General Psychiatry, 57,* 894–902. (15)

Sullivan, P. F., Kendler, K. S., & Neale, M. C. (2003). Schizophrenia as a complex trait: Evidence from a meta-analysis of twin studies. *Archives of General Psychiatry, 60,* 1187–1192. (15)

Suls, J., Martin, R., & Wheeler, L. (2002). Social comparisons: Why, with whom, and with what effect? *Current Directions in Psychological Science, 11,* 159–163. (13)

Sun, Q., Townsend, M. K., Okereke, O. I., Rimm, E. B., Hu, F. B., Stampfer, M. J., . . . Grodstein, F. (2011). Alcohol consumption at midlife and successful ageing in women: A prospective cohort analysis in the Nurses' Health Study. *PLoS Medicine, 8,* e1001090. (2)

Sun, Y.-G., Zhao, Z.-Q., Meng, X.-L., Yin, J., Liu, X.-Y., & Chen, Z.-F. (2009). Cellular basis of itch sensation. *Science, 325,* 1531–1534. (4)

Sundet, J. M., Barlaug, D. G., & Torjussen, T. M. (2004). The end of the Flynn effect? A study of secular trends in mean intelligence test scores of Norwegian conscripts during half a century. *Intelligence, 32,* 349–362. (9)

Sundet, J. M., Eriksen, W., Borren, I., & Tambs, K. (2010). The Flynn effect in sibships: Investigating the role of age differences between siblings. *Intelligence, 38,* 38–44. (9)

Sundet, J. M., Eriksen, W., & Tambs, K. (2008). Intelligence correlations between brothers decrease with increasing age difference. *Psychological Science, 19,* 843–847. (9)

Suschinsky, K. D., & Lalumière, M. L. (2011). Prepared for anything? An investigation of female genital arousal in response to rape cues. *Psychological Science, 22,* 159–165. (11)

Susskind, J. M., Lee, D. H., Cusi, A., Feiman, R., Grabski, W., & Anderson, A. K. (2008). Expressing fear enhances sensory acquisition. *Nature Neuroscience, 11,* 843–850. (12)

Suvisaari, J. M., Haukka, J. K., Tanskanen, A. J., & Lönnqvist, J. K. (1999). Decline in the incidence of schizophrenia in Finnish cohorts born from 1954 to 1965. *Archives of General Psychiatry, 56,* 733–740. (15)

Suwazono, Y., Dochi, M., Sakata, K., Okubo, Y., Oishi, M., Tanaka, K., . . . Nogawa, K. (2008). A longitudinal study on the effect of shift work on weight gain in male Japanese workers. *Obesity, 16,* 1887–1893. (10)

Swan, S. H., Liu, F., Hines, M., Kruse, R. L., Wang, C., Redmon, J. B., . . . Weiss, B. (2010). Prenatal phthalate exposure and reduced masculine play in boys. *International Journal of Andrology, 33,* 259–269. (5)

Swinton, S. S. (1987). *The predictive validity of the restructured GRE with particular attention to older students* (GRE Board Professional Rep. No. 83-25P. ETS Research Rep. 87-22). Princeton, NJ: Educational Testing Service. (9)

Swoboda, H., Amering, M., Windhaber, J., & Katschnig, H. (2003). The long-term course of panic disorder—an 11 year follow-up. *Journal of Anxiety Disorders, 17,* 223–232. (15)

Szymanski, H. V., Simon, J. C., & Gutterman, N. (1983). Recovery from schizophrenic psychosis. *American Journal of Psychiatry, 140,* 335–338. (15)

Takano, Y., & Osaka, E. (1999). An unsupported common view: Comparing Japan and the U.S. on individualism/collectivism. *Asian Journal of Social Psychology, 2,* 311–341. (13)

Tamietto, M., Castelli, L., Vighetti, S., Perozzo, P., Geminiani, G., Weiskrantz, L., . . . de Gelder, B. (2009). Unseen facial and bodily expressions trigger fast emotional reactions. *Proceedings of the National Academy of Sciences, 106,* 17661–17666. (3)

Tanaka, J. W., Curran, T., & Sheinberg, D. L. (2005). The training and transfer of real-world perceptual expertise. *Psychological Science, 16,* 145–151. (8)

Taris, T. W. (2006). Is there a relationship between burnout and objective performance? *Work and Stress, 20,* 316–334.(11)

Tarr, M. J., & Gauthier, I. (2000). FFA: A flexible fusiform area for subordinate-level visual processing automatized by experience. *Nature Neuroscience, 3,* 764–769. (3)

Taylor, C. B., Bryson, S., Luce, K. H., Cunning, D., Doyle, A. C., Abascal, L. B., . . . Wilfley, D. E. (2006). Prevention of eating disorders in at-risk college-age women. *Archives of General Psychiatry, 63,* 881–888. (15)

Taylor, J., Roehrig, A. D., Hensler, B. S., Connor, C. M., & Schatschneider, C. (2010). Teacher quality moderates the genetic effects on early reading. *Science, 328,* 512–514. (9)

Teasdale, T. W., & Owen, D. R. (2005). A long-term rise and recent decline in intelligence test performance: The Flynn effect in reverse. *Personality and Individual Differences, 39,* 837–843. (9)

Teasdale, T. W., & Owen, D. R. (2008). Secular declines in cognitive test scores: A reversal of the Flynn effect. *Intelligence, 36,* 121–126. (9)

Teesson, M., Ross, J., Darke, S., Lynskey, M., Ali, R., Ritter, A., & Cooke, R. (2006). One year outcomes for heroin dependence: Findings from the Australian Treatment Outcome Study (ATOS). *Drug and Alcohol Dependence, 83,* 174–180. (15)

Teff, K. L., Elliott, S. S., Tschöp, M., Kieffer, T. J., Rader, D., Heiman, M., . . . Havel, P. J. (2004). Dietary fructose reduces circulating insulin and leptin, attenuates postprandial suppression of ghrelin, and increases triglycerides in women. *Journal of Clinical Endocrinology and Metabolism, 89,* 2963–2972. (11)

ten Have, M., de Graaf, R., & Monshouwer, K. (2011). Physical exercise in adults and mental health status: Findings from the Netherlands Mental Health Survey and Incidence Study (NEMESIS). *Journal of Psychosomatic Research, 71,* 342–348. (15)

Terr, L. (1988). What happens to early memories of trauma? A study of twenty children under age five at the time of documented traumatic events. *Journal of the American Academy of Child and Adolescent Psychiatry, 27,* 96–104. (7)

Terracciano, A., Abdel-Khalek, A. M., Ádám, N., Admaovová, L., Ahn, C.-k., Ahn, H.-n., . . . McCrae, R. R. (2005). National character does not reflect mean personality levels in 49 cultures. *Science, 310,* 96–100. (14)

Terracciano, A., Sanna, S., Uda, M., Deiana, B., Usala, G., . . . Costa, P. T. Jr. (2010). Genome-wide association scan for five major dimensions of personality. *Molecular Psychiatry, 15,* 647–656. (14)

Terrace, H. S., Petitto, L. A., Sanders, R. J., & Bever, T. G. (1979). Can an ape create a sentence? *Science, 206,* 891–902. (8)

Testa, M., Livingston, J. A., Vanzile-Tamsen, C., & Frone, M. R. (2003). The role of women's substance use in vulnerability to forcible and incapacitated rape. *Journal of Studies on Alcohol, 64,* 756–764. (13)

Tetlock, P. E. (1992). Good judgment in international politics: Three psychological perspectives. *Political Psychology, 13,* 517–539. (8)

Tett, R. P., & Burnett, D. D. (2003). A personality trait-based interactionist model of job performance. *Journal of Applied Psychology, 88,* 500–517. (11)

Tett, R. P., & Palmer, C. A. (1997). The validity of handwriting elements in relation to self-report personality trait measures. *Personality and Individual Differences, 22,* 11–18. (14)

Thanickal, T. C., Moore, R. Y., Nienhuis, R., Ramanathan, L., Gulyani, S., Aldrich, M., . . . Siegel, J. M. (2000). Reduced number of hypocretin neurons in human narcolepsy. *Neuron, 27,* 469–474. (10)

"The medals and the damage done." (2004). *Nature, 430,* 604. (3)

Thieman, T. J. (1984). A classroom demonstration of encoding specificity. *Teaching of Psychology, 11,* 101–102. (7)

Thierry, G., & Wu, Y. J. (2007). Brain potentials reveal unconscious translation during foreign-language comprehension. *Proceedings of the National Academy of Sciences, USA, 104,* 12530–12535. (8)

Thomas, C., Avidan, G., Humphreys, K., Jung, K., Gao, F., & Behrmann, M. (2009). Reduced structural connectivity in ventral visual cortex in congenital prosopagnosia. *Nature Neuroscience, 12,* 29–31. (3)

Thompson, C. R., & Church, R. M. (1980). An explanation of the language of a chimpanzee. *Science, 208,* 313–314. (8)

Thomsen, L., Frankenhuis, W. E., Ingold-Smith, M., & Carey, S. (2011). Big and mighty: Preverbal infants mentally represent social dominance. *Science, 331,* 477–480. (5)

Thoresen, C. J., Kaplan, S. A., Barsky, A. P., Warren, C. R., & de Chermont, K. (2003). The affective underpinnings of job perceptions and attitudes: A meta-analytic review and integration. *Psychological Bulletin, 129,* 914–945. (11)

Thorleifsson, G., Walters, G. B., Gudbjartsson, D. F., Steinthorsdottir, V., Sulem, P., Helgadottir, A., . . . Stefansson, K. (2009). Genome-wide association yields new sequence variants at seven loci that associate with measures of obesity. *Nature Genetics, 41,* 18–24. (11)

Thorndike, E. L. (1918). The nature, purposes, and general methods of measurements of educational products. In E. J. Ashbaugh, W. A. Averill, L. P. Ayres, F. W. Ballou, E. Bryner, B. R. Buckingham, et al. (Eds.), *The seventeenth yearbook of the National Society for the Study of Education. Part II: The measurement of educational products* (pp. 16–24). Bloomington, IL: Public School Publishing Company. (9)

Thorndike, E. L. (1970). *Animal intelligence.* Darien, CT: Hafner. (Original work published 1911) (6)

Timberlake, W., & Farmer-Dougan, V. A. (1991). Reinforcement in applied settings: Figuring out ahead of time what will work. *Psychological Bulletin, 110,* 379–391. (6)

Tinbergen, N. (1951). *The study of instinct.* Oxford, England: Oxford University Press. (3)

Tinbergen, N. (1958). *Curious Naturalists.* New York: Basic Books. (3)

Titchener, E. B. (1910). *A textbook of psychology.* New York: Macmillan. (1)

Todd, J. J., Fougnie, D., & Marois, R. (2005). Visual short-term memory load suppresses temporo-parietal junction activity and induces inattentional blindness. *Psychological Science, 16,* 965–972. (8)

Toh, K. L., Jones, C. R., He, Y., Eide, E. J., Hinz, W. A., Virshup, D. M., . . . Fu, Y. H. (2001). An hPer2 phosphorylation site mutation in familial advanced sleep phase syndrome. *Science, 291,* 1040–1043. (10)

Tolman, E. C. (1938). The determinants of behavior at a choice point. *Psychological Review, 45,* 1–41. (1)

Tolstoy, L. (1978). *Tolstoy's letters: Vol. I. 1828–1879.* New York: Charles Scribner's Sons. (Original works written 1828–1879) (5)

Tombaugh, C. W. (1980). *Out of the darkness, the planet Pluto.* Harrisburg, PA: Stackpole. (4)

Torrey, E. F. (1986). Geographic variations in schizophrenia. In C. Shagass, R. C. Josiassen, W. H. Bridger, K. J. Weiss, D. Stoff, & G. M. Simpson (Eds.), *Biological psychiatry 1985* (pp. 1080–1082). New York: Elsevier. (15)

Torrey, E. F., & Miller, J. (2001). *The invisible plague: The rise of mental illness from 1750 to the present.* New Brunswick, NJ: Rutgers University Press. (15)

Torrey, E. F., & Yolken, R. H. (2005). *Toxoplasma gondii* as a possible cause of schizophrenia. *Biological Psychiatry, 57,* 128S. (15)

Townshend, J. M., & Duka, T. (2003). Mixed emotions: Alcoholics' impairments in the recognition of specific emotional facial expressions. *Neuropsychologia, 41,* 773–782. (12)

Tracy, J. L., & Beall, A. T. (2011). Happy guys finish last: The impact of emotion expressions on sexual attraction. *Emotion, 11,* 1379–1387. (13)

Tracy, J. L., & Robins, R. W. (2004). Show your pride: Evidence for a discrete emotion expression. *Psychological Science, 15,* 194–197. (12)

Tracy, J. L., Robins, R. W., & Lagattuta, K. H. (2005). Can children recognize pride? *Emotion, 5,* 251–257. (12)

Trawalter, S., & Richeson, J. A. (2006). Regulatory focus and executive function after interracial interactions. *Journal of Experimental Social Psychology, 42,* 406–412. (13)

Treisman, A. (1999). Feature binding, attention and object perception. In G. W. Humphreys, J. Duncan, & A. Treisman (Eds.), *Attention, space and action* (pp. 91–111). Oxford, England: Oxford University Press. (3)

Treisman, A., & Souther, J. (1985). Search asymmetry: A diagnostic for preattentive processing of separable features. *Journal of Experimental Psychology: General, 114,* 285–310. (8)

Trevena, J. A., & Miller, J. (2002). Cortical movement preparation before and after a conscious decision to move. *Consciousness and Cognition, 11,* 162–190. (10)

Trickett, E. J. (2009). Community psychology: Individuals and interventions in community context. *Annual Review of Psychology, 60,* 395–419. (15)

Trimmer, C. G., & Cuddy, L. L. (2008). Emotional intelligence, not music training, predicts recognition of emotional speech prosody. *Emotion, 8,* 838–849. (12)

Tronick, E. Z., Morelli, G. A., & Ivey, P. K. (1992). The Efe forager infant and toddler's pattern of social relationships: Multiple and simultaneous. *Developmental Psychology, 28,* 568–577. (5)

True, W. R., Xian, H., Scherer, J. F., Madden, P. A. F., Bucholz, K. K., Heath, A. C., . . . Tsuang, M. (1999). Common genetic vulnerability for nicotine and alcohol dependence in men. *Archives of General Psychiatry, 56,* 655–661. (15)

Tsankova, N., Renthal, W., Kumar, A., & Nestler, E. J. (2007). Epigenetic regulation in psychiatric disorders. *Nature Reviews Neuroscience, 8,* 355–367. (3)

Tucker-Drob, E. M., Rhemtulla, M., Harden, K. P., Turkheimer, E., & Fask, D. (2011). Emergence of a gene x socioeconomic status interaction on infant mental ability between 10 months and 2 years. *Psychological Science, 22,* 125–133. (9)

Tuerk, P. W. (2005). Research in the high-stakes era. *Psychological Science, 16,* 419–425. (9)

Tugade, M. M., & Fredrickson, B. L. (2004). Resilient individuals use positive emotions to bounce back from negative emotional

experiences. *Journal of Personality and Social Psychology, 86,* 320–333. (12)

Tuiten, A., Van Honk, J., Koppeschaar, H., Bernaards, C., Thijssen, J., & Verbaten, R. (2000). Time course of effects of testosterone administration on sexual arousal in women. *Archives of General Psychiatry, 57,* 149–153. (11)

Tulving, E. (1989). Remembering and knowing the past. *American Scientist, 77,* 361–367. (7)

Tulving, E., & Thomson, D. M. (1973). Encoding specificity and retrieval processes in episodic memory. *Psychological Review, 80,* 352–373. (7)

Tuntiya, N. (2007). Free-air treatment for mental patients: The deinstitutionalization debate of the nineteenth century. *Sociological Perspectives, 50,* 469–488. (15)

Tups, A. (2009). Physiological models of leptin resistance. *Journal of Neuroendocrinology, 21,* 961–971. (11)

Turkheimer, E., Haley, A., Waldron, M., D'Onofrio, B., & Gottesman, I. I. (2003). Socioeconomic status modifies heritability of IQ in young children. *Psychological Science, 14,* 623–628. (9)

Tversky, A., & Kahneman, D. (1981). The framing of decisions and the psychology of choice. *Science, 211,* 453–458. (8)

Tversky, A., & Kahneman, D. (1983). Extensional versus intuitive reasoning: The conjunctional fallacy in probability judgment. *Psychological Review, 90,* 293–315. (8)

Twenge, J. M. (2000). The age of anxiety? Birth cohort change in anxiety and neuroticism, 1952–1993. *Journal of Personality and Social Psychology, 79,* 1007–1021. (14)

Twenge, J. M. (2006). *Generation me.* New York: Free Press. (5)

Twenge, J. M. (2009). Change over time in obedience: The jury's still out, but it might be decreasing. *American Psychologist, 64,* 28–31. (13)

Twenge, J. M., & Campbell, W. K. (2008). Increases in positive self-views among high-school students. *Psychological Science, 19,* 1082–1086. (5)

Twenge, J. M., Konrath, S., Foster, J. D., Campbell, W. K., & Bushman, B. J. (2008). Egos inflating over time: A cross-temporal meta-analysis of the narcissistic personality inventory. *Journal of Personality, 76,* 875–901. (14)

U.S. Department of Labor. (2008). *Occupational outlook handbook* (2008–2009 ed.). Retrieved November 9, 2008, from www.bls.gov/oco/ocos056.htm. (1)

Uchino, B. N., Cacioppo, J. T., & Kiecolt-Glaser, J. K. (1996). The relationship between social support and physiological processes: A review with emphasis on underlying mechanisms and implications for health. *Psychological Bulletin, 119,* 488–531. (12)

Udolf, R. (1981). *Handbook of hypnosis for professionals.* New York: Van Nostrand Reinhold. (10)

Udry, J. R., & Chantala, K. (2006). Masculinity-femininity predicts sexual orientation in men but not in women. *Journal of Biosocial Science, 38,* 797–809. (11)

Uhlhaas, P. J., Linden, D. E. J., Singer, W., Haenschel, C., Lindner, M., Maurer, K., & Rodriguez, E. (2006). Dysfunctional long-range coordination of neural activity during Gestalt perception in schizophrenia. *Journal of Neuroscience, 26,* 8168–8175. (15)

Ulrich, R. E., Stachnik, T. J., & Stainton, N. R. (1963). Student acceptance of generalized

personality interpretations. *Psychological Reports, 13,* 831–834. (14)

Ulrich, R. S. (1984). View through a window may influence recovery from surgery. *Science, 224,* 420–421. (4)

Unsworth, N., Heitz, R. P., & Parks, N. A. (2008). The importance of temporal distinctiveness for forgetting over the short term. *Psychological Science, 19,* 1078–1081. (7)

Vacic, V., McCarthy, S., Malhotra, D., Murray, F., Chou, H.-H., Peoples, A, . . . Sebat, J. (2011). Duplications of the neuropeptide receptor gene *VIPR2* confer significant risk for schizophrenia. *Nature, 471,* 499–503. (15)

Vaillant, G. E., & Milofsky, E. S. (1982). The etiology of alcoholism: A prospective viewpoint. *American Psychologist, 37,* 494–503. (15)

Valli, K., Strandholm, T., Sillanmäki, L., & Revonsuo, A. (2008). Dreams are more negative than real life: Implications for the function of dreaming. *Cognition and Emotion, 22,* 833–861. (10)

Vallines, I., & Greenlee, M. W. (2006). Saccadic suppression of retinotopically localized blood oxygen level-dependent responses in human primary visual area V1. *Journal of Neuroscience, 26,* 5965–5969. (8)

van Anders, S. M., & Watson, N. V. (2006). Relationship status and testosterone in North American heterosexual and non-heterosexual men and women: Cross-sectional and longitudinal data. *Psychoneuroendocrinology, 31,* 715–723. (11)

van Anders, S. M., Hamilton, L. D., & Watson, N. V. (2007). Multiple partners are associated with higher testosterone in North American men and women. *Hormones and Behavior, 51,* 454–459. (11)

Van Cantfort, T. E., Gardner, B. T., & Gardner, R. A. (1989). Developmental trends in replies to Wh-questions by children and chimpanzees. In R. A. Gardner, B. T. Gardner, & T. E. Van Cantfort (Eds.), *Teaching sign language to chimpanzees* (pp. 198–239). Albany: State University of New York Press. (8)

van den Hout, M., & Kindt, M. (2003). Repeated checking causes memory distrust. *Behaviour Research and Therapy, 41,* 301–316. (15)

van der Pligt, J., de Vries, N. K., Manstead, A. S. R., & van Harreveld, F. (2000). The importance of being selective: Weighing the role of attribute importance in attitudinal judgment. *Advances in Experimental Social Psychology, 32,* 135–200. (13)

van der Pligt, J., & Eiser, J. R. (1983). Actors' and observers' attributions, self-serving bias, and positivity. *European Journal of Social Psychology, 13,* 95–104. (13)

Van der Werf, Y. D., Altena, E., Schoonheim, M. M., Sanz-Arigita, E. J., Vis, J. C., De Rijke, W., & Van Someren, E. J. (2009). Sleep benefits subsequent hippocampal functioning. *Nature Neuroscience, 12,* 122–123. (10)

Van Der Zee, K. I., Huet, R. C. G., Cazemier, C., & Evers, K. (2002). The influence of the premedication consult and preparatory information about anesthesia on anxiety among patients undergoing cardiac surgery. *Anxiety, Stress, and Coping, 15,* 123–133. (12)

van IJzendoorn, M. H., Juffer, F., & Poelhuis, C. W. K. (2005). Adoption and cognitive development: A meta-analytic comparison of adopted and nonadopted children's IQ and school performance. *Psychological Bulletin, 131,* 301–316. (9)

Vandello, J. A., Bosson, J. K., Cohen, D., Burnaford, R. M., & Weaver, J. R. (2008). Precarious manhood. *Journal of Personality and Social Psychology, 95,* 1325–1339. (5)

Vartanian, L. R., Herman, C. P., & Wansink, B. (2008). Are we aware of the external factors that influence our food intake? *Health Psychology, 27,* 533–538. (11)

Vasey, P. L., & VanderLaan, D. P. (2010). An adaptive cognitive dissociation between willingness to help kin and nonkin in Samoan *Fa'afafine. Psychological Science, 21,* 292–297. (11)

Vasterling, J., Duke, L. M., Brailey, K., Constans, J. I., Allain, A. N., & Sutker, P. B. (2002). Attention, learning, and memory performances and intellectual resources in Vietnam veterans: PTSD and no disorder comparisons. *Neuropsychology, 16,* 5–14. (9)

Vega, V., & Malamuth, N. M. (2007). Predicting sexual aggression: The role of pornography in the context of general and specific risk factors. *Aggressive Behavior, 33,* 104–117. (13)

Verona, E., & Sullivan, E. A. (2008). Emotional catharsis and aggression revisited: Heart rate reduction following aggressive responding. *Emotion, 8,* 331–340. (14)

Verplanken, B., & Faes, S. (1999). Good intentions, bad habits, and effects of forming implementation intentions on healthy eating. *European Journal of Social Psychology, 29,* 591–604. (11)

Verrey, F., & Beron, J. (1996). Activation and supply of channels and pumps by aldosterone. *News in Physiological Sciences, 11,* 126–133. (1)

Vetencourt, J. F. M., Sale, A., Viegi, A., Baroncelli, L., DePasquale, R., . . . Maffei, L. (2008). The antidepressant fluoxetine restores plasticity in the adult visual cortex. *Science, 320,* 385–388. (15)

Viglione, D. J., & Taylor, N. (2003). Empirical support for interrater reliability of Rorschach Comprehensive System scoring. *Journal of Clinical Psychology, 59,* 111–121. (14)

Viken, R. J., Rose, R. J., Kaprio, J., & Koskenvuo, M. (1994). A developmental genetic analysis of adult personality: Extraversion and neuroticism from 18 to 59 years of age. *Journal of Personality and Social Psychology, 66,* 722–730. (5, 14)

Vinci, C., Copeland, A. L., & Carrigan, M. H. (2011). Exposure to negative affect cues and urge to smoke. *Experimental and Clinical Psychopharmacology, 20,* 47–55. (15)

Visser, B. A., Ashton, M. C., & Vernon, P. A. (2006). Beyond *g*: Putting multiple intelligences theory to the test. *Intelligence, 34,* 487–502. (9)

Vitacco, M. J., Van Rybroek, G. J., Erickson, S. K., Rogstad, J. E., Tripp, A., Harris, L., & Miller, R. (2008). Developing services for insanity acquittees conditionally released into the community: Maximizing success and minimizing recidivism. *Psychological Services, 5,* 118–125. (15)

Vohs, K. D., & Schooler, J. W. (2008). The value of believing in free will: Encouraging a belief in determinism increases cheating. *Psychological Science, 19,* 49–54. (1)

Voineagu, I., Wang, X., Johnston, P., Lowe, J. K., Tian, Y., . . . Geschwind, D. H. (2011). Transcriptomic analysis of autistic brain reveals convergent molecular pathology. *Nature, 474,* 380–384. (15)

Vokey, J. R., & Read, J. D. (1985). Subliminal messages: Between the devil and the media. *American Psychologist, 40,* 1231–1239. (4)

Volkow, N. D., Wang, G.-J., & Fowler, J. S. (1997). Imaging studies of cocaine in the human brain and studies of the cocaine addict. *Annals of the New York Academy of Sciences, 820,* 41–55. (3)

Volkow, N. D., Wang, G.-J., Fowler, J. S., Tomasi, D., & Telang, F. (2011). Addiction: Beyond dopamine reward circuitry. *Proceedings of the National Academy of Sciences (U.S.A.), 108,* 15037–15042. (15)

Volkow, N. D., Wang, G.-J., Fowler, J., Gatley, S. J., Logan, J., Ding, Y.-S., . . . Pappas. N. (1998). Dopamine transporter occupancies in the human brain induced by therapeutic doses of oral methylphenidate. *American Journal of Psychiatry, 155,* 1325–1331. (3)

Volkow, N. D., Wang, G.-J., Telang, F., Fowler, J. S., Logan, J., Childress, A.-R., . . . Wong, C. (2006). Cocaine cues and dopamine in dorsal striatum: Mechanism of craving in cocaine addiction. *Journal of Neuroscience, 26,* 6583–6588. (15)

von Hippel, W., Brener, L., & von Hippel, C. (2008). Implicit prejudice toward injecting drug users predicts intentions to change jobs among drug and alcohol nurses. *Psychological Science, 19,* 7–11. (14)

von Stumm, S., Hell, B., & Chamorro-Premuzic, T. (2011). The hungry mind: Intellectual curiosity is the third pillar of academic performance. *Perspectives on Psychological Science, 6,* 574–588. (9)

Vorauer, J. D., Gagnon, A., & Sasaki, S. J. (2009). Salient intergroup ideology and intergroup interaction. *Psychological Science, 20,* 838–845. (13)

Vrij, A., Granhag, P. A., & Porter, S. (2010). Pitfalls and opportunities in nonverbal and verbal lie detection. *Psychological Science in the Public Interest, 11,* 89–121. (12)

Vroom, V. H., & Jago, A. G. (2007). The role of the situation in leadership. *American Psychologist, 62,* 17–24. (11)

Vyazovskiy, V. V., Cirelli, C., Pfister-Genskow, M., Faraguna, U., & Tononi, G. (2008). Molecular and electrophysiological evidence for net synaptic potentiation in wake and depression in sleep. *Nature Neuroscience, 11,* 200–208. (10)

Vyazovskiy, V. V., Olcese, U., Hanlon, E. C., Nir, Y., Cirelli, C., . . . Tononi, G. (2011). Local sleep in awake rats. *Nature, 472,* 443–447. (10)

Vygotsky, L. S. (1978). *Mind in society.* Cambridge, MA: Harvard University Press. (5)

Wachholtz, A. B., & Pargament, K. I. (2008). Migraines and meditation: Does spirituality matter? *Journal of Behavioral Medicine, 31,* 351–366. (10)

Wachtel, P. L. (2000). Psychotherapy in the twenty-first century. *American Journal of Psychotherapy, 54,* 441–450. (15)

Wade, K. A., Garry, M., Read, J. D., & Lindsay, D. S. (2002). A picture is worth a thousand lies: Using false photographs to create false childhood memories. *Psychonomic Bulletin and Review, 9,* 597–603. (7)

Wager, T. D., Scott, D. J., & Zubieta, J.-K. (2007). Placebo effects on human µ-opioid activity during pain. *Proceedings of the National Academy of Sciences (U.S.A.), 104,* 11056–11061. (4)

Wagner, A. D., Desmond, J. E., Demb, J. B., Glover, G. H., & Gabrieli, J. D. E. (1997). Semantic repetition priming for verbal and pictorial knowledge: A functional MRI study of left inferior prefrontal cortex. *Journal of Cognitive Neuroscience, 9,* 714–726. (3)

Wagstaff, G. F., Brunas-Wagstaff, J., Cole, J., Knapton, L., Winterbottom, J., Crean, V., & Wheatcroft, J. (2004). Facilitating memory with hypnosis, focused meditation, and eye closure. *International Journal of Clinical and Experimental Hypnosis, 52,* 434–455. (10)

Wai, J., & Putallaz, M. (2011). The Flynn effect puzzle: A 30-year examination from the right tail of the ability distribution provides some missing pieces. *Intelligence, 39,* 443–455. (9)

Wainright, J. L., Russell, S. T., & Patterson, C. J. (2004). Psychosocial adjustment, school outcomes, and romantic relationships of adolescents with same-sex parents. *Child Development, 75,* 1886–1898. (5)

Wald, G. (1968). Molecular basis of visual excitation. *Science, 162,* 230–239. (4)

Waldherr, M., & Neumann, I. D. (2007). Centrally released oxytocin mediates mating-induced anxiolysis in male rats. *Proceedings of the National Academy of Sciences, U.S.A., 104,* 16681–16684. (11)

Waller, N. G., Kojetin, B. A., Bouchard, T. J., Jr., Lykken, D. T., & Tellegen, A. (1990). Genetic and environmental influences on religious interests, attitudes, and values: A study of twins reared apart and together. *Psychological Science, 1,* 138–142. (5)

Walsh, R., & Shapiro, S. L. (2006). The meeting of meditative disciplines and Western psychology. *American Psychologist, 61,* 227–239. (10)

Walster, E., Aronson, E., Abrahams, D., & Rottman, L. (1966). Importance of physical attractiveness in dating behavior. *Journal of Personality and Social Psychology, 4,* 508–516. (13)

Walters, E. T. (2009). Chronic pain, memory, and injury: Evolutionary clues from snail and rat nociceptors. *International Journal of Comparative Psychology, 22,* 127–140. (4)

Walton, G. M., & Spencer, S. J. (2009). Latent ability. *Psychological Science, 20,* 1132–1139. (9)

Wampold, B. E., Mondin, G. W., Moody, M., Stich, F., Benson, K., & Ahn, H. (1997). A meta-analysis of outcome studies comparing bona fide psychotherapies: Empirically, "All must have prizes." *Psychological Bulletin, 122,* 203–215. (15)

Wandersman, A., & Florin, P. (2003). Community interventions and effective prevention. *American Psychologist, 58,* 441–448. (15)

Wang, P. S., Lane, M., Olfson, M., Pincus, H. A., Wells, K. B., & Kessler, R. C. (2005). Twelve-month use of mental health services in the United States. *Archives of General Psychiatry, 62,* 629–640. (15)

Wansink, B., & Kim, J. (2005). Bad popcorn in big buckets: Portion size can influence intake as much as taste. *Journal of Nutrition Education and Behavior, 37,* 242–245. (11)

Wansink, B., & Payne, C. R. (2009). The joy of cooking too much: 70 years of calorie increases in classic recipes. *Annals of Internal Medicine, 150,* 291. (11)

Wansink, B., Payne, C. R., & North, J. (2007). Fine as North Dakota wine: Sensory expectations and the intake of companion foods. *Physiology & Behavior, 90,* 712–716. (11)

Wansink, B., & van Ittersum, K. (2003). Bottoms up! The influence of elongation on pouring and consumption volume. *Journal of Consumer Research, 30,* 455–463. (5)

Wansink, B., van Ittersum, K., & Painter, J. E. (2006). Ice cream illusions—Bowls, spoons, and self-served portion sizes. *American Journal of Preventive Medicine, 31,* 240–243. (11)

Wansink, B., & Wansink, C. S. (2010). The largest Last Supper: Depictions of food portions and plate size increased over the millennium. *International Journal of Obesity, 34,* 943–944. (11)

Warneken, F., Lohse, K., Melis, A. P., & Tomasello, M. (2011). Young children share the spoils after collaboration. *Psychological Science, 22,* 267–273. (5)

Warren, R. M. (1970). Perceptual restoration of missing speech sounds. *Science, 167,* 392–393. (4, 8)

Warren, R. M. (1999). *Auditory perception.* Cambridge, England: Cambridge University Press. (4)

Washington, E. (2006). *Female socialization: How daughters affect their legislator fathers' voting on women's issues* (Working Paper No. 11924). Cambridge, MA: National Bureau of Economic Research. (2)

Wason, P. C. (1960). On the failure to eliminate hypotheses in a conceptual task. *Quarterly Journal of Experimental Psychology, 12,* 129–140. (8)

Waters, E., Merrick, S., Treboux, D., Crowell, J., & Albersheim, L. (2000). Attachment security in infancy and early adulthood: A twenty-year longitudinal study. *Child Development, 71,* 684–689. (5)

Watson, D., & Clark, L. A. (2006). Clinical diagnosis at the crossroads. *Clinical Psychology, 13,* 210–215. (15)

Watson, D., Wiese, D., Vaidya, J., & Tellegen, A. (1999). The two general activation systems of affect: Structural findings, evolutionary considerations, and psychobiological evidence. *Journal of Personality and Social Psychology, 76,* 820–838. (12)

Watson, J. B. (1913). Psychology as the behaviorist views it. *Psychological Review, 20,* 158–177. (1)

Watson, J. B. (1919). *Psychology from the standpoint of a behaviorist.* Philadelphia: Lippincott. (1)

Watson, J. B. (1925). *Behaviorism.* New York: W. W. Norton. (1, 6)

Watson, J. B., & Rayner, R. (1920). Conditioned emotional reactions. *Journal of Experimental Psychology, 3,* 1–14. (15)

Watson, J. M., Balota, D. A., & Roediger, H. L., III (2003). Creating false memories with hybrid lists of semantic and phonological associates: Over-additive false memories produced by converging associative networks. *Journal of Memory and Language, 49,* 95–118. (7)

Weaver, I. C. G., Cervoni, N., Champagne, F. A., D'Alessio, A. C., Sharma, S., Seckl, J. R., . . . Meaney, M. J. (2004). Epigenetic programming by maternal behavior. *Nature Neuroscience, 7,* 847–854. (3)

Weeden, J., & Sabini, J. (2005). Physical attractiveness and health in Western societies: A review. *Psychological Bulletin, 131,* 635–653. (13)

Wegner, D. M. (2002). *The illusion of conscious will.* Cambridge, MA: MIT Press. (1, 10)

Wegner, D. M. (2009). How to think, say, or do precisely the worst thing for any occasion. *Science, 325,* 48–50. (13)

Weinberger, D. R. (1996). On the plausibility of "the neurodevelopmental hypothesis" of schizophrenia. *Neuropsychopharmacology, 14,* 1S–11S. (15)

Weinberger, D. R. (1999). Cell biology of the hippocampal formation in schizophrenia. *Biological Psychiatry, 45,* 395–402. (15)

Weiskrantz, L., Warrington, E. K., Sanders, M. D., & Marshall, J. (1974). Visual capacity in the hemianopic field following a restricted occipital ablation. *Brain, 97,* 709–728. (3)

Weissman, M. M., Leaf, P. J., & Bruce, M. L. (1987). Single parent women: A community study. *Social Psychiatry, 22,* 29–36. (5)

Weissman, M. M., Warner, V., Wickramaratne, P., Moreau, D., & Olfson, M. (1997). Offspring of depressed parents. *Archives of General Psychiatry, 54,* 932–940. (15)

Wellings, K., Field, J., Johnson, A., & Wadsworth, J. (1994). *Sexual behavior in Britain: The national survey of sexual attitudes and lifestyles.* New York: Penguin. (11)

Wellman, H. M., Cross, D., & Watson, J. (2001). Meta-analysis of theory-of-mind development: The truth about false beliefs. *Child Development, 72,* 655–684. (5)

Wells, G. L., Malpass, R. S., Lindsay, R. C. L., Fisher, R. P., Turtle, J. W., & Fulero, S. M. (2000). From the lab to the police station. *American Psychologist, 55,* 581–598. (7)

Wells, G. L., Memon, A., & Penrod, S. D. (2006). Eyewitness evidence: Improving its probative value. *Psychological Science in the Public Interest, 7,* 45–75. (7)

Wells, G. L., Olson, E. A., & Charman, S. D. (2003). Distorted retrospective eyewitness reports as functions of feedback and delay. *Journal of Experimental Psychology: General, 9,* 42–52. (7)

Wender, P. H., Wolf, L. E., & Wasserstein, J. (2001). Adults with ADHD. *Annals of the New York Academy of Sciences, 931,* 1–16. (8)

Werker, J. F., & Tees, R. C. (2005). Speech perception as a window for understanding plasticity and commitment in language systems of the brain. *Developmental Psychology, 46,* 233–251. (8)

Werle, C. O. C., Wansink, B., & Payne, C. R. (2011). Just thinking about exercise makes me serve more food. Physical activity and calorie compensation. *Appetite, 56,* 332–335. (11)

Westen, D. (1998). The scientific legacy of Sigmund Freud: Toward a psychodynamically informed psychological science. *Psychological Bulletin, 124,* 333–371. (14)

Westerberg, C. E., & Marsolek, C. J. (2006). Do instructional warnings reduce false recognition? *Applied Cognitive Psychology, 20,* 97–114. (7)

Wethington, E., Kessler, R. C., & Pixley, J. E. (2004). Turning points in adulthood. In O. G. Brim, C. D. Ryff, & R. C. Kessler (Eds.), *How healthy are we?* (pp. 586–613). Chicago: University of Chicago Press. (5)

Wexler, B. E., Zhu, H., Bell, M. D., Nicholls, S. S., Fulbright, R. K., Gore, J. C., . . . Peterson, B. S. (2009). Neuropsychological near normality and brain abnormality in schizophrenia. *American Journal of Psychiatry, 166,* 189–195. (15)

Whalen, P. J. (1998). Fear, vigilance, and ambiguity: Initial neuroimaging studies of the human amygdala. *Current Directions in Psychological Science, 7,* 177–188. (12)

Wheeler, D. D. (1970). Processes in word recognition. *Cognitive Psychology, 1,* 59–85. (8)

Wheeler, M. E., & Treisman, A. M. (2002). Binding in short-term visual memory. *Journal of Experimental Psychology: General, 131,* 48–64. (3)

White, M. P., & Dolan, P. (2009). Accounting for the richness of daily activities. *Psychological Science, 20,* 1000–1008. (12)

White, S. J., Johnson, R. L., Liversedge, S. P., & Rayner, K. (2008). Eye movements when reading transposed text: The importance of word-beginning letters. *Journal of Experimental Psychology: Human Perception and Performance, 34,* 1261–1276. (8)

White, S., O'Reilly, H., & Frith, U. (2009). Big heads, small details and autism. *Neuropsychologia, 47,* 1274–1281. (15)

Whitson, J. A., & Galinsky, A. D. (2008). Lacking control increases illusory pattern perception. *Science, 322,* 115–117. (12)

Wichman, A. L., Rodgers, J. L., & MacCallum, R. C. (2006). A multilevel approach to the relationship between birth order and intelligence. *Personality and Social Psychology Bulletin, 32,* 117–127. (5)

Wicklund, R. A., & Brehm, J. W. (1976). *Perspectives on cognitive dissonance.* Hillsdale, NJ: Erlbaum. (13)

Wig, N. N., Menon, D. K., Bedi, H., Leff, J., Kuipers, L., Ghosh, A., . . . Sartorius, N. (1987). Expressed emotion and schizophrenia in North India: II. Distribution of expressed emotion components among relatives of schizophrenic patients in Aarhus and Chandigarh. *British Journal of Psychiatry, 151,* 160–165. (15)

Wilensky, A. E., Schafe, G. E., Kristensen, M. P., & LeDoux, J. E. (2006). Rethinking the fear circuit. *Journal of Neuroscience, 26,* 12387–12396. (12)

Wilkins, L., & Richter, C. P. (1940). A great craving for salt by a child with corticoadrenal insufficiency. *Journal of the American Medical Association, 114,* 866–868. (1)

Willems, R. M., Labruna, L., D'Esposito, M., Ivry, R., & Casasanto, D. (2011). A functional role for the motor system in language understanding: Evidence from theta-burst transcranial magnetic stimulation. *Psychological Science, 22,* 849–854. (8)

Williams, C. L., Barnett, A. M., & Meck, W. H. (1990). Organizational effects of early gonadal secretions on sexual differentiation in spatial memory. *Behavioral Neuroscience, 104,* 84–97. (5)

Williams, K. D., & Karau, S. J. (1991). Social loafing and social compensation: The effects of expectations of co-worker performance. *Journal of Personality and Social Psychology, 61,* 570–581. (1)

Williams, L. E., & Bargh, J. A. (2008). Experiencing physical warmth promotes interpersonal warmth. *Science, 322,* 606–607. (1)

Williams, L. M. (1994). Recall of childhood trauma: A prospective study of women's memories of child sexual abuse. *Journal of Consulting and Clinical Psychology, 61,* 1167–1176. (7)

Williams, R. W., & Herrup, K. (1988). The control of neuron number. *Annual Review of Neuroscience, 11,* 423–453. (3)

Williamson, D. A., Ravussin, E., Wong, M.-L., Wagner, A., DiPaoli, A., Caglayan, S., . . . Licinio, J. (2005). Microanalysis of eating behavior of three leptin deficient adults treated with leptin therapy. *Appetite, 45,* 75–80. (11)

Wilson, D. S., Near, D., & Miller, R. R. (1996). Machiavellianism: A synthesis of the evolutionary and psychological literatures. *Psychological Bulletin, 119,* 285–299. (13)

Wilson, G. T., Grilo, C. M., & Vitousek, K. M. (2007). Psychological treatment of eating disorders. *American Psychologist, 62,* 199–216. (11)

Wilson, J. R., & the editors of *Life.* (1964). *The mind.* New York: Time. (4)

Wilson, R. I., & Nicoll, R. A. (2002). Endocannabinoid signaling in the brain. *Science, 296,* 678–682. (3)

Wilson, R. S. (1987). Risk and resilience in early mental development. In S. Chess & A. Thomas (Eds.), *Annual progress in child psychiatry and child development 1986* (pp. 69–85). New York: Brunner/Mazel. (5)

Wimmer, H., & Perner, J. (1983). Beliefs about beliefs: Representation and constraining function of wrong beliefs in young children's understanding of deception. *Cognition, 13,* 103–128. (5)

Winer, G. A., & Cottrell, J. E. (1996). Does anything leave the eye when we see? Extramission beliefs of children and adults. *Current Directions in Psychological Science, 5,* 137–142. (4)

Winer, G. A., Cottrell, J. E., Gregg, V., Fournier, J. S., & Bica, L. A. (2002). Fundamentally misunderstanding visual perception: Adults' belief in visual emissions. *American Psychologist, 57,* 417–424. (4)

Winner, E. (1986, August). Where pelicans kiss seals. *Psychology Today,* 24–35. (5)

Winner, E. (2000). Giftedness: Current theory and research. *Current Directions in Psychological Science, 9,* 153–156. (9)

Winocur, G., & Hasher, L. (1999). Aging and time-of-day effects on cognition in rats. *Behavioral Neuroscience, 113,* 991–997. (10)

Winocur, G., & Hasher, L. (2004). Age and time-of-day effects on learning and memory in a non-matching-to-sample test. *Neurobiology of Aging, 25,* 1107–1115. (10)

Winocur, G., Moscovitch, M., & Sekeres, M. (2007). Memory consolidation or transformation: Context manipulation and hippocampal representations of memory. *Nature Neuroscience, 10,* 555–557. (7)

Witkiewitz, K., & Marlatt, G. A. (2004). Relapse prevention for alcohol and drug problems: That was Zen, this is Tao. *American Psychologist, 59,* 224–235. (15)

Wolfe, J. M., Horowitz, T. S., & Kenner, N. M. (2005). Rare items often missed in visual searches. *Nature, 435,* 439–440. (4)

Wolkin, A., Rusinek, H., Vaid, G., Arena, L., Lafargue, T., Sanfilipo, M., . . . Rotrosen, J. (1998). Structural magnetic resonance image averaging in schizophrenia. *American Journal of Psychiatry, 155,* 1064–1073. (15)

Wolman, B. B. (1989). *Dictionary of behavioral science* (2nd ed.). San Diego, CA: Academic Press. (9)

Wolpe, J. (1961). The systematic desensitization treatment of neuroses. *Journal of Nervous and Mental Disease, 132,* 189–203. (15)

Wolraich, M. L., Lindgren, S. D., Stumbo, P. J., Steglink, L. D., Appelbaum, M. I., & Kiritsy, M. C. (1994). Effects of diets high in sucrose or aspartame on the behavior and cognitive performance of children. *New England Journal of Medicine, 330,* 301–307. (2)

Wood, J. M., Nezworski, T., Lilienfeld, S. O., & Garb, H. N. (2003). *What's wrong with the Rorschach?* San Francisco: Jossey-Bass. (14)

Wood, J. V., Perunovic, W. Q. E., & Lee, J. W. (2009). Positive self-statements: Power for some, peril for others. *Psychological Science, 20,* 860–866. (13)

Wood, S., Hanoch, Y., Barnes, A., Liu, P.-J., Cummings, J., Bhattacharya, C., & Rice, T. (2011). Numeracy and Medicare Part D: The importance of choice and literacy for numbers in optimizing decision making for Medicare's prescription drug program. *Psychology & Aging, 26,* 295–307. (8)

Wood, W., & Eagly, A. H. (2002). A cross-cultural model of the behavior of women and men: Implications for the origins of sex differences. *Psychological Bulletin, 128,* 699–727. (5)

Wood, W., Lundgren, S., Ouellette, J. A., Busceme, S., & Blackstone, T. (1994). Minority influence: A meta-analytic review of social influence processes. *Psychological Bulletin, 115,* 323–345. (13)

Wood, W., & Quinn, J. M. (2003). Forewarned and forearmed? Two meta-analytic syntheses of forewarnings of influence appeals. *Psychological Bulletin, 129,* 119–138. (13)

Wooding, S., Kim, U., Bamshad, M. J., Larsen, J., Jorde, L. B., & Drayna, D. (2004). Natural selection and molecular evolution in *PTC*, a bitter-taste receptor gene. *American Journal of Human Genetics, 74,* 637–646. (1)

Woods, J. H., & Winger, G. (1997). Abuse liability of flunitrazepam. *Journal of Clinical Psychopharmacology, 17*(Suppl. 3), S1–S57. (3)

Woods, S. C. (1991). The eating paradox: How we tolerate food. *Psychological Review, 98,* 488–505. (11)

Wooley, A. W., Chabris, C. F., Pentland, A., Hashmi, N., & Malone, T. W. (2010). Evidence for a collective intelligence factor in the performance of human groups. *Science, 330,* 686–688. (13)

Worthington, E. L., Jr., Kurusu, T. A., McCullough, M. E., & Sandage, S. J. (1996). Empirical research on religion and psychotherapeutic processes and outcomes: A 10-year review and research prospectus. *Psychological Bulletin, 119,* 448–487. (15)

Woychyshyn, C. A., McElheran, W. G., & Romney, D. M. (1992). MMPI validity measures: A comparative study of original with alternative indices. *Journal of Personality Assessment, 58,* 138–148. (14)

Wright, D. B., & Skagerberg, E. M. (2007). Postidentification feedback affects real eyewitnesses. *Psychological Science, 18,* 172–178. (7)

Wright, I. C., Rabe-Hesketh, S., Woodruff, P. W. R., David, A. S., Murray, R. M., & Bullmore, E. T. (2000). Meta-analysis of regional brain volumes in schizophrenia. *American Journal of Psychiatry, 157,* 16–25. (15)

Wright, L. (1994). *Remembering Satan.* New York: Knopf. (7)

Writing Group for the Women's Health Initiative Investigators. (2002). Risks and benefits of estrogen plus progestin in healthy postmenopausal women. *Journal of the American Medical Association, 288,* 321–333. (2)

Wu, K., Lindsted, K. D., Tsai, S.-Y., & Lee, J. W. (2007). Chinee NEO-PI-R in Taiwanese adolescents. *Personality and Individual Differences, 44,* 656–667. (14)

Wulff, K., Gatti, S., Wettstein, J. G., & Foster, R. G. (2010). Sleep and circadian rhythm disruption in psychiatric and neurodegenerative disease. *Nature Neuroscience, 11,* 589–599. (10)

Wundt, W. (1902). *Outlines of psychology* (C. H. Judd, Trans.). New York: Gustav Sechert. (Original work published 1896) (1)

Wundt, W. (1961). Contributions to the theory of sensory perception. In T. Shipley (Ed.), *Classics in psychology* (pp. 51–78). New York: Philosophical Library. (Original work published 1862) (1)

Wyart, C., Webster, W. W., Chen, J. H., Wilson, S. R., McClary, A., Khan, R. M., & Sobel, N. (2007). Smelling a single component of male sweat alters levels of cortisol in women. *Journal of Neuroscience, 27,* 1261–1265. (4)

Xu, A. J., & Wyer, R. S., Jr. (2008). The comparative mind set. *Psychological Science, 19,* 859–864. (11)

Yamagata, S., Suzuki, A., Ando, J., One, Y., Kijima, N., Yoshimura, K., . . . Jang, K. L. (2006). Is the genetic structure of human personality universal? A cross-cultural twin study from North America, Europe, and Asia. *Journal of Personality and Social Psychology, 90,* 987–998. (14)

Yamagishi, T., Hashimoto, H., & Schug, J. (2008). Preferences versus strategies as explanations for culture-specific behavior. *Psychological Science, 19,* 579–584. (5)

Yang, K.-S. (2003). Beyond Maslow's culture-bound linear theory: A preliminary statement of the double-Y model of basic human needs. *Nebraska Symposium on Motivation, 49,* 175–255. (11)

Yarsh, T. L., Farb, D. H., Leeman, S. E., & Jessell, T. M. (1979). Intrathecal capsaicin depletes substance P in the rat spinal cord and produces prolonged thermal analgesia. *Science, 206,* 481–483. (4)

Yehuda, R. (1997). Sensitization of the hypothalamic-pituitary-adrenal axis in posttraumatic stress disorder. *Annals of the New York Academy of Sciences, 821,* 57–75. (12)

Yeomans, M. R., Tepper, B. J., Rietzschel, J., & Prescott, J. (2007). Human hedonic responses to sweetness: Role of taste genetics and anatomy. *Physiology & Behavior, 91,* 264–273. (1)

Yik, M., Russell, J. A., & Steiger, J. H. (2011). A 12-point circumplex structure of core affect. *Emotion, 11,* 705–731. (12)

Ying, Y.-W., Han, M., & Wong, S. L. (2008). Cultural orientation in Asian American adolescents: Variation by age and ethnic density. *Youth and Society, 39,* 507–523. (5)

Yoo, S.-S., Hu, P. T., Gujar, N., Jolesz, F. A., & Walker, M. P. (2007). A deficit in the ability to form new human memories without sleep. *Nature Neuroscience, 10,* 385–392. (10)

Yoon, K. L., Hong, S. W., Joormann, J., & Kang, P. (2009). Perception of facial expressions of emotion during binocular rivalry. *Emotion, 9,* 172–182. (12)

Yunesian, M., Aslani, A., Vash, J. H., & Yazdi, A. B. (2008). Effects of transcendental meditation on mental health: A before-after study. *Clinical Practice and Epidemiology in Mental Health, 4,* 25. (10)

Zaccaro, S. J. (2007). Trait-based perspectives of leadership. *American Psychologist, 62,* 6–16. (11)

Zahavi, A., & Zahavi, A. (1997). *The handicap principle.* New York: Oxford University Press. (13)

Zahn, T. P. Rapoport, J. L., & Thompson, C. L. (1980). Autonomic and behavioral effects of dextroamphetamine and placebo in normal and hyperactive prepubertal boys. *Journal of Abnormal Child Psychology, 8,* 145–160. (8)

Zajonc, R. B. (1968). Attitudinal effects of mere exposure. *Journal of Personality and Social Psychology, 9*(Monograph Suppl. 2, Pt. 2). (13)

Zaragoza, M. S., Payment, K. E., Ackil, J. K., Drivdahl, S. B., & Beck, M. (2001). Interviewing witnesses: Forced confabulation and confirmatory feedback increase false memories. *Psychological Science, 12,* 473–477. (7)

Zarkadi, T., Wade, K. A., & Stewart, N. (2009). Creating fair lineups for suspects with distinctive features. *Psychological Science, 20,* 1448–1453. (7)

Zehr, D. (2000). Portrayals of Wundt and Titchener in introductory psychology texts: A content analysis. *Teaching of Psychology, 27,* 122–126. (1)

Zepelin, H., & Rechtschaffen, A. (1974). Mammalian sleep, longevity, and energy metabolism. *Brain, Behavior, and Evolution, 10,* 425–470. (10)

Zhang, T.-Y., & Meaney, M. J. (2010). Epigenetics and the environmental regulation of the genome and its function. *Annual Review of Psychology, 61,* 439–466. (3)

Zhang, W., & Luck, S. J. (2008). Discrete fixed-resolution representations in visual working memory. *Nature, 453,* 233–235. (8)

Zhang, X., & Firestein, S. (2002). The olfactory receptor gene superfamily of the mouse. *Nature Neuroscience, 5,* 124–133. (4)

Zhong, C.-B., Bohns, V. K., & Gino, F. (2010). Good lamps are the best police: Darkness increases dishonesty and self-interested behavior. *Psychological Science, 21,* 311–314. (13)

Zhong, C.-B., & DeVoe, S. E. (2010). You are how you eat: Fast food and impatience. *Psychological Science, 21,* 619–622. (8)

Zhou, W., & Chen, D. (2009). Fear-related chemosignals modulate recognition of fear in ambiguous facial expressions. *Psychological Science, 20,* 177–183. (12)

Zietsch, B. P., Morley, K. I., Shekar, S. N., Verwej, K. J. H., Keller, M. C., Macgregor, S., . . . Martin, N. G. (2008). Genetic factors predisposing to homosexuality may increase mating success in heterosexuals. *Evolution and Human Behavior, 29,* 424–433. (11)

Zihl, J., von Cramon, D., & Mai, N. (1983). Selective disturbance of movement vision after bilateral brain damage. *Brain, 106,* 313–340. (3)

Zolotor, A. J., & Puzia, M. E. (2010). Bans against corporal punishment: A systematic review of the laws, changes in attitudes and behaviours. *Child Abuse Review, 19,* 229–247. (6)

Zucker, K. J., Bradley, S. J., Oliver, G., Blake, J., Fleming, S., & Hood, J. (1996). Psychosexual development of women with congenital adrenal hyperplasia. *Hormones and Behavior, 30,* 300–318. (11)

Zuriff, G. E. (1995). Continuity over change within the experimental analysis of behavior. In J. T. Todd & E. K. Morris (Eds.), *Modern perspectives on B. F. Skinner and contemporary behaviorism* (pp. 171–178). Westport, CT: Greenwood Press. (6)

Attention-deficit hyperactivity disorder (ADHD) condition marked by easy distraction, impulsiveness, moodiness, and failure to follow through on plans, plus excessive activity and "fidgetiness," 263–264

Attention tendency to respond to and to remember some stimuli more than others, 258–263
    attention-deficit disorder, 263–264
    and bilingualism, 284
    limits of, 260–261, *261*
    and memory, 233, 251
    preattentive *vs.* attentive processes, 259–*260*

Attentive process procedure that requires searching through the items in a series, 259, *259*

Attitudes likes or dislikes that influences behavior, 437–438. See also **Persuasion**

Attraction
    equity theory, 447
    and mate selection, 445–446
    and physical attractiveness, 445–447, *446*
    and proximity, 445
    and relationships, 445–448
    and similarity, 447
    and technology, 447–448

Attribution set of thought processes we use to assign causes to our own behavior and that of others, 431–435
    actor-observer effect, 432–433
    and culture, 433–434
    fundamental attribution error, 433
    and self-perception, 434–435

Atypical antipsychotic drugs drugs that relieve schizophrenia without causing tardive dyskinesia, 522

Audition. *See* Hearing

Aura, 345–346

Authoritarian parents those who tend to be emotionally more distant from the child; they set rules without explaining the reasons behind them, 178

Authoritative parents those who set high standards and impose controls, but they are also warm and responsive to the child's communications, 178

Authority, obedience to, 452–455, *453*, *454*

Autism lifelong condition characterized by impaired social contact, 522–523

Autonomic nervous system section of the nervous system that controls the organs, 75, *75*, 84, 385–386, *386*, 388

Availability heuristic tendency to assume that if we easily think of examples of a category, then that category must be common, 271–272, *272*

Avoidance learning learning to make a response that avoids pain or some similar outcome, 202, 203, 502, 505

Axon single, long, thin, straight fiber with branches near its tip, 59, *60*

Bait-and-switch technique method of eliciting compliance whereby a person first offers an extremely favorable deal, gets the other person to commit to the deal, and then makes additional demands, 440–441

Barnum effect tendency to accept vague descriptions of one's own personality, 482

Base-rate information data about how common two categories are, 270–271

Basic emotions, 391–395

Basic research study that seeks theoretical knowledge for its own sake, 20

Before-and-after study, 44–46, *45*

Behavioral neuroscientist. *See* Biopsychologist

Behaviorism the position that psychology should concern itself only with what people and other animals do, and the circumstances in which they do it, 187–188
    history of, 19–20
    and humanistic psychology, 470–471
    and psychotherapy, 502–503

Behavior modification (or applied behavior analysis) procedure in which a psychologist removes reinforcement for unwanted behaviors and provides reinforcement for more acceptable behaviors, 208

Behavior therapy treatment that begins with clear, well-defined behavioral goals, such as eliminating test anxiety, and then attempts to achieve those goals through learning, *527*, 527–528

Belief in a just world idea that life is fair and people usually get what they deserve, 474–475

Benzodiazepines, 70, *73*

Bias tendency for test scores to overstate or understate the true performance of one or more groups, 311–315

Biculturalism partial identification with two cultures, 176–177, *177*

Big Five personality traits neuroticism, extraversion, agreeableness, conscientiousness, and openness to new experience, 476–477, *477*

Bilingual understanding two languages, 284

Bimodal distribution, 50

Binding problem question of how separate brain areas combine to produce a unified perception of an object, 86–88, *87*

Binet, Alfred, 18

Binocular cues visual cues that depend on both eyes, 137

Binocular rivalry alteration between seeing the pattern in the left retina and the pattern in the right retina, *323*, 323–324

Biopsychologist (or behavioral neuroscientist) specialist who explains behavior in terms of biological factors, such as activities of the nervous system, the effects of drugs and hormones, genetics, and evolutionary pressures, 10–11, *12*

Biopsychosocial model concept that emphasizes three aspects of abnormal behavior: biological, psychological, and sociological, 496

Bipolar cells, *106*, 107

Bipolar disorder condition previously known as manic-depressive disorder, in which someone alternates between mood extremes, 514–515

Biracialism, 177, *177*

Birdsong learning, 212–213, *213*

Birth order, 177–178, *178*

Bisexuality attraction to both sexes, 378. *See also* Sexual orientation

Blind observer someone who records data without knowing the researcher's predictions, 43

Blindsight ability to point to or otherwise indicate the direction to a visual stimulus, without conscious perception of seeing anything at all, 76–77

Blind spot retinal area where the optic nerve exits, 104, 108, *108*, *109*

Blocking effect phenomenon in which the previously established association to one stimulus blocks the formation of an association to an added stimulus, 194

Bobo doll experiment, 215

Body mass index, 366

Body weight, 366–370

Bonobos, *280*, 280–281, *281*

Bottom-up-process perceptual activity in which individual sensory elements combine to produce larger items, 132, 258, 259

Brain
    and anxiety, *401*, 401–402
    and autism, 523
    and autonomic nervous system, 86–88, *87*
    binding problem, 86–88, *87*
    cerebral cortex, 75–80
    and circadian rhythms, 330, *331*
    and consciousness, 321–324, *322*, *323*
    and cutaneous senses, 118–119
    and depression, 515–516
    development of, 94, 150, 520, 521, 532
    and dreaming, 76
    and emotions, 78, 387, *387*, 396–397
    and hearing, 85–86
    hemispheric connections, 80–81, *82*
    and hunger, 362, 363, *363*
    and hypnosis, 342, *342*
    and language, 77, *282*, 282–283
    measurement techniques, 82–83
    and memory, 83, *249*, 249–251
    mind-brain problem, 5–6
    and motor control, 83
    and nervous system, 75, *75*, 387, *387*
    and olfaction, 123, *123*
    and pain, 118–119
    plasticity of, 84–86
    and reading, 85
    and schizophrenia, 521, *521*
    and sexual orientation, 380, *380*
    and sleep, 76, 333–*334*, 336
    and spatial attention, 78
    subcortical areas, 83–84, *84*
    and substance-related disorders, *508*, 508–509
    and vision, 76, 77

Brain death condition in which the brain shows no activity and no response to any stimulus, 321

Breuer, Josef, 462

Brief therapy, 525

Brightness contrast increase or decrease in an object's apparent brightness by comparison to objects around it, 130, *130*

Broaden-and-build hypothesis idea that a happy mood increases your readiness to explore new ideas and opportunities, 396

Broca's aphasia condition characterized by difficulties in language production, 282, *282*

Bulimia nervosa a condition in which people alternate between self-deprivation and periods of excessive eating, with a feeling of loss of control, 369–370

Buprenorphine, 512

Burden of proof obligation to present evidence to support one's claim, 28–29

Burton, Lance, 31

Bystander responses, 424–425, *425*

Caffeine, *73*

Calkins, Mary, 20

Cancer, 41, 43, 71, 95, 201, 212, 366, 440

Capsaicin chemical that stimulates receptors that respond to painful heat, 119

Case history a thorough description of a person, including abilities and disabilities, medical condition, life history, unusual experiences, and whatever else seems relevant, 37, *43*

Cataract, *105*

Categorization, 264–266

Catharsis release of pent-up emotional tension, 462

Causation *vs.* correlation, 41–42

Cell body part of the neuron that contains the nucleus of the cell, 59

Central executive, 277

Central nervous system brain and spinal cord, 75, *75*

Central route to persuasion process in which people who take a decision seriously invest the necessary effort to evaluate the evidence and logic, 439

Cerebellum (Latin for "little brain") part of the hindbrain, 83

Cerebral cortex outer covering of the forebrain, 75–80, *76*

Chaining procedure for reinforcing each behavior with the opportunity to engage in the next response, 205, *205*

Change blindness failure to detect changes in parts of a scene, 261, *262*, 263

Channels (gates), 61, *62*, *64*, 119

Chemical senses, 120–124

Child, as eye witness, 225–226

Child care, 179–180

Childhood amnesia (or infant amnesia) scarcity of early episodic memories, 252

Chimpanzees, *280*, 280–281, *281*

Choice-delay task opportunity to choose between a small immediate reward and a larger delayed reward, 263

Chomsky, Noam, 228, 279, 281

Chromosome strands of hereditary material, 90, 95

Chunking grouping items into meaningful sequences or clusters, 228

Circadian rhythm rhythm of activity and inactivity lasting approximately one day, 328–330, *329*, *330*, *331*

Circumplex model of emotions, 395, *395*

Classical conditioning (or Pavlovian conditioning) process by which an organism learns a new association between a neutral stimulus and one that already evokes a reflexive response, 187–196
and drug tolerance, 192–193
examples of, 190
explanations of, 194–196
Pavlov's studies, *188*, 188–189
phenomena of, 190–192
vs. operant conditioning, *203*

Clever Hans, 29–*30*

Climax (orgasm) stage of sexual arousal, *374*, 375

Clinical psychologist someone with an advanced degree in psychology (master's degree, PhD, or PsyD), with a specialty in understanding and helping people with psychological problems, 7, *8*, *12*

Clinical psychology, 20

Clinical social worker someone similar to a clinical psychologist but with different training, 7, *8*

Closure in Gestalt psychology, tendency to imagine the rest of an incomplete, familiar figure, 133–134, *134*, 135

Cocaine, 68, *73*

Cochlea fluid-filled canals of the snail-shaped organ, which contains the receptors for hearing, 113, *114*, *115*

Codeine, 71

Coercive persuasion, 443

Cognition thought and knowledge, 10
and aggression, 426
and depression, 516–517
and emotions, 398
errors in, 270–274, *272*

expertise, 274–277
heuristics, 269–270
research examples, *257*, 257–258, *258*
See also Cognitive development; Intelligence

Cognitive-behavior therapy treatment in which therapists set explicit behavioral goals, but also try to change people's interpretation of situations, 528

Cognitive development
concrete operations stage, 161, *162*
formal operations stage, 161, *162*
preoperational stage, 156–161, *157*, *158*, *159*, *160*–*161*, *162*
sensorimotor stage, 154–156, *162*
Vygotsky on, 162–163

Cognitive dissonance state of unpleasant tension that people experience when they hold contradictory attitudes or when their behavior contradicts their stated attitudes, especially if the inconsistency distresses them, 437–439

Cognitive psychologist specialist who studies thought and knowledge processes, 10, *11*, *12*

Cognitive psychology, 20, 256–258

Cognitive therapy procedure that seeks to improve psychological well-being by changing people's interpretation of events, 528

Cohort group of people born at a particular time or a group of people who enter an organization at a particular time, 149, *149*, 478–480

Collective unconscious according to Jung, inborn thoughts and images that relate to the cumulative experience of preceding generations, 467–468

Collectivism, 176, 452, *452*

Color constancy tendency of an object to appear nearly the same color under a variety of lighting conditions, 110, *111*

Color vision, 108–*109*

Color vision deficiency, 110–111, *111*

Coma condition in which the brain shows a steady but low level of activity and no response to any stimulus, 321

Common fate tendency to perceive objects as part of the same group if they change or move in similar ways at the same time, 134, *134*

Community psychologists those who try to help people change their environment, both to prevent disorders and to promote a positive sense of mental well-being, *12*, 532

Companionate love stage in a relationship marked by sharing, care, and protection, 449

Comparative psychologist specialist who compares different animal species, 18

Compulsion repetitive, almost irresistible action, 505, 506

Conditional positive regard, 471

Conditioned reflex, 188

Conditioned response (CR) whatever response the conditioned stimulus elicits as a result of the conditioning (training) procedure, 189, *189*, *527*

Conditioned stimulus (CS) response that depends on the preceding conditions, 189, *189*, 190, 192–193, 194–196, *195*, 210, 527, *527*

Conditioned taste aversion association of a food with illness, 210–212, *211*, *212*

Conduction deafness hearing impairment because the bones connected to the

eardrum fail to transmit sound waves properly to the cochlea, 113

Cones visual receptors adapted for color vision, daytime vision, and detailed vision, 105, *106*, *107*, 108

Confabulations attempts by amnesic patients to fill in the gaps in their memory, 250–251

Confidence intervals, 52–*53*

Confirmation bias tendency to accept a hypothesis and then look for evidence to support it instead of considering other possibilities, 272–273

Conformity altering one's behavior to match other people's behavior or expectation, *450*, 450–452, *451*, *452*

Conscientiousness tendency to show self-discipline, to be dutiful, and to strive for achievement and competence, 476–477

Consciousness subjective experience of perceiving oneself and one's surroundings, 321
and action, 324–325
and brain, 321–324, *322*, *323*
as construction, 324
déjà vu experiences, 345–346
and meditation, 345
purpose of, 326
unconscious perception, 324
See also Hypnosis; Sleep

Consensus information how a person's behavior compares with other people's behavior, 432

Conservation concept that objects conserve such properties as number, length, volume, area, and mass after changes in the shape or arrangement of the objects, *160*, 160–161, *161*

Consistency information how a person's behavior varies from one time to the next, 432

Consolidation converting a short-term memory into a long-term memory, 229, 239

Contempt reaction to a violation of community standards, 403

Contingency management, 512

Continuation in Gestalt psychology, a filling in of the gaps, 133, *134*, 135

Continuous reinforcement procedure providing reinforcement for every correct response, 205–206

Contrast effects, 440

Control group set of individuals treated in the same way as the experimental group except for the procedure that the experiment is designed to test, 42

Convenience sample group chosen because of its ease of study, *35*, *36*

Convergence degree to which the eyes turn in to focus on a close object, 137

Cooperation
altruistic behavior, *422*, 422–423
bystander responses, 423–424
social loafing, 424

Copy number variants deletions and duplications of tiny parts of a chromosome, 520

Cornea rigid, transparent structure on the surface of the eyeball, 104, *104*

Corpus callosum set of axons that connect the left and right hemispheres of the cerebral cortex, 80, *81*

Correlation coefficient mathematical estimate of the relationship between two variables, 39–40, *43*

Correlation the degree of relationship between two variables, 39–42, *43*

Correspondence bias, 433

Cortical blindness, 76

Cortisol hormone that enhances metabolism and increases the supply of sugar and other fuels to the cells, 410

Counseling psychologist specialist who helps people with educational, vocational, marriage, health-related, and other decisions, 8, *12*

Crack cocaine, 68

Creativity, 403, 472, 475

Criminal profiling, 488–490, *490*

Critical thinking careful evaluation of evidence for and against any conclusion, 272

Cross-cultural psychology field that compares the behavior of people from different cultures, 11

Cross-cultural sample groups of people from at least two cultures, 35, *36*

Cross-sectional study procedure that compares groups of individuals of different ages at the same time, 147–148, *148*

CR (conditioned response) whatever response the conditioned stimulus begins to elicit as a result of the conditioning procedure, 189, *189*, *527*

Crying, 406

Crystallized intelligence acquired skills and knowledge and the ability to apply that knowledge in specific situations, 297, 299, *299*

CS (conditioned stimulus) stimulus that comes to evoke a particular response after being paired with the unconditioned stimulus, 189, *189*, 190, 192–193, 194–196, *195*, 210, 527, *527*

Cued recall method to test memory by providing significant hints about the material, 222, *222*, *223*

Culture
    and abnormal behavior, 496–497
    and aggression, 425, 426
    and alcoholism, 510, *510*
    and anxiety, 501, *501*
    and attention, 284
    and attributions, 433–434
    and conformity, 451–452
    and cooperation, 431
    and eating disorders, 367, 368
    and emotions, 391, 393, 395
    and family, 179–180
    and gender differences, 176, *177*
    and gender roles, 470, *470*
    and happiness, 404
    and health, *366*
    and human needs, 353
    and hunger, 364–365, *365*
    and intelligence testing, 311–315
    and Jungian theory, 466–468
    and memory, 233
    and moral reasoning, 421
    and personality, 467, 477, 479, 484
    and persuasion, 207–208
    and schizophrenia, 519
    and sexuality, 372–374
    and social support, 413
    and stereotypes, 313–315

Culture-reduced testing, 300–301

Cumulative record, 206–207

Cutaneous senses skin senses, *118*, 118–120, *119*

Dahmer, Jeffrey, 534

Dark adaptation gradual improvement in the ability to see in dim light, 107, *107*

Darwin, Charles, 18, 45, 96

Data analysis
    descriptive statistics, 49–52
    inferential statistics, 52–53

Data collection, 27–28

Date rape drugs, 70

Daylight savings time, 330

Deadlines, 355

Death, 171–172

Declarative memory memories we can readily state in words, 223, 250

Defense mechanism method employed by ego to defend itself against anxieties, 464–465

Dehumanization, 426

Deindividualization, 426

Deinstitutionalization removal of patients from mental hospitals, 533

Déjà vu experience feeling that an event is uncannily familiar, 345–346

Delayed-response problem, *18*

Delay of gratification declining a pleasant activity now in order to get greater pleasure later, 356

Delusion of grandeur false belief that you are unusually important, 519

Delusion of persecution false belief that enemies are persecuting you, 519

Delusion of reference a tendency to take all sorts of messages personally, 519

Delusions beliefs that are strongly held despite a lack of evidence for them, 519

Demand characteristics cues that tell participants what is expected of them and what the experimenter hopes to find, 43–*44*

Dement, William, 332, 333

Dendrites widely branching structures of a neuron that receive input from other neurons, 59, *60*

Denial refusal to believe unpleasant information, 465

Dependence (or addiction) inability to quit a self-destructive habit, 508

Dependent variable item that an experimenter measures to determine the effect of the independent variable, 42

Depressants drugs that decrease arousal, 70, *70*, *73*

Depression
    and cognition, 516–517
    and genetics, 515
    seasonal affective disorder, 514
    and sleep, 332, 514
    and stress, 401–402, 411–412
    treatments for, 515–518

Depth-of-processing principle idea that how easily you retrieve a memory depends on the number and types of associations you form, 235, *235*

Depth perception perception of distance, 136–139, *137*, *138*, 139–140, *141*

Descriptive statistics mathematical summaries of results, 49–52

Determinism idea that every event has a cause, or determinant, that one could observe or measure, 4, *5*, 470

Detour problem, *18*

Development
    language, 279–290
    prenatal, 70, 150–151, 375, 376, 521, 532
    research methods, 147–149
    sexual, 375–377, *376*
    See also Cognitive development; Social/ emotional development

Developmental psychologist specialist who studies how behavior changes with age, 9, *10*, *12*

Diagnostic and Statistical Manual of Mental Disorders (DSM) book that sets specific criteria for each psychological diagnosis, 497–499, *498*, *499*

Diazepam (Valium), 70

Diffusion of responsibility tendency to feel less responsibility to act when other people are equally able to act, 423–424

Direct memory (or explicit memory) a memory that someone can state, recognizing it as a memory, 223, 250, 487

DISC1 gene that is disrupted in schizophrenia, 520

Discrimination (a) in classical conditioning, to respond differently to stimuli that predict different outcomes; (b) in operant conditioning, a response to one stimulus and not the other; (c) in social behavior, unequal treatment of different groups of people, 192, 204, 429

Discriminative stimulus item that indicates whether a response is appropriate or inappropriate, 204

Disequilibrium principle idea that anything that decreases opportunity for an activity produces disequilibrium, and an opportunity to return to equilibrium will be reinforcing, 200

Disgust reaction to something that would make you feel contaminated if it got into your mouth, 403

Dishabituation increase in a previously habituated response as a result of a change in stimulation, 152–153

Disordered thinking, 251, 534

Displacement diversion of a behavior or thought away from its natural target toward a less threatening target, 465

Dispositional attributions, 432

Dissociation memory that one has stored but cannot retrieve, 246

Dissociative identity disorder, 518

Distinctiveness how a person's behavior varies from one situation to another, 432

Distraction, and stress, 414

Disulfiram. *See* Antabuse

Divorce, 148, 180–181, 404, 448

Dizygotic twins those who share only half their genes because they developed from two eggs, 93, *94*, 302. *See also* Twin studies

DNA, 90, *92*

Dominant gene of which a single copy is sufficient to produce its effect, 91

Dopamine hypothesis of schizophrenia idea that the underlying cause of schizophrenia is excessive stimulation of certain types of dopamine synapses, 522

Dopamine neurotransmitter that promotes activity levels and reinforcement, 65, 66, 507–508

Double-blind study research in which neither the observer nor the subjects know which subjects received which treatment, 43, *44*

Down syndrome condition marked by a variety of physical and mental impairments as a result of having an extra copy of chromosome #21, 306–307, *307*

Dream analysis seeks to understand symbolism in reported dreams, 527

Dreaming, 336–338, *337*

Drive-reduction theory, 351

Drive state of unrest or irritation that energizes one behavior after another until one of them removes the irritation, 351, *352*

Drugs
    and aggression, 70
    chart, *73*
    depressants, 70, *70*
    hallucinogens, *69*, 69–70
    marijuana, *71*, 71–72

narcotics, 71
psychoactive, 68
stimulants, 68–69
tolerance, 192–193
See also Substance-related disorders
Drug tolerance weakened effects of a drug after someone has taken the drug repeatedly, 192–193, *193*
DSM (*Diagnostic and Statistical Manual of Mental Disorders*) book that sets specific criteria for each psychological diagnosis, 497
Dualism view that the mind is separate from the brain but somehow controls the brain and therefore the rest of the body, 5–6, 75
Duchenne smile full expression including the muscles around the eyes, 392, *392*

Ear, 113, 117, *117. See also* Hearing
Eating disorders, 368–370
Ebbinghaus, Hermann, *221*, 221–222, *222*, 244, 244–245
Eclectic therapy treatment that uses a combination of methods and approaches, 528
Ecstasy (MDMA), 69–70, *73*
ECT (electroconvulsive therapy) treatment in which a brief electrical shock is administered across a patient's head to induce a convulsion, 517–518, *518*
Educational psychologist, *12*
EEG (electroencephalograph) device that measures and amplifies tiny electrical changes on the scalp that reflect brain activity, 333, *333*
Ego according to Freud, the rational, decision-making aspect of the personality, 464
Egocentric seeing the world as centered around oneself, with difficulty taking another person's perspective, 156–157, 163
Electroconvulsive therapy (ECT) treatment in which a brief electrical shock is administered across a patient's head to induce a convulsion, 517–518, *518*
Electroencephalograph (EEG) device that measures and amplifies tiny electrical changes on the scalp that reflect brain activity, 82
Electromagnetic spectrum continuum of all the frequencies of radiated energy, 103
Embarrassment emotional reaction to mistakes, being the center of attention, or "sticky situations," 406
Emotional intelligence ability to perceive, imagine, and understand emotions and to use that information in making decisions, 398
Emotion-focused coping regulating one's emotional reaction, 412, 413–414
Emotions
anger, 395, *395*, 403
anxiety, 401–403
basic, 391–395
and culture, 391, 393, 395
emotional intelligence, 398
and facial expressions, *391*, 391–395, *392*, *393*, *394*, *395*
happiness, 403–406
and hunger, 366–367
impaired, 396–397, *397*
James-Lange theory, 387–389, *388*
measurement, 385–387
and memory, 233, 506
and moral reasoning, 396, *397*
sadness, 394, *394*, 406
Schachter and Singer's theory, *389*, 389–390
self-conscious, 406

usefulness of, 396
See also Stress
Empirically supported treatments therapies demonstrated to be helpful, 525
Encoding, 232–236
Encoding specificity principle idea that the associations you form at the time of learning will be the most effective retrieval cues later, 235–236, *236*
Endocrine system glands that produce hormones and release them into the blood, 84, *86*
Endorphins chemicals produced by the brain that bind to opiate receptors, *65*, 71, 119, *120*
Entropy, 103
Environment
influence on depression, 515
influence on intelligence, 303–304
See also Nature-nurture issue
Environmental psychologist, *12*
Epigenetics changes in gene expression as a result of environmental influences, without modification of the DNA sequence, 92
Epilepsy condition in which cells somewhere in the brain emit abnormal rhythmic, spontaneous impulses, 80
Epinephrine (adrenaline), 233, 386, 389–390, *390*
Episodic memory memory for specific events in your life, 227, 252
Equilibration establishment of harmony or balance between assimilation and accommodation, 154
Equity theories (or exchange theories) theories maintaining that social relationships are transactions in which partners exchange goods and services, 447
Ergonomist. *See* Human factors specialist
Erikson, Erik, *166*, 166–171
ESP (extrasensory perception) claim that some people, some of the time, acquire information without receiving energy through any sense organ, 30–*31*
Estrogen hormone present in higher quantities in females than in males, 375
Estrogens, 42–43, 84
Ethics
concerns with nonhuman, 46–*47*
informed consent, 46, 455
surveyor bias, 38–*39*
Ethnic background, 176–177
Evidence
and falsifiability, 28–29
and parsimony, 29–32
and replicability, 28
and scientific method, 27
See also Data analysis; Research; Research example
Evolution gradual change in the frequency of various genes from one generation to the next
and attraction, 446
and genetics, 45–46, 96
and preparedness, 210, 211
and sexual orientation, 379
Evolutionary psychologist one who tries to explain behavior in terms of the evolutionary history of the species, including why evolution might have favored a tendency to act in particular ways, 11. *See also* Evolution
Evolutionary psychology, 20, 96–98
Exchange (or equity) theories maintain that social relationships are transactions in which partners exchange goods and service, 447
Excitation, 60–61, 151. *See also* Action potential
Excitement stage of sexual arousal, *374*, 374–375

Executive functioning cognitive process that governs shifts of attention, 229–230
Exercise, and stress, 414
Experimental group the group that receives the treatment that an experiment is designed to test, 42
Experimenter bias tendency of an experimenter (unintentionally, as a rule) to misperceive the results, 43
Experiments studies in which the investigator manipulates at least one variable while measuring at least one other variable, 42–46, *43. See also* Research; Research examples
Expertise, 274–277
Explanatory style, 516–517
Explicit memory (or direct memory) a memory that someone can state, recognizing it as a memory, 223, 250, 487
External attributions explanations based on the situation, including events that would influence almost anyone, 431, 432
Extinction (a) in classical conditioning, the process that weakens a conditioned response by presenting the conditioned stimulus without the unconditioned stimulus; (b) in operant conditioning, the process that weakens a response when it no longer leads to reinforcement, 190, *191*, 203, 207
Extrasensory perception (ESP) claim that some people, some of the time, acquire information without receiving energy through any sense organ, 30–*31*
Extraversion tendency to seek stimulation and to enjoy the company of other people, 476, *479*
Eye, 103–*105*, *104. See also* Vision
Eye movements, and reading, 289
Eyewitness memory, 224–226, *225*

Face recognition, 77, 151–152
Facial expressions, *391*, 391–395, *392*, *393*, *394*, *395*
False memory inaccurate report that someone believes to be a memory, 246–248
Falsifiable stated in such clear, precise terms that we can see what evidence would count against it, 28–29
Family
and alcoholism, 510
and anorexia nervosa, 368
birth order, 177–178, *178*
divorce, 180–181
nontraditional, 180
parental employment, 179–180
parenting style, 178–179, 478
and schizophrenia, 520, *520*
Family systems therapy treatment based on the assumption that most people's problems develop in a family setting and that the best way to deal with them is to improve family relationships and communication, 528, *529*
Far transfer benefit from practicing something not similar to it, 276–277
Fear, 401. *See also* Anxiety
Fear messages, 441
Feature detector specialized neuron in the visual cortex that responds to the presence of a simple feature, such as a line, 130–132, *131*, *132*
Fetal alcohol syndrome condition marked by physical deformities or mental impairments, caused by alcohol consumed by the mother during pregnancy, *150*, 150–151

Fetus organism more developed than an embryo but not yet born (from about 8 weeks after conception until birth in humans), 150–151

Figure and ground distinguishing an object from its background, 132

First impressions, 428

Fixation (a) in vision, a period when the eyes are stationary; (b) in Freud's theory, a persisting preoccupation with the pleasure area associated with that stage of psychosexual development, 289, 463

Fixed-interval schedule procedure that provides reinforcement for the first response after a specific time interval, 206, 206–207

Fixed-ratio schedule rule that provides reinforcement only after a certain (fixed) number of correct responses, 206, 206

Flashbulb memories, 233

Fluid intelligence power of reasoning, using information, and solving new problems, 297, 299, 299

Flunitrazepam (Rohypnol), 70

Flynn effect tendency for performance on IQ tests to improve from one generation to the next, 307–309

fMRI (functional magnetic resonance imaging) procedure that uses magnetic detectors outside the head to compare the amounts of hemoglobin with and without oxygen in different brain areas, 6, 82, 82–83, 321, 324

Footbridge Dilemma, 396, 397

Foot-in-the-door technique method of eliciting compliance whereby someone starts with a modest request, which you accept, and follows with a larger request, 440

Forebrain, 75, 75–76, 78

Forensic psychologist one who provides advice and consultation to police, lawyers, and courts, 8, 8

Forewarning effect phenomenon that informing people that they are about to hear a persuasive speech activates their resistance and weakens the persuasion, 442

Forgetting, 244–252
    and Alzheimer's disease, 251–252
    amnesia, 227
    and interference, 229, 245
    recovered memory, 246

Fovea central area of the human retina, 104, 104, 105, 107

Framing effect tendency to answer a question differently when it is worded differently, 273–274, 274

Free association procedure in which a client says everything that comes to mind, 527

Freebase cocaine, 44

Free recall describing what you remember, as you do on essay tests, 222, 222, 223

Free will belief that behavior is caused by a person's independent decisions, 4–5

Frequency principle concept that a sound wave through the fluid of the cochlea vibrates all the hair cells, which produce action potentials in synchrony with the sound waves, 114–115, 115

Freud, Anna, 464–465

Freud, Sigmund, 7, 20, 29, 246, 338, 461–466

Frontal lobe the anterior (forward) pole of the brain, which includes the primary motor cortex, important for controlling fine movements, 79–80

Frustration-aggression hypothesis theory in which the main cause of anger and aggression is an obstacle that stands in the way of doing something or obtaining something, 425

Functional fixedness tendency to adhere to a single approach or a single way of using an item, 273

Functionalism emphasis on studying what the mind does, instead of the structures that compose it, 16

Functional magnetic resonance imaging (fMRI) procedure that uses magnetic detectors outside the head to compare the amounts of hemoglobin with and without oxygen in different brain areas, 6, 82–83, 83, 321, 324

Fundamental attribution error tendency to make internal attributions for people's behavior even when we see evidence for an external influence on behavior, 433

Fusiform gyrus, 77

GABA (gamma-amino-butyric acid), 65, 71, 151

GAD (generalized anxiety disorder) disorder in which people have frequent and exaggerated worries, 501

Gage, Phineas, 396–397, 397

Galton, Francis, 18

Ganglion cells neurons in the eye that receive input from bipolar cells, which in turn receive input from the visual receptors, 107–108

Ganzfeld procedure, 32

Gardner, Randy, 332

Gates (channels), 61, 62, 64, 119

Gate theory idea that pain messages must pass through a gate, presumably in the spinal cord, that can block the messages, 118–119

Gender differences, 173, 173–175, 174, 175
    and attraction, 447
    and culture/ethnicity, 176–177, 177
    and gender roles, 469–470, 470
    and hormones, 375–376
    and intelligence, 18, 307
    and sex roles, 175
    and sexual orientation, 378

Gender identity sex that someone regards himself or herself as being, 375

Gender role pattern of behavior that a person is expected to follow because of being male or female, 469–470, 470

Generalization, 203

Generalized anxiety disorder (GAD) disorder in which people have frequent and exaggerated worries, 501

Genes structures that control the chemical reactions that direct development, 90–93, 91. See also Genetics

Genetics
    and alcoholism, 510
    and autism, 523
    and behavior, 95–96
    and circadian rhythms, 328
    and depression, 515
    and evolution, 45–46
    heritability, 93–95
    and intelligence, 18, 302–303
    and obesity, 367
    principles of, 90–95
    and schizophrenia, 520
    and sexual orientation, 354
    See also Nature-nurture issue

Genital stage according to Freud, period when someone becomes sexually interested in other people, 463, 463

Gestalt psychology a field that emphasizes perception of overall patterns, 132–135

g factor, 295, 295–296, 296

GHB (gamma hydroxybutyrate), 70, 73

Ghrelin, 362

Giftedness, 307

Glaucoma, 105

Glia cells that support the neurons in many ways such as insulating them, synchronizing activity among neighboring neurons, and removing waste materials, 59

Glucagon, 362

Glucose most abundant sugar in the blood, an important source of energy for the body and almost the only source the brain uses, 362–363

Glutamate, 65, 71, 151

Goal-setting, 353–355

Goodall, Jane, 37

Good figure in Gestalt psychology, the tendency to perceive simple, symmetrical figures, 134, 134–135

Grasp reflex, 96, 97

Group decision making, 455–456

Group polarization tendency for people who lean in the same direction on a particular issue to become more extreme in that position after discussing it with one another, 455–456

Group therapy treatment that is administered to several people at once, 529, 529

Groupthink tendency for people to suppress their doubts about a group's decision for fear of making a bad impression or disrupting group harmony, 456

Guilt, 391, 406

Guilty-knowledge test modified version of the polygraph test, produces more accurate results by asking questions that should be threatening only to someone who knows the facts of a crime, 403

Habituate, 78

Habituation decreased response to a repeated stimulus, 152

Hair cells, 113–115, 114, 115, 117

Hallucinations perceptions that do not correspond to anything in the real world, 518–519

Hallucinogens drugs that induce sensory distortions, 69, 69–70, 73

Handwriting analysis, 487

Happiness, 403–406

Harm reduction approach to drug abuse that concentrates on decreasing the frequency of drug use and minimizing the harmful consequences to health and well-being

Health
    and emotions, 405
    and physical attractiveness, 446

Health maintenance organizations (HMOs), 525

Health psychology addresses how people's behavior influences health, 408

Hearing, 85–86, 113–114, 113–116, 115, 116, 135, 152–153, 153

Heart disease, 410–411

Helmholtz, Hermann von, 108

Hemisphere (brain), 75–76, 76

Heredity. See Genetics; Nature-nurture issue

Hering, Ewald, 109

Heritability estimate of the variance within a population that is due to heredity, 93–95. See also Genetics

Heroin, 71, 73, 102, 509, 512, 512

Hertz (Hz) cycles (vibrations) per second, 113

Heterosexuality. See Sexual orientation

Heuristics strategy for simplifying a problem and generating a satisfactory guess, 269–272, 272

Hierarchical models of intelligence, 297

Hierarchies, 264, 297